GUN TRADER'S GUIDE™

Thirty-Sixth Edition

A Comprehensive, Fully Illustrated Guide to Modern Collectible Firearms with Current Market Values

Edited by Robert A. Sadowski

Skyhorse Publishing

Contents

Skyhorse Publishing books may be purchased in bulk at special discounts for sales promotion, corporate gifts, fund-raising, or educational purposes. Special editions can also be created to specifications. For details, contact the Special Sales Department, Skyhorse Publishing, 307 West 36th Street, 11th Floor, New York, NY 10018 or info@skyhorsepublishing.com.

Skyhorse® and Skyhorse Publishing® are registered trademarks of Skyhorse Publishing, Inc.®, a Delaware corporation.

Visit our website at www.skyhorsepublishing.com.

10 9 8 7 6 5 4 3 2 1

Library of Congress Cataloging-in-Publication Data is available on file.
Print ISBN: 978-1-62914-752-9
Ebook ISBN: 978-1-62914-973-8

Printed in Canada

Front cover images courtesy Beretta.

Introduction

The 36th edition of Skyhorse Publishing's *Gun Trader's Guide* (*GTG*) has been ehanced to provide the professional and amateur firearms enthusiast with even more firearm specifications and photographs. Also new in this edition is additional information covering online trading and curios and relics.

CURRENT AND UP-TO-DATE

The *GTG* is revised annually to ensure that its wealth of information is both current and detailed. In the past fifty years, *GTG* has grown to over six hundred pages and more than six thousand standard firearms and their variations, evolving into one of the most complete catalogs of modern smokeless-powder rifles, shotguns, and handguns from the late 19th century, through the 20th century, to the 21st century. We have made every effort to ensure the information between these covers is current and up to date. Not every gun ever manufactured can be listed in a catalog of this size, but we have made every effort to include the makes and models that are most popular with American owners and collectors. Please note *GTG* does not include antique or recently manufactured blackpowder firearms.

EASY TO USE FORMAT

GTG's reference guide format is simple and straightforward. Tabbed sections and a complete index offer ease of use. Entries are alphebetized by manufacturer and model with specifications that include:

- Manufacturer
- Model Name
- Model Number
- Caliber or Gauge
- Barrel Length
- Overall Length
- Weight
- Distinguishing features
- Variations of different models
- Dates of manufacture (when they can be accurately determined)
- Date of discontinuation (if applicable)
- Current value for condition
- Photos (or illustrations)

EXTENSIVE PHOTOGRAPHS

Unique to *GTG* are photographs to help identify and compare firearms. The exclusive and extensive pictorial format along with accompanying comprehensive specifications provide a complete resource for identifying firearms and their current value.

ACCURATE FIREARM VALUES

Values shown are based on national averages obtained by conferring with knowledgeable gun dealers, traders, collectors, and auctioneers around the country, not by applying an arbitrary mathematical formula that could produce unrealistic figures. The values listed accurately reflect the nationwide average at the time of publication and are updated annually. Keep in mind that the stated values are averages based on a wide spectrum of variables. No price given in any such catalog should be considered the one and only value for a particular firearm. Value is ultimately determined by the buyer and seller.

In the case of rare or one-of-a-kind items, such as the Winchester Model 1873 One of One Thousand rifle or the Parker AA1 Special shotgun in 28 gauge, where little trading takes place, active gun collectors were consulted to obtain current market values.

In researching data for this edition, some manufacturers' records were unavailable and at times information was unobtainable. Some early firearms manufacturers' production records have been destroyed in fires, lost, or were simply not maintained accurately. These circumstances resulted in some minor deviations in the presentation format of certain model listings. For example, production dates may not be listed when manufacturing records are unclear or unavailable. As an alternative, approximate dates of manufacture may be listed to reflect the availability of guns from a manufacturer or distributor. These figures may represent disposition dates indicating when that particular model was shipped to a distributor or importer. Frequently, and especially with foreign manufacturers, production records are unavailable. Therefore, availability information is often based on importation records that reflect domestic distribution only.

This is meant to explain the procedure and policy used regarding these published dates and to establish the distinction between production dates, which are based on manufacturers' records, and availability dates, which are based on distribution records in the absence of recorded production data.

To ensure *GTG* has the most accurate information available, we encourage and solicit users to contact our research staff at the Skyhorse Publishing, Inc., offices and to forward any verifiable information they may have, especially in relation to older out-of-production models.

ACKNOWLEDGMENTS

The publisher wishes to express special thanks to the many collectors, dealers, manufacturers, shooting editors, firearm firms and distributors' public relations and production personnel, research personnel who provide us with specifications and updates throughout the year, and other industry professionals. We are especially grateful for their assistance and cooperation in compiling information for this edition, as well as allowing *GTG* to reproduce photographs and illustrations of their collectible firearms. Special thanks to Neil Delmonico of Brooklyn Trading Post (brooklyntradingpost.com) in Brooklyn, Connecticut, for use of the pre-'64 Winchester Model 94 in the "How to Use *GTG*" section.

Finally, *GTG* thanks to all the dedicated readers who take the time to write to us with comments, suggestions, and queries about collectible firearms. We appreciate and value your input.

Readers may send comments or suggestions to: info@skyhorsepublishing.com

How to Use *GTG*

Are you planning on buying or selling a used rifle, shotgun, or handgun? Perhaps you just want to establish the value of a favorite rifle, shotgun, or handgun in your collection. No matter what your interest in collectible modern, smokeless-powder firearms, today's enthusiast inevitably turns to the *Gun Trader's Guide (GTG)* to determine specifications, date of manufacture, and the average value (in the United States) of a specific modern firearm.

Opening the book, the collector asks him- or herself the first obvious question: "How much is my used gun worth?"

Gun prices contained in this book should be considered retail; that is, the average price a collector anywhere in the United States may expect to pay for a firearm in similar condition. Don't leap to the instant conclusion that your firearm will bring top dollar! There is no right or wrong price for any collectible firearm. The listings shown here are based on national averages and may be higher or lower depending on where you live and the strength of the market in your area. There is a market for everything from folk art to xylophones, but the range of values can be extreme and only items in perfect condition will bring top dollar.

Many variables must be considered when buying or selling a used gun. Scarcity, demand, geographic location, the buyer's position, and the gun's condition ultimately govern the selling price of a particular firearm. Sentiment often shades the value of a particular gun in the seller's mind, but the market value of Grandpa's old .30/30 cannot be logically cataloged nor effectively marketed—except possibly to someone else in the family!

GRANDPA'S DEER GUN

To illustrate how the price of a particular gun may fluctuate, let us consider the popular Winchester Model 94 (it was discontinued in 2006, after 110 years of continuous production, then reintroduced in 2010) and see what its value might be.

The Model 1894 (or Model 94) is a lever-action, solid-frame repeater. Round or octagon barrels of twenty-six inches were standard when the rifle was first introduced in 1894. However, half-octagon barrels were offered for a slight increase in price. Various magazine lengths were also available.

Fancy grade versions in all Model 94 calibers were available with twenty-six-inch round, nickel steel barrels. This grade featured a checkered fancy walnut pistol grip stock and forearm and was available with either shotgun or rifle-type butt plates.

In addition, Winchester produced this model in a carbine style with a saddle ring on the left side of the receiver. The carbine had a twenty inch round barrel and a full or half magazine. Some carbines were supplied with standard-grade barrels while others were made of nickel steel. Trapper models were also available with shorter fourteen-, sixteen-, or eighteen-inch barrels.

In later years, the Rifle and Trapper models were discontinued, and only the carbine remained. Eventually, the saddle ring was eliminated from this model and the carbine butt stock was replaced with a shotgun-type butt stock and shortened forend.

After World War II, the finish on Winchester Model 94 carbines changed to strictly hot caustic bluing; thus, prewar models usually demand a premium over postwar models.

In 1964 (a turning point for many American firearms manufacturers), beginning with serial number 2,700,000, the action on the Winchester Model 94 was redesigned for easier manufacture. Many collectors and firearms enthusiasts considered this and other design changes to be inferior to former models. Therefore, the term pre-'64 has become the watchword for collectors when it comes to setting values on Winchester-made firearms. This will likely be the case in the future, as the now-discontinued models 70, 94, and 1300 Winchester reach the collectible market.

Whether this evaluation is correct or not is unimportant. The justification for an immediate increase in the value of pre-'64 models was that they were no longer available. This diminished availability placed them in the scarce class, making them more desirable to collectors.

Shortly after the 1964 transition, Winchester began producing Model 94 commemorative models in great numbers, which added confusion to the concept of limited production. Increased availability adversely affected the annual appreciation and price stability of these commemorative models. The negative response generated by this marketing practice was increased when Winchester was sold in the 1980s. The name of this long-established American firearms manufacturer was changed to U.S. Repeating Arms Company, which manufactured the Model 94 in standard, carbine, and big-bore models until 2006. Later, the Angle-Eject model was introduced, a design change that allowed for the mounting of scope sights directly above the action. Currently the Model 94 in various configurations are in production in Japan; originals were built in New Haven, Connecticut.

With the above facts in mind, let's explore *GTG* to establish the approximate value of your particular Model 94. We will assume that you recently inherited the rifle, which has "Winchester Model 94" inscribed on the barrel. Turn to the "Rifle" section of the book and look under "Winchester." The index at the back of the book is another way to locate your rifle.

This is a pre-'64 Winchester Model 94 as Grandpa would have hunted whitetails with; its conditions rate fair at 75% to 70%.

The listings in the *GTG* are arranged within each manufacturer's entry, first by model numbers in consecutive order followed by model names in alphabetical order. At first glance, you see that there are two model designations that may apply: the original designation (Model 1894) or the revised, shorter designation (Model 94). Which of these designations applies to your recently acquired Winchester?

The next step in the process is to try to match the appearance of your model with an illustration in the book. The photos may all look alike at first glance, but close evaluation and careful attention to detail will enable you to eliminate models that are not applicable. Further examination of your gun might reveal a curved or crescent-shaped butt plate. By careful observation of your gun's characteristics and close visual comparison of the photographic examples, you may logically conclude that your gun is the Winchester Model 94 Lever-Action Rifle. (Please note that the guns shown in the *GTG* are not always shown in proportion to one another; that is, a carbine barrel might not appear to be shorter than a rifle barrel.)

Here a pre-'64 Winchester Model 94 (left) is compared to a newer Winchester Model 94 Short Rifle (right) made in 2011. Note the differences in ejection port, hammer, thumb safety (the pre-'64 has no thumb safety), and finish.

You have now tentatively determined your model, but to be sure, you should read through the specifications for that model and establish that the barrel on the pictured rifle is twenty-six inches long and round, octagonal, or half-octagonal.

The pre-'64 Winchester Model 94 (top) has a barrel band at the muzzle and sports a front sight with removable hood (the hood is long gone from this specimen); the newer Short Rifle (bottom) has a retro-looking marbles front sight with a brass bead.

Upon measuring, you find that the barrel on your rifle

is approximately twenty-six inches, perhaps a trifle under, and it is round. Additionally, your rifle is marked .38-55. The caliber offerings listed in the specifications include .38-55, so you are further convinced that this is your gun. You may read on to determine that this rifle was manufactured from 1894 to 1937. After that date, only the shorter-barreled carbine was offered by Winchester, and then only in .25-35, .30-30, and .32 Special.

The older Winchester Model 94 (top) has a band at the end of the forearm, while the newer Winchester Model 94 (bottom) has a forearm cap.

At this point, you know you have a Winchester Model 94 rifle manufactured before World War II. You read the value and take the rifle to your dealer to initiate a sale.

Here is a look at some of the trades or deals you may encounter for Grandpa's deer rifle:

DEAL 1
If the rifle is truly in excellent condition—that is, if it retains at least 95 percent of its original finish on both the metal and wood and has a perfect bore—then the gun does, in fact, have a collectible value as noted. However, keep in mind that the dealer is in business to make a profit. If

he pays you the full value of the gun, he will have to charge more than this when he sells it to make a reasonable profit. If more than the fair market value is charged, the gun will not sell or someone will pay more than the gun it is actually worth.

Therefore, expect a reputable dealer to offer you less than the published maximum value for the gun in its present condition. The exact amount will vary for a variety of reasons. For example, if the dealer already has a dozen or so of the same model on his shelf and they do not sell well, his offer will be considerably lower. On the other hand, if the dealer does not have any of this model in stock and knows several collectors who want it, chances are his offer will be considerably higher.

DEAL 2
Perhaps you overestimated the true state of the rifle's condition. Suppose the gun's finish is flawed and not much of the original bluing remains. There are several shiny, bare metal spots mixed with a brown patina over the remaining metal. Also, much of the original varnish on the wood has been worn off from extended use. Consequently, the rifle is not considered to be in excellent condition and is worth proportionately less than the value shown in this book.

DEAL 3
Your Winchester Model 94 rifle looks nearly new, as if it were just out of the box,

and the rifle works perfectly. Therefore, you are convinced that the dealer should pay you the full value of the gun—less a reasonable profit of 25 to 35 percent. When the dealer offers you about half what you expect, you are shocked!

Although the rifle looks new to you, the experienced dealer has detected that the gun (or parts of it) has been refinished. Perhaps you did not notice the rounding of the formerly sharp edges on the receiver or the slight funneling of some screw holes—all dead giveaways that the rifle has been refinished. If so, your rifle is not in excellent condition as you originally assumed and is therefore worth less than high book value.

A knowledgeable gun dealer will check each firearm to determine that it functions properly, and the condition of interior parts may also be a factor in determining the value of any firearm. Even when a collectible firearm has been expertly refinished to excellent condition, it is no longer original, and a rule of thumb is to deduct 50 percent from the value listed in this book. If the job is poorly done, deduct 80 percent or more.

Now, if you are somewhat of an expert and know for certain that your rifle has never been refinished or otherwise repaired or damaged it has at least 95 percent of its original finish left, and you believe you have a firearm that is truly worth full book value, understand that a dealer will still only offer you from 25 to 50 percent less for it due to profit margins, over-stocked goods, and so forth.

TOP-DOLLAR OPTIONS

One alternative for getting top dollar for your gun is to advertise your item in a local newspaper or go online and list it with one of several online gun auction websites, and sell the firearm directly to a private collector. Many collectors have a special interest in certain models, manufacturers, or product lines and will happily pay full price and sometimes more for a hard-to-find piece. However, these approaches may prove time-consuming, frustrating, and expensive. Online auction websites charge fees, and you have to package and ship the firearm to your buyer's FFL dealer. In addition, there may be federal and local restrictions on the sale of firearms in your area, so be sure to check with the local police chief or sheriff before you proceed with a private sale.

If you experience such complications, chances are the next time you have a firearm to sell, you will be more than happy to take it to a dealer and let them take their fair share of profit!

STANDARDS OF CONDITION

The condition of a firearm is an important factor in determining its value. In some rare and unusual models, a variation in condition from excellent to very good can mean a value difference of 50 percent or more in some models. Therefore, you must be able to determine the gun's condition before you can accurately evaluate the value of the firearm.

Several sets of value standards have been used in gun trading, but the National Rifle Association Standards of Condition of Modern Firearms are probably the most popular. In recent years, condition has been established by the percentage of original finish remaining on the wood and metal of the firearm.

Here's a look at how these standards are applied:

EXCELLENT

For the purpose of assigning comparative values as a basis for trading, firearms listed in this book are assumed to be in excellent condition if they have 95 percent or more remaining original finish, no noticeable marring of wood or metal, and the bore has no pits or rust.

To the novice, this translates to meaning a practically new gun, almost as though it had just been removed from its shipping box. The trained eye, however, will see the difference between new or mint condition and merely excellent.

VERY GOOD

Any other defects, no matter how minor, diminish the value of a firearm below those listed in this book. For example, if more than 5 percent of the original finish is gone and there are minor surface dents or scratches, regardless of how small, the gun is no longer in excellent condition. Instead, it is considered to be in very good condition, provided the gun is in perfect working order. Despite the minor defects, the gun will still look relatively new to the untrained buyer.

GOOD

If the gun is in perfect working condition and functions properly but has minor wear on working surfaces (perhaps some deep scratches on the wood or metal), the gun is considered to be in good condition, one grade below very good according to NRA standards. Again, the price shown in this book for that particular firearm must be reduced to reflect its true value.

The two remaining NRA conditions fall under the headings of fair and poor. These guns normally have little value unless they are of historical importance or an aficionado simply must have them to complete his collection. The value of such guns is then determined by the price the buyer is willing to pay.

In any case, do not sell any gun until you have researched its history and value. Many plain-looking guns have sold for thousands of dollars for a variety of reasons. Many an innocent widow has given away her deceased husband's guns without knowing that were of extremely high value. Avoid buyers who are in a hurry to make a purchase or who quickly offer what seems to be more money than the gun is worth. Not every gun is priceless, but many of them are nearly so!

Previous editions of *GTG* offered multiplication factors to use for firearms in other than excellent condition. These factors are listed below. Be aware that the figures given are not etched in stone. Instead, they are simply another rough means of establishing the value of a particular firearm.

For guns in other than excellent condition, multiply the price shown in this book for the model in question by the following factors:

Multiplication Factors for Guns Not in Excellent Condition:

Condition	X	Factor
Mint or New (NIB)		1.25
Excellent (Ex)		1.00
Very Good (VG)		.85
Good (Gd)		.68
Fair		.45
Poor		.15

UNIQUE SERIAL NUMBERS

The serial number on a firearm can increase the value if it is unique, and consecutive serial numbers can boost value to a set of firearms.

Here is a brace of Glock 36 .45 ACP pistols with consecutive serial numbers 044 and 045.
(Courtesy Stanley Ruselowski, Jr. collection.)

PROVENANCE

Provenance means place or source of origin. In gun trading, it means who owned the gun and to a certain extent, when or where the gun was used. Beware of Jesse James six-shooters or else I may want to sell you the Brooklyn Bridge. Make sure the gun has documentation stating prior ownership. It can mean the difference between a really valuable firearm or a really expensive fake.

The unique serial number of this 1911 makes this Wilson Combat CQB more valuable.

Bill Wilson displays his Wilson Combat CQB.

PARTING THOUGHTS

Remember, the word "guide" in *Gun Trader's Guide* should be taken literally. This book is meant to be a reference only and is not the gospel of the collectible trade. We sincerely hope, however, that you find this publication useful when you decide to buy or sell a used collectible modern firearm. Study all available references, manufacturers' histories, visit state and regional auction houses and dealers, and go online to develop an accurate assessment of your firearm's true value before you sell it.

Also, keep in mind that gun values vary from region to region. For example, lever-action deer rifles are more popular among collectors and hunters in the east, while bolt-action bean field rifles bring higher prices in the south and west. For this reason, we recommend that you attend regional gun shows, auctions, and look online to develop a better understanding of local gun values and pricing. And, whenever you travel, check the prices of guns you're familiar with to compare their values in other parts of the country. The difference can be surprising!

Finally, beware of guns that have been refinished or refurbished by amateurs or even expert gunsmiths. A century-old gun that looks brand new has probably been refinished and will actually be worth far less than a time-worn original. Every new screw, pin, or spring added to an original firearm diminishes its value—the worn, pitted original parts of a firearm enhance its value far more than modern replacements. Refinishing a gun may improve its looks and satisfy the final owner, but it will lose collectible value that will never be recovered.

Colt Model 1911
Semi-Automatic Pistol

Adopted by the U.S. Ordnance Department in 1911, the Colt semi-automatic pistol was originally manufactured by Colt and the government's Springfield Armory. In 1917, with the US entry into World War I, the government contracted with Colt for one million pistols and contracts were signed for the production of a total of two million more pistols with Remington-UMC, North American Arms, Savage, Winchester, National Cash Register Co., Burroughs Adding Machine, Lamston Monotype, and Caron Bros. A total of 629,000 pistols were completed by the war's end in1918. Production was resumed in 1924 with a series of design modifications introduced during the inter-war period resulting in the Model 1911 A1. From the onset of World War II until its end in 1945 Colt, Remington UMC, Remington-Rand, Ithaca, Singer, and Union Switch and Signal Company manufactured nearly 2 million M1911A1s.

NRA Perfect Condition is 100 percent original condition. This Colt 1911 has all original parts and commands the same price with or without the box. The frame and receiver are in perfect condition with no wear or damage. The checkering on the grip is in "as new" condition and the wood shows no wear, scratches, or stains.

NRA Good Condition ranges from 60 to 80 percent original condition. There are no replacement parts. This 1911 has worn, rounded edges on the frame with slight pitting and scratches. The bluing is thinning on the working surfaces and stampings show minor wear in areas. The checkering on the grips is slightly rounded with minor nicks. The wood is in good condition, not cracked or stained. A good condition pistol must be in safe working condition.

NRA Fair Condition ranges from 20 to 60 percent original condition. This Model 1911 is in well-worn condition with the frame retaining only 40 percent of its original finish. Some major and minor parts have been replaced and scratches and pitting from rust and corrosion are evident on the frame and slide. Serial numbers and other markings are shallow and difficult to identify. While the grips on this pistol are not badly scratched or soiled, they show worn checkering and several large and small dents. The gun must function and shoot properly.

Winchester Model 94

Winchester produced approximately 2,550,000 Model 94 lever action rifles between 1894 and 1962. The Model 94 was manufactured in both rifle and carbine versions with several configurations that included pistol- and straight-grip stocks, various grades of wood, and several different barrel lengths and magazine capacities. Crescent and shotgun style buttstocks and takedown barrels were also offered. The Model 94 was produced in 25-35, 30, 30-30, 32-40 and 38-55 calibers.

NRA Perfect Condition ranges from 95 to 100 percent original condition. This Model 94 shows very little use and looks in new condition with 96 percent of its original finish remaining. All parts are original and in excellent condition. There is no noticeable wear with the wood and metal showing no stains, scratches or nicks. The bluing is in near-perfect condition. The action functions smoothly and the rifle is in perfect working condition.

NRA Good Condition ranges from 60 to 80 percent original condition. There are no replacement parts. The gun has all original parts and shows no corrosive rusting or pitting. The edges of the action are slightly rounded and the bluing is beginning to wear thin on the working surfaces. The stampings show minor wear in areas. There are no broken parts and the stock fits smoothly to the metal with only minor nicking. The gun must be in safe working condition.

NRA Fair Condition ranges from 20 to 60 percent original condition. This Model 94 is in well-worn condition with some minor parts replaced or requiring restoration or adjustment. The serial numbers and descriptive stampings are shallow and hard to read. The wood is badly scratched and dented with evident repairs. There is corrosive pitting and scratches but the gun remains in safe firing condition.

Winchester Model 12

When introduced in 1912, the hammerless Model 12 slide-action shotgun was offered only in 20-gauge with a 2½-inch chamber. In 1914 12- and 16-gauge versions were introduced followed by a 28-gauge in 1937. The Model 12 was available with various chokes and with walnut, straight or pistol grip stock and forearm. Winchester sold more than 1,900,000 Model 1912s during the shotgun's 51-year history.

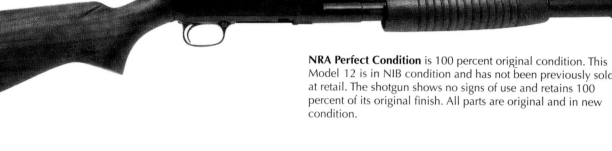

NRA Perfect Condition is 100 percent original condition. This Model 12 is in NIB condition and has not been previously sold at retail. The shotgun shows no signs of use and retains 100 percent of its original finish. All parts are original and in new condition.

NRA Good Condition ranges from 60 to 80 percent original condition. This gun has all original parts in good condition. There is no corrosive pitting or rusting and the action displays only slightly rounded edges. The gun retains 70 percent of its original finish with bluing beginning to wear on the working surfaces. The stock fits smoothly to the metal and has only minor nicking. The shotgun must be in good working order.

NRA Fair Condition ranges from 20 to 60 percent original condition. Showing a well-worn condition, this gun may require minor parts to be replaced or adjusted. The serial numbers and descriptive stamping are shallow and difficult to read. The wood is badly scratched and dented with evident repairs. Corrosive pitting and scratches in the metal, while considerable, do not render the gun unsafe.

The Art of Gun Trading

No matter if you are trading bottle caps, marbles, or fine firearms, there is an art and a science to the process that beginners often fail to realize and seasoned experts rely on. In other words, if you do not know what you are doing, you can expect to be burned—badly, in some cases.

Trading in guns is as unique and specialized as any other item of interest from stamps to furniture and pottery to weather vanes. Most trades or sales are simple and direct when both parties are aware of the facts and knowledgeable about the gun type. Some sales are unusual because they involve rare pieces, high prices, or individuals (often agents representing absentee buyers) who know what they want and are prepared to pay any price for it. This is great if you are selling what they are buying, but not so great if you want to buy what they have.

GUN TRADING BASICS

As is the case when selling any collectible item, there is no substitute for research.

The first step in shrewd gun trading is to know your firearm, its condition, and its value in your market—meaning your part of the country. A Marlin .30/30 lever-action rifle, for example, will not carry as high a value in California, Georgia, or Texas as it will in Pennsylvania, Maine,

New York, or elsewhere in the east, where short-range brush-country guns are most popular.

Next, study the NRA Standards of Condition (see pages X thru XII) and get a feel for such terms as New In Box, Excellent, and Good and what they mean to a collector. Condition is only partially relevant, of course, because an ardent collector who wants or needs a specific gun model to complete his or her collection—because complete collections are worth more than partial collections—will pay the extra dollar to fill that vacant space on the wall or in the gun safe.

DICKERING DOS AND DON'TS

When it comes to "horse trading" there are no rules, but the conflict is always the same: Each party wants to come out a winner. Armed (pun intended) with your knowledge of your firearm, its condition, and its value, the only thing left to do is convince your buyer that the item is worth the price you are asking. This is where the fun begins.

Below are a few tips for the new gun trader to consider.

DON'T SAY TOO MUCH

It's great to be enthusiastic, but don't spill all your beans at once. Present the gun to the prospective buyer and let him or her make all the comments and ask

all the questions. Be sure, however, that you can explain away the tarnish, the pitted metal, the worn bluing, and so forth, and be sure that you can counter questions about replaced, repaired, cracked, worn, or broken parts.

DECIDE ON A PRICE

This is complicated territory and often requires a little of the poker player's panache. If you name a price and the buyer pounces on it, you may have undersold yourself. Set the price too high and he or she will start to bargain with you or just walk away because it's more than he or she wants to pay.

The right price will keep a buyer interested, which is why knowing your gun and its value is important. Two knowledgeable gun buffs can strike a deal and walk away feeling satisfied with the transaction, and that's as good as it gets in the collectible gun trade.

DON'T LIE OR EMBELLISH

Gun collectors generally know their guns as well as anyone and are quick to spot a fraud. If your gun is not in its original condition, has been refurbished, or is not what it appears to be, be honest and say so. If you don't know the answer to an important question, take the time to find out. Remember that there is no rush in selling any collectible item. A week or two will not matter to a buyer who truly wants the item you are trying to sell. However, attempting to sell a knowledgeable buyer a junker will not work and will only tarnish your reputation. Word gets out among those who buy and sell guns, and one mistake—intended or not—can taint your business dealings for years to come.

KNOW WHEN TO QUIT

All collectible guns have their value, and all collectors have instincts. Trust your instincts when a buyer seems overeager to buy your gun, tells you its value is much less than you know it is worth, or tries to tell you the gun is illegal, a fake, or otherwise not what you say it is. Remember, any sale may be postponed until the details are cleaned up. If you feel that you are being tricked—while either buying or selling—back away, do more research, and come back next time armed with new knowledge and a different offer.

LEARN AS YOU GO

If you spend time buying and selling guns, or any collectible for that matter, you are going to make some great sales and unfortunately, you are also going to be beaten in price by a buyer or dealer who has been in the game longer than you have. Generally, the best advice is to never sell a gun for less than you paid for it. Good research will keep you from selling a $10,000 gun for $100—it happens!—or from paying thousands more than a gun is worth, which also happens. No gun catalog on the market today contains the top current value of every firearm ever made, so study as many sources as possible (beginning with old manufacturer's catalogs) so you can be at least as well versed in your negotiations as your counterpart.

If you have reservations, questions, or uncertainties, postpone the transaction until you can find out more details about that particular firearm. If necessary, take the time to contact the gun's manufacturer or a certified archivist. The NRA is a great place to start.

There is no absolute value for any firearm because it's impossible to gauge what a rabid, avid collector will pay for a piece he or she desperately wants or needs. However, the general, standard market value of any gun may be calculated if you take advantage of all of the tools available to you, including the *GTG*, which offers market prices based on national averages.

The ultimate value of a firearm depends on the rarity of the model, the region, and the buyer's needs; rare, unusual, or one-of-a-kind guns can be worth substantially more than the standard model. It's in your best interest to find out what kind of gun you have and what it is worth before you offer it for sale.

Gun Shows

The majority of private non-commercial firearms transactions in the United States take place in living rooms and garages—spur-of-the-moment deals that involve a seller who needs cash and a buyer who wants to acquire a particular firearm. The seller simply wants as much money as he or she can get for the piece and the buyer just wants a good deal for a firearm to resell at a profit. In most such one-time purchases, both parties go away happy with the outcome. But before one enters the world of serious firearms collecting, it's important to do some homework.

Start by attending organized gun shows. This is where gun lovers converge on hundreds of booths containing thousands of firearms ranging in value from less than $10 to $100,000 or more. Learn the differences between them, study the trends, and increase your knowledge of the firearms and values that interest you the most.

GO TO THE SHOW!

The best classroom for learning about the value and condition of used firearms is the weekend gun show. Dealers from throughout the region and often across the country will be on hand to show, sell, buy, trade, and talk about new and used guns of every make and model. Some dealers specialize in firearms made by a specific manufacturer (Beretta, Benelli, Winchester, Remington, Savage, Ruger, Stevens, etc.), while some deal in just one model of firearm (pre-'64 Winchester Model 70s, for example). Others may offer custom guns or firearms made by European or Asian manufacturers, while others offer a variety of collectibles including swords, knives, and ancient weaponry.

Gun buyers, collectors, and dealers benefit from attending gun shows because it is a chance to see a wide variety of firearms, their condition, and their value at the local level. This is the place to really learn about guns and how their value is determined. Most dealers will gladly explain the nuances of gun condition, why perfectly refurbished guns are worth so much less than a rusted, beat-up original, and what makes one gun worth so much while another seemingly similar model is worth so much less.

GUN SHOW ETIQUETTE

Unless otherwise noted, all gun shows in the United States are open to the public. Ticket prices are reasonable and food and beverages are usually available. Of course, there are security requirements that must be met and procedures that must be followed. In general, anyone attending a gun show may bring guns for appraisal, sale, or trade. Laws vary from state to state, so be sure to check with show promoters or local law enforcement personnel before bringing a gun to any show!

Most guns shows are well attended, often crowded, and sales can be brisk. Be patient while moving between booths. If a particular dealer or booth is overrun with customers, come back later to talk. There are always slow periods at gun shows, such as early in the day, around lunchtime, and just before closing, so schedule your visits to dealers and make the most of the time you have available.

In general, do not bring a gun to a commercial show and expect to get top dollar for it. Show dealers often work in volume sales and may have a dozen or more of your model on the table. This is especially true of the cheaper imports, WWII Japanese and Italian rifles, and other by-the-barrel items.

Specialty guns, of course, will draw any dealer's attention, and once in a while you will get far more than you expected from a particular firearm. However, it is best to bring your gun in for appraisal only. See what the dealer is willing to give you for it and compare that to the prices listed in the *GTG* and other collectible gun books. If he or she is offering you a much higher price than you expected, tell him you'll think about it and then conduct some more research because you may have a unique model with a higher value.

In most cases, there will be too much confusion, conversation, and diversion at gun show booths to allow you to make a serious sale or trade. If you are feeling rushed or pressured, move on to another dealer or ask for his or her card and plan to make a one-on-one visit later in the week or month. Most gun dealers follow the gun show circuit and may be found again in a week or two at another location or at their shop or home, so don't be rushed into a sale. Work the shows, study the guns and prices, and make your best deal when you are ready to commit to a final transaction.

WORK THE CROWD

While huge crowds at gun shows can be a hindrance when you are trying to buy or sell a gun, you can use the crowd to your advantage by carrying your locked and tagged for sale gun with you as you move around the arena. There will be a wide variety of gun buyers, dealers, and fans in the crowd who may stop you and want to discuss your firearm. A buyer who needs a particular piece to complete

his collection could easily offer you more than the gun is listed for, more than the dealer offered, and more than you ever expected to get for it.

Remember, everyone attending a gun show is in the market to trade, buy, or sell. Even if you do not make a sale while you are there, you can make valuable contacts that may come in handy for future transactions. For example, you may encounter a dealer who trades only in vintage Savage rifles, and on your next trip to the family farm you find that your grandfather left his trusty Model 99 in .303 Savage in an upstairs closet. Or you may find a pre-'64 Winchester Model 70 Super Grade in a corner of your uncle's attic. Having met the right people at the local gun show, you can buy, sell, or trade your new collectibles quickly and profitably because you took the time to find the right people.

Commercial gun shows are ongoing events that occur weekly, monthly, or annually in various towns and cities around the country. Some shows are sponsored by the same organizations in the same location each time, so it is easy to keep track of them.

It is possible to attend a different gun show every weekend somewhere in the United States. For a complete, updated list of gun shows near you, go to gunshows-usa.com. This useful website includes a listing of all the gun shows presently scheduled in every state and the list is updated weekly.

Be sure to call ahead to verify show times, dates, ticket fees, and regulations, including tips on identification requirements, security procedures, and how to prepare firearms for trade, sale, or appraisal.

Online Buying and Selling

There is not a facet of our lives that isn't touched by technology. I am old enough to have seen telephone communications hardware evolve from rotary dial phones to smart phones that not only allow me to make a simple phone call but just about everything else—pay bills, watch videos, map driving directions—even trade guns. Time was you visited a gun shop, looked through the glass cases and racks, and you might be lucky to find that firearm you always wanted or desired. You were limited to the selection your dealer had on hand or what they were able to order from their distributor. Today, auction websites such as gunbroker.com, gunsamerica.com, and others, as well as online dealers such as impactguns.com and galleryofguns.com offer gun buyers a vast selection of firearms to choose from. You can buy and sell guns using your computer.

Buyers can easily search for that one rare gun to complete their collection or look for a new rifle for next deer season. The internet allows buyers to search for new and used firearms, as well as curios and relics, surplus guns, gun parts, ammunition, reloading equipment, and just about anything firearm related.

The online auction websites enable sellers to reach buyers they might not have normally reached. A small one-room gun store in Maine can now sell to buyers across the country, let alone the next town over. If you are a private individual with a gun to sell, all you need to do is create an account, type in a description, take a few digital pictures of the item, and list it. It's that simple and that easy.

All the same federal, state, and local gun laws apply when selling and purchasing a gun online as when purchasing a gun at a brick-and-mortar retailer. In fact, the transfer of the firearm is the same. When a buyer purchases a firearm on say gunsamerica.com, the buyer must provide the seller with a copy of their gun shop's FFL (Federal Firearms License) or arrange to have the seller ship the firearm to one of the FFL located near the buyer that is listed on the website. The seller then ships the gun to the gun shop with the FFL holder—not directly to the buyer—and the buyer then fills out the necessary state and local paperwork to take transfer of the gun. Gun shops usually charge the buyer a fee to transfer the gun, typically $45 to $65. It is up to the buyer to be aware of state and local laws. For example, a buyer in Connecticut cannot take ownership of a Bushmaster AR-15 M4-style carbine that is offered by a seller in Georgia or Texas. The gun laws in Connecticut forbid sales of any assault-style rifles. Know your local and state laws before buying. If you bid on it and win, you own.

Online gun auctions are big business. Gunbroker.com celebrated their 15th anniversary in March of 2014. It is among the top 400 US websites, and in January of 2014 recorded nearly $3 billion in cumulative merchandise sales. On any given day, Gunbroker.com has 650,000 active listings allowing both sellers and buyers 24/7 access. Monthly visitor traffic averages about 5.5 million and 80 percent of the website traffic is repeat visitors. They also have a mobile app for iPhone and Android devices so you can watch your auctions or bid on others.

Auction sites charge a fee, a small percentage of the sale, to all sellers. The fee is only charged if the seller actually sells the gun through an auction. There is no charge to list a firearm. When setting up an account with online auction websites, a seller needs to provide a credit card. Once an auction closes with a sale, the fee is automatically charged to the seller's credit card.

Online gun dealers, such as galleryofguns.com, are not auction sites, but they allow users to purchase guns that are then shipped to an FFL-holding retailer in or near the buyer's zip code.

Finding a specific firearm is easy for buyers because of search functionality built into auction websites. Once a user has an account, they can click off search criteria to zero in on a specific manufacturer, model, caliber, barrel length, magazine capacity, and other criteria. The user then has the ability to save the search and have e-mail alerts sent to their e-mail inbox with search results. For example, if you are looking for Winchester Model 70, you can input the following search information: Winchester > Model 70 > pre-'64 > .270 Winchester. Your search results will then include a list of rifles from across the country by gun retailers that fit your search criteria.

Many online auctions also offer services for after the sale with shipping profiles, FFL look up, and others tools to smoothly complete the transaction.

Most sellers and buyers online strive to ensure all parties are satisfied with the transaction. Like any aspect in a buying and selling situation, there are some who will try to take advantage. Do your due diligence and contact the seller prior to making a bid, get as much information as you can about the item, and finally look at the seller's rating. Most sellers do their best to keep their rating high, and most will be willing to go the distance to satisfy a customer. The auction websites have a system in place to deal with buyer and seller protection. Like in anything, the old dictum "buyer beware" applies. If the deal seems too good to be true, then it probably is.

I have used online gun auctions to bid on and purchase firearms I would never had seen at my local gun dealer. With online auctions, there is an excitement about bidding against other buyers—remember your budget, and remember what the firearm is worth. You do not want to get caught up in a bidding war and overpay for the item. On the other hand, you may be inclined to pay slightly more for an item that is less popular in your geographic area or for an item that is no longer manufactured. Technology has opened up gun trading 24/7/365.

TYPES OF ONLINE AUCTIONS

Basic: In a basic auction, the seller's starting price is the amount the seller is willing to take for the item.

Dutch: In a Dutch Auction, a seller is auctioning two or more identical items, and a buyer bids on the per-item cost for a total of however many items the seller is auctioning. If you bid $1 and there are ten items, the total price is $10.

Absolute or Penny: An Absolute or Penny Auction starts out at $.01 with no reserve with the item selling for the last bid after the auction closes.

Reserve: In a Reserve Auction, a seller has a minimum reserve price set for the item. This amount is hidden.

ONLINE AUCTION GLOSSARY

10- or 15-minute Rule: After the last bid activity and when an auction is ready to close, there is a time interval of 10 to 15 minutes, depending on the website, that must pass to allow any last bids to be entered. Think of it as the "going, going, gone" statement made by an auctioneer. If a bid is entered during the last 10 or 15 minutes, the 10- or 15-minute interval resets. Only when the entire 10 or 15 minutes has passed is the auction considered closed.

Auto Bid or Proxy Bid: A buyer bids the maximum amount they are willing to pay for an item, and Auto Bid automatically enters the least amount to win and continues to automatically bid to the specified maximum. For example, buyer one sets up an Auto Bid for $500, yet the current bid on the item is $450. Buyer two bids $475, and buyer one's Auto Bid bids according to the bid increment of the auction and the maximum amount specified buyer one. Once Auto Bid hits the maximum amount, it stops bidding.

Bid: Amount a buyer is willing to pay for an item.

Bid History: Shows the bids of buyers, time, and date of bid. During a live auction, the bid amounts are hidden, but after the auction closes bid amounts per shown.

Bid Increment: Amount the bid is increased by as specified by the seller.

BuyNow: Displayed price the seller is willing to accept to end the auction.

FFL: Federal Firearms License—a holder of an FFL is required to transfer a firearm from a seller to a buyer.

Feedback: Buyers and sellers can leave feedback on the auction transaction for public viewing. Typically both sellers and buyers are rated on a scale of how well the transaction went.

Fixed Price: An item that sells at a set price with no bidding.

Inspection Period: Some auction websites require the seller to give the buyer a set time limit, usually three days, to inspect the item. If the buyer declines the item, the buyer is entitled a full refund on the auction price. Return shipping of the item to the seller is paid for by the buyer.

Minimum Bid: Total amount of the current high bid plus the bid increment.

Reserve Price: Lowest price the seller is willing to accept; typically the reserve price is hidden.

Reserve Price Not Met/Reserve

Price Met: In a reserve auction, whether the reserve price is met is indicated on a item depending on if bidding has not or has met the price.

Starting Bid: Least amount a bidder is allowed to bid; this is set by the seller.

Watch List: A buyer can use a watch list to track items they are interested in and bid or not bid on the item. Items stay in a user's watch list until deleted by a user, even if the item's auction has closed.

ATF Notes

HIGH CAPACITY MAGAZINE MODELS

An amendment to the Gun Control Act of 1968 prohibited the manufacture, transfer, or possession of firearms intended for disposition to the general public designed to accept large capacity ammunition feeding devices. Manufacturers who produced such arms were required to redesign those models to limit their capacities to ten rounds or fe or discontinue production or importation. The law applied to all such devices manufactured after October 13, 1994. Postban feeding devices must meet the capacity limit requirements. However, the grandfather clause of this amendment exempts all such devices lawfully possessed at the time the legislation became law. Pre-ban arms (manufactured before October 13, 1994) may therefore be bought, sold, or traded with no additional restrictions imposed by this law, which was ultimately rescinded in 2004 under the sunset provision and is no longer in effect. Any student of firearms should study the provisions of the Gun Control Act of 1968 for more information on firearms ownership, sales, and transfers in the United States. For updates and current firearms regulations, contact the Bureau of Alcohol, Tobacco, Firearms, and Explosives at www.atf.gov.

For the purposes of this book, models previously designed to accept high capacity feeding devices will be listed at their original specifications and capacities if only the feeding device was modified to reduce that capacity.

Regarding shotguns, the reader should be aware that shotgun barrels must be eighteen inches or longer except when used by military or law enforcement personnel. A special permit from the Bureau of Alcohol, Tobacco, Firearms, and Explosives is required to possess shotguns with barrel lengths that are shorter than eighteen inches.

Because state and federal laws vary and may change annually, it is in the collector's best interest to inquire about the legality of ownership, concealment, or display of specific firearms in his or her state, town, or county. Firearms restrictions are not universal and ignorance of the law is not a legal defense. Protect yourself by knowing which guns you may own, purchase, and transport under the laws of your state.

CURIOS AND RELICS

Curios and relics (C&R) represent a segment of gun trading and collecting. Firearms designated as a C&R have slightly different classifications than newly manufactured firearms. Collectors often apply for a C&R license, which allows them to collect certain firearms. The ATF website (atf.gov) has a complete list of firearms that are classified as C&R firearms. According to the ATF website: "Firearm curios or relics include firearms which have special value to collectors because they possess some qualities not ordinarily associated with firearms intended for sporting use or as offensive or defensive weapons. To be recognized as curios or relics, firearms must fall within one of the following categories:

1. Have been manufactured at least 50 years prior to the current date, but not including replicas thereof; or

2. Be certified by the curator of a municipal, State, or Federal museum which exhibits firearms to be curios or relics of museum interest; or

3. Derive a substantial part of their monetary value from the fact that they are novel, rare, bizarre, or from the fact of their association with some historical figure, period, or event.

The definition for C&R firearms found in 27 CFR § 478.11 does not specifically state that a firearm must be in its original condition to be classified as a C&R firearm. However, ATF Ruling 85-10, which discusses the importation of military C&R firearms, notes that they must be in original configuration and adds that a receiver is not a C&R item. Combining this ruling and the definition of C&R firearms, the Firearms Technology Branch

(FTB) has concluded that a firearm must be in its original condition to be considered a C&R weapon.

"It is also the opinion of FTB, however, that a minor change such as the addition of scope mounts, non-original sights, or sling swivels would not remove a firearm from its original condition. Moreover, we have determined that replacing particular firearms parts with new parts that are made to the original design would also be acceptable—for example, replacing a cracked M1 Grand stock with a new wooden stock of the same design, but replacing the original firearm stock with a plastic stock would change its classification as a C&R item."

Firearms automatically attain C&R status when they are fifty years old. Below is a list of firearms classified as C&R but still subject to provisions of the Gun Control Act of 1968. For a complete list and more information, go to atf.gov.

- Johnson, Model 1941 semiautomatic rifles, .30 caliber, all serial numbers, with the collective markings, "CAL .30–06 SEMI-AUTO, JOHNSON AUTOMATICS, MODEL 1941, MADE IN PROVIDENCE. R.I., U.S.A., and Cranston Arms Co." —the latter enclosed in a triangle on the receiver

- Polish, Model P64 pistols, 9 x 18mm Makarov caliber, all serial numbers

- Springfield Armory, M1 Garand semiautomatic rifle, .30 caliber, S/N 2502800

- Walther, Model P38 semiautomatic pistols, bearing the Norwegian Army Ordnance crest on the slide, 9mm Luger caliber, S/N range 369001-370000

- Colt, New Service Revolver, .44-40 caliber, serial number 325333, with factory-fitted, smooth-bored barrel

- Marlin, Model 1894, caliber .44-40, "Policias Fiscales Chile," S/N 383384, with 15-inch barrel

- Marlin, Model 1894, caliber .44-40, "Policias Fiscales Chile," S/N 386503, with 15-inch barrel

- Marlin, Model 1894, caliber .32-20, S/N 417837, with 15-inch barrel

- Winchester, Model 1892, caliber .44WCF, S/N 597676, with 15-inch barrel

- Winchester, Model 1892, caliber .44WCF, S/N 691600, with 14-inch barrel

State Gun Purchasing Permit Requirements

Gun laws are subject to change. This information is to be used a guide.
Always consult your state and local authorities for details on all gun laws in your state and local area.

Permit Required for purchase:

STATE	Long Guns (Rifles and Shotguns)	Handguns	Notes:
Alabama	No	No	
Alaska	No	No	
Arizona	No	No	
Arkansas	No	No	
California	No	No	A valid California Driver's License or California Identification Card and purchaser's right thumbprint required.
Colorado	No	No	
Connecticut	Yes	Yes	Long guns require a valid long gun eligibility certificate, a valid permit to carry a handgun, a valid eligibility certificate for a handgun, or a valid permit to sell a handgun at retail. Handguns require a permit to carry a handgun, a handgun eligibility certificate, or a permit to sell handguns.
Delaware	No	No	
District of Columbia	No	No	
Florida	No	No	
Georgia	No	No	Handguns require a photo ID.
Hawaii	Yes	Yes	Long guns and handguns require a local police chief to issue a permit prior to taking ownership of firearm.
Idaho	No	No	
Illinois	Yes	Yes	Long guns and handguns require FOID (Federal Owner's Identification Card).
Indiana	No	No	
Iowa	No	Yes	Handguns require a permit to purchase a handgun.
Kansas	No	No	
Kentucky	No	No	
Louisiana	No	No	
Maine	No	No	
Maryland	No	No	

Massachusetts	Yes	Yes	Long guns require a valid FID (Firearms Identification); Class A carry license is required for a large capacity firearm (rifle, shotgun, or handgun); Class B carry license required for a non-large capacity firearm (rifle, shotgun, or handgun).
Michigan	No	Yes	Handguns require a license to purchase issued by a local chief of police or county sheriff.
Minnesota	No	Yes	Handguns and semiautomatic military-style assault weapons require a handgun transferee permit, carry permit, or a transfer report after a seven day waiting period.
Mississippi	No	No	
Missouri	No	No	
Montana	No	No	
Nebraska	No	Yes	Handguns require a certificate from local sheriff or police chief.
Nevada	No	No	
New Hampshire	No	No	
New Jersey	Yes	Yes	Long guns require a valid FID (Firearms Purchasers Identification Card). Handguns require a Permit to Purchase issued by state police or a local police chief for each handgun.
New Mexico	No	No	
New York	No	Yes	Handguns require a license to carry or posses. New York City requires a permit to purchase and possess for any firearm (rifle, shotgun, or handgun).
North Carolina	No	Yes	Handguns require a permit issued by a county sheriff.
North Dakota	No	No	
Ohio	No	No	
Oklahoma	No	No	
Oregon	No	No	
Pennsylvania	No	No	
Rhode Island	No	No	Long guns require a Purchase of a Shotgun or Rifle Application Form. Handguns require a hunter safety course card or pistol safety course card.
South Carolina	No	No	
South Dakota	No	No	
Tennessee	No	No	All firearms (rifle, shotgun, or handgun) require an ID.
Texas	No	No	
Utah	No	No	
Vermont	No	No	
Virginia	No	No	
Washington	No	No	
West Virginia	No	No	
Wisconsin	No	No	
Wyoming	No	No	

36th Edition
GUN TRADER'S GUIDE

Handguns

NOTE: *Abbreviations used throughout the Handgun section:*

ACP = Automatic Colt Pistol
Adj. = Adjustable
Avail. = Available
Bbl. = Barrel
c. = circa
DA = Double Action
Disc. = Discontinued

LC = Long Colt
LR = Long Rifle
Mag. = Magnum
Mfg. = Manufacture
NiB = New In Box
NM = National Match
Reintro. = Reintroduced

SA = Single Action
S/N = serial number
TH = Target Hammer
TT = Target Trigger
Win = Winchester
WMR = Winchester Magnum Rimfire

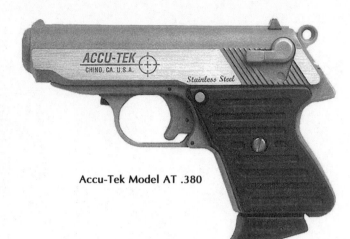

Accu-Tek Model AT .380

Accu-Tek Model BL-9

Accu-Tek HC-380SS

A.A. ARMS — Monroe, North Carolina

AP-9 SERIES
Semiautomatic recoil-operated pistol w/polymer integral grip/frame design. Fires from a closed bolt. Caliber: 9mm Parabellum. 10- or 20-round magazine, 3- , 5- or 11-inch bbl., 11.8 inches overall w/5-inch bbl., Weight: 3.5 lbs. Fixed blade, protected post front sight adjustable for elevation, winged square notched rear. Matte phosphate/blue or nickel finish. Checkered polymer grip/frame. Made from 1988-99.
AP9 model
(pre-94 w/ventilated bbl., shroudNiB $445 Ex $369 Gd $267
AP9 Mini model
(post-94 w/o bbl., shroud). . . . NiB $265 Ex $250 Gd $195
AP9 Target model
(pre-94 w/11-inch bbl.). . . . . . NiB $550 Ex $425 Gd $315
Nickel finish, add $40

ACCU-TEK — Ontario, California (accu-tekfirearms.com)

MODEL AT-9 AUTO PISTOL
Caliber: 9mm Para. 8-round magazine, Double action only. 3.2-inch bbl., 6.25 inches overall. Weight: 28 oz. Fixed blade front sight, adj. rear w/3-dot system. Firing pin block with no External safety. Stainless or black over stainless finish. Checkered black nylon grips. Announced 1992, but made from 1995-99.
Satin stainless model . . . . NiB $347 Ex $275 Gd $210
Matte black stainless. . . . . NiB $311 Ex $250 Gd $200

MODEL AT-25 AUTO PISTOL
Similar to Model AT380 except chambered .25 ACP w/7-round magazine, Made from 1992-96.
Lightweight w/aluminum frame NiB $164 Ex $135 Gd $115
Bright stainless (disc. 1991) . . NiB $164 Ex $135 Gd $115
Satin stainless model . . . . NiB $164 Ex $135 Gd $115
Matte black stainless. . . . . NiB $164 Ex $135 Gd $115

MODEL AT-32 AUTO PISTOL
Similar to Model AT-.380 except chambered .32 ACP. Made from 1990-2003.
Lightweight w/aluminum
Frame (disc. 1991) . . . . NiB $215 Ex $160 Gd $110
Satin stainless model . . . . NiB $215 Ex $160 Gd $110
Matte black stainless. . . . . NiB $225 Ex $170 Gd $120

MODEL AT-40 DA AUTO PISTOL
Caliber: .40 S&W. 7-round magazine, 3.2-inch bbl., 6.25 inches overall. Weight: 28 oz. Fixed blade front sight, adj. rear w/3-dot system. Firing pin block with no External safety. Stainless or black over stainless finish. Checkered black nylon grips. Announced 1992, but made from 1995-96.
Satin stainless model . . . . NiB $290 Ex $166 Gd $129
Matte black stainless. . . . . NiB $295 Ex $177 Gd $140

MODEL AT-380 AUTO PISTOL
Caliber: .380 ACP. Five-round magazine, 2.75-inch bbl., 5.6 inches overall. Weight: 20 oz. External hammer w/slide safety. Grooved black composition grips. Alloy or stainless frame w/steel slide. Black, satin aluminum or stainless finish. Made from 1992-2003.
Standard alloy frame (disc. 1992) NiB $291 Ex $165 Gd $145
AT-380II Satin stainless (Avail. 1990) NiB$291 Ex$165 Gd$145
Matte black stainless. . . . . NiB $279 Ex $188 Gd $129

MODELS BL-9, BL 380 . . . . . NiB $200 Ex $155 Gd $130
Ultra compact DAO semiautomatic pistols. Calibers: .380 ACP, 9mm Para. 5-round magazine, 3-inch bbl., 5.6 inches overall. Weight: 24 oz. Fixed sights. Carbon steel frame and slide w/black finish. Polymer grips. Made 1997 to 1999.

MODELS CP-9, CP-40, CP-45
Compact, double action only, semiautomatic pistols. Calibers: 9mm Parabellum, .40 S&W, .45 ACP, 8-, 7- or 6-round magazine, 3.2-inch bbl., 6.25 inches overall. Weight: 28 oz. Fixed blade front sight, adj. rear w/3-dot system. Firing-pin block with no External safety. Stainless or black over stainless finish. Checkered black nylon grips. Made1997-2002 (CP-9), 1999 (CP-40), 1996 (CP-45.
Black stainless model . . . . NiB $255 Ex $190 Gd $140
Satin stainless model . . . . NiB $255 Ex $190 Gd $140

MODEL HC-380 AUTO PISTOL. .NiB $280 Ex $235 Gd $220
Caliber: .380 ACP. 13-round magazine, 2.75-inch bbl., 6 inches overall. Weight: 28 oz. External hammer w/slide safety. Checkered black composition grips. Stainless finish. Made 1993 to 2003, Reintro. 2007..

Action Arms AT-84 with Prototype of Model AT-84P in background

ACTION ARMS—Philadelphia, Pennsylvania
See also listings under CZ pistols. Action Arms stopped importing firearms in 1994.

AT-84S DA AUTOMATIC PISTOL NiB $530 Ex $380 Gd $320
Caliber: 9mm Para. 15-round magazine, 4.75-inch bbl., 8 inches overall. Weight: 35 oz. Fixed front sight, drift-adj. rear. Checkered walnut grips. Blued finish. Made in Switzerland from 1988 to 1989.

AT-84P DA AUTO PISTOL . . . NiB $510 Ex $365 Gd $320
Compact version of the Model AT-84. Only a few prototypes were manufactured in 1985.

AT-88P DA AUTO PISTOL . . . NiB $530 Ex $479 Gd $377
Compact version of the AT-88S w/3.7-inch bbl. Only a few prototypes of this model were manufactured in 1985. Note: The AT-88 pistol series was later manufactured by Sphinx-Muller as the AT-2000 series.

AT-88S DA AUTOMATIC PISTOL NiB $550 Ex $479 Gd $377
Calibers: 9mm Para. or .41 Action Express, 10-round magazine, 4.6-inch bbl., 8.1 inches overall. Weight: 35.3 oz. Fixed blade front sight, adj. rear. Checkered walnut grips. Imported 1989 to 1991.

ADVANTAGE ARMS — St. Paul, Minnesota

MODEL 422 DERRINGER . . . . NiB $175 Ex $115 Gd $110
Hammerless, top-break, 4-bbl., derringer w/rotating firing pin. Calibers: .22 LR and .22 Mag., 4-round capacity, 2.5 inch bbl., 4.5 inches overall. Weight: 15 oz. Fixed sights. Walnut grips. Blued, nickel or PDQ matte black finish. Made from 1985 to 1987.

S. A. ALKARTASUNA FABRICA DE ARMAS — Guernica, Spain

"RUBY" AUTOMATIC PISTOL. NiB $355 Ex $283 Gd $225
Caliber: .32 Automatic (7.65mm), 9-round magazine, 3.63-inch bbl., 6.38 inches overall. Weight: About 34 oz. Fixed sights. Blued finish. Checkered wood or hard rubber grips. Made from 1917-22. Note: Mfd. by a number of Spanish firms, the Ruby was a secondary standard service pistol of the French Army in World Wars I and II. Specimens made by Alkartasuna bear the "Alkar" trademark.

AMERICAN ARMS — Kansas City, Missouri
Importer of Spanish and Italian shotguns, pistols, and rifles. Acquired by TriStar Sporting Arms, Ltd., in 2000.

BISLEY SA REVOLVER. . . . . . . NiB $490 Ex $400 Gd $315
Uberti reproduction of Colt's Bisley. Caliber: .45 LC, 6-round cylinder, 4.75-, 5.5- or 7.7-inch bbl., Case-hardened steel frame. Fixed blade front sight, grooved top strap rear. Hammer block safety. Imported from 1997 to 1998

CX-22 CLASSIC DA AUTOMATIC PISTOL
Similar to Model PX-.22 except w/8-round magazine, 3.33-inch bbl., 6.5 inches overall. Weight: 22 oz. Made from 1990 to 1995.
CX-22 Classic. . . . . NiB $200 Ex $145 Gd $125
CXC-22 w/chrome
Slide (disc. 1990) . . . . NiB $195 Ex $140 Gd $120

EP-380 DA AUTOMATIC PISTOL NiB $410 Ex $299 Gd $160
Caliber: .380 Automatic. 7-round magazine, 3.5-inch bbl., 6.5 inches overall. Weight: 25 oz. Fixed front sight, square notch adj. rear. Stainless finish. Checkered wood grips. Made 1989 to 1991.

ESCORT DA AUTO PISTOL . . NiB $315 Ex $225 Gd $155
Caliber: .380 ACP, 7-round magazine, 3.38-inch bbl., 6.13 inches overall. Weight: 19 oz. Fixed, low-profile sights. Stainless steel frame, slide, and trigger. Nickel-steel bbl., Soft polymer grips. Loaded chamber indicator. Made from 1995 to 1997.

MATEBA AUTO REVOLVER
Unique combination action design allows both slide and cylinder to recoil together causing cylinder to rotate. Single or double action. Caliber: .357 Mag, 6-round cylinder, 4- or 6-inch bbl., 8.77 inches overall w/4-inch bbl., Weight: 2.75 lbs. Steel/alloy frame. Ramped blade front sight, adjustable rear. Blue finish. Smooth walnut grips. Imported from 1997-99.
Mateba model (w/4-inch bbl.) NiB $1630 Ex $1130 Gd $775
Mateba model (w/6-inch bbl.) NiB $1695 Ex $1195 Gd $870

P-98 CLASSIC DA AUTOMATIC NiB $215 Ex $140 Gd $105
Caliber: .22 LR, 8-round magazine, 5-inch bbl., 8.25 inches overall. Weight: 25 oz. Fixed front sight, square notch adj. rear. Blued finish. Serrated black polymer grips. Made 1989 to 1996.

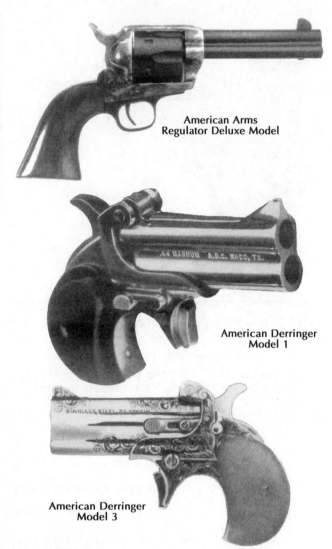

American Arms
Regulator Deluxe Model

American Derringer
Model 1

American Derringer
Model 3

PK-22 CLASSIC DA
AUTOMATIC PISTOL . . . . . . NiB $190 Ex $145 Gd $120
Caliber: .22 LR. 8-round magazine, 3.33-inch bbl., 6.33 inches overall. Weight: 22 oz. Fixed front sight, V-notch rear. Blued finish. Checkered black polymer grips. Made from 1989 t5o 1996.

PX-22 DA AUTOMATIC PISTOL NiB $245 Ex $177 Gd $155
Caliber: .22 LR. 7-round magazine, 2.75-inch bbl., 5.33 inches overall. Weight: 15 oz. Fixed front sight, V-notch rear. Blued finish. Checkered black polymer grips. Made from 1989-96.

PX-25 DA AUTOMATIC PISTOL NiB $255 Ex $220 Gd $190
Same general specifications as the Model PX-22 except chambered for .25 ACP. Made from 1991-92.

REGULATOR SA REVOLVER
Similar in appearance to the Colt Single-Action Army. Calibers: .357 Mag., .44-.40, .45 Long Colt. Six-round cylinder, 4.75- or 7.5-inch bbl., blade front sight, fixed rear. Brass trigger guard/backstrap on Standard model. Casehardened steel on Deluxe model. Made from 1992 to 2000.
Standard model . . . . NiB $279 Ex $210 Gd $125
Standard combo set
(45 LC/.45 ACP & .44-.40/.44 Spec.) NiB $445 Ex $375 Gd $275
Deluxe model . . . . NiB $375 Ex $315 Gd $225

Deluxe combo set (.45 LC/.45
ACP & .44-40/.44 Spec.). . . . . NiB $445 Ex $389 Gd $260
Stainless steel . . . . NiB $425 Ex $355 Gd $250

BUCKHORN SA REVOLVER
Similar to Regulator model except chambered .44 Mag. w/4.75-, 6- or 7.7-inch bbl., Fixed or adjustable sights. Hammer block safety. Imported 1993 to 1996.
Buckhorn model (standard sights) NiB $425 Ex $315 Gd $255
w/adjustable sights, add $40

SPECTRE DA AUTO PISTOL
Blowback action, fires closed bolt. Calibers: 9mm Para., .40 S&W, .45 ACP, 30-round magazine, 6-inch bbl., 13.75 inches overall. Weight: 4 lbs. 8 oz. Adj. post front sight, fixed U-notch rear. Black nylon grips. Matte black finish. Imported 1990 to 1994.
9mm Para. . . . . NiB $545 Ex $450 Gd $260
.40 S&W (disc. 1991) . . . . NiB $515 Ex $400 Gd $300
.45 ACP . . . . NiB $560 Ex $445 Gd $315

WOODMASTER SA AUTO PISTOL NiB $300 Ex $250 Gd $195
Caliber: .22 LR. 10-round magazine, 5.88-inch bbl., 10.5 inches overall. Weight: 31 oz. Fixed front sight, square-notch adj. rear. Blued finish. Checkered wood grips. Disc. 1989.

454 SSA REVOLVER . . . . NiB $795 Ex $680 Gd $530
Umberti SSA chambered 454. 6-round cylinder, 6-inch solid raised rib or 7.7-inch top-ported bbl., satin nickel finish, adj. rear sight. Hammer block safety. Imported from 1996 to 1997.

AMERICAN DERRINGER CORPORATION — Waco, Texas (amderringer.com)

MODEL 1 STAINLESS
Single-action similar to the Remington O/U derringer, 2-shot capacity. More than 60 calibers from .22 LR to .45-70, 3-inch bbl., 4.82 inches overall, weight: 15 oz. Automatic bbl., selection. Satin or high-polished stainless steel. Rosewood grips. Made from 1980 to date.
.45 Colt, .44-40 Win., .44
Special, .410 . . . . NiB $575 Ex $420 Gd $300
.45-70, .44 Mag., 41 Mag.,
.30-30 Win., .223 Rem. . . . . . NiB $650 Ex $550 Gd $458
.357 Max., .357 Mag., .45 Win.
Mag., 9mm Para. . . . . NiB $655 Ex $555 Gd $460
.38 Special, .38 Super, .32 Mag.,
.22 LR, .22 WRM. . . . . NiB $655 Ex $560 Gd $455

MODEL 2 STEEL "PEN" PISTOL
Calibers: .22 LR, .25 Auto, .32 Auto. Single-shot, 2-inch bbl., 5.6 inches overall (4.2 inches in pistol format). Weight: 5 oz. Stainless finish. Made from 1993 to 1994.
.22 LR . . . . NiB $500 Ex $430 Gd $337
.25 Auto. . . . . NiB $600 Ex $530 Gd $430
.32 Auto. . . . . NiB $650 Ex $580 Gd $480

MODEL 3 STAINLESS STEEL . . . . NiB $125 Ex $90 Gd $75
Single-shot. Calibers: .32 Mag. or .38 Special. 2.5-inch bbl., 4.9 inches overall. Weight: 8.5 oz. Rosewood grips. Made from 1984 to 1995.

MODEL 4 DOUBLE DERRINGER
Calibers: .357 Mag., .357 Max., .44 Mag., .45 LC, .45 ACP (upper bbl., and 3-inch .410 shotshell (lower bbl.). 4.1-inch bbl, 6 inches overall. Weight: 16.5 oz. Stainless steel. Staghorn grips. Made from 1984 to date. (.44 Mag.and .45-70 disc. 2003.)
.357 Mag., .357 Max . . . . NiB $789 Ex $525 Gd $345
.44 Mag., .45 LC, .45 ACP . . . NiB $899 Ex $555 Gd $489
Engraved, add $150

MODEL 4 ALASKAN SURVIVAL MODEL... NiB $880 Ex $570 Gd $340
Similar specifications as Model 4 except upper bbl., chambered for .45-70 or 3-inch .410 and .45 LC lower bbl. Also available in .45 Auto, .45 LC, .44 Special, .357 Mag. and .357 Max. Made from 1985 to date.

MODEL 6 . . . . NiB $785 Ex $625 Gd $499
Caliber: .22 Mag., .357 Mag., .45 LC, .45 ACP or .45 LC/.410 or .45 Colt. Bbl.: 6 inches, 8.2 inches overall. Weight: .22 oz. Satin or high-polished stainless steel w/rosewood grips. Made 1986 to date.
Engraved, add $150

MODEL 7
Same general specifications as the Model 1 except high-strength aircraft aluminum used to reduce its weight to 7.5 oz. Made from 1986 to date. (.44 Special disc. then reintroduced in 2008.)
.22 LR, .22 WMR.. . . . . NiB $575 Ex $440 Gd $280
.44 Special, add $150

MODEL 8. . . . . NiB $920 Ex $530 Gd $280
Calibers: .45 LC/.410, 8-inch bbl., 9.8 inches overall. Weight: 24 oz. Rosewood grips. New 1997.
Engraved (Made from 1997 to 1998), add $1000

MODEL 10
Same general specifications as the Model 7 except chambered for .38 Special, .45 ACP or .45 LC with aluminum grip frame
.38 Special or .45 ACP . . . . . NiB $559 Ex $365 Gd $295
.45 LC . . . . NiB $500 Ex $395 Gd $279

Model 11 . . . . NiB $559 Ex $490 Gd $369
Same general specifications as Model 7 except with a matte gray finish only, weight: 11 oz. Made from 1980 to 2003.

25 AUTOMATIC PISTOL
Calibers: .25 ACP or .250 Mag. Bbl.: 2.1 inches, 4.4 inches overall. Weight: 15.5 oz. Smooth rosewood grips. Limited production.
**.25 ACP blued
(est. production 50)** . . . . NiB $650 Ex $540 Gd $385
**.25 ACP stainless
(est. production 400)** . . . . NiB $510 Ex $425 Gd $380
**.250 Mag. stainless
(est. production 100)** . . . . . . NiB $675 Ex $530 Gd $407

DA 38 DOUBLE ACTION DERRINGER
Hammerless, double action, double bbl (o/u). Calibers: .22LR, .357 Mag., .38 Special, 9mm Para., .40 S&W. 3-inch bbls., satin stainless with aluminum grip frame. DA trigger, hammerblock thumb safety. Weight: 14.5 oz. Made from 1990 to date.
.22LR (1996-03), .38 Special, 9mm Para., **NiB $615 Ex $415 Gd $230**
.357 Mag. or .40 cal. (Disc. 2012) NiB $710 Ex $445 Gd $265
Lady Derringer (faux ivory grips, made from 1992-94 **), add** $40

COP DA DERRINGER . . . . . . NiB $660 Ex $510 Gd $291
Hammerless, double-action, 4-bbl., derringer. Caliber: .357 Mag. 3.15-inch bbl., 5.5 inches overall. Weight: 16 oz. Blade front sight, open notched rear. Rosewood grips. Intro. 1990, disc. 1994.

LM-5 AUTOMATIC PISTOL
Calibers: .25 ACP, .32 H&R Mag. or .380 Automatic. Bbl.: 2 inches, 3 inches overall. Weight: 15 oz. Stainless steel construction, smooth wood grips. Limited production.
.25 ACP or 32 H&R Mag. . . . . NiB $650 Ex $540 Gd $385
.380 Automatic (Disc. 1999). . NiB $425 Ex $380 Gd $300

LADY DERRINGER . . . . NiB $769 Ex $610 Gd $499
Similar specifications as Model 1 except w/custom-tuned action fitted w/scrimshawed synthetic ivory grips. Calibers: .32 H&R Mag., .32 Special, .38 Special (additional calibers on request). Deluxe Grade

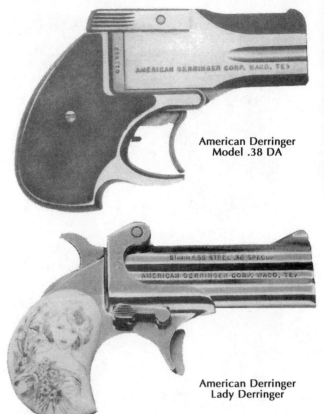

American Derringer
Model .38 DA

American Derringer
Lady Derringer

engraved and highly polished w/French fitted jewelry box. Made from 1991 to date.

Deluxe Engraved (Disc. 1994) .NiB $699 Ex $470 Gd $355
Gold Engraved (Disc. 1994) . . . . .Rare
Lady II (aluminum frame, made 1999-03) NiB $400 Ex $350 Gd $255

MINI-COP DA DERRINGER . . NiB $325 Ex $200 Gd $145
Similar general specifications as the COP except chambered for .22 WMR. Made from 1990 to 1995.

SEMMERLING LM-4
Manually operated repeater. Calibers: .45 ACP or 9mm, 4-round (.45 ACP) or 6-round magazine (9mm), 3.6-inch bbl., 5.2 inches overall. Weight: 24 oz. Made from 1997 to date. Limited availability.
Blued or Stainless steel . . NiB $4350 Ex $3200 Gd $2020

TEXAS COMMEMORATIVE . . .NiB $380 Ex $350 Gd $300
Same general specifications as Model 1 except w/solid brass frame, stainless bbls. and stag grips. Calibers: .22 LR, .32 Mag., .38 Special, .44-40 Win. or .45 LC. Made from 1991 to date.
.44-40 Win. or .45 LC . . . . . . NiB $800 Ex $750 Gd $695

125TH ANNIVERSARY . . . .
Same general specifications as Model 1 except w/solid brass frame, stainless bbls. and stag grips. Calibers: .38 Special, .44-40 Win. or .45 LC. Disc. 1993. Limited production.
.38 Special . . . . NiB $337 Ex $320 Gd $295
.44-40 Win. or .45 LC . . . . .NiB $400 Ex $395 Gd $375

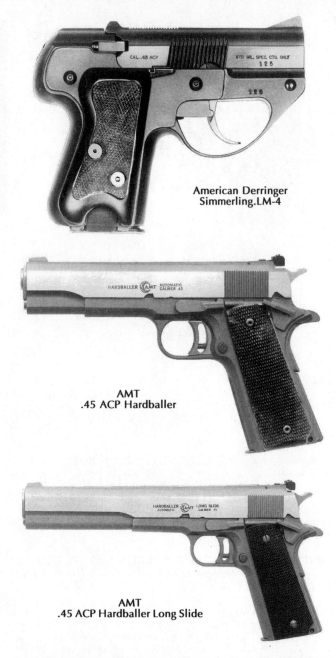

American Derringer Simmerling.LM-4

AMT .45 ACP Hardballer

AMT .45 ACP Hardballer Long Slide

AMERICAN FIREARMS MFG. CO., INC. — San Antonio, Texas

25 AUTO PISTOL
Caliber: .25 Auto. 8-round magazine, 2.1-inch bbl., 4.4 inches overall. Weight: 14.5 oz. Fixed sights. Stainless or blued ordnance steel. Smooth walnut grips. Made from 1966 to 1974.
Stainless steel model. . . . . . . NiB $215 Ex $190 Gd $110
Blued steel model. . . . . NiB $200 Ex $145 Gd $110

380 AUTO PISTOL . . . . NiB $735 Ex $540 Gd $389
Caliber: .380 Auto. 8-round magazine, 3.5-inch bbl., 5.5 inches overall. Weight: 20 oz. Stainless steel. Smooth walnut grips. Made from 1972 to 1974.

AMT (ARCADIA MACHINE & TOOL) — Trademark owed by Crusader Gun Company Houston TX (previously Galena Industries, Strugis, SD; and Irwindale Arms, Inc., Irwindale, CA)

NOTE: *The AMT Backup II automatic pistol was introduced in 1993 as a continuation of the original .380 backup with the traditional double action function and a redesigned double safety.*

45 ACP HARDBALLER . . . . . . NiB $545 Ex $430 Gd $345
Colt 1991 style. Caliber: .45 ACP, 7-round magazine, 5-inch bbl., 8.5 inches overall. Weight: 39 oz. Adj. or fixed sights. Serrated matte slide rib w/loaded chamber indicator. Extended combat safety, adj. trigger and long grip safety. Wraparound Neoprene grips. Stainless steel. Made 1978-2001.
Long slide conversion kit (disc. 1997), add $315

45 ACP HARDBALLER LONG SLIDE
Similar to the standard Hardballer except w/2-inch-longer bbl. and slide. Also chambered for .400 Cor-Bon. Made from 1980-2001
.45 ACP long slide . . . . NiB $529 Ex $435 Gd $320
.400 Cor-Bon long slide (Intro.1998)NiB$535 Ex$425 Gd$300
5-inch conversion kit (disc. 1997), add $315

45 ACP STANDARD GOVERNMENT MODEL
AUTO PISTOL . . . . NiB $460 Ex $395 Gd $339
Caliber: .45 ACP, 7-round magazine, 5-inch bbl., 8.5 inches overall. Weight: 38 oz. Fixed sights. Wraparound Neoprene grip. Made from 1979 to date.

AUTOMAG II
AUTOMATIC PISTOL . . . . NiB $845 Ex $575 Gd $360
Caliber: .22 Mag., 7- or 9-round magazine, bbl., lengths: 3.38-4.5-, 6-inch. Weight: 32 oz. Fully adj. Millett sights. Stainless finish. Smooth black composition grips. Made from 1986 to 2001, reintro 2004.

AUTOMAG III
AUTOMATIC PISTOL . . . . NiB $600 Ex $495 Gd $365
Calibers: .30 M1 or 9mm Win. Mag., 8-round magazine., 6.38-inch bbl., 10.5 inches overall. Weight: 43 oz. Millet adj. sights. Stainless finish. Carbon fiber grips. Made from 1992 to 2001.

AUTOMAG IV
AUTOMATIC PISTOL . . . . NiB $610 Ex $520 Gd $395
Calibers: 10mm or .45 Win. Mag., 8- or 7-round magazine, 6.5- or 8.63-inch bbl., 10.5 inches overall. Weight: 46 oz. Millet adj. sights. Stainless finish. Carbon fiber grips. Made from 1992-2001.

AUTOMAG V
AUTOMATIC PISTOL . . . . . . NiB $1000 Ex $855 Gd $775
Caliber: .50 A.E., 5-round magazine, 7-inch bbl., 10.5 inches overall. Weight: 46 oz. Custom adj. sights. Stainless finish. Carbon fiber grips. Made from 1994 to 1995.

BACKUP (SMALL FRAME) AUTOMATIC PISTOL
Caliber: .22 LR, .380 ACP, 8-round (.22LR) or 5-round (.380 ACP) magazine, 2.5-inch bbl., 5 inches overall. Weight: 18 oz. (.380 ACP). Open sights. Carbon fiber or walnut grips. Stainless steel finish. Made from 1990 to 1987.
.22 LR (disc. 1987). . . . . NiB $495 Ex $335 Gd $188
.380 ACP (disc. 2000, reintro. 2004, disc. 2010). . NiB $450
Ex $305 . . . . Gd $171

BACKUP II
AUTOMATIC PISTOL . . . . NiB $300 Ex $260 Gd $200
Caliber: .380 ACP, 5-round magazine, 2.5-inch bbl., 5 inches overall. Weight: 18 oz. Single action. Open sights. Stainless steel finish. Carbon-fiber grips. Made from 1993 to 1998.

BACKUP (LARGE FRAME) AUTO PISTOL
Calibers: .357 SIG, .38 Super, 9mm Para., .40 Cor-Bon, .40 S&W, .45 ACP. Six-round (.357 SIG, .38 Super 9mm) or 5-round (.40 Cor-Bon, .40 S&W, .45 ACP) magazine, 2.5-inch bbl., 5.75-inches overall. Weight: 23 oz. Double action only. Open fixed sights. Stainless steel finish. Carbon fiber grips. Made from 1992 to date.
.357 SIG, .38 Super, 9mm.40 S&W, .45 ACPNiB $530 Ex $400 Gd $300
.40 Cor-Bon (disc. 2010). . . . . NiB $630 Ex $500 Gd $400

BULL'S EYE TARGET MODEL .NiB $695 Ex $550 Gd $415
Similar to the standard Hardballer. Caliber: .40 S&W, 8-round magazine, 5-inch bbl., 8.5 inches overall. Weight: 38 oz. Millet adjustable sights. Wide adj. trigger. Wraparound Neoprene grips. Made from 1990 to 1991.

JAVELINA. . . . . NiB $695 Ex $550 Gd $420
Caliber: 10mm, 8-round magazine, 7-inch bbl., 10.5 inches overall. Weight: 48 oz. Long grip safety, beveled magazine well, wide adj. trigger. Millet adj. sights. Wraparound Neoprene grips. Stainless finish. Made from 1991 to 1993.

LIGHTNING AUTO PISTOL
Caliber: .22 LR. 10-round magazine, 5-, 6.5-, 8.5-, 10-inch bbl., 10.75 inches overall (6.5-inch bbl.). Weight: 45 oz. (6.5-inch bbl.). Millett adj. sights. Checkered rubber grips. Stainless finish. Made from 1984 to 1987.
Standard model . . . . NiB $455 Ex $315 Gd $210
Bull's-Eye model (6.5-inch bull bbl.)NiB $520 Ex $355 Gd $240

ON DUTY DA PISTOL
Calibers: .40 S&W, 9mm Para., .45 ACP. 15-round (9mm), 13-shot (.40 S&W) or 9-round (.45 ACP) magazine, 4.5-inch bbl., 7.75 inches overall. Weight: 32 oz. Hard anodized aluminum frame. Stainless steel slide and bbl., Carbon fiber grips. Made from 1991 to 1994.
9mm or .40 S&W . . . . NiB $465 Ex $316 Gd $235
.45 ACP . . . . NiB $515 Ex $400 Gd $265

SKIPPER AUTO PISTOL . . . . . NiB $465 Ex $359 Gd $325
Calibers: .40 S&W or .45 ACP, 7-round magazine, 4.25-inch bbl., 7.5 inches overall. Weight: 33 oz. Millet adj. sights. Walnut grips. Matte finish stainless steel. Made from 1990 to 1992.

ANSCHUTZ PISTOLS — Ulm, Germany. Mfd. by J.G. Anschutz GmbH Jagd und Sportwaffenfabrik

Currently imported by Accuracy International, Boseman, MT and AcuSport Corporation, Bellefontaine, OH

MODEL 64P
Calibers: .22 LR or .22 WMR, 5- or 4-round magazine, 10-inch bbl., 64MS action w/two-stage trigger. Target sights optional. Rynite black synthetic stock. Imported from 1998 to 2003.
.22 LR . . . . NiB $490 Ex $305 Gd $225
.22 WMR . . . . NiB $515 Ex $249 Gd $195
w/tangent sights, add $100

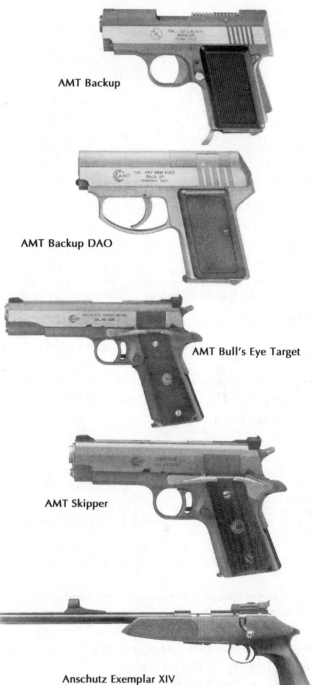

AMT Backup

AMT Backup DAO

AMT Bull's Eye Target

AMT Skipper

Anschutz Exemplar XIV

EXEMPLAR (1416P/1451P) BOLT-ACTION PISTOL
Caliber: .22 LR, single-shot or 5-round magazine, 7- or 10-inch bbl., 19 inches overall (10-inch bbl.). Weight: 3.33 lbs. Match 64 action. Slide safety. Hooded ramp post front sight, adjustable open notched rear. European walnut contoured grip. Exemplar made from 1987-95 and 1400 series made from 1997. Disc. 1997. Note: The .22 WMR chambering was advertised but never manufactured.
Exemplar w/7- or 10-inch bbl NiB $420 Ex $295 Gd $185

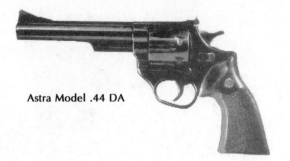

Astra Model .44 DA

Left-hand model (disc. 1997) . NiB $535 Ex $455 Gd $365
Model 1451P (single-shot) . . . NiB $450 Ex $365 Gd $285
Model 1416P (5-round repeater) . . NiB $1150 Ex $869 Gd $610

EXEMPLAR HORNET . . . . . . NiB $1015 Ex $815 Gd $700
Based on the Anschutz Match 54 action, tapped and grooved for scope mounting with no open sights. Caliber: .22 Hornet, 5-round magazine, 10-inch bbl., 20 inches overall. Weight: 4.35 lbs. Checkered European walnut grip. Winged safety. Made from 1990 to 1995.

EXEMPLAR XIV . . . . NiB $875 Ex $560 Gd $465
Same general specifications as the standard Exemplar bolt-action pistol except with 14-inch bbl., weight: 4.15 lbs. Made from 1989 to 1995.

ARMALITE, INC. — Genesco, IL (formerly Costa Mesa, CA)

AR-24 AUTOMATIC PISTOL . . NiB $550 Ex $380 Gd $300
Full size automatic, mfg. by Sarzsilmaz in Turkey. Caliber: 9mm Para, 15-round magazine, 4.67-inch bbl., 8.3 inches overall. Parkerized finish, checkered synthetic grips. Imported from 2007 to 2013.
AR-24-15C Combat Custom
(adj. rear sight) . . . . NiB $630 Ex $430 Gd $375
AR-24K-13 Compact
(3.89-inch bbl.) . . . . NiB $560 Ex $400 Gd $380
AR-24K-13 Combat Custom Compact (adj. rear sight, 3.89-inch bbl.) . . . . NiB $630 Ex $430 Gd $375

ARMSCOR (Arms Corp.) — Manila, Philippines. Currently imported by Armscor Precision Int'l. Pahrump, NV (Previously Imported by K.B.I., Harrisburg, PA., 1991–95 by Ruko Products, Inc., Buffalo NY., Armscor Precision, San Mateo, CA.)

MODEL M1911-A1
AUTOMATIC PISTOL . . . . . . NiB $400 Ex $320 Gd $275
Caliber: .45 ACP. Eight-round magazine, 5-inch bbl., 8.75 inches overall. Weight: 38 oz. Blade front sight, drift adjustable rear w/3-dot system. Skeletonized tactical hammer and trigger. Extended slide release and beavertail grip safety. Parkerized finish. Checkered composition or wood stocks. Imported from 1996 to 1997. Reintro. 2001 to 2008.

MODEL M1911-A1
COMMANDER . . . . NiB $410 Ex $300 Gd $220
Caliber: .45 ACP. Similar to M1911-A-1 except with Commander configuration and 4-inch bbl. Rear slide serrations only. Disc. 1991.
Two-tone finish, add $50
Stainless, add $95

MODEL M1911-A1 OFFICER . . NiB $425 Ex $350 Gd $265
Caliber: .45 ACP. Similar to M1911-A-1 except with Combat configuration. Bbl.:3.5 inches. Checkered hardwood grips. Weight: 2.16 pounds. Disc. 1991.
Two-tone finish, add. $50
Stainless, add $95

MODEL M1911-A1
MEDALLION SERIES . . . . NiB $495 Ex $360 Gd $285
Caliber: 9mm Para., .40 S&W, .45ACP. Standard or Tactical, blue finish standard. Bbl.: 5 inches. Custom model with match barrel, checkered wood Pachmayr grips. Disc. 1991.
Two-tone finish (Tactical), add $200
Chrome (Tactical), add $250

MODEL200 DC/TC
DA REVOLVER . . . . NiB $240 Ex $160 Gd $110
Caliber: .38 Special. Six-round cylinder, 2.5-, 4-, or 6-inch bbl.; 7.3, 8.8, or 11.3 inches overall. Weight: 22, 28, or 34 oz. Ramp front and fixed rear sights. Checkered mahogany or rubber grips. Disc. 1991.

MODEL 202A REVOLVER . . . . NiB $165 Ex $110 Gd $95
Caliber: .38 Special. Similar to Model 200 (DC) revolver except does not have barrel shroud. Disc. 1991.

MODEL 206 REVOLVER . . . . . NiB $250 Ex $203 Gd $170
Caliber: .38 Special. Similar to Model 200 (DC) revolver except has a 2-7/8-inch bbl. Weight: 24 oz. Disc. 1991.

MODEL 210 REVOLVER . . . . . NiB $219 Ex $170 Gd $135
Caliber: .38 Special. Similar to Model 200 (DC) except has a 4-inch ventilated rib bbl., adj. rear sight. Weight: 28 oz. Disc. 1991.

ASAI AG — Advanced Small Arms Industries Solothurn, Switzerland

Currently imported by Magnum Research Inc., Minneapolis, MN.

See listings under Magnum Research Pistols

ASTRA PISTOLS — Guernica, Spain. Manufactured by Unceta y Compania

(Currently not imported to U.S., previously imported by E.A.A. Corporation, Sharpes, FL.)

MODEL 357 DA REVOLVER . . NiB $385 Ex $299 Gd $230
Caliber: .357 Magnum. Six-round cylinder. 3-, 4-, 6-, 8.5-inch bbl., 11.25 inches overall (with 6-inch bbl.). Weight: 42 oz. (with 6-inch bbl.). Ramp front sight, adj. rear sight. Blued finish. Checkered wood grips. Imported from 1972 to 1988.

MODEL 44 DA REVOLVER
Similar to Astra ..357 except chambered for .44 Magnum. Six- or 8.5-inch bbl., 11.5 inches overall (6-inch bbl.). Weight: 44 oz. (6-inch bbl.). Imported from 1980 to 1993.
Blued finish (disc. 1987) . . . . . NiB $375 Ex $290 Gd $245
Stainless finish (disc. 1993) . . . NiB $395 Ex $320 Gd $255

MODEL 41 DA REVOLVER . . .NiB $375 Ex $295 Gd $235
Same general specifications as Model 44 except in .41 Mag. Imported from 1980-85.

MODEL 45 DA REVOLVER . . . NiB $366 Ex $275 Gd $215
Similar to Astra .357 except chambered for .45 LC or .45 ACP. Six- or 8.5-inch bbl., 11.5 inches overall (with 6-inch bbl.). Weight: 44 oz. (6-inch bbl.). Imported from 1980-87.

MODEL 200 FIRECAT
VEST POCKET AUTO PISTOL. .NiB $320 Ex $260 Gd $205
Caliber: .25 Automatic (6.35mm). Six-round magazine, 2.25-inch bbl., 4.38 inches overall. Weight: 11.75 oz. Fixed sights. Blued finish. Plastic grips. Made 1920 to date. U.S. importation disc. in 1968.

MODEL 202 FIRECAT
VEST POCKET AUTO PISTOL . NiB $590 Ex $475 Gd $400
Same general specifications as the Model 200 except chromed and engraved w/pearl grips. U.S. importation disc. 1968.

MODEL 400 AUTO PISTOL . . NiB $725 Ex $595 Gd $350
Caliber: 9mm Bayard Long (.38 ACP, 9mm Browning Long, 9mm Glisenti, 9mm Para. and 9mm Steyr cartridges may be used interchangeably in this pistol because of its chamber design). Nine-round magazine., 6-inch bbl., 10 inches overall. Weight: 35 oz. Fixed sights. Blued finish. Plastic grips. Made 1922-45. Note: This pistol, as well as Astra Models 600 and 3000, is a modification of the Browning Model 1912.
Nazis Mfg. (S/N range 92,850-98,850), add **100%**

MODEL 600 MIL./POLICE-TYPE
AUTO PISTOL . . . . NiB $565 Ex $425 Gd $300
Calibers: .32 Automatic (7.65mm), 9mm Para. Magazine: 10-round (.32 cal.) or 8-round (9mm)., 5.25-inch bbl., 8 inches overall. Weight: About 33 oz. Fixed sights. Blued finish. Checkered wood or plastic grips. Made from 1944 to 1945.
Nazis markings, add **100%**

MODEL 800 CONDOR
MILITARY AUTO PISTOL . NiB $2101 Ex $1754 Gd $1512
Similar to Models 400 and 600 except has an External hammer. Caliber: 9mm Para. Eight-round magazine, 5.25-inch bbl., 8.25 inches overall. Weight: 32.5 oz. Fixed sights. Blued finish. Plastic grips. Imported from 1958 to 1965.

MODEL 2000 CAMPER
AUTOMATIC PISTOL . . . . NiB $395 Ex $279 Gd $215
Same as Model 2000 Cub except chambered for .22 Short only, has 4-inch bbl., overall length, 6.25 inches, weight: 11.5 oz. Imported from 1955 to 1960.

MODEL 2000 CUB
POCKET AUTO PISTOL . . . . . NiB $363 Ex $297 Gd $214
Calibers: .22 Short, .25 Auto. Six-round magazine, 2.25-inch bbl., 4.5 inches overall. Weight: About 11 oz. Fixed sights. Blued or chromed finish. Plastic grips. Made 1954 to date. U.S. importation disc. in 1968.

MODEL 3000
POCKET AUTO PISTOL . . . . NiB $1001 Ex $654 Gd $467
Calibers: .22 LR, .32 Automatic (7.65mm), .380 Auto (9mm Short). Ten-round magazine (.22 cal.), 7-round (.32 cal.), 6-round (.380 cal.). Four-inch bbl., 6.38 inches overall. Weight: About 22 oz. Fixed sights. Blued finish. Plastic grips. Made from 1947 to 1956.

MODEL 3003 POCKET AUTO PISTOL . . NiB $2420 Ex $1419 Gd $880
Same general specifications as the Model 3000 except chromed and engraved w/pearl grips. Disc. 1956.

Astra Model 3003 Pocket

Astra Model 4000 Falcon

MODEL 4000 FALCON AUTO PISTOL . . NiB $675 Ex $495 Gd $320
Similar to Model 3000 except has an External hammer. Calibers: .22 LR, .32 Automatic (7.65mm), .380 Auto (9mm Short). Ten-round magazine (.22 LR), 8-round (.32 Auto), 7-round (.380 Auto), 3.66-inch bbl., 6.5-inches overall. Weight: 20 oz. (.22 cal.) or 24.75 oz. (.32 and .380). Fixed sights. Blued finish. Plastic grips. Made from 1956 to 1971.

CONSTABLE DA AUTO PISTOL
Calibers: .22 LR, .32 Automatic (7.65mm), .380 Auto (9mm Short). Magazine capacity: 10-round (.22 LR), 8-round (.32), 7-round (.380). 3.5-inch bbl., 6.5 inches overall. Weight: about 24 oz. Blade front sight, windage adj. rear. Blued or chromed finish. Imported from 1965 to 1992.
Stainless finish . . . . NiB $395 Ex $290 Gd $229
Blued engraved finish . . . . NiB $605 Ex $419 Gd $297
Chrome finish (disc. 1990) . . . NiB $500 Ex $335 Gd $234

MODEL A-60 DA AUTOMATIC PISTOL NiB $415 Ex $285 Gd $210
Similar to the Constable except in .380 only, w/13-round magazine and slide-mounted ambidExtrous safety. Blued finish only. Imported from 1980 to 1991.

MODEL A-70 COMPACT AUTO PISTOL
Calibers: 9mm Para., .40 S&W. Eight-round (9mm) or 7-round (.40 S&W) magazine., 3.5-inch bbl., 6.5 inches overall. Blued, nickel or stainless finish. Weight: 29.3 oz. Imported from 1992 to 1996.
Blued finish . . . . NiB $414 Ex $295 Gd $210
Nickel finish. . . . . NiB $424 Ex $345 Gd $229
Stainless finish . . . . NiB $593 Ex $430 Gd $372

MODEL A-75 ULTRALIGHT . . NiB $400 Ex $299 Gd $234
Similar to the standard Model 75 except 9mm only w/24-oz. aluminum alloy frame. Imported from 1994 to 1997.

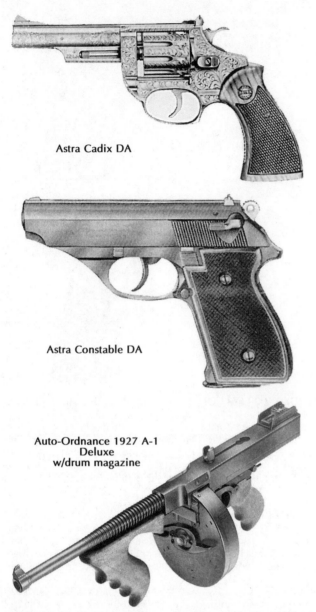

Astra Cadix DA

Astra Constable DA

Auto-Ordnance 1927 A-1
Deluxe
w/drum magazine

MODEL A-80 AUTO PISTOL. . NiB $450 Ex $404 Gd $265
Calibers: 9mm Para., .38 Super, .45 ACP. 15-round or 9-round (.45 ACP). magazine. Bbl.: 3.75 inches., 7 inches overall. Weight: 36 oz. Imported from 1982 to 1989.

MODEL A-90 DA
AUTOMATIC PISTOL. . . . . . . .NiB $505 Ex $400 Gd $245
Calibers: 9mm Para., .45 ACP. 15-round (9mm) or 9-round (.45 ACP) magazine, 3.75-inch bbl., 7 inches overall. Weight: about 40 oz. Fixed sights. Blued finish. Checkered plastic grips. Imported 1985 to 1990.

MODEL A-100 DA AUTO PISTOL
Same general specifications as the Model A-90 except selective double action chambered for 9mm Para., .40 S&W or .45 ACP. Imported from 1991 to 1997.
Blued finish . . . . NiB $470 Ex $310 Gd $249
Nickel finish. . . . . NiB $495 Ex $340 Gd $287
For night sights, add. $100

CADIX DA REVOLVER

Calibers: .22 LR, .38 Special. Nine-round (.22 LR) or 5-round (.38 cal.) cylinder. Four- or 6-inch bbl., Weight: About 27 oz. (6-inch bbl.). Ramp front sight, adj. rear sight. Blued finish. Plastic grips. Imported from 1960-68.
Standard model . . . . NiB $275 Ex $229 Gd $160
Lightly engraved model . . . . . NiB $380 Ex $255 Gd $200
Heavily engraved model (shown). NiB $700 Ex $515 Gd $395

MODEL A-75 DECOCKER AUTO PISTOL
Similar to the Model 70 except in 9mm, .40 S&W and .45 ACP w/decocking system and contoured pebble-tExtured grips. Imported from 1993-97.
Blued finish, 9mm or .40 S&W NiB $395 Ex $320 Gd $235
Nickel finish, 9mm or .40 S&WNiB $405 Ex $330 Gd $245
Stainless, 9mm or .40 S&W. . . NiB $410 Ex $305 Gd $197
Blued finish, .45 ACP . . . . NiB $395 Ex $315 Gd $235
Nickel finish, .45 ACP . . . . . . NiB $405 Ex $350 Gd $275
Stainless, .45 ACP . . . . NiB $420 Ex $365 Gd $290

AUTAUGA ARMS — Prattville, Alabama

MODEL 32 (MK II)
DAO AUTOMATIC PISTOL. . . .NiB $367 Ex $309 Gd $267
Caliber: .32 ACP. Six-round magazine, 2-inch bbl., weight: 11.36 oz.. Double action only. Stainless steel. Black polymer grips. Made from 1996 to 2000.

AUTO-ORDNANCE CORPORATION — Division of Kahr Arms, Worchester, MA (previously West Hurley, New York)

1911 A1 GOVERNMENT AUTO . NIB $515 EX $375 GD $300
Copy of Colt 1911 A1 semiautomatic pistol. Calibers: 9mm Para., .38 Super, 10mm, .45 ACP. 9-round (9mm, .38 Super) or 7-round 10mm, .45 ACP) magazine. Five-inch bbl., 8.5 inches overall. Weight: 39 oz. Fixed blade front sight, rear adj. Blued, satin nickel or Duo-Tone finish. Checkered plastic grips. Made 1983 to 1999.
1911 A1 WWII (parkerized finish)NiB $540 Ex $393 Gd $315
1911 A1 100th Anniversary (laser engraved), add 20%

1911A1 .40 S&W PISTOL . . . . NiB $498 Ex $399 Gd $309
Similar to the Model 1911 A1 except has 4.5-inch bbl., w/7.75-inch overall length. Eight-round magazine, weight: 37 oz. Blade front and adj. rear sights w/3-dot system. Checkered black rubber wraparound grips. Made from 1991 to 1999.

1911 A1 "THE GENERAL". . . . NiB $441 Ex $351 Gd $253
Caliber: .45 ACP. Seven-round magazine, 4.5-inch bbl., 7.75 inches overall. Weight: 37 oz. Blued nonglare finish. Made 1992 to 1999.

1927 A-1 DELUXE SEMIAUTOMATIC PISTOL
Similar to Thompson Model 1928A submachine gun except has no provision for automatic firing and does not have detachable buttstock. Caliber: .45 ACP, 5-, 15-, 20- and 30-round detachable box magazines. 30-round drum also available. 13-inch finned bbl., 26 inches overall. Weight: About 6.75 lbs. Adj. rear sight, blade front. Blued finish. Walnut grips. Made from 1977 to 1994.
w/box magazine . . . . NiB $1412 Ex $1078 Gd $764
w/drum magazine, add $300

ZG-51 PIT BULL
AUTOMATIC PISTOL . . . . NiB $435 Ex $325 Gd $288
Caliber: .45 ACP. Seven-round magazine, 3.5-inch bbl., 7 inches overall. Weight: 32 oz. Fixed front sight, square-notch rear. Blued finish. Checkered plastic grips. Made from 1991 to 1999.

LES BAER — LECLAIRE, IOWA (PREVIOUSLY Hillsdale, Illinois)

1911 CONCEPT SERIES AUTOMATIC PISTOL

Similar to Government 1911 built on steel or alloy full-size or compact frame. Caliber: .45 ACP. Seven-round magazine, 4.25- or 5-inch bbl. Weight: 34 to 37 oz. Adjustable low mount combat or BoMar target sights. Blued, matte black, Two-Tone or stainless finish. Checkered wood grips. Made from 1996 to date.

Concept models I & II	NiB $1402	Ex $1116	Gd $797
Concept models III, IV & VII	NiB $1556	Ex $1414	Gd $1204
Concept models V, VI & VIII	NiB $1538	Ex $1369	Gd $863
Concept models IX & X . . .	NiB $1529	Ex $1237	Gd $1045

1911 PREMIER SERIES AUTOMATIC PISTOL

Similar to the Concept series except also chambered for .38 Super, 9x23 Win., .400 Cor-Bon and .45 ACP. 5- or 6-inch bbl. Weight: 37 to .40 oz. Made from 1996 to date.

Premier II (9x23 w/5-inch bbl.)	NiB $1760	Ex $1479	Gd $1331
Premier II (.400 Cor-Bon w/5-inch bbl.) . . .	NiB $1540	Ex $1369	Gd $1292
Premier II (.45 ACP w/5-inch bbl.)	NiB $1446	Ex $1314	Gd $1098
Premier II (.45 ACP S/S w/5-inch bbl.)	NiB $1531	Ex $1265	Gd $875
Premier II (.45/.400 combo w/5-inch bbl.) . . .	NiB $1749	Ex $1457	Gd $1281
Premier II (.38 Super w/6-inch bbl.) . . .	NiB $1996	Ex $1864	Gd $1490
Premier II (.400 Cor-Bon w/6-inch bbl.) . . .	NiB $1798	Ex $1529	Gd $1364
Premier II (.45 ACP w/6-inch bbl.)	NiB $1672	Ex $1501	Gd $1408

S.R.P. AUTOMATIC PISTOL

Similar to F.B.I. Contract "Swift Response Pistol" built on a (customer-supplied) Para-Ordance over-sized frame or a 1911 full-size or compact frame. Caliber: .45 ACP. Seven-round magazine, 5-inch bbl., weight: 37 oz. Ramp front and fixed rear sights, w/Tritium Sight insert.

SRP 1911 Government or Commanche model . . .	NiB $2295	Ex $2084	Gd $1905
SRP P-12 model	NiB $2619	Ex $2346	Gd $2199
SRP P-13 model	NiB $2404	Ex $2178	Gd $2021
SRP P-14 model	NiB $2320	Ex $2109	Gd $1317

1911 ULTIMATE MASTER COMBAT SERIES AUTOMATIC PISTOL

Model 1911 in Combat Competition configuration. Calibers: .38 Super, 9x23 Win., .400 Cor-Bon and .45 ACP. Five- or 6-inch NM bbl., weight: 37 to 40 oz. Made from 1996 to date.

Ultimate MC (.38 or 9x23 w/5-inch bbl.)	NiB $2580	Ex $2010	Gd $1400
Ultimate MC (.400 Cor-Bon w/5-inch bbl.)	NiB $2480	Ex $1835	Gd $1300
Ultimate MC (.45 ACP w/5-inch bbl.)	NiB $2430	Ex $1910	Gd $1300
Ultimate MC (.38 or 9x23 w/6-inch bbl.)	NiB $2680	Ex $2025	Gd $1495
Ultimate MC (.400 Cor-Bon w/6-inch bbl.)	NiB $2630	Ex $2060	Gd $1450
Ultimate MC (.45 ACP w/6-inch bbl.)	NiB $2580	Ex $2010	Gd $1400
Ultimate "Steel Special" (.38 Super Bianchi SPS) . .	NiB $2855	Ex $2310	Gd $1661
Ultimate "PARA" (.38, 9x23 or .45 IPSC comp) . . .	NiB $2871	Ex $2326	Gd $1650
w/Triple-Port Compensator, add			$100

1911 CUSTOM CARRY SERIES AUTOMATIC PISTOL

Auto-Ordnance
ZG-51 Pit Bull

Model 1911 in Combat Carry configuration built on steel or alloy full-size or compact frame. 4.5- or 5-inch NM bbl., chambered for .45 ACP. Weight: 34 to 37 oz.

Custom carry (steel frame w/4.24- or 5-inch bbl.) . . .	NiB $1728	Ex $1555	Gd $1166
Custom carry (alloy frame w/4.24-inch bbl.)	NiB $2039	Ex $2029	Gd $1521

BAUER FIREARMS CORPORATION — Fraser, Michigan

.25 AUTOMATIC PISTOL . . . . . NiB $175 Ex $125 Gd $95
Stainless steel. Caliber: .25 Automatic. Six-round magazine, 2.13-inch bbl., 4 inches overall. Weight: 10 oz. Fixed sights. Checkered walnut or simulated pearl grips. Made from 1972 to 1984.

BAYARD PISTOLS — Herstal, Belgium. Mfd. by Anciens Etablissements Pieper

MODEL 1908
POCKET AUTOMATIC PISTOL NiB $455 Ex $300 Gd $195
Calibers: .25 Automatic (6.35mm). .32 Automatic (7.65mm), .380 Automatic (9mm Short). Six-round magazine, 2.25-inch bbl., 4.88 inches overall. Weight: About 16 oz. Fixed sights. Blued finish. Hard rubber grips. Intro. 1908. Disc. 1923.

MODEL 1923 POCKET
.25 AUTOMATIC PISTOL . . . . NiB $393 Ex $300 Gd $170
Caliber: .25 Automatic (6.35mm). 2.13-inch bbl., 4.31 inches overall. Weight: 12 oz. Fixed sights. Blued finish. Checkered hard-rubber grips. Intro. 1923. Disc. 1930.

MODEL 1923 POCKET
AUTOMATIC PISTOL . . . . NiB $429 Ex $313 Gd $218
Calibers: .32 Automatic (7.65mm), .380 Automatic (9mm Short). Six-round magazine, 3.31-inch bbl., 5.5 inches overall. Weight: About 19 oz. Fixed sights. Blued finish. Checkered hard-rubber grips. Intro. 1923. Disc. 1940.

MODEL 1930 POCKET
.25 AUTOMATIC PISTOL . . . . NiB $395 Ex $255 Gd $195
This is a modification of the Model 1923, which it closely resembles.

BEEMAN PRECISION ARMS, INC. — Santa Rosa, California

P08 AUTOMATIC PISTOL . . . . . NiB $420 Ex $335 Gd $245
Luger toggle action. Caliber: .22 LR. 10-round magazine, 3.8-inch bbl., 7.8 inches overall. Weight: 25 oz. Fixed sights. Blued finish. Checkered hardwood grips. Imported from 1969 to 1991.

GRADING: **NiB** = New in Box   **Ex** = Excellent or NRA 95%   **Gd** = Good or NRA 68%

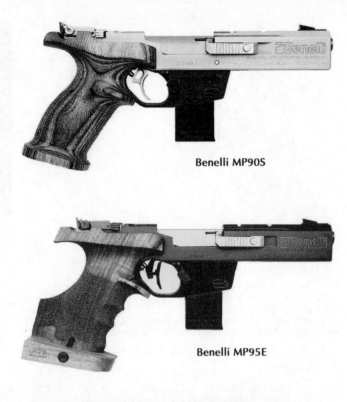

Benelli MP90S

Benelli MP95E

Beretta Model 21

MINI P08 AUTOMATIC PISTOL NiB $470 Ex $375 Gd $295
Caliber: Same general specifications as P08 except shorter 3.5-inch bbl., 7.4 inches overall. Weight: 20 oz. Imported 1986 to 1991.

SP METALLIC SILHOUETTE PISTOLS
Caliber: .22 LR. Single-shot. Bbl. lengths: 6-, 8-, 10- or 15-inches. Adj. rear sight. Receiver contoured for scope mount. Walnut target grips w/adj. palm rest. Models SP made 1985 to 1986 and SPX 1993-94.

SP Standard w/8-or 10-inch bbl.	NiB $285	Ex $235	Gd $172
SP Standard w/12-inch bbl.	NiB $330	Ex $266	Gd $191
SP Standard w/15-inch bbl.	NiB $344	Ex $286	Gd $200
SP Deluxe w/8-or 10-inch bbl.	NiB $346	Ex $276	Gd $199
SP Deluxe w/12-inch bbl.	NiB $355	Ex $291	Gd $209
SP Deluxe w/15-inch bbl.	NiB $374	Ex $306	Gd $215
SPX Standard w/10-inch bbl.	NiB $679	Ex $548	Gd $387
SPX Deluxe w/10-inch bbl.	NiB $925	Ex $744	Gd $524

BEHOLLA PISTOL — Suhl, Germany. Mfd. by both Becker and Holländer and Stenda-Werke GmbH

POCKET AUTOMATIC PISTOL NiB $272 Ex $227 Gd $191
Caliber: .32 Automatic (7.65mm). Seven-round magazine, 2.9-inch bbl., 5.5 inches overall. Weight: 22 oz. Fixed sights. Blued finish. Serrated wood or hard rubber grips. Made by Becker and Hollander 1915 to 1920, by Stenda-Werke circa 1920 to 1925. Note: Essentially the same pistol was manufactured w/the Stenda version as the "Leonhardt" by H. M. Gering and as the "Menta" by August Menz.

BENELLI PISTOLS — Urbino, Italy. *Imported by Larry's Guns in Gray, ME since 2003 (Previously imported by EEA in Sharpes, FL; Sile Dist. New York, NY; Saco, Arlington, VA)*

MP90S WORLD CUP TARGET PISTOL
Semiautomatic blowback action.   Calibers: .22 Short, .22 LR, .32 W.C. Five-round magazine, 4.33-inch fixed bbl. 6.75 inches overall. Weight: 36 oz. Post front sight, adjustable rear. Blue finish. Anatomic shelf-style grip. Imported from 1992 to 2001.

MP90S (.22 LR) . . . . NiB $1430 Ex $1221 Gd $1095
MP90S (.22 Short, disc. 1995) NiB $1314 Ex $1155 Gd $984
MP90S (.32 S&W) . . . . . . NiB $1562 Ex $1364 Gd $1221
w/conversion kit, add $80

MODEL B-76 . . . . NiB $441 Ex $326 Gd $257
Semi-auto, SA/DA. Cal.: 9 mm Para. Bbl.: 4.25 inches. 8-round mag. Weight: 34 oz. Disc. 1990.

MODEL B-765 TARGET . . . . . . NiB $604 Ex $475 Gd $665
Cal.: 9 mm Para. Similar to B-76 model but w/5.5-inch bbl., target grips, adj. rear sight. Disc. 1990.

MODEL B-77 . . . . NiB $405 Ex $309 Gd $220
Semi-auto, SA/DA. Cal.: 32 ACP. Bbl.: Steel, 4.25 inches. 8-round mag. Disc. 1995.

MODEL B-80 . . . . NiB $425 Ex $315 Gd $245
Semi-auto, SA/DA. Cal.: .30 Luger. Bbl.: Steel, 4.25 inches. 8-round mag. Weight: 34 oz. Disc. 1995.

B-80s Target, add $126

MODEL B-82 . . . . NiB $813 Ex $551 Gd $414
Limited production Italian police model; serial no. with "D" suffix. Cal.: .30 Luger, .32 ACP, 9 mm Ultra.

MODEL MP3S . . . . NiB $603 Ex $467 Gd $336
Semi-auto, target model. Cal.: .32 S&W Long Wadcutter. Bbl.: 5.5 inches. High gloss blued finish, target grips. Adj. rear sight. Disc. 1995.

MP95E SPORT TARGET PISTOL
Similar to the MP90S except with 5- or 9-round magazine, 4.25- inch bbl., Blue or chrome finish. Checkered target grip. Imported from1994 to date.
Blue MP95 (.22 LR) . . . . NiB $892 Ex $708 Gd $467
Blue MP95 (.32 WC). . . . . NiB $981 Ex $840 Gd $640
Chrome, add $80

BERETTA USA CORP. — Accokeek, Maryland (berettausa.com)

Beretta firearms are manufactured by Fabbrica D'Armi Pietro Beretta S. p. A. in the Gardone Val Trompia (Brescia), Italy. This prestigious firm has been in business since 1526. In 1977, Beretta U.S.A. Corp., a manufacturing and importing facility, opened in Accokeek, MD. (Previously imported by Garcia Corp., J.L. Galef & Son, Inc. and Berben Corporation.) Note: Beretta also owns additional firearms manufacturing companies including: Benelli, Franchi, Sako, Stoeger, Tikka and Uberti.

MODEL 20 DA AUTO PISTOL . . NiB $257 Ex $203 Gd $136
Caliber: .25 ACP. Eight-round magazine, 2.5-inch bbl., 4.9 inches overall. Weight: 10.9 oz. Plastic or walnut grips. Fixed sights. Made 1984 to 1985.

MODEL 21 DA AUTO PISTOL
Calibers: .22 LR and .25 ACP. Seven-round (.22 LR) or 8-round (..25 ACP) magazine, 2.5-inch bbl., 4.9 inches overall. Weight: About 12 oz. Blade front sight, V-notch rear. Walnut grips. Made from 1985 to date. Model 21EL disc. 2000.

Blued finish . . . . NiB $285 Ex $210 Gd $165
Nickel finish (.22 LR only) . . . NiB $300 Ex $225 Gd $177
Model 21EL engraved model. . NiB $375 Ex $310 Gd $230

MODEL 70
AUTOMATIC PISTOL . . . . .NiB $278 Ex $199 Gd $131
Improved version of Model 1935. Steel or lightweight alloy. Calibers: .32 Auto (7.65mm), .380 Auto (9mm Short). Eight-round (.32) or 7-round (.380) magazine, 3.5-inch bbl., 6.5 inches overall. Weight: Steel, 22.25 oz.; alloy, 16 oz. Fixed sights. Blued finish. Checkered plastic grips. Made 1959 to 1985. Note: Formerly marketed in U.S. as "Puma" (alloy model in .32) and "Cougar" (steel model in .380). Disc.

MODEL 70S . . . . NiB $420 Ex $288 Gd $210
Similar to Model 70T except chambered for .22 Auto and .380 Auto. Longer bbl. guide and safety lever blocking hammer. Front blade and rear sight fixed on breechblock. Weight: 1 lb., 7 oz. Made 1977 to 1985.

MODEL 70T
AUTOMATIC PISTOL . . . . NiB $315 Ex $231 Gd $189
Similar to Model 70. Caliber: .32 Automatic (7.65mm). Nine-round magazine, 6-inch bbl., 9.5 inches overall. Weight: 19 oz. adj. rear sight, blade front sight. Blued finish. Checkered plastic grips. Intro. in 1959. Disc.

MODEL 71
AUTOMATIC PISTOL . . . . NiB $268 Ex $199 Gd $142
Same general specifications as alloy Model 70. Caliber: .22 LR. Six-inch bbl., 8-round magazine, Adj. rear sight frame. Single action. Made 1959 to 1989. Note: Formerly marketed in U.S. as the "Jaguar Plinker."

MODEL 72 . . . . NiB $315 Ex $231 Gd $190
Same as Model 71 except has 6-inch bbl., w eight: 18 oz. Intro. in 1959. Disc. Note: Formerly marketed in U.S as "Jaguar Plinker."

MODEL 76 AUTO TARGET PISTOL
Caliber: .22 LR. 10-round magazine, 6-inch bbl., 8.8 inches overall. Weight: 33 oz. adj. rear sight, front sight w/interchangeable blades. Blued finish. Checkered plastic or wood grips. Made from 1966 to 1985. Note: Formerly marketed in the U.S. as the "Sable."
Model 76 w/plastic grips. . . . . NiB $393 Ex $315 Gd $257
Model 76W w/wood grips. . . . NiB $430 Ex $357 Gd $299

MODEL 81 DA AUTO PISTOL NiB $341 Ex $247 Gd $199
Caliber: .32 Automatic (7.65mm). 12-round magazine, 3.8-inch bbl., 6.8 inches overall. Weight: 23.5 oz. Fixed sights. Blued finish. Plastic grips. Made principally for the European market 1975 to 1984, w/similar variations as implemented on the Model 84.

MODEL 82W DA AUTO PISTOL NiB $330 Ex $231 Gd $178
Caliber: .32 ACP. Similar to the Model 81 except with a slimmer-profile frame designed to accept a single column 9-round magazine. Matte black finish. Importation disc. 1984.

MODEL 84B DA AUTO PISTOL NiB $325 Ex $222 Gd $173
Same as Model 81 except made in caliber .380 Automatic w/13-round magazine, 3.82-inch bbl., 6.8 inches overall. Weight: 23 oz. Fixed front and rear sights. Made from 1975 to 1982.

MODEL 84B DA AUTO PISTOL NiB $335 Ex $230 Gd $184
Improved version of Model 84 w/strengthened frame a nd slide, and firing-pin block safety added. AmbidExtrous reversible magazine release. Blued or nickel finish. Checkered black plastic or wood grips. Other specifications same. Made circa 1982 to 1984.

Beretta Model 71

Beretta Model 72

Beretta Model 84

Beretta Model 84
Cheetah (Nickel finish)

MODEL 84(BB) DA AUTO PISTOL
Improved version of Model 84B w/further-strengthened slide, frame and recoil spring. Caliber: .380 ACP. 13-round magazine, 3.82-inch bbl., 6.8 inches overall. Weight: 23 oz. Checkered black plastic or wood grips. Blued or nickel finish. Notched rear and blade front sight. Made circa 1984-94.
Blued w/plastic grips . . . . . . NiB $393 Ex $241 Gd $152
Blued w/wood grips . . . . NiB $446 Ex $372 Gd $270
Nickel finish w/wood grips . . . NiB $630 Ex $493 Gd $383

Beretta Model 85

Beretta Model 85BB

Beretta Model 86 Cheetah

MODEL 84 CHEETAH SEMI-AUTO PISTOL
Similar to the Model 84 BB except with required design changes as mandated by regulation, including reduced magazine capacity (10-round magazine) and marked as 9mm short (.380) as a marketing strategy to counter increased availability of 9mm chamberings from other manufacturers. Made from 1994 to 2002, reintro. 2004.
Blued w/plastic grips . . . . NiB $650 Ex $520 Gd $360
Blued w/wood grips . . . . NiB $667 Ex $551 Gd $367
Nickel finish w/wood grips . . . NiB $735 Ex $498 Gd $372

MODEL 85
DA AUTO PISTOL . . . . NiB $660 Ex $460 Gd $330
Similar to the Model 84 except designed with a slimmer-profile frame to accept a single column 8-round magazine, no

ambidExtrous magazine release. Matte black finish. Weight: 21.8 oz. Introduced in 1977 following the Model 84.

MODEL 85B DA AUTO PISTOLNiB $430 Ex $330 Gd $210
Improved version of the Model 85. Imported from 1982-85.

MODEL 85BB DA PISTOL
Improved version of the Model 85B w/strengthened frame and slide. Caliber: .380 ACP. Eight-round magazine, 3.82 inch bbl., 6.8 inches overall. Weight: 21.8 oz. Blued or nickel finish. Checkered black plastic or wood grips. Imported from 1985 to 1994.
Blued finish
w/plastic grips . . . . NiB $520 Ex $395 Gd $280
Blued finish
w/wood grips . . . . NiB $530 Ex $404 Gd $295
Nickel finish
w/wood grips . . . . NiB $582 Ex $430 Gd $315

MODEL 85 CHEETAH SEMI-AUTO PISTOL
Similar to the Model 85 BB except with required design changes as mandated by regulation and marked as 9mm short (.380) as a marketing strategy to counter increased availability of 9mm chamberings from other manufacturers. Made from 1994 to date.
Blued finish
w/plastic grips . . . . NiB $656 Ex $470 Gd $310
Blued finish
w/wood grips . . . . NiB $680 Ex $490 Gd $330
Nickel finish
w/wood grips . . . . NiB $719 Ex $525 Gd $393

MODEL 85F DA PISTOL
Similar to the Model 85BB except has re-contoured trigger guard and manual ambidExtrous safety w/decocking device. Bruniton finish. Imported in 1990 only.
Matte black Bruniton
finish w/plastic grips. . . . . . . NiB $390 Ex $315 Gd $255
Matte black Bruniton
finish w/wood grips . . . . NiB $420 Ex $344 Gd $283

MODEL 86 CHEETAH
DA AUTO PISTOL . . . . NiB $628 Ex $493 Gd $278
Caliber: .380 auto. Eight-round magazine, 4.4- inch bbl., 7.3 inches overall. Weight: 23.3 oz. Bruniton finish w/wood grips. Made from 1986-89. (Reintroduced 1990 in the Cheetah series.)

MODEL 87 CHEETAH AUTOMATIC PISTOL
Similar to the Model 85 except in .22 LR w/8- or 10- round magazine (Target) and optional Extended 6-inch bbl. (Target in single action). Overall length: 6.8 to 8.8 inches. Weight: 20.1 oz. to 29.4 oz (Target). Checkered wood grips. Made from 1987 to date.
Blued finish
(double-action). . . . . NiB $735 Ex $550 Gd $430
Target model
(single action). . . . . NiB $765 Ex $580 Gd $467

MODEL 89 GOLD STANDARD TARGET
AUTOMATIC PISTOL . . . . . . NiB $703 Ex $556 Gd $467
Caliber: .22 LR. Eight-round magazine, 6-inch bbl., 9.5 inches overall. Weight: 41 oz. Adj. target sights. Blued finish. Target-style walnut grips. Made from 1988 to 2000.

MODEL 90
DA AUTO PISTOL . . . . NiB $325 Ex $235 Gd $195
Caliber: .32 Auto (7.65mm). Eight-round magazine, 3.63-inch bbl., 6.63 inches overall. Weight: 19.5 oz. Fixed sights. Blued finish. Checkered plastic grips. Made from 1969 to 1983.

MODEL 92 DA AUTO
PISTOL (1ST SERIES). . . . . . . NiB $824 Ex $640 Gd $445
Caliber: 9mm Para. 15-round magazine, 4.9-inch bbl., 8.5 inches overall. Weight: 33.5 oz. Fixed sights. Blued finish. Plastic grips. Initial production of 5,000 made in 1976.

MODEL 92D DA AUTO PISTOL

Same general specifications as Model 92F except DA only w/ bobbed hammer and 3-dot sight. Made from 1992 to 1998.
Model 92D . . . . **NiB $667 Ex $470 Gd $364**
With Tritium
sight system, add **$100**

MODEL 92F COMPACT

DA AUTOMATIC PISTOL . . . . **NiB $630 Ex $560 Gd $279**
Caliber: 9mm Para. 12-round magazine, 4.3-inch bbl., 7.8 inches overall. Weight: 31.5 oz. Wood grips. Square-notched rear sight, blade front integral w/slide. Made from 1990-93.

MODEL 92F COMPACT L TYPE M DA AUTOMATIC PISTOL

Same general specifications as the original 92F Compact except 8-round magazine, Weight: 30.9 oz. Bruniton matte finish. Made from 1998 to 2003.
Model 92F
Compact L Type M . . . . **NiB $660 Ex $580 Gd $390**
Model 92F
Compact L Type M Inox . . . . . **NiB $656 Ex $583 Gd $393**
w/Tritium
sight system, add **$100**

MODEL 92F DA AUTOMATIC PISTOL

Same general specifications as Model 92 except w/slide-mounted safety and repositioned magazine release. Replaced Model 92SB. Blued or stainless finish. Made from 1992 to 1998.
Blued finish . . . . **NiB $630 Ex $493 Gd $341**
Stainless finish . . . . **NiB $619 Ex $477 Gd $325**
Model 92F-EL gold, add **$200**

MODEL 92FS DA AUTOMATIC PISTOL

Calibers: 9mm, 9mmx19 and .40 S&W. 15- round magazine, 4.9-inch bbl., 8.5 inches overall. Weight: 34.4 to 35.3 oz. AmbidExtrous safety/decock lever. Chrome-lined bore w/combat trigger guard. Bruniton finish w/plastic grips or Inox finish w/rubber grips. Made from 1999 to 2003.
Model 92FS . . . . **NiB $630 Ex $520 Gd $325**
Model 92FS, B-lok . . . . **NiB $640 Ex $477 Gd $330**
Model 92FS — Brigadier
(Made 1999 to date) . . . . **NiB $760 Ex $556 Gd $395**
Model 92FS —
Brigadier Inox . . . . **NiB $766 Ex $630 Gd $477**
Model 92FS — Centurion
(Made 1992 to date) . . . . **NiB $525 Ex $404 Gd $289**
Model 92FS — 470th Anniver.
(Made 1999) . . . . **NiB $2205 Ex $1900 Gd $1690**

MODEL 92S DA AUTO

PISTOL (2ND SERIES) . . . . **NiB $645 Ex $520 Gd $370**
Revised version of Model 92 w/ambidExtrous slide-mounted safety modification intended for both commercial and military production. Evolved to Model 92S-1 for U.S. Military trials. Made from 1980 to 1985.

MODEL 92SB DA

AUTO PISTOL (3RD SERIES) . . **NiB $598 Ex $430 Gd $345**
Same general specifications as standard Model 92 except has slide-mounted safety and repositioned magazine release. Made 1981 to 1985.

MODEL 92 SB-F

DA AUTO PISTOL . . . . **NiB $735 Ex $598 Gd $404**
Caliber: 9mm Para. 15-round magazine, bbl.: 4.9 inches, 8.5 inches overall. Weight: 34 oz. Plastic or Beretta Model 92 SB-F DA Auto Pistol wood grips. Square-notched rear sight, blade front sight integral w/slide. This model, also called Model 92S-1, was the standard-issue sidearm for the U.S. Armed Forces. Disc. 1985.

Beretta Model 92F

Beretta Model 92
Compact L Type M

Beretta Model 92FS
Brigadier Inox

Beretta Model 96

Beretta Model 949 Olimpionico

Beretta Model 950BS Jetfire

MODEL 96 DA AUTO PISTOL
Same general specifications as Model 92F except in .40 S&W. 10-round magazine (9-round in Compact model). Made from 1992 to 1998.
Model 96 D (DA only) . . . . . . NiB $475 Ex $355 Gd $300
Model 96 Centurion (compact) NiB $550 Ex $460 Gd $310
w/Tritium sights, add $110
w/Tritium sights system, add $115

MODEL 101 . . . . NiB $270 Ex $200 Gd $155
Same as Model 70T except caliber .22 LR, has 10-round magazine, Intro. in 1959. Disc.

MODEL 318 (1934) AUTO PISTOL . . . NiB $270 Ex $200 Gd $155
Caliber: .25 Automatic (6.35mm). Eight-round magazine, 2.5-inch bbl., 4.5 inches overall. Weight: 14 oz. Fixed sights. Blued finish. Plastic grips. Made from 1934 to c. 1939.

MODEL 949
OLYMPIC TARGET AUTO PISTOL . . NiB $708 Ex $577 Gd $456
Calibers: .22 Short, .22 LR. Five-round magazine, 8.75-inch bbl., 12.5 inches overall. Weight: 38 oz. Target sights. Adj. bbl., weight. Muzzle brake. Checkered walnut grips w/thumbrest. Made from 1959 to 1964.

MODEL 950B AUTO PISTOL . NiB $225 Ex $168 Gd $115
Same general specifications as Model 950CC except caliber .25 Auto, has 7-round magazine, Made from 1959 to date. Note: Formerly marketed in the U.S. as "Jetfire."

MODEL 950B JETFIRE SA PISTOL
Calibers: .25 ACP or .22 Short (disc.1992). Seven- or 8-round magazine, 2.4- or 4- inch bbl., 4.5 to 4.7 inches overall. Weight: 9.9 oz. Fixed blade front and V-notch rear sights. Matte Blue or Inox (Stainless) finish. Checkered black plastic grips. Made from 1987 to date.
Blued finish . . . . NiB $168 Ex $99 Gd $84
Nickel finish. . . . . NiB $225 Ex $173 Gd $147
Inox finish . . . . NiB $257 Ex $204 Gd $160
w/4-inch bbl., (.22 Short) . . . . NiB $256 Ex $207 Gd $157

MODEL 950CC
AUTO PISTOL . . . . NiB $157 Ex $126 Gd $104
Caliber: .22 Short. Six-round magazine, hinged 2.38-inch bbl., 4.75 inches overall. Weight: 11 oz. Fixed sights. Blued finish. Plastic grips. Made from 1959 to date. Note: Formerly marketed in the U.S. as "Minx M2."

MODEL 950CC
SPECIAL AUTO PISTOL . . . . . . NiB $155 Ex $103 Gd $88
Same general specifications as Model 950CC Auto except has 4-inch bbl. Made from 1959 to date. Note: Formerly marketed in the U.S. as "Minx M4."

MODEL 951 (1951)
MILITARY AUTO PISTOL . . . . NiB $330 Ex $251 Gd $200
Caliber: 9mm Para. Eight-round magazine, 4.5-inch bbl., 8 inches overall. Weight: 31 oz. Fixed sights. Blued finish. Plastic grips. Made from 1952 to date. Note: This is the standard pistol of the Italian Armed Forces, also used by Egyptian and Israeli armies and by the police in Nigeria. Egyptian and Israeli models usually command a premium. Formerly marketed in the U.S. as the "Brigadier."

MODEL 1915
AUTO PISTOL . . . . NiB $1587 Ex $1386 Gd $1087
Calibers: 9mm Glisenti and .32 ACP (7.65mm). Eight-round magazine, 4-inch bbl., 6.7 inches overall (9mm), 5.7 inches (.32 ACP). Weight: 30 oz. (9mm), 20 oz. (.32 ACP). Fixed sights. Blued finish. Wood grips. Made 1915-1922. An improved postwar 1915/1919 version in caliber .32 ACP was later offered for sale in 1922 as the Model 1922.

MODEL 1923 AUTO PISTOL NiB $2136 Ex $2094 Gd $1669
Caliber: 9mm Glisenti (Luger). Eight-round magazine, 4-inch bbl., 6.5 inches overall. Weight: 30 oz. Fixed sights. Blued finish. Plastic grips. Made circa 1923 to 1936.

MODEL 1934 AUTO PISTOL
Caliber: .380 Automatic (9mm Short). Seven-round magazine, 3.38-inch bbl., 5.88 inches overall. Weight: 24 oz. Fixed sights. Blued finish. Plastic grips. Official pistol of the Italian Armed Forces. Wartime pieces not as well made and finished as commercial models. Made from 1934 to 1959.
Commercial model . . . . . . NiB $2340 Ex $2100 Gd $1333
War model . . . . NiB $598 Ex $383 Gd $299

MODEL 1935 AUTO PISTOL
Caliber: .32 ACP (7.65mm). Eight-round magazine, 3.5-inch bbl., 5.75 inches overall. Weight: 24 oz. Fixed sights. Blued finish. Plastic grips. A roughly-finished version of this pistol was produced during WW II. Made from 1935 to 1959.

Commercial model . . . . . . NiB $1806 Ex $1465 Gd $1078
War model . . . . NiB $598 Ex $383 Gd $299

MODEL 3032 DA SEMIAUTOMATIC TOMCAT
Caliber: .32 ACP. Seven-round magazine, 2.45-inch bbl., 5 inches overall. Weight: 14.5 oz. Fixed sights. Blued or stainless finish. Made from 1996 to date.

Matte blue . . . . NiB $329 Ex $262 Gd $180
Polished blue . . . . NiB $386 Ex $329 Gd $252
Stainless. . . . . NiB $412 Ex $365 Gd $252

Beretta
Model 3032 Tomcat

MODEL 8000/8040/8045 COUGAR DA PISTOL
Calibers: 9mm, .40 S&W and .45 Auto. Eight- or 10- shot magazine, 3.6 to 3.7- inch bbl., 7- to 7.2 inches overall. Weight: 32 to 32.6 oz. Short recoil action w/rotating barrel. Fixed sights w/3-dot Tritium system. TExtured black composition grips. Matte black Bruniton finish w/alloy frame. Made from 1995 to 2005.

8000 Cougar D
(9mm DAO) . . . . NiB $715 Ex $649 Gd $400
8000 Cougar F
(9mm DA) . . . . NiB $750 Ex $644 Gd $388
8040 Cougar D
(.40 S&W DAO) . . . . NiB $685 Ex $618 Gd $373
8040 Cougar F
(.40 S&W DA) . . . . NiB $685 Ex $618 Gd $373
8045 Cougar D
(.45 Auto DAO) . . . . NiB $736 Ex $637 Gd $400
8045 Cougar F
(.357 Sig SA/DA) . . . . NiB $685 Ex $536 Gd $386

Beretta
Model 8000 Cougar D

MODEL 8000/8040/8045 MINI COUGAR DA PISTOL
Calibers: 9mm, .40 S&W and .45 Auto. Six- 8- or 10-round magazine, 3.6- to 3.7- inch bbl., 7 inches overall. Weight: 27.4 to 30.4 oz. Fixed sights w/3-dot Tritium system. AmbidExtrous safety/decocker lever. Matte black Bruniton finish w/anodized aluminum alloy frame. Made from 1995 to 2008.

8000 Mini
Cougar D (9mm DAO) . . . . . . NiB $654 Ex $577 Gd $326
8000 Mini
Cougar F (9mm DA) . . . . NiB $654 Ex $577 Gd $326
8040 Mini
Cougar D (.40 S&W DAO) . . . NiB $654 Ex $577 Gd $326
8040 Mini
Cougar F (.40 S&W DA) . . . . . NiB $654 Ex $577 Gd $326
8045 Mini
Cougar D (.45 Auto DAO) . . . .NiB $654 Ex $577 Gd $326
8045 Mini
Cougar F (.45 Auto DA) . . . . . NiB $654 Ex $577 Gd $326

Beretta
Model 8000 Cougar F

MODEL 9000S SUBCOMPACT PISTOL SERIES
Calibers: 9mm, .40 S&W. 10-round magazine, 3.5- inch bbl., 6.6 inches overall. Weight: 25.7 to 27.5 oz. Single/double and double-action only. Front and rear dovetail sights w/3- dot system. Chrome-plated barrel w/Techno-polymer frame. Geometric locking system w/tilt barrel. Made from 2000 to 2005.

Type D (9mm) . . . . .NiB $432 Ex $366 Gd $304
Type D (.40 S&W) . . . . NiB $432 Ex $366 Gd $304
Type F (9mm) . . . . NiB $432 Ex $366 Gd $304
Type F (.40 S&W) . . . . NiB $432 Ex $366 Gd $304

Beretta
Model 8040 Mini Cougar D

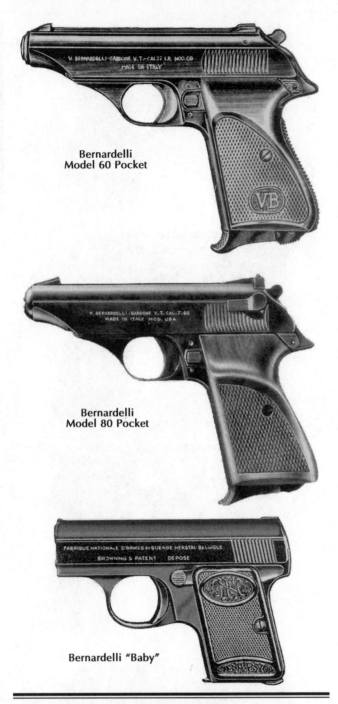

Bernardelli
Model 60 Pocket

Bernardelli
Model 80 Pocket

Bernardelli "Baby"

BERNARDELLI, VINCENZO S.P.A.—
Gardone V. T. (Brescia), Italy

MODEL 60 POCKET
AUTOMATIC PISTOL . . . . NiB $247 Ex $221 Gd $190
Calibers: .22 LR, .32 Auto (7.65mm), .380 Auto (9mm Short). Eight-round magazine (.22 and .32), 7-round (.380). 3.5-inch bbl., 6.5 inches overall. Weight: About 25 oz. Fixed sights. Blued finish. Bakelite grips. Made from 1959 to 1990.

MODEL 68 AUTOMATIC PISTOL . . NiB $180 Ex $128 Gd $92
Caliber: 6.35. Five- and 8-round magazine, 2.13-inch bbl., 4.13 inches overall. Weight: 10 oz. Fixed sights. Blued or chrome finish. Bakelite or pearl grips. This model, like its .22-caliber counterpart, was known as the "Baby" Bernardelli. Disc. 1970.

MODEL 69 AUTOMATIC
TARGET PISTOL . . . . NiB $693 Ex $570 Gd $383
Caliber: .22 LR. 10-round magazine, 5.9-inch bbl., 9 inches overall. Weight: 2.2 lbs. Fully adj. target sights. Blued finish. Stippled right- or left-hand wraparound walnut grips. Made from 1987 to date. This was previously Model 100; not imported to the U.S.

MODEL 80
AUTOMATIC PISTOL . . . . NiB $204 Ex $128 Gd $92
Calibers: .22 LR, .32 ACP (7.65mm), .380 Auto (9mm Short). Magazine capacity: 10-round (.22), 8-round (.32), 7-round (.380). 3.5-inch bbl., 6.5 inches overall. Weight: 25.6 oz. adj. rear sight, white dot front sight. Blued finish. Plastic thumbrest grips. Note: Model 80 is a modification of Model 60 designed to conform w/U.S. import regulations. Made from 1968 to 1988.

MODEL 90
SPORT TARGET . . . . NiB $245 Ex $199 Gd $148
Same as Model 80 except has 6-inch bbl., 9 inches overall, weight: 26.8 oz. Made from 1968 1990.

MODEL 100 TARGET
AUTOMATIC PISTOL . . . . NiB $428 Ex $362 Gd $291
Caliber: .22 LR. 10-round magazine, 5.9-inch bbl., 9 inches overall. Weight: 37.75 oz. Adj. rear sight, interchangeable front sights. Blued finish. Checkered walnut thumbrest grips. Made from 1969-86. Note: Formerly Model 69.

MODEL AMR AUTO PISTOL . . NiB $433 Ex $321 Gd $270
Simlar to Model USA except with 6-inch bbl. and target sights. Imported from 1992 to 1994.

"BABY" AUTOMATIC PISTOL . NiB $321 Ex $235 Gd $179
Calibers: .22 Short, .22 Long. Five-round magazine, 2.13-inch bbl., 4.13 inches overall. Weight: 9 oz. Fixed sights. Blued finish. Bakelite grips. Made from 1949 to 1968.

MODEL P010
AUTOMATIC PISTOL . . . . NiB $712 Ex $520 Gd $341
Caliber: .22 LR. Five- and 10-round magazine, 5.9-inch bbl. w/7.5-inch sight radius. Weight: 40 oz. Interchangeable front sight, adj. rear. Blued finish. TExtured walnut grips. Made from 1988 to 1992 and 1995 to 1997.

P018 COMPACT MODEL . . . . NiB $571 Ex $461 Gd $385
Slightly smaller version of the Model P018 standard DA automatic except has 14-round magazine and 4-inch bbl., 7.68 inches overall. Weight: 33 oz. Walnut grips only. Imported from 1987 to 1996.

P018 DOUBLE-ACTION
AUTOMATIC PISTOL
Caliber: 9mm Para. 16-round magazine, 4.75-inch bbl., 8.5 inches overall. Weight: 36 oz. Fixed combat sights. Blued finish. Checkered plastic or walnut grips. Imported from 1987 to 1996.
w/plastic grips . . . . NiB $510 Ex $405 Gd $305
w/walnut grips . . . . NiB $551 Ex $428 Gd $342

P-ONE DA AUTO PISTOL
Caliber: 9mm Parabellum or .40 S&W. 10- or 16-round magazine, 4.8-inch bbl., 8.35 inches overall. Weight: 34 oz. Blade front sight, adjustable rear w/3-dot system. Matte black or chrome finish. Checkered walnut or black plastic grips. Imported from 1993 to 1997.
Model P-One blue finish.... NiB $622 Ex $525 Gd $357
Model P-One chrome finish .. NiB $693 Ex $556 Gd $393
w/walnut grips, add $50

P-ONE PRACTICAL VB AUTO PISTOL
Similar to Model P One except chambered for 9x21mm w/2-, 4- or 6-port compensating system for IPSC competition. Imported 1993 to 1997.
**Model P One
Practical (2 port)**......... NiB $1148 Ex $1068 Gd $785
**Model P One
Practical (4 port)**......... NiB $1259 Ex $1054 Gd $782
**Model P One
Practical (6 port)**......... NiB $1678 Ex $1393 Gd $995
w/chrome finish, add $75

SPORTER AUTOMATIC PISTOL. NiB $332 Ex $245 Gd $133
Caliber .22 LR. Eight-round magazine, bbl., lengths: 6-, 8- and 10-inch, 13 inches overall (10-inch bbl.). weight: About 30 oz. (10-inch bbl.) Target sights. Blued finish. Walnut grips. Made 1949 to 1968.

MODEL USA AUTO PISTOL
Single-action, blowback. Calibers: .22 LR, .32 ACP, .380 ACP. Seven-round magazine or 10-round magazine (.22 LR). 3.5-inch bbl., 6.5 inches overall. Weight: 26.5 oz. Ramped front sight, adjustable rear. Blue or chrome finish. Checkered black bakelite grips w/ thumbrest. Imported from 1991 to 1997.
Model USA blue finish...... NiB $420 Ex $330 Gd $265
Model USA chrome finish.... NiB $469 Ex $385 Gd $219

VEST POCKET
AUTOMATIC PISTOL .... NiB $275 Ex $199 Gd $148
Caliber: .25 Auto (6.35mm). Five- or 8-round magazine, 2.13-inch bbl., 4.13 inches overall. Weight: 9 oz. Fixed sights. Blued finish. Bakelite grips. Made from 1945 to 1968.

BERSA PISTOLS — Argentina.
Currently imported by Eagle Imports, Wanamassa, NJ (previously by Interarms & Outdoor Sports)

MODEL 83 DA AUTO PISTOL
Similar to the Model 23 except for the following specifications: Caliber: .380 ACP. Seven-round magazine, 3.5-inch bbl., Front blade sight integral on slide, square-notch rear adj. for windage. Blued or satin nickel finish. Custom wood grips. Imported from 1988 to 1994.
Blued finish .... NiB $275 Ex $201 Gd $126
Satin nickel .... NiB $321 Ex $271 Gd $194

MODEL 85 DA AUTO PISTOL
Same general specifications as Model 83 except 13-round magazine, Imported from 1988 to 1994.
Blued finish .... NiB $326 Ex $235 Gd $128
Satin nickel .... NiB $377 Ex $286 Gd $179

MODEL 86 DA AUTO PISTOL
Same general specifications as Model 85 except available in matte blued finish and w/Neoprene grips. Imported from 1992 to 1994.
Matte blued finish .... NiB $347 Ex $270 Gd $219
Nickel finish.............. NiB $362 Ex $262 Gd $199

Bernardelli P010

Bernardelli P018

Bersa Model 85

Bersa Model 383

Bersa Thunder .380

Bersa Thunder .380 Deluxe

MODEL 95 DA AUTOMATIC PISTOL

Caliber: .380 ACP. Seven-round magazine, 3.5-inch bbl., weight: 23 oz. Wraparound rubber grips. Blade front and rear notch sights. Imported from 1995 to date.

Blued finish . . . . NiB $329 Ex $214 Gd $158
Nickel finish. . . . . NiB $318 Ex $204 Gd $143

MODEL 97 AUTO PISTOL . . . NiB $389 Ex $332 Gd $219

Caliber: .380 ACP. Seven-round magazine, 3.3-inch bbl., 6.5 inches overall. Weight: 28 oz. Intro. 1982. Disc.

MODEL 223

Same general specifications as Model 383 except in .22 LR w/10-round magazine capacity. Disc. 1987.

Double-action . . . . NiB $243 Ex $213 Gd $143
Single-action . . . . NiB $224 Ex $168 Gd $125

MODEL 224

Caliber: .22 LR. 10-round magazine, 4-inch bbl., weight: 26 oz. Front blade sight, square-notched rear adj. for windage. Blued finish. Checkered nylon or custom wood grips. Made 1984. SA. disc. 1986.

Double-action . . . . NiB $240 Ex $204 Gd $143
Single-action . . . . NiB $204 Ex $179 Gd $122

MODEL 226

Same general specifications as Model 224 but w/6-inch bbl. Disc. 1987.

Double-action . . . . NiB $240 Ex $204 Gd $143
Single-action . . . . NiB $204 Ex $179 Gd $122

MODEL 383 AUTO PISTOL

Caliber: .380 Auto. Seven-round magazine, 3.5-inch bbl. Front blade sight integral on slide, square-notched rear sight adj. for windage. Custom wood grips on double-action, nylon grips on single action. Blued or satin nickel finish. Made 1984. SA. disc. 1989.

Double-action . . . . NiB $235 Ex $150 Gd $102
Single-action . . . . NiB $219 Ex $158 Gd $122

MODEL 622 AUTO PISTOL . . NiB $204 Ex $138 Gd $100

Caliber: .22 LR. Seven-round magazine, 4- or 6-inch bbl., 7 or 9 inches overall. Weight: 2.25 lbs. Blade front sight, square-notch rear adj. for windage. Blued finish. Nylon grips. Made from 1982 to 1987.

MODEL 644 AUTO PISTOL . . NiB $286 Ex $240 Gd $168

Caliber: .22 LR. 10-round magazine, 3.5-inch bbl., weight: 26.5 oz. 6.5 inches overall. Adj. rear sight, blade front. Contoured black nylon grips. Made from 1980 to 1988.

THUNDER 9 AUTO PISTOL . . NiB $408 Ex $272 Gd $168

Caliber: 9mm Para. 15-round magazine, 4-inch bbl., 7.38 inches overall. Weight: 30 oz. Blade front sight, adj. rear w/3-dot system. AmbidExtrous safety and decocking device. Matte blued finish. Checkered black polymer grips. Made from 1993 to 1996.

THUNDER .22 AUTO PISTOL (MODEL 23)

Caliber: .22 LR, 10-round magazine, 3.5-inch bbl., 6.63 inches overall. Weight: 24.5 oz. Notched-bar dovetailed rear, blade integral w/slide front. Black polymer grips. Made from 1988 to 1998.

Blued finish . . . . NiB $254 Ex $214 Gd $168
Nickel finish. . . . . NiB $260 Ex $220 Gd $177

THUNDER .380 AUTO PISTOL
Caliber: .380 ACP. Seven-round magazine, 3.5-inch bbl., 6.63 inches overall. Weight: 25.75 oz. Notched-bar dovetailed rear, blade integral w/slide front. Blued, satin nickel, or Duo-Tone finish. Made from 1995 to 1998.
Blued finish . . . . NiB $306 Ex $230 Gd $183
Satin nickel finish. . . . . NiB $333 Ex $255 Gd $204
Duo-Tone finish . . . . NiB $306 Ex $230 Gd $168

THUNDER .380 PLUS AUTO PISTOL
Same general specifications as standard Thunder .380 except has 10-round magazine and weight: 26 oz. Made from 1995 to 1997.
Matte finish . . . . NiB $306 Ex $230 Gd $168
Satin nickel finish. . . . . NiB $321 Ex $245 Gd $194
Duo-Tone finish, add $40

BROLIN ARMS — La Verne, California

"LEGEND SERIES" SA AUTOMATIC PISTOL
Caliber: .45 ACP. Seven-round magazine, 4- or 5-inch bbl., weight: 32-36 oz. Walnut grips. Single action, full size, compact, or full size frame compact slide. Matte blued finish. Lowered and flared ejection port. Made from 1995 to 1998.
Model L45 . . . . NiB $469 Ex $398 Gd $306
Model L45C . . . . NiB $487 Ex $366 Gd $305
Model L45T . . . . NiB $487 Ex $366 Gd $305

"PATRIOT SERIES" SA AUTOMATIC PISTOL
Caliber: .45 ACP. Seven-round magazine, 3.25- and 4-inch bbl., weight: 33-37 oz. Wood grips. Fixed rear sights. Made 1996 to 1997.
Model P45 . . . . NiB $627 Ex $469 Gd $301
Model P45C (disc. 1997) . . . . NiB $638 Ex $479 Gd $311
Model P45T (disc. 1997). . . . . NiB $658 Ex $551 Gd $372

"PRO-STOCK AND PRO-COMP" SA PISTOL
Caliber: .45 ACP. Eight-round magazine, 4- or 5-inch bbl., weight: 37 oz. Single action, blued or two-tone finish. Wood grips. Bomar adjustable sights. Made from 1996 to 1997.
Model Pro comp. . . . . NiB $872 Ex $663 Gd $566
Model Pro stock . . . . NiB $714 Ex $551 Gd $475

TAC SERIES
Caliber: .45 ACP. Eight-round magazine, 5-inch bbl., 8.5 inches overall. Weight: 37 oz. Low profile combat or Tritium sights. Beavertail grip safety. Matte blue, chrome or two-tone finish. Checkered wood or contoured black rubber grips. Made from 1997 to 1998.
Model TAC 11 service . . . . . NiB $643 Ex $510 Gd $398
Model TAC 11 compact . . . . NiB $653 Ex $531 Gd $419
w/Tritium sights, add $100

BANTAM MODEL. . . . . .NiB $403 Ex $283 Gd $ 204
Caliber: 9mmPara., .40 S&W. Single or double-action, super compact size, concealed hammer, all steel construction; 3-dot sights; royal blue or matte finish. Manufactured 1999 only.

BRONCO PISTOL — Eibar, Spain.
Manufactured by Echave y Arizmendi

MODEL 1918 POCKET
AUTOMATIC PISTOL . . . . NiB $204 Ex $129 Gd $92
Caliber: .32 ACP (7.65mm). Six-round magazine 2.5-inch bbl., 5 inches overall. Weight: 20 oz. Fixed sights. Blued finish. Hard rubber grips. Made circa 1918- to 1925.

Browning
Model 25 Automatic

VEST POCKET AUTO PISTOL . . NiB $203 Ex $128 Gd $66
Caliber: .25 ACP, 6-round magazine, 2.13-inch bbl., 4.13 inches overall. Weight: 11 oz. Fixed sights. Blued finish. Hard rubber grips. Made from 1919 to 1935.

BROWNING PISTOLS — Morgan, Utah

The following Browning pistols have been manufactured by Fabrique Nationale d'Armes de Guerre (now Fabrique Nationale Herstal) of Herstal, Belgium, by Arms Technology Inc. of Salt Lake City and by J. P. Sauer & Sohn of Eckernforde, W. Germany. (See also FN Browning and J.P. Sauer & Sohn listings.)

.25 AUTOMATIC PISTOL
Same general specifications as FN Browning Baby (see separate listing). Standard Model, blued finish, hard rubber grips. Light Model, nickel-plated, Nacrolac pearl grips. Renaissance Engraved Model, nickel-plated, Nacrolac pearl grips. Made by FN from 1955 to 1969.
Standard model . . . . NiB $587 Ex $534 Gd $283
Lightweight model . . . . NiB $592 Ex $540 Gd $294
Renaissance model. . . . . NiB $1121 Ex $867 Gd $539

.32 AND .380 AUTOMATIC PISTOL, 1955 TYPE
Same general specifications as FN Browning .32 (7.65mm) and .380 Pocket Auto. Standard Model, Renaissance Engraved Model as furnished in .25 Automatic. Made by FN from 1955 to 1969.
Standard model (.32 ACP). . . . NiB $507 Ex $386 Gd $291
Standard model (.380 ACP). . . NiB $454 Ex $376 Gd $283
Renaissance model. . . . . NiB $1121 Ex $918 Gd $740

.380 AUTOMATIC PISTOL, 1971 TYPE
Same as .380 Automatic, 1955 Type except has longer slide, 4.44-inch bbl., is 7.06 inches overall, weight: 23 oz. Rear sight adj. for windage and elevation, plastic thumbrest grips. Made 1971 to 1975.
Standard model . . . . NiB $509 Ex $387 Gd $294
Renaissance model. . . . . NiB $1132 Ex $913 Gd $616

BDA DA AUTOMATIC PISTOL
Similar to SIG-Sauer P220. Calibers: 9mm Para., .38 Super Auto, .45 Auto. Nine-round magazine (9mm and .38), 7-round (.45 cal), 4.4-inch bbl., 7.8 inches overall. Weight: 29.3 oz. Fixed sights. Blued finish. Plastic grips. Made from 1977 to 1980 by J. P. Sauer.
BDA model, 9mm, .45 ACP . . NiB $611 Ex $464 Gd $326
BDA model, .38 Super . . . . . NiB $741 Ex $465 Gd $437

**Browning
BDA .380 Nickel Finish**

**Browning
Buck Mark 22 Field (5.5)**

**Browning
Buck Mark 22 Bullseye**

**Browning
Buck Mark 22 Plus**

**Browning
BDM 9mm DA**

BDA .380 DA AUTOMATIC PISTOL
Caliber: .380 Auto. 10- or 13-round magazine, bbl. length: 3.81 inches., 6.75 inches overall. Weight: 23 oz. Fixed blade front sight, square-notch drift-adj. rear sight. Blued or nickel finish. Smooth walnut grips. Made from 1982 to 1997 by Beretta.
Blued finish. . . . . .NiB $602 Ex $454 Gd $284
Nickel finish. . . . . NiB $692 Ex $524 Gd $377

BDM SERIES AUTOMATIC PISTOLS
Calibers: 9mm Para., 10-round magazine, 4.73-inch bbl., 7.85 inches overall. Weight: 31 oz., windage adjustable sights w/3-dot system. Low profile removable blade front sights. Matte blued, Bi-Tone or silver chrome finish. Selectable shooting mode and decocking safety lever. Made from 1991 to 1997.
BDM Standard . . . . NiB $622 Ex $499 Gd $333
BDM Practical . . . . NiB $598 Ex $490 Gd $373
BDM-D Silver Chrome . . . . . . NiB $693 Ex $509 Gd $384

BUCK MARK .22 AUTOMATIC PISTOL
Caliber: .22 LR. 10-round magazine, 5.5-inch bbl., 9.5 inches overall. Weight: 32 oz. Black molded grips. Adj. rear sight. Blued or nickel finish. Made from 1985 to date.
Blued finish . . . . NiB $342 Ex $221 Gd $143
Nickel finish. . . . . NiB $403 Ex $285 Gd $203

BUCK MARK .22 BULLSEYE PISTOL
Same general specifications as the standard Buck Mark 22 except w/7.25-inch fluted barrel, 11.83 inches overall. Weight: 36 oz. Adjustable target trigger. Undercut post front sight, click-adjustable Pro-Target rear. Laminated, Rosewood, black rubber or composite grips. Made from 1996 to 2006.
Standard model (composite grips)NiB $487 Ex $344 Gd $249
Target model . . . . NiB $475 Ex $316 Gd $219

BUCK MARK .22
BULLSEYE TARGET. . . . . NiB $487 Ex $344 Gd $249
Caliber: .22 LR. 10-round magazine, 7.25-inch fluted bbl., 11.83 inches overall. Weight: 31 oz. Rosewood wrap-around finger groove grips w/matte blued finish. Made from 1996 to 2005.

BUCK MARK .22 FIELD
(5.5) AUTO PISTOL . . . . NiB $487 Ex $344 Gd $249
Calibers: .22 LR. 10-round magazine, 5.5-inch bbl., 9.58 inches overall. Weight: 35.5 oz. Standard sights. Matte Blue finish. Made from 1991 to date.

BUCK MARK .22 MICRO AUTOMATIC PISTOL
Same general specifications as standard Buck Mark .22 except w/4-inch bbl., 8 inches overall. Weight: 32 oz. Molded composite grips. Ramp front sight, Pro Target rear sight. Made from 1992 to date.
Blued finish . . . . NiB $367 Ex $271 Gd $181
Nickel finish. . . . . NiB $418 Ex $321 Gd $244

**Browning
Buck Mark .22 Silhouette**

BUCK MARK .22 MICRO PLUS AUTO PISTOL
Same specifications as the Buck Mark .22 Micro except ambidextrous, laminated wood grips. Made from 1996 to 2001.
Blued finish . . . . NiB $285 Ex $234 Gd $192
Nickel finish. . . . . NiB $382 Ex $321 Gd $204

BUCK MARK .22 PLUS AUTO PISTOL
Same general specifications as standard Buck Mark .22 except for black molded, impregnated hardwood grips. Made from 1987 to 2001.
Blued finish . . . . NiB $383 Ex $321 Gd $204
Nickel finish. . . . . NiB $404 Ex $329 Gd $223

BUCK MARK .22 TARGET (5.5) AUTO PISTOL
Caliber: .22 LR. 10-round magazine, 5.5-inch bbl., 9.6 inches overall. Weight: 35.5 oz. Pro target sights. Wrap-around walnut or contoured finger groove grips. Made from 1990 to 2009.
Matte blue finish . . . . NiB $455 Ex $374 Gd $223
Nickel finish (1994 to date) . . NiB $499 Ex $395 Gd $245
Gold finish (1991-99) . . . . NiB $385 Ex $270 Gd $184

BUCK MARK .22 SILHOUETTE NiB $544 Ex $372 Gd $220
Same general specifications as standard Buck Mark .22 except for 9.88-inch bbl. Weight: 53 oz. Target sights mounted on full-length scope base, and laminated hardwood grips and forend. Made from 1987 to 1999.

BUCK MARK .22
UNLIMITED SILHOUETTE. . . . NiB $547 Ex $431 Gd $285
Same general specifications as standard Buck Mark .22 Silhouette except w/14-inch bbl., 18.69 inches overall. Weight: 64 oz. Interchangeable post front sight and Pro Target rear. Nickel finish. Made from 1991 to 1999.

BUCK MARK .22
VARMINT AUTO PISTOL . . . . NiB $346 Ex $282 Gd $230
Same general specifications as standard Buck Mark .22 except for 9.88-inch bbl. Weight: 48 oz. No sights, full-length scope base, and laminated hardwood grips. Made from 1987 to 1999.

CHALLENGER AUTOMATIC PISTOL
Caliber: .22 LR. 10-round magazine, bbl. lengths: 4.5 and 6.75-inches. 11.44 inches overall (with 6.75-inch bbl.). Weight: 38 oz. (6.75-inch bbl.). Removable blade front sight, screw adj. rear. Standard finish, blued, also furnished gold inlaid (Gold model) and engraved and chrome-plated (Renaissance model). Checkered walnut grips. Finely figured and carved grips on Gold and Renaissance models. Standard made by FN 1962-75, higher grades. Intro. 1971. Disc.
Standard model . . . . NiB $590 Ex $427 Gd $285
Gold model . . . . NiB $3172 Ex $2448 Gd $1742
Renaissance model. . . . . . NiB $3058 Ex $2445 Gd $1744

CHALLENGER II
AUTOMATIC PISTOL . . . . NiB $363 Ex $259 Gd $164
Same general specifications as Challenger Standard model w/6.75-inch bbl. except changed grip angle and impregnated hardwood grips. Original Challenger design modified for lower production costs. Made by ATI from 1976 to 1983.

**Browning
Buck Mark .22 Target (5.5)**

**Browning
Buck Mark .22 Micro Plus**

**Browning Challenger
Standard Model**

**Browning Challenger
Renaissance Model**

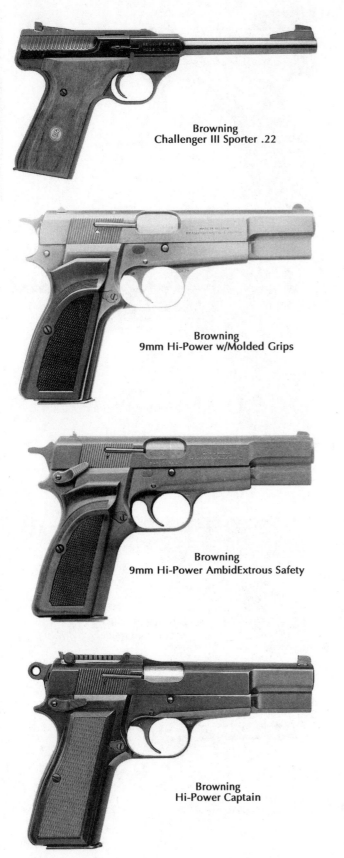

Browning
Challenger III Sporter .22

Browning
9mm Hi-Power w/Molded Grips

Browning
9mm Hi-Power AmbidExtrous Safety

Browning
Hi-Power Captain

Browning
Hi-Power Mark III

CHALLENGER III
AUTOMATIC PISTOL . . . . NiB $266 Ex $217 Gd $153
Same general description as Challenger II except has 5.5 inch bull bbl., alloy frame and new sight system. Weight: 35 oz. Made from 1982-84. Sporter Model w/6.75-inch bbl.. Made from 1982-85.

HI-POWER AUTOMATIC PISTOL
Same general specifications as FN Browning Model 1935 except chambered for 9mm Para., .30 Luger or .40 S&W. 10- or 13-round magazine, 4.63-inch bbl., 7.75 inches overall. Weight: 32 oz. (9mm) or 35 oz. (.40 S&W). Fixed sights, also available w/rear sight adj. for windage and elevation, and ramp front sight. AmbidExtrous safety added after 1989. Standard model blued, chrome-plated or Bi-Tone finish. Checkered walnut, contour-molded Polyamide or wraparound rubber grips. Renaissance Engraved model chrome-plated, w/Nacrolac pearl grips. Made by FN from 1954 to 2002.

Standard model,
fixed sights, 9mm . . . . NiB $895 Ex $689 Gd $510
Standard model, fixed sights,
.40 S&W (intro. 1986) . . . . . . NiB $784 Ex $683 Gd $582
Standard model,
.30 Luger (1986-89) . . . . NiB $942 Ex $702 Gd $489
Renaissance model,
fixed sights. . . . . NiB $4098 Ex $3651 Gd $2688
w/adjustable
rear sight, add $75
w/ambidExtrous
safety, add $110
w/moulded grips,
deduct $50
w/tangent rear sight
(1965-78), add* $315
w/T-Slot grip &
tangent sight
(1965-78), add* $620
*Check FN agent to certify value

HI-POWER CAPTAIN
AUTOMATIC PISTOL . . . . NiB $804 Ex $605 Gd $429
Similar to the standard Hi-Power except fitted w/adj. 500-meter tangent rear sight and rounded serrated hammer. Made from 1993 to 2000.

HI-POWER MARK III
AUTOMATIC PISTOL . . . . NiB $793 Ex $498 Gd $398
Calibers: 9mm or .40 S&W. 10-round magazine, 4.75-inch bbl., 7.75 inches overall. Weight: 32 oz. Fixed sights with molded grips. Durable non-glare matte blue finish. Made from 1985 to 2000.

**Browning
Hi-Power Practical**

**Browning
Hi-Power Silver Chrome**

HI-POWER PRACTICAL AUTOMATIC PISTOL

Similar to the standard Hi-Power except has silver-chromed frame and blued slide w/Commander-style hammer. Made from 1991 to 2006.

w/fixed sights . . . . NiB $729 Ex $533 Gd $385
w/adj. sights, add $75

HI-POWER SILVER CHROME

AUTOMATIC PISTOL . . . . NiB $792 Ex $650 Gd $407
Calibers: 9mm or .40 S&W. 10-round magazine, 4.75-inch bbl., 7.75 inches overall. Weight: 36 oz. Adjustable sights with Pachmayer grips. Silver-chromed finish. Made from 1991 to 2000.

HI-POWER 9MM CLASSIC

Limited Edition 9mm Hi-Power, w/silver-gray finish, high-grade engraving and finely-checkered walnut grips w/double border. Proposed production of the Classic was 5000 w/less than half that number produced. Gold Classic limited to 500 w/two-thirds proposed production in circulation. Made from 1985 to 1986.

Gold classic . . . . NiB $5401 Ex $4999 Gd $3495
Standard classic . . . . NiB $895 Ex $657 Gd $542

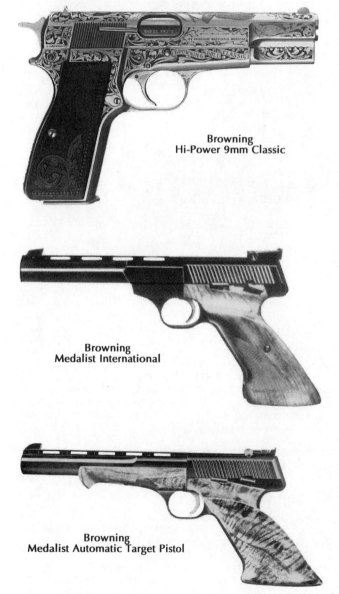

**Browning
Hi-Power 9mm Classic**

INTERNATIONAL MEDALIST EARLY MODEL

TARGET PISTOL . . . . NiB $1197 Ex $992 Gd $804
Modification of Medalist to conform w/International Shooting Union rules. 5.9-inch bbl., Smaller grip with no forearm. Weight: 42 oz. Made from 1970-73. Subtract 30% for post 1974 models

MEDALIST AUTOMATIC TARGET PISTOL

Caliber: .22 LR. 10-round magazine, 6.75-inch bbl. w/vent rib, 11.94 inches overall. Weight: 46 oz. Removable blade front sight, click-adj. micrometer rear. Standard finish, blued also furnished gold-inlaid (Gold Model) and engraved and chrome-plated (Renaissance Model). Checkered walnut grips w/thumbrest (for right- or left-handed shooter). Finely figured and carved grips on Gold and Renaissance Models. Made by FN from 1962 to 1975. Higher grades. Intro. 1971.

Standard model . . . . NiB $1552 Ex $1333 Gd $1072
Gold model . . . . NiB $3071 Ex $1835 Gd $1032
Renaissance model. . . . . . NiB $2631 Ex $2183 Gd $1426

**Browning
Medalist International**

NOMAD

AUTOMATIC PISTOL . . . . NiB $486 Ex $328 Gd $227
Caliber: .22 LR. 10-round magazine, bbl. lengths: 4.5 and 6.75-inches, 8.94 inches overall (4.5-inch bbl.). Weight: 34 oz. (with 4.5-inch bbl.). Removable blade front sight, screw adj. rear. Blued finish. Plastic grips. Made by FN from 1962 to 1974.

**Browning
Medalist Automatic Target Pistol**

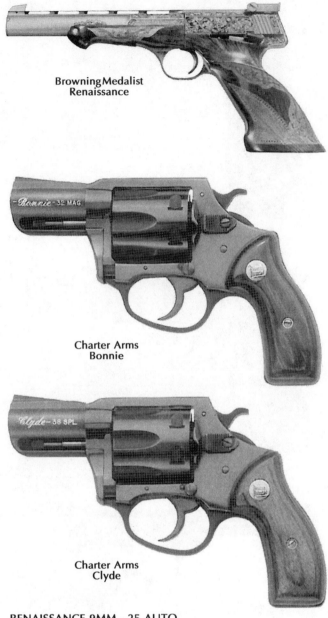

Browning Medalist Renaissance

Charter Arms Bonnie

Charter Arms Clyde

RENAISSANCE 9MM, .25 AUTO
AND .380 AUTO (1955) ENGRAVED
MODELS, CASED SET . . . . NiB $4080 Ex $3565 Gd $3160
One pistol of each of the three models in a special walnut carrying case, all chrome-plated w/Nacrolac pearl grips. Made by FN from 1964 to 1975. Options and engraving varies.

BRYCO ARMS INC. — Irvine, California. Distributed by Jennings Firearms. Inc. Carson City, NV

MODELS J22, J25 AUTO PISTOL
Calibers: .22 LR, .25 ACP. Six-round magazine, 2.5-inch bbl., about 5 inches overall. Weight: 13 oz. Fixed sights. Chrome, satin nickel or black Teflon finish. Walnut, grooved black Cycolac or resin-impregnated wood grips. Made from 1981 to 1985.
Model J-22 (disc. 1985) . . . . NiB $73 Ex $56 Gd $45
Model J-25 (disc. 1995) . . . . NiB $123 Ex $90 Gd $75

MODELS M25, M32, M38 AUTO PISTOL
Calibers: .25 ACP, .32 ACP, .380 ACP. Six-round magazine, 2.81-inch bbl., 5.31 inches overall. Weight: 11oz. to 15 oz. Fixed sights. Chrome, satin nickel or black Teflon finish. Walnut, grooved, black Cycolac or resin-impregnated wood grips. Made from 1988 to 2000.
Model M25 (disc.) . . . . NiB $119 Ex $92 Gd $74
Model M32 . . . . NiB $143 Ex $102 Gd $77
Model M38 . . . . NiB $147 Ex $108 Gd $91

MODEL M48
AUTO PISTOL . . . . NiB $128 Ex $102 Gd $81
Calibers: .22 LR, .32 ACP, .380 ACP. Seven-round magazine, 4-inch bbl., 6.69 inches overall. Weight: 20 oz. Fixed sights. Chrome, satin nickel or black Teflon finish. Smooth wood or black Teflon grips. Made from 1989 to 1995.

MODEL M58
AUTO PISTOL . . . . NiB $132 Ex $108 Gd $90
Caliber: .380 ACP. 10-round magazine, 3.75-inch bbl., 5.5 inches overall. Weight: 30 oz. Fixed sights. Chrome, satin nickel, blued or black Teflon finish. Smooth wood or black Teflon grips. Made 1993 to 1995.

MODEL M59
AUTO PISTOL . . . . NiB $128 Ex $102 Gd $82
Caliber: 9mm Para. 10-round magazine, 4-inch bbl., 6.5 inches overall. Weight: 33 oz. Fixed sights. Chrome, satin nickel, blued or black Teflon finish. Smooth wood or black Teflon grips. Made 1994 to 1996.

MODEL NINE SA
AUTO PISTOL . . . . NiB $171 Ex $136 Gd $112
Similar to Bryco/Jennings Model M59 except w/redesigned slide w/ loaded chamber indicator and frame mounted ejector. Weight: 30 oz. Made from 1997 to 2003.

MODEL 5 AUTO PISTOL . . . . . . NiB $102 Ex $69 Gd $46
Caliber: .380 ACP, 9mm Para.; 10- or 12-shot magazine. Bbl: 3.25 inches. Blue or nickel finish, black synthetic grips. Weight: 36 oz. Disc. 1995.

BUDISCHOWSKY PISTOL — Mt. Clemens, Michigan. Mfd. by Norton Armament Corporation

TP-70 DA AUTOMATIC PISTOL
Calibers: .22 LR, .25 Auto. Six-round magazine, 2.6-inch bbl., 4.65 inches overall. Weight: 12.3 oz. Fixed sights. Stainless steel. Plastic grips. Made from 1973 to 1977.
.22 LR . . . . NiB $487 Ex $361 Gd $372
.25 ACP . . . . NiB $362 Ex $249 Gd $192

CALICO LIGHT WEAPONS SYSTEM — Hillsboro, Oregon

MODEL 110 AUTO PISTOL . . NiB $635 Ex $576 Gd $486
Caliber: .22 LR. 100-round magazine, 6-inch bbl., 17.9 inches overall. Weight: 3.75 lbs. Adj. post front sight, fixed U-notch rear. Black finish aluminum frame. Molded composition grip. Made from 1986 to 1994.

MODEL M-950 AUTO PISTOL NiB $850 Ex $479 Gd $362
Caliber 9mm Para. 50- or 100-round magazine, 7.5-inch bbl., 14 inches overall. Weight: 2.25 lbs. Adj. post front sight, fixed U-notch rear. Glass-filled polymer grip. Made from 1989 to 1994.

CHARTER ARMS CORPORATION—Shelton, Connecticut (charterfirearms.com)

MODEL 40 AUTOMATIC PISTOL. NiB $283 Ex $224 Gd $171
Caliber: .22 LR. Eight-round magazine, 3.3-inch bbl., 6.3 inches overall. Weight: 21.5 oz. Fixed sights. Checkered walnut grips. Stainless steel finish. Made from 1985 to 1986.

MODEL 79K
DA AUTOMATIC PISTOL . . . . NiB $362 Ex $286 Gd $230
Calibers: .380 or .32 Auto. Seven-round magazine, 3.6-inch bbl., 6.5 inches overall. Weight: 24.5 oz. Fixed sights. Checkered walnut grips. Stainless steel finish. Made from 1985 to 1986.

BONNIE AND CLYDE SET . . . NiB $454 Ex $342 Gd $297
Matching pair of shrouded 2.5-inch bbl., revolvers chambered for .32 Magnum (Bonnie) and .38 Special (Clyde). Blued finish w/scrolled name on bbls.. Made 1989 to 1990.

BULLDOG .44 DA REVOLVER
Caliber: .44 Special. Five-round cylinder, 2.5- or 3-inch bbl., 7 or 7.5 inches overall. Weight: 19 or 19.5 oz. Fixed sights. Blued, nickel-plated or stainless finish. Checkered walnut Bulldog or square buttgrips. Made from 1973 to 1996.
Blued finish/
Pocket Hammer (2.5-inch) . . . NiB $260 Ex $192 Gd $134
Blued finish/
Bulldog grips (3-inch disc. 1988)NiB $244 Ex $206 Gd $147
Electroless nickel . . . . NiB $274 Ex $223 Gd $146
Stainless steel/
Bulldog grips (disc. 1992) . . . . NiB $220 Ex $193 Gd $132
Neoprene grips/
Pocket Hammer . . . . NiB $242 Ex $203 Gd $148

BULLDOG .357 DA REVOLVERNiB $214 Ex $169 Gd $129
Caliber: .357 Magnum. Five-round cylinder, 6-inch bbl., 11 inches overall. Weight: 25 oz. Fixed sights. Blued finish. Square, checkered walnut grips. Made from 1977 to 1996.

BULLDOG NEW POLICE DA REVOLVER
Same general specifications as Bulldog Police except chambered for .44 Special. Five-round cylinder, 2.5- or 3.5-inch bbl. Made from 1990 to 1992.
Blued finish . . . . NiB $263 Ex $201 Gd $148
Stainless finish (2.5-inch bbl. only) NiB $202 Ex $166 Gd $114

BULLDOG POLICE DA REVOLVER
Caliber: .38 Special or .32 H&R Magnum. Six-round cylinder, 4-inch bbl., 8.5 inches overall. Weight: 20.5 oz. Adj. rear sight, ramp front. Blued or stainless finish. Square checkered walnut grips. Made from 1976-93. No shroud on new models.
Blued finish . . . . NiB $272 Ex $204 Gd $158
Stainless finish . . . . NiB $234 Ex $194 Gd $147
.32 H&R Magnum (disc.1992). NiB $270 Ex $204 Gd $142

BULLDOG PUG DA REVOLVER
Caliber: .44 Special. Five-round cylinder, 2.5 inch bbl., 7.25 inches overall. Weight: 20 oz. Blued or stainless finish. Fixed ramp front sight, fixed square-notch rear. Checkered Neoprene or walnut grips. Made from 1988 to 1993.
Blued finish . . . . NiB $262 Ex $224 Gd $183
Stainless finish . . . . NiB $224 Ex $172 Gd $121

BULLDOG TARGET DA REVOLVER
Calibers: .357 Magnum, .44 Special (latter intro. in 1977). Four-inch bbl., 8.5 inches overall. Weight: 20.5 oz. in .357. Adj. rear sight, ramp front. Blued finish. Square checkered walnut grips. Made 1976 to 1992.
Stainless steel . . . . NiB $271 Ex $203 Gd $147

Charter Arms
Bulldog Police

Charter Arms
Bulldog Police

Charter Arms
Bulldog Target

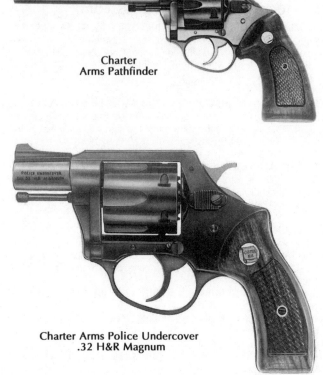

Charter Arms Explorer II

Charter Arms Explorer II Silvertone w/optional barrels

Charter Arms Pathfinder

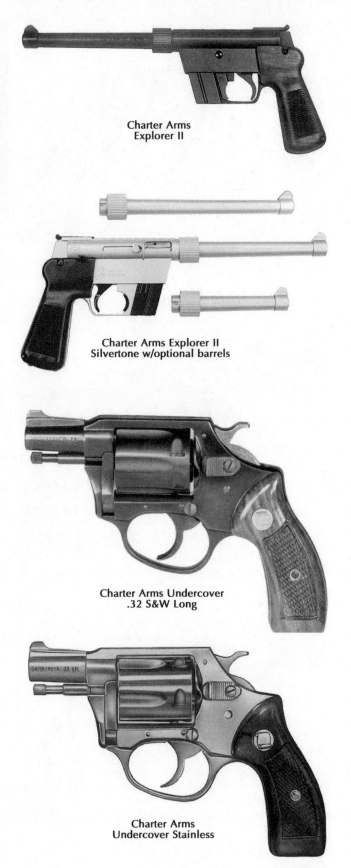

Charter Arms Undercover .32 S&W Long

Charter Arms Undercover Stainless

Charter Arms Police Undercover .32 H&R Magnum

BULLDOG TRACKER
DA REVOLVER . . . . **NiB $207 Ex $134 Gd $102**
Caliber: .357 Mag. Five-round cylinder, 2.5-, 4- or 6-inch bbl., 11 inches overall (6-inch bbl.). Weight: 21 oz. (2.5-inch bbl.). Adj. rear sight, ramp front. Checkered walnut grips. Blued finish. 4- or 6-inch bbl., Disc.1986. Reintroduced 1989 to 1992.

EXPLORER II SEMIAUTO SURVIVAL PISTOL
Caliber: .22 LR, 8-round magazine, 6-, 8- or 10-inch bbl., 13.5 inches overall (6-inch bbl.). Weight: 28 oz. finishes: Black, heat cured, semi-gloss textured enamel or silvertone anticorrosion. Disc. 1987.
Standard model . . . . **NiB $158 Ex $100 Gd $66**
**Silvertone (w/optional
6- or 10-inch bbl.)** . . . . **NiB $143 Ex $123 Gd $83**

OFF-DUTY DA REVOLVER
Calibers: .22 LR or .38 Special. Six-round (.22 LR) or 5-round (.38 Special) cylinder. Two-inch bbl., 6.25 inches overall. Weight: 16 oz. Fixed rear sight, Partridge-type front sight. Plain walnut grips. Matte black, nickel or stainless steel finish. Made from 1992 to 1996.
Matte black finish . . . . **NiB $185 Ex $153 Gd $112**
Nickel finish. . . . . **NiB $230 Ex $194 Gd $150**
Stainless steel. . . . . **NiB $260 Ex $194 Gd $128**

PATHFINDER DA REVOLVER
Calibers: .22 LR, .22 WMR. Six-round cylinder, bbl. lengths: 2-, 3-, 6-inches, 7.13 inches overall (in 3-inch bbl.), and regular grips. Weight: 18.5 oz. (3-inch bbl.). Adj. rear sight, ramp front. Blued or stainless finish. Plain walnut regular, checkered Bulldog or square buttgrips. Made 1970 to date. Note: Originally designated "Pocket Target," name was changed in 1971 to "Pathfinder." Grips changed in 1984. Disc. 1990.
Blued finish . . . . **NiB $203 Ex $148 Gd $112**
Stainless finish . . . . **NiB $240 Ex $192 Gd $128**

CHARTER ARMS PIT BULL DA REVOLVER

Calibers: 9mm, .357 Magnum, .38 Special. Five-round cylinder, 2.5-, 3.5- or 4-inch bbl., 7 inches overall (2.5-inch bbl.). Weight: 21.5 to 25 oz. All stainless steel frame. Fixed ramp front sight, fixed square-notch rear. Checkered Neoprene grips. Blued or stainless finish. Made from 1989 to 1991.

Blued finish . . . . NiB $261 Ex $223 Gd $137
Stainless finish . . . . .NiB $270 Ex $ 230 Gd $143

CHARTER ARMS UNDERCOVER DA REVOLVER

Caliber: .38 Special. Five-round cylinder,. bbl., lengths: 2-, 3-, 4-inches, 6.25 inches overall (2-inch bbl.), and regular grips. Weight: 16 oz. (2-inch bbl.). Fixed sights. Plain walnut, checkered Bulldog or square buttgrips. Made from 1965 to 1996.

Blued or nickel-plated finish. . NiB $216 Ex $120 Gd $101
Stainless finish . . . . NiB $281 Ex $230 Gd $148

CHARTER ARMS UNDERCOVER

Same general specifications as standard Undercover except chambered for .32 H&R Magnum or .32 S&W Long, has 6-round cylinder and 2.5-inch bbl.

.32 H&R Magnum (blued). . . . NiB $316 Ex $253 Gd $170
.32 H&R Magnum nickel . . . . NiB $212 Ex $171 Gd $109
.32 H&R Magnum (stainless). . NiB $332 Ex $268 Gd $187
.32 S&W Long (blued) disc. 1989. NiB $303 Ex $225 Gd $179

CHARTER ARMS UNDERCOVER POCKET POLICE DA REVOLVER

Same general specifications as standard Undercover except has 6-round cylinder and pocket-type hammer. Blued or stainless steel finish. Made from 1969 to 1981.

Blued finish . . . . .NiB $342 Ex $283 Gd $ 214
Stainless steel. . . . . NiB $356 Ex $290 Gd $219

CHARTER ARMS UNDERCOVER POLICE DA REVOLVER

Same general specifications as standard Undercover except has 6-round cylinder. Made from 1984 to 1989. Reintroduced 1993.

Blued, .38 Special . . . . .NiB $337 Ex $ 279 Gd $204
Stainless, .38 Special . . . . . . NiB $270 Ex $204 Gd $158
.32 H&R Magnum. . . . . NiB $250 Ex $200 Gd $143

CHARTER ARMS UNDER-COVERETTE DA REVOLVER . . NiB $179 Ex $130 Gd $101

Same as Undercover model w/2-inch bbl. except caliber .32 S&W Long, 6-round cylinder, blued finish only. Weight: 16.5 oz. Made 1972 to 1983.

CIMARRON F.A. CO. — Fredricksburg, Texas

CIMARRON EL PISTOLERO
SINGLE-ACTION REVOLVER. . NiB $444 Ex $336 Gd $260
Calibers: .357 Mag., .45 Colt. Six-round cylinder, 4.75- 5.5- or 7.5-inch bbl., polished brass backstrap and triggerguard. Otherwise, same as Colt Single-Action Army revolver w/parts being interchangeable. Made from 1997 to 1998.

COLT'S MANUFACTURING CO., INC. — Hartford, Connecticut

Previously Colt Industries, Firearms Division. Production of some Colt handguns spans the period before World War II to the postwar years. Values shown for these models are for earlier production. Those manufactured c. 1946 and later generally are less desirable to collectors and values are approximately 30 percent lower.

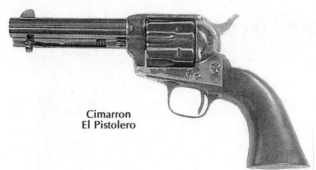

Cimarron
El Pistolero

NOTE: *For ease in finding a particular firearm, Colt handguns are grouped into three sections: Automatic Pistols, Single-Shot Pistols & Derringers. and Revolvers. For a complete listing, please refer to the IndEx.*

AUTOMATIC PISTOLS

COLT MODEL 1900 .38 AUTOMATIC PISTOL

Caliber: .38 ACP (modern high-velocity cartridges should not be used in this pistol). Seven-round magazine, 6-inch bbl., 9 inches overall. Weight: 35 oz. Fixed sights. Blued finish. Hard rubber and plain or checkered walnut grips. Sharp-spur hammer. Combination rear sight and safety unique to the Model 1900 (early production). In mid-1901 a solid rear sight was dovetailed into the slide. (S/N range 1-4274) Made 190003. Note: 250 models were sold to the military (50 Navy and 200 Army).

Early commercial model
(w/sight/safety) . . . . NiB $15,810 Ex $14,586 Gd $11,220
Late commercial model
(w/dovetailed sight) . . . . . . NiB $15,810 Ex $14,586 Gd $11,220
Army Model w/U.S. inspector
marks (1st Series - S/N 90-150
w/inspector mark J.T.T.) . . . . NiB $32,130 Ex $27,540 Gd $22,185
(2nd Series - S/N 1600-1750
w/inspector mark R.A.C.) . . . . .NiB $11,577 Ex $9736 Gd $6700
Navy model (Also marked
w/USN-I.D. number). . . . . . NiB $18,967 Ex $13,107 Gd $10,200

COLT MODEL 1902 MILITARY .38 AUTOMATIC PISTOL

Caliber: .38 ACP (modern high-velocity cartridges should not be used in this pistol). Eight-round magazine, 6-inch bbl., 9 inches overall. Weight: 37 oz. Fixed sights w/blade front and V-notch rear. Blued finish. Checkered hard rubber grips. Round back hammer, changed to spur type in 1908. No safety but fitted w/standard military swivel. About 18,000 produced with split S/N ranges. The government contract series (15,001-15,200) and the commercial sales series (15,000 receding to 11,000) and (30,200-47,266). Made from 1902 to 1929.

Early military model (w/front
slide serrations) . . . . .NiB $6,120 Ex $3871 Gd $3528
Late military model (w/rear
slide serrations) . . . . NiB $6115 Ex $3732 Gd $2525
Marked "U.S. Army" (S/N 15,001-
15,200) . . . . .NiB $19,635 Ex $17,340 Gd $15,402

COLT MODEL 1902 SPORTING
.38 AUTOMATIC PISTOL . NiB $5008 Ex $3213 Gd $2443
Caliber: .38 ACP (modern high-velocity cartridges should not be used in this pistol). Seven-round magazine, 6-inch bbl., 9 inches overall. Weight: 35 oz. Fixed sights w/blade front and V-notch rear. Blued finish. Checkered hard rubber grips. Round back hammer was standard but some spur hammers were installed during late production. No safety and w/o swivel as found on military model. Total production about 7,500 w/split S/N ranges (4275-10,999) and (30,000-30,190) Made from 1902 to 1908.

Colt
Model 1902 Military

Colt
1903 Early Hammer

Colt
Model 1903 Pocket Hammerless

MODEL 1903 POCKET .32 AUTOMATIC PISTOL
FIRST ISSUE - COMMERCIAL SERIES

Caliber: .32 Auto. Eight-round magazine, 4-inch bbl., 7 inches overall. Weight: 23 oz. Fixed sights. Blued or nickel finish. Checkered hard rubber grips. Hammerless (concealed hammer). Slide lock and grip safeties. Fitted w/barrel bushing but early models have no magazine safety. Total production of the Model 1903 reached 572,215. The First Issue maded from 1903 to 1908 (S/N range 1-72,000).

Blued finish . . . . NiB $1132 Ex $806 Gd $587
Nickel finish. . . . . NiB $1153 Ex $826 Gd $602

MODEL 1903 POCKET .32 AUTOMATIC PISTOL
SECOND ISSUE - COMMERCIAL SERIES

Same as First Issue but with 3.75-inch bbl. and small Extractor. Made from 1908 to 1910 (S/N range 72,001 -105,050).

Blued finish . . . . NiB $816 Ex $602 Gd $474
Nickel finish. . . . . NiB $842 Ex $689 Gd $498

MODEL 1903 POCKET .32 AUTOMATIC PISTOL,
THIRD ISSUE - COMMERCIAL SERIES

Caliber: .32 Auto. Similar to Second Issue w/3.75-inch bbl. except with integral barrel bushing and locking lug at muzzle end of bbl. Production occurred 1910 to 1926 (S/N range 105,051-468,096).

Blued finish . . . . NiB $1326 Ex $1030 Gd $813
Nickel finish. . . . . NiB $1474 Ex $1234 Gd $918

MODEL 1903 POCKET .32 AUTOMATIC PISTOL
FOURTH ISSUE - COMMERCIAL SERIES

Caliber: .32 Auto. Similar to Third Issue except a slide lock safety change was made when a Tansley-style disconnector was added on all pistols above S/N 468,097, which prevents firing of cartridge in chamber when the magazine is removed. Blued or nickel finish. Checkered walnut grips. These design changes were initiated 1926 to 1945 (S/N range 105,051-554,446).

Blued finish . . . . NiB $1331 Ex $1020 Gd $804
Nickel finish. . . . . NiB $1535 Ex $1132 Gd $945

MODEL 1903 POCKET (HAMMER) .38 AUTOMATIC PISTOL

Caliber: .38 ACP (modern high-velocity cartridges should not be used in this pistol). Similar to Model 1902 Sporting .38 but w/shorter frame, slide and 4.5-inch bbl. Overall dimension reduced to 7.5 inches. Weight: 31 oz. Fixed sights w/blade front and V-notch rear. Blued finish. Checkered hard rubber grips. Round back hammer, changed to spur type in 1908. No safety. (S/N range 16,001-47,226 with some numbers above 30,200 assigned to 1902 Military). Made from 1903 to 1929.

**Early model
(round hammer)** . . . . NiB $2030 Ex $1713 Gd $1418
**Late model
(spur hammer)** . . . . NiB $2254 Ex $1953 Gd $1641

MODEL 1903 POCKET HAMMERLESS (CONCEALED HAMMER) .32 AUTOMATIC PISTOL - MILITARY

Caliber: .32 ACP. Eight-round magazine, Similar to Model 1903 Pocket .32 except concealed hammer and equipped w/magazine safety. Parkerized or blued finish. (S/N range with "M" prefix M1-M200,000) Made from 1941 to 1945.

**Blued service model (marked
"U.S. Property")** . . . . NiB $1333 Ex $1179 Gd $852
**Parkerized service model (marked
"U.S. Property")** . . . . NiB $2162 Ex $1821 Gd $1520
**Blued documented
Officer's model** . . . . NiB $3182 Ex $2880 Gd $1760
**Parkerized documented
Officer's model** . . . . NiB $3182 Ex $2880 Gd $1760

MODEL 1905 .45 AUTOMATIC PISTOL

Caliber: .45 (Rimless) Automatic. Seven-round magazine, 5-inch bbl., 8 inches overall. Weight: 32.5 oz. Fixed sights w/blade front and V-notch rear. Blued finish. Checkered walnut, hard rubber or pearl grips. Predecessor to Model 1911 Auto Pistol and contributory to the development of the .45 ACP cartridge. (S/N range 1-6100) Made from 1905 to 1911.

Commercial model . . . . . NiB $7461 Ex $5579 Gd $3784
**w/slotted backstrap
(500 produced)** . . . . NiB $10,761 Ex $8966 Gd $7359
w/shoulder stock/holster, add . . . .$7650 to $10,200

MODEL 1905 .45 (1907)

CONTRACT PISTOL NiB $22,440 Ex $17,340 Gd $10,200
Variation of the Model 1905 produced to U.S. Military specifications, including loaded chamber indicator, grip safety and lanyard loop. Only 201 were produced, but 200 were delivered and may be identified by the chief inspector's initials "K.M." (S/N range 1-201) Made from 1907 to 1908.

MODEL 1908 POCKET .25 HAMMERLESS AUTO PISTOL

Caliber: .25 Auto. Six-round magazine, 2-inch bbl., 4.5 inches overall. Weight: 13 oz. Flat-top front, square-notch rear sight in groove. Blued, nickel or Parkerized finish. Checkered hard rubber grips on early models, checkered walnut on later type, special pearl grips illustrated. Both a grip safety and slide lock safety are included on all models. The Tansley-style safety disconnector was added in 1916 at pistol No. 141000. (S/N range 1-409,061) Made 1908 to 1941.

Blued finish . . . . NiB $1734 Ex $1415 Gd $1137
Nickel finish, add $125
Marked "U.S. Property"
(w/blued finish) . . . . NiB $3213 Ex $2861 Gd $2560

MODEL 1908 POCKET .380 AUTOMATIC PISTOL

Similar to Pocket .32 Auto w/3.75-inch bbl. except chambered for .380 Auto w/seven-round magazine. Weight: 23 oz. Blue, nickel or Parkerized finish. (S/N range 1-138,009) Made from 1908 to 1945.

First Issue (made 1908-11, w/bbl.,
lock and bushing, w/S/N 1-6,250) NiB $1734 Ex $1528 Gd $1312
Second Issue (made 1911-28,
w/o bbl., lock and bushing,
w/S/N 6,251-92,893) . . . . NiB $2017 Ex $1693 Gd $1528
Third Issue (made 1928-45,
w/safety disconnector,
w/S/N 92,894-138,009) . . . NiB $1734 Ex $1528 Gd $1312
Parkerized service model
(Marked "U.S. Property" made
1942-45, w/S/N "M" prefix.) NiB $2649 Ex $1972 Gd $1723
Documented officer's model
(service model w/military
assignment papers) . . . . . . NiB $3162 Ex $2557 Gd $1804

NOTE: *During both World Wars, Colt licensed other firms to make these pistols under government contract, including Ithaca Gun Co., North American Arms Co., Ltd. (Canada), Remington-Rand Co., Remington-UMC, Singer Sewing Machine Co., and Union Switch & Signal Co. M1911 also produced at Springfield Armory.*

MODEL 1911 AUTOMATIC PISTOL

Caliber: .45 Auto. Seven-round magazine, 5-inch bbl., 8.5 inches overall. Weight: 39 oz. Fixed sights. Blued finish on Commercial model. Parkerized or similar finish on most military pistols. Checkered walnut grips (early production), plastic grips (later production). Checkered, arched mainspring housing and longer grip safety spur adopted in 1923 (on M1911A1).

Model 1911
commercial (C-series) NiB $15,300 Ex $13,255 Gd $11,424
Model 1911A1 commercial
(Pre-WWII) . . . . NiB $3886 Ex $3172 Gd $2240

U.S. GOVERNMENT MODEL 1911

Colt manufacture . . . . . . NiB $10,353 Ex $8975 Gd $6849
North American Arms Co.
manufacture . . . . NiB $36,720 Ex $29,580 Gd $24,990
Remington-UMC manufacture NiB $6120 Ex $4070 Gd $2458
Springfield manufacture . . NiB $6120 Ex $4070 Gd $2458
Navy Model M1911 type . NiB $8771 Ex $6654 Gd $4995

U.S. GOVERNMENT MODEL 1911A1

Singer manufacture . . NiB $45,900 Ex $39,015 Gd $25,455
Colt, Ithaca, Remington-
Rand manufacture . . . . . . NiB $2647 Ex $2254 Gd $1902
Union Switch &
Signal manufacture . . . . . . NiB $6727 Ex $6847 Gd $6047

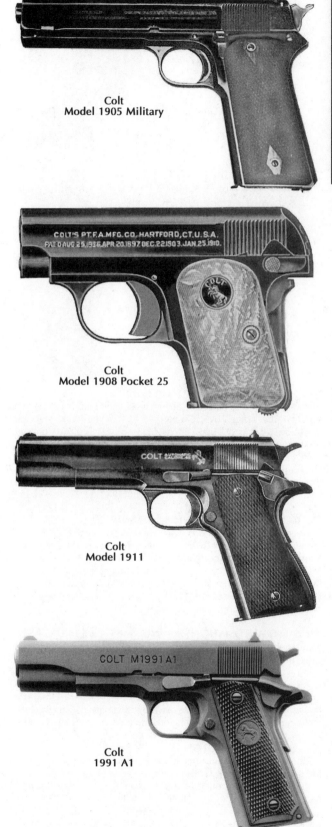

Colt
Model 1905 Military

Colt
Model 1908 Pocket 25

Colt
Model 1911

Colt
1991 A1

Colt Cadet .22

Colt All American
Model 2000

MODEL M1991 A1 SEMIAUTO PISTOL

Reissue of Model 1911A1 (see above) w/a continuation of the original serial number range 1945. Caliber: .45 ACP. Seven-round magazine, 5-inch bbl., 8.5 inches overall. Weight: 39 oz. Fixed blade front sight, square notch rear. Parkerized finish. Black composition grips. Made from 1991 to date. (Commander and Compact variations intro. 1993).
Standard model . . . . **NiB $1913 Ex $1566 Gd $1367**
Commander w/4.5-inch bbl., ... **NiB $1209 Ex $984 Gd $842**
Compact w/3.5-inch bbl., (six-round) NiB $882 Ex $760 Gd $589

.22 CADET AUTOMATIC PISTOL NiB $479 Ex $343 Gd $270

Caliber: 22 LR. 10-round magazine, 4.5-inch vent rib bbl., 8.63 inches overall. Weight: 33.5 oz. Blade front sight, dovetailed rear. Stainless finish. TExtured black polymer grips w/Colt medallion. Made 1993 to 1995. Note: The Cadet Model name was disc. under litigation but the manufacturer continued to produce this pistol configuration as the Model "Colt 22". For this reason the "Cadet" model will command slight premiums.

.22 SPORT AUTOMATIC PISTOL NiB $485 Ex $345 Gd $270

Same specifications as Cadet Model except renamed Colt .22 w/composition monogrip or wraparound black rubber grip. Made 1994 to 1998.

.22 TARGET PISTOL . . . . NiB $464 Ex $321 Gd $204

Similar to Colt 22 Sport Model except w/6-inch vent rib bbl., 10.12 inches overall. Weight: 40.5 oz. Partridge style front sight, adjustable white outline rear on full length grooved rib. Made from 1995 to 1999.

ACE AUTOMATIC PISTOL

Caliber: .22 LR (regular or high speed). 10-round magazine. Built on the same frame as the Government Model .45 Auto w/same safety features, etc. Hand-honed action, target bbl., adj. rear sight. 4.75-inch bbl., 8.25. inches overall. Weight: 38 oz. Made 1930 to 1940.
Commercial model . . . . . . **NiB $4650 Ex $3783 Gd $3264**
Service model (1938-42) . . **NiB $7710 Ex $5498 Gd $4769**

ALL AMERICAN

MODEL 2000 DA PISTOL . . . . NiB $785 Ex $566 Gd $408
Hammerless semiautomatic w/blued slide and polymer or alloy receiver fitted w/roller-bearing trigger. Caliber: 9mm Para. 15-round magazine, 4.5-inch bbl., 7.5 inches overall. Weight: 29 oz. (Polymer) or 33 oz (Alloy). Fixed blade front sight, square-notch rear w/3-dot system. Matte blued slide w/black polymer or anodized aluminum receiver. Made from 1992 to 1994.

AUTOMATIC .25 PISTOL

As a result of the 1968 Firearms Act restricting the importation of the Colt Pocket Junior that was produced in Spain, Firearms International was contracted by Colt to manufacture a similar blowback action with the same Exposed hammer configuration. Both the U.S. and Spanish-made. .25 automatics were recalled to correct an action malfunction. Returned firearms were fitted with a rebounding firing pin to prevent accidental discharges. Caliber: .25 ACP. Six-round magazine, 2.25-inch bbl., 4.5 inches overall. Weight: 12.5 oz. Integral blade front, square-notch rear sight groove. Blued finish. Checkered wood grips w/Colt medallion. Made from 1970 to 1975.
Model as issued . . . . **NiB $386 Ex $316 Gd $198**
Model recalled
& refitted . . . . **NiB $386 Ex $316 Gd $198**

CHALLENGER

AUTOMATIC PISTOL . . . . NiB $734 Ex $478 Gd $282
Same basic design as Woodsman Target, Third Issue but lacks some of the refinements. Fixed sights. Magazine catch on butt as in old Woodsman. Does not stay open on last shot. Lacks magazine safety. 4.5- or 6-inch bbl., 9 to 10.5 inches overall. Weight: 30 oz. (4.5-inch bbl.) or 31.5 oz. (6-inch bbl.) Blued finish. Checkered plastic grips. Made from 1950 to 1955.

COMBAT COMMANDER AUTOMATIC PISTOL

Same as Lightweight Commander except has steel frame w/blued or nickel-plated finish. Weight: 36 oz. Made from 1950 to 1976.
9mm Para. . . . . **NiB $736 Ex $590 Gd $444**
.38 Super, .45 ACP . . . . **NiB $852 Ex $691 Gd $486**

COMMANDER LIGHTWEIGHT AUTOMATIC PISTOL

Same basic design as Government Model except w/shorter 4.25-inch bbl., and a special lightweight "Coltalloy" receiver and mainspring housing. Calibers: .45 Auto, .38 Super Auto, 9mm Para. Seven-round magazine (.45 cal.), nine-round (.38 Auto and 9mm), 8 inches overall. Weight: 26.5 oz. Fixed sights. Round spur hammer. Improved safety lock. Blued finish. Checkered plastic or walnut grips. Made from 1950 to 1976.
9mm Para. . . . . **NiB $1091 Ex $812 Gd $542**
.38 Super, .45 ACP . . . . **NiB $1152 Ex $871 Gd $613**

CONVERSION

UNIT—.22-.45 . . . . **NiB $306 Ex $255 Gd $179**
Converts Service Ace .22 to National Match .45 Auto. Unit consists of match-grade slide assembly and bbl., bushing, recoil spring, recoil spring guide and plug, magazine and slide stop. Made from 1938 to 1942.

CONVERSION

UNIT — .45-.22 . . . . **NiB $617 Ex $489 Gd $362**
Converts Government Model .45 Auto to a .22 LR target pistol. Unit consists of slide assembly, bbl., floating chamber (as in Service Ace), bushing, ejector, recoil spring, recoil spring guide and plug, magazine and slide stop. The component parts differ and are not interchangable between post war, series 70, series 80, ACE I and ACE II units. Made from 1938 to 1984.

DELTA ELITE SEMIAUTO PISTOL

Caliber: 10 mm. Five-inch bbl., 8.5 inches overall. Eight-round magazine, Weight: 38 oz. Checkered Neoprene combat grips w/ Delta medallion. Three-dot, high-profile front and rear combat sights. Blued or stainless finish. Made from 1987 to 1996.

First Edition

(500 Ltd. edition)	NiB $975	Ex $784	Gd $551
Blued finish	NiB $923	Ex $626	Gd $468
Matte stainless finish	NiB $975	Ex $784	Gd $551
Ultra stainless finish, add	$100		

DELTA GOLD CUP SEMIAUTO PISTOL

Same general specifications as Delta Elite except w/Accro adjustable rear sight. Made 1989 to 1993 and 1995 to 1996.

Blued finish (disc. 1991).	NiB $997	Ex $693	Gd $474
Stainless steel finish	NiB $1076	Ex $792	Gd $576

GOLD CUP MARK III

NATIONAL MATCH . . . . . . NiB $1241 Ex $1020 Gd $704
Similar to Gold Cup National Match .45 Auto except chambered for .38 Special Mid Range. Five-round magazine, Made 1961 to 1974.

GOLD CUP NATIONAL

MATCH .45 AUTO . . . . NiB $1122 Ex $989 Gd $631
Match version of Government Model .45 Auto w/same general specifications except: match grade bbl., w/new design bushing, flat mainspring housing, long wide trigger w/adj. stop, hand-fitted slide w/improved ejection port, adj. rear sight, target front sight, checkered walnut grips w/gold medallions. Weight: 37 oz. Made 1957 to 1970.

GOVERNMENT MODEL 1911/1911A1

See Colt Model 1911.

HUNTSMAN . . . . NiB $683 Ex $453 Gd $348
Same specifications as the Challenger. Made from 1955 to 1976.

MK I & II/SERIES '90 DOUBLE

EAGLE COMBAT COMMANDER NiB $2080 Ex $1832 Gd $1433
Calibers: .40 S&W, .45 ACP. Seven-round magazine, 4.25-inch bbl., 7.75 inches overall. Weight: 36 oz. Fixed blade front sight, square-notch rear. Checkered Xenoy grips. Stainless finish. Made from 1992 to 1996.

MK II/SERIES '90 DOUBLE EAGLE DA SEMIAUTO PISTOL

Calibers: .38 Super, 9mm, .40 S&W, 10mm, .45 ACP. Seven-round magazine. Five-inch bbl., 8.5 inches overall. Weight: 39 oz. Fixed or Accro adj. sights. Matte stainless finish. Checkered Xenoy grips. Made from 1991 to 1996.

.38 Super, 9mm, .40

S&W (fixed sights)	NiB $760	Ex $581	Gd $425
.45 ACP (adjustable sights) . . .	NiB $729	Ex $577	Gd $428
.45 ACP (fixed sights)	NiB $714	Ex $546	Gd $407
10mm (adjustable sights)	NiB $729	Ex $576	Gd $434
10mm (fixed sights)	NiB $714	Ex $550	Gd $407

MK II/SERIES '90 DOUBLE

EAGLE OFFICER'S ACP . . . NiB $2141 Ex $1641 Gd $1448
Same general specifications as Double Eagle Combat Commander except chambered for .45 ACP only, 3.5-inch bbl., 7.25 inches overall. Weight: 35 oz. Also available in lightweight (25 oz.) w/blued finish (same price). Made from 1990 to 1993.

MK IV/SERIES '70 COMBAT COMMANDER

Same general specifications as the Lightweight Commander except made from 1970 to 1983.

Blued finish	NiB $1020	Ex $903	Gd $750
Nickel finish.	NiB $1193	Ex $974	Gd $815

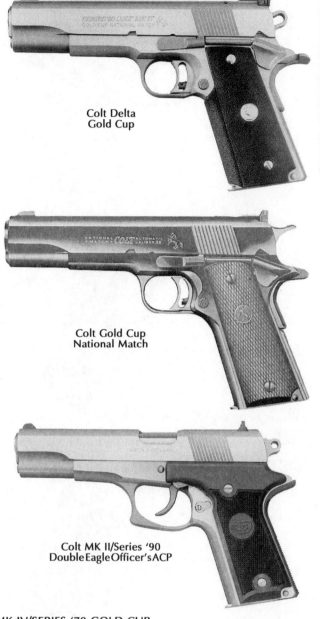

Colt Delta Gold Cup

Colt Gold Cup National Match

Colt MK II/Series '90 Double Eagle Officer's ACP

MK IV/SERIES '70 GOLD CUP

NATIONAL MATCH .45 AUTO . . . . NiB $1743 Ex $1356 Gd $1153
Match version of MK IV/Series '70 Government Model. Caliber: .45 Auto only. Flat mainspring housing. Accurizor bbl., and bushing. Solid rib, Colt-Elliason adj. rear sight undercut front sight. Adj. trigger, target hammer. 8.75 inches overall. Weight: 38.5 oz. Blued finish. Checkered walnut grips. Made from 1970 to 1984.

MK IV/SERIES '70 GOV'T.

AUTO PISTOL . . . . NiB $1120 Ex $815 Gd $570
Calibers: .45 Auto, .38 Super Auto, 9mm Para. Seven-round magazine in .45, 9-round in .38 and 9mm. Five-inch bbl., 8.38 inches overall. Weight: 38 oz., (.45); 39 oz. in .38 and 9mm. Fixed rear sight and ramp front sight. Blued or nickel-plated finish. Checkered walnut grips. Made from 1970 to 1984.

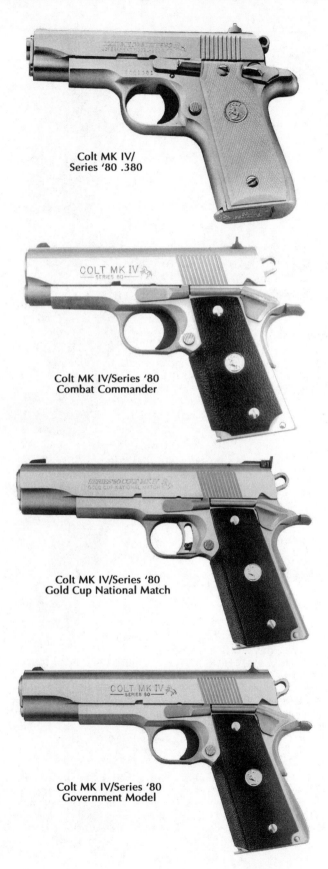

Colt MK IV/ Series '80 .380

Colt MK IV/Series '80 Combat Commander

Colt MK IV/Series '80 Gold Cup National Match

Colt MK IV/Series '80 Government Model

MK IV/SERIES 80 .380 AUTOMATIC PISTOL
Caliber: .380 ACP, 3.29-inch bbl., 6.15 inches overall. Weight: 21.8 oz. Composition grips. Fixed sights. Made since 1983 to 1996.
Blued finish
(disc.1997). . . . . NiB $1132 Ex $918 Gd $712
Bright nickel
(disc.1995). . . . . NiB $1181 Ex $974 Gd $729
Satin nickel
Coltguard (disc.1989) . . . . . NiB $1219 Ex $1016 Gd $751
Stainless finish . . . . NiB $1173 Ex $974 Gd $755

MK IV/SERIES '80 COMBAT COMMANDER
Updated version of the MK IV/Series '70 w/same general specifications. Blued, two-tone or stainless steel w/"pebbled" black Neoprene wraparound grips. Made 1998.
Blued finish
(disc.1996). . . . . NiB $1122 Ex $882 Gd $781
Satin nickel
(disc.1987). . . . . NiB $1234 Ex $979 Gd $862
Stainless finish . . . . NiB $1122 Ex $882 Gd $781
Two-tone finish . . . . NiB $1301 Ex $1086 Gd $954

MK IV/SERIES '80 COMBAT ELITE
Same general specifications as MK IV/Series '80 Combat Commander except w/Elite enhancements. Calibers: .38 Super, .40 S&W, .45 ACP. Stainless frame w/blued steel slide. Accro adj. sights and beavertail grip safety. Made from 1986 to 1996.
.38 Super,
.45 ACP . . . . NiB $1028 Ex $755 Gd $434
.40 S&W . . . . NiB $1028 Ex $755 Gd $434

MK IV/SERIES '80 GOLD CUP NATIONAL MATCH
Same general specifications as Match '70 version except w/additional finishes and "pebbled" wraparound Neoprene grips. Made from 1983 to 1996.
Blued finish . . . . NiB $1071 Ex $714 Gd $490
Bright blued
finish . . . . NiB $1071 Ex $714 Gd $490
Stainless finish . . . . NiB $1148 Ex $867 Gd $638

MK IV/SERIES '80 GOVERNMENT MODEL
Same general specifications as Government Model Series '70 except also chambered in .40 S&W, w/"pebbled" wraparound Neoprene grips, blued or stainless finish. Made 1983 to 1998.
Blued finish . . . . NiB $1117 Ex $755 Gd $520
Bright blued
finish . . . . NiB $1117 Ex $755 Gd $520
Bright stainless
finish . . . . NiB $1117 Ex $755 Gd $520
Matte stainless finish . . . . . . NiB $1117 Ex $755 Gd $520

MK IV/SERIES '80 LIGHT-
WEIGHT COMMANDER . . . . NiB $1071 Ex $714 Gd $490
Updated version of the MK IV/Series '70 w/same general specifications.

MK IV/SERIES '80
MUSTANG .380 AUTOMATIC
Caliber: .380 ACP. Five- or 6-round magazine, 2.75-inch bbl., 5.5 inches overall. Weight: 18.5 oz. Blued, nickel or stainless finish. Black composition grips. Made from 1983 to 1998.
Blued finish . . . . NiB $638 Ex $437 Gd $296
Nickel finish
(disc.1994). . . . . NiB $770 Ex $479 Gd $308
Satin nickel
Coltguard (disc.1988) . . . . NiB $740 Ex $474 Gd $306
Stainless finish . . . . NiB $709 Ex $397 Gd $306

MK IV/SERIES '80 MUSTANG PLUS II

Caliber: .380 ACP, 7-round magazine, 2.75-inch bbl., 5.5 inches overall. Weight: 20 oz. Blued or stainless finish w/checkered black composition grips. Made from 1988 to 1996.

Blued finish . . . . NiB $693   Ex $407   Gd $302
Stainless finish . . . . NiB $693   Ex $407   Gd $302

MK IV/SERIES '80 MUSTANG POCKETLITE

Same general specifications as the Mustang 30 except weight: 12.5 oz. w/aluminum alloy receiver. Blued, chrome or stainless finish. Optional wood grain grips. Made since 1987.

Blued finish . . . . NiB $683   Ex $405   Gd $305
Lady Elite
(two-tone) finish. . . . . NiB $683   Ex $405   Gd $305
Stainless finish . . . . NiB $683   Ex $405   Gd $305
Teflon/stainless finish . . . . NiB $683   Ex $405   Gd $305

MK IV/SERIES '80 OFFICER'S ACP AUTOMATIC PISTOL

Calibers: .40 S&W and .45 ACP, 3.63-inch bbl., 7.25 inches overall. Weight: 34 oz. Made from 1984 to 1997. .40 S&W, disc.1992.

Blued finish
(disc.1996). . . . . NiB $605   Ex $500   Gd $357
Matte finish . . . . NiB $581   Ex $474   Gd $349
Satin nickel finish. . . . . NiB $669   Ex $544   Gd $378
Stainless steel. . . . . NiB $630   Ex $514   Gd $367

MK IV/SERIES '80
SA LIGHTWEIGHT CONCEALED
CARRY OFFICER . . . . NiB $741   Ex $581   Gd $415

Caliber: .45 ACP. Seven-round magazine, 4.25-inch bbl., 7.75 inches overall. Weight: 35 oz. Aluminum alloy receiver w/stainless slide. Dovetailed low-profile sights w/3-dot system. Matte stainless finish w/blued receiver. Wraparound black rubber grip w/finger grooves. Made in 2000.

MK IV/SERIES '90 DEFENDER
SA LIGHTWEIGHT . . . . NiB $918   Ex $576   Gd $398

Caliber: .45 ACP. Seven-round magazine, 3-inch bbl., 6.75 inches over-all. Weight: 22.5 oz. Aluminum alloy receiver w/stainless slide. Dovetailed low-profile sights w/3-dot system. Matte stainless finish w/Nickel-Teflon receiver. Wraparound black rubber grip w/ finger grooves. Made since 1998.

MK IV/SERIES 90
PONY DAO PISTOL . . . . NiB $772   Ex $567   Gd $396

Caliber: .380 ACP. Six-round magazine, 2.75-inch bbl., 5.5 inches overall. Weight: 19 oz. Ramp front sight, dovetailed rear. Stainless finish. Checkered black composition grips. Made 1997 to 1998.

MK IV/SERIES 90
PONY POCKETLITE . . . . NiB $794   Ex $577   Gd $396

Similar to standard weight Pony Model except w/aluminum frame. Brushed stainless and Teflon finish. Made from 1997 to 1999.

NATIONAL MATCH AUTOMATIC PISTOL

Identical to the Government Model .45 Auto but w/hand-honed action, match-grade bbl., adj. rear and ramp front sights or fixed sights. Made from 1932 to 1940.

w/adjustable
sights. . . . . NiB $1723   Ex $1456   Gd $1203
w/fixed sights. . . . . NiB $1523   Ex $1280   Gd $1059

NRA CENTENNIAL .45 GOLD CUP

NATIONAL MATCH . . . . . . NiB $1321   Ex $1024   Gd $841
Only 2500 produced in 1971.

Colt MK IV/Series
'80 Mustang Plus II

Colt MK IV/Series '80
Mustang Pocketlite

Colt MK IV/Series '80
Officer's ACP

Colt Pocket Junior

Colt Super Match .38

Colt Targetsman

Colt Woodsman
Match Target First Issue

POCKET JUNIOR MODEL
AUTOMATIC PISTOL . . . . NiB $464 Ex $344 Gd $260
Made in Spain by Unceta y Cia (Astra). Calibers: .22 Short, .25 Auto. Six-round magazine, 2.25 inch bbl., 4.75 inches overall. Weight: 12 oz. Fixed sights. Checkered walnut grips. Note: In 1980, this model was subject to recall to correct an action malfunction. Returned firearms were fitted with a rebounding firing pin to prevent accidental discharges. Made from 1958 to 1968.

SUPER .38 AUTOMATIC PISTOL
Identical to Government Model .45 Auto except for caliber and magazine capacity. Caliber: .38 Automatic. Nine-round magazine, Made from 1928 to 1970.
Pre-war . . . . NiB $6125 Ex $4429 Gd $3010
Post-war. . . . . NiB $2709 Ex $2199 Gd $2008

SUPER MATCH .38 AUTOMATIC PISTOL
Identical to Super .38 Auto but w/hand-honed action, match grade bbl., adjustable rear sight and ramp front sight or fixed sights. Made from 1933 to 1946.
w/adjustable sights . . . . . NiB $11,595 Ex $6125 Gd $3162
w/fixed sights . . . . NiB $10,125 Ex $5125 Gd $2125

TARGETSMAN . . . . NiB $831 Ex $668 Gd $357
Similar to Woodsman Target but has "economy" adj. rear sight, lacks automatic slide stop. Made from 1959 to 1976.

WOODSMAN MATCH TARGET AUTOMATIC PISTOL
FIRST ISSUE . . . . NiB $3356 Ex $1947 Gd $1039
Same basic design as other Woodsman models. Caliber: .22 LR. 10-round magazine, 6.5-inch bbl., slightly tapered w/flat sides, 11 inches overall. Weight: 36 oz. Adjustable rear sight. Blued finish. Checkered walnut one-piece grip w/Extended sides. Made from 1938 to 1942.

WOODSMAN MATCH TARGET AUTO PISTOL,
SECOND ISSUE . . . . NiB $1029 Ex $765 Gd $632
Same basic design as Woodsman Target Third Issue. Caliber: .22 LR (reg. or high speed). 10-round magazine, Six-inch flat-sided heavy bbl., 10.5 inches overall. Weight: 40 oz. Click adj. rear sight, ramp front. Blued finish. Checkered plastic or walnut grips. Made from 1948 to 1976.

WOODSMAN MATCH TARGET "4 1/2"
AUTOMATIC PISTOL. . . . . . NiB $714 Ex $453 Gd $316
Same as Match Target second issue except w/4.5-inch bbl., 9 inches overall. Weight: 36 oz. Made from 1950 to 1976.

WOODSMAN SPORT MODEL AUTOMATIC PISTOL,
FIRST ISSUE . . . . NiB $1066 Ex $893 Gd $621
Caliber: .22 LR (reg. or high speed). Same as Woodsman Target second issue except has 4.5-inch bbl., adjustable rear sight w/ fixed or adjustable front sight. Weight: 27 oz., 8.5 inches overall. Made from 1933 to 1948.

WOODSMAN SPORT MODEL AUTOMATIC
PISTOL, SECOND ISSUE. . NiB $2064 Ex $1418 Gd $1145
Same as Woodsman Target third Issue but w/4.5-inch bbl., 9 inches overall. Weight: 30 oz. Made from 1948 to 1976.

WOODSMAN TARGET MODEL
AUTOMATIC, FIRST ISSUE . NiB $1729 Ex $1097 Gd $785
Caliber: .22 LR (reg. velocity). 10-round magazine, 6.5-inch bbl., 10.5 inches overall. Weight: 28 oz. Adjustable sights. Blued finish. Checkered walnut grips. Made 1915 to 1932. Note: The mainspring housing of this model is not strong enough to permit safe use of high-speed cartridges. Change to a new heat-treated mainspring housing was made at pistol No. 83,790. Many of the old models were converted by installation of new housings. The new housing may be distinguished from the earlier type by the checkering in the curve under the breech. The new housing is grooved straight across, while the old type bears a diagonally-checkered oval.

WOODSMAN TARGET MODEL
AUTOMATIC, SECOND ISSUE NiB $954 Ex $561 Gd $444
Caliber: .22 LR (reg. or high speed). Same as original model except has heavier bbl., and high-speed mainspring housing. (See note under Woodsman, First Issue). Weight: 29 oz. Made from 1932 to 1948.

WOODSMAN TARGET MODEL
AUTOMATIC, THIRD ISSUE . . NiB $836 Ex $515 Gd $326
Same basic design as previous Woodsman pistols but w/longer grip, magazine catch on left side, larger thumb safety, slide stop, slide stays open on last shot, magazine disconnector thumbrest grips. Caliber: .22 LR (reg. or high speed). 10-round magazine, 6-inch bbl., 10.5 inches overall. Weight: 32 oz. Click adjustable rear sight, ramp front sight. Blued finish. Checkered plastic or walnut grips. Made 1948 to 1976.

WORLD WAR I 50TH ANNIVERSARY COMMEMORATIVE SERIES
Limited production replica of Model 1911 .45 Auto engraved w/battle scenes, commemorating Battles at Chateau Thierry, Belleau Wood Second Battle of the Marne, Meuse Argonne. In special presentation display cases. Production: 7,400 Standard model, 75 Deluxe, 25 Special Deluxe grade. Match numbered sets offered. Made 1967 to 1969. Values indicated are for commemoratives in new condition.
Standard grade . . . . NiB $1046 Ex $780 Gd $638
Deluxe grade . . . . NiB $2152 Ex $1743 Gd $1220
Special Deluxe grade . . . . NiB $4687 Ex $3890 Gd $2448

WORLD WAR II COMMEMORATIVE
.45 AUTO . . . . NiB $1047 Ex $774 Gd $562
Limited production replica of Model 1911A1 .45 Auto engraved w/ respective names of locations where historic engagements occurred during WW II, as well as specific issue and theater identification. European model has oak leaf motif on slide, palm leaf design frames the Pacific issue. Cased. 11,500 of each model were produced. Made in 1970. Value listed is for gun in new condition.

WORLD WAR II 50TH ANNIVERSARY
COMMEMORATIVE . . . . . NiB $2647 Ex $2064 Gd $1629
Same general specifications as the Colt World War II Commemorative .45 Auto except slightly different scroll engraving, 24-karat gold-plate trigger, hammer, slide stop, magazine catch, magazine catch lock, safety lock and four grip screws. Made in 1995 only.

WORLD WAR II D-DAY
INVASION COMMEMORATIVE. . NiB $1550 Ex $1436 Gd $1138
High-luster and highly decorated version of the Colt Model 1911A1. Caliber: .45 ACP. Same general specifications as the Colt Model 1911 except for 24-karat gold-plated hammer, trigger, slide stop, magazine catch, magazine catch screw, safety lock and four grip screws. Also has scrolls and inscription on slide. Made in 1991 only.

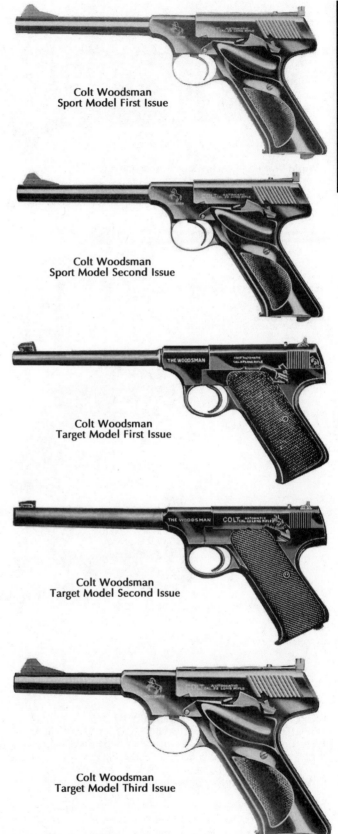

Colt Woodsman
Sport Model First Issue

Colt Woodsman
Sport Model Second Issue

Colt Woodsman
Target Model First Issue

Colt Woodsman
Target Model Second Issue

Colt Woodsman
Target Model Third Issue

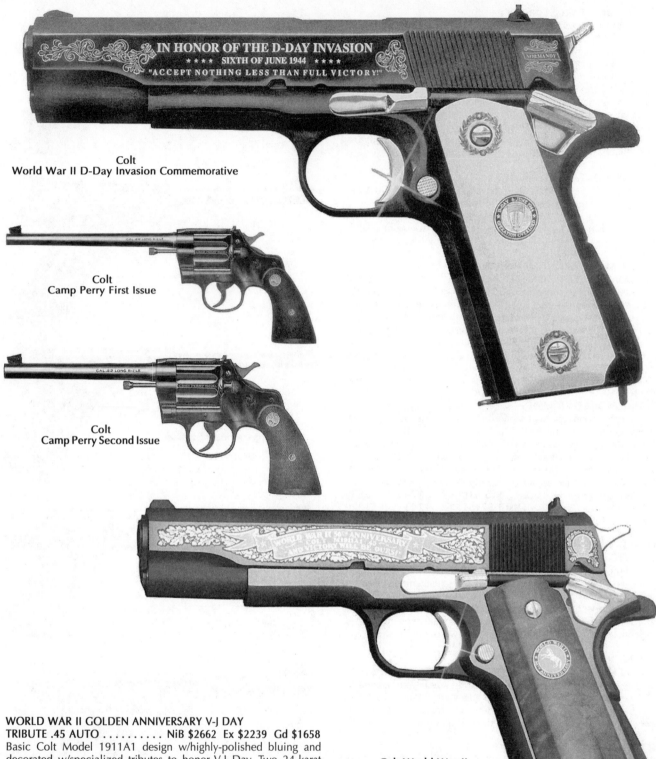

Colt
World War II D-Day Invasion Commemorative

Colt
Camp Perry First Issue

Colt
Camp Perry Second Issue

Colt World War II
50th Anniversary Commemorative

**WORLD WAR II GOLDEN ANNIVERSARY V-J DAY
TRIBUTE .45 AUTO** . . . . **NiB $2662 Ex $2239 Gd $1658**
Basic Colt Model 1911A1 design w/highly-polished bluing and
decorated w/specialized tributes to honor V-J Day. Two 24-karat
gold scenes highlight the slide. 24-karat gold-plated hammer.
Checkered wood grips w/gold medallion on each side. Made 1995.

NOTE: *For ease in finding a particular firearm, Colt handguns are grouped
into three sections: Automatic Pistols (which precedes this one), this section,
and Revolvers, which follows. For a complete listing, please refer to the indEx.*

SINGLE-SHOT PISTOLS & DERRINGERS

CAMP PERRY MODEL SINGLE-
SHOT PISTOL, FIRST ISSUENiB $1892 Ex $1540 Gd $1097
Built on Officers' Model frame. Caliber: .22 LR (embedded head chamber for high-speed cartridges after 1930). 10 inch bbl., 13.75 inches overall. Weight: 34.5 oz. Adj. target sights. Hand-finished action. Blued finish. Checkered walnut grips. Made 1926 to 1934.

CAMP PERRY MODEL
SECOND ISSUE . . . . NiB $1647 Ex $1392 Gd $998
Same general specifications as First Issue except has shorter hammer fall and 8-inch bbl., 12 inches overall. Weight: 34 oz. Made from 1934 to 1941 (about 440 produced).

CIVIL WAR CENTENNIAL MODEL PISTOL
Single-shot replica of Colt Model 1860 Army Revolver. Caliber: .22 Short. Six-inch bbl., weight: 22 oz. Blued finish w/gold-plated frame, grip frame, and trigger guard, walnut grips. Cased. 24,114 were produced. Made in 1961.
Single pistol . . . . NiB $362 Ex $265 Gd $204
Pair w/consecutive serial numbers NiB $689 Ex $541 Gd $408

DERRINGER NO. 4
Replica of derringer No. 3 (1872 Thuer Model). Single-shot w/side-swing bbl., Caliber: .22 Short, 2.5-inch bbl., 4.9 inches overall. Weight: 7.75 oz. Fixed sights. Gold-plated frame w/blued bbl., and walnut grips or completely nickel- or gold-plated w/simulated ivory or pearl grips. Made 1959 to 1963. 112,000 total production. (S/N w/D or N suffix)
Single pistol (gun only) . . . . NiB $128 Ex $88 Gd $61
Single pistol (cased w/accessories) . . NiB $408 Ex $281 Gd $189

DERRINGER NO. 4 COMMEMORATIVE MODELS
Limited production version of .22 derringers issued, w/appropriate inscription, to commemorate historical events. Additionally, non-firing models (w/unnotched bbls.) were furnished in books, picture frames and encased in plExiglass as singles or in cased pairs.
No. 4 Presentation Derringers
(Non-firing w/accessories) . . . . NiB $408 Ex $281 Gd $189
Ltd. Ed. Book Series
(w/nickel-plated derringers) . . . NiB $388 Ex $255 Gd $143
1st Presentation Series
(Leatherette covered metal case)NiB $408 Ex $281 Gd $189
2nd Presentation Series
(Single wooden case) . . . . NiB $408 Ex $281 Gd $189
2nd Presentation Series
(Paired wooden case) . . . . NiB $423 Ex $291 Gd $198
1961 Issue Geneseo, Illinois,
125th Anniversary (104 produced)NiB $729 Ex $556 Gd $388
1962 Issue Fort McPherson,
Nebraska, Centennial (300 produced)NiB $729 Ex $556 Gd $388

LORD AND LADY DERRINGERS (NO. 5)
Same as Derringer No. 4. Lord model with blued bbl., w/gold-plated frame and walnut grips. Lady model is gold-plated w/simulated pearl grips. Sold in cased pairs. Made from 1970 to 1972. (S/N w/Der suffix)
Lord derringer, pair in case. . . NiB $577 Ex $408 Gd $301
Lady derringer, pair in case . . NiB $577 Ex $408 Gd $301
Lord and Lady derringers,
one each, in case . . . . NiB $577 Ex $408 Gd $301

ROCK ISLAND ARSENAL
CENTENNIAL PISTOL . . . . NiB $520 Ex $489 Gd $332
Limited production (550 pieces) version of Civil War Centennial Model single-shot .22 pistol, made Exclusively for Cherry's Sporting Goods, Geneseo, Illinois, to commemorate the centennial of the Rock Island Arsenal in Illinois. Cased. Made in 1962.

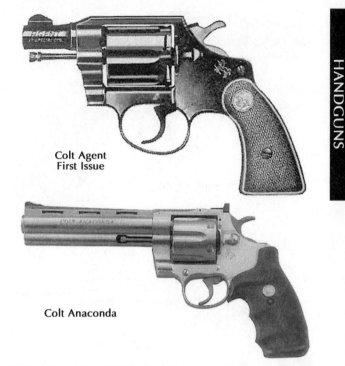

**Colt Agent
First Issue**

Colt Anaconda

NOTE: *This section of Colt handguns contains only revolvers. For automatic pistols or single-shot pistols and derringers, please see the two sections that precede this. For a complete listing, please refer to the IndEx.*

REVOLVERS

.38 DS II REVOLVER . . . . NiB $540 Ex $437 Gd $306
Caliber: .38 Special. Six-round cylinder, 2-inch bbl., 7 inches overall. Weight: 21 oz. Ramp front sight, fixed notch rear. Satin stainless finish. Black rubber combat grip w/finger grooves. Made from 1997 to 1998.

AGENT DA REVOLVER,
FIRST ISSUE . . . . NiB $556 Ex $468 Gd $326
Same as Cobra, first issue except has short-grip frame .38 Special only, weight: 14 oz. Made from 1955 to 1972.

AGENT (LW) DA REVOLVER,
SECOND ISSUE . . . . NiB $541 Ex $444 Gd $270
Same as Colt Agent, first issue except has shrouded ejector rod and alloy frame. Made from 1973 to 1986.

ANACONDA DA REVOLVER
Calibers: .44 Mag., .45 Colt., bbl. lengths: 4, 6 or 8 inches; 11.63 inches overall (with 6-inch bbl.). Weight: 53 oz. (6-inch bbl.). Adj. white outline rear sight, red insert ramp-style front. Matte stainless or Realtree gray camo finish. Black Neoprene combat grips w/finger grooves. Made 1990 to 1999 and 2002 to 2006.
Matte stainless . . . . NiB $1100 Ex $714 Gd $487
Realtree gray camo
finish (disc. 1996). . . . . . . NiB $1632 Ex $1357 Gd $1151
Custom model
(.44 Mag. w/ported bbl.) . . . . NiB $1203 Ex $816 Gd $587
First Edition model
(Ltd. Edition 1000) . . . . NiB $1100 Ex $714 Gd $487
Hunter model
(.44 Mag. w/2x scope) . . . NiB $1652 Ex $1357 Gd $1151

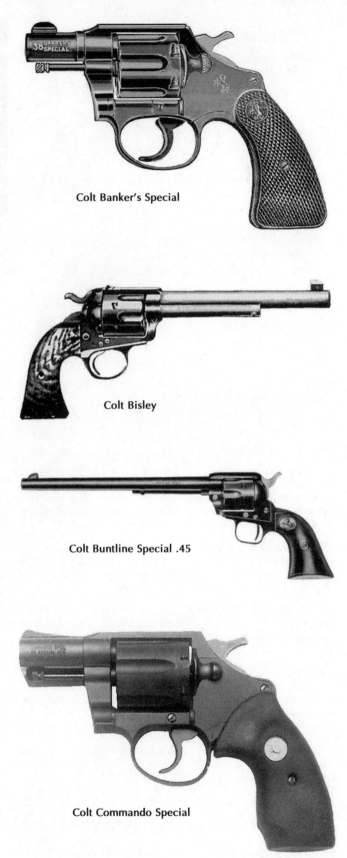

Colt Banker's Special

Colt Bisley

Colt Buntline Special .45

Colt Commando Special

ANACONDA TITANIUM DA REVOLVER
Same general specifications as the standard Anaconda except chambered .44 Mag. only w/titanium-plated finish, gold-plated trigger, hammer and cylinder release. Limited edition of 1,000 distributed by American Historical Foundation w/personalized inscription. Made in 1996.
One of 1000 . . . . **NiB $2744 Ex $2242 Gd $1624**
Presentation case, add **$255**

ARMY SPECIAL DA REVOLVER . NiB $1015 Ex $831 Gd $530
.41-caliber frame. Calibers: .32-20, .38 Special (.41 Colt). Six-round cylinder, right revolution. Bbl., lengths: 4-, 4.5, 5-, and 6-inches, 9.25 inches overall (4-inch bbl.). Weight: 32 oz. (4-inch bbl.). Fixed sights. Blued or nickel-plated finish. Hard rubber grips. Made 1908-27. Note: This model has a somewhat heavier frame than the New Navy, which it replaced. Serial numbers begin w/300,000. The heavy .38 Special High velocity loads should not be used in .38 Special arms of this model.

BANKER'S SPECIAL DA REVOLVER
This is the Police Positive w/a 2-inch bbl., otherwise specifications same as that model, rounded butt intro. in 1933. Calibers: .22 LR (embedded head-cylinder for high speed cartridges intro. 1933), .38 New Police. 6.5 inches overall. Weight: 23 oz. (.22 LR), 19 oz. (.38). Made from 1926 to 1940.
.38 caliber . . . . **NiB $1566 Ex $1352 Gd $203**
.22 caliber . . . . **NiB $2651 Ex $2387 Gd $2152**

BISLEY MODEL SA REVOLVER
Variation of the Single-Action Army, developed for target shooting w/modified grips, trigger and hammer. Calibers: General specifications same as SA Army. Target Model made w/flat-topped frame and target sights. Made 1894 to 1915.
Standard model . . . . **NiB $8578 Ex $6945 Gd $4723**
Target model (flat-top) NiB $12,470 Ex $10,277 Gd $7166

BUNTLINE SPECIAL .45 . . . NiB $1448 Ex $1137 Gd $816
Same as standard SA Army except has 12-inch bbl., caliber .45 Long Colt. Made from 1957 to 1975.

COBRA DA REVOLVER,
ROUND BUTT, FIRST ISSUE . . NiB $599 Ex $489 Gd $357
Lightweight Detective Special w/same general specifications as that model except w/Colt-alloy frame. Two-inch bbl., calibers: .38 Special, .38 New Police, .32 New Police. Weight: 15 oz., (.38 cal.). Blued finish. Checkered plastic or walnut grips. Made 1951 to 1973.

COBRA DA REVOLVER,
SECOND ISSUE . . . . **NiB $643 Ex $577 Gd $388**
Lightweight version of Detective Special, Second Issue has aluminum alloy frame. 16.5 oz. Made from 1973-81.

COBRA DA REVOLVER
SQUARE BUTT . . . . **NiB $530 Ex $425 Gd $304**
Lightweight Police Positive Special w/same general specifications except has Colt-alloy frame, 4-inch bbl., Calibers: .38 Special, .38 New Police, .32 New Police. Weight: 17 oz. in .38 caliber. Blued finish. Checkered plastic or walnut grips. Made from 1951-73.

COMMANDO SPECIAL
DA REVOLVER . . . . **NiB $546 Ex $423 Gd $329**
Caliber: .38 Special. Six-round cylinder, 2-inch bbl., 6.88 inches overall. Weight: 21.5 oz. Fixed sights. Low-luster blued finish. Made from 1982-86.

DETECTIVE SPECIAL DA REVOLVER, FIRST ISSUE
Similar to Police Positive Special w/2-inch bbl., otherwise specifications same as that model, rounded butt intro. 1933. .38 Special only in pre-war issue. Blued or nickel-plated finish. Weight: 17 oz. 6.75 inches overall. Made 1926-46.
Blued finish . . . . **NiB $530 Ex $464 Gd $342**
Nickel finish. . . . . **NiB $1030 Ex $811 Gd $610**

**Colt Cobra
Round Butt First Issue**

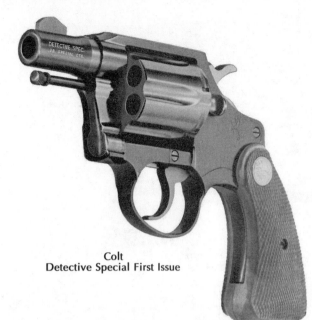

**Colt
Detective Special First Issue**

DETECTIVE SPECIAL DA REVOLVER, 2ND ISSUE

Similar to Detective special first issue except w/2- or 3-inch bbl., and also chambered .32 New Police, .38 New Police. Wood, plastic or over-sized grips. Made from 1947 to 1972.

Blued finish . . . . NiB $556 Ex $459 Gd $346
Nickel finish. . . . . NiB $648 Ex $509 Gd $362
w/three-inch bbl., add $110

DETECTIVE SPECIAL DA REVOLVER, 3RD ISSUE

"D" frame, shrouded ejector rod. Caliber: .38 Special. Six-round cylinder, 2-inch bbl., 6.88 inches overall. Weight: 21.5 oz. Fixed rear sight, ramp front. Blued or nickel-plated finish. Checkered walnut wraparound grips. Made from 1973 to 1984.

Blued finish . . . . NiB $561 Ex $443 Gd $316
Nickel finish. . . . . NiB $571 Ex $464 Gd $342
w/three-inch bbl., add $90

DETECTIVE SPECIAL DA REVOLVER, 4TH ISSUE

Similar to Detective Special, Third Issue except w/alloy frame. Blued or chrome finish. Wraparound black neoprene grips w/Colt medallion. Made from 1993 to 1995.

Blued finish . . . . NiB $500 Ex $362 Gd $296
Chrome finish. . . . . NiB $525 Ex $377 Gd $306
DAO model (bobbed hammer) NiB $658 Ex $497 Gd $347

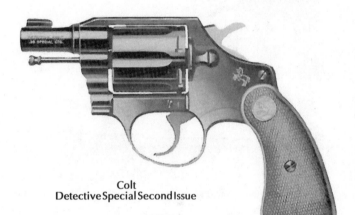

**Colt
Detective Special Second Issue**

DIAMONDBACK DA REVOLVER

"D" frame, shrouded ejector rod. Calibers: .22 LR, .22 WRF, .38 Special. Six-round cylinder, 2.5-, 4- or 6-inch bbl., w/vent rib, 9 inches overall (with 4-inch bbl). Weight: 31.75 oz. (.22 cal., 4-inch bbl.), 28.5 oz. (.38 cal.). Ramp front sight, adj. rear. Blued or nickel finish. Checkered walnut grips. Made from 1966 to 1984.

Blued finish . . . . NiB $1336 Ex $1127 Gd $826
Nickel finish. . . . . NiB $1545 Ex $1231 Gd $986
.22 Mag. model . . . . NiB $2118 Ex $1937 Gd $1754
w/2.5-inch bbl., add. $90

DA ARMY (1878) REVOLVER NiB $6140 Ex $4524 Gd $3177

Also called DA Frontier. Similar in appearance to the smaller Lightning Model but has heavier frame of different shape, round disc on left side of frame, lanyard loop in butt. Calibers: .38-40, .44-40, .45 Colt. Six-round cylinder, bbl. lengths: 3.5- and 4-inches (w/o ejector), 4.75-, 5.5- and 7.5-inches w/ejector. 12.5 inches overall (7.5-inch bbl.). Weight: 39 oz. (.45 cal., 7.5-inch bbl.). Fixed sights. Hard rubber bird's-head grips. Blued or nickel finish. Made from 1878 to 1905.

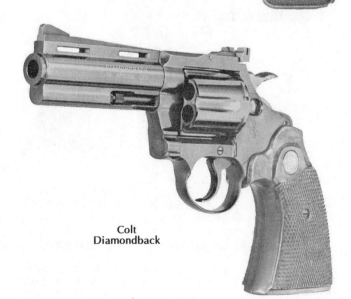

**Colt
Diamondback**

Colt Lightning/Thunderer
1877-1912

Colt Idaho Territorial
Centennial 1963 Issue

Colt New Jersey Tercentenary 1964 issue

Colt General Hood
Centennial 1964 issue

FRONTIER SCOUT REVOLVER
SA Army replica, scale. Calibers: .22 Short, Long, LR or .22 WMR (interchangeable cylinder available). Six-round cylinder, 4.75-inch bbl., 9.9 inches overall. Weight: 24 oz. Fixed sights. Plastic grips. Originally made w/bright alloy frame. Since 1959 w/steel frame and blued finish or all-nickel finish w/composition, wood or Staglite grips. Made 1958 to 1971.

Blued finish, plastic grips . . . . NiB $464 Ex $395 Gd $272
Nickel finish, wood grips . . . . .NiB $499 Ex $407 Gd $286
Buntline model, add. $75

Extra interchangeable
cylinder, add $100

FRONTIER SCOUT REVOLVER COMMEMORATIVE MODELS
Limited production versions of Frontier Scout issued, w/appropriate inscription, to commemorate historical events. Cased, in new condition.

1961 ISSUES
Kansas Statehood Centennial
(6201 produced). . . . . NiB $536
Pony Express Centennial
(1007 produced). . . . . NiB $638
1962 ISSUES
Columbus, Ohio, Sesquicentennial
(200 produced) . . . . .NiB $638
Fort Findlay, Ohio, Sesqui-
centennial (130 produced) . . . . .NiB $913
Fort Findlay Cased Pair, .22 Long
Rifle and .22 Magnum (20 produced) . . . . .NiB $2627
New MExico Golden Anniversary. . . . . .NiB $638
West Virginia Statehood
Centennial (3452 produced). . . . . .NiB $6130

1963 ISSUES
Arizona Territorial Centennial
(5355 produced) . . . . NiB $638
Battle of Gettysburg Centennial
(1019 produced) . . . . NiB $638
Carolina Charter Tercentenary
(300 produced) . . . . NiB $2270
Fort Stephenson, Ohio, Sesquicentennial
(200 produced) . . . . NiB $638
General John Hunt Morgan Indiana Raid . . . . NiB $689
Idaho Territorial Centennial (902 produced). . . . . .NiB $638

1964 ISSUES
California Gold Rush
(500 produced) . . . . NiB $638
Chamizal Treaty (450 produced) . . . . NiB $638
General Hood Centennial
(1503 produced) . . . . NiB $638
Montana Territorial Centennial
(2300 produced) . . . . NiB $638
Nevada "Battle Born"
(981 produced) . . . . NiB $597
Nevada Statehood Centennial
(3984 produced) . . . . NiB $2678
New Jersey Tercentenary
(1001 produced) . . . . NiB $577
St. Louis Bicentennial
(802 produced) . . . . NiB $638
Wyoming Diamond Jubilee
(2357 produced) . . . . NiB $638

1965 ISSUES
Appomattox Centennial
(1001 produced) . . . . NiB $577
Forty-Niner Miner
(500 produced) . . . . NiB $638
General Meade Campaign
(1197 produced) . . . . NiB $1647
Kansas Cowtown Series—Wichita
500 produced) . . . . NiB $577
Old Fort Des Moines Reconstruction
(700 produced) . . . . NiB $2280
Oregon Trail (1995 produced) . . . . NiB $638
St. Augustine Quadricentennial
(500 produced) . . . . NiB $638

1966 ISSUES
Colorado Gold Rush
(1350 produced)..........................NiB $638
Dakota Territory (1000 produced)..............NiB $638
Indiana Sesquicentennial
(1500 produced)..........................NiB $638
Kansas Cowtown Series—Abilene
(500 produced) .... NiB $577
Kansas Cowtown Series—Dodge City
(500 produced)......................... NiB $577
Oklahoma
Jubilee (1343 produced) .... NiB $638

1967 ISSUES
Alamo (4500 produced) .... NiB $577
Kansas Cowtown Series—Coffeyville
(500 produced)......................... NiB $561
Kansas Trail Series—Chisholm
Trail (500 produced)..................... NiB $577
Lawman Series—
Bat Masterson (3000 produced)............. NiB $570

1968 ISSUES
Kansas Cowtown Series—Santa Fe Trail
(501 produced)......................... NiB $577
Kansas Trail Series—Pawnee Trail
(501 produced)......................... NiB $577
Lawman Series—Pat Garrett
(3000 produced)........................ NiB $638
Nebraska Centennial
(7001 produced)........................ NiB $577

1969 ISSUES
Alabama Sesquicentennial
(3001 produced)........................ NiB $577
Arkansas Territory Sesquicentennial
(3500 produced)........................ NiB $561
California Bicentennial (5000 produced)............ NiB $577
General Nathan Bedford Forrest
(3000 produced)........................ NiB $577
Golden Spike (11,000 produced)................ NiB $577
Kansas Trail Series—Shawnee Trail
(501 produced)......................... NiB $577
Lawman Series—Wild Bill Hickock
(3000 produced)........................ NiB $638

1970 ISSUES
Kansas Fort Series—Fort Larned
(500 produced)......................... NiB $577
Kansas Fort Series—Fort Hays
(500 produced)......................... NiB $577
Kansas Fort Series—Fort Riley
(500 produced)......................... NiB $577
Lawman Series—Wyatt Earp
(3000 produced) .... NiB $780
Maine Sesquicentennial
(3000 produced)........................ NiB $577
Missouri Sesquicentennial (3000 produced) ..... NiB $577

1971 ISSUES
Kansas Fort Series—Fort Scott (500 produced).... NiB $577

1972 ISSUES
Florida Territory Sesquicentennial (2001 produced) NiB $638

1973 ISSUES Arizona ranger
(3001 produced) .... NiB $638

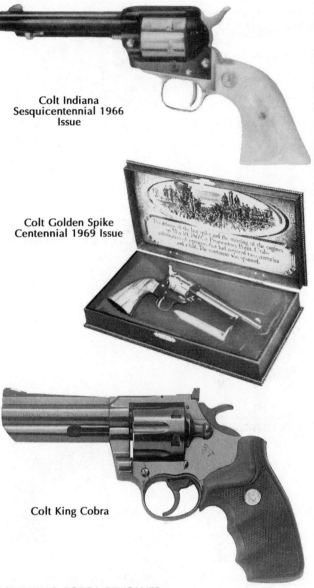

Colt Indiana
Sesquicentennial 1966
Issue

Colt Golden Spike
Centennial 1969 Issue

Colt King Cobra

COLT KING COBRA REVOLVER
Caliber: .357 Mag., bbl. lengths: 2.5-, 4-, 6- or 8-inches, 9 inches overall (with 4-inch bbl.). Weight: 42 oz., average. Matte stainless steel finish. Black Neoprene combat grips. Made 1986 to date. 2.5-inch bbl. and "Ultimate" bright or blued finish. Made from 1988 to 1992.
Matte stainless .... NiB $658 Ex $447 Gd $321
Ultimate bright stainless ..... NiB $780 Ex $468 Gd $362
Blued................... NiB $587 Ex $475 Gd $321

LAWMAN MK III DA REVOLVER
"J" frame, shrouded ejector rod on 2-inch bbl., only. Caliber: .357 Magnum. Six-round cylinder, bbl. lengths: 2-, 4-inch. 9.38 inches overall (w/4-inch bbl.), Weight: (with 4-inch bbl.), 35 oz. Fixed rear sight, ramp front. Service trigger and hammer or target trigger and wide-spur hammer. Blued or nickel-plated finish. Checkered walnut service or target grips. Made from 1969 to 1982.
Blued finish .... NiB $499 Ex $402 Gd $265
Nickel finish.............. NiB $546 Ex $412 Gd $274

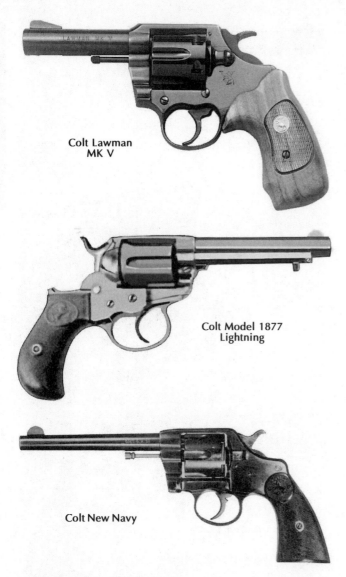

Colt Lawman
MK V

Colt Model 1877
Lightning

Colt New Navy

LAWMAN MK V DA REVOLVER

Similar to Trooper MK V. Caliber: .357 Mag. Six-round cylinder, 2- or 4-inch bbl., 9.38 inches overall (4-inch bbl.). Weight: 35 oz. (4-inch bbl.). Fixed sights. Checkered walnut grips. Made 1984 and 1991.
Blued finish . . . . **NiB $362 Ex $295 Gd $214**
Nickel finish. . . . . **NiB $397 Ex $304 Gd $228**

MAGNUM CARRY DA REVOLVER . . **NiB $489 Ex $373 Gd $296**
Similar to Model DS II except chambered for .357 Magnum. Made from 1998 to date.

MARINE CORPS MODEL (1905) DA REVOLVER

General specifications same as New Navy Second Issue except has round butt, was supplied only in .38 caliber (.38 Short & Long Colt, .38 Special) w/6-inch bbl. (S/N range 10,001-10,926) Made 1905 to 1909.
Marine Corps model NiB $15,606 Ex $14,050 Gd $13,260
Marked "USMC". . . . . **NiB $7803 Ex $5636 Gd $3886**

METROPOLITAN MK III
DA REVOLVER. . . . . **NiB $536 Ex $423 Gd $316**
Same as Official Police MK III except has 4-inch bbl. w/service or target grips. Weight: 36 oz. Made from 1969 to 1972.

MODEL 1877
LIGHTNING REVOLVER . . **NiB $4197 Ex $3264 Gd $2973**
Also called Thunderer Model. Calibers: .38 and .41 centerfire. Six-round cylinder, bbl. lengths: 2.5-, 3.5-, 4.5- and 6-inch without ejector, 4.5- and 6-inch w/ejector, 8.5 inches overall (3.5-inch bbl.). Weight: 23 oz. (.38 cal., with 3.5-inch bbl.) Fixed sights. Blued or nickel finish. Hard rubber bird's-head grips. Made 1877 to 1909.

NEW FRONTIER BUNTLINE SPECIAL
Same as New Frontier SA Army except has 12-inch bbl.,
Second generation (1962-75)NiB $2570 Ex $2028 Gd $1392
Third generation (1976-92) . **NiB $1352 Ex $1120 Gd $861**

NEW FRONTIER SA ARMY REVOLVER
Same as SA Army except has flat-top frame, adj. target rear sight, ramp front sight, smooth walnut grips. 5.5- or 7.5-inch bbl., Calibers: .357 Magnum, .44 Special, .45 Colt. Made 1961 to 1992.
Second generation (1961-75)NiB $2902 Ex $2647 Gd $2458
Third generation (1976-92) . **NiB $1362 Ex $1118 Gd $857**

NEW FRONTIER SA .22 REVOLVER . **NiB $532 Ex $342 Gd $235**
Same as Peacemaker .22 except has flat-top frame, adj. rear sight, ramp front sight. Made from 1971-76; reintro. 1982 to 1986.

NEW NAVY (1889) DA, FIRST ISSUE
Also called New Army. Calibers: .38 Short & Long Colt, .41 Short & Long Colt. Six-round cylinder, left revolution. Bbl. lengths: 3-, 4.5- and 6-inches, 11.25 inches overall (with 6-inch bbl.). Weight: 32 oz. with 6-inch bbl. Fixed sights, knife-blade and V-notch. Blued or nickel-plated finish. Walnut or hard rubber grips. Made 1889 to 1994. Note: This model, which was adopted by both the Army and Navy, was Colt's first revolver of the solid frame, swing-out cylinder type. It lacks the cylinder-locking notches found on later models made on this .41 frame; ratchet on the back of the cylinder is held in place by a double projection on the hand.
First issue. . . . . **NiB $2018 Ex $1644 Gd $1182**
First issue w/3-inch bbl. . . **NiB $2539 Ex $2040 Gd $1484**
Navy contract, marked
"U.S.N.(S/N 1-1500) . . . . . **NiB $3682 Ex $2981 Gd $2121**

NEW NAVY (1892) DA, SECOND ISSUE
Also called New Army. General specifications same as First Issue except has double cylinder notches and double locking bolt. Calibers: .38 Special added in 1904 and .32-20 in 1905. Made 1892 to 1907. Note: The heavy .38 Special High Velocity loads should not be used in .38 Special arms of this model.
Second issue . . . . **NiB $1750 Ex $1446 Gd $1020**
Second issue w/3-inch bbl. NiB $2746 Ex $2264 Gd $1619
Navy contract, marked "U.S.N". . **NiB $2865 Ex $2344 Gd $1644**

NEW POCKET DA REVOLVER **NiB $770 Ex $620 Gd $464**
Caliber: .32 Short & Long Colt. Six-round cylinder. bbl. lengths: 2.5, 3.5- and 6-inches. 7.5 inches overall w/3.5-inch bbl., Weight: 16 oz., with 3.5-inch bbl. Fixed sights, knife-blade and V-notch. Blued or nickel finish. Rubber grips. Made from 1893 to 1905.

NEW POLICE DA REVOLVER **NiB $1020 Ex $638 Gd $445**
Built on New Pocket frame but w/larger grip. Calibers: .32 Colt New Police, .32 Short & Long Colt. Bbl. lengths: 2.5-, 4- and 6-inches; 8.5 inches overall (with 4-inch bbl.). Weight: 17 oz., with 4-inch bbl. Fixed knife-blade front sight, V-notch rear. Blued or nickel finish. Rubber grips. Made from 1896 to 1905.

NEW POLICE TARGET DA REVOLVER **NiB $1258 Ex $1111 Gd $893**
Target version of the New Police w/same general specifications. Target sights. Six-inch bbl., blued finish only. Made 1896 to 1905.

NEW SERVICE DA REVOLVER

Calibers: .38 Special, .357 Magnum (intro. 1936), .38-40, .44-40, .44 Russian, .44 Special, .45 Auto, .45 Colt, .450 Eley, .455 Eley, .476 Eley. Six-round cylinder, bbl. lengths: 4-, 5- and 6-inch in .38 Special and .357 Magnum, 4.5-, 5.5- and 7.5 inches in other calibers; 9.75 inches overall (with 4.5-inch bbl.). Weight: 39 oz. (.45 cal. with 4.5-inch bbl.). Fixed sights. Blued or nickel finish. Checkered walnut grips. Made 1898-42. Note: More than 500,000 of this model in caliber .45 Auto (designated "Model 1917 Revolver") were purchased by the U.S. Gov't. during WW I. These arms were later sold as surplus to National Rifle Association members through the Director of Civilian Marksmanship. Price was $16.15 plus packing charge. Supply Exhausted during the early 1930s.

Commercial model	NiB $1851	Ex $1507	Gd $1086
Magnum	NiB $1223	Ex $1018	Gd $729
1917 Army	NiB $1188	Ex $683	Gd $597

NEW SERVICE TARGET . . . . NiB $1336 Ex $1188 Gd $770

Target version of the New Service. Calibers: Originally chambered for .44 Russian, .450 Eley, .455 Eley and .476 Eley, later models in .44 Special, .45 Colt and .45 Auto. Six- or 7.5-inch bbl., 12.75 inches overall (7.5-inch bbl.). Adj. target sights. Hand-finished action. With blued finish. Checkered walnut grips. Made 1900 to 1940.

OFFICERS' MODEL MATCH . . NiB $852 Ex $714 Gd $425

Same general design as Officers' Model revolvers. Has tapered heavy bbl., wide hammer spur, Adjustable rear sight ramp front sight, large target grips of checkered walnut. Calibers: .22 LR, .38 Special. Six-inch bbl., 11.25 inches overall. Weight: 43 oz. (in .22 cal.), 39 oz. (.38 cal.). Blued finish. Made from 1953 to 1970.

OFFICERS' MODEL SPECIAL . . NiB $894 Ex $621 Gd $423

Target version of Officers' Model Second Issue w/similar characters except w/heavier, nontapered bbl. redesigned hammer. Ramp front sight, Colt Officers' Model Special "Coltmaster" rear sight adj. for windage and elevation. Calibers: .22 LR, .38 Special. Six-inch bbl. 11.25 inches overall. Weight: 39 oz. (in .38 cal.), 43 oz., (.22 cal.). Blued finish. Checkered plastic grips. Made from 1949 to 1953.

OFFICERS' MODEL TARGET

DA REVOLVER, FIRST ISSUE NiB $1343 Ex $1099 Gd $791

Caliber: .38 Special. Six-inch bbl., hand-finished action, adj. target sights. Checkered with walnut grips. General specifications same as New Navy, Second Issue. Made from 1904 to 1908.

OFFICERS' MODEL TARGET, SECOND ISSUE

Calibers: .22 LR (intro. 1930, embedded head-cylinder for high-speed cartridges after 1932), .32 Police Positive (made 1932-1942), .38 Special. Six-round cylinder, bbl. lengths: 4-, 4.5-, 5-, 6- and 7.5-inch (in .38 Special) or 6-inch only (.22 LR and .32 PP), 11.25 inches overall (6-inch bbl. in .38 Special). Adj. target sights. Blued finish. Checkered walnut grips. Hand-finished action. General features same as Army Special and Official Police of same date. Made from 1908 to 1949 (w/exceptions noted).

Second issue (.38 caliber)	NiB $1130	Ex $930	Gd $653
Second issue (.32 caliber)	NiB $1744	Ex $1426	Gd $984
Second issue (.22 caliber)	NiB $1232	Ex $1018	Gd $729
w/shorter bbls. (4-, 4.5- or 5-inches), add			.50%

OFFICIAL POLICE DA REVOLVER

Calibers: .22 LR (intro. 1930, embedded head-cylinder for high-speed cartridges after 1932), .32-20 (disc. 1942), .38 Special, .41 Long Colt (disc. 1930). Six-round cylinder, bbl. lengths: 4-, 5-, and 6-inch or 2-inch and 6-inch heavy bbl. in .38 Special only; .22 LR w/4- and 6-inch bbls. only; 11.25 inches overall. Weight: 36

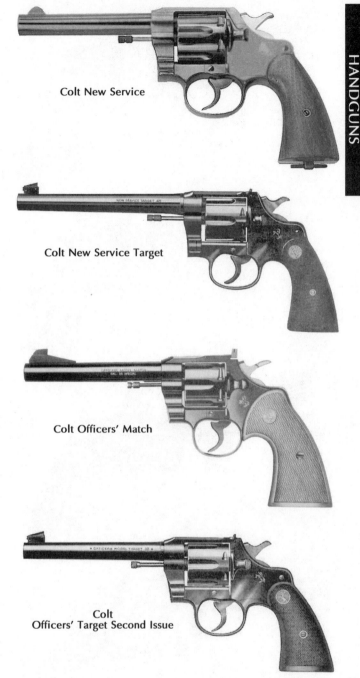

Colt New Service

Colt New Service Target

Colt Officers' Match

Colt
Officers' Target Second Issue

oz. (standard 6-inch bbl.) in .38 Special. Fixed sights. Blued or nickel-plated finish. Checkered walnut grips on all revolvers of this model except some of postwar production had checkered plastic grips. Made 1927-69. Note: This model is a refined version of the Army Special, which it replaced in 1928 at about serial number 520,000. The Commando .38 Special was a wartime adaptation of the Official Police made to government specifications. Commando can be identified by its sandblasted blued finish. Serial numbers start w/number 1-50,000 (Made 1942 to 1945).

Commercial model (pre-war)	NiB $638	Ex $510	Gd $388
Commercial model (post-war)	NiB $557	Ex $476	Gd $362
Commando model	NiB $669	Ex $564	Gd $398

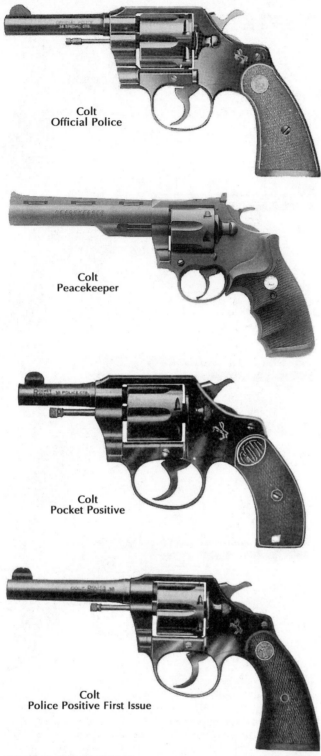

Colt
Official Police

Colt
Peacekeeper

Colt
Pocket Positive

Colt
Police Positive First Issue

OFFICIAL POLICE MK III
DA REVOLVER . . . . NiB $321 Ex $262 Gd $198
"J" frame, without shrouded ejector rod. Caliber: .38 Special. Six-round cylinder. bbl., lengths: 4-, 5-, 6-inches, 9.25 inches overall w/4-inch bbl., weight: 34 oz. (4-inch bbl.). Fixed rear sight, ramp front. Service trigger and hammer or target trigger and wide-spur hammer. Blued or nickel-plated finish. Checkered walnut service grips. Made 1969 to 1975.

PEACEKEEPER DA REVOLVER. NiB $499 Ex $418 Gd $220
Caliber: .357 Mag. Six-round cylinder, 4- or 6-inch bbl., 11.25 inches overall (6-inch bbl.). Weight: 46 oz. (with 6-inch bbl.). Adj. white outline rear sight, red insert ramp-style front. Non-reflective matte blued finish. Made from 1985 to 1989.

PEACEMAKER .22 SECOND AMENDMENT
COMMEMORATIVE . . . . NiB $660 Ex $544 Gd $286
Caliber: .22, revolver w/7.5-inch bbl., nickel-plated frame, bbl. ejector rod assembly, hammer and trigger, blued cylinder, backstrap and trigger guard. Black pearlite grips. bbl., inscribed "The Right to Keep and Bear Arms." Presentation case. Limited edition of 3000 issued in 1977. Top value is for revolver in new condition.

PEACEMAKER .22 SA REVOLVER NiB $423 Ex $332 Gd $275
Calibers: .22 LR and .22 WMR. Furnished w/cylinder for each caliber, 6-round. Bbl.: 4.38-, 6- or 7.5-inches, 11.25 inches overall (with 6-inch bbl.). Weight: 30.5 oz. (with 6-inch bbl.). Fixed sights. Black composite grips. Made from 1971 to 1976.

POCKET POSITIVE DA REVOLVER
General specifications same as New Pocket except this model has positive lock feature (see Police Positive). Calibers: .32 Short & Long Colt (disc. 1914), .32 Colt New Police (.32 S&W Short & Long). Fixed sights, flat top and square notch. Blue or nickel finish. Made from 1905 to 1940.
Blue finish . . . . NiB $635 Ex $577 Gd $388
Nickel finish. . . . . NiB $699 Ex $571 Gd $435

POLICE POSITIVE DA, FIRST ISSUE
Improved version of the New Police w/the "Positive Lock," which prevents the firing pin coming in contact w/the cartridge except when the trigger is pulled. Calibers: .32 Short & Long Colt (disc. 1915), .32 Colt New Police (.32 S&W Short & Long), .38 New Police (.38 S&W). Six-round cylinder, bbl. lengths: 2.5- (.32 cal. only), 4- 5- and 6-inches; 8.5 inches overall (with 4-inch bbl.). Weight 20 oz. (with 4-inch bbl.). Fixed sights. Blued or nickel finish. Rubber or checkered walnut grips. Made from 1905 to 1947.
Blue finish . . . . NiB $529 Ex $439 Gd $351
Nickel finish. . . . . NiB $581 Ex $475 Gd $340

POLICE POSITIVE DA, SECOND ISSUE
Same as Detective Special second issue except has 4-inch bbl., 9 inches overall, weight: 26.5 oz. Intro. in 1977. Note: Original Police Positive (First Issue) has a shorter frame, is not chambered for .38 Special.
Blue finish . . . . NiB $524 Ex $437 Gd $351
Nickel finish. . . . . NiB $581 Ex $469 Gd $342

POLICE POSITIVE SPECIAL
DA REVOLVER . . . . NiB $581 Ex $498 Gd $356
Based on the Police Positive w/frame lengthened to permit longer cylinder. Calibers: .32-20 (disc. 1942), .38 Special, .32 New Police and .38 New Police (intro. 1946). Six-round cylinder; bbl. lengths: 4-(only length in current production), 5- and 6-inch; 8.75 inches overall (with 4-inch bbl.). Weight: 23 oz. (with 4-inch bbl. in .38 Special). Fixed sights. Checkered grips of hard rubber, plastic or walnut. Made 1907 to 1973.

COLT POLICE POSITIVE TARGET
DA REVOLVER . . . . NiB $884 Ex $724 Gd $523
Target version of the Police Positive. Calibers: .22 LR (intro. 1910, embedded-head cylinder for high-speed cartridges after 1932), .22 WRF (1910-35), .32 Short & Long Colt, (1915), .32 New Police (.32 S&W Short & Long). Six-inch bbl., blued finish only, 10.5 inches overall. Weight: 26 oz. in .22 cal. Adj. target sights. Checkered walnut grips. Made from 1905 to 1940.

PYTHON DA REVOLVER

"I" frame, shrouded ejector rod. Calibers: .357 Magnum, .38 Special. Six-round cylinder, 2.5-, 4-, 6- or 8-inch vent rib bbl., 11.25 inches overall (with 6-inch bbl.). Weight: 44 oz. (6-inch bbl.). Adj. rear sight, ramp front. Blued, nickel or stainless finish. Checkered walnut target grips. Made from 1955 to 1996. Ultimate stainless finish made in 1985.

Blued finish	NiB $1316	Ex $924	Gd $437
Royal blued finish	NiB $1316	Ex $924	Gd $437
Nickel finish.	NiB $1316	Ex $924	Gd $437
Stainless finish	NiB $1357	Ex $975	Gd $479
Ultimate stainless finish	NiB $1357	Ex $975	Gd $479
Hunter model (w/2x scope).	NiB $1907	Ex $1510	Gd $926
Silhouette model (w/2x scope).	NiB $2152	Ex $1803	Gd $1039

SHOOTING MASTER DA REVOLVER

Deluxe target arm based on the New Service model. Calibers: Originally made only in .38 Special, .44 Special, .45 Auto and .45 Colt added in 1933, .357 Magnum in 1936. Six-inch bbl., 11.25 inches overall. Weight: 44 oz., in (.38 cal.), adj. target sights. Hand-finished action. Blued finish. Checkered walnut grips. Rounded butt. Made from 1932 to 1941.

Shooting Master .38 Special.	NiB $1507	Ex $1344	Gd $915
Shooting Master .357 Mag.	NiB $1533	Ex $1269	Gd $908
Shooting Master .44 Special, .45 ACP, .45LC	NiB $4092	Ex $3773	Gd $2285

SINGLE ACTION ARMY (SAA) REVOLVER

Also called Frontier Six-Shooter and Peacemaker. Available in more than 30 calibers including: .22 Rimfire (Short, Long, LR), .22 WRF, .32 Rimfire, .32 Colt, .32 S&W, .32-20, .38 Colt, .38 S&W, .38 Special, .357 Magnum, .38-40, .41 Colt, .44 Rimfire, .44 Russian, .44 Special, .44-40, .45 Colt, .45 Auto, .450 Boxer, 450 Eley, .455 Eley, .476 Eley. Six-round cylinder. Bbl. lengths: 4.75, 5 .5 and 7.5 inches w/ejector or 3 and 4 inches w/o ejector. 10.25 inches overall (with 4.75-inch bbl.). Weight: 36 oz. (.45 cal. w/4.75-inch bbl.). Fixed sights. Also made in Target Model w/flat top-strap and target sights. Blued finish w/casehardened frame or nickel-plated. One-piece smooth walnut or checkered black rubber grips. Note: S.A. Army Revolvers w/serial numbers above 165,000 (circa 1896) are adapted to smokeless powder and cylinder pin screw was changed to spring catch at about the same time. The "First Generation" of SA Colts included both blackpowder and smokeless configurations and were manufactured from 1873 to 1940. Production resumed in 1955 w/serial number 1001SA and continued through 1975 to complete the second series, which is referred to as the "Second Generation." In 1976, the "Third Generation" of production began and continues to to date. However, several serial number rollovers occurred at 99,999. For Example, in 1978 the "SA" suffix became an "SA" prefix and again in 1993, when the serial number SA99,999 was reached, the serialization format was changed again to include both an "S" prefix and an "A" suffix. Although the term "Fourth Generation" is frequently associated with this rollover, no series change actually occurred, therefore, the current production is still a "Third Generation" series. Current calibers: .357 Magnum, .44 Special, .45 Long Colt.

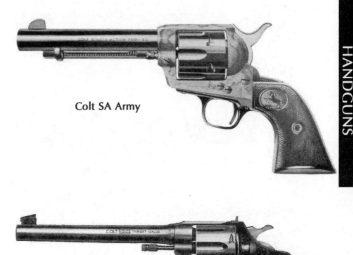

Colt SA Army

Colt
Police Positive Target

Colt Python

Pinched frame (1873 only)	NiB $84,558	Ex $68,034	Gd $46,138
Early commercial (1873-77).	NiB $43,631	Ex $34,945	Gd $23,792
Early military (1873-77).	NiB $50,184	Ex $39,984	Gd $27,335
Large bore rimfire (1875-80).	NiB $40,565	Ex $33,558	Gd $22,313
Small bore rimfire (1875-80) . . .	NiB $31,391	Ex $25,169	Gd $17,151
Frontier six-shooter, .44-40 (1878-82).	NiB $47,323	Ex $37,964	Gd $25,875
Storekeeper's model, no ejector (1883-98).	NiB $49,980	Ex $40,025	Gd $27,311
Sheriff's model (1883-98).	NiB $47,226	Ex $37,954	Gd $25,760
Target model, flat top strap, target sights	NiB $26,204	Ex $20,808	Gd $14,229
U.S. Cavalry model, .45 (1873-92).	NiB $45,890	Ex $36,705	Gd $25,194

Colt SA Army — 125th Anniversary

Colt 150th Anniversary Deluxe

Colt 150th Anniversary Engraving Sampler

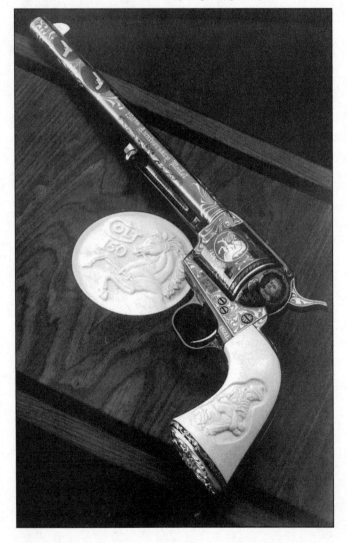

In the previous section the GTG deviates from the observed practice of listing only the value of firearms produced after 1900. This deliberate departure from the standard format is intended to provide a general reference and establish proper orientation for the reader, because the Colt SSA had its origins in the last quarter of the 19th century. Consequently, antique firearms produced prior to 1898 have been listed as a preface and introduction to the first series of production (what is now recognized as "1st Generation") in order to systematically demonstrate the progressive and sequential development of the multi-generation Colt SAA. Therefore, the previous general values have been provided to establish a point of reference to allow a more comprehensive Examination of the evolution of the Colt SAA. However, please note that the following values apply only to original models, not to similar S.A.A. revolvers of more recent manufacture.

Standard model, pre-war
(1st generation) . . . . $13,770 to $66,810
Standard model (1955-75)
(2nd generation) . . . . NiB $2509 Ex $2050 Gd $1499
Standard model (1976 to date)NiB $1275 Ex $1122 Gd $824

SA ARMY — 125TH ANNIVERSARY NiB $1668 Ex $1438 Gd $1239
Limited production deluxe version of SA Army issued in commemoration of Colt's 125th Anniversary. Caliber: .45 Long Colt., 7.5-inch bbl., cold-plated frame trigger, hammer, cylinder pin, ejector rod tip, and grip medallion. Presentation case w/anniversary medallion. Serial numbers "50AM." 7368 were made in 1961.

SA ARMY COMMEMORATIVE MODELS

Limited production versions of SA Army .45 issued, w/appropriate inscription to commemorate historical events. Cased. Note: Values indicated are for commemorative revolvers in new condition.

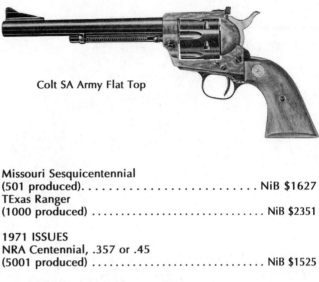

Colt SA Army Flat Top

1963 ISSUES
Arizona Territorial Centennial
(1280 produced). . . . . NiB $1663
West Virginia Statehood
Centennial (600 produced) . . . . NiB $1663

1964 ISSUES
Chamizal Treaty (50 produced). . . . . NiB $1867
Colonel Sam Colt Sesquicentennial
Presentation (4750 produced) . . . . NiB $1663
Deluxe Presentation
(200 produced). . . . . NiB $3621
Special Deluxe Presentation
(50 produced). . . . . NiB $5687
Montana Territorial Centennial
(851 produced). . . . . NiB $1724
Nevada "Battle Born"
(100 produced). . . . . NiB $2672
Nevada Statehood Centennial
(1877 produced). . . . . NiB $2275
New Jersey Tercentenary
(250 produced). . . . . NiB $1663
Pony Express Presentation
(1004 produced). . . . . NiB $1836
St. Louis Bicentennial
(450 produced). . . . . NiB $1663
Wyatt Earp Buntline
(150 produced). . . . . NiB $2809

1965 ISSUES
Appomattox Centennial
(500 produced). . . . . NiB $1454
Old Fort Des Moines Recon-
struction (200 produced). . . . . NiB $1454

1966 ISSUES
Abercrombie & Fitch Trailblazer
—Chicago (100 produced) . . . . NiB $1423
Abercrombie & Fitch Trailblazer
—New York (200 produced) . . . . NiB $1423
Abercrombie & Fitch Trailblazer
—San Francisco (100 produced) . . . . NiB $1423
California Gold Rush
(130 produced) . . . . NiB $1423
General Meade (200 produced) . . . . NiB $1663
Pony Express Four Square (4 guns) . . . . NiB $7268

1967 ISSUES
Alamo (1000 produced) . . . . NiB $1663
Lawman Series—Bat Masterson
(500 produced). . . . . NiB $1760

1968 ISSUES
Lawman Series—Pat Garrett (500 produced) . . . . NiB $1663
1969 ISSUES
Lawman Series—Wild Bill Hickok
(500 produced). . . . . NiB $1663

1970 ISSUES
Lawman Series—Wyatt Earp
(501 produced) . . . . NiB $2907

Missouri Sesquicentennial
(501 produced). . . . . NiB $1627
TExas Ranger
(1000 produced) . . . . NiB $2351

1971 ISSUES
NRA Centennial, .357 or .45
(5001 produced) . . . . NiB $1525

1975 ISSUES
Peacemaker Centennial .45
(1501 produced) . . . . NiB $1872
Peacemaker Centennial .44-40
(1501 produced). . . . . NiB $1872
Peacemaker Centennial Cased
Pair (501 produced) . . . . NiB $1872

1979 ISSUES
Ned Buntline .45
(3000 produced) . . . . NiB $1367

1986 ISSUES
Colt 150th Anniversary (standard). . . . . NiB $2064
Colt 150th Anniversay (engraved). . . . . NiB $3647

COLT SA COWBOY REVOLVER NiB $632 Ex $468 Gd $363
SA variant designed for "Cowboy Action Shooting." Caliber: .45 Colt. Six-round cylinder, 5.5-inch bbl., 11 inches overall. Weight: 42 oz. Blade front sight, fixed V-notch rear. Blued finish w/color casehardened frame. Smooth walnut grips. Made from 1999 to 2003.

SA SHERIFF'S MODEL .45
Limited edition replica of Storekeeper's Model in caliber .45 Colt, made Exclusively for Centennial Arms Corp. Chicago, Illinois. Numbered "1SM." Blued finish w/casehardened frame or nickel-plated. Walnut grips. Made in 1961.
Blued finish (478 produced) NiB $2152 Ex $1780 Gd $1454
Nickel finish (25 produced) NiB $8155 Ex $5763 Gd $4024

THREE-FIFTY-SEVEN DA REVOLVER
Heavy frame. Caliber: .357 Magnum. Six-shot cylinder, 4 or 6-inch bbl. Quickdraw ramp front sight, Accro rear sight. Blued finish. Checkered walnut grips. 9.25 or 11.25 inches overall. Weight: 36 oz. (4-inch bbl.), 39 oz. (6 inch bbl.). Made from 1953 to 1961.
w/standard hammer and service grips NiB $711 Ex $601 Gd $431
w/wide-spur hammer and target grips NiB $733 Ex $612 Gd $444

TROOPER DA REVOLVER
Same specifications as Officers' Model Match except has 4-inch bbl. w/quick-draw ramp front sight, weight: 34 oz. in .38 caliber. Made from 1953 to 1969.
w/standard hammer and service grips NiB $536 Ex $ 464 Gd $357
w/wide-spur hammer and target grips NiB $632 Ex $525 Gd $408

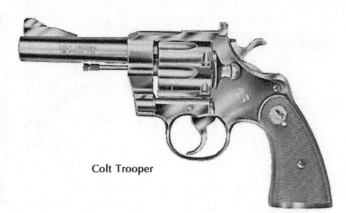

Colt Trooper

Colt Trooper MK V

TROOPER MK III DA REVOLVER
"J"frame, shrouded ejector rod. Calibers: .22 LR, .22 Magnum, .38 Special, .357 Magnum. Six-round cylinder. bbl. lengths: 4-, 6-inches. 9.5 inches overall (with 4-inch bbl.). Weight: 39 oz. (4-inch bbl.). Adj. rear sight, ramp front. Target trigger and hammer. Blued or nickel-plated finish. Checkered walnut target grips. Made 1969 to 1978.
Blued finish . . . . NiB $587 Ex $418 Gd $224
Nickel finish. . . . . NiB $643 Ex $452 Gd $224

TROOPER MK V REVOLVER
Re-engineered Mark III for smoother, faster action. Caliber: .357 Magnum. Six-round cylinder, bbl. lengths: 4-, 6-, 8-inch w/vent rib. Adj. rear sight, ramp front, red insert. Checkered walnut grips. Made from 1982 to 1986.
Blued finish . . . . NiB $562 Ex $437 Gd $321
Nickel finish. . . . . NiB $577 Ex $499 Gd $316

VIPER DA REVOLVER . . . . NiB $760 Ex $602 Gd $356
Same as Cobra, Second Issue except has 4-inch bbl., 9 inches overall, weight: 20 oz. Made from 1977 to 1984.

U.S. BICENTENNIAL
COMMEMORATIVE SET . . . . NiB $3290
Replica Colt 3rd Model Dragoon revolver w/accessories, Colt SA Army revolver, and Colt Python revolver. Matching roll-engraved unfluted cylinders, blued finish and rosewood grips w/Great Seal of the United States silver medallion. Dragoon revolver has silver grip frame. Serial numbers 0001 to 1776. All revolvers in set have same number. Deluxe drawer-style presentation case of walnut w/book compartment containing a reproduction of "Armsmear." Issued in 1976. Value is for revolvers in new condition.

COONAN ARMS, INC. — Maplewood, Minnesota (formerly St. Paul, Minnesota)

MODEL .357 MAGNUM AUTO PISTOL
Caliber: .357 Mag. Seven-round magazine, 5- or 6-inch bbl., 8.3 inches overall (with 5-inch bbl.). Weight: 42 oz. Front ramp interchangeable sight, fixed rear sight, adj. for windage. Black walnut grips. Made from 1983 to 1999.
Model A Std. grade w/o grip
safety (disc. 1991) . . . . NiB $1221 Ex $1056 Gd $869
Model B Std. grade w/5-inch bbl.,. . . NiB $944 Ex $703 Gd $500
Model B Std. grade w/6-inch bbl.,. . . NiB $714 Ex $601 Gd $437
Model B w/5-inch
compensated bbl., (Classic). . . . . . NiB $1336 Ex $1122 Gd $923
Model B w/6-inch
compensated bbl . . . . NiB $1016 Ex $789 Gd $561

.357 MAGNUM CADET COMPACT
Similar to the standard .357 Magnum model except w/3.9-inch bbl., on compact frame. Six-round (Cadet), 7- or 8-round magazine (Cadet II). Weight: 39 oz., 7.8 inches overall. Made 1993 to 1999.
Cadet model. . . . . NiB $897 Ex $653 Gd $497
Cadet II model . . . . NiB $897 Ex $653 Gd $497

CZ PISTOLS — Uhersky Brod (formerly Strakonice), Czechoslovakia. Mfd. by Ceska Zbrojovka-Nardoni Podnik (formerly Bohmische Waffenfabrik A. G.)

Currently imported by CZ-USA, Kansas City, KS. Previously by Magnum Research and Action Arms. Vintage importation is by Century International Arms. Also, see Dan Wesson Firearms listings.

Colt U.S. Bicentennial Commemorative Set

CZ P-01 . . . . NiB $658 Ex $406 Gd $305
Caliber: 9mm Para. Based on CZ-75 design but with improved metals, aluminum alloy frame, hammer forged bbl. (3.8 inches), checkered rubber grips, matte black polycoat finish. Imported 2003.

CZ 40 . . . . NiB $530 Ex $372 Gd $321
Caliber: .40 S&W. M1911-style frame, CZ-75B operating mechanism; single or double-action; black polycoat finish. Fixed sights; 10-round mag.

MODEL 27 AUTO PISTOL . . . . NiB $653 Ex $555 Gd $385
Caliber: .32 Automatic (7.65mm). Eight-round magazine, 4-inch bbl., 6 inches overall. Weight: 23.5 oz. Fixed sights. Blued finish. Plastic grips. Made from 1927 to 1951. Note: After the German occupation (March 1939), Models 27 and 38 were marked w/manufacturer code "fnh." Designation of Model 38 was changed to "Pistole 39(t)."

MODEL .38 AUTO PISTOL (VZ SERIES)
Caliber: .380 Automatic (9mm). Nine-round magazine, 3.75-inch bbl., 7 inches overall. Weight: 26 oz. Fixed sights. Blued finish. Plastic grips. After 1939 designated as T39. Made 1938 to 1945.
CZ DAO model . . . . NiB $518 Ex $442 Gd $358
CZ SA/DA model . . . . NiB $1451 Ex $1144 Gd $825

MODEL 50 DA AUTO PISTOL NiB $265 Ex $191 Gd $153
Similar to Walther Model PP except w/frame-mounted safety and trigger guard not hinged. Caliber: .32 ACP (7.65mm), 8-round magazine, 3.13-inch bbl., 6.5 inches overall. Weight: 24.5 oz. Fixed sights. Blued finished. Intro. in 1950. disc. Note: "VZ50" is the official designation of this pistol used by the Czech National Police ("New Model .006" was the Export designation but very few were released).

MODEL 52 SA AUTO PISTOL . NiB $248 Ex $202 Gd $137
Roller-locking breech system. Calibers: 7.62mm or 9mm Para. Eight-round magazine, 4.7-inch bbl., 8.1 inches overall. Weight: 31 oz. Fixed sights. Blued finish. Grooved composition grips. Made 1952 to 1956.

MODEL 70 DA AUTO PISTOL NiB $530 Ex $420 Gd $296
Similar to Model 50 but redesigned to improve function and dependability. Made from 1962 to 1983.

MODEL 75 DA/DAO AUTOMATIC PISTOL
Calibers: 9mm Para. or .40 S&W w/selective action mode. 10-, 13- or 15-round magazine, 3.9-inch bbl., (Compact) or 4.75-inch bbl., (Standard), 8 inches overall (Standard). Weight: 35 oz. Fixed sights. Blued, nickel, Two-Tone or black polymer finish. Checkered wood or high-impact plastic grips. Made from 1994 to date.
Black polymer finish . . . . NiB $459 Ex $385 Gd $284
High-polish blued finish . . . . . NiB $526 Ex $453 Gd $347
Matte blued finish . . . . NiB $499 Ex $398 Gd $295
Nickel finish. . . . . NiB $541 Ex $442 Gd $330
Two-tone finish . . . . NiB $530 Ex $431 Gd $325
w/.22 Kadet conversion, add. $281
Compact model, add $65

MODEL 82 DA AUTO PISTOL NiB $407 Ex $306 Gd $221
Similar to the standard CZ 83 model except chambered in 9x18 Makarov. This model currently is the Czech military sidearm.

MODEL 83 DA AUTOMATIC PISTOL
Calibers: .32 ACP, .380 ACP. 15-round (.32 ACP) or 13-round (.380 ACP) magazine, 3.75-inch bbl., 6.75 inches overall. Weight: 26.5 oz. Fixed sights. Blued (standard); chrome and nickel (optional special edition) w/brushed, matte or polished finish. Checkered black plastic grips. Made from 1985 to date.
Standard finish . . . . NiB $434 Ex $357 Gd $221
Special edition . . . . NiB $580 Ex $453 Gd $322
Engraved . . . . NiB $1234 Ex $1017 Gd $718

MODEL 85 AUTOMATIC DA PISTOL
Same as CZ 75 except w/ambidExtrous slide release and safety.

CZ Model 75 Compact

CZ Model 75 Kadet

CZ Model 83

Calibers: 9mm Para., 7.65mm. Made 1986 to date.
Black polymer finish . . . . NiB $478 Ex $388 Gd $274
High-polish blued finish . . . . . . NiB $576 Ex $477 Gd $319
Matte blued finish . . . . NiB $529 Ex $372 Gd $267

85

CZ Model 85 Combat

CZ Model 97B

CZ Model 100

Daewoo DH40

MODEL 85 COMBAT DA AUTOMATIC PISTOL
Similar to the standard CZ 85 model except w/13-round magazine, combat-style hammer, fully adj. rear sight and walnut grips. Made from 1986 to date.

Black polymer
finish . . . . NiB $569 Ex $489 Gd $306
High-polished
blued finish . . . . NiB $610 Ex $498 Gd $373
Matte blued
finish . . . . NiB $614 Ex $486 Gd $366

MODEL 97B DA
AUTOLOADING PISTOL . . . . NiB $629 Ex $540 Gd $344
Similar to the CZ Model 75 except chambered for the .45 ACP cartridge. 10-round magazine, Frame-mounted thumb safety that allows single-action, cocked-and-locked carry. Made from 1998 to date.

MODEL 100 DA
AUTOMATIC PISTOL . . . . NiB $488 Ex $398 Gd $265
Caliber: 9mm, .40 S&W. 10-round magazine, 3.8-inch bbl., Weight: 25 oz. Polymer grips w/fixed low-profile sights. Made from 1996 to 2007. Reintroduced 2009.

MODEL 1945 DA
POCKET AUTO PISTOL . . . . . NiB $328 Ex $241 Gd $183
Caliber: .25 Auto (6.35mm). Eight-round magazine, 2.5-inch bbl., 5 inches overall. Weight: 15 oz. Fixed sights. Blued finish. Plastic grips. Intro. 1945. disc.

DUO POCKET
AUTO PISTOL . . . . NiB $328 Ex $252 Gd $174
Caliber: .25 Automatic (6.35mm). Six-round magazine, 2.13 inch bbl., 4.5 inches overall. Weight: 14-.5 oz. Fixed sights. Blued or nickel finish. Plastic grips. Made circa 1926 to 1960.

DAEWOO PISTOLS — Seoul, Korea.
Mfd. by Daewoo Precision Industries Ltd.

Imported by Daewoo Precision Industries, Southhampton, PA, Previously by Nationwide Sports Distributors and KBI, Inc.

DH40 AUTO PISTOL . . . . NiB $357 Ex $255 Gd $172
Caliber: .40 S&W. 12-round magazine, 4.25-inch bbl., 7 inches overall. Weight: 28 oz. Blade front sight, dovetailed rear w/3-dot system. Blued finish. Checkered composition grips. DH/DP series feature a patented "fastfire" action w/5-6 lb. trigger pull. Made from 1994 to 1996.

DH45 AUTO PISTOL . . . . NiB $346 Ex $248 Gd $189
Caliber: .45 ACP. 13-round magazine, 5-inch bbl., 8.1 inches overall. Weight: 35 oz. Blade front sight, dovetailed rear w/3-dot system. Blued finish. Checkered composition grips. Announced 1994, but not imported.

DP51 AUTO PISTOL . . . . NiB $330 Ex $221 Gd $148
Caliber: 9mm Para. 13-round magazine, 4.1-inch bbl., 7.5 inches overall. Weight: 28 oz. Blade front and square-notch rear sights. Matte black finish. Checkered composition grips. Made from 1991 to 1996.

DP52 AUTO PISTOL . . . . NiB $358 Ex $255 Gd $172
Caliber: .22 LR. 10-round magazine, 3.8-inch bbl., 6.7 inches overall. Weight: 23 oz. Blade front sight, dovetailed rear w/3-dot system. Blued finish. Checkered wood grips. Made from 1994 to 1996.

Dakota Hartford
Engraved Model

DAKOTA/E.M.F. CO. — Santa Ana, California

MODEL 1873 SA REVOLVER
Calibers: .22 LR, .22 Mag., .357 Mag., .45 Long Colt, .30 M1 carbine, .38-40, .32-20, .44-40. Bbl. lengths: 3.5, 4.75, 5.5, 7.5 inches. Blued or nickel finish. Engraved models avail.
Standard model . . . . **NiB $347 Ex $305 Gd $229**
Nickel finish, add. **40%**

MODEL 1875 OUTLAW
SA REVOLVER . . . . **NiB $525 Ex $420 Gd $293**
Calibers: .45 Long Colt, .357 Mag., .44-40. 7.5-inch bbl. Casehardened frame, blued finish. Walnut grips. This is an Exact replica of the Remington Number 3 revolver produced 1875 to 1889.

MODEL 1890 REMINGTON POLICE
Calibers: .357 Mag., .44-40, .45 Long Colt, 5.75-inch bbl., blued or nickel finish. Similar to Outlaw w/lanyard ring and no bbl. web .
Standard model . . . . **NiB $560 Ex $441 Gd $332**
Nickel model . . . . **NiB $637 Ex $523 Gd $371**
Engraved model . . . . **NiB $780 Ex $603 Gd $444**

BISLEY SA REVOLVER
Calibers: .44-40, .45 Long Colt, .357 Mag, 5.5- or 7.5-inch bbl., disc. 1992. Reintroduced 1994.
Standard model . . . . **NiB $459 Ex $378 Gd $272**
Engraved model . . . . **NiB $638 Ex $509 Gd $283**

HARTFORD SA REVOLVER
Calibers: .22 LR, .32-20, .357 Mag., .38-40, .44-40, .44 Special, .45 Long Colt. These are Exact replicas of the original Colts w/steel backstraps, trigger guards and forged frames. Blued or nickel finish. Imported from 1990 to 2008.
Standard model . . . . **NiB $444 Ex $367 Gd $274**
Engraved model . . . . **NiB $734 Ex $546 Gd $499**
Hartford Artillery,
U.S. Cavalry models . . . . **NiB $484 Ex $401 Gd $267**

SHERIFF'S MODEL
SA REVOLVER . . . . **NiB $437 Ex $377 Gd $271**
Calibers: .32-20, .357 Mag., .38-40, .44 Special, .44-40, .45 LC. 3.5-inch bbl. Reintroduced 1994.

TARGET SA REVOLVER . . . . . **NiB $478 Ex $351 Gd $279**
Calibers: .45 Long Colt, .357 Mag., .22 LR; 5.5- or 7.5-inch bbl. Polished, blued finish, casehardened frame. Walnut grips. Ramp front, blade target sight, adj. rear sight.

CHARLES DALY HANDGUNS — Currently imported by K.B.I., Harrisburg, Pennsylvania

MODEL M1911-A1 FIELD FS AUTOMATIC PISTOL
Caliber: .45 ACP. Eight- or 10-round magazine (Hi-Cap), 5-inch bbl., 8.75 inches overall. Weight: 38 oz. Blade front sight, drift adjustable rear w/3-dot system. Skeletonized tactical hammer and trigger. Extended slide release and beavertail grip safety. Matte blue, stainless or Duo finish. Checkered composition or wood stocks. Imported from 1999 to 2000.
Matte blue (Field FS) . . . . . . **NiB $525 Ex $479 Gd $326**
Stainless (Empire EFS) . . . . . . **NiB $560 Ex $459 Gd $361**
Duo (Superior FS) . . . . **NiB $653 Ex $497 Gd $363**
w/.22 conversion kit, add **$204**

DAVIS INDUSTRIES, INC. — Chino, California

MODEL D DERRINGER
Single-action double derringer. Calibers: .22 LR, .22 Mag., .25 ACP, .32 Auto, .32 H&R Mag., 9mm, .38 Special. Two-round capacity, 2.4-inch or 2.75-inch bbl., 4 inches overall (2.4-inch bbl.). Weight: 9 to 11.5 oz. Laminated wood grips. Black Teflon or chrome finish. Made from 1987 to 2001.
.22 LR or .25 ACP . . . . **NiB $192 Ex $109 Gd $88**
.22 Mag., .32 H&R Mag., .38 Spec. **NiB $204 Ex $128 Gd $91**
.32 Auto . . . . **NiB $214 Ex $115 Gd $91**
9mm Para. . . . . **NiB $170 Ex $122 Gd $96**

LONG BORE DERRINGER . . . . . **NiB $219 Ex $122 Gd $97**
Similar to Model D except in calibers .22 Mag., .32 H&R Mag., .38 Special, 9mm Para. 3.75-inch bbl., weight: 16 oz. Made from 1995 to 2001.

MODEL P-.32 . . . . **NiB $152 Ex $101 Gd $78**
Caliber: .32 Auto. Six-round magazine, 2.8-inch bbl., 5.4 inches overall. Weight: 22 oz. Black Teflon or chrome finish. Laminated wood grips. Made from 1987 to 2001.

MODEL P-.380 . . . . **NiB $192 Ex $115 Gd $89**
Caliber: .380 Auto. Five-round magazine, 2.8-inch bbl., 5.4 inches overall. Weight: 22 oz. Black Teflon or chrome finish. Made from 1990 to 2001.

DESERT INDUSTRIES, INC. — Las Vegas, Nevada (previously Steel City Arms, Inc.)

DOUBLE DEUCE DA PISTOL . **NiB $386 Ex $286 Gd $225**
Caliber: .22 LR. Six-round magazine, 2.5-inch bbl., 5.5 inches overall. Weight: 15 oz. Matte-finish stainless steel. Rosewood grips.

TWO-BIT SPECIAL PISTOL . . . **NiB $431 Ex $326 Gd $237**
Similar to the Double Deuce model except chambered in .25 ACP w/5-shot magazine.

DETONICS FIREARMS IND. — Phoenix, Arizona (previously Detonics Firearms Industries, Bellevue, WA)

COMBATMASTER
Calibers: .45 ACP, .451 Detonics Mag. Six-round magazine, 3.5-inch bbl., 6.75 inches overall. Combat-type w/fixed or adjustable sights. Checkered walnut grip. Stainless steel construction. Disc. 1992.
MK I, matte stainless,
fixed sights (disc. 1981) . . . . **NiB $1097 Ex $963 Gd $893**
MK II polished finish, (disc. 1979) **NiB $1494 Ex $1370 Gd $1133**

Detonics Combatmaster

Detonics Scoremaster

Dreyse Model 1907

MK III chrome,
(disc. 1980) . . . . NiB $551 Ex $443 Gd $328
MK IV polished blued,
adj. sights, (disc. 1981) . . . . . NiB $612 Ex $500 Gd $373
MK V matte stainless,
fixed sights, (disc. 1985) . . . . NiB $762 Ex $621 Gd $499
MK VI polished stainless, fixed
sights, (disc. 1985) . . . . NiB $831 Ex $666 Gd $509
MK VI in .451 Magnum,
(disc. 1986) . . . . NiB $1199 Ex $979 Gd $695
MK VII matte stainless steel,
no sights, (disc. 1985) . . . . . . NiB $1037 Ex $845 Gd $591
MK VII in .451 Magnum,
(disc. 1980) . . . . NiB $1380 Ex $1131 Gd $806

POCKET 9 . . . . NiB $668 Ex $541 Gd $426
Calibers: 9mm Para., .380. Six-round magazine, three-inch bbl., 5.88 inches overall. Fixed sights. Double- and single-action trigger mechanism. Disc. 1986.

SCOREMASTER . . . . NiB $1550 Ex $1257 Gd $1120
Calibers: .45 ACP, .451 Detonics Mag. Seven-round magazine. Five- or 6-inch heavyweight match bbl., 8.75 inches overall. Weight: 47 oz. Stainless steel construction, self-centering bbl., system. Disc. 1992.

SERVICEMASTER . . . . NiB $1117 Ex $780 Gd $530
Caliber: .45 ACP. Seven-round magazine, 4.25-inch bbl., weight: 39 oz. Interchangeable front sight, Millett rear sight. Disc. 1986.

SERVICEMASTER II . . . . NiB $1117 Ex $780 Gd $530
Same general specifications as standard Service Master except comes in polished stainless steel w/self-centering bbl., system. Disc. 1992.

DOWNSIZER CORPORATION — Santee, California

MODEL WSP
DAO PISTOL . . . . NiB $499 Ex $381 Gd $264
Single-round, tip-up pistol. Calibers: .22 Mag., .32 Mag., .380 ACP. 9mm Parabellum, .357 Mag., .40 S&W, .45 ACP. Six-round cylinder, 2.10-inch bbl. w/o Extractor, 3.25 inches overall. Weight: 11 oz. No sights. Stainless finish. Synthetic grips. Made from 1994 to 2007.

DREYSE PISTOLS — Sommerda, Germany. Mfd. by Rheinische Metallwaren und Maschinenfabrik ("Rheinmetall")

MODEL 1907
AUTOMATIC PISTOL . . . . NiB $273 Ex $224 Gd $179
Caliber: .32 Auto (7.65mm). Eight-round magazine, 3.5-inch bbl., 6.25 inches overall. Weight: About 24 oz. Fixed sights. Blued finish. Hard rubber grips. Made circa 1907 to 1914.

VEST POCKET
AUTOMATIC PISTOL . . . . NiB $357 Ex $293 Gd $204
Conventional Browning type. Caliber: .25 Auto (6.35mm). Six-round magazine, 2-inch bbl., 4.5 inches overall. Weight: About 14 oz. Fixed sights. Blued finish. Hard rubber grips. Made 1909 to 1914.

DWM PISTOL — Berlin, Germany. Mfd. by Deutsche Waffen-und-Munitionsfabriken

POCKET AUTOMATIC PISTOL NiB $1050 Ex $918 Gd $713
Similar to the FN Browning Model 1910. Caliber: .32 Automatic (7.65mm). 3.5-inch bbl., 6 inches overall. Weight: About 21 oz. Blued finish. Hard rubber grips. Made circa 1921 to 1931.

ED BROWN — Perry, Montana

CLASS A LTD SA
AUTOMATIC PISTOL . . . . NiB $2312 Ex $2152 Gd $1041
Caliber: .38 Super, 9mm, 9x23, .45 ACP. Seven-round magazine, 4.25- or 5-inch bbl., weight: 34-39 oz. Rubber checkered or optional Hogue Exotic wood grip. M1911 style single action pistol. Fixed front and rear Novak Lo-mount or fully adjustable sights.

CLASSIC CUSTOM SA
AUTOMATIC PISTOL . . . . NiB $3231 Ex $2553 Gd $1527
Caliber: .45 ACP. Seven-round magazine, 4.25- or 5-inch bbl., weight: 39 oz. Exotic Hogue wood grip w/modified ramp or post front and rear adjustable sights.

SPECIAL FORCES SA
AUTOMATIC PISTOL . . . . NiB $2240 Ex $1918 Gd $1437
Caliber: .45 ACP. Seven-round magazine, 4.25- or 5-inch bbl., weight: 34-39 oz. Rubber checkered, optional exotic wood grips. Single action M1911 style pistol.

ENFIELD REVOLVER — Enfield Lock, Middlesex, England. Manufactured by Royal Small Arms Factory

(BRITISH SERVICE) NO. 2 MK 1
DA REVOLVER . . . . NiB $362 Ex $271 Gd $221
Webley pattern. Hinged frame. Double action. Caliber: .380 British Service (.38 S&W w/200-grain bullet). Six-round cylinder, 5-inch bbl., 10.5 inches overall. Weight: About 27.5 oz. Fixed sights. Blued finish. Vulcanite grips. First issued in 1932, this was the standard revolver of the British Army in WW II. Now obsolete. Note: This model also produced w/spurless hammer as No. 2 Mk 1* and Mk 1**.

ENTREPRISE ARMS — Irwindale, California

ELITE SERIES SA
AUTO PISTOL . . . . NiB $661 Ex $498 Gd $401
Single action M1911 style pistol. Caliber: .45 ACP. 10-round magazine, 3.25-, 4.25-, 5-inch bbl., (models P325, P425, P500). Weight: 36-40 oz. Ultraslim checkered grips, Tactical 2 high profile sights w/3-dot system. Lightweight adjustable trigger. Blued or matte black oxide finish. Made from 1997 to date.

MEDALIST SA AUTOMATIC PISTOL
Similar to Elite model except machined to match tolerances and target configuration. Caliber: .45 ACP, .40 S&W. 10-round magazine, 5-inch compensated bbl. w/dovetail front and fully adjustable rear Bo-Mar sights. Weight: 40 oz. Made from 1997 to date.
.40 S&W model . . . . NiB $1015 Ex $862 Gd $689
.45 ACP model . . . . NiB $893 Ex $740 Gd $577

TACTICAL SA AUTOMATIC PISTOL
Similar to Elite model except in combat carry configuration. De-horned frame and slide w/ambidExtrous safety. Caliber: .45 ACP. 10-round magazine, 3.25-, 4.25-, 5-inch bbl., weight: 36-40 oz. Tactical 2 Ghost Ring or Novak Lo-mount sights.
Tactical 2 ghost
ring sights . . . . NiB $917 Ex $724 Gd $571
Novak Lo-Mount . . . . NiB $917 Ex $724 Gd $571
Tactical plus model . . . . NiB $917 Ex $724 Gd $571

BOXER SA
AUTOMATIC PISTOL . . . . . NiB $1243 Ex $1122 Gd $831
Similar to Medalist model except w/profiled slide configuration and fully adjustable target sights. weight: 42 oz. Made from 1997 to date.

TOURNAMENT SHOOTER MODEL SA AUTOMATIC PISTOL
Similar to Elite model except in IPSC configuration. Caliber: .45 ACP, .40 S&W. 10-round magazine, 5-inch compensated bbl., w/ dovetail front and fully adjustable rear Bo-Mar sights. Weight: 40 oz. Made from 1997 to date.

**Enfield
(British Service) No. 2 MK 1 Revolver**

**Erma
Model ER-772 Match Revolver**

TSM I model	NiB $2145	Ex $1986	Gd $1637
TSM II model	NiB $1834	Ex $1687	Gd $1331
TSM III model	NiB $2575	Ex $1403	Gd $1661

ERMA-WERKE — Dachau, Germany

MODEL ER-772
MATCH REVOLVER . . . . . . NiB $1132 Ex $1071 Gd $655
Caliber: .22 LR. Six-round cylinder, 6-inch bbl., 12 inches overall. Weight: 47.25 oz. Adjustable micrometer rear sight and front sight blade. Adjustable trigger. Interchangeable walnut sporter or match grips. Polished blued finish. Made from 1991 to 1994.

MODEL ER-773
MATCH REVOLVER . . . . NiB $957 Ex $831 Gd $587
Same general specifications as Model 772 except chambered for .32 S&W. Made from 1991 to 1995.

MODEL ER-777
MATCH REVOLVER . . . . NiB $923 Ex $785 Gd $623
Caliber: .357 Magnum. Six-round cylinder. 4- or 5.5-inch bbl., 9.7 to 11.3 inches overall. Weight: 43.7 oz. (with 5.5-inch bbl.). Micrometer adj. rear sight. Checkered walnut sporter or match-style grip (interchangeable). Made from 1991 to 1995.

MODEL ESP-85A COMPETITION PISTOL
Calibers: .22 LR and .32 S&W Wadcutter. Eight- or 5-round magazine, 6-inch bbl., 10 inches overall. Weight: 40 oz. Adj. rear sight, blade front sight. Checkered walnut grip w/thumbrest. Made from 1991 to 1997.
Match model . . . . NiB $1280 Ex $1128 Gd $716
Chrome match . . . . NiB $1540 Ex $1330 Gd $998
Sporting model . . . . NiB $1251 Ex $1049 Gd $735
Conversion unit .22 LR . . . NiB $1566 Ex $1212 Gd $1030
Conversion unit .32 S&W . NiB $1566 Ex $1212 Gd $1030

European American Armory
Big Bore Bounty Hunter

MODEL KGP68
AUTOMATIC PISTOL . . . . NiB $484 Ex $306 Gd $239
Luger type. Calibers: .32 Auto (7.65mm), .380 Auto (9mm Short).
Six-round magazine (.32 Auto), 5-round (.380 Auto), 4-inch bbl.,
7.38 inches overall. Weight: 22.5 oz. Fixed sights. Blued finish.
Checkered walnut grips. Made from 1968 to 1993.

MODEL KGP69
AUTOMATIC PISTOL . . . . NiB $357 Ex $291 Gd $214
Luger type. Caliber: .22 LR. Eight-round magazine, 4-inch bbl.,
7.75 inches overall. Weight: 29 oz. fixed sights. Blued finish.
Checkered walnut grips. Imported from 1969 to 1993.

EUROPEAN AMERICAN ARMORY —
Rockledge, Florida

See also listings under Astra Pistols.

EUROPEAN MODEL AUTO PISTOL
Calibers: .32 ACP (SA only), .380 ACP (SA or DA), 3.85-inch bbl.,
7.38 overall, 7-round magazine, Weight: 26 oz. Blade front sight,
drift-adj. rear. Blued, chrome, blue/chrome, blue/gold, Duo-Tone or
Wonder finish. Imported 1991 to date.
Blued .32 ACP (disc. 1995) . . . NiB $140 Ex $101 Gd $81
Blue/chrome .32 caliber
(disc. 1995) . . . . NiB $204 Ex $117 Gd $81
Chrome .32 caliber
(Disc. 1995). . . . . NiB $137 Ex $101 Gd $81
Blued .380 caliber . . . . NiB $158 Ex $116 Gd $88
Blue/chrome .380 caliber
(disc. 1993) . . . . NiB $204 Ex $136 Gd $91
DA .380 caliber (disc. 1994). . NiB $398 Ex $267 Gd $167
Lady .380 caliber (disc. 1995). NiB $270 Ex $203 Gd $143
Wonder finish .380 caliber . . . NiB $275 Ex $186 Gd $131

BIG BORE BOUNTY HUNTER SA REVOLVER
Calibers: .357 Mag., .41 Mag., .44-40, .44 Mag., .45 Colt. Bbl.,
lengths: 4.63, 5.5, 7.5 inches. Blade front and grooved topstrap rear
sights. Blued or chrome finish w/color casehardened or gold-plated
frame. Smooth walnut grips. Imported 1992.
Blued finish . . . . NiB $377 Ex $255 Gd $189
Blued w/color-
casehardened frame . . . . NiB $388 Ex $265 Gd $190
Blued w/gold-plated frame . . . NiB $403 Ex $281 Gd $214
Chrome finish. . . . . NiB $408 Ex $286 Gd $219
Gold-plated frame, add. $110

Erma-Werke
Model KGP69

Model ESP-85A
Competition Pistol

BOUNTY HUNTER SA REVOLVER
Calibers: .22 LR, .22 Mag. Bbl. lengths: 4.75, 6 or 9 inches. Blade front and dovetailed rear sights. Blued finish or blued w/gold-plated frame. European hardwood grips. Imported from 1997 to date.
Blued finish (4.75-inch bbl.) . . **NiB $281 Ex $191 Gd $128**
**Blued .22 LR/.22 WRF combo
(4.75-inch bbl.)** . . . . **NiB $281 Ex $191 Gd $128**
**Blued .22 LR/.22 WRF combo
(6-inch bbl.)** . . . . **NiB $281 Ex $191 Gd $128**
**Blued .22 LR/.22 WRF combo
(9-inch bbl.)** . . . . **NiB $281 Ex $191 Gd $128**

EA22 TARGET . . . . **NiB $398 Ex $281 Gd $214**
Caliber: .22 LR. 12-round magazine, 6-inch bbl., 9.10 inches overall. Weight: 40 oz. Ramp front sight, fully adj. rear. Blued finish. Checkered walnut grips w/thumbrest. Made from 1991 to 1994.

FAB 92 AUTO PISTOL
Similar to the Witness model except chambered in 9mm only w/ slide-mounted safety and no cock-and-lock provision. Imported 1992 to 1995.
FAB 92 standard. . . . . **NiB $437 Ex $342 Gd $223**
FAB 92 compact. . . . . **NiB $437 Ex $342 Gd $223**

STANDARD GRADE REVOLVER
Calibers: .22 LR, .22 WRF, .32 H&R Mag., .38 Special. Two-, 4- or 6-inch bbl., blade front sight, fixed or adj. rear. Blued finish. European hardwood grips w/finger grooves. Imported 1991 to date.
.22 LR (4-inch bbl.) . . . . **NiB $215 Ex $171 Gd $128**
.22 LR (6-inch bbl.) . . . . **NiB $228 Ex $181 Gd $133**
.22 LR combo (4-inch bbl.) . . . **NiB $301 Ex $237 Gd $171**
.22 LR combo (6-inch bbl.) . . . **NiB $337 Ex $265 Gd $187**
.32 H&R, .38 Special (2-inch bbl.) **NiB $231 Ex $174 Gd $128**
.38 Special (4-inch bbl.) . . . . . **NiB $235 Ex $187 Gd $132**
.357 Mag . . . . **NiB $242 Ex $206 Gd $144**

TACTICAL GRADE REVOLVER
Similar to the Standard model except chambered in .38 Special only. Two- or 4-inch bbl., fixed sights. Available w/compensator. Imported from 1991-93.
Tactical revolver . . . . **NiB $229 Ex $185 Gd $109**
Tactical revolver w/compensator. **NiB $316 Ex $270 Gd $192**

WINDICATOR TARGET REVOLVER. . **NiB $444 Ex $381 Gd $255**
Calibers: .22 LR, .38 Special, .357 Magnum. Eight-round cylinder in .22 LR, 6-round in .38 Special and .357 Magnum. Six-inch bbl. w/bbl. weights. 11.8 inches overall. Weight: 50.2 oz. Interchangeable blade front sight, fully adj. rear. Walnut competition-style grips. Imported from 1991-93.

WITNESS DA AUTO PISTOL
Similar to the Brno CZ-75 w/a cocked-and-locked system. Double or single action. Calibers: 9mm Para. .38 Super, .40 S&W, 10mm; .41 AE and .45 ACP. 16-round magazine (9mm), 12 shot (.38 Super/.40 S&W), or 10-round (10mm/.45 ACP), 4.75-inch bbl., 8.10 inches overall. Weight: 35.33 oz. Blade front sight, rear sight adj. for windage w/3-dot sighting system. Steel or polymer frame. Blued, satin chrome, blue/chrome, stainless or Wonder finish. Checkered rubber grips. EA Series imported 1991 to date.
9mm blue . . . . **NiB $475 Ex $337 Gd $249**
9mm chrome or blue/chrome . . . . . . **NiB $475 Ex $337 Gd $249**
9mm stainless. . . . . **NiB $469 Ex $337 Gd $283**
9mm Wonder finish . . . . **NiB $500 Ex $356 Gd $265**
.38 Super and .40 S&W blued. . . . . . **NiB $475 Ex $337 Gd $237**
**.38 Super and .40 S&W chrome
or blue/chrome.** . . . . **NiB $469 Ex $388 Gd $273**
.38 Super and .40 S&W stainless. . . . **NiB $546 Ex $425 Gd $292**
.38 Super and .40 S&W Wonder finish **NiB $577 Ex $340 Gd $296**

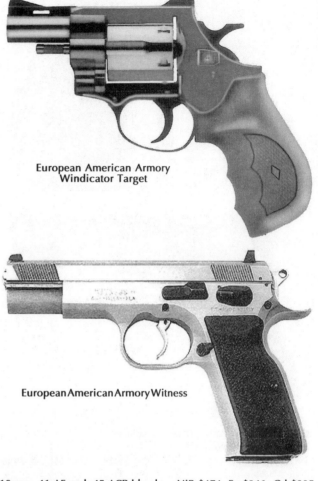

European American Armory
Windicator Target

European American Armory Witness

10mm, .41 AE and .45 ACP blued. . . **NiB $474 Ex $346 Gd $235**
**10mm, .41 AE and .45 ACP
chrome or blue/chrome** . . . . **NiB $546 Ex $437 Gd $316**
10mm, .41 AE and .45 ACP stainless. **NiB $577 Ex $464 Gd $337**
**10mm, .41 AE and
.45 ACP Wonder finish.** . . . . **NiB $562 Ex $439 Gd $321**

COMPACT WITNESS DA AUTO PISTOL (L SERIES)
Similar to the standard Witness series except more compact w/ 3.625-inch bbl., and polymer or steel frame. Weight: 30 oz. Matte blued or Wonder finish. EA Compact series imported 1999 to date.
9mm blue . . . . **NiB $468 Ex $330 Gd $235**
9mm Wonder finish . . . . **NiB $468 Ex $330 Gd $235**
.38 Super and .40 S&W blued. . . . . . **NiB $468 Ex $330 Gd $235**
.38 Super and .40 S&W Wonder finish **NiB $468 Ex $330 Gd $235**
10mm, .41 AE and .45 ACP blued. . . **NiB $549 Ex $369 Gd $273**
10mm, .41 AE and .45 ACP Wonder fin. . . . **NiB $549 Ex $369 Gd $273**
w/ported bbl., add **$50**

WITNESS CARRY COMP
Double/Single action. Calibers: .38 Super, 9mm Parabellum, .40 S&W, 10mm, .45 ACP. 10-, 12- or 16-round magazine, 4.25-inch bbl., w/1-inch compensator. Weight: 33 oz., 8.10 inches overall. Black rubber grips. Post front sight, drift adjustable rear w/3-dot system. Matte blue, Duo-Tone or Wonder finish. Imported 1992 to 2004.
9mm, .40 S&W . . . . **NiB $453 Ex $359 Gd $273**
.38 Super, 10mm, .45 ACP . . . **NiB $453 Ex $359 Gd $273**
w/Duo-Tone finish (disc.), add **$40**
w/Wonder finish, add **$20**

Feather Guardian Angel Derringer

FEG Mark II AP-.22

WITNESS LIMITED
CLASS AUTO PISTOL . . . . . . NiB $909 Ex $734 Gd $559
Single action. Calibers: .38 Super, 9mm Parabellum, .40 S&W, .45 ACP. 10-round magazine, 4.75-inch bbl., Weight: 37 oz. Checkered competition-style walnut grips. Long slide w/post front sight, fully adj. rear. Matte blue finish. Imported 1994 to 1998.

WITNESS SUBCOMPACT DA AUTO PISTOL
Calibers: 9mm Para., .40 S&W, 41 AK, .45 ACP. 13-round magazine in 9mm, 9-round in .40 S&W, 3.66-inch bbl., 7.25 inches overall. Weight: 30 oz. Blade front sight, rear sight adj. for windage. Blued, satin chrome or blue/chrome finish. Imported from 1995 to 1997.
9mm blue . . . . NiB $408 Ex $281 Gd $204
9mm chrome or blue/chrome . NiB $453 Ex $306 Gd $225
.40 S&W blue. . . . . NiB $453 Ex $306 Gd $225
.40 S&W chrome or blue/chrome NiB $497 Ex $366 Gd $229
.41 AE blue . . . . NiB $525 Ex $429 Gd $308
.41 AE chrome or blue/chrome NiB $577 Ex $448 Gd $319
.45 ACP blued . . . . NiB $525 Ex $336 Gd $308
.45 ACP chrome or blue/chrome NiB $500 Ex $439 Gd $321

WITNESS TARGET PISTOLS
Similar to standard Witness model except fitted w/2- or 3-port compensator, competition frame and S/A target trigger. Calibers: 9mm Para., 9x21, .40 S&W, 10mm and .45 ACP, 5.25-inch match bbl., 10.5 inches overall. Weight: 38 oz. Square post front sight, fully adj. rear or drilled and tapped for scope. Blued or hard chrome finish. Low-profile competition grips. Imported 1992 to date.
Silver Team (blued w/2-port
compensator) . . . . NiB $895 Ex $785 Gd $561
Gold Team (chrome
w/3-port compensator) . . . NiB $1810 Ex $1632 Gd $1331

FAS PISTOLS — Malino, Italy.
Currently imported by Nygord Precision Products (previously by Beeman Precision Arms and Osborne's, Cheboygan, MI)

OP601 SEMIAUTOMATIC MATCH TARGET PISTOL
Caliber: .22 Short. Five-round top-loading magazine, 5.6-inch ported and ventilated bbl., 11 inches overall. Weight: 41.5 oz. Removable, adj. trigger group. Blade front sight, open-notch fully adj. rear. Stippled walnut wraparound or adj. target grips.
Right-hand model . . . . NiB $1076 Ex $930 Gd $714
Left-hand model . . . . NiB $1153 Ex $985 Gd $755

602 SEMIAUTOMATIC MATCH TARGET PISTOL
Similar to Model FAS 601 except chambered for .22 LR. Weight: 37 oz.
Right-hand model . . . . NiB $960 Ex $705 Gd $581
Left-hand model . . . . NiB $1030 Ex $830 Gd $691

CF603 SEMIAUTOMATIC
MATCH TARGET PISTOL . . . NiB $1030 Ex $816 Gd $647
Similar to Model FAS 601 except chambered for .32 S&W (wadcutter).

SP607 SEMIAUTOMATIC
MATCH TARGET PISTOL . . . NiB $1030 Ex $804 Gd $658
Similar to Model FAS 601 except chambered for .22 LR, w/removable bbl. weights. Imported 1995 to date.

FEATHER INDUSTRIES — Boulder, Colorado

GUARDIAN ANGEL DERRINGER
Double-action over/under derringer w/interchangeable drop-in loading blocks. Calibers: .22 LR, .22 WMR, 9mm, .38 Spec. Two-round capacity, 2-inch bbl., 5 inches overall. weight: 12 oz. Stainless steel. Checkered black grip. Made from 1988 to 1995.
.22 LR, .22 WMR . . . . NiB 165 Ex $101 Gd $81
9mm, .38 Special (disc. 1989). NiB $233 Ex $189 Gd $150

FEG (FEGYVERGYAN) PISTOLS — Budapest, Soroksariut, Hungary. Currently imported by KBI, Inc. and Century International Arms (previously by Interarms)

MARK II AP-.22 DA AUTOMATIC PISTOL NiB $271 Ex $219 Gd $179
Caliber: .22 LR. Eight-round magazine, 3.4-inch bbl., Weight: 23 oz. Drift-adj. sights. Double action, all-steel pistol. Imported 1997 to 1998.

MARK II AP-.380 DA AUTOMATIC PISTOL NiB $271 Ex $219 Gd $179
Caliber: .380. Seven-round magazine, 3.9-inch bbl., weight 27 oz. Drift-adj. sights. Double action, all-steel pistol. Imported 1997 to 1998.

MARK II APK-.380 DA
AUTOMATIC PISTOL. . . . . NiB $271 Ex $219 Gd $179
Caliber: .380. Seven-round magazine, 3.4-inch bbl., weight: 25 oz. Drift-adj. sights. Double action, all-steel pistol. Imported 1997 to 1998.

MODEL GKK-9 (92C) AUTO PISTOL . . . NiB $321 Ex $240 Gd $204
Improved version of the double-action FEG Model MBK. Caliber: 9mm Para. 14-round magazine, 4-inch bbl., 7.4 inches overall. Weight: 34 oz. Blade front sight, rear sight adj. for windage. Checkered wood grips. Blued finish. Imported from 1992 to 1993.

MODEL GKK-.45 AUTO PISTOL
Improved version of the double-action FEG Model MBK. Caliber: .45 ACP. Eight-round magazine, 4.1-inch bbl., 7.75 inches overall. Weight: 36 oz. Blade front sight, rear sight adj. for windage w/3-dot system. Checkered walnut grips. Blued or chrome finish. Imported 1993 to 1996.
Blued model (disc. 1994) . . . . NiB $325 Ex $265 Gd $204
Chrome model . . . . NiB $362 Ex $281 Gd $220

MODEL MBK-9HP
AUTO PISTOL . . . . NiB $469 Ex $306 Gd $281
Similar to the double-action Browning Hi-Power. Caliber: 9mm Para. 14-round magazine, 4.6-inch bbl., 8 inches overall. Weight: 36 oz. Blade front sight, rear sight adj. for windage. Checkered wood grips. Blued finish. Imported from 1992 to 1993.

MODEL PJK-9HP AUTO PISTOL
Similar to the single-action Browning Hi-Power. Caliber: 9mm Para. 13-round magazine, 4.75-inch bbl., 8 inches overall. Weight: 21 oz. Blade front sight, rear sight adj. for windage w/3-dot system. Checkered walnut or rubber grips. Blued or chrome finish. Imported 1992 to 2003.
Blued model . . . . NiB $469 Ex $388 Gd $265
Chrome model . . . . NiB $500 Ex $408 Gd $316

MODEL PSP-.25 AUTO PISTOL
Similar to the Browning .25. Caliber: .25 ACP. Six-round magazine, 2.1-inch bbl., 4.1 inches overall. Weight: 9.5 oz. Fixed sights. Checkered composition grips. Blued or chrome finish.
Blued model . . . . NiB $316 Ex $204 Gd $150
Chrome model . . . . NiB $316 Ex $204 Gd $150

MODEL SMC-.22 AUTO PISTOL NiB $222 Ex $130 Gd $79
Same general specifications as FEG Model SMC-.380 except in .22 LR. Eight-round magazine, 3.5-inch bbl., 6.1 inches overall. Weight: 18.5 oz. Blade front sight, rear sight adj. for windage. Checkered composition grips w/thumbrest. Blued finish.

MODEL SMC-.380 AUTO PISTOL NiB $222 Ex $130 Gd $79
Similar to the Walther DA PPK w/alloy frame. Caliber: .380 ACP. Six-round magazine, 3.5-inch bbl., 6.1 inches overall. Weight: 18.5 oz. Blade front sight, rear sight adj. for windage. Checkered composition grips w/ thumbrest. Blued finish. Imported 1993 to 1997.

MODEL SMC-918 AUTO PISTOL NiB $203 Ex $120 Gd $90
Same general specifications as FEG Model SMC-.380 except chambered in 9x18mm Makarov. Imported from 1994 to 1997.

FIALA OUTFITTERS, INC. — New York

REPEATING PISTOL . . . . NiB $689 Ex $479 Gd $365
Hand-operated, not semi-auto. Caliber: .22 LR. 10-round magazine, bbl. lengths: 3-, 7.5- and 20-inch. 11.25 inches overall (with 7.5-inch bbl.). Weight: 31 oz. (with 7.5-inch bbl.). Target sights. Blued finish. Plain wood grips. Shoulder stock was originally supplied for use w/20-inch bbl. Made from 1920 to 1923. Value shown is for pistol w/one bbl., no shoulder stock. Three bbl. cased sets start at $3,030.

F.I.E. CORPORATION — Hialeah, Florida.
The F.I.E. Corporation became QFI (Quality Firearms Corp.) of Opa Locka, Fl., about 1990, when most of F.I.E.'s models were discontinued.

FEG Model PJK-9HP

F.I.E. Model A27BW

F.I.E. Arminius

MODEL A27 "THE BEST" SEMIAUTO NiB $140 EX $95 GD $55
Caliber: .25 ACP. Six-round magazine, 2.5-inch bbl., 6.75 inches overall. Weight: 13 oz. Fixed sights. Checkered walnut grip. Discontinued in 1990.

ARMINIUS DA STANDARD REVOLVER
Calibers: .22 LR, .22 combo w/interchangeable cylinder, .32 S&W, .38 Special, .357 Magnum. Six, 7 or 8 rounds depending on caliber. Swing-out cylinder. bbl., lengths: 2-, 3-, 4, 6-inch. Vent rib on calibers other than .22, 11 inches overall (with 6-inch bbl.). Weight: 26 to 30 oz. Fixed or micro-adj. sights. Checkered plastic or walnut grips. Blued finish. Made in Germany. Disc.
.22 LR . . . . NiB $130 Ex $89 Gd $67
.22 Combo . . . . NiB $198 Ex $148 Gd $101
.32 S&W . . . . NiB $207 Ex $149 Gd $101
.38 Special . . . . NiB $161 Ex $95 Gd $70
.357 Magnum . . . . NiB $240 Ex $179 Gd $135

F.I.E. Titan Tiger

F.I.E. Titan II

F.I.E. Model TZ75

BUFFALO SCOUT SA REVOLVER
Calibers: .22 LR, .22 WRF, .22 combo w/interchangeable cylinder. 4.75-inch bbl., 10 inches overall. Weight: 32 oz. Adjustable sights. Blued or chrome finish. Smooth walnut or black checkered nylon grips. Made in Italy. Disc.

Blued standard	NiB $84	Ex $62	Gd $40
Blued convertible	NiB $91	Ex $62	Gd $40
Chrome standard	NiB $91	Ex $62	Gd $40
Chrome convertible	NiB $91	Ex $62	Gd $40

HOMBRE SA REVOLVER . . . . . NiB $230 Ex $179 Gd $105
Calibers: .357 Magnum, .44 Magnum, .45 Colt. Six-round cylinder. bbl. lengths: 6 or 7.5 inches, 11 inches overall (with - inch bbl.). Weight: 45 oz. (6-inch bbl.). Fixed sights. Blued bbl., w/color-casehardened receiver. Smooth walnut grips. Made from 1979 to 1990.

SUPER TITAN II
Caliber: .32 ACP or .380 ACP, 3.25-inch bbl., weight: 28 oz. Blued or chrome finish. Disc. 1990.

.32 ACP blue;	NiB $138	Ex $95	Gd $70
.32 ACP chrome.	NiB $138	Ex $95	Gd $70
.380 ACP blue;	NiB $138	Ex $95	Gd $70
.380 ACP chrome.	NiB $138	Ex $95	Gd $70

TEXAS RANGER SINGLE-ACTION REVOLVER
Calibers: .22 LR, .22 WRF, .22 combo w/interchangeable cylinder. bbl., lengths: 4.75-, 6.5-, 9-inch. 10 inches overall (with 4.75-inch bbl.). Weight: 32 oz. (with 4.75-inch bbl.). Fixed sights. Blued finish. Smooth walnut grips. Made from 1983 to 1990.

Standard	NiB $97	Ex $75	Gd $55
Convertible	NiB $97	Ex $75	Gd $55

LITTLE RANGER SA REVOLVER
Same as the TExas Ranger except w/3.25-inch bbl. and bird's-head grips. Made from 1986 to 1990.

Standard.	NiB $97	Ex $75	Gd $55
Convertible	NiB $109	Ex $81	Gd $61

TITAN TIGER DOUBLE-
ACTION REVOLVER . . . . NiB $78 Ex $47 Gd $35
Caliber: .38 Special. Six-round cylinder, 2- or 4-inch bbl., 8.25 inches overall (with 4-inch bbl.). Weight: 30 oz. (4-inch bbl.). Fixed sights. Blued finish. Checkered plastic or walnut grips. Made in the U.S. Disc. 1990.

TITAN II SEMIAUTOMATIC
Caiibers: .22 LR, .32 ACP, .380 ACP. 10-round magazine, integral tapered post front sight, windage-adjustable rear sight. European walnut grips. Blued or chrome finish. Disc. 1990.

.22 LR in blue	NiB $140	Ex $108	Gd $88
.32 ACP in blued	NiB $211	Ex $170	Gd $128
.32 ACP in chrome	NiB $221	Ex $176	Gd $141
.380 ACP in blue	NiB $221	Ex $176	Gd $141
.380 ACP in chrome	NiB $235	Ex $181	Gd $158

MODEL TZ75 DA SEMIAUTOMATIC
Double action. Caliber: 9mm. 15-round magazine, 4.5-inch bbl., 8.25 inches overall. Weight: 35 oz. Ramp front sight, windage-adjustable rear sight. European walnut or black rubber grips. Imported from 1988 to 1990.

Blued finish	NiB $387	Ex $302	Gd $214
Satin chrome	NiB $425	Ex $321	Gd $255

YELLOW ROSE SA REVOLVER
Same general specifications as the Buffalo Scout except in .22 combo w/interchangeable cylinder and plated in 24-karat gold. Limited Edition w/scrimshawed ivory polymer grips and American walnut presentation case. Made from 1987 to 1990.

Yellow Rose .22 combo	NiB $140	Ex $93	Gd $59
Yellow Rose Limited Edition	NiB $292	Ex $229	Gd $188

FIREARMS INTERNATIONAL CORP. — Washington, D.C.

MODEL D
AUTOMATIC PISTOL . . . . NiB $219 Ex $179 Gd $95
Caliber: .380 Automatic. Six-round magazine, 3.3-inch bbl., 6.13 inches overall. Weight: 19.5 oz. Blade front sight, windage-adjustable rear sight. Blued, chromed, or military finish. Checkered walnut grips. Made from 1974 to 1977.

REGENT
DA REVOLVER . . . . NiB $189 Ex $130 Gd $101
Calibers: .22 LR, .32 S&W Long. Eight-round cylinder (.22 LR), or 7-round (.32 S&W). Bbl. lengths: 3-, 4-, 6-inches (.22 LR) or 2.5-, 4-inches (.32 S&W). Weight: 28 oz.(with 4-inch bbl.). Fixed sights. Blued finish. Plastic grips. Made from 1966 to 1972.

FN BROWNING PISTOLS — Liege, Belgium. Mfd. by Fabrique Nationale Herstal

See also Browning Pistols.

6.35MM POCKET AUTO PISTOL
(See FN Browning Baby Auto Pistol)

MODEL 1900 POCKET
AUTO PISTOL . . . . NiB $842 Ex $702 Gd $485
Caliber: .32 Automatic (7.65mm). Seven-round magazine, 4-inch bbl., 6.75 inches overall. Weight: 22 oz. Fixed sights. Blued finish. Hard rubber grips. Made from 1899 to 1910.

MODEL 1903 MILITARY AUTO PISTOL
Caliber: 9mm Browning Long. Seven-round magazine, 5-inch bbl., 8 inches overall. Weight: 32 oz. Fixed sights. Blued finish. Hard rubber grips. Note: Aside from size, this pistol is of the same basic design as the Colt Pocket .32 and .380 Automatic pistols. Made from 1903 to 1939.
Model 1903
Standard. . . . . NiB $1285 Ex $1152 Gd $880
Model 1903
(w/slotted backstrap). . . . . . NiB $1285 Ex $1152 Gd $880
Model 1903 (w/slotted backstrap, shoulder stock and Extended magazine). . NiB $2525 Ex $2270 Gd $1790

MODEL 1910
POCKET AUTO PISTOL . . . . . NiB $577 Ex $431 Gd $286
Calibers: .32 Auto (7.65mm), .380 Auto (9mm). Seven-round magazine (.32 cal.), or 6-round (.380 cal.), 3.5-inch bbl., 6 inches overall. Weight: 20.5 oz. Fixed sights. Blued finish. Hard rubber grips. Made from 1910 to 1954.

MODEL 1922 (10/.22) POLICE/MILITARY AUTO
Calibers: .32 Auto (7.65mm), .380 Auto (9mm). Nine-round magazine (.32 cal.), or 8-round (.380 cal.), 4.5-inch bbl., 7 inches overall. Weight: 25 oz. Fixed sights. Blued finish. Hard rubber grips. Made from 1922 to 1959.
Model 1922
commercial . . . . NiB $459 Ex $326 Gd $265
Model 1922
Military contract. . . . . NiB $414 Ex $301 Gd $204
Model 1922 (w/Nazi proofs) . . NiB $414 Ex $326 Gd $265

Firearms International
Model D

Firearms
International Regent

FN Browning
6.35mm Pocket

FN Browning
1900 Pocket

FN Browning 1910
Pocket

FN Browning 1922
Police/Military

FN Browning 1935
Military Hi-Power

FN Browning
Baby

MODEL 1935 MILITARY HI-POWER PISTOL

Variation of the Browning-Colt .45 Auto design. Caliber: 9mm Para.13-round magazine, 4.63-inch bbl., 7.75 inches overall. Weight: About 35 oz. Adjustable rear sight and fixed front, or both fixed. Blued finish (Canadian manufacture Parkerized). Checkered walnut or plastic grips. Note: Above specifications in general apply to both the original FN production and the pistols made by John Inglis Company of Canada for the Chinese government. A smaller version, w/shorter bbl. and slide and 10-round magazine, was made by FN for the Belgian and Rumanian Governments about 1937 to 191940. Both types were made at the FN plant during the German occupation of Belgium.

Pre-war commercial (w/fixed sights) NiB $1152 Ex $918 Gd $729
Pre-war commercial
(w/tangent sight only) . . . . NiB $2040 Ex $1347 Gd $712
Pre-war commercial
(w/tangent sight, slotted backstrap)NiB $3014 Ex $2652 Gd $1448
Pre-war Belgian military contract . NiB $1234 Ex $1020 Gd $704
Pre-war Foreign military contract NiB $2212 Ex $1785 Gd $1225
War production (w/fixed sights). . . . . NiB $861 Ex $674 Gd $485
War production (w/tangent sight only)NiB $1405 Ex $1133 Gd $783
War production
(w/tangent sight and slotted backstrap)NiB $3488 Ex $2770 Gd $1913
Post-war/pre-BAC (w/fixed sights) . . . NiB $842 Ex $577 Gd $392
Post-war/pre-BAC (w/tangent sight only)NiB $893 Ex $577 Gd $392
Post-war/pre-BAC
(w/tangent sight, slotted backstrap) . . NiB $663 Ex $784 Gd $756
Inglis manufacture
Canadian military (w/fixed sights) . . NiB $1015 Ex $743 Gd $571
Canadian military
(w/fixed sight, slotted). . . . . NiB $1871 Ex $1494 Gd $1021
Canadian military
(w/tangent sight, slotted). . . . . . . NiB $1533 Ex $1235 Gd $884
Canadian military
(marked w/Inglis logo) . . . . NiB $2654 Ex $2149 Gd $1462
Chinese military contract
(w/tangent sight, slotted). . . . . . . NiB $3421 Ex $2754 Gd $1876
Canadian military
(w/fixed sight, slotted backstrap) . NiB $1879 Ex $1503 Gd $1029
Canadian military
(marked w/Inglis logo) . . . . NiB $2642 Ex $2147 Gd $1460
w/issue wooden holster, add. $408

BABY AUTO PISTOL . . . . . . NiB $638 Ex $530 Gd $377
Caliber: .25 Automatic (6.35mm). Six-round magazine, 2.13-inch bbl., 4 inches overall. Weight: 10 oz. Fixed sights. Blued finish. Hard rubber grips. Made from 1931 to 1983.

FOREHAND & WADSWORTH — Worcester, Massachusetts

REVOLVERS
See listings of comparable Harrington & Richardson and Iver Johnson revolvers for values.

FORTWORTH FIREARMS—FortWorth, Texas

MATCH MASTER STANDARD. . . . . . NiB $499 Ex $283 Gd $225
Semi-automatic. Caliber: .22LR. Equipped with 3 7/8-, 4 1/2-, 5 1/2-, 7 1/2- or 10-inch bull bbl., double Extractors, includes upper push button and standard magazine release, angled grip, low profile frame. Made from 1995 to 2000.

MATCH MASTER

DOVETAIL . . . . NiB $500 Ex $408 Gd $321
Similar to Match Master except has 3 7/8-, 4 1/2-, or 5 1/2-inch bbl. with dovetail rib.

MATCH MASTER DELUXE . . . . NiB $581 Ex $464 Gd $367
Similar to Match master Standard except has Weaver rib on bbl.
w/10-inch bbl, add. $128

SPORT KING . . . . NiB $601 Ex $321 Gd $270
Semi-automatic. Caliber: .22 LR. Equipped with 4 1/2- or 5 1/2-inch bbl., blued finish, military grips, drift sights, 10 round magazine. Made from 1995 to 2000.

CITATION . . . . NiB $439 Ex $319 Gd $265
Semi-automatic. Caliber: .22 LR. Equipped with 5 1/2-inch bull bbl. or 7 1/2-inch fluted bbl., military grips, 10-round magazine.

TROPHY . . . . NiB $433 Ex $332 Gd $270
Semi-automatic. Caliber: .22 LR. Equipped with 5 1/2- or 7 1/2-inch bull bbl. blued finish, military grips, 10-round magazine.
w/LH action (5 1/2-inch bbl. only), add. $65

VICTOR . . . . NiB $499 Ex $398 Gd $301
Semi-automatic. Caliber: .22LR. Equipped with 3 7/8-, 4 1/2- (VR or Weaver rib), 8- (Weaver rib) or 10-inch (Weaver rib) bbls.; blued finish, military grips, 10-round magazine.
w/4 1/2- or 4 1/2-inch Weaver rib bbls, add $100
w/8- or 10-inch Weaver rib bbls, add $190

OLYMPIC . . . . NiB $668 Ex $525 Gd $410
Semi-automatic. Caliber: .22 LR or Short. Equipped with 6 1/2-inch fluted bbl., blued finish, military grips, 10-round magazine.

SHARPSHOOTER . . . . NiB $499 Ex $365 Gd $259
Semi-automatic. Caliber: .22 LR. Equipped with 5 1/2-inch bull bbl.,blued finish, military grips, 10-round magazine.

LE FRANCAIS PISTOLS — St. Etienne, France. Produced by Manufacture Francaise d'Armes et Cycles

ARMY MODEL
AUTOMATIC PISTOL . . . . NiB $1749 Ex $1305 Gd $842
Similar in operation to the Le Francais .25 Automatics. Caliber: 9mm Browning Long. Eight-round magazine, 5-inch bbl., 7.75 inches overall. Weight: About 34 oz. Fixed sights. Blued finish. Checkered walnut grips. Made from 1928 to 1938.

POLICEMAN MODEL
AUTOMATIC PISTOL . . . . . . NiB $1020 Ex $917 Gd $416
DA. Hinged bbl., Caliber: .25 Automatic (6.35mm). Seven-round magazine, 3.5-inch bbl., 6 inches overall. Weight: About 12 oz. Fixed sights. Blued finish. Hard rubber grips. Introduced in 1914. disc.

STAFF OFFICER MODEL
AUTOMATIC PISTOL . . . . NiB $388 Ex $301 Gd $205
Caliber: .25 Automatic. Similar to the "Policeman" model except does not have cocking-piece head, barrel, is about an inch shorter and weight is an ounce less. Introduced in 1914. disc.

FREEDOM ARMS — Freedom, Wyoming

MODEL 97 PREMIER GRADE SA REVOLVER
Calibers: .357 Mag., .41 Mag. or .45 LC. Five- or 6-round cylinder, 4.25, 5, 5.5, 6 or 7.5-inch bbl., removable front blade with adjustable or fixed rear sight. Hardwood or black Micarta grips. Satin stainless finish. Made from 1997 to date.
Premier grade 97 . . . . NiB $1732 Ex $1414 Gd $890
w/Extra cylinder, add $225
w/fixed sights, deduct. $150

MODEL FA-.44 (83-44) SA REVOLVER
Similar to Model 454 Casull except chambered in .44 Mag. Made from 1988 to date.
Field Grade . . . . NiB $1545 Ex $1148 Gd $890
Premier Grade . . . . NiB $1854 Ex $1345 Gd $830
Silhouette class (w/10-inch bbl.)NiB $1528 Ex $1135 Gd $895
Silhouette pack
(10-inch bbl., access.) . . . . NiB $1550 Ex $1120 Gd $880
w/fixed sights, deduct. $100

MODEL FA-.45 (83-85) SA REVOLVER
Similar to Model 454 Casull except chambered in .45 Long Colt. Made from 1988 to 1990.
Field Grade . . . . NiB $1372 Ex $1022 Gd $685
Premier Grade . . . . NiB $1212 Ex $975 Gd $689
w/fixed sights, deduct. $100

MODEL FA-252 (83-22) SA REVOLVER
Calibers: .22 LR w/optional .22 Mag. cylinder. Bbl. lengths: 5.13 and 7.5 (Varmint Class), 10 inches (Silhouette Class). Adjustable Express or competition silhouette sights. Brushed or matte stainless finish. Black Micarta (Silhouette) or black and green laminated hardwood grips (Varmint). Made from 1991 to date.
Silhouette class . . . . NiB $2038 Ex $1713 Gd $730
Silhouette class
w/Extra .22 Mag. cyl. . . . . . NiB $1612 Ex $1279 Gd $898
Varmint class . . . . NiB $1232 Ex $979 Gd $705
Varmint class
w/Extra .22 Mag. cyl. . . . . . NiB $1515 Ex $1209 Gd $862

MODEL FA-353 (83-357) SA REVOLVER
Caliber: .357 Mag., bbl. lengths: 4.75, 6, 7.5 or 9 inches. Removable blade front sight, adjustable rear. Brushed or matte stainless finish. Pachmayr Presentation or impregnated hardwood grips.
Field Grade . . . . NiB $1048 Ex $864 Gd $597
Premier Grade . . . . NiB $1695 Ex $1562 Gd $712
Silhouette class
(w/9-inch bbl.) . . . . NiB $1080 Ex $862 Gd $612

MODEL FA-454AS (83-454) REVOLVER
Caliber: .454 Casull (w/optional .45 ACP, .45 LC, .45 Win. Mag. cylinders). Five-round cylinder, bbl. lengths: 4.75, 6, 7.5 or 10 inches. Adjustable Express or competition silhouette sights. Pachmayr presentation or impregnated hardwood grips. Brushed or matte stainless steel finish.
Field Grade . . . . NiB $1725 Ex $1276 Gd $638
Premier Grade . . . . NiB $2201 Ex $1824 Gd $760
Silhouette class (w/10-inch bbl.)NiB $1234 Ex $899 Gd $634
For Extra cylinder, add $255

MODEL FA-454FS REVOLVER
Same general specifications as Model FA-454AS except w/fixed sight.
Field grade. . . . . NiB $1762 Ex $1566 Gd $950
Premier grade. . . . . NiB $1807 Ex $1566 Gd $984

Freedom Arms
FA-252

Freedom Arms
FA-454AS

MODEL FA-454 GAS REVOLVER. . NiB $1705 Ex $1540 Gd $940
Field Grade version of Model FA-454AS except not made w/12-inch bbl., Matte stainless finish, Pachmayr presentation grips. Adj. Sights or fixed sight on 4.75-inch bbl.

MODEL FA-555 REVOLVER
Similar to Model .454 Casull except chambered in .50 AK. Made 1994.
Field Grade . . . . NiB $1595 Ex $1153 Gd $918
Premier Grade . . . . NiB $1955 Ex $1424 Gd $1040

MODEL FA-BG-22LR
MINI-REVOLVER . . . . NiB $237 Ex $165 Gd $128
Caliber: .22 LR. Three-inch tapered bbl., partial high-gloss stainless steel finish. Disc. 1987.

MODEL FA-BG-22M
MINI-REVOLVER . . . . NiB $246 Ex $180 Gd $143
Same general specifications as model FA-BG-22LR except in caliber .22 WMR. Disc. 1987.

MODEL FA-BG-22P
MINI-REVOLVER . . . . NiB $237 Ex $198 Gd $128
Same general specifications as Model FA-BG-22LR except in .22 percussion. Disc. 1987.

MODEL FA-L-22LR MINI-REVOLVERNiB $204 Ex $159 Gd $103
Caliber: .22 LR, 1.75-inch contoured bbl., partial high-gloss stainless steel finish. Bird's-head-type grips. Disc. 1987.

MODEL FA-L-22M
MINI-REVOLVER . . . . NiB $204 Ex $159 Gd $103
Same general specifications as Model FA-L-22LR except in caliber .22 WMR. Disc. 1987.

MODEL FA-L-22P MINI-REVOLVERNiB $235 Ex $160 Gd $121
Same general specifications as Model FA-L-22LR except in .22 percussion. Disc. 1987.

MODEL FA-S-22LR MINI-REVOLVERNiB $214 Ex $189 Gd $105
Caliber: .22 LR. One-inch contoured bbl., partial high-gloss stainless steel finish. Disc. 1988.

MODEL FA-S-22M MINI-REVOLVERNiB $189 Ex $135 Gd $101
Same general specifications as Model FA-S-22LR except in caliber .22 WMR. Disc. 1988.

MODEL FA-S-22P MINI-REVOLVERNiB $207 Ex $179 Gd $128
Same general specifications as Model FA-S-22LR except in .22 percussion. Disc. 1988.

FRENCH MILITARY PISTOLS — Cholet, France.

Manufactured originally by Société Alsacienne de Constructions Mécaniques (S.A.C.M.). Currently made by Manufacture d'Armes Automatiques, Lotissement Industriel des Pontots, Bayonne

MODEL 1935A AUTOMATIC PISTOL . NiB $377 Ex $274 Gd $143
Caliber: 7.65mm Long. Eight-round magazine, 4.3-inch bbl., 7.6 inches overall. Weight: 26 oz. Two-lug locking system similar to the Colt U.S. M1911A1. Fixed sights. Blued finish. Checkered grips. Made 1935-45. Note: This pistol was used by French troops during WW II and in Indo-China 1945 to 1954.

MODEL 1935S AUTOMATIC PISTOL. . NiB $342 Ex $281 Gd $135
Similar to Model 1935A except shorter (4.1-inch bbl., and 7.4 inches overall) and heavier (28 oz.). Single-step lug locking system.

MODEL 1950 AUTOMATIC PISTOL. . . NiB $485 Ex $397 Gd $270
Caliber: 9mm Para. Nine-round magazine, 4.4-inch bbl., 7.6 inches overall. Weight: 30 oz. Fixed sights, tapered post front and U-notched rear. Similar in design and function to the U.S. .45 service automatic except no bbl. bushing.

MODEL MAB F1 AUTOMATIC PISTOL NiB $653 Ex $587 Gd $270
Similar to Model MAB P-15 except w/6-inch bbl. and 9.6 inches overall. Adjustable target-style sights. Parkerized finish.

MODEL MAB P-8 AUTOMATIC PISTOL NiB $576 Ex $464 Gd $342
Similar to Model MAB P-15 except w/8-round magazine,

MODEL MAB P-15 AUTOMATIC PISTOLNiB $632 Ex $474 Gd $385
Caliber: 9mm Para. 15-round magazine, 4.5-inch bbl., 7.9 inches overall. Weight: 38 oz. Fixed sights, tapered post front and U-notched rear.

FROMMER PISTOLS — Budapest, Hungary. Manufactured by Fémáru-Fegyver-és Gépgyár R.T.

LILIPUT POCKET
AUTOMATIC PISTOL . . . . NiB $437 Ex $362 Gd $240
Caliber: .25 Automatic (6.35mm). Six-round magazine, 2.14-inch bbl., 4.33 inches overall. Weight: 10.13 oz. Fixed sights. Blued finish. Hard rubber grips. Made during early 1920s. Note: Although similar in appearance to the Stop and Baby, this pistol is designed for blowback operation.

STOP POCKET AUTOMATIC PISTOLNiB $414 Ex $321 Gd $165
Locked-breech action, outside hammer. Calibers: .32 Automatic (7.65mm), .380 Auto (9mm short). Seven-round (.32 cal.) or 6-round (.380 cal.) magazine, 3.88-inch bbl., 6.5 inches overall. Weight: About 21 oz. Fixed sights. Blued finish. Hard rubber grips. Made 1912 to 1920.

BABY POCKET AUTOMATIC PISTOLNiB $321 Ex $262 Gd $143
Similar to Stop model except has 2-inch bbl., 4.75 inches overall. Weight 17.5 oz. Magazine capacity is one round less than Stop Model. Intro. shortly after WW I.

GALENA INDUSTRIES INC. — Sturgis, South Dakota

Galena Industries purchased the rights to use the AMT trademark in 1998. Many, but not all, original AMT designs were included in the transaction.

AMT BACKUP . . . . **NiB $474 Ex $291 Gd $219**
Caliber: .380 (small frame, 2.5-inch bbl. only), .38 Super, .357 Sig, .40 S&W, .400 CorBon, .45 ACP, 9mm; magazine capacity: 5 or 6 rounds. Double action, 3-inch bbl., weight: 18 oz. (in .380), or 23 oz.
.38 Super, .357 Sig, .400 CorBon, add. **$75**

AUTOMAG II SEMI AUTO . . . **NiB $831 Ex $587 Gd $321**
Caliber: .22 WMR, 9-round magazine (except 7-round in 3.38-inch bbl.); 3.38- 4.5- or 6-inch bbls.; weight: About 32 oz.

AUTOMAG III . . . . **NiB $561 Ex $500 Gd $377**
Similar to Automag II except chambered for the .30 Carbine cartridge, 6.38-inch bbl., stainless steel finish, weight: About 43 oz.

AUTOMAG IV . . . . **NiB $561 Ex $500 Gd $377**
Caliber: .45 Winchester Magnum; 7-round magazine, 6.5-inch bbl., weight: 46 oz.

AUTOMAG .440 CORBON. . . **NiB $816 Ex $689 Gd $571**
Semiautomatic, 7.5-inch bbl., 5-round magazine, checkered walnut grips, matte black finish, weight: 46 oz. Intro. in 2000.

HARDBALLER II . . . . **NiB $505 Ex $347 Gd $235**
Based on the Colt Model 1911 frame. Caliber: .45 ACP, .40 S&W, .400 CorBon, 7-round magazine capacity, 5-inch bbl., weight: About 38 oz.

HARDBALLER II LONGSLIDE . **NiB $530 Ex $431 Gd $342**
Similar to Hardballer model except caliber: .45 ACP, 7-inch bbl., 7-round magazine capacity, stainless steel finish, weight: About 46 ounces.

HARDBALLER ACCELERATOR NiB $587 Ex $437 Gd $332
Similar to Hardballer model except caliber: .400 CorBon, 7-inch bbl., 7-round magazine capacity, stainless steel finish, weight: About 46 ounces.

COMMANDO . . . . **NiB $474 Ex $326 Gd $220**
Similar to Hardballer model except caliber: .40 S&W, 4-inch bbl., 8-round magazine capacity, stainless steel finish, weight: About 38 ounces.

GALESI PISTOLS — Collebeato (Brescia), Italy. Manufactured by Industria Armi Galesi

MODEL 6
POCKET AUTOMATIC PISTOL NiB $227 Ex $179 Gd $128
Calibers: .22 Long, .25 Automatic (6.35mm). Six-round magazine, 2.25-inch bbl., 4.38 inches overall. Weight: About 11 oz. Fixed sights. Blued finish. Plastic grips. Made from 1930 to date.

MODEL 9 POCKET AUTOMATIC PISTOL
Calibers: .22 LR, .32 Auto (7.65mm), .380 Auto (9mm Short). Eight-round magazine, 3.25-inch bbl., 5.88 inches overall. Weight: About 21 oz. Fixed sights. Blued finish. Plastic grips. Made from 1930 to date.

AUTOMATIC PISTOL
Note: Specifications vary, but those shown for .32 Automatic are common.
.22 LR or
.380 Auto. . . . . **NiB $273 Ex $191 Gd $135**
.32 Auto. . . . . **NiB $265 Ex $180 Gd $110**

Galesi
Model 6 Pocket

GLISENTI PISTOL — Carcina (Brescia), Italy. Mfd. by Societa Siderurgica Glisenti

MODEL 1910 ITALIAN
SERVICE AUTOMATIC . . . **NiB $1397 Ex $1214 Gd $1015**
Caliber: 9mm Glisenti. Seven-round magazine, 4-inch bbl., 8.5 inches overall. Weight: About 32 oz. Fixed sights. Blued finish. Hard rubber or plastic grips. Adopted 1910 and used through WWII.

BRIXIA MODEL . . . . **NiB $1627 Ex $1122 Gd $943**
Similar to Glisenti Model 1910 except mass produced using simplified mfg. techniques for the civilian market.

SOSSO MODEL . . . . **EXTREMELY RARE**
Experimental semi-auto. Cal.: 9 mm Para. Double action (marked "Sosso"), later single action. Mag.: 19 or 21 rounds. Made by FNA. Fewer than 10 made.

GLOCK, INC. — Smyrna, Georgia

NOTE: *Models: 17, 19, 20, 21, 22, 23, 24, 31, 32, 33, 34 and 35 were fitted with a redesigned grip-frame in 1998. Models: 26, 27, 29, 30 and all "C" guns (compensated models) retained the original frame design.*

MODEL 17 STRIKER FIRE AUTOMATIC PISTOL
Caliber: 9mm Parabellum. 10-, 17- or 19-round magazine, 4.5-inch bbl., 7.2 inches overall. Weight: 22 oz. w/o magazine, Polymer frame, steel bbl., slide and springs. Fixed or adj. rear sights. Matte, nonglare finish. Made of only 35 components, including three internal safety devices. Imported from 1985 to date.
Model 17 (w/fixed sights) . . . . . **NiB $505 Ex $385 Gd $301**
Model 17C (compensated bbl.) NiB $672 Ex $562 Gd $398
w/adjustable sights, add **$75**
w/Meprolight sights, add. **$100**
w/Trijicon sights, add **$120**

MODEL 17L COMPETITION STRIKER FIRE
Same general specifications as Model 17 except weight: 23.35 oz. with 6-inch bbl. 8.85 inches overall. Imported 1988 to 1999.
Model 1 L7 (w/fixed sights) . . . **NiB $714 Ex $577 Gd $396**
w/ported bbl., (early production), add **$75**
w/adjustable sights, add **$50**

GRADING: **NiB** = New in Box   **Ex** = Excellent or NRA 95%   **Gd** = Good or NRA 68%   **79**

**Glock Model 19
Compact**

**Glock
Model 30**

MODEL 19 COMPACT STRIKER FIRE

Same general specifications as Model 17 except smaller version with 4-inch bbl., 6.85 inches overall and weight: 21 oz. Imported from 1988 to date.

Model 19 (w/fixed sights) .... NiB $499 Ex $395 Gd $255
Model 19C (compensated bbl.) .... NiB $602 Ex $498 Gd $362
w/adjustable sights, add $75
w/Meprolight sights, add. $95
w/Trijicon sights, add $120

MODEL 20 STRIKER FIRE AUTO PISTOL

Caliber: 10mm. 15-round, hammerless, 4.6-inch bbl., 7.59 inches overall. Weight: 26.3 oz. Fixed or adj. sights. Matte, non-glare finish. Made from 1990 to date.

Model 20 (w/fixed sights) .... NiB $530 Ex $377 Gd $270
Model 19C (compensated bbl.) NiB $632 Ex $485 Gd $377
w/adjustable sights, add $75
w/Meprolight sights, add. $95
w/Trijicon sights, add $120

MODEL 21 STRIKER FIRE AUTOMATIC PISTOL

Same general specifications as Model 17 except chambered in .45 ACP. 13-round magazine, 7.59 inches overall. Weight: 25.2 oz. Imported from 1990 to date.

Model 21 (w/fixed sights) .... NiB $530 Ex $377 Gd $270
Model 21C (compensated bbl.) NiB $632 Ex $485 Gd $377
w/adjustable sights, add $75
w/Meprolight sights, add. $95
w/Trijicon sights, add $120

MODEL 22 STRIKER FIRE AUTOMATIC PISTOL

Same general specifications as Model 17 except chambered for .40 S&W. 15-round magazine, 7.4 inches overall. Imported from 1990 to date.

Model 22 (w/fixed sights) .... NiB $505 Ex $348 Gd $270
Model 22C
(compensated bbl.). . . . . NiB $612 Ex $362 Gd $281
w/adjustable sights, add $75
w/Meprolight sights, add. $95
w/Trijicon sights, add $120

MODEL 23 STRIKER FIRE AUTOMATIC PISTOL

Same general specifications as Model 19 except chambered for .40 S&W. 13-round magazine, 6.97 inches overall. Imported from 1990 to date.

Model 23 (w/fixed sights) .... NiB $505 Ex $348 Gd $270
Model 23C (compensated bbl.) NiB $586 Ex $434 Gd $357
w/adjustable sights, add $50
w/Meprolight sights, add. $80
w/Trijicon sights, add $105

MODEL 24 STRIKER FIRE AUTOMATIC PISTOL

Caliber: .40 S&W, 10- and 15-round magazines (the latter for law enforcement and military use only), 8.85 inches overall. Weight: 26.5 oz. Manual trigger safety; passive firing block and drop safety. Made from 1994 to 1999.

Model 24 (w/fixed sights) .... NiB $617 Ex $530 Gd $431
Model 24C (compensated bbl.) NiB $816 Ex $648 Gd $500
w/adjustable sights, add $75

MODEL 26 STRIKER FIRE AUTOMATIC PISTOL

Caliber: 9mm, 10-round magazine, 3.47-inch bbl., 6.3 inches overall. Weight: 19.77 oz. Imported from 1995 to date.

Model 26 (w/fixed sights) .... NiB $505 Ex $357 Gd $306
Model 26C (compensated bbl.) NiB $635 Ex $541 Gd $388
w/adjustable sights, add $75

MODEL 27 STRIKER FIRE AUTO PISTOL

Similar to the Glock Model .22 except subcompact. Caliber: .40 S&W, 10-round magazine, 3.5-inch bbl., Weight: 21.7 oz. Polymer stocks, fixed or fully adjustable sights. Imported from 1995 to date.

Model 27 (w/fixed sights) .... NiB $505 Ex $389 Gd $290
w/adjustable sights, add $75
w/Meprolight sights, add. $95
w/Trijicon sights, add $120

MODEL 28 COMPACT (LAW ENFORCEMENT ONLY)

Same general specifications as Model 25 except smaller version. Caliber: .380 ACP; 3.5-inch bbl. Weight: 20 ozs. Imported 1999 to date.

MODEL 29 STRIKER FIRE AUTO PISTOL

Similar to the Glock Model 20 except subcompact. Caliber: 10mm. 10-round magazine, 3.8-inch bbl., weight: 27.1 oz. Polymer stocks, fixed or fully adjustable sights. Imported from 1997 to date.

Model 29 (w/fixed sights) .... NiB $546 Ex $365 Gd $270
w/adjustable sights, add $75
w/Meprolight sights, add. $95
w/Trijicon sights, add $120

MODEL 30 STRIKER FIRE AUTO PISTOL

Similar to the Glock Model 21 except subcompact. Caliber: .45 ACP. 10-round magazine, 3.8-inch bbl., weight: 26.5 oz. Polymer stocks, fixed or fully adjustable sights. Imported from 1997 to date.

Model 30 (w/fixed sights) .... NiB $546 Ex $365 Gd $270
w/adjustable sights, add $75
w/Meprolight sights, add. $90
w/Trijicon sights, add $120

MODEL 31 STRIKER FIRE AUTOMATIC PISTOL
Caliber: .357 Sig., safe action system. 10- 15- or 17-round magazine, 4.49-inch bbl., weight: 23.28 oz. Safe Action trigger system w/3 safeties. Imported from 1998 to date.
Model 31
(w/fixed sights) . . . . NiB $546 Ex $357 Gd $270
Model 31C
(compensated bbl.) . . . . .NiB $612 Ex $464 Gd $270
w/adjustable sights, add $75
w/Meprolight sights, add. $95
w/Trijicon sights, add $120

MODEL 32 STRIKER FIRE AUTOMATIC PISTOL
Caliber: .357 Sig., safe action system. 10- 13- or 15-round magazine, 4.02-inch bbl., weight: 21.52 oz. Imported from 1998 to date.
Model 32
(w/fixed sights) . . . . NiB $546 Ex $357 Gd $270
Model 32C . . . . NiB $648 Ex $485 Gd $395
w/adjustable sights, add $75
w/Meprolight sights, add. $95
w/Trijicon Sights, add. $120

MODEL 33 STRIKER FIRE AUTOMATIC PISTOL
Caliber: .357 Sig., safe action system. Nine- or 11-round magazine, 3.46-inch bbl. Weight: 19.75 oz. Imported from 1998 to date.
Model 33
(w/fixed sights) . . . . NiB $530 Ex $357 Gd $286
w/adjustable sights, add $75
w/Meprolight sights, add. $95
w/Trijicon sights, add $120

MODEL 34 AUTO PISTOL . . . NiB $577 Ex $485 Gd $377
Similar to Model 17 except w/redesigned grip-frame and Extended slide-stop lever and magazine release. 10-, 17- or 19-round magazine, 5.32- inch bbl. Weight: 22.9 oz. Fixed or adjustable sights. Imported from 1998 to date.

MODEL 35 AUTO PISTOL . . . NiB $581 Ex $469 Gd $362
Similar to Model 34 except .40 S&W. Imported from 1998 to date.

MODEL 36 STRIKER FIRE AUTOMATIC PISTOL
Caliber: .45 ACP., safe action system. Six-round magazine, 3.78-inch bbl., weight: 20.11 oz. Safe Action trigger system w/3 safeties. Imported from 1999 to date.
Model 36
(w/fixed sights) . . . . NiB $536 Ex $444 Gd $342
w/adjustable sights, add $75
w/Meprolight sights, add. $95
w/Trijicon sights, add $120

DESERT STORM
COMMEMORATIVE . . . . . NiB $1525 Ex $1375 Gd $1225
Same specifications as Model 17 except "Operation Desert Storm, January 16-February 27, 1991" engraved on side of slide w/list of coalition forces. Limited issue of 1,000 guns. Made in 1991.

GREAT WESTERN ARMS CO. — North Hollywood, California

NOTE: *Values shown are for improved late model revolvers early Great Westerns are variable in quality and should be evaluated accordingly. It should also be noted that, beginning about July 1956, these revolvers were offered in kit form. Values of guns assembled from these kits will, in general, be of less value than factory-completed weapons.*

DOUBLE BARREL DERRINGER NiB $884 Ex $780 Gd $536
Replica of Remington Double Derringer. Caliber: .38 S&W, .38 S&W Spl. . Double bbls. (superposed), 3-inch bbl. Overall length: 5 inches. Fixed sights. Blued finish. Checkered black plastic grips. Made 1953 to 1962 in various configurations.

Grendel Model P-12

SA FRONTIER REVOLVER. . . . NiB $793 Ex $530 Gd $388
Replica of the Colt Single Action Army Revolver. Calibers: .22 LR, .22 WMR, .357 Magnum, .38 Special, .44 Special, .44 Magnum .45 Colt. Six-round cylinder, bbl. lengths: 4.75- 5.5 and 7.5-inches. Weight: 40 oz. in .22 cal. w/5.5-inch bbl. Overall length: 11.13 inches w/5.5-inch bbl. Fixed sights. Blued finish. Imitation stag grips. Made from 1951 to 1962.

SHERIFF'S MODEL . . . . NiB $791 Ex $638 Gd $500
Reportedly made from old Colt parts inventory. Cal.: .45 Long Colt. Blue, nickel, or case-colored finish. Plastic staghorn grips.

FAST DRAW MODEL . . . . NiB $714 Ex $601 Gd $439
Similar to Frontier Six Shooter. Bbl.: 4.75 inches. Brass backstrap and trigger guard; blue finish; plastic staghorn grips. Longer, turned-up hammer spur.

TARGET MODEL . . . . NiB $740 Ex $616 Gd $474
Similar to Frontier Six Shooter. Cal.: .22 LR. Adj. rear sights, Micro front blade. Blue or case colored frame. Bbl.: Various lengths.

DEPUTY MODEL . . . . NiB $831 Ex $709 Gd $500
Cal.: .22 LR, .38 Spl., .357 Mag. Bbl.: 4 inches. Deluxe blue finish, walnut grips. Adj. rear sight. Fewer than 100 made.

GRENDEL, INC. — Rockledge, Florida

MODEL P-10 AUTOMATIC PISTOL
Hammerless, blow-back action. DAO with no external safety. Caliber: .380 ACP. 10-round box magazine integrated in grip. Three-inch bbl., 5.3 inches overall. Weight: 15 oz. Matte blue, nickel or green Teflon finish. Made from 1988 to 1991.
Blued finish . . . . NiB $219 Ex $160 Gd $105
Nickel finish. . . . . NiB $227 Ex $179 Gd $120
Green finish . . . . NiB $227 Ex $179 Gd $105
w/compensated bbl., add $65

MODEL P-12 DA AUTOMATIC PISTOL
Caliber: .380 ACP. 11-round Zytel magazine, 3-inch bbl., 5.3 inches overall. Weight: 13 oz. Fixed sights. Polymer DuPont ST-800 grip. Made from 1991 to 1995.
Standard model . . . . NiB $214 Ex $135 Gd $105
Electroless nickel . . . . NiB $219 Ex $135 Gd $105

MODEL P-30 AUTOMATIC PISTOL
Caliber: .22 WMR. 30-round magazine, 5-or 8-inch bbl., 8.5 inches overall w/5-inch bbl., weight: 21 oz. Blade front sight, fixed rear sight. Made from 1991 to 1995.
w/5-inch bbl., ... NiB $337 Ex $255 Gd $214
w/8-inch bbl., ... NiB $337 Ex $255 Gd $214

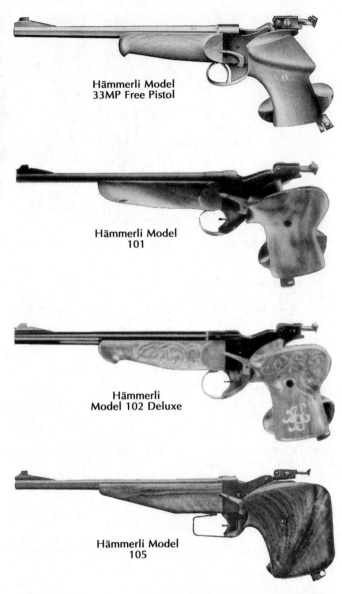

Hämmerli Model 33MP Free Pistol

Hämmerli Model 101

Hämmerli Model 102 Deluxe

Hämmerli Model 105

MODEL P-31
AUTOMATIC PISTOL . . . . **NiB $474 Ex $352 Gd $281**
Caliber: .22 WMR. 30-round Zytel magazine, 11-inch bbl., 17.3 inches overall. Weight: 48 oz. Adjustable blade front sight, fixed rear. Checkered black polymer DuPont ST-800 grip and forend. Made from 1991 to 1995.

GUNSITE — Paulden, Arizona

"ADVANCED TACTICAL" SA AUTO PISTOL
Manufactured w/Colt 1911 or Springfield 1911 parts. Caliber: .45 ACP. Eight-round magazine, 3.5-, 4.25-, 5-inch bbl. Weight: 32-38 oz. Checkered or laser-engraved walnut grips. Fixed or Novak Lo-mount sights.
Stainless finish . . . . **NiB $1193 Ex $974 Gd $704**
Blued finish . . . . **NiB $1030 Ex $836 Gd $621**

"CUSTOM CARRY" SA AUTO PISTOL
Caliber: .45 ACP. Eight-round magazine, 3.5-, 4.25-, 5-inch bbl., Weight: 32-38 oz. Checkered or laser-engraved walnut grips. Fixed

Novak Lo-mount sights. Single action, manufactured based on enhanced colt models.
Stainless finish . . . . **NiB $1219 Ex $990 Gd $740**
Blued finish . . . . **NiB $1151 Ex $927 Gd $709**

H&R 1871, INC. — Gardner, Massachusetts
NOTE: *In 1991, H&R 1871, Inc. was formed from the residual of the parent company, Harrington & Richardson, and then took over the New England Firearms facility. H&R 1871 produced firearms under both their logo and the NEF brand name until 1999, when the Marlin Firearms Company acquired the assets of H&R 1871. See listings under Harrington & Richardson, Inc.*

HÄMMERLI — Lenzburg, Switzerland.
Currently imported by Sigarms, Inc., Exeter, NH. Previously by Hammerli, USA; Beeman Precision Arms & Mandall Shooting Supplies
MODEL 33MP FREE PISTOL . . **NiB $964 Ex $863 Gd $577**
System Martini single-shot action, set trigger. Caliber: .22 LR. 11.5-inch octagon bbl., 16.5 inches overall. Weight: 46 oz. Micrometer rear sight, interchangeable front sights. Blued finish. Walnut grips, forearm. Imported from 1933 to 1949.

MODEL 100 FREE PISTOL
Same general specifications as Model 33MP. Improved action and sights, redesigned stock. Standard model has plain grips and forearm, deluxe model has carved grips and forearm. Imported 1950 to 1956.
Standard model . . . . **NiB $938 Ex $775 Gd $556**
Deluxe model. . . . . **NiB $1020 Ex $893 Gd $612**

MODEL 101 . . . . **NiB $913 Ex $791 Gd $612**
Similar to Model 100 except has heavy round bbl. w/matte finish, improved action and sights, adj. grips. Weight: About 49 oz. Imported from 1956 to 1960.

MODEL 102
Same as Model 101 except bbl., has highly polished blued finish. Deluxe model (illustrated) has carved grips and forearm. Made from 1956 to 1960.
Standard model . . . . **NiB $928 Ex $760 Gd $561**
Deluxe model. . . . . **NiB $1035 Ex $791 Gd $602**

MODEL 103 . . . . **NiB $969 Ex $826 Gd $536**
Same as Model 101 except has lighter octagon bbl. (as in Model 100) w/highly polished blued finish, grips and forearm of select French walnut. Weight: About 46 oz. Imported 1956 to 1960.

MODEL 104 . . . . **NiB $804 Ex $673 Gd $439**
Similar to Model 102 except has lighter round bbl., improved action redesigned grips and forearm. Weight: 46 oz. Imported 1961 to 1965.

MODEL 105 . . . . **NiB $960 Ex $779 Gd $500**
Similar to Model 103 except has improved action, redesigned grips and forearm. Imported from 1961 to 1965.

MODEL 106 . . . . **NiB $933 Ex $796 Gd $464**
Similar to Model 104 except has improved trigger and grips. Made from 1966 to 1971.

MODEL 107
Similar to Model 105 except has improved trigger and stock. Deluxe model (illustrated) has engraved receiver and bbl., carved grips and forearm. Imported from 1966 to 1971.
Standard model . . . . **NiB $1034 Ex $831 Gd $462**
Deluxe model. . . . . **NiB $1025 Ex $826 Gd $474**

Hämmerli
Model 106

Hämmerli
Model 107 Deluxe

MODEL 120 HEAVY BARREL
Same as Models 120-1 and 120-2 except has 5.7-inch heavy bbl., weight: 41 oz. Avail. w/standard or adj. grips. 1,000 made. Imported from 1972.
w/standard grips . . . . NiB $627 Ex $459 Gd $388
w/adj. grips . . . . NiB $761 Ex $588 Gd $377

MODEL 120-1 SINGLE-
SHOT FREE PISTOL . . . . NiB $658 Ex $536 Gd $385
Side lever-operated bolt action. Adj. single-stage or two-stage trigger. Caliber: .22 LR, 9.9-inch bbl., 14.75 inches overall. Weight: 44 oz. Micrometer rear sight, front sight on high ramp. Blued finish bbl., and receiver, lever and grip frame anodized aluminum. Checkered walnut thumbrest grips. Imported from 1972 to date.

MODEL 120-2 . . . . NiB $734 Ex $648 Gd $377
Same as Model 120-1 except has hand-contoured grips w/adj. palm rest (available for right or left hand). Imported from 1972 to date.

MODELS 150/151 FREE PISTOLS
Improved Martini-type action w/lateral-action cocking lever. Set trigger adj. for weight, length and angle of pull. Caliber: .22 LR, 11.3-inch round free-floating bbl., 15.4 inches overall. Weight: 43 oz. (w/Extra weights, 49.5 oz.). Micrometer rear sight, front sight on high ramp. Blued finish. Select walnut forearm and grips w/adj. palm shelf. Imported from 1972 to 1993.
Model 150 (disc. 1989). . . NiB $1938 Ex $1709 Gd $1020
Model 151 (disc. 1993). . . NiB $1938 Ex $1709 Gd $1020

MODEL 152 ELECTRONIC PISTOL
Same general specifications as Model 150 except w/electronic trigger. Made from 1990 to 1992
Right hand . . . . NiB $1812 Ex $1700 Gd $1036
w/adj. grips, add $306

MODELS 160/162 FREE PISTOLS
Caliber: .22 LR. Single-shot. 11.31-inch bbl., 17.5 inches overall. Weight: 46.9 oz. Interchangeable front sight blades, fully adj. match rear. Match-style stippled walnut grips w/adj. palm shelf and polycarbon fiber forend. Imported from 1993 to 2002.
Model 160 w/mechanical
set trigger (disc. 2000) . . . NiB $1812 Ex $1681 Gd $1005
Model 162 w/electronic triggerNiB $1982 Ex $1622 Gd $1132

MODEL 208 STANDARD
AUTO PISTOL . . . . NiB $1802 Ex $1488 Gd $959
Caliber: .22 LR. Eight-round magazine, 5.9-inch bbl., 10 inches overall. Weight: 35 oz. (bbl. weight adds 3 oz.). Micrometer rear sight, ramp front. Blued finish. Checkered walnut grips w/adj. heel plate. Imported from 1966 to 1988.

MODEL 208S TARGET PISTOL NiB $2540 Ex $2232 Gd $2066
Caliber: .22 LR. Eight-round magazine, 6-inch bbl., 10.2 inches overall. Weight: 37.3 oz. Micrometer rear sight, ramp front sight. Blued finish. Stippled walnut grips w/adj. heel plate. Imported from 1988 to 2000.

MODEL 211. . . . . NiB $1601 Ex $1458 Gd $847
Same as Model 208 except has standard. Thumbrest grips. Imported from 1966 to 1990.

Hämmerli
Model 120 Heavy Barrel

Hämmerli
Model 120-1

Hämmerli
Model 150

Hämmerli
Model 160

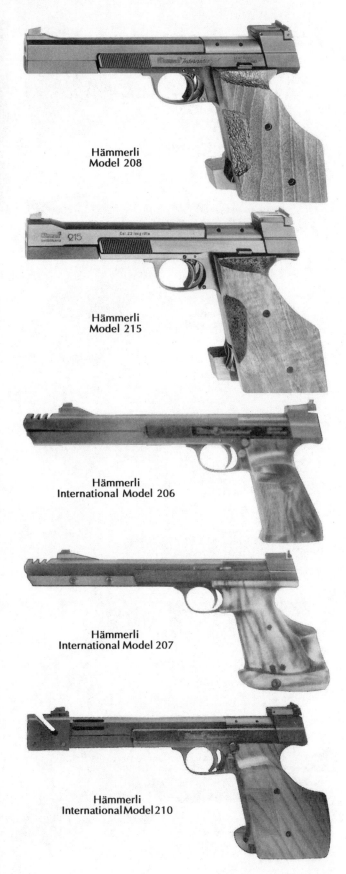

Hämmerli
Model 208

Hämmerli
Model 215

Hämmerli
International Model 206

Hämmerli
International Model 207

Hämmerli
International Model 210

Hämmerli
Model 232 Rapid Fire

MODEL 212
HUNTER'S PISTOL . . . . . . **NiB $2146 Ex $1816 Gd $1436**
Caliber: .22 LR, 4.88-inch bbl., 8.5 inches overall. Weight: 31 oz. Blade front sight, square-notched fully adj. rear. Blued finish. Checkered walnut grips. Imported from 1984 to 1993.

MODEL 215 . . . . **NiB $2368 Ex $2035 Gd $1734**
Similar to the Model 208 except w/heavier bbl. and fewer deluxe features. Imported from 1990 to 1993.

MODEL 230-1 RAPID FIRE
AUTO PISTOL . . . . **NiB $755 Ex $576 Gd $478**
Caliber: .22 Short. Five-round magazine, 6.3-inch bbl., 11.6 inches overall. Weight: 44 oz. Micrometer rear sight, post front. Blued finish. Smooth walnut thumbrest grips. Imported from 1970 to 1983.

MODEL 230-2 RAPID FIRE
AUTO PISTOL . . . . **NiB $785 Ex $601 Gd $444**
Same as Model 230-1 except has checkered walnut grips w/adj. heel plate. Imported from 1970 to 1983.

MODEL 232 RAPID FIRE
AUTO PISTOL . . . . **NiB $1454 Ex $1256 Gd $780**
Caliber: .22 Short. Six-round magazine, 5.1-inch ported bbl., 10.5 inches overall. Weight: 44 oz. Fully adj. target sights. Blued finish. Stippled walnut wraparound target grips. Imported 1984 to 1993.

INTERNATIONAL MODEL 206
AUTO PISTOL . . . . **NiB $709 Ex $469 Gd $306**
Calibers: .22 Short, .22 LR. Six-round (.22 Short) or 8-round (.22 LR) magazine, 7.1-inch bbl. w/muzzle brake, 12.5 inches overall. Weight: 33 oz. (.22 Short), 39 oz. (.22 LR) (supplementary weights add 5 and 8 oz.). Micrometer rear sight, ramp front. Blued finish. Standard thumbrest grips. Imported from 1962 to 1969.

INTERNATIONAL MODEL 207
AUTO PISTOL . . . . **NiB $760 Ex $621 Gd $469**
Same as Model 206 except has grips w/adj. heel plate, weight: 2 oz. more. Made from 1962 to 1969.

INTERNATIONAL MODEL 209
AUTO PISTOL . . . . **NiB $825 Ex $672 Gd $562**
Caliber: .22 Short. Five-round mag., 4.75-inch bbl., w/muzzle brake and gas-escape holes, 11 inches overall. Weight: 39 oz. (interchangeable front weight adds 4 oz.). Micrometer rear sight, post front. Blued finish. Standard thumbrest grips of checkered walnut. Imported from 1966 to 1970.

INTERNATIONAL MODEL 210 NiB $827 Ex $676 Gd $530
Same as Model 209 except has grips w/adj. heel plate, is 0.8-inch longer and weighs 1 ounce more. Made from 1966 to 1970.

MODEL 280 TARGET PISTOL

Carbon-reinforced synthetic frame and bbl., housing. Calibers: .22 LR, .32 S&W Long WC. Six-round (.22 LR) or 5-round (.32 S&W) magazine, 4.5-inch bbl. w/interchangeable metal or carbon fiber counterweights. 11.88 inches overall. Weight: 39 oz. Micro-adj. match sights w/interchangeable elements. Imported from 1988 to 2000.

.22 LR . . . . NiB $1550 Ex $1295 Gd $627
.32 S&W
Long WC . . . . NiB $1729 Ex $1550 Gd $842
.22/.32
Conversion
kit, add $816

VIRGINIAN SA REVOLVER . . . NiB $780 Ex $602 Gd $ 440

Similar to Colt Single-Action Army except has base pin safety system (SWISSAFE). Calibers: .357 Magnum, .45 Colt. Six-round cylinder. 4.63-, 5.5- or 7.5-inch bbl., 11 inches overall (with 5.5-inch bbl.). Weight: 40 oz. (with 5.5-inch bbl.). Fixed sights. Blued bbl. and cylinder, casehardened frame, chrome-plated grip frame and trigger guard. One-piece smooth walnut stock. Imported from 1973 to 1976 by Interarms, AlExandria, Va.

WALTHER OLYMPIA MODEL 200
AUTOMATIC PISTOL, 1952-TYPE NiB $704 Ex $598 Gd $479

Similar to 1936 Walther Olympia Funfkampf model. Calibers: .22 Short, .22 LR. Six-round (.22 Short) or 10-round (.22 LR) magazine, 7.5-inch bbl., 10.7 inches overall. Weight: 27.7 oz. (.22 Short, light alloy breechblock), 30.3 oz. (.22 LR). Supplementary weights provided. Adj. target sights. Blued finish. Checkered walnut thumbrest grips. Imported 1952 to 1958.

WALTHER
OLYMPIA MODEL 200,1958-TYPE NiB $780 Ex $632 Gd $530

Same as Model 200 1952 type except has muzzle brake, 8-round magazine (.22 LR). 11.6 inches overall. Weight: 30 oz. (.22 Short), 33 oz. (.22 LR). Imported 1958 to 1963.

WALTHER
OLYMPIA MODEL 201 . . . . . . NiB $704 Ex $546 Gd $437

Same as Model 200,1952-Type except has 9.5-inch bbl. Imported from 1955 to 1957.

WALTHER
OLYMPIA MODEL 202 . . . . . . NiB $780 Ex $632 Gd $530

Same as Model 201 except has grips w/adjustable heel plate. Imported from 1955 to 1957.

WALTHER OLYMPIA MODEL 203

Same as corresponding Model 200 (1955 type lacks muzzle brake) except has grips w/adjustable heel plate. Imported 1955 to 1963.

1955 type. . . . . NiB $794 Ex $638 Gd $479
1958 type. . . . . NiB $842 Ex $709 Gd $475

WALTHER OLYMPIA MODEL 204

American model. Same as corresponding Model 200 (1956-Type lacks muzzle brake) except in .22 LR only, has slide stop and micrometer rear sight. Imported from 1956 to 1963.

1956-type . . . . NiB $760 Ex $606 Gd $464
1958-type . . . . NiB $816 Ex $680 Gd $556

WALTHER OLYMPIA MODEL 205

American model. Same as Model 204 except has grips w/adjustable heel plate. Imported from 1956 to 1963.

1956-type . . . . NiB $842 Ex $714 Gd $610
1958-type . . . . NiB $893 Ex $727 Gd $556

Hämmerli-Walther
Olympia Model 203 1958-Type

Hämmerli-Walther
Olympia Model 205

SIG-Hämmerli
Model P240 Target

MODEL P240 TARGET AUTO PISTOL

Calibers: .32 S&W Long (wadcutter), .38 Special (wadcutter). Five-round magazine, 5.9-inch bbl., 10 inches overall. Weight: 41 oz. Micrometer rear sight, post front. Blued finish/smooth walnut thumbrest grips. Accessory .22 LR conversion unit available. Imported from 1975 to 1986.

.32 S&W Long . . . . NiB $1540 Ex $1329 Gd $755
.38 Special. . . . . NiB $2545 Ex $2353 Gd $2025
.22 LR conversion
unit, add $561

Harrington & Richardson SL .32

Harrington & Richardson USRA
Model Single-Shot Target Pistol

Harrington & Richardson Model 4

Harrington & Richardson Model 5

HARRINGTON & RICHARDSON, INC. — Gardner, Massachusetts (now H&R 1871, Inc., Gardner, MA)

Formerly Harrington & Richardson Arms Co. of Worcester, Mass. One of the oldest and most distinguished manufacturers of handguns, rifles and shotguns, H&R suspended operations on January 24, 1986. In 1987, New England Firearms was established as an independent company producing selected H&R models under the NEF logo. In 1991, H&R 1871, Inc., was formed from the residual of the parent company and then took over the New England Firearms facility. H&R 1871 produced firearms under both its logo and the NEF brand name until 1999, when the Marlin Firearms Company acquired the assets of H&R 1871.

NOTE: *For ease in finding a particular firearm, H&R handguns are grouped into Automatic/Single-Shot Pistols, followed by Revolvers. For a complete listing, please refer to the index.*

AUTOMATIC/SINGLE-SHOT PISTOLS

SL .25 PISTOL . . . . **NiB $587 Ex $405 Gd $290**
Modified Webley & Scott design. Caliber: .25 Auto. Six-round magazine, 2-inch bbl., 4.5 inches overall. Weight: 12 oz. Fixed sights. Blued finish. Black hard rubber grips. Made from 1912 to 1916.

SL .32 PISTOL . . . . **NiB $562 Ex $321 Gd $205**
Modified Webley & Scott design. Caliber: .32 Auto. Eight-round magazine, 3.5-inch bbl., 6.5 inches overall. Weight: About 20 oz. Fixed sights. Blued finish. Black hard rubber grips. Made from 1916 to 1924.

**USRA MODEL SINGLE-
SHOT TARGET PISTOL**. . . . . . **NiB $548 Ex $500 Gd $288**
Hinged frame. Caliber: .22 LR, bbl. lengths: 7-, 8- and 10-inch. Weight: 31 oz. w/10-inch bbl., Adj. target sights. Blued finish. Checkered walnut grips. Made from 1928 to 1941.

REVOLVERS

**MODEL 4
(1904) DA** . . . . **NiB $255 Ex $180 Gd $90**
Solid frame. Calibers: .32 S&W Long, .38 S&W. Six-round cylinder (.32 cal.), or 5-round (.38 cal.), bbl. Lengths: 2.5-, 4.5- and 6-inch. Weight: About 16 oz. (in .32 cal.) Fixed sights. Blued or nickel finish. Hard rubber grips. Disc. prior to 1942.

MODEL 5 (1905) DA . . . . **NiB $237 Ex $159 Gd $77**
Solid frame. Caliber: .32 S&W. Five-round cylinder, bbl., lengths: 2.5-,4.5- and 6-inch. Weight: About 11 oz. Fixed sights. Blued or nickel finish. Hard rubber grips. Disc. prior to 1942.

MODEL 6 (1906) DA . . . . **NiB $198 Ex $115 Gd $75**
Solid frame. Caliber: .22 LR. Seven-round cylinder, bbl. lengths: 2.5, 4.5- and 6-inches. Weight: About 10 oz. Fixed sights. Blued or nickel finish. Hard rubber grips. Disc. prior to 1942.

.22 SPECIAL DA . . . . **NiB $351 Ex $197 Gd $101**
Heavy hinged frame. Calibers: .22 LR, .22 Mag. Nine-round cylinder, 6-inch bbl., weight: 23 oz. Fixed sights, front gold-plated. Blued finish. Checkered walnut grips. Recessed safety cylinder on later models for high-speed ammunition. Disc. prior to 1942.

MODEL 199 SPORTSMAN
SA REVOLVER . . . . **NiB $347 Ex $291 Gd $158**
Hinged frame. Caliber: .22 LR. Nine-round cylinder, 6-inch bbl., 11 inches overall. Weight: 30 oz. Adj. target sights. Blued finish. Checkered walnut grips. Disc. 1951.

MODEL 504 DA . . . . **NiB $255 Ex $189 Gd $143**
Caliber: .32 H&R Magnum. Five-round cylinder, 4- or 6-inch bbl., (square butt), 3- or 4-inch bbl., round butt. Made 1984 to 1986.

MODEL 532 DA . . . . **NiB $179 Ex $129 Gd $88**
Caliber: .32 H&R Magnum. Five-round cylinder, 2.5- or 4-inch bbl., weight: Approx. 20 and 25 oz. respectively. Fixed sights. American walnut grips. Lustre blued finish. Made 1984 to 1986.

MODEL 586 DA . . . . **NiB $290 Ex $188 Gd $130**
Caliber: .32 H&R Magnum. Five-round cylinder. bbl. lengths: 4.5, 5.5, 7.5, 10 inches. Weight: 30 oz. average. Adj. rear sight, blade front. Walnut finished hardwood grips. Made from 1984 to 1986.

MODEL 603 TARGET . . . . . **NiB $219 Ex $158 Gd $115**
Similar to Model 903 except in .22 WMR. Six-round capacity w/ unfluted cylinder. Made from 1980 to 1983.

MODEL 604 TARGET . . . . . **NiB $219 Ex $158 Gd $115**
Similar to Model 603 except w/6-inch bull bbl., weight: 38 oz. Made from 1980 to 1983.

MODEL 622/623 DA . . . . . . **NiB $170 Ex $128 Gd $79**
Solid frame. Caliber: .22 Short, Long, LR, 6-round cylinder. bbl., lengths: 2.5-, 4-, 6-inches. Weight: 26 oz. (with 4-inch bbl.). Fixed sights. Blued finish. Plastic grips. Made from 1957 to 1986. Note: Model 623 is same except chrome or nickel finish.

MODEL 632/633
GUARDSMAN DA REVOLVER NiB $171 Ex $128 Gd $79
Solid Frame. Caliber: .32 S&W Long. Six-round cylinder, bbl., lengths: 2.5- or 4-inch. Weight: 19 oz. (with 2.5-inch bbl.). Fixed sights. Blued or chrome finish. Checkered Tenite grips (round butt on 2.5-inch, square butt on 4-inch). Made from 1953 to 1986. Note: Model 633 is the same except for chrome or nickel finish.

MODEL 649/650 DA . . . . . . **NiB $265 Ex $158 Gd $95**
Solid frame. Side loading and ejection. Convertible model w/ two 6-round cylinders. Calibers: .22 LR, .22 WMR. 5.5-inch bbl., Weight: 32 oz. Adj. rear sight, blade front. Blued finish. One-piece, Western-style walnut grip. Made from 1976 to 1986. Note: Model 650 is same except nickel finish.

MODEL 666 DA . . . . **NiB $151 Ex $104 Gd $64**
Solid frame. Convertible model w/two 6-round cylinders. Calibers: .22 LR, .22 WMR. Six-inch bbl., weight: 28 oz. Fixed sights. Blued finish. Plastic grips. Made from 1976 to 1978.

MODEL 676 DA . . . . **NiB $283 Ex $200 Gd $104**
Solid frame. Side loading and ejection. Convertible model w/two 6-round cylinders. Calibers: .22 LR, .22 WMR, bbl. lengths: 4.5, 5.5, 7.5, 12-inches. Weight: 32 oz. (with 5.5-inch bbl.). Adj. rear sight, blade front. Blued finish, color-casehardened frame. One-piece, Western-style walnut grip. Made from 1976 to 1980.

MODEL 686 DA . . . . **NiB $306 Ex $205 Gd $128**
Caliber: .22 LR and .22 WMR. Six-round magazine, 4.5, 5.5, 7.5, 10 or 12-inch bbl. Adj. rear sight, ramp and blade front. Blued, color-casehardened frame. Weight: 31 oz. (with 4.5-inch bbl.). Made from 1980 to 1986.

Harrington & Richardson
Model 6

Harrington & Richardson
.22 Special

Harrington & Richardson
Model 199 Sportsman

Harrington & Richardson
Model 622

Harrington & Richardson
Model 649

Harrington & Richardson
Model 650

Harrington & Richardson
Model 666

Harrington & Richardson
Model 676

Harrington & Richardson
Model 830

Harrington & Richardson
Model 686

Harrington & Richardson
Model 733

MODEL 732/733 DA . . . . NiB $198 Ex $129 Gd $83
Solid frame, swing-out 6-round cylinder. Calibers: .32 S&W, .32 S&W
Long. bbl., lengths: 2.5 and 4-inch. Weight: 26 oz. (with 4-inch bbl.).
Fixed sights (windage adj. rear on 4-inch bbl. model). Blued finish.
Plastic grips. Made from 1958 to 1986. Note: Model 733 is the same
except with nickel finish.

MODEL 826 DA . . . . NiB $200 Ex $135 Gd $88
Caliber: .22 WMR. Six-round magazine, 3-inch bull bbl., ramp and
blade front sight, adj. rear. American walnut grips. Weight: 28 oz.
Made from 1981 to 1983.

MODEL 829/830 DA
Same as Model 826 except in .22 LR caliber. Nine round capacity.
Made from 1981 to 1983.
Model 829, blued. . . . . NiB $189 Ex $143 Gd $94
Model 830, nickel . . . . NiB $181 Ex $135 Gd $90

MODEL 832/833 DA
Same as Model 826 except in .32 SW Long. Blued or nickel finish.
Made from 1981 to 1983.
Model 832, blued. . . . . NiB $199 Ex $112 Gd $77
Model 833, nickel . . . . NiB $199 Ex $112 Gd $77

MODEL 900/901 DA . . . . NiB $179 Ex $105 Gd $70
Solid frame, snap-out cylinder. Calibers: .22 Short, Long, LR. Nine-
round cylinder, bbl. lengths: 2.5, 4, and 6-inches. Weight: 26 oz.
(with 6-inch bbl.). Fixed sights. Blued finish. Cycolac grips. Made
from 1962 to 1973. Note: Model 901 (disc. in 1963) is the same
except has chrome finish and white Tenite grips.

MODEL 903 TARGET . . . . NiB $240 Ex $177 Gd $112
Caliber: .22 LR. Nine round capacity. SA/DA, 6-inch target-weight
flat-side bbl., swing-out cylinder. Weight: 35 oz. Blade front sight,
adj. rear. American walnut grips. Made from 1980- to 1983.

MODEL 904 TARGET . . . . NiB $265 Ex $177 Gd $116
Similar to Model 903 except 4 or 6-inch bull bbl. Weight: 32 oz.
with 4-inch bbl. Made from 1980 to 1986.

Harrington & Richardson
Model 900

Harrington & Richardson
Model 925

Harrington & Richardson
Model 903

Harrington & Richardson
Model 905

Harrington & Richardson
Model 922, First Issue

Harrington & Richardson
Model 922, Second Issue

Harrington & Richardson
Model 926

MODEL 905

TARGET . . . . **NiB $270 Ex $183 Gd $137**
Same as Model 904 except w/4-inch bbl. only. Nickel finish. Made from 1981 to 1983.

MODEL 922 DA REVOLVER

FIRST ISSUE . . . . **NiB $232 Ex $189 Gd $148**
Solid frame. Caliber: .22 LR. Nine-round cylinder, 10-inch octagon bbl., (early model) or 6-inches, round bbl. (later production). Weight: 26 oz. (with 6-inch bbl.). Fixed sights. Blued finish. Checkered walnut grips. Safety cylinder on later models. Disc. prior to 1942.

MODEL 922/923 DA REVOLVER,

SECOND ISSUE . . . . **NiB $220 Ex $112 Gd $88**
Solid frame. Caliber: .22 LR. Nine-round cylinder, bbl. lengths: 2.5, 4, and 6-inches. Weight: 24 oz. (with 4-inch bbl.). Fixed sights. Blued finish. Plastic grips. Made 1950 to 1986. Note: Second Issue Model 922 has a different frame from that of the First Issue. Model 923 is same as Model 922, Second Issue except for nickel finish.

MODEL 925

DEFENDER . . . . **NiB $255 Ex $148 Gd $110**
DA. Hinged frame. Caliber: .38 S&W. Five-round cylinder, 2.5-inch bbl., weight: 22 oz. Adj. rear sight, fixed front. Blued finish. One-piece wraparound grip. Made from 1964 to 1978.

MODEL 926 DA . . . . **NiB $255 Ex $158 Gd $110**
Hinged frame. Calibers: .22 LR, .38 S&W. Nine-round (.22 LR) or 5-round (.38) cylinder, 4-inch bbl., weight: 31 oz. Adj. rear sight, fixed front. Blued finish. Checkered walnut grips. Made 1968 to 1978.

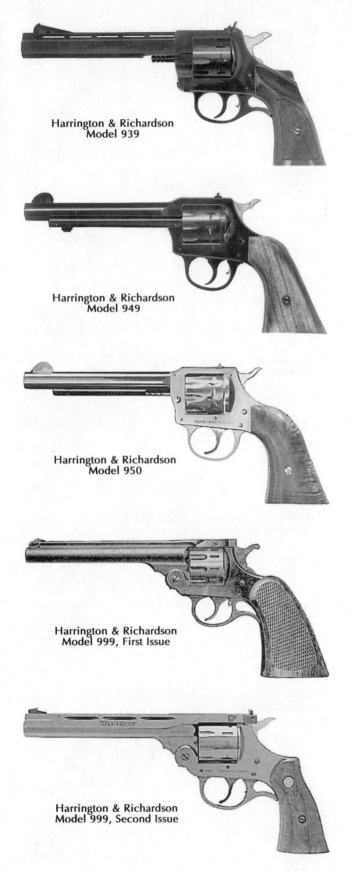

Harrington & Richardson
Model 939

Harrington & Richardson
Model 949

Harrington & Richardson
Model 950

Harrington & Richardson
Model 999, First Issue

Harrington & Richardson
Model 999, Second Issue

Harrington & Richardson
Model 929

MODEL 929/930
SIDEKICK DA REVOLVER . . . . NiB $219 Ex $130 Gd $95
Caliber: .22 LR. Solid frame, swing-out 9-round cylinder, bbl. lengths: 2.5-, 4-, 6-inches. Weight: 24 oz. (with 4-inch bbl.). Fixed sights. Blued finish. Checkered plastic grips. Made from 1956 to 1986. Note: Model 930 is same except with nickel finish.

MODEL 939/940 ULTRA SIDEKICK
DA REVOLVER . . . . NiB $290 Ex $187 Gd $112
Solid frame, swing-out 9-round cylinder. Safety lock. Calibers: .22 Short, Long, LR. Flat-side 6-inch bbl. w/vent rib. Weight: 33 oz. Adj. rear sight, ramp front. Blued finish. Checkered walnut grips. Made 1958 to 1986, reintroduced by H&R 1871 in 1992. Note: Model 940 is same except has round bbl.

MODEL 949/950 FORTY-NINER
DA REVOLVER . . . . NiB $270 Ex $190 Gd $110
Solid frame. Side loading and ejection. Calibers: .22 Short, Long, LR. Nine-round cylinder, 5.5- or 7.5 inch bbl., weight: 31 to 38 oz. Adj. rear sight, blade front. Blued or nickel finish. One-piece, Western-style walnut grip. Made 1960 to 1986, reintroduced by H&R 1871 in 1992 to 1999. Note: Model 950 is same except has nickel finish.

MODEL 976 DA . . . . NiB $310 Ex $197 Gd $109
Same as Model 949 except has color-casehardened frame, 7.5-inch bbl. Weight: 36 oz. Intro. 1977. Disc.

MODEL 999 SPORTSMAN DA REVOLVER,
FIRST ISSUE . . . . NiB $499 Ex $316 Gd $200
Hinged frame. Calibers: .22 LR, .22 Mag. Same specifications as Model 199 Sportsman Single Action. Disc. before 1942.

MODEL 999 SPORTSMAN DA REVOLVER
SECOND ISSUE . . . . NiB $464 Ex $309 Gd $197
Hinged frame. Caliber: .22 LR. Nine-round cylinder, 6-inch bbl. w/ vent rib. Weight: 30 oz. Adj. sights. Blued finish. Checkered walnut grips. Made from 1950 to 1986.

(NEW) MODEL 999 SPORTSMAN
DA REVOLVER . . . . NiB $499 Ex $316 Gd $197
Hinged frame. Caliber: .22 Short, Long, LR. Nine-round cylinder. Six-inch bbl. w/vent rib. Weight: 30 oz. Blade front sight adj. for elevation, square-notched rear adj. for windage. Blued finish. Checkered hardwood grips. Reintroduced by H&R 1871 in 1992.

AMERICAN DA. . . . . NiB $245   Ex $115   Gd $79
Solid frame. Calibers: .32 S&W Long, .38 S&W. Six-round (.32 cal.) or 5-round (.38 cal.) cylinder, bbl. lengths: 2.5-,4.5- and 6-inches. Weight: About 16 oz. Fixed sights. Blued or nickel finish. Hard rubber grips. Disc. prior to 1942.

AUTOMATIC EJECTING DA REVOLVER NiB $231   Ex $174   Gd $120
Hinged frame. Calibers: .32 S&W Long, .38 S&W. Six-round (.32 cal.) or 5-round (.38 cal.) cylinder, bbl. lengths: 3.25-, 4-, 5- and 6-inches. Weight: 16 oz. (.32 cal.), 15 oz. (.38 cal.). Fixed sights. Blued or nickel finish. Black hard rubber grips. Disc. prior to 1942.

BOBBY DA. . . . . NiB $316   Ex $219   Gd $160
Hinged frame. Calibers: .32 S&W, .38 S&W. Six-round cylinder (.32 cal.) or 5-round (.38 cal.). Four-inch bbl., 9 inches overall. Weight: 23 oz. Fixed sights. Blued finish. Checkered walnut grips. Disc. 1946. Note: Originally designed and produced for use by London's bobbies.

DEFENDER .38 DA . . . . NiB $346   Ex $219   Gd $110
Hinged frame. Based on the Sportsman design. Caliber: .38 S&W. Bbl. lengths: 4- and 6-inches, 9 inches overall (with 4-inch bbl.). Weight: 25 oz. with 4-inch bbl. Fixed sights. Blued finish. Black plastic grips. Disc. 1946. Note: This model was manufactured during WW II as an arm for plant guards, auxiliary police, etc.

EXPERT MODEL DA . . . . NiB $499   Ex $283   Gd $110
Same specifications as .22 Special except has 10-inch bbl., weight: 28 oz. Disc. prior to 1942.

HAMMERLESS DA, LARGE FRAME . . NiB $206   Ex $137   Gd $115
Hinged frame. Calibers: .32 S&W Long 38 S&W. Six-round (.32 cal.), or 5-round (.38 cal.) cylinder, bbl. lengths: 3.25, 4, and 6-inches. Weight: About 17 oz. Fixed sights. Blued or nickel finish. Hard rubber grips. Disc. prior to 1942.

HAMMERLESS DA, SMALL FRAME . . NiB $189   Ex $130   Gd $101
Hinged frame. Calibers: .22 LR, .32 S&W. Seven-round (.22 cal.) or 5-round (.32 cal.) cylinder, bbl. lengths: 2, 3, 4, 5 and 6-inches. Weight: About 13 oz. Fixed sights. Blued or nickel finish. Hard rubber grips. Disc. prior to 1942.

HUNTER MODEL DA . . . . NiB $601   Ex $410   Gd $309
Solid frame. Caliber: .22 LR. Nine-round cylinder, 10-inch octagon bbl., weight: 26 oz. Fixed sights. Blued finish. Checkered walnut grips. Safety cylinder on later models. Note: An earlier Hunter Model was built on the smaller 7-round frame. Disc. prior to 1942.

NEW DEFENDER DA . . . . NiB $346   Ex $244   Gd $189
Hinged frame. Caliber: .22 LR. Nine-round cylinder, 2-inch bbl., 6.25 inches overall. Weight: 23 oz. Adj. sights. Blued finish. Checkered walnut grips, round butt. Note: Basically, this is the Sportsman DA w/a short bbl., Disc. prior to 1942.

PREMIER DA . . . . NiB $306   Ex $198   Gd $109
Small hinged frame. Calibers: .22 LR, .32 S&W. Seven-round (.22 LR) or 5-round (.32) cylinder. Bbl. Lengths: 2, 3, 4, 5, and 6-inches. Weight: 13 oz. (in .22 LR), 12 oz. (in .32 S&W). Fixed sights. Blued or nickel finish. Black hard rubber grips. Disc. prior to 1942.

MODEL STR 022 BLANK REVOLVER. . . NiB $143   Ex $90   Gd $70
Caliber: .22 RF blanks. Nine-round cylinder, 2.5-inch bbl. Weight: 19 oz. Satin blued finish.

MODEL STR 032 BLANK REVOLVER. . . NiB $148   Ex $95   Gd $75
Same general specifications as STR 022 except chambered for .32 S&W blank cartridges.

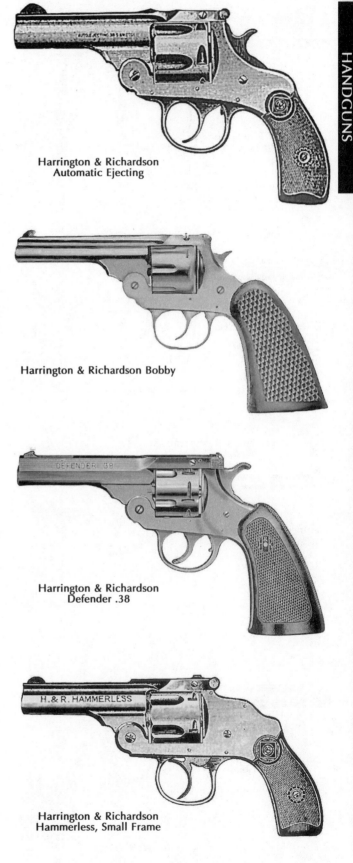

Harrington & Richardson
Automatic Ejecting

Harrington & Richardson **Bobby**

Harrington & Richardson
Defender .38

Harrington & Richardson
Hammerless, Small Frame

Harrington & Richardson
Premier

Harrington & Richardson
Vest Pocket

Harrington & Richardson
Target

Harrington & Richardson
Young American

Harrington & Richardson
Trapper

Harrington & Richardson
Ultra Sportsmen

TARGET MODEL DA . . . . **NiB $237 Ex $166 Gd $120**
Small hinged frame. Calibers: .22 LR, .22 W.R.F. Seven-round cylinder, 6-inch bbl., weight: 16 oz. Fixed sights. Blued finish. Checkered walnut grips. Disc. prior to 1942.

TRAPPER MODEL DA . . . . . . **NiB $388 Ex $219 Gd $130**
Solid frame. Caliber: .22 LR. Seven-round cylinder, 6-inch octagon bbl., weight: 12.5 oz. Fixed sights. Blued finish. Checkered walnut grips. Safety cylinder on later models. Disc. prior to 1942.

ULTRA SPORTSMAN . . . . **NiB $321 Ex $219 Gd $165**
SA. Hinged frame. Caliber: .22 LR. Nine-round cylinder, 6-inch bbl., weight: 30 oz. Adj. target sights. Blued finish. Checkered walnut grips. This model has short action, wide hammer spur, cylinder is length of a .22 LR cartridge. Disc. prior to 1942.

VEST POCKET DA . . . . **NiB $138 Ex $95 Gd $70**
Solid frame. Spurless hammer. Calibers: .22 Rimfire, .32 S&W. Seven-round (.22 cal.) or 5-round (.32 cal.) cylinder, 1.13-inch bbl., weight: About 9 oz. Blued or nickel finish. Hard rubber grips. Disc. prior to 1942.

YOUNG AMERICA DA . . . . **NiB $241 Ex $109 Gd $81**
Solid frame. Calibers: .22 Long, .32 S&W. Seven-round (.22 cal.) or 5-round (.32 cal.) cylinder. Bbl. lengths: 2-, 4.5- and 6-inches. Weight: About 9 oz. Fixed sights. Blued or nickel finish. Hard rubber grips. Disc. prior to 1942.

HARTFORD ARMS & EQUIPMENT CO. — Hartford, Connecticut

Hartford pistols were the forebearer of the original High Standard line. High Standard Mfg. Corp. acquired Hartford Arms & Equipment Co. in 1932. The High Standard Model B is essentially the same as the Hartford Automatic.

AUTOMATIC TARGET PISTOL NiB $648 Ex $534 Gd $431
Caliber. .22 LR. 10-round magazine, 6.75-inch bbl., 10.75 inches overall. Weight: 31 oz. Target sights. Blued finish. Black rubber grips. This gun closely resembles the early Colt Woodsman and High Standard pistols. Made 1929 to 1930.

REPEATING PISTOL . . . . NiB $785 Ex $576 Gd $342
Check for authenticity. This model is a hand-operated repeating pistol similar to the Fiala and Schall pistols Made from 1929 to 1930.

SINGLE-SHOT TARGET PISTOLNiB $785 Ex $577 Gd $342
Similar in appearance to the Hartford Automatic. Caliber: .22 LR, 6.75-inch bbl., 10.75 inches overall. Weight: 38 oz. Target sights. Mottled frame and slide, blued bbl., Black rubber or walnut grips. Made from 1929 to 1930.

HASKELL MANUFACTURING — Lima, Ohio
See listings under Hi-Point.

HAWES FIREARMS — Van Nuys, California

DEPUTY MARSHAL SA REVOLVER
Calibers: .22 LR, also .22 WMR in two-cylinder combination. Six-round cylinder, 5.5-inch bbl., 11 inches overall. Weight: 34 oz. Adj. rear sight, blade front. Blued finish. Plastic or walnut grips. Imported 1973 to 1981.
.22 LR (plastic grips). . . . . NiB $219 Ex $120 Gd $88
Combination, .22 LR/.22 WMR (plastic)NiB $293 Ex $219 Gd $130
Walnut grips, add $20

DEPUTY DENVER MARSHAL
Same as Deputy Marshal SA except has brass frame. Imported 1973 to 1981.
.22 LR (plastic grips). . . . . NiB $265 Ex $212 Gd $110
Combination, .22 LR/.22 WMR (plastic)NiB $293 Ex $219 Gd $130
Walnut grips add $10

DEPUTY MONTANA MARSHAL
Same as Deputy Marshal except has brass grip frame. Walnut grips only. Imported from 1973 to 1981.
.22 LR . . . . NiB $283 Ex $198 Gd $118
Combination, .22 LR/.22 WMR NiB $321 Ex $235 Gd $128

DEPUTY SILVER CITY MARSHAL
Same as Deputy Marshal except has chrome-plated frame, brass grip frame, blued cylinder and bbl., Imported from 1973 to 1981.
.22 LR (plastic grips). . . . . .NiB $281 Ex $209 Gd $158
Combination, .22 LR/.22 WMR (plastic)NiB $306 Ex $205 Gd $115
Walnut grips, add $15

DEPUTY TEXAS MARSHAL
Same as Deputy Marshal except has chrome finish. Imported 1973 to 1981.
.22 LR (plastic grips). . . . . NiB $293 Ex $205 Gd $110
Combination, .22 LR/.22 WMR (plastic)NiB $306 Ex $190 Gd $110
Walnut grips, add. $15

FAVORITE SINGLE-SHOT TARGET PISTOLNiB $219 Ex $128 Gd $90
Replica of Stevens No. 35. Tip-up action. Caliber: .22 LR. Eight-inch bbl., 12 inches overall. Weight: 24 oz. Target sights. Chrome-plated frame. Blued bbl., Plastic or rosewood grips (add $5). Imported 1972- to 1976.

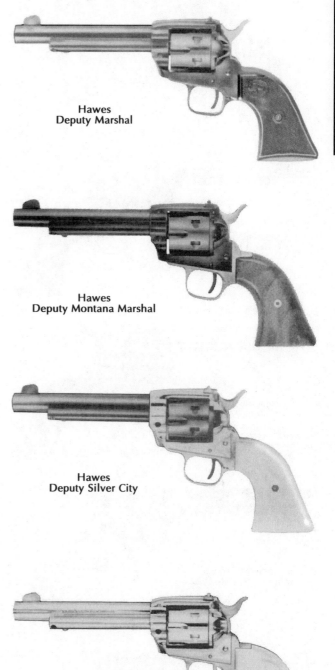

Hawes
Deputy Marshal

Hawes
Deputy Montana Marshal

Hawes
Deputy Silver City

Hawes
Deputy Texas Marshal

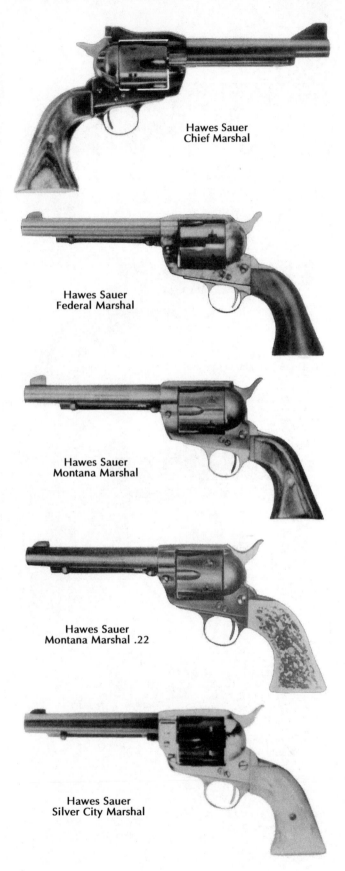

Hawes Sauer
Chief Marshal

Hawes Sauer
Federal Marshal

Hawes Sauer
Montana Marshal

Hawes Sauer
Montana Marshal .22

Hawes Sauer
Silver City Marshal

Hawes Sauer
Texas Marshal

SAUER CHIEF MARSHAL SA TARGET REVOLVER
Same as Western Marshal except has adjustable rear sight and front sight, oversized rosewood grips. Not made in .22 caliber. Imported from 1973 to 1981.

.357 Magnum or .45 Colt . . . . NiB $326 Ex $254 Gd $189
.44 Magnum. . . . . NiB $362 Ex $282 Gd $214
Combination .357 Magnum
and 9mm Para.
.45 Colt and .45 Auto. . . . . NiB $362 Ex $282 Gd $214
Combination
.44 Magnum and .44-40 . . . . NiB $369 Ex $290 Gd $225

SAUER FEDERAL MARSHAL
Same as Western Marshal except has color-casehardened frame, brass grip frame, one-piece walnut grip. Not made in .22 caliber. Imported from 1973 to 1981.

.357 Magnum or .45 Colt . . . . NiB $321 Ex $235 Gd $198
.44 Magnum. . . . . NiB $362 Ex $235 Gd $198
Combination
.357 Magnum and 9mm Para.,
.45 Colt and .45 Auto. . . . . NiB $362 Ex $290 Gd $198
Combination .44 Magnum and .44-40 NiB $369 Ex $305 Gd $189

SAUER MONTANA MARSHAL
Same as Western Marshal except has brass grip frame. Imported from 1973 to 1981.

.357 Magnum or .45 Colt . . . . NiB $326 Ex $270 Gd $190
.44 Magnum. . . . . NiB $357 Ex $281 Gd $214
Combination .357 Magnum and 9mm Para.,
.45 Colt and .45 Auto. . . . . NiB $377 Ex $301 Gd $219
Combination .44 Magnum and .44-40 NiB $385 Ex $309 Gd $220
.22 LR . . . . NiB $306 Ex $240 Gd $180
Combination .22 LR and .22 WMR . . NiB $332 Ex $281 Gd $190

SAUER SILVER CITY MARSHAL
Same as Western Marshal except has nickel plated frame, brass grip frame, blued cylinder and barrel, pearlite grips. Imported from 1973 to 1981.

.44 Magnum. . . . . NiB $377 Ex $289 Gd $219
Combination .357 Magnum and 9mm Para.
.45 Colt and .45 Auto. . . . . NiB $362 Ex $270 Gd $180
Combination .44 Magnum and .44-40 NiB $365 Ex $270 Gd $214

SAUER TEXAS MARSHAL
Same as Western Marshal except nickel plated, has pearlite grips. Imported from 1973 to 1981.

.357 Magnum or .45 Colt . . . . NiB $362 Ex $270 Gd $204
.44 Magnum. . . . . NiB $365 Ex $303 Gd $214
Combination .357 Magnum and 9mm Para.,
.45 Colt and .45 Auto. . . . . NiB $388 Ex $321 Gd $225
Combination .44 Magnum and .44-40 NiB $395 Ex $332 Gd $239
.22 LR . . . . NiB $321 Ex $244 Gd $189
Combination .22 LR and .22 WMR . . NiB $336 Ex $265 Gd $189

SAUER WESTERN MARSHAL SA REVOLVER
Calibers: .22 LR (disc.), .357 Magnum, .44 Magnum, .45 Auto. Also in two-cylinder combinations: .22 WMR (disc.), 9mm Para., .44-40, .45 Auto. Six-round cylinder, bbl. lengths: 5.5-inch (disc.), 6-inch, 11.75 inches overall (with 6-inch bbl.). Weight: 46 oz. Fixed sights. Blued finish. Originally furnished w/simulated stag plastic grips. Recent production has smooth rosewood grips. Made from 1968 by J. P. Sauer & Sohn, Eckernforde, Germany. Imported from 1973 to 1981.

.357 Magnum or .45 LC	NiB $357	Ex $265	Gd $200
.44 Magnum	NiB $377	Ex $290	Gd $219
Combination .357 Magnum and 9mm Para., .45 Colt and .45 Auto	NiB $385	Ex $270	Gd $214
Combination .44 Magnum and .44-40	NiB $385	Ex $270	Gd $214
.22 LR	NiB $281	Ex $198	Gd $160
Combination .22 LR and .22 WMR	NiB $281	Ex $198	Gd $160

Hawes Sauer
Western Marshal

HECKLER & KOCH — Oberndorf am Neckar, Germany, and Chantilly, Virginia

MODEL HK4 DA AUTO PISTOL
Calibers: .380 Automatic (9mm Short), .22 LR, .25 Automatic (6.35mm), .32 Automatic (7.65mm) w/conversion kits. Seven-round magazine (.380 Auto), 8-round in other calibers, 3.4-inch bbl., 6.19 inches overall. Weight: 18 oz. Fixed sights. Blued finish. Plastic grip. Disc. 1984.

.22 LR or .380 units to kit	NiB $536	Ex $388	Gd $265
.25 ACP or .32 ACP units to kit	NiB $536	Ex $377	Gd $255
.380 units to kit w/.22 conversion unit	NiB $530	Ex $357	Gd $225
.380 units to kit w/.22, .25, .32 conversion units	NiB $530	Ex $357	Gd $225

Heckler & Koch
Model HK4

MODEL MARK 23
DA AUTO PISTOL . . . . . . NiB $2356 Ex $1831 Gd $1290
Short-recoil semiautomatic pistol w/polymer frame and steel slide. Caliber: .45 ACP. 10-round magazine, 5.87-inch bbl., 9.65 inches overall. Weight: 43 oz. Seven interchangeable rear sight adjustment units w/3-dot system. Developed primarily in response to specifications by the Special Operations Command (SOCOM) for a Special Operations Forces Offensive Handgun Weapon System. Imported from 1996 to date.

Heckler & Koch
Mark 23

MODEL P7 K3 DA
AUTO PISTOL
Caliber: .380 ACP. Eight-round magazine, 3.8 inch-bbl., 6.3 inches overall. Weight: About 26 oz. Adj. rear sight. Imported 1988 to 1994.

P7K3 in .380 Cal.	NiB $954	Ex $785	Gd $546
.22 LR conversion kit	NiB $713	Ex $611	Gd $434
.32 ACP conversion kit	NiB $388	Ex $328	Gd $228

MODEL P7 M8 . . . . NiB $1295 Ex $804 Gd $577
Squeeze-cock SA semiautomatic pistol. Caliber: 9mm Para. Eight-round magazine, 4.13-inch bbl., 6.73 inches overall. Weight: 29.9 oz. Matte black or nickel finish. Adjustable rear sight. Imported from 1985 to 2005.

MODEL P7 M10
Caliber: .40 S&W. Nine-round magazine, 4.2-inch bbl., 6.9 inches overall. Weight: 43 oz. Fixed front sight blade, adj. rear w/3-dot system. Imported from 1992 to 1994.

Blued finish	NiB $1163	Ex $879	Gd $643
Nickel finish	NiB $1163	Ex $879	Gd $643

Heckler & Koch
Model P7K3

Heckler & Koch
Model P7M13

Heckler & Koch USP45

Heckler & Koch
Model P7 (PSP)

Heckler & Koch
Model P9S DA

MODEL P7 M13 . . . . **NiB $2219 Ex $1848 Gd $1632**
Caliber: 9mm. 13-round magazine, 4.13-inch bbl., 6.65 inches
overall. Weight: 34.42 oz. Matte black finish. Adj. rear sight.
Imported 1985 to 1994.

MODEL P7 (PSP)
AUTO PISTOL . . . . **NiB $917 Ex $701 Gd $510**
Caliber: 9mm Para. Eight-round magazine, 4.13-inch bbl., 6.54
inches overall. DA. Weight: About 33.5 oz. Blued finish. Imported
1983 to 1985 and again in 1990 with limited availability.

MODEL P9S
DA AUTOMATIC PISTOL
Calibers: 9mm Para., .45 Automatic. Nine-round (9mm) or 7-round
(.45 Auto) magazine. Four-inch bbl., 7.63 inches overall. Weight:
32 ounces. Fixed sights. Blued finish. Contoured plastic grips. This
model disc. 1986.
9mm . . . . **NiB $893 Ex $663 Gd $486**
.45 Automatic . . . . **NiB $918 Ex $713 Gd $500**

MODEL P9S TARGET COMPETITION KIT
Same as Model P9S Target except comes w/Extra 5.5-inch bbl. and
bbl. weights. Also available w/walnut competition grip.
w/standard grip . . . . **NiB $1061 Ex $973 Gd $745**
Competition grip . . . . **NiB $1199 Ex $1121 Gd $891**

MODEL SP89 . . . . **NiB $4023 Ex $3224 Gd $2227**
Semiautomatic, recoil-operated, delayed roller-locked bolt system.
Caliber: 9mm Para. 15-round magazine, 4.5-inch bbl., 13 inches
overall. Weight: 68 oz. Hooded front sight, adj. rotary-aperture rear.
Imported 1989 to 1993.

MODEL USP AUTO PISTOL
Polymer integral grip/frame design w/recoil reduction system.
Calibers: 9mm Para., .40 S&W or .45 ACP. 15-round (9mm) or
13-round (.40 S&W and .45ACP) magazine, 4.13- or 4.25-inch
bbl., 6.88 to 7.87 inches overall. Weight: 26.5-30.4 oz. Blade
front sight, adj. rear w/3-dot system. Matte black or stainless
finish. Stippled black polymer grip. Available in SA/DA or DAO.
Imported 1993 to date.
Matte
Black finish . . . . **NiB $928 Ex $627 Gd $468**
Stainless. . . . . **NiB $816 Ex $510 Gd 332**
w/Tritium sights, add **$100**
w/ambidExtrous decocking lever, add **$30**

**Heckler & Koch Model USP45
Compact 50th Anniversary**

**Heckler & Koch
Model USP9 Compact (Stainless)**

**Heckler & Koch
Model USP357 Compact**

**Heckler & Koch
Model USP Expert**

**Heckler & Koch
Model USP Tactical**

MODEL USP9 COMPACT

Caliber: 9mm. 10-round magazine, 4.25-inch bbl., 7.64 inches overall. Weight: 25.5 oz. Short recoil w/modified Browning action. 3-dot sighting system. Polymer frame w/integral grips. Imported from 1993 to date.

Blued finish . . . . NiB $1301 Ex $1193 Gd $1029
Stainless finish . . . . NiB $1301 Ex $1193 Gd $1029
w/ambidExtrous
decocking lever, add $75

MODEL USP40 COMPACT

Caliber: .40 S&W. 10-round magazine, 3.58- inch bbl., 6.81 inches overall. Weight: 27 oz. Short recoil w/modified Browning action. 3-dot sighting system. Polymer frame w/integral grips. Imported from 1993 to date.

Blued finish . . . . NiB $857 Ex $615 Gd $437
Stainless finish . . . . NiB $774 Ex $627 Gd $431
w/ambidExtrous
decocking lever, add $50

MODEL USP45 COMPACT

Caliber: .45 ACP. Eight-round magazine, 3.8- inch bbl., 7.09 inches overall. Weight: 28 oz. Short recoil w/modified Browning action. 3-dot sighting system. Polymer frame w/integral grips. Imported from 1998 to date.

Blued finish . . . . NiB $918 Ex $615 Gd $410
Stainless finish . . . . NiB $816 Ex $639 Gd $431
w/ambidExtrous
decocking lever, add $50
50th Anniversary
(1 of 1,000) . . . . NiB $1199 Ex $947 Gd $709

MODEL
USP EXPERT. . . . . NiB $1301 Ex $1142 Gd $842
Caliber: .45 ACP. 10-round magazine, 6.2- inch bbl., 9.65 inches overall. Weight: 30 oz. Adjustable 3-dot target sights. Short recoil modified Browning action w/recoil reduction system. Reinforced polymer frame w/integral grips and match-grade slide. Imported from 1999 to 2009.

MODEL USP
TACTICAL . . . . NiB $1178 Ex $933 Gd $638
SOCOM Enhanced version of the USP Standard Model, w/4.92-inch threaded bbl. Chambered for .45 ACP only. Imported from 1998 to date.

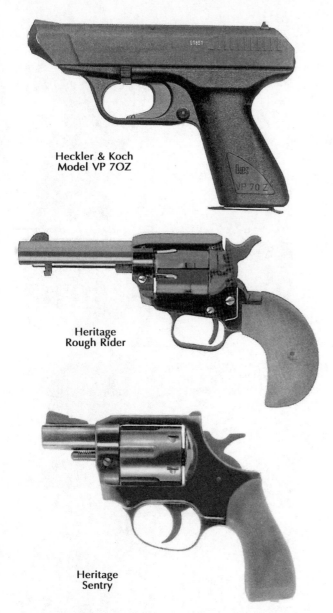

**Heckler & Koch
Model VP 7OZ**

**Heritage
Rough Rider**

**Heritage
Sentry**

MODEL VP 70Z AUTO PISTOL NiB $791 Ex $536 Gd $377
Caliber: 9mm Para. 18-round magazine, 4.5-inch bbl., 8 inches overall. Weight: 32.5 oz. DA Fixed sights. Blued slide, polymer receiver and grip. Disc. 1986.

HELWAN PISTOLS
See listings under Interarms.

HERITAGE MANUFACTURING—Opa Locka, Florida (sold to Taurus Int'l. 2012)

MODEL H-25 AUTO PISTOL
Caliber: .25 ACP. Six-round magazine, 2.5-inch bbl., 4.63 inches overall. Weight: 12 oz. Fixed sights. Blued or chrome finish. Made 1995 to 1999.
Blued. . . . . NiB $136 Ex $95 Gd $75
Nickel, add $20

ROUGH RIDER SA REVOLVER
Calibers: .22 LR, .22 Mag. Six-round cylinder. bbl. lengths: 2.75, 3.75, 4.75, 6.5 or 9 inches. Weight: 31-38 oz. Blade front sight, fixed rear. High-polished blued finish w/gold accents. Smooth walnut grips. Made from 1993 to date.
.22 LR . . . . NiB $247 Ex $115 Gd $95
.22 LR/.22 Mag. combo . . . . . NiB $291 Ex $179 Gd $110

SENTRY DA REVOLVER
Calibers: .22 LR, .22 Mag., .32 Mag., 9mm or .38 Special. Six- or 8-round (rimfire) cylinder, 2- or 4-inch bbl., 6.25 inches overall (2-inch bbl.). Ramp front sight, fixed rear. Blued or nickel finish. Checkered polymer grips. Made from 1993 to 1997.
Blued. . . . . NiB $131 Ex $95 Gd $75
Nickel, add $15

STEALTH DA AUTO PISTOL . . NiB $241 Ex $179 Gd $101
Calibers: 9mm, .40 S&W. 10-round magazine, 3.9-inch bbl., weight: 20.2 oz. Gas-delayed blowback, double action only. AmbidExtrous trigger safety. Blade front sight, drift-adj. rear. Black chrome or stainless slide. Black polymer grip frame. Made from 1996 to 2000.

HI-POINT FIREARMS — Mansfield, Ohio

MODEL JS-9MM
AUTO PISTOL . . . . NiB $158 Ex $101 Gd $75
Caliber: 9mm Para. Eight-round magazine, 4.5-inch bbl., 7.75 inches overall. Weight: 39 oz. Fixed low-profile sights w/3-dot system. Matte blue, matte black or chrome finish. Checkered synthetic grips. Made from 1990 to 2000.

MODEL JS-9MM COMPETITION PISTOL
(STALLARD) . . . . NiB $151 Ex $90 Gd $69
Similar to standard JS-9 except w/4-inch compensated bbl. w/ shortened slide and adj. sights. 10-round magazine, 7.25 inches overall. Weight: 30 oz. Made from 1998 to 2006.

MODEL JS-9MM/C-9MM COMPACT PISTOL
(BEEMILLER). . . . . NiB $148 Ex $90 Gd $75
Similar to standard JS-9 except w/3.5-inch bbl. and shortened slide w/alloy or polymer frame. 6.72 inches overall. Weight: 29 oz. or 32 oz. Three-dot-style sights. Made from 1993 to date.

MODEL CF-.380
POLYMER . . . . NiB $158 Ex $88 Gd $61
Caliber: .380 ACP. Eight-round magazine, 3.5-inch bbl., 6.72 inches overall. Weight: 32 oz. Three-dot sights. Made from 1994 to date.

MODEL JS-.40/JC-.40 AUTO PISTOL
(IBERIA) . . . . NiB $171 Ex $110 Gd $75
Similar to Model JS-9mm except in caliber .40 S&W.

MODEL JS-.45/JH-.45 AUTO PISTOL
(HASKELL) . . . . NiB $150 Ex $101 Gd $70
Similar to Model JS-9mm except in caliber .45 ACP w/7-round magazine and two-tone Polymer finish.

J. C. HIGGINS

See Sears, Roebuck & Company

HIGH STANDARD SPORTING FIREARMS — East Hartford, Connecticut. Formerly High Standard Mfg. Co., Hamden, Connecticut

A long-standing producer of sporting arms, High Standard disc. its operations in 1984. See new High Standard models under separate entry, HIGH STANDARD MFG. CO., INC.

NOTE: *For ease in finding a particular firearm, High Standard handguns are grouped into three sections: Automatic pistols (below), derringers and revolvers. For a complete listing, please refer to the IndEx.*

AUTOMATIC PISTOLS

MODEL A
HAMMERLESS . . . . **NiB $847 Ex $748 Gd $497**
Caliber: .22 LR. 10-round magazine, bbl. lengths: 4.5-, 6.75-inch. 11.5 inches overall (6.75-inch bbl.). Weight: 36 oz. (in 6.75-inch bbl.). Adj. target sights. Blued finish. Checkered walnut grips. Made from 1938 to 1942.

MODEL B
AUTOMATIC PISTOL . . . . **NiB $668 Ex $444 Gd $367**
Original Standard pistol. Hammerless. Caliber: .22 LR. 10-round magazine, bbl. lengths: 4.5-, 6.75-inch, 10.75 inches overall (with 6.75-inch bbl.). Weight: 33 oz. (6.75-inch bbl.). Fixed sights. Blued finish. Hard rubber grips. Made from 1932 to 1942.

MODEL C
AUTOMATIC PISTOL . . . . **NiB $979 Ex $826 Gd $549**
Same as Model B except in .22 Short. Made from 1935 to 1942.

MODEL D
AUTOMATIC PISTOL . . . . . . **NiB $1020 Ex $774 Gd $544**
Same general specifications as Model A but heavier bbl., weight: 40 oz. (6.75-inch bbl.). Made from 1937 to 1942.

DURA-MATIC
AUTOMATIC PISTOL . . . . **NiB $362 Ex $301 Gd $204**
Takedown. Caliber: .22 LR. 10-round magazine, 4.5 or 6.5 inch interchangeable bbl., 10.88 inches overall (6.5-inch bbl.). Weight: 35 oz. (in 6.5-inch bbl.). Fixed sights. Blued finish. Checkered grips. Made from 1952 to 1970.

MODEL E
AUTOMATIC PISTOL . . . . . **NiB $1275 Ex $1051 Gd $929**
Same general specifications as Model A but w/Extra heavy bbl. and thumbrest grips. Weight: 42 oz. (6.75-inch bbl.). Made 1937 to 1942.

FIELD-KING AUTOMATIC PISTOL FIRST MODEL
Same general specifications as Sport-King but w/heavier bbl. and target sights. Late model 6.75-inch bbls. have recoil stabilizer and lever take-down feature. Weight: 43 oz. (6.75-inch bbl.). Made from 1951 to 1958.
w/one bbl. . . . . **NiB $683 Ex $529 Gd $408**
w/both bbls., add **$204**

FIELD-KING AUTOMATIC PISTOL SECOND MODEL
Same general specifications as First Model Field-King but w/button take-down and marked FK 100 or FK 101.
w/one bbl. . . . . **NiB $852 Ex $588 Gd $324**
w/both bbls., add **$204**

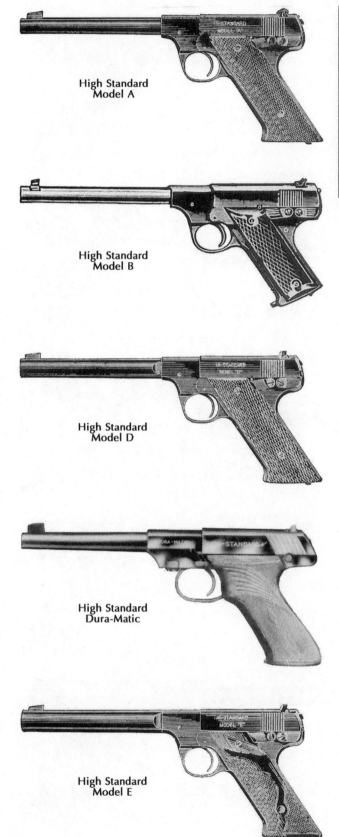

High Standard
Model A

High Standard
Model B

High Standard
Model D

High Standard
Dura-Matic

High Standard
Model E

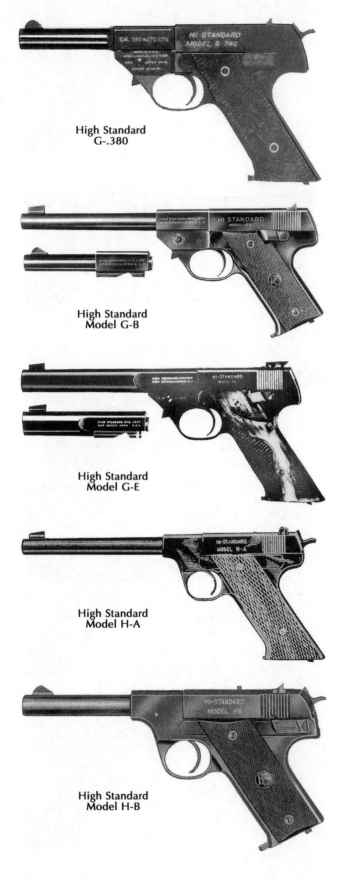

High Standard
G-.380

High Standard
Model G-B

High Standard
Model G-E

High Standard
Model H-A

High Standard
Model H-B

FLITE-KING AUTOMATIC PISTOL — FIRST MODEL
Same general specifications as Sport-King except in .22. Short w/ aluminum alloy frame and slide and marked FK 100 or FK 101. Weight: 26 oz. (6.5-inch bbl.). Made from 1953 to 1958.

w/one bbl. . . . . NiB $668 Ex $469 Gd $342
w/both bbls. . . . . NiB $872 Ex $660 Gd $546

FLITE-KING AUTOMATIC PISTOL — SECOND MODEL
Same as Flite-King—First Model except w/steel frame and marked in the 102 or 103 series. Made from 1958 to 1966.

Model 102 . . . . NiB $556 Ex $398 Gd $265
Model 103 . . . . NiB $536 Ex $388 Gd $219

MODEL G-.380
AUTOMATIC PISTOL . . . . NiB $668 Ex $571 Gd $408
Lever takedown. Visible hammer. Thumb safety. Caliber: .380 Automatic. Six-round magazine, 5-inch bbl., weight: 40 oz. Fixed sights. Blued finish. Checkered plastic grips. Made 1943 to 1950.

MODEL G-B AUTOMATIC PISTOL
Lever takedown. Hammerless. Interchangeable bbls. Caliber: .22 LR. 10-round magazine, bbl. lengths: 4.5, 6.75 inches, 10.75 inches overall (with 6.75-inch bbl.). Weight: 36 oz. (with 6.75-inch bbl.). Fixed sights. Blued finish. Checkered plastic grips. Made 1948 to 1951.

w/one bbl. . . . . NiB $689 Ex $500 Gd $365
w/both bbls. . . . . NiB $893 Ex $704 Gd $576

MODEL G-D AUTOMATIC PISTOL
Lever takedown. Hammerless. Interchangeable bbls. Caliber: .22 LR. 10-round magazine, bbl. lengths: 4.5, 6.75 inches. 11.5 inches overall (with 6.75-inch bbl.). Weight: 41 oz. (6.75-inch bbl.). Target sights. Blued finish. Checkered walnut grips. Made 1948 to 1951.

w/one bbl. . . . . NiB $1076 Ex $917 Gd $709
w/both bbls. . . . . NiB $1275 Ex $1048 Gd $898

MODEL G-E AUTOMATIC PISTOL
Same general specifications as Model G-D but w/Extra heavy bbl. and thumbrest grips. Weight: 44 oz. (with 6.75-inch bbl.). Made from 1949 to 1951.

w/one bbl. . . . . NiB $1488 Ex $1266 Gd $1015
w/both bbls. . . . . NiB $1692 Ex $1470 Gd $1200

MODEL H-A
AUTOMATIC PISTOL . . . . . NiB $2230 Ex $1355 Gd $859
Same as Model A but w/visible hammer, no thumb safety. Made from 1939 to 1942.

MODEL H-B
AUTOMATIC PISTOL . . . . NiB $816 Ex $590 Gd $433
Same as Model B but w/visible hammer, no thumb safety. Made from 1940 to 1942.

MODEL H-D
AUTOMATIC PISTOL . . . . . NiB $1282 Ex $1122 Gd $806
Same as Model D but w/visible hammer, no thumb safety. Made from 1939 to 1942.

MODEL H-DM
AUTOMATIC PISTOL . . . . NiB $663 Ex $524 Gd $429
Also called H-D Military. Same as Model H-D but w/thumb safety. Made from 1941 to 1951.

MODEL H-E
AUTOMATIC PISTOL . . . . NiB $2275 Ex $2142 Gd $1197
Same as Model E but w/visible hammer, no thumb safety. Made from 1939 to 1942.

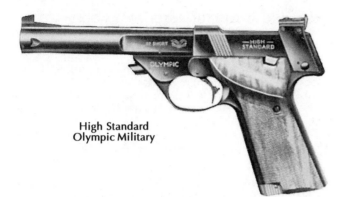

High Standard
Olympic Military

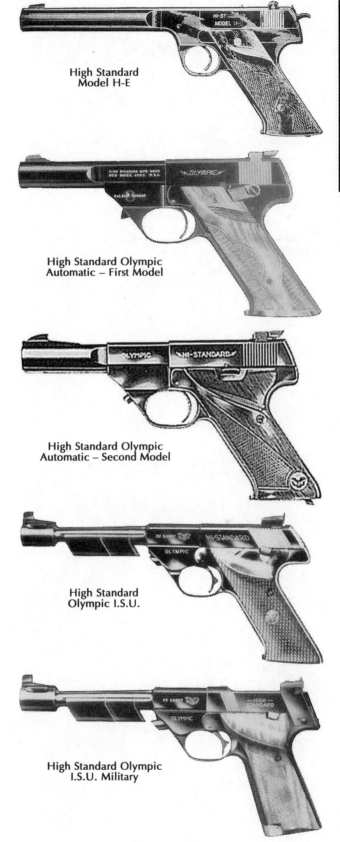

High Standard
Model H-E

High Standard Olympic
Automatic – First Model

High Standard Olympic
Automatic – Second Model

High Standard
Olympic I.S.U.

High Standard Olympic
I.S.U. Military

OLYMPIC AUTOMATIC PISTOL FIRST MODEL (G-O)
Same general specifications as Model G-E but in .22 Short w/light alloy slide. Made from 1950 to 1951.
w/one bbl. . . . . NiB $1785 Ex $1153 Gd $629
w/both bbls, add. $408

OLYMPIC AUTOMATIC
SECOND MODEL
Same general specifications as Supermatic but in .22 Short w/light alloy slide. Weight: 39 oz. (6.75-inch bbl.). Made 1951 to 1958.

OLYMPIC AUTOMATIC PISTOL,
SECOND MODEL
w/one bbl. . . . . NiB $1325 Ex $1076 Gd $730
w/both bbls, add. $306

OLYMPIC AUTOMATIC PISTOL,
THIRD MODEL. . . . . NiB $1213 Ex $984 Gd $734
Same as Supermatic Trophy w/bull bbl. except in .22 Short. Made from 1963 to 1966.

OLYMPIC COMMEMORATIVE
Limited edition of Supermatic Trophy Military issued to commemorate the only American-made rimfire target pistol ever to win an Olympic gold medal. Highly engraved w/Olympic rings inlaid in gold. Deluxe presentation case. Two versions issued: In 1972 (.22 LR) and 1980 (.22 Short).
1972 issue . . . . NiB $6523 Ex $5416 Gd $3550
1980 issue . . . . NiB $2243 Ex $1877 Gd $1215

OLYMPIC I.S.U . . . . NiB $1316 Ex $1020 Gd $798
Same as Supermatic Citation except caliber .22 Short, 6.75- or 8-inch tapered bbl. w/stabilizer, detachable weights. Made from 1958 to 1977. Eight-inch bbl. disc. in 1966.

OLYMPIC I.S.U. MILITARY . . NiB $1120 Ex $940 Gd $702
Same as Olympic I.S.U. except has military grip and bracket rear sight. Intro. in 1965. Disc.

OLYMPIC MILITARY. . . . . . . NiB $1142 Ex $932 Gd $755
Same as Olympic — Third Model except has military grip and bracket rear sight. Made in 1965.

SHARPSHOOTER
AUTOMATIC PISTOL . . . . NiB $385 Ex $267 Gd $197
Takedown. Hammerless. Caliber: .22 LR. 10-round magazine, 5.5-inch bull bbl., 9 inches overall. Weight: 42 oz. Micrometer rear sight, blade front sight. Blued finish. Plastic grips. Made from 1971 to 1983.

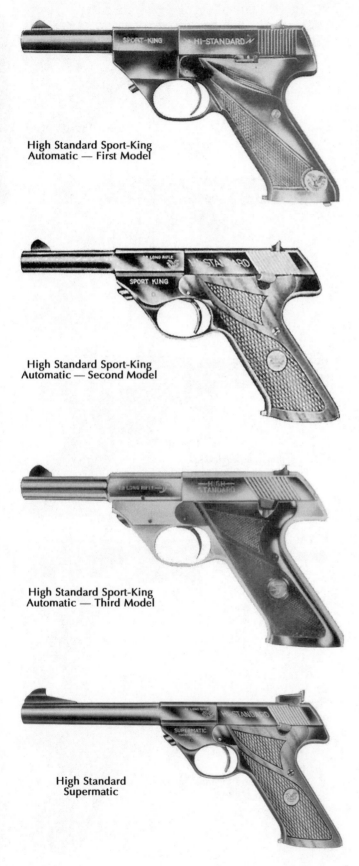

High Standard Sport-King Automatic — First Model

High Standard Sport-King Automatic — Second Model

High Standard Sport-King Automatic — Third Model

High Standard Supermatic

SPORT-KING AUTOMATIC PISTOL FIRST MODEL
Takedown. Hammerless. Interchangeable barrels. Caliber: .22 LR. 10-round magazine, barrel lengths: 4.5-, 6.75-inches. 11.5 inches overall (with 6.75-inch barrel). Weight: 39 oz. (with 6.75-inch barrel). Fixed sights. Blued finish. Checkered plastic thumbrest grips. Made from 1951 to 1958. Note: 1951 to 1954 production has lever takedown as in "G" series. Later version (illustrated at left) has push-button takedown.
w/one bbl.............. NiB $388 Ex $306 Gd $220
w/both bbls. .... NiB $590 Ex $500 Gd $408

SPORT-KING AUTOMATIC PISTOL
SECOND MODEL .... NiB $357 Ex $279 Gd $204
Caliber: .22 LR. 10-round magazine, 4.5- or 6.75 inch interchangeable bbl. 11.25 inches overall (with 6.75-inch barrel). Weight: 42 oz. (with 6.75-inch barrel). Fixed sights. Blued finish. Checkered grips. Made from 1958 to 1970.

SPORT-KING AUTOMATIC PISTOL
THIRD MODEL. .... NiB $305 Ex $204 Gd $135
Similar to Sport-King — Second Model with same general specifications for weight and length. Blued or nickel finish. Introduced in 1974. Disc.

SPORT-KING LIGHTWEIGHT
Same as standard Sport-King except lightweight has forged aluminum alloy frame. Weight: 30 oz. with 6.75-inch barrel Made from 1954 to 1965.
w/one bbl. .... NiB $590 Ex $380 Gd $255
w/both bbls................ NiB $791 Ex $602 Gd $453

SUPERMATIC AUTOMATIC PISTOL
Takedown. Hammerless. Interchangeable bbls. Caliber: .22 LR. 10-round magazine, barrel lengths: 4.5-, 6.75-inches. Late model 6.75-inch barrel have recoil stabilizer feature. Weight: 43 oz. (with 6.75-inch barrel) 11.5 inches overall (with 6.75-inch barrel). Target sights. Elevated serrated rib between sights. Adjustable barrel weights add 2 or 3 oz. Blued finish. Checkered plastic thumb-rest grips. Made from 1951 to 1958.
w/one bbl. .... NiB $872 Ex $683 Gd $509
w/both bbls.............. NiB $1070 Ex $893 Gd $714

SUPERMATIC CITATION
Same as Supermatic Tournament except 6.75-, 8- or 10-inch tapered bbl. with stabilizer and two removable weights. Also furnished with Tournament's 5.5-inch bull barrel, adjustable trigger pull, recoil-proof click-adjustable rear sight (barrel-mounted on 8- and 10-inch barrels), checkered walnut thumbrest grips on bull barrel model. Currently manufactured with only bull barrel. Made from 1958 to 1966.
With 5.5-inch
bull bbl................... NiB $893 Ex $612 Gd $377
With 6.75-inch
tapered bbl. .... NiB $893 Ex $612 Gd $377
With 8-inch
tapered bbl. .... NiB $1066 Ex $760 Gd $536
With 10-inch
tapered bbl. .... NiB $1099 Ex $811 Gd $571

High Standard Victor
Solid Rib Barrel

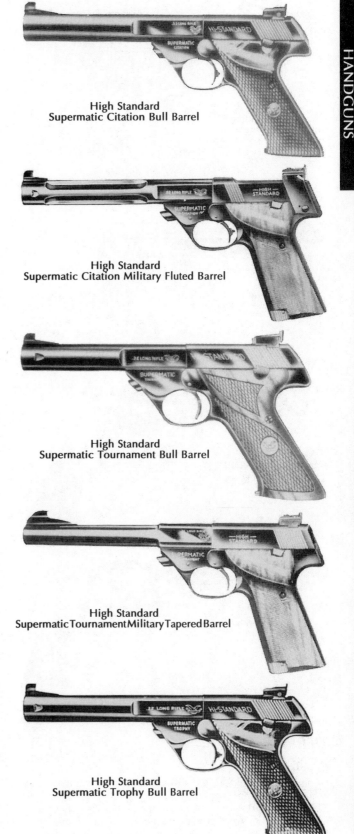

High Standard
Supermatic Citation Bull Barrel

High Standard
Supermatic Citation Military Fluted Barrel

High Standard
Supermatic Tournament Bull Barrel

High Standard
Supermatic Tournament Military Tapered Barrel

High Standard
Supermatic Trophy Bull Barrel

SUPERMATIC CITATION MILITARY

Same as Supermatic Citation except has military grip and bracket
rear sight as in Supermatic Trophy. Made from 1965 to 1973.
w/bull bbl................ NiB $897 Ex $581 Gd $499
w/fluted bbl............... NiB $964 Ex $806 Gd $602

SUPERMATIC
TOURNAMENT .... NiB $734 Ex $587 Gd $362
Takedown. Caliber: .22 LR. 10-round magazine, interchangeable
5.5-inch bull or 6.75-inch heavy tapered bbl., notched and drilled
for stabilizer and weights. 10 inches overall (with 5.5-inch bbl.).
Weight: 44 oz. (5.5-inch bbl.). Click adj. rear sight, undercut ramp
front. Blued finish. Checkered grips. Made from 1958 to 1966.

SUPERMATIC TOURNAMENT
MILITARY.............. NiB $1305 Ex $997 Gd $836
Same as Supermatic Tournament except has military grip. Made
from 1965 to 1971.

SUPERMATIC TROPHY

Same as Supermatic Citation except with 5.5-inch bull bbl., or
7.25-inch fluted bbl., w/detachable stabilizer and weights, Extra
magazine, High-luster blued finish, checkered walnut thumbrest
grips. Made from 1963 to 1966.
w/bull bbl.............. NiB $1305 Ex $1090 Gd $638
w/fluted bbl............ NiB $1305 Ex $1090 Gd $638

SUPERMATIC TROPHY MILITARY

Same as Supermatic Trophy except has military grip and bracket
rear sight. Made from 1965 to 1984.
w/bull bbl.............. NiB $1357 Ex $1060 Gd $760
w/fluted bbl............. NiB $1408 Ex $1120 Gd $813

THE VICTOR
AUTOMATIC .... NiB $3299 Ex $2798 Gd $2550
Takedown. Caliber: .22 LR. 10-round magazine, 4.5-inch solid or
vent rib and 5.5-inch vent rib, interchangeable bbl., 9.75 inches
overall (with 5.5-inch bbl.). Weight: 52 oz. (with 5.5-inch bbl.). Rib
mounted target sights. Blued finish. Checkered walnut thumbrest
grips. Standard or military grip configuration. Made from 1972 to
1984 (standard-grip model made from1974 to 1975).

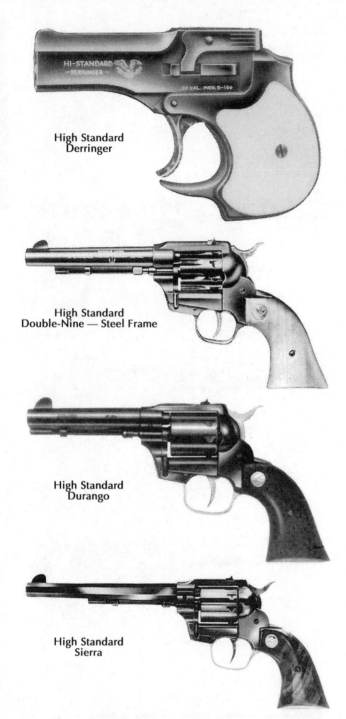

High Standard
Derringer

High Standard
Double-Nine — Steel Frame

High Standard
Durango

High Standard
Sierra

NOTE: *High Standard automatic pistols can be found in the preceding section, while revolvers immediately follow this derringer listing.*

DERRINGERS

DERRINGER
Hammerless, double action, two-round, double bbl. (over/under). Calibers: .22 Short, Long, LR or .22 Magnum Rimfire, 3.5-inch bbls., 5 inches overall. Weight: 11 oz. Standard model has blued or nickel finish w/plastic grips. Presentation model is goldplated in walnut case. Standard model made from 1963 (.22 S-L-LR) and 1964 (.22 MRF) to 1984. Gold model, made from 1965 to 1983.

Standard model (blue). . . . . . . NiB $332 Ex $225 Gd $204
Standard model (nickel) . . . . . NiB $332 Ex $225 Gd $204
Standard model
(Electroless nickel) . . . . NiB $337 Ex $291 Gd $230
Gold Presentation
One Derringer . . . . NiB $541 Ex $362 Gd $286
Silver Presentation
One Derringer . . . . NiB $592 Ex $431 Gd $342
Presentation Set, Matched pair,
consecutive numbers
(1965 only) . . . . NiB $1392 Ex $1180 Gd $836

REVOLVERS

NOTE: *Only High Standard revolvers can be found in this section. See the preceding sections for automatic pistols and derringers. For a complete listing of High Standard handguns, please refer to the IndEx.*

CAMP GUN . . . . NiB $270 Ex $220 Gd $189
Same as Sentinel Mark I/Mark IV except has 6-inch bbl., adj. rear sight, target-style checkered walnut grips. Caliber: .22 LR or .22 WMR. Made from 1976 to 1983.

DOUBLE-NINE DA REVOLVER —ALUMINUM FRAME
Western-style version of Sentinel. Blued or nickel finish w/simulated ivory, ebony or stag grips, 5.5-inch bbl., 11 inches overall. Weight: 27.25 oz. Made from 1959 to 1971.
Blue model . . . . NiB $255 Ex $190 Gd $150

DOUBLE-NINE—STEEL FRAME
Similar to Double-Nine—Aluminum Frame, w/same general specifications except w/steel frame and has Extra cylinder for .22 WMR, walnut grips. Intro. in 1971. Disc.
Blue model . . . . NiB $291 Ex $225 Gd $179
Nickel model . . . . NiB $306 Ex $225 Gd $190

DOUBLE-NINE DELUXE . . . . . NiB $326 Ex $240 Gd $198
Same as Double-Nine Steel Frame except has adj. target rear sight. Intro. in 1971. Disc.

DURANGO
Similar to Double-Nine—Steel Frame except .22 LR only, available w/4.5- or 5.5-inch bbl. Made from 1971 to 1973.
Blue model . . . . NiB $275 Ex $189 Gd $150
Nickel model . . . . NiB $301 Ex $219 Gd $170

HIGH SIERRA DA REVOLVER
Similar to Double-Nine—Steel Frame except has 7-inch octagon bbl., w/gold-plated grip frame, fixed or adj. sights. Made 1973 to 1983.
w/fixed sights . . . . NiB $352 Ex $286 Gd $214
w/adj. sights . . . . NiB $362 Ex $306 Gd $230

HOMBRE
Similar to Double-Nine—Steel Frame except .22 LR only, lacks single-action type ejector rod and tube, has 4.5-inch bbl. Made from 1971 to 1973.
Blue model . . . . NiB $281 Ex $204 Gd $143
Nickel model . . . . NiB $306 Ex $220 Gd $165

KIT GUN DA REVOLVER . . . . NiB $275 Ex $214 Gd $150
Solid frame, swing-out cylinder. Caliber: .22 LR. Nine-round cylinder, 4-inch bbl., 9 inches overall. Weight: 19 oz. Adj. rear sight, ramp front. Blued finish. Checkered walnut grips. Made from 1970 to 1973.

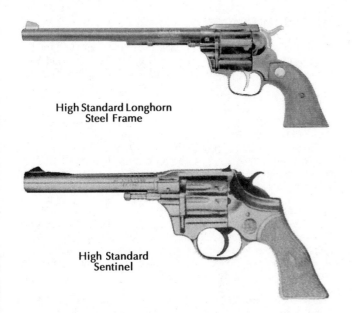

High Standard Longhorn
Steel Frame

High Standard
Sentinel

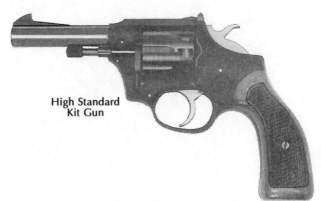

High Standard
Kit Gun

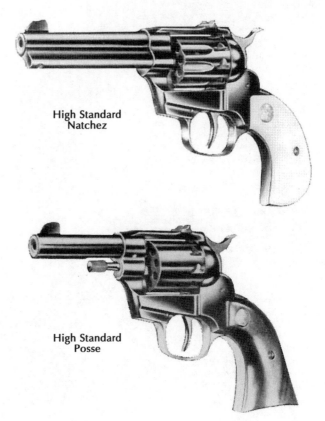

High Standard
Longhorn Aluminum Frame

High Standard
Natchez

High Standard
Posse

LONGHORN ALUMINUM FRAME
Similar to Double-Nine—Aluminum Frame except has Longhorn hammer spur, 4.5-, 5.5- or 9.5-inch bbl., Walnut, simulated pearl or simulated stag grips. Blued finish. Made from 1960 to 1971.
w/4.5- or 5.5-inch bbl. . . . . . . NiB $357 Ex $254 Gd $190
w/9.5-inch bbl . . . . NiB $357 Ex $254 Gd $190

LONGHORN STEEL FRAME
Similar to Double-Nine — Steel Frame except has 9.5-inch bbl. w/ fixed or adj. sights. Made from 1971 to 1983
w/fixed sights . . . . NiB $362 Ex $270 Gd $204
w/adj. sights . . . . NiB $377 Ex $316 Gd $229

NATCHEZ . . . . NiB $418 Ex $270 Gd $209
Similar to Double-Nine — Aluminum Frame except 4.5-inch bbl., 10 inches overall, weight: 25.25 oz., blued finish, simulated ivory bird's-head grips. Made 1961-66.

POSSE . . . . NiB $281 Ex $180 Gd $148
Similar to Double-Nine — Aluminum Frame except 3.5-inch bbl., 9 inches overall, weight: 23.25 oz. Blued finish, brass-grip frame and trigger guard, walnut grips. Made from 1961 to 1966.

SENTINEL DA REVOLVER
Solid frame, swing-out cylinder. Caliber: .22 LR. Nine-round cylinder, 3- 4- or 6-inch bbl. Nine inches overall (with 4-inch-bbl.). Weight: 19 oz. (with 4-inch bbl.). Fixed sights. Aluminum frame. Blued or nickel finish. Checkered grips. Made from 1955 to 1956.
Blue model . . . . NiB $302 Ex $156 Gd $120
Blue/green model . . . . NiB $577 Ex $439 Gd $319
Gold model . . . . NiB $555 Ex $397 Gd $317
Nickel model . . . . NiB $270 Ex $214 Gd $158
Pink model. . . . . NiB $536 Ex $306 Gd $180

SENTINEL DELUXE
Same as Sentinel except w/4- or 6-inch bbl., wide trigger, drift-adj. rear sight, two-piece square-butt grips. Made from 1957 to 1974. Note: Designated Sentinel after 1971.
Blue model . . . . NiB $270 Ex $170 Gd $128
Nickel model . . . . NiB $296 Ex $189 Gd $160

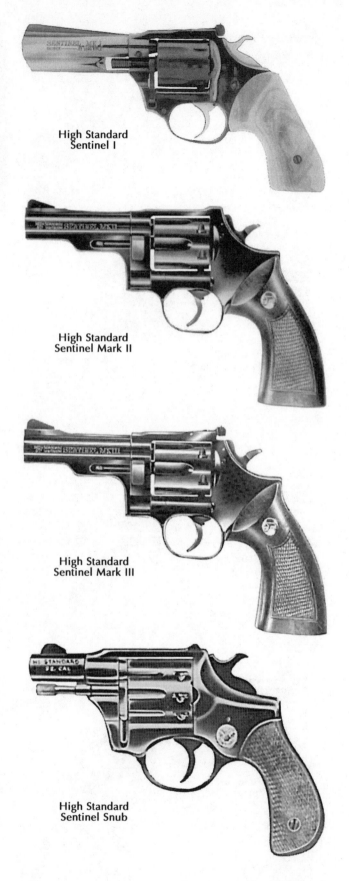

High Standard
Sentinel I

High Standard
Sentinel Mark II

High Standard
Sentinel Mark III

High Standard
Sentinel Snub

SENTINEL IMPERIAL
Same as Sentinel except has onyx-black or nickel finish, two-piece checkered walnut grips, ramp front sight. Made from 1962 to 1965.
Blue model . . . . NiB $270 Ex $179 Gd $130
Nickel model . . . . NiB $281 Ex $189 Gd $143

SENTINEL MARK 1 DA REVOLVER
Steel frame. Caliber: .22 LR. Nine-round cylinder, bbl. lengths: 2-, 3-, 4-inch, 6.88 inches overall (with 2-inch bbl.). Weight: 21.5 oz. (2-inch bbl.). Ramp front sight, fixed or adj. rear. Blued or nickel finish. Smooth walnut grips. Made from 1974 to 1983.
Blue model . . . . NiB $265 Ex $219 Gd $179
Nickel model . . . . NiB $296 Ex $255 Gd $190
w/adj. sights. . . . . NiB $337 Ex $270 Gd $225

SENTINEL MARK II
DA REVOLVER . . . . NiB $326 Ex $255 Gd $179
Caliber: .357 Magnum. Six-round cylinder, bbl. lengths: 2.5-, 4-, 6-inch, 9 inches overall w/4-inch bbl., weight: 38 oz. (with 4-inch bbl.). Fixed sights. Blued finish. Walnut service or combat-style grips. Made from 1974 to 1976.

SENTINEL MARK III . . . . NiB $326 Ex $255 Gd $175
Same as Sentinel Mark II except has ramp front and adj. rear sights. Weight: 40 oz. (with 4-inch bbl.). Blued finish. Made 1974 to 1976.

SENTINEL MARK IV
Same as Sentinel Mark I except in .22 WMR. Made 1974 to 1983.
Blue model . . . . NiB $301 Ex $230 Gd $175
Nickel model . . . . NiB $326 Ex $265 Gd $198
w/adj. sights. . . . . NiB $352 Ex $255 Gd $220

SENTINEL SNUB
Same as Sentinel Deluxe except w/2.75-inch bbl., (7.25 inches overall, weight: 15 oz.), checkered bird's head-type grips. Made 1957 to 1974.
Blued finish . . . . NiB $255 Ex $190 Gd $148
Nickel finish. . . . . NiB $274 Ex $160 Gd $109

HIGH STANDARD MFG. CO., INC. — Houston, Texas.
Distributed from Hartford, Connecticut

VICTOR 10X AUTO PISTOL . NiB $1120 Ex $840 Gd $540
Caliber: .22 LR. 10-round magazine, 5.5-inch bbl., 9.5 inches overall. Weight: 45 oz. Checkered walnut grips. Blued finish. Made from 1994 to date.

OLYMPIC I.S.U. AUTOMATIC PISTOL
Same specifications as the 1958 I.S.U. issue. See listing under previous High Standard Section.
Olympic I.S.U. model. . . . . . NiB $592 Ex $345 Gd $270
Olympic I.S.U. military model NiB $816 Ex $577 Gd $336

SPORT KING AUTO PISTOL. . . . . . NiB $694 Ex $434 Gd $305
Caliber: .22 LR. 10-round magazine, 4.5- or 6.75-inch bbl., 8.5 or 10.75 inches overall. Weight: 44 oz. (with 4.5-inch bbl.), 46 oz. (with 6.75-inch bbl.). Fixed sights, slide mounted. Checkered walnut grips. Parkerized finish. Manufactured in limited quantities.

SUPREME CITATION AUTO PISTOLNiB $536 Ex $399 Gd $254
Caliber: .22 LR. 10-round magazine, 5.5- or 7.75-inch bbl., 9.5 or 11.75 inches overall. Weight: 44 oz. (with 5.5-inch bbl.), 46 oz. (with 7.75-inch bbl.). Frame-mounted, micro-adj. rear sight, undercut ramp front sight. Blued or Parkerized finish. Made from 1994 to 2003.
.22 Short conversion. . . . . . . NiB $408 Ex $337 Gd $255

CITATION MS AUTO PISTOL . NiB $821 Ex $638 Gd $474
Similar to the Supermatic Citation except has 10-inch bbl., 14 inches overall. Weight: 49 oz. Made from 1994 to date.

SUPERMATIC TOURNAMENT. NiB $745 Ex $377 Gd $274
Caliber: .22 LR. 10-round magazine, bbl. lengths: 4.5, 5.5, or 6.75 inches, overall length: 8.5, 9.5 or 10.75 inches. Weight: 43, 44 or 45 oz. depending on bbl. length. Micro-adj. rear sight, undercut ramp front sight. Checkered walnut grips. Parkerized finish. Made from 1995 to 1997.

SUPERMATIC TROPHY. . . . . . NiB $719 Ex $356 Gd $220
Caliber: .22 LR. 10-round magazine, 5.5 or 7.25-inch bbl., 9.5 or 11.25 inches overall. Weight: 44 oz. (with 5.5-inch bbl.). Micro-adj. rear sight, undercut ramp front sight. Checkered walnut grips w/thumbrest. Blued or Parkerized finish. Made from 1994 to date.
.22 Short Conversion . . . . . . NiB $1301 Ex $890 Gd $779

VICTOR AUTOMATIC . . . . . . NiB $723 Ex $475 Gd $270
Caliber: .22 LR.10-round magazine, 4.5- or 5.5-inch ribbed bbl., 8.5 or 9.5 inches overall. Weight: 45 oz. (with 4.5-inch bbl.), 46 oz. (with 5.5-inch bbl.). Micro-adj. rear sight, post front. Checkered walnut grips. Blued or Parkerized finish. Made from 1994 to date.
.22 Short conversion. . . . . . . NiB $1193 Ex $925 Gd $780

HOPKINS & ALLEN ARMS CO. — Norwich, Connecticut

HOPKINS & ALLEN REVOLVERS
See listings of comparable Harrington & Richardson and Iver Johnson models for values.

INGRAM — Mfd. by Military Armament Corp.

See listings under M.A.C. (Military Armament Corp.)

Note: *Military Armament Corp. ceased production of the select-fire automatic, M10 (9mm & .45 ACP) and M11 (.380 ACP) in 1977. Commercial production resumed on semiautomatic versions under the M.A.C. banner until 1982.*

INTERARMS — Alexandria, Virginia
See also Bersa Pistol.

HELWAN BRIGADIER
AUTO PISTOL . . . . NiB $265 Ex $203 Gd $143
Caliber: 9mm Para. Eight-round magazine, 4.25-inch bbl., 8 inches overall. Weight: 32 oz. Blade front sight, dovetailed rear. Blued finish. Grooved plastic grips. Imported from 1987 to 1995.

VIRGINIAN DRAGOON SA REVOLVER
Calibers: .357 Magnum, .44 Magnum, .45 Colt. Six-round cylinder. Bbls.: 5- (not available in .44 Magnum), 6-, 7.5-, 8.38-inch (latter only in .44 Magnum w/adj. sights), 11.88 inches overall with (6-inch bbl.). Weight: 48 oz. (with 6-inch bbl.). Fixed sights or micrometer rear and ramp front sights. Blued finish w/color-casetreated frame. Smooth walnut grips. SWISSAFE base pin safety system. Mfg. by Interarms Industries Inc., Midland, VA. from 1977 to 1984.
Standard Dragoon. . . . . NiB $388 Ex $281 Gd $214
Engraved Dragoon . . . . NiB $785 Ex $530 Gd $362
Deputy model . . . . NiB $377 Ex $274 Gd $179
Stainless. . . . . NiB $398 Ex $265 Gd $165

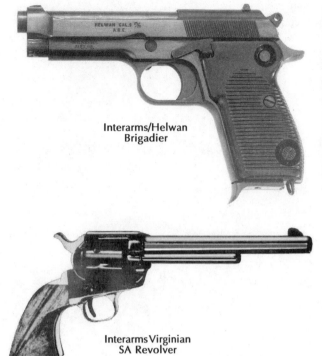

Interarms/Helwan
Brigadier

Interarms Virginian
SA Revolver

VIRGINIAN REVOLVER
SILHOUETTE MODEL. . . . . . . NiB $385 Ex $274 Gd $244
Same general specifications as regular model except designed in stainless steel w/untapered bull bbl., lengths of 7.5, 8.38 and 10.5 inches. Made from 1985 to 1986.

VIRGINIAN SA REVOLVER . . . NiB $388 Ex $270 Gd $265
Similar to Colt Single Action Army except has base pin safety system. Imported from 1973-76. (See also listing under Hämmerli.)

INTRATEC U.S.A., INC. — Miami, Florida

CATEGORY 9 DAO
SEMIAUTOMATIC . . . . NiB $270 Ex $177 Gd $120
Blowback action w/polymer frame. Caliber: 9mm Par Eight-round magazine, 3-inch bbl., 7.7 inches overall. Weight: 18 oz. TExtured black polymer grips. Matte black finish. Made from 1993 to 2000.

CATEGORY 40
DAO SEMIAUTOMATIC . . . . . NiB $270 Ex $177 Gd $120
Locking-breech action w/polymer frame. Caliber: .40 S&W. Seven-round magazine, 3.25-inch bbl., 8 inches overall. Weight: 21 oz. TExtured black polymer grips. Matte black finish. Made from 1994 to 2000.

CATEGORY 45
DAO SEMIAUTOMATIC . . . . . NiB $295 Ex $184 Gd $133
Locking-breech action w/polymer frame. Caliber: .45 ACP. Six-round magazine, 3.25-inch bbl., 8 inches overall. Weight: 21 oz. TExtured black polymer grips. Matte black finish. Made from 1994 to 2000.

Japanese
Model 14 (1925)

Japanese
Model 26 DAO Revolver

MODEL PROTEC .25 ACP DA SEMIAUTOMATIC
Caliber: .25 ACP. 10-round magazine, 2.5-inch bbl., 5 inches overall. Weight: 14 oz. Wraparound composition grips. Black Teflon, satin grey or Tec-Kote finish. Disc. 2000..
ProTec .25 standard..................NiB $128 Ex $88 Gd $61
ProTec .25 w/satin or Tec-Kote ....NiB $130 Ex $90 Gd $65

MODEL TEC-DC9 SEMIAUTOMATIC
Caliber: 9mm Para. 20- or 36-round magazine, 5-inch bbl., weight: 50-51 oz. Open fixed front sight, adj. rear. Military nonglare blued or stainless finish.
Tec-9 w/blued finish........ NiB $510 Ex $332 Gd $270
Tec-9 w/Tec Kote finish ..... NiB $546 Ex $342 Gd $301
Tec 9S w/stainless finish..... NiB $576 Ex $398 Gd $301

MODEL TEC-DC9M SEMIAUTOMATIC
Same specifications as Model Tec-9 except has 3-inch bbl. without shroud and 20-round magazine, blued or stainless finish.
Tec-9M w/blued finish ...... NiB $546 Ex $337 Gd $281
Tec-9MS w/stainless finish ... NiB $622 Ex $398 Gd $255

MODEL TEC-22T SEMIAUTOMATIC
Caliber: .22 LR. 10/.22-type 30-round magazine, 4-inch bbl., 11.19 inches overall. Weight: 30 oz. Protected post front sight, adj. rear sight. Matte black or Tec-Kote finish. Made from 1991 to 1994.
Tec-22T standard .... NiB $434 Ex $220 Gd $189
Tec-22TK Tec-Kote, add $50

TEC-38
DERRINGER............. NiB $183 Ex $129 Gd $101
Calibers: .22 Mag., .32 H&R Mag., .357 Mag., .38 Special. Two-round capacity, 3-inch blued bbl., 4.63 inches overall. Weight: 13 oz. Fixed sights. Synth. black frame. Double-action. Made from 1986 to 1988.

ISRAEL ARMS — Kfar Sabs, Israel. Imported by Israel Arms International, Houston TX

MODEL BUL-M5 LOCKED
BREECH (2000) AUTO PISTOL NiB $398 Ex $235 Gd $148
Similar to the M1911 U.S. Government model. Caliber: .45 ACP. Seven-round magazine, 5-inch bbl., 8.5 inches overall. Weight: 38 oz. Blade front and fixed, low-profile rear sights.

KAREEN MK II (1500) AUTO PISTOL
Single-action only. Caliber: 9mm Para. 10-round magazine, 4.75-inch bbl., 8 inches overall. Weight: 33.6 oz. Blade front sight, rear adjustable for windage. TExtured black composition or rubberized grips. Blued, two-tone, matte black finish. Imported from 1997 to 1998.
Blued or matte black finish... NiB $386 Ex $301 Gd $219
Two-tone finish .... NiB $556 Ex $386 Gd $304
Meprolite sights, add $50

KAREEN MK II COMPACT
(1501) AUTO PISTOL....... NiB $386 Ex $290 Gd $204
Similar to standard Kareen MKII except w/3.85-inch bbl., 7.1 inches overall. Weight: 32 oz. Imported 1999 to 2000.

GOLAN MODEL (2500) AUTO PISTOL
Single or double action. Caliber: 9mm Para., .40 S&W. 10-round magazine, 3.85-inch bbl., 7.1 inches overall. Weight: 34 oz. Steel slide and alloy frame w/ambidExtrous safety and decocking lever. Matte black finish. Imported 1999.
9mm Para................ NiB $954 Ex $755 Gd $536
.40 S&W .... NiB $954 Ex $755 Gd $536

GAL MODEL
(5000) AUTO PISTOL....... NiB $437 Ex $289 Gd $220
Caliber: .45 ACP. Eight-round magazine, 4.25-inch bbl., 7.25 inches overall. Weight: 42 oz. Low profile 3-dot sights. Combat-style black rubber grips. Imported from 1999 to 2001.

JAPANESE MILITARY PISTOLS — Tokyo, Japan. Manufactured by Government Plant

MODEL 14 (1925)
AUTOMATIC PISTOL ..... NiB $1423 Ex $1009 Gd $658
Modification of the Nambu Model 1914, changes chiefly intended to simplify mass production. Standard round trigger guard or oversized guard for use w/gloves. Caliber: 8mm Nambu. Eight-round magazine, 4.75-inch bbl., 9 inches overall. Weight: About 29 oz. Fixed sights. Blued finish. Grooved wood grips. Intro. 1925 and mfd. through WW II.

MODEL 26 DAO REVOLVER NiB $1586 Ex $1120 Gd $779
Top-break frame. Caliber: 9mm. Six-round cylinder w/automatic Extractor/ejector, 4.7-inch bbl., adopted by the Japanese Army from 1893 to 1914, replaced by the Model 14 Automatic Pistol but remained in service through World War II.

MODEL 94 (1934)
AUTOMATIC PISTOL . . . . NiB $780 Ex $464 Gd $342
Poorly designed and constructed, this pistol is unsafe and can be fired merely by applying pressure on the sear, which is Exposed on the left side. Caliber: 8mm Nambu. Six-round magazine, 3.13-inch bbl., 7.13 inches overall. Weight: About 27 oz. Fixed sights. Blued finish. Hard rubber or wood grips. Intro. in 1934, principally for Export to Latin American countries, production continued thru WW II.

NAMBU MODEL
1914 AUTOMATIC PISTOL. . NiB $1389 Ex $989 Gd $785
Original Japanese service pistol, resembles Luger in appearance and Glisenti in operation. Caliber: 8mm Nambu. Seven-round magazine, 4.5-inch bbl., 9 inches overall. Weight: About 30 oz. Fixed front sight, adj. rear sight. Blued finish. Checkered wood grips. Made from 1914 to 1925.

Japanese Model 94 (1934)

JENNINGS FIREARMS INC. — Currently Manufactured by Bryco Arms, Irvine, California. Previously by Calwestco, Inc. & B.L. Jennings
See additional listings under Bryco Arms.

MODEL J-22 AUTO PISTOL
Calibers: .22 LR, .25 ACP. Six-round magazine, 2.5-inch bbl., about 5 inches overall. Weight: 13 oz. Fixed sights. Chrome, satin nickel or black Teflon finish. Walnut, grooved black Cycolac or resin-impregnated wood grips. Made from 1981-85 under Jennings and Calwestco logos; disc. 1985 by Bryco Arms.
Model J-22. . . . . NiB $81 Ex $50 Gd $40
Model J-25. . . . . NiB $91 Ex $61 Gd $50

Jennings Model J Auto Pistol

IVER JOHNSON ARMS, INC. — Jacksonville, Arkansas

Operation of this company dates back to 1871, when Iver Johnson and Martin Bye partnered to manufacture metallic cartridge revolvers. Johnson became the sole owner and changed the name to Iver Johnson's Arms & Cycle Works, which it was known as for almost 100 years. Modern management shortened the name, and after several owner changes the firm was moved from Massachusetts, its original base, to Jacksonville, Arkansas. In 1987, the American Military Arms Corporation (AMAC) acquired the operation, which subsequently ceased in 1993.

NOTE: *For ease in finding a particular firearm, Iver Johnson handguns are divided into two sections: Automatic Pistols (below) and Revolvers, which follow. For the complete handgun listing, please refer to the Index.*

AUTOMATIC PISTOLS

9MM DA AUTOMATIC. . . . . NiB $474 Ex $357 Gd $265
Caliber: 9mm. Six-round magazine, 3-inch bbl., 6.5 inches overall. Weight: 26 oz. Blade front sight, adj. rear. Smooth hardwood grip. Blued or matte blued finish. Intro. 1986.

COMPACT .25 ACP . . . . NiB $273 Ex $190 Gd $148
Bernardelli V/P design. Caliber: .25 ACP. Five-round magazine, 2.13-inch bbl., 4.13 inches overall. Weight: 9.3 oz. Fixed sights. Checkered composition grips. Blued slide, matte blued frame and color-casehardened trigger. Made from 1991 to 1993.

Iver Johnson Enforcer

ENFORCER. . . . . NiB $893 Ex $643 Gd $431
Semiautomatic. Caliber: .30 U.S. Carbine. Five-, 15-, or 30-round magazine, 9.5- inch bbl., weight: 5.5 lbs. Adj. sights. Walnut stock. Made 1986.

I.J. SUPER
ENFORCER AUTOMATIC . . . . NiB $893 Ex $643 Gd $431
Caliber: .30 U.S. Carbine. Fifteen- or 30-round magazine, 9.5-inch bbl., 17 inches overall. Weight: 4 pounds. Adj. peep rear sight, blade front. American walnut stock. Made from 1978 to 1993.

PONY AUTOMATIC PISTOL
Caliber: .380 Auto. Six-round magazine, 3.1-inch bbl., 6.1 inches overall. Blue, matte blue, nickel finish or stainless. Weight: 20 oz. Wooden grips. Smallest of the locked breech automatics. Made from 1982-88. Reintroduced from 1989 to 1991.
Blue or matte
blue model. . . . . NiB $434 Ex $342 Gd $270
Nickel model . . . . NiB $464 Ex $345 Gd $290
Deluxe model. . . . . NiB $464 Ex $377 Gd $281

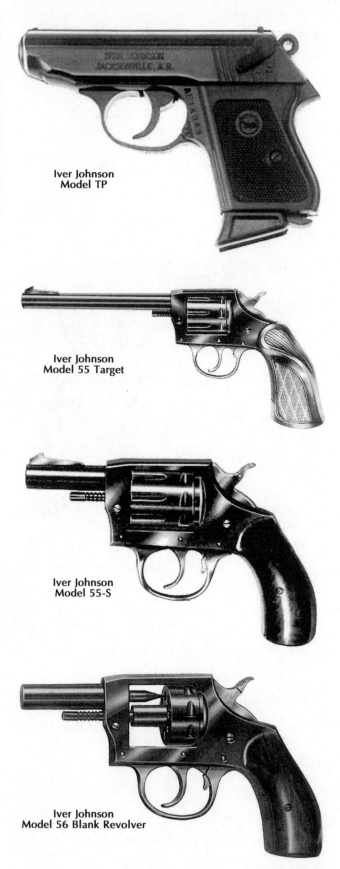

Iver Johnson
Model TP

Iver Johnson
Model 55 Target

Iver Johnson
Model 55-S

Iver Johnson
Model 56 Blank Revolver

Iver Johnson
Model 57A Target

MODEL TP-22 DA
AUTOMATIC . . . . NiB $316   Ex $219   Gd $160
Calibers: .22 LR, Seven-round magazine, 2.85-inch bbl., 5.39 inches overall. Blued finish. Weight: 14.46 oz. Made from 1982 to 1989.

MODEL TP25 DA
POCKET PISTOL . . . . NiB $271   Ex $190   Gd $143
Double-action automatic. Caliber: .25 ACP. Seven-round magazine, 3-inch bbl., 5.5 inches overall. Weight: 12 oz. Black plastic grips and blued finish. Made from 1981 to 1982.

TRAILSMAN AUTOMATIC PISTOL
Caliber: .22 LR. 10-round magazine, 4.5 or 6-inch bbl., 8.75 inches overall (with 4.5-inch bbl.). Weight: 46 oz. Fixed target-type sights. Checkered composition grips. Made from 1985 to 1991.
Standard model . . . . NiB $306   Ex $220   Gd $160
Deluxe model. . . . . NiB $321   Ex $230   Gd $170

REVOLVERS

MODEL 55 TARGET DA REVOLVER . NiB $237   Ex $160   Gd $115
Solid frame. Caliber: .22 LR. Eight-round cylinder, bbl. lengths: 4.5-, 6-inches. 10.75 inches overall (with 6-inch bbl.). Weight: 30.5 oz. (with 6-inch bbl.). Fixed sights. Blued finish. Walnut grips. Note: Original model designation was 55; changed to 55A when loading gate was added in 1961. Made from 1955 to 1960.

MODEL 55-S REVOLVER . . . . NiB $265   Ex $165   Gd $110
Same general specifications as the Model 55 except for 2.5-inch bbl. and small, molded pocket-size grip.

MODEL 56
BLANK REVOLVER . . . . NiB $128   Ex $81   Gd $55
Solid frame. Caliber: .22 blanks only. Eight-round cylinder, 2.5-inch solid bbl., 6.75 inches overall. Weight: 10 oz.

MODEL 57A
TARGET DA REVOLVER . . . . . NiB $255   Ex $143   Gd $101
Solid frame. Caliber: .22 LR. Eight-round cylinder, bbl. lengths: 4.5, and 6-inches. 10.75 inches overall. Weight: 30.5 oz. with 6-inch bbl. Adj. sights. Blued finish. Walnut grips. Note: Original model designation was 57, changed to 57A when loading gate was added in 1961. Made from 1961 to 1978.

TRAILSMAN
DA REVOLVER . . . . NiB $306   Ex $209   Gd $160
Hinged frame. Rebounding hammer. Caliber: .22 LR. Eight-round cylinder, 6-inch bbl., 11 inches overall. Weight: 34 oz. Adj. sights. Blued finish. Walnut grips. Made from 1985 to 1991.

Iver Johnson
Model 66 Trailsman

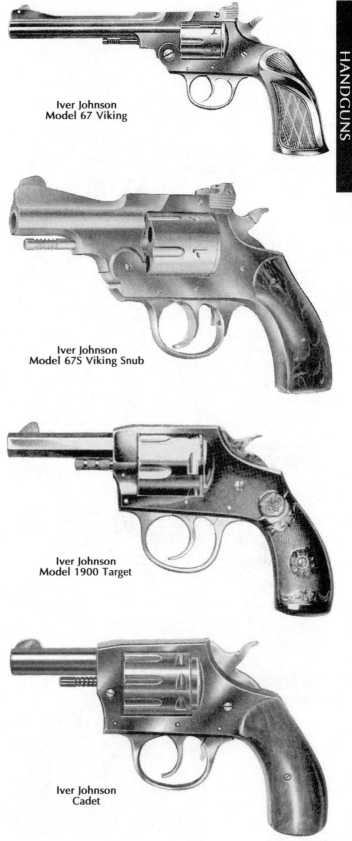

Iver Johnson
Model 67 Viking

Iver Johnson
Model 67S Viking Snub

Iver Johnson
Model 1900 Target

Iver Johnson
Cadet

MODEL 67 VIKING DA REVOLVER. . NiB $273 Ex $165 Gd $110
Hinged frame. Caliber: .22 LR. Eight-round cylinder, bbl. lengths: 4.5-
and 6-inches, 11 inches overall (with 6-inch bbl.). Weight: 34 oz. (with
6-inch bbl.). Adj. sights. Walnut grips w/thumbrest. Made 1964 to 1978.

**MODEL 67S VIKING
SNUB REVOLVER. . . . . NiB $286 Ex $189 Gd $179**
DA. Hinged frame. Calibers: .22 LR, .32 S&W Short and Long, .38 S&W.
Eight-round cylinder in .22, 5-round in .32 and .38 calibers; 2.75-inch
bbl. Weight: 25 oz. Adj. sights. Tenite grips. Made from 1964 to 1978.

MODEL 1900 DA REVOLVER . . . NiB $158 Ex $90 Gd $65
Solid frame. Calibers: .22 LR, .32 S&W, .32 S&W Long, .38 S&W.
Seven-round cylinder in .22 cal. , 6-round (.32 S&W), 5-round (.32
S&W Long, .38 S&W); bbl. lengths: 2.5-, 4.5- and 6-inches. Weight:
12 oz. (in .32 S&W w/2.5-inch bbl.). Fixed sights. Blued or nickel
finish. Hard rubber grips. Made from 1900 to 1941.

**MODEL 1900
TARGET DA REVOLVER . . . . . NiB $222 Ex $175 Gd $135**
Solid frame. Caliber: .22 LR. Seven-round cylinder, bbl. lengths: 6-
and 9.5-inches. Fixed sights. Blued finish. Checkered walnut grips.
(This earlier model does not have counterbored chambers as in the
Target Sealed 8. Made from 1925 to 1942.)

AMERICAN BULLDOG DA REVOLVER
Solid frame. Calibers: .22 LR, .22 WMR, .38 Special. Six-round
cylinder in .22, 5-round in .38. Bbl. lengths: 2.5-, 4-inch. 9 inches
overall (with 4-inch bbl.). Weight: 30 oz. (with 4-inch bbl.). Adj.
sights. Blued or nickel finish. Plastic grips. Made from 1974 to 1976.
.38 Special. . . . . NiB $464 Ex $286 Gd $204
Other calibers . . . . NiB $464 Ex $286 Gd $204

ARMSWORTH MODEL 855 SA NiB $464 Ex $290 Gd $198
Hinged frame. Caliber: .22 LR. Eight-round cylinder, 6-inch bbl., 10.75
inches overall. Weight: 30 oz. Adj. sights. Blued finish. Checkered walnut one-piece grip. Adj. finger rest. Made from 1955 to 1957.

CADET DA REVOLVER . . . . . . NiB $255 Ex $165 Gd $101
Solid frame. Calibers: .22 LR, .22 WMR, .32 S&W Long, .38 S&W, .38
Special. Six- or 8-round cylinder in .22, 5-round in other calibers, 2.5-
inch bbl., 7 inches overall. Weight: 22 oz. Fixed sights. Blued finish or
nickel finish. Plastic grips. Note: Loading gate added in 1961, .22 cylinder capacity changed from 8 to 6 rounds in 1975. Made 1955 to 1977.

CATTLEMAN SA REVOLVER . . NiB $369 Ex $301 Gd $170
Patterned after the Colt Army SA revolver. Calibers: .357 Magnum, .44
Magnum, .45 Colt. Six-round cylinder. Bbl. lengths: 4.75-, 5.5- (not available in .44), 6- (.44 only), 7.25-inch. Weight: About 41 oz. Fixed sights.
Blued bbl., and cylinder color-casehardened frame, brass grip frame. One-
piece walnut grip. Made by Aldo Uberti, Brescia, Italy, from 1973 to 1978.
.44 Magnum, add. $50

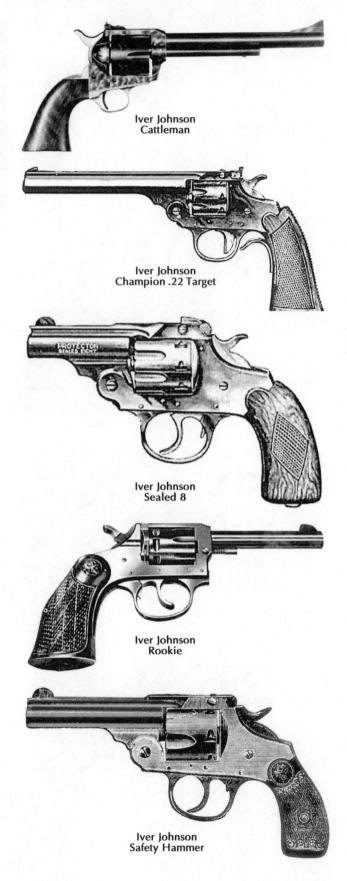

Iver Johnson
Cattleman

Iver Johnson
Champion .22 Target

Iver Johnson
Sealed 8

Iver Johnson
Rookie

Iver Johnson
Safety Hammer

CATTLEMAN BUCKHORN SA REVOLVER
Same as standard Cattleman except has adj. rear and ramp front sights. Bbl. lengths: 4.75- (.44 only), 5.75- (not available in .44), 6- (.44 only), 7.5- or 12-inches bbl., weight: About 44 oz. Made from 1973 to 1978.

.357 Magnum or .45
Colt w/12-inch bbl. . . . . NiB $439 Ex $326 Gd $219
.357 Magnum or .45
Colt w/5.75- or 7.5-inch bbl. . NiB $342 Ex $255 Gd $158
.44 Magnum, w/12-inch bbl. . . NiB $459 Ex $367 Gd $279
.44 Magnum, other bbls. . . . . . NiB $439 Ex $326 Gd $219

CATTLEMAN BUNTLINE SA REVOLVER
Same as Cattleman Buckhorn except has 18-inch bbl., walnut shoulder stock w/brass fittings. Weight: About 56 oz. Made from 1973 to 1978.

.44 Magnum. . . . . NiB $443 Ex $332 Gd $225
Other calibers . . . . NiB $443 Ex $332 Gd $225

CATTLEMAN
TRAIL BLAZER . . . . NiB $377 Ex $274 Gd $189
Similar to Cattleman Buckhorn except .22 caliber has interchangeable .22 LR and .22 WMR cylinders, 5.5- or 6.5-inch bbl., weight: About 40 oz. Made from 1973 to 1978.

CHAMPION 822
.22 TARGET SA . . . . NiB $499 Ex $326 Gd $175
Hinged frame. Caliber: .22 LR. Eight-round cylinder. Single action. Counterbored chambers as in Sealed 8 model, 6-inch bbl., 10.75 inches overall. Weight: 28 oz. Adj. target sights. Blued finish. Checkered walnut grips, adj. finger rest. Made from 1938 to 1948.

DELUXE TARGET . . . . NiB $305 Ex $225 Gd $175
Same as Sportsman except has adj. sights. Made from 1975 to 1976.

PROTECTOR SEALED 8
DA REVOLVER. . . . . NiB $453 Ex $337 Gd $204
Hinged frame. Caliber: .22 LR. Eight-round cylinder, 2.5-inch bbl., 7.25 inches overall. Weight: 20 oz. Fixed sights. Blued finish. Checkered walnut grips. Made from 1933 to 1949.

ROOKIE
DA REVOLVER. . . . . NiB $270 Ex $204 Gd $90
Solid frame. Caliber: .38 Special. Five-round cylinder, 4-inch bbl., 9-inches overall. Weight: 30 oz. Fixed sights. Blued or nickel finish. Plastic grips. Made from 1975 to 1977.

SAFETY HAMMER
DA REVOLVER. . . . . NiB $342 Ex $170 Gd $105
Hinged frame. Calibers: .22 LR, .32 S&W, .32 S&W Long, .38 S&W. Seven-round cylinder in .22 cal.,or 6-round (.32 S&W Long), 5-round (.32 S&W, .38 S&W). bbl. lengths: 2, 3, 3.25, 4, 5 or 6 inches. Weight w/4-inch bbl.: 15 oz. (.22, .32 S&W), 19.5 oz. (.32 S&W Long) or 19 oz. (.38 S&W). Fixed sights. Blued or nickel finish. Hard rubber, round butt grips or square butt, rubber or walnut grips available. Note: .32 S&W Long and .38 S&W models built on heavy frame. Made from 1892 to 1950.

SAFETY HAMMERLESS
DA REVOLVER. . . . . NiB $337 Ex $219 Gd $129
Similar to the Safety Hammer Model except w/shrouded hammerless frame. Made from 1895 to 1950.

SIDEWINDER
DA REVOLVER . . . . **NiB $281 Ex $179 Gd $110**
Solid frame. Caliber: .22 LR. Six- or 8-round cylinder, bbl. lengths: 4.75, 6 inches; 11.25 inches overall (with 6-inch bbl.). Weight: 31 oz. (with 6-inch bbl.). Fixed sights. Blued or nickel finish w/plastic staghorn grips or color-casehardened frame w/ walnut grips. Note: Cylinder capacity changed from 8 to 6 rounds in 1975. Made from1961 to 1978

SIDEWINDER "S"
. . . . **NiB $281 Ex $179 Gd $110**
Same as Sidewinder except has interchangeable cylinders in .22 LR and .22 WMR, adj. sights. Intro. 1974. Disc.

SPORTSMAN
DA REVOLVER . . . . **NiB $222 Ex $165 Gd $109**
Solid frame. Caliber: .22 LR. Six-round cylinder. Bbl. lengths: 4.75-, 6-inches, 10.75 inches overall (with 6-inch bbl.). Weight: 30.5 oz. (with 6-inch bbl.). Fixed sights. Blued finish. Plastic grips. Made 1974 to 1976.

SUPERSHOT .22 DA REVOLVER
NiB $273 Ex $175 Gd $119
Hinged frame. Caliber: .22 LR. Seven-round cylinder, 6-inch bbl. Fixed sights. Blued finish. Checkered walnut grips. This earlier model does not have counterbored chambers as in the Supershot Sealed 8. Made from 1929 to 1949.

SUPERSHOT 9
DA REVOLVER . . . . **NiB $273 Ex $175 Gd $119**
Same as Supershot Sealed 8 except has nine non-counterbored chambers. Made from 1929 to 1949.

SUPERSHOT MODEL 844 DA
NiB $336 Ex $204 Gd $129
Hinged frame. Caliber: .22 LR. Eight-round cylinder, bbl. lengths: 4.5- or 6-inch, 9.25 inches overall (with 4.5-inch bbl.). Weight: 27 oz. (4.5-inch bbl.). Adj. sights. Blued finish. Checkered walnut one-piece grip. Made from 1955 to 1956.

SUPERSHOT SEALED
8 DA REVOLVER . . . . **NiB $316 Ex $180 Gd $140**
Hinged frame. Caliber: .22 LR. Eight-round cylinder, 6-inch bbl., 10.75 inches overall. Weight: 24 oz. Adj. target sights. Blued finish. Checkered walnut grips. Postwar model does not have adj. finger rest as earlier version. Made from 1931 to 1957.

SWING-OUT DA REVOLVER
Calibers: .22 LR, .22 WMR, .32 S&W Long, .38 Special. Six-round cylinder in .22, 5-round in .32 and .38. Two, 3-, 4-inch plain bbl., or 4- 6-inch vent rib bbl., 8.75 inches overall (with 4-inch bbl.). Fixed or adj. sights. Blue or nickel finish. Walnut grips. Made in 1977.
w/plain barrel, fixed sights . . . **NiB $220 Ex $158 Gd $115**
w/vent rib, adj. sights . . . . **NiB $204 Ex $148 Gd $110**

TARGET 9 DA REVOLVER
. . . . **NiB $265 Ex $180 Gd $135**
Same as Target Sealed 8 except has nine non-counterbored chambers. Made from 1929 to 1946.

TARGET SEALED 8 DA REVOLVER
. . **NiB $273 Ex $166 Gd $135**
Solid frame. Caliber: .22 LR. Eight-round cylinder, bbl. lengths: 6- and 10-inches. 10.75 inches overall (with 6-inch bbl.). Weight: 24 oz. (with 6-inch bbl.). Fixed sights. Blued finish. Checkered walnut grips. Made from 1931 to 1957.

TRIGGER-COCKING SA TARGET
. . . **NiB $321 Ex $239 Gd $187**
Hinged frame. First pull on trigger cocks hammer, second pull releases hammer. Caliber: .22 LR. Eight-round cylinder, counterbored chambers, 6-inch bbl., 10.75 inches overall. Weight: 24 oz. Adj. target sights. Blued finish. Checkered walnut grips. Made 1940 to 1947.

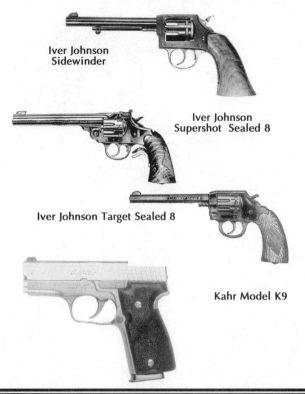

Iver Johnson Sidewinder

Iver Johnson Supershot Sealed 8

Iver Johnson Target Sealed 8

Kahr Model K9

KAHR ARMS — Worcester, Massachusetts
FORMERLY Pearl River, New York

MODEL K9 DAO AUTO PISTOL
Caliber: 9mm Para. Seven-round magazine, 3.5-inch bbl., 6 inches overall. Weight: 24 oz. Fixed sights. Matte black, electroless nickel, Birdsong Black-T or matte stainless finish. Wraparound textured polymer or hardwood grips. Made from 1994 to 2003.

Duo-Tone finish	NiB $587	Ex $464	Gd $321
Electroless nickel finish	NiB $657	Ex $577	Gd $395
Black-T finish	NiB $740	Ex $602	Gd $464
Matte stainless finish	NiB $785	Ex $631	Gd $453
Kahr Lady K9 model	NiB $530	Ex $345	Gd $270
Elite model	NiB $836	Ex $610	Gd $399
Tritium Night Sights, add			$100

MODEL K40 DAO AUTO PISTOL
Similar to Model K9 except chambered .40 S&W w/5- or 6-round magazine, Weight: 26 oz. Made from 1997 to 2003.

Matte black finish	NiB $590	Ex $433	Gd $321
Electroless nickel finish	NiB $668	Ex $595	Gd $395
Black-T finish	NiB $740	Ex $562	Gd $362
Matte black stainless finish . . .	NiB $653	Ex $485	Gd $345
Covert model (shorter grip-frame)	NiB $536	Ex $395	Gd $306
Elite model	NiB $826	Ex $602	Gd $437
Tritium Night Sights, add			$100

MODEL K9 DAO AUTO PISTOL
Similar to Model K9 except w/Micro-Compact frame. Six- or 7-round magazine, 3- inch bbl., 5.5 inches overall. Weight: 22 oz. Stainless or Duo-Tone finish. Made from 1993 to 2003.

Duo-Tone finish	NiB $665	Ex $530	Gd $398
Matte stainless finish	NiB $437	Ex $347	Gd $301
Elite model	NiB $830	Ex $544	Gd $429
Tritium Night Sights, add			$100

Kel-Tec Model P-11

Kimber Model Classic .45

CW series DAO Auto Pistol. . . NiB $425 Ex $325 Gd $250
Caliber: 9mm Para., .40 S&W, .45 ACP. Seven-round magazine (9mm Para), 3.6-inch bbl., 6 inches overall. Weight: 15.8 oz. Fixed sights. Textured black polymer frame, matte stainless steel slide. Made from 2005 (9mm para), 2008 (.40 S&W, .45 ACP).

CM series DAO Auto Pistol. . . NiB $450 Ex $350 Gd $250
Caliber: 9mm Para., .40 S&W, .45 ACP. Six-round magazine (9mm Para), 3-inch bbl., 6 inches overall. Weight: 15.8 oz. Fixed sights. Textured black polymer frame, matte stainless steel slide. Made from 2011 (9mm para), 2012 (.40 S&W), 2013 (.45 ACP).

E9 DAO Auto Pistol . . . . NiB $425 Ex $340 Gd $250
Caliber: 9mm Para. Seven-round magazine, 3.5-inch bbl., 6 inches overall. Weight: 15.8 oz. Fixed sights. Textured black polymer frame. Made from 1997, reintro. 2003.

MK Micro series DAO Auto PistolNiB $450 Ex $350 Gd $250
Caliber: 9mm Para., .40 S&W. Six-round magazine (9mm para), 3-inch bbl., 5.5 inches overall. Weight: 15.8 oz. Fixed sights., Matte stainless steel slide and frame. Made from 1998-99 (9mm para), intro. 1999 (.40 S&W).

T series DAO Auto Pistol . . . . NiB $600 Ex $450 Gd $290
Caliber: 9mm Para., .40 S&W. 8-round magazine (9mm para), 4-inch bbl., 6.5 inches overall. Weight: 26 oz. Fixed sights., Matte stainless steel slide and frame, wood grips. Made from 2002 (9mm para), 2004 (.40 S&W).

TP series DAO Auto Pistol . . . NiB $500 Ex $430 Gd $285
Similar to T series except polymer frame and matte stainless steel slide. Made from 2004.

KBI, INC — Harrisburg, Pennsylvania

MODEL PSP-.25 AUTO PISTOLNiB $308 Ex $244 Gd $157
Caliber: .25 ACP. Six-round magazine, 2.13-inch bbl., 4.13 inches overall. Weight: 9.5 oz. All-steel construction w/dual safety system. Made 1994.

KEL-TECCNCINDUSTRIES,INC.—Cocoa,Florida

MODEL P-11 DAO PISTOL
Caliber: 9mm Parabellum or .40 S&W. 10-round magazine, 3.1-inch bbl., 5.6 inches overall. Weight: 14 oz. Blade front sight, drift adjustable rear. Aluminum frame w/steel slide. Checkered black, gray, or green polymer grips. Matte blue, nickel, stainless steel or Parkerized finish. Made from 1995 to date.
9mm . . . . NiB $305 Ex $214 Gd $156
.40 S&W . . . . NiB $590 Ex $399 Gd $243

Parkerized finish, add $75
Nickel finish (disc. 1995) add $75
Stainless finish, (1996 to date) add $75
Tritium Night Sights, add $90
.40 S&W conversion kit, add $204

P-32 . . . . NiB $291 Ex $170 Gd $90
Semi-auto, double-action. Cal.: .32 ACP. Internal block safety. 7-round mag. Bbl.: 2.68 inches; Parkerized, blue, or chrome finish. Choice of ivory or colored grips. Weight: 6.6 oz.

P-3AT . . . . NiB $301 Ex $180 Gd $95
Similar to P-32. Cal.: .380 ACP. Bbl.: 2.76 inches. 6-round mag. Black composite frame with Parkerized steel slide. Weight: 8.3 oz.

P-40 . . . . NiB $290 Ex $175 Gd $88
Semi-auto, double-action. 9- or 10-round mag. Composite frame with steel slide. Bbl.: 3.3 inches. Parkerized, blue, or chrome finish. Made from 1999 to 2001.
Parkerized finish, add $50
Hard chrome finish, add. $70

PLR-16 . . . . NiB $638 Ex $495 Gd $281
M-16-type gas operated. Cal.: .223 Rem., 10-round mag. Bbl.: 9.2 inches. Upper w/Picatinny accessory rail. Black composite frame. Weight: 3.2 lbs.

PLR-22 . . . . NiB $357 Ex $265 Gd $170
Similar to PLR-16 except in .22 LR; 26-round mag. Weight: 2.8 lbs.

PF-9 . . . . NiB $306 Ex $198 Gd $143
Similar to P-11, cal.: 9 mm Para. Bbl.: 3.1 inches. 7-round mag., lower accessory rail. Black finish. Weight: 12.7 oz. Limited production in 2006, reintro. 2008.
Parkerized finish, add. $50
Hard chrome finish, add. $65

PMR-30 . . . . NiB $408 Ex $301 Gd $189
Cal.: .22 Mag. Bbl.: 4.3 inches. 30-round mag, blowback action, manual safety. Black finished aluminum frame. Lower Picatinny accessory rail. Steel slide and bbl., fiber optic sights. Weight: 19.5 oz.

KIMBERMANUFACTURING,INC.—Yonkers, New York (formerly Kimber of America, Inc.)

MODEL CLASSIC .45
Similar to Government 1911 built on steel, polymer or alloy full-size or compact frame. Caliber: .45 ACP. Seven-, 8-, 10- or 14-round magazine, 4- or 5-inch bbl., 7.7 or 8.75 inches overall. Weight: 28 oz. (Compact LW), 34 oz. (Compact or Polymer) or .38 oz. (Custom FS). McCormick low-profile combat or Kimber adj. target sights. Blued, matte black oxide or stainless finish. Checkered custom wood or black synthetic grips. Made from 1994 to date.
Custom (matte black) . . . . NiB $882 Ex $599 Gd $431
Custom Royal (polished blue) . NiB $774 Ex $612 Gd $443
Custom stainless (satin stainless)NiB $737 Ex $577 Gd $439
Custom Target (matte black) . . NiB $755 Ex $581 Gd $453
Target Gold Match
(polished blue) . . . . NiB $1020 Ex $755 Gd $587
Target stainless Match
(polished stainless) . . . . NiB $852 Ex $669 Gd $474
Polymer (matte black) . . . . NiB $852 Ex $669 Gd $474
Polymer Stainless
(satin stainless slide) . . . . NiB $967 Ex $784 Gd $577
Polymer Target
(matte black slide) . . . . NiB $918 Ex $744 Gd $536
Compact (matte black) . . . . . . NiB $644 Ex $541 Gd $377
Compact stainless (satin stainless) . . . NiB $714 Ex $559 Gd $437
Compact LW (matte
black w/alloy frame) . . . . NiB $733 Ex $577 Gd $408

SERIES II MODELS

Similar to Classic 1911 models except includes firing pin block safety and denoted with "II" following all model names. Size configurations vary per model and include from smallest to largest: Micro (2.75-in. bbl., micro frame), Ultra (3-in. bbl., short frame), Ultra+ (3-in. bbl., full size frame), Compact (4-in. bbl., short frame), Pro (4-in. bbl., full size frame), Custom (5-in. bbl., full size frame). Made from 2001 to date.

Model	NiB	Ex	Gd
Aegis II (intro. 2006)	$1200	$1140	$840
CDP II (intro. 2000)	$1150	$1095	$805
Compact II	$960	$912	$500
Covert II (intro. 2007)	$1450	$1100	$650
Crimson Cary II (laser grip)	$1050	$900	$735
Custom II	$730	$525	$330
Custom II Stainless	$855	$655	$365
Custom Royal II	$1900	$1000	$580
Eclipse II (intro. 2002)	$1100	$1045	$570
Gold Match II	$1300	$1000	$580
Master Carry II (intro. 2013)	$1330	$1265	$931
Micro Carry (intro. 2013, .380 ACP)	$580	$475	$375
Raptor II (intro. 2004)	$1300	$1235	$910
Super Carry II (intro. 2010)	$1350	$1285	$945
Tactical II (intro. 2003)	$1130	$1075	$795
Ultra Carry II (intro. 1999)	$800	$760	$560
Custom Royal II	$1900	$1000	$580

KORTH PISTOLS — Lollar Germany. Previously Ratzeburg, Germany.

Currently imported by Korth USA (Earl's Repair Service, Tewkberry, MA). Previously by Keng's Firearms Specialty, Inc., Beeman Precision Arms; Osborn Beeman Precision Arms; Osborne's and Mandall Shooting Supply

REVOLVERS COMBAT, SPORT, TARGET

Calibers: .357 Mag. and .22 LR w/interchangeable combination cylinders of .357 Mag./9mm Para. or .22 LR/.22 WMR also .22 Jet, .32 S&W and .32 H&R Mag. Bbls: 2.5-, 3-, 4-inch (combat) and 5.25- or 6-inch (target). Weight: 33 to 42 oz. Blued, stainless, matte silver or polished silver finish. Checkered walnut grips. Imported 1967 to date.

Model	NiB	Ex	Gd
Standard rimfire model	$4590	$2735	$1895
Standard centerfire model	$6899	$5100	$4029
ISU Match Target model	$7429	$5433	$3329
Custom stainless finish, add			$485
Matte silver finish, add			$689
Polished silver finish, add			$950

SEMIAUTOMATIC PISTOL

Calibers: 30 Luger, 9mm Para., .357 SIG, .40 S&W, 9x21mm. 10- or 14-round magazine, 4- or 5-inch bbl., all-steel construction, recoil-operated. Ramp front sight, adj. rear. Blued, stainless, matte silver or polished silver finish. Checkered walnut grips. Limited import from 1988.

Model	NiB	Ex	Gd
Standard model	$6495	$5040	$3934
Matte silver finish, add			$332
Polished silver finish, add			$791

LAHTI PISTOLS — Mfd. by Husqvarna Vapenfabriks A. B. Huskvarna, Sweden, and Valtion Kivaar Tedhas ("VKT") Jyväskyla, Finland

AUTOMATIC PISTOL

Caliber: 9mm Para. Eight-round magazine, 4.75-inch bbl., weight: About 46 oz. Fixed sights. Blued finish. Plastic grips. Specifications given are those of the Swedish Model 40 but also apply in general to the Finnish Model L-35, which differs only slightly. A considerable

Lahti Automatic Pistol

L.A.R. Mark I Grizzly

Laseraim Series I

Laseraim Series II

number of Swedish Lahti pistols were imported and sold in the U.S. The Finnish model, somewhat better made, is rare. Finnish Model L-35 adopted 1935. Swedish Model 40 adopted 1940, mfd. through 1944.

Model	NiB	Ex	Gd
Finnish L-35 model (1st Variation)	$4120	$3020	$2455
Swedish 40 model	$648	$449	$332

L.A.R. MANUFACTURING, INC. — West Jordan, Utah

MARK I GRIZZLY WIN. MAG. AUTOMATIC PISTOL

Calibers: .357 Mag., .45 ACP, .45 Win. Mag. Seven-round magazine, 6.5-inch bbl., 10.5 inches overall. Weight: 48 oz. Fully adj. sights. Checkered rubber combat-style grips. Blued finish. Made from 1983 to date. 8- or 10-inch bbl., Made from 1987 to 1999.

Model	NiB	Ex	Gd
.357 Mag. (6.5 inch barrel)	$918	$643	$434
.45 Win. Mag.(6.5 inch barrel)	$918	$740	$444
8-inch barrel	$1237	$1040	$943
10-inch barrel	$1320	$1118	$1029

MARK 4 GRIZZLY

AUTOMATIC PISTOL . . . . . . NiB $918 Ex $740 Gd $629

Same general specifications as the L.A.R. Mark I except chambered for .44 Magnum, has 5.5- or 6.5-inch bbl., beavertail grip safety, matte blued finish. Made from 1991 to 1999.

MARK 5 AUTO PISTOL. . . . . . NiB $918 Ex $734 Gd $631

Similar to the Mark I except chambered in 50 Action Express. Six-round magazine, 5.4- or 6.5-inch bbl., 10.6 inches overall (with 5.4-inch bbl.). Weight: 56 oz. Checkered walnut grips. Made 1993 to 1999.

**Laseraim Series III
w/LA93 Illusion III Scope**

**Llama Model IIIA
Deluxe Chrome Engraved First Issue**

**Llama Model IIIA
Deluxe Blue Engraved Second Issue**

LASERAIM TECHNOLOGIES, INC. — Little Rock, Arkansas

SERIES I SA AUTO PISTOL
Calibers: .40 S&W, .45 ACP, 10mm. Seven or 8- round magazine, 3.875- or 5.5-inch dual-port compensated bbl., 8.75 or 10.5 inches overall. Weight: 46 or 52 oz. Fixed sights w/Laseraim or adjustable Millet sights. TExtured black composition grips. Extended slide release, ambidExtrous safety and beveled magazine well. Stainless or matte black Teflon finish. Made from 1993 to 1999.
Series I w/adjustable sights . . . NiB $362 Ex $255 Gd $188
Series I w/fixed sights . . . . . . NiB $362 Ex $255 Gd $188
Series I w/fixed sights (HotDot) NiB $479 Ex $270 Gd $203
Series I Dream Team (RedDot) NiB $479 Ex $ 270 Gd $203
Series I Illusion (Laseraim) . . . NiB $479 Ex $270 Gd $203

SERIES II SA AUTO PISTOL
Similar to Series I except w/stainless finish and no bbl., compensator. Made from 1993 to 1996.
Series II w/adjustable sights . . NiB $530 Ex $365 Gd $265
Series II w/fixed sights . . . . . . NiB $530 Ex $365 Gd $265
Series II Dream Team . . . . NiB $602 Ex $437 Gd $279
Series II Illusion . . . . NiB $540 Ex $439 Gd $321

SERIES III SA AUTO PISTOL
Similar to Series II except w/serrated slide and 5-inch compensated bbl., only. Made 1994. Disc.
Series III w/adjustable sights . . NiB $632 Ex $536 Gd $398
Series III w/fixed sights . . . . . . NiB $632 Ex $599 Gd $362

VELOCITY SERIES SA AUTO PISTOL
Similar to Series I except chambered for .357 Sig. or .400 Cor-Bon, 3.875-inch unported bbl., (compact) or 5.5-inch dual-port compensated bbl. Made from 1993 to 1999. See illustration previous page.
Compact model (unported) . . . NiB $362 Ex $290 Gd $204
Government model (ported) . . NiB $362 Ex $290 Gd $204
w/wireless laser (HotDot), add $175

LIGNOSE PISTOLS — Suhl, Germany. Aktien-Gesellschaft "Lignose" Abteilung

The following Lignose pistols were manufactured from 1920 to the mid-1930s. They were also marketed under the Bergmann name.

EINHAND MODEL 2A
POCKET AUTO PISTOL . . . . . NiB $434 Ex $305 Gd $209
As the name implies, this pistol is designed for one-hand operation, pressure on a "trigger" at the front of the guard retracts the slide. Caliber: .25 Auto. (6.35 mm). Six-round magazine, 2-inch bbl., 4.75 inches overall. Weight: About 14 oz. Blued finish. Hard rubber grips.

MODEL 2 POCKET
AUTO PISTOL . . . . NiB $362 Ex $237 Gd $175
Conventional Browning type. Same general specifications as Einhand Model 2A but lacks the one-hand operation.

EINHAND MODEL
3A POCKET AUTO PISTOL . . . NiB $479 Ex $369 Gd $270
Same as the Model 2A except has longer grip, 9-round magazine, weight: About 16 oz.

LLAMA HANDGUNS — Manufactured by Gabilondo y Cia, Vitoria, Spain (imported by S.G.S., Wanamassa, New Jersey)

NOTE: *For ease in finding a particular Llama handgun, the listings are divided into two groupings: Automatic Pistols (below) and Revolvers, which follow. For a complete listing of Llama handguns, please refer to the index.* www.skyhorsepublishing.com

AUTOMATIC PISTOLS

MODEL IIIA
AUTOMATIC PISTOL . . . . . . **NiB $337 Ex $170 Gd $109**
Caliber: .380 Auto. Seven-round magazine, 3.69-inch bbl., 6.5 inches overall. Weight: 23 oz. Adj. target sights. Blued finish. Plastic grips. Intro. 1951. Disc.

MODELS IIIA, XA, XV DELUXE
Same as standard Model IIIA, XA and XV except engraved w/blued or chrome finish and simulated pearl grips.
Chrome-engraved finish . . . . . **NiB $365 Ex $306 Gd $219**
Blue-engraved finish. . . . . . . **NiB $356 Ex $290 Gd $204**

MODEL VIII
AUTOMATIC PISTOL . . . . . . **NiB $377 Ex $306 Gd $255**
Caliber: .38 Super. Nine-round magazine, 5-inch bbl., 8.5 inches overall. Weight: 40 oz. Fixed sights. Blued finish. Wood grips. Intro. in 1952. Disc.

MODELS VIII, IXA, XI DELUXE
Same as standard Models VIII, IXA and XI except finish (chrome engraved or blued engraved) and simulated pearl grips. Disc. 1984.
Chrome-engraved finish . . . . . **NiB $377 Ex $290 Gd $190**
Blue-engraved finish. . . . . . . **NiB $377 Ex $290 Gd $190**

MODEL IXA AUTOMATIC PISTOL**NiB $377 Ex $290 Gd $190**
Same as model VIII except .45 Auto, 7-round magazine,

MODEL XA AUTOMATIC PISTOL**NiB $377 Ex $290 Gd $190**
Same as model IIIA except .32 Auto, 8-round magazine,

MODEL XI AUTOMATIC PISTOL**NiB $377 Ex $290 Gd $190**
Same as model VIII except 9mm Para.

MODEL XV AUTOMATIC PISTOL**NiB $321 Ex $255 Gd $170**
Same as model XA except .22 LR.

MODELS BE-IIIA, BE-XA, BE-XV **NiB $530 Ex $332 Gd $235**
Same as models IIIA, XA and XV except w/blued-engraved finish. Made from 1977-84.

MODELS BE-VIII,
BE-IXA, BE-XI DELUXE . . . . . . **NiB $530 Ex $398 Gd $281**
Same as models VIII, IXA and XI except w/blued-engraved finish. Made from 1977 to 1984.

MODELS C-IIIA, C-XA, C-XV. . **NiB $408 Ex $365 Gd $259**
Same as models IIIA, XA and XV except in satin chrome.

MODELS C-VIII, C-IXA, C-XI. . **NiB $475 Ex $357 Gd $244**
Same as models VIII, IXA and XI except in satin chrome.

MODELS CE-IIIA,
CE-XA, CE-XV. . . . . **NiB $398 Ex $347 Gd $230**
Same as models IIIA, XA and XV except w/chrome engraved finish. Made from 1977 to 1984.

MODELS CE-VIII,
CE-IXA, CE-XI. . . . . **NiB $475 Ex $357 Gd $244**
Same as models VIII, IXA and XI, w/except chrome engraved finish. Made from 1977 to 1984.

COMPACT FRAME
AUTO PISTOL . . . . **NiB $345 Ex $270 Gd $204**
Calibers: 9mm Para., .38 Super, .45 Auto. Seven-, 8- or 9-round magazine, 5-inch bbl., 7.88 inches overall. Weight: 34 oz. Blued, satin-chrome or Duo-Tone finishes. Made from 1986 to 1997. Duo-Tone disc. 1993.

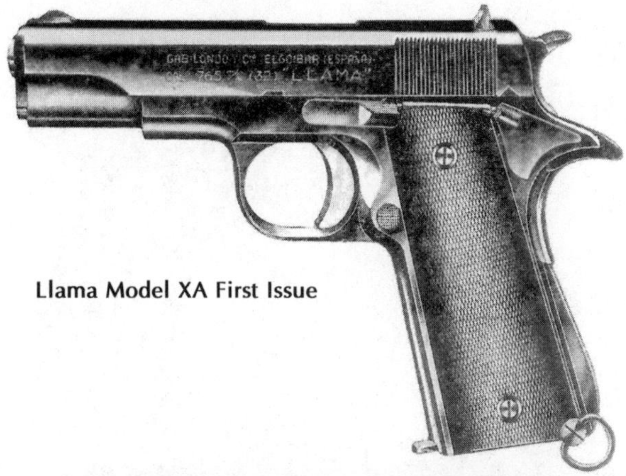

Llama Model XA First Issue

Llama Model C-XI

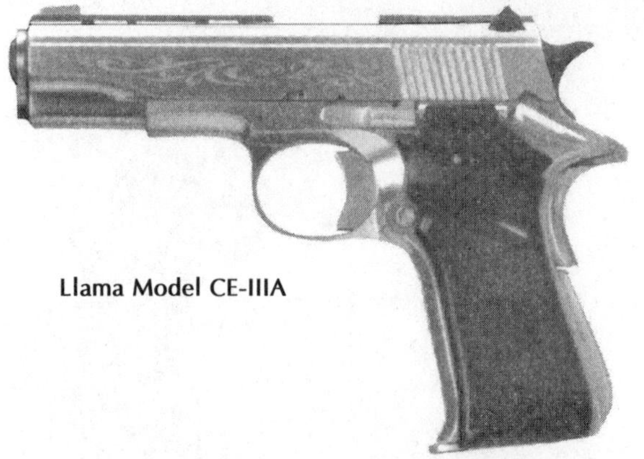

Llama Model CE-IIIA

Llama Model Compact

GRADING: **NiB** = New in Box   **Ex** = Excellent or NRA 95%   **Gd** = Good or NRA 68%

**Llama Duo-Tone
Large Frame**

**Llama M-82
DA Auto**

Llama MINI-MAX II

Llama MAX-I

DUO-TONE LARGE
FRAME AUTO PISTOL . . . . . . NiB $449 Ex $368 Gd $305
Caliber: .45 ACP. Seven-round magazine, 5-inch bbl., 8.5 inches overall. Weight: 36 oz. Adj. rear sight. Blued finished w/satin chrome. Polymer black grips. Made from 1991 to 1993.

DUO-TONE SMALL
FRAME AUTO PISTOL . . . . . . NiB $306 Ex $209 Gd $150
Calibers: .22 LR, .32 and .380 Auto. Seven- or 8-round magazine, 3.69 inch bbl., 6.5 inches overall. Weight: 23 oz. Square-notch rear sight, Partridge-type front. Blued finish w/chrome. Made from 1990 to 1993.

MODEL G-IIIA DELUXE . . NiB $2520 Ex $1944 Gd $1659
Same as Model IIIA except gold damascened w/simulated pearl grips. Disc. 1982.

LARGE-FRAME AUTOMATIC PISTOL (IXA)
Caliber: .45 Auto. Seven-round magazine, 5-inch bbl., weight: 2 lbs., 8 oz. Adj. rear sight, Partridge-type front. Walnut grips or teakwood on satin chrome model. Later models w/polymer grips.
Blued finish . . . . NiB $369 Ex $258 Gd $198
Satin chrome finish. . . . . NiB $538 Ex $444 Gd $290

M-82 DA AUTOMATIC PISTOL. . . . . NiB $587 Ex $398 Gd $270
Caliber: 9mm Para. 15-round magazine, 4.25-inch bbl., 8 inches overall. Weight: 39 oz. Drift-adj. rear sight. Matte blued finish. Matte black polymer grips. Made from 1988 to 1993.

M-87 COMPETITION PISTOL NiB $1029 Ex $816 Gd $634
Caliber: 9mm Para. 15-round magazine, 5.5-inch bbl., 9.5 inches overall. Weight: 40 oz. Low-profile combat sights. Satin nickel finish. Matte black grip panels. Built-in ported compensator to minimize recoil and muzzle rise. Made from 1989 to 1993.

MICRO-MAX SA AUTOMATIC PISTOL
Caliber: .380 ACP. Seven-round magazine, 3.125-inch bbl., weight: 23 oz. Blade front sight, drift adjustable rear w/3-dot system. Matte blue or satin chrome finish. Checkered polymer grips. Imported from 1997 to 2005.
Matte blue finish . . . . NiB $281 Ex $204 Gd $165
Satin chrome finish. . . . . NiB $288 Ex $230 Gd $219

MINI-MAX SA AUTOMATIC PISTOL
Calibers: 9mm, .40 S&W or .45 ACP. Six- or 8-round magazine, 3.5-inch bbl., 8.3 inches overall. Weight: 35 oz. Blade front sight, drift adjustable rear w/3-dot system. Matte blue, Duo-Tone or satin chrome finish. Checkered polymer grips. Imported 1996 to 2005.
Duo-Tone finish . . . . NiB $290 Ex $204 Gd $158
Matte blue finish . . . . NiB $306 Ex $220 Gd $170
Satin chrome finish. . . . . NiB $326 Ex $240 Gd $190
Stainless (disc.). . . . . NiB $359 Ex $301 Gd $235

MINI-MAX II SA AUTOMATIC PISTOL
Cal: .45 ACP only. 10-round mag., 3.625 inch bbl., 7.375 inch overall. Wt: 37 oz. Blade front sight, drift adj. rear w/3-dot system. Shortened barrel and grip. Matte and Satin Chrome finish. Imp. 2005.
Matte blue finish . . . . NiB $290 Ex $225 Gd $170
Satin chrome finish. . . . . NiB $316 Ex $255 Gd $189

MAX-I SA AUTOMATIC PISTOL
Calibers: 9mm or .45 ACP. 7- or 9-round magazine, 4.25- to 5.125 inch bbl., weight: 34 or 36 oz. Blade front sight, drift adj. rear w/3-dot system. Matte blue, Duo-Tone or satin chrome finish. Checkered black rubber grips. Imported from 1995 to 1999.
Duo-Tone finish . . . . NiB $306 Ex $265 Gd $198
Matte blue finish . . . . NiB $301 Ex $240 Gd $189
Satin chrome finish. . . . . NiB $316 Ex $270 Gd $219

MAX-II SA AUTOMATIC PISTOL
Same as the MAX-I with 4.25 bbl. except w/10-round mag. Weight 40 oz., made 2005.
Matte blue finish . . . . NiB $306 Ex $265 Gd $198
Satin chrome finish. . . . . NiB $332 Ex $270 Gd $219

OMNI 45 DOUBLE-ACTION
AUTOMATIC PISTOL . . . . NiB $437 Ex $291 Gd $220
Caliber: .45 Auto. Seven-round magazine, 4.25-inch bbl., 7.75 inches overall. Weight: 40 oz. Adj. rear sight, ramp front. Highly polished deep blued finish. Made from 1984-86.

OMNI 9MM DOUBLE-ACTION
AUTOMATIC . . . . NiB $469 Ex $347 Gd $290
Same general specifications as .45 Omni except chambered for 9mm w/13-round magazine. Made from 1983-86.

SINGLE-ACTION
AUTOMATIC PISTOL . . . . NiB $485 Ex $386 Gd $270
Calibers: .38 Super, 9mm, .45 Auto. Nine-round magazine (7-round for .45 Auto), 5-inch bbl., 8.5 inches overall. Weight: 2 lbs., 8 oz. Intro. in 1981.

SMALL-FRAME AUTOMATIC PISTOL
Calibers: .380 Auto (7-round magazine), .22 RF (8-round magazine), 3.69-inch bbl., weight: 23 oz. Partridge-blade front sight, adj. rear. Blued or satin-chrome finish. Disc. 1997.
Blued finish . . . . NiB $255 Ex $204 Gd $165
Satin-chrome finish. . . . . NiB $270 Ex $220 Gd $175

REVOLVERS

MARTIAL DOUBLE-
ACTION REVOLVER . . . . NiB $255 Ex $170 Gd $120
Calibers: .22 LR, .38 Special. Six-round cylinder, bbl. lengths: 4-inch (.38 Special only) or 6-inch; 11.25 inches overall (w/6-inch bbl.). Weight: About 36 oz. w/6-inch bbl. Target sights. Blued finish. Checkered walnut grips. Made from 1969 to 1976.

MARTIAL DOUBLE-ACTION DELUXE
Same as standard Martial except w/satin chrome, chrome-engraved, blued engraved or gold damascened finish. Simulated pearl grips. Made from 1969 to 1976.
Satin-chrome finish. . . . . NiB $306 Ex $225 Gd $165
Chrome-engraved finish . . . . . NiB $581 Ex $431 Gd $286
Blue-engraved finish. . . . . NiB $638 Ex $453 Gd $332
Gold-damascened finish . . NiB $2810 Ex $2647 Gd $2299

COMANCHE I DOUBLE-ACTION
REVOLVER. . . . . NiB $270 Ex $204 Gd $160
Same general specifications as Martial .22. Made 1977 to 1982.

COMANCHE II
. . . . NiB $265 Ex $189 Gd $150
Same general specifications as Martial .38. Made 1977 to 1982.

COMANCHE III DOUBLE-ACTION
REVOLVER. . . . . NiB $306 Ex $219 Gd $144
Caliber: .357 Magnum. Six-round cylinder, 4-inch bbl., 9.25 inches overall. Weight: 36 oz. Adj. rear sight, ramp front. Blued finish. Checkered walnut grips. Made from 1975 to 1995. Note: Prior to 1977, this model was designated "Comanche."

COMANCHE III
CHROME. . . . . NiB $362 Ex $270 Gd $204
Same gen. specifications as Comanche III except has satin chrome finish, 4- or 6-inch bbl. Made from 1975 to 1995.

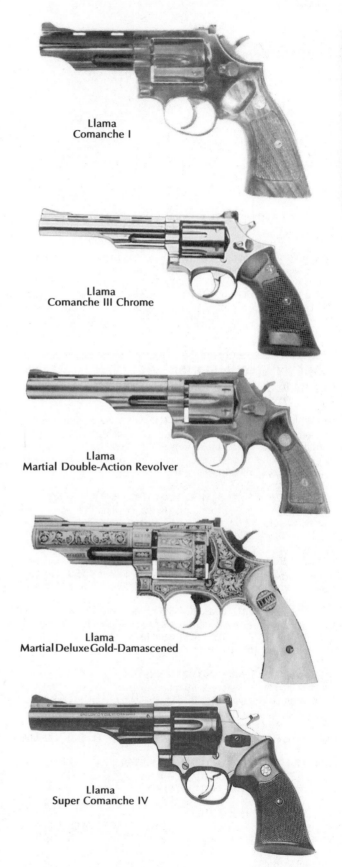

Llama
Comanche I

Llama
Comanche III Chrome

Llama
Martial Double-Action Revolver

Llama
Martial Deluxe Gold-Damascened

Llama
Super Comanche IV

Luger 1900
American Eagle

SUPER COMANCHE IV DA REVOLVER . . . . NiB $388 Ex $301 Gd $204
Caliber: .44 Magnum. Six-round cylinder, 6-inch bbl., 11.75 inches overall. Weight: 50 oz. Adj. rear sight, ramp front. Polished deep blued finish. Checkered walnut grips. Disc. 1998.

SUPER COMANCHE V DA REVOLVER NiB $362 Ex $270 Gd $214
Caliber: .357 Mag. Six-round cylinder, 4-, 6- or 8.5-inch bbl., weight: 48 ozs. Ramped front blade sight, click-adj. Rear. Made from 1980 to 1988.

LORCIN ENGINEERING CO., INC. — Mira Loma, California

MODEL L-22 SEMIAUTOMATIC PISTOL NiB $120 Ex $90 Gd $70
Caliber: 22 LR. Nine-round magazine, 2.5-inch bbl., 5.25 inches overall. Weight: 16 oz. Blade front sight, fixed notch rear w/3-dot system. Black Teflon or chrome finish. Black, pink or pearl composition grips. Made from 1990 to 1998.

MODEL L-25, LT-.25 SEMIAUTOMATIC PISTOL
Caliber: 25 ACP. Seven-round magazine, 2.4-inch bbl., 4.8 inches overall. Weight: 12 oz. (LT-25) or 14.5 oz. (L-25). Blade front sight, fixed rear. Black Teflon or chrome finish. Black, pink or pearl composition grips. Made from 1989-98.
Model L-25 . . . . NiB $89 Ex $61 Gd $40
Model LT-25 . . . . NiB $79 Ex $50 Gd $35
Model Lady Lorcin . . . . NiB $81 Ex $55 Gd $35

MODEL L-32 SEMIAUTOMATIC PISTOL NiB $90 Ex $65 Gd $50
Caliber: 32 ACP. Seven-round magazine, 3.5-inch bbl., 6.6 inches overall. Weight: 27 oz. Blade front sight, fixed notch rear. Black Teflon or chrome finish. Black composition grips. Made from 1992 to 1998.

MODEL L-380 SEMIAUTOMATIC PISTOL
Caliber: .380 ACP. Seven- or 10-round magazine, 3.5-inch bbl., 6.6 inches overall. Weight: 23 oz. Blade front sight, fixed notch rear. Matte Black finish. Grooved black composition grips. Made 1994 to 1998.
Model L-380 (10-round) . . . . . . NiB $158 Ex $95 Gd $65
Model L-380 (13-round) . . . . . . NiB $128 Ex $90 Gd $61

MODEL L9MM SEMIAUTOMATIC PISTOL
Caliber: 9mm Parabellum. 10- or 13-round magazine, 4.5-inch bbl., 7.5 inches overall. Weight: 31 oz. Blade front sight, fixed notch rear w/3-dot system. Black Teflon or chrome finish. Black composition grips. Made from 1992 to 1998.
Model L-9mm (7-round) . . . . . . NiB $158 Ex $95 Gd $65
Model L-9mm (10-round) . . . . . . NiB $158 Ex $95 Gd $65

O/U DERRINGER . . . . NiB $198 Ex $105 Gd $70

Caliber: .38 Special/.357 Mag., .45LC. Two-round derringer. 3.5-inch bbls. 6.5 inches overall. Weight: 12 oz. Blade front sight, fixed notch rear. Stainless finish. Black composition grips. Made from 1996-98.

LUGER PISTOLS — Manufactured by Deutsche Waffen und Munitionsfabriken (DWM), Berlin, Germany

1900 AMERICAN EAGLE . . NiB $6900 Ex $6555 Gd $4830
Caliber: 7.65 mm. Eight-round magazine; thin, 4.75-inch; tapered bbl.; 9.5 inches overall. Weight: 32 oz. Fixed rear sight, dovetailed front sight. Grip safety. Checkered walnut grips. Early-style toggle, narrow trigger, wide guard, no stock lug. American Eagle over chamber. Estimated 8,000 production.

1900 COMMERCIAL . . . . . NiB $6910 Ex $6565 Gd $4837
Same specifications as Luger 1900 American Eagle except DWM on early-style toggle, no chamber markings. Estimated 8000 production.

1900 SWISS . . . . NiB $6700 Ex $6365 Gd $4700
Same specifications as Luger 1900 American Eagle except Swiss cross in sunburst over chamber. Estimated 9,000 production.

1902 AMERICAN EAGLE NiB $16,650 Ex $14,000 Gd $12,990
Caliber: 9mm Para. Eight-round magazine, 4-inch heavy tapered bbl., 8.75 inches overall. Weight: 30 oz. Fixed rear sight, dovetailed front sight. Grip safety. Checkered walnut grips. American Eagle over chamber, DWM on early-style toggle, narrow trigger, wide guard, no stock lug. Estimated 700 production.

1902 CARBINE
Caliber: 7.65mm. Eight-round magazine, 11.75-inch tapered bbl., 16.5 inches overall. Weight: 46 oz. Adj. 4-position rear sight, long ramp front sight. Grip safety. Checkered walnut grips and forearm. DWM on early-style toggle, narrow trigger, wide guard, no chamber markings, stock lug. Estimated 3,200 production.
Model 1902 carbine (gun only) . NiB $12,245 Ex $11,353 Gd $7015
Model 1902 carbine
(gun only, American Eagle), add 45%
w/issued stock and matching numbers, add 20%
w/original stock and non-matching numbers, deduct 20%

1902 CARTRIDGE COUNTER . NiB $45,200 Ex $38,990 Gd $29,900
Caliber: 9mm Para. Eight-round magazine, Heavy, tapered 4-inch bbl., 8.75 inches overall. Weight: 30 oz. Fixed rear sight, dovetailed front sight. Grip safety. Checkered walnut grips. DWM on dished toggle w/lock, American Eagle over chamber when marked. No stock lug. Estimated production unknown.

1902 COMMERCIAL . . NiB $13,600 Ex $10,895 Gd $5,500
Same basic specifications as Luger 1902 Cartridge Counter except DWM on early-style toggle, narrow trigger, wide guard, no chamber markings, no stock lug. Estimated 400 production.

1902 AMERICAN EAGLE NiB $16,600 Ex $13,995 Gd $7,900
Same basic specifications as Luger 1902 Commercial except American Eagle over chamber, DWM on early-style toggle, narrow trigger, wide guard, no stock lug. Estimated 700 production.

1902 AMERICAN EAGLE
CARTRIDGE COUNTER . . . . . . NiB $45,200 Ex $38,650 Gd $15,088
Same basic specifications as Luger 1902 Cartridge Counter except American Eagle over chamber, DWM on early-style toggle, narrow trigger, wide guard, no stock lug. Estimated 700 production.

1904 GL "BABY" NiB $197,500 Ex $166,000 Gd $110,000
Caliber: 9mm Para. Seven-round magazine, 3.25-inch bbl., 7.75 inches overall. Weight: Approx. 20 oz. Serial number 10077B. "GL" marked on rear of toggle. Georg Luger's personal sidearm. Only one made in 1904.

1904 NAVAL (REWORKED) . NiB $14,000 Ex $11,000 Gd $8,250
Caliber: 9mm Para. Eight-round magazine, bbl., length altered to 4 inches., 8.75 inches overall. Weight: 30 oz. Adj. two-position rear sight, dovetailed front sight. Thumb lever safety. Checkered walnut grips. Heavy tapered bbl., DWM on new-style toggle w/lock, 1902 over chamber. w/or without grip safety and stock lug. Estimated 800 production. Untouched original (rare) worth $50,000.

1906 (11.35MM) . . NiB $119,000 Ex $95,900 Gd $66,500
Caliber: .45 ACP. Six-round magazine, 5-inch bbl., 9.75 inches overall. Weight: 36 oz. Fixed rear sight, dovetailed front sight. Grip safety. Checkered walnut grips. GL monogram on rear toggle link, larger frame w/altered trigger guard and trigger, no proofs, no markings over chamber. No stock lug. Only two were known to be made. Note: This version of the Luger pistol is the most valuable nExt to the "GL" Baby Luger.

1906 AMERICAN EAGLE
(7.65MM). . . . . NiB $4235 Ex $3300 Gd $2200
Caliber: 7.65mm. Eight-round magazine, thin 4.75-inch tapered bbl., 9.5 inches overall. Weight: 32 oz. Fixed rear sight, dovetailed front sight. Grip safety. Checkered walnut grips. DWM on new-style toggle, American Eagle over chamber. No stock lug. Estimated 8,000 production.

1906 AMERICAN EAGLE (9MM) . NiB $4600 Ex $4370 Gd $2000
Same basic specifications as the 7.65mm 1906 except in 9mm Para. w/4-inch barrel, 8.75 inches overall, weight: 30 oz. Estimated 3,500 production.

1906 BERN (7.65MM). . . . NiB $4430 Ex $2520 Gd $1996
Same basic specifications as the 7.65mm 1906 American Eagle except checkered walnut grips w/.38-inch borders, Swiss Cross on new-style toggle, Swiss proofs, no markings over chamber, no stock lug. Estimated 17,874 production.

1906 BRAZILIAN (7.65MM) . . . . NiB $3550 Ex $3375 Gd $1910
Same general specifications as the 7.65mm 1906 American Eagle except w/Brazilian proofs, no markings over chamber, no stock lug. Estimated 4,500 produced.

1906 BRAZILIAN (9MM). . NiB $1691 Ex $1390 Gd $1039
Same basic specifications as the 9mm 1906 American Eagle except w/Brazilian proofs, no markings over chamber, no stock lug. Production fewer than 4,000 estimated.

1906 COMMERCIAL. . . . . NiB $4000 Ex $3400 Gd $1500
Calibers: 7.65mm or 9mm. Same specifications as the 1906 American Eagle versions (above) except no chamber markings and no stock lug. Estimated production: 6,000 (7.65mm) and 3,500 (9mm).

1906 DUTCH. . . . . NiB $4200 Ex $3699 Gd $2809
Caliber: 9mm Para. Same specifications as the 9mm 1906 American Eagle except tapered bbl., w/proofs, no markings over chamber, no stock lug. Arsenal rework. Estimated 3,000 production.
Original finish, add 100%

1906 LOEWE AND COMPANY . . NiB $4823 Ex $3899 Gd $2744
Caliber: 7.65mm. Eight-round magazine, 6-inch tapered bbl., 10.75 inches overall. Weight: 35 oz. Adj. two-position rear sight, dovetailed front sight. Grip safety. Checkered walnut grips. Loewe & Company over chamber, Naval proofs, DWM on new-style toggle, no stock lug. Estimated production unknown.

1906 NAVY
Caliber: 9mm Para. Eight-round magazine, 6-inch tapered bbl., 10.75 inches overall. Weight: 35 oz. Adj. two-position rear sight, dovetailed front sight. Grip safety and thumb safety w/lower marking (1st issue), higher marking (2nd issue). Checkered walnut grips. No chamber markings, DWM on new-style toggle w/o lock, but w/stock lug. Est. production: 9,000 (lst issue); 2,000 (2nd issue).
First issue. . . . . NiB $7020 Ex $5630 Gd $4490

1906 NAVY COMMERCIAL NiB $5600 Ex $5320 Gd $2350
Same as the 1906 Navy except lower marking on thumb safety, no chamber markings. DWM on new-style toggle, w/stock lug and commercial proofs. Estimated ,3000 production.

1906 PORTUGUESE ARMY NiB $3400 Ex $3230 Gd $1720
Same specifications as the 7.65mm 1906 American Eagle except w/Portuguese proofs, crown and crest over chamber. No stock lug. Estimated 3,500 production.

1906 PORTUGUESE NAVAL . . . NiB $11,560 Ex $9260 Gd $7300
Same as the 9mm 1906 American Eagle except w/Portuguese proofs, crown and anchor over chamber, no stock lug.

1906 RUSSIAN. . . . . NiB $18,650 Ex $15,767 Gd $12,890
Same general specifications as the 9mm 1906 American Eagle except thumb safety has markings concealed in up position, DWM on new-style toggle, DWM bbl., proofs, crossed rifles over chamber. Estimated production unknown.

1906 SWISS . . . . NiB $3900 Ex $2709 Gd $2100
Same general specifications as the 7.65mm 1906 American Eagle Luger except Swiss Cross in sunburst over chamber, no stock lug. Estimated 10,300 production.

1906 SWISS (REWORK) . . NiB $3750 Ex $3250 Gd $2000
Same basic specifications as the 7.65mm 1906 Swiss except in bbl. lengths of 3.63, 4 and 4.75 inches, overall length 8.38 inches (with 4-inch bbl.). Weight 32 oz. (with 4-inch bbl.). DWM on new-style toggle, bbl., w/serial number and proof marks, Swiss Cross in sunburst or shield over chamber, no stock lug. Estimated production unknown.

1906 SWISS POLICE. . . . . NiB $3189 Ex $2910 Gd $2397
Same general specifications as the 7.65mm 1906 Swiss except DWM on new-style toggle, Swiss Cross in matted field over chamber, no stock lug. Estimated 10,300 production.

1908 BULGARIAN . . . . . . NiB $3860 Ex $2450 Gd $2600
Caliber: 9mm Para. Eight-round magazine, 4-inch tapered bbl., 8.75 inches overall. Weight: 30 oz. Fixed rear sight dovetailed front sight. Thumb safety w/lower marking concealed. Checkered walnut grips. DWM chamber marking, no proofs, crown over shield on new-style toggle lanyard loop, no stock lug. Estimated production unknown.

1908 COMMERCIAL. . . . . NiB $2560 Ex $2010 Gd $1713
Same basic specifications as the 1908 Bulgarian except higher marking on thumb safety. No chamber markings, commercial proofs, DWM on new-style toggle, no stock lug. Estimated 4,000 production.

1908 ERFURT MILITARY. . NiB $2555 Ex $2055 Gd $1824
Caliber: 9mm Para. Eight-round magazine, 4-inch tapered bbl., 8.75 inches overall. Weight: 30 oz. Fixed rear sight dovetailed front sight. Thumb safety w/higher marking concealed. Checkered walnut grips. Serial number and proof marks on barrel, crown and Erfurt on new-style toggle, dated chamber, but no stock lug. Estimated production unknown.

Luger 1923 Stoeger

1908 MILITARY
Same general specifications as the 9mm 1908 Erfurt Military Luger except first and second issue have thumb safety w/higher marking concealed, serial number on bbl., no chamber markings, proofs on frame, DWM on new-style toggle but no stock lug. Estimated production: 10,000 (first issue) and 5000 (second issue). Third issue has serial number and proof marks on barrel, dates over chamber, DWM on new-style toggle but no stock lug. Estimated 3,000 production.

First issue . . . . NiB $2460 Ex $2160 Gd $1645
Second issue . . . . NiB $2010 Ex $1605 Gd $1320
Third issue . . . . NiB $2299 Ex $1897 Gd $1645

1908 NAVY . . . . NiB $8405 Ex $79849 Gd $3475
Same basic specifications as the 9mm 1908 military Lugers except w/6-inch bbl, adj. two-position rear sight, no chamber markings, DWM on new-style toggle, w/stock lug. Estimated 26,000 production.

1908 NAVY (COMMERCIAL)NiB $6600 Ex $6270 Gd $4620
Same specifications as the 1908 Naval Luger except no chamber markings or date. Commercial proofs, DWM on new-style toggle, w/stock lug. Estimated 1,900 produced.

1914 ERFURT ARTILLERY . NiB $4670 Ex $4435 Gd $3040
Caliber: 9mm Para. Eight-shot magazine, 8-inch tapered bbl., 12.75 inches overall. Weight: 40 oz. Artillery rear sight, Dovetailed front sight. Thumb safety w/higher marking concealed. Checkered walnut grips. Serial number and proof marks on barrel, crown and Erfurt on new-style toggle, dated chamber, w/stock lug. Estimated production unknown.

1914 ERFURT MILITARY . . NiB $2170 Ex $2061 Gd $1190
Same specifications as the 1914 Erfurt Artillery except w/4-inch bbl., and corresponding length, weight, etc.; fixed rear sight. Estimated 3,000 production.

1914 NAVY . . . . NiB $6000 Ex $5700 Gd $3000
Same specifications as 9mm 1914 Lugers except has 6-inch bbl. w/corresponding length and weight, adj. two-position rear sight. Dated chamber, DWM on new-style toggle, w/stock lug. Estimated 40,000 produced.

1914 1918 DWM ARTILLERY .NiB $3600 Ex $3090 Gd $1997
Caliber: 9mm Para. Eight-shot magazine, 8-inch tapered bbl., 12.75 inches overall. Weight: 40 oz. Artillery rear sight, dovetailed front sight. Thumb safety w/higher marking concealed. Checkered walnut grips. Serial number and proof marks on barrel, DWM on new-style toggle, dated chamber, w/stock lug. Estimated 3,000 production.

1914–1918 DWM MILITARY . . . .NiB $2200 Ex $1899 Gd $1100
Same specifications as the 9mm 1914-1918 DWM Artillery except w/4-inch tapered bbl., and corresponding length, weight, etc., and fixed rear sight. Production unknown.

1920 CARBINE
Caliber: 7.65mm. Eight-round magazine, 11.75-inch tapered bbl., 15.75 inches overall. Weight: 44 oz. Four-position rear sight, long ramp front sight. Grip (or thumb) safety. Checkered walnut grips and forearm. Serial numbers and proof marks on barrel, no chamber markings, various proofs, DWM on new-style toggle, w/stock lug. Estimated production unknown.
(gun only) . . . . NiB $7430 Ex $7058 Gd $3000
(w/shoulder stock), add 35%

1920 NAVY CARBINE. . . . NiB $4800 Ex $4560 Gd $3360
Caliber: 7.65mm. Eight-round magazine, 11.75-inch tapered bbl., 15.75 inches overall. Two-position sliding rear sight. Naval military proofs and no forearm. Production unknown.

1920 COMMERCIAL . . . . . NiB $1450 Ex $1250 Gd $1018
Calibers: 7.65mm, 9mm Para. Eight-round magazine, 3.63-, 3.75-, 4-, 4.75-, 6-, 8-, 10-, 12-, 16-, 18- or 20-inch tapered bbl., overall length: 8.375 to 24.75 inches. Weight: 30 oz. (with 3.63-inch bbl.). Varying rear sight configurations, dovetailed front sight. Thumb safety. Checkered walnut grips. Serial numbers and proof marks on barrel, no chamber markings, various proofs, DWM or crown over Erfurt on new-style toggle, w/stock lug. Production not documented.

1920 POLICE . . . . NiB $1410 Ex $1200 Gd $931
Same specifications as 9mm 1920 DWM w/some dated chambers, various proofs, DWM or crown over Erfurt on new-style toggle, identifying marks on grip frame, w/stock lug. Estimated 3,000 production.

1923 COMMERICAL . . . . . NiB $1600 Ex $1520 Gd $1120
Calibers: 7.65mm and 9mm Para. Eight-round magazine, 3.63, 3.75, 4, 6, 8, 12 or 16-inch tapered bbl., overall length: 8.38 inches (with 3.63-inch bbl.). Weight: 30 oz. (with 3.63-inch bbl.). Various rear sight configurations, dovetailed front sight. Thumb lever safety. Checkered walnut grips. DWM on new-style toggle, serial number and proofs on barrel, no chamber markings, w/stock lug. Estimated 15,000 production.

1923 DUTCH COMMERICAL . . . NiB $2320 Ex $2088 Gd $1872
Same basic specifications as 1923 Commercial Luger w/same caliber offerings, but only 3.63 or 4-inch bbl. Fixed rear sight, thumb lever safety w/arrow markings. Production unknown.

1923 KRIEGHOFF COMMERCIAL NiB $2340 Ex $2223 Gd $1638
Same specifications as 1923 Commercial Luger, w/same caliber offerings but bbl., lengths of 3.63, 4, 6, and 8 inches. "K" marked on new-style toggle. Serial number, proofs and Germany on barrel. No chamber markings, but w/ stock lug. Production unknown.

1923 SAFE AND LOADED NiB $2460 Ex $2337 Gd $1722
Same caliber offerings, bbl., lengths and specifications as the 1923 Commercial except thumb lever safety, "safe" and "loaded" markings, w/stock lug. Estimated 10,000 production.

1923 STOEGER
Same general specifications as the 1923 Commercial Luger with the same caliber offerings and bbl., lengths of 3.75, 4, 6, 8 and up to 24 inches. Thumb lever safety. DWM on new-style toggle, serial number and/or proof marks on barrel. American Eagle over chamber but no stock lug. Estimated production less than 1000 (also see Stoeger listings). Note: Qualified appraisals should be obtained on all Stoeger Lugers with bbl. lengths over 8 inches to ensure accurate values.
3.75-, 4-, or 6-inch bbl. . . NiB $5660 Ex $5377 Gd $2730
8-inch bbl. . . . . NiB $6350 Ex $6035 Gd $2255

1926 "BABY" PROTOTYPE NiB $112,750 Ex $90,295 Gd $62,355
Calibers: 7.65mm Browning and 9mm Browning (short). Five-round magazine, 2.31-inch bbl., about 6.25 inches overall. Small-sizedframe and toggle assembly. Prototype for a Luger "pocket pistol," but never manufactured commercially. Checkered walnut grips, slotted for safety. Only four known to Exist, but as many as a dozen could have been made.

1929 SWISS . . . . NiB $2017 Ex $1486 Gd $989
Caliber: 7.65mm. Eight-round magazine, 4.75-inch tapered bbl., 9.5 inches overall. Weight: 32 oz. Fixed rear sight, dovetailed front sight. Long grip safety and thumb lever w/S markings. Stepped receiver and straight grip frame. Checkered plastic grips. Swiss Cross in shield on new-style toggle. Serial numbers and proofs on barrel, no markings over chamber and no stock lug. Estimated 1,900 production.

1934 KRIEGHOFF
COMMERCIAL (SIDE FRAME) . . . NiB $ 7100 Ex $6350 Gd $2895
Caliber: 7.65mm or 9mm Para. Eight-round magazine, bbl. lengths: 4, 6, and 8 inches, overall length: 8.75 (with 4-inch bbl.). Weight: 30 oz. (with 4-inch bbl.). Various rear sight configurations w/dovetailed front sight. Thumb lever safety. Checkered brown plastic grips. Anchor w/H K Krieghoff Suhl on new-style toggle, but no chamber markings. Tapered bbl., w/serial number and proofs; w/stock lug. Estimated 1,700 production.

1934 KRIEGHOFF S CODE MODELS
Caliber: 9mm Para. Eight-round magazine, 4-inch tapered bbl., 8.75 inches overall. Weight: 30 oz. Fixed rear sight, dovetailed front sight. Thumb lever safety. Anchor w/H K Krieghoff Suhl on new-style toggle, S dated chamber, bbl., proofs and stock lug. Early model: Checkered walnut or plastic grips. Estimated 2,500 production. Late model: Checkered brown plastic grips. Estimated 1,200 production.
Early model . . . . NiB $4660 Ex $4077 Gd $2976
Late model . . . . NiB $4460 Ex $3900 Gd $1464

1934 BYF . . . . NiB $2170 Ex $1950 Gd $1000
Caliber: 9mm Para. Eight-round magazine, 4-inch tapered bbl., 8.75 inches overall. Weight: 30 oz. Fixed rear sight, dovetailed front sight. Thumb lever safety. Checkered walnut or plastic grips. "byf" on new-style toggle, serial number and proofs on bbl., 41-42 dated chamber and w/stock lug. Estimated 3,000 productlon.

1934 MAUSER S/42 K . . . . NiB $7950 Ex $6800 Gd $3500
Caliber: 9mm Para. Eight-round magazine, 4-inch tapered bbl., 8.75 inches overall. Weight: 30 oz. Fixed rear sight dovetailed front sight. Thumb lever safety. Checkered walnut or plastic grips. "42" on new-style toggle, serial number and proofs on barrel, 1939-40 dated chamber markings and w/stock lug. Estimated 10,000 production.

1934 MAUSER S/42 (DATED) NiB $2244 Ex $2117 Gd $1599
Same specifications as Luger 1934 Mauser 42 except 41 dated chamber markings and w/stock lug. Production unknown.

Luger S42

1934 MAUSER BANNER (MILITARY) NiB $4190 Ex $3455 Gd $3097
Same specifications as Luger 1934 Mauser 42 except Mauser in banner on new-style toggle, tapered bbl., w/serial number and proofs usually, dated chamber markings and w/stock lug. Production unknown.

1934 MAUSER BANNER COMMERCIAL NiB $4400 Ex $3760 Gd $3156
Same specifications as Luger 1934 Mauser 42 except checkered walnut grips. Mauser in banner on new-style toggle, tapered bbl., usually w/serial number and proofs, no chamber markings, but w/stock lug. Production unknown.

1934 MAUSER BANNER DUTCH . NiB $3787 Ex $3375 Gd $3099
Same specifications as Luger 1934 Mauser 42 except checkered walnut grips. Mauser in banner on new-style toggle, tapered bbl., w/caliber, 1940 dated chamber markings and w/stock lug. Production unknown.

1934 MAUSER LATVIAN . . NiB $3260 Ex $2355 Gd $1989
Caliber: 7.65mm. Eight-round magazine, 4-inch tapered bbl., 8.75 inches overall. Weight: 30 oz. Fixed square-notched rear sight, dovetailed Partridge front sight. Thumb lever safety. Checkered walnut stocks. Mauser in banner on new-style toggle, 1937 dated chamber markings and w/stock lug. Production unknown.

1934 MAUSER (OBERNDORF) . . NiB $3155 Ex $2535 Gd $1733
Same as 1934 Mauser 42 except checkered walnut grips. Oberndorf 1934 on new-style toggle, tapered bbl., w/proofs and caliber, Mauser banner over chamber and w/stock lug (also see Mauser).

1934 SIMSON-S TOGGLE. NiB $4459 Ex $4188 Gd $3799
Same as 1934 Mauser 42 except checkered walnut grips, "S" on new-style toggle, tapered bbl., w/serial number and proofs, no chamber markings; w/stock lug. Estimated 10,000 production.

42 MAUSER BANNER (BYF) NiB $3877 Ex $3078 Gd $2689
Same specifications as Luger 1934 Mauser 42 except weight: 32 oz. Mauser in banner on new-style toggle, tapered bbl., w/serial number and proofs usually, dated chamber markings and w/stock lug. Estimated 3,500 production.

ABERCROMBIE AND FITCH . . . . NiB $5465 Ex $4876 Gd $2879
Calibers: 7.65mm and 9mm Para. Eight-round magazine, 4.75-inch tapered bbl., 9.5 inches overall. Weight: 32 oz. Fixed rear sight, dovetailed front sight. Grip safety. Checkered walnut grips. DWM on new-style toggle Abercrombie & Fitch markings on barrel, Swiss Cross in sunburst over chamber, no stock lug. Est. 100 production.

Luna Model 200
Free Pistol

DUTCH ROYAL AIR FORCE NiB $3324 Ex $2190 Gd $998
Caliber: 9mm Para. Eight-round magazine, 4-inch tapered bbl., 8.75 inches overall. Weight: 30 oz. Fixed rear sight dovetailed front sight. Grip safety and thumb safety w/markings and arrow. Checkered walnut grips. DWM on new-style toggle, bbl., dated w/serial number and proofs, no markings over chamber, no stock lug. Estimated 4,000 production.

DWM (G DATE) . . . . NiB $2189 Ex $1953 Gd $1645
Caliber: 9mm Para. Eight-round magazine, 4-inch tapered bbl., 8.75 inches overall. Weight: 30 oz. Fixed rear sight, dovetailed front sight. Thumb lever safety. Checkered walnut grips. DWM on new-style toggle, serial number and proofs on barrel, G (1935 date) over chamber and w/stock lug. Production unknown.

DWM AND ERFURT . . . . . . NiB $1357 Ex $1134 Gd $876
Caliber: 9mm Para. Eight-round magazine, 4- or 6-inch tapered bbl., overall length: 8.75 or 10.75 inches. Weight: 30 or 38 oz. Fixed rear sight, dovetailed front sight. Thumb safety. Checkered walnut grips. Serial numbers and proof marks on barrel, double dated chamber, various proofs, DWM or crown over Erfurt on new-style toggle and w/stock lug. Production unknown.

KRIEGHOFF 36 . . . . NiB $4550 Ex $3799 Gd $1899
Caliber: 9mm Para. Eight-round magazine, 4-inch tapered bbl., 8.75 inches overall. Weight: 30 oz. Fixed rear sight, dovetailed front sight. Thumb lever safety. Checkered brown plastic grips. Anchor w/H K Krieghoff Suhl on new-style toggle, 36 dated chamber, serial number and proofs on barrel and w/stock lug. Estimated 700 production.

KRIEGHOFF DATED (1936 - 1945)
Same specifications as Luger Krieghoff 36 except 1936-45 dated chamber, bbl. proofs. Est. 8,600 production.
1936, 1937 and 1940 . . . . NiB $5500 Ex $4779 Gd $2735
1938 and 1941 . . . . NiB $6500 Ex $5779 Gd $2735
1942 thru 1943, ADD 60%
1945, ADD 110%

KRIEGHOFF (GRIP SAFETY)NiB $4977 Ex $3965 Gd $2790
Same specifications as Luger Krieghoff 36 except grip safety and thumb lever safety. No chamber markings, tapered bbl., w/serial number, proofs and caliber, no stock lug. Production unknown.

MAUSER BANNER (GRIP SAFETY) NiB $2874 Ex $2050 Gd $1465
Caliber: 7.65mm. Eight-round magazine, 4.75-inch tapered bbl., 9.5 inches overall. Weight: 30 oz. Fixed rear sight, dovetailed front sight. Grip safety and thumb lever safety. Checkered walnut grips. Mauser in banner on new-style toggle, serial number and proofs on barrel, 1939 dated chamber markings, but no stock lug. Production unknown.

MAUSER BANNER 42 (DATED) NiB 2170 Ex $1196 Gd $100
Caliber: 9mm Para. Eight-round magazine, 4-inch tapered bbl., 8.75 inches overall. Weight: 30 oz. Fixed rear sight, dovetailed front sight. Thumb lever safety. Checkered walnut or plastic grips. Mauser in ban-

ner on new-style toggle serial number and proofs on bbl., (usually) 1942 dated chamber markings and stock lug. Production unknown.

MAUSER BANNER (SWISS PROOF)NiB $3460 Ex $2830 Gd $1540
Same specifications as Luger Mauser Banner 42 except checkered walnut grips and 1939 dated chamber.

MAUSER FREISE . . . . NiB $4960 Ex $4090 Gd $2866
Same specifications as Mauser Banner 42 except checkered walnut grips, tapered bbl. w/proofs on sight block and Freise above chamber. Production unknown.

S/42
Caliber: 9mm Para. Eight-round magazine, 4-inch tapered barrel. 8.75 inches overall. Weight: 30 oz. Fixed rear sight, dovetailed front sight. Thumb lever safety. Checkered walnut grips. S/42 on new-style toggle, serial number and proofs on barrel and w/stock lug. Dated Model: Has dated chamber; estimated 3000 production. G Date: Has G (1935 date) over chamber; estimated 3000 production. K Date: Has K (1934 date) over chamber; production unknown.
Dated model . . . . NiB $6780 Ex $5977 Gd $4538
G date model . . . . NiB $2669 Ex $2380 Gd $2010
K date model . . . . NiB $6876 Ex $5986 Gd $4610

RUSSIAN COMMERCIAL . . NiB $3146 Ex $2548 Gd $1713
Caliber: 7.65mm. Eight-round magazine, 3.63-inch tapered bbl., 8.38 inches overall. Weight: 30 oz. Fixed rear sight, dovetailed front sight. Thumb lever safety. Checkered walnut grips. DWM on new-style toggle, Russian proofs on barrel, no chamber markings but w/stock lug. Production unknown.

SIMSON AND COMPANY
Calibers: 7.65mm and 9mm Para. Eight-round magazine, Weight: 32 oz. Fixed rear sight, dovetailed front sight. Thumb lever safety. Checkered walnut grips. Simson & Company Suhl on new-style toggle, serial number and proofs on barrel, date over chamber and w/stock lug. Estimated 10,000 production.
Simson and Company
(9mm w/1925 date) . . . . . . NiB $6300 Ex $5300 Gd $300
Simson and Company
(undated) . . . . NiB $4300 Ex $3650 Gd $200
Simson and Company
(S code) . . . . NiB $5600 Ex $4800 Gd $2389

VICKERS-DUTCH . . . . NiB $4375 Ex $3968 Gd $3316
Caliber: 9mm Para. Eight-round magazine, 4-inch tapered bbl., 8.75 inches overall. Weight: 30 oz. Fixed rear sight, dovetailed front sight. Grip safety and thumb lever w/arrow markings. Checkered walnut grips (coarse). Vickers LTD on new-style toggle, no chamber markings, dated barrel but no stock lug. Estimated 10,000 production.

LUNA FREE PISTOL—Zella-Mehlis, Germany. Originally mfd. by Ernst Friedr. Buchel and later by Udo Anschutz

MODEL 200 FREE PISTOL . . NiB $1198 Ex $1027 Gd $784
Single-shot. System Aydt action. Set trigger. Caliber: .22 LR. Eleven-inch bbl., weight: 40 oz. Target sights. Blued finish. Checkered and carved walnut grip and forearm; improved design w/adj. hand base on later models of Udo Anschutz manufacture. Made prior to WWII.

M.A.C. (Military Armament Corp.) — Ducktown, Tennessee

Ingram Model 10 Auto Pistol Select fire (NFA-Title II-Class III) SMG based on Ingram M10 blowback system using an open bolt design with or without telescoping stock. Calibers: 9mm or .45 ACP. Cyclic rate: 750 RPM (9mm) or 900 RPM (.45 ACP). 32- or 30-round magazine, 5.75-inch threaded bbl. (to accept muzzle brake) bbl. Extension or suppressor, 10.5 inches overall w/o stock or 10.6 (w/telescoped stock) and 21.5 (w/Extended stock). Weight: 6.25 pounds. Front protected post sight, fixed aperture rear sight.

9mm model	NiB $1113	Ex $920	Gd $669
ACP model	NiB $998	Ex $877	Gd $668
w/bbl. extension, add			$255
w/suppressor, add			$587

INGRAM MODEL 10A1S SEMIAUTOMATIC
Similar to the Model 10 except (Class I) semiautomatic w/closed bolt design to implement an interchangable component system to easily convert to fire 9mm and .45 ACP.

9mm model	NiB $408	Ex $332	Gd $225
.45 ACP model	NiB $431	Ex $342	Gd $235
w/bbl. extension, add			$204
w/fake suppressor, add			$225

INGRAM MODEL 11 SEMIAUTOMATIC
Similar to the Model 10A1 except (Class I) semiautomatic chambered .380 ACP.

.380 ACP model	NiB $862	Ex $714	Gd $536
w/bbl. extension, add			$204
w/fake suppressor, add			$225

MAGNUM RESEARCH, INC. (MRI) —
Minneapolis, Minnesota. Originally mfd. by IMI (Isreal Military Industries). MRI purchased by Kahr Arms in 2010.

BABY EAGLE SEMIAUTOMATIC . . . . NiB $577   Ex $479   Gd $365
DA. Calibers: 9mm, .40 S&W, .41 AE. 15-shot magazine (9mm), 9-round magazine (.40 S&W), 10-round magazine (.41 AE), 4.75-inch bbl., 8.15 inches overall. Weight: 35.4 oz. Combat sights. Matte blued finish. Imported from 1991-96 and 1999 to 2007.

DESERT EAGLE MK VII SEMIAUTOMATIC
Gas-operated. Calibers: .357 Mag., .41 Mag., .44 Mag., .50 Action Express (AE). Eight- or 9-round magazine, 6-inch w/standard bbl., or 10- and 14-inch w/polygonal bbl., 10.6 inches overall (with 6-inch bbl.). Weight: 52 oz. (w/alum. alloy frame) or 67 oz. (w/steel frame). Fixed or adj. combat sights. Combat-type trigger guard. finish: Military black oxide, nickel, chrome, stainless or blued. Wraparound rubber grips. Made from 1983 to 1995 and 1998 to 2001.

.357 standard (steel) or alloy (6-inch bbl.)	NiB $903	Ex $658	Gd $562
.357 stainless steel (6-inch bbl.)	NiB $940	Ex $704	Gd $536
.41 Mag. standard (steel) or alloy 6-inch bbl.)	NiB $1099	Ex $831	Gd $638
.41 Mag. stainless steel (6-inch bbl.)	NiB $1145	Ex $984	Gd $780
.44 Mag. standard (steel) or alloy (6-inch bbl.)	NiB $1015	Ex $798	Gd $567
.44 Mag. stainless steel (6-inch bbl.)	NiB $991	Ex $806	Gd $559
.50 AE Magnum standard	NiB $1135	Ex $968	Gd $689
For 10-inch bbl., add	NiB $204	Ex $148	Gd $110
For 14-inch bbl., add	NiB $225	Ex $175	Gd $128

MODEL DESERT EAGLE MARK XIX SEMI-AUTOMATIC PISTOL
Interchangeable component system based on .50-caliber frame.

Magnum Research Model Desert Eagle Mark XIX (Shown w/Optional Leupold Scope

Magnum Research Model One Pro .45

Calibers: .357 Mag., .44 Mag., .50 AE. Nine-, 8-, 7-round magazine, 6- or 10-inch bbl. w/dovetail design and cross slots to accept scope rings. Weight: 70.5 oz. (6-inch bbl.) or 79 oz. 10.75 or 14.75 inches overall. Sights: Post front and adjustable rear. Blue, chrome or nickel finish; available brushed, matte or polished. Hogue soft rubber grips. Made from 1995 to 1998..

.357 Mag. and .44 Mag. (w/6-inch bbl.)	NiB $1400	Ex $1150	Gd $900
.50 AE (w/6-inch bbl.)	NiB $1435	Ex $1164	Gd $989
w/10-inch bbl., add			$100
Two caliber conversion (bbl., bolt & mag.), add			$444

XIX Platform System

(three-caliber conversion kit w/six bbls.)	NiB $4335	Ex $3799	Gd $3260
XIX6 System (two-caliber conversion kit w/two 6-inch bbls.)	NiB $2675	Ex $2254	Gd $1969
XIX10 System (two-caliber conversion kit w/two 10-inch bbls.)	NiB $2150	Ex $1720	Gd $1196
Custom shop finish, add			$20%
24K gold finish, add			$40%

(ASAI) MODEL ONE PRO .45 PISTOL
Calibers: .45 ACP or .400 COR-BON, 3.75- inch bbl., 7.04 or 7.83 (IPSC Model) inches overall. Weight: 23.5 (alloy frame) or 31.1 oz. 10-round magazine. Short recoil action. SA or DA mode w/de-cocking lever. Steel or alloy grip-frame. TExtured black polymer grips. Imported from 1998.

Model 1P45	NiB $740	Ex $567	Gd $399
Model 1C45/400 (compensator kit), add			$204
Model 1C400NC (400 conversion kit), add			$150

Magnum Research SSP-91 Lone Eagle Pistol
(w/Optional Leupold Scope)

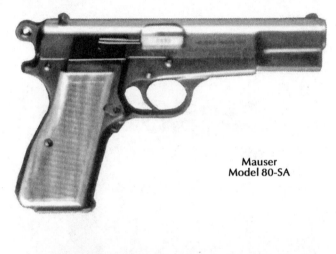

Mauser
Model 80-SA

Mauser
Model 90-DA

MOUNTAIN EAGLE SEMIAUTOMATIC
Caliber: .22 LR. 15-round polycarbonate resin magazine, 6.5-inch injection-molded polymer and steel bbl., 10.6 inches overall. Weight: 21 oz. Ramp blade front sight, adj. rear. Injection-molded, checkered and tExtured grip. Matte black finish. Made 1992 to 1996.
Standard, w/6-inch bb. . . . . NiB $214 Ex $160 Gd $143
Compact, w/ 4.5-inch bbl. . . . . NiB $190 Ex $143 Gd $110

SSP-91 LONE EAGLE PISTOL
Single-shot action w/interchangeable rotating breech bbl., assembly. Calibers: .22 LR, .22 Mag., .22 Hornet, .22-250, .223 Rem., .243 Win., 6mm BR, 7mm-08, 7mm BR, .30-06, .30-30, .308 Win., .35 Rem., .357 Mag., .44 Mag., .444 Marlin. 14-inch interchangeable bbl. assembly, 15 inches overall. Weight: 4.5 lbs. Black or chrome finish. Made from

1991 to 2001.
Black finish . . . . .NiB $434 Ex $321 Gd $165
Chrome finish . . . . .NiB $464 Ex $342 Gd $186
Extra 14-inch bbl., black finish $150
Extra 14-inch bbl., chrome finish, ...$175
Ambidextrous stock assembly (only) $220
w/muzzle brake, add $408
w/open sights, add $45

MAUSER PISTOLS — Oberndorf, Germany, Waffenfabrik Mauser of Mauser-Werke A.G.

MODEL 80-SA AUTOMATIC. . NiB $577 Ex $395 Gd $255
Caliber: 9mm Para. 13-round magazine, 4.66-inch bbl., 8 inches overall. Weight: 31.5 oz. Blued finish. Hardwood grips. Made 1992 to 1996.

MODEL 90 DA AUTOMATIC . NiB $530 Ex $354 Gd $234
Caliber: 9mm Para. 14-round magazine, 4.66-inch bbl., 8 inches overall. Weight: 35 oz. Blued finish. Hardwood grips. Made 1992 to 1996.

MODEL 90 DAC COMPACT . . NiB $571 Ex $405 Gd $270
Caliber: 9mm Para. 14-round magazine, 4.13-inch bbl., 7.4 inches overall. Weight: 33.25 oz. Blued finish. Hardwood grips. Made 1992 to 1996.

MODEL 1898 (1896) "BROOMHANDLE" MILITARY AUTO PISTOL
Caliber: 7.63mm Mauser, but also chambered for 9mm Mauser and 9mm Para. w/the latter being identified by a large red "9" in the grips. 10-round box magazine, 5.25-inch bbl., 12 inches overall. Weight: 45 oz. Adj. rear sight. Blued finish. Walnut grips. Made from 1897 to 1939. Note: Specialist collectors recognize a number of variations at significantly higher values. Price here is for more common commercial and military types with original finish.
Commercial model (pre-war) . . . . . . NiB $3520 Ex $2735 Gd $1096
Commercial model (wartime) . . . . . . NiB $3015 Ex $2512 Gd $1040
Red 9 Commercial model (fixed sight)NiB $3265 Ex $2979 Gd $1049
Red 9 WWI Contract (tangent sight) . NiB $3300 Ex $2670 Gd $1300
w/stock sssembly (matching S/N), add $1300

MODEL HSC DA AUTO PISTOL
Calibers: .32 Auto (7.65mm), .380 Auto (9mm Short). Eight-round (.32) or 7-round (.380) magazine, 3.4-inch bbl., 6.4 inches overall. Weight: 23.6 oz. Fixed sights. Blued or nickel finish. Checkered walnut grips. Made from 1938 to 1945 and from 1968 to 1996.
Military model (low grip screw) . . . . NiB $6200 Ex $5110 Gd $2820
Commercial model (wartime). . . . . NiB $536 Ex $398 Gd $249
Nazi military model (pre-war) . . . . NiB $1148 Ex $974 Gd $632
Nazi military model (wartime) . . . . NiB $600 Ex $499 Gd $270
French production (postwar) . . . . NiB $474 Ex $398 Gd $239
Mauser production (postwar) . . . . NiB $497 Ex $377 Gd $235
Recent importation (Armes De Chasse) . NiB $478 Ex $398 Gd $270
Recent importation (Interarms) . . . . NiB $388 Ex $289 Gd $230
Recent importation (European Amer. Arms)NiB $328 Ex $196 Gd $115
Recent importation (Gamba, USA) . . . . . NiB $431 Ex $316 Gd $194
American Eagle model (1 of 5000) . . . . . NiB $562 Ex $433 Gd $319

LUGER LANGE PISTOL 08
Caliber: 9mm Para. Eight-inch bbl., Checkered grips. Blued finish. Accessorized w/walnut shoulder stock, front sight tool, spare magazine, leather case. Currently in production. Commemorative version made in limited quantities w/ivory grips and 14-carat gold monogram plate.
Commemorative model (100 produced)NiB $2855 Ex $2330 Gd $1875
Commemorative matched pair . . NiB $5423 Ex $4412 Gd $3099
Cartridge counter model . . . . NiB $4010 Ex $2907 Gd $2017
Carbine model (w/matching buttstock)NiB $8025 Ex $6309 Gd $3718

**Mauser Model 1898
(1896) Military**

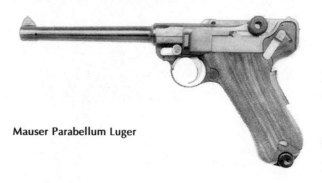

Mauser Parabellum Luger

PARABELLUM LUGER AUTO PISTOL
Current commercial model. Swiss pattern with grip safety. Calibers: 7.65mm Luger, 9mm Para. Eight-round magazine, bbl. lengths: 4-, 6-inch, 8.75 inches overall (with 4-inch bbl.). Weight: 30 oz. (with 4-inch bbl.). Fixed sights. Blued finish. Checkered walnut grips. Made from 1970 to date. Note: Pistols of this model sold in the U.S. have the American Eagle stamped on the receiver.
Standard model (blue). . . . . NiB $1603 Ex $1230 Gd $704

POCKET MODEL 1910 AUTO PISTOL
Caliber: .25 Auto (6.35mm). Nine-round magazine, 3.1-inch bbl., 5.4 inches overall. Weight: 15 oz. Fixed sights. Blued finish. Checkered walnut or hard rubber grips. Made from 1910 to 1934.
Model 1910 (standard) . . . . . . NiB $691 Ex $461 Gd $306
Model 1910 (w/side latch) . . . NiB $546 Ex $431 Gd $309

POCKET MODEL 1914 AUTOMATIC. . . NiB $691 Ex $485 Gd $314
Similar to Pocket Model 1910. Caliber: .32 Auto (7.65mm). Eight-round magazine, 3.4-inch bbl., 6 inches overall. Weight: 21 oz. Fixed sights. Blued finish. Checkered walnut or hard rubber grips. Made 1914 to 1934

POCKET MODEL 1934 . . . . . . NiB $816 Ex $595 Gd $410
Similar to Pocket Models 1910 and 1914 in the respective calibers. Chief difference is in the more streamlined, one-piece grips. Made from 1934 to 1939.

WTP MODEL I AUTO PISTOL. NiB $779 Ex $610 Gd $413
"Westentaschen-Pistole" (Vest Pocket Pistol). Caliber: .25 Automatic (6.35mm). Six-round magazine, 2.5-inch bbl., 4 inches overall. Weight: 11.5 oz. Blued finish. Hard rubber grips. Made from 1922 to 1937.

WTP MODEL II AUTO PISTOL NiB $1398 Ex $1137 Gd $895
Similar to Model I but smaller and lighter. Caliber: .25 Automatic (6.35mm). Six-round magazine, 2-inch bbl., 4 inches overall. Weight: 9.5 oz. Blued finish. Hard rubber grips. Made from 1938 to 1940.

MERWIN HULBERT & CO. — New York
FIRST MODEL
FRONTIER ARMY . . . . NiB $9679 Ex $8023 Gd $6029
Single action, .44 caliber, 7.5-inch bbl. Square butt, open top, scoop flutes on cylinder, two screws above trigger guard

SECOND MODEL
FRONTIER ARMY . . . . NiB $8617 Ex $7608 Gd $6138
Similar to First Model except has only one screw above trigger guard.

SECOND MODEL
POCKET ARMY. . . . . NiB $7740 Ex $ 6487 Gd $5009

Similar to Second Model except has bird's-head butt instead of square butt, 3.5- or 7-inch (scarce) bbl. Some models may be marked "Pocket Army."

THIRD MODEL
FRONTIER ARMY . . . . NiB $6995 Ex $3429 Gd $2152
Caliber: .44, 7-inch round bbl. with no rib, single action. Square butt, top strap, usually has conventional fluting on cylinder but some have scoop flutes.

THIRD MODEL DA
FRONTIER ARMY . . . . NiB $6775 Ex $5254 Gd $4890
Similar to Third Model Frontier Army SA except is double action.

THIRD MODEL POCKET ARMY NiB $7610 Ex $5366 Gd $4997
Caliber: .44, 3.5- or 7.5-inch bbl. with no rib. Single action, bird's-head butt, top strap.

THIRD MODEL POCKET ARMY DA NiB $6648 Ex $5096 Gd $3930
Similar to Third Model Pocket Army SA except is double action.

FOURTH MODEL
FRONTIER ARMY . . . . NiB $9010 Ex $8188 Gd $4992
Caliber: .44, 3.5- 5- or 7-inch unique ribbed bbl. Single action, square butt, top strap, conventional flutes on cylinder.

FOURTH MODEL FRONTIER
ARMY DA . . . . NiB $8189 Ex $5883 Gd $5409
Similar to Fourth Model Frontier Army SA except is double action.

(The following handguns are foreign copies of Merwin Hulbert Co. guns and may be marked as such, or as "Sistema Merwin Hulbert," but rarely with the original Hopkins & Allen markings. These guns will usually bring half or less of a comparable genuine Merwin Hulbert product.)

FIRST POCKET MODEL. . . NiB $2270 Ex $1996 Gd $1416
Caliber: .38 Special, 5-round cylinder (w/cylinder pin Exposed at front of frame), single action. Spur trigger; round loading hole in recoil shield, no loading gate.

SECOND POCKET MODEL NiB $1815 Ex $1595 Gd $1416
Similar to First Pocket Model except has sliding loading gate.

THIRD POCKET MODEL . . NiB $1633 Ex $1270 Gd $1111
Similar to First Pocket Model except has enclosed cylinder pin.

THIRD POCKET
MODEL W/TRIGGER GUARD NiB $1517 Ex $1319 Gd $1133
Similar to First Pocket Model except w/conventional trigger guard.

Mitchell Arms
Citation II

Mitchell Arms
Sharpshooter II

SMALL FRAME
POCKET MODEL . . . . **NiB $1360 Ex $1120 Gd $601**
Caliber: .38 Spec., 5-round cylinder, DA, may have hammer spur.

SMALL FRAME
POCKET MODEL 32 . . . . . . **NiB $1377 Ex $1190 Gd $979**
Similar to Medium Frame Pocket Model except .32 caliber, 7-round cylinder, double action.

TIP-UP MODEL 22 . . . . . **NiB $1579 Ex $1367 Gd $1056**
Similar to S&W Model One except .22 caliber, 7-round cylinder, spur trigger. Scarce.

MITCHELL ARMS, INC. — Santa Ana, California

MODEL 1911 GOLD SIGNATURE
Caliber: .45 ACP. Eight-round mag, 5-inch bbl., 8.75 inches overall. Weight: 39 oz. Interchangeable blade front sight, drift-adj. combat or fully adj. rear. Smooth or checkered walnut grips. Made 1994 to 1996.
Blued model w/fixed sights . . . **NiB $512 Ex $393 Gd $301**
Blued model w/adj. sights . . . . **NiB $554 Ex $456 Gd $412**
Stainless model w/fixed sights . **NiB $709 Ex $549 Gd $464**
Stainless model w/adj. sights . . **NiB $755 Ex $601 Gd $530**

ALPHA MODEL AUTO PISTOL
Dual action w/interchangeable trigger modules. Caliber: .45 ACP. Eight-round magazine, 5-inch bbl., 8.75 inches overall. Weight: 39 oz. Interchangeable blade front sight, drift-adj. rear. Smooth or checkered walnut grips. Blued or stainless finish. Made in 1994 . Advertised in 1995 but not manufactured.

AMERICAN EAGLE LUGER PISTOL NiB $900 Ex $678 Gd $369
Stainless-steel re-creation of the American Eagle Parabellum auto pistol. Caliber: 9mm Para. Seven-round magazine, 4-inch bbl., 9.6 inches overall. Weight: 26.6 oz. Blade front sight, fixed rear. Stainless finish. Checkered walnut grips. Made from 1993 to 1994.

CITATION II AUTO PISTOL . . **NiB $433 Ex $309 Gd $228**
Re-creation of the High Standard Supermatic Citation Military.

Caliber: .22 LR. 10-round magazine, 5.5-inch bull bbl. or 7.25 fluted bbl., 9.75 inches overall (5.5-inch bbl.). Weight: 44.5 oz. Ramp front sight, slide-mounted micro-adj. rear. Satin blued or stainless finish. Checkered walnut grips w/thumbrest. Made 1992 to 1996.

OLYMPIC I.S.U.
AUTO PISTOL . . . . **NiB $659 Ex $556 Gd $434**
Similar to the Citation II model except chambered in .22 Short, 6.75-inch round tapered bbl. w/stabilizer and removable counterweights. Made from 1992 to 1996.

SHARPSHOOTER I
AUTO PISTOL . . . . **NiB $362 Ex $288 Gd $212**
Re-creation of the High Standard Sharpshooter. Caliber: .22 LR. 10-round magazine, 5-inch bull bbl., 10.25 inches overall. Weight: 42 oz. Ramp front sight, slide-mounted micro-adj. rear. Satin blued or stainless finish. Checkered walnut grips w/thumbrest. Made 1992 to 1996.

MODEL SA SPORT KING II . . . **NiB $304 Ex $226 Gd $170**
Caliber: .22 LR. 10-round magazine, 4.5- or 6.75-inch bbl., 9 or 11.25 inches overall. Weight: 39 or 42 oz. Checkered walnut or black plastic grips. Blade front sight and drift adjustable rear. Made 1993 to 1994.

SA ARMY REVOLVER
Calibers: .357 Mag., .44 Mag., .45 Colt/.45 ACP. Six-round cylinder. bbl., lengths: 4.75, 5.5, 7.5 inches, weight: 40-43 oz. Blade front sight, grooved top strap or adj. rear. Blued or nickel finish w/color-casehardened frame. Brass or steel backstrap/trigger guard. Smooth one-piece walnut grips. Imported from 1987-94 and 1997. Disc.
Standard model w/blued finish . . . . . **NiB $431 Ex $319 Gd $235**
Standard model w/nickel finish . . . . . **NiB $464 Ex $398 Gd $303**
Standard model w/steel backstrap . . . **NiB $541 Ex $422 Gd $317**
.45 Combo w/blued finish. . . . . **NiB $544 Ex $429 Gd $346**
.45 Combo w/nickel finish . . . . **NiB $601 Ex $562 Gd $433**

TROPHY II
AUTO PISTOL . . . . **NiB $464 Ex $337 Gd $270**
Similar to the Citation II model except w/gold-plated trigger and gold-filled markings. Made 1992 to 1996.

VICTOR II AUTO PISTOL . . . . **NiB $544 Ex $419 Gd $342**
Re-creation of the High Standard Victor w/full-length vent rib. Caliber: .22 LR. 10-round magazine, 4.5- or 5.5-inch bbl., 9.75 inches overall (with 5.5-inch bbl.). Weight: 52 oz. (with 5.5-inch bbl.). Rib-mounted target sights. Satin blued or stainless finish. Checkered walnut grips w/thumbrest. Made from 1992 to 1996.

GUARDIAN ANGEL
DERRINGER . . . . **NiB $158 Ex $120 Gd $101**
Hammerless, double-action O/U derringer w/interchangeable drop-in breech block. Calibers: .22 LR, .22 WRM. Two-round capacity. Two-inch bbl., 5 inches overall. Weight: 12 oz. Blue, nickel or gold finish. Blade front and fixed rear sights. Checkered black grips. Made from 1996 to 1997.

GUARDIAN II. . . . . **NiB $327 Ex $235 Gd $169**
Caliber: .38 Special, Six-round cylinder, 2-, 4- or 6-inch bbl., 8.5 inches overall (with 4-inch bbl.). Weight: 32 oz (with 4-inch bbl.). Blade ramp front and fixed rear sights. Checkered combat or target grips. Blued finish. Made in 1995.

GUARDIAN III . . . . **NiB $369 Ex $272 Gd $181**
Same specifications as Guardian II model except w/adjustable rear sights. Made in 1995.

TITAN II DA. . . . . **NiB $295 Ex $259 Gd $175**
Caliber: .357 Mag. Six-round cylinder. 2-, 4- or 6-inch bbl., 7.75 inches overall (with 4-inch bbl.). Weight: 38 oz (with 4-inch bbl.). Blade front and fixed rear sights. Crane mounted cylinder release. Blued or stainless finish. Made in 1995.

TITAN III DA . . . . **NiB $345 Ex $204 Gd $119**
Same specification as the Titan II except w/adjustable rear sight. Made in 1995.

MKE PISTOL — Ankara, Turkey.
Manufactured by Makina ve Kimya Endüstrisi Kurumu

KIRIKKALE DA
AUTOMATIC PISTOL . . . . **NiB $399 Ex $283 Gd $212**
Similar to Walther PP. Calibers: .32 Auto (7.65mm), .380 Auto (9mm Short). Seven-round magazine, 3.9-inch bbl., 6.7 inches overall. Weight: 24 oz. Fixed sights. Blued finish. Checkered plastic grips. Made from 1948 to 1988. Note: This is a Turkish Army standard service pistol.

MOA CORPORATION — Dayton, Ohio

MAXIMUM SINGLE-SHOT PISTOL
Calibers: .22 Hornet to .454 Casull Mag. Armoloy, Chromoloy or stainless falling block action fitted w/blued or stainless 8.75-, 10- or 14-inch Douglas bbl., weight: 60-68 oz. Smooth walnut grips. Made from 1986.
Chromoloy receiver
(blued bbl.) . . . . **NiB $806 Ex $588 Gd $475**
Armoloy receiver (blued bbl.) . **NiB $933 Ex $836 Gd $497**
Stainless receiver (blued bbl.) **NiB $1028 Ex $916 Gd $689**
w/stainless bbl., add **$306**
w/Extra bbl., add **$388**

MAXIMUM CARBINE PISTOL
Similar to Maximum Pistol except w/18-inch bbl. Made intermittently from 1986-88 and from 1994 to date.
MOA Maximum (blued bbl.) . . **NiB $984 Ex $780 Gd $601**
MOA Maximum (stainless bbl.) **NiB $1100 Ex $890 Gd $597**

Mitchell Arms SA
Army Revolver

Mitchell Arms
Victor II

MKE Kirikkale

MOA Maximum
Carbine Pistol

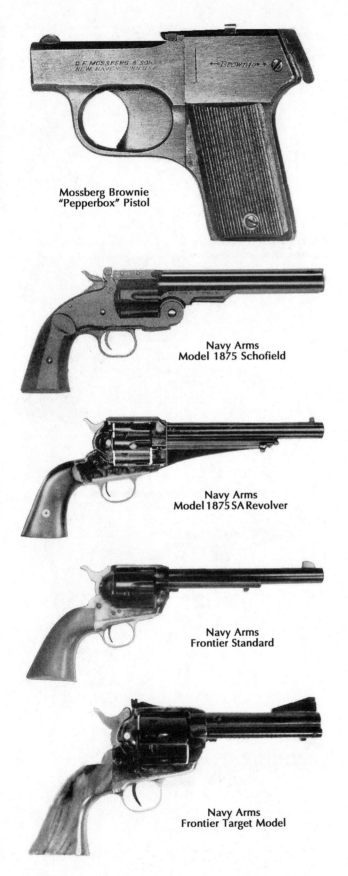

Mossberg Brownie
"Pepperbox" Pistol

Navy Arms
Model 1875 Schofield

Navy Arms
Model 1875 SA Revolver

Navy Arms
Frontier Standard

Navy Arms
Frontier Target Model

O.F. MOSSBERG & SONS, INC. — North Haven, Connecticut

BROWNIE "PEPPERBOX" PISTOL . . . NiB $816 Ex $562 Gd $375
Hammerless, top-break, double-action, four bbls. w/revolving firing pin. Caliber: .22 LR, 2.5-inch bbls., weight: 14 oz. Blued finish. Serrated grips. Approximately 37,000 made from 1919-32.

NAMBU PISTOLS

See Listings under Japanese Military Pistols.

NAVY ARMS COMPANY — Martinsburg, West Virginia

MODEL 1873 SA REVOLVER
Calibers: .44-40, .45 Colt. Six-round cylinder, bbl. lengths: 3, 4.75, 5.5, 7.5 inches, 10.75 inches overall (with 5.5-inch bbl.). Weight: 36 oz. Blade front sight, grooved topstrap rear. Blued w/color-casehardened frame or nickel finish. Smooth walnut grips. Made from 1991 to 2009.
Blued finish w/brass backstrap NiB $468 Ex $357 Gd $235
U.S. Artillery model w/5-inch bbl.NiB $544 Ex $386 Gd $270
U.S. Cavalry model w/7-inch bblNiB $544 Ex $386 Gd $270
Bisley model . . . . NiB $536 Ex $359 Gd $225
Sheriff's model (disc. 1998). . . NiB $434 Ex $356 Gd $220

MODEL 1875 SCHOFIELD REVOLVER
Replica of S&W Model 3, top-break single-action w/auto ejector. Calibers: .44-40 or .45 LC. Six-round cylinder, 5- or 7-inch bbl., 10.75 or 12.75 inches overall. Weight: 39 oz. Blade front sight, square-notched rear. Polished blued finish. Smooth walnut grips. Made from 1999 to 2009.
Cavalry model (7-inch bbl.) . . NiB $668 Ex $544 Gd $336
Deluxe Cavalry model
(engraved) . . . . NiB $1720 Ex $1398 Gd $1176
Wells Fargo model (5-inch bbl.)NiB $840 Ex $636 Gd $447
Deluxe Wells Fargo
model (engraved) . . . . NiB $1479 Ex $1266 Gd $1122
Hideout model (3.5-inch bbl.). NiB $748 Ex $590 Gd $398

1875 REMINGTON SA REVOLVERNiB $398 Ex $283 Gd $194
Replica of Remington Model 1875. Calibers: .357 Magnum, .44-40, .45 Colt. Six-round cylinder, 7.5-inch bbl., 13.5 inches overall. Weight: About 48 oz. Fixed sights. Blued or nickel finish. Smooth walnut grips. Made in Italy c.1955-1980 and 1994 to 2000. Originally marketed in the U.S. as Replica Arms Model 1875 (that firm was acquired by Navy Arms Co).

FRONTIER SA REVOLVER. . . . NiB $397 Ex $290 Gd $224
Calibers: .22 LR, .22 WMR, .357 Mag., .45 Colt. Six-round cylinder, bbl. lengths: 4.5-, 5.5-, 7.5-inches, 10.25 inches overall (with 4.5-inch bbl.). Weight: About 36 oz. (with 4.5-inch bbl.). Fixed sights. Blued bbl., and cylinder, color-casehardened frame, brass grip frame. One-piece smooth walnut grip. Imported from 1975 to 1979.

FRONTIER TARGET MODEL . . NiB $416 Ex $312 Gd $225
Same as standard Frontier except has adj. rear sight and ramp front sight. Imported from 1975 to 1979.

BUNTLINE FRONTIER . . . . . . NiB $569 Ex $467 Gd $342
Same as Target Frontier except has detachable shoulder stock and 16.5-inch bbl. Calibers: .357 Magnum and .45 Colt only. Made from 1975 to 1979.

LUGER AUTOMATIC . . . . NiB $166 Ex $112 Gd $88
Caliber: .22 LR, standard or high velocity. 10-round magazine, bbl. length: 4.5 inches, 8.9 inches overall. Weight: 1 lb., 13.5 oz. Square blade front sight w/square notch, stationary rear sight. Walnut checkered grips. Non-reflecting black finish. Made 1986 to 1988.

ROLLING BLOCK
SINGLE-SHOT PISTOL . . . . . . NiB $418 Ex $345 Gd $231
Calibers: .22 LR, .22 Hornet, .357 Magnum. Eight-inch bbl., 12 inches overall. Weight: About 40 oz. Adjustable sights. Blued bbl., color-casehardened frame, brass trigger guard. Smooth walnut grip and forearm. Imported from 1965 to 1980.

TT-OLYMPIA PISTOL . . . . NiB $283 Ex $214 Gd $170
Reproduction of the Walther Olympia Target Pistol. Caliber: .22 LR. Eight inches overall 4.6-inch bbl., weight: 28 oz. Blade front sight, adj. rear. Blued finish. Checkered hardwood grips. Imported 1992 to 1994.

NEW ENGLAND FIREARMS — Gardner, Massachusetts

In 1987, New England Firearms was established as an independent company producing select H&R models under the NEF logo. In 1991, H&R 1871, Inc. was formed from the residual of the parent company and took over the New England Firearms facility. H&R 1871 produced firearms under both their logo and the NEF brand name until 1999, when the Marlin Firearms Company acquired the assets of H&R 1871. Purchased by Freedom Group in 2008.

MODEL R73 REVOLVER . . . . . . NiB $158 Ex $98 Gd $67
Caliber: .32 H&R Mag. Five-round cylinder, 2.5- or 4-inch bbl., 8.5 inches overall (with 4-inch bbl.). Weight: 26 oz. (with 4 inch bbl.). Fixed or adjustable sights. Blued or nickel finish. Walnut-finish hardwood grips. Made from 1988 to 1999.

MODEL R92 REVOLVER . . . . NiB $137 Ex $90 Gd $64
Same general specifications as Model R73 except chambered for .22 LR. Nine-round cylinder. Weight: 28 oz. w/4 inch bbl., Made 1988 to 1999.

MODEL 832 STARTER PISTOL . NiB $148 Ex $101 Gd $75
Calibers: .22 Blank, .32 Blank. Nine- and 5-round cylinders, respectively. Push-pin swing-out cylinder. Solid wood grips w/NEF medallion insert.

ULTRA REVOLVER . . . . NiB $170 Ex $109 Gd $70
Calibers: .22 LR, .22 Mag. Nine-round cylinder in .22 LR, 6-round cylinder in .22 Mag., 4- or 6-inch ribbed bull bbl., 10.75 inches overall (with 6-inch bbl.). Weight: 36 oz. (with 6-inch bbl.). Blade front sight, adj. square-notched rear. Blued or nickel finish. Walnut-finish hardwood grips. Made from 1989 to 1999.

LADY ULTRA REVOLVER . . . . NiB $169 Ex $144 Gd $106
Same basic specifications as the Ultra except in .32 H&R Mag. w/5-round cylinder and 3-inch ribbed bull bbl., 7.5 inches overall. Weight: 31 oz. Made from 1992 to 1999.

NORTH AMERICAN ARMS — Provo, Utah

MODEL NAA .22LR . . . . NiB $175 Ex $149 Gd $70
Same as Model 22S except chambered for .22 LR., is 3.88-inches overall, weight: 4.5 oz. Made from 1975 to date.

MODEL NAA 22S MINI REVOLVER NiB $170 Ex $150 Gd $70
Single-Action. Caliber: .22 Short. Five-round cylinder, 1.13-inch bbl., 3.5-inches overall. Weight: 4 oz. Fixed sights. Stainless steel.

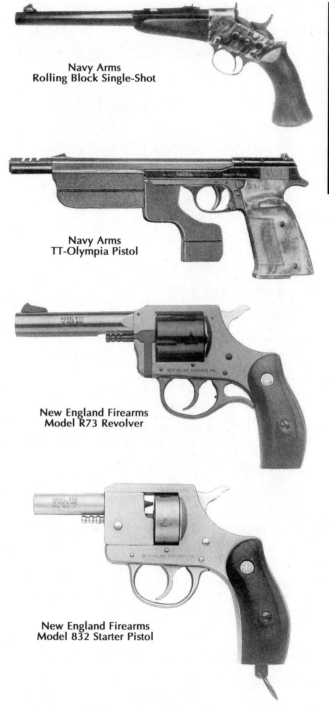

Navy Arms
Rolling Block Single-Shot

Navy Arms
TT-Olympia Pistol

New England Firearms
Model R73 Revolver

New England Firearms
Model 832 Starter Pistol

Plastic grips. Made from 1975 to date.

MODEL 450 MAGNUM EXPRESS
Single-Action. Calibers: .450 Magnum Express, .45 Win. Mag. Five-round cylinder, 7.5- or 10.5-inch bbl., matte or polished stainless steel finish. Walnut grips. Presentation case. Disc. 1984.
Matte stainless model . . . . . NiB $1259 Ex $1066 Gd $808
Polished stainless model . . . NiB $1528 Ex $1234 Gd $856
w/10-inch bbl., add $281
w/combo cylinder, add $255

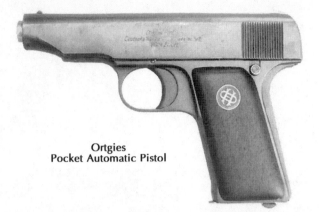

Ortgies
Pocket Automatic Pistol

BLACK WIDOW REVOLVER

SA. Calibers: .22 LR., .22 WMR. Five-round cylinder, 2-inch heavy vent bbl., 5.88-inches overall. Weight: 8.8 oz. Fixed or adj. sights. Full-size black rubber grips. Stainless steel brush finish. Made from 1990 to date.

Adj. sight model. . . . . NiB $257 Ex $188 Gd $135
Adj. sight combo model, add $45
Fixed sight model. . . . . NiB $257 Ex $188 Gd $135
Fixed sight combo model, add $40

GUARDIAN DAO PISTOL. . . . NiB $377 Ex $286 Gd $198

Caliber: .25 ACP, .32 ACP or .380. Six-round magazine (.32 ACP), 2-inch bbl., 4.4 inches overall. Weight: 13.5 oz. Fixed sights. Black synthetic grips. Stainless steel. Made from 1997 to date.

MINI-MASTER TARGET REVOLVER

SA. Calibers: .22 LR., .22 WMR. Five-round cylinder, 4-inch heavy vent rib bbl., 7.75-inches overall. Weight: 10.75 oz. Fixed or adj. sights. Black rubber grips. Stainless steel brush finish. Made from 1990 to date.

Adj. sight model. . . . . NiB $270 Ex $214 Gd $165
Adj. sight combo model, add $35
Fixed sight model. . . . . NiB $270 Ex $214 Gd $165
Fixed sight combo model, add $35

NORWEGIAN MILITARY PISTOLS — Manufactured by Kongsberg Vaapenfabrikk, Government Arsenal at Kongsberg, Norway

MODEL 1914

AUTOMATIC PISTOL . . . . NiB $511 Ex $378 Gd $283
Similar to Colt Model 1911 .45 Automatic w/same general specifications except has lengthened slide stop. Made 1919-46.

NORWEGIAN

MODEL 1912. . . . . NiB $2885 Ex $2289 Gd $1588
Same as the model 1914 except has conventional slide stop. Only 500 were made.

OLYMPIC ARMS, INC. — Olympia, Washington

OA-93 AR SEMIAUTOMATIC PISTOL

AR-15 style receiver with no buffer tube or charging handle. Caliber: .223 Rem. or 7.62x39mm. Five-, 20- or 30-round detachable magazine, 6-, 9- or 14-inch stainless steel bbl., 15.75 inches over-

all w/6-inch bbl., weight: 4 lbs., 3 oz. Flattop upper with no open sights. VortEx flash suppressor. A2 stowaway pistol grip and forward pistol grip. Made 1993-94. Note: All post-ban versions of OA-93 style weapons are classified by BATF as "Any Other Weapon" and must be transferred by a Class III dealer. Values listed here are for limited-production, pre-ban guns.

Model OA-93
(.223 Rem.) . . . . NiB $1134 Ex $871 Gd $687
Model OA-93
(7.62x39mm) . . . . NiB $2234 Ex $1669 Gd $1378

OA-96 AR SEMI-
AUTOMATIC PISTOL . . . . NiB $904 Ex $804 Gd $637
Similar to Model OA-93 AR except w/6.5-inch bbl. only chambered for .223 Rem. Additional compliance modifications include a fixed (nonremovable) well-style magazine and no forward pistol grip. Made from 1996 to 2000.

ORTGIES PISTOLS — Erfurt, Germany. Manufactured by Deutsche Werke A.G.

POCKET-

AUTOMATIC PISTOL . . . . NiB $399 Ex $305 Gd $225
Calibers: .32 Auto (7.65mm), .380 Auto (9mm). Seven-round magazine (.380 cal.), 8-round (.32 cal.), 3.25-inch bbl., 6.5-inches overall. Weight: 22 oz. Fixed sights. Blued finish. Plain walnut grips. Made in 1920's.

VEST POCKET

AUTOMATIC PISTOL . . . . .NiB $365 Ex $289 Gd $203
Caliber: .25 Auto (6.35mm). Six-round magazine, 2.75-inch bbl., 5.19 inches overall. Weight: 13.5 oz. Fixed sights. Blued finish. Plain walnut grips. Made in 1920's.

PARA USA, INC. — Pineville, North Carolina (Purchased by Freedom Group in 2012)

LIMITED EDITION SERIES

Custom-tuned and fully accessorized "Limited Edition" versions of standard "P" Models. Enhanced-grip frame and serrated slide fitted w/match-grade bbl., and full-length recoil spring guide system. Beavertail grip safety and skeletonized hammer. Ambidextrous safety and trigger-stop adjustment. Fully adjustable or contoured low-mount sights. For pricing see individual models.

MODEL P-10 SA AUTO PISTOL

Super compact. Calibers: .40 S&W, .45 ACP. 10-round magazine, 3-inch bbl., weight: 24 oz. (alloy frame) or 31 oz. (steel frame). Ramp front sight and drift adjustable rear w/3-dot system. Steel or alloy frame. Matte black, Duo-Tone or stainless finish. Made from 1997 to 2002.

Alloy model . . . . NiB $637 Ex $540 Gd $413
Duo-Tone model . . . . NiB $688 Ex $581 Gd $464
Stainless steel model. . . . . NiB $693 Ex $577 Gd $447
Steel model . . . . NiB $648 Ex $536 Gd $410
Limited model (tuned & accessorized), add $150

P-12 COMPACT AUTO PISTOL

Calibers: .45 ACP. 11-round magazine, 3.5-inch bbl., 7-inches overall. Weight: 24 oz. (alloy frame). Blade front sight, adj. rear w/3-dot system. TExtured composition grips. Matte black alloy or steel finish. Made from 1990 to 2003.

Model P1245 (alloy) . . . . . . NiB $779 Ex $606 Gd $530
Model P1245C (steel) . . . . . NiB $857 Ex $686 Gd $541
Limited model (tuned & accessorized), add $150

P-13 AUTO PISTOL
Same general specifications as Model P-12 except w/12-round magazine, 4.5-inch bbl., 8-inches overall. Weight: 25 oz. (alloy frame). Blade front sight, adj. rear w/3-dot system. TExtured composition grips. Matte black alloy or steel finish. Made from 1993 to 2003.

Model P1345 (alloy) . . . . . . NiB $779 Ex $606 Gd $530
Model P1345C (steel) . . . . NiB $772 Ex $586 Gd $337
Limited model
(tuned & accessorized), add $150

P-14 AUTO PISTOL
Caliber: .45 ACP. 13-round magazine, 5-inch bbl., 8.5 inches overall. Weight: 28 oz. Alloy frame. Blade front sight, adj. rear w/3-dot system. TExtured composition grips. Matte black alloy or steel finish. Made from 1990 to 2003.

Model P1445 (alloy) . . . . . . NiB $685 Ex $474 Gd $332
Model P1445C (stainless) . . . . NiB $755 Ex $546 Gd $395
Limited model (tuned & accessorized), add $128

MODEL P-15 AUTO PISTOL
Caliber: .40 S&W. 10-round magazine, 4.25-inch bbl., 7.75 inches overall. Weight: 28 to 36 oz. Steel, alloy or stainless receiver. Matte black, Duotone or stainless finish. Made 1996 to 1999.

Model P1540 (alloy) . . . . . . NiB $740 Ex $495 Gd $362
Model P1540C (steel) . . . . NiB $665 Ex $544 Gd $468
Duotone stainless model . . . NiB $740 Ex $495 Gd $362
Stainless model. . . . . NiB $700 Ex $602 Gd $536

MODEL P-16 SA AUTO PISTOL
Caliber: .40 S&W. 10- or 16-round magazine, 5-inch bbl., 8.5 inches overall. Weight: 40 oz. Ramp front sight and drift adjustable rear w/3-dot system. Carbon steel or stainless frame. Matte black, Duotone or stainless finish. Made from 1995 to 2002.

Blue steel model. . . . . NiB $683 Ex $536 Gd $437
Duotone model. . . . . NiB $709 Ex $572 Gd $362
Stainless model. . . . . NiB $740 Ex $576 Gd $485
Limited model (tuned & accessorized), add $175

MODEL P-18 SA AUTO PISTOL
Caliber: 9mm Parabellum. 10- or 18-round magazine, 5-inch bbl., 8.5 inches overall. Weight: 40 oz. Dovetailed front sight and fully adjustable rear. Bright stainless finish. Made from 1998 to 2003.

Stainless model. . . . . NiB $816 Ex $652 Gd $523
Limited model (tuned & accessorized), add $150

PXT SINGLE STACK SERIES AUTO PISTOL
Caliber: 9mm Para. , .38 Super or .45 ACP. Eight- or 9-round (9mm Para) magazine, 3-, 3.5-, 4.25-, 5- or 6-inch bbl., 8.5 inches overall (5-in. bbl.). Weight: 30 oz. (5-in. bbl.). Steel or stainless frame. Blade front sight, adj. rear w/3-dot system. Textured composition grips. Matte black alloy or steel finish. Made from 2004 to date.

1911 OPS (disc. 2008) . . . . . . NiB $980 Ex $931 Gd $450
1911 LTC (intro. 2009) . . . . . . NiB $780 Ex $741 Gd $330
1911 Wild Bunch (intro. 2011) NiB $660 Ex $550 Gd $340
GI Expert (intro. 2009) . . . . . . NiB $580 Ex $440 Gd $355
Slim Hawg (.45 ACP, 3-in. bbl.)NiB $860 Ex $670 Gd $400

PXT HIGH CAPACITY SERIES AUTO PISTOL
Similar to PXT Single Stack series except 10-, 14-, or 18-round magazine.Made from 2004 to date.
P14.45 (.45 ACP, 14-rnd. magazine) . . . .
NiB $880 Ex $650 Gd $410
P18.9 (9mm Para, 18-rnd. magazine) . . . .
NiB $1030 Ex $840 Gd $470
Warthog (.45 ACP, 10-rnd. magazine) . NiB $900 Ex $700
Gd $400

Para-Ordnance
P-12 Compact

Para-Ordnance
P-14 Auto Pistol

PHOENIX ARMS — Ontario, California

MODEL HP22/HP25 SA
AUTO PISTOLS. . . . . NiB $170 Ex $95 Gd $66
Caliber: .22 LR, .25 ACP. 10-round magazine, 3-inch bbl., 5.5 inches overall. Weight: 20 oz. Checkered synthetic grips. Blade front sight, adj. rear. Blue, chrome or nickel finish. Made from 1994 to date.

MODEL HP RANGE-MASTER TARGET SA
AUTO PISTOL . . . . NiB $170 Ex $95 Gd $66
Similar to Model HP .22 except w/5.5-inch target bbl. and Extended magazine, Ramp front sight, adj. notch rear on vent rib. Checkered synthetic grips. Blue or satin nickel finish. Made from 1998 to date.

MODEL HP RANGE-MASTER DELUXE TARGET
SA AUTO PISTOL . . . . NiB $204 Ex $165 Gd $110
Similar to Model HP Rangemaster Target model except w/dual-2000 laser sight and custom wood grips. Made from 1998 to date.

RAVEN SA AUTO PISTOL . . . . . . NiB $88 Ex $61 Gd $45
Caliber: .25 ACP. Six-round magazine, 2.5 inch bbl., 4.75 inches overall. Weight: 15 oz. Ivory, pink pearl, or black slotted stocks. Fixed sights. Blue, chrome or nickel finish. Made from 1993 to 1998.

GRADING: NiB = New in Box   Ex = Excellent or NRA 95%   Gd = Good or NRA 68%

Plainfield Model 71

Plainfield Model 72

Radom P-35

PLAINFIELD MACHINE COMPANY — Dunellen, New Jersey

This firm disc. operation about 1982.

MODEL 71 AUTOMATIC PISTOL
Calibers: .22 LR, .25 Automatic w/conversion kit available. 10-round magazine (.22 LR) or 8-round (.25 Auto), 2.5-inch bbl., 5.13 inches overall. Weight: 25 oz. Fixed sights. Stainless steel frame/slide. Checkered walnut grips. Made from 1970-82.

.22 LR or .25 Auto . . . . NiB $200 Ex $177 Gd $128
w/conversion kit. . . . . NiB $222 Ex $188 Gd $119

MODEL 72 AUTOMATIC PISTOL
Same as Model 71 except has aluminum slide, 3.5-inch bbl., 6 inches overall. Made from 1970 to 1982
.22 LR or .25 Auto only . . . . . NiB $220 Ex $177 Gd $101
w/conversion kit. . . . . NiB $235 Ex $166 Gd $128

PROFESSIONAL ORDNANCE, INC. — Lake Havasu City, Arizona

MODEL CARBON-15 TYPE 20
SEMIAUTOMATIC PISTOL . . . NiB $944 Ex $819 Gd $581
Similar to Carbon-15 Type 97 except w/unfluted barrel. Weight: 40 oz. Matte black finish. Made from 1999 to 2000.

MODEL CARBON-15 TYPE 97
SEMIAUTOMATIC PISTOL . . NiB $1030 Ex $927 Gd $588
AR-15 operating system w/recoil reduction system. Caliber: .223 Rem. 10-round magazine, 7.25-inch fluted bbl., 20 inches overall. Weight: 46 oz. Ghost ring sights. Carbon-fiber upper and lower receivers w/Chromoly bolt carrier. Matte black finish. Checkered composition grip. Made from 1996 to 2003.

RADOM PISTOL — Radom, Poland. Manufactured by the Polish Arsenal

P-35 AUTOMATIC PISTOL
Variation of the Colt Government Model .45 Auto. Caliber: 9mm Para. Eight-round magazine, 4.75-inch bbl., 7.75 inches overall. Weight: 29 oz. Fixed sights. Blued finish. Plastic grips. Made from 1935 thru WWII.
Commercial model
(Polish Eagle) . . . . NiB $4599 Ex $4370 Gd $2555
Nazi military model
(w/slotted backstrap). . . . . . NiB $1629 Ex $1199 Gd $877
Nazi military model
(w/takedown lever). . . . . . . NiB $1300 Ex $1000 Gd $431
Nazi military model
(No takedown lever or slot). . . NiB $459 Ex $356 Gd $232
Nazi military model (Parkerized), add $357

RANDALL FIREARMS COMPANY — Sun Valley, California

The short-lived Randall firearms Company (1982 to 1984) was a leader in the production of stainless steel semi-autimatic handguns, particularly in left-handed configurations. Prices shown are for production models. Add 50% for prototype models (t-prefix on serial numbers) and $125 for guns with serial numbers below 2000. Scare models (C311, C332, etc., made in lots of four pieces or less) valued substantially higher to avid collectors.

MODEL A111 . . . . NiB $791 Ex $479 Gd $316
Caliber: .45 Auto. Barrel: 5 inches. Round-slide top; right-hand model. Sights: Fixed. Total production: 3,431 pieces.

MODEL A112 . . . . NiB $920 Ex $689 Gd $581
Calibers: 9mm. Barrel: 5 inches. Round-slide top; right-hand model. Sights: Fixed.

MODEL A121 . . . . NiB $734 Ex $643 Gd $377
Caliber: .45 Auto. Barrel: 5 inches. Flat-slide top; right-hand model. Sights: Fixed.

MODEL A211. . . . . NiB $785 Ex $571 Gd $479
Caliber: .45 Auto. Barrel: 4.25 inches. Round-slide top; right-hand model. Sights: Fixed.

MODEL A232. . . . . NiB $1560 Ex $1357 Gd $1100
Caliber: 9mm. Barrel: 4.25 inches. Flat-slide top; right-hand model. Sights: Fixed.

MODEL A331. . . . . NiB $1808 Ex $1566 Gd $1234
Caliber: .45 Auto. Barrel: 4.25 inches. Flat-slide top; right-hand model. Sights: Fixed.

MODEL B111. . . . . NiB $1270 Ex $1124 Gd $890
Caliber: .45 Auto. Barrel: 5 inches. Round-slide top; left-hand model. Sights: Fixed. Toatal production: 297 pieces

MODEL B131. . . . . NiB $1470 Ex $1326 Gd $1152
Caliber: .45 Auto. Barrel: 5 inches. Flat-slide top; left-hand model. Sights: Millet. Total production: 225 pieces.

MODEL B311. . . . . NiB $1632 Ex $1418 Gd $1206
Caliber: .45 Auto. Barrel: 4.25 inches. Round-slide top; left-hand model. Sights: Fixed. Total production: 52 pieces.

MODEL B312 LEMAY. . . . NiB $5170 Ex $1669 Gd $3090
Caliber: 9mm. Barrel: 4.25 inches. Round-slide top; left-hand model. Sights: Fixed. Total production: 9 pieces.

MODEL B331. . . . . NiB $1800 Ex $1589 Gd $1356
Caliber: .45 Auto. Barrel: 4.25 inches. Flat-slide top; left-hand model. Sights: Millet. Total production: 45 pieces.

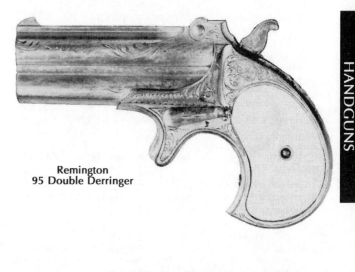

Remington
95 Double Derringer

RECORD-MATCH PISTOLS — Zella-Mehlis, Germany. Manufactured by Udo Anschütz

MODEL 200 FREE PISTOL. . . . NiB $1039 Ex $760 Gd $616
Basically the same as Model 210 except w/different stock design and conventional set trigger, spur trigger guard. Made prior to WW II.

MODEL 210 FREE PISTOL. . NiB $1355 Ex $1206 Gd $919
System Martini action, set trigger w/button release. Caliber: .22 LR. Single-shot, 11-inch bbl., weight: 46 oz. Target sights micrometer rear. Blued finish. Carved and checkered walnut forearm and stock w/adj. hand base. Also made w/dual action (Model 210A); weight 35 oz. Made prior to WWII.

Record-Match
Model 200 Free Pistol

REISING ARMS CO. — Hartford, Connecticut

TARGET AUTOMATIC PISTOL NiB $1132 Ex $862 Gd $587
Hinged frame. Outside hammer. Caliber: .22 LR. 12-round magazine, 6.5-inch bbl., fixed sights. Blued finish. Hard rubber grips. Made 1921 to 1924.

REMINGTON ARMS COMPANY — Ilion, New York

MODEL 51 AUTOMATIC PISTOL
Calibers: .32 Auto, .380 Auto. Seven-round magazine, 3.5-inch bbl., 6.63 inches overall. Weight: 21 oz. Fixed sights. Blued finish. Hard rubber grips. Made from 1918 to 1926.
.32 ACP. . . . . NiB $887 Ex $780 Gd $453
.380 ACP. . . . . NiB $899 Ex $790 Gd $495

MODEL 95 DOUBLE DERRINGER
SA. Caliber: 41 Short Rimfire. Three-inch double bbls. (superposed), 4.88 inches overall. Early models have long ham-

mer spur and two-armed Extractor, but later guns have short hammer spur and sliding Extractor (a few have no Extractor). Fixed blade front sight and grooved rear. finish: Blued, blued w/nickel-plated frame or fully nickel-plated; also w/factory engraving. Grips: Walnut, checkered hard rubber, pearl, ivory. Weight: 11 oz. Made 1866-1935. Approximately 150,000 were manufactured. Note: During the 70 years of its production, serial numbering of this model was repeated two or three times. Therefore, aside from hammer and Extractor differences between the earlier and later models, the best clue to the age of a Double Derringer is the stamping of the company's name on the top of the bbl., or side rib. Prior to 1888, derringers were stamped "E. Remington & Sons, Ilion, N.Y." on one side rib and "Elliot's Patent Dec. 12, 1865" on the other (Type I-early & mid-production) and on the top rib (Type I-late production). In 1888-1911, "Remington Arms Co., Ilion, N.Y." and patent date were stamped on the top rib (Type II) and from 1912-35 "Remington Arms - U.M.C. Co., Ilion, N.Y." and patent date were stamped on the top rib.
Model 95 (Early Type I,
w/o Extractor). . . . . NiB $6600 Ex $5000 Gd $3800
Model 95 (Mid Type I,
w/Extractor) . . . . .NiB $11,000 Ex $8000 Gd $4000
Model 95 (Late Type I,
w/Extractor) . . . . NiB $5000 Ex $4219 Gd $1000
M95 (TYPE II
PRODUCED 1888-1911). . . NiB $3700 Ex $2588 Gd $909
Model 95 (Type III,
produced 1912-35). . . . . . NiB $3600 Ex $3000 Gd $1099
Factory-engraved model w/ivory
or pearl grips, add 40%

NEW MODEL SINGLE-SHOT TARGET PISTOL
Also called Model 1901 Target. Rolling-block action. Calibers: .22 Short & Long, .25 Stevens, .32 S&W, .44 S&W Russian. 10-inch half-octagon bbl., 14 inches overall. Weight: 45 oz. (.22 cal.). Target sights. Blued finish. Checkered walnut grips and forearm. Made from 1901 to 1909.

Model 1901 (.22 caliber) . NiB $3750 Ex $2550 Gd $1203
Model 1901
(.25 Stevens, .32 S&W) . . . NiB $3449 Ex $2988 Gd $1380
Model 1901 (.44 Russian) . NiB $3969 Ex $2709 Gd $1190

MODEL XP-100
SINGLE-SHOT PISTOL. . . . . .NiB $984 Ex $622 Gd $464
Bolt action. Caliber: 221 Rem. Fireball. 10.5-inch vent rib bbl., 16.75 inches overall. Weight: 3.75 lbs. Adj. rear sight, blade front, receiver drilled and tapped for scope mounts. Blued finish. One-piece brown nylon stock. Made from 1963 to 1988.

MODEL XP-100 CUSTOM PISTOL . . NiB $1096 Ex $755 Gd $596
Bolt-action, single-shot, long-range pistol. Calibers: .223 Rem., 7mm-08 or .35 Rem. 14.5-inch bbl., standard contour or heavy. Weight: About 4.25 lbs. Currently in production.

MODEL XP-100 SILHOUETTE . NiB $984 Ex $622 Gd $464
Same general specifications as Model XP-100 except chambered for 7mm BR Rem. and 35 Rem. 14.75-inch bbl., weight: 4.13 lbs. Made from 1987 to 1992.

MODEL XP-100
VARMINT SPECIAL . . . . NiB $984 Ex $622 Gd $464
Bolt-action, single-shot, long-range pistol. Calibers: .223 Rem., 7mm BR. 14.5-inch bbl., 21.25 inches overall. Weight: About 4.25 lbs. One-piece Du Pont nylon stock w/universal grips. Made from 1986 to 1992.

MODEL XP-100R
CUSTOM REPEATER
Same general specifications as Model XP-100 Custom except 4- or 5- round repeater chambered for .22-250, .223 Rem., .250 Savage, 7mm-08 Rem., .308 Win., .35 Rem. and .350 Rem. Mag. Kevlar-reinforced synthetic or fiberglass stock w/blind magazine and sling swivel studs. Made from 1992-94 and from 1998 to 1999.

Model XP-100R (fiberglass stock) . . . NiB $984 Ex $622 Gd $464
Model XP-100R KS (kevlar stock) . . . NiB $984 Ex $622 Gd $464
NOTE: *The following Remington derringers were produced from the mid-1860s through the mid-1930s. The Zig-Zag model is reputed to be the first cartridge handgun ever produced at the Remington plant. Few if any Remington derringers Exiswt in "new" or "in box" condition, therefore, guns in 90-percent condition command top price.*

ZIG-ZAG DERRINGER . . . NiB $6155 Ex $5875 Gd $4145
Caliber: .22S, L, LR. Six shot, six-barrel (rotating) cluster. 3-inch bbl., blued, ring trigger. Two-piece rubber grips. Fewer than 1,000 pieces produced from 1861 to 1863.

ELIOT'S FIVE-SHOT
DERRINGER . . . . .NiB $1897 Ex $1268 Gd $1091
Caliber: .22S, L, LR. Five shot, five-barrel fixed cluster. 3-inch bbl., ring trigger, blue and/or nickel finish. Two-piece rubber, walnut, ivory or pearl grips.

ELIOT'S FOUR-SHOT
DERRINGER . . . . .NiB $5000 Ex $4275 $3795
Caliber: .32. Four shot, four-barrel fixed cluster. 3-3/8 inch bbl., ring trigger, blue and/or nickel finish. Two-piece rubber, walnut, ivory or pearl grips. Approx. 25,000 pieces (.22 and .32) produced.

VEST POCKET DERRINGER NiB $3255 Ex $2920 Gd $2635
Caliber: .22, .30, .32, .41 rimfire . Two shot, various bbl. lengths, blue or nickel finish. Two-piece walnut grips. Spur trigger. Made from 1865 to 1888.

OVER AND UNDER DERRINGERNiB $6270 Ex $4720 Gd $3955
Caliber: .41 rimfire. Two shot, 3-inch super imposed bbl., spur trigger, blue and/or nickel finish. Two-piece rubber, walnut, ivory or pearl grips. Oscillating firing pin. Produced 1866-1934. Also known as Double Derringer or Model 95. Type 1 and variatitons bear maker's name, patent data stamped between the barrels, with or without Extractor. Types Two and Three marked "Remington Arms Company, Ilion, NY." Type Four marked on top of barrel, "Remington Arms-U.M.C. Co. Ilion, NY."

MODEL 1866
ROLLING BLOCK PISTOL . NiB $6210 Ex $4329 Gd $3144
Caliber: .50 rimfire. Single-shot, 8-1/2 inch round, blue finish. Walnut grip and forearm. Spur trigger. Made from 1866-67. Mistakenly designated as Model 1865 Navy. Top values are for military-marked, pristine pieces. Very few of these guns remain in original condition.

MODEL 1870 NAVY
ROLLING BLOCK PISTOL . NiB $4225 Ex $3199 Gd $1905
Caliber: .50 centerfire. Single shot, 7-inch round bbl. Standard trigger with trigger guard, walnut grip and forearm. Approx. 6,400 pieces made from 1870-75. Modified for the Navy from Model 1866. Higher values are for 8--inch commercial version without proof marks.

RIDER'S
MAGAZINE PISTOL . . . . . .NiB $3577 Ex $2885 Gd $2389
Caliber: .32. Five shot, 3-inch octagon bbl. blued (add 50 percent for case-hardened receiver). Walnut, rosewood, ivory or pearl grips. Spur trigger. Made from 1871 to 1888.

ELIOT'S VEST POCKET
SINGLE-SHOT DERRINGER NiB $3387 Ex $1109 Gd $879
Caliber: .41 rimfire. Single-shot, 2-1/2-inch round bbl., blue and/or nickel finish. Also known as "Mississippi Derringer." Two-piece walnut grips. Spur trigger. Approx. 10,000 made from 1867 to 1888.

MODEL 1890 SINGLE-ACTION
REVOLVER . . . . NiB $15,210 Ex $14,070 Gd $7680
Caliber: .41 centerfire . Six shot, 5-3/4 or 7-1/2-inch round bbl., blue or nickel finish. Standard trigger with trigger guard. Two-piece ivory or pearl grips with Remington monogram. nickel finish valued about 15 percent less.

MODEL 1911
REMINGTON UMC . . . . . .NiB $7000 Ex $5550 Gd $1650
Caliber: .45 ACP. WWII military contract production. Blued finish. Made from 1918 to 1919, with serial numbers 1 to 21,676.

MODEL 1911A1
REMINGTON RAND . . . . .NiB $2500 Ex $2079 Gd $1086
Caliber: .45 ACP. Parkerized finish. Two-piece walnut grips. Made from 1943-45 by Remington Rand Co., not Remington Arms Co.

RG REVOLVERS — Manufactured by Rohm Gmbh, Germany (imported by R.G. Industries, Miami, FL)

MODEL 23 . . . . **NiB $115 Ex $88 Gd $70**
SA/DA. 6-round magazine, swing-out cylinder. Caliber: .22 LR. 1.75- or 3.38-inch bbl., Overall length: 5.13 and 7.5 inches. Weight: 16-17 oz. Fixed sights. Blued or nickel finish. Disc. 1986.

MODEL 385
SA/DA. Caliber: .38 Special. Six-round magazine, swing-out cylinder. Three- or 4-inch bbl., overall length: 8.25 and 9.25 inches. Weight: 32-34 oz. Windage-adj. rear sight. Blued finish. Disc. 1986.
w/plastic grips . . . . **NiB $177 Ex $140 Gd $101**
w/wood grips . . . . **NiB $212 Ex $130 Gd $95**

ROSSI REVOLVERS — Sáo Leopoldo, Brazil. Manufactured by Amadeo Rossi S.A. (imported by Interarms, Alexandria, VA)

MODEL 31 DA REVOLVER . . . . . **NiB $144 Ex $78 Gd $62**
Caliber: .38 Special. Five-round cylinder, 4-inch bbl., weight: 20 oz. Blued or nickel finish. Disc. 1985.

MODEL 51 DA REVOLVER . . . . . **NiB $147 Ex $82 Gd $61**
Caliber: .22 LR. Six-round cylinder, 6-inch bbl., weight: 28 oz. Blued finish. Disc. 1985.

MODEL 68 . . . . **NiB $177 Ex $147 Gd $101**
Caliber: .38 Special. Five-round magazine, 2- or 3-inch bbl., overall length: 6.5 and 7.5 inches. Weight: 21-23 oz. Blued finish. Nickel finish available w/3-inch bbl. Disc. 1998.

MODEL 84 DA REVOLVER . . . **NiB $209 Ex $160 Gd $110**
Caliber: .38 Special. Six-round cylinder, 3-inch bbl., 8 inches overall. Weight: 27.5 oz. Stainless steel finish. Imported 1984 to 1986.

MODEL 85 DA REVOLVER . . . **NiB $209 Ex $160 Gd $110**
Same as Model 84 except has vent rib. Imported from 1985 to 1986.

MODEL 88 DA REVOLVER
Caliber: .38 Special. Five-round cylinder, 2- or 3-inch bbl., weight: 21 oz. Stainless steel finish. Imported from 1988 to 1998.
Model 88 (disc.) . . . . **NiB $219 Ex $180 Gd $148**
Model 88 Lady Rossi
(round butt) . . . . **NiB $225 Ex $189 Gd $152**

MODEL 88/2 DA REVOLVER . **NiB $219 Ex $180 Gd $140**
Caliber: .38 Special. Five-round cylinder, 2- or 3-inch bbl., 6.5 inches overall. Weight: 21 oz. Stainless steel finish. Imported 1985 to 1987.

MODEL 89 DA REVOLVER . . . . **NiB $184 Ex $110 Gd $75**
Caliber: .32 S&W. Six-round cylinder, 3-inch bbl., 7.5 inches overall. Weight: 17 oz. Stainless steel finish. Imported 1989 to 1990.

MODEL 94 DA REVOLVER . . . .**NiB $175 Ex $109 Gd $88**
Caliber: .38 Special. Six-round cylinder, 3-inch bbl., 8 inches overall. Weight: 29 oz. Imported from 1985 to 1988.

MODEL 95 (951) REVOLVER . **NiB $219 Ex $175 Gd $141**
Caliber: .38 Special. Six-round magazine, 3-inch bbl., 8 inches overall. Weight: 27.5 oz. Vent rib. Blued finish. Imported 1985 to 1990.
MODEL 351/352 REVOLVERS

Caliber: .38 Special. Five-round cylinder, 2-inch bbl., 6.87 inches overall. Weight: 22 oz. Ramp front and rear adjustable sights. Stainless or matte blued finish. Imported from 1999 to date.
Model 351 (matte blue finish) . **NiB $362 Ex $255 Gd $186**
Model 352 (stainless finish). . . **NiB $437 Ex $326 Gd $265**

MODEL 461/462 REVOLVERS
Caliber: .357 Magnum. Six-round cylinder, 2-inch heavy bbl., 6.87 inches overall. Weight: 26 oz. Rubber grips w/ serrated ramp front sight. Stainless or matte blued finish. Imported 1999 to date.
Model 461 (matte blue finish) . **NiB $365 Ex $265 Gd $188**
Model 462 (stainless finish). . . **NiB $439 Ex $290 Gd $219**

MODEL 511 DA REVOLVER . . . **NiB $195 Ex $170 Gd $75**
Similar to the Model 51 except in stainless steel. Imported 1986 to 1990.

MODEL 515 DA REVOLVER . . . **NiB $214 Ex $105 Gd $70**
Calibers: .22 LR, .22 Mag. Six-round cylinder, 4-inch bbl., 9 inches overall. Weight: 30 oz. Red ramp front sight, adj. square-notched rear. Stainless finish. Checkered hardwood grips. Imported from 1994 to 1998.

MODEL 518 DA REVOLVER . . . **NiB $214 Ex $105 Gd $70**
Similar to the Model 515 except in caliber .22 LR. Imported from 1993 to 1998.

MODEL 677 DA REVOLVER . . **NiB $225 Ex $180 Gd $128**
Caliber: .357 Mag. Six-round cylinder, 2-inch bbl., 6.87 inches overall. Weight: 26 oz. Serrated front ramp sight, channel rear. Matte blue finish. Contoured rubber grips. Imported from 1997 to 1998.

MODEL 720 DA REVOLVER . . **NiB $235 Ex $170 Gd $141**
Caliber: .44 Special. Five-round cylinder, 3-inch bbl., 8 inches overall. Weight: 27.5 oz. Red ramp front sight, adj. square-notched rear. Stainless finish. Checkered Neoprene combat-style grips. Imported from 1992 to 1998.

MODEL 841 DA REVOLVER . . **NiB $319 Ex $225 Gd $160**
Same general specifications as Model 84 except has 4-inch bbl., (9 inches overall), weight: 30 oz. Imported from 1985 to 1986.

MODEL 851 DA REVOLVER . . **NiB $336 Ex $259 Gd $158**
Same general specifications as Model 85 except w/3-or 4-inch bbl., 8 inches overall (with 3-inch bbl.). Weight: 27.5 oz. (with 3-inch bbl.). Red ramp front sight, adj. square-notched rear. Stainless finish. Checkered hardwood grips. Imported from 2001 to 2009 to date.

MODEL 877 DA REVOLVER . . **NiB $230 Ex $160 Gd $110**
Same general specifications as Model 677 except stainless steel. Made from 1996 to date.

MODEL 941 DA REVOLVER . . . **NiB $214 Ex $109 Gd $82**
Caliber: .38 Special. Six-round cylinder, 4-inch bbl., 9 inches overall. Weight: 30 oz. Blued finish. Imported from 1985-86.

MODEL 951 DA REVOLVER . . . **NiB $214 Ex $109 Gd $82**
Previous designation M95 w/same general specifications.

MODEL 971 DA REVOLVER
Caliber: .357 Magnum. Six-round cylinder, 2.5-, 4- or 6-inch bbl., 9 inches overall (with 4-inch bbl.). Weight: 36 oz. (with 4-inch bbl.). Blade front sight, adj. square-notched rear. Blued or stainless finish. Checkered hardwood grips. Imported from 1988 to 1998.
Blued finish . . . . **NiB $219 Ex $166 Gd $129**
Stainless finish . . . . **NiB $240 Ex $175 Gd $101**
w/compensated bbl., add **$25**

Ruger Mark I Target w/5.5-inch Untapered Bull Barrel

Ruger Mark II

Ruger Mark II .22/.45

MODEL 971 VRC
DA REVOLVER . . . . NiB $321 Ex $270 Gd $175
Same general specifications as Model 971 stainless except w/ventilated rib and compensated bbl. Made 1988 to 1998.

CYCLOPS DA REVOLVER . . . . NiB $425 Ex $362 Gd $274
Caliber: .357 Mag. Six-round cylinder, 6- or 8-inch compensated slab-sided bbl., 11.75 or 13.75 inches overall. Weight: 44 oz. or 51 oz. Undercut blade front sight, fully adjustable rear. B-Square scope mount and rings. Stainless steel finish. Checkered rubber grips. Made from 1997 to 1998.

DA REVOLVER . . . . NiB $220 Ex $170 Gd $124
Calibers: .22 LR, .32 S&W Long, .38 Special. Five-round (.38) or 6-round cylinder (other calibers), bbl. lengths: 3-, 6-inches. Weight: 22 oz. (3-inch bbl.). Adj. Rear sight, ramp front. Blued or nickel finish. Wood or plastic grips. Imported from 1965-91.

SPORTSMAN'S .22 . . . . NiB $279 Ex $219 Gd $170
Caliber: .22 LR. Six-round magazine, 4-inch bbl., 9 inches overall. Weight: 30 oz. Stainless steel finish. Disc. 1991.

RUBY PISTOL — Manufactured by Gabilondo y Urresti, Eibar, Spain, and others

7.65MM
AUTOMATIC PISTOL . . . . . . NiB $342 Ex $255 Gd $129
Secondary standard service pistol of the French Army in world wars I and II. Essentially the same as the Alkartasuna (see separate listing). Other manufacturers: Armenia Elgoibarresa y Cia., Eceolaza y Vicinai y Cia., Hijos de Angel Echeverria y Cia., Bruno Salaverria y Cia., Zulaika y Cia., all of Eibar, Spain-Gabilondo y Cia., Elgoibar Spain; Ruby Arms Company, Guernica, Spain. Made from 1914 to 1922.

RUGER — Southport, Connecticut. Manufactured by Sturm, Ruger & Co.

Rugers made in 1976 are designated "Liberty" in honor of the U.S. Bicentennial and bring a premium of approximately 25% in value over regular models.

NOTE: *For ease in finding a particular Ruger handgun, the listings are divided into two groups: Automatic/Single-Shot Pistols (below) and Revolvers, which follow. For a complete listing, please refer to the index.*

AUTOMATIC/SINGLE-SHOT PISTOLS

HAWKEYE SINGLE-SHOT PISTOL NiB $2555 Ex $2427 Gd $1000
Built on a SA revolver frame w/cylinder replaced by a swing-out breechblock and fitted w/a bbl., w/integral chamber. Caliber: .256 Magnum. 8.5-inch bbl., 14.5 inches overall. Weight: 45 oz. Blued finish. Ramp front sight, click adj. rear. Smooth walnut grips. Made from 1963 to 1965 (3,300 produced).

MARK I TARGET MODEL AUTOMATIC PISTOL
Caliber: .22 LR. 10-round magazine, 5.25- and 6.88-inch heavy tapered or 5.5-inch untapered bull bbl., 10.88 inches overall (with 6.88-inch bbl.). Weight: 42 oz. (in 5.5- or 6.88-inch bbl.). Undercut target front sight, adj. rear. Blued finish. Hard rubber grips or checkered walnut thumbrest grips. Made from 1952 to 1982.
Standard model . . . . NiB $877 Ex $791 Gd $612
w/red medallion . . . . NiB $975 Ex $859 Gd $712
Walnut grips, add $434

MARK II AUTOMATIC PISTOL
Caliber: .22 LR, standard or high velocity 10-round magazine, 4.75- or 6-inch tapered bbl., 8.31 inches overall (with 4.75-inch bbl.). Weight: 36 oz. Fixed front sight, square notch rear. Blued or stainless finish. Made from 1982 to 2004.
Blued . . . . NiB $265 Ex $305 Gd $158
Stainless . . . . NiB $321 Ex $265 Gd $204
Bright stainless (ltd.
prod. 5,000 in 1982) . . . . NiB $590 Ex $479 Gd $346

MARK II .22/.45 AUTOMATIC PISTOL

Same general specifications as Ruger Mark II .22 LR except w/blued or stainless receiver and bbl., in four lengths: 4-inch tapered w/adj. sights (P4), 4.75-inch tapered w/fixed sights (KP4), 5.25-inch tapered w/adj. sights (KP 514) and 5.5-inch bull (KP 512). Fitted w/Zytel grip frame of the same design as the Model 1911 45 ACP. Made from 1993 to 2004.

Model KP4 (4.75-inch bbl.)........ NiB $255 Ex $177 Gd $140

Model KP512, KP514

(w/5.5- or 5.25-inch bbl.)........ NiB $365 Ex $229 Gd $126

Model P4, P512

(Blued w/4- or 5.5-inch bbl.)...... NiB $270 Ex $216 Gd $160

MARK II BULL BARREL MODEL

Same as standard Mark II except for bull bbl. (5.5- or 10-inch). Weight: About 2.75 lbs.

Blued finish .... NiB $319 Ex $237 Gd $175

Stainless finish (intro. 1985) .. NiB $430 Ex $379 Gd $128

MARK II GOVERNMENT MODEL AUTO PISTOL

Civilian version of the Mark II used by U.S. Armed Forces. Caliber: .22LR. 10-round magazine, 6.88-inch bull bbl., 11.13 inches overall. Weight: 44 oz. Blued or stainless finish. Made from 1986 to 1999.

Blued model (MK687G commercial) . NiB $388 Ex $286 Gd $198

Stainless steel model

(KMK678G commercial) .... NiB $444 Ex $337 Gd $270

w/U.S. markings (military model) .. NiB $1148 Ex $910 Gd $629

MARK II TARGET MODEL

Caliber: .22 LR. 10-round magazine, 4-, 5.5- and 10-inch bull bbl. or 5.25- and 6.88-inch heavy tappered bbl., weight: 38 oz. to 52 oz. 11.13 inches overall (with 6.88-inch bbl.). Made 1982 to 2004.

Blued.................. NiB $375 Ex $303 Gd $128

Stainless steel............. NiB $444 Ex $377 Gd $290

MODEL P-85 AUTOMATIC PISTOL

Caliber: 9mm. DA, recoil-operated. 15-round capacity, 4.5 inch bbl., 7.84 inches overall. Weight: 32 oz. Fixed rear sight, square-post front. Available w/decocking levers, ambidExtrous safety or in DA only. Blued or stainless finish. Made from 1987 to 1992.

Blued finish .... NiB $332 Ex $214 Gd $110

Stainless steel finish .... NiB $439 Ex $365 Gd $291

MODEL P-89 AUTOMATIC PISTOL

Caliber: 9mm. DA w/slide-mounted safety levers. 15-round magazine, 4.5-inch bbl., 7.84 inches overall. Weight: 32 oz. Square-post front sight, adj. rear w/3-dot system. Blued or stainless steel finish. Grooved black Xenoy grips. Made from 1992 to 2007.

P-89 blued.............. NiB $434 Ex $321 Gd $225

P-89 stainless .... NiB $546 Ex $453 Gd $388

MODEL P-89 DAC/DAO AUTO PISTOLS

Similar to the standard Model P-89 except the P-89 DAC has ambidExtrous decocking levers. The P-89 DAO operates in double-action-only mode. Made from 1991 to 2009.

P-89 DAC blued........... NiB $431 Ex $316 Gd $225

P-89 DAC/DAO stainless .... NiB $530 Ex $431 Gd $316

MODEL P-90, KP90 DA AUTOMATIC PISTOL

Caliber: .45 ACP. Seven-round magazine, 4.5-inch bbl., 7.88 inches overall. Weight: 33.5 oz. Square-post front sight adj. square-notched rear w/3-dot system. Grooved black Xenoy composition grips. Blued or stainless finish. DAC model has ambidExtrous decocking levers. Made from 1991 to 2010.

Model P-90 blued......... NiB $530 Ex $342 Gd $240

Model P-90 DAC (decocker) .. NiB $530 Ex $342 Gd $240

Model KP-90 DAC stainless .. NiB $536 Ex $367 Gd $270

Model KP-90 DAC (decocker). NiB $536 Ex $367 Gd $270

Ruger P-89 DAC/ DAO

Ruger P-90

Ruger P-93 Compact

Ruger Bearcat SA
(Old Model)

Ruger Bisley
Colt .45 Long (New Model)

Ruger Bisley
Single-Six Small Frame

Ruger Blackhawk

Ruger Blackhawk
SA .44

Ruger P-97

MODEL KP-91 DA AUTOMATIC PISTOL
Same general specifications as the Model P-90 except chambered for .40 S&W w/12-round double-column magazine, Made 1992 to 1994.
Model P-91 DAC (decockers) . NiB $444 Ex $289 Gd $225
Model P-91 DAO (DA only) . . NiB $444 Ex $289 Gd $225

MODEL P-93D AUTO PISTOL
Similar to the standard Model P-89 except w/3.9-inch bbl., (7.3 inches overall) and weight: 31 oz. Stainless steel finish. Made from 1993 to 2004.
Model P-93 DAC (decocker) (disc. 1994)NiB $444 Ex $289 Gd $225
Model P-93 Stainless . . . . NiB $485 Ex $357 Gd $283

MODEL P-94 AUTOMATIC PISTOL
Similar to the Model P-91 except w/4.25-inch bbl., Calibers: 9mm or .40 S&W. Blued or stainless steel finish. Made 1994 to 2004.
Model KP-94 DAC (S/S decocker) . . . . . NiB $444 Ex $289 Gd $225
Model KP-94 DAO (S/S dble. action only)NiB $444 Ex $289 Gd $225
Model P-94 DAC (Blued decocker) . . . . NiB $444 Ex $289 Gd $225
Model P-94 DAO (blued dble. action only)NiB $395 Ex $290 Gd $198

MODEL P-95PR AUTO PISTOL
Caliber: 9mm Parabellum. 10-round magazine, 3.9-inch bbl., 7.3 inches overall. Weight: 27 oz. Square-post front sight, drift adjustable rear w/3-dot system. Molded polymer grip-frame fitted w/stainless or chrome-moly slide. AmbidExtrous decocking levers (P-95D) or double action only (DAO). Matte black or stainless finish. Made from 1997 to date.
P-95 blued . . . . NiB $444 Ex $289 Gd $225
KP-95PR stainless . . . . NiB $398 Ex $270 Gd $190

MODEL P-97D AUTOMATIC PISTOL
Caliber: .45 ACP. Eight-round magazine, 4.5- inch bbl., 7.25 inches overall. Weight: 30.5 oz. Square-post front sight adj. square-notched rear w/3-dot system. Grooved black Xenoy composition grips. Blued or stainless finish. DAC model has ambidExtrous decocking levers. Made from 2002 to 2004.
Model KP-97
DAO stainless . . . . NiB $444 Ex $289 Gd $225
Model P-97D
DAC (decockers) . . . . NiB $377 Ex $306 Gd $219

STANDARD MODEL AUTOMATIC PISTOL
Caliber: .22 LR. Nine-round magazine, 4.75- or 6-inch bbl., 8.75 inches overall (with 4.75-inch bbl.). Weight: 36 oz. (with 4.75 inch bbl.). Fixed sights. Blued finish. Hard rubber or checkered walnut grips.

Made from 1949 to 1952. Known as the "Red Eagle Automatic," this early type is now a collector's item. Note: After the death of Alexander Sturm in 1951, the color of the eagle on the grip medallion was changed from red to black as a memorial. Made from 1952 to 1981.

w/red eagle medallion . . . . . . NiB $689 Ex $536 Gd $431
w/black eagle medallion. . . . . NiB $430 Ex $379 Gd $170
Walnut grips, add. $40

NOTE: *This section contains only Ruger revolvers. Automatic and single-shot pistols may be found on the preceding pages. For a complete listing of Ruger handguns, please refer to the index.*

REVOLVERS

BEARCAT, SUPER (OLD MODEL) . . . NiB $602 Ex $365 Gd $291
Same general specifications as Bearcat except has steel frame. Weight: 25 oz. Made from 1971 to 1974.

NEW MODEL BEARCAT REVOLVER
Same general specifications as Super Bearcat except all steel frame and trigger guard. Interlocked mechanism and transfer bar. Calibers: .22 LR and .22WMR. Interchangeable 6-round cylinders (disc. 1996). Smooth walnut stocks w/Ruger medallion. Made from 1994 to date.
Convertible model (disc.
1996 after factory recall) . . . . NiB $469 Ex $362 Gd $291
Standard model (.22 LR only). . . . . NiB $485 Ex $326 Gd $225

BISLEY SA REVOLVER, LARGE FRAME
Calibers: .357 Mag., .41 Mag. .44 Mag., .45 Long Colt. 7.5-inch bbl., 13 inches overall. Weight: 48 oz. Non-fluted or fluted cylinder, no engraving. Ramp front sight, adj. rear. Satin blued or stainless. Made from 1986 to date.
Blued finish . . . . NiB $485 Ex $365 Gd $270
Vaquero/Bisley (blued w/case colored fr.) NiB $612 Ex $474 Gd $398
Vaquero/Bisley (stainless steel) NiB $587 Ex $434 Gd $357
w/ivory grips, add. $50

BISLEY SINGLE-SIX REVOLVER, SMALL FRAME
Calibers: .22 LR and .32 Mag. Six-round cylinder, 6.5-inch bbl., 11.5 inches overall. Weight: 41 oz. Fixed rear sight, blade front. Blue finish. Goncalo Alves grips. Made from 1986 to date.
.22 caliber . . . . NiB $485 Ex $365 Gd $270
.32 H&R Mag. . . . . NiB $693 Ex $601 Gd $479

BLACKHAWK SA CONVERTIBLE (OLD MODEL)
Same as Blackhawk except has Extra cylinder. Caliber combinations: .357 Magnum and 9mm Para., .45 Colt and .45 Automatic. Made 1967 to 1972.
.357/9mm combo (early w/o prefix S/N).NiB $556 Ex $437 Gd $290
.357/9mm combo (late w/prefix S/N). NiB $556 Ex $437 Gd $290
.45 LC/.45 ACP combo
(1967-85 & 1999 to date) . . . . NiB $556 Ex $437 Gd $290

BLACKHAWK SA REVOLVER (OLD MODEL)
Calibers: .30 Carbine, .357 Magnum, .41 Magnum, .45 Colt. Six-round cylinder, bbl. lengths: 4.63-inch (.357, .41, .45 caliber), 6.5-inch (.357, .41 caliber), 7.5-inch (.30, .45 caliber). 10.13 inches overall (.357 Mag. w/4.63-inch bbl.). Weight: 38 oz. (.357 w/4.63-inch bbl.). Ramp front sight, adj. rear. Blued finish. Checkered hard rubber or smooth walnut grips. Made from 1955 to 1962.
.30 Carbine, .357 Mag. . . . . . . NiB $510 Ex $432 Gd $325
.41 Mag. . . . . NiB $760 Ex $660 Gd $265
.45 Colt . . . . .NiB $875 Ex $532 Gd $255

BLACKHAWK SA "FLAT-TOP" REVOLVER (OLD MODEL)
Similar to standard Blackhawk except w/"Flat Top" cylinder strap. Calibers: .357 or .44 Magnum. Six-round fluted cylinder, 4.625-, 6.5-, 7.5- or 10-inch bbl., adj. rear sight, ramp front. Blued finish. Black rubber or smooth walnut grips. Made from 1955 to 1962.

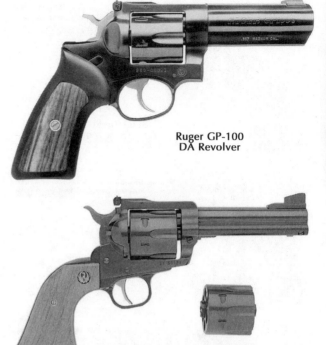

Ruger GP-100
DA Revolver

Ruger New Model Blackhawk Convertible

Ruger Blackhawk High-Gloss Stainless
(New Model) .357 Magnum

.357 Mag. (w/4.625-inch bbl.) . . . NiB $1235 Ex $1148 Gd $975
.357 Mag. (w/6.5-inch bbl.) . . . . NiB $479 Ex $342 Gd $198
.357 Mag. (w/10-inch bbl.) . . . . . NiB $2540 Ex $1650 Gd $1030
.44 Mag. (w/fluted cylinder/ 4.625-inch bbl.) NiB $1336 Ex $1270 Gd $1030
.44 Mag. (w/fluted cylinder/ 6.5-inch bbl.)NiB $1020 Ex $666 Gd $408
.44 Mag. (w/fluted cylinder/ 10-inch bbl.) NiB $2540 Ex $1945 Gd $1779

GP-100 DA REVOLVER
Caliber: .357 Magnum. Three- to 4-inch heavy bbl., or 6-inch standard or heavy bbl., Overall length: 9.38 or 11.38 inches. Cushioned grip panels. Made from 1986 to date.
Blued finish . . . . NiB $590 Ex $434 Gd $274
Stainless steel finish . . . . NiB $570 Ex $410 Gd $290

NEW MODEL BLACKHAWK CONVERTIBLE
Same as New Model Blackhawk except has Extra cylinder. Blued finish only. Caliber combinations: .357 Magnum/9mm Para., .44 Magnum/.44-40, .45 Colt/.45 ACP. (Limited Edition Buckeye Special .32-20/.32 H&R Mag. or .38-40/10mm). Made from 1973 to 1985. Reintro. 1999.
.32-20/.32 H&R Mag. (1989-90) . . . . NiB $556 Ex $386 Gd $259
.38-40/10mm (1990-91) . . . . NiB $556 Ex $386 Gd $259
.357/9mm combo. . . . . NiB $556 Ex $386 Gd $259
.44/.44-40 combo (disc.1982). . . . . . NiB $834 Ex $579 Gd $389
.45 LC/.45 ACP combo (disc. 1985) . NiB $556 Ex $386 Gd $259

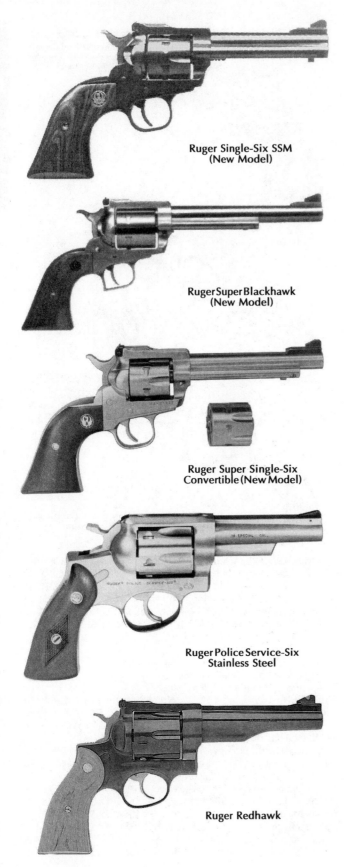

Ruger Single-Six SSM
(New Model)

Ruger Super Blackhawk
(New Model)

Ruger Super Single-Six
Convertible (New Model)

Ruger Police Service-Six
Stainless Steel

Ruger Redhawk

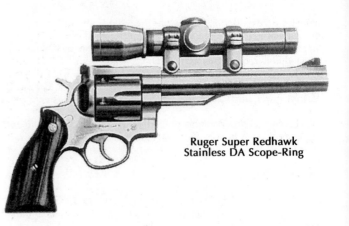

Ruger Super Redhawk
Stainless DA Scope-Ring

NEW MODEL BLACKHAWK SA REVOLVER

Interlocked mechanism. Calibers: .30 Carbine, .357 Magnum, .357 Maximum, .41 Magnum, .44 Magnum, .44 Special, .45 Colt. Six-round cylinder, bbl. lengths: 4.63-inch (.357, .41, .45 Colt); 5.5 inch (.44 Mag., .44 Spec.); 6.5-inch (.357, .41, .45 Long Colt); 7.5-inch (.30, .45, .44 Special, .44 Mag.); 10.5-inch in .44 Mag; 10.38 inches overall (.357 Mag. w/4.63-inch bbl.). Weight: 40 oz. (.357 w/4.63-inch bbl.). Adj. rear sight, ramp front. Blued finish or stainless steel; latter only in .357 or .45 LC. Smooth walnut grips. Made from 1973.
Blued finish . . . . NiB $464 Ex $326 Gd $203
High-gloss stainless (.357 Mag., .45 LC)NiB $459 Ex$316 Gd$190
Satin stainless (.357 Mag., .45 LC) . NiB $418 Ex $332 Gd $265
.357 Maximum SRM (1984-85) . . . NiB $452 Ex $357 Gd $226

NEW MODEL SUPER SINGLE-SIX SSM

SA REVOLVER . . . . NiB $555 Ex $480 Gd $209
Same general specifications as standard Single-Six except chambered for .32 H&R Magnum cartridge. Bbl. lengths: 4.63, 5.5, 6.5 or 9.5 inches.

NEW MODEL SUPER BLACKHAWK SA REVOLVER

Interlocked mechanism. Caliber: .44 Magnum. Six-round cylinder, 5.5-inch, 7.5-inch and 10.5-inch bull bbl. 13.38 inches overall. Weight: 48 oz. Adj. rear sight, ramp front. Blued and stainless steel finish. Smooth walnut grips. Made 1973 to date, 5.5-inch bbl. made from 1973 to date.
Blued finish . . . . NiB $570 Ex $477 Gd $281
High-gloss stainless
(1994-96) . . . . NiB $580 Ex $486 Gd $290
Satin stainless steel . . . . NiB $570 Ex $480 Gd $295
Stainless steel Hunter (intro. 2002) NiB $780 Ex $490 Gd $295

NEW MODEL SUPER SINGLE-SIX CONVERTIBLE REVOLVER

SA w/interlocked mechanism. Calibers: .22 LR and .22 WMR. Interchangeable 6-round cylinders. Bbl. lengths: 4.63, 5.5, 6.5, 9.5 inches. 10.81 inches overall (with 4.63 inch bbl.). Weight: 33 oz. (with 4.63-inch bbl.). Adj. rear sight, ramp front. Blued finish or stainless steel; latter only w/5.5- or 6.5-inch bbl., smooth walnut grips. Made from 1994 to 2004.
Blued finish . . . . NiB $500 Ex $306 Gd $190
Stainless steel . . . . NiB $530 Ex $316 Gd $219
Stainless steel Hunter (intro. 2002) NiB $660 Ex $560 Gd $295
Stainless steel Hunter 17HMR/17 Mach 2 (made from 2005 to 2006)
. . . . NiB $760 Ex $560 Gd $295

POLICE SERVICE-SIX

Same general specifications as Speed-Six except has square butt. Stainless steel models and 9mm Para. caliber available w/only 4-inch bbl., Made from 1971 to 1988.

.38 Special, blued finish . . . . . NiB $434 Ex $306 Gd $230
.38 Special, stainless steel . . . NiB $345 Ex $290 Gd $270
.357 Magnum or 9mm Para.,
blued finish . . . . NiB $444 Ex $309 Gd $235
.357 Magnum, stainless steel . NiB $439 Ex $306 Gd $225

REDHAWK DA REVOLVER

Calibers: .357 Mag., .41 Mag., .45 LC, .44 Mag. Six-round cylinder, 5.5-and 7.5-inch bbl., 11 and 13 inches overall, respectively. Weight: About 52 oz. Adj. rear sight, interchangeable front sights. Stainless finish. Made from 1979 to 2009; .357 Mag. disc. 1986. Alloy steel model w/blued finish intro. in 1986 in .41 Mag. and .44 Mag. calibers.

Blued finish . . . . NiB $620 Ex $450 Gd $270
Stainless steel . . . . NiB $789 Ex $499 Gd $300

SUPER REDHAWK STAINLESS DA SCOPE-RING REVOLVER

Calibers: .44 Mag., .454 Casull and .480 Ruger. Six-round cylinder, 7.5- to 9.5- inch bbl., 13 to 15 inches overall. Weight: 53 to 58 oz. Integral scope mounting system w/stainless rings. Adjustable rear sight. Cushioned grip panels. Made from 1987 to date.

Model .44 Mag. 7.5- inch
bbl., stainless . . . . NiB $795 Ex $546 Gd $434
Model .44 Mag. 9.5- inch
bbl., stainless . . . . NiB $830 Ex $577 Gd $444
Model .454 Casull & .480 Ruger
Stainless/target gray stainless. . NiB $862 Ex $590 Gd $474
Alaskan (intro. 2005) . . . . NiB $880 Ex $590 Gd $480

SECURITY-SIX DA REVOLVER

Caliber: .357 Magnum, handles .38 Special. Six-round cylinder, bbl. lengths: 2.25-, 4-, 6-inch, 9.25 inches overall (with 4-inch bbl.). Weight: 33.5 oz. (with 4-inch bbl.). Adj. rear sight, ramp front. Blued finish or stainless steel. Square butt. Checkered walnut grips. Made 1971 to 1985.

Blued finish . . . . NiB $410 Ex $280 Gd $214
Stainless steel . . . . NiB $420 Ex $300 Gd $265

SINGLE-SIX REVOLVER (OLD MODEL)

Calibers: .22 LR, .22 WMR. Six-round cylinder. bbl., lengths: 4.63, 5.5, 6.5, 9.5 inches, 10.88 inches overall (with 5.5-inch bbl.). Weight: About 35 oz. Fixed sights. Blued finish. Checkered hard rubber or smooth walnut grips. Made 1953-73. Note: Pre-1956 model w/flat loading gate is worth about twice as much as later version.

Standard. . . . . NiB $879 Ex $602 Gd $439
Convertible (w/two cylinders,
.22 LR/.22 WMR) . . . . NiB $561 Ex $398 Gd $272

SINGLE-SIX — LIGHTWEIGHT NiB $1086 Ex $816 Gd $530

Same general specifications as Single-Six except has 4.75-inch bbl., lightweight alloy cylinder and frame, 10 inches overall length, weight: 23 oz. Made in 1956.

SP101 DA REVOLVER

Calibers: .22 LR, .32 Mag., 9mm, .38 Special+P, .357 Mag. Five- or 6-round cylinder, 2.25-, 3.06- or 4-inch bbl., weight: 25-34 oz. Stainless steel finish. Cushioned grips. Made from 1989 to date.

Standard model . . . . NiB $530 Ex $321 Gd $204
DAO model (DA only, spurless hammer) NiB $530 Ex $321 Gd $204

SPEED-SIX DA REVOLVER

Calibers: .38 Special, .357 Magnum, 9mm Para. Six-round cylinder, 2.75-, 4-inch bbl., (9mm available only w/2.75-inch bbl.). 7.75 inches overall (2.75-inch bbl.). Weight: 31 oz. (with 2.75-inch bbl.).

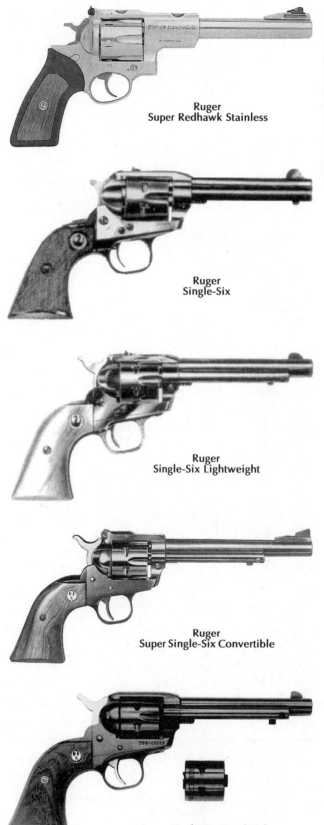

Ruger
Super Redhawk Stainless

Ruger
Single-Six

Ruger
Single-Six Lightweight

Ruger
Super Single-Six Convertible

Ruger Single-Six Fixed Sight

Ruger Vaquero Stainless Steel

Ruger Vaquero Blued

Fixed sights. Blued or stainless steel finish; latter available in .38 Special (with 2.75 inch bbl.), .357 Magnum and 9mm w/either bbl., Round butt. Checkered walnut grips. Made from 1973 to 1987.

blued finish	NiB $439	Ex $272	Gd $190
stainless steel	NiB $449	Ex $303	Gd $214
9mm Para., blued finish	NiB $689	Ex $522	Gd $440
9mm Para., stainless steel	NiB $690	Ex $540	Gd $442

SUPER BLACKHAWK
SA .44 MAGNUM REVOLVER (OLD MODEL)
SA w/heavy frame and unfluted cylinder. Caliber: .44 Magnum. Six-round cylinder. 6.5- or 7.5-inch bbl., Adj. rear sight, ramp front. Steel or brass grip frame w/square-back trigger guard. Smooth walnut grips. Blued finish. Made from 1956 to 1973.

w/6.5-inch bbl.,	NiB $1316	Ex $1148	Gd $918
w/7.5-inch bbl.,	NiB $806	Ex $385	Gd $281
w/brass gripframe	NiB $1599	Ex $1316	Gd $1153

VAQUERO SA REVOLVER
Calibers: .357 Mag., .44-40, .44 Magnum, .45 Colt. Six-round cylinder. Bbl. lengths: 4.625, 5.5, 7.5 inches, 13.63 inches overall (with 7.5-inch bbl.). Weight: 41 oz. (with 7.5-inch bbl.). Blade front sight, grooved topstrap rear. Blued w/color casehardened frame or polished stainless finish. Smooth rosewood grips w/Ruger medallion. Made from 1993 to 2004.

Blued w/color-case

hardened frame	NiB $590	Ex $431	Gd $316
Stainless finish	NiB $590	Ex $431	Gd $316
w/ivory grips	NiB $590	Ex $431	Gd $316

RUSSIAN SERVICE PISTOLS—Manufactured by Government plants at Tula and elsewhere

Tokarev-type pistols have also been made in Hungary, Poland, Yugoslavia, People's Republic of China, N. Korea.

MODEL TT30 TOKAREV SERVICE AUTOMATIC
Modified Colt-Browning type. Caliber: 7.62mm Russian Auto (also uses 7.63mm Mauser Auto cartridge). Eight-round magazine, 4.5-inch bbl., 7.75 inches overall. Weight: About 29 oz. Fixed sights. Made from 1930 to mid-1950s. Note: A slightly modified version w/ improved locking system and different disconnector was adopted in 1933.

Standard Service Model TT30	NiB $1239	Ex $1127	Gd $918
Standard Service Model TT33	NiB $2490	Ex $2285	Gd $1879

Recent imports (distinguished
by importer marks)	NiB $209	Ex $158	Gd $109

MODEL PSM
MAKAROV AUTO PISTOL NiB $3000 Ex $2445 Gd $2000
Double-action, blowback design. Caliber: 9mm Makarov. Eight-round magazine, 3.8-inch bbl., 6.4 inches overall. Weight: 26 oz. Blade front sight, square-notched rear. Checkered composition grips.

Standard Service Model PM
(Pistole Makarov)	NiB $3595	Ex $3125	Gd $2890

Recent imports (distinguished
by importer marks)	NiB $434	Ex $306	Gd $170

SAKO HANDGUNS — Riihimaki, Finland. Manufactured by Oy Sako Ab

.22-.32 OLYMPIC PISTOL (TRIACE)
Calibers: .22 LR, .22 Short, .32 S&W Long. Five-round magazine, 6- or 8.85- (.22 Short) inch bbl., weight: About 46 oz. (.22 LR); 44 oz. (.22 Short); 48 oz. (.32). Steel frame. ABS plastic, anatomically designed grip. Non-reflecting matte black upper surface and chromium-plated slide. Equipped w/carrying case and tool set. Limited importation from 1983 to 1989.

Sako .22 or .32
Single pistol	NiB $1355	Ex $1240	Gd $1090

Sako Triace, triple-barrel set
w/wooden grip	NiB $2647	Ex $2279	Gd $2045

SAUER HANDGUNS — Manufactured through WW II by J. P. Sauer & Sohn, Suhl, Germany. Now manufactured by J. P. Sauer & Sohn, GmbH, Ecmernförde, West Germany

See also listings under Sig Sauer.

MODEL 1913 POCKET
AUTOMATIC PISTOL . . . . NiB $342 Ex $240 Gd $179
Caliber: .32 Automatic (7.65mm). Seven-round magazine, 3-inch bbl., 5.88 inches overall. Weight: 22 oz. Fixed sights. Blued finish. Black hard rubber grips. Made from 1913 to 1930.

MODEL 1930 POCKET AUTOMATIC PISTOL
Authority Model (Behorden Model). Successor to Model 1913, has improved grip and safety. Caliber: .32 Auto (7.65mm). Seven-round magazine, 3-inch bbl., 5.75 inches overall. Weight: 22 oz. Fixed sights. Blued finish. Black hard rubber grips. Made from 1930-38. Note: Some pistols made w/indicator pin showing when cocked. Also mfd. w/dual slide and receiver; this type weight: about 7 oz. less than the standard model.
Steel model . . . . NiB $405 Ex $290 Gd $203
Dural (alloy) model . . . . . NiB $1454 Ex $1367 Gd $1209

MODEL 38H DA AUTOMATIC PISTOL
Calibers: .25 Auto (6.35mm), .32 Auto (7.65mm), .380 Auto (9mm). Specifications shown are for .32 Auto model. Seven-round magazine, 3.25-inch bbl., 6.25 inches overall. Weight: 20 oz. Fixed sights. Blued finish. Black plastic grips. Also made in dual model weighing about 6 oz. less. Made 1938-1945. Note: This pistol, designated Model .38, was mfd. during WW II for military use. Wartime models are inferior in design to earlier production, as some lack safety lever.
.22 caliber . . . . NiB $5625 Ex $3410 Gd $2200
.32 ACP . . . . NiB $643 Ex $410 Gd $281
.32 ACP (w/Nazi proofs) . . . . . NiB $709 Ex $453 Gd $326
.380 ACP . . . . NiB $4500 Ex $4255 Gd $3975

POCKET .25 (1913)
AUTOMATIC PISTOL . . . . NiB $398 Ex $286 Gd $214
Smaller version of Model 1913, issued about same time as .32 caliber model. Caliber: .25 Auto (6.35mm). Seven-round magazine, 2.5-inch bbl., 4.25 inches overall. Weight: 14.5 oz. Fixed sights. Blued finish. Black hard rubber grips. Made 1913 to 1930.

SINGLE-ACTION REVOLVERS
See listings under Hawes.

SAVAGE ARMS CO. — Utica, New York

MODEL 101 SA
SINGLE-SHOT PISTOL . . . . . . NiB $255 Ex $170 Gd $105
Barrel integral w/swing-out cylinder. Calibers: .22 Short, Long, LR. 5.5-inch bbl. Weight: 20 oz. Blade front sight, slotted rear, adj. for windage. Blued finish. Grips of compressed, impregnated wood. Made 1960 to 1968.

MODEL 501/502F "STRIKER" SERIES PISTOLS
Calibers: .22 LR., and .22 WMR. 5- or 10- round magazine, 10-inch bbl., 19 inches overall. Weight: 4 lbs. Drilled and tapped sights for scope mount (installed). AmbidExtrous rear grip. Made from 2000 to 2005.
Model 501F, .22 LR . . . . NiB $359 Ex $206 Gd $165
Model 502F, .22 WMR . . . . . . NiB $301 Ex $190 Gd $158

MODEL 510/516 "STRIKER" SERIES PISTOLS
Calibers: 223 Rem., .22-250 Rem., .243 Win., 7mm-08 Rem., .260 Rem., and .308 Win. Three-round magazine, 14-inch bbl., .22.5

Sako Model .22-.32 Olympic

Sauer 1930 Pocket

Savage Model 101

inches overall. Drilled and tapped for scope mounts. Left hand bolt with right hand ejection. Stainless steel finish. Made from 1998 to 2005.

Model 510F . . . . NiB $495 Ex $395 Gd $235
Model 516FSAK . . . . NiB $546 Ex $474 Gd $230
Model 516FSS . . . . NiB $546 Ex $474 Gd $230
Model 516FSAK . . . . NiB $704 Ex $468 Gd $408
Model 516BSS . . . . NiB $755 Ex $500 Gd $437

MODEL 1907 AUTOMATIC PISTOL
Caliber: .32 ACP, 10-round magazine, 3.25-inch bbl., 6.5 inches overall. Weight: 19 oz. Checkered hard rubber or steel grips marked "Savage Quality," circling an Indian-head logo. Optional pearl grips. Blue, nickel, silver or gold finish. Made from 1910 to 1917.
Blued model (.32 ACP) . . . . . NiB $610 Ex $430 Gd $175
Blued model (.380 ACP) . . . . . NiB $709 Ex $495 Gd $326

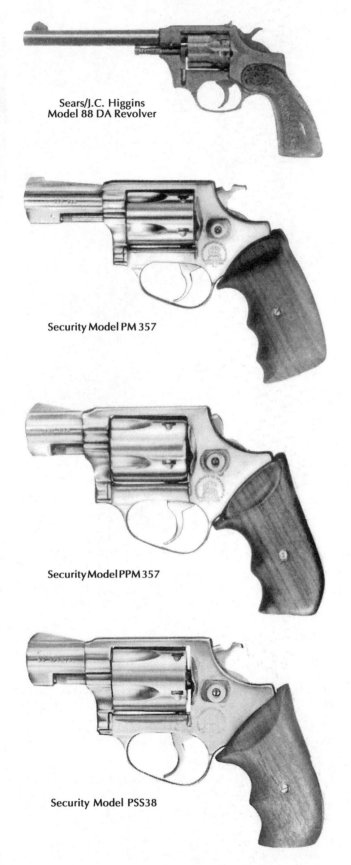

Sears/J.C. Higgins
Model 88 DA Revolver

Security Model PM 357

Security Model PPM 357

Security Model PSS38

MODEL 1907 AUTOMATIC PISTOL

Calibers: .32 Auto, .380 Auto. 10-round magazine (.32 cal.), 9-round (.380 cal.). 3.75-inch bbl., (.32 cal.), 4.25-inch (.380 cal.). 6.5 inches overall (.32 cal.), 7 inches (.380 cal.). Weight: About 23 oz. Fixed sights. Blued finish. Hard rubber grips. Made in hammerless type w/ grip safety or w/Exposed hammer spur. Made from 1910 to 1917.

.32 ACP . . . . NiB $601 Ex $457 Gd $270
.380 ACP . . . . NiB $700 Ex $560 Gd $499

MODEL 1915 AUTOMATIC PISTOL

Same general specifications as the Savage Model 1907 except the Model 1915 is hammerless and has a grip safety. It is also chambered for both the .32 and .380 ACP. Made froim 1915 to 1917.

.32 ACP . . . . NiB $930 Ex $729 Gd $500
.380 ACP . . . . NiB $1400 Ex $857 Gd $643

U.S. ARMY TEST MODEL . . . . NiB $12,650 Ex $8990 Gd $653
Caliber: .45 ACP, Seven-round magazine w/Exposed hammer. An enlarged version of the Model 1910 manufactured for military trials between 1907 and 1911. Note: Most "Trial Pistols" were refurbished and resold as commercial models. Values are for original Government Test Issue models.

MODEL 1917 AUTOMATIC PISTOL

Same specifications as 1910 Model except has spur-type hammer and redesigned, heavier grip. Made from 1917 to 1928.

.32 ACP . . . . NiB $564 Ex $445 Gd $279
.380 ACP . . . . NiB $646 Ex $486 Gd $336

SEARS, ROEBUCK & COMPANY — Chicago, Illinois

J.C. HIGGINS MODEL 80
AUTO PISTOL . . . . NiB $281 Ex $165 Gd $109
Caliber: .22 LR. 10-round magazine, 4.5- or 6.5-inch interchangeable bbl., 10.88 inches overall (with 6.5-inch bbl.). Weight: 41 oz. (with 6.5-inch bbl.). Fixed Partridge sights. Blued finish. Checkered grips w/thumbrest.

J.C. HIGGINS MODEL 88
DA REVOLVER . . . . NiB $209 Ex $105 Gd $75
Caliber: .22 LR. Nine-round cylinder, 4- or 6-inch bbl., 9.5 inches (with 4-inch bbl.). Weight: 23 oz. (with 4-inch bbl.). Fixed sights. Blued or nickel finish. Checkered plastic grips.

J.C. HIGGINS RANGER
DA REVOLVER . . . . NiB $219 Ex $137 Gd $88
Caliber: .22 LR. Nine-round cylinder, 5.5-inch bbl., 10.75 inches overall. Weight: 28 oz. Fixed sights. Blued or chrome finish. Checkered plastic grips.

SECURITY INDUSTRIES OF AMERICA — Little Ferry, New Jersey

MODEL PM 357 DA REVOLVER . .NiB $255 Ex $198 Gd $160
Caliber: .357 Magnum. Five-round cylinder, 2.5-inch bbl., 7.5 inches overall. Weight: 21 oz. Fixed sights. Stainless steel. Walnut grips. Made 1975. Disc..

MODEL PPM357 DA REVOLVER. .NiB $255 Ex $198 Gd $160
Caliber: .357 Magnum. Five-round cylinder, 2-inch bbl., 6.13 inches overall. Weight: 18 oz. Fixed sights. Stainless steel. Walnut grips. Made in 1975. Note: Spurless hammer (illustrated) was disc. in 1975; this model has the same conventional hammer as other Security revolvers.

MODEL PSS 38

DA REVOLVER . . . . **NiB $197 Ex $112 Gd $90**
Caliber: .38 Special. Five-round cylinder, 2-inch bbl., 6.5 inches overall. Weight: 18 oz. Fixed sights. Stainless steel. Walnut grips. Intro. 1973. disc.

R. F. SEDGLEY. INC. — Philadelphia, Pennsylvania

BABY HAMMERLESS
EJECTOR REVOLVER . . . . **NiB $704 Ex $556 Gd $290**
DA. Solid frame. Folding trigger. Caliber: .22 Long. Six-round cylinder, 4 inches overall. Weight: 6 oz. Fixed sights. Blued or nickel finish. Rubber grips. Made 1930 to 1939.

L. W. SEECAMP, INC. — Milford, Connecticut

MODEL LWS .25
DAO PISTOL . . . . **NiB $439 Ex $398 Gd $281**
Caliber: .25 ACP. Seven-round magazine, 2-inch bbl., 4.125 inches overall. Weight: 12 oz. Checkered black polycarbonate grips. Matte stainless finish. No sights. Made from 1981 to 1985.

MODEL LWS .32 DAO PISTOL
Caliber: .32 ACP. Six-round magazine, 2-inch bbl., 4.25 inches overall. Weight: 12.9 oz. Ribbed sighting plane with no sights. Checkered black LExon grips. Stainless steel. Made from 1985 to date. Limited production results in inflated resale values.
Matte stainless finish . . . . **NiB $464 Ex $398 Gd $272**
Polished stainless finish, add. **$128**

SHERIDAN PRODUCTS, INC. — Racine, Wisconsin

KNOCKABOUT
SINGLE-SHOT PISTOL . . . . . . **NiB $305 Ex $189 Gd $108**
Tip-up type. Caliber: .22 LR, Long, Short; 5-inch bbl., 6.75 inches overall. Weight: 24 oz. Fixed sights. Checkered plastic grips. Blued finish. Made from 1953 to 1960.

SIG PISTOLS — Neuhausen am Rheinfall, Switzerland

See also listings under SIG-Sauer.

MODEL P210-1
AUTOMATIC PISTOL . . . . **NiB $2878 Ex $2662 Gd $2288**
Calibers: .22 LR, 7.65mm Luger, 9mm Para. Eight-round magazine, 4.75-inch bbl., 8.5 inches overall. Weight: 33 oz. (.22 cal.) or 35 oz. (7.65mm, 9mm). Fixed sights. Polished blued finish. Checkered wood grips. Made from 1949 to 1986.

MODEL P210-2 . . . . **NiB $1835 Ex $1590 Gd $1409**
Same as Model P210-1 except has sandblasted finish, plastic grips. Not avail. in .22 LR. Disc. 2002.

MODEL P210-5
TARGET PISTOL . . . . **NiB $2330 Ex $2190 Gd $1902**
Same as Model P210-2 except has 6-inch bbl., micrometer adj. rear sight, target front sight, adj. trigger stop, 9.7 inches overall. Weight: About 38.3 oz. Disc. 2007.

SIG
Model P210-1

SIG
Model P210-6 Target Pistol

MODEL P210-6 TARGET PISTOL NiB $1910 Ex $1720 Gd $1525
Same as Model P210-2 except has micrometer adj. rear sight, target front sight, adj. trigger stop. Weight: About 37 oz. Disc. 1987.

P210 .22 CONVERSION UNIT, add **$1525**
Converts P210 pistol to .22 LR. Consists of bbl., w/recoil spring, slide and magazine,

SIG SAUER HANDGUNS — Manufactured by J. P. Sauer & Sohn of Germany, SIG of Switzerland, and other manufacturers

MODEL P220 DA/DAO AUTOMATIC PISTOL
Calibers: 22LR, 7.65mm, 9mm Para., .38 Super, .45 ACP. Seven-round in .45 ACP, 9-round in other calibers, 4.4-inch bbl., 8 inches overall. Weight: 26.5 oz. (9mm). Fixed sights. Blue, electroless nickel, K-Kote, Duo/nickel or Ilaflon finish. Alloy frame. Checkered plastic grips. Imported from 1976 to date. Note: Also sold in U.S. as Browning BDA.
Blue finish . . . . **NiB $918 Ex $734 Gd $499**
Duo/nickel finish . . . . **NiB $1030 Ex $712 Gd $523**
Nickel finish. . . . . **NiB $988 Ex $784 Gd $546**
K-Kote finish . . . . **NiB $974 Ex $693 Gd $474**
Ilaflon finish. . . . . **NiB $969 Ex $689 Gd $507**
.22 LR conversion kit, add **$434**
w/Siglite sights, add **$100**

MODEL P220 SPORT AUTOMATIC NiB $1415 Ex $1119 Gd $1016
Similar to Model P220 except .45 ACP only w/4.5-inch compensated bbl., 10-round magazine, adj. target sights. Weight: 46.1 oz. Stainless finish. Made from 1999 to date.

SIG Sauer
P220

SIG Sauer
P225

SIG Sauer
P230

MODEL P225 DA AUTOMATIC
Caliber: 9mm Para. Eight-round magazine, 3.85-inch bbl., 7 inches overall. Weight: 26.1 oz. Blue, nickel, K-Kote, Duo/nickel or Ilaflon finish.
Blued finish . . . . NiB $628 Ex $556 Gd $431
Duo/nickel finish . . . . NiB $669 Ex $588 Gd $500
Nickel finish. . . . . NiB $700 Ex $612 Gd $478
K-Kote finish . . . . NiB $700 Ex $612 Gd $478
w/Siglite sights, add $128

MODEL P226 DA/DAO AUTOMATIC
Caliber: .357 SIG, 9mm Para., .40 S&W, 10- or 15-round magazine, 4.4-inch bbl., 7.75 inches overall. Weight: 29.5 oz. Alloy frame. Blue, electroless nickel, K-Kote, Duo/nickel or Nitron finish. Imported from 1983 to date.
Blued finish . . . . NiB $882 Ex $724 Gd $444
Duo/nickel finish . . . . NiB $898 Ex $809 Gd $496
Nickel finish. . . . . NiB $804 Ex $659 Gd $478
K-Kote finish . . . . NiB $804 Ex $639 Gd $485
Nitron finish
(blackened stainless). . . . . NiB $826 Ex $658 Gd $479
w/Siglite sights, add $100

MODEL P228 DA AUTOMATIC
Same general specifications as Model P226 except w/3.86-inch bbl., 7.13 inches overall. 10- or 13-round magazine, Imported 1990 to 1997.
Blued finish . . . . NiB $831 Ex $709 Gd $455
Duo/nickel finish . . . . NiB $860 Ex $755 Gd $499
Electroless nickel finish . . . . . NiB $895 Ex $780 Gd $530
K-Kote finish . . . . NiB $882 Ex $743 Gd $541
w/Siglite night sights, add $130

MODEL P229 DA/DAO AUTOMATIC
Same general specifications as Model P228 except w/3.86-inch bbl., 10- or 12-round magazine, weight: 32.5 oz. Nitron or Satin Nickel finish. Imported from 1991 to date.
Nitron finish
(Blackened stainless). . . . . NiB $860 Ex $755 Gd $464
Satin nickel finish. . . . . NiB $890 Ex $791 Gd $500
For Siglite nite sights, add. $128

MODEL P229
SPORT AUTOMATIC . . . . . NiB $1292 Ex $1035 Gd $871
Similar to Model P229 except .357 SIG only w/4.5-inch compensated bbl., adj. target sights. Weight: 43.6 oz. Stainless finish. Made from 1998 to 2003. Reintroduced 2003 to 2005.

MODEL P230 DA AUTOMATIC PISTOL
Calibers: .22 LR, .32 Auto (7.65mm), .380 Auto (9mm Short), 9mm Ultra. 10-round magazine in .22, 8-round in .32, 7-round in 9mm; 3.6-inch bbl., 6.6 inches overall. Weight: 18.2 oz. or 22.4 oz. (steel frame). Fixed sights. Blued or stainless finish. Plastic grips. Imported 1976 to 1996.
Blued finish . . . . NiB $530 Ex $408 Gd $308
Stainless finish (P230SL) . . . . . NiB $602 Ex $500 Gd $367

MODEL P232 DA/DAO AUTOMATIC PISTOL
Caliber: .380 ACP. Seven-round magazine, 3.6-inch bbl., 6.6 inches overall. Weight: 16.2 oz. or 22.4 oz. (steel frame). Double/single action or double action only. Blade front and notch rear drift adjustable sights. Alloy or steel frame. Automatic firing pin lock and heel-mounted magazine release. Blue, Duo or stainless finish. Stippled black composite stocks. Imported 1997 to date.
Blued finish . . . . NiB $576 Ex $467 Gd $316
Duo finish . . . . NiB $601 Ex $498 Gd $321
Stainless finish . . . . NiB $588 Ex $523 Gd $433
w/Siglite night sights, add. $65

MODEL P239 DA/DAO AUTOMATIC PISTOL
Caliber: .357 SIG, 9mm Parabellum or .40 S&W. Seven- or 8-round magazine, 3.6-inch bbl., 6.6 inches overall. Weight: 28.2 oz. Double/single action or double action only. Blade front and notch rear adjustable sights. Alloy frame w/stainless slide. AmbidExtrous frame- mounted magazine release. Matte black or Duo finish. Stippled black composite stocks. Made from 1996 to date.
Matte black finish. . . . . NiB $590 Ex $524 Gd $301
DAO finish. . . . . NiB $638 Ex $530 Gd $365
w/Siglite night sights, add $128

SMITH & WESSON, INC. — Springfield, Massachusetts

NOTE: *For ease in locating a particular S&W handgun, the listings are divided into two groupings: Automatic/Single-Shot Pistols (below) and Revolvers (page 155). For a complete handgun listing, please refer to the index.*

AUTOMATIC/SINGLE-SHOT PISTOLS

MODEL 35 (1913) AUTOMATIC PISTOL NiB $979 Ex $780 Gd $469
Caliber: 35 S&W Auto. Seven-round magazine, 3.5-inch bbl., (hinged to frame). 6.5 inches overall. Weight: 25 oz. Fixed sights. Blued or nickel finish. Plain walnut grips. Made from 1913 to 1921.

MODEL .32 AUTOMATIC PISTOL NiB $3097 Ex $2315 Gd $1699
Caliber: .32 Automatic. Same general specifications as .35 caliber model, but barrel is fastened to the receiver instead of hinged. Made from 1924 to 1937.

MODEL .22A SPORT SERIES
Caliber: .22 LR. 10-round magazine, 4-, 5.5- or 7-inch standard (A-series) or bull bbl., (S-series). Single action. Eight, 9.5 or 11 inches overall. Weight: 28 oz. to 33 oz. Partridge front sight, fully adjustable rear. Alloy frame w/stainless slide. Blued finish. Black polymer or Dymondwood grips. Made from 1997 to date.
Model 22A (w/4-inch bbl.) . . . NiB $255 Ex $190 Gd $105
Model 22A (w/5.5-inch bbl.). . NiB $265 Ex $204 Gd $120
Model 22A (w/7-inch bbl.) . . . NiB $265 Ex $204 Gd $120
Model 22S (w/5.5-inch bbl.) . . NiB $362 Ex $290 Gd $214
Model 22S (w/7-inch bbl.) . . . NiB $395 Ex $337 Gd $265
w/bull bbl., add $65
w/Dymondwood grips, add. $100

MODEL 39 9MM DA AUTO PISTOL
Calibers: 9mm Para. Eight-round magazine, 4-inch barrel. Overall length: 7.44-inches. Steel or alloy frames. Weight: 26.5 oz. (w/alloy frame). Click adjustable rear sight, ramp front. Blued or nickel finish. Checkered walnut grips. Made 1954-82. Note: Between 1954 and 1966, 927 pistols were produced w/steel instead of alloy. In 1970, Model 39-1 w/alloy frame and steel slide. In 1971, Model 39-2 was introduced as an improved version of the original Model 39 w/ modified Extractor.
Model 39 (early production) 1954-70
First series (S/N 1000-2600) . . . . NiB $1566 Ex $1418 Gd $1299
9mm blue (w/steel frame & slide,
produced 1966) . . . . NiB $1866 Ex $1618 Gd $1299
9mm blue (w/alloy frame) . . . . NiB $622 Ex $437 Gd $225
Nickel finish, add $45
Models 39-1, 39-2 (late production,
1970-82), 9mm blue (w/alloy frame) . NiB $534 Ex $331 Gd $220
Nickel finish, add $50

MODEL 41 .22 AUTOMATIC PISTOL
Caliber: .22 LR, .22 Short (not interchangeably). 10-round magazine, bbl. lengths: 5-, 5.5-, 7.75-inches; latter has detachable muzzle brake, 12 inches overall (with 7.75-inch bbl.). Weight: 43.5 oz. (with 7.75-inch bbl.). Click adj. rear sight, undercut Partridge front. Blued finish. Checkered walnut grips w/thumbrest. 1957 to date.
.22 LR model . . . . NiB $1200 Ex $870 Gd $529
.22 Short model
(w/counter-
weights & muzzle brake) . NiB $2700 Ex $1299 Gd $1120
w/Extended sight, add. $128
w/muzzle brake, add $50

**Smith & Wesson
Model 22A Sport Series**

**Smith & Wesson
Model 22S Sport Series
w/Dymondwood Grips**

**Smith & Wesson
Model 41 .22 w/ muzzle brake**

MODEL 46 .22 AUTO PISTOL NiB $1225 Ex $765 Gd $448
Caliber: .22 LR. 10-round magazine, bbl. lengths: 5-, 5.5-, 7-inches. 10.56 inches overall (with 7-inch bbl.). Weight: 42 oz. (with 7-inch bbl.). Click adj. rear sight, undercut Partridge front. Blued finish. Molded nylon grips w/thumbrest. Only 4,000 produced. Made from 1957 to 1966.

MODEL 52 .38 MASTER AUTO
Caliber: .38 Special (midrange wadcutter only). Five-round magazine, 5-inch bbl., overall length: 8.63 inches. Weight: 41 oz. Micrometer click rear sight, Partridge front on ramp base. Blued finish. Checkered walnut grips. Made from 1961 to 1963.
Model 52 (1961-63) . . . . NiB $1109 Ex $915 Gd $546
Model 52-1 (1963-71) . . . . . NiB $1029 Ex $915 Gd $546
Model 52-2 (1971-93) . . . . . NiB $1029 Ex $915 Gd $546
Model 52-A USA Marksman
(fewer than 100 mfg.) . . . . NiB $3820 Ex $3470 Gd $3139

Smith & Wesson
Model 41

Smith & Wesson
Model 52

Smith & Wesson
Model 59

Smith & Wesson
Model 422

Smith & Wesson
Model 439

MODEL 59 9MM DA AUTO
Similar specifications as Model 39 except has 14-round staggered column magazine, checkered nylon grips. Made 1971 to 1981.
Model 59, blue. . . . . NiB $549 Ex $431 Gd $290
Model 59, nickel . . . . NiB $600 Ex $444 Gd $326
Model 59
(early production
w/smooth grip frame) . . . . NiB $1647 Ex $1508 Gd $1015

MODEL 61 ESCORT POCKET AUTOMATIC PISTOL
Caliber: .22 LR. Five-round magazine, 2.13-inch bbl., 4.69 inches overall. Weight: 14 oz. Fixed sights. Blued or nickel finish. Checkered plastic grips. Made from 1970 to 1974.
Model 61, blue. . . . . NiB $380 Ex $270 Gd $165
Model 61, nickel . . . . NiB $431 Ex $316 Gd $220

MODEL 410
AUTO PISTOL . . . . NiB $561 Ex $444 Gd $244
Caliber: .40 S&W. Double action. 10-round magazine, 4-inch bbl., 7.5 inches overall. Weight: 28.5 oz. Alloy frame w/steel slide. Post front sight, fixed rear w/3-dot system. Matte blue finish. Checkered synthetic grips w/straight backstrap. Made from 1996 to 2007.

MODEL 411
AUTO PISTOL . . . . NiB $530 Ex $433 Gd $386
Similar to S&W Model 915 except in caliber .40 S&W. 11-round magazine, made from 1994 to 1996.

MODEL 422 SA AUTO PISTOL
Caliber: .22 LR. 10-round magazine, 4.5- or 6-inch bbl., 7.5 inches overall (with 4.5-inch bbl.). Weight: 22-23.5 oz. Fixed or adjustable sights. Checkered plastic or walnut grips. Blued finish. Made from 1987 to 1996.
Standard model . . . . NiB $220 Ex $175 Gd $150
Target model . . . . NiB $274 Ex $198 Gd $170

MODEL 439 9MM AUTOMATIC
DA. Caliber: 9mm Para. Two 8-round magazines, 4-inch bbl., 7.44 inches overall. Alloy frame. Weight: 30 oz. Serrated ramp square front sight, square notch rear. Checkered walnut grips. Blued or nickel finish. Made from 1979 to 1988.
Model 439, blue . . . . NiB $530 Ex $368 Gd $306
Model 439, nickel . . . . NiB $529 Ex $386 Gd $316
w/adjustable sights, add $40

Smith & Wesson
Model 645

Smith & Wesson
Model 459

MODEL 457
COMPACT AUTO PISTOL. . . . **NiB $571 Ex $434 Gd $265**
Caliber: .45 ACP. Double action. Seven-round magazine, 3.75-inch bbl., 7.25 inches overall. Weight: 29 oz. Alloy frame w/steel slide. Post front sight, fixed rear w/3-dot system. Bobbed hammer. Matte blue finish. Wraparound synthetic grip w/straight backstrap. Made from 1996 to 2006.

MODEL 459 DA AUTOMATIC
Caliber: 9mm Para. Two 14-round magazines, 4-inch bbl., 7.44 inches overall. Alloy frame. Weight: 28 oz. Blued or nickel finish. Made from 1979 to 1987.

Model 459, blue.	NiB $485	Ex $431	Gd $319
Model 459, nickel	NiB $527	Ex $475	Gd $377
FBI Model (brushed finish) . . .	NiB $733	Ex $599	Gd $437

MODEL 469
(MINI) AUTOMATIC. . . . . **NiB $485 Ex $388 Gd $270**
DA. Caliber: 9mm Para. Two 12-round magazines, 3.5-inch bbl., 6.88 inches overall. Weight: 26 oz. Yellow ramp front sight, dovetail mounted square-notch rear. Sandblasted blued finish. Optional ambidExtrous safety. Made from 1982 to 1988.

Smith & Wesson
Model 469

MODEL 539 DA AUTOMATIC
Similar to Model 439 except w/steel frame. Caliber: 9mm Para. Two 8-round magazines, 4-inch bbl., 7.44 inches overall. Weight: 36 oz. Blued or nickel finish. Made from 1980 to 1983.

Model 539, blue.	NiB $590	Ex $486	Gd $368
Model 539, nickel	NiB $601	Ex $530	Gd $408
w/adjustable sights, add			$50

MODEL 559 DA AUTOMATIC
Similar to Model 459 except w/steel frame. Caliber: 9mm Para. Two 14-round magazines, 4-inch bbl., 7.44 inches overall. Weight: 39.5 oz. Blued or nickel finish. (3750 produced) Made 1980 to 1983.

Model 559, blue.	NiB $612	Ex $536	Gd $408
Model 559, nickel	NiB $648	Ex $561	Gd $444
w/adjustable sights, add			$50

MODEL 622 SA AUTO PISTOL
Same general specifications as Model 422 except w/stainless finish. Made from 1989 to 1996.

Standard model	NiB $265	Ex $197	Gd $120
Target model	NiB $309	Ex $212	Gd $146

MODEL 639 AUTOMATIC . . . NiB $530 Ex $377 Gd $304
Caliber: 9mm Para. Stainless. Two 12-round magazines, 3.5-inch bbl., 6.9 inches overall. Weight: 36 oz. Made from 1986 to 1988.

Smith & Wesson
Model 639

**Smith & Wesson
Model 659**

**Smith & Wesson
Model 745**

**Smith & Wesson
Model 1026**

MODEL 645 DA AUTOMATIC
Caliber: .45 ACP. Eight-round. 5-inch bbl., overall length: 8.5 inches. Weight: Approx. 38 oz. Red ramp front, fixed rear sights. Stainless. Made from 1986-88.
Model 645 (w/fixed sights) . . . NiB $601 Ex $433 Gd $346
Model 645 (w/adjustable sights)NiB $638 Ex $464 Gd $366

MODEL 659 9MM AUTOMATIC
DA. Similar to S&W Model 459 except weight: 39.5 oz. and finish is satin stainless steel finish. Made from 1983-88.
Model 659 (w/fixed sights) . . . NiB $517 Ex $419 Gd $326
Model 659 (w/adjustable sights)NiB $528 Ex $444 Gd $356

MODEL 669 AUTOMATIC . . . NiB $559 Ex $345 Gd $274
Caliber: 9mm. 12-round magazine, 3.5 inch bbl., 6.9 inches overall. Weight: 26 oz. Serrated ramp front sight w/red bar, fixed rear. Non-glare stainless steel finish. Made from 1986-88.

MODEL 745 AUTOMATIC PISTOL
Caliber: .45 ACP. Eight-round magazine, 5-inch bbl., 8.63 inches overall. Weight: 38.75 oz. Fixed sights. Blued slide, stainless frame. Checkered walnut grips. Similar to the model 645, but w/o DA capability. Made from 1987-90.
w/standard competition features . . . . NiB $760 Ex $549 Gd $433
IPSC Commemorative (first 5,000). . . NiB $798 Ex $638 Gd $429

MODEL 908/910 AUTO PISTOLS
Caliber: 9mm Parabellum. Double action. Eight-round (Model 908), 9-round (Model 909) or 10-round (Model 910) magazine; 3.5- or 4-inch bbl.; 6.83 or 7.38 inches overall. Weight: 26 oz. to 28.5 oz. Post front sight, fixed rear w/3-dot system. Matte blue steel slide w/alloy frame. Delrin synthetic wrap-around grip w/straight backstrap. Made from 1994 to date.
Model 908 . . . . NiB $541 Ex $397 Gd $272
Model 909 (disc 1996) . . . . . . NiB $479 Ex $347 Gd $239
Model 910 . . . . NiB $497 Ex $348 Gd $255

MODEL 915 AUTO PISTOL . . NiB $434 Ex $306 Gd $220
DA. Caliber: 9mm Para. 15-round magazine, 4-inch bbl., 7.5 inches overall. Weight: 28.5 oz. Post front sight, fixed square-notched rear w/3-dot system. Xenoy wraparound grip. Blued steel slide and alloy frame. Made from 1992-94.

MODEL 1000 SERIES DA AUTO
Caliber: 10mm. Nine-round magazine, 4.25- or 5-inch bbl., 7.88 or 8.63 inches overall. Weight: About 38 oz. Post front sight, adj. or fixed square-notched rear w/3-dot system. One-piece Xenoy wraparound grips. Stainless slide and frame. Made from 1990-94.
Model 1006 (fixed sights, 5-inch bbl.) NiB $724 Ex $530 Gd $433
Model 1006 (adj. sights, 5-inch bbl.). NiB $740 Ex $544 Gd $479
Model 1026 (fixed sights, 5-inch bbl., decocking lever). . . . . NiB $724 Ex $530 Gd $433
Model 1066 (fixed sights, 4.25 inch bbl.) . . . . NiB $678 Ex $530 Gd $362
Model 1076 (fixed sights, 4.25 inch bbl., frame-mounted decocking lever,. . . . NiB $730 Ex $536 Gd $439
Model 1076 (same as above w/Tritium night sight) . . . . NiB $730 Ex $536 Gd $439
Model 1086 (same as model 1076 in DA only) . . . . NiB $760 Ex $544 Gd $429

MODEL 2206 SA AUTOMATIC PISTOL
Similar to Model 422 except w/stainless-steel slide and frame, weight: 35-39 oz. Partridge front sight on adj. sight model; post w/ white dot on fixed sight model. Plastic grips. Made from 1990-96.
Standard model . . . . NiB $342 Ex $227 Gd $130
Target model . . . . NiB $377 Ex $239 Gd $178

MODEL 2213
SPORTSMAN AUTO. . . . . NiB $279 Ex $180 Gd $119
Caliber: .22 LR. Eight-round magazine, 3-inch bbl., 6.13 inches overall. Weight: 18 oz. Partridge front sight, fixed square-notched rear w/3-dot system. Black synthetic molded grips. Stainless steel slide w/alloy frame. Made from 1992-99.

MODEL 2214
SPORTSMAN AUTO. . . . . NiB $362 Ex $190 Gd $126
Same general specifications as Model 2214 except w/blued slide and matte black alloy frame. Made from 1990-99.

MODEL 3904/3906 DA AUTO PISTOL

Caliber: 9mm. Eight-round magazine, 4-inch bbl., 7.5 inches over-all. Weight: 25.5 oz. (Model 3904) or 34 oz. (Model 3906). Fixed or adj. sights. Delrin one-piece wraparound checkered grips. Alloy frame w/blued carbon steel slide (Model 3904) or satin stainless (Model 3906). Made from 1989 to 1991.

Model 3904 w/adjustable sights . . . . NiB $536 Ex $362 Gd $287
Model 3904 w/fixed sights . . . . NiB $497 Ex $328 Gd $249
Model 3904 w/Novak LC sight . . . . . NiB $536 Ex $362 Gd $287
Model 3906 w/adjustable sights . . . . NiB $576 Ex $497 Gd $431
Model 3906 w/Novak LC sight . . . . . NiB $546 Ex $499 Gd $366

MODEL 3913/3914 DA AUTOMATIC

Caliber: 9mm Parabellum (Luger). Eight-round magazine, 3.5-inch bbl., 6.88 inches overall. Weight: 25 oz. Post front sight, fixed or adj. square-notched rear. One-piece Xenoy wraparound grips w/straight backstrap. Alloy frame w/stainless or blued slide. Made from 1990 to 1999.

Model 3913 stainless . . . . NiB $577 Ex $449 Gd $346
Model 3913LS Lady Smith stainless
w/contoured trigger guard. . . . . NiB $755 Ex $588 Gd $479
Model 3913TSW (intro. 1998). . . . . . NiB $739 Ex $596 Gd $479
Model 3914 blued compact
(disc 1995). . . . . NiB $559 Ex $467 Gd $386

MODEL 3953/3954 DA AUTO PISTOL

Same general specifications as Model 3913/3914 except double action only. Made from 1990 to 2002.

Model 3953 stainless,
double action only . . . . NiB $590 Ex $444 Gd $396
Model 3954 blued, double
action only (disc. 1992). . . . . NiB $530 Ex $431 Gd $340

MODEL 4000 SERIES DA AUTO

Caliber: .40 S&W. 11-round magazine, 4-inch bbl., 7.88 inches overall. Weight: 28-30 oz. w/alloy frame or 36 oz. w/stainless frame. Post front sight, adj. or fixed square-notched rear w/2 white dots. Straight backstrap. One-piece Xenoy wraparound grips. Blued or stainless finish. Made between 1991 to 1993.

Model 4003 stainless w/alloy frame . NiB $658 Ex $498 Gd $388
Model 4003 TSW w/
S&W Tactical options . . . . NiB $870 Ex $779 Gd $608
Model 4004 blued w/alloy frame . . . NiB $601 Ex $449 Gd $397
Model 4006 stainless
frame, fixed sights . . . . NiB $711 Ex $562 Gd $431
Model 4006 stainless
frame, Adj. sights . . . . NiB $744 Ex $634 Gd $498
Model 4006 TSW w/
S&W Tactical options . . . . NiB $855 Ex $760 Gd $475
Model 4013 stainless frame,
fixed sights. . . . . NiB $622 Ex $419 Gd $377
Model 4013 TSW w/
S&W Tactical options . . . . NiB $855 Ex $760 Gd $475
Model 4014 blued, fixed sights
(disc. 1993) . . . . NiB $581 Ex $419 Gd $398
Model 4026 w/decocking
Lever (disc. 1994). . . . . NiB $659 Ex $562 Gd $449
Model 4043 DA only, stainless
w/alloy frame. . . . . NiB $693 Ex $580 Gd $497
Model 4044 DA only,
blued w/alloy frame . . . . NiB $569 Ex $448 Gd $346
Model 4046 DA only, stainless
frame, fixed sights . . . . NiB $739 Ex $668 Gd $499
Model 4046 TSW w/
S&W Tactical options . . . . NiB $700 Ex $632 Gd $485
Model 4046 DA only, stainless
frame, Tritium night sight . . . . NiB $724 Ex $634 Gd $475

Smith & Wesson
Model 3906

Smith & Wesson
Model 3953

Smith & Wesson
Model 4013

Smith & Wesson
Model 4046

Smith & Wesson
Model 4053

Smith & Wesson
Model 4586

Smith & Wesson Model 5904 w/
Adjustable Sights

MODEL 4013/4014 DA AUTOMATIC
Caliber: .40 S&W. Eight-round capacity, 3.5-inch bbl., 7 inches overall. Weight: 26 oz. Post front sight, fixed Novak LC rear w/3-dot system. One-piece Xenoy wraparound grips. Stainless or blued slide w/alloy frame. Made from 1991 to 1996.
Model 4013 w/stainless slide (disc. 1996)NiB $643 Ex $536 Gd $327
Model 4013 Tactical w/stainless slide . . NiB $860 Ex $693 Gd $588
Model 4014 w/blued slide (disc. 1993) NiB $587 Ex $464 Gd $328

MODEL 4053/4054 DA AUTO PISTOL
Same general specifications as Model 4013/4014 except double action only. Alloy frame fitted w/blued steel slide. Made from 1991 to 1997.

Model 4053 DA only w/stainless slide . . NiB $668 Ex $530 Gd $458
Model 4053 TSW w/ S&W Tactical optionsNiB $760 Ex $648 Gd $541
Model 4054 DA only w/blued slide
(disc. 1992) . . . . NiB $709 Ex $464 Gd $378

MODEL 4500 SERIES DA AUTOMATIC
Caliber: .45 ACP. Six-, 7- or 8-round magazine, bbl. lengths: 3.75, 4.25 or 5 inches; 7.13 to 8.63 inches overall. Weight: 34.5 to 38.5 oz. Post front sight, fixed Novak LC rear w/3-dot system or adj. One-piece Xenoy wraparound grips. Satin stainless finish. Made from 1991 to 1997.
Model 4505 w/fixed sights, 5-inch bbl. . NiB $693 Ex $597 Gd $386
Model 4505 w/Novak LC sight, 5-inch bbl.NiB $653 Ex $578 Gd $431
Model 4506 w/fixed sights, 5-inch bbl. . NiB $744 Ex $581 Gd $523
Model 4506 w/Novak LC sight, 5-inch bbl.NiB $755 Ex $590 Gd $500
Model 4513T (TSW) w/3.75-inch bbl.
Tactical Combat. . . . . NiB $781 Ex $633 Gd $499
Model 4516 w/3.75-inch bbl . . . . NiB $724 Ex $622 Gd $479
Model 4526 w/5-inch bbl., alloy frame,
decocking lever, fixed sights . . . . NiB $734 Ex $590 Gd $500
Model 4536, decocking lever . . . . NiB $734 Ex $590 Gd $500
Model 4546, w/3.75-inch bbl., DA only NiB $734 Ex $590 Gd $500
Model 4553T (TSW) w/3.75-inch bbl.
Tactical Combat. . . . . NiB $780 Ex $665 Gd $459
Model 4556, w/3.75-inch bbl., DA only NiB $700 Ex $601 Gd $397
Model 4563 TSW w/4.25-inch bbl.
Tactical Combat. . . . . NiB $779 Ex $658 Gd $499
Model 4566 w/4.25-inch bbl.,
ambidExtrous safety, fixed sights . . . . . . NiB $693 Ex $536 Gd $453
Model 4566 TSW w/4.25-inch bbl.
Tactical Combat. . . . . NiB $693 Ex $536 Gd $453
Model 4576 w/4.25-inch bbl.,
decocking lever . . . . NiB $691 Ex $607 Gd $449
Model 4583T TSW w/4.25-inch bbl.
Tactical Combat. . . . . NiB $780 Ex $665 Gd $459
Model 4586 w/4.25-inch bbl., DA only NiB $780 Ex $610 Gd $500
Model 4586 TSW w/4.25-inch bbl.
Tactical Combat. . . . . NiB $734 Ex $590 Gd $500

MODEL 5900 SERIES DA AUTOMATIC
Caliber: 9mm. 15-round magazine, 4-inch bbl., 7.5 inches overall. Weight: 26-38 oz. Fixed or adj. sights. One-piece Xenoy wraparound grips. Alloy frame w/stainless-steel slide (Model 5903) or blued slide (Model 5904) stainless-steel frame and slide (Model 5906). Made from 1990 to 1997.
Model 5903 w/adjustable sights . . . . . . NiB $693 Ex $556 Gd $386
Model 5903 w/Novak LC rear sight . . . . NiB $780 Ex $691 Gd $386
Model 5903 TSW w/4-inch bbl.,
Tactical Combat. . . . . NiB $767 Ex $658 Gd $497
Model 5904 w/adjustable sights . . . . . . NiB $581 Ex $468 Gd $376
Model 5904 w/Novak LC rear sight . . . . NiB $599 Ex $474 Gd $398
Model 5905 L/C Adjustable Sights   . . . . NiB $693 Ex $549 Gd $398
Model 5905 w/Novak LC rear sight . . . . NiB $733 Ex $634 Gd $464
Model 5906 w/adjustable sights . . . . . . NiB $658 Ex $544 Gd $439
Model 5906 w/Novak LC rear sight . . . . NiB $658 Ex $544 Gd $439
Model 5906 w/Tritium night sight . . . . . NiB $755 Ex $650 Gd $562
Model 5906 TSW w/4-inch bbl.,
Tactical Combat. . . . . NiB $862 Ex $733 Gd $544
Model 5924 w/anodized frame, blued slide NiB $659 Ex $508 Gd $337
Model 5926 w/stainless frame, decocking leverNiB $644 Ex $543 Gd$444
Model 5943 w/alloy frame/
stainless slide, DA only . . . . NiB $601 Ex $444 Gd $351
Model 5943 TSW w/4-inch bbl., DA onlyNiB $650 Ex $546 Gd $429
Model 5944 w/alloy frame/
blued slide, DA only . . . . NiB $689 Ex $556 Gd $456
Model 5946 w/stainless frame/slide, DA onlyNiB $658 Ex $534 Gd $376
Model 5946 TSW w/4-inch bbl., DA onlyNiB $774 Ex $632 Gd $337

MODEL 6900 COMPACT SERIES
Double action. Caliber: 9mm. 12-round magazine, 3.5-inch bbl., 6.88 inches overall. Weight: 26.5 oz. AmbidExtrous safety. Post front sight, fixed Novak LC rear w/3-dot system. Alloy frame w/blued carbon steel slide (Model 6904) or stainless steel slide (Model 6906). Made 1989 to 1997.

Model 6904	NiB $601	Ex $499	Gd $377
Model 6906 w/fixed sights	NiB $621	Ex $546	Gd $499
Model 6906 w/Tritium night sight	NiB $843	Ex $621	Gd $500
Model 6926			
w/decocking lever	NiB $691	Ex $587	Gd $374
Model 6944			
in DA only	NiB $612	Ex $546	Gd $342
Model 6946			
in DA only ,fixed sights	NiB $709	Ex $577	Gd $395
Model 6946 w/Tritium night sight	NiB $709	Ex $544	Gd $433

SIGMA SW380 AUTOMATIC PISTOL NiB $536 Ex $357 Gd $290
Caliber: .380 ACP. Double-action only. Six-round magazine, 3-inch bbl., weight: 14 oz. Black integral polymer gripframe w/checkered back and front straps. Fixed channel sights. Polymer frame w/hammerless steel slide. Made from 1994 to 1996.

SIGMA SW9 SERIES AUTOMATIC PISTOL
Caliber: 9mm Parabellum. Double action only. 10-round magazine, 3.25-, 4- or 4.5-inch bbl., weight: 17.9 oz. to 24.7 oz. Polymer frame w/hammerless steel slide. Post front sight and drift adjustable rear w/3-dot system. Gray or black integral polymer gripframe w/checkered back and front straps. Made from 1994 to 1996.

Model SW9C (compact w/3.25-inch bbl.)	NiB $500	Ex $425	Gd $326
Model SW9F (blue slide w/4.5-inch bbl.)	NiB $500	Ex $425	Gd $326
Model SW9M (compact w/3.25-inch bbl.)	NiB $342	Ex $255	Gd $165
Model SW9V (stainless slide w/4-inch bbl.)	NiB $408	Ex $304	Gd $229
Tritium night sight, add			$25

SW40 SERIES AUTOMATIC PISTOL
Same general specifications as SW9 series except chambered for .40 S&W w/4- or 4.5-inch bbl., weight: 24.4 to 26 oz. Made 1994 to 1998.

Model SW40C (compact w/4-inch bbl.)	NiB $497	Ex $346	Gd $249
Model SW40F (blue slide w/4.5-inch bbl.)	NiB $497	Ex $346	Gd $249
Model SW40V (stainless slide w/4-inch bbl.)	NiB $497	Ex $346	Gd $249
w/Tritium night sight, add			$25

MODEL 1891 SINGLE-SHOT TARGET PISTOL, FIRST MODEL
Hinged frame. Calibers: .22 LR, .32 S&W, .38 S&W. Bbl. lengths: 6-, 8- and 10-inches, approx. 13.5 inches overall (with 10-inch bbl.). Weight: About 25 oz. Target sights, barrel catch rear adj. for windage and elevation. Blued finish. Square butt, hard rubber grips. Made 1893-1905. Note: This model was available also as a combination arm w/accessory .38 revolver bbl. and cylinder enabling conversion to a pocket revolver. It has the frame of the .38 SA revolver Model 1891 w/side flanges, hand and cylinder stop slots.

Single-shot pistol, .22 LR	NiB $2890	Ex $2643	Gd $2425
Single-shot pistol, .32 S&W or .38 S&W	NiB $2320	Ex $1996	Gd $1748
Combination set, revolver and single-shot barrel	NiB $3635	Ex $3145	Gd $2869

MODEL 1891 SINGLE-SHOT TARGET PISTOL, SECOND MODEL. NiB $2797 Ex $2466 Gd $1580
Similar to the First Model except side flanges, hand and stop slots eliminated, cannot be converted to revolver, redesigned rear sight. Caliber: .22 LR only, 10-inch bbl. only. Made from 1905 to 1909.

PERFECTED SINGLE-SHOT TARGET PISTOL
Similar to Second Model except has double-action lockwork. Caliber: .22 LR only, 10-inch bbl. Checkered walnut grips, Extended square-butt target type. Made 1909-23. Note: In 1920 and thereaf-

Smith & Wesson
Model 1

ter, this model was made w/barrels having bore diameter of .223 instead of .226 and tight, short chambering. The first group of these pistols was produced for the U.S. Olympic Team of 1920, thus the designation Olympic Model.

Pre-1920 type.	NiB $2314	Ex $1945	Gd $1566
Olympic model	NiB $2665	Ex $2380	Gd $2235

STRAIGHT LINE SINGLE-SHOT TARGET PISTOL. NiB $3345 Ex $3267 Gd $3095
Frame shaped like that of an automatic pistol, barrel swings to the left on pivot for Extracting and loading, straight-line trigger and hammer movement. Caliber: .22 LR. 10-inch bbl., 11.25 inches overall. Weight: 34 oz. Target sights. Blued finish. Smooth walnut grips. Supplied in metal case w/screwdriver and cleaning rod. Made from 1925 to 1936.

NOTE: *The following section contains only S&W Revolvers. For a complete listing of S&W handguns, please refer to the indEx.*

REVOLVERS

MODEL 1 HAND EJECTOR
DA REVOLVER. NiB $2670 Ex $2000 Gd $1289
First Model. Forerunner of the .32 Hand Ejector and Regulation Police models, this was the first S&W revolver of the solid-frame, swing-out cylinder type. Top strap of this model is longer than those of later models, and it lacks the usual S&W cylinder latch. Caliber: .22 Long. Bbl., lengths: 3.25-, 4.25-, and 6-inches. Fixed sights. Blued or nickel finish. Round butt, hard rubber stocks. Made from 1896 to 1903.

NO. 3 SA FRONTIER. NiB $5170 Ex $4350 Gd $3095
Caliber: .44-40 WCF. Bbl., lengths: 4-, 5- and 6.5-inch. Fixed or target sights. Blued or nickel finish. Round, hard rubber or checkered walnut grips. Made from 1885 to 1908.

NO. 3 SA (NEW MODEL). NiB $7245 Ex $6095 Gd $4270
Hinged frame. Six-round cylinder. Caliber: .44 S&W Russian. Bbl., lengths: 4-, 5-, 6-, 6.5-, 7.5- and 8-inches. Fixed or target sights. Blued or nickel finish. Round, hard rubber or checkered walnut grips. Made from 1878 to 1908. Note: Value shown is for standard model. Specialist collectors recognize numerous variations w/a range of higher values.
Performance Center Schofield Model of 2000 (modern repro) . NiB $1800

NO. 3 SA TARGET. NiB $6996 Ex $3890 Gd $3175
Hinged frame. Six-round cylinder. Calibers: .32/.44 S&W, .38/.44 S&W Gallery & Target. 6.5-inch bbl. only. Fixed or target sights. Blued or nickel finish. Round, hard rubber or checkered walnut grips. Made from 1887 to 1910.

Smith & Wesson
Model 10 (Two-inch Barrel)

Smith & Wesson
Model 12 (Two-inch Barrel)

Smith & Wesson Model 13
(Heavy Barrel)

Smith & Wesson
Model 14

MODEL 10 .38 MILITARY & POLICE DA

Also called Hand Ejector Model of 1902, Hand Ejector Model of 1905, Model K. Manufactured substantially in its present form since 1902, this model has undergone numerous changes, most of them minor. Round- or square-butt models, the latter intro. in 1904. Caliber: .38 Special. Six-round cylinder, bbl. lengths: 2-(intro. 1933), 4-, 5-, 6- and 6.5-inch (latter disc. 1915) also 4-inch heavy bbl., (intro. 1957); 11.13 inches overall (square-butt model w/6-inch bbl.). Round-butt model is 1/4-inch shorter, weight: About 1/2 oz. less. Fixed sights. Blued or nickel finish. Checkered walnut grips, hard rubber available in round-butt style. Current Model 10 has short action. Made 1902 to date. Note: S&W Victory Model, wartime version of the M & P .38, was produced for the U.S. Government from 1940 to the end of the war. A similar revolver, designated .38/200 British Service Revolver, was produced for the British Government during the same period. These arms have either brush-polish or sandblast blued finish, and most of them have plain, smooth walnut grips, lanyard swivels.

Model of 1902 (1902-05) . . . . NiB $639 Ex $536 Gd $362
Model of 1905 (1905-40) . . . NiB $1165 Ex $910 Gd $602
.38/200 British Service (1940-45)NiB $1165 Ex $910 Gd $602
Victory Model (1942-45). . . . . NiB $643 Ex $529 Gd $425
Model of 1944 (1945-48) . . . . NiB $785 Ex $431 Gd $319
Model 10 (1948-date). . . . . . . NiB $530 Ex $437 Gd $319

MODEL 10 .38 MILITARY
& POLICE HEAVY BARREL . . . NiB $632 Ex $499 Gd $337
Same as standard Model 10 except has heavy 4-inch bbl., weight: 34 oz. Made from 1957 to 1986.

MODEL 12 .38 M&P
AIRWEIGHT . . . . NiB $544 Ex $388 Gd $290
Same as standard Military & Police except has light alloy frame, f8rnished w/2- or 4-inch bbl. only, weight: 18 oz. (w/2-inch bbl.). Made from 1952 to 1986.

MODEL 12/13 (AIR FORCE MODEL)
DA REVOLVER . . . . NiB $536 Ex $439 Gd $265
Special "Air Force" Model designed with alloy cylinder and frame to be used as a "Survival Weapon" for air crews. Athough this weapon was actually a first-series Model 12, the Air Force stamped "M13" on the top strap. Issued 1953 but recalled for function problems in 1954.

MODEL 13 .357
MILITARY/POLICE . . . . NiB $487 Ex $318 Gd $204
Same as Model 10 .38 Military & Police Heavy Barrel except chambered for .357 Magnum and .38 Special w/3- or 4-inch bbl. Round or square butt configuration. Made from1974 to 1998.

MODELS 14 (K-38) AND 16 (K-32) MASTERPIECE REVOLVERS
Calibers: .22 LR, .22 Magnum Rimfire, .32 S&W Long, .38 Special. Six-round cylinder. DA/SA. Bbl. lengths: 4- (.22 WMR only), 6-, 8.38-inch (latter not available in K32), 11.13 inches overall (with 6-inch bbl.). Weight: 38.5 oz. (with 6-inch bbl.). Click adj. rear sight, Partridge front. Blued finish. Checkered walnut grips. Made from 1947 to date. (Model 16 disc. 1974; 3,630 produced; reissued 1990 to 1993.)

Model 14 (K-38 double-
action) . . . . NiB $577 Ex $318 Gd $209
Model 14 (K-38 single action,
6-inch bbl.) . . . . NiB $693 Ex $366 Gd $220
Model 14 (K-38 single action,
8.38-inch bbl.) . . . . NiB $474 Ex $351 Gd $259
Model 16 (K-32 double-
action) 1st Issue . . . . NiB $3500 Ex $3316 Gd $889
Model 16 (K-32 double-
action) . . . . NiB $2579 Ex $1138 Gd $974

MODELS 15 (.38) AND 18 (.22) COMBAT MASTERPIECE DA REVOLVERS

Same as K-22 and K-38 Masterpiece but w/2- (.38) or 4-inch bbl., and Baughman quick-draw front sight. 9.13 inches overall w/4-inch bbl., Weight: 34 oz. (.38 cal.). Made from 1950 to 1999.

Model 15 . . . . NiB $805 Ex $602 Gd $456
Model 18 (disc. 1985) . . . . . . NiB $691 Ex $523 Gd $487
w/target options TH & TT, add $50

MODEL 17 K-22 MASTERPIECE DA REVOLVER

Caliber: 22 LR. Six-round cylinder, Bbl lengths: 4, 6 or 8.38 inches. 11.13 inches overall (with 6-inch bbl.). Weight: 38 oz. (with 8-inch bbl.). Partridge-type front sight, S&W micrometer click rear. Checkered walnut Service grips with S&W momogram. S&W blued finish. Made from 1947-93 and from 1996-98.

Model 17 (4-inch bbl.). . . . . . .NiB $632 Ex $453 Gd $347
Model 17 (6-inch bbl.) . . . . . . NiB $632 Ex $453 Gd $347
Model 17 (8.38-inch bbl.). . . . NiB $823 Ex $546 Gd $479
w/target options TH & TT, add $50

MODEL 19 .357 COMBAT MAGNUM DA REVOLVER

Caliber: .357 Magnum. Six-round cylinder, bbl. lengths: 2.5 (round butt), 4, or 6 inches, 9.5 inches overall (with 4-inch bbl.). Weight: 35 oz. (with 4-inch bbl.). Click adj. rear sight, ramp front. Blued or nickel finish. Target grips of checkered Goncalo Alves. Made from 1956 to date (2.5- and 6-inch bbls. were disc. in 1991).

Model 19 (2.5-inch bbl.). . . . . NiB $601 Ex $431 Gd $319
Model 19 (4-inch bbl.) . . . . . . NiB $601 Ex $431 Gd $319
Model 19 (6-inch bbl.) . . . . . . NiB $601 Ex $431 Gd $319
Model 19 (8.38-inch bbl.). . . . NiB $601 Ex $431 Gd $319
w/target options TH & TT, add $75

MODEL 20 .38/44 HEAVY DUTY DA

Caliber: .38 Special. Six-round cylinder, bbl. lengths: 4, 5 and 6.5 inches;10.38 inches overall (with 5-inch bbl.). Weight: 40 oz. (with 5-inch bbl.). Fixed sights. Blued or nickel finish. Checkered walnut grips. Short action after 1948. Made from 1930-56 and from 1957 to 67.

Pre-World War II . . . . NiB $1970 Ex $1770 Gd $525
Post-war. . . . . NiB $2270 Ex $1620 Gd $910

MODEL 21 .44 MILITARY DA REVOLVER

Postwar version of the 1926 Model 44 Military. Caliber: .44 Special, 6-round cylinder. Bbl. lengths: 4-, 5- and 6.5-inches. 11.75 inches overall (w/6.5-inch bbl.) Weight: 39.5 oz. (w/6.5-inch bbl.). Fixed front sight w/square-notch rear sight; target model has micrometer click rear sight adj. for windage and elevation. Checkered walnut grips w/S&W monogram. Blued or nickel finish. Made 1950 to 1967.

Model 21 (4- or 5-inch bbl.) . . . . . NiB $2979 Ex $2035 Gd $809
Model 21 (6.5-inch bbl.), add. 50%

MODEL 22 1950 ARMY DA . . .NiB $2025 Ex $1735 Gd $816

Postwar version of the 1917 Army w/same general specifications except redesigned hammer. Made from 1950 to 1967.

.22/.32 TARGET DA REVOLVER

Also known as the "Bekeart Model." Design based upon ".32 Hand Ejector." Caliber: .22 LR (recessed head cylinder for high-speed cartridges intro. 1935). Six-round cylinder, 6-inch bbl., 10.5 inches overall. Weight: 23 oz. Adj. target sights. Blued finish. Checkered walnut grips. Made from 1911-53. Note: In 1911, San Francisco gun dealer Phil Bekeart, who suggested this model, received 292 pieces. These are the true "Bekeart Model" revolvers and are marked with separate identification numbers on the base of the wooden grip.

.22/.32 TARGET DA REVOLVER . . . . . NiB $1160 Ex $760 Gd $498
.22/.32 (early prod. 1-3000), add. 20%
.22/.32 Bekeart model . . . . NiB $1565 Ex $1329 Gd $752

.22/.32 KIT GUN . . . . NiB $850 Ex $580 Gd $319

Same as .22/.32 Target except has 2- or 4-inch bbl., round grips, 6 or 8 inches overall, weight: 19-21oz. Made from 1935 to 1953.

Smith & Wesson
Model 15

Smith & Wesson
Model 17 K-22

Smith & Wesson
Model 18 (See Model 15 for description)

Smith & Wesson
Model 19 (Round Butt)

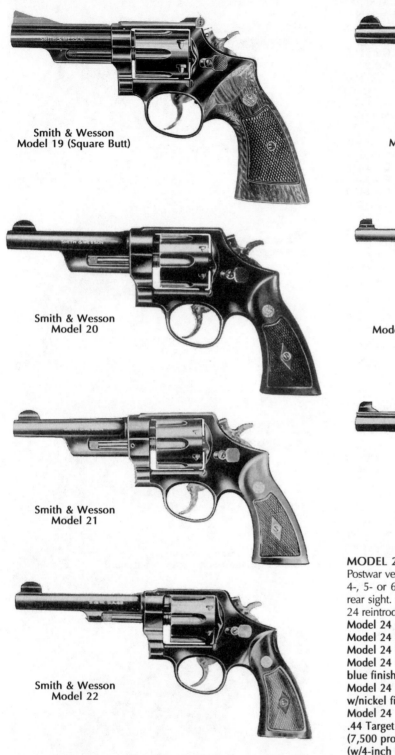

Smith & Wesson
Model 19 (Square Butt)

Smith & Wesson
Model 20

Smith & Wesson
Model 21

Smith & Wesson
Model 22

Smith & Wesson
Model 22/32 Kit Gun

Smith & Wesson
Model 22/32 Target Revolver

Smith & Wesson
Model 23

MODEL 23 .38-44 OUTDOORSMAN DA REVOLVER

Target version of the .38/44 Heavy Duty. 6.5- or 8.75-inch bbl., weight: 41.75 oz. Target sights, micrometer-click rear on postwar models. Blued or nickel finish. 1950 transition model has ribbed barrel, redesigned hammer. Made from 1930 to 1967.
Pre-war model (plain bbl.) NiB $2555 Ex $1958 Gd $1278
Post-war (ribbed bbl.). . . . . NiB $1724 Ex $1398 Gd $780

MODEL 24 1950 .44 TARGET DA REVOLVER

Postwar version of the 1921 Model .44 Hand Ejector. .44 Special with 4-, 5- or 6.5-inch ribbed bbl., redesigned hammer, micrometer click rear sight. Matte or polished blue finish. Made from 1950-67. Model 24 reintroduced in 1983 only.
Model 24 (1950 w/6.5-inch bbl.. . NiB $2770 Ex $1696 Gd $897
Model 24 (1950) w/4-inch bbl., add. .20%
Model 24 (1950) w/5-inch bbl., add 100%
Model 24 (1950) w/polished
blue finish, add 25%
Model 24 (1950)
w/nickel finish, add 65%
Model 24
.44 Target reintroduced
(7,500 produced in 1983-84)
(w/4-inch bbl.) . . . . NiB $760 Ex $560 Gd $402
Model 24 (w/6.5-inch bbl.). . . . . NiB $730 Ex $553 Gd $365
Model 24-3 .44
Lew Horton Special
w/3-inch bbl. (produced in 1983) . . . NiB $860 Ex $654 Gd $380
Classics w/6.5-inch bbl. (produced 2008-2012)NiB $770 Ex $554 Gd $370
Classics w/ nickel finish, add 8%

MODEL 25 1955 .45 TARGET DA REVOLVER
Same as 1950 Model .44 Target, but chambered for .45 ACP, .45 Auto Rim or .45 LC w/4-, 6- or 6.5-inch bbl. Made from 1955 to 1991 in several variations. Note: In 1961, the .45 ACP was designated Model 25-2, and in 1978 the .45 LC was designated Model 25-5.
Model 25 1955 .45 Target
.45 ACP w/4- or 6-inch bbl. . . . . NiB $780 Ex $587 Gd $434
.45 ACP w/6.5-inch pinned bbl.. . . . . . . NiB $767 Ex $660 Gd $449
.45 LC early production . . . . NiB $4245 Ex $4040 Gd $3779
Model 25-2 .45 ACP
Lew Horton Specialw/3-inch bbl. . . . . . . NiB $541 Ex $453 Gd $346
Model 25-2 (w/4-inch bbl.) . . . . NiB $601 Ex $485 Gd $402
Model 25-3 (w/6.5-inch bbl.). . . . . NiB $734 Ex $544 Gd $429
Model 25-5 .45 LC w/4-inch bbl. . . . . . NiB $601 Ex $484 Gd $377
Model 25-3 (w/6.5-inch bbl.). . . . . NiB $648 Ex $530 Gd $362
Model 25 Classics (reintro. 2008). . . . . . NiB $980 Ex $530 Gd $362

MODEL 26 1950 .45 LIGHT TARGET DA REVOLVER
Similar to 1950 Model Target except w/lighter bbl. Note: Lighter profile was not well received. (Only 2,768 produced)
Model 26 (.45 ACP or .45 Auto Rim
w/6.5-inch bbl.) . . . . NiB $4590 Ex $4295 Gd $3988
Model 26 .45 LC, (200 produced) . . NiB $4590 Ex $4295 Gd $3988
w/4- or 5-inch bbl., ...$50

MODEL 27 .357 MAGNUM DA
Caliber: .357 Magnum. Six-round cylinder, bbl. lengths: 3.5-, 4-, 5-, 6-, 6.5-and 8.38-inches, 11.38 inches overall (with 6-inch bbl.). Weight: 44 oz. (with 6-inch bbl.). Adj. target sights, Baughman quick-draw ramp front sight on 3.5-inch bbl., Blued or nickel finish. Checkered walnut grips. Made from 1935-94. Note: Until 1938, the .357 Magnum was custom made in any barrel length from 3.5-inch to 8.75-inch. Each of these revolvers was accompanied by a registration certificate and has its registration number stamped on the inside of the yoke. Postwar magnums have a redesigned hammer w/ shortened fall and the new S&W micrometer click rear sight.
Pre-war model
(Reg number on yoke) . . . . NiB $893 Ex $730 Gd $615
Pre-war model w/out reg number. . . . . . NiB $862 Ex $653 Gd $612
Early model w/pinned bbl., recessed cyl. NiB $895 Ex $755 Gd $624
Late model w/8. 38-inch bbl.. . . . . NiB $895 Ex $755 Gd $624
Late model w/3.5 to 5-inch bbl.. . . . . . . NiB $895 Ex $755 Gd $624
Late model, other bbl. lengths . . . . NiB $915 Ex $785 Gd $612

MODEL 28 HIGHWAY PATROLMAN
Caliber: .357 Magnum. Six-round cylinder, bbl. lengths: 4- or 6-inches, 11.25 inches overall (with 6-inch bbl.). Weight: 44 oz. (with 6-inch bbl.). Adj. rear sight, ramp front. Blued finish. Checkered walnut grips, Magna or target type. Made from 1954 to 1986.
Pre-war registered model
(reg number on yoke). . . . . NiB $893 Ex $780 Gd $610
Pre-war model without registration numberNiB $1190 Ex $975 Gd $700
Early model w/pinned bbl.,
recessed cylinder, 5-screws . . . . NiB $895 Ex $734 Gd $632
Late model, all bbl. lengths . . . . NiB $536 Ex $362 Gd $255

MODEL 29 .44 MAGNUM DA REVOLVER
Caliber: .44 Magnum. Six-round cylinder. bbl., lengths: 4-, 5-, 6.5-, 8.38-inches. 11.88 inches overall (with 6.5-inch bbl.). Weight: 47 oz. (with 6.5-inch bbl.). Click adj. rear sight, ramp front. Blued or nickel finish. Checkered Goncalo Alves target grips. Made from 1956 to 1998. Early Production Standard Series (disc. 1983)
3-Screw model (1962-83) . . . . NiB $970 Ex $843 Gd $686
4-Screw model (1957-61) . . . . NiB $2200 Ex $1693 Gd $880
5-Screw model (1956-57) . . . . NiB $3497 Ex $2895 Gd $2630
w/5-inch bbl., 3- or 4-screw models, add 100%

Smith & Wesson
Model 24 Target

Smith & Wesson
Model 25 Target

Smith & Wesson
Model 27

Smith & Wesson
Model 28

Late Production standard series (disc. 1998)
Model 29 (w/4- or 6.5-inch bbl.) . . . . . . NiB $870 Ex $669 Gd $432
Model 29 (w/3-inch bbl., Lew Horton Special) . NiB $920 Ex $689 Gd $432
Model 29 (w/8.38-inch bbl.) . . . . NiB $895 Ex $679 Gd $432
Model 29 Classic (w/5- or 6.5-inch bbl.) NiB $610 Ex $539 Gd $332
Model 29 Classic (w/8.38-inch bbl.) . . . NiB $630 Ex $540 Gd $345
Model 29 Classic DX (w/6.5-in. and 8.38-in. bbl.)NiB $1260 Ex $648 Gd $556
Model 29 Classic DX (w/5-inch bbl.) . . NiB $1410 Ex $798 Gd $656
Model 29 Magna Classic
(w/7.5-inch ported bbl.) . . . . NiB $1170 Ex $859 Gd $537
Model 29 Silhouette (w/10.63-inch bbl.) NiB $860 Ex $656 Gd $437

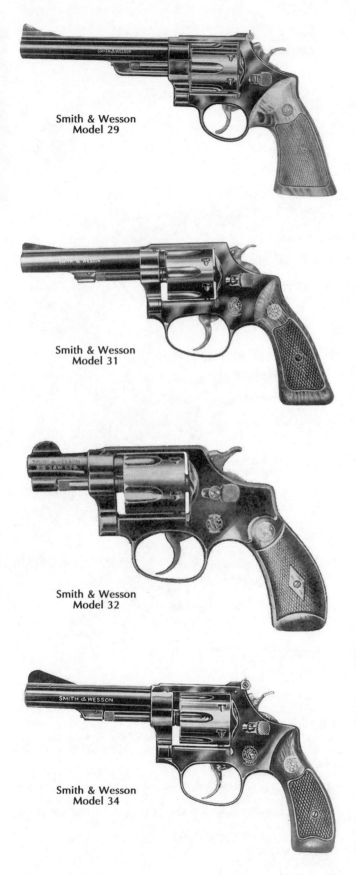

Smith & Wesson
Model 29

Smith & Wesson
Model 31

Smith & Wesson
Model 32

Smith & Wesson
Model 34

MODEL 30 .32 HAND EJECTOR
DA REVOLVER . . . . **NiB $554 Ex $469 Gd $356**
Caliber: .32 S&W Long. Six-round cylinder, bbl. lengths: 2- (intro. 1949), 3-, 4- and 6-inches, 8 inches overall (with 4-inch bbl.). Weight: 18 oz. (with 4-inch bbl.). Fixed sights. Blued or nickel finish. Round, checkered walnut or hard rubber grips. Made from 1903-76.

MODELS 31 & 33 REGULATION POLICE DA REVOLVER
Same basic type as .32 Hand Ejector except has square butt-grips. Calibers: .32 S&W Long (Model 31) .38 S&W (Model 33). Six-round cylinder in .32 cal., 5-round in .38 caliber. Bbl., lengths: 2- (intro. 1949), 3-, 4- and 6-inches in .32 cal., 4-inch only in .38 cal., 8.5 inches overall (with 4-inch bbl.). Weight: 18 oz. (.38 cal. w/4-inch bbl.), 18.75 oz. (.32 cal. w/4-inch bbl.). Fixed sights. Blued or nickel finish. Checkered walnut grips. Made from 1917. Model 33 disc. in 1974; Model 31 disc. in 1992.
Model 31 . . . . **NiB $546 Ex $306 Gd $255**
Model 33 . . . . **NiB $448 Ex $283 Gd $198**

MODEL 32 DA REVOLVER . . **NiB $546 Ex $467 Gd $219**
Hinged frame. Caliber: .32 S&W. Five-round cylinder, bbl. lengths: 3-, 3.5- and 6-inches. Fixed sights. Blued or nickel finish. Hard rubber grips. Made from 1880-1919. Note: Value shown applies generally to the several varieties. exception is the rare first issue of 1880 (identified by squared sideplate and serial no. 1 to 30) valued up to $2,500.

MODEL 32 TERRIER DA . . . . . **NiB $479 Ex $342 Gd $255**
Caliber: .38 S&W. Five-round cylinder, 2-inch bbl., 6.25 inches overall. Weight: 17 oz. Fixed sights. Blued or nickel finish. Checkered walnut or hard rubber grips. Built on .32 Hand Ejector frame. Made from 1936-74.

MODEL 33 .32-20 MILITARY & POLICE
DA REVOLVER . . . . **NiB $2845 Ex $2719 Gd $2530**
Same as M&P 38 except chambered for .32-20 Winchester cartridge. First intro. in the 1899 model, M&P revolvers were produced in this caliber until about 1940. Values same as M&P .38 models.

MODEL 34
DA REVOLVER . . . . **NiB $756 Ex $408 Gd $305**
Caliber: .22 LR. Six-shot cylinder, 2-inch or 4-inch bbl. and round or square grips, blued or nickel finish. Made from 1936-91.

MODEL 35 1953
.22/.32 TARGET . . . . **NiB $772 Ex $590 Gd $362**
Same general specifications as previous model .22/.32 Target except has micrometer-click rear sight. Magna type target grips. Weight: 25 oz. Made from 1953-74.

MODEL 36 CHIEFS SPECIAL DA
Based on .32 Hand Ejector w/frame lengthened to permit longer cylinder for .38 Special cartridge. Caliber: .38 Special. Five-round cylinder, bbl. lengths: 2- or 3-inches, 6.5 inches overall (with 2-inch bbl.). Weight: 19 oz. Fixed sights. Blued or nickel finish. Checkered walnut grips, round or square butt. Made from 1952 to date.
Blued model . . . . **NiB $638 Ex $425 Gd $255**
Nickel model . . . . **NiB $648 Ex $437 Gd $265**
**Early model (5-screw, small trigger
guard, S/N 1-2500)** . . . . **NiB $668 Ex $541 Gd $386**
Model 36 Ladysmith (1990-2008) **NiB $480 Ex $290 Gd $186**

MODEL 37 AIRWEIGHT
CHIEFS SPECIAL . . . . **NiB $500 Ex $366 Gd $225**
Same general specifications as standard Chiefs Special except has light alloy frame, weight: 12.5 oz. w/2-inch bbl., blued finish only. Made from 1954 to 1995

MODEL 38 BODYGUARD AIRWEIGHT DA REVOLVER
Shrouded hammer. Light alloy frame. Caliber: .38 Special. Five-round cylinder, 2- or 3-inch bbl., 6.38 inches overall (w/2-inch bbl). Weight: 14.5 oz. Fixed sights. Blued or nickel finish. Checkered walnut grips. Made from 1955 to 1998.
Blued model. . . . . **NiB $479 Ex $347 Gd $235**
Nickel model . . . . **NiB $500 Ex $362 Gd $274**
Early model (pinned bbl. &
recessed cyl., pre-1981) . . . . . **NiB $485 Ex $342 Gd $243**

.38 DA REVOLVER . . . . **NiB $945 Ex $734 Gd $544**
Hinged frame. Caliber: .38 S&W. Five-round cylinder, bbl. lengths: 4-, 4.25-, 5-, 6-, 8- and 10-inch. Fixed sights. Blued or nickel finish. Hard rubber grips. Made from 1880-1911. Note: Value shown applies generally to the several varieties. exceptions are the first issue of 1880 (identified by squared sideplate and serial no. 1 to 4,000) and the 8- and 10-inch bbl. models of the third issue (1884 to 1995).

MODEL .38 HAND EJECTOR DA
Military & Police — First Model. Resembles Colt New Navy in general appearance, lacks bbl., lug and locking bolt common to all later S&W hand ejector models. Caliber: .38 Long Colt. Six-round cylinder, bbl. lengths: 4-, 5-, 6- and 6.5-inch, 11.5 inches overall (with 6.5-inch bbl.). Fixed sights. Blued or nickel finish. Round, checkered walnut or hard rubber grips. Made from 1899 to 1902.
Standard model
(civilian issue) . . . . **NiB $1870 Ex $1322 Gd $1132**
Army Model (marked U.S.
Army Model, 1000 issued) NiB $3725 Ex $3397 Gd $2935
Navy Model (marked USN,
1000 issued) . . . . **NiB $4495 Ex $3800 Gd $3412**

.38 MILITARY & POLICE
TARGET DA . . . . **NiB $3725 Ex $3397 Gd $2740**
Target version of the Military & Police w/standard features of that model. Caliber: .38 Special, six-inch bbl. Weight: 32.25 oz. Adj. target sights. Blued finish. Checkered walnut grips. Made from 1899 to 1940. For values, add $175 for corresponding M&P 38 models.

MODEL .38 PERFECTED DA **NiB $1465 Ex $1336 Gd $1145**
Hinged frame. Similar to earlier .38 DA Model but heavier frame, side latch as in solid-frame models, improved lockwork. Caliber: .38 S&W. Five-round cylinder, bbl. lengths: 3.25, 4, 5 and 6 inches. Fixed sights. Blued or nickel finish. Hard rubber grips. Made 1909 to 1920.

MODEL 40 CENTENNIAL
DA HAMMERLESS REVOLVER
Similar to Chiefs Special but has Safety Hammerless-type mechanism w/grip safety. Two-inch bbl. Weight: 19 oz. Made from 1953 to 1974.
Blued model. . . . . **NiB $633 Ex $437 Gd $398**
Nickel model . . . . **NiB $1319 Ex $1109 Gd $895**

MODEL 42 CENTENNIAL AIRWEIGHT
Same as standard Centennial model except has light alloy frame, weight: 13 oz. Made from 1954 to 1974.
Blued model . . . . **NiB $648 Ex $429 Gd $351**
Nickel model . . . . **NiB $1250 Ex $1062 Gd $884**

MODEL 43 1955 .22/.32
KIT GUN AIRWEIGHT . . . . . . **NiB $760 Ex $543 Gd $274**
Same as Model 34 Kit Gun except has light alloy frame, square grip. Furnished w/3.5-inch bbl., weight: 14.25 oz. Made 1954 to 1974.

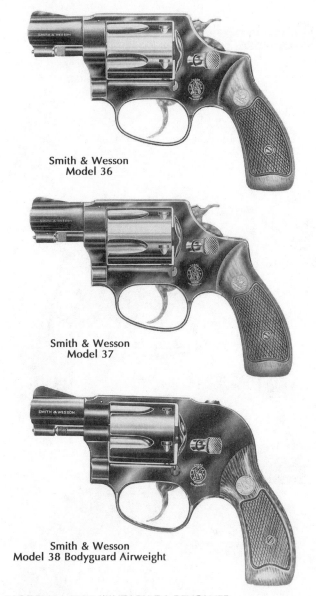

Smith & Wesson
Model 36

Smith & Wesson
Model 37

Smith & Wesson
Model 38 Bodyguard Airweight

MODEL 44 1926 MILITARY DA REVOLVER
Same as the early New Century model with Extractor rod casing but lacking the "Triple Lock" feature. Caliber: .44 S&W Special. Six-round cylinder, bbl. lengths: 4, 5 and 6.5 inches, 11.75 inches overall (with 6.5-inch bbl.). Weight: 39.5 oz. (with 6.5-inch bbl.). Fixed sights. Blued or nickel finish. Checkered walnut grips. Made 1926 to 1941.
Standard model . . . . **NiB $3715 Ex $3409 Gd $3135**
Target model w/6.5-inch bbl.,
target sights, blued . . . . . **NiB $3715 Ex $3409 Gd $3095**

.38 AND .44 DA REVOLVERS
Also called Wesson Favorite (lightweight model), Frontier (caliber .44-40). Hinged frame. Six-round cylinder. Calibers: .44 S&W Russian, .38-40, .44-40. Bbl. lengths: 4-, 5-, 6- and 6.5-inch. Weight: 37.5 oz. (with 6.5-inch bbl.). Fixed sights. Blued or nickel finish. Hard rubber grips. Made from 1881 to 1913, Frontier disc. 1910.
Standard model, .44 Russian NiB $10,930 Ex $9795 Gd $6579
Standard model, .38-40 . . **NiB $6030 Ex $5095 Gd $1479**
Frontier model . . . . **NiB $5089 Ex $3240 Gd $1939**
Favorite model . . . . **NiB $10,600 Ex $8499 Gd $2977**

Smith & Wesson
Model 48

Smith & Wesson
Model 49 Bodyguard

Smith & Wesson
Model 57

Smith & Wesson
Model 60

Smith & Wesson
Model 63

Smith & Wesson
Model 64

.44 HAND EJECTOR MODEL DA REVOLVER

First Model, New Century, also called "Triple Lock" because of its third cylinder lock at the crane. Six-round cylinder. Calibers: .44 S&W Special, .450 Eley, .455 Mark II. Bbl. lengths: 4-, 5-, 6.5- and 7.5-inch. Weight: 39 oz. (with 6.5-inch bbl.). Fixed sights. Blued or nickel finish. Checkered walnut grips. Made 1907 to 1966.

Second Model is basically the same as New Century except crane lock ("Triple Lock" feature) and Extractor rod casing eliminated. Calibers: .44 S&W Special .44-40 Win. .45 Colt. Bbl. lengths: 4-, 5-, 6.5- and 7.5-inch; 11.75 inches overall (with 6.5-inch bbl.). Weight: 38 oz. (with 6.5-inch bbl.). Fixed sights. Blued or nickel finish. Checkered walnut grips. Made from 1915 to 1937.

First Model w/triple lock (1907-15)
Standard model,
.44 S&W Special . . . . NiB $4735 Ex $4380 Gd $4335
Standard model
other calibers . . . . NiB $2865 Ex $2555 Gd $2339
British .455
Target model . . . . NiB $3520 Ex $3299 Gd $1135
Second Model
w/o triple lock (1915-37) . NiB $3520 Ex $3266 Gd $1117
.44 S&W Special . . . . NiB $2420 Ex $2119 Gd $1972
Second model,
other calibers . . . . NiB $5200 Ex $4190 Gd $3977

.44 HAND EJECTOR, SECOND MODEL

DA REVOLVER . . . . NiB $2425 Ex $2174 Gd $1981
Basically the same as New Century except crane lock ("Triple Lock" feature) and Extractor rod casing eliminated. Calibers: .44 S&W Special .44-40 Win. .45 Colt. Bbl. lengths: 4-, 5-, 6.5- and 7.5-inches, 11.75 inches overall (with 6.5-inch bbl.). Weight: .38 oz. (with 6.5-inch bbl.). Fixed sights. Blued or nickel finish. Checkered walnut grips. Made from 1915 to 1937.

MODEL 48 (K-22) MASTERPIECE M.R.F. DA REVOLVER
Caliber: .22 Mag. and .22 LR. Six-round cylinder, bbl. lengths: 4, 6 and 8.38 inches, 11.13 inches overall (w/ 6-inch bbl.). Weight: 39 oz. Adj. rear sight, ramp front. Made from 1959 to 1986.
Model 48 (4- or 6-inch bbl.) . . NiB $862 Ex $668 Gd $495
Model 48 (8.38-inch bbl.). . . . NiB $826 Ex $612 Gd $439
w/target options TH & TT, add $75

MODEL 49 BODYGUARD
Same as Model 38 Bodyguard Airweight except has steel frame, weight: 20.5 oz. Made from 1959 to 1996.
Blued model . . . . NiB $478 Ex $337 Gd $244
Nickel model . . . . NiB $530 Ex $377 Gd $270

MODEL 51 1960 .22/.32 KIT GUN . . NiB $755 Ex $549 Gd $319
Same as Model 34 Kit Gun except chambered for .22 WMR 3.5-inch bbl., weight: 24 oz. Made from 1960 to 1974.

MODEL 53 .22 REM. JET DA
Caliber: .22 Rem. Jet C.F. Magnum. Six-round cylinder (inserts permit use of .22 Short, Long, or LR cartridges). Bbl. lengths: 4, 6, 8.38 inches, 11.25 inches overall (with 6-inch bbl.). Weight: 40 oz. (with 6-inch bbl.). Micrometer-click rear sight ramp front. Checkered walnut grips. Made from 1960 to 1974.
Model 53 (4- or 6-inch bbl.) . . NiB $933 Ex $749 Gd $633
Model 53 (8.38-inch bbl.). . . NiB $1040 Ex $844 Gd $704
w/target options TH & TT, add $75

MODEL 57 .41 MAGNUM DA REVOLVER
Caliber: 41 Magnum. Six-round cylinder, bbl. lengths: 4-, 6-, 8.38-inch. Weight: 40 oz. (with 6-inch bbl.). Micrometer click rear sight, ramp front. Target grips of checkered Goncalo Alves. Made from 1964 to 1993.
Model 57 (w/4- or 6-inch bbl.) . . . . . NiB $812 Ex $627 Gd $429
Model 57 (w/8.63-inch bbl.). . . . . . . NiB $852 Ex $677 Gd $449
Model 57 (w/pinned bbl., recessed cylinder), add 10%
Model 57 Classics (reintro. 2009) . . . NiB $780 Ex $577 Gd $400

MODEL 58 .41 MILITARY& POLICE
DA REVOLVER . . . . NiB $855 Ex $709 Gd $576
Caliber: 41 Magnum. Six-round cylinder, 4-inch bbl. 9.25 inches overall. Weight: 41 oz. Fixed sights. Checkered walnut grips. Made from 1964 to 1982.

MODEL 60 STAINLESS DA
Caliber: .38 Special or .357 Magnum. Five-round cylinder, bbl. lengths: 2, 2.1 or 3 inches, 6.5 or 7.5 inches overall. Weight: 19 to 23 oz. Square-notch rear sight, ramp front. Satin finish stainless steel. Made from 1965-96 (.38 Special) and from 1996 to date (.357/.38).
.38 Special (disc. 1996) . . . . . NiB $474 Ex $346 Gd $270
.357 Mag. . . . . NiB $498 Ex $366 Gd $283
Lady Smith (w/smaller grip). . . . NiB $544 Ex $377 Gd 280

MODEL 63 (1977) KIT GUN DA . . . . NiB $474 Ex $319 Gd $265
Caliber: .22 LR. Six-round cylinder, 2- or 4-inch bbl., 6.5 or 8.5 inches overall. Weight: 19 to 24.5 oz. Adj. rear sight, ramp front. Stainless steel. Checkered walnut or synthetic grips.

MODEL 64 .38 M&P STAINLESS . . . . NiB $498 Ex $362 Gd $287
Same as standard Model 10 except satin-finished stainless steel, square butt w/4-inch heavy bbl., or round butt w/2-inch bbl. Made from 1970 to date.

MODEL 65 .357 MILITARY/
POLICE STAINLESS. . . . . .NiB $499 Ex $357 Gd $290
Same as Model 13 except satin-finished stainless steel. Made 1974 to 2004.
Model 65 Lady Smith (w/smaller grip) . . NiB $540 Ex $377 Gd $302

**Smith & Wesson
Model 66 Combat Magnum**

**Smith & Wesson
Model 67 Combat Masterpiece**

MODEL 66 .357 COMBAT MAGNUM STAINLESS
Same as Model 19 except satin-finished stainless steel. Made from 1971 to date.
Model 66 (2.5-inch bbl.). . . . . NiB $536 Ex $439 Gd $328
Model 66 (3-inch bbl.) . . . . . . NiB $536 Ex $431 Gd $303
Model 66 (4-inch bbl.) . . . . . . NiB $536 Ex $431 Gd $303
Model 66 (6-inch bbl.) . . . . . . NiB $562 Ex $456 Gd $346
w/target options TH & TT, add $65

MODEL 67 .38 COMBAT
MASTERPIECE STAINLESS. . . . NiB $597 Ex $440 Gd $337
Same as Model 15 except satin-finished stainless steel available only w/4-inch bbl. Made from 1972-1988 and from 1991-1998.

MODEL 68 .38 COMBAT
MASTERPIECE STAINLESS. . . . NiB $831 Ex $668 Gd $601
Same as Model 66 except w/4- or 6-inch bbl., chambered for .38 Special. Made to accommodate CA Highway Patrol because they were not authorized to carry .357 magnums. Made from 1976 yo 1983. (7,500 produced)

125th Anniversary Commemorative
Issued to celebrate the 125th anniversary of the 1852 partnership of Horace Smith and Daniel Baird Wesson. Standard Edition is a Model 25 revolver in .45 Colt w/6.5-inch bbl., bright blued finish, gold-filled bbl., roll mark "Smith & Wesson 125th Anniversary," sideplate marked w/gold-filled Anniversary seal, smooth Goncalo Alves grips, in presentation case w/nickel silver Anniversary medallion and book, "125 Years w/Smith & Wesson," by Roy Jinks. Deluxe Edition is same except revolver is Class A engraved w/gold-filled seal on sideplate, ivory grips, Anniversary medallion is sterling silver and book is leather bound. Limited to 50 units. Total issue is 10,000 units, of which 50 are Deluxe Edition and two are a Custom Deluxe Edition and not for sale. Made in 1977.
Standard edition. . . . . NiB $648 Ex $377 Gd $305
Deluxe edition . . . . NiB $2579 Ex $2365 Gd $2094

**Smith & Wesson
Model 629 Classic**

**Smith & Wesson
Model 586 Distinguished Combat Magnum**

**Smith & Wesson
Model 625**

**Smith & Wesson
Model 629**

317 AIRLITE DA REVOLVER
Caliber: .22 LR. Eight-round cylinder, 1.88- or 3-inch bbl., 6.3 or 7.2 inches overall. Weight: 9.9 oz. or 11 oz. Ramp front sight, notched frame rear. Aluminum, carbon fiber, stainless and titanium construction. Brushed aluminum finish. Synthetic or Dymondwood grips. Made from 1997 to date.
Model 317 (w/1.88-inch bbl.) . NiB $590 Ex $380 Gd $306
Model 317 (w/3-inch bbl.) . . . NiB $683 Ex $453 Gd $356
Model 317 (w/Dymondwood grips), add $100

MODEL 500
Caliber: .500 S&W Magnum. Uses S&W's largest revolver frame: X-frame. 5-round cylinder, bbl. lengths: 4, 6.5 and 8.38 inches, ported barrel, overall length: 15 inches (8.38-inch bbl.). Weight: 71.9 oz. (8.38-inch bbl.). Interchangeable front sight, micrometer-click adj. rear. Synthetic grip. Satin stainless finish. Made from 2003 to date.
w/6- or 8.38-inch bbl. . . . . . NiB $1299 Ex $740 Gd $459
w/4-inch bbl. , add $70
w/ factory HI-VIZ sights (8.38-in. bbl.), add $70

MODEL 520
DA REVOLVER . . . . NiB $556 Ex $410 Gd $321
Caliber: .357 Mag. Six-round cylinder. N-Frame w/4-inch bbl. Weight: 40 oz. Fixed sights. In 1980, 3000 pieces were made for the N.Y. State Police but that agency did not purchase those firearms. so they werte sold commercially.

MODEL 547
DA REVOLVER . . . . NiB $816 Ex $709 Gd $499
Caliber: 9mm. Six-round cylinder, bbl. length: 3 or 4 inches, 7.31 inches overall. Weight: 32 oz. Square-notch rear sight, ramp front. Disc. 1986.

MODEL 581 REVOLVER
Caliber: .357 Magnum. Bbl. lengths: 4 inches, weight: 34 oz. Serrated ramp front sight, square notch rear. Checkered walnut grips. Made from 1985 to 1992.
Blued finish . . . . NiB $648 Ex $500 Gd $357
Nickel finish. . . . . NiB $704 Ex $536 Gd $385

MODEL 586 DISTINGUISHED COMBAT MAGNUM
Caliber: .357 Magnum. Six-round cylinder, bbl. lengths: 4, 6 and 8.38 inches, overall length: 9.75 inches (with 4-inch bbl.). Weight: 42, 46, 53 oz., respectively. Red ramp front sight, micrometer-click adj. rear. Checkered grip. Blued or nickel finish. Made 1980 to 1999.
Model 586 (w/4- or 6-inch bbl.)NiB $691 Ex $479 Gd $345
Model 586 (w/8.63-inch bbl.) . NiB $709 Ex $499 Gd $359
Model 586 (w/adjustable front sight), add $50
Model 586 (w/nickel finish), add. $65

MODEL 610 DA REVOLVER . . NiB $755 Ex $612 Gd $500
Similar to Model 625 except in caliber 10mm. Magna classic grips. Made from 1990 to 1991 and from 1998 to 2004.

MODEL 617 DA REVOLVER
Similar to Model 17 except in stainless. Made from 1990 to date.
Semi-target model w/4- or 6-inch bbl. . . NiB $648 Ex $530 Gd $362
Target model w/6-inch bbl. . . . . NiB $648 Ex $530 Gd $362
Target model w/8.38-inch bbl. . . . . NiB $615 Ex $485 Gd $332
w/10-round cylinder, add $128

MODEL 624 DOUBLE-ACTION REVOLVER
Same general specifications as Model 24 except satin finished stainless steel. Limited production of 10,000. Made from 1986 to 1987.
Model 624 w/4-inch bbl. . . . . NiB $500 Ex $335 Gd $306
Model 624 w/6 1/2--inch bbl) . . . . . . NiB $524 Ex $335 Gd $229

Smith & Wesson
Model 642 Centennial Airweight

Smith & Wesson
Model 640

MODEL 625 DA REVOLVER . . NiB $866 Ex $733 Gd $569
Same general specifications as Model 25 except 3-, 4- or 5-inch bbl., round-butt Pachmayr grips and satin stainless steel finish. Made 1989 to 20087.

MODEL 627 DA REVOLVER . . NiB $730 Ex $427 Gd $337
Same general specifications as Model 27 except satin stainless steel finish. Made from 1989 to 1991.

MODEL 629 DA REVOLVER
Same as Model 29 in .44 Magnum except in stainless steel. Classic made from 1990 to date.

w/ 3-inch bbl.(Backpacker model). . .	NiB $774	Ex $567	Gd $408
w/4- or 6-inch bbls.	NiB $774	Ex $567	Gd $408
w/8.38-inch bbl..	NiB $774	Ex $567	Gd $408
Classic model (w/5- or 6.5-inch bbl.)	NiB $829	Ex $581	Gd $444
Classic model (w/8.38-inch bbl.) . . .	NiB $685	Ex $576	Gd $469
Classix DX model (w/6.5-inch bbl.) .	NiB $685	Ex $576	Gd $469
Classic DX model (w/8.38-inch bbl.)	NiB $685	Ex $576	Gd $469
Magna Classic model	NiB $979	Ex $680	Gd $530

MODEL 631 DA REVOLVER
Similar to Model 31 except chambered for .32 H&R Mag. Goncalo Alves combat grips. Made in 1991 to 1992.

Fixed sights, 2-inch bbl.	NiB $800	Ex $659	Gd $246
Adjustable sights, 4-inch bbl., add 10%			
Lady Smith, 2-inch bbl.	NiB $410	Ex $329	Gd $246
Lady Smith, 2-inch bbl. (black stainless).	NiB $420	Ex $329	Gd $246

MODEL 632 CENTENNIAL DA REVOLVER
Same general specifications as Model 640 except chambered for .32 H&R Mag. 2- or 3-inch bbl., weight: 15.5 oz. Stainless slide w/alloy frame. Fixed sights. Santoprene combat grips. Made 1991 to 1992.

w/2-inch bbl..	NiB $693	Ex $408	Gd $321
w/3-inch bbl..	NiB $789	Ex $485	Gd $930

MODEL 637 CHIEFS SPECIAL AIRWEIGHT
DA REVOLVER. . . . . NiB $485 Ex $357 Gd $289
Same general specifications as Model 37 except w/clear anodized fuse alloy frame and stainless cylinder. 560 made in 1991 and reintroduced in 1996.

MODEL 638 BODYGUARD
AIRWEIGHT DA. . . . . NiB $468 Ex $367 Gd $326
Same general specifications as Model .38 except w/clear anodized fuse alloy frame and stainless cylinder. 1,200 made in 1990 and reintroduced in 1998.

MODEL 640 CENTENNIAL DA NiB $648 Ex $398 Gd $326
Caliber: .38 Special. Five-round cylinder, 2, 2.1 or 3-inch bbl., 6.31 inches overall. Weight: 20-22 oz. Fixed sights. Stainless finish. Smooth hardwood service grips. Made from 1990 to date.

MODEL 642 CENTENNIAL AIRWEIGHT
DA REVOLVER . . . . NiB $479 Ex $365 Gd $290
Same general specifications as Model 640 except w/stainless steel/aluminum alloy frame and finish. Weight 15.8 oz. Santoprene combat grips. Made from 1990-93 and reintroduced 1996.
Lady Smith model

(w/smaller grip)	NiB $648	Ex $478	Gd $377
2.125-in. bbl. w/ PowerPort (2009-2010), add.			$150
Pro Series w/ full moon clips (intro. 2010), add.			$30

MODEL 648
DA REVOLVER. . . . . NiB $695 Ex $506 Gd $450
Same general specifications as Models 17/617 except in stainless and chambered for .22 Mag. Made from 1990 to 1993.
Model 648-2 (2003-2005). . . . . . .NiB $660 Ex $500 Gd $390

MODEL 649 BODYGUARD
DA REVOLVER. . . . . NiB $644 Ex $369 Gd $290
Caliber: .38 Special. Five-round cylinder, bbl. length: 2 inches, 6.25 inches overall. Weight: 20 oz. Square-notch rear sight ramp front. Stainless frame and finish. Made from 1986 to date.

MODEL 650
REVOLVER. . . . . .NiB $856 Ex $680 Gd $525
Caliber: .22 Mag. Six-round cylinder, 3-inch bbl., 7 inches overall. Weight: 23.5 oz. Serrated ramp front sight, fixed square-notch rear. Round butt, checkered walnut monogrammed grips. Stainless steel finish. Made from 1983 to 1986.

Smith & Wesson
Model 696

Smith & Wesson
Model K-22 Outdoorsman

Smith & Wesson
Lady Smith First Model

Smith & Wesson
Lady Smith Second Model

MODEL 651 STAINLESS DA

Caliber: .22 Mag. Rimfire. Six-round cylinder, bbl. length: 3 and 4 inches, 7 and 8.63 inches, respectively, overall. Weight: 24.5 oz. Adj. rear sight, ramp front. Made from 1983 to 1987 and from 1990 to 1998. Note: .22 LR cylinder available during early production.

w/3- or 4-inch bbl. . . . . NiB $561 Ex $366 Gd $345
w/Extra cylinder . . . . NiB $862 Ex $386 Gd $365

MODEL 657 REVOLVER

Caliber: 41 Mag. Six-round cylinder. Bbl. lengths: 4, 6 or 8.4 inches; 9.6, 11.4, and 13.9 inches overall. Weight: 44.2, 48 and 52.5 oz. Serrated black ramp front sight on ramp base click rear, adj. for windage and elevation. Satin finished stainless steel. Made from 1986 to 2008.

w/4- or 6-inch bbl. . . . . NiB $601 Ex $433 Gd $398
w/8.4-inch bbl. . . . . NiB $882 Ex $464 Gd $377

MODEL 681 DSM. . . . . NiB $464 Ex $329 Gd $255

Same as S&W Model 581 except in stainless finish only. Made 1991 to 1993.

MODEL 686

Same as S&W Model 586 Distinguished Combat Magnum except in stainless finish w/additional 2.5-inch bbl. Made from 1991 to date.

w/2.5-inch bbl. . . . . NiB $639 Ex $434 Gd $332
w/4- or 6-inch bbl. . . . . NiB $639 Ex $434 Gd $332
w/8.63-inch bbl. . . . . NiB $639 Ex $434 Gd $332
Model 686 (w/adjustable
front sight), add $50

MODEL 686 PLUS

Same as standard Model 686 Magnum except w/7-round cylinder and 2.5-, 4- or 6-inch bbl. Made from 1996 to date.

w/2.5-inch bbl. . . . . NiB $689 Ex $617 Gd $499
w/4-inch bbl. . . . . NiB $704 Ex $595 Gd $408
w/6-inch bbl. . . . . NiB $700 Ex $631 Gd $429

MODEL 696 . . . . NiB $546 Ex $386 Gd $337

Caliber: .44 S&W Special. L-Frame w/five-round cylinder, 3-inch shrouded bbl., 8.38 inches overall. Weight: 48 oz. Red ramp front sight, micrometer-click adj. rear. Checkered synthetic grip. Satin stainless steel. Made from 1997 to 2002.

MODEL 940 CENTENNIAL DA NiB $479 Ex $367 Gd $290

Same general specifications as Model 640 except chambered for 9mm. Two- or 3-inch bbl., Weight: 23-25 oz. Santoprene combat grips. Made from 1991 to 1998.

MODEL 1891 SA REVOLVERNiB $2779 Ex $2465 Gd $2190

Hinged frame. Caliber: .38 S&W. Five-round cylinder, bbl. lengths: 3.25, 4, 5 and 6-inches. Fixed sights. Blued or nickel finish. Hard rubber grips. Made 1891-1911. Note: Until 1906, an accessory single-shot target bbl. (see Model 1891 Single-Shot Target Pistol) was available for this revolver.

w/Extra .22 single-shot bbl. NiB $5300 Ex $4220 Gd $3690

MODEL 1917 ARMY DA REVOLVER

Caliber: .45 Automatic, using 3-cartridge half-moon clip or .45 Auto Rim, without clip. Six-round cylinder, 5.5-inch bbl., 10.75 inches overall. Weight: 36.25 oz. Fixed sights. Blued finish (blue-black finish on commercial model, brush polish on military). Checkered walnut grips (commercial model, smooth on military). Made under U.S. Government contract 1917-19 and produced commercially 1919-1941. Note: About 175,000 of these revolvers were produced during WW I. The DCM sold these to NRA members during the 1930s at $16.15 each.

Commercial model . . . . . . NiB $2500 Ex $2168 Gd $1870
Military model . . . . NiB $1860 Ex $1640 Gd $1389

K-22 MASTERPIECE DA .. NiB $5100 Ex $4390 Gd $2724
Improved version of K-22 Outdoorsman w/same specifications but w/micrometer-click rear sight, short action and antibacklash trigger. Fewer than 1,100 manufactured in 1940.

K-22 OUTDOORSMAN DA NiB $2552 Ex $1906 Gd $1392
Design based on the .38 Military & Police Target. Caliber: .22 LR. Six-round cylinder, 11.13 inches overall. Weight: 35 oz. Adj. target sights. Blued finish. Checkered walnut grip. Made 1931 to 1940.

K-32 AND K-38 HEAVY MASTERPIECES
Same as K32 and K38 Masterpiece but w/heavy bbl. Weight: 38.5 oz. Made 1950-53. Note: All K32 and K38 revolvers made after September 1953 have heavy bbls. and the "Heavy Masterpiece" designation was disc. Values for Heavy Masterpiece models are the same as shown for Models 14 and 16. (See separate listing).

K-32 TARGET DA REVOLVER NiB $18,600 Ex $15,400 Gd $9900
Same as .38 Military & Police Target except chambered for .32 S&W Long cartridge, slightly heavier bbl., weight: 34 oz. Only 98 produced. Made from 1938 to 1940.

LADY SMITH (MODEL M HAND EJECTOR) DA REVOLVER
Caliber: .22 LR. Seven-round cylinder, bbl. length: 2.25-, 3-, 3.5- and 6-inch (Third Model only), approximately 7 inches overall w/3.5-inch bbl., weight: About 9.5 oz. Fixed sights, adj. target sights available on Third Model. Blued or nickel finish. Round butt, hard rubber grips on First and Second models; checkered walnut or hard rubber square buttgrips on Third Model. First Model —1902-06: Cylinder locking bolt operated by button on left side of frame, no bbl., lug and front locking bolt. Second Model —1906-11: Rear cylinder latch eliminated, has bbl. lug, forward cylinder lock w/draw-bolt fastening. Third Model —1911-21: Same as Second Model except has square grips, target sights and 6-inch bbl. available. Note: Legend has it that a straight-laced D.B. Wesson ordered discontinuance of the Lady Smith when he learned of the little revolver's reputed popularity w/ladies of the evening. The story, which undoubtedly has enhanced the appeal of this model to collectors, is not true: The Lady Smith was disc. because of difficulty of manufacture and high frequency of repairs.
First model . . . . NiB $3140 Ex $2130 Gd $1696
Second model . . . . NiB $2315 Ex $1779 Gd $1015
Third model, w/fixed sights,
2.25- or 3.5-inch bbl. . . . . NiB $2315 Ex $1779 Gd $1015
Third model, w/fixed sights,
6-inch bbl. . . . . NiB $2315 Ex $1779 Gd $1015
Third model, w/adj. sights,
6-inch bbl. . . . . NiB $2215 Ex $1888 Gd $934

REGULATION POLICE
DA (I FRAME). . . . . NiB $811 Ex $602 Gd $434
Calibers: .32 S&W (6-round) or .38 S&W (5-round) built on .32 Hand Ejector frames. Two-, 3-, 3.25-, 4-, 4.25- or 6-inch bbl., weight: 20-24 oz. Fixed sights. Blue or nickel finish. Checkered walnut grips. Made 1917-57. Note: After 1957 "J" Frames replaced the older "I" Frames and designations changed to Model 31 and 33 respectively.
Regulation Police, .32 S&W . NiB $1097 Ex $920 Gd $599
Regulation Police, .38 S&W . NiB $1097 Ex $920 Gd $599

REGULATION POLICE TARGET DA
Target version of the Regulation Police w/standard features of that model. Calibers: .32 S&W Long or .38 S&W. 6-inch bbl., 10.25 inches overall. Weight: 20 oz. Adjustable target sights. Blue or nickel finish. Checkered walnut grips. Made from about 1917 to 1957.
Regulation Police Target, .32 S&W NiB $2600 Ex $2470 Gd $780
Regulation Police Target, .38 S&W (pre-war) NiB $3000 Ex $2855 Gd $900

Smith & Wesson
Regulation Police Target

Smith & Wesson
Safety Hammerless

SAFETY HAMMERLESS
REVOLVER . . . . NiB $1396 Ex $1178 Gd $1024
Also called New Departure Double Action. Hinged frame. Calibers: .32 S&W, .38 S&W. Five-round cylinder, bbl. lengths: 2, 3- and 3.5-inch (.32 cal.) or 2-, 3.25-, 4-, 5- and 6-inch (.38 cal.); 6.75 inches overall (.32 cal. w/3-inch bbl.) or 7.5 inches (.38 cal. w/3.25-inch bbl.). Weight: 14.25 oz. (.32 cal. w/3-inch bbl.) or 18.25 oz. (.38 cal. 2.5-inch bbl.). Fixed sights. Blued or nickel finish. Hard rubber grips. Made from 1888 to 1937 (.32 cal.); 1887 to 1941 (.38 cal. w/various minor changes.)

TEXAS RANGER
COMMEMORATIVE . . . . NiB $658 Ex $359 Gd $270
Issued to honor the 150th anniversary of the TExas Rangers. Model 19 .357 Combat Magnum w/4-inch bbl., sideplate stamped w/TExas Ranger Commemorative Seal, smooth Goncalo Alves grips. Special Bowie knife in presentation case. 8,000 sets made in 1973. Top value is for set in new condition.

SPHINX ENGINEERING S.A. — Matten b. Interlaken, Switzerland

MODEL AT-380 DA PISTOL
Caliber: .380 ACP. 10-round magazine, 3.27- inch bbl., 6.03 inches overall. Weight: 25 oz. Stainless steel frame w/blued slide or Palladium finish. Slide latch w/ambidExtrous magazine release. Imported from 1993 to 1996.
Two-tone (w/blued slide) . . . . NiB $474 Ex $336 Gd $240
w/Palladium finish . . . . NiB $561 Ex $431 Gd $336

NOTE: *The AT-88 pistol series was previously manufactured by ITM in Switzerland and imported by Action Arms before Sphinx-Muller resumed production of these firearms, now designated as the AT-2000 series.*

Springfield Armory
1911-A1 Post '90 Series Trophy Model

Springfield Armory
1911-A1 PDP Series Defender

Springfield Armory
1911-A1 Champion

Springfield Armory
1911-A1 Compact

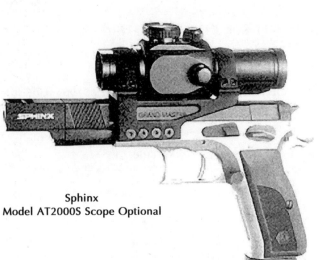

Sphinx
Model AT2000S Scope Optional

MODEL 2000S DA AUTOMATIC PISTOL
Calibers: 9mm Parabellum, .40 S&W. 15- or 11-round magazine respectively, 4.53-inch bbl., (S-standard), 3.66-inch bbl., (P-compact), 3.34-inch bbl., (H-subcompact), 8.25 inches overall. Weight: 36.5 oz. Fixed sights w/3-dot system. Stainless frame w/ blued slide or Palladium finish. AmbidExtrous safety. Checkered walnut or neoprene grips. Imported 1993 to 1996.
Standard model . . . . .NiB $990 Ex $903 Gd $581
Compact model . . . . .NiB $890 Ex $755 Gd $536
Sub-compact model . . . . .NiB $890 Ex $755 Gd $536
.40 S&W, add. $50
Palladium finish, add $100

MODEL AT2000C/2000CS COMPETITOR
Similar to the Model AT2000S except also chambered for 9x21mm. 10-round magazine, 5.31-inch compensated bbl., 9.84 inches overall. Weight: 40.56 oz. Fully adjustable BoMar or ProPoint sights. Made 1993 to 1996.
w/Bomar sight . . . . NiB $1844 Ex $1599 Gd $1418
w/ProPoint sight. . . . . NiB $2254 Ex $1923 Gd $1690

MODEL AT2000GM/GMS GRAND MASTER
Similar to the AT2000C except single action only w/square trigger guard and Extended beavertail grip. Imported 1993 to 1996.
w/BoMar sight . . . . NiB $1872 Ex $1624 Gd $1375
w/ProPoint sight. . . . . NiB $2179 Ex $1919 Gd $1699

SPRINGFIELD, INC. — Geneseo, Illinois (formerly Springfield Armory)
MODEL M1911 SERIES AUTO PISTOL
Springfield builds the "PDP" (Personal Defense Pistol) Series based on the self-loading M 1911-A1 pistol (military specifications model) as adopted for a standard service weapon by the U.S. Army. With enhancements and modifications they produce a full line of firearms including Ultra-Compacts, Lightweights, Match Grade and Competition Models. For values see specific models.

MODEL 1911-A1 GOVERNMENT
Calibers: 9mm Para., .38 Super, .40 S&W, 10mm or .45 ACP., 7-, 8-, 9- or 10-round magazine, 4- or 5-inch bbl., 8.5 inches overall. Weight: 36 oz. Fixed combat sights. Blued, Parkerized or Duo-Tone finish. Checkered walnut grips. Note: This is an Exact duplicate of the Colt M1911-A1 that was used by the U.S. Armed Forces as a service weapon.
Blued finish . . . . NiB $453 Ex $347 Gd $265
Parkerized finish. . . . . NiB $453 Ex $347 Gd $265

MODEL 1911-A1 (PRE '90 SERIES)
Calibers: 9mm Parabellum, .38 Super, 10mm, .45 ACP. Seven-, 8-, 9- or 10-round magazine, bbl. length: 3.63, 4, 4.25 or 5 inches, 8.5 inches overall. Weight: 36 oz. Fixed combat sights. Blued, Duo-Tone or Parkerized finish. Checkered walnut stocks. Made 1985 to 1990.

Government model (blued) . . . NiB $453 Ex $347 Gd $265
Government model (Parkerized)NiB $621 Ex $436 Gd $362
Bullseye model (wadcutter). . NiB $1474 Ex $1345 Gd $866
Combat Commander model (blued)NiB $474 Ex $386 Gd $321
Combat Commander model
(Parkerized) . . . . NiB $650 Ex $475 Gd $353
Commander model (blued) . . . NiB $479 Ex $306 Gd $219
Commander model (Duo-Tone) NiB $567 Ex $473 Gd $397
Commander model (Parkerized)NiB $650 Ex $536 Gd $386
Compact model (blued) . . . . .NiB $ 470 Ex $347 Gd $265
Compact model (Duo-Tone) . . NiB $559 Ex $500 Gd $434
Compact model (Parkerized). . NiB $668 Ex $500 Gd $342
Defender model (blued) . . . . . NiB $546 Ex $434 Gd $290
Defender model (Parkerized). . NiB $704 Ex $556 Gd $377
Defender model (Custom Carry)NiB $540 Ex $429 Gd $326
National Match model (Hardball)NiB $829 Ex $709 Gd $546
Trophy Master (Competition) NiB $1355 Ex $1265 Gd $918
Trophy Master (Distinguished)NiB $2152 Ex $2030 Gd $1234
Trophy Master (Expert) . . . NiB $1723 Ex $1528 Gd $1322

MODEL 1911-A1 (CUSTOM LOADED SERIES)
1911 style operating system w/steel or alloy frame. Calibers: 9mm Parabellum, .38 Super, .40 S&W, 10mm, .45 ACP. Seven-, 8-, 9- or 10-round magazine, bbl. length: 3.63, 4, 4.25 or 5 inches; 8.5 inches overall. Weight: 28 oz. to 36 oz. Fixed combat sights. Blued, Duo-Tone, Parkerized or stainless finish. Checkered composition or walnut stocks. Made from 1990 to 1998.

Mil-Spec model (blued) . . . . . NiB $595 Ex $419 Gd $340
Mil-Spec model (Parkerized). . NiB $809 Ex $644 Gd $444
Standard model (blued). . . . . NiB $879 Ex $689 Gd $499
Standard model (Parkerized) . NiB $1068 Ex $998 Gd $826
Standard model (stainless). . . . NiB $806 Ex $699 Gd $497
Trophy model (blued) . . . . . NiB $1440 Ex $1240 Gd $989
Trophy model (Hi-Tone) . . NiB $1437 Ex $1245 Gd $1029
Trophy model (stainless) . . . . . NiB $709 Ex $577 Gd $429

MODEL 1911-A1 PDP SERIES
PDP Series (Personal Defense Pistol). Calibers: .38 Super, .40 S&W, .45 ACP. Seven-, 8-, 9-, 10-, 13- or 17-round magazine, bbl. length: 4, 5, 5.5 or 5.63 inches, 9 to 11 inches overall w/compensated bbl. Weight: 34.5 oz. to 42.8 oz. Post front sight, adjustable rear w/3-dot system. Blued, Duo-Tone, Parkerized or stainless finish. Checkered composition or walnut stocks. Made from 1991 to 1998.

Defender model (blued) . . . . . NiB $910 Ex $780 Gd $586
Defender model (Duo-Tone) . . NiB $910 Ex $780 Gd $586
Defender model (Parkerized). . NiB $910 Ex $780 Gd $586
.45 ACP Champion Comp model (blued) NiB $780 Ex $562 Gd $431
.45 ACP Compact Comp HC model (blued) . . . NiB $602 Ex $453 Gd $398
.380 Sup Factory Comp model (blued)NiB $740 Ex $546 Gd $431
.45 ACP Factory Comp model (blued) NiB $866 Ex $780 Gd $544
.380 Sup Factory Comp HC model (blued) . . . NiB $740 Ex $546 Gd $398
.45 ACP Factory Comp HC model (blued) NiB $733 Ex $789 Gd $556

MODEL M1911-A1 CHAMPION
Calibers: .380 ACP, 9mm Para., .45 ACP. Six- or 7-round magazine, 4-inch bbl. Weight: 26.5 to 33.4 oz. Low profile post front sight and drift adjustable rear w/3-dot sighting system. Commander-style hammer and slide. Checkered walnut grips. Blue, Bi-Tone, Parkerized or stainless finish. Made from 1992 to 2002.

.380 ACP standard
(disc. 1995) . . . . NiB $850 Ex $807 Gd $479
.45 ACP (parkerized or blued) NiB $700 Ex $665 Gd $480

Springfield Armory
M1911-A1 Ultra
Compact Parkerized

.45 ACP (Bi-Tone) (B/H Model) . . . .
NiB $912 Ex $790 Gd $386
.45 ACP (stainless) . . . . NiB $742 Ex $707 Gd $522
.45 ACP Super Tuned (1997-1999) NiB $850 Ex $807 Gd $479

MODEL M1911-A1 COMPACT
Similar to the standard M1911 w/champion length slide on a steel or alloy frame w/a shortened grip. Caliber: .45 ACP. Six- or 7-round magazine (10+ law enforcement only), 4-inch bbl. weight: 26.5 to 32 oz. Low profile sights w/3-dot system. Checkered walnut grips. Matte blue, Duo-Tone or Parkerized finish. Made 1991 to 1996.

Compact (Parkerized) . . . . NiB $464 Ex $380 Gd $290
Compact (blued). . . . . NiB $464 Ex $380 Gd $290
Compact (Duo-Tone) . . . . NiB $577 Ex $500 Gd $434
Compact (stainless). . . . . NiB $556 Ex $376 Gd $270
Compact Comp (ported) . . . . . NiB $882 Ex $792 Gd $587
High capacity (blued). . . . . NiB $595 Ex $369 Gd $321
High capacity (stainless). . . . . NiB $831 Ex $638 Gd $499

MODEL M1911-A1 ULTRA COMPACT
Similar to M1911 Compact except chambered for .380 ACP or .45 ACP. 6- or 7-round magazine, 3.5-inch bbl., weight: 22 oz. to 30 oz. Matte Blue, Bi-Tone, Parkerized (military specs) or stainless finish. Made from 1995 to 2003.

.380 ACP Ultra (disc. 1996) . . NiB $740 Ex $585 Gd $388
.45 ACP Ultra (Parkerized or blued)NiB $740 Ex $585 Gd $388
.45 ACP Ultra (Bi-Tone) . . . . . NiB $844 Ex $709 Gd $500
.45 ACP (stainless) . . . . NiB $740 Ex $585 Gd $388
.45 ACP ultra high capacity (Parkerized) . NiB $740 Ex $585 Gd $388
.45 ACP ultra high capacity (blued). NiB $780 Ex $615 Gd $499
.45 ACP ultra high capacity (stainless) .NiB $780 Ex $615 Gd $499
.45 ACP V10 ultra comp (Parkerized) . . .NiB $979 Ex $806 Gd $495
.45 ACP V10 ultra comp (blued) NiB $979 Ex $806 Gd $495
.45 ACP V10 ultra comp (stainless)NiB $979 Ex $806 Gd $495
.45 ACP V10 ultra (super tuned) NiB $1090 Ex $974 Gd $577

MODEL 1911-A1 TRP (TACITCAL RESPONSE PISTOL) OPERATOR
SA AUTO PISTOL . .   NIB $1620   EX $1460   GD $780
1911 style operating system w/steel frame. Caliber: .45 ACP. Seven-round magazine, bbl. length: 5 inches; 8.5 inches overall. Weight: 36 oz. Fixed combat sights. Black Armory Kote or stainless finish. Checkered front strap, composition stocks. Made from 2008 to date.

MODEL 1911-A1 LONG SLIDE CUSTOM LOADED
SA AUTO PISTOL . . .   NIB $1100   EX $960   GD $480
1911 style operating system w/steel frame. Caliber: .45 ACP or .45 Super. Seven-round magazine, bbl. length: 6 inches; 8.5 inches overall. Weight: 36 oz. Fixed combat sights. Black Armory Kote or stainless finish. Checkered wood stocks. Made from 2001 to 2012.

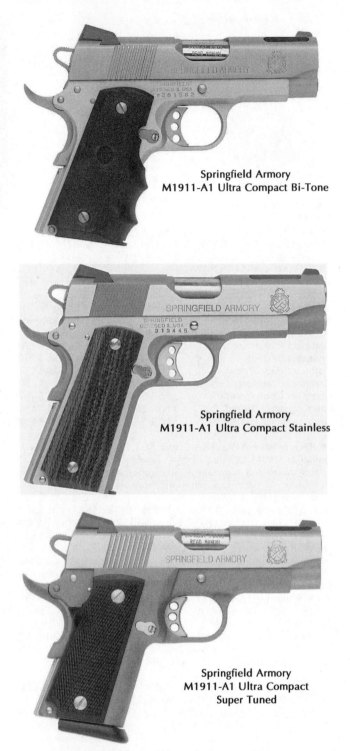

Springfield Armory
M1911-A1 Ultra Compact Bi-Tone

Springfield Armory
M1911-A1 Ultra Compact Stainless

Springfield Armory
M1911-A1 Ultra Compact
Super Tuned

Springfield Armory
P9 Combat

Springfield Armory Panther

FIRECAT AUTOMATIC PISTOL
Calibers: 9mm, .40 S&W. Eight-round magazine (9mm) or 7-round magazine (.40 S&W), 3.5-inch bbl., 6.5 inches overall. Weight: 25.75 oz. Fixed sights w/3-dot system. Checkered walnut grip. Matte blued finish. Made from 1991 to 1993.
9mm . . . . NiB $556 Ex $408 Gd $289
.40 S&W . . . . NiB $556 Ex $408 Gd $289

PANTHER
AUTO PISTOL . . . . NiB $606 Ex $453 Gd $346
Calibers: 9mm, .40 S&W. 15-round magazine (9mm) or 11-round magazine (.40 S&W), 3.8-inch bbl., 7.5 inches overall. Weight: 28.95 oz. Blade front sight, rear adj. for windage w/3-dot system. Checkered walnut grip. Matte blued finish. Made from 1991 to 1993.

MODEL P9 DA COMBAT SERIES
Calibers: 9mm, .40 S&W, .45 ACP. Magazine capacity: 15-round (9mm), 11-round (.40 S&W) or 10-round (.45 ACP), 3.66-inch bbl., (Compact and Sub-Compact), or 4.75-inch bbl., (Standard), 7.25 or 8.1 inches overall. Weight: 32 to 35 oz. Fixed sights w/3-dot system. Checkered walnut grip. Matte blued, Parkerized, stainless or Duo-Tone finish. Made from 1990 to 1994.
Compact model (9mm,
Parkerized). . . . . NiB $464 Ex $342 Gd $279
Sub-Compact model (9mm,
Parkerized). . . . . NiB $433 Ex $309 Gd $235
Standard model (9mm,
Parkerized). . . . . NiB $498 Ex $377 Gd $304
w/blued finish, add. $50
w/Duo-Tone finish, add $100
w/stainless finish, add. $128
.40 S&W, add. $35
.45 ACP add. $50

MODEL P9 COMPETITION SERIES

Same general specifications as Model P9 except in target configuration w/5-inch bbl., (LSP Ultra) or 5.25-inch bbl. Factory Comp model w/dual port compensator system, Extended safety and magazine release.

Factory Comp model (9mm Bi-Tone)	NiB $648	Ex $444	Gd $337
Factory Comp model (9mm stainless)	NiB $733	Ex $431	Gd $281
IPSC Ultra model (9mm Bi-Tone)	NiB $689	Ex $431	Gd $270
LSP Ultra model (9mm stainless)	NiB $785	Ex $580	Gd $425
.40 S&W, .45 ACP: add			$128

STALLARD ARMS — Mansfield, Ohio

See listings under Hi-Point.

STAR PISTOLS — Eibar, Spain, Star, Bonifacio Echeverria, S.A.

MODEL 30M DA AUTO PISTOL . . . NiB $431 Ex $288 Gd $189

Caliber: 9mm Para. 15-round magazine, 4.38-inch bbl., 8 inches overall. Weight: 40 oz. Steel frame w/combat features. Adj. sights. Checkered composition grips. Blued finish. Made from 1984 to 1991.

MODEL 30PK DA AUTO PISTOL . . . NiB $431 Ex $288 Gd $189

Same gen. specifications as Star Model 30M except 3.8-inch bbl., weight: 30 oz. Alloy frame. Made from 1984 to 1989.

MODEL 31P DA AUTO PISTOL

Same general specifications as Model 30M except removable backstrap houses complete firing mechanism. Weight: 39.4 oz. Made from 1990 to 1994.

Blued finish	NiB $431	Ex $288	Gd $189
Starvel finish, add.			$50

MODEL 31 PK DA AUTO PISTOL . . . NiB $431 Ex $288 Gd $189

Same general specifications as Model 31P except w/alloy frame. Weight: 30 oz. Made from 1990 to 1997.

MODEL A AUTOMATIC PISTOL NiB $365 Ex $259 Gd $169

Modification of the Colt Government Model .45 Auto, which it closely resembles, but lacks grip safety. Caliber: .38 Super. Eight-round magazine, 5-inch bbl., 8 inches overall. Weight: 35 oz. Fixed sights. Blued finish. Checkered grips. Made from 1934-97. (No longer imported.)

MODELS AS, BS, PS . . . . NiB $500 Ex $380 Gd $279

Same as Models A, B and P except have magazine safety. Made in 1975.

MODEL B . . . . NiB $498 Ex $365 Gd $259

Same as Model A except in 9mm Para. Made from 1934 to 1975.

MODEL BKM . . . . NiB $398 Ex $306 Gd $225

Similar to Model BM except has aluminum frame weight: 25.6 oz. Made from 1976 to 1992.

MODEL BKS STARLIGHT

AUTOMATIC PISTOL . . . . NiB $431 Ex $279 Gd $209

Light alloy frame. Caliber: 9mm Para. Eight-round magazine, 4.25-inch bbl., 7 inches overall. Weight: 25 oz. Fixed sights. Blued or chrome finish. Plastic grips. Made from 1970 to 1981.

Star Model 30M

Star Model 30PK

Star Model AS

Star Model BKS

Star Model F

Star Model F
Olympic Rapid-Fire

Star Model FS

MODEL BM AUTOMATIC PISTOL
Caliber: 9mm. Eight-round magazine, 3.9-inch bbl., 6.95 inches overall. Weight: 34.5 oz. Fixed sights. Checkered walnut grips. Blued or Starvel finish. Made from 1976 to 1992.
Blued finish . . . . NiB $367 Ex $279 Gd $220
Starvel finish . . . . NiB $380 Ex $304 Gd $240

MODEL CO POCKET
AUTOMATIC PISTOL . . . . . . NiB $316 Ex $217 Gd $126
Caliber: .25 Automatic (6.35mm), 2.75-inch bbl., 4.5 inches overall. Weight: 13 oz. Fixed sights. Blued finish. Plastic grips. Made from 1941 to 197.

MODEL CU STARLET
POCKET PISTOL. . . . . NiB $291 Ex $198 Gd $124
Light alloy frame. Caliber: .25 Auto (6.35mm). Eight-round magazine, 2.38-inch bbl., 4.75 inches overall. Weight: 10.5 oz. Fixed sights. Blued or chrome-plated slide w/frame anodized in black,

blue, green, gray or gold. Plastic grips. Made from 1957 to 1997. (U.S. importation disc. 1968.)

MODEL F
AUTOMATIC PISTOL . . . . . . NiB $362 Ex $268 Gd $130
Caliber: .22 LR. 10-round magazine, 4.5-inch bbl., 7.5 inches overall. Weight: 25 oz. Fixed sights. Blued finish. Plastic grips. Made from 1942 to 1967.

MODEL F
OLYMPIC RAPID-FIRE . . . . . . NiB $556 Ex $408 Gd $230
Caliber: .22 Short. Nine-round magazine, 7-inch bbl., 11.06 inches overall. Weight: 52 oz. w/weights. Adj. target sight. Adj. 3-piece bbl. weight. Aluminum alloy slide. Muzzle brake. Plastic grips. Made from 1942 to 1967.

MODEL FM . . . . NiB $362 Ex $279 Gd $171
Similar to Model FR except has heavier frame w/web in front of trigger guard, 4.25-inch heavy bbl., Weight: 32 oz. Made from 1972 to 1991.

MODEL FR. . . . . NiB $362 Ex $279 Gd $171
Similar to Model F w/same general specifications but restyled, has slide stop and adj. rear sight. Made from 1967 to 1972.

MODEL FR SPORT . . . . NiB $398 Ex $306 Gd $229
Same as Model FR except has 6-inch bbl., weight: 28 oz. Also avail. in chrome finish. Made from 1967 to 1991.

MODEL FS . . . . NiB $362 Ex $309 Gd $165
Same as regular Model F but w/6-inch bbl. and adj. sights. Weight: 27 oz. Made from 1942 to 1967.

MODEL HK LANCER
AUTOMATIC PISTOL . . . . . . NiB $319 Ex $225 Gd $249
Similar to Starfire w/same general specifications except .22 LR. Made from 1955 to 1968.

MODEL HN
AUTOMATIC PISTOL . . . . . . NiB $431 Ex $279 Gd $220
Caliber: .380 Auto (9mm Short). Six-round magazine, 2.75-inch bbl., 5.56 inches overall. Weight: 20 oz. Fixed sights. Blued finish. Plastic grips. Made from 1934 to 1941.

MODEL H . . . . NiB $357 Ex $281 Gd $165
Same as Model HN except .32 Auto (7.65mm), 7-round magazine, weight: 20 oz. Made from 1934 to 1941.

MODEL I
AUTOMATIC PISTOL . . . . . . NiB $398 Ex $302 Gd $177
Caliber: .32 Auto (7.65mm). Nine-round magazine, 4.81-inch bbl., 7.5 inches overall. Weight: 24 oz. Fixed sights. Blued finish. Plastic grips. Made from 1934 to 1936.

MODEL IN. . . . . NiB $434 Ex $290 Gd $175
Same as Model I except caliber .380 Auto (9mm Short), 8-round magazine, weight: 24.5 oz. Made from 1934-36.

MODEL M MILITARY
AUTOMATIC PISTOL . . . . . . NiB $398 Ex $337 Gd $219
Modification of the Model M without grip safety. Calibers: 9mm Bergmann (Largo), .45 ACP, 9mm Para. Eight-round magazine except 7-shot in .45 caliber, 5-inch bbl., 8.5 inches overall. Weight: 36 oz. Fixed sights. Blued finish. Checkered grips. Made from 1934 to 1939.

MODELS M40, M43, M45 FIRESTAR AUTO PISTOLS

Calibers: 9mm, .40 S&W, .45 ACP. Seven-round magazine (9mm) or 6-round (other calibers). 3.4-inch bbl., 6.5 inches overall. Weight: 30.35 oz. Blade front sight, adj. rear w/3-dot system. Checkered rubber grips. Blued or Starvel finish. Made 1990 to 1997.

M40 blued (.40 S&W)	NiB $367	Ex $289	Gd $232
M40 Starvel (.40 S&W)	NiB $398	Ex $304	Gd $239
M43 blued (9mm)	NiB $365	Ex $294	Gd $237
M43 Starvel (9mm)	NiB $398	Ex $304	Gd $239
M45 blued (.45 ACP)	NiB $357	Ex $270	Gd $120
M45 Starvel (.45 ACP)	NiB $377	Ex $290	Gd $143

MEGASTAR AUTOMATIC PISTOL

Calibers: 10mm, .45 ACP. 12-round magazine, 4.6-inch bbl., 8.44 inches overall. Weight: 47.6 oz. Blade front sight, adj. rear. Checkered composition grip. finishes: Blued or Starvel. Made from 1992 to 1997.

Blued finish, 10mm or .45 ACP	NiB $500	Ex $397	Gd $274
Starvel finish, 10mm or .45 ACP	NiB $544	Ex $416	Gd $305

MODEL P . . . . NiB $464 Ex $345 Gd $283
Same as Model A except caliber .45 Auto, has 7-round magazine. Made from 1934 to 1975.

MODEL PD AUTOMATIC PISTOL

Caliber: .45 Auto. Six-round magazine, 3.75-inch bbl., 7 inches overall. Weight: 25 oz. Adj. rear sight, ramp front. Blued or Starvel finish. Checkered walnut grips. Made from 1975 to 1992.

Blued finish	NiB $398	Ex $304	Gd $224
Starvel finish	NiB $422	Ex $342	Gd $270

MODEL S . . . . NiB $319 Ex $220 Gd $159
Same as Model SI except caliber .380 Auto (9mm), 7-round magazine, weight: 19 oz. Made from 1941 to 1965.

MODEL SI AUTOMATIC PISTOL. . . . NiB $316 Ex $225 Gd $130
Reduced-size modification of the Colt Government Model .45 Auto, lacks grip safety. Caliber: .32 Auto (7.65mm). Eight-round magazine, 4-inch bbl., 6.5 inches overall. Weight: 20 oz. Fixed sights. Blued finish. Plastic grips. Made from 1941 to 1965.

STARFIRE DK AUTOMATIC PISTOL . NiB $453 Ex $337 Gd $255
Light alloy frame. Caliber: .380 Automatic (9mm Short). Seven-round magazine, 3.13-inch bbl.. 5.5 inches overall. Weight: 14.5 oz. Fixed sights. Blued or chrome-plated slide w/frame anodized in black, blue, green, gray or gold. Plastic grips. Made 1957-97. U.S. importation disc. 1968.

MODEL SUPER A AUTOMATIC PISTOL NiB $499 Ex $431 Gd $220
Caliber: .38 Super. Improved version of Model A but has disarming bolt permitting easier takedown, cartridge indicator, magazine safety, take-down magazine, improved sights w/luminous spots for aiming in darkness. This is the standard service pistol of the Spanish Armed Forces, adopted 1946.

MODEL SUPER B AUTOMATIC PISTOL

Caliber: 9mm Para. Similar to Model B except w/improvements described under Model Super A. Made 1946 to 1990.

Super blued finish	NiB $453	Ex $342	Gd $225
Starvel finish	NiB $456	Ex $366	Gd $249

MODELS SUPER M, SUPER P . NiB $852 Ex $685 Gd $478
Calibers: .45 ACP, 9mm Parabellum or 9mm Largo, (Super M) and 9mm Parabellum (Super P). Improved versions of the Models M & P w/same general specifications, but has disarming bolt permitting easier takedown, cartridge indicator, magazine safety, take-down magazine, improved sights w/luminous spots for aiming in darkness.

MODELS SUPER SI, SUPER S . NiB $332 Ex $239 Gd $274
Same general specifications as the regular Model SI and S except w/improvements described under Super Star. Made 1946 to 1972.

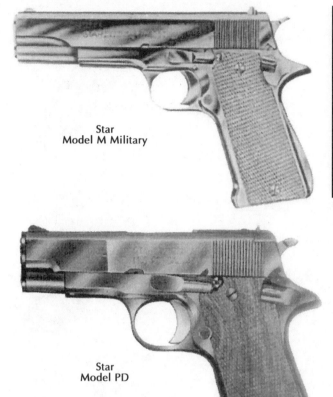

Star
Model M Military

Star
Model PD

MODEL SUPER SM . . . . NiB $398 Ex $386 Gd $204
Similar to Model Super S except has adj. rear sight, wood grips. Made from 1973 to 1981.

SUPER TARGET MODEL . . NiB $1595 Ex $1396 Gd $1309
Same as Super Star model except w/adj. target rear sight. (Disc.)

ULTRASTAR DA AUTOMATIC PISTOL NiB $365 Ex $290 Gd $200
Calibers: 9mm Parabellum or .40 S&W. Nine-round magazine, 3.57-inch bbl., 7 inches overall. Weight: 26 oz. Blade front, adjustable rear w/3-dot system. Polymer frame. Blue metal finish. Checkered black polymer grips. Imported from 1994 to 1997.

STENDA-WERKE PISTOL — Suhl, Germany

POCKET AUTOMATIC PISTOL NiB $337 Ex $279 Gd $160
Essentially the same as the Beholla (see listing of that pistol for specifications). Made circa 1920-.25. Note: This pistol may be marked "Beholla" along w/the Stenda name and address.

STERLING ARMS CORPORATION—Gasport, New York

MODEL 283 TARGET 300
AUTO PISTOL . . . . NiB $189 Ex $109 Gd $90
Caliber: .22 LR. 10-round magazine, bbl. lengths: 4.5-, 6- 8-inch. 9 inches overall w/4.5-inch bbl., Weight: 36 oz. w/4.52-inch bbl. Adj. sights. Blued finish. Plastic grips. Made from 1970 to 1971.

Sterling
Model 283 Target 300

Sterling
Model 284 Target 300L

Sterling
Model 285 Husky

Sterling
Model 286 Trapper

Sterling
Model 300

Sterling
Model 400

MODEL 284 TARGET 300L . . . . NiB $179 Ex $115 Gd $90
Same as Model 283 except has 4.5- or 6-inch Luger-type bbl. Made from 1970 to 1971.

MODEL 285 HUSKY . . . . NiB $179 Ex $115 Gd $90
Same as Model 283 except has fixed sights, 4.5-inch bbl only. Made from 1970 to 1971.

MODEL 286 TRAPPER . . . . NiB $129 Ex $115 Gd $90
Same as Model 284 except w/fixed sights. Made from 1970 to 1971.
MODEL 287 PPL-.380

AUTOMATIC PISTOL . . . . NiB $179 Ex $115 Gd $90
Caliber: .380 Auto. Six-round magazine, 1-inch bbl., 5.38 inches overall. Weight: 22.5 oz. Fixed sights. Blued finish. Plastic grips. Made from 1971- to 1972.

MODEL 300
AUTOMATIC PISTOL . . . . NiB $150 Ex $90 Gd $75
Caliber: .25 Auto. Six-round magazine, 2.33-inch bbl., 4.5 inches overall. Weight: 13 oz. Fixed sights. Blued or nickel finish. Plastic grips. Made from 1972 to 1983.

MODEL 300S . . . . NiB $179 Ex $115 Gd $90
Same as Model 300 except in stainless steel. Made 1976 to 1983.

MODEL 302 . . . . NiB $179 Ex $115 Gd $90
Same as Model 300 except in .22 LR. Made from 1973 to 1983.

MODEL 302S . . . . NiB $179 Ex $115 Gd $90
Same as Model 302 except in stainless steel. Made 1976 to 1983.

MODEL 400 DA
AUTOMATIC PISTOL . . . . NiB $309 Ex $214 Gd $129
Caliber: .380 Auto. Seven-round magazine, 3.5-inch bbl., 6.5 inches overall. Weight: 24 oz. Adj. rear sight. Blued or nickel finish. Checkered walnut grips. Made from 1975 to 1983.

MODEL 400S . . . . NiB $309 Ex $214 Gd $129
Same as Model 400 except stainless steel. Made from 1977 to 1983.

MODEL 450 DA
AUTO PISTOL . . . . NiB $309 Ex $214 Gd $129
Caliber: .45 Auto. Eight-round magazine, 4-inch bbl., 7.5 inches overall. Weight: 36 oz. Adj. rear sight. Blued finish. Smooth walnut grips. Made from 1977 to 1983.

MODEL PPL-22
AUTOMATIC PISTOL . . . . . . NiB $309 Ex $214 Gd $129
Caliber: .22 LR. 10-round magazine, 1-inch bbl., 5.5 inches overall. Weight: About 24 oz. Fixed sights. Blued finish. Wood grips. Only 382 made in 1970 to 1971.

J. STEVENS ARMS & TOOL CO. — Chicopee Falls, Massachusetts

This firm was established in Civil War era by Joshua Stevens, for whom the company was named. In 1999 Savage Arms began manufacture of Stevens designs..

NO. 10 SINGLE-SHOT
TARGET PISTOL . . . . NiB $249 Ex $207 Gd $160
Caliber: .22 LR. 8-inch bbl., 11.5 inches overall. Weight: 37 oz. Target sights. Blued finish. Hard rubber grips. In External appearance this arm resembles an automatic pistol but it has a tip-up action. Made from 1919 to 1939.

NO. 35 OFFHAND MODEL SINGLE-SHOT
TARGET PISTOL . . . . NiB $377 Ex $301 Gd $255
Tip-up action. Caliber: .22 LR. Bbl. lengths: 6, 8, 10, 12.25 inches. Weight: 24 oz. w/6-inch bbl. Target sights. Blued finish. Walnut grips. Note: This pistol is similar to the earlier "Gould" model. Made from 1907 to 1939.

OFFHAND NO. 35 SINGLE-SHOT
PISTOL/SHOTGUN . . . . NiB $377 Ex $301 Gd $255
Same general specifications as the standard No. 35 pistol except chambered for the .410 shotshell. Six-, 8-, 10-, or 12-inch half-ocatagonal bbl., iron frame either blued, nickel plated, or casehardened. BATF Class 3 license required to purchase. Made from 1923 to 1942.

NO. 36
SINGLE-SHOT PISTOL . . . . . . NiB $842 Ex $577 Gd $439
Tip-up action. Calibers: .22 Short and LR, .22 WRF, .25 Stevens, .32 Short Colt, .38 Long Colt, .44 Russian. 10- or 12-inch half-octagonal bbl., iron or brass frame w/nickel plated finish. Blued bbl. Checkered walnut grips. Made from 1880 to 1911.

NO. 37
SINGLE-SHOT PISTOL . . . . . NiB $1020 Ex $836 Gd $544
Similar specifications to the No. 38 except the finger spur on the trigger guard has been omitted. Made from 1889 to 1919.

NO. 38
SINGLE-SHOT PISTOL . . . . . . NiB $536 Ex $437 Gd $247
Tip-up action. Calibers: .22 Short and LR, .22 WRF, .25 Stevens, .32 Stevens, .32 Short Colt. Iron or brass frame. Checkered grips. Made from 1884 to 1903.

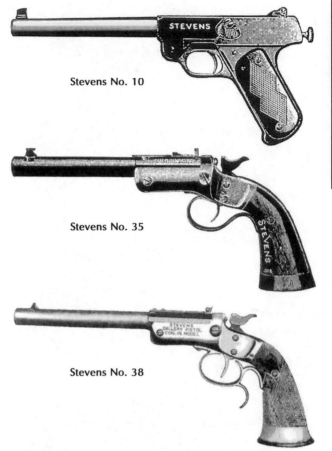

Stevens No. 10

Stevens No. 35

Stevens No. 38

NO. 41 TIP-UP
SINGLE-SHOT PISTOL . . . . . . NiB $342 Ex $281 Gd $204
Tip-up action. Caliber: .22 Short, 3.5-inch half-octagonal bbl. Blued metal parts w/optional nickel frame. Made from 1896 to 1915.

STEYR PISTOLS — Steyr, Austria

GB SEMIAUTOMATIC PISTOL
Caliber: 9mm Para. 18-round magazine, 5.4-inch bbl., 8.9 inches overall. Weight: 2.9 lbs. Post front sight, fixed, notched rear. Double, gas-delayed, blow-back action. Made from 1981 to 1988.
Commercial model . . . . NiB $680 Ex $530 Gd $337
Military model
(Less than 1000 imported) . . . . NiB $800 Ex $652 Gd $377

STEYR-HAHN (M12) AUTOMATIC PISTOL
Caliber: 9mm Steyr. Eight-round fixed magazine, charger loaded; 5.1-inch bbl., 8.5 inches overall. Weight: 35 oz. Fixed sights. Blued finish. Checkered wood grips. Made from 1911-19. Adopted by the Austro-Hungarian Army in 1912. Note: Confiscated by the Germans in 1938, an estimated 250,000 of these pistols were converted to 9mm Para. and stamped w/an identifying "08" on the left side of the slide. Mfd. by Osterreichische Waffenfabrik-Gesellschaft.
Commercial model (9mm Steyr) NiB $544 Ex $468 Gd $377
Military model (9mm Steyr-
Austro-Hungarian Army) . . . . . NiB $568 Ex $479 Gd $229
Military model (9mm Parabellum
Conversion marked "08") . . . NiB $1033 Ex $879 Gd $498

Stoeger
American Eagle Luger P08 Stainless

Stoeger
American Eagle Luger Navy Model

Stoeger
Standard Luger .22

Targa
Model GT380XE

STOEGER LUGERS —
Formerly manufactured by Stoeger Industries, So. Hackensack, New Jersey; later by Classic Arms, Union City, New Jersey

AMERICAN EAGLE LUGER
Caliber: 9mm Para. Seven-round magazine, 4- or 6-inch bbl., 8.25 inches overall (with 4-inch bbl.). or 10.25 inches (with 6-inch bbl.). Weight: 30 or 32 oz. Checkered walnut grips. Stainless steel w/ brushed or matte black finish. Intro. 1994. Disc.
Model P-08
stainless
(4-inch bbl.) . . . . NiB $774 Ex $499 Gd $366
Navy model
(6-inch bbl.) . . . . NiB $854 Ex $811 Gd $400
w/matte black
finish, add $85

STANDARD LUGER .22
AUTOMATIC PISTOL . . . . NiB $299 Ex $137 Gd $101
Caliber: .22 LR. 10-round magazine, 4.5- or 5.5-inch bbl., 8.88 inches overall (with 4.5-inch bbl.). Weight: 29.5 oz. (with 4.5-inch bbl.). Fixed sights. Black finish. Smooth wood grips. Made 1969 to 1986.

STEEL FRAME LUGER
.22 AUTO PISTOL . . . . NiB $290 Ex $133 Gd $95
Caliber: .22 LR. 10-round magazine, 4.5-inch bbl., 8.88 inches overall. Blued finish. Checkered wood grips. Features one piece forged and machined steel frame. Made from 1980 to 1986.

TARGET LUGER
.22 AUTO PISTOL . . . . NiB $227 Ex $160 Gd $110
Same as Standard Luger .22 except has target sights 9.38 inches overall w/4.5-inch bbl., Checkered wood grips. Made from 1975 to 1986.

TARGA PISTOLS — Italy.
Manufactured by Armi Tanfoglio Guiseppe

MODEL GT26S
AUTO PISTOL . . . . NiB $166 Ex $98 Gd $79
Caliber: .25 ACP. Six-round magazine, 2.5-inch bbl., 4.63 inches overall. Weight: 15 oz. fixed sights. Checkered composition grips. Blued or chrome finish. Disc. 1990.

MODEL GT32 AUTO PISTOL
Caliber: .32 ACP. Six-round magazine, 4.88-inch bbl., 7.38 inches overall. Weight: 26 oz. fixed sights. Checkered composition or walnut grips. Blued or chrome finish.
Blued finished . . . . NiB $166 Ex $109 Gd $88
Chrome finish. . . . . NiB $179 Ex $118 Gd $89

MODEL GT380 AUTOMATIC PISTOL
Same as the Targa GT32 except chambered for .380 ACP.
Blued finish . . . . NiB $179 Ex $118 Gd $89
Chrome finish. . . . . NiB $197 Ex $137 Gd $101

MODEL GT380XE
AUTOMATIC PISTOL . . . . NiB $220 Ex $165 Gd $101
Caliber: .380 ACP. 11-round magazine, 3.75-inch bbl., 7.38 inches overall. Weight: 28 oz. Fixed sights. Blued or satin nickel finish. Smooth wooden grips. Made from 1980 to 1990.

Taurus Model .44

TAURUS INT'L. MFG. — Manufactured by
FORJAS TAURUS S.A. Porto Alegre, Brazil; imported Miami, FL

MODEL 44 DA REVOLVER
Caliber: .44 Mag. Six-round cylinder, 4-, 6.5-, or 8.38-inch bbl. Weight: 44.75 oz., 52.5 or 57.25 oz. Brazilian hardwood grips. Blued or stainless steel finish. Made from 1994 to 2004.
Blued finish . . . . NiB $433 Ex $327 Gd $220
Model 44SS Stainless finish (intro. 1994) NiB $600 Ex $487 Gd $274

MODEL 65 DA REVOLVER
Caliber: .357 Magnum. 6-round cylinder, 3- or 4-inch bbl., weight: 32 oz. Front ramp sight, square notch rear. Checkered walnut target grip. Royal blued or satin nickel finish. Imported 1992 to 1997 and from 1999 to date.
Blue finish . . . . NiB $398 Ex $289 Gd $171
Stainless finish . . . . NiB $427 Ex $351 Gd $212

MODEL 66 DA REVOLVER
Calibers: .357 Magnum, .38 Special. Six-round cylinder, 3-, 4- and 6-inch bbl., weight: 35 oz. Serrated ramp front sight, rear click adj. Checkered walnut grips. Royal blued or nickel finish. Imported 1992-1997 and from 1999 to date.
Blue finish . . . . NiB $500 Ex $351 Gd $212
Model 66SS Stainless finish. . . NiB $550 Ex $398 Gd $229

MODEL 73 DA REVOLVER . . . NiB $211 Ex $121 Gd $101
Caliber: .32 Long. Six-round cylinder, 3-inch heavy bbl., weight: 20 oz. Checkered grips. Blued or satin nickel finish. Disc. 1993.

MODEL 76 TARGET
GRADE DA REVOLVER. . . . . . NiB $244 Ex $279 Gd $118
Caliber: .32 S&W Long. Six-round cylinder, 3-inch bbl., 8.25 inches overall. Weight: 20 oz. Adj. rear sight, ramp front. Blued or nickel finish. Checkered walnut grips. Made from 1971 to 1990.

MODEL 80 DA REVOLVER
Caliber: .38 Special. Six-round cylinder, bbl. lengths: 3, 4 inches, 9.25 inches overall (with 4-inch bbl.). Weight: 30 oz. (with 4-inch bbl.) Fixed sights. Blued or nickel finish. Checkered walnut grips. Made 1996 to 1997.
Blued finish . . . . NiB $214 Ex $140 Gd $98
Model 80SS Stainless finish. . . NiB $431 Ex $337 Gd $258

MODEL 82 HEAVY BARREL
Same as Model 80 except has heavy bbl., weight: 33 oz. w/4-inch bbl., Made from 1971 to date.
Blued finish . . . . NiB $366 Ex $290 Gd $212
Model 82SS Stainless finish (intro. 1993). . NiB $437 Ex $327 Gd $259

MODEL 83 HEAVY BARREL TARGET GRADE
Same as Model 84 except has heavy bbl., weight: 34.5 oz. Made from 1977 to date.
Blued finish . . . . NiB $255 Ex $160 Gd $105
Model 83SS Stainless finish. . . NiB $281 Ex $198 Gd $128

Taurus Model 66

Taurus
Model 74 Target Grade

Taurus Model 80

Taurus Model 82

Taurus Model 83

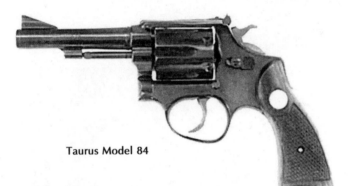

Taurus Model 84

Taurus
Model 85 Concealed Hammer

Taurus Model 86

Taurus
Model 85 w/Spur Hammer

MODEL 84 TARGET
GRADE REVOLVER . . . . NiB $312 Ex $235 Gd $170
Caliber: .38 Special. Six-round cylinder, 4-inch bbl., 9.25 inches overall. Weight: 31 oz. Adj. rear sight, ramp front. Blued or nickel finish. Checkered walnut grips. Made from 1971 to 1989.

MODEL 85 DA REVOLVER
Caliber: .38 Special. Five-round cylinder, 2- or 3-inch. bbl., weight: 21 oz. Fixed sights. Checkered walnut grips. Blued, satin nickel or stainless-steel finish. Currently in production. Model 85CH is the same as the standard version except for concealed hammer.
Blued or satin nickel finish . . . NiB $377 Ex $302 Gd $143
Stainless steel finish . . . . NiB $437 Ex $362 Gd $189

MODEL 86 CUSTOM TARGET
DA REVOLVER . . . . NiB $301 Ex $208 Gd $110
Caliber: .38 Special. Six-round cylinder, 6-inch bbl., 11.25 inches overall. Weight: 34 oz. Adj. rear sight, Partridge-type front. Blued finish. Checkered walnut grips. Made from 1971 to 1994.

MODEL 94 DA REVOLVER
Same as Model 74 except .22 LR. w/9-round cylinder, 3- or 4-inch bbl., weight: 25 oz. Blued or stainless finish. Made from 1971 to date.
Blued finish . . . . NiB $362 Ex $306 Gd $219
Model 94SS Stainless finish. . . NiB $386 Ex $348 Gd $255

MODEL 96 TARGET SCOUT . . NiB $301 Ex $209 Gd $112
Same as Model 86 except in .22 LR. Made from 1971 to 1998.

MODEL 431 DA REVOLVER
Caliber: .44 Spec. Five-round cylinder, 3- or 4-inch solid-rib bbl. w/ ejector shroud. Weight: 35 oz. w/4-inch bbl., Serrated ramp front sight, notched topstrap rear. Blued or stainless finish. Made 1992 to 1997.
Blued finish . . . . NiB $239 Ex $198 Gd $144
Stainless finish . . . . NiB $434 Ex $306 Gd $265

MODEL 441 DA REVOLVER
Similar to the Model 431 except w/6-inch bbl. and fully adj. target sights. Weight: 40 oz. Made from 1991 to 1997.
Blued finish . . . . NiB $306 Ex $237 Gd $144
Stainless finish . . . . NiB $434 Ex $306 Gd $225

MODEL 445 DA REVOLVER
Caliber: .44 Special. Five-round cylinder, 2-inch bbl., 6.75 inches overall. Weight: 28.25 oz. Serrated ramp front sight, notched frame rear. Standard or concealed hammer. Santoprene I grips. Blue or stainless finish. Imported from 1997 to 2003.
Blued finish . . . . NiB $306 Ex $239 Gd $190
Stainless finish . . . . NiB $342 Ex $265 Gd $204

MODEL 454 DA RAGING BULL REVOLVER
Caliber: .454 Casull. Five-round cylinder, ported 6.5- or 8.4-inch vent rib bbl., 12 inches overall (w/6.5-inch bbl.). Weight: 53 or 63 oz. Partridge front sight, micrometer adj. rear. Santoprene I or walnut grips. Blue or stainless finish. Imported from 1997 to date.

Blued finish . . . . **NiB $862 Ex $730 Gd $587**
Stainless finish . . . . **NiB $877 Ex $791 Gd $648**

MODEL 669/669VR DA REVOLVER
Caliber: .357 Mag. Six-round cylinder, 4- or 6-inch solid-rib bbl. w/ejector shroud Model 669VR has vent rib bbl., weight: 37 oz. w/4-inch bbl., Serrated ramp front sight, micro-adj. rear. Royal blued or stainless finish. Checkered Brazilian hardwood grips. Made from 1989 to 1998.

Blued finish . . . . **NiB $283 Ex $214 Gd $165**
Stainless finish . . . . **NiB $362 Ex $286 Gd $240**
Model 669VR, blued finish . . . **NiB $301 Ex $225 Gd $175**
Model 669VR, stainless finish . **NiB $362 Ex $286 Gd $255**

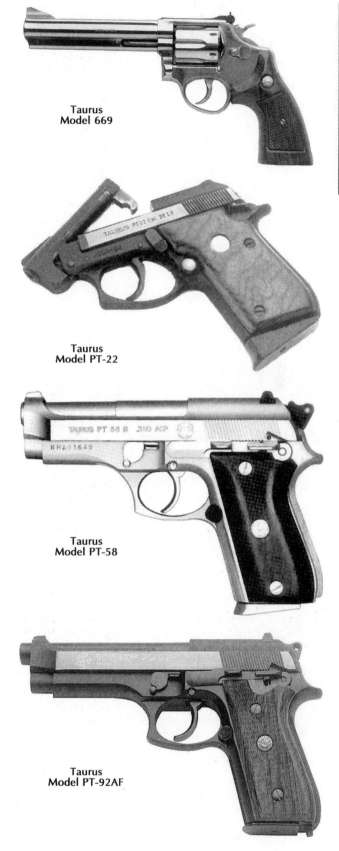

Taurus Model 669

MODEL 741/761 DA REVOLVER
Caliber: .32 H&R Mag. Six-round cylinder, 3- or 4-inch solid-rib bbl. w/ejector shroud. Weight: 20 oz. w/3-inch bbl., Serrated ramp front sight, micro-adj. rear. Blued or stainless finish. Checkered Brazilian hardwood grips. Made from 1991 to 1997.

Blued finish . . . . **NiB $225 Ex $129 Gd $90**
Stainless finish . . . . **NiB $291 Ex $204 Gd $150**
MODEL 761
(6-inch bbl.,
34 oz., blued finish) . . . . **NiB $281 Ex $204 Gd $143**

MODEL 941 TARGET REVOLVER
Caliber: .22 Magnum. Eight-round cylinder. Solid-rib bbl. w/ejector shroud. Micro-adj. rear sight. Brazilian hardwood grips. Blued or stainless finish.

Blued finish . . . . **NiB $357 Ex $306 Gd $204**
Stainless finish . . . . **NiB $408 Ex $365 Gd $274**

Taurus Model PT-22

MODEL PT-22 DA
AUTOMATIC PISTOL . . . . **NiB $285 Ex $177 Gd $101**
Caliber: .22 LR. Nine-round magazine, 2.75-inch bbl., weight: 12.3 oz. Fixed open sights. Brazilian hardwood grips. Blued finish. Made from 1991 to date.

MODEL PT-25 DA
AUTOMATIC PISTOL . . . . **NiB $285 Ex $170 Gd $92**
Same general specifications as Model PT 22 except in .25 ACP w/ eight-round magazine. Made from 1992 to date.

Taurus Model PT-58

MODEL PT-58 SEMI-
AUTOMATIC PISTOL . . . . **NiB $408 Ex $332 Gd $240**
Caliber: .380 ACP. Twelve-round magazine, 4-inch bbl., 7.2 inches overall. Weight: 30 oz. Blade front sight, rear adj. for windage w/3-dot sighting system. Blued, satin nickel or stainless finish. Made from 1988 to 1996.

MODEL PT-92AF SEMIAUTOMATIC PISTOL
Similar to Beretta M92 SB-F. Double action. Caliber: 9mm Para. Fifteen-round magazine, 5-inch bbl., 8.5 inches overall. Weight: 24 oz. Blade front sight, notched bar rear. Smooth Brazilian walnut grips. Blued, satin nickel or stainless finish. Made from 1991 to date.

Blued finish . . . . **NiB $670 Ex $377 Gd $286**
Satin nickel finish . . . . **NiB $720 Ex $418 Gd $319**
Stainless finish . . . . **NiB $679 Ex $398 Gd $306**
Deluxe (blue/gold or stainless/gold)NiB $520 Ex $390 Gd $300

Taurus Model PT-92AF

Taurus
Model PT-99AF

Taurus
Model PT-908

MODEL PT-92AFC COMPACT PISTOL
Same general specs as Model PT-92AF except w/13-round magazine, 4.25-inch bbl., 7.5 inches overall. Weight: 31 oz. Made 1991 to 1996
Blued finish . . . . NiB $362 Ex $283 Gd $214
Satin nickel finish. . . . . NiB $408 Ex $328 Gd $266
Stainless finish . . . . NiB $434 Ex $346 Gd $220

MODEL PT-99AF
SEMI-AUTOMATIC PISTOL . . . NiB $530 Ex $437 Gd $301
Same general specifications as Model PT-92AF except rear sight is adj. for elevation and windage, and finish is blued or satin nickel.

MODEL PT-100 DA AUTOMATIC PISTOL
Caliber: .40 S&W. Eleven-round magazine, 5-inch bbl., weight: 34 oz. Fixed front sight, adj. rear w/3-dot system. Smooth hardwood grip. Blued, satin nickel or stainless finish. Made from 1991 to 1997.
Blued finish . . . . NiB $500 Ex $444 Gd $362
Satin finish. . . . . NiB $546 Ex $469 Gd $377
Stainless finish . . . . NiB $536 Ex $444 Gd $367

MODEL PT-101 DA AUTOMATIC PISTOL
Same general specifications as Model 100 except w/micrometer click adj. sights. Made from 1992 to 1996.
Blued finish . . . . NiB $536 Ex $444 Gd $367
Satin nickel finish. . . . . NiB $576 Ex $453 Gd $367
Stainless finish . . . . NiB $536 Ex $444 Gd $367

MODEL PT-111 MILLENNIUM DAO PISTOL
Caliber: 9mm Parabellum. 10-round magazine, 3.12-inch bbl., 6 inches overall. Weight: 19.1 oz. Fixed low-profile sights w/3-dot system. Black polymer grip/frame. Blue or stainless slide. Imported from 1998 to 2004.
Blue finish . . . . NiB $362 Ex $265 Gd $130
Stainless finish . . . . NiB $380 Ex $286 Gd $185

MODEL PT-908 SEMIAUTOMATIC PISTOL
Caliber: 9mm Para. Eight-round magazine, 3.8-inch bbl., 7 inches overall. Weight: 30 oz. Post front sight, drift-adj. combat rear w/3-dot system. Blued, satin nickel or stainless finish. Made 1993 to 1997.
Blued finish . . . . NiB $357 Ex $286 Gd $204
Satin nickel finish. . . . . NiB $388 Ex $316 Gd $205
Stainless finish . . . . NiB $431 Ex $321 Gd $265

MODEL PT-911 COMPACT SEMIAUTOMATIC PISTOL
Caliber: 9mm Parabellum. 10-round magazine, 3.75-inch bbl., 7.05 inches overall. Weight: 28.2 oz. Fixed low-profile sights w/3-dot system. Santoprene II grips. Blue or stainless finish. Imported from 1997 to date.
Blued finish . . . . NiB $546 Ex $408 Gd $270
Stainless finish . . . . NiB $546 Ex $408 Gd $270

MODEL PT-938 COMPACT SEMIAUTOMATIC PISTOL
Caliber: 380 ACP. 10-round magazine, 3.72-inch bbl., 6.75 inches overall. Weight: 27 oz. Fixed low-profile sights w/3-dot system. Santoprene II grips. Blue or stainless finish. Imported 1997 to 2005.
Blue finish . . . . NiB $499 Ex $357 Gd $265
Stainless finish . . . . NiB $469 Ex $377 Gd $286

MODEL PT-940 COMPACT SEMIAUTOMATIC PISTOL
Caliber: .40 S&W. 10-round magazine, 3.75-inch bbl., 7.05 inches overall. Weight: 28.2 oz. Fixed low-profile sights w/3-dot system. Santoprene II grips. Blue or stainless finish. Imported from 1997 to date.
Blue finish . . . . NiB $546 Ex $437 Gd $290
Stainless finish . . . . NiB $571 Ex $499 Gd $316

MODEL PT-945 COMPACT SEMIAUTOMATIC PISTOL
Caliber: .45 ACP. Eight-round magazine, 4.25-inch bbl., 7.48 inches overall. Weight: 29.5 oz. Fixed low-profile sights w/3-dot system. Santoprene II grips. Blue or stainless finish. Imported from 1995 to date.
Blue finish . . . . NiB $601 Ex $530 Gd $377
Stainless finish . . . . NiB $587 Ex $437 Gd $316

TEXAS ARMS — Waco, Texas

DEFENDER DERRINGER . . . . . NiB $306 Ex $218 Gd $120
Calibers: 9mm, .357 Mag., .44 Mag., .45 ACP, .45 Colt/.410. Three-inch bbl., 5 inches overall. Weight: 21 oz. Blade front sight, fixed rear. Matte gun-metal gray finish. Smooth grips. Made from 1993 to 1999.

TEXAS LONGHORN ARMS — Richmond, Texas

"THE JEZEBEL" PISTOL . . . . . . **NiB $337 Ex $265 Gd $200**
Top-break, single-shot. Caliber: .22 Short, Long or LR. Six-inch half-round bbl., 8 inches overall. Weight: 15 oz. Bead front sight, adj. rear. One-piece walnut grip. Stainless finish. Intro. in 1987.

SA REVOLVER CASED SET
Set contains one each of the TExas Longhorn Single Actions. Each chambered in the same caliber and w/the same serial number. Intro. in 1984.
Standard set . . . . NiB $1620 Ex $1400 Gd $1000
Engraved set . . . . NiB $1820 Ex $1615 Gd $1219

SOUTH TEXAS ARMY LIMITED
EDITION SA REVOLVER . . **NiB $1840 Ex $1418 Gd $1120**
Calibers: All popular centerfire pistol calibers. Six-round cylinder, 4.75-inch bbl.,10.25 inches overall. Weight: 40 oz. Fixed sights. Color casehardened frame. One-piece deluxe walnut grips. Blued bbl., Intro. in 1984.

SESQUICENTENNIAL SA REVOLVER NiB $2613 Ex $2114 Gd $1489
Same as South TExas Army Limited Edition except engraved and nickel-plated w/one-piece ivory grip. Intro. in 1986.

TEXAS BORDER SPECIAL
SA REVOLVER . . . . **NiB $1744 Ex $1316 Gd $954**
Same as South TExas Army Limited Edition except w/3.5-inch bbl. and bird's-head grips. Intro. in 1984.

WEST TEXAS FLAT TOP
TARGET SA REVOLVER . . . **NiB $1633 Ex $1316 Gd $896**
Same as South TExas Army Limited Edition except w/choice of bbl. lengths from 7 .5 to 15 inches. Same special features w/flat-top style frame and adj. rear sight. Intro. in 1984.

THOMPSON PISTOL — West Hurley, New York. Manufactured by Auto-Ordnance Corporation

MODEL 1927A-5
SEMIAUTO PISTOL . . . . .NiB $1071 Ex $855 Gd $668
Similar to Thompson Model 1928A submachine gun except has no provision for automatic firing, does not have detachable buttstock. Caliber: .45 Auto, 20-round detachable box magazine (5-, 15- and 30-round box magazines, 39-round drum also available), 13-inch finned bbl., overall length: 26 inches. Weight: About 6.75 lbs. Adj. rear sight, blade front. Blued finish. Walnut grips. Intro. in 1977. See Auto-Ordnance in Handgun Section.

THOMPSON/CENTER ARMS — Rochester, New Hampshire. Acquired by Smith & Wesson in 2006

CONTENDER SINGLE-SHOT PISTOL
Break frame, underlever action. Calibers: (rimfire) .22 LR. .22 WMR, 5mm RRM; (standard centerfire), .218 Bee, .22 Hornet, .22 Rem. Jet, .221 Fireball, .222 Rem., .25-35, .256 Win. Mag., .30 M1 Carbine, .30-30, .38 Auto, .38 Special .357 Mag./Hot Shot, 9mm Para., .45 Auto, .45 Colt, .44 Magnum/Hot Shot; (wildcat centerfire) .17 Ackley Bee, .17 Bumblebee, .17 Hornet, .17 K Hornet, .17 Mach IV, .17-.222, .17-.223, .22 K Hornet, .30 Herrett, .357 Herrett, .357-4 B&D. Interchangeable bbls.: 8.75- or 10-inch standard octagon (.357 Mag., .44 Mag. and .45 Colt available w/detachable choke for

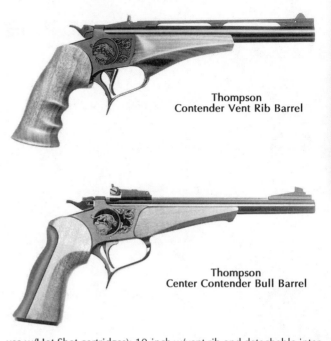

Thompson
Contender Vent Rib Barrel

Thompson
Center Contender Bull Barrel

use w/Hot Shot cartridges); 10-inch w/vent rib and detachable internal choke tube for Hot Shots, .357 and .44 Magnum only; 10-inch bull bbl., .30 or .357 Herrett only. 13.5 inches overall w/10-inch bbl., Weight: 43 oz. (w/standard 10-inch bbl.). Adj. rear sight, ramp front; vent rib model has folding rear sight, adj. front; bull bbl., available w/ or w/o sights. Lobo 1.5/ scope and mount (add $40 to value). Blued finish. Receiver photoengraved. Checkered walnut thumbrest grip and forearm (pre-1972 model has different grip w/silver grip cap). Made from 1967 to date, w/the following revisions and variations.
Standard model . . . . .NiB $419 Ex $321 Gd $204
Vent rib model . . . . .NiB $439 Ex $342 Gd $230
Bull bbl. model, w/sights . . . . . . .NiB $434 Ex $326 Gd $214
Bull bbl. model, without sights . . .NiB $431 Ex $316 Gd $204
Extra standard bbl, add. $255
Extra vent rib or bull bbl, add. $306

CONTENDER BULL BARREL . . **NiB $408 Ex $321 Gd $204**
Caliber offerings of the bull bbl. version Expanded in 1973 and 1978, making it the Contender model w/the widest range of caliber options: .22 LR, .22 Win. Mag., .22 Hornet, .223 Rem., 7mm T.C.U., 7x30 Waters, .30 M1 Carbine, .30-30 Win., .32 H&R Mag., .32-20 Win., .357 Rem. Max., .357 Mag., 10mm Auto, .44 Magnum, .445 Super Magnum. 10-inch heavy bbl., Partridge-style iron sights. Contoured Competitor grip. Blued finish.

CONTENDER INTERNAL
CHOKE MODEL . . . . **NiB $434 Ex $347 Gd $225**
Originally made in 1968-69 w/octagonal bbl., this Internal Choke version in .45 Colt/.410 caliber only was reintroduced in 1986 w/10-inch bull bbl. Vent rib also available. Fixed iron rear sight, bead front. Detachable choke screws into muzzle. Blued finish. Contoured American black walnut Competitor grip, also since 1986, has nonslip rubber insert permanently bonded to back of grip.
w/bull bbl, add. $50
w/vent rib, add $61

CONTENDER OCTAGON BARREL . . **NiB $388 Ex $290 Gd $204**
The original Contender design, this octagonal bbl., version began to see the discontinuance of caliber offerings in 1980. Now it is available in .22 LR only, 10-inch octagonal bbl., Partridge-style iron sights. Contoured Competitor grip. Blued finish.

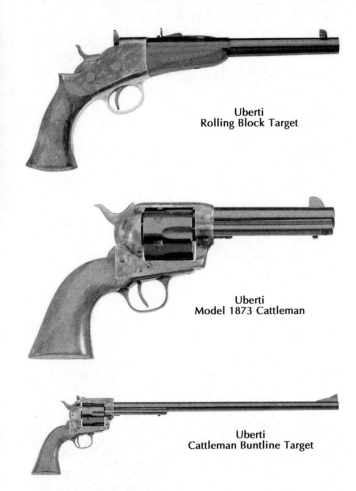

**Uberti
Rolling Block Target**

**Uberti
Model 1873 Cattleman**

**Uberti
Cattleman Buntline Target**

CONTENDER STAINLESS

Similar to the standard Contender models except stainless steel w/ blued sights. Black Rynite forearm and ambidExtrous finger-groove grip. Made from 2006 to date.

Standard SS model (10-inch bbl.) . . .	NiB $469	Ex $386	Gd $306
SS Super 14	NiB $377	Ex $291	Gd $143
SS Super 16	NiB $377	Ex $291	Gd $143

CONTENDER SUPER (14 IN./16 IN.)

Calibers: .22 LR, .222 Rem., .223 Rem., 6mm T.C.U., 6.5mm T.C.U., 7mm T.C.U., 7x30 Waters, .30 Herrett, .30-30 Win., .357 Herrett, .357 Rem. Max., .35 Rem., 10mm Auto, .44 Mag., .445 Super Mag. 14- or 16.25-inch bull bbl., 18 or 20.25 inches overall. Weight: 43-65 oz. Partridge-style ramp front sight, adj. target rear. Blued finish. Made from 1978 to 1997.

Super 14	NiB $380	Ex $306	Gd $204
Super 16	NiB $380	Ex $306	Gd $204

CONTENDER TC ALLOY II

Calibers: .22 LR, .223 Rem., .357 Magnum, .357 Rem. Max., .44 Magnum, 7mm T.C.U., .30-30 Win., .45 Colt/.410 (w/internal choke), .35 Rem. and 7-30 Waters (14-inch bbl.). 10- or 14-inch bull bbl. or 10-inch vent rib bbl. (w/internal choke). All metal parts permanently electroplated w/T/C Alloy II, which is harder than stainless steel, ensuring smoother action, 30 percent longer bbl. life. Other design specifications the same as late model Contenders. Made from 1986 to 1989.

w/10-inch bull bbl.	NiB $377	Ex $306	Gd $214
w/vent rib bbl. and choke.	NiB $464	Ex $377	Gd $286
Super 14	NiB $388	Ex $306	Gd $219

ENCORE SINGLE-SHOT PISTOL

Similar to the standard Contender models except w/10-, 12- or 15-inch bbl., Calibers: .22-250 Rem., .223 Rem., .243 Win., .260 Rem., .270 Win., 7mm BR Rem., 7mm-08 Rem., 7.62x39mm, .308 Win., .30-06 Spfd., .44 Rem. Mag., .444 Marlin, .45-70 Govt., .45 LC/410. Blue or stainless finish. Walnut or composition, ambidExtrous finger-groove grip. Hunter Model w/2.5-7x pistol scope. Note: Encore bbls. are not interchangeable with Contender models. Made from 1998 to date.

w/10-inch

bbl. (blue, disc.).	NiB $561	Ex $499	Gd $270
w/12-inch bbl., blued.	NiB $561	Ex $499	Gd $270
w/15-inch bbl., blued.	NiB $576	Ex $464	Gd $286
Hunter model w/2,5-7x scope.	NiB $755	Ex $546	Gd $365
Encore model (stainless finish), add.			$25

UBERTI HANDGUNS — Mfd. by Aldo Uberti, Ponte Zanano, Italy (imported by Uberti USA, Inc.)

MODEL 1871 ROLLING BLOCK

TARGET PISTOL . . . . NiB $418 Ex $321 Gd $230
Single shot. Calibers: .22 LR, .22 Magnum, .22 Hornet and .357 Magnum; 9.5-inch bbl., 14 inches overall. Weight: 44 oz. Ramp front sight, fully adjustable rear. Smooth walnut grip and forearm. Color casehardened frame w/brass trigger guard. Blued half-octagon or full round barrel. Made 2002 to 2006.

MODEL 1873 CATTLEMAN SA REVOLVER

Calibers: .357 Magnum, .38-40, .44-40, .44 Special, .45 Long Colt, .45 ACP. Six-round cylinder, Bbl length: 3.5, 4.5, 4.75, 5.5, 7.5 or 18 inches; 10.75 inches overall (5.5-inch bbl.). Weight: 38 oz. (5.5-inch bbl.). Color casehardened steel frame w/steel or brass back strap and trigger guard. Nickel-plated or blued barrel and cylinder. Imported from 1997 to 2010.

First issue	NiB $459	Ex $386	Gd $235
Bisley	NiB $459	Ex $386	Gd $235
Bisley (flattop)	NiB $459	Ex $386	Gd $235
Buntline (reintroduced 1992)	NiB $500	Ex $395	Gd $244
Quick Draw	NiB $459	Ex $386	Gd $235
Sabre (bird head)	NiB $459	Ex $386	Gd $235
Sheriff's model	NiB $459	Ex $386	Gd $235
Convertible cylinder, add			$75
Stainless steel, add			$150
Steel backstrap and trigger guard, add			$75
Target sights, add			$75

MODEL 1875 REMINGTON OUTLAW

Replica of Model 1875 Remington. Calibers: .357 Mag., .44-40, .45 ACP, .45 Long Colt. Six-round cylinder, 5.5- to 7.5-inch bbl., 11.75 to 13.75 inches overall. Weight: 44 oz. (with 7.5 inch bbl). Color casehardened steel frame w/steel or brass back strap and trigger guard. Blue or nickel finish.

Blue finish	NiB $479	Ex $366	Gd $219
Nickel finish (disc. 1995)	NiB $541	Ex $473	Gd $321
Convertible cylinder			
(.45 LC/.45 ACP), add.			$50

MODEL 1890 REMINGTON POLICE

Similar to Model 1875 Remington except without the web under the ejector housing.

Blue Model	NiB $464	Ex $346	Gd $198
Nickel finish (disc. 1995).	NiB $862	Ex $704	Gd $345
Convertible Cylinder (.45 LC/.45 ACP), add.			$50

ULTRA LIGHT ARMS, INC — Granville, West Virginia
MODEL 20 SERIES PISTOLS
Calibers: .22-250 thru .308 Win. Five-round magazine, 14-inch bbl., weight: 4 lbs. Composite Kevlar, graphite reinforced stock. Benchrest grade action available in right- or left-hand models. Timney adjustable trigger w/three function safety. Bright or matte finish. Made 1987 to 1999.
Model 20 Hunter's Pistol (disc. 1989) NiB $1295 Ex $1057 Gd $974
Model 20 Reb Pistol (disc. 1999) NiB $1508 Ex $1345 Gd $1199

UNIQUE PISTOLS — Hendaye, France. Manufactured by Manufacture d'Armes des Pyrénées. Currently imported by Nygord Precision Products (previously by Beeman Precision Arms)

MODEL B/CF AUTOMATIC PISTOL... NiB $220 Ex $115 Gd $70
Calibers: .32 ACP, .380 ACP. Nine-round (.32) or 8-round (.38) magazine, 4-inch bbl., 6.6 inches overall. Weight: 24.3 oz. Blued finish. Plain or thumbrest plastic grips. Intro. in 1954. Disc.

MODEL D2 . . . . NiB $326 Ex $219 Gd $177
Same as Model D6 except has 4.5-inch bbl., 7.5 inches overall, weight: 24.5 oz. Made from 1954. Disc.

MODEL D6 AUTOMATIC PISTOL . . . NiB $332 Ex $239 Gd $118
Caliber: .22 LR. 10-round magazine, 6-inch bbl., 9.25 inches overall. Weight: About 26 oz. Adj. sights. Blued finish. Plain or thumbrest plastic grips. Intro. in 1954. Disc.

MODEL DES/32U RAPID FIRE PISTOL
Caliber: .32 S&W Long (wadcutter). Five- or 6-round magazine, 5.9-inch bbl., weight: .40.2 oz. Blade front sight, micro-adj. rear. Trigger adj. for weight and position. Blued finish. Stippled handrest grips. Imported from 1990 to date.
Right-hand model . . . . NiB $1418 Ex $1316 Gd $1155
Left-hand model . . . . NiB $1486 Ex $1366 Gd $1220

MODEL DES/69-U STANDARD MATCH PISTOL
Caliber: .22 LR. Five-round magazine, 5.9-inch bbl., w/250 gm counterweight. 10.6 inches overall. Trigger adjusts for position and pull. Weight: 35.3 oz. Blade front sight, micro-adj. rear. Checkered walnut thumbrest grips w/adj. handrest. Blued finish. Imported from 1969 to 1999.
Right-hand model . . . . NiB $1234 Ex $1138 Gd $909
Left-hand model . . . . NiB $1240 Ex $1144 Gd $941

MODEL DES 823U RAPID FIRE
MATCH AUTOMATIC PISTOL. . . . . NiB $1122 Ex $950 Gd $836
Caliber: .22 Short. Five-round magazine, 5.9-inch bbl., 10.4 inches overall. Weight: 43 oz. Click adj. rear sight blade front. Checkered walnut thumbrest grips w/adj. handrest. Trigger adj. for length of pull. Made from 1974 to 1998.

KRIEGSMODELL L AUTOMATIC PISTOL NiB $362 Ex $255 Gd $180
Caliber: .32 Auto (7.65mm). Nine-round magazine, 3.2-inch bbl., 5.8 inches overall. Weight: 26.5 oz. Fixed sights. Blued finish. Plastic grips. Mfd. during German occupation of France 1940 to 194545. Note: Bears the German military acceptance marks and may have grips marked "7.65m/m 9 SCHUSS."

MODEL L AUTOMATIC PISTOL . . . . NiB $283 Ex $204 Gd $149
Calibers: .22 LR, .32 Auto (7.65mm), .380 Auto (9mm Short). 10-round magazine in .22, 7 in .32, 6 in .380; 3.3-inch bbl.; 5.8 inches overall. Weight: 16.5 oz. (.380 Auto w/light alloy frame), 23 oz. (w/steel frame). Fixed sights. Blued finish. Plastic grips. Intro. in 1955. Disc.

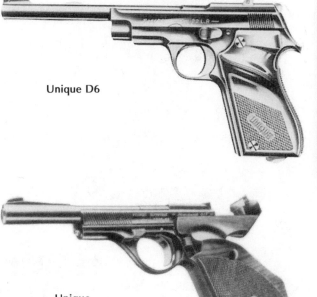

Unique D6

Unique
DES/69 Standard Match

Unique
Model DES/VO Rapid Fire Match

MODEL MIKROS POCKET
AUTOMATIC PISTOL . . . . NiB $225 Ex $150 Gd $97
Calibers: .22 Short, .25 Auto (6.35mm). Six-round magazine, 2.25-inch bbl., 4.44 inches overall. Weight: 9.5 oz. (light alloy frame), 12.5 oz. (steel frame.). Fixed sights. Blued finish. Plastic grips. Intro. in 1957. Disc.

MODEL RR
AUTOMATIC PISTOL . . . . NiB $218 Ex $109 Gd $68
Postwar commercial version of WWII Kriegsmodell w/same general specifications. Intro. in 1951. Disc.

MODEL 2000-U MATCH PISTOL
Caliber: .22 Short. Designed for U.I.T. rapid fire competition. Five-round top-inserted magazine, 5.5-inch bbl., w/five vents for recoil reduction. 11.4 inches overall. Weight: 43.4 oz. Special light alloy frame, solid steel slide and shock absorber. Stippled French walnut w/adj. handrest. Imported from 1990 to 1996.
Right-hand model . . . . NiB $1367 Ex $1199 Gd $1122
Left-hand model . . . . NiB $1398 Ex $1250 Gd $1196

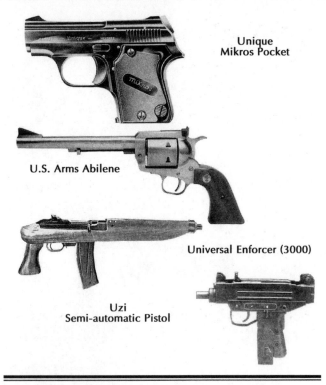

Unique
Mikros Pocket

U.S. Arms Abilene

Universal Enforcer (3000)

Uzi
Semi-automatic Pistol

UNITED STATES ARMS CORPORATION — Riverhead, New York

ABILENE SA REVOLVER
Safety Bar action. Calibers: .357 Mag., .41 Mag., .44 Mag., .45 Colt and .357/9mm convertible model w/two cylinders. Six-round cylinder, bbl. lengths: 4.63-, 5.5-, 6.5-inch, 7.5- and 8.5-inches in .44

Mag. only. Weight: About 48 oz. Adj. rear sight, ramp front. Blued finish or stainless steel. Smooth walnut grips. Made 1976 to 1983.

.44 Magnum, blued finish....	NiB $365	Ex $306	Gd $225
Magnum, stainless steel	NiB $437	Ex $336	Gd $265
Other calibers, blued finish...	NiB $327	Ex $209	Gd $200
.357 Magnum, stainless steel .	NiB $433	Ex $342	Gd $266

Convertible, .357 Mag./9mm
Para., blued finish .... NiB $362 Ex $224 Gd $207

UNITED STATES FIRE ARMS MFG CO., INC. — Hartford, CT

(Manufacturer of high quality reproduction Colt SAA revolver and Colt 1911 pistols from 1995 to 2012)

1910 COMMERCIAL MODEL
AUTOMATIC PISTOL ..... NiB $1650 Ex $1300 Gd $800
Full size 1911-style pistol. Caliber: .45 ACP, 7-round magazine, 5-inch bbl., 8.3 inches overall. High polish Armory Blue finish, checkered walnut grips. Made from 2006 to 2009.
1911 Military Model
(similar Colt 1911 rollmarks) NiB $1650 Ex $1300 Gd $800
1911 Super 38 (.38 Super) . NiB $1650 Ex $1300 Gd $800

SINGLE ACTION ARMY REVOLVER PREMIUM GRADE . .NIB $910 EX $660 GD $400
Calibers: .22 LR, .22 WMR, .32-20, .357 Mag., .38 Special, .38-40, .41 Colt, .44-40, .44 Special, .45 Long Colt, .45 ACP. Six-round cylinder, Bbl length: 3, 4, 4.75, 5.5, 7.5 or 10 inches. Dome Blue,

Old Armory, Bone Case or nickel finish.
Flat Top (adj. sights) ..... NiB $1509 Ex $1186 Gd $710
U.S. Pre-War .... NiB $1400 Ex $1000 Gd $610
New Buntline Special ....
(16-in. bbl., skeleton stock) NiB $1900 Ex $1550 Gd $990
Bisley .... NiB $1560 Ex $1210 Gd $710
Sheriff's Model .... NiB $1060 Ex $900 Gd $500
Rodeo (matte finish) ...... NiB $700 Ex $500 Gd $350
Cowboy
(Dome Blue finish, brown rubber grips) NiB $775 Ex $600 Gd $400
Omni-Potent (Bisley style grip) NiB $1500 Ex $1060 Gd $675

UNIVERSAL FIREARMS CORPORATION — Hialeah, Florida

This company was purchased by Iver Johnson Arms in the mid-1980s, when the Enforcer listed below was disc. An improved version was issued under the Iver Johnson name (see separate listing).

ENFORCER (3000)
SEMIAUTOMATIC PISTOL ... NiB $479 Ex $337 Gd $265
M-1 Carbine-type action. Caliber: 30 Carbine. Five-, 15- or 30-round clip magazine, 10.25-inch bbl., 17.75 inches overall. Weight: 4.5 lbs. (with 30-round magazine). Adj. rear sight, blade front. Blued finish. Walnut stock w/pistol grip and handguard. Made from 1964 to 1983.

UZI PISTOLS — Manufactured by Israel Military Industries, Israel (currently imported by UZI America)
SEMIAUTOMATIC PISTOL . . NiB $1044 Ex $855 Gd $658
Caliber: 9mm Para. 20-round magazine, 4.5-inch bbl., about 9.5 inches overall. Weight: 3.8 lbs. Front post-type sight, rear open-type, both adj. Disc. in 1993.

"EAGLE" SERIES SEMIAUTOMATIC DA PISTOL
Caliber: 9mm Parabellum, .40 S&W, .45 ACP (Short Slide). 10-round magazine, 3.5-, 3.7- and 4.4-inch bbl., weight: 32 oz. to 35 oz. Blade front sight, drift adjustable tritium rear. Matte blue finish. Black synthetic grips. Imported from 1997 to 1998.
Compact model
(DA or DAO) .... NiB $540 Ex $406 Gd $317
Polymer compact model .... NiB $540 Ex $496 Gd $317
Full-size model .... NiB $540 Ex $496 Gd $317
Short slide model .... NiB $540 Ex $496 Gd $317

WALTHER PISTOLS — Manufactured by German, French, Swiss and U.S. firms

The following Walther pistols were made before and during World War II by Waffenfabrik Walther, Zella-Mehlis (Thür.), Germany.

MODEL 1
AUTOMATIC PISTOL .... NiB $900 Ex $581 Gd $316
Caliber: .25 Auto (6.35mm). Six-round. 2.1-inch bbl., 4.4 inches overall. Weight: 12.8 oz. Fixed sights. Blued finish. Checkered hard rubber grips. Intro. in 1908.

MODEL 2 AUTOMATIC PISTOL
Caliber: .25 Auto (6.35mm). Six-round, 2.1-inch bbl., 4.2 inches overall. Weight: 9.8 oz. Fixed sights. Blued finish. Checkered hard rubber grips. Intro. in 1909.
Standard model .... NiB $663 Ex $468 Gd $227
Pop-up sight model ..... NiB $1950 Ex $1345 Gd $1188

MODEL 3 AUTOMATIC PISTOL . NiB $4010 Ex $3286 Gd $1005
Caliber: .32 Auto (7.65mm). Six-round magazine, 2.6-inch bbl.,
5 inches overall. Weight: 16.6 oz. Fixed sights. Blued finish.
Checkered hard rubber grips. Intro. in 1910.

MODEL 4 AUTOMATIC PISTOL .... NiB $556 Ex $425 Gd $235
Caliber: .32 Auto (7.65mm). Eight-round magazine, 3.5-inch bbl.,
5.9 inches overall. Weight: 18.6 oz. Fixed sights. Blued finish.
Checkered hard rubber grips. Made from 1910 to 1918.

MODEL 5 AUTOMATIC PISTOL .... NiB $660 Ex $541 Gd $204
Improved version of Model 2 w/same general specifications, distinguished chiefly by better workmanship and appearance. Intro. in
1913.

MODEL 6 AUTOMATIC PISTOL . NiB $9570 Ex $7933 Gd $5420
Caliber: 9mm Para. Eight-round magazine, 4.75-inch bbl., 8.25 inches
overall. Weight: 34 oz. Fixed sights. Blued finish. Checkered hard rubber
grips. Made from 1915-17. Note: The 9mm Para. cartridge is too powerful
for the simple blow-back system of this pistol, so firing is not recommended.

MODEL 7 AUTOMATIC PISTOL .... NiB $759 Ex $553 Gd $301
Caliber: .25 Auto. (6.35mm). Eight-round magazine, 3-inch bbl.,
5.3 inches overall. Weight: 11.8 oz. Fixed sights. Blued finish.
Checkered hard rubber grips. Made from 1917 to 1918.

MODEL 8 AUTOMATIC PISTOL .... NiB $770 Ex $639 Gd $240
Caliber: .25 Auto. (6.35mm). Eight-round magazine, 2.88-inch bbl.,
5.13 inches overall. Weight: 12.38 oz. Fixed sights. Blued finish.
Checkered plastic grips. Made from 1920 to 1945.

MODEL 8 LIGHTWEIGHT
AUTOMATIC PISTOL .... NiB $733 Ex $530 Gd $422
Same as standard Model Eight except about 25 percent lighter due
to use of aluminum alloys.

MODEL 9 VEST POCKET
AUTOMATIC PISTOL .... NiB $779 Ex $577 Gd $396
Caliber: .25 Auto (6.35mm). Six-round magazine, 2-inch bbl., 3.94
inches overall. Weight: 9 oz. Fixed sights. Blued finish. Checkered
plastic grips. Made from 1921 to 1945.

MODEL HP DOUBLE-ACTION AUTOMATIC
Prewar commercial version of the P38 marked with an "N" proof over an
"Eagle" or "Crown." The "HP" is an abbreviation of "Heeres Pistole" (Army
Pistol). Caliber: 9mm Para. 8-round magazine, 5-inch bbl., 8.38 inches
overall. Weight: About 34.5 oz. Fixed sights. Blued finish. Checkered wood
or plastic grips. The Model HP is distinguished by its notably fine material
and workmanship. Made from 1937 to 1944. (S/N range 1000-25900)
First production (Swedish Trials
model H1000-H2000)......... NiB $3595 Ex $2765 Gd $2064
Standard commercial production
(2000-24,000) .... NiB $2152 Ex $1825 Gd $1743
War production - marked "P38"
(24,000-26,000) .... NiB $1722 Ex $1550 Gd $1289
w/Nazi proof "Eagle/359," add $270

OLYMPIA FUNFKAMPF
MODEL AUTOMATIC.... NiB $3266 Ex $2430 Gd $2220
Caliber: .22 LR. 10-round magazine, 9.6-inch bbl., 13 inches overall. Weight: 33 oz., less weight. Set of 4 detachable weights. Adj.
target sights. Blued finish. Checkered grips. Intro. in 1936.

OLYMPIA HUNTING
MODEL AUTOMATIC.... NiB $2762 Ex $2430 Gd $2220
Same general specifications as Olympia Sport Model but w/4-inch
bbl., Weight: 28.5 oz.

Walther Model 5

Walther Model 8

Walther Model 9

OLYMPIA RAPID FIRE AUTO NiB $2550 Ex $1620 Gd $1244
Caliber: .22 Short. Six-round magazine, 7.4-inch bbl., 10.7 inches
overall. Weight: (without 12.38 oz. detachable muzzle weight,) 27.5
oz. Adj. target sights. Blued finish. Checkered grips. Made 1936 to
1940.

OLYMPIA SPORT
MODEL AUTOMATIC.... NiB $2090 Ex $1398 Gd $1269
Caliber: .22 LR. 10-round magazine, 7.4-inch bbl., 10.7 inches
overall. Weight: 30.5 oz., less weight. Adj. target sights. Blued finish. Checkered grips. Set of four detachable weights was supplied
at Extra cost. Made about 1936 to 1940.

Walther PP
(Prewar)

P38 MILITARY DA AUTOMATIC
Modification of the Model HP adopted as an official German Service arm in 1938 and produced throughout WW II by Walther (code "ac"), Mauser (code "byf") and a few other manufacturers. General specifications and appearance same as Model HP, but w/a vast difference in quality, the P38 being a mass-produced military pistol. Some of the late wartime models were very roughly finished and tolerances were quite loose.

War Production w/Walther banner (1940)
Zero S/N 1st issue (S/N01-01,000) . . . .NiB $8130 Ex $6160 Gd $2445
Zero S/N. 2nd issue (S/N 01,000-03,500)NiB $6515 Ex $5125 Gd $2309
Zero S/N. 3rd issue (S/N 03,500-013,000)NiB $3130 Ex $2112 Gd $1021

WALTHER CONTRACT PISTOLS (LATE 1940-44)
"480" code Series (S/N 1-7,600) . . . . . .NiB $5745 Ex $3937 Gd $1590
"ac" code Ser. w/no date (S/N 7,350-9,700)NiB $6079 Ex $4390 Gd $2244
"ac" code Ser. w/.40 below
code (S/N 9,700-9,900A) . . . . .NiB $4435 Ex $3866 Gd $1879
"ac40" code inline Ser. (S/N 1-9,900B) . .NiB $2360 Ex $1966 Gd $909
"ac" code Ser. w/41 below code (S/N 1-4,5001)NiB $1897 Ex $1633 Gd $974
"ac" code Ser. w/42 below code
(S/N 4,500I-9,300K). . . . . .NiB $1610 Ex $1364 Gd $869
"ac" code Ser. w/43 date (inline or below). NiB $831 Ex $633 Gd $478
"ac" code Ser. w/45 (inline or below) . . . . NiB $780 Ex $599 Gd $439

MAUSER CONTRACT PISTOLS (LATE 1942-44)
"byf" code Ser. w/42 date (19,000 prod.) NiB $1418 Ex $1023 Gd $816
"bcf" code Ser. w/43, 44 or 45 date
(inline or below) . . . . NiB $984 Ex $744 Gd $612
"svw" code Ser. (French prod. w/Nazi proofs)NiB $1316 Ex$1066 Gd$693
"svw" code Ser. (French prod. w/star proof) NiB $576 Ex $500 Gd $376

SPREEWERKE CONTRACT PISTOLS (LATE 1942-45)
"cyq" code Ser 1st Ser. w/Eagle over
359 (500 prod.) . . . . .NiB $1866 Ex $1598 Gd $1135
"cyq" code Standard Ser. (300,000 prod.) . NiB $989 Ex $590 Gd $478
"cyq" code "0" Ser. (5,000 prod.) . . . . . . NiB $1132 Ex $741 Gd $562

MODEL PP DA AUTOMATIC PISTOL
Polizeipistole (Police Pistol). Calibers: .22 LR (5.6mm), .25 Auto (6.35mm), .32 Auto (7.65mm), .380 Auto (9mm). Eight-round magazine, (7-round in .380), 3.88-inch bbl., 6.94 inches overall. Weight: 23 oz. Fixed sights. Blued finish. Checkered plastic grips. 1929-45. Post-War production and importation 1963 to 2000.

NOTE: Wartime models are inferior in quality to prewar commercial pistols.

COMMERICAL MODEL WITH CROWN "N" PROOF
.22 cal. . . . . .NiB $1599 Ex $1033 Gd $713
.25 cal. . . . . .NiB $8554 Ex $3390 Gd $1729
.32 cal. . . . . .NiB $890 Ex $568 Gd $376
.32 cal. (w/Dural alloy frame) . . . . .NiB $1025 Ex $979 Gd $377

.32 cal. (w/Verchromt Fin., pre-war) . . .NiB $3560 Ex $2533 Gd $907
.32 cal. (A.F.Stoeger Contract, pre-war) . NiB $2550 Ex $1656 Gd $691
.32 cal. (Allemagne French contract,
pre-war). . . . . .NiB $1489 Ex $1189 Gd $712
.380 cal. (w/Comm. Crown "N" proof). . NiB $1578 Ex $1266 Gd $831
.380 cal. (w/Verchromt Fin., pre-war) . NiB $2779 Ex $2465 Gd $1109

WARTIME MODEL WITH EAGLE "N" PROOF
.32 cal. (w/Waffenampt proofs) . . . . .NiB $980 Ex $544 Gd $475
.32 cal. (w/Eagle "C" Nazi Police markings)NiB $1056 Ex $744 Gd $496
.32 cal. (w/Eagle "F" Nazi Police markings)NiB $1060 Ex $748 Gd $500
.32 cal. (w/NSKK markings) . . . . .NiB $3277 Ex $3417 Gd $1100
.32 cal. (w/NSDAP Gruppe markings) . NiB $2660 Ex $2245 Gd $1033
.380 cal. (w/Waffenampt proofs). . . .NiB $1440 Ex $1187 Gd $899

COMMERCIAL MODEL (POST-WAR)
.22 cal. (German manufacture) . . . . . . .NiB $1203 Ex $1032 Gd $601
.32 cal. (German manufacture) . . . . .NiB $1044 Ex $806 Gd $577
.380 cal. (German manufacture). . . . . . .NiB $1181 Ex $1099 Gd $444
.22 cal. (French manufacture) . . . . .NiB $601 Ex $498 Gd $290
.32 cal. (French manufacture) . . . . .NiB $601 Ex $498 Gd $290
.380 cal. (French manufacture) . . . . .NiB $610 Ex $567 Gd $289
.22, .32 or .380 Cal. (other foreign manuf.) NiB $449 Ex $346 Gd $240

MODEL PP SPORT DA AUTOMATIC PISTOL
Target version of the Model PP. Caliber: .22 LR. Eight-round magazine, 5.75- to 7.75 inch bbl. w/adjustable sights. Blue or nickel finish. Checkered plastic grips w/thumbrest. Made from 1953 to 1970.
Walther manufacture. . . . . .NiB $1233 Ex $730 Gd $464
Manurhin manufacture. . . . . .NiB $990 Ex $834 Gd $561
C Model (comp./SA). . . . . .NiB $1294 Ex $920 Gd $668
w/nickel finish, add $204
w/matched bbl., weights, add $100

MODEL PP DELUXE ENGRAVED
These elaborately engraved models are available in blued finish, silver- or gold-plated.
Blued finish . . . . .NiB $ 1667 Ex $1462 Gd $1230
Silver-plated. . . . . NiB $1922 Ex $1530 Gd $1306
Gold-plated . . . . NiB $2130 Ex $1830 Gd $1488
w/ivory grips, add. $281
w/presentation case, add $4750
.22 caliber, add $75
.380 caliber, add 100%

MODEL PP LIGHTWEIGHT
Same as standard Model PP except about 25 percent lighter due to use of aluminum alloys (Dural). Values 40 percent higher. (See individual listings).

MODEL PP SUPER
DA PISTOL. . . . . NiB $1066 Ex $831 Gd $623
Caliber: 9x18mm. Seven-round magazine, 3.6-inch bbl., 6.9 inches overall. Weight: 30 oz. Fixed sights. Blued finish. Checkered plastic grips. Made from 1973 to 1979.

MODEL PP 7.65MM
PRESENTATION . . . . NiB $2100 Ex $1596 Gd $1214
Made of soft aluminum alloy in green-gold color, these pistols were not intended to be fired.

MODEL PPK DOUBLE-ACTION AUTOMATIC PISTOL
Polizeipistole Kriminal (Detective Pistol). Calibers: .22 LR (5.6mm), .25 Auto (6.35mm), .32 Auto (7.65mm), .380 Auto (9mm). Seven-round magazine, (6-round in .380), 3.25-inch bbl., 5.88 inches overall. Weight: 19 oz. Fixed sights. Blued finish. Checkered plastic grips. *Note: Wartime models are inferior in workmanship to prewar commercial pistols. Made 1931 to 1945.*

NOTE: *After both World Wars, the Walther manufacturing facility was required to cease the production of "restricted" firearms as part of the armistice agreements. Following WW II, Walther moved its manufacturing facility from the original location in Zella/Mehilis, Germany to Ulm/Donau. In 1950, the firm Manufacture de Machines du Haut Rhine at Mulhouse, France was licensed by Walther and started production of PP and PPK models at the Manurhin facility in 1952. The MK II Walthers as produced at Manurhin were imported into the U.S. until 1968 when CGA importation requirements restricted the PPK firearm configuration from further importation. As a result, Walther developed the PPK/S to conform to the new regulations and licensed Interarms to produce the firearm in the U.S. from 1986-99. From 1984-86, Manurhin imported PP and PPK/S type firearms under the Manurhin logo. Additional manufacturing facilities (both licensed & unlicensed) that produced PP and PPK type firearms were established after WW II in various locations and other countries including: China, France, Hungary, Korea, Romania and Turkey. In 1996, Walther was sold to UmarEx Sportwaffen GmbH and manufacturing facilities were relocated in Arnsberg, Germany. In 1999, Walther formed a partnership with Smith and Wesson and selected Walther firearms were licensed for production in the U.S.*

Walther PPK (WW II)

Walther PPK Silver-Plated

COMMERCIAL MODEL W/EAGLE PROOF (PREWAR)
.22 cal. . . . . NiB $2560 Ex $1735 Gd $1509
.25 cal. . . . . .NiB $10,620 Ex $6387 Gd $4960
.32 cal. . . . . NiB $1533 Ex $831 Gd $567
.380 cal. . . . . NiB $4530 Ex $3789 Gd $3320

WARTIME MODEL W/EAGLE "N" PROOF
.22 cal. . . . . NiB $2522 Ex $1733 Gd $1458
.22 cal. (w/Dural frame). . . . . NiB $1920 Ex $1779 Gd $1357
.32 cal. . . . . NiB $1599 Ex $1022 Gd $879
.32 cal. (w/Dural frame). . . . . NiB $1199 Ex $ 1022 Gd $879
.32 cal. (w/Verchromt Fin., Pre-War) . NiB $1199 Ex $1022 Gd $879
.380 cal. . . . . NiB $3885 Ex $2345 Gd $2097
.380 cal. (w/Dural frame). . . . . NiB $3885 Ex $2345 Gd $2097
.380 cal. (w/Verchromt Fin., Pre-War)NiB $3885 Ex $2345 Gd $2097
.32 cal. (w/Waffenampt proofs) . . . . . NiB $2132 Ex $882 Gd $453
.32 cal. (w/Eagle "C" Nazi Police markings)NiB $2132 Ex $882 Gd $453
.32 cal. (w/Eagle "F" Nazi Police markings)NiB $2566 Ex $1145 Gd $650
.32 cal. (w/NSKK markings) . . . . NiB $2366 Ex $1918 Gd $1333
.32 cal. (w/NSDAP Gruppe markings)NiB $8560 Ex $5788 Gd $1225
.380 cal. (w/Waffenampt proofs) . . . NiB $1474 Ex $1198 Gd $1029

COMMERCIAL MODEL (POST-WAR)
.22 cal. (German manufacture). . . . . . NiB $1076 Ex $945 Gd $411
.32 cal. (German manufacture). . . . . .NiB $850 Ex $601 Gd $383
.380 cal. (German manufacture). . . . . .NiB $1091 Ex $591 Gd $498
.22 cal. (French manufacture) . . . . . . .NiB $2212 Ex $924 Gd $538
.32 cal. (French manufacture) . . . . . . .NiB $857 Ex $651 Gd $437
.380 cal. (French manufacture). . . . . . NiB $1173 Ex $839 Gd $452
.22, .32 or .380 cal. (other foreign manuf.)NiB $332 Ex $281 Gd $201

COMMERCIAL MODEL (U.S. PRODUCTION 1986-2001)
.380 cal. (w/blue finish) . . . . NiB $658 Ex $499 Gd $403
.380 cal. (w/nickel finish). . . . . NiB $658 Ex $499 Gd $403
.32 or .380 Cal. (stainless steel) . . . . . NiB $658 Ex $499 Gd $403

MODEL PPK DELUXE ENGRAVED
These elaborately engraved models are available in blued finish, chrome-, silver- or gold-plated.
Blued finish . . . . .NiB $1932 Ex $1543 Gd $1199
Chrome-plated . . . . .NiB $3087 Ex $2156 Gd $1779
Silver-plated. . . . . .NiB $2234 Ex $1789 Gd $1418

Gold-plated. . . . . NiB $2567 Ex $1979 Gd $1598
w/ivory grips, add. $306
w/Presentation case, add $791
.22 cal, add. $75
.25 cal, add $128
.380 cal, add $110

MODEL PPK LIGHTWEIGHT
Same as standard Model PPK except about 25 percent lighter due to aluminum alloys. Values 50 percent higher.

MODEL PPK 7.65MM
PRESENTATION . . . . NiB $1856 Ex $1418 Gd $966
Made of soft aluminum alloy in green-gold color, these pistols were not intended to be fired.

MODEL PPK/S DA AUTOMATIC PISTOL
Designed to meet the requirements of the U.S. Gun Control Act of 1968, this model has the frame of the PP and the shorter slide and bbl., of the PPK. Overall length: 6.1 inches. Weight: 23 oz. Other specifications are the same as those of standard PPK except steel frame only. German, French and U.S. production 1971 to date. U.S. version made by Interarms 1978-1999, Smith & Wesson production from 2002-2009..
.22 cal. (German manufacture)NiB $1336 Ex $1016 Gd $660
.32 cal. (German manufacture) NiB $997 Ex $789 Gd $497
.380 cal. (German manufacture)NiB $1321 Ex $997 Gd $577
.22 cal. (French manufacture) . NiB $968 Ex $760 Gd $561
.32 cal. (French manufacture) . NiB $973 Ex $781 Gd $577
.380 cal. (French manufacture) NiB $944 Ex $632 Gd $500
.22, .32 or .380 cal., blue
(U.S. manufacture) . . . . NiB $638 Ex $508 Gd $398
.22, .32 or .380 cal., stainless
(U.S. manuf.) . . . . NiB $638 Ex $508 Gd $398

NOTE: *Interarms (Interarmco) acquired a license from Walther in 1978 to manufacturer PP and PPK models at the Ranger Manufacturing Co., Inc. in Gadsden, Alabama. In 1988 the Ranger facility was licensed as EMCO and continued to produce Walther firearms for Interarms until 1996. From 1996-99, Black Creek in Gadsden, Alabama produced Walther pistols for Interarms. In 1999, Smith & Wesson acquired manufacturing rights for Walther firearms at the Black Creek facility.*

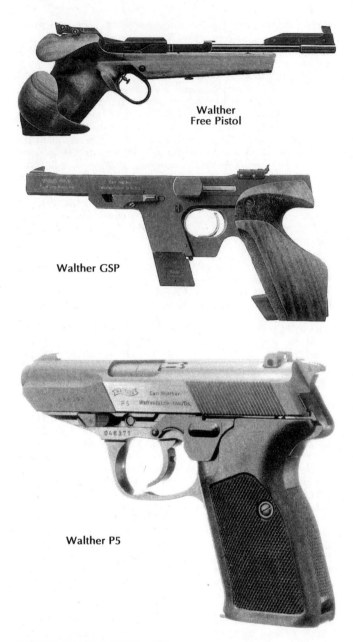

Walther
Free Pistol

Walther GSP

Walther P5

MODELS PPK/S DELUXE ENGRAVED
These elaborately engraved models are available in blued finish, chrome-, silver- or gold-plated.

Blued finish . . . . NiB $1634 Ex $1216 Gd $1094
Chrome-plated . . . . NiB $1552 Ex $1268 Gd $976
Silver-plated. . . . . NiB $1755 Ex $1296 Gd $966
Gold-plated . . . . NiB $1889 Ex $1566 Gd $1034

NOTE: *The following Walther pistols are now manufactured by Carl Walther, Waffenfabrik, Ulm/Donau, Germany.*

SELF-LOADING
SPORT PISTOL. . . . . NiB $866 Ex $856 Gd $546
Caliber: .22 LR. 10-round magazine, bbl. lengths: 6- and 9-inch, 9.88 inches overall w/6-inch bbl. Target sights. Blued finish. One-piece, wood or plastic grips, checkered. Intro. in 1932.

MODEL FREE PISTOL . . . . NiB $1533 Ex $1367 Gd $1159
Single-Shot. Caliber: .22 LR. 11.7-inch heavy bbl., Weight: 48 oz. Adj. grips and target sights w/electronic trigger. Importation disc. 1991.

MODEL GSP TARGET AUTOMATIC PISTOL
Calibers: .22 LR, .32 S&W Long Wadcutter. Five-round magazine, 4.5-inch bbl., 11.8 inches overall. Weights: 44.8 oz. (.22 cal.) or 49.4 oz. (.32 cal.). Adj. target sights. Black finish. Walnut thumbrest grips w/adj. handrest. Made from 1969 to 1994.
.22 LR . . . . NiB $1598 Ex $1432 Gd $889
.32 S&W Long
Wadcutter . . . . NiB $2773 Ex $2513 Gd $2122
Conversion unit.
.22 Short
or .22 LR, add $1071

MODEL OSP RAPID
FIRE TARGET PISTOL . . . . NiB $1744 Ex $1509 Gd $1345
Caliber: .22 Short. Five-round magazine, 4.5-inch bbl., 11.8 inches overall. Weight: 42.3 oz. Adj. target sights. Black finish. Walnut thumbrest grips w/adj. handrest. .22 LR conversion unit available (add $281). Made from 1968 to 1994.

MODEL P4 (P38-LV)
DA PISTOL. . . . . NiB $844 Ex $712 Gd $448
Similar to P38 except has an uncocking device instead of a manual safety. Caliber: 9mm Para. 4.3-inch bbl., 7.9 inches overall. Other general specifications same as for current model P38. Made from 1974 to 1982.

MODEL P5 DA PISTOL. . . . . NiB $1654 Ex $804 Gd $543
Alloy frame w/frame-mounted decocking levers. Caliber: 9mm Para. Eight-round magazine, 3.5-inch bbl., 7 inches overall. Weight: 28 oz. blued finish. Checkered walnut or synthetic grips. Made from 1997 to date.

MODEL P5 COMPACT
DA PISTOL. . . . . NiB $1693 Ex $988 Gd $497
Similar to model P5 except w/3.1-inch bbl. and weight: 26 oz. Imported from 1987.

MODEL P1 DA AUTOMATIC
Postwar commercial version of the P38, has light alloy frame. Calibers: .22 LR, 7.65mm Luger, 9mm Para. Eight-round magazine, bbl., lengths: 5.1-inch in .22 caliber, 4.9- inch in 7.65mm and 9mm, 8.5 inches overall. Weight: 28.2 oz. Fixed sights. Nonreflective black finish. Checkered plastic grips. Made from 1957 to 1989. Note: The "P1" was W. German Armed Forces official pistol.
.22 LR . . . . NiB $805 Ex $644 Gd $433
Other calibers . . . . NiB $806 Ex $610 Gd $398

MODEL P38 DELUXE ENGRAVED PISTOL
Elaborately engraved, available in blued or chrome-, silver- or gold-plated finish.
Blued finish . . . . NiB $2077 Ex $1566 Gd $1028
Chrome-plated . . . . NiB $1776 Ex $1432 Gd $998
Silver-plated. . . . . NiB $1712 Ex $1429 Gd $1043
Gold-plated . . . . NiB $1987 Ex $1603 Gd $1163

MODEL P38K . . . . NiB $886 Ex $781 Gd $468
Short-barreled version of current P38, the "K" standing for "kurz" (meaning short). Same general specifications as standard model except 2.8-inch bbl., 6.3 inches overall, weight: 27.2 oz. Front sight is slide mounted. Caliber: 9mm Para. Made from 1974 to 1980.

MODEL P88 DA AUTOMATIC
PISTOL . . . . NiB $1132 Ex $988 Gd $774
Caliber: 9mm Para. 15-round magazine, 4-inch bbl., 7.38 inches overall. Weight: 31.5 oz. Blade front sight, adj. rear. Checkered black synthetic grips. External hammer w/ambidExtrous decocking levers. Alloy frame w/matte blued steel slide. Made 1987 to 1993.

MODEL P88 DA COMPACT
Similar to the standard P88 Model except w/10- or 13-round magazine, 3.8-inch bbl., 7.1 inches overall. Weight: 29 oz. Imported from 1993 to 2003.
Model P88
(early importation) . . . . NiB $1088 Ex $975 Gd $648
Model P88
(post 1994 importation) . . . . NiB $1088 Ex $975 Gd $648

MODEL P99 DA
AUTOMATIC PISTOL . . . . NiB $756 Ex $576 Gd $486
Calibers: 9mm Para., .40 S&W or 9x21mm. 10-round magazine, 4-inch bbl., 7.2 inches overall. Weight: 22-25 oz. AmbidExtrous magazine release, decocking lever and 3-function safety. Interchangeable front post sight, micro-adj. rear. Polymer grip-frame w/blued slide. Imported from 1995 to date.

MODEL TPH DA POCKET PISTOL
Light alloy frame. Calibers: .22 LR, .25 ACP (6.35mm). Six-round magazine, 2.25-inch bbl., 5.38 inches overall. Weight: 14 oz. Fixed sights. Blued finish. Checkered plastic grips. Made 1968 to date. Note: Few Walther-made models reached the U.S. because of import restrictions. A U.S.-made version was mfd. by Interarms from 1986 to 1999.
German model . . . . NiB $1100 Ex $756 Gd $602
U.S. model . . . . NiB $900 Ex $743 Gd $436

NOTE: The Walther Olympia Model pistols were manufactured 1952-1963 by Hämmerli AG Jagd-und Sportwaffenfabrik, Lenzburg, Switzerland, and marketed as "Hämmerli-Walther." See Hämmerli listings for specific data.

OLYMPIA MODEL 200 AUTO PISTOL,
1952 TYPE . . . . NiB $729 Ex $612 Gd $453
Similar to 1936 Walther Olympia Funfkampf Model.

For the following Hammerli-Walther Models
(200, 201, 202, 203, 204, and 205)
See listings under Hammerli Section.

WARNER PISTOL — Norwich, Connecticut, Warner Arms Corp. (or Davis-Warner Arms Co.)

INFALLIBLE POCKET
AUTOMATIC PISTOL . . . . NiB $507 Ex $356 Gd $253
Caliber: .32 Auto. Seven-round magazine, 3-inch bbl., 6.5 inches overall. Weight: About 24 oz. Fixed sights. Blued finish. Hard rubber grips. Made from 1917 to 1919.

Walther P38

Walther P38K

Walther P88

Walther TPH

**Webley 9MM
Military Police Automatic**

**Webley Mark III
38 Military & Police Revolver**

WEBLEY & SCOTT LTD. — London and Birmingham, England

MODEL 1909 9MM MILITARY
& POLICE AUTOMATIC . . . NiB $2090 Ex $1465 Gd $1288
Caliber: 9mm Browning Long. Eight-round magazine, 8 inches overall. Weight: 32 oz. Fixed sights. Blued finish. Checkered Vulcanite grips. Made from 1909 to 1930.

MODEL 1907 HAMMER
AUTOMATIC . . . . NiB $1006 Ex $866 Gd $207
Caliber: .25 Automatic. Six-round magazine, overall length: 4.75 inches. Weight: 11.75 oz. No sights. Blued finish. Checkered Vulcanite grips. Made from 1906 to 1940.

MODEL 1912 HAMMERLESS
AUTOMATIC . . . . NiB $1500 Ex $1306 Gd $1233
Caliber: .25 Automatic. Six-round magazine, overall length: 4.25 inches, weight: 9.75 oz. Fixed sights. Blued finish. Checkered Vulcanite grips. Made from 1909 to 1940.

MARK I 455
AUTOMATIC PISTOL . . . . NiB $2505 Ex $1988 Gd $1600
Caliber: .455 Webley Auto. Seven-round magazine, 5-inch bbl., 8.5 inches overall. Weight: About 39 oz. Fixed sights. Blued finish. Checkered Vulcanite grips. Made 1913-31. Reissued during WWII. Total production about 9,300. Note: Mark I No. 2 is same pistol w/ adj. rear sight and modified manual safety.

MARK III 38 MILITARY & POLICE
DA REVOLVER . . . . NiB $974 Ex $789 Gd $633
Hinged frame. DA. Caliber: .38 S&W. Six-round cylinder, bbl. lengths: 3- and 4-inches. 9.5 inches overall (with 4-inch bbl.). Weight: 21 oz. (with 4-inch bbl.). Fixed sights. Blued finish. Checkered walnut or Vulcanite grips. Made from 1897 to 1945.

MARK IV 22 CALIBER
TARGET REVOLVER . . . . NiB $806 Ex $691 Gd $386
Same frame and general appearance as Mark IV .38. Caliber: .22 LR. Six-round cylinder, 6-inch bbl., 10.13 inches overall. Weight: 34 oz. Target sights. Blued finish. Checkered grips. Disc. in 1945.

MARK IV 38 MILITARY & POLICE
DA REVOLVER . . . . NiB $806 Ex $691 Gd $386
Identical in appearance to the double-action Mark IV .22 w/hinged frame except chambered for .38 S&W. Six-round cylinder, bbl. length: 3-, 4- and 5-inches; 9.13 inches overall (with 5-inch bbl.). Weight: 27 oz. (with 5-inch bbl.). Fixed sights. Blued finish. Checkered grips. Made from 1929 to 1957.

MARK VI NO. 1 BRITISH SERVICE
DA REVOLVER . . . . NiB $691 Ex $567 Gd $478
Hinged frame. Caliber: 455 Webley. Six-round cylinder, bbl. lengths: 4-, 6- and 7.5-inches; 11.25 inches overall (with 6-inch bbl.). Weight: 38 oz. (with 6-inch bbl.). Fixed sights. Blued finish. Checkered walnut or Vulcanite grips. Made from 1915 to 1947.

MARK VI 22
TARGET REVOLVER . . . . . . NiB $1266 Ex $1096 Gd $909
Same frame and general appearance as the Mark VI 455. Caliber: .22 LR. Six-round cylinder, 6-inch bbl., 11.25 inches overall. Weight: 40 oz. Target sights. Blued finish. Checkered walnut or Vulcanite grips. Disc. in 1945.

METROPOLITAN POLICE
AUTOMATIC PISTOL . . . . NiB $1629 Ex $1528 Gd $1266
Calibers: .32 Auto, .380 Auto. Eight-round (.32) or 7-round (.380) magazine, 3.5-inch bbl., 6.25 inches overall. weight: 20 oz. Fixed sights. Blued finish. Checkered Vulcanite grips. Made from 1906-40 (.32) and 1908 to 1920 (.380).

R.I.C. MODELS DA REVOLVER NiB $950 Ex $700 Gd $500
Royal Irish Constabulary or Bulldog Model. Solid frame. Caliber: .455 Webley. Five-round cylinder, 2.25-inch bbl., weight: 21 oz. Fixed sights. Blued finish. Checkered walnut or vulcanite grips. Made from 1897-1939 .

SEMIAUTOMATIC
SINGLE-SHOT PISTOL . . . . .NiB $1090 Ex $ 916 Gd $617
Similar in appearance to the Webley Metropolitan Police Automatic, this pistol is "semiautomatic" in the sense that the fired case is Extracted and ejected and the hammer cocked as in a blow-back automatic pistol; it is loaded singly and the slide manually operated in loading. Caliber: .22 Long, 4.5- or 9-inch bbl., 10.75 inches overall (with 9-inch bbl.). Weight: 24 oz. (with 9-inch bbl.). Adj. sights. Blued finish. Checkered Vulcanite grips. Made from 1911 to 1927.

SINGLE-SHOT TARGET PISTOL NiB $1588 Ex $1469 Gd $1190
Hinge frame. Caliber: .22 LR. 10-inch bbl., 15 inches overall. Weight: 37 oz. Fixed sights on earlier models, current production has adj. rear sight. Blued finish. Checkered walnut or Vulcanite grips. Made from 1909.

WEBLEY-FOSBERY AUTOMATIC REVOLVER
Hinged frame. Recoil action revolves cylinder and cocks hammer. Caliber: 455 Webley. Six-round cylinder, 6-inch bbl., 12 inches overall. Weight: 42 oz. Fixed or adjustable sights. Blued finish. Checkered walnut grips. Made 1901-1939. Note: A few were produced in caliber .38 Colt Auto w/an 8-shot cylinder (very rare).
1901 model . . . . .NiB $12,600 Ex $8600 Gd $5500
1902 model .38 Colt (8-round), add, add 300%
1903 model . . . . .NiB $10,000 Ex $7600 Gd $4600
Target model w/adjustable sights, add. 20%

WESSON FIREARMS CO., INC. — Palmer, Massachusetts. Formerly Dan Wesson Firearms, Inc. Acquired by CZ-USA in 2005

MODEL 8 SERVICE
Same general specifications as Model 14 except caliber .38 Special. Made from 1971 to 1975. Values same as for Model 14.

MODEL 8-2 SERVICE
Same general specifications as Model 14-2 except caliber .38 Special. Made from 1975 to date. Values same as for Model 14-2.

MODEL 9 TARGET
Same as Model 15 except caliber .38 Special. Made from 1971 to 1975. Values same as for Model 15.

MODEL 9-2 TARGET
Same as Model 15-2 except caliber .38 Special. Made from 1975 to date. Values same as for Model 15-2.

MODEL 9-2H HEAVY BARREL
Same general specifications as Model 15-2H except caliber .38 Special. Made from 1975 to date. Values same as for Model 15-2H. Disc. 1983.

MODEL 9-2HV VENT RIB HEAVY BARREL
Same as Model 15-2HV except caliber .38 Special. Made from 1975 to date. Values same as for Model 15-2HV.

MODEL 9-2V VENT RIB
Same as Model 15-2V except caliber .38 Special. Made from 1975 to date. Values same as for Model 15-2H.

MODEL 11 SERVICE DA REVOLVER
Caliber: .357 Magnum. Six-round cylinder. bbl. lengths: 2.5-, 4-, 6-inches interchangeable bbl. assemblies, 9 inches overall (with 4-inch bbl.). Weight: 38 oz. (with 4-inch bbl.). Fixed sights. Blued finish. Interchangeable grips. Made from 1970-71. Note: The Model 11 has an External bbl. nut.

w/one bbl. assembly and grip . NiB $274 Ex $180 Gd $101
Extra bbl. assembly, add $75
Extra grip, add $50

MODEL 12 TARGET
Same general specifications as Model 11 except has adj. sights. Made from 1970-71.

w/one-bbl. assembly and grip . NiB $290 Ex $204 Gd $135
Extra bbl. assembly, add $75
Extra grip, add $50

MODEL 14 SERVICE DA REVOLVER
Caliber: .357 Magnum. Six-round cylinder, bbl. length: 2.25-, 3.75, 5.75-inches; interchangeable bbl. assemblies, 9 inches overall (with 3.75-inch bbl.). Weight: 36 oz. (with 3.75-inch bbl.). Fixed sights. Blued or nickel finish. Interchangeable grips. Made from 1971 to 1975. Note: Model 14 has recessed bbl. nut.

w/one-bbl. assembly and grip . . NiB $225 Ex $158 Gd $101
Extra bbl. assembly, add $61
Extra grip, add $25

MODEL 14-2 SERVICE DA REVOLVER
Caliber: .357 Magnum. Six-round cylinder, bbl. lengths: 2.5-, 4-, 6-, 8-inch; interchangeable bbl. assemblies, 9.25 inches overall (with 4-inch bbl.) Weight: 34 oz. (with 4-inch bbl.). Fixed sights. Blued finish. Interchangeable grips. Made from 1975 to 1995. Note: Model 14-2 has recessed bbl. nut.

Dan Wesson
Model 14-2 Service

Dan Wesson
Model 15-2H Interchangeable Heavy

w/one bbl. assembly
(8 inch) and grip . . . . NiB $270 Ex $204 Gd $158
w/one bbl. assembly
(other lengths) and grip . . . . . . NiB $270 Ex $204 Gd $158
Extra bbl. assembly, 8 inch, add $75
Extra bbl. assembly,
other lengths, add $75
Extra grip, add $50

MODEL 15 TARGET
Same general specifications as Model 14 except has adj. sights. Made from 1971 to 1975.

w/one bbl. assembly
and grip . . . . NiB $306 Ex $230 Gd $190
Extra bbl. assembly, add $75
Extra grip, add $50

MODEL 15-2 TARGET
Same general specifications as Model 14-2 except has adj. rear sight and interchangeable blade front; also avail. w/10-, 12- or 15-inch bbl., Made from 1975 to 1995.

w/one bbl. assembly (8 inch) and grip NiB $362 Ex $289 Gd $187
w/one bbl. assembly (10 inch) and grip NiB $362 Ex $289 Gd $187
w/one bbl. assembly
(12 inch)/grip. Disc . . . . NiB $362 Ex $289 Gd $187
w/one bbl. assembly
(15 inch)/grip. Disc . . . . NiB $362 Ex $289 Gd $187
w/one-bbl. assembly
(other lengths)/grip . . . . NiB $244 Ex $159 Gd $133
Extra bbl. assembly, add $75
Extra grip, add $50

MODEL 15-2H HEAVY BARREL
Same as Model 15-2 except has heavy bbl., assembly weight: with 4-inch bbl., 38 oz. Made from 1975 to 1983.

w/one bbl. assembly . . . . NiB $500 Ex $345 Gd $235
Extra bbl. assembly, add $75
Extra grip, add $50

MODEL 15-2HV VENT RIB HEAVY BARREL
Same as Model 15-2 except has vent rib heavy bbl. assembly; weight: (w/4-inch bbl.) 37 oz. Made from 1975 to 1995.

w/one bbl. assembly (8 inch) and gripNiB $303 Ex $240 Gd $162
w/one bbl. assembly (10 inch) and gripNiB $303 Ex $240 Gd $162
w/one bbl. assembly (12 inch) and gripNiB $303 Ex $240 Gd $162
w/one bbl. assembly
(15 inch) and grip . . . . NiB $321 Ex $273 Gd $192
w/one bbl. assembly (other
lengths) and grip . . . . NiB $198 Ex $241 Gd $163
Extra bbl. assembly (8 inch), add $75
Extra bbl. assembly (10 inch), add. $75
Extra bbl. assembly (12 inch), add. $75
Extra bbl. assembly (15 inch), add. $75
Extra bbl. assembly
(other lengths), add. $75
Extra grip, add $50

MODEL 15-2V VENT RIB
Same as Model 15-2 except has vent rib bbl. assembly, weight: 35 oz. (with 4-inch bbl.). Made from 1975 to date. Values same as for 15-2H.

HUNTER PACS
Dan Wesson Hunter Pacs are offered in all Magnum calibers and include heavy vent rib 8-inch shrouded bbl., Burris scope mounts, bbl. changing tool in a case.

Model	NiB	Ex	Gd
HP22M-V	$893	$660	$473
HP22M-2	$733	$612	$447
HP722M-V	$843	$632	$439
HP722M-2	$806	$612	$408
HP32-V	$785	$571	$395
HP32-2	$691	$530	$425
HP732-V	$816	$597	$434
HP732-2.	$755	$608	$449
HP15-V	$755	$608	$449
HP15-2	$780	$601	$437
HP715-V	$831	$654	$479
HP715-2.	$755	$657	$478
HP41-V	$688	$556	$425
HP741-V	$841	$689	$495
HP741-2	$739	$607	$439
HP44-V	$884	$700	$536
HP44-2	$739	$607	$439
HP744-V	$933	$781	$576
HP744-2	$897	$738	$546
HP40-V	$616	$497	$366
HP40-2	$827	$691	$496
HP740-V	$988	$816	$590
HP740-2.	$918	$729	$526
HP375-V	$595	$500	$356
HP375-2	$944	$786	$590
HP45-V	$734	$626	$439

WHITNEY FIREARMS COMPANY — Hartford, Connecticut

WOLVERINE AUTOMATIC PISTOL
Dural frame/shell contains all operating components. Caliber: .22 LR. 10-round magazine, 4.63-inch bbl., 9 inches overall. Weight: 23 oz. Partridge-type sights. Blued or nickel finish. Plastic grips. Made from 1955 to 1962.
Blue finish . . . . NiB $680 Ex $575 Gd $383
Nickel finish. . . . . .NiB $1330 Ex $1080 Gd $610

WICHITA ARMS — Wichita, Kansas

CLASSIC PISTOL
Caliber: Chambered to order. Bolt-action, single-shot. 11.25-inch octagonal bbl., 18 inches overall. Weight: 78 oz. Open micro sights. Custom-grade checkered walnut stock. Blued finish. Made from 1980 to 1997.
Standard . . . . .NiB $3310 Ex $2546 Gd $2245
Presentation grade
(engraved) . . . . .NiB $5379 Ex $3916 Gd $2166

HIUNTER PISTOL . . . . . . .NiB $1433 Ex $1096 Gd $872
Bolt-action, single-shot. Calibers: .22 LR, .22 WRF, 7mm Super Mag., 7-30 Waters, .30-30 Win., .32 H&R Mag., .357 Mag., .357 Super Mag. 10.5-inch bbl., 16.5 inches overall, weight: 60 oz. No sights (scope mount only). Stainless steel finish. Walnut stock. Made from 1983 to 1994.

INTERNATIONAL PISTOL . . NiB $733 Ex $567 Gd $453
Top-break, single-shot. SA. Calibers: 7-30 Waters, 7mm Super Mag., 7R (.30-30 Win. necked to 7mm), .30-30 Win. .357 Mag., .357 Super Mag., .32 H&R Mag., .22 Mag., .22 LR. 10- and 14-inch bbl. (10.5 inch for centerfire calibers). Weight: 50-71 oz. Partridge front sight, adj. rear. Walnut forend and grips.

MK-40 SILHOUETTE PISTOLNiB $1613 Ex $1407 Gd $1206
Calibers: .22-250, 7mm IHMSA, .308 Win. Bolt-action, single-shot. 13-inch bbl., 19.5 inches overall. Weight: 72 oz. Wichita Multi-Range sight system. Aluminum receiver w/blued bbl., gray Fiberthane glass stock. Made from 1981 to 1994.

SILHOUETTE
PISTOL (WSP) . . . . NiB $1587 Ex. . $1453 Gd $1356
Calibers: .22-250, 7mm IHMSA 308 Win. Bolt-action, single-shot. 14.94-inch bbl., 21.38 inches overall. Weight: 72 oz. Wichita Multi-Range sight system. Blued finish. Walnut or gray Fiberthane glass stock. Walnut center or rear grip. Made from 1979 to 1994.

WILKINSON ARMS — Parma, Idaho (2000-2005)

LINDA SEMI-AUTOMATIC PISTOLNiB $680 Ex $557 Gd $360
Caliber: 9mm Para. 31-round magazine, 8.25-inch bbl., 12.25 inches overall. Weight: 77 oz. Rear peep sight w/blade front. Blued finish. Checkered composition grips.

SHERRY SEMI-AUTOMATIC PISTOLNiB $274 Ex $188 Gd $126
Caliber: .22 LR. Eight-round magazine, 2.13-inch bbl., 4.38 inches overall. Weight: 9.25 oz. Crossbolt safety. Fixed sights. Blued or blue-gold finish. Checkered composition grips.

DIANE SEMI-AUTOMATIC PISTOLNiB $160 Ex $97 Gd $55
Caliber: .25 ACP, 6-round magazine, 2.125-inch bbl., matte blue.nches overall. Weight: 77 oz. Rear peep sight w/blade front. Blued finish. Checkered composition grips.

36th Edition
GUN TRADER'S GUIDE

Rifles

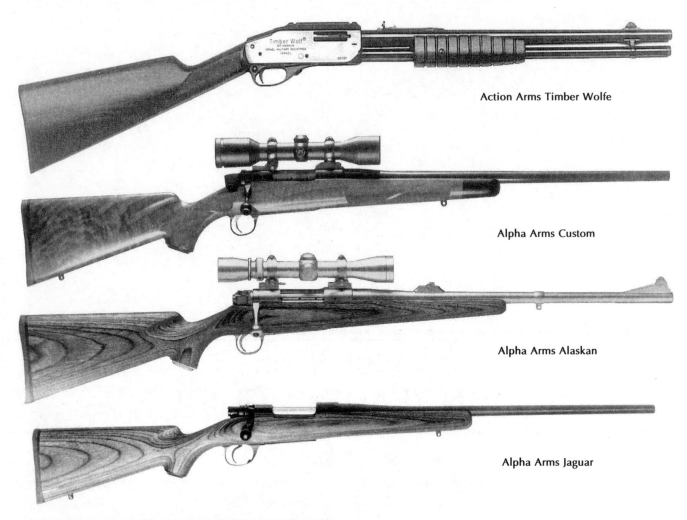

Action Arms Timber Wolfe

Alpha Arms Custom

Alpha Arms Alaskan

Alpha Arms Jaguar

A.A. ARMS — Monroe, North Carolina

AR-9 SEMIAUTOMATIC CARBINE NiB $805 Ex $641 Gd $439
Semiautomatic recoil-operated rifle w/side-folding metal stock design. Fires from a closed bolt. Caliber: 9mm Parabellum. 20-round magazine. 16.25-inch bbl., 33 inches overall. Weight: 6.5 lbs. Fixed blade, protected postfront sight adjustable for elevation, winged square notched rear. Matte phosphate/blue or nickel finish. Checkered polymer grip/frame. Made 1991 to 1994 (banned)

ACTION ARMS — Philadelphia, Pennsylvania

MODEL B SPORTER
SEMI-AUTOMATIC CARBINE . NiB $650 Ex $572 Gd $380
Similar to Uzi Carbine (see separate listing) except w/thumbhole stock. Caliber: 9mm Parabellum, 10-round magazine. 16-inch bbl. Weight: 8.75 lbs. Post front sight; adj. rear. Imported 1994.

TIMBERWOLF REPEATING RIFLE
Calibers: .357 Mag./.38 Special and .44 Mag. slide-action. Tubular magazine holds 10 and 8 rounds, respectively. 18.5-inch bbl. 36.5 inches overall. Weight: 5.5 lbs. Fixed blade front sight; adj. rear. Receiver w/integral scope mounts. Checkered walnut stock. Imported from 1989 to 1993, later by I.M.I. Israel.

Blued model. . . . . NiB $338 Ex $271 Gd $190
Chrome model, add $75
.44 Mag., add. $126

ALPHA ARMS, INC. — Dallas, Texas

CUSTOM BOLT-ACTION RIFLE. . . NiB $1707 Ex $1335 Gd $876
Calibers: .17 Rem. thru .338 Win. Mag. Right or left-hand action in three action lengths w/three-lug locking system and 60-degree bolt rotation. 20- to 24-inch round or octagonal bbl. Weight: 6 to 7 lbs. No sights. Presentation-grade California Claro walnut stock w/hand-rubbed oil finish, custom inletted sling swivels and ebony forend tip. Made from 1984 to 1987.

ALASKAN BOLT-ACTION RIFLE . . NiB $1706 Ex $1337 Gd $869
Similar to Custom model but w/stainless-steel bbl. and receiver w/all other parts coated w/Nitex. Weight: 6.75 to 7.25 lbs. Open sights w/ bbl-band sling swivel. Classic-style Alpha wood stock w/Niedner-style steel grip cap and solid recoil pad. Made from 1985 to 1987.

GRAND SLAM
BOLT-ACTION RIFLE . . . . . NiB $1322 Ex $1065 Gd $795
Same as Custom model but has Alphawood (fiberglass and wood) classic-style stock featuring Niedner-style grip cap. Wt: 6.5 lbs. Left-hand models same value. Made 1985 to 1987.

CUSTOM BOLT-ACTION RIFLE
Same as Custom Rifle except designed on Mauser-style action w/ claw extractor drilled and tapped for scope. Originally designated Alpha Model 1. Calibers: .243, 7mm-08, .308 original chambering (1984 to 1985) up to .338 Win. Mag. in standard model; .338 thru .458 Win. Mag. in Big Five model (1987). Teflon-coated trigger guard/floorplate assembly. Made from1984 to 1987.

Jaguar Grade I . . . . NiB $1035 Ex $855 Gd $624
Jaguar Grade II . . . . NiB $1268 Ex $684 Gd $707
Jaguar Grade III . . . . NiB $1319 Ex $1046 Gd $756
Jaguar Grade IV . . . . NiB $1424 Ex $1056 Gd $755
Big Five model . . . . NiB $1717 Ex $1198 Gd $977

AMERICAN ARMS — N. Kansas City, Missouri

1860 HENRY . . . . NiB $926 Ex $698 Gd $530
Replica of 1860 Henry rifle. Calibers: .44-40 or .45 LC. 24.25-inch half-octagonal bbl. 43.75 inches overall. Weight: 9.25 lbs. Brass frame and appointments. Straight-grip walnut buttstock.

1866 WINCHESTER
Replica of 1866 Winchester. Calibers: .44-40 or .45 LC. 19-inch round tapered bbl. (carbine) or 24.25-inch tapered octagonal bbl. (rifle). 38 to 43.25 inches overall. Weight: 7.75 or 8.15 lbs. Brass frame, elevator and buttplate. Walnut buttstock and forend.
Carbine . . . . NiB $743 Ex $625 Gd $409
Rifle. . . . . NiB $743 Ex $625 Gd $409

1873 WINCHESTER
Replica of 1873 Winchester rifle. Calibers: .44-40 or .45 LC. 24.25-inch tapered octagonal bbl. w/tubular magazine. Color casehardened steel frame w/brass elevator and ejection port cover. Walnut buttstock w/steel buttplate.
Standard model . . . . NiB $876 Ex $710 Gd $419
Deluxe model. . . . . NiB $1141 Ex $924 Gd $640

AMERICAN SPIRIT ARMS CORP. — Scottsdale, Arizona

ASA BULL BARREL FLATTOP RIFLE NiB $1043 Ex $709 Gd $533
Semi-automatic. Caliber: ..223 Rem. Patterned after AR-15. Forged steel lower receiver, aluminum flattop upper receiver, 24-inch stainless bull barrel, free-floating aluminum hand guard, includes Harris bipod.

ASA BULL BARREL A2 RIFLE. . . . NiB $989 Ex $733 Gd $535
Similar to Flattop Rifle except has A2 upper receiver with carrying handle and sights. Introduced 1999.

OPEN MATCH RIFLE . . . . NiB $1471 Ex $1097 Gd $745
Caliber: .223 Rem. Bbl.: 16-inch fluted and ported stainless steel match with round shroud. Flattop without sights, forged upper and lower receiver, match trigger. Introduced 2001.

LIMITED MATCH RIFLE . . . . . . NiB $1411 Ex $909 Gd $579
Caliber: .223 Rem. Bbl.: 16-inch fluted stainless steel match with round shroud. National Match front and rear sights; match trigger.

DCM SERVICE RIFLE. . . . . NiB $1412 Ex $915 Gd $618
Caliber: .223 Rem. Bbl.: 20-inch stainless steel match type with free-floating shroud. National Match front and rear sights; match trigger; pistol grip.

ASA M4 RIFLE . . . . NiB $944 Ex $679 Gd $482
Caliber: .223 Rem. Non-collapsible stock, M4 hand guard, 16-inch bbl. w/muzzle brake; aluminum flattop upper receiver.

ASA A2 RIFLE. . . . . NiB $926 Ex $633 Gd $509
Caliber: .223 Rem. A2 receiver; 20-inch National Match barrel. Intro. 1999.

ASA CARBINE . . . . NiB $1077 Ex $707 Gd $589
Caliber: .223 Rem. or Short. Side-charging, flattop receiver; M4 hand guard; 16-inch National Match bbl. w/slotted muzzle brake.

POST-BAN CARBINE . . . . NiB $909 Ex $690 Gd $482
Caliber: .223 Rem. Wilson 16-inch National Match bbl.; non-collapsible stock. Introduced 1999.

BULL BARREL A2 INVADER . . . . NiB $1032 Ex $710 Gd $544
Caliber: .223 Rem. Similar to ASA 24-inch bull bbl. rifle except has 16-inch stainless steel bbl.. Introduced 1999.

A2 CAR CARBINE. . . . . NiB $1041 Ex $703 Gd $544
Caliber: 9mm Parabellum. Forged receiver, non-collapsible stock. Bbl.: 16-inch Wilson w/o muzzle brake, bird cage flash hider (pre-ban) or muzzle brake (post-ban).

FLATTOP CAR RIFLE . . . . NiB $1041 Ex $703 Gd $544
Caliber: 9mm Parabellum. Similar to A2 CAR Rifle except flattop design w/o sights. Introduced 2002.

ASA TACTICAL RIFLE . . . . NiB $1788 Ex $1096 Gd $780
Caliber: .308 Win. Bbl.: 16-inch stainless steel regular or match; side-charging handle; pistol grip.
Match model (w/fluted bbl. match trigger, chrome finish) Add $525

ASA 24-INCH MATCH RIFLE . . NiB $1806 Ex $1106 Gd $789
Caliber: .308 Win. Bbl.: 24-inch stainless steel match with or w/o fluting/porting. Side-charging handle; pistol grip. Introduced 2002.

AMT (ARCADIA MACHINE & TOOL) — Irwindale, California (1998)

BOLT-ACTION REPEATING RIFLE
Winchester-type push-feed or Mauser-type controlled-feed short-, medium- or long-action. Calibers: .223 Remington, .22-250 Remington, .243 A, .243 Winchester, 6mm PPC, .25-06 Remington, 6.5x08, .270 Winchester, 7x57 Mauser, 7mm-08 Remington, 7mm Remington Mag., 7.62x39mm, .308 Winchester, .30-06, .300 Winchester Mag., .338 Winchester Mag., .375 H&H, .416 Remington, .416 Rigby, .458 Winchester Mag. 22- to 28-inch number 3 contour bbl. Weight: 7.75 to 8.5 lbs. Sights: None furnished; drilled and tapped for scope mounts. Classic composite or Kevlar stock. Made from 1996 to 1997.
Standard model . . . . NiB $899 Ex $720 Gd $531
Deluxe model. . . . . NiB $1087 Ex $830 Gd $529

BOLT-ACTION SINGLE-SHOT RIFLE
Winchester-type cone breech push-feed or Mauser-type controlled-feed action. Calibers: .22 Hornet, .22 PPC, .222 Remington, .223 Remington, .22-250 Remington, .243 A, .243 Winchester, 6mm PPC, 6.5x08, .270 Win., 7mm-08 Remington, .308 Winchester 22- to 28-inch #3 contour bbl. Weight: 7.75 to 8.5 lbs. Sights: None furnished; drilled and tapped for scope mounts. Classic composite or Kevlar stock. Made from1996.
Standard model . . . . NiB $865 Ex $733 Gd $520
Deluxe model. . . . . NiB $1077 Ex $744 Gd $500

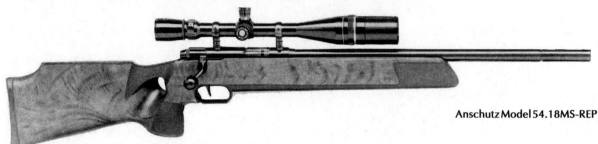

Anschutz Model 54.18MS-REP

CHALLENGER AUTOLOADING TARGET RIFLE SERIES I, II & III
Similar to Small Game Hunter except w/McMillan target fiberglass stock. Caliber: .22 LR. 10-round magazine. 16.5-, 18-, 20- or 22-inch bull bbl. Drilled and tapped for scope mount; no sights. Stainless steel finish. Made from 1994 to 1998.
Challenger I Standard . . . . NiB $822 Ex $577 Gd $409
Challenger II w/muzzle brake . NiB $926 Ex $755 Gd $554
Challenger III w/bbl extension . NiB $976 Ex $588 Gd $452
W/jeweled trigger, add $227

LIGHTNING 25/22
AUTOLOADING RIFLE . . . . . . NiB $316 Ex $237 Gd $170
Caliber: .22 LR. 25-round magazine. 18-inch tapered or bull bbl. Weight: 6 lbs. 37 inches overall. Sights: Adj. rear; ramp front. Folding stainless-steel stock w/matte finish. Made 1986 to 1993.

SMALL GAME HUNTER SERIES
Similar to AMT 25/22 except w/conventional matte black fiberglass/nylon stock. 10-round rotary magazine. 22-inch bbl. 40.5 inches overall. Weight: 6 lbs. Grooved for scope; no sights. Made from 1986 to 1994 (Series I), and 1993 (Series II).
Hunter I . . . . NiB $333 Ex $218 Gd $155
Hunter II (w/22-inch
heavy target bbl.) . . . . NiB $269 Ex $223 Gd $159

MAGNUM HUNTER AUTO RIFLE . . NiB $495 Ex $455 Gd $240
Similar to Lightning Small Game Hunter II model except chambered in .22 WRF w/22-inch match-grade bbl. Made from 1995 to 1998.

ANSCHUTZ RIFLES — Ulm, Germany.
Currently imported by Merkel USA.

Anschutz models 1407 ISU, 1408-ED, 1411, 1413, 1418, 1432, 1433, 1518 and 1533 were marketed in the U.S. by Savage Arms. Further, Anschutz models 1403, 1416, 1422D, 1441, 1516 and 1522D were sold as Savage/Anschutz with Savage model designations (see also listings under Savage Arms)

MODEL 54.18MS . . . . NiB $1300 Ex $899 Gd $469
Bolt-action, single-shot, Caliber: .22 LR. 22-inch bbl. European hardwood stock w/cheekpiece. Stipple-checkered forend and Wundhammer swell pistol-grip. Receiver grooved, drilled and tapped for scope blocks. Weight: 8.4 lbs. Imported 1982 to 1997.

MODEL 54.18MS-REP REPEATING RIFLE
Same as model 54.18MS except w/repeating action and 5-round magazine. 22- to 30-inch bbl. 41-49 inches overall. Avg. weight: 7 lbs., 12 oz. Hardwood or synthetic gray thumbhole stock. Imported from 1989 to 1997.
Standard MS-REP model . . . NiB $2050 Ex $1569 Gd $880
Left-hand model . . . . NiB $2070 Ex $1579 Gd $790

MODEL 64S BOLT-ACTION SINGLE-SHOT RIFLE
Bolt-action, single-shot. Caliber: .22 LR. 26-inch bbl. Checkered European hardwood stock w/Wundhammer swell pistol-grip and adj. buttplate. Single-stage trigger. Aperture sights. Weight: 8.25 lbs. Imported from 1963 to 1981.
Standard . . . . NiB $480 Ex $370 Gd $250
Left-hand model . . . . NiB $480 Ex $370 Gd $250

MODEL 64MS BOLT-ACTION SINGLE-SHOT RIFLE
Bolt-action, single-shot. Caliber: .22 LR. 21.25-inch bbl. European hardwood silhouette-style stock w/cheekpiece. Forend base and Wundhammer swell pistol-grip, stipple-checkered. Adj. two-stage trigger. Receiver grooved, drilled and tapped for scope blocks. Weight: 8 lbs. Imported from 1982 to 1996.
Standard or Featherweight
(disc. 1988) . . . . NiB $1133 Ex $780 Gd $620
Left-hand model . . . . NiB $1133 Ex $780 Gd $620

MODEL 64MSR BOLT-ACTION REPEATER
Similar to Anschutz Model 64MS except repeater w/5-round magazine. Imported from 1996.
Standard model . . . . NiB $1045 Ex $789 Gd $603
Left-hand model . . . . NiB $1045 Ex $789 Gd $603

MODEL 520/61 SEMIAUTOMATIC . . NiB $331 Ex $270 Gd $167
Caliber: .22 LR. 10-round magazine. 24-inch bbl. Sights: Folding leaf rear, hooded ramp front. Receiver grooved for scope mounting. Rotary-style safety. Monte Carlo stock and beavertail forend, checkered. Weight: 6.5 lbs. Imported from 1982 to 1983.

MODEL 525 AUTOLOADER
Caliber: .22 LR. 10-round magazine. 20- or 24-inch bbl. 39 to 43 inches overall. Weight: 6.1 to 6.5 lbs. Adj. folding rear sight; hooded ramp front. Checkered European hardwood Monte Carlo style buttstock and beavertail forend. Sling swivel studs. Imported 1984 to 1995.
Carbine model
(disc. 1986) . . . . NiB $430 Ex $324 Gd $227
Rifle model (24-inch bbl.) . . . . NiB $500 Ex $443 Gd $319

MODEL 1403B . . . . NiB $904 Ex $745 Gd $440
A lighter-weight model designed for Biathlon competition. Caliber: .22 LR. 21.5-inch bbl. Adj. two-stage trigger. Adj. grooved wood buttplate, stipple-checkered deep thumb-rest flute and straight pistol-grip. Weight: 9 lbs. w/sights. Imported from 1990 to 1992.

MODEL 1403D MATCH SINGLE-SHOT TARGET RIFLE
Caliber: .22 LR. 25-inch bbl. 43 inches overall. Weight: 8.6 lbs. No sights, receiver grooved for Anschutz target sights. Walnut-finished hardwood target stock w/adj. buttplate. Importation disc. 1992.
Standard model . . . . NiB $707 Ex $567 Gd $417
W/match sights . . . . NiB $988 Ex $779 Gd $555

Anschutz Model 1416D

Anschutz Model 1418

Anschutz Model 1422D

MODEL 1407 I.S.U. MATCH 54 RIFLE
Bolt-action, single-shot, caliber: .22 LR. 26.88-inch bbl. Scope bases. Receiver grooved for Anschutz sights. Single-stage adj. trigger. Select walnut target stock w/deep forearm for position shooting, adj. buttplate, hand stop and swivel. Weight: 10 lbs. Imported 1970 to 1981.

Standard model	NiB $653	Ex $535	Gd $291
Left-hand model	NiB $653	Ex $535	Gd $291
W/international sights, add			$75

MODEL 1408 . . . . NiB $466 Ex $408 Gd $370
Bolt-action, single-shot, caliber: .22 LR. 23.5-inch bbl. w/sliding weights. No metallic sights. Receiver drilled and tapped for scope-sight bases. Single-stage adj. trigger. Oversize bolt knob. Select walnut stock w/thumbhole, adj. comb and buttplate. Weight: 9.5 lbs. Intro. 1976. Disc. Add $175 for ED model.

MODEL 1411 MATCH 54 RIFLE
Bolt-action, single-shot. Caliber: .22 LR. 27.5-inch extra heavy bbl. w/mounted scope bases. Receiver grooved for Anschutz sights. Single-stage adj. trigger. Select walnut target stock w/cheekpiece (adj. in 1973 and later production), full pistol-grip, beavertail fore-arm, adj. buttplate, hand stop and swivel. Model 1411-L has left-hand stock. Weight: 11 lbs. Disc.

W/Non-adj. cheekpiece	NiB $678	Ex $423	Gd $269
W/adj. cheekpiece	NiB $703	Ex $532	Gd $402
with Anschutz			
International Sight set, add			$300

MODEL 1413 SUPER MATCH 54 RIFLE
Freestyle international target rifle w/specifications similar to those of Model 1411, except w/special stock w/thumbhole, adj. pistol grip, adj. cheekpiece in 1973 and later production, adj. hook buttplate, adj. palmrest. Model 1413-L has left-hand stock. Weight: 15.5 lbs. Disc.

W/non-adj. cheekpiece	NiB $830	Ex $733	Gd $400
W/adj. cheekpiece	NiB $704	Ex $572	Gd $399
With Anschutz			
International sight set, add			$300

MODEL 1416D . . . . NiB $790 Ex $577 Gd $368
Bolt-action sporter. Caliber: .22 LR. 22.5-inch bbl. Sights: Folding leaf rear; hooded ramp front. Receiver grooved for scope mounting. Select European stock w/cheekpiece, skip-checkered pistol grip and forearm. Weight: 6 lbs. Imported 1982 to 2007.

MODEL 1416D CLASSIC/CUSTOM SPORTERS
Same as Model 1416D except w/American classic-style stock (Classic) or modified European-style stock w/Monte Carlo roll-over cheekpiece and Schnabel forend (Custom). Weight: 5.5 lbs. (Classic); 6 lbs. (Custom). Imported 1986 to 2007.

Model 1416D Classic	NiB $995	Ex $549	Gd $380
Model 1416D Classic, "True" left-hand	NiB $1095	Ex $577	Gd $419
Model 1416D Custom	NiB $980	Ex $750	Gd $380
Model 1416D fiberglass (1991-92)	NiB $760	Ex $623	Gd $445

MODEL 1418 BOLT-ACTION
SPORTER . . . . NiB $452 Ex $352 Gd $200
Caliber: .22 LR. 5- or 10-round magazine. 19.75-inch bbl. Sights: Folding leaf rear; hooded ramp front. Receiver grooved for scope mounting. Select walnut stock, Mannlicher type w/cheekpiece, pistol-grip and forearm skip checkered. Weight: 5.5 lbs. Intro. 1976. Disc.

MODEL 1418D BOLT-ACTION
SPORTER . . . . NiB $1008 Ex $886 Gd $533
Caliber: .22 LR. 5- or 10-round magazine. 19.75-inch bbl. European walnut Monte Carlo stock, Mannlicher type w/cheekpiece, pistol-grip and forend skip-line checkered, buffalo horn Schnabel tip. Weight: 5.5 lbs. Imported from 1982 to 1995 and 1998 to 2003.

MODEL 1422D CLASSIC/CUSTOM RIFLE
Bolt-action sporter. Caliber: .22 LR. Five-round removable straight-feed clip magazine. 24-inch bbl. Sights: Folding leaf rear; hooded ramp front. Select European walnut stock, classic type (Classic); Monte Carlo w/hand-carved rollover cheekpiece (Custom). Weight: 7.25 lbs. (Classic) 6.5 lbs. (Custom). Imported 1982 to 1989.

Model 1422D Classic	NiB $833	Ex $670	Gd $432
Model 1422D Custom	NiB $896	Ex $833	Gd $479

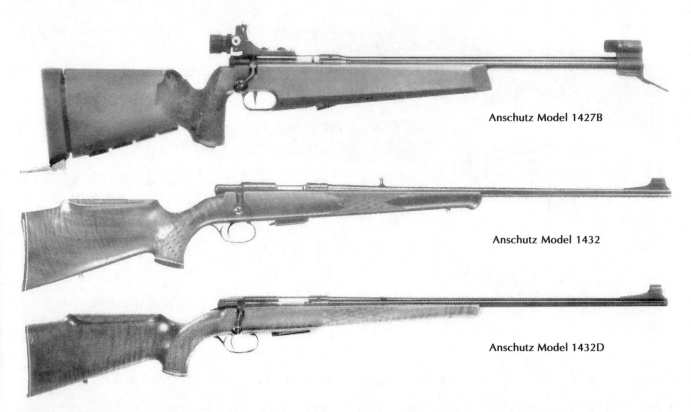

Anschutz Model 1427B

Anschutz Model 1432

Anschutz Model 1432D

MODEL 1827B BIATHLON RIFLE NiB $1943 Ex $1377 Gd $937
Bolt-action clip repeater. Caliber: .22 LR. 21.5-inch bbl. Two-stage trigger w/wing-type safety. Hardwood stock w/deep fluting, pistol grip and deep forestock with adj. hand stop rail. Target sights w/adjustable weights. Advertised in 1981 but imported from 1982 to date as Model 1827B.

MODEL 1430D MATCH . . . . . NiB $976 Ex $650 Gd $429
Improved version of Model 64S. Bolt-action, single-shot. Caliber: .22 LR. 26-inch medium-heavy bbl. Walnut Monte Carlo stock w/cheekpiece, adj. buttplate, deep midstock tapered to forend. Pistol-grip and contoured thumb groove w/stipple checkering. Single-stage adj. trigger. Target sights. Weight: 8.38 lbs. Imported from 1982 to 1990.

MODEL 1432 BOLT-ACTION SPORTER
Caliber: .22 Hornet. 5-round box magazine. 24-inch bbl. Sights: Folding leaf rear, hooded ramp front. Receiver grooved for scope mounting. Select walnut stock w/Monte Carlo comb and cheekpiece, pistol-grip and forearm skip-checkered. Weight: 6.75 lbs. Imported from 1974 to 1987. (Reintroduced as 1707/1730 series)
Early model
(1974-85). . . . . NiB $1347 Ex $988 Gd $721
Late model
(1985-87). . . . . NiB $1145 Ex $933 Gd $631

MODEL 1432D CLASSIC/CUSTOM RIFLE
Bolt-action sporter similar to Model 1422D except chambered for Caliber: .22 Hornet. 4-round magazine. 23.5-inch bbl. Weight: 7.75 lbs. (Classic); 6.5 lbs. (Custom). Classic stock on Classic model; fancy-grade Monte Carlo w/hand-carved rollover cheekpiece (Custom). Imported from 1982 to 1987. (Reintroduced as 1707/1730 series)
Model 1432D Classic . . . . . . NiB $1347 Ex $982 Gd $733
Model 1432D Custom. . . . . . NiB $1175 Ex $923 Gd $634

MODEL 1433 BOLT-ACTION SPORTER NiB $1131 Ex $916 Gd $650
Caliber: .22 Hornet. 5-round box magazine. 19.75-inch bbl. Sights: Folding leaf rear, hooded ramp front. Receiver grooved for scope mounting. Single-stage or double-set trigger. Select walnut Mannlicher stock; cheekpiece, pistol-grip and forearm skip-checkered. Weight: 6.5 lbs. Imported from 1976 to 1986.

MODEL 1448D. . . . . NiB $421 Ex $324 Gd $236
Similar to Model 1449 except chambered for Caliber: .22 LR. w/22.5-inch smooth bore bbl. and no sights. Walnut-finished hardwood stock. Imported from 1999 to 2001.

MODEL 1449D YOUTH SPORTERNiB $300 Ex $233 Gd $177
Bolt-action sporter version of Model 2000. Caliber: .22 LR. 5-round box magazine. 16.25-inch bbl. Weight: 3.5 lbs. Hooded ramp front sight, addition. Walnut-finished hardwood stock. Imported from 1990 to 1991.

MODEL 1450B TARGET RIFLE . . . . . NiB $703 Ex $533 Gd $397
Biathlon rifle developed on 2000 Series action. 19.5-inch bbl. Weight: 5.5 lbs. Adj. buttplate. Target sights. Imported from 1993 to 1994.

MODEL 1451 E/R SPORTER/TARGET
Bolt-action, single-shot (1451E) or repeater (1451R). Caliber: .22 LR. 22- or 22.75-inch bbl. w/o sights. Select hardwood stock w/stippled pistolgrip and vented forearm. beavertail forend, adj. cheekpiece, and deep thumb flute. Weight: 6.5 lbs. Imported from 1996 to 2001.
Model 1451E (disc. 1997) . . . NiB $487 Ex $370 Gd $254
Model 1451R . . . . NiB $479 Ex $455 Gd $310

MODEL 1451D CLASSIC/CUSTOM RIFLE
Same as Model 1451R except w/walnut-finished hardwood stock (Classic) or modified European-style walnut stock w/Monte Carlo rollover cheekpiece and Schnabel forend (Custom). Weight: 5 lbs. Imported from 1998 to 2001.
Model 1451D Classic (Super) . NiB $367 Ex $288 Gd $199
Model 1451D Custom. . . . . . . NiB $488 Ex $455 Gd $321

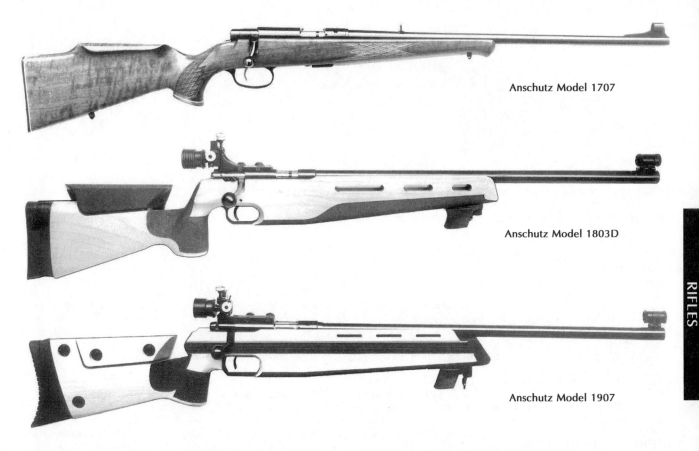

Anschutz Model 1707

Anschutz Model 1803D

Anschutz Model 1907

MODEL 1451 ST- R RIFLE. . . . NiB $499 Ex $454 Gd $342
Same as Model 1451R except w/two-stage trigger and walnut-finished hardwood uncheckered stock. Imported 1996 to 2001.

MODEL 1516D CLASSIC/CUSTOM RIFLE
Same as Model 1416D except chambered for Caliber: .22 Magnum RF, with American classic-style stock (Classic) or modified European-style stock w/Monte Carlo rollover cheekpiece and Schnabel forend (Custom). Weight: 5.5 lbs. (Classic), 6 lbs. (Custom). Imported from 1986 to 2003.
Model 1516D Classic . . . . NiB $704 Ex $572 Gd $379
Model 1516D Custom. . . . . . . NiB $639 Ex $600 Gd $423

MODELS 1516D/1518D LUXUS RIFLES
The alpha designation for these models was changed from Custom to Luxus in 1996 to 1998. (See Custom listings for Luxus values.)

MODELS 1518/1518D SPORTING RIFLES
Same as Model 1418 except chambered for .22 Magnum RF, 4-round box magazine. Model 1518 intro. 1976. Disc. Model 1518D has full Mannlicher-type stock. Imported from 1982 to 2001.
Model 1518 . . . . NiB $766 Ex $650 Gd $423
Model 1518D. . . . . NiB $974 Ex $788 Gd $544
W/set trigger, add. $150

MODEL 1522D CLASSIC/CUSTOM RIFLE
Same as Model 1422D except chambered for .22 Magnum RF, 4-round magazine. Weight: 6.5 lbs. (Custom). Fancy-grade Classic or Monte Carlo stock w/hand-carved rollover cheekpiece. Imported 1982 to 1989. (Reintroduced as 1707D/1730D series)
Model 1522D Classic . . . . . . NiB $1197 Ex $869 Gd $633
Model 1522D Custom. . . . . . NiB $1197 Ex $869 Gd $633

MODEL 1532D CLASSIC/CUSTOM RIFLE
Same as Model 1432D except chambered for .222 Rem. Three-round mag. Weight: 6.5 lbs. (Custom). Classic stock on Classic Model; fancy-grade Monte Carlo stock w/handcarved rollover cheekpiece (Custom). Imported from 1982 to 1989. (Reintroduced as 1707D/174 D0 series)
Model 1532D Classic . . . . . . NiB $1019 Ex $795 Gd $448
Model 1532D Custom. . . . . . NiB $1297 Ex $996 Gd $698

MODEL 1533 . . . . NiB $1090 Ex $844 Gd $589
Same as Model 1433 except chambered for .222 Rem. Three-shot box magazine. Imported from 1976 to 1994.

MODEL 1707 SERIES BOLT-ACTION REPEATER
Match 54 Sporter. Calibers: .22 LR, .22 Mag., .22 Hornet, .222 Rem. Five-shot removable magazine 24-inch bbl. 43 inches overall. Weight: 7.5 lbs. Folding leaf rear sight, hooded ramp front. Select European walnut stock w/cheekpiece and Schnabel forend tip. Imported from 1989 to 2001.
Standard Model 1707
Bavarian — rimfire cal. . . . . NiB $1018 Ex $933 Gd $580
Standard Model 1707
Bavarian — centerfire cal. . . . . NiB $1342 Ex $1056 Gd $697
Model 1707D Classic (Classic
stock, 6.75 lbs.) rimfire cal. . . . . NiB $1179 Ex $994 Gd $698
Model 1707D Classic — centerfire cal.NiB $1279 Ex $1044 Gd $748
Model 1707D Custom — rimfire cal. . . NiB $1094 Ex $893 Gd $633
Model 1707D Custom — centerfire cal.NiB $1332 Ex $1088 Gd $775
Model 1707D Graphite Cust. (McMillan graphite
reinforced stock, 22-inch bbl., intro. 1991)NiB $1156 Ex $985 Gd $641
Select walnut and gold trigger, add $200
Model 1707 FWT (featherweight, 6.5 lbs.) –
rimfire cal. . . . . NiB $1122 Ex $909 Gd $641
Model 1707 FWT — centerfire cal. . . NiB $1289 Ex $1136 Gd $703

Anschutz Model 2013

MODEL 1733D MANNLICHER . . . NiB $1370 Ex $1168 Gd $860
Same as Model 1707D except w/19-inch bbl. and Mannlicher-style stock. 39 inches overall. Weight: 6.25 lbs. Imported from 1993 to 1995 (Reintroduced in 1998, disc. 2001).

MODEL 1740 MONTE CARLO SPORTER
Caliber: .22 Hornet or .222 Rem. Three and 5-round magazines respectively. 24-inch bbl. 43.25 inches overall. Weight: 6.5 lbs. Hooded ramp front, folding leaf rear. Drilled and tapped for scope mounts. Select European walnut stock w/roll-over cheekpiece, checkered grip and forend. Imported from 1998 to 2006.
Model 1740 Classic
(Meistergrade) . . . . NiB $1504 Ex $1237 Gd $866
Model 1740 Custom . . . . . NiB $1370 Ex $1089 Gd $733

MODEL 1743 MONTE CARLO
SPORTER . . . . NiB $1370 Ex $1132 Gd $769
Similar to Model 1740 except w/Mannlicher full stock. Imported from 1997 to 2001.

MODEL 1903D MATCH SINGLE-SHOT TARGET RIFLE
Caliber: .22 LR. 25.5-inch bbl. 43.75 inches overall. Weight: 8.5 lbs. No sights; receiver grooved, drilled and tapped for scope mounts. Blonde or walnut-finished hardwood stock w/adj. cheekpiece, stippled grip and forend. Left-hand version. Imported 1987 to 1993.
Right-hand model
(Reintroduced as 1903D) . . . NiB $1006 Ex $844 Gd $544
Left-hand model . . . . NiB $1108 Ex $866 Gd $633

MODEL 1807 ISU
STANDARD MATCH. . . . . NiB $1359 Ex $1094 Gd $708
Bolt-action single-shot. Caliber: 22 LR. 26-inch bbl. Improved Super Match 54 action. Two-stage match trigger. Removable cheekpiece, adj. buttplate, thumbpiece and forestock w/stipple-checkered. Weight: 10 lbs. Imported 1982 to 1988. (Reintroduced as 1907 ISU)

MODEL 1808ED SUPER RUNNING TARGET
Bolt-action single-shot. Caliber: .22 LR. 23.5-inch bbl. w/sliding weights. Improved Super Match 54 action. Heavy beavertail forend w/adj.cheekpiece and buttplate. Adj. single-stage trigger. Weight: 9.5 lbs. Imported from 1982 to 1998.
Right-hand model . . . . NiB $1677 Ex $1328 Gd $869
Left-hand model . . . . NiB $1688 Ex $1377 Gd $973

MODEL 1808MS-R
METALLIC SILHOUETTE . . . NiB $2021 Ex $1565 Gd $932
Bolt-action repeater. Caliber: .22 LR. 19.2-inch bbl. w/o sights. Thumbhole Monte Carlo stock w/grooved forearm enhanced w/ "Anschutz" logo. Weight: 8.2 lbs. Imported from 1998 to date.

MODEL 1810 SUPER MATCH II . . NiB $1979 Ex $1440 Gd $937
A less detailed version of the Super Match 1813 model. Tapered forend w/deep receiver area. Select European hardwood stock. Weight: 13.5 lbs. Imported from 1982 to 1988 (reintroduced as 1910 series).

MODEL 1811 PRONE MATCH . . . NiB $1843 Ex $1623 Gd $877
Bolt-action single-shot. Caliber: .22 LR. 27.5-inch bbl. Improved Super Match 54 action. Select European hardwood stock w/ beavertail forend, adj. cheekpiece, and deep thumb flute. Thumb groove and pistol grip w/stipple checkering. Adj. buttplate. Weight: 11.5 lbs. Imported 1982 to 1988. (Reintroduced as 1911 Prone Match)

MODEL 1813 SUPER MATCH. . . . NiB $2281 Ex $1951 Gd $869
Bolt-action single-shot. Caliber: .22 LR. 27.5-inch bbl. Improved Super Match 54 action w/light firing pin, one-point adj. trigger. European walnut thumbhole stock, adj. palm rest, forend and pistol grip stipple checkered. Adj. cheekpiece and hook buttplate. Weight: 15.5 lbs. Imported from 1979 to 1988. (Reintroduced as 1913 Super Match)

MODEL 1827B BIATHLON RIFLE
Bolt-action clip repeater. Caliber: .22 LR. 21.5-inch bbl. 42.5 inches overall. Weight: 8.5 to 9 lbs. Slide safety. Adj. target sight set w/ snow caps. European walnut stock w/cheekpiece, stippled pistol grip and forearm w/adj. weights. Fortner straight pull bolt option offered in 1986. Imported from 1982 to date.
Mdl. 1827B w/Sup. Mat. 54 action NiB $2359 Ex $2153 Gd $1020
Model 1827B, left-hand . . . . . . NiB $2101 Ex $1716 Gd $1224
Model 1827BT w/Fortner
Option, right-hand . . . . NiB $2467 Ex $2261 Gd $1032
Model 1827BT, left-hand . . . . . NiB $2604 Ex $2127 Gd $1513
Model 1827BT w/laminated stock, add $175
W/stainless steel bbl., add $205

MODEL 1907 ISU INTERNATIONAL MATCH RIFLE
Updated version of Model 1807 w/same general specifications as Model 1913 except w/26-inch bbl. 44.5 inches overall. Weight: 11 lbs. Designed for ISU 3-position competition. Fitted w/vented beechwood or walnut, blonde or color-laminated stock. Imported from 1989 to date.
Right-hand model . . . . NiB $1544 Ex $1353 Gd $838
Left-hand model . . . . NiB $1730 Ex $1415 Gd $1012
W/laminated stock, add $135
W/walnut stock, add $100
W/stainless steel bbl., add $130

MODEL 1910 INTERNATIONAL SUPER MATCH RIFLE
Updated version of Model 1810 w/same general specifications Model 1913 except w/less-detailed hardwood stock w/tapered forend. Weight: 13.5 lbs. Imported from 1989 to 1998.
Right-hand model . . . . NiB $2566 Ex $2077 Gd $1103
Left-hand model . . . . NiB $2560 Ex $2097 Gd $1506

MODEL 1911 PRONE MATCH RIFLE
Updated version of Model 1811 w/same general specifications Model 1913 except w/specialized prone match hardwood stock w/ beavertail forend. Weight: 11.5 lbs. Imported from 1989 to date.
Right-hand model . . . . NiB $1854 Ex $1764 Gd $849

Anschutz Achiever

MODEL 1912
LADIES' SPORT RIFLE. . . . . NiB $1837 Ex $1932 Gd $865
Similar to the Model 1907 designed for ISU 3-position competition w/same general U.I.T. specifications except w/shorter dimensions to accomodate smaller competitors. Weight: 11.4 lbs. Imported from 1999 to date.

MODEL 1913 STANDARD RIFLE. . NiB $1611 Ex $1235 Gd $909
Similar to 1913 Super Match w/economized appointments. Imported from 1997 to date.

MODEL 1913 SUPER MATCH RIFLE
Bolt-action single-shot Super Match (updated version of Model 1813). Caliber: .22 LR. 27.5-inch bbl. Weight: 14.2 lbs. Adj. two-stage trigger. Vented International thumbhole stock w/adj. cheek-piece, hand and palm rest, fitted w/10-way butthook. Imported from 1989 to date.
Right-hand model . . . . NiB $3310 Ex $1989 Gd $879
Left-hand model . . . . NiB $2370 Ex $1909 Gd $1343
W/laminated stock, add $150
W/stainless steel bbl., add $175

MODEL 2007 ISU STANDARD RIFLE
Bolt-action single-shot. Caliber: .22 LR. 19.75-inch bbl. 43.5 to 44.5 inches overall. Weight: 10.8 lbs. Two-stage trigger. Standard ISU stock w/adj. cheekpiece. Imported from 1992 to date.
Right-hand model . . . . NiB $1997 Ex $1529 Gd $909
Left-hand model . . . . NiB $2040 Ex $1719 Gd $1244
W/stainless steel bbl., add $175

MODEL 2013
LADIES' SPORT RIFLE. . . . . NiB $2197 Ex $2021 Gd $933
Similar to the Model 2007 designed for ISU 3-position competition w/ same general U.I.T. specifications except w/shorter dimensions to accomo-date smaller competitors. Weight: 11.4 lbs. Imported from 1999 to date.

MODEL 2013
BENCHREST RIFLE (BR-50) . NiB $1889 Ex $1624 Gd $877
Bolt-action single-shot. Caliber: .22 LR. 19.6-inch bbl. 43 inches overall. Weight: 10.3 lbs. Adjustable trigger for single or two-stage function. Benchrest-configuration stock. Imported from 1999 to date.

MODEL 2013 SILHOUETTE RIFLE . . . NiB $2187 Ex $1675 Gd $944
Bolt-action single-shot. Caliber: .22 LR. 20-inch bbl. 45.5 inches overall. Weight: 11.5 lbs. Two-stage trigger. Thumbhole black synthetic or laminated stock w/adj. cheekpiece, hand and palm rest. Imported from 1994 to date.

MODEL 2013 SUPER MATCH RIFLE
Bolt-action single-shot. Caliber: .22 LR. 19.75- or 27.1-inch bbl. 43 to 50.1 inches overall. Weight: 15.5 lbs. Two-stage trigger. International thumbhole, black synthetic or laminated stock w/ adj. cheekpiece, hand and palm rest; fitted w/10-way butthook. Imported from 1992 to date.
Right-hand model . . . . NiB $3566 Ex $2317 Gd $1149

Left-hand model . . . . NiB $2588 Ex $1290 Gd $1482
W/laminated stock, add $200

ACHIEVER BOLT-ACTION RIFLE. . . . NiB $422 Ex $337 Gd $219
Caliber: .22 LR. 5-round magazine. Mark 2000-type repeating action. 19.5-inch bbl. 36.5 inches overall. Weight: 5 lbs. Adj. open rear sight; hooded ramp front. Plain European hardwood target-style stock w/vented forend and adj. buttplate. Imported 1987 to 1995.

ACHIEVER ST-SUPER TARGET NiB $559 Ex $431 Gd $269
Same as Achiever except single-shot w/22-inch bbl. and adj. stock. 38.75 inches overall. Weight: 6.5 lbs. Target sights. Imported since 1994 to 1995.

BR-50 BENCH REST RIFLE NiB $2123 Ex $1707 Gd $1026
Single-shot. Caliber: .22 LR. 19.75-inch bbl. (23 inches w/muzzle weight). 37.75-42.5 inches overall. Weight: 11 lbs. Grooved receiver, no sights. Walnut-finished hardwood or synthetic ben-chrest stock w/adj. cheekpiece. Imported from 1994 to 1997. (Reintroduced as Model 2013 BR-50)

KADETT BOLT-ACTION
REPEATING RIFLE . . . . NiB $370 Ex $241 Gd $198
Caliber: .22 LR. 5-round detachable box magazine. 22-inch bbl. 40 inches overall. Weight: 5.5 lbs. Adj. folding leaf rear sight; hooded ramp front. Checkered European hardwood stock w/walnut-finish. Imported 1987.

MARK 2000 MATCH. . . . . NiB $448 Ex $355 Gd $221
Takedown, bolt-action single-shot. Caliber: .22 LR. 26-inch heavy bbl. Walnut stock w/deep-fluted thumb-groove, Wundhammer swell pistol grip, beavertail forend. Adj. buttplate, single-stage adj. trigger. Weight: 8 lbs. Imported from 1982 to 1988.

ARMALITE, INC. — Geneseo, Illinois (formerly Costa Mesa, California)
Armalite was in Costa Mesa, California from 1959-73. Following the acquisition by Eagle Arms in 1995, production resumed under the Armalite, Inc. Logo in Geneseo, Illinois.
Production by ARMALITE

AR-7 EXPLORER SURVIVAL RIFLE NiB $469 Ex $345 Gd $290
Takedown. Semiautomatic. Caliber: .22 LR. Eight-round box maga-zine. 16-inch cast aluminum bbl. w/steel liner. Sights: Peep rear; blade front. Brown plastic stock, recessed to stow barrel, action, and magazine. Weight: 2.75 lbs. Will float stowed or assembled. Made from 1959-1973 by Armalite; from 1974-90 by Charter Arms; from 1990-97 by Survival Arms, Cocoa, FL.; from 1997 to date by Henry Repeating Arms Co., Brooklyn, NY.

AR-7 EXPLORER CUSTOM RIFLE . NiB $325 Ex $270 Gd $199
Same as AR-7 Survival Rifle except w/deluxe walnut stock w/cheek-piece and pistol grip. Weight: 3.5 lbs. Made from 1964 to 1970.

RIFLES

Armalite AR-10

Armalite AR-10 (T) Target Carbine

Armalite M-15A2 National Match

Armalite M-15A2 HBAR

AR-180 SEMIAUTOMATIC RIFLE

Commercial version of full automatic AR-18 Combat Rifle. Gas-operated semiautomatic. Caliber: .223 Rem. (5.56mm). 5-, 20-, 30-round magazines. 18.25-inch bbl. w/flash hider/muzzle brake. Sights: Flip-up "L" type rear, adj. for windage; post front, adj. for elevation. Accessory: 3x scope and mount (add $60 to value). Folding buttstock of black nylon, rubber buttplate and pistol grip, heat dissipating fiberglass forend (hand guard), swivels, sling. 38 inches overall, 28.75 inches folded. Weight: 6.5 lbs. Note: Made by Armalite Inc. 1969 to 1972, manufactured for Armalite by Howa Machinery Ltd., Nagoya, Japan, from 1972 to 1973; by Sterling Armament Co. Ltd., Dagenham, Essex, England, from 1976 to 1994. Importation disc.

Armalite AR-180 (Mfg. by
Armalite-Costa Mesa) . . . . NiB $2189 Ex $1543 Gd $1043

Armalite AR-180 (Mfg. by Howa) . NiB $2109 Ex $1535 Gd $990
Armalite AR-180 (Mfg. by Sterling) NiB $1809 Ex $1404 Gd $933
W/3x scope and mount, add $250

AR-10 SEMIAUTOMATIC SERIES

Gas-operated semiautomatic action. Calibers: .243 Win. or .308 Win. (7.62 x 51mm). 10-round magazine. 16- or 20-inch bbl. 35.5 or 39.5 inches overall. Weight: 9 to 9.75 lbs. Post front sight, adj. aperature rear. Black or green composition stock. Made from 1995 to date.

AR-10 A2 (Std. carbine) . . . NiB $1190 Ex $1088 Gd $707
AR-10 A2 (Std. rifle) . . . . . . NiB $1190 Ex $1088 Gd $707
AR-10 A4 (S.P. carbine) . . . . NiB $1080 Ex $905 Gd $600
AR-10 A4 (S.P. rifle) . . . . NiB $1080 Ex $905 Gd $600
W/stainless steel bbl., add $150

Armi Jager AP-74 Wood Stock

AR-10 T (TARGET)
Similar to AR-10A except in National Match configuration w/ three-slot short Picatinny rail system and case deflector. Additional calibers: .260 Rem., .300 RUM, 7mm-08 Rem., .338 Fed. 16- or 24-inch bbl. Weight: 8.25 to 10.4 lbs. Composite stock and handguard. No sights. Optional National Match carry handle and detachable front sight. Made from 1995 to date.

AR-10 T (Rifle)	NiB $1579	Ex $1289	Gd $1043
AR-10 T (Carbine)	NiB $1479	Ex $1289	Gd $1043

MODEL AR-50 SS BOLT-ACTION
RIFLE . . . . NiB $3198 Ex $2645 Gd $1370
Caliber: .50 BMG. 31-inch bbl. w/muzzle brake. 59 inches overall. Weight: 41 lbs. Modified octagonal-form receiver, drilled and slotted for scope rail. Single-stage trigger. Triple front-locking bolt lug w/ spring-loaded plunger for automatic ejection. Magnesium phosphate steel, hard-anodized aluminum finish. Made from 1999 to date.

M15 SERIES
Gas-operated semiautomatic w/A2-style forward-assist mechanism and push-type pivot pin for easy takedown. Caliber: .223 Rem., 5.56 NATO or 6.8 SPC. 7-round magazine. 16-, 20- or 24-inch bbl. Weight: 7-9.2 lbs. Composite or retractable stock. Fully adj. sights. Black anodized finish. Made from 1995 to date.

M-15A2 (Carbine)	NiB $927	Ex $800	Gd $647
M-15A2 (Service Rifle)	NiB $989	Ex $845	Gd $655
M-15A2 (National Match)	NiB $1350	Ex $1123	Gd $770
M-15A2 (Golden Eagle heavy bbl.)	NiB $1332	Ex $1086	Gd $730
M-15A2 M4C (retractable stock, disc. 1997)	NiB $1299	Ex $1021	Gd $698
M-15A4 (Action Master, disc. 1997)	NiB $1139	Ex $934	Gd $670
M-15A4 (Predator)	NiB $977	Ex $855	Gd $654
M-15A4 S.P. R. (Special Purpose Rifle)	NiB $956	Ex $799	Gd $535
M-15A4 (S.P. Carbine)	NiB $875	Ex $720	Gd $463
M-15A4T (Eagle Eye Carbine)	NiB $1326	Ex $1090	Gd $775
M-15A4T (Eagle Eye Rifle)	NiB $1377	Ex $1030	Gd $755

ARMI JAGER — Turin, Italy

AP-74 COMMANDO . . . . NiB $322 Ex $248 Gd $166
Similar to standard AP-74 but styled to resemble original version of Uzi 9mm submachine gun w/wood buttstock. Lacks carrying handle and flash suppressor. Has different type front sight mount and guards, wood stock, pistol grip and forearm. Intro. 1976. Disc.

AP-74 SEMIAUTOMATIC RIFLE
Styled after U.S. M16 military rifle. Caliber: .22 LR, .32 Auto (pistol cartridge). Detachable clip magazine; capacity: 14 rounds caliber .22 LR, 9 rounds .32 ACP. 20-inch bbl. w/flash suppressor. Weight: 6.5 lbs. M16 type sights. Stock, pistol-grip and forearm of black plastic, swivels and sling. Intro. 1974. Disc.
.22 LR. . . . . NiB $359 Ex $290 Gd $200

.32 Auto. . . . . NiB $379 Ex $322 Gd $209

AP-74 WOOD STOCK MODEL
Same as standard AP-74 except w/wood stock, pistol-grip and forearm weight: 7 lbs. Disc.

.22 LR	NiB $448	Ex $380	Gd $250
.32 Auto	NiB $448	Ex $380	Gd $250

ARMSCOR (Arms Corp.)—Manila, Philippines (imported by Armscor Precision Int'l.)

MODEL 20 AUTO RIFLE
Caliber: .22 LR. 15-round magazine. 21-inch bbl. 39.75 inches overall. Weight: 6.5 lbs. Sights: Hooded front; adj. rear. Checkered or plain walnut finished mahogany stock. Blued finish. Imported 1990 to 1991. (Reinstated by Ruko in the M series.)

Model 20 (checkered stock)	NiB $167	Ex $130	Gd $97
Model 20C (carbine-style stock)	NiB $144	Ex $122	Gd $98
Model 20P (plain stock)	NiB $126	Ex $100	Gd $78

MODEL 1600 AUTO RIFLE
Caliber: .22 LR. 15-round magazine. 19.5-inch bbl. 38 inches overall. Weight: 6 lbs. Sights: Post front; aperture rear. Plain mahogany stock. Matte black finish. Imported 1987 to 1991. (Reinstated by Ruko in the M series.)

Standard model	NiB $180	Ex $155	Gd $100
Retractable stock model	NiB $190	Ex $167	Gd $110

MODEL AK22 AUTO RIFLE
Caliber: .22 LR. 15- or 30-round magazine. 18.5-inch bbl. 36 inches overall. Weight: 7 lbs. Sights: Post front; adj. rear. Plain mahogany stock. Matte black finish. Imported 1987 to 1991.

Standard model	NiB $179	Ex $150	Gd $110
Folding stock model	NiB $269	Ex $220	Gd $166

MODEL M14 SERIES BOLT-ACTION RIFLE
Caliber: .22 LR. 10-round magazine. 23-inch bbl. Weight: 6.25 lbs. Open sights. Walnut or mahogany stock. Imported 1991 to 1997.

M14P Standard model	NiB $129	Ex $98	Gd $70
M14D Deluxe model (checkered stock, disc. 1995)	NiB $149	Ex $110	Gd $90

MODEL M20 SERIES SEMIAUTOMATIC RIFLE
Caliber: .22 LR. 10- or 15-round magazine. 18.25- or 20.75-inch bbl. Weight: 5.5 to 6.5 lbs. 38 to 40.5 inches overall. Hooded front sight w/ windage adj. rear. Walnut finished mahogany stock. Imported 1990 to 1997.

M20C (carbine model)	NiB $144	Ex $109	Gd $80
M20P (standard model)	NiB $128	Ex $100	Gd $78
M20S Sporter Deluxe (w/checkered mahogany stock)	NiB $167	Ex $150	Gd $97
M20SC Super Classic (w/checkered walnut stock)	NiB $281	Ex $227	Gd $108

RIFLES

A-Square — Hannibal

MODEL M1400 BOLT-ACTION RIFLE
Similar to Model 14P except w/checkered stock w/Schnabel forend. Weight: 6 lbs. Imported from 1990 to 1997.
M1400LW (Lightweight, disc. 1992) . NiB $239 Ex $199 Gd $137
M1400S (Sporter) . . . . NiB $177 Ex $150 Gd $100
M1400SC (Super Classic) . . . . NiB $300 Ex $255 Gd $179

MODEL M1500 BOLT-ACTION RIFLE
Caliber: .22 Mag. 5-round magazine. 21.5-inch bbl. Weight: 6.5 lbs. Open sights. Checkered mahogany stock. Imported 1991 to 1997.
M1500 (standard) . . . . NiB $198 Ex $137 Gd $105
M1500LW (Euro-style walnut
stock, disc. 1992) . . . . NiB $219 Ex $188 Gd $135
M1500SC (Monte Carlo stock) . . . . . NiB $224 Ex $190 Gd $140

MODEL M1600 AUTO RIFLE
Rimfire replica of Armalite Model AR 180 (M16) except chambered for Caliber .22 LR. 15-round magazine. 18-inch bbl. Weight: 5.25 lbs. Composite or retractable buttstock w/composite handguard and pistol grip. Carrying handle w/adj. aperture rear sight and protected post front. Black anodized finish. Imported from 1991 to 1997.
M-1600 (standard w/fixed stock) . .NiB $190 Ex $149 Gd $110
M-1600R (retractable stock) . . . . .NiB $200 Ex $161 Gd $120

MODEL M1800 BOLT-ACTION RIFLE
Caliber: .22 Hornet. 5-round magazine. 22-inch bbl. Weight: 6.6 lbs. Checkered hardwood or walnut stock. Sights: Post front; adj. rear. Imported from 1996 to 1997.
M-1800 (standard) . . . . NiB $310 Ex $233 Gd $175
M-1800SC (checkered walnut stock) . NiB $400 Ex $327 Gd $255

MODEL M2000 BOLT-ACTION RIFLE
Similar to Model 20P except w/checkered mahogany stock and adj. sights. Imported from 1991 to 1997.
M2000S (standard) . . . . NiB $177 Ex $139 Gd $100
M2000SC (w/checkered walnut stock) NiB $279 Ex $220 Gd $167

ARNOLD ARMS — Arlington, Washington

AFRICAN SAFARI
Calibers: .243 to .458 Win. Mag. and proprietary cartridges. 22- to 26-inch bbl. Weight: 7-9 lbs. Scope mount standard or w/optional M70 Express sights. Chrome-moly in four finishes. "A" and "AA" Fancy Grade English walnut stock with number 5 standard wraparound checkering pattern. Ebony forend tip. Made from 1994 to 2001.
With "A" Grade English
walnut stock, blue finish. . . . . . . NiB $4732 Ex $3841 Gd $2690
Std. polish . . . . NiB $4969 Ex $4000 Gd $2821
Hi-Luster . . . . NiB $5189 Ex $4290 Gd $2950
Stainless steel matte . . . . NiB $4733 Ex $3847 Gd $2993
With "AA" Grade English
walnut stock, C-M matte blue finishNiB $4707 Ex $3810 Gd $2688
Std. polish . . . . NiB $4988 Ex $4037 Gd $2835
Hi-Luster . . . . NiB $5188 Ex $4200 Gd $2969
Stainless steel matte finish . . . . . NiB $4707 Ex $3875 Gd $2710

ALASKAN TROPHY
Calibers: .300 Magnum to .458 Win. Magnum. 24- to 26-inch bbl. Weight: 7-9 lbs. Scope mount w/Express sights standard. Stainless steel or chrome-moly Apollo action w/fibergrain or black synthetic stock. Barrel band on 357 H&H and larger magnums. Made from 1996 to 2000.
Matte finish . . . . NiB $3330 Ex $2689 Gd $1900
Std. polish . . . . NiB $3559 Ex $2900 Gd $2044
Stainless steel. . . . . NiB $3386 Ex $2744 Gd $1935

A-SQUARE COMPANY INC.—Glenrock, Wyoming

CAESAR BOLT-ACTION RIFLE
Custom rifle built on Remington's 707 receiver. Calibers: Same as Hannibal, Groups I, II and III. 20- to 26-inch bbl. Weight: 8.5 to 11 lbs. Express 3-leaf rear sight, ramp front. Synthetic or classic Claro oil-finished walnut stock w/flush detachable swivels and Coil-Chek recoil system. Three-way adj. target trigger; 3-position safety. Right- or left-hand. Made from 1986 to 2012.
Synthetic stock modelNiB $3512 Ex $2790 Gd $1947
Walnut stock model. .NiB $4044 Ex $2379 Gd $1756

GENGHIS KHAN BOLT-ACTION RIFLE
Custom varmint rifle developed on Winchester's M70 receiver; fitted w/heavy tapered bbl. and Coil-Chek stock. Calibers: .22-250 Rem., .243 Win., .25-06 Rem., 6mm Rem. Weight: 8-8.5 lbs. Made from 1995 to 2012.
Synthetic stock model. . . . NiB $3566 Ex $2312 Gd $2044
Walnut stock model . . . . . NiB $3482 Ex $2854 Gd $2023

HAMILCAR BOLT-ACTION RIFLE
Similar to Hannibal Model except lighter. Calibers: .25-06, .257 Wby., 6.5x55 Swedish, .270 Wby., 7x57, 7mm Rem., 7mm STW, 7mm Wby., .280 Rem., .30-06, .300 Win., .300 Wby., .338-06, 9.3x62. Weight: 8-8.5 lbs. Made from 1994 to 2012.
Synthetic stock model. . . . NiB $3554 Ex $2909 Gd $2011
Walnut stock model . . . . . NiB $3508 Ex $2866 Gd $2009

HANNIBAL BOLT-ACTION RIFLE
Custom rifle built on reinforced P-17 Enfield receiver. Calibers: Group I: 30-06; Group II: 7mm Rem. Mag., .300 Win. Mag., .416 Taylor, .425 Express, .458 Win. Mag.; Group III: .300 H&H, .300 Wby. Mag., 8mm Rem. Mag., .340 Wby. Mag., .375 H&H, .375 Wby. Mag., .404 Jeffery, .416 Hoffman, .416 Rem Mag., .450 Ackley, .458 Lott; Group IV: .338 A-Square Mag., .375 A-Square Mag., .378 Wby. Mag., .416 Rigby, .416 Wby. Mag., .460 Short Square Mag., .500 A-Square Mag. 20- to 26-inch bbl. Weight: 9 to 11.75 lbs. Express 3-leaf rear sight, ramp front. Classic Claro oil-finished walnut stock or synthetic stock w/flush detachable swivels and Coil-Chek recoil system. Adj. trigger w/2-position safety. Made from 1986 to 2012.
Synthetic stock model. . . . NiB $3614 Ex $2870 Gd $1921
Walnut stock model . . . . . NiB $3707 Ex $2795 Gd $2021

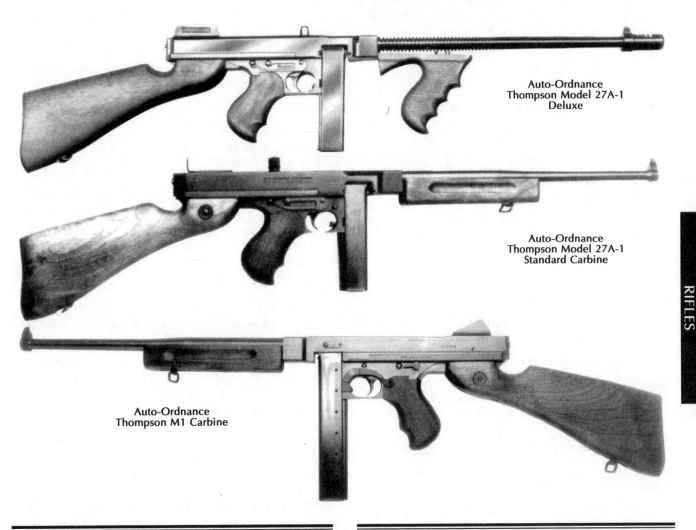

Auto-Ordnance
Thompson Model 27A-1
Deluxe

Auto-Ordnance
Thompson Model 27A-1
Standard Carbine

Auto-Ordnance
Thompson M1 Carbine

RIFLES

AUSTRIAN MILITARY RIFLES—Steyr, Austria
Manufactured at Steyr Armory

MODEL 90
STEYR-MANNLICHER RIFLE . . NiB $337 Ex $189 Gd $139
Straight-pull bolt action. Caliber: 8mm. 5-round magazine. Open sights. 10-inch bayonet. Cartridge clip forms part of the magazine mechanism. Some of these rifles were provided with a laced canvas hand guard, others were of wood.

MODEL 90
STEYR-MANNLICHER CARBINE NiB $339 Ex $228 Gd $139
Same general specifications as Model 90 rifle except w/19.5-inch bbl., weight 7 lbs. No bayonet stud or supplemental forend grip.

MODEL 95
STEYR-MANNLICHER CARBINE NiB $329 Ex $250 Gd $141
Same general specifications as Model 95 rifle except w/19.5-inch bbl., weight 7 lbs. Post front sight; adj. rear carbine sight.

MODEL 95 STEYR-MANNLICHER
SERVICE RIFLE . . . . NiB $299 Ex $190 Gd $137
Straight-pull bolt action. Caliber: 8x50R Mannlicher (many of these rifles were altered during World War II to use the 7.9mm German service ammunition). 5-round Mannlicher-type box magazine. 30-inch bbl. Weight: 8.5 lbs. Sights: Blade front; rear adj. for elevation. Military-type full stock.

AUTO-ORDNANCE CORPORATION — Worcester, Massachusetts (division of Kahr Arms)

THOMPSON
MODEL 22-27A-3. . . . . NiB $997 Ex $754 Gd $498
Similar as Deluxe Model 27A-1 except 22 LR w/lightweight alloy receiver, weight 6.5 lbs. Magazines include 5-, 20-, 30- and 50-round box types, 80-round drum. Made from 1977 to 1994.

THOMPSON MODEL 27A-1 DELUXE   NiB $1100 Ex $879 Gd $530
Same as Standard Model 27A-1 except w/finned bbl. w/compensator, adj. rear sight, pistol-grip forestock. Caliber: .22 LR, l0mm (1991 to 1993) or 45 ACP. Weight: 11.5 lbs. Made from 1976 to 1999.

.22 LR (Limited production) NiB $1190 Ex $1000 Gd $770
10-round stick magazine, add. $70
20- or 30-round stick magazine, add. $80
10-round drum magazine, add $200
50-round drum magazine, add $300
100-round drum magazine, add $600
Violin carrying case, add $227
Hard carrying case, add $200
Detacable stock/horizontal grip (2007), add $440

GRADING: **NiB** = New in Box   **Ex** = Excellent or NRA 95%   **Gd** = Good or NRA 68%

THOMPSON MODEL 27A-1 STANDARD
SEMIAUTO CARBINE. . . . . NiB $689 Ex $641 Gd $440
Similar to Thompson submachine gun ("Tommy Gun") except has no provision for automatic firing. Caliber: .45 ACP. 20-round detachable box magazine (5-,15- and 30-round box magazines, 39-round drum also available). 16-inch plain bbl. Weight: 14 lbs. Sights: Aperture rear; blade front. Walnut buttstock, pistol grip and grooved forearm, sling swivels. Made from 1976-86.

THOMPSON 27A-1C LIGHTWEIGHT NiB $1090 Ex $900 Gd $707
Similar to Model 27A-1 except w/lightweight alloy receiver. Weight: 9.25 lbs. Made 1984 to date.

THOMPSON M1 . . . . NiB $1070 Ex $660 Gd $479
Similar to Model 27A-1 except in M-1 configuration w/side cocking lever and horizontal forearm. Weight: 11.5 lbs. Made from 1986 to date.
M1-C (lightweight) . . . . NiB $1080 Ex $860 Gd $570

THOMPSON 27A-1 COMMANDO . . . . NiB $1098 Ex $860 Gd $579
Similar to Model 27A-1 except parkerized finish and black stock. 13 lbs. Made from 1997 to date.

BAIKAL — Izhevsk, Russia
(Imported by RWC, Tullytown, PA. Formerly imported by EAA, Corp., Rockledge, FL)

MP221 Side By Side . . . . NiB $910 Ex $700 Gd $300
Double barrel, boxlock, break action. Caliber: .223 Rem., .270 Win., .30-06, .308 Win., or .45-70. 23.5-inch bbl., 40 inches overall. Matte blue finish, checkered walnut stock. Imported from 2003 to 2009, reintro. 2011 to date.

MP161K Semi Automatic . . . . NiB $330 Ex $250 Gd $170
Caliber: .17 HMR, .22 LR or .22 WMR. 10-round magazine. 19.5-inch bbl., 39 inches overall. Matte blue finish, polymer thumbhole stock. Imported from 2009 to date.
.17 HMR or .22 WMR, add. 20%

IZH-18MN Single Shot . . . . . . NiB $250 Ex $190 Gd $110
Boxlock, break action. Caliber: .222 Rem., .223 Rem., .243 Win., .270 Win., 7.62x39mm, .308 Win., .30-06, or .45-70. 23.5-inch bbl., 40 inches overall. Matte blue finish, checkered walnut stock. Imported from 2003 to 2009.

Ballard Arms, Inc. — Onsted, MI

Formerly Ballard Rifle LLC, Cody WY. Firearms manufactured since 1996.

BALLARD 1-1/2 HUNTER'S RIFLE. . . . . NiB $3200 Ex $2440 Gd $1833
Calibers: Seven calibers from .22 LR to .50-70. Single trigger, S-style lever action; uncheckered stock. Weight: 10.5 lbs.

BALLARD 1-3/4 FAR WEST RIFLE. . . . . NiB $2902 Ex $2045 Gd $1471
Calibers: Eight calibers from .32-40 WCF to .50-90 SS. Patterned after original Ballard Far West model. 30 or 32-inch bbl., standard or heavyweight octagon; double set triggers; ring-style lever. Weight: 9.75 to 10.5 lbs.

BALLARD NO. 5 PACIFIC NiB $3208 Ex $2460 Gd $1996
Calibers: Nine calibers between .32-40 WCF and .50-90 SS. Similar to No. 1-3/4 Far West model but with under-barrel wiping rod.

BALLARD NO. 4-1/2
MID-RANGE RIFLE . . . . NiB $2900 Ex $2080 Gd $1765
Calibers: .Five calibers between .32-40 WCF and .45-110. Designed for black powder silhouette shooting. 30 or 32-inch bbl., half-octagonal heavyweight; single or double set triggers; pistol grip stock; full loop lever; hard rubber Ballard buttplate; Vernier tang sight. Weight: 10.75 to 11.5 lbs.

BALLARD NO. 7
LONG-RANGE RIFLE. . . NiB $3369 Ex $2390 Gd $1479
Caliber: Five calibers between .40-65 Win. and .45-110. Similar to No. 4-1/2 Mid-Range Rifle; designed for long-range shooting. 32 or 34-inch half-octagon standard or heavyweight bbl.

MODEL 1885
HIGH WALL RIFLE . . . . NiB $3190 Ex $2444 Gd $1954
Calibers: Various. Exact replica of Winchester Model 1885 (parts are interchangeable). 30 or 32-inch bbl., octagon; case-colored receiver, uncheckered straight-grip stock and forearm. Weight: Approx. 9 lbs. Introduced 2001.
Deluxe model, add $1717
Sporting model, add $250
Shuetzen model, add. $400

BANSNER'S ULTIMATE RIFLES, LLC — Established in 1981 in Adamstown, Pennsylvania, as Basner's Gunsmithing Specialties. Company name changed in 2000

ULTIMATE
ONE RIFLE . . . . NiB $5540 Ex $3766 Gd $3060
Calibers: Various. Bolt-action, modeled on Winchester M70 and Remington 707 actions. Various metal finishes; muzzle brake; custom trigger; custom stock; Pachmayer decelerator pad; custom scope mounts and bases.
Three-position safety, add $250

HIGH TECH
SERIES RIFLE. . . . . NiB $1032 Ex $790 Gd $641
Calibers: Various. Steel or stainless steel action with factory bbl. Bansner's synthetic stock and Pachmayer decelerator pad.
Stainless steel model, add $300

SAFARI
HUNTER RIFLE . . . . NiB $6200 Ex $4396 Gd $2398
Calibers: Various dangerous game calibers. Based on Model 70 Classic action; muzzle brake; Lilja Precision stainless steel barrel; synthetic stock; matte black Teflon metal finish. Introduced 2003.

WORLD SLAM LIMITED EDITION
RIFLE . . . . NiB $5345 Ex $3850 Gd $2300
Calibers: Various. Customized Model 707 action; fluted bold body. jeweled trigger. three-position safety; synthetic stock. Only 25-50 of limited edition models were made beginning in 2003.

BARRETT FIREARMS MFG., INC. — Murfreesboro, Tennessee

MODEL 82A1
SEMI-AUTOMATIC RIFLE . NiB $8900 Ex $7760 Gd $5100
Caliber: .50 BMG. 10-round detachable box magazine. 29-inch recoiling bbl. w/muzzle brake. 57 inches overall. Weight: 28.5 lbs. Open iron sights and 10x scope. Composit stock w/Sorbothance recoil pad and self-leveling bipod. Blued finish. Made in various configurations from 1985 to date.

MODEL 90 BOLT-ACTION RIFLENiB $3530 Ex $3099 Gd $2020
Caliber: .50 BMG. Five round magazine. 29-inch match bbl. 45 inches overall. Weight: 22 lbs. Composite stock w/retractable bipod. Made from 1990 to 1995.

Model 95 Bolt-Action . . . . NiB $6635 Ex $4890 Gd $3530
Similar to Model 90 bullpup design chambered for .50 BMG except w/ improved muzzle brake and extendable bipod. Made from 1995 to date.

Model 98B Bolt-Action . . . NiB $4699 Ex $4400 Gd $2530
Caliber: .338 Lapua Mag. 20-, 26-, or 27-inch bbl. Weight: 13.5 lbs. 10-round magazine. Muzzle brake, adj. stock. Made from 2009 to date.

Model M4468 semi-Automatic . . NiB $2100 Ex $1707 Gd $1000
AR-style rifle. Caliber: 6.8 SPC. 16-inch bbl. Weight: 8 lbs. 5-, 10-, 30-round magazine. Made from 2005 to 2008.

BEEMAN PRECISION ARMS INC. — Santa Rosa, California

Since 1993 all European firearms imported by Beeman have been distributed by Beeman Outdoor Sports, Div., Roberts Precision Arms, Inc., Santa Rosa, CA.

WEIHRAUCH HW MODELS 60J AND 60J-ST BOLT-ACTION RIFLES
Calibers: .22 LR (60J-ST), .222 Rem. (60J). 22.8-inch bbl. 41.7 inches overall. Weight: 6.5 lbs. Sights: Hooded blade front; open adj. rear. Blued finish. Checkered walnut stock w/cheekpiece. Made from 1988 to 1994.
Model 60J . . . . NiB $835 Ex $746 Gd $615
Model 60J-ST . . . . NiB $655 Ex $539 Gd $398

Weihrauch HW Model 60M
Small Bore Rifle . . . . NiB $690 Ex $579 Gd $389
Caliber: .22 LR. Single-shot. 26.8-inch bbl. 45.7 inches overall. Weight: 10.8 lbs. Adj. trigger w/push-button safety. Sights: Hooded blade front on ramp, precision aperture rear. Target-style stock w/stippled forearm and pistol grip. Blued finish. Made from 1988 to 1994.

WEIHRAUCH HW
MODEL 660 MATCH RIFLE. . NiB $1023 Ex $855 Gd $445
Caliber: .22 LR. 26-inch bbl. 45.3 inches overall. Weight: 10.7 lbs. Adj. match trigger. Sights: globe front, precision aperture rear. Match-style walnut stock w/adj. cheekpiece and buttplate. Made from 1988 to 1994.

FEINWERKBAU MODEL 2600 SERIES TARGET RIFLE
Caliber: .22 LR. Single-shot. 26.3-inch bbl. 43.7 inches overall. Weight: 10.6 lbs. Match trigger w/fingertip weight adjustment dial. Sights: Globe front; micrometer match aperture rear. Laminated hardwood stock w/adj. cheekpiece. Made from 1988 to 1994.

Standard Model 2600 (left-hand) NiB $1733 Ex $1360 Gd $944
Standard Model 2600
(right-hand) . . . . NiB $1560 Ex $1239 Gd $816
Free Rifle Model 2602
(left-hand) . . . . NiB $2196 Ex $1755 Gd $1024
Free Rifle Model 2602
(right-hand) . . . . NiB $2196 Ex $1755 Gd $1024

BELGIAN MILITARY RIFLES — Mfd. by Fabrique Nationale D'Armes de Guerre, Herstal, Belgium; Fabrique D'Armes de L'Etat, Lunich, Belgium

Hopkins & Allen Arms Co. of Norwich, Conn., as well as contractors in Birmingham, England, also produced these guns during World War I.

MODEL 1889 MAUSER
MILITARY RIFLE . . . . NiB $279 Ex $230 Gd $156
Caliber: 7.65mm Belgian Service (7.65mm Mauser). 5-round projecting box magazine. 30.75-inch bbl. w/jacket. Weight: 8.5 lbs. Adj. rear sight, blade front. Straight-grip military stock. This, and the carbine version, was the principal weapon of the Belgian Army at the start of WWII. Made from 1889 to c.1935.

MODEL 1916
MAUSER CARBINE . . . .
NiB $300 Ex $240 Gd $190
Same as Model 1889 Rifle except w/20.75-inch bbl. Weighs 8 lbs. and has minor differences in the rear sight graduations, lower band closer to the muzzle and swivel plate on side of buttstock.

MODEL 1935 MAUSER
MILITARY RIFLE . . . .
NiB $370 Ex $292 Gd $169
Same general specifications as F.N. Model 1924; minor differences. Caliber: 7.65mm Belgian Service. Mfd. by Fabrique Nationale D'Armes de Guerre.

MODEL 1936 MAUSER
MILITARY RIFLE . . . . NiB $378 Ex $290 Gd $166
An adaptation of Model 1889 w/German M/98-type bolt, Belgian M/89 protruding box magazine. Caliber: 7.65mm Belgian Service. Mfd. by Fabrique Nationale D'Armes de Guerre.

BENELLI — Urbino, Itay
(Imported by Benelli USA, Accokeek, MD)

R1 Semi-Automatic . . . . NiB $910 Ex $700 Gd $500
Caliber: .270 WSM, .308 Win., .30-06, .300 WSM, .300 Win. Mag. or .338 Win. Mag. 20-, 22- or 24-inch bbl. Matte black finish, checkered walnut or polymer stock. Designated Argo in Europe. Imported from 2002 to date.
ComforTech stock, add $125

BENTON & BROWN FIREARMS, INC. — Fort Worh, Texas

MODEL 93 BOLT-ACTION RIFLE
Similar to Blaser Model R84 (the B&B rifle is built on the Blaser action, see separate listing) with an interchangeable bbl. system. Calibers: .243 Win., 6mm Rem., .25-06, .257 Wby., .264 Win., .270 Win., .280 Rem., 7mm Rem Mag., .30-06, .308, .300 Wby., .300 Win. Mag., .338 Win., .375 H&H. 22- or 24-inch bbl. 41 or 43 inches overall. Bbl.-mounted scope rings and one-piece base; no sights. Two-piece walnut or fiberglass stock. Made from 1993 to 1996.
Walnut stock model . . . . NiB $1896 Ex $1744 Gd $1012
Fiberglass stock model add $227
Extra bbl. assembly, add $525
Extra bolt assembly, add $450

RIFLES

Beretta 501
Bolt-Action Sporter

Beretta AR-70

BERETTA U.S.A. CORP. — Accokeek, Maryland. Manufactured by Fabbrica D'Armi Pietro Beretta, S.P.A., Gardone Val Trompia (Brescia), Italy

455 SIDE BY SIDE EXPRESS DOUBLE RIFLE
Sidelock action w/removable sideplates. Calibers: .375 H&H, .458 Win. Mag., .470 NE, .500 NE (3 inches), .416 Rigby. Bbls.: 23.5 or 25.5-inch. Weight: 11 lbs. Double triggers. Sights: Blade front; V-notch folding leaf rear. Checkered European walnut forearm and buttstock w/recoil pad. Color casehardened receiver w/blued bbls. Various grades of engraving. Custom built. Made from 1990 to date.
Model 455 . . . . .NiB $100,000
Model 455EELL . . . . .NiB $150,000

500 BOLT-ACTION SPORTER
Centerfire bolt-action rifle w/Sako A I short action. Calibers: .222 Rem., .223 Rem. Five round magazine. 23.63-inch bbl. Weight: 6.5 lbs. Available w/ or w/o iron sights. Tapered dovetailed receiver. European walnut stock. Disc. 1998.
Standard . . . . NiB $707 Ex $590 Gd $475
DL Model. . . . . NiB $1590 Ex $1288 Gd $909
500 EELL
Engraved . . . . NiB $1670 Ex $1465 Gd $990
W/iron sights, add 10%

501 BOLT-ACTION SPORTER
Same as Model 500 except w/Sako A II medium action. Calibers: .243 Win., .308 Win. Weight: 7.5 lbs. Disc. 1986.
Standard. . . . . NiB $625 Ex $466 Gd $420
Standard
w/iron sights. . . . . NiB $707 Ex $650 Gd $430
DL model. . . . . NiB $1386 Ex $1097 Gd $944
501 EELL (engraved) . . . . . . NiB $1607 Ex $1329 Gd $989
W/iron sights, add 10%

502 BOLT-ACTION SPORTER
Same as Model 500 except w/Sako A III long action. Calibers: .270 Win., 7mm Rem. Mag., .30/06, 375 H&H. Weight: 8.5 lbs. Disc. 1986.
Standard model . . . . NiB $675 Ex $534 Gd $460
DL model. . . . . NiB $1565 Ex $1299 Gd $980
502 EELL (engraved) . . . . . NiB $1607 Ex $1347 Gd $1088
W/iron sights, add 10%

AR-70 SEMIAUTOMATIC RIFLE. . NiB $2020 Ex $1788 Gd $1077
Caliber: .223 Rem. (5.56mm). 30-round magazine. 17.75-inch bbl. Weight: 8.25 lbs. Sights: Rear peep adj. for windage and elevation; blade front. High-impact synthetic buttstock. Imported 1984 to 1989.

EXPRESS S686/S689 SILVER SABLE O/U RIFLE
Calibers: .30-06 Spfld., 9.3x74R, and .444 Marlin. 24-inch bbl. Weight: 7.7 lbs. Drilled and tapped for scope mount. European-style cheek rest and ventilated rubber recoil pad. Imported 1995.
Model S686/S689 Silver Sable II . NiB $4720 Ex $3800 Gd $2244
Model S689 Gold Sable . . . . NiB $6347 Ex $5329 Gd $3144
Model S686/S689 EELL
Diamond Sable. . . . . NiB $13,325 Ex $9765 Gd $6479
W/extra bbl. set, add $350
W/detachable claw mounts, add $645

EXPRESS SSO O/U EXPRESS DOUBLE RIFLE
Sidelock. Calibers: .375 H&H Mag., .458 Win. Mag., 9.3 x 74R. 23-24- or 25.5-inch blued bbls. Weight: 11 lbs. Double triggers. Express sights w/blade front and V-notch folding leaf rear. Optional Zeiss scope w/claw mounts. Color casehardened receiver w/scroll engraving, game scenes and gold inlays on higher grades. Checkered European walnut forearm and buttstock w/cheekpiece and recoil pad. Imported 1985 to 1989.
Model SS0 (disc. 1989). . . . . NiB $15,800 Ex $10,600 Gd $6545
Model SS05 (disc. 1990). . . . . NiB $18600 Ex $14,300 Gd $7600
Model SS06 Custom . . . . .NiB $75,000
Model SS06 EELL Gold Custom . . . . .NiB $125,000
Extra bbl. assembly, add. $7070
Claw mounts, add $800

Blaser Model R84

in Italy. Introduced in 1969, discontinued 1989.

MATO. . . . . NIB $1015 EX $733 GD $533
Calibers: .270 Win., .280 Rem., 7mm Rem. Mag., .300 Win. Mag., .338 Win. Mag., .375 H&H. 23.6-inch bbl. Weight: 8 lbs. Adjustable trigger. Drop-out box magazine. Drilled and tapped for scope w/ w/o adj. sights. Walnut or synthetic stock. Manufactured based on Mauser 98 action. Made from 1997 to 2002.
Deluxe model. . . . . NiB $2015 Ex $1723 Gd $976
.375 H&H w/iron sights, add $350

SMALL BORE SPORTING CARBINE/TARGET RIFLE
Semiautomatic w/bolt handle in raised or conventional single-shot bolt-action w/handle in lowered position. Caliber: .22 LR. Four, 5-, 8-, 10- or 20-round magazines. 20.5-inch standard or heavy bbl. Sights: 3-leaf folding rear, partridge front. Target or sporting stock w/checkered pistol grip and forend and sling swivels. Weight: 5.5 to 6 lbs.
Sporter model (Super Sport X). NiB $460 Ex $355 Gd $256
Target model (Olympia X). . . . NiB $340 Ex $520 Gd $345

BERNARDELLI, VINCENZO — Brescia, Italy

Currently headquartered in Brescia, Italy, Bernardelli arms were manufactured from 1721 to 1997 in Gardone, Italy. Imported and distributed by Armsport, Inc., Miami, Florida. Also handled by Magnum Research, Inc., Quality Arms, Inc., Armes De Chasse, Stoeger and Action Arms.

EXPRESS VB . . . . NiB $5768 Ex $4755 Gd $3690
Double barrel. Calibers: Various. Side-by-side sidelock action. Ejectors, double triggers. Imported from 1990 to1997.
Deluxe model (w/double triggers), add $1125

EXPRESS 2000 . . . . NiB $2707 Ex $2025 Gd $1580
Calibers: .30-06, 7x65R, 8x57JRS, 9.3x74R. Over/under boxlock design. Single or double triggers, extractors. Checkered walnut stock and forearm. Imported from 1994 to 1997.
Single trigger, add $200

MINERVA EXPRESS . . . . . NiB $5200 Ex $3890 Gd $4098
Caliber: Various. Exposed hammers. Extractors, double triggers. Moderate engraving. Imported from 1995 to 1997.

CARBINA .22 . . . . NiB $580 Ex $300 Gd $170
Semi-auto. Caliber: .22 rimfire. Blow-back action. Imported from 1990 to 1997.

MODEL 120 . . . . NiB $2120 Ex $1587 Gd $1100
Combination gun; over-under boxlock; 12 gauge over .22 Hornet, .222 Rem., 5.6x50R Mag., .243 Win., 6.5x57R, .270 Win., 7x57R, .308 Win., .30-06, 6.5x55, 7x65R, 8x57JRS, 9.3x74R. Iron sights. Checkered walnut stock and forearm. Double triggers, automatic ejectors or extractors. Ventilated recoil pad. Engraved action. Made in Italy. Discontinued.

MODEL 190 . . . . NiB $1489 Ex $1129 Gd $1069
Combination gun; over-under boxlock. Calibers: 12, 16 or 20 ga. Over .222 Rem., .243 Win., .30-06, .308 Win., 5.6x50R Mag., .5.6x57R, 6.5x55, 6.5x57R, 7x57R, 7x65R, 8x57JRS, 9.3x74R. Iron sights. Checkered walnut stock. Double triggers; extractors. Made

MODEL 2000 . . . . NiB $2713 Ex $1866 Gd $1390
Combination gun; over-under boxlock action. Calibers: 12, 16 or 20 ga. Over .222 Rem., .22 Hornet, 5.6x50R Mag., .243 Win., 6.5x55, 6.5x57R, .270 Win., 7x57R, .308 Win., .30-06, 8x57JRS, 9.3x74R. Bbl: 23 inches. Sights: Blade front, open rear. Hand checkered, oil-finished select European walnut stock, double-set triggers, auto ejectors. Silvered, engraved action. Made in Italy. Introduced in 1990, disconti nued 1991.
Extra bbl. assembly, add $595

BLASER U.S.A., INC. — Fort Worth, Texas. Manufactured by Blaser Jagdwaffen GmbH, Germany (imported by Sigarms, Exeter, NH; Autumn Sales, Inc., Fort Worth, TX)

MODEL R-84 BOLT-ACTION RIFLE
Calibers: .22-250, .243, 6mm Rem., .25-06, .270, .280 Rem., .30-06- .257 Wby. Mag., .264 Win. Mag., 7mm Rem Mag., .300 Win. Mag., .300 Wby. Mag., .338 Win. Mag., .375 H&H. Interchangeable bbls. w/standard or Magnum bolt assemblies. Bbl. length: 23 inches (standard); 24 inches (Magnum). 41 to 42 inches overall. Weight: 7 to 7.25 lbs. No sights. Bbl.-mounted scope system. Two-piece Turkish walnut stock w/solid black recoil pad. Imported from 1989 to 1994.
Model R84 Standard . . . . NiB $2245 Ex $1725 Gd $1190
Model R84 Deluxe
(engraved game scene) . . . . NiB $2400 Ex $2021 Gd $1200
Model R84 Super Deluxe
(Gold and silver inlays). . . . . NiB $2449 Ex $1990 Gd $1590
Left-hand model, add $150
Extra bbl. assembly, add $600

MODEL R-93 SAFARI SERIES BOLT-ACTION REPEATER
Similar to Model R-84 except restyled action w/straight-pull bolt, unique safety and searless trigger mechanism. Additional chamberings: 6.5x55, 7x57, .308, .416 Rem. Optional open sights. Imported 1994 to 1998.
Model R93 Safari . . . . NiB $3598 Ex $2277 Gd $1844
Model R93 Safari Deluxe . . . . . . NiB $3943 Ex $4134 Gd $3297
Model R84 Safari
Super Deluxe . . . . NiB $4854 Ex $4326 Gd $3458
Extra bbl. assembly, add $600

MODEL R-93 CLASSIC SERIES BOLT-ACTION REPEATER
Similar to Model R-93 Safari except w/expanded model variations. Imported from 1998 to 2002.
Model R93 Attache
(Premium wood, fluted bbl.) . . . . NiB $3566 Ex $3887 Gd $3110
Model R93 Classic
(.22-250 to .375 H&H) . . . . NiB $3525 Ex $2889 Gd $2009
Model R93 Classic Safari (.416 Rem.) NiB $3535 Ex $3279 Gd $2270
Model R93 LX (.22-250 to .416 Rem.) NiB $1799 Ex $1445 Gd $996
Model R93 Synthetic (.22-250
to .375 H&H). . . . . NiB $1908 Ex $1235 Gd $855
Extra bbl. assembly, add $600

RIFLES

Brno Model II

Brno Model 21H
Bolt-Action Sporting Rifle

Brno Model 22F

Brno Hornet
Bolt-Action Sporting Rifle

BRITISH MILITARY RIFLES —
Manufactured at Royal Small Arms Factory, Enfield Lock, Middlesex, England, private contractors

RIFLE NO. 1 MARK III . . . . . . **NiB $338 Ex $209 Gd $144**
Short magazine Lee-Enfield (S.M.L.E.). Bolt action. Caliber: .303 British. 10-round box magazine. 25.25-inch bbl. Weight: 8.75 lbs. Sights: Adj. rear; blade front w/guards. Two-piece, full-length military stock. Note: The earlier Mark III (approved 1907) is virtually the same as Mark III (adopted 1918) except for sights and different magazine cut-off that was eliminated on the latter.

RIFLE NO. 3 MARK I (PATTERN 14) . **NiB $347 Ex $255 Gd $160**
Modified Mauser-type bolt action. Except for caliber .303 British and long-range sight, this rifle is the same as U.S. Model 1917 Enfield. See listing of the latter for general specifications.

RIFLE NO. 4 MARK I . . . . **NiB $278 Ex $230 Gd $155**
Post-World War I modification of the S.M.L.E. intended to simplify mass production. General specifications same as Rifle No. 1 Mark III except w/aperture rear sight and minor differences in construction and weighs 9.25 lbs.

LIGHT RIFLE NO. 4 MARK I . . **NiB $227 Ex $170 Gd $133**
Modification of the S.M.L.E. Caliber: .303 British. 10-round box magazine. 23-inch bbl. Weight: 6.75 lbs. Sights: Micrometer click rear peep; blade front. One-piece military-type stock w/recoil pad. Made during WWII.

RIFLE NO. 5 MARK I . . . . . . **NiB $369 Ex $244 Gd $175**
Jungle Carbine. Modification of the S.M.L.E. similar to Light Rifle No. 4 Mark I except w/20.5-inch bbl. w/flash hider, carbine-type stock. Made during WWII, originally designed for use in the Pacific Theater.

BRNO SPORTING RIFLES — Brno, Czech Republic. Manufactured by Ceska Zbrojovka; Imported by Euro-Imports, El Cajon, CA (previously by Bohemia Arms & Magnum Research)

See also CZ rifles.

MODEL I BOLT-ACTION
SPORTING RIFLE . . . . **NiB $689 Ex $615 Gd $437**
Caliber: .22 LR. Five round detachable magazine. 22.75-inch bbl. Weight: 6 lbs. Sights: three-leaf open rear; hooded ramp front. Sporting stock w/checkered pistol grip, swivels. Made 1946 to 1973.

MODEL II BOLT-ACTION
SPORTING RIFLE . . . . **NiB $641 Ex $543 Gd $444**
Same as Model I except w/deluxe grade stock. Made 1949 to 1957.

MODEL III BOLT-ACTION
TARGET RIFLE . . . . **NiB $707 Ex $567 Gd $495**
Same as Model I except w/heavy bbl. and target stock. Made from 1948-56.

MODEL IV BOLT-ACTION
TARGET RIFLE . . . . **NiB $755 Ex $587 Gd $488**
Same as Model III except w/improved target trigger mechanism. Made 1956 to 1962.

MODEL V BOLT-ACTION
SPORTING RIFLE . . . . **NiB $789 Ex $633 Gd $456**
Same as Model I except w/improved trigger mechanism. Made from 1956 to 1973.

Brno Model-ZKM 611

Brown Precision High Country Youth Rifle

MODEL 21H BOLT-ACTION
SPORTING RIFLE . . . . NiB $1590 Ex $1325 Gd $1009
Mauser-type action. Calibers: 6.5x57mm, 7x57mm 8x57mm. Five round box magazine. 20.5-inch bbl. Double set trigger. Weight: 6.75 lbs. Sights: Two-leaf open rear-hooded ramp front. Half-length sporting stock w/cheekpiece, checkered pistol-grip and forearm, swivels. Made from 1946 to 1955.

MODEL 22F . . . . NiB $1408 Ex $1010 Gd $679
Same as Model 21H except w/full-length Mannlicher-type stock, weight: 6 lbs., 14 oz. Disc.

MODEL 98 STANDARD
Calibers: .243 Win., .270 Win., .30-06, .308 Win., .300 Win. Mag., 7x57mm, 7x64mm, or 9.3x62mm. 23.8-inch bbl. Overall 34.5 inches. Weight: 7.25 lbs. Checkered walnut stock w/Bavarian cheekpiece. Imported from 1998. Disc.
Standard calibers . . . . NiB $560 Ex $439 Gd $300
Calibers .300 Win., Mag., 9.3x62mm NiB $580 Ex $469 Gd $386
W/single set trigger, add $150

MODEL 98 MANNLICHER
Similar to Model 98 Standard except full length stock and set triggers. Imported from 1998. Disc.
Standard calibers . . . . NiB $724 Ex $545 Gd $390
Calibers .300 Win. Mag., 9.3x62mm. NiB $755 Ex $600 Gd $445

ZKB-110 SINGLE-SHOT
Calibers: .22 Hornet, .222 Rem., 5.6x52R, 5.6x50 Mag., 6.5x57R, 7x57R, and 8x57JRS. 23.8-inch bbl. Weight: 6.1 lbs. Walnut checkered buttstock and forearm w/Bavarian cheekpiece. Imported from 1998 to 2003.
Standard model . . . . NiB $279 Ex $218 Gd $177
Lux model . . . . NiB $448 Ex $333 Gd $266
Calibers 7x57R and 8x57 JRS, add $50
W/interchangeable 12 ga.
shotgun bbl., add $150

HORNET BOLT-ACTION
SPORTING RIFLE . . . . NiB $1278 Ex $1043 Gd $689
Miniature Mauser action. Caliber: .22 Hornet. Five-round detachable box magazine. 23-inch bbl. Double set trigger. Weight: 6.25 lbs.

Sights: Three-leaf open rear hooded ramp front. Sporting stock w/ checkered pistol grip and forearm, swivels. Made 1949-74. Note: This rifle was also marketed in U.S. as "Z-B Mauser Varmint Rifle." (Reintroduced as Model ZKB 689)

MODEL ZKB 689
BOLT-ACTION RIFLE . . . . NiB $482 Ex $345 Gd $296
Calibers: .22 Hornet, .222 Rem. Five-round detachable box magazine. 23.5-inch bbl. Weight: 5.75 lbs. Double-set triggers. Adj. open rear sight, hooded ramp front. Walnut stock. Imported from 1985 to 1992.

MODEL ZKM 611 SEMIAUTOMATIC RIFLE
Caliber: .22 WMR. Six-round magazine. 20-inch bbl. 37 inches overall. Weight: 6.2 lbs. Hooded front sight; mid-mounted rear sight. Checkered walnut or beechwood stock. Single thumb-screw takedown. Grooved receiver for scope mounting. Imported from 2006 to date.
Standard beechwood model . . NiB $508 Ex $412 Gd $389
Deluxe walnut model . . . . NiB $600 Ex $482 Gd $328

BROWN PRECISION COMPANY — Los Molinos, California

MODEL 7 SUPER LIGHT SPORTER NiB $1128 Ex $1086 Gd $775
Lightweight sporter built on a Remington Model 7 barreled action w/18-inch factory bbl. Weight: 5.25 lbs. Kevlar stock. Made from 1984 to 1992.

HIGH COUNTRY BOLT-ACTION SPORTER
Custom sporting rifles built on Blaser, Remington 707, Ruger 77 and Winchester 70 actions. Calibers: .243 Win., .25-06, .270 Win., 7mm Rem. Mag., .308 Win., .30-06. Five-round magazine (4-round in 7mm Mag.). 22- or 24-inch bbl. Weight: 6.5 lbs. Fiberglass stock w/recoil pad, sling swivels. No sights. Made from 1975 to 1992.
Standard High Country . . . . NiB $1624 Ex $1043 Gd $855
Custom High Country . . . . NiB $4490 Ex $3124 Gd $1876
Left-hand action, add $250
Stainless bbl., add $250
70, 77 or Blaser actions, add $150
70 SG action, add $400

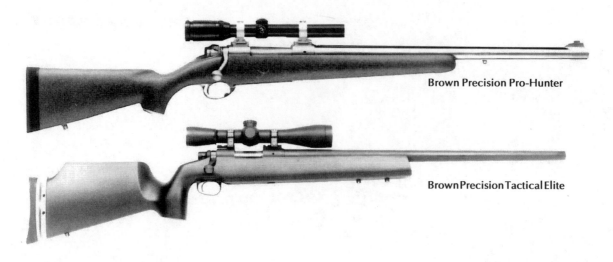

Brown Precision Pro-Hunter

Brown Precision Tactical Elite

HIGH COUNTRY YOUTH RIFLE. . NiB $1336 Ex $1023 Gd $688
Similar to standard Model 7 Super Light except w/Kevlar or graphite stock, scaled-down to youth dimensions. Calibers: .223, .243, 6mm, 7mm-08, .308. Made from 1993 to 2000.

PRO-HUNTER BOLT-ACTION RIFLE
Custom sporting rifle built on Remington 707 or Winchester 70 SG action fitted w/match-grade Shilen bbl. chambered in customer's choice of caliber. Matte blued, nickel or Teflon finish. Express-style rear sight hooded ramp front. Synthetic stock. Made from 1989 to date
Standard Pro-Hunter . . . . NiB $4597 Ex $3150 Gd $2370
Pro-Hunter Elite (1993 to date) . NiB $6066 Ex $3886 Gd $2125

PRO-VARMINTER BOLT-ACTION RIFLE
Custom varminter built on a Remington 707 or 40X action fitted w/ Shilen stainless steel benchrest bbl. Varmint or benchrest-style stock. Made from 1993 to date.
Standard Pro-Varminter. . . . . NiB $3735 Ex $2966 Gd $969
Pro-Hunter w/Rem 40X action add $650

SELECTIVE TARGET MODEL . NiB $1044 Ex $835 Gd $590
Tactical law-enforcement rifle built on a Remington 707V action. Caliber: .308 Win. 20-, 22- or 24-inch bbl. Synthetic stock. Made from 1989 to 1992.

TACTICAL ELITE RIFLE . . NiB $4566 Ex $3290 Gd $1977
Similar to Selective Target Model except fitted w/select match-grade Shilen benchrest heavy stainless bbl. Calibers: .223, .308, .300 Win. Mag. Black or camo Kevlar/graphite composite fiberglass stock w/adj. buttplate. Non-reflective black Teflon metal finish. Made from 1997 to date.

BROWNING RIFLES — Morgan, Utah.
Manufactured for Browning by Fabrique Nationale d'Armes de Guerre (now Fabrique Nationale Herstal), Herstal, Belgium; Miroku Firearms Mfg. Co., Tokyo, Japan; A.T.I., Salt Lake City, UT; Oy Sako Ab, Riihimaki, Finland

.22 AUTOMATIC RIFLE, GRADE I
Similar to discontinued Remington Model 241A. Autoloading. Take-down.

Calibers: .22 LR. .22 Short (not interchangeably). Tubular magazine in buttstock holds 11 LR. 16 Short. Bbl. lengths: 19.25 inches (.22 LR), 22.25 inches (.22 Short). Weight: 4.75 lbs. (.22 LR); 5 lbs. (.22 Short). Receiver scroll engraved. Open rear sight, bead front. Checkered pistol-grip buttstock, semibeavertail forearm. Made from 1956 to 1972 by FN; from 1972 to date by Miroku. Note: Illustrations are of rifles manufactured by FN.
FN manufacture . . . . NiB $899 Ex $500 Gd $265
Miroku manufacture . . . . NiB $650 Ex $398 Gd $327

.22 AUTOMATIC RIFLE, GRADE II
Same as Grade I except satin chrome-plated receiver engraved w/ small game animal scenes, gold-plated trigger select walnut stock and forearm. .22 LR only. Made from 1972 to 1984.
FN manufacture . . . . NiB $1200 Ex $909 Gd $369
Miroku manufacture . . . . NiB $554 Ex $439 Gd $300

.22 AUTOMATIC RIFLE, GRADE III
Same as Grade I except satin chrome-plated receiver elaborately hand-carved and engraved w/dog and game-bird scenes, scrolls and leaf clusters: gold-plated trigger, extra-fancy walnut stock and forearm, skip-checkered. .22 LR only. Made from 1972 to 1984.
FN manufacture . . . . NiB $1500 Ex $1125 Gd $880
Miroku manufacture . . . . NiB $822 Ex $590 Gd $480

.22 AUTOMATIC, GRADE VI NiB $1190 Ex $798 Gd $600
Same general specifications as standard .22 Automatic except for engraving, high-grade stock w/checkering and glossy finish. Made by Miroku from 1986 to date.

MODEL 52 BOLT-ACTION RIFLE . . . NiB $800 Ex $655 Gd $443
Limited edition of Winchester Model 52C Sporter. Caliber: .22 LR. Five-round magazine. 24-inch bbl. Weight: 7 lbs. Micro-Motion trigger. No sights. Checkered select walnut stock w/rosewood forend and metal grip cap. Blued finish. 5000 made from 1991 to 1992.

MODEL 53 LEVER-ACTION RIFLE . . . NiB $833 Ex $724 Gd $480
Limited edition of Winchester Model 53. Caliber: .32-20. Seven-round tubular half-magazine. 22-inch bbl. Weight: 6.5 lbs. Adj. rear sight, bead front. Select walnut checkered pistol-grip stock w/high-gloss finish. Classic-style forearm. Blued finish. 5000 made in 1990.

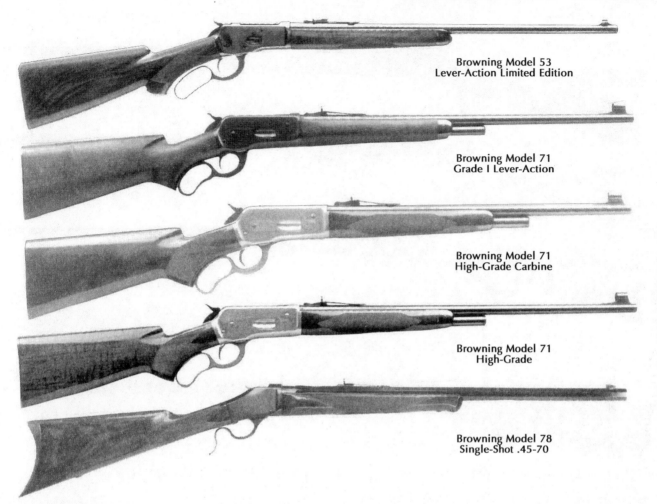

Browning Model 53
Lever-Action Limited Edition

Browning Model 71
Grade I Lever-Action

Browning Model 71
High-Grade Carbine

Browning Model 71
High-Grade

Browning Model 78
Single-Shot .45-70

MODEL 65 GRADE I
LEVER-ACTION RIFLE . . . . . NiB $730 Ex $445 Gd $370
Caliber: .218 Bee. 7-round tubular half-magazine. 24-inch bbl. Weight: 6.75 lbs. Sights: Adj. buckhorn-style rear, hooded bead front. Select walnut pistol-grip stock w/high-gloss finish. Semibeavertail forearm. Limited edition of 3500 made in 1989.

MODEL 65 HIGH GRADE RIFLE . . . NiB $1009 Ex $733 Gd $528
Same general specifications as Model 65 Grade I except w/engraving and gold-plated animals on grayed receiver. Cut checkering on pistol grip and forearm. Limited edition of 1500 made in 1989.

MODEL 71 GRADE I CARBINE . . . . NiB $880 Ex $640 Gd $455
Same general specifications as Model 71 Grade I Rifle except carbine w/20-inch round bbl. and weighs 8 lbs. Limited edition of 4000 made in 1986 to 1987.

MODEL 71 GRADE I
LEVER-ACTION RIFLE . . . . . . NiB $916 Ex $710 Gd $497
Caliber: .348 Win. 4-round magazine. 24-inch round bbl. Weight: 8 lbs., 2 oz. Open buckhorn sights. Select walnut straight grip stock w/satin finish. Classic-style forearm, flat metal buttplate. Limited edition of 3000 made in 1986 to 1987.

MODEL 71 HIGH-GRADE CARBINE NiB $1332 Ex $1123 Gd $765
Same general specifications as Model 71 High Grade Rifle, except carbine w/20-inch round bbl. Limited edition of 3000 made 1986 to 1988.

MODEL 71 HIGH-GRADE RIFLE . . NiB $1440 Ex $1110 Gd $823
Caliber: .348 Win. Four round magazine. 24-inch round bbl. Weight: 8 lbs., 2 oz. Engraved receiver. Open buckhorn sights. Select walnut checkered pistol-grip stock w/high-gloss finish. Classic-style forearm, flat metal buttplate. Limited edition of 3000 made in 1987.

M-78 BICENTENNIAL SET. NiB $3866 Ex $3121 Gd $2140
Special Model 78 .45-70 w/same specifications as standard type, except sides of receiver engraved w/bison and eagle, scroll engraving on top of receiver, lever, both ends of bbl. and buttplate; high-grade walnut stock and forearm. Accompanied by an engraved hunting knife and stainless steel commemorative medallion, all in an alder wood presentation case. Each item in set has matching serial number beginning with "1776" and ending with numbers 1 to 1,000. Edition limited to 1,000 sets. Made in 1976.

MODEL 78 SINGLE-SHOT RIFLE
Falling-block lever-action similar to Winchester 1885 High Wall single-shot rifle. Calibers: .22-250, 6mm Rem., .243 Win., .25-06, 7mm Rem. Mag., .30-06, .45-70 Govt. 26-inch octagon or heavy round bbl.; 24-inch octagon bull bbl. on .45-70 model. Weight: 7.75 lbs. w/octagon bbl.; w/round bbl., 8.5 lbs.; .45-70, 8.75 lbs. Furnished w/o sights except .45-70 model w/open rear sight, blade front. Checkered fancy walnut stock and forearm. .45-70 model w/straight-grip stock and curved buttplate; others have Monte Carlo comb and cheekpiece, pistol-grip w/cap, recoil pad. Made from 1973 to 1983 by Miroku. Reintroduced in 1985 as Model 1885.
All calibers except .45-70. NiB $1500 Ex $1274 Gd $1010
.45-70 . . . . NiB $970 Ex $766 Gd $523

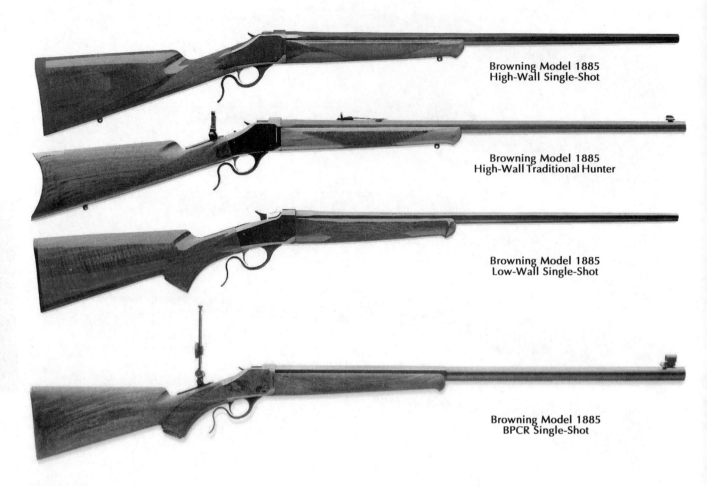

Browning Model 1885
High-Wall Single-Shot

Browning Model 1885
High-Wall Traditional Hunter

Browning Model 1885
Low-Wall Single-Shot

Browning Model 1885
BPCR Single-Shot

MODEL 1885 SINGLE-SHOT RIFLE

Calibers: .22 Hornet, .223, .243, (Low Wall); .357 Mag., .44 Mag., .45 LC (L/W Traditional Hunter); .22-250, .223 Rem., .270 Win., 7mm Rem. Mag., .30-06, .454 Casull Mag., .45.70 (High Wall); .30.30 Win., .38-55 WCF, .45 Govt. (H/W Traditional Hunter); .40-65, .45 Govt. and .45.90 (BPCR). 24-, 28-, 30 or 34-inch round, octagonal or octagonal and round bbl. 39.5, 43.5, 44.25 or 46.125 inches overall. Weight: 6.25, 8.75, 9, 11, or 11.75 lbs. respectively. Blued or color casehardened receiver. Gold-colored adj. trigger. Drilled and tapped for scope mounts w/no sights or vernier tang rear sight w/globe front and open sights on .45-70 Govt. Walnut straight-grip stock and Schnabel forearm w/cut checkering and high-gloss or oil finish. Made from 1985 to 2001.

Low Wall model w/o sights (Intro. 1995) .. NiB $1400 Ex $976 Gd $540
Traditional Hunter model (Intro. 1998)NiB $1450 Ex $990 Gd $575
High Wall model w/o sights (Intro. 1985) NiB $1390 Ex $1020 Gd $770
Traditional Hunter model (Intro. 1997)NiB $1390 Ex $1020 Gd $770
BPCR model w/no
ejector (Intro. 1996) . . . . NiB $1933 Ex $1442 Gd $1041
BPCR Creedmoor Model .45-90
(Intro. 1998). . . . . NiB $1933 Ex $1442 Gd $1041

MODEL 1886 MONTANA

CENTENNIAL RIFLE . . . . . NiB $2120 Ex $1670 Gd $1097
Same general specifications as Model 1886 High Grade lever-action except w/specially engraved receiver designating Montana Centennial; also different stock design. Made in 1986 in limited issue by Miroku.

MODEL 1886 GRADE I

LEVER-ACTION RIFLE. . . . . NiB $1255 Ex $712 Gd $495
Caliber: .45-70 Govt., 8-round magazine. 26-inch octagonal bbl. 45 inches overall. Weight: 9 lbs., 5 oz. Deep blued finish on receiver. Open buckhorn sights. Straight-grip walnut stock. Classic-style forearm. Metal buttplate. Satin finish. Made in 1986 in limited issue 7070 by Miroku.

MODEL 1886 HIGH-

GRADE LA RIFLE . . . . NiB $2055 Ex $1359 Gd $933
Same general specifications as the Model 1886 Grade I except receiver is grayed, steel embellished w/scroll; elk and American bison engraving. High-gloss stock. Made in 1986 in limited issue of 3000 by Miroku.

MODEL 1895 GRADE I LA RIFLE . . . NiB $979 Ex $911 Gd $765

Caliber: .30-06, .30-40 Krag. Four round magazine. 24-inch round bbl. 42 inches overall. Weight: 8 lbs. French walnut stock and Schnabel forend. Sights: Rear buckhorn; gold bead on elevated ramp front. Made in 1984 in limited issue of 8,000 (2,000 chambered for .30-40 Krag and 6,000 chambered for .30-06). Mfd. by Miroku.

MODEL 1895 HIGH-

GRADE LA RIFLE . . . . NiB $1630 Ex $1379 Gd $996
Same general specifications as Model 1895 Grade I except engraved receiver and Grade III French walnut stock and forend w/fine checkering. Made in 1985 in limited issue of 1000 in each caliber by Miroku.

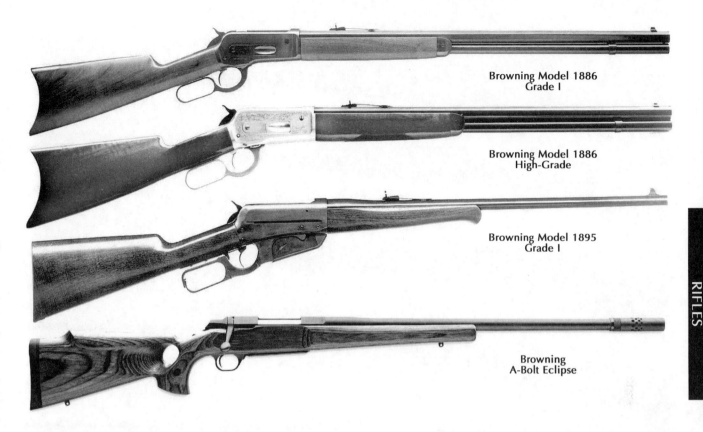

Browning Model 1886
Grade I

Browning Model 1886
High-Grade

Browning Model 1895
Grade I

Browning
A-Bolt Eclipse

MODEL A-BOLT .22 RIFLE
Calibers: .22 LR, .22 Magnum. Five- and 15-round magazines. 22-inch round bbl. 40.25 inches overall. Weight: 5 lbs., 9 oz. Gold-colored adj. trigger. Laminated walnut stock w/checkering. Rosewood forend grip cap; pistol grip. With or w/o sights. Ramp front and adj. folding leaf rear on open sight model. 22 LR made 1985 to 1996; 22 Magnum, 1990 to 1996.

Grade I .22 LR	NiB $575	Ex $340	Gd $255
Grade I .22 Magnum	NiB $600	Ex $423	Gd $269
Deluxe Grade			
Gold Medallion	NiB $620	Ex $479	Gd $354

MODEL A-BOLT ECLIPSE BOLT RIFLE
Same general specifications as Hunter Grade except fitted w/gray and black laminated thumbhole stock. Available in both short and long action w/two bbl. configurations w/BOSS. Mfd. by Miroku 1996 to 2006.

Eclipse w/standard bbl.	NiB $955	Ex $821	Gd $677
Eclipse Varmint w/heavy bbl.	NiB $1123	Ex $978	Gd $720
Eclipse M-1000			
Target (.300 Win. Mag.).	NiB $1304	Ex $1038	Gd $796

MODEL A-BOLT EURO-BOLT RIFLE
Same general specifications as Hunter Grade except w/checkered satin-finished walnut stock. W/continental-style cheekpiece, palm-swell grip and Schnabel forend. Mannlicher-style spoon bolt handle and contoured bolt shroud. 22- or 26-inch bbl. w/satin blued finish. Weight: 6.8 to 7.4 lbs. Calibers: .22-250 Rem., .243 Win., .270 Win., .30.06, .308 Win., 7mm Rem. Mag. Mfd. by Miroku 1993 to 1994; 1994 to 1996 (Euro-Bolt II).

Euro-Bolt	NiB $679	Ex $536	Gd $369
Euro-Bolt II.	NiB $755	Ex $640	Gd $470
BOSS option, add.			$100

MODEL A-BOLT HUNTER GRADE RIFLE
Calibers: .22 Hornet, .223 Rem., .22-250 Rem., .243 Win., .257 Roberts, 7mm-08 Rem., .308 Win., (short action) .25-06 Rem., .270 Win., .280 Rem., .284 Win., .30-06, 7mm Rem. Mag., .300 Win. Mag., .338 Win. Mag. Four-round magazine (standard), 3-round (magnum). 22-inch bbl. (standard), 24-inch (magnum). Weight: 7.5 lbs. (standard), 8.5 lbs. (magnum). With or w/o sights. Classic-style walnut stock. Produced in two action lengths w/nine locking lugs, fluted bolt w/60 degree rotation. Mfd. by Miroku from 1985 to 1993; from 1994 to 2007 (Hunter II).

Hunter	NiB $489	Ex $333	Gd $269
Hunter II	NiB $590	Ex $389	Gd $310
Hunter Micro	NiB $596	Ex $395	Gd $317
BOSS option, add.			$100
Open sights, add			$75

MODEL A-BOLT MEDALLION GRADE RIFLE
Same as Hunter Grade except w/high-gloss deluxe stock rosewood grip cap and forend; high-luster blued finish. Also in .375 H&H w/open sights. Left-hand models available in long action only. Mfd. by Miroku from 1988 to 1993; from 1994 to 2009 (Medallion II). Bighorn Sheep Ltd. Ed.

.270 Win. (600 made 1986)	NiB $1412	Ex $1096	Gd $790
Gold Medallion Deluxe Grade	NiB $679	Ex $500	Gd $346
Gold Medallion II Deluxe Grade	NiB $670	Ex $525	Gd $380
Medallion, Standard Grade	NiB $633	Ex $488	Gd $354
Medallion II, Standard Grade	NiB $655	Ex $500	Gd $397
Medallion, .375 H&H.	NiB $999	Ex $770	Gd $488
Medallion II, .375 H&H	NiB $1012	Ex $790	Gd $497
Micro Medallion.	NiB $690	Ex $557	Gd $367
Micro Medallion II	NiB $707	Ex $569	Gd $415
Pronghorn Antelope Ltd. Ed. 243 Win.			
(500 made 1987,).	NiB $1266	Ex $1139	Gd $923
W/BOSS option, add.			$100
W/Open sights, add			$75

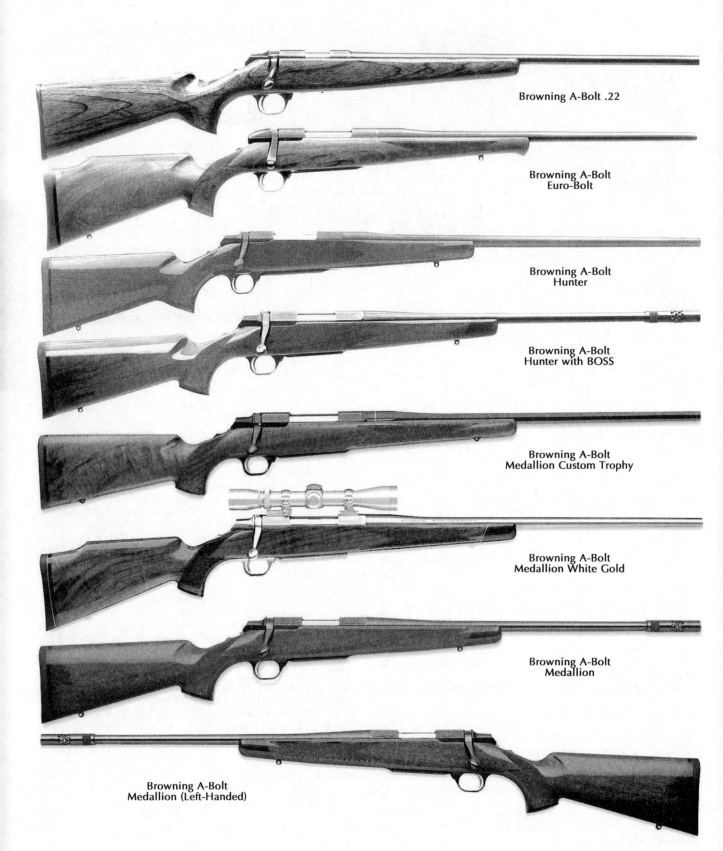

Browning A-Bolt .22

Browning A-Bolt
Euro-Bolt

Browning A-Bolt
Hunter

Browning A-Bolt
Hunter with BOSS

Browning A-Bolt
Medallion Custom Trophy

Browning A-Bolt
Medallion White Gold

Browning A-Bolt
Medallion

Browning A-Bolt
Medallion (Left-Handed)

Browning A-Bolt
Composite Stalker

Browning A-Bolt
Stainless Stalker

Browning BAR, Grade IV

Browning BAR, Grade V

MODEL A-BOLT STALKER RIFLE

Same general specifications as Model A-Bolt Hunter Rifle except w/ checkered graphite-fiberglass composite stock and matte blued or stainless metal. Non-glare matte finish of all exposed metal surfaces. 3 models: Camo Stalker orig. w/multi-colored laminated wood stock, matte blued metal; Composite Stalker w/graphite-fiberglass stock, matte blued metal; w/composite stock, stainless metal. Made by Miroku from 1987 to 1993; 1994 to date. (Stalker II).

Camo Stalker (orig. laminated stock) .	NiB $960	Ex $709	Gd $350
Composite Stalker.	NiB $990	Ex $656	Gd $433
Composite Stalker II	NiB $990	Ex $656	Gd $433
Stainless Stalker	NiB $1045	Ex $745	Gd $500
Stainless Stalker II.	NiB $876	Ex $655	Gd $571
Stainless Stalker, .375 H&H	NiB $909	Ex $808	Gd $667
W/BOSS option, add.			$100
Left-hand model, add			$100

MODEL A-BOLT
VARMINT II RIFLE . . . . NiB $805 Ex $723 Gd $577

Same general specifications as Stalker model except w/22-inch heavy bbl. w/BOSS system and varmint-style black laminated wood stock. Calibers: .22-250, .223 or .308. No sights. Bright blue or satin finish. Made by Miroku from 2002 to 2008.

MODEL B-92 LEVER-ACTION RIFLE . NiB $534 Ex $467 Gd $288

Calibers: .357 Mag. and .44 Rem. Mag. 11-round magazine. 20-inch round bbl. 37.5 inches overall. Weight: 5.5 to 6.4 lbs. Seasoned French walnut stock w/high gloss finish. Cloverleaf rear sight; steel post front. Made from1979 to 1989 by Miroku.

BAR AUTOMATIC RIFLE,
GRADE I, STANDARD CALIBERS NiB $805 Ex $ 623 Gd $455

Gas-operated semiautomatic. Calibers: .243 Win., .270 Win., .280 Rem., .308 Win., .30-06. Four-round box magazine. 22-inch bbl. Weight: 7.5 lbs. Folding leaf rear sight, hooded ramp front. French walnut stock and forearm checkered, QD swivels. Made from 1967 to 1992 by FN.

BAR, GRADE I, MAGNUM CALIBERS . . NiB $809 Ex $733 Gd $590

Same as BAR in standard calibers, except w/24-inch bbl. 7mm Rem. Mag. or .300 Win. Mag. .338 Win. Mag. w/3-round box magazine and recoil pad. Weight: 8.5 lbs. Made 1969 to 1992 by FN.

BAR, GRADE II

Same as Grade I except receiver engraved w/big-game heads (deer and antelope on standard-caliber rifles, ram and grizzly on Magnum-caliber) and scrollwork, higher grade wood. Made 1967 to 1974 by FN.

Standard calibers	NiB $1229	Ex $976	Gd $657
Magnum calibers	NiB $1338	Ex $875	Gd $617

BAR, GRADE III

Same as Grade I except receiver of grayed steel engraved w/big-game heads (deer and antelope on standard-caliber rifles, moose and elk on Magnum-caliber) framed in fine-line scrollwork, gold-plated trigger, stock and forearm of highly figured French walnut, hand-checkered and carved. Made from 1971 to 1974 by FN.

Standard calibers	NiB $1554	Ex $993	Gd $591
Magnum calibers	NiB $1617	Ex $1230	Gd $725

BAR, GRADE IV

Same as Grade I except receiver of grayed steel engraved w/full detailed rendition of running deer and antelope on standard-caliber rifles, moose and elk on Magnum-caliber gold-plated trigger, stock and forearm of highly figured French walnut, hand checkered and carved. Made frm 1971 to 1986 by FN.

Standard calibers	NiB $2490	Ex $1546	Gd $1110
Magnum calibers	NiB $2669	Ex $1721	Gd $1300

BAR, GRADE V

Same as Grade I except receiver w/complete big-game scenes executed by a master engraver and inlaid w/18K gold (deer and antelope on standard-caliber rifles, moose and elk on Magnum caliber), gold-plated trigger, stock and forearm of finest French walnut, intricately hand-checkered and carved. Made from 1971 to 1974 by FN.

Standard calibers	NiB $6457	Ex $4707	Gd $2897
Magnum calibers	NiB $6844	Ex $5110	Gd $3194

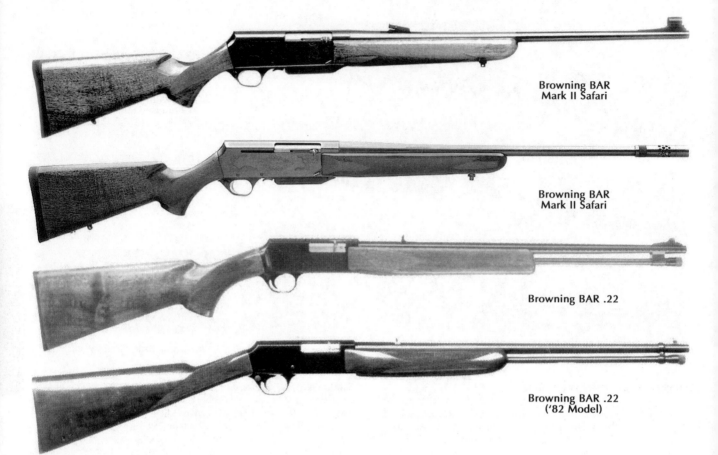

Browning BAR
Mark II Safari

Browning BAR
Mark II Safari

Browning BAR .22

Browning BAR .22
('82 Model)

BAR MARK II SAFARI AUTOMATIC RIFLE
Same general specifications as standard BAR semiautomatic rifle, except w/redesigned gas and buffer systems, new bolt release lever, and engraved receiver. Made from 1993 to date.

Standard calibers . . . . NiB $1019 Ex $707 Gd $505
Magnum calibers . . . . NiB $1040 Ex $808 Gd $617
Lightweight (Alloy receiver
w/20-inch bbl.). . . . . NiB $765 Ex $588 Gd $380
BAR Mk II Grade III (intro. 1996) NiB $3520 Ex $2377 Gd $1290
BAR Mk II Grade IV (intro. 1996) NiB $3609 Ex $2303 Gd $1829
W/BOSS option, add $75
W/open sights, add $25

BAR .22 AUTOMATIC RIFLE
Semiautomatic. Caliber: .22 LR. Tubular magazine holds 15 rounds. 20.25-inch bbl. Weight: 6.25 lbs. Sights: Folding-leaf rear, gold bead front on ramp. Receiver grooved for scope mounting. French walnut pistol-grip stock and forearm checkered. Made from 1977 to 1985.

Grade I . . . . NiB $641 Ex $369 Gd $322
Grade II . . . . NiB $1011 Ex $555 Gd $375

BBR LIGHTNING BOLT-ACTION RIFLE NiB $606 Ex $495 Gd $400
Bolt-action rifle w/short bolt throw of 60 degrees. Calibers: .25-06 Rem., .270 Win., .30-06, 7mm Rem. Mag., .300 Win. Mag. 24-inch bbl. Weight: 8 lbs. Made from 1979 to 1984.

BL-.22 LEVER-ACTION REPEATING RIFLE
Short-throw lever-action. Caliber: .22 LR, Long, Short. Tubular magazine holds 15 LR, 17 Long 22 Short rounds. 20-inch bbl. Weight: 5 lbs. Sights: Folding leaf rear; bead front. Receiver grooved for scope

mounting. Walnut straight-grip stock and forearm, bbl. band. Made from 1970 to date by Miroku.

Grade I . . . . NiB $445 Ex $379 Gd $290
Grade II
(w/scroll engraving) . . . . NiB $498 Ex $390 Gd $300

BLR LEVER-ACTION REPEATING RIFLE
Calibers: (short action only) .243 Win., .308 Win., .358 Win. Four round detachable box magazine. 20-inch bbl. Weight: 7 lbs. Sights: Windage and elevation adj. open rear; hooded ramp front. Walnut straight-grip stock and forearm, checkered, bbl. band, recoil pad. Made in 1966 by BAC/USA; from 1969 to 1973 by FN; from 1974 to 1980 by Miroku. Note: USA manufacture of this model was limited to prototypes and pre-production guns only and may be identified by the "MADE IN USA" roll stamp on the bbl.

FN model. . . . . NiB $1000 Ex $699 Gd $554
Miroku model. . . . . NiB $690 Ex $500 Gd $398
USA model. . . . . NiB $1245 Ex $1097 Gd $686

BLR LIGHTNING MODEL
Lightweight version of the Browning BLR '81 w/forged alloy receiver and redesigned trigger group. Calibers: Short Action— .22-250 Rem., .223 Rem., .243 Win., 7mm-08 Rem., .308 Win.; Long Action— .270 Win., 7mm Rem. Mag., .30-06, .300 Win. Mag. Three or 4-round detachable box magazine. 20-, 22- or 24-inch bbl. Weight: 6.5 to 7.75 lbs. Pistol-grip style walnut stock and forearm, cut checkering and recoil pad. Made by Miroku from 1995 to 2002.

Short action model . . . . NiB $690 Ex $586 Gd $390
Long action model . . . . NiB $707 Ex $596 Gd $400

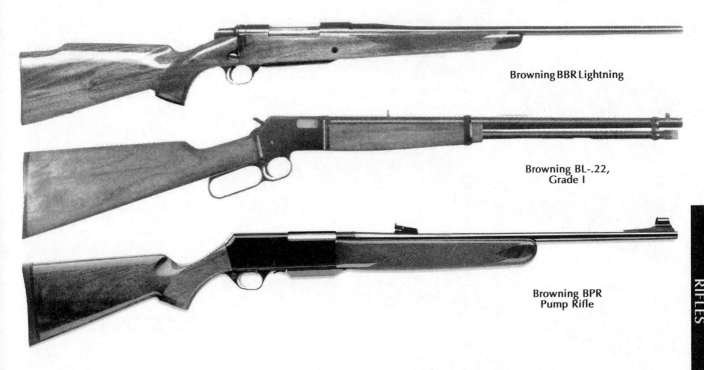

Browning BBR Lightning

Browning BL-.22, Grade I

Browning BPR Pump Rifle

BLR MODEL '81

Redesigned version of the Browning BLR. Calibers: .222-50 Rem., .243 Win., .308 Win., .358 Win; Long Action— .270 Win., 7mm Rem. Mag., .30-06. Fourround detachable box magazine. 20-inch bbl. Weight: 7 lbs. Walnut straight-grip stock and forearm, cut checkering, recoil pad. Made by Miroku from 1981 to 1995; Long Action intro. 1991.

Short action model . . . . NiB $780 Ex $592 Gd $396
Long action model . . . . NiB $850 Ex $505 Gd $390

BPR-22 PUMP RIFLE

Hammerless slide-action repeater. Specifications same as for BAR-.22, except also available chambered for .22 Magnum RF; magazine capacity, 11 rounds. Made from 1977 to 1982 by Miroku.

Model I . . . . NiB $355 Ex $274 Gd $200
Model II . . . . NiB $425 Ex $437 Gd $262

BPR PUMP RIFLE

Slide-action repeater based on proven BAR designs w/forged alloy receiver and slide that cams down to clear bbl. and receiver. Calibers: .243 Win., .308 Win., .270 Win., .30-06, 7mm Rem. Mag. .300 Win. Mag. Three or 4-round detachable box magazine. 22- or 24-inch bbl. w/ramped front sight and open adj. rear. Weight: 7.2 to 7.4 lbs. Made from 1997 to 2001 by Miroku.

BPR Model standard calibers. . NiB $743 Ex $533 Gd $390
BPR Model magnum calibers add $75

HIGH-POWER BOLT-ACTION
RIFLE, MEDALLION GRADE . . . . NiB $3877 Ex $3488 Gd $1967

Same as Safari Grade except receiver and bbl. scroll engraved, ram's head engraved on floorplate; select walnut stock w/rosewood forearm tip, grip cap. Made from 1961 to 1974.

HIGH-POWER BOLT-ACTION
RIFLE, OLYMPIAN GRADE . . . . . NiB $3831 Ex $3435 Gd $1925

Same as Safari Grade except bbl. engraved; receiver, trigger guard and floorplate satin chrome-plated and engraved w/game scenes appropriate to caliber; finest figured walnut stock w/rosewood forearm tip and grip cap, latter w/18K-gold medallion. Made from 1961 to 1974.

HIGH-POWER BOLT-ACTION RIFLE,
SAFARI GRADE, MEDIUM ACTION NiB $1443 Ex $988 Gd $733

Same as Standard except medium action. Calibers: .22-250, .243 Win., .264 Win. Mag., .284 Win. Mag., .308 Win. Bbl.: 22-inch lightweight bbl.; .22-250 and .243 also available w/24-inch heavy bbl. Weight: 6 lbs., 12 oz. w/lightweight bbl.; 7 lbs. 13 oz. w/heavy bbl. Made 1963 to 1974 by Sako.

HIGH-POWER BOLT-ACTION RIFLE,
SAFARI GRADE, SHORT ACTION . . NiB $1722 Ex $933 Gd $747

Same as Standard except short action. Calibers: .222 Rem., .222 Rem. Mag. 22-inch lightweight or 24-inch heavy bbl. No sights. Weight: 6 lbs., 2 oz. w/lightweight bbl.; 7.5 lbs. w/heavy bbl. Made from 1963 to 1974 by Sako.

HIGH-POWER BOLT-ACTION RIFLE,
SAFARI GRADE, STANDARD ACTION NiB $1523 Ex $1133 Gd $944

Mauser-type action. Calibers: .270 Win., .30-06, 7mm Rem. Mag., .300 H&H Mag., .300 Win. Mag., .308 Norma Mag. .338 Win. Mag., .375 H&H Mag., .458 Win. Mag. Cartridge capacity: 6 rounds in .270, .30-06; 4 in Magnum calibers. Bbl. length: 22 in., in .270, .30-06; 24 in., in Magnum calibers. Weight: 7 lbs., 2 oz., in .270, .30-06; 8.25 lbs. in Mag. calibers. Folding leaf rear sight, hooded ramp front. Checkered stock w/pistol grip, Monte Carlo cheekpiece, QD swivels; recoil pad on Magnum models. Made from 1959 to 1974 by FN.

T-BOLT T-1 .22 REPEATING RIFLE

Straight-pull bolt action. Caliber: .22 LR. Five round clip magazine. 24-inch bbl. Peep rear sight w/ramped blade front. Plain walnut stock w/pistol grip and laquered finish. Weight: 6 lbs. Also left-hand model. Made from 1965 to 1974 by FN.

Right-hand model . . . . NiB $650 Ex $469 Gd $300
Left-hand model . . . . NiB $675 Ex $512 Gd $409

T-BOLT T-2

Same as T-1 Model except w/checkered fancy figured walnut stock. Made from 1966-74 by FN. (Reintroduced briefly during the late 1980's with oil-finished stock)

Original model . . . . NiB $909 Ex $579 Gd $289
Reintroduced model . . . . NiB $589 Ex $433 Gd $266

Browning
BL-22 II

Browning
BLR Model '81

Browning High-Power
Bolt-Action Rifle, Medallion Grade

Browning High-Power
Safari Grade Medium Action, Heavy Barrel

Browning High-Power
Safari Grade Short Action, Heavy Barrel

Browning High-Power
Safari Grade Standard Action

F.N. BROWNING FAL SEMIAUTOMATIC RIFLE
Same as F.N. FAL Semiautomatic Rifle. See F.N. listing for specifications. Sold by Browning for a brief period c. 1960.
F.N. FAL standard
model (G-series). . . . . NiB $4977 Ex $3677 Gd $2928
F.N. FAL lightweight
model (G-series). . . . . NiB $5310 Ex $4400 Gd $3090
F.N. FAL heavy bbl..
model (G-series). . . . . NiB $7175 Ex $6230 Gd $4956
BAC FAL model . . . . NiB $5320 Ex $4952 Gd $4915

BSA GUNS LTD. — Birmingham, England
(previously imported by Samco Global Arms, BSA Guns Ltd and Precision Sports)

NO. 12 MARTINI SINGLE-SHOT
TARGET RIFLE . . . . NiB $766 Ex $567 Gd $433
Caliber .22 LR. 29-inch bbl. Weight: 8.75 lbs. Parker-Hale Model 7 rear sight and Model 2 front sight. Straight-grip stock, checkered forearm. Note: This model was also available w/open sights or w/BSA No. 20 and 30 sights. Made before WWII.

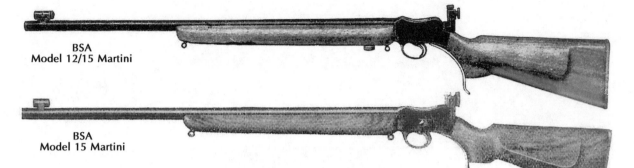

BSA
Model 12/15 Martini

BSA
Model 15 Martini

MODEL 12/15 MARTINI HEAVY . . . . **NiB $765 Ex $544 Gd $379**
Same as Standard Model 12/15 except w/extra heavy bbl., weighs 11 lbs.

MODEL 12/15 MARTINI
SINGLE-SHOT TARGET RIFLE . **NiB $650 Ex $479 Gd $355**
Caliber: .22 LR. 29-inch bbl. Weight: 9 lbs. Parker-Hale No. PH-7A rear sight and No. FS-22 front sight. Target stock w/high comb and cheekpiece, beavertail forearm. Note: This is a post-WWII model; however, a similar rifle, the BSA-Parker Model 12/15, was produced c. 1938.

NO. 13 MARTINI SINGLE-SHOT
TARGET RIFLE . . . . **NiB $756 Ex $579 Gd $443**
Caliber: .22 LR. Lighter version of the No.12 w/same general specifications except w/25-inch bbl., weighs 6.5lbs. Made before WWII.

NO. 13 SPORTING RIFLE
Same as No. 13 Target except fitted w/Parker-Hale "Sportarget" rear sight and bead front sight. Also available in .22 Hornet. Made before WWII.
.22 Long Rifle. . . . . **NiB $756 Ex $579 Gd $443**
.22 Hornet . . . . **NiB $976 Ex $800 Gd $579**

MODEL 15 MARTINI
SINGLE-SHOT TARGET RIFLE. . . . . . **NiB $765 Ex $577 Gd $338**
Caliber: .22 LR. 29-inch bbl. Weight: 9.5 lbs. BSA No. 30 rear sight and No. 20 front sight. Target stock w/cheekpiece and pistol-grip, long, semi-beavertail forearm. Made before WWII.

CENTURION MODEL
MATCH RIFLE . . . . **NiB $522 Ex $423 Gd $320**
Same general specifications as Model 15 except w/Centurion match bbl. Made before WWII.

CF-2 BOLT-ACTION
HUNTING RIFLE . . . . **NiB $543 Ex $399 Gd $265**
Mauser-type action. Calibers: 7mm Rem. Mag., .300 Win. Mag. Three-round magazine. 23.6-inch bbl. Weight: 8 lbs. Sights: Adj. rear; hooded ramp front. Checkered walnut stock w/Monte Carlo comb, rollover cheekpiece, rosewood forend tip, recoil pad, sling swivels. Made 1975 to 1987.

CF-2 STUTZEN RIFLE . . . . **NiB $577 Ex $437 Gd $333**
Calibers: .222 Rem., .22-250, .243 Win., .270 Win., .308 Win. .30-06. Four round capacity (5 in 222 Rem.). 20.6-inch bbl. 41.5 inches (approx.) overall length. Weight: 7.5 to 8 lbs. Williams front and rear sights. Hand-finished European walnut stock. Monte Carlo cheekpiece and Wundhammer palm swell. Double-set triggers. Importation disc. 1987.

CFT TARGET RIFLE. . . . . **NiB $926 Ex $735 Gd $533**
Single-shot bolt action. Caliber: 7.62mm. 26.5-inch bbl. About 47.5 inches overall. Weight: 11 lbs., incl. accessories. Bbl. and action weight: 6 lbs., 12 oz. Importation disc. 1987.

MAJESTIC DELUXE FEATHERWEIGHT BOLT-ACTION HUNTING RIFLE
Mauser-type action. Calibers: .243 Win., .270 Win., .308 Win., .30-06, .458 Win. Mag. Four round magazine. 22-inch bbl. w/BESA recoil reducer. Weight: 6.25 lbs.; 8.75 lbs. in 458. Folding leaf rear sight, hooded ramp front. Checkered European-style walnut stock w/cheekpiece, pistol-grip, Schnabel forend, swivels, recoil pad. Made from 1959 to 1965.
.458 Win. Mag. caliber. . . . . . **NiB $650 Ex $508 Gd $380**
Other calibers . . . . **NiB $506 Ex $433 Gd $298**

BSA MAJESTIC DELUXE
STANDARD WEIGHT . . . . **NiB $508 Ex $332 Gd $255**
Same as Featherweight model except heavier bbl. w/o recoil reducer. Calibers: .22 Hornet, .222 Rem., .243 Win., 7x57mm, .308 Win., .30-06. Weight: 7.25 to 7.75 lbs. Disc.

MARTINI-INTERNATIONAL
ISU MATCH RIFLE . . . . **NiB $944 Ex $708 Gd $577**
Similar to MK III, but modified to meet International Shooting Union "Standard Rifle" specifications. 28-inch standard weight bbl. Weight: 10.75 lbs. Redesigned stock and forearm, latter attached to bbl. w/"V" section alloy strut. Intro. 1968. Disc.

MARTINI-INTERNATIONAL
MARK V MATCH RIFLE. . . . . **NiB $1077 Ex $897 Gd $623**
Same as ISU model except w/heavier bbl. Weight: 12.25 lbs. Intro. 1976. Disc.

MARTINI-INTERNATIONAL MATCH
RIFLE SINGLE-SHOT HEAVY PATTERN NiB $866 Ex $630 Gd $443
Caliber: .22 LR. 29-inch heavy bbl. Weight: 14 lbs. Parker-Hale "International" front and rear sights. Target stock w/full cheekpiece and pistol-grip, broad beavertail forearm, handstop, swivels. Right- or left-hand models. Made from 1950 to 1953.

MARTINI-INTERNATIONAL
MATCH RIFLE — LIGHT PATTERN . . . . **NiB $775 Ex $584 Gd $455**
Same general specifications as Heavy Pattern except w/26-inch lighter weight bbl. Weight: 11 lbs. Disc.

MARTINI-INTERNATIONAL
MK II MATCH RIFLE. . . . . . . **NiB $1043 Ex $720 Gd $630**
Same general specifications as original model. Heavy and Light Pattern. Improved trigger mechanism and ejection system. Redesigned stock and forearm. Made from 1953 to 1959.

MARTINI-INTERNATIONAL
MK III MATCH RIFLE . . . . . . **NiB $1044 Ex $812 Gd $613**
Same general specifications as MK II Heavy Pattern. Longer action frame w/I-section alloy strut to which forearm is attached; bbl. is fully floating. Redesigned stock and forearm. Made 1959 to 1967.

BSA CFT Target

BSA
Martini-International ISU Match

BSA
Martini-International Mark V Match

BSA
Martini-International MK III Match

BSA
Monarch Deluxe Varmint

MONARCH DELUXE BOLT-ACTION
HUNTING RIFLE . . . . **NiB $714 Ex $349 Gd $260**
Same as Majestic Deluxe Standard Weight model except w/redesigned stock of U.S. style w/contrasting hardwood forend tip and grip cap. Calibers: .222 Rem., .243 Win., .270 Win., 7mm Rem. Mag., .308 Win., .30-06. 22-inch bbl. Weight: 7 to 7.25 lbs. Made 1965 to 1974.

MONARCH DELUXE
VARMINT RIFLE . . . . **NiB $710 Ex $420 Gd $290**
Same as Monarch Deluxe except w/24-inch heavy bbl. and weighs 9 lbs. Calibers: .222 Rem., .243 Win.

BUSHMASTER FIREARMS —
(Quality Parts Company) Currently Ilion, NY, formerly Windham, Maine. Purchased by Freedom Group Inc. 2011

M17S BULLPUP . . . . **NiB $735 Ex $600 Gd $466**
Caliber: .223. 21.5-inch bbl. Weight: 8.2 lbs. Polymer stocks. Handle w/fixed open sights w/Weaver-type rail for any optics. Semi-auto, self-compensating short stroke gas piston. Forward trigger/grip w/rear chamber. Bullpup style. Alloy receiver. Synthetic lower receiver is hinged to upper w/hinged takedown system. Accepts M-16 type magazines. Made from 1992 to 2005.

MODEL XM15 E2S SERIES
Caliber: .223. 16-, 20-, 24- or 26-inch bbl. Weight: 7 to 8.6 lbs. Polymer stocks. Adjustable sights w/dual flip-up aperture; optional flattop rail accepts scope. Direct gas-operated w/rotating bolt. Forged alloy receiver. All steel-coated w/manganese phosphate. Accepts M-16 type magazines. Made from 1989 to date.
XM15 E2S Carbine . . . . **NiB $1210 Ex $989 Gd $750**
XM15 E2S Target Rifle . . . . **NiB $1244 Ex $1018 Gd $707**

CABELA'S, INC. — Sidney, Nebraska

Cabela's is a sporting goods dealer and catalog company headquartered in Sidney, Nebraska. Cabela's imports black powder cartridge Sharps replicas, revolvers and other reproductions and replicas manufactured in Italy by A. Uberti, Pedersoli, Pietta and others.

1858 HENRY REPLICA . . . . . . **NiB $707 Ex $599 Gd $524**
Lever-action. Modeled after the original Henry rifle. Caliber: .44-40. Thirteen-round magazine; Bbl: 24 inches. Overall length: 43 inches. Weight: 9 pounds. European walnut stock. Sights: Bead front, open adjustable rear. Brass receiver and buttplate. Introduced 1994.

1866 WINCHESTER REPLICA . **NiB $599 Ex $425 Gd $347**
Lever-action modeled after the original Model 1866 rifle. Caliber: .44-40. Thirteen-round magazine. Bbl: 24 inches, octagonal; overall length: 43 inches. Weight: 9 pounds. European walnut stock, brass receiver, butt plate and forend cap. Sights: Bead front, open adjustable rear.

1873 WINCHESTER REPLICA . **NiB $525 Ex $455 Gd $390**
Lever-action modeled after the original Model 1873 rifle. Caliber: .44-40, .45 Colt. Thirteen-round magazine. Bbl: 30 inches. Overall length: 43 inches. Weight: 8 pounds. European walnut stock. Sights: Bead front, open adjustable rear or globe front and tang rear. Color case-hardened steel receiver. Introduced 1994.
W/tang rear sight, globe front, add $175

**1873 SPORTING
MODEL REPLICA** . . . . **NiB $655 Ex $577 Gd $500**
Same as 1873 Winchester except with 30-inch bbl.
W/half-round, half-octagonal bbl., half magazine, add $126

CATTLEMAN CARBINE . . . . . . **NiB $355 Ex $290 Gd $227**
Revolver with shoulder stock. Caliber: .44-40; six-round cylinder. Bbl: 18 inches. Overall length: 34 inches. Weight: 4 pounds. European walnut stock. Sights: Blade front, notch rear. Color case-hardened frame, remainder blued. Introduced 1994.

SHARPS SPORTING RIFLE . . . **NiB $879 Ex $779 Gd $576**
Single-shot. Caliber: .45-70. Bbl: Tapered octagon, 32 inches. Overall length: 47 inches. Weight: 9 pounds. Checkered walnut stock. Sights: Blade front, open adjustable rear. Color case-hardened receiver and hammer; remainder blued. Introduced 1995.

CALICO LIGHT WEAPONS SYSTEMS — Cornelius, OR, formerly Bakersville, California

LIBERTY 50/100 SEMIAUTOMATIC RIFLE
Retarded blowback action. Caliber: 9mm. 50- or 100-round helical-feed magazine. 16.1-inch bbl. 34.5 inches overall. Weight: 7 lbs. Adjustable post front sight and aperture rear. Ambidextrous rotating safety. Glass-filled polymer or thumbhole-style wood stock. Made 1995 to 2001; reintro. 2007.
Model Liberty 50 . . . . **NiB $800 Ex $668 Gd $410**
Model Liberty 100 . . . . **NiB $909 Ex $869 Gd $495**

MODEL M-100 SEMIAUTOMATIC SERIES
Similar to the Liberty 100 Model except chambered for .22 LR. Weight: 5 lbs. 34.5 inches overall. Folding or glass-filled polymer stock and forearm. Made from 1986 to 1994; reintro. 2007.
Model M-100 w/folding
stock (disc. 1994). . . . . **NiB $600 Ex $355 Gd $300**
Model M-100 FS w/fixed
stock disc. 1996. . . . . **NiB $400 Ex $379 Gd $320**

**MODEL M-105 SEMI-AUTOMATIC
SPORTER** . . . . **NiB $688 Ex $492 Gd $333**
Similar to the Liberty 100 Model except fitted w/walnut buttstock

and forearm. Made from 1989 to 1994.

MODEL M-900 SEMIAUTOMATIC CARBINE
Caliber: 9mm Parabellum. 50- or 100-round magazine. 16.1-inch bbl. 28.5 inches overall. Weight: 3.7 lbs. Post front sight adj. for windage and elevation, fixed notch rear. Collapsible steel buttstock and glass-filled polymer grip. Matte black finish. Made from 1989 to 1990, 1992 to 1993 and 2007.
Model M-100 w/folding
stock (disc. 1994). . . . . **NiB $808 Ex $497 Gd $338**
Model M-100 FS w/fixed
stock (intro. 1996) . . . . **NiB $677 Ex $533 Gd $390**

MODEL M-951 TACTICAL CARBINE
Similar to Model 900 except w/long compensator and adj. forward grip. Made from 1990 to 1994.
Model 951 . . . . **NiB $725 Ex $533 Gd $445**
Model 951-S . . . . **NiB $725 Ex $533 Gd $445**

CANADIAN MILITARY RIFLES — Quebec, Canada. Manufactured by Ross Rifle Co.

**MODEL 1907 MARK II
ROSS MILITARY RIFLE** . . . . . . **NiB $409 Ex $299 Gd $277**
Straight-pull bolt action. Caliber: .303 British. Five-round box magazine. 28-inch bbl. Weight: 8.5 lbs. Sights: adj. rear; blade front. Military-type full stock. Note: The Ross was originally issued as a Canadian service rifle in 1907. There were several variations; it was the official weapon at the start of WWI, but has been obsolete for many years. For Ross sporting rifle, see listing under Ross Rifle company.

CENTURY INTERNATIONAL ARMS, INC. — Delray Beach, Florida

CENTURION M38/M96 BOLT-ACTION SPORTER
Sporterized Swedish M38/96 Mauser action. Caliber: 6.5x55mm. Five-round magazine. 24-inch bbl. 44 inches overall. Adj. rear sight. Blade front. Black synthetic or checkered European hardwood Monte Carlo stock. Holden Ironsighter see-through scope mount. Imported from 1987 to date.
W/hardwood stock . . . . **NiB $277 Ex $190 Gd $133**
W/synthetic stock . . . . **NiB $280 Ex $198 Gd $144**

CENTURION M98 BOLT-ACTION SPORTER
Sporterized VZ24 or 98 Mauser action. Calibers: .270 Win., 7.62x39mm, .308 Win., .30-06. Five round magazine. 22-inch bbl. 44 inches overall. Weight: 7.5 lbs. W/Millet or Weaver scope base(s), rings and no iron sights. Classic or Monte Carlo laminated hardwood, black synthetic or checkered European hardwood stock. Imported from 1992 to date.
M98 Action W/black
synthetic stock (w/o rings) . . . . **NiB $300 Ex $220 Gd $167**
M98 Action W/hardwood Stock(w/o rings). . . . NiB $290 Ex $190 Gd $126
VZ24 action w/laminated
hardwood stock (Elite) . . . . . . **NiB $355 Ex $289 Gd $188**
VZ24 action w/black
synthetic stock . . . . **NiB $338 Ex $269 Gd $175**
W/Millet base and rings, add $45

CENTURION P-14 SPORTER
Sporterized P-14 action. Caliber: 7mm Rem. Mag., .300 Win. Mag. Five-round magazine. 24-inch bbl. 43.4 inches overall. Weight: 8.25 lbs. Weaver-type scope base. Walnut stained hardwood or fiberglass stock. Imported from 1987 to date.

RIFLES

W/hardwood stock . . . . NiB $269 Ex $211 Gd $157
W/fiberglass stock. . . . . NiB $299 Ex $223 Gd $167

ENFIELD SPORTER 4 BOLT-ACTION RIFLE
Sporterized Lee-Enfield action. Caliber: .303 British. 10-round magazine. 25.25-inch bbl. 44.5 inches overall. Blade front sight, adj. aperture rear. Sporterized beechwood military stock or checkered walnut Monte Carlo stock. Blued finish. Imported from 1987 to date.
W/sporterized military stock . . . .NiB $169 Ex $128 Gd $90
W/checkered walnut stock . . . NiB $223 Ex $190 Gd $135

L1A1 FAL SPORTER . . . . NiB $944 Ex $749 Gd $588
Sporterized L1A1 FAL semiautomatic. Caliber: .308 Win. 20.75-inch bbl. 41 inches overall. Weight: 9.75 lbs. Protected front post sight, adj. aperture rear. Matte blued finish. Black or camo Bell & Carlson thumbhole sporter stock w/rubber buttpad. Imported from 1988-98.

M-14 SPORTER . . . . NiB $460 Ex $338 Gd $255
Sporterized M-14 gas operated semiautomatic action. Caliber: .308 Win. 10-round magazine. 22-inch bbl. 41 inches overall. Weight: 8.25 lbs. Blade front sight, adj. aperture rear sight. Parkerized finish. Walnut stock w/rubber recoil pad. Forged receiver. Imported from 1991 to date.

TIGER DRAGUNOV . . . . NiB $1023 Ex $790 Gd $545
Russian SVD semiautomatic sniper rifle. Caliber: 7.62x54R. Five-round magazine. 21-inch bbl. 43 inches overall. Weight: 8.5 lbs. Blade front sight, open rear adj. for elevation. Blued finish. European laminated hardwood thumbhole stock. 4x range-finding scope w/lighted reticle and sunshade. Quick detachable scope mount. Imported from 1994 to 1995.

GAMESTALKER. . . . . NiB $1399 Ex $1088 Gd $946
Cal.: .243 WSSM, .25 WSSM, .300 WSSM. Bbl.: 22 inches, stainless steel, flattop upper, free-floating aluminum hand guard. ACE skeleton stock with ERGO Sure Grip. 100% camo. Weight: 7 lbs.

G-3 SPORTER. . . . . NiB $866 Ex $633 Gd $425
Semi-auto. Cal.: .308 Win. Made from G3 parts, American-made receiver with integrated scope rail. Bbl.: 19 inches. 20-round mag. Pistol grip stock, matte black finish. Weight: 9.3 pounds. Imported 1999 to 2006.

CETME SPORTER . . . . NiB $754 Ex $577 Gd $387
Cal.: .308 Win. Bbl.: 19.5 inches. 20-round mag. Blue or Mossy Oak Break-Up camo finish, wood or synthetic stock w/pistol grip. Vented forearm. Weight: 9.7 lbs.

S.A.R. 1 . . . . NiB $835 Ex $600 Gd $380
AK-47-type by Romarm. Cal.: 7.62x39mm. Bbl.: 16 inches. Wood stock and forearm. Includes one 10 and one 30-round double-stack magazine. Disc. 2003
S.A.R. 2 (5.45x39mm). . . . . . . NiB $835 Ex $600 Gd $380
S.A.R. 3 (.223 Rem.). . . . . NiB $835 Ex $600 Gd $380

MODEL B-82 . . . . NiB $835 Ex $600 Gd $380
Limited production Italian police model; serial no. with "D" suffix. Cal.: .30 Luger, .32 ACP, 9 mm Ultra.

GP WASR-10 . . . . NiB $555 Ex $370 Gd $244
AK-47 type by Romarm. Cal.: 7.62x39mm. Bbl.: 16.25 inches. Wood stock and forearm, includes one 5- and one 10-round mag. Weight: 7.5 lbs.
High-Cap series . . . . NiB $529 Ex $345 Gd $221

L1A1/R1A1 SPORTER . . . . . . NiB $1044 Ex $835 Gd $229
Modeled after British L1A1. Cal.: .308 Win. Bbl.: 22.5 inches. Carrying handle, synthetic furn. 20-round mag. Folding rear sight. Weight: 9.5 lbs.

GOLANI SPORTER . . . . NiB$835 Ex$650 Gd$456
Made in Israel. Cal.: .223 Rem. Bbl.: 21 inches. Folding stock, opt. bayonet lug., 35-round mag. Weight: 8 lbs.

Century International Arms GP WASR-10

Century International Arms Tantal Sporter

Century International Arms VZ 2008 Sporter

Century International Arms GP 1975

Century International Arms Degtyarev DP28

Century International Arms Sterling SA

TANTAL SPORTER . . . . NiB $735 Ex $555 Gd $455
Cal.: 5.45x39mm. Bbl.: 18 inches, flash hider. Folding wire stock. Parkerized finish. Includes extra mag. Weight. 8 lbs.

VZ 2008 SPORTER . . . . NiB $865 Ex $645 Gd $465
Copy of the Czech V258. Cal.: 7.62x39mm. Bbl.: 16.25 inches; steel receiver w/matte finish; wood or plastic stock. Weight: 7 lbs.

M-76 SNIPER . . . . NiB $1956 Ex $1538 Gd $967
Semi-auto version of Yugoslav M76. Cal.: 8mm Mauser. Bbl.: 21.5 inches. U.S.-made receiver. Includes scope, mount and 10-round mag. Weight: 11.3 lbs.

GP 1975 . . . . NiB $650 Ex $440 Gd $300
Cal.: 7.62x39mm. Bbl.: 16.25 inches. Black synthetic furniture, U.S.-made receiver and bbl. Weight: 7.4 lbs.

DEGTYAREV DP28 . . . . . NiB $4125 Ex $3155 Gd $2390
Semi-auto, top-mounted magazine. Cal.: 7.62x54R. Gas operated. Full stock. 47- to 50-round mag. Weight: 10 lbs.
DPM 28 (pistol grip) . . NiB $3970 Ex $3289 Gd $2410
DPX Tank Model . . . . . NiB $3970 Ex $3289 Gd $2410

STERLING SA . . . . NiB $745 Ex $560 Gd $380
Semi-auto version of Sterling sub-machine gun. Cal.: 9mm Para., 34-round mag. Bbl.: 16 inches. U.S.-made receiver and bbl., crinkle finish; folding stock.

PAR 1 . . . . NiB $439 Ex $300 Gd $218
AK-47 receiver, made by PAR. Cal.: 7.62x39mm; 10-round mag. Bbl.: 20.9 inches. Weight: 7.6 lbs. Imported 2002 to 2009.
PAR 3 (.223 Rem.) . . . . NiB $439 Ex $300 Gd $218

CHARTER ARMS CORPORATION—Shelton, Connecticut

AR-7 EXPLORER
SURVIVAL RIFLE . . . . NiB $139 Ex $120 Gd $99
Same as Armalite AR-7, except w/black, instead of brown, "wood grain" plastic stock. See listing of that rifle for specifications. Made from 1973 to 1990.

CHIPMUNK RIFLES — Milltown, PA, formerly Prospect, Oregon. Manufactured by Rogue Rifle Company (formerly Oregon Arms Company and Chipmunk Manufacturing, Inc.)

BOLT-ACTION SINGLE-SHOT RIFLE
Calibers: .22 LR. or .22 WMR. 16.13-inch standard or 18.13-inch bull bbl. Weight: 2.5 lbs. (standard) or 4 lbs. (Bull bbl.) Peep sight rear; ramp front. Plain or checkered American walnut, laminated or black hardwood stock. Made from 1982 to 2007.
Standard model
w/plain walnut stock . . . . NiB $235 Ex $156 Gd $103
Standard model
w/black hardwood stock . . . . . . NiB $195 Ex $155 Gd $99
Standard model
w/camouflage stock . . . . NiB $227 Ex $170 Gd $130
Standard model
w/laminated stock . . . . NiB $200 Ex $160 Gd $126
Deluxe grade
w/checkered walnut stock . . . . NiB $289 Ex $227 Gd $144
.22 WMR, add $40

CHURCHILL RIFLES — Manufactured in High Wycombe, England imported by Elliot Brothers, Chapin, SC.

HIGHLANDER
BOLT-ACTION RIFLE . . . . NiB $439 Ex $367 Gd $298
Calibers: .243 Win., .25-06 Rem., .270 Win., .308 Win., .30-06, 7mm Rem. Mag., .300 Win. Mag. Four round magazine (stan-

dard); 3-round (magnum). Bbl. length: 22-inch (standard); 24-inch (magnum). 42.5 to 44.5 inches overall. Weight: 7.5 lbs. Adj. rear sight, blade front. Checkered European walnut pistol-grip stock. Imported from 1986 to 1991.

"ONE OF ONE THOUSAND"
RIFLE . . . . NiB $4220 Ex $2535 Gd $1966
Made for Interarms to commemorate that firm's 20th anniversary. Mauser-type action. Calibers: .270, 7mm Rem. Mag., .308, .30-06, .300 Win. Mag., .375 H&H Mag., .458 Win. Mag. Five round magazine (3-round in Magnum calibers). 24-inch bbl. Weight: 8 lbs. Classic-style French walnut stock w/cheekpiece, black forend tip, checkered pistol grip and forearm, swivel-mounted recoil pad w/cartridge trap, pistol-grip cap w/trap for extra front sight, barrel-mounted sling swivel. Limited issue of 1,000 rifles made in 1973. See illustration next page.

REGENT
BOLT-ACTION RIFLE . . . . NiB $577 Ex $423 Gd $290
Calibers: .243 Win., .25-06 Rem., .270 Win., .308 Win., .30-06, 7mm Rem. Mag., .300 Win. Mag. Four round magazine. 22-inch round bbl. 42.5 inches overall. Weight: 7.5 lbs. Ramp front sight w/gold bead; adj. rear. Hand-checkered Monte Carlo-style stock of select European walnut; recoil pad. Made from 1986 to 1988.

CIMARRON ARMS — Fredericksburg, Texas

1860 HENRY LEVER-ACTION REPLICA
Replica of 1860 Henry w/original Henry loading system. Calibers: .44-40, .44 Special, .45 Colt. 13-round magazine. 22-inch bbl. (carbine) or 24.25-inch bbl. (rifle). 43 inches overall (rifle). Weight: 9.5 lbs. (rifle). Bead front sight, open adj. rear. Brass receiver and buttplate. Smooth European walnut buttstock. Imported from 1991.
Carbine model . . . . NiB $1460 Ex $1096 Gd $735
Rifle model . . . . NiB $1390 Ex $1087 Gd $675
Civil War model
(U.S. issue martially marked) NiB $1466 Ex $1100 Gd $709
W/ standard engraving add $2550
W/standard engraving, deluxe wood, add $3150
W/Lincoln hand engraving (disc. 2009), add $4500
W/Lincoln hand engraving,
deluxe wood (disc. 2009), add $5000

1866 YELLOWBOY LEVER-ACTION
Replica of 1866 Winchester. Calibers: .22 LR, 22WMR, .38 Special, .44-40, .45 Colt. 16-inch round bbl. (Trapper), 19-inch round bbl. (Carbine) or 24.25-inch ocatagonal bbl. (rifle). 43 inches overall (rifle). Weight: 9 lbs. (rifle). Bead front sight, open adj. rear. Brass receiver, buttplate and forend cap. Smooth European walnut stock. Imported 1991 to date.
Carbine . . . . NiB $1075 Ex $787 Gd $581
Rifle . . . . NiB $1050 Ex $612 Gd $406
Indian model (disc.) . . . . NiB $895 Ex $585 Gd $379
Trapper Model (.44-40 WCF only, disc.) NiB $995 Ex $756 Gd $502
W/A-engraving, add $2025
W/B-engraving, add $2500
W/C-engraving, add $3000

1873 LEVER-ACTION
Replica of 1873 Winchester. Calibers: .22 LR. .22WMR, .357 Magnum, .44-40 or .45 Colt. 16-inch round bbl. (Trapper), 19-inch round bbl. (SRC), 20-inch octagonal bbl. (short rifle), 24.25-inch octagonal bbl. (sporting rifle) and 30-inch octagonal bbl. (express rifle). 43 inches overall (sporting rifle). Weight: 8 lbs. Fixed blade front sight, adj. semi-buckhorn rear or tang peep sight. Walnut stock and forend. Color case-hardened receiver. Imported from 1989 to date.

RIFLES

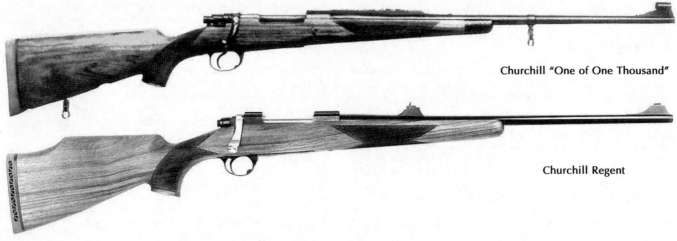

Churchill "One of One Thousand"

Churchill Regent

Express Rifle	NiB $1235	Ex $960	Gd $677
Short Rifle (disc.)	NiB $1235	Ex $960	Gd $677
Sporting Rifle	NiB $1235	Ex $960	Gd $677
SRC Carbine	NiB $1235	Ex $960	Gd $677
Trapper (disc.)	NiB $1268	Ex $980	Gd $697
One of 1000 engraved model	NiB $2409	Ex $2033	Gd $1354

1874 FALLING BLOCK SPORTING RIFLE
Replica of 1874 Sharps Sporting Rifle. Calibers: .45-65, .45-70, .45-90 or .45-120. 32- or 34-inch round or octagonal bbl. Weight: 9.5 to 10 lbs. Blade or globe front sight w/adj. open rear or sporting tang peep sight. Single or double set triggers. Checkered walnut stock and forend w/nose cap. Color case-hardened receiver. Imported from 1997 to date.

1874 Sporting Rifle - Billy Dixon Model	NiB $1754	Ex $1289	Gd $1100
1874 Sporting Rifle - Quigley Model	NiB $1556	Ex $1178	Gd $909
Sharps Sporting No. 1 Silhoette Rifle	NiB $1577	Ex $1133	Gd $926

1883 BURGESS RIFLE . . . . . NiB $1489 Ex $1077 Gd $744
Caliber: .45 Long Colt. Bbl.: 20 or 25 ½ inches. Reproduction. Importation began in 2010.

LIGHTNING
MAGAZINE RIFLE . . . . NiB $1488 Ex $1088 Gd $755
Reproduction of Colt Lightning Rifle. Cal.: .357 Mag., .44-40 WCF or .45 Long Colt. Bbl.: round; 20 or 24 inches; octagon: 20, 24, or 26 inches. Blue or case-colored frame.

W/octagon bbl., add	$150
Color case-hardened frame, add	$300

MODEL 1871 ROLLING BLOCK
BABY CARBINE . . . . NiB $379 Ex $290 Gd $195
Remington repro. Caliber: .22 LR, .22 Hornet, .22 Mag. Or .357 Mag. Bbl: 22 inches. Walnut stock and forearm. Brass trigger guard and buttplate. Disc. 1990.

Deluxe model. . . . . NiB $785 Ex $580 Gd $338

LONG RANGE CREEDMOOR . . . NiB $1279 Ex $899 Gd $655
Cal.: .45-70 Gov't. Barrel: 30-inch octagon. Deluxe checkered walnut stock.

ADOBE WALLS FALLING
BLOCK RIFLE . . . . NiB $1754 Ex $1310 Gd $976
Cal.: .45-70 Gov't. Bbl.: 30 inches, octagon. Case hardened receiver, hand checkered walnut stock, German silver nose cap. Optional Creedmoor sights.

SHARPS NO. 1 RIFLE . . . . . . NiB $1087 Ex $755 Gd $544
Sharps reproduction. Cal.: .40-65 Win. or .45-70 Gov't. Bbl.: 32 inches, octagon; pistol grip stock. Imported 2000 to 2002.

No. 1 Silhouette . . . . NiB $1588 Ex $1011 Gd $744

MODEL 1874 SPORTING RIFLE . . . NiB $1377 Ex $986 Gd $650
Armi-Sport Billy Dixon model. Cal.: .38-55 WCF, .45-70 Gov't., .45-90 Win., .45-110, .50-90. Bbl.: 32 inches. Checkered deluxe walnut stock. Double set triggers.

Pedersoli model	NiB $1809	Ex $1335	Gd $1088
Quigley II model	NiB $1569	Ex $1104	Gd $854
Pedersoli Quigley	NiB $2188	Ex $1598	Gd $1077
Big 50 model	NiB $2769	Ex $1988	Gd $1369
Sharps Pride model	NiB $2240	Ex $1674	Gd $1290
Pride II model	NiB $1544	Ex $1068	Gd $909
Professional Hunter	NiB $1357	Ex $1068	Gd $909
Texas Ranger	NiB $1271	Ex $933	Gd $730

SHARPS ROCKY MOUNTAIN II
MODEL 74 . . . . NiB $1498 Ex $1043 Gd $677
Repro. Cal.: .45-70 Gov't. Bbl.: 30 inches, octagon. Silver receiver, checkered walnut stock. Optional 6x Malcolm rifle scope.

W/scope, add	$650

MODEL 1860 SPENCER RIFLE NiB $1560 Ex $1154 Gd $933
By Armi Sport. Cal.: 56-50. Bbl.: 30 inches. Plain walnut stock and forearm. Case hardened receiver, trigger guard and hammer. Three barrel bands.

MODEL 1865 SPENCER
REPEATING RIFLE . . . . NiB $1490 Ex $1167 Gd $770
By Armi Sport. Cal.: .44-40 WCF, .45 Schofield, .45 Long Colt, .56-50. Bbl.: 20 or 30 inches (in 56-50 only, disc. 2009). Blue finish, color case hardened frame. Straight grip walnut stock.

W/30-inch bbl., add	$227

CIVIL WAR HENRY RIFLE . . NiB $1344 Ex $1269 Gd $976
By Uberti. Cal.: .44-40 WCF or .45 Long Colt. Bbl.: 24 inches. Includes military inspector's marks and cartouche; military-type sling swivels.

1866 YELLOWBOY CARBINE NiB $1192 Ex $1054 Gd $593
By Uberti. Cal.: .32-20 WCF, .38 SP, .38-55 WCF, .44 SP, .44-40 WCF, .45 Long Colt. Similar to Model 1866 Sporting Rifle except w/19-inch round bbl., two barrel bands, saddle ring, smooth walnut stock, and forearm.

Trapper model	NiB $1167	Ex $866	Gd $546
Indian Carbine model	NiB $1056	Ex $679	Gd $496
Red Cloud model	NiB $1056	Ex $679	Gd $496

1873 SADDLE RING CARBINE NiB $1355 Ex $1089 Gd $733
Cal.: .22 LR, .22 Mag., .32-20 WCF, .357 Mag./.38 SP, .38-40 WCF, .44 SP., .44-40 WCF, .45 Long Colt. Bbl.: 19 inches, round. Blued receiver, saddle ring.

Trapper Carbine . . . . NiB $1490 Ex $1100 Gd $977

1876 CENTENNIAL
SPORTING RIFLE . . . . NiB $1525 Ex $1260 Gd $995
Cal.: .40-60 WCF, .45-60 WCF, .45-70 WCF,.50-95 WCF; bbl.: 22 or 28 inches, octagon. Blue finish, case hardened frame. Full-length magazine, iron sights, walnut stock, and forearm.

1876 CARBINE. . . . . NiB $1788 Ex $1388 Gd $1100
By Uberti. Cal.: .45-60 WCF, .45-75. Bbl.: 22 inches, round. Full length fore end and barrel band. Canadian NWMP model has blued frame and saddle ring.

1885 HI-WALL RIFLE . . . . . . NiB $1169 Ex $977 Gd $749
Cal.: .30-40 Krag, .348 Win., .38-55 Win., .405 Win., .40-65 WCF, .45-70 Gov't., .45-90 WCF, .45-120 WCF. Bbl.: 28 or 30 inches, octagon. Case hardened finish frame. Iron sights standard or optional aperture rear and globe front offered.
Pedersoli mode. . . . . NiB $2378 Ex $1956 Gd $1100

1885 LOW-WALL RIFLE . . . . NiB $1077 Ex $800 Gd $654
Cal.: .22 LR, .22 Hornet, .22 Mag., .30-30 Win., .32-20 WCF, .357 Mag., .38-40 WCF, .44 Mag., .38-55, .44-40 WCF, .45-70 Gov't., .45 Long Colt. Bbl.: 30 inches. Hand checkered walnut stock, single- or double-set trigger.
Deluxe model, add. $200
Standard custom engraving, add $1750
Double set triggers, add $400

1892 RIFLE. . . . . NiB $1288 Ex $800 Gd $643
Cal.: .357 Mag., .44 Mag., .44-40 WCF, .45 Long Colt. Bbl.: 20 or 24 inches. Solid or take-down frame, smooth walnut stock and forearm, case colored receiver.
W/take-down frame, add $200
.44-40 WCF, .44 Mag., add $50

1892 CARBINE. . . . . NiB $1235 Ex $866 Gd $650
Cal.: .357 Mag., .44 Mag., .44-40 WCF, .45 Long Colt. Bbl.: 16 (Trapper model) or 20 inches. Solid frame, choice of big loop lever (El Dorado) or standard with 20-inch bbl. Saddle ring with 20-inch bbl. only.

CLERKE RECREATION PRODUCTS — Santa Monica, California

DELUXE HI-WALL . . . . NiB $337 Ex $290 Gd $219
Same as standard model, except w/adj. trigger, half-octagon bbl., select wood, stock w/cheekpiece and recoil pad. Made 1972 to 1974.

HI-WALL
SINGLE-SHOT RIFLE. . . . . . . NiB $310 Ex $234 Gd $177
Falling-block lever-action similar to Winchester 1885 High Wall S.S. Color casehardened investment-cast receiver. Calibers: .222 Rem., .22-250, .243 Rem., 6mm Rem., .25-06, .270 Win., 7mm Rem. Mag., .30-06, .45-70 Govt. 26-inch medium-weight bbl. Weight: 8 lbs. Furnished w/o sights. Checkered walnut pistol-grip stock and Schnabel forearm. Made from 1972 to 1974.

CLIFTON ARMS — Medina, Texas

SCOUT BOLT-ACTION RIFLE
Custom rifle built on the Dakota .76, Ruger .77 or Winchester .70 action. Shilen match-grade barrel cut and chambered to customer's specification. Clifton composite stock fitted and finished to customer's preference. Made from 1992 to 1997.
African
Scout . . . . NiB $3175 Ex $2690 Gd $2310

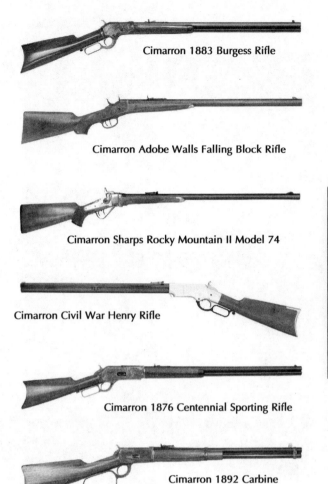

Cimarron 1883 Burgess Rifle

Cimarron Adobe Walls Falling Block Rifle

Cimarron Sharps Rocky Mountain II Model 74

Cimarron Civil War Henry Rifle

Cimarron 1876 Centennial Sporting Rifle

Cimarron 1892 Carbine

Pseudo
Scout . . . . NiB $3160 Ex $2211 Gd $1589
Standard
Scout . . . . NiB $3122 Ex $2520 Gd $1443
Super
Scout . . . . NiB $3145 Ex $2175 Gd $1590

COLT'S MFG. CO., INC. — West Hartford, Connecticut

NOTE: *Add $200 to pre-ban models made prior to 10/13/94.*

AR-15 A2 DELTA
MATCH H-BAR RIFLE. . . . . NiB $2300 Ex $1977 Gd $1492
Similar to AR-15A2 Government Model except w/standard stock and heavy refined bbl. Furnished w/3-9x rubber armored scope and removeable cheekpiece. Made from 1986 to 1991.

AR-15 A2 GOVERNMENT
MODEL CARBINE. . . . . NiB $1945 Ex $1044 Gd $813
Caliber: .223 Rem., Five-round magazine. 16-inch bbl. w/flash suppressor. 35 inches overall. Weight: 5.8 lbs. Telescoping aluminum buttstock; sling swivels. Made from 1985 to 1991.

Colt AR-15 A2

Colt AR-15 A2 Delta Match H-BAR

Colt AR-15 A2 Government Model

Colt AR-15 Sporter Competition H-BAR

AR-15 A2 SPORTER II. . . . NiB $1937 Ex $1347 Gd $1136
Same general specifications as standard AR-15 Sporter except heavier bbl., improved pistol-grip. Weight 7.5 lbs.; optional 3x or 4x scope. Made from 1985 to 1989.

AR-15 COMPACT 9MM CARBINE NiB $2255 Ex $1990 Gd $1176
Semiautomatic. Caliber: 9mm NATO. 20-round detachable magazine. Bbl.: 16-inch round. Weight: 6.3 lbs. Adj. rear and front sights. Adj. buttstock. Ribbed round handguard. Made from 1985 to 1986.

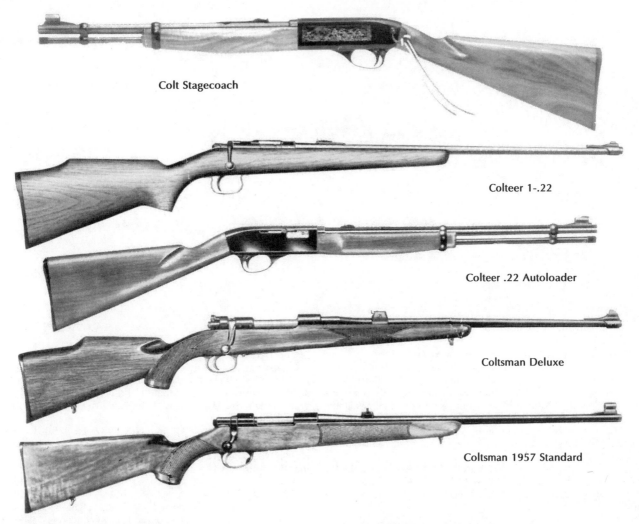

Colt Stagecoach

Colteer 1-.22

Colteer .22 Autoloader

Coltsman Deluxe

Coltsman 1957 Standard

RIFLES

AR-15 SEMIAUTOMATIC SPORTER

Commercial version of U.S. M16 rifle. Gas-operated. Takedown. Caliber: .223 Rem. (5.56mm). 20-round magazine w/spacer to reduce capacity to 5 rounds. 20-inch bbl. w/flash suppressor. Sights: Rear peep w/windage adjustment in carrying handle; front adj. for windage. 3x scope and mount optional. Black molded buttstock of high-impact synthetic material, rubber buttplate. Barrel surrounded by handguard of black fiberglass w/heat-reflecting inner shield. Swivels, black web sling strap. Weight: w/o accessories, 6.3 lbs. Made from 1964 to 1994.
Standard Sporter . . . . NiB $1951 Ex $1447 Gd $1133
W/adj. stock, redesigned
forearm (disc. 1988), add $227
W/3x scope and mount, add $126

AR-15 SPORTER COMPETITION
H-BAR RIFLE . . . . NiB $1997 Ex $1126 Gd $766
Similar to AR-15 Sporter Target model except w/integral Weaver-type mounting system on a flat-top receiver. 20-inch bbl. w/counter-bored muzzle and 1:9 rifling twist. Made from 1991 to date.

AR-15 SPORTER
COMPETITION H-BAR (RS). NiB $2009 Ex $1143 Gd $931
Similar to AR-15 Sporter Competition H-BAR Model except "Range Selected" for accuracy w/3x9 rubber-clad scope w/mount. Carrying handle w/iron sights. Made from 1992 to 1994.

AR-15 SPORTER MATCH TARGET LIGHTWEIGHT

Calibers: .223 Rem., 7.62x39mm, 9mm. Five-round magazine. 16-inch bbl. (non-threaded after 1994). 34.5-35.5 inches overall. Weight: 7.1 lbs. Redesigned stock and shorter handguard. Made from 1991 to 2002.
Standard LW Sporter (except 9mm) . . NiB $976 Ex $755 Gd $612
Standard LW Sporter, 9mm . . . . . . NiB $1077 Ex $776 Gd $556
.22 LR conversion (disc. 1994), add $200

AR-15 SPORTER TARGET RIFLE

Caliber: .223 Rem. Five-round magazine. 20-inch bbl. w/flash suppressor (non-threaded after 1994). 39 inches overall. Weight: 7.5 lbs. Black composition stock, grip and handguard. Sights: post front; adj. aperture rear. Matte black finish. Made from 1993 to date.
Sporter Target Rifle . . . . NiB $1244 Ex $1087 Gd $722
.22 LR conversion (disc. 1994), add $227

LIGHTNING MAGAZINE RIFLE - LARGE FRAME

Similar to Medium Frame model except w/large frame to accommodate larger calibers: .38-56, .44-60, .45-60, .45-65, .45-85, or .50-95 Express. Standard 22-inch (carbine & baby carbine) or 28-inch round or octagonal bbl. (rifle). Note: Additional bbl. lengths optional. Weight: 8 to 10.5 lbs. Sights: Open rear; bead or blade front. Walnut stock and checkered forearm. Made 1887 to 1994. (6,496 produced)
Rifle . . . . NiB $11,765 Ex $7390 Gd $3469
Carbine . . . . NiB $10,576 Ex $7798 Gd $4479
Baby Carbine . . . . NiB $14,475 Ex $9077 Gd $5796
.50-95 Express, add 40%

Coltsman 1961 Custom

Coltsman 1961 Standard

Colt-Sauer Grand African

LIGHTNING MAGAZINE RIFLE – MEDIUM FRAME
Slide-action w/12-round tubular magazine Carbine & Baby Carbine) or 15-round tubular magazine (rifle). Calibers: .32-20, .38-40, .44-40. Standard 20-inch (Carbine & Baby Carbine) or 26-inch round or octagonal bbl.(rifle). Note: Additional bbl. lengths optional. Weight: 5.5 lbs. (Baby Carbine), 6.25 lbs. (carbine) or 7 to 9 lbs. (rifle). Sights: Open rear; bead or blade front. Walnut stock and checkered forearm. Blue finish w/color casehardened hammer. Made from 1884 to 1902. (89,777 produced)

Rifle	NiB $6096	Ex $3822	Gd $2274
Carbine	NiB $7778	Ex $4966	Gd $2988
Baby Carbine	NiB $9380	Ex $5246	Gd $4012

Military model
w/bayonet
lug & sling swivels . . . . . NiB $5250   Ex $3844   Gd $2691

LIGHTNING MAGAZINE RIFLE – SMALL FRAME
Similar to Medium Frame model except w/smaller frame and chambered for .22 caliber only. Standard 24-inch round or octagonal bbl. w/half magazine. Note: Additional bbl. lengths optional. Weight: 6 lbs. Sights: Open rear; bead or blade front. Walnut stock and checkered forearm. Made from 1884 to 1902. (89,912 produced)

Standard Rifle model . . . . NiB $5599   Ex $4125   Gd $2889
W/Deluxe or optional features, add. 25%

STAGECOACH .22 AUTOLOADER . . NiB $395   Ex $298   Gd $200
Same as Colteer .22 Autoloader except w/engraved receiver, saddle ring, 16.5-inch bbl. Weight: 4 lbs., 10 oz. Made from 1965 to 1975.

COLTEER 1-.22 SINGLE-SHOT
BOLT-ACTION RIFLE . . . . NiB $403   Ex $397   Gd $159
Caliber: .22 LR. Long, Short. 20- or 22-inch bbl. Sights: Open rear; ramp front. Pistol-grip stock w/Monte Carlo comb. Weight: 5 lbs. Made from 1957 to 1967.

.22 AUTOLOADER . . . . NiB $390   Ex $288   Gd $227
Caliber: .22 LR. 15-round tubular magazine. 19.38-inch bbl. Sights: Open rear; hooded ramp front. Straight-grip stock, Western carbine-style forearm w/bbl. band. Weight: 4.75 lbs. Made 1964 to 1975.
CUSTOM BOLT-ACTION

SPORTING RIFLE . . . . NiB $600   Ex $498   Gd $338
FN Mauser action, side safety, engraved floorplate. Calibers: .30-06, .300 H&H Mag. Five round box magazine. 24-inch bbl., rampfront sight. Fancy walnut stock. Monte Carlo comb, cheekpiece, pistol-grip, checkered, QD swivels. Weight: 7.25 lbs. Made 1957 to 1961.

DELUXE RIFLE . . . . NiB $977   Ex $798   Gd $569
FN Mauser action. Same as Custom model, except plain floorplate, plainer wood and checkering. Made from 1957-61. Value shown is for rifle as furnished by manufacturer w/o rear sight.

1957 SERIES RIFLES
Sako medium action. Calibers: .243, .308. Weight: 6.75 lbs. Other specifications similar to those of models w/FN actions. Made from 1957 to 1961.

Standard.	NiB $755	Ex $486	Gd $417
Custom	NiB $944	Ex $697	Gd $488
Deluxe.	NiB $944	Ex $697	Gd $488

1961 MODEL
CUSTOM RIFLE . . . . NiB $733   Ex $568   Gd $422
Sako action. Calibers: .222, .222 Mag., .223, .243, .264, .270, .308, .30-06, .300 H&H. 23-, 24-inch bbl. Sights: Folding leaf rear; hooded ramp front. Fancy French walnut stock w/Monte Carlo comb, rosewood forend tip and grip cap skip checkering, recoil pad, sling swivels. Weight: 6.5 - 7.5 lbs. Made from 1963 to 1965.

1961 MODEL,
STANDARD RIFLE . . . . NiB $744   Ex $578   Gd $432
Same as Custom model except plainer, American walnut stock. Made from 1963 to 1965.

STANDARD RIFLE . . . . NiB $689   Ex $533   Gd $390
FN Mauser action. Same as Deluxe model except in .243, .30-06, .308, .300 Mag. and stock w/o cheekpiece, bbl. length 22 inches. Made from 1957 to 1961. Value shown is for rifle as furnished by manufacturer w/o rear sight.

COLT-SAUER DRILLINGS   See Colt shotgun listings.

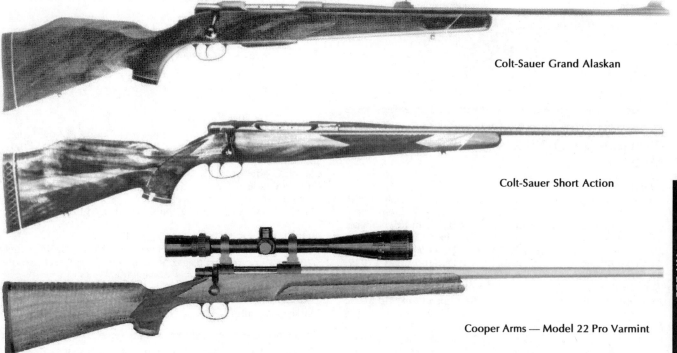

Colt-Sauer Grand Alaskan

Colt-Sauer Short Action

Cooper Arms — Model 22 Pro Varmint

GRAND AFRICAN . . . . . . NiB $2656 Ex $1966 Gd $1049
Same specifications as standard model except .458 Win. Mag., weight: 9.5 lbs. Sights: Adj. leaf rear; hooded ramp front. Magnum-style stock of Bubinga. Made from 1973 to 1985.

GRAND ALASKAN . . . . . . NiB $2606 Ex $1989 Gd $1008
Same specifications as standard model except .375 H&H, weight: 8.5 lbs. Sights: Adj. leaf rear; hooded ramp front. Magnum-style stock of walnut.

MAGNUM . . . . NiB $2506 Ex $1923 Gd $778
Same specifications as standard model except calibers 7mm Rem. Mag., .300 Win. Mag., .300 Weatherby. Weight: 8.5 lbs. Made from 1973 to 1985.

SHORT ACTION. . . . . NiB $2390 Ex $1613 Gd $766
Same specifications as standard model except shorter action chambered for the following calibers: .22-250, .243 Win., .308 Win. and similar length cartridges. Weight: 7.5 1bs.; 8.25 lbs. (.22-250). Drilled and tapped for scope mount. No front or rear open sights. Made from 1973 to 1988.

SPORTING RIFLE,
STANDARD MODEL. . . . . . . NiB $2077 Ex $1405 Gd $766
Sauer 80 non-rotating bolt action. Calibers: .25-06, .270 Win., .30-06. Three-round detachable box magazine. 24-inch bbl. Weight: 7.75 lbs., 8.5 lbs. (.25-06). Furnished w/o sights. American walnut stock w/Monte Carlo cheekpiece, checkered pistol grip and forearm, rosewood forend tip and pistol-grip cap, recoil pad. Made from 1973 to 1988.

COMMANDO ARMS — Knoxville, Tennessee (formerly Volunteer Enterprises, Inc.)

MARK III SEMIAUTOMATIC CARBINE
Blow-back action, fires from closed bolt. Caliber: .45 ACP. 15- or 30-round magazine. 16.5-inch bbl. w/cooling sleeve and muzzle brake. Weight: 8 lbs. Sights: peep rear; blade front. "Tommy Gun" style stock and forearm or grip. Made from 1969 to 1976.
W/horizontal forearm . . . . . . NiB $510 Ex $399 Gd $277

MARK 9
Same specifications as Mark III and Mark 45 except caliber 9mm Luger. Made from 1976 to 1981.
W/horizontal forearm . . . . . . NiB $545 Ex $439 Gd $333
W/vertical foregrip . . . . NiB $650 Ex $565 Gd $389

MARK 45
Same specifications as Mark III. Has redesigned trigger housing and magazines. Made from 1976 to 1988.
W/horizontal forearm . . . . . . NiB $499 Ex $438 Gd $293
W/vertical foregrip . . . . NiB $596 Ex $484 Gd $341

CONTINENTAL RIFLES — Manufactured in Belgium for Continental Arms Corp., New York, New York

DOUBLE RIFLE
Calibers: .270, .303 Sav., .30-40, .348 Win., .30-06, .375 H&H, .400 Jeffrey, .465, .470, .475 No. 2, .500, .600. Side-by-side. Anson-Deeley reinforced boxlock action w/triple bolting lever work. Two triggers. Non-automatic safety. 24- or 26-inch bbls. Sights: Express rear; bead front. Checkered cheekpiece stock and forend. Weight: From 7 lbs., depending on caliber. Imported from 1956 to 1975.
.270 to .348 Win. . . . . NiB $5077 Ex $3966 Gd $3095
.375 H&H & larger calibers, add. $60%

CZ Model ZKK 600

COOPER FIREARMS of MONTANA, INC. — (Previously COOPER ARMS) Stevensville, Montana

MODEL 21
Similar to Model 36C except in calibers .17 Rem., .17 Mach IV, .221 Fireball, .222, .223, 6x45, 6x47. 24-inch stainless or chrome-moly bbl. 43.5 inches overall. Weight: 8.75 lbs. Made from 1994 to date.
21 Benchrest . . . . NiB $1513 Ex $1207 Gd $943
21 Classic . . . . NiB $2223 Ex $1766 Gd $1007
21 Custom Classic . . . . . . NiB $2178 Ex $1859 Gd $1032
21 Western Classic. . . . . . NiB $3030 Ex $1956 Gd $1043
21 Varminter . . . . NiB $1408 Ex $976 Gd $800
21 Varmint Extreme . . . . . . NiB $1944 Ex $1244 Gd $976

MODEL 22
Bolt-action, single-shot. Calibers: .22 BR. .22-250 Rem., .220 Swift, .243 Win., 6mm PPC, 6.5x55mm, 25-06 Rem., 7.62x39mm 26-inch bbl, 45.63 inches overall. Weight: 8 lbs., 12 oz. Single-stage trigger. AAA Claro walnut stock. Made from 1999 to date.
22 Benchrest . . . . NiB $1533 Ex $1377 Gd $1079
22 Classic . . . . NiB $2176 Ex $1312 Gd $755
22 Custom Classic . . . . NiB $1370 Ex $1244 Gd $879
22 Western Classic. . . . . . . NiB $2244 Ex $1359 Gd $954
22 Varminter . . . . NiB $1468 Ex $934 Gd $650
22 Pro-Varmint Extreme . . . NiB $2011 Ex $1143 Gd $836
22 Black Jack. . . . . NiB $1895 Ex $1154 Gd $846

MODEL 36 RF/BR 50 . . . . . NiB $1608 Ex $1266 Gd $880
Caliber: .22 LR. Bolt-action. Single-shot. 22-inch bbl. 40.5 inches overall. Weight: 6.8 lbs. No sights. Fully-adj. match-grade trigger. Stainless barrel. McMillan benchrest stock. Three mid-bolt locking lugs. Made from 1993 to 1999.

MODEL 36 CF BOLT-ACTION RIFLE
Calibers: .17 CCM, .22 CCM, .22 Hornet. Four-round mag. 23.75 inch bbl. 42.5 inch overall. Weight: 7 lbs. Walnut or synthetic stock. Made from 1992 to 1994.
Marksman . . . . NiB $1635 Ex $880 Gd $654
Sportsman . . . . NiB $730 Ex $544 Gd $343
Classic Grade . . . . NiB $1863 Ex $1154 Gd $866
Custom Grade . . . . NiB $1744 Ex $937 Gd $665
Custom Classic Grade. . . . . NiB $1706 Ex $1266 Gd $876

MODEL 36 RF BOLT-ACTION RIFLE
Similar to Model 36CF except in caliber .22 LR. Five round magazine. Weight: 6.5-7 lbs. Made from 1992 to 1994.
BR-50 (22-inch stainless bbl.)NiB $1755 Ex $1139 Gd $768
Custom Grade . . . . NiB $1756 Ex $906 Gd $675
Custom Classic Grade. . . . . NiB $1670 Ex $951 Gd $688
Featherweight. . . . . NiB $1617 Ex $988 Gd $709

MODEL 36 TRP-1 SERIES
Similar to Model 36RF except in target configuration w/ ISU or silhouette-style stock. Made from 1992 to 1993.
TRP-1 (ISU single-shot). . . . . NiB $944 Ex $778 Gd $533
TRP-1S (Silhouette). . . . . NiB $944 Ex $778 Gd $533

MODEL 38 SINGLE SHOT
Similar to Model 36CF except in calibers .17 or .22 CCM w/3-round magazine. Weight: 8 lbs. Walnut or synthetic stock. Made 1992 to 1993.
Standard Sporter. . . . . NiB $1544 Ex $1023 Gd $688
Classic Grade. . . . . NiB $2239 Ex $1836 Gd $989
Custom Grade . . . . .NiB $3035 Ex $1997 Gd $977
Custom
Classic Grade. . . . . NiB $1570 Ex $1267 Gd $855

MODEL 40 CLASSIC BOLT-ACTION RIFLE
Calibers: .17 CCM, .17 Ackley Hornet, .22 Hornet, .22K Hornet, .22 CCM, 4- or 5-round magazine. 23.75-inch bbl. Checkered oil-finished AAA Claro walnut stock. Made from 1995 to 1996.
Classic. . . . . NiB $1644 Ex $1233 Gd $886
Custom Classic. . . . . NiB $1844 Ex $1450 Gd $1139
Classic Varminter . . . . NiB $1844 Ex $1450 Gd $1139

CUMBERLAND MOUNTAIN ARMS — Winchester, Tennessee

PLATEAU RIFLE
Falling block action w/underlever. Calibers: .40-65, and .45-70. 32-inch round bbl. 48 inches overall. Weight: 10.5 lbs. American walnut stock. Bead front sight, adj. buckhorn rear. Blued finish. Lacquer finish walnut stock w/crescent buttplate. Made from 1993 to 1999.
Standard model . . . . NiB $1133 Ex $829 Gd $631
Deluxe model, add. $375

CZ RIFLES — Strankonice, Czechoslovakia
(currently CZ USA Kansas City, KS formerly Czechpoint, Inc.)

See also listings under Brno Sporting Rifles and Springfield, Inc.

ZKK 600 BOLT-ACTION RIFLE
Calibers: .270 Win., 7x57, 7x64, .30-06. Five round magazine. 23.5- inch bbl. Weight: 7.5 lbs. Adj. folding-leaf rear sight, hooded ramp front. Pistol-grip walnut stock. Imported from 1990 to 1995.
Standard model . . . . NiB $613 Ex $479 Gd $350
Deluxe model. . . . . NiB $688 Ex $554 Gd $400

ZKK 601 BOLT-ACTION RIFLE
Similar to Model ZKK 600 except w/short action in calibers .223 Rem., .243 Win., .308 Win. 43 inches overall. Weight: 6 lbs., 13 oz. Checkered walnut pistol-grip stock w/Monte Carlo cheekpiece. Imported from 1990 to 1995.
Standard model . . . . NiB $570 Ex $495 Gd $443
Deluxe model. . . . . NiB $641 Ex $567 Gd $423

ZKK 602 BOLT-ACTION RIFLE
Similar to Model ZKK 600 except w/Magnum action in calibers .300 Win. Mag., 8x68S, .375 H&H, .458 Win. Mag. 25-inch bbl. 45.5 inches overall. Weight: 9.25 lbs. Imported from 1990 to 1997.
Standard model . . . . NiB $727 Ex $650 Gd $468
Deluxe model. . . . . NiB $896 Ex $744 Gd $505

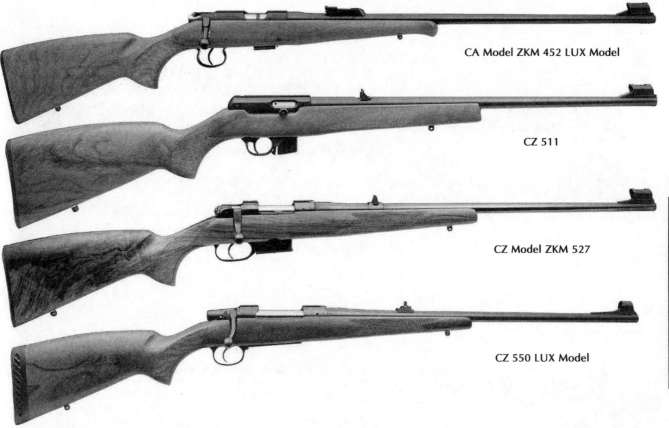

CA Model ZKM 452 LUX Model

CZ 511

CZ Model ZKM 527

CZ 550 LUX Model

CZ 452 BOLT-ACTION REPEATING RIFLE
Calibers: .22 LR. or .22 WMR. Five, 6- or 10-round magazine. 25-inch bbl. 43.5 inches overall. Weight: 6 lbs. Adj. rear sight, hooded bead front. Oil-finished beechwood or checkered walnut stock w/Schnabel forend. Imported 1995 and 2007.

Standard model (22 LR)	NiB $455	Ex $338	Gd $200
Deluxe model (22 LR)	NiB $455	Ex $338	Gd $200
Varmint model (22 LR)	NiB $458	Ex $370	Gd $215
.22 WMR, add			$50

CZ 527 BOLT-ACTION RIFLE
Calibers: .22 Hornet, .222 Rem., .223 Rem., 7.62x39mm. Five round magazine. 23.5-inch bbl. 42.5 inches overall. Weight: 6.75 lbs. Adj. rear sight, hooded ramp front. Grooved receiver. Adj. double-set triggers. Oil-finished beechwood or checkered walnut stock . Imported 1995.

Standard model	NiB $650	Ex $465	Gd $340
Classic model	NiB $655	Ex $470	Gd $338
Carbine model (shorter configuration)	NiB $600	Ex $466	Gd $345
Deluxe model	NiB $657	Ex $572	Gd $373

CZ 537 SPORTER BOLT-ACTION RIFLE
Calibers: .243 Win., .270 Win., 7x57mm, .308 Win., .30-06. Four or 5-round magazine. 19- or 23.5-inch bbl. 40.25 or 44.75 inches overall. Weight: 7 to 7.5 lbs. Adj. folding leaf rear sight, hooded ramp front. Shrouded bolt. Standard or Mannlicher-style checkered walnut stock. Imported 1995.

Standard model	NiB $529	Ex $460	Gd $345
Mountain Carbine model	NiB $555	Ex $439	Gd $326

CZ-511 SEMI-AUTO RIFLE ... NiB $355 Ex $252 Gd $155
Mannlicher model, ... add $126
Caliber: .22 LR. 8-round magazine. 22- inch bbl., 38.6 inches overall. Weight: 5.39 lbs. Receiver top fitted for telescopic sight mounts. Walnut wood-lacquered checkering stock. Imported 1996, 1998 to 2001, 2005 to 2006.

CZ 550 BOLT-ACTION SERIES
Calibers: .243 Win., 6.5x55mm, .270 Win., 7mm Mag., 7x57, 7x64, .30-06, .300 Win Mag., .375 H&H, .416 Rem., .416 Rigby, .458 Win. Mag., 9.3x62. Four or 5-round detachable magazine. 20.5- or 23.6-inch bbl. Weight: 7.25 to 8 lbs. No sights or Express sights on magnum models. Receiver drilled and tapped for scope mount. Standard or Mannlicher-style checkered walnut stock w/buttpad. Imported 1995 to 2000.

Standard	NiB $510	Ex $423	Gd $326
Magnum	NiB $855	Ex $633	Gd $465
Lux	NiB $530	Ex $456	Gd $355
Battue Lux (1998)	NiB $500	Ex $426	Gd $325
Mannlicher	NiB $817	Ex $579	Gd $370
Calibers .416 Rem., .416 Rigby, .458 Win. Mag., add			$100

CZECHOSLOVAKIAN MILITARY RIFLES —
Brno, Czechoslovakia. Manufactured by Ceska Zbrojovka

MODEL 1924 (VZ24)
MAUSER MILITARY RIFLE. . . . NiB $331 Ex $243 Gd $176
Basically same as German Kar., 98k and F.N. (Belgian Model 1924.) Caliber: 7.9mm Mauser. Five round box magazine. 23.25-inch bbl. Weight: 8.5 lbs. Sights: Adj. rear; blade front w/guards. of Belgian-type military stock, full handguard. Made from 1924 thru WWII. Many of these rifles were made for export. As produced during the German occupation, this model was known as Gewehr 24t.

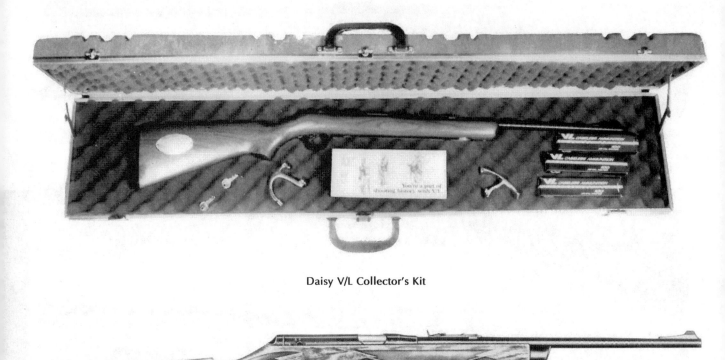

Daisy V/L Collector's Kit

Daisy V/L Standard

MODEL 1933 (VZ33) MAUSER
MILITARY CARBINE . . . . NiB $380 Ex $300 Gd $227
Modification of German M/98 action w/smaller receiver ring. Caliber: 7.9mm Mauser. 19.25-inch bbl. Weight: 7.5 lbs. Sights: Adj. rear; blade front w/guards. Military-type full stock. Mfd. 1933 thru WWII. A similar model, produced during the German occupation, was designated Gew. 33/40.

DAEWOO PRECISION INDUSTRIES — Manufactured in Korea (previously imported by Kimber of America; Daewoo Precision Industries; Nationwide Sports and KBI, Inc.)

DR200 SA SEMIAUTOMATIC SPORTER
Caliber: .223 Rem. (5.56mm). Six or 10-round magazine. 18.4-inch bbl. 39.25 inches overall. Weight: 9 lbs. Protected post front sight, fully-adj. aperture rear. Forged aluminum receiver w/rotating locking bolt assembly. Synthetic sporterized thumbhole stock. Imported from 1994 to 1996.
Sporter model. . . . . NiB $679 Ex $545 Gd $459
Varmint model . . . . NiB $650 Ex $579 Gd $356

DR300 SA SEMIAUTO-
MATIC SPORTER . . . . NiB $670 Ex $602 Gd $421
Similar to Model Daewoo DR200 except chambered for 7.62x39mm. Imported from 1994 to 1996.

DAISY RIFLES — Rogers, Arkansas

Daisy V/L rifles carry the first and only commercial caseless cartridge system. These rifles are expected to appreciate considerably in future years. The cartridge, no longer made, is also a collector's item. Production was discontinued following BATF ruling the V/L model to be a firearm.

COLLECTOR'S KIT . . . . NiB $590 Ex $427 Gd $304
Presentation-grade rifle w/gold plate inscribed w/owner's name and gun serial number mounted on the stock. Also includes a special gun case, pair of brass gun cradles for wall-hanging, 300 rounds of 22 V/L ammunition and a certificate signed by Daisy president Cass S. Hough. Approx. 1,000 manufactured from 1968 to 1969.

PRESENTATION
GRADE . . . . NiB $347 Ex $296 Gd $245
Same specifications as standard model except w/walnut stock. Approx. 4,000 manufactured from 1968 to 1969.

STANDARD RIFLE . . . . NiB $269 Ex $224 Gd $175
Single-shot under-lever action. Caliber: .22 V/L (caseless cartridge, propellant ignited by jet of hot air). 18-inch bbl. Weight: 5 lbs. Sights: Adj. open rear, ramp w/blade front. Wood-grained Lustran stock (foam-filled). About 19,000 manufactured from 1968 to 1969.

Dakota Model 10 Single-Shot Rifle

Dakota Arms Model 76 African Grade

Dakota Arms Model 76 Classic Grade

Dakota Arms Model 97 Hunter

DAKOTA ARMS, INC.—Sturgis, South Dakota, currently owned by Freedom Arms Inc.

MODEL 10 SINGLE-SHOT RIFLE
Chambered for most commercially-loaded calibers. 23-inch bbl. 39.5 inches overall. Weight: 5.5 lbs. Top tang safety. No sights. Checkered pistol-grip buttstock and semi-beavertail forearm, QD swivels, rubber recoil pad. Made from 1992 to date.
Standard calibers . . . . NiB $4679 Ex $3066 Gd $1977
Deluxe model, add $1,375

MODEL 22 BOLT-ACTION
SPORTER RIFLE . . . . NiB $2735 Ex $1217 Gd $823
Calibers: .22 LR. .22 Hornet. Five round magazine. 22-inch bbl. Weight: 6.5 lbs. Adj. trigger. Checkered classic-style Claro or English walnut stock w/black recoil pad. Made from 2003 to 2004.

MODEL 76 AFRICAN
BOLT-ACTION RIFLE . . . . NiB $7998 Ex $4056 Gd $2597
Same general specifications as Model 76 Safari. Calibers: .404 Jeffery, .416 Rigby, .416 Dakota, .450 Dakota. 24-inch bbl. Weight: 8 lbs. Checkered select walnut stock w/two cross bolts. "R" prefix on ser. nos. Intro. 1989.

MODEL 76 ALPINE
BOLT-ACTION RIFLE . . . . NiB $5634 Ex $2789 Gd $2009
Same general specifications as Model 76 Classic except short action w/blind magazine. Calibers: .22-250, .243, 6mm Rem., .250-3000, 7mm-08, .308. 21-inch bbl. Weight: 7.5 lbs. Made from 1989 to 1992.

MODEL 76 CLASSIC
BOLT-ACTION RIFLE . . . . NiB $5629 Ex $3467 Gd $2240
Calibers: .257 Roberts, .270 Win., .280 Rem., .30-06, 7mm Rem. Mag., .300 Win. Mag., .338 Win. Mag., .375 H&H Mag., .458 Win.

Mag. 21- or 23-inch bbl. Weight: 7.5 lbs. Receiver drilled and tapped for sights. Adj. trigger. Classic-style checkered walnut stock w/steel grip cap and solid recoil pad. Right- and left-hand models. Made from 1987 to date.

MODEL 76 LONGBOW TACTICAL
BOLT-ACTION RIFLE . . . . NiB $4466 Ex $3459 Gd $2390
Calibers: .300 Dakota Mag., .330 Dakota Mag., .338 Lapua Mag. Blind magazine. Ported 28-inch bbl. 50 to 51 inches overall. Weight: 13.7 lbs. Black or oliver green fiberglass stock w/adj. cheekpiece and buttplate. Receiver drilled and tapped w/one-piece rail mount and no sights. Made from 1997 to 2009.

MODEL 76 SAFARI
BOLT-ACTION RIFLE . . . . NiB $7533 Ex $5416 Gd $2307
Calibers: .300 Win. Mag., .338 Win. Mag., .375 H&H Mag. .458 Win. Mag. 23-inch bbl. w/bbl. band swivel. Weight: 8.5 lbs. Ramp front sight, standing leaf rear. Checkered fancy walnut stock w/ ebony forend tip and solid recoil pad. Made from 1987 to date.

MODEL 76 TRAVELER SERIES RIFLES
Threadless take-down action w/interchangeable bbl. capability based on the Dakota 76 design. Calibers: .257 through .458 Win (Standard-Classic & Safari) and .416 Dakota, .404 Jeffery, .416 Rigby, .338 Lapua and .450 Dakota Mag. (E/F Family-African Grade). 23- to 24- inch bbl. Weight: 7.5 to 9.5 lbs. Right or left-hand action. X grade (Classic) or XXX grade (Safari or African) oil finish English Bastogne or Claro walnut stock. Made from 1999 to date.
Classic Grade . . . . NiB $6644 Ex $5428 Gd $2380
Safari Grade . . . . NiB $8577 Ex $6502 Gd $2866
African Grade . . . . NiB $9233 Ex $7544 Gd $3209
Interchangeable bbl. assemblies
Standard calibers, add $2500
Safari calibers, add $2700
African calibers, add $2970

MODEL 76 VARMINT
BOLT-ACTION RIFLE .... NiB $2710 Ex $1988 Gd $1165
Similar to Model 76 Classic except single-shot action w/ heavy bbl. chambered for .17 Rem. to 6mm PPC. Weight: 13.7 lbs. Checkered walnut or synthetic stock. Receiver drilled and tapped for scope mounts and no sights. Made from 1994 to 1998.

MODEL 97 HUNTER BOLT-ACTION SERIES
Calibers: .22-250 Rem. to .330 Dakota Mag.(Lightweight), .25-06 to .375 Dakota Mag. (Long Range). 22-, 24- or 26-inch bbl. 43 to 46 inches overall. Weight: 6.16 lbs. to 7.7 lbs. Black composite fiberglass stock w/recoil pad. Fully adj. match trigger. Made from 1997 to 2004.
Lightweight .... NiB $2744 Ex $1675 Gd $944
Long Range .... NiB $3440 Ex $2475 Gd $1755

MODEL 97 VARMINT HUNTER
BOLT-ACTION RIFLE .... NiB $3734 Ex $2566 Gd $1896
Similar to Model 97 Hunter except single-shot action w/ heavy bbl. chambered .22-250 Rem. to .308 Win. Checkered walnut stock. Receiver drilled and tapped for scope mounts and no sights. Made from 1998 to 2004.

CHARLES DALY RIFLE — Harrisburg, Pennsylvania. Imported by K.B.I., Inc., Harrisburg, PA (previously by Outdoor Sports Headquarters, Inc.)

EMPIRE GRADE BOLT-ACTION RIFLE (RF)
Similar to Superior Grade except w/checkered California walnut stock w/rosewood grip cap and forearm cap. High polished blued finish and damascened bolt. Made from 1998. Disc.
Empire Grade (.22 LR) ...... NiB $370 Ex $324 Gd $223
Empire Grade (.22WMR).... NiB $406 Ex $322 Gd $235
Empire Grade (.22 Hornet) ... NiB $556 Ex $444 Gd $320

FIELD GRADE BOLT-ACTION RIFLE (RF)
Caliber: .22 LR. 16.25-, 17.5- or 22.63-inch bbl. 32 to 41 inches overall. Single-shot (True Youth) and 6- or 10-round magazine. Plain walnut-finished hardwood or checkered polymer stock. Blue or stainless finish. Imported from 1998. Disc.
Field Grade (Standard w/22.63-inch bbl.)NiB $157 Ex $128 Gd $95
Field Grade (Youth w/17.5-inch bbl.) . NiB $170 Ex $139 Gd $99
Field Grade (True Youth
w/16.25-inch bbl.) .... NiB $188 Ex $155 Gd $131
Field Grade (Polymer w/stainless action)NiB $158 Ex $130 Gd $100

FIELD GRADE HUNTER BOLT-ACTION RIFLE
Calibers: .22 Hornet, .223 Rem., .243 Win., .270 Win., 7mm Rem. Mag. .308 Win., .30-06, .300 Win. Mag., .300 Rem. Ultra Mag., .338 Win. Mag. Three, 4-, or 5-round magazine. 22- or 24-inch bbl. w/o sights. Weight: 7.2 to 7.4 lbs. Checkered walnut or black polymer stock. Receiver drilled and tapped. Blue or stainless finish. Imported from 1998. Disc.
Field Grade Hunter (walnut stock)... NiB $572 Ex $457 Gd $339
Field Grade Hunter (polymer stock). . NiB $589 Ex $478 Gd $339
w/Left-hand model, add $35

HAMMERLESS DRILLING
See listing under Charles Daly shotguns.

HORNET RIFLE......... NiB $1299 Ex $1088 Gd $759
Same as Herold Rifle. See listing of that rifle for specifications. imported during the 1930s. Disc.

MAUSER 98
Calibers: .243 Win., .270 Win., 7mm Rem. Mag. .308 Win., .30-06, .300 Win. Mag., .375 H&H, or .458 Win. Mag. Three, 4-, or 5-round magazine. 23-inch bbl. 44.5 inches overall. Weight: 7.5 lbs. Checkered European walnut (Superior) or fiberglass/graphic (Field) stock w/recoil pad. Ramped front sight, adj. rear. Receiver drilled and tapped w/side saftey. Imported from 1998. Disc.
Field Grade (standard calibers) Disc.. NiB $466 Ex $423 Gd $155
Field Grade (375 H&H
and 458 Win. Mag.) .... NiB $669 Ex $572 Gd $354
Superior Grade (standard calibers) Disc.NiB $669 Ex $572 Gd $454
Superior Grade (magnum calibers) Disc.NiB $903 Ex $766 Gd $641

MINI-MAUSER 98
Similar to Mauser 98 except w/19.25-inch bbl. chambered for .22 Hornet, .22-250 Rem., .223 Rem., or 7.62x39mm. Five round magazine. Imported from 1998. Disc.
Field Grade .... NiB $409 Ex $358 Gd $233
Superior Grade........... NiB $533 Ex $447 Gd $259

SUPERIOR GRADE BOLT-ACTION RIFLE
Calibers: .22 LR. .22 WMR, .22 Hornet. 20.25- to 22.63-inch bbl. 40.5 to 41.25 inches overall. Five, 6-, or 10-round magazine. Ramped front sight, adj. rear w/grooved receiver. Checkered walnut stock. Made from 1998. Disc.
Superior Grade (.22 LR) ..... NiB $179 Ex $150 Gd $100
Superior Grade (.22WMR).... NiB $244 Ex $190 Gd $145
Superior Grade (.22 Hornet) .. NiB $399 Ex $345 Gd $239

SEMIAUTOMATIC RIFLE
Caliber: .22 LR. 20.75-inch bbl. 40.5 inches overall. 10-round magazine. Ramped front sight, adj. rear w/grooved receiver. Plain walnut-finished hardwood stock (Field), checkered walnut (Superior), checkered polymer stock or checkered California walnut stock w/rosewood grip cap and forearm cap (Empire). Blue or stainless finish. Imported from 1998. Disc.
Field Grade .... NiB $145 Ex $126 Gd $85
Field Grade (Polymer
w/stainless action) .... NiB $161 Ex $136 Gd $92
Superior Grade............ NiB $215 Ex $188 Gd $132
Empire Grade............. NiB $355 Ex $290 Gd $200

BOLT ACTION RIFLE .... NiB $922 Ex $659 Gd $560
Calibers: .22 Hornet. Bbl.: 24 inches. Five round box magazine, hinged floorplate. Sights: Ramp front, leaf rear. Walnut stock, checkered grip and forearm. Early version rifle, introduced 1931 by Franz Jaeger Co. Discontinued 1939. Imported by Charles Daly but same model was imported by A. F. Stoeger as Herold Rifle.

SUPERIOR
COMBINATION GUN. . . . NiB $1354 Ex $1149 Gd $1013
Calibers: 12-guage shotgun over .22 Hornet, .223 Remington, .22-250, .243 Win., .270 Win., or .30-06. Barrels: 23 1/2 inches. Shotgun choked Imp. Cyl. Weight: About 7.5 pounds. Checkered walnut, pistol grip, semi-beavertail forend. Silvered, engraved receiver. Chrome-moly steel barrels, double triggers, extractors. Gold bead front sight. Introduced 1997, imported by K.B.I.

EMPIRE COMBINATION GUNNiB $1743 Ex $1540 Gd $1179
Similar to Superior Combination Gun but with fancy grade wood, European style comb and cheekpiece, slimmer forend. Introduced 1997, imported by K.B.I.

FIELD GRADE AUTO RIFLE. . . . NiB $167 Ex $109 Gd $94
Calibers: .22 LR. Semiautomatic, 10-round magazine, shell deflector. Bbl.: 20 3/4 inches. Weight: 6.5 pounds. Overall length: 40.5

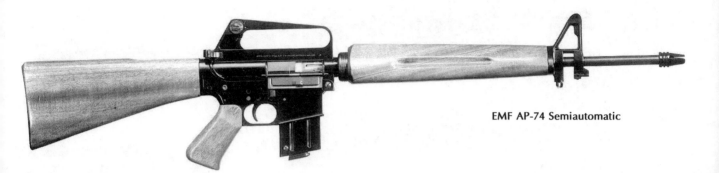

EMF AP-74 Semiautomatic

inches. Stock: Hardwood, walnut-finished, Monte Carlo style. Sights: Hooded front, adjustable open rear. Grooved for scope mounting. Blued finish. Introduced 1998. Imported by K. B. I.

EMPIRE GRADE AUTO RIFLE .NiB $210 Ex $166 Gd $135
Similar to Field Grade Auto Rifle but with select California walnut stock, hand checkering. Contrasting forend and grip caps. Damascened bolt, high-polish blued finish. Introduced 1998; discontinued.

TRUE YOUTH
BOLT-ACTION RIFLE . . . . . . NiB $156 Ex $100 Gd $75
Caliber: .22 LR. Single-shot., bolt-action. Bbl.: 16.25 inches. Weight: 3 pounds. Overall length: 32 inches. Walnut-finished hardwood stock. Sights: Blade front, adjustable rear. Blued finish. Introduced 1998. Imported by K. B. I.

EAGLE ARMS INC. — Geneseo, Illinois (previously Coal Valley, Illinois)

In 1995, Eagle Arms Inc., became a division of ArmaLite and reintroduced that logo. For current ArmaLite production see models under that listing.

MODEL EA-15 CARBINE
Caliber: .223 Rem. (5.56mm). 30-round magazine. 16-inch bbl. and collapsible buttstock. Weight: 5.75 lbs. (E1); 6.25 lbs. (E2 w/ heavy bbl. & National Match sights). Made 1990 to 1995; reintro. 2002 to 2005.
E1 Carbine . . . . .NiB $976 Ex $739 Gd $510
E2 Carbine . . . . .NiB $976 Ex $739 Gd $510

MODEL EA-15 GOLDEN
EAGLE MATCH RIFLE . . . . . .NiB $1244 Ex $977 Gd $657
Same general specifications as EA-15 Standard, except w/E2-style National Match sights. 20-inch Douglas Heavy Match bbl. NM trigger and bolt-carrier group. Weight: 12.75 lbs. Made 1991 to 1995, reintro. 2002.

MODEL EA-15
SEMIAUTOMATIC RIFLE . . . . .NiB $1221 Ex $722 Gd $504
Same as EA-15 Carbine except 20-inch bbl., 39 inches overall and weighs 7 lbs. Made from 1990 to 1993; reintro. 2002 to 2005.

EMF COMPANY, INC.—Santa Ana, California

MODEL AP-74
SEMI-AUTOMATIC CARBINE .NiB $397 Ex $300 Gd $221

Calibers: .22 LR or .32 ACP, 15-round magazine. 20-inch bbl. w/ flash reducer. 38 inches overall. Weight: 6.75 lbs. Protected pin front sight; protected rear peep sight. Lightweight plastic buttstock; ventilated snap-out forend. Importation disc. 1989.

MODEL AP74-W
SPORTER CARBINE. . . . . .NiB $419 Ex $321 Gd $213
Sporterized version of AP-74 w/wood buttstock and forend. Importation disc. 1989.

MODEL AP74 PARATROOPER NiB $433 Ex $260 Gd $242
Same general specifications as Model AP74-W except w/folding tubular buttstock. Made in .22 LR. only. Importation disc. 1987.

MODEL 1860 HENRY RIFLE
Calibers: .44-40 and .45 LC. 24.25-inch bbl.; upper-half octagonal w/magazine tube in one-piece steel. 43.75-inches overall. Weight: 9.25 lbs. Varnished American walnut wood stock. Polished brass frame and brass buttplate. Original rifle was patented by B. Tyler Henry and produced by the New Haven Arms Company, when Oliver Winchester was president. Imported 1987 to 2008.
Deluxe model . . . . .NiB $968 Ex $688 Gd $347
Engraved model . . . . .NiB $1123 Ex $832 Gd $560

MODEL 1866
YELLOW BOY RIFLE . . . . .NiB $754 Ex $558 Gd $359
Calibers: .44-40, .45 LC and .38 Special. Lever-action. Bbl: 24 inches, 43 inches overall. Bead front sight. Offered w/blued finish, walnut stock and brass frame 2005 to 2008.

MODEL 1866 YELLOW BOY CARBINE
Same features as 1866 Yellow Boy Rifle except carbine.
Standard carbine . . . . .NiB $933 Ex $465 Gd $333
Engraved carbine . . . . .NiB $933 Ex $465 Gd $333

MODEL 1873 SPORTING RIFLE
Calibers: .22 LR. .22 WMR, .357 Mag., .44-40 and .45 LC. 24.25-inch octagonal bbl. 43.25 inches overall. Weight: 8.16 lbs. Color casehardened frame w/blued steel magazine tube. Walnut stock and forend.
Standard Rifle. . . . . .NiB $922 Ex $707 Gd $459
Engraved Rifle . . . . .NiB $1007 Ex $657 Gd $482
Boy's Rifle
(Youth Model, .22 LR). . . . . .NiB $674 Ex $558 Gd $369

MODEL 1873 SPORTING RIFLE CARBINE
Same features as 1873 sporting rifle except w/19-inch bbl. Overall length: 38.25 inches. Weight: 7.38 lbs. Color casehardened or blued frame. Made 1988 to 1989.
Standard carbine . . . . .NiB $904 Ex $689 Gd $466

Erma — EG712

Erma — EGM1

Erma — EM1 22

ERMA-WERKE — Dachau, Germany (previously imported by Precision Sales International; Nygord Precision Products; Mandall's Shooting Supplies)

MODEL EG72
PUMP-ACTION REPEATER . . . . NiB $158 Ex $110 Gd $98
Visible hammer. Caliber: .22 LR. 15-round magazine. 18.5-inch bbl. Weight: 5.25 lbs. Sights: open rear; hooded ramp front. Receiver grooved for scope mounting. Straight-grip stock, grooved slide handle. Imported from 1970 to 1976.

MODEL EG73 . . . . NiB $288 Ex $223 Gd $172
Same as Model EG712 except chambered for .22 WMR w/12-round tubular magazine, 19.3-inch bbl. Imported from 1973 to 1997.

MODEL EG712 LEVER-ACTION
REPEATING CARBINE . . . . NiB $297 Ex $229 Gd $167
Styled after Winchester Model 94. Caliber: .22 LR. Long, Short. Tubul33 magazine holds 15 LR, 17 Long, 21 Short. 18.5-inch bbl. Weight: 5.5 lbs. Sights: Open rear; hooded ramp front. Receiver grooved for scope mounting. Western carbine-style stock and forearm w/bbl. band. Imported 1976 to 1997. Note: A similar carbine of Erma manufacture is marketed in U.S. as Ithaca Model 72 Saddle Gun.

MODEL EGM1 . . . . NiB $290 Ex $247 Gd $180
Same as Model EM1 except w/unslotted buttstock, ramp front sight, 5-round magazine standard. Imported from 1970 to 1995.

MODEL EM1 .22
SEMIAUTOMATIC CARBINE . . NiB $387 Ex $320 Gd $222
Styled after U.S. Carbine cal. 30 M1. Caliber: .22 LR. 10- or 15-round magazine. 18-inch bbl. Weight: 5.5 lbs. Carbine-type sights. Receiver grooved for scope mounting. Military stock/handguard. Imported 1966 to 1997.

EUROPEAN AMERICAN ARMORY — Sharpes, Florida

MODEL HW 660 BOLT-ACTION
SINGLE-SHOT RIFLE . . . . NiB $909 Ex $745 Gd $495
Caliber: .22 LR. 26.8-inch bbl., 45.7 inches overall. Weight: 10.8 lbs. Match-type aperture rear sight; Hooded ramp front. Stippled walnut stock. Imported from 1992 to 1996.

MODEL HW BOLT-ACTION
SINGLE-SHOT TARGET RIFLE . NiB $895 Ex $740 Gd $485
Same general specification as Model HW 660 except equipped w/ target stock. Imported from 1995 to 1996.

MODEL SABITTI SP1822
Caliber: .22 LR. 10-round detachable magazine. 18.5 inch bbl. 37.5 inches overall. Weight: 5.25 to 7.15 lbs. No sights. Hammer-forged heavy non-tapered bbl. Scope-mounted rail. Flush-mounted magazine release. Alloy receiver w/non-glare finish. Manual bolt lock. Wide claw extractor. Blowback action. Cross-trigger safety. Imported 1994 to 1996.
Traditional Sporter model . . . . NiB $259 Ex $206 Gd $149
Thumbhole Sporter
model (synthetic stock) . . . . NiB $379 Ex $312 Gd $221

FABRIQUE NATIONALE HERSTAL — Herstal & Liege, Belgium (formerly Fabrique Nationale d'Armes de Guerre)

MODELS 1924, 1934/30 AND
1930 MAUSER MILITARY RIFLES . . . NiB $445 Ex $337 Gd $241
Similar to German Kar. 98k w/straight bolt handle. Calibers: 7mm, 7.65mm and 7.9mm Mauser. Five round box magazine. 23.5-inch bbl. Weight: 8.5 lbs. Sights: Adj. rear; blade front. Military stock of M/98 pattern w/slight modification. Model differences are minor. Also produced in a short carbine model w/17.25-inch bbl. Note: These rifles were manufactured under contract for Abyssinia, Argentina, Belgium, Bolivia, Brazil, Chile, China, Colombia, Ecuador, Iran, Luxembourg, Mexico, Peru, Turkey, Uruguay and Yugoslavia. Such arms usually bear the coat of arms of the country for which they were made together with the contractor's name and date of manufacture. Also sold commercially and exported to all parts of the world.

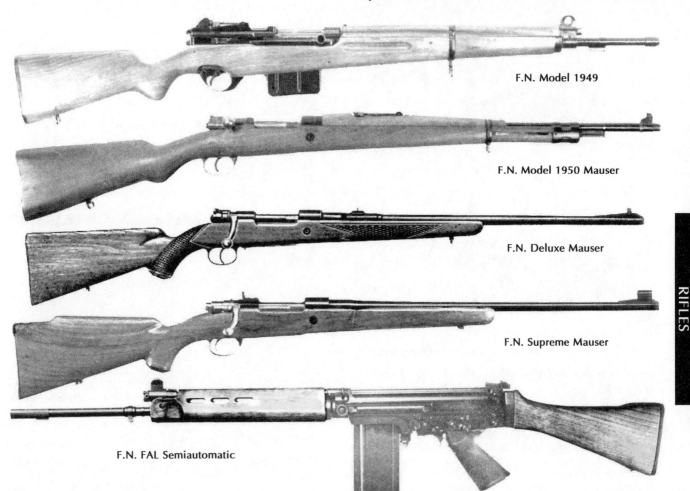

F.N. Model 1949

F.N. Model 1950 Mauser

F.N. Deluxe Mauser

F.N. Supreme Mauser

F.N. FAL Semiautomatic

RIFLES

MODEL 1949 SEMIAUTOMATIC
MILITARY RIFLE . . . . **NiB $799 Ex $647 Gd $328**
Gas-operated. Calibers: 7mm, 7.65mm, 7.92mm, .30-06. 10-round box magazine, clip fed or loaded singly. 23.2-inch bbl. Weight: 9.5 lbs. Sights: Tangent rear-shielded post front. Pistol-grip stock, handguard. Note: Adopted by Belgium in 1949; also by Belgian Congo, Brazil, Colombia, Luxembourg, Netherlands, East Indies, and Venezuela. Approx. 160,000 were made.

MODEL 1950 MAUSER
MILITARY RIFLE . . . . **NiB $533 Ex $360 Gd $287**
Same as previous F.N. models of Kar. 98k type except chambered for .30-06.

DELUXE MAUSER BOLT-ACTION
SPORTING RIFLE . . . . **NiB $799 Ex $689 Gd $443**
American calibers: .220 Swift, .243 Win., .244 Rem., .250/3000, .257 Roberts, .270 Win., 7mm, .300 Sav., .308 Win. .30-06. European calibers: 7x57, 8x57JS, 8x60S, 9.3x62, 9.5x57, 10.75x68mm. Five round box magazine. 24-inch bbl. Weight: 7.5-8.25 lbs. American model is standard w/hooded ramp front sight and Tri-Range rear; Continental model w/two-leaf rear. Checkered stock w/cheekpiece, pistol-grip, swivels. Made from 1947 to 1963.

DELUXE MAUSER —
PRESENTATION GRADE . . . **NiB $1337 Ex $1096 Gd $752**
Same as regular model except w/select grade stock; engraving on receiver, trigger guard, floorplate and bbl. breech. Disc. 1963.
FAL/FNC/LAR SEMIAUTOMATIC

Same as standard FAL military rifle except w/o provision for automatic firing. Gas-operated. Calibers: 7.62mm NATO (.308 Win.) or 5.56mm (.223 Rem.). 10- or 20-round box magazine. 25.5-inch bbl. (including flash hider). Weight: 9 lbs. Sights: Post front; aperture rear. Fixed wood or folding buttstock, pistol-grip, forearm/handguard w/carrying handle and sling swivels. Disc. 1988.

**F.N. FAL/LAR model (Light
Automatic Rifle)** . . . . **NiB $2594 Ex $2216 Gd $1402**
F.N. FAL/HB model (heavy bbl.) . **NiB $2955 Ex $2343 Gd $1644**
F.N. FAL/PARA (Paratrooper) . . . . **NiB $3566 Ex $2886 Gd $1854**
**F.N. FNC Carbine
model (.223 cal.)** . . . . **NiB $2715 Ex $1954 Gd $1294**
**F.N. FNC Carbine model w/flash
suppresser (.223 cal.)** . . . . **NiB $2790 Ex $2033 Gd $1387**

SUPREME MAUSER BOLT-ACTION
SPORTING RIFLE . . . . **NiB $808 Ex $865 Gd $443**
Calibers: .243, .270, 7mm, .308, .30-06. Four round magazine in .243 and .308; 5-round in other calibers. 22-inch bbl. in .308; 24-inch in other calibers. Sights: Hooded ramp front, Tri-Range peep rear. Checkered stock w/ Monte Carlo cheekpiece, pistol-grip, swivels. Weight: 7.75 lbs. Made from 1957 to 1975.

SUPREME MAGNUM MAUSER . . . . **NiB $865 Ex $689 Gd $474**
Calibers: .264 Mag., 7mm Mag., .300 Win. Mag. Specifications same as for standard caliber model except 3-round magazine capacity.

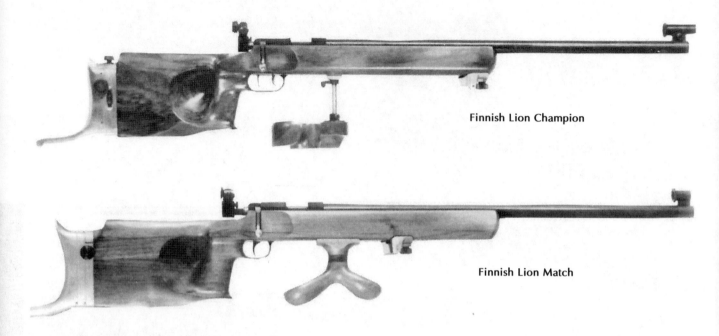

Finnish Lion Champion

Finnish Lion Match

FEATHER INDUSTRIES, INC. — Boulder, Colorado

See MITCHELL ARMS. for current production.

MODEL AT-9 SEMIAUTOMATIC RIFLE
Caliber: 9mm Parabellum. 10-, 25-, 32-, or 100-round magazine. 17-inch bbl. 35 inches overall (extended). Hooded post front sight, adj. aperture rear. Weight: 5 lbs. Telescoping wire stock w/composition pistol-grip and barrel-shroud handguard. Matte black finish. Made from 1988 to 1995.

Model AT-9 . . . . NiB $898	Ex $714	Gd $479
W/32-round magazine, add. $100
W/100-round drum magazine, add $300

MODEL AT-22 . . . . NiB $355 Ex $232 Gd $171
Caliber: .22 LR. 20-round magazine. 17-inch bbl. 35 inches overall (extended). Hooded post front sight; adj. aperture rear. Weight: 3.25 lbs. Telescoping wire stock w/composition pistol-grip and barrel shroud handguard. Matte black finish.

MODEL F2 SA CARBINE. . . . . NiB $331 Ex $258 Gd $149
Similar to AT-22, except w/fixed Polymer stock and pistol-grip. Made from 1992 to 1995.

MODEL F9 SA CARBINE. . . . . NiB $758 Ex $599 Gd $400
Similar to AT-9, except w/fixed Polymer stock and pistol-grip. Made from 1992 to 1995.

FINNISH LION RIFLES — Jyväkylylä, Finland. Manufactured by Valmet Oy, Tourula Works

CHAMPION FREE RIFLE . . . . . NiB $688 Ex $545 Gd $390
Bolt-action single-shot target rifle. Double-set trigger. Caliber: .22 LR. 28.75-inch heavy bbl. Weight: 16 lbs. Sights: Extension rear peep; aperture front. Walnut free-rifle stock w/full pistol-grip, thumbhole, beavertail forend, hook buttplate, palm rest, hand stop, swivel. Made from 1965 to 1972.

STANDARD ISU
TARGET RIFLE . . . . NiB $421 Ex $337 Gd $213
Bolt-action, single-shot. Caliber: .22 LR. 27.5-inch bbl. Weight: 10.5 lbs. Sights: extension rear peep; aperture front. Walnut target stock w/full pistol-grip, checkered beavertail forearm, adj. buttplate, sling swivel. Made from 1966 to 1977.

MATCH RIFLE . . . . NiB $569 Ex $510 Gd $343
Bolt-action, single-shot. Caliber: .22 LR. 28.75-inch heavy bbl. Weight: 14.5 lbs. Sights: Extension rear peep; aperture front. Walnut free-rifle stock w/full pistol-grip, thumbhole, beavertail forearm, hook buttplate, palm rest, hand stop, swivel. Made from 1937 to 1972.

STANDARD TARGET RIFLE
Bolt-action, single-shot. Caliber: .22 LR. 27.5-inch bbl. 44.5 inches overall. Weight: 10.5 lbs. No sights; micrometer rear and globe front International-style sights available. Select walnut stock in target configuration. Made 1966 to 1997..

Standard model . . . . NiB $808	Ex $679	Gd $448
Thumbhole stock model . . . . NiB $893	Ex $733	Gd $533
Deluxe model. . . . . NiB $439	Ex $350	Gd $259

LUIGI FRANCHI, S.P.A. — Brescia, Italy

CENTENNIAL AUTOMATIC RIFLE
Commemorates Franchi's 100th anniversary (1868-1968). Centennial seal engraved on receiver. Semiautomatic. Take-down. Caliber: .22 LR. 11-round magazine in buttstock. 21-inch bbl. Weight: 5.13 lbs. Sights: Open rear; gold bead front on ramp. Checkered walnut stock and forend. Deluxe model w/fully engraved receiver, premium grade wood. Made in 1968.

Standard model . . . . NiB $433	Ex $321	Gd $224
Engraved model . . . . NiB $478	Ex $379	Gd $270

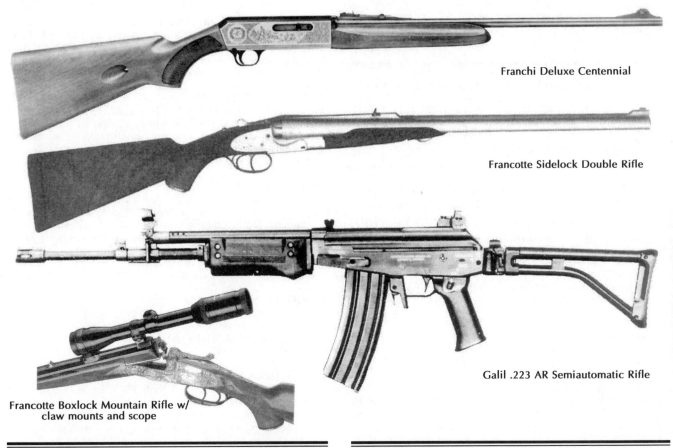

Franchi Deluxe Centennial

Francotte Sidelock Double Rifle

Galil .223 AR Semiautomatic Rifle

Francotte Boxlock Mountain Rifle w/
claw mounts and scope

RIFLES

FRANCOTTE RIFLES — Leige, Belgium. Imported by Armes de Chasse, Hertford, NC (previously by Abercrombie & Fitch)

BOLT-ACTION RIFLE
Custom rifle built on Mauser style bolt action. Available in three action lengths. Calibers: .17 Bee to .505 Gibbs. Barrel length: 21- to 24.5-inches. Weight: 8 to 12 lbs. Stock dimensions, wood type and style to customer's specifications. Engraving, appointments and finish to customer's preference. Note: Deduct 25% for models w/o engraving.

Short action . . . . NiB $9770 Ex $7725 Gd $4690
Standard action . . . . NiB $7859 Ex $6233 Gd $3834
Magnum Francotte action NiB $14,000 Ex $11,770 Gd $7690

BOXLOCK MOUNTAIN RIFLE
Custom single-shot rifle built on Anson & Deeley style boxlock or Holland & Holland style sidelock action. 23- to 26-inch barrels chambered to customer's specification. Stock dimensions, wood type and style to customer's specifications. Engraving, appointments and finish to customer's preference. Note: Deduct 30% for models w/o engraving.

Boxlock . . . . NiB $14,299 Ex $12,200 Gd $7800
Sidelock. . . . . NiB $22,438 Ex $17,950 Gd $12,206

DOUBLE RIFLE
Custom side-by-side rifle. Built on Francotte system boxlock or back-action sidelock. 23.5- to 26-inch barrels chambered to customer's specification. Stock dimensions, wood type and style to customer's specifications. Engraving, appointments and finish to customer's preference. Note: Deduct 30% for models w/o engraving.

Boxlock . . . . NiB $26,750 Ex $16,875 Gd $10,270
Sidelock. . . . . NiB $31,760 Ex $26,900 Gd $16,975

FRENCH MILITARY RIFLE — Saint Etienne, France

MODEL 1936
MAS MILITARY RIFLE . . . . NiB $209 Ex $170 Gd $103
Bolt-action. Caliber: 7.5mm MAS. Five-round box magazine. 22.5-inch bbl. Weight: 8.25 lbs. Sights: Adj. rear; blade front. Two-piece military-type stock. Bayonet carried in forend tube. Made from 1936 to 1940 by Manufacture Francaise d'Armes et de Cycles de St. Etienne (MAS).

GALIL RIFLES — Manufactured by Israel Military Industries, Israel. Imported by UZI America Inc., North Haven, CT (previously by Action Arms, Springfield Armory and Magnum Research, Inc.)

AR SEMIAUTOMATIC RIFLE
Calibers: .308 Win. (7.62 NATO), .223 Rem. (5.56mm). 25-round (.308) or 35-round (.223) magazine. 16-inch (.223) or 18.5-inch (.308) bbl. w/flash suppressor. Weight: 9.5 lbs. Folding aperture rear sight, post front. Folding metal stock w/carrying handle. Imported 1982 to 1994. Currently select fire models available to law enforcement only.

Model .223 AR. . . . . NiB $3233 Ex $1998 Gd $1200
Model .308 AR. . . . . NiB $3233 Ex $1998 Gd $1200
Model .223 ARM . . . . NiB $3227 Ex $2290 Gd $1669
Model .308 ARM . . . . NiB $3227 Ex $2290 Gd $1669

SPORTER SEMIAUTOMATIC RIFLE NiB $1723 Ex $1009 Gd $707
Same general specifications as AR Model except w/hardwood thumbhole stock and 5-round magazine. Weight: 8.5 lbs. Imported 1991 to 1994.

GARCIA CORPORATION—Teaneck, New Jersey

BRONCO 22 SINGLE-SHOT RIFLE . . . NiB $151 Ex $112 Gd $88
Swing-out action. Takedown. Caliber: .22 LR, Long, Short. 16.5-inch bbl. Weight: 3 lbs. Sights: Open rear-blade front. One-piece stock and receiver, crackle finish. Intro. 1967. Discontinued.

GERMAN MILITARY RIFLES — Manufactured by Ludwig Loewe & Co., Berlin, other contractors and by German arsenals and various plants under German government control

MODEL 24T (GEW. 24T) MAUSER RIFLE NiB $598 Ex $443 Gd $300
Same general specifications as Czech Model 24 (VZ24) Mauser Rifle w/minor modification and laminated wood stock. Weight: 9.25 lbs. Made in Czechoslovakia during German occupation; adopted 1940.

MODEL 29/40 (GEW. 29/40)
MAUSER RIFLE. . . . . NiB $433 Ex $329 Gd $244
Same general specifications as Kar. 98K w/minor differences. Made in Poland during German occupation; adopted 1940.

MODEL 33/40 (GEW. 33/40)
MAUSER RIFLE. . . . . NiB $1030 Ex $799 Gd $515
Same general specifications as Czech Model 33 (VZ33) Mauser Carbine w/minor modifications and laminated wood stock as found in war-time Model 98K carbines. Made in Czechoslovakia during German occupation; adopted 1940.

MODELS 41 AND 41-W (GEW. 41, GEW. 41-W)
SEMIAUTOMATIC MILITARY RIFLES
Gas-operated, muzzle cone system. Caliber: 7.9mm Mauser. Ten-round box magazine. 22.5-inch bbl. Weight: 10.25 lbs. Sights: Adj. leaf rear; blade front. Military-type stock w/semi-pistol grip, plastic handguard. Note: Model 41 lacks bolt release found on Model 41-W; otherwise, the models are the same. These early models were mfd. in Walther's Zella-Mehlis plant. Made c.1941 to 1943.
Model 41 . . . . NiB $4460 Ex $3588 Gd $2510
Model 41-W . . . . NiB $3488 Ex $2789 Gd $1809

MODEL 43 (GEW. 43, KAR. 43)
SEMIAUTO MILITARY RIFLES . . . . NiB $1399 Ex $1125 Gd $848
Gas-operated, bbl. vented as in Russian Tokarev. Caliber: 7.9mm Mauser. 10-round detachable box magazine. 22- or 24-inch bbl. Weight: 9 lbs. Sights: Adj. rear; hooded front. Military-type stock w/semi-pistol-grip, wooden handguard. Note: These rifles are alike except for minor details, have characteristic late WWII mfg. short cuts: cast receiver and bolt cover, stamped steel parts, etc. Gew. 43 may have either 22- or 24-inch bbl. The former length was standardized in late 1944, when weapon designation was changed to "Kar. 43." Made from 1943 to 1945.

MODEL 1888 (GEW. 88) MAUSER-
MANNLICHER SERVICE RIFLE. . . . . . NiB $433 Ex $265 Gd $221
Bolt-action w/straight bolt handle. Caliber: 7.9mm Mauser (8x57mm). Five round Mannlicher box magazine. 29-inch bbl. w/jacket. Weight: 8.5 lbs. Fixed front sight, adj. rear. Military-type full stock. Mfd. by Ludwig Loewe & Co., Haenel, Schilling and other contractors.

MODEL 1888 (KAR. 88) MAUSER-
MANNLICHER CARBINE. . . . . NiB $337 Ex $249 Gd $245
Same general specifications as Gew. 88 except w/18-inch bbl., w/o jacket, flat turned-down bolt handle, weight: 6.75 lbs. Mfd. by Ludwig Loewe & Co., Haenel, Schilling and other contractors.

MODEL 1898 (GEW. 98)
MAUSER MILITARY RIFLE. . . . NiB $572 Ex $434 Gd $270
Bolt action with straight bolt handle. Caliber: 7.9mm Mauser (8x57mm). Five round box magazine. 29-inch stepped bbl. Weight: 9 lbs. Sights: Blade front; adj. rear. Military-type full stock w/rounded bottom pistol grip. Adopted 1898.

MODEL 1898A (KAR. 98A)
MAUSER CARBINE . . . . NiB $521 Ex $433 Gd $329
Same general specifications as Model 1898 (Gew.98) Rifle except has turned-down bolt handle, smaller receiver ring, light 23.5-inch-straight taper bbl., front sight guards, sling is attached to left side of stock, weight: 8 lbs. Note: Some of these carbines are marked "Kar. 98;" the true Kar. 98 is the earlier original M/98 carbine w/17-inch bbl. and is rarely encountered.

MODEL 1898B (KAR. 98B)
MAUSER CARBINE . . . . NiB $475 Ex $397 Gd $294
Same general specifications as Model 1898 (Gew.98) Rifle except has turned-down bolt handle and sling attached to left side of stock. This is post-WWI model.

MODEL 1898K (KAR. 98K)
MAUSER CARBINE . . . . NiB $515 Ex $423 Gd $320
Same general specifications as Model 1898 (Gew.98) Rifle except has turned-down bolt handle, 23.5-inch bbl., may have hooded front sight, sling attached to left side of stock, weighs about 8.5 lbs. Adopted in 1935, this was the standard German service rifle of WWII. Note: Late-war models had stamped sheet steel trigger guards and many of the Model 98K carbines made during WWII had laminated wood stocks These weigh .5 to .75 pound more than the previous Model 98K. Value shown is for earlier type.

MODEL VK 98
PEOPLE'S RIFLE ("VOLKSGEWEHR") NiB $290 Ex $233 Gd $166
Kar. 98K-type action. Caliber: 7.9mm. Single-shot or repeater (latter w/rough hole-in-the-stock 5-round "magazine" or fitted w/10-round clip of German Model 43 semiauto rifle). 20.9-inch bbl. Weight: 7 lbs. Fixed V-notch rear sight dovetailed into front receiver ring; front blade welded to bbl. Crude, unfinished, half-length stock w/o buttplate. Last ditch weapon made in 1945 for issue to German civilians. Note: Of value only as a military arms collector's item, this hastily-made rifle should be regarded as unsafe to shoot.

GÉVARM RIFLE — Saint Etienne, France. Manufactured by Gevelot

E-1 AUTOLOADING RIFLE . . . NiB $234 Ex $190 Gd $150
Caliber: .22 LR. Eight-round clip magazine. 19.5-inch bbl. Sights: Open rear; post front. Pistol-grip stock and forearm of French walnut.

GOLDEN EAGLE RIFLES — Houston, Texas. Manufactured by Nikko Firearms Ltd., Tochigi, Japan

MODEL 7070 GRADE I AFRICAN . . NiB $743 Ex $578 Gd $468
Same as Grade I Big Game except: Caliber: .375 H&H Mag. and .458 Win. Mag. Two-round magazine in .458, weight: 8.75 lbs. in .375 and 10.5 lbs. in .458, furnished w/sights. Imported 1976 to 1981.

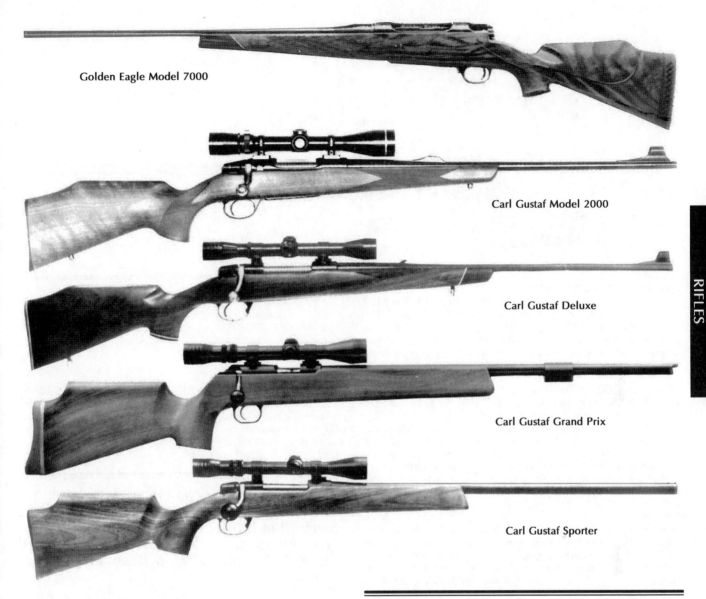

Golden Eagle Model 7000

Carl Gustaf Model 2000

Carl Gustaf Deluxe

Carl Gustaf Grand Prix

Carl Gustaf Sporter

MODEL 7070 BIG GAME SERIES

Bolt action. Calibers: .22-250, .243 Win., .25-06, .270 Win., Weatherby Mag., 7mm Rem. Mag., .30-06, .300 Weatherby Mag., .300 Win. Mag., .338 Win. Mag. Magazine capacity: 4 rounds in .22-250, 3 rounds in other calibers. 24- or 26-inch bbl. (26-inch only in 338). Weight: 7 lbs., .22-250; 8.75, lbs., other calibers. Furnished w/o sights. Fancy American walnut stock, skip checkered, contrasting wood forend tip and grip cap w/gold eagle head, recoil pad. Imported 1976 to 1981.

Model 7070 Grade I . . . . NiB $722 Ex $630 Gd $455
Model 7070 Grade II . . . . . . NiB $755 Ex $689 Gd $479

GREIFELT & CO. — Suhl, Germany

SPORT MODEL 22 HORNET

BOLT-ACTION RIFLE . . . . NiB $2388 Ex $1907 Gd $1412
Caliber: .22 Hornet. Five round box magazine. 22-inch Krupp steel bbl. Weight: 6 lbs. Sights: Two-leaf rear; ramp front. Walnut stock, checkered pistol-grip and forearm. Made before WWII.

CARL GUSTAF RIFLES — Eskilstuna, Sweden. Manufactured by Carl Gustaf Stads Gevärsfaktori

MODEL 2000 BOLT-ACTION RIFLE

Calibers: .243, 6.5x55, 7x64, .270, .308 Win., .30-06, 7mm Rem. Mag., .300 Win. Mag. Three round magazine. 24-inch bbl. 44 inches overall. Weight: 7.5 lbs. Receiver drilled and tapped. Hooded ramp front sight, open rear. Adj. trigger. Checkered European walnut stock w/Monte Carlo cheekpiece and Wundhammer palmswell grip. Imported 1991 to 1995

Model 2000
w/o sights. . . . . NiB $1443 Ex $1235 Gd $879
Model 2000 w/sights . . . . NiB $1790 Ex $1390 Gd $1009
Model 2000 LUXE . . . . . . NiB $1744 Ex $1689 Gd $1035

DELUXE . . . . NiB $707 Ex $579 Gd $522
Same specifications as Monte Carlo Standard. Calibers: 6.5x55, 308 Win., .30-06, 9.3x62. Four round magazine in 9.3x62. Jeweled bolt. Engraved floorplate and trigger guard. Deluxe French walnut stock w/rosewood forend tip. Imported 1970 to 1977.

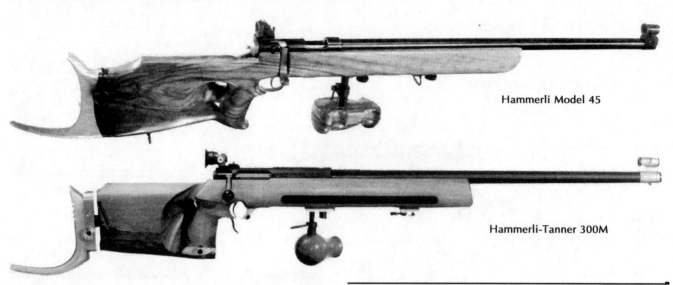

Hammerli Model 45

Hammerli-Tanner 300M

GRAND PRIX SINGLE-SHOT
TARGET RIFLE . . . . **NiB $577 Ex $459 Gd $202**
Special bolt action with "world's shortest lock time." Single-stage trigger adjusts down to 18 oz. Caliber: .22 LR. 26.75-inch heavy bbl. w/adj. trim weight. Weight: 9.75 lbs. Furnished w/o sights. Target-type Monte Carlo stock of French walnut, adj. cork buttplate. Imported from 1970 to 1977.

MONTE CARLO STANDARD
BOLT-ACTION SPORTING RIFLE . . . **NiB $507 Ex $422 Gd $370**
Carl Gustaf 1900 action. Calibers: 6.5x55, 7x64, .270 Win., 7mm Rem. Mag., .308 Win., .30-06, 9.3x62. Five round magazine, except 4-round in 9.3x62 and 3-round in 7mm Rem. Mag. 23.5-inch bbl. Weight: 7 lbs. Sights: Folding leaf rear; hooded ramp front. French walnut Monte Carlo stock w/cheekpiece, checkered forearm and pistol grip, sling swivels. Also available in left-hand model. Imported from 1970 to 1977.

SPECIAL
. . . . **NiB $575 Ex $401 Gd $376**
Also designated "Grade II" in U.S. and "Model 9000" in Canada. Same specifications as Monte Carlo Standard. Calibers: .22-250, .243 Win., .25-06, .270 Win., 7mm Rem. Mag., .308 Win., .30-06, .300 Win. Mag. Three round magazine in magnum calibers. Select wood stock w/rosewood forend tip. Left-hand model avail. Imported from 1970 to 1977.

SPORTER
. . . . **NiB $512 Ex $355 Gd $291**
Also designated "Varmint-Target" in U.S. Fast bolt action w/large Bakelite bolt knob. Trigger pull adjusts down to 18 oz. Calibers: .222 Rem., .22-250, .243 Win., 6.5x55. Five round magazine except 6-round in .222 Rem. 26.75-inch heavy bbl. Weight: 9.5 lbs. Furnished w/o sights. Target-type Monte Carlo stock of French walnut. Imported from 1970 to 1977.

STANDARD
. . . . **NiB $512 Ex $355 Gd $291**
Same specifications as Monte Carlo Standard. Calibers: 6.5x55, 7x64, .270 Win., .308 Win., .30-06, 9.3x62. Classic-style stock w/o Monte Carlo. Imported from 1970 to 1977.

TROFÉ
. . . . **NiB $588 Ex $479 Gd $382**
Also designated "Grade III" in U.S. and "Model 8000" in Canada. Same specifications as Monte Carlo Standard. Calibers: .22-250, .25-06, 6.5x55, .270 Win., 7mm Rem. Mag., .308 Win., .30-06, .300 Win. Mag. Three round magazine in magnum calibers. Furnished w/o sights. Fancy wood stock w/rosewood forend tip, high-gloss lacquer finish. Imported from 1970 to 1977.

C.G. HAENEL — Suhl, Germany

'88 MAUSER SPORTER . . . . . . **NiB $813 Ex $508 Gd $380**
Same general specifications as Haenel Mauser-Mannlicher except w/Mauser 5-round box magazine.

MAUSER-MANNLICHER
BOLT-ACTION SPORTING RIFLE **NiB $821 Ex $572 Gd $400**
Mauser M/88-type action. Calibers: 7x57, 8x57, 9x57mm. Mannlicher clip-loading box magazine, 5-round. 22- or 24-inch half or full octagon bbl. w/raised matted rib. Double-set trigger. Weight: 7.5 lbs. Sights: Leaf-type open rear; ramp front. Sporting stock w/cheekpiece, checkered pistol-grip, raised side-panels, Schnabel tip, swivels.

HÄMMERLI AG JAGD-UND-SPORTWAFFENFABRIK — Lenzburg, Switzerland. Imported by Sigarms, Exetre, NH (previously by Hammerli USA; Mandall Shooting Supplies, Inc. & Beeman Precision Arms)

MODEL 45 SMALLBORE BOLT-ACTION
SINGLE-SHOT MATCH RIFLE . . . . **NiB $765 Ex $654 Gd $453**
Calibers: .22 LR. 22 Extra Long. 27.5-inch heavy bbl. Weight: 15.5 lbs. Sights: Micrometer peep rear; globe front. Free-rifle stock w/ cheekpiece, full pistol-grip, thumbhole, beavertail forearm, palm-rest, Swiss-type buttplate, swivels. Made from 1945 to 1957.

MODEL 54 SMALLBORE
MATCH RIFLE . . . . **NiB $709 Ex $544 Gd $423**
Bolt-action, single-shot. Caliber: .22 LR. 27.5-inch heavy bbl. Weight: 15 lbs. Sights: Micrometer peep rear; globe front. Free-rifle stock w/cheekpiece, thumbhole, adj. hook buttplate, palm rest, swivel. Made from 1954 to 1957.

MODEL 508 FREE RIFLE
. . . . . **NiB $707 Ex $546 Gd $413**
Bolt-action, single-shot. Caliber: .22 LR. 27.5-inch heavy bbl. Weight: 15 lbs. Sights: Micrometer peep rear; globe front. Free-rifle stock w/cheekpiece, thumbhole, adj. hook buttplate, palm rest, swivel. Made from 1957 to 1962.

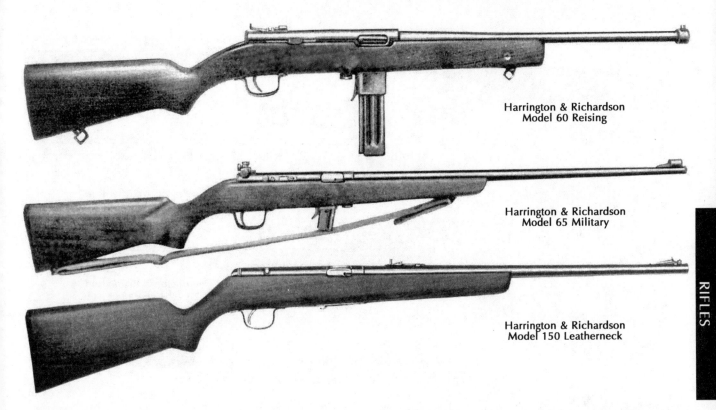

Harrington & Richardson
Model 60 Reising

Harrington & Richardson
Model 65 Military

Harrington & Richardson
Model 150 Leatherneck

MODEL 506 SMALLBORE MATCH RIFLE NiB $769 Ex $650 Gd $439
Bolt-action, single-shot. Caliber: .22 LR. 26.75-inch heavy bbl. Weight: 16.5 lbs. Sights: Micrometer peep rear; globe front. Free-rifle stock w/cheekpiece, thumbhole adj. hook buttplate, palmrest, swivel. Made from 1963 to 1966.

**MODEL OLYMPIC 300 METER BOLT-ACTION
SINGLE-SHOT FREE RIFLE** . . . . NiB $905 Ex $755 Gd $556
Calibers: .30-06, .300 H&H Magnum for U.S.A.; ordinarily produced in 7.5mm, other calibers available on special order. 29.5-inch heavy bbl. Double-pull or double-set trigger. Sights: Micrometer peep rear, globe front. Free-rifle stock w/cheekpiece, full pistol grip, thumbhole, beavertail forend, palmrest, Swiss-type buttplate, swivels. Made 1945 to 1959.

TANNER 300 METER FREE RIFLE. . . . NiB $937 Ex $740 Gd $534
Bolt-action, single-shot. Caliber: 7.5mm standard, available in most popular centerfire calibers. 29.5-inch heavy bbl. Weight: 16.75 lbs. Sights: Micrometer peep rear; globe front. Free-rifle stock w/cheekpiece, thumbhole, adj. hook buttplate, palmrest, swivel. Intro. 1962. Disc. See Illustration previous page.

HARRINGTON & RICHARDSON, INC. —
Gardner, Massachusetts (now H&R 1871)

Formerly Harrington & Richardson Arms Co. of Worcester, Mass. One of the oldest and most distinguished manufacturers of handguns, rifles and shotguns, H&R suspended operations on January 24, 1986. In 1987, New England Firearms was established as an independent company producing selected H&R models under the NEF logo. In 1991, H&R 1871, Inc. was formed from the residual of the parent company and that took over the New England Firearms facility. H&R 1871 produced firearms under both its logo and the NEF brand name until 1999, when the Marlin Firearms Company acquired the assets of H&R 1871. Marlin was purchased by the Freedom Group Inc. in 2008.

**MODEL 60 REISING SEMI-
AUTOMATIC RIFLE** . . . . NiB $1266 Ex $899 Gd $598
Caliber: .45 Automatic. 12- and 20-round detachable box magazines. 18.25-inch bbl. Weight: 7.5 lbs. Sights: Open rear; blade front. Plain pistol-grip stock. Made from 1944 to 1946.

**MODEL 65 MILITARY
AUTOLOADING RIFLE** . . . . . . NiB $496 Ex $322 Gd $208
Also called "General." Caliber: .22 LR. 10-round detachable box magazine. 23-inch heavy bbl. Weight: 9 lbs. Sights: Redfield 70 rear peep, blade front w/protecting "ears." Plain pistol-grip stock, "Garand" dimensions. Made from 1944 to 1946. Note: This model was used as a training rifle by the U.S. Marine Corps.

**MODEL 150
LEATHERNECK AUTOLOADER** . . . . . . NiB $338 Ex $234 Gd $110
Caliber: .22 LR. only. Five round detachable box magazine. 22-inch bbl. Weight: 7.25 lbs. Sights: Open rear; blade front, on ramp. Plain pistol-grip stock. Made from 1949 to 1953.

MODEL 151 . . . . NiB $338 Ex $234 Gd $110
Same as Model 150 except w/Redfield 70 rear peep sight.

**MODEL 155
SINGLE-SHOT RIFLE.** . . . . NiB $279 Ex $178 Gd $126
Model 158 action. Calibers: .44 Rem. Mag., .45-70 Govt. 24- or 28-inch bbl. (latter in .44 only). Weight: 7 or 7.5 lbs. Sights: Folding leaf rear; blade front. Straight-grip stock, forearm w/bbl. band, brass cleaning rod. Made from 1972 to 1982.

**MODEL 157
SINGLE-SHOT RIFLE.** . . . . NiB $333 Ex $154 Gd $121
Model 158 action. Calibers: .22 WMR, .22 Hornet, .30-30. 22-inch bbl. Weight: 6.25 lbs. Sights: Folding leaf rear; blade front. Pistol-grip stock, full-length forearm, swivels. Made from 1976 to 1986.

RIFLES

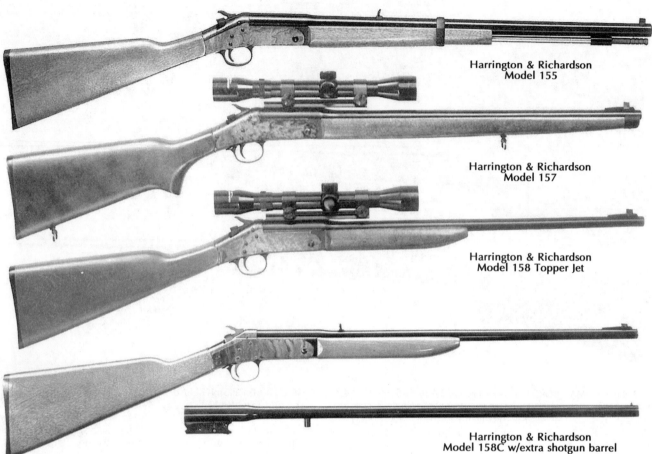

Harrington & Richardson
Model 155

Harrington & Richardson
Model 157

Harrington & Richardson
Model 158 Topper Jet

Harrington & Richardson
Model 158C w/extra shotgun barrel

MODEL 158 TOPPER JET SINGLE-SHOT COMBINATION RIFLE
Shotgun-type action w/visible hammer, side lever, auto ejector. Caliber: .22 Rem. Jet. 22-inch bbl. (interchanges with .30-30, .410 ga., 20 ga. bbls.). Weight: 5 lbs. Sights: Lyman folding adj. open rear; ramp front. Plain pistol-grip stock and forearm, recoil pad. Made from 1963 to 1967.
Rifle only . . . . **NiB $250 Ex $171 Gd $126**
Interchangeable bbl.
.30-30, shotgun, add **$75**

MODEL 158C. . . . . **NiB $250 Ex $171 Gd $126**
Same as Model 158 Topper Jet except calibers .22 Hornet, .30-30, .357 Mag., .357 Mag., .44 Mag. Straight-grip stock. Made 1963 to 1986.

MODEL 163 MUSTANG
SINGLE-SHOT RIFLE. . . . . **NiB $250 Ex $168 Gd $124**
Same as Model 158 Topper except w/gold-plated hammer and trigger, straight-grip stock and contoured forearm. Made 1964 to 1967.

MODEL 165
LEATHERNECK AUTOLOADER . . . . **NiB $250 Ex $170 Gd $126**
Caliber: .22 LR. 10-round detachable box magazine. 23-inch bbl. Weight: 7.5 lbs. Sights: Redfield 70 rear peep; blade front, on ramp. Plain pistol-grip stock, swivels, web sling. Made from 1945 to 1961.

MODEL 171. . . . . **NiB $633 Ex $466 Gd $257**
Model 1873 Springfield Cavalry Carbine replica. Caliber: .45-70. 22-inch bbl. Weight: 7 lbs. Sights: Leaf rear; blade front. Plain walnut stock. Made from 1972 to 1981.

MODEL 171 DELUXE . . . . . . **NiB $776 Ex $523 Gd $309**
Same as Model 171 except engraved action and different sights. Made from 1972-86. See illustration next page.

MODEL 172. . . . . **NiB $759 Ex $588 Gd $454**
Same as Model 171 Deluxe except silver-plated, w/fancy walnut stock, checkered, w/grip adapter; tang-mounted aperture sight. Made from 1972 to 1986.

MODEL 173. . . . . **NiB $1663 Ex $963 Gd $538**
Model 1873 Springfield Officer's Model replica, same as 100th Anniversary Commemorative except w/o plaque on stock. Made from 1972 to 1986.

MODEL 174. . . . . **NiB $1266 Ex $1009 Gd $633**
Little Big Horn Commemorative Carbine. Same as Model 171 Deluxe except w/tang-mounted aperture sight, grip adapter. Made from 1972 to 1984.

MODEL 178. . . . . **NiB $735 Ex $422 Gd $328**
Model 1873 Springfield Infantry Rifle replica. Caliber: .45-70. 32-inch bbl. Weight: 8 lbs. 10 oz. Sights: Leaf rear; blade front. Full-length stock w/bbl. bands, swivels, ramrod. Made 1973 to 1986.

MODEL 250 SPORTSTER BOLT-ACTION
REPEATING RIFLE . . . . **NiB $220 Ex $111 Gd $80**
Caliber: .22 LR. Five-round detachable box magazine. 23-inch bbl. Weight: 6.5 lbs. Sights: Open rear; blade front, on ramp. Plain pistol-grip stock. Made from 1948 to 1961.

Harrington & Richardson
Model 171

Harrington & Richardson
Model 171 Deluxe

Harrington & Richardson
Model 172

Harrington & Richardson
Model 173

Harrington & Richardson
Model 174 Little Big Horn Commemorative

Harrington & Richardson
Model 178

MODEL 251 . . . . **NiB $255 Ex $128 Gd $90**
Same as Model 250 except w/Lyman No. 55H rear sight.

MODEL 265 "REG'LAR" BOLT-
ACTION REPEATING RIFLE. . . . NiB $337 Ex $140 Gd $98
Caliber: .22 LR. 10-round detachable box magazine. 22-inch bbl.
Weight: 6.5 lbs. Sights: Lyman No. 55 rear peep; blade front, on
ramp. Plain pistol-grip stock. Made from 1946 to 1949.

MODEL 300 ULTRA

BOLT-ACTION RIFLE . . . . **NiB $572 Ex $521 Gd $302**
Mauser-type action. Calibers: .22-250, .243 Win., .270 Win., .30-06,
.308 Win., 7mm Rem. Mag., .300 Win. Mag. Three round magazine
in 7mm and .300 Mag. calibers, 5-round in others. 22- or 24-inch bbl.
Sights: Open rear; ramp front. Checkered stock w/rollover cheekpiece
and full pistol grip, contrasting wood forearm tip and pistol grip, rubber buttplate, sling swivels. Weight: 7.25 lbs. Made 1965 to 1982.

Harrington & Richardson
Model 300

Harrington & Richardson
Model 301 Carbine

Harrington & Richardson
Model 317P

Harrington & Richardson
Model 330

Harrington & Richardson
Model 360 Ultra

Harrington & Richardson
Model 370 Ultra Medalist

MODEL 301 CARBINE . . . . . . **NiB $523 Ex $412 Gd $287**
Same as Model 300 except w/18-inch bbl., Mannlicher-style stock,
weighs 7.25 lbs.; not available in caliber .22-250. Made 1967 to 1982.

MODEL 308 AUTOMATIC RIFLE NiB $531 Ex $390 Gd $277
Original designation of the Model 360 Ultra. Made 1965 to 1967.

MODEL 317 ULTRA WILDCAT
BOLT-ACTION RIFLE . . . . **NiB $650 Ex $495 Gd $380**
Sako short action. Calibers: .17 Rem. 17/.223 (handload), .222 Rem.,

.223 Rem. Six round magazine. 20-inch bbl. No sights, receiver
dovetailed for scope mounts. Checkered stock w/cheekpiece and
full pistol grip, contrasting wood forearm tip and pistol-grip cap,
rubber buttplate. Weight: 5.25 lbs. Made from 1968 to 1976.

MODEL 317P
PRESENTATION GRADE . . . . . **NiB $710 Ex $546 Gd $488**
Same as Model 317 except w/select grade fancy walnut stock w/
basket weave carving on forearm and pistol-grip. Made from 1968
to 1976.

Harrington & Richardson
Model 700 Deluxe

Harrington & Richardson
Model 750 Pioneer

Harrington & Richardson
"New" Model 750

Harrington & Richardson
Model 755

MODEL 330 HUNTER'S RIFLE NiB $439 Ex $326 Gd $244
Similar to Model 300, but w/plainer stock. Calibers: .243 Win., .270 Win., .30-06, .308 Win., 7mm Rem. Mag., .300 Win. Mag. Weight: 7.13 lbs. Made from 1967 to 1972.

MODEL 333 . . . . NiB $439 Ex $326 Gd $244
Plainer version of Model 300 w/uncheckered walnut-finished hardwood stock. Calibers: 7mm Rem. Mag. and .30-06. 22-inch bbl. Weight: 7.25 lbs. No sights. Made in 1974.

MODEL 340 . . . . NiB $450 Ex $341 Gd $259
Mauser-type action. Calibers: .243 Win., .308 Win., .270 Win., .30-06, 7x57. 22-inch bbl. Weight: 7.25 lbs. Hand-checkered American walnut stock. Made from 1982 to 1984.

MODEL 360
ULTRA AUTOMATIC RIFLE . . . NiB $534 Ex $380 Gd $300
Gas-operated semiautomatic. Calibers: .243 Win., .308 Win. Three round detachable box magazine. 22-inch bbl. Sights: Open rear; ramp front. Checkered stock w/rollover cheekpiece, full pistol grip, contrasting wood forearm tip and pistol-grip cap, rubber buttplate, sling swivels. Weight: 7.25 lbs. Made from 1967 to 1978.

MODEL 361 . . . . NiB $556 Ex $439 Gd $333
Same as Model 360 except w/full rollover cheekpiece for right- or left-hand shooters. Made from 1970 to 1973.

MODEL 369 ACE BOLT-ACTION

SINGLE-SHOT RIFLE . . . . NiB $178 Ex $140 Gd $96
Caliber: .22 LR. 22-inch bbl. Weight: 6.5 lbs. Sights: Lyman No. 55 rear peep, blade front, on ramp. Plain pistol-grip stock. Made 1946 to 1947.

MODEL 370 ULTRA MEDALIST NiB $555 Ex $423 Gd $320
Varmint and target rifle based on Model 300. Calibers: .22-250, .243 Win., 6mm Rem. Three round magazine. 24-inch varmint weight bbl. No sights. Target-style stock w/semibeavertail forearm. Weight: 9.5 lbs. Made from 1968 to 1973.

MODEL 422 SLIDE-ACTION
REPEATER . . . . NiB $375 Ex $234 Gd $141
Caliber: .22 LR. Long, Short. Tubular magazine holds 21 Short, 17 Long, 15 LR. 24-inch bbl. Weight: 6 lbs. Sights: Open rear; ramp front. Plain pistol-grip stock grooved slide handle. Made 1956 to 1958.

MODEL 450 . . . . NiB $403 Ex $221 Gd $130
Same as Model 451 except w/o front and rear sights.

MODEL 451 MEDALIST
BOLT-ACTION TARGET RIFLE NiB $433 Ex $222 Gd $130
Caliber: .22 LR. Five round detachable box magazine. 26-inch bbl. Weight: 10.5 lbs. Sights: Lyman No. 524F extension rear; Lyman No. 77 front, scope bases. Target stock w/full pistol-grip and forearm, swivels and sling. Made from 1948 to 1961.

Harrington & Richardson
Model 760

Harrington & Richardson
Model 866

Harrington & Richardson
Model 1873 — 100th Anniversary

Harrington & Richardson
Model 5200 Sporter

Harrington & Richardson
Ultra Varmint

**MODEL 465 TARGETEER SPECIAL
BOLT-ACTION REPEATER. . . . NiB $423 Ex $233 Gd $144**
Caliber: .22 LR. 10-round detachable box magazine. 25-inch
bbl. Weight: 9 lbs. Sights: Lyman No. 57 rear peep; blade front,
on ramp. Plain pistol-grip stock, swivels, web sling strap. Made
from 1946 to 1947.

**MODEL 707
AUTOLOADER. . . . . NiB $456 Ex $321 Gd $188**
Caliber: .22 WMR. Five-round magazine. 22-inch bbl. Weight: 6.5
lbs. Sights: Folding leaf rear; blade front, on ramp. Monte Carlo-style
stock of American walnut. Made from 1977 to 1986.

MODEL 707 DELUXE . . . . NiB $508 Ex $381 Gd $285
Same as Model 707 Standard except w/select custom polished
and blued finish, select walnut stock, hand checkering, and
no iron sights. Fitted w/H&R Model 432 4x scope. Made from
1980 to 1986.

**MODEL 750 PIONEER BOLT-ACTION
SINGLE-SHOT RIFLE. . . . . NiB $145 Ex $104 Gd $80**
Caliber: .22 LR, Long, Short. 22- or 24-inch bbl. Weight: 5 lbs.
Sights: Open rear; bead front. Plain pistol-grip stock. Made from
1954 to 1981; redesigned 1982; disc. 1985.

MODEL 751 SINGLE-SHOT RIFLE. . . . . NiB $170 Ex $95 Gd $77
Same as Model 750 except w/Mannlicher-style stock. Made in 1971.

**MODEL 755 SAHARA
SINGLE-SHOT RIFLE. . . . . NiB $166 Ex $90 Gd $67**
Blow-back action, automatic ejection. Caliber: .22 LR, Long,
Short. 18-inch bbl. Weight: 4 lbs. Sights: Open rear; military-
type front. Mannlicher-style stock. Made from 1963 to 1971.

MODEL 760 SINGLE-SHOT . . . NiB $188 Ex $100 Gd $80
Same as Model 755 except w/conventional sporter stock. Made
from 1965 to 1970.

**MODEL 765 PIONEER BOLT-ACTION
SINGLE-SHOT RIFLE . . . . NiB $188 Ex $97 Gd $66**
Caliber: .22 LR, Long, Short. 24-inch bbl. Weight: 5 lbs. Sights: Open
rear; hooded bead front. Plain pistol-grip stock. Made 1948 to 1954.

MODEL 800 LYNX
AUTOLOADING RIFLE . . . . . . NiB $407 Ex $224 Gd $119
Caliber: .22 LR. Five or 10-round clip magazine. 22-inch bbl. Open sights. Weight: 6 lbs. Plain pistol-grip stock. Made 1958 to1960.

MODEL 852 FIELDSMAN
BOLT-ACTION REPEATER . . . . . NiB $198 Ex $101 Gd $89
Caliber: .22 LR, Long, Short. Tubular magazine holds 21 Short, 17 Long, 15 LR. 24-inch bbl. Weight: 5.5 lbs. Sights: Open rear; bead front. Plain pistol-grip stock. Made from 1952 to 1953.

MODEL 865 PLAINSMAN
BOLT-ACTION REPEATER . . . . . NiB $167 Ex $115 Gd $80
Caliber .22 LR, Long, Short. Five round detachable box magazine. 22- or 24-inch bbl. Weight: 5.25 lbs. Sights: Open rear, bead front. Plain pistol-grip stock. Made from 1949 to 1986.

MODEL 866
BOLT-ACTION REPEATER . . . . . NiB $197 Ex $115 Gd $80
Same as Model 865, except w/Mannlicher-style stock. Made 1971.

MODEL 1873 100TH ANNIVERSARY
(1871-1971) COMMEMORATIVE
OFFICER'S SPRINGFIELD REPLICA NiB $866 Ex $659 Gd $475
Model 1873 "trap door" single-shot action. Engraved breech block, receiver, hammer, lock, band and buttplate. Caliber: .45-70. 26-inch bbl. Sights: Peep rear; blade front. Checkered walnut stock w/anniversary plaque. Ramrod. Weight: 8 lbs. 10,000 made in 1971.

MODEL 5200 SPORTER . . . . . NiB $677 Ex $376 Gd $277
Turn-bolt repeater. Caliber: .22 LR. 24-inch bbl. Classic-style American walnut stock. Adj. trigger. Sights: Peep receiver; hooded ramp front. Weight: 6.5 lbs. Disc. 1983.

MODEL 5200 MATCH RIFLE. . NiB $590 Ex $495 Gd $368
Same action as 5200 Sporter. Caliber: .22 LR. 28-inch target weight bbl. Target stock of American walnut. Weight: 11 lbs. Made 1982 to 1986.

CUSTER MEMORIAL ISSUE
Limited Edition Model 1873 Springfield Carbine replica, richly engraved and inlaid w/gold, fancy walnut stock, in mahogany display case. Made in 1973.
Officers' Model
Limited to 25 pieces . . . . NiB $4125 Ex $2990 Gd $12423
Enlisted Men's model,
limited to 243 pieces . . . . NiB $2033 Ex $1021 Gd $690

TARGETEER JR. BOLT-ACTION RIFLE NiB $227 Ex $177 Gd $145
Caliber: .22 LR. Five-round detachable box magazine. 20-inch bbl. Weight: 7 lbs. Sights: Redfield 70 rear peep; Lyman No. 17A front. Target stock, junior-size w/pistol grip, swivels and sling. Made 1948 to 1951.

ULTRA SINGLE-SHOT RIFLE
Side-lever single-shot. Calibers: .22-250 Rem., .223 Rem., .25-06 Rem., .308 Win. 22- to 26-inch bbl. Weight: 7-8 lbs. Curly maple or laminated stock. Barrel-mounted scope mount, no sights. Made from 1993 to date.
Ultra Hunter (.25-06, .308). . . NiB $257 Ex $166 Gd $167
Ultra Varmint . . . . NiB $288 Ex $230 Gd $188

HARRIS GUNWORKS — Phoenix, Arizona (formerly McMillan Gun Works)

Sporting line of firearms discontinued, now specializes in sniper and tactical arms.

SIGNATURE ALASKAN
BOLT-ACTION RIFLE . . . . NiB $3510 Ex $3108 Gd $2110
Same general specifications as Classic Sporter except w/match-grade bbl. Rings and mounts. Sights: Single-leaf rear, bbl. band front. Checkered Monte Carlo stock w/palmswell and solid recoil pad. Nickel finish. Calibers: LA (long): .270 Win., .280 Rem., .30-06, MA (Magnum): 7mm Rem. Mag., .300 Win. Mag., .300 Wby. Mag., .340 Wby. Mag., .358 Win., .375 H&H Mag. Made from 1990. Disc.

SIGNATURE CLASSIC SPORTER
The prototype for Harris' Signature Series, this bolt-action rifle is available in three lengths: SA (standard/ short) — from .22-250 to .350 Rem Mag.; LA (long) — .25-06 to .30-06; MA (Magnum) — 7mm STW to .416 Rem. Mag. Four-round or 3-round (Magnum) magazine. Bbl. lengths: 22, 24 or 26 inches. Weight: 7 lbs. (short action). No sights; rings and bases provided. Harris fiberglass stock, Fibergrain or wood stock optional. Stainless, matte black or black chrome sulfide finish. Available in right- and left-hand models. Made from 1987. Disc. Has pre-64 Model 70-style action for dangerous game.
Classic Sporter, standard. . NiB $2565 Ex $2347 Gd $1424
Classic Sporter, stainless . . NiB $2565 Ex $2347 Gd $1424
Talon Sporter . . . . NiB $2613 Ex $2092 Gd $1474

SIGNATURE MOUNTAIN RIFLE . NiB $3037 Ex $2977 Gd $1609
Same general specifications as Harris (McMillan) Classic Sporter except w/titanium action and graphite-reinforced fiberglass stock. Weight: 5.5 lbs. Calibers: .270 Win., .280 Rem., .30-06, 7mm Mag., .300 Win. Mag. Other calibers on special order. Made from 1995. Disc.

SIGNATURE SUPER VARMINTER NiB $2512 Ex $2233 Gd $1429
Same general specifications as Harris (McMillan) Classic Sporter except w/heavy, contoured bbl., adj. trigger, fiberglass stock and field bipod. Calibers: .223, .22-250, .220 Swift, .244 Win., 6mm Rem., .25-06, 7mm-08, .308 Win., .350 Win. Mag. Made from 1995. Disc.

TALON SAFARI RIFLE
Same general specifications as Harris (McMillan) Classic Sporter except w/Harris Safari-grade action, match-grade bbl. and "Safari" fiberglass stock. Calibers: Magnum — .300 H&H Mag., .300 Win Mag., .300 Wby. Mag., .338 Win. Mag., .340 Wby. Mag., .375 H&H Mag., .404 Jeffrey, .416 Rem. Mag., .458 Win., Super Mag. — .300 Phoenix, .338 Lapua, .378 Wby. Mag., .416 Rigby, .416 Wby. Mag., .460 Wby. Mag. Matte black finish. Other calibers available on special order, and at a premium, but the "used gun" value remains the same. Imported 1989. Disc.
Safari Magnum . . . . NiB $3809 Ex $3166 Gd $2179
Safari Super Magnum . . . . NiB $4322 Ex $3561 Gd $2574

HECKLER & KOCH, GMBH — Oberndorf am Neckar, Germany.
Imported by Heckler & Koch, Inc., Sterling, VA

MODEL 911 SEMIAUTO RIFLE . . NiB $1970 Ex $1723 Gd $1019
Caliber: .308 (7.62mm). Five-round magazine. 19.7-inch bull bbl. 42.4 inches overall. Sights: Hooded post front; adj. aperture rear. Weight: 11 lbs. Kevlar-reinforced fiberglass thumbhole-stock. Imported 1989 to 1993.

MODEL HK91 A-2 SEMIAUTO . . NiB $2634 Ex $2133 Gd $1388
Delayed roller-locked blow-back action. Caliber: 7.62mmx51 NATO (308 Win.) 5- or 20-round box magazine. 19-inch bbl. Weight: W/o magazine, 9.37 lbs. Sights L "V" and aperture rear, post front. Plastic buttstock and forearm. Disc. 1991.

RIFLES

Heckler & Koch
Model HK91 A-2

Heckler & Koch
Model HK91 A-3

Heckler & Koch
Model HK93 A-2

Heckler & Koch
Model HK940 Carbine

MODEL HK91 A-3 . . . . . . NiB $2721 Ex $2490 Gd $1665
Same as Model HK91 A-2 except w/retractable metal buttstock, weighs 10.56 lbs. Disc. 1991.

MODEL HK93 SEMIAUTOMATIC
Delayed roller-locked blow-back action. Caliber: 5.56mm x 45 (.223 Rem.). 5- or 20-round magazine. 16.13-inch bbl. Weight: W/o magazine, 7.6 lbs. Sights: "V" and aperture rear; post front. Plastic buttstock and forearm. Disc. 1991.
HK93 A-2. . . . . NiB $2835 Ex $2177 Gd $1198
HK93 A-3 w/retractable stock . . . NiB $3590 Ex $2816 Gd $2021

MODEL HK94 SEMIAUTOMATIC CARBINE
Caliber: 9mm Para. 15-round magazine. 16-inch bbl. Weight: 6.75 lbs. Aperture rear sight, front post. Plastic buttstock and forend or retractable metal stock. Imported from 1983 to 1991.

HK94-A2 w/standard stock . . . . . NiB $4054 Ex $3209 Gd $2775
HK94-A3 w/retractable stock, add 20%

MODEL HK300
SEMIAUTOMATIC . . . . NiB $1423 Ex $955 Gd $600
Caliber: .22 WMR. Five- or 15-round box magazine. 19.7-inch bbl. w/polygonal rifling. Weight: 5.75 lbs. Sights: V-notch rear; ramp front. High-luster polishing and bluing. European walnut stock w/ cheekpiece, checkered forearm and pistol-grip. Disc. 1989.

MODEL HK630
SEMIAUTOMATIC . . . . NiB $1733 Ex $1277 Gd $1009
Caliber: .223 Rem. Four- or 10-round magazine. 24-inch bbl. Overall length: 42 inches. Weight: 7 lbs. Sights: Open rear; ramp front. European walnut stock w/Monte Carlo cheekpiece. Imported from 1983 to 1990.

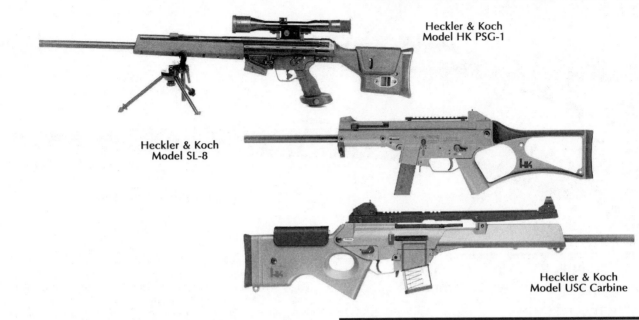

Heckler & Koch
Model HK PSG-1

Heckler & Koch
Model SL-8

Heckler & Koch
Model USC Carbine

MODEL HK770 SEMIAUTOMATIC . NiB $2244 Ex $1703 Gd $1099
Caliber: .308 Win. Three- or 10-round magazine. Overall length: 44.5 inches. Weight: 7.92 lbs. Sights: Open rear; ramp front. European walnut stock w/Monte Carlo cheekpiece. Imported from 1983 to 1986.

MODEL HK940 SEMIAUTOMATIC . NiB $2055 Ex $1833 Gd $1079
Caliber: .30-06 Springfield. Three- or 10-round magazine. Overall length: 47 inches. Weight: 8.8 lbs. Sights: Open rear; ramp front. European walnut stock w/Monte Carlo cheekpiece. Imported from 1983 to 1986.

MODEL HK PSG-1
MARKSMAN'S RIFLE. . NiB $12,790 Ex $10,879 Gd $8966
Caliber: .308 (7.62mm). Five- and 20-round magazine. 25.6-inch bbl. 47.5 inches overall. Hensoldt 6x42 telescopic sight. Weight: 17.8 lbs. Matte black composite stock w/pistol-grip. Imported from 1988 to 1998.

MODEL SL8-1 RIFLE. . . . . . NiB $2006 Ex $1409 Gd $987
Caliber: .223 Win. Ten-round magazine. 20.80- inch bbl. 38.58 inches overall. Weight: 8.6 lbs. Gas-operated, short-stroke piston w/rotary locking bolt. Rear adjustable sight w/ambidextrous safety selector lever. Polymer receiver w/adjustable buttstock. Introduced in 1999.

MODEL SR-9
SEMIAUTO RIFLE . . . . NiB $2130 Ex $1850 Gd $1044
Caliber: .308 (7.62mm). Five round magazine. 19.7-inch bull bbl. 42.4 inches overall. Hooded post front sight; adj. aperture rear. Weight: 11 lbs. Kevlar-reinforced fiberglass thumbhole-stock w/ wood grain finish. Imported from 1989 to 1993.

MODEL SR-9
TARGET RIFLE . . . . NiB $2844 Ex $2166 Gd $1482
Same general specifications as standard SR-9 except w/ PSG-1 trigger group and adj. buttstock. Imported from 1992 to 1994.

MODEL USC
CARBINE RIFLE . . . . NiB $1675 Ex $1133 Gd $790
Caliber: 45 ACP. 10-round magazine. 16- inch bbl., 35.43 inches overall. Weight: 6 lbs. Blow-back operating system. Polymer receiver w/integral grips. Rear adjustable sight w/ambidextrous safety selector lever. Introduced in 1999.

Henry Repeating Arms — Bayonne, NJ

Mini Bolt . . . . NiB $260 Ex $215 Gd $90
Caliber: .22 Short, LR. Single shot. 16.25-inch bbl. Stainless steel receiver, synthetic stock. Made 2002 to date.

Acu-Bolt. . . . . NiB $335 Ex $225 Gd $120
Caliber: .17 HMR, .22 LR or .22 WMR. Single shot. 20-inch bbl. Stainless steel receiver, synthetic stock. Made 2004 to date.

Lever Action. . . . . NiB $335 Ex $225 Gd $120
Caliber: .17 HMR, .22 Short, Long, LR or .22 WMR. Lever action, 15-round (.22 LR) tube magazine. 16.12-, 18.25-, 19.25-, or 20-inch round or octagon bbl. Blued receiver, American walnut stock. Made 1997 to date.
Carbine Large Loop . . . . NiB $290 Ex $186 Gd $130
Golden Boy (brass receiver) . . NiB $430 Ex $275 Gd $160

"Big Boy" Lever Action. . . . . . NiB $335 Ex $225 Gd $120
Caliber: .38 Special/.357 Mag., 17 HMR, .44 Special/.44 Mag. or .45 LC. Lever action, 10-round tube magazine. 20-inch octagon bbl. Brass receiver, American walnut stock. Made 2003 to date.
Deluxe II (hand engraved). . NiB $1725 Ex $1230 Gd $710

.30-30 Lever Action . . . . NiB $335 Ex $225 Gd $120
Caliber: .30-30 Win. Lever action, 6-round tube magazine. 20-inch round or octagon bbl. Blued receiver, American walnut stock. Made 2008 to date.
Brass receiver/octagon bbl., add $220

Pump Action . . . . NiB $335 Ex $225 Gd $120
Caliber: .22 Short, Long, LR or .22 WMR. Pump action, 16-round (.22 LR) tube magazine. 18.25- or 20.5-inch round bbl. Blued receiver, American walnut stock. Made 1999 to date.

U.S. Survival .22 Semi-Automatic. . NiB $225 Ex $170 Gd $115
Similar to Armalite AR-7 takedown rifle. Caliber: .22 LR. Semi-auto action, 8-round magazine. Made 1997 to date.

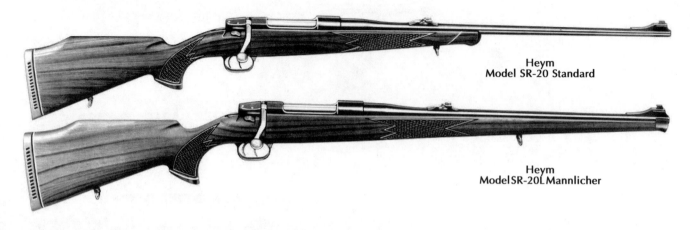

Heym
Model SR-20 Standard

Heym
Model SR-20L Mannlicher

HEROLD RIFLE — Suhl, Germany.
Made by Franz Jaeger & Company

BOLT-ACTION REPEATING
SPORTING RIFLE . . . . **NiB $1044 Ex $800 Gd $634**
"Herold-Repetierbüchse." Miniature Mauser-type action w/unique 5-round box magazine on hinged floorplate. Double-set triggers. Caliber: .22 Hornet. 24-inch bbl. Sights: Leaf rear; ramp front. Weight: 7.75 lbs. Fancy checkered stock. Made before WWII. Note: These rifles were imported by Charles Daly and A.F. Stoeger Inc. of New York City and sold under their names.

HEYM RIFLES AMERICA, INC. — Manufactured by Heym, GmbH & Co JAGWAFFEN KD., Gleichamberg, Germany (previously imported by Heym America, Inc.; Heckler & Koch; JagerSport, Ltd.)

MODEL 55B DOUBLE RIFLE
Kersten boxlock action w/double cross bolt and cocking indicators. Calibers: .308 Win., .30-06, .375 H&H, .458 Win. Mag., .470 N.E. 25-inch bbl. 42 inches overall. Weight: 8.25 lbs. Sights: fixed V-type rear; front ramp w/silver bead. Engraved receiver w/optional sidelocks, interchangeable bbls. and claw mounts. Checkered European walnut stock. Imported from Germany.
Model 55 (boxlock) . . . . . **NiB $6677 Ex $6488 Gd $5745**
Model 55 (sidelock . . . . . . **NiB $9544 Ex $7890 Gd $6791**
W/Extra rifle bbls., add $6000
W/Extra shotgun bbls., add $3000

MODEL 88B DOUBLE RIFLE
Modified Anson & Deeley boxlock action w/standing gears, double underlocking lugs and Greener extension w/crossbolt. Calibers: 8x57 JRS, 9.3x74R, .30-06, .375 H&H, .458 Win. Mag., .470 Nitro Express, .500 Nitro Express. Other calibers available on special order. Weight: 8 to 10 lbs. Top tang safety and cocking indicators. Double triggers w/front set. Fixed or 3-leaf express rear sight, front ramp w/silver bead. Engraved receiver w/ optional sidelocks. Checkered French walnut stock. Imported from Germany.
Model 88B Boxlock . . . . **NiB $11,669 Ex $8875 Gd $6067**
Model 88B/SS Sidelock . . . . . **NiB $15,538 Ex $10,850 Gd $7410**
Model 88B Safari (Magnum) . **NiB $15,038 Ex $12,050 Gd $8226**

EXPRESS BOLT-ACTION RIFLE
Same general specifications as Model SR-20 Safari except w/modified magnum Mauser action. Checkered AAA-grade European walnut stock w/cheekpiece, solid rubber recoil pad, rosewood forend tip and grip cap. Calibers: .338 Lapua Magnum, .375 H&H, .378 Wby. Mag., .416 Rigby .450 Ackley, .460 Wby. Mag., .500 A-Square, .500 Nitro Express, .600 Nitro Express. Other calibers available on special order, but no change in used gun value. Imported from Germany 1989 to 1995.
Standard Express Magnum . . . . . **NiB $5644 Ex $4490 Gd $3230**
600 Nitro Express . . . . **NiB $5895 Ex $5133 Gd $3190**
Left-hand models, add $750

SR-20 BOLT-ACTION RIFLE
Calibers: .243 Win., .270 Win., .308 Win., .30-06, 7mm Rem. Mag., .300 Win. Mag., .375 H&H. Five round (standard) or 3-round (Magnum) magazine. Bbl. length: 20.5-inch (SR-20L); 24-inch (SR-20N); 26-inch (SR-20G). Weight: 7.75 lbs. Adj. rear sight, blade front. Checkered French walnut stock in Monte Carlo style (N&G Series) or full Mannlicher (L Series). Imported from Germany. Disc. 1992.
SR-20L . . . . **NiB $2316 Ex $1832 Gd $1209**
SR-20N . . . . **NiB $2279 Ex $1856 Gd $1200**
SR-20G . . . . **NiB $2865 Ex $2379 Gd $1600**

SR-20 CLASSIC BOLT-ACTION RIFLES
Same as SR-20 except w/.22-250 and .338 Win. Mag. plus metric calibers on request. 24-inch (standard) or 25-inch (Magnum) bbl. Checkered French walnut stock. Left-hand models. Imported from Germany since 1985; Sporter version 1989 to 1993.
Classic (Standard) . . . . **NiB $1860 Ex $1875 Gd $1423**
Classic (Magnum) . . . . **NiB $2355 Ex $2216 Gd $1466**
Classic Sporter (Std.
w/22-inch bbl.) . . . . **NiB $2556 Ex $2203 Gd $1499**
Classic Sporter (Mag.
w/24-inch bbl.) . . . . **NiB $1899 Ex $2288 Gd $1633**
Left-hand models, add $350

SR-20 ALPINE, SAFARI AND TROPHY SERIES
Same general specifications as Model SR-20 Classic Sporter except Alpine Series w/20-inch bbl., Mannlicher stock, chambered in standard calibers only; Safari Series w/24-inch bbl., 3-leaf express sights and magnum action in calibers .375 H & H, .404 Jeffrey, .425 Express, .458 Win. Mag.; Trophy Series w/Krupp-Special tapered octagon bbl. w/quarter rib and open sights, standard and Magnum calibers. Imported from Germany from 1989 to 1993.
Alpine Series . . . . **NiB $1969 Ex $1812 Gd $1492**
Safari Series . . . . **NiB $2308 Ex $2177 Gd $1545**
Trophy Series (Stand. calibers) . . **NiB $2589 Ex $2115 Gd $1904**
Trophy Series
(Magnum calibers) . . . . . . **NiB $2733 Ex $2118 Gd $1944**

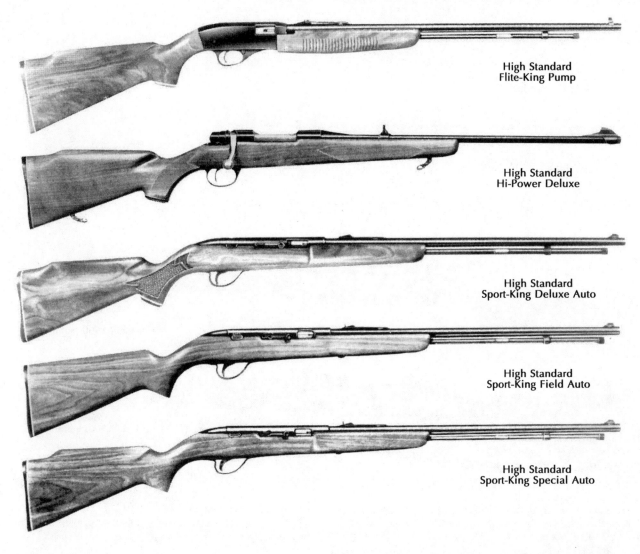

High Standard
Flite-King Pump

High Standard
Hi-Power Deluxe

High Standard
Sport-King Deluxe Auto

High Standard
Sport-King Field Auto

High Standard
Sport-King Special Auto

J.C. HIGGINS RIFLES

See Sears, Roebuck & Company.

HI-POINT FIREARMS — Dayton, Ohio

MODEL 995 CARBINE

Semiautomatic recoil-operated carbine. Calibers: 9mm Parabellum or 40 S&W. 10-round magazine. 16.5-inch bbl. 31.5 inches overall. Protected post front sight, aperture rear w/integral scope mount. Matte blue, chrome or Parkerized finish. Checkered polymer grip/frame. Made from 1996 to date.

Model 995, 9mm (blue or Parkerized) NiB $233 Ex $179 Gd $130
Model 995, .41 S&W (blue or Parkerized)NiB $248 Ex $211 Gd $146
W/laser sights, add $50
W/chrome finish, add $25

HIGH STANDARD SPORTING FIREARMS — East Hartford, Connecticut (formerly High Standard Mfg. Co., Hamden, CT)

A long-standing producer of sporting arms, High Standard discontinued its operations in 1984.

SPORT-KING PUMP RIFLE . . . . NiB $207 Ex $144 Gd $98
Hammerless slide-action. Caliber: .22 LR, .22 Long, .22 Short. Tubular mag. holds 17 LR, 19 Long, or 24 Short. 24-inch bbl. Weight: 5.5 lbs. Sights: Partridge rear; bead front. Monte Carlo stock w/pistol grip, serrated semibeavertail forearm. Made from 1963 to 1976.

HI-POWER DELUXE RIFLE NiB $475 Ex $315 Gd $221
Mauser-type bolt action, sliding safety. Calibers: .270, .30-06. Four round magazine. 22-inch bbl. Weight: 7 lbs. Sights: Folding open rear; ramp front. Walnut stock w/checkered pistol-grip and forearm, Monte Carlo comb, QD swivels. Made from 1962 to 1965.

Holland & Holland
Best Quality Magazine

Holland & Holland
Royal Deluxe Double

Howa
Model 1500 Hunter

Howa
Model 1500 Lightning

HI-POWER FIELD BOLT-ACTION RIFLE NiB $255 Ex $179 Gd $126
Same as Hi-Power Deluxe except w/plain field style stock. Made
from 1962 to 1966.

SPORT-KING AUTO-
LOADING CARBINE . . . . NiB $379 Ex $318 Gd $200
Same as Sport-King Field Autoloader except w/18.25-inch bbl.,
Western-style straight-grip stock w/bbl. band, sling and swivels.
Made from 1964 to 1973.

SPORT-KING DELUXE AUTOLOADER. . NiB $280 Ex $213 Gd $100
Same as Sport-King Special Autoloader except w/checkered stock.
Made from 1966 to 1975.

SPORT-KING FIELD AUTOLOADER . . . . NiB $229 Ex $130 Gd $90
Calibers: .22 LR, .22 Long, .22 Short (high speed). Tubular magazine
holds 15 LR, 17 Long, or 21 Short. 22.25-inch bbl. Weight: 5.5 lbs.
Sights: Open rear; beaded post front. Plain pistol-grip stock. Made
from 1960 to 1966.

SPORT-KING SPECIAL AUTOLOADER . NiB $210 Ex $166 Gd $106
Same as Sport-King Field except stock w/Monte Carlo comb and
semibeavertail forearm. Made from 1960 to 1966.

HOLLAND & HOLLAND, LTD. — London, England. Imported by Holland & Holland, New York, NY

NO. 2 MODEL HAMMERLESS
EJECTOR DOUBLE RIFLE . . NiB $15,650 Ex $12,800 Gd $10,770
Same general specifications as Royal Model except plainer finish. Disc. 1960.

BEST QUALITY MAGAZINE RIFLE NiB $15,300 Ex $12,000 Gd $9890
Mauser or Enfield action. Calibers: .240 Apex, .300 H&H Mag.,
.375 H&H Magnum. Four round box magazine. 24-inch bbl.
Weight: 7.25 lbs., 240 Apex; 8.25 lbs., .300 Mag. and .375 Mag.
Sights: Folding leaf rear; hooded ramp front. Detachable French
walnut stock w/cheekpiece, checkered pistol-grip and forearm,
swivels. Currently mfd. Specifications given apply to most models.

DE LUXE MAGAZINE RIFLE . NiB $16,780 Ex $13,966 Gd $9566
Same specifications as Best Quality except w/exhibition-grade stock
and special engraving. Currently mfd.

ROYAL HAMMERLESS
EJECTOR RIFLE . . . . . NiB $43,000 Ex $33,900 Gd $24,775
Sidelock. Calibers: .240 Apex, 7mm H&H Mag., .300 H&H Mag., .300
Win. Mag., .30-06, .375 H&H Mag., .458 Win. Mag., .465 H&H Mag.
24- to 28-inch bbls. Weight: From 7.5 lbs. Sights: Folding leaf rear, ramp
front. Cheekpiece stock of select French walnut, checkered pistol-grip and
forearm. Currently mfd. Same general specifications apply to prewar model.

ROYAL DELUXE DOUBLE RIFLE NiB $57,956 Ex $47,888 Gd $32,600
Formerly designated "Modele Deluxe." Same specifications as
Royal Model except w/exhibition-grade stock and special engrav-
ing. Currently mfd.

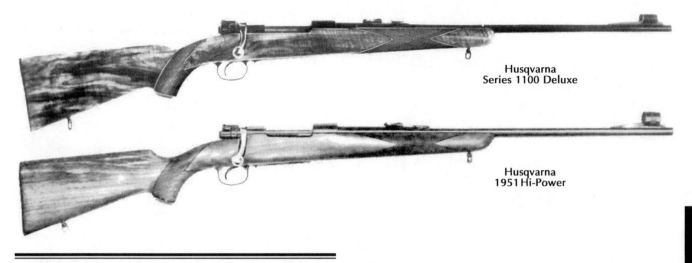

Husqvarna
Series 1100 Deluxe

Husqvarna
1951 Hi-Power

HOWA RIFLES — Tokyo, Japan. Imported by Legacy Sports Int., Reno, NV

See also Mossberg (1500) Smith & Wesson (1500 & 1707) and Weatherby (Vanguard).

MODEL 1500 HUNTER
Similar to Trophy Model except w/standard walnut stock. No Monte Carlo cheekpiece or grip cap. Imported from 1988 to 1989.
Standard calibers . . . . NiB $508 Ex $455 Gd $337
Magnum calibers . . . . NiB $520 Ex $466 Gd $350
Stainless steel, add $100

MODEL 1500 LIGHTNING BOLT-ACTION RIFLE
Similar to Hunter Model except fitted w/black Bell & Carlson Carbelite stock w/checkered grip and forend. Weight: 7.5 lbs. Imported 1988.
Standard calibers . . . . NiB $479 Ex $336 Gd $269
Magnum calibers . . . . NiB $482 Ex $410 Gd $312

MODEL 1500 PCS BOLT-ACTION RIFLE
Similar to Hunter Model except in Police Counter Sniper configuration and chambered for .308 Win. only. Walnut or synthetic stock w/checkered grip and forend. Receiver drilled and tapped but w/o sights. Weight: 8.5 to 9.3 lbs. Imported from 1999 to 2000.
PCS Model w/walnut stock . . NiB $433 Ex $337 Gd $249
PCS Model w/synthetic stock . NiB $479 Ex $388 Gd $307
Stainless steel, add $100

MODEL 1500 REALTREE
CAMO RIFLE . . . . NiB $546 Ex $489 Gd $333
Similar to Trophy Model except fitted w/Camo Bell & Carlson Carbelite stock w/checkered grip and forend. Weight: 8 lbs. Stock, action and barrel finished in Realtree camo. Available in standard calibers only. Imported 1993 to 1994.

MODEL 1500 TROPHY/VARMINT BOLT-ACTION RIFLE
Calibers: .22-250, .223, .243 Win., .270 Win., .308 Win., .30-06, 7mm Mag., .300 Win. Mag.,. .338 Win. Mag. 22-inch bbl. (standard); 24-inch bbl. (Magnum). 42.5 inches overall (standard). Weight: 7.5 lbs. Adj. rear sight hooded ramp front. Checkered walnut stock w/ Monte Carlo cheekpiece. Varmint Model w/24-inch heavy bbl., weight of 9.5 lbs. in calibers .22-250, .223 and .308 only. Imported 1988 to 1992 and 2001 to 2008.
Trophy Standard . . . . NiB $575 Ex $499 Gd $370
Trophy Magnum . . . . NiB $590 Ex $508 Gd $379
Varmint (Parkerized finish) . . . NiB $602 Ex $488 Gd $380
Stainless steel, add $100

MODEL 1500 WOODGRAIN LIGHTNING RIFLE
Calibers: .243, .270, 7mm Rem. Mag., .30-06. Mag. Five round magazine 22-inch. 42 inches overall. Weight: 7.5 lbs. Receiver drilled and tapped for scope mount, no sights. Checkered woodgrain synthetic polymer stock. Imported from 1993 to 1994.
Standard calibers . . . . NiB $488 Ex $419 Gd $374
Magnum calibers . . . . NiB $500 Ex $443 Gd $399

H-S PRECISION — Rapid City, South Dakota

PRO-SERIES
Custom rifle built on Remington 707 bolt action. Calibers: .22 to .416, 24- or 26-inch bbl. w/fluted option. Aluminum bedding block system w/take-down option. Kevlar/carbon fiber stock to customer's specifications. Appointments and options to customer's preference. Made from 1990 to date.
Sporter model . . . . NiB $2180 Ex $1830 Gd $1100
Pro-Hunter model (PHR) . . . . . . NiB $2866 Ex $2033 Gd $1108
Long-Range Model . . . . NiB $4597 Ex $3766 Gd $2080
Long-Range
takedown model . . . . NiB $2355 Ex $1944 Gd $1390
Marksman model . . . . NiB $2966 Ex $1830 Gd $1106
Marksman takedown model . . . . NiB $2977 Ex $2133 Gd $1490
Varmint takedown model (VTD) . NiB $4369 Ex $2835 Gd $2000
Left-hand models, add $227

HUNGARIAN MILITARY RIFLES — Budapest, Hungary. Manufactured at government arsenal

MODEL 1935M MANNLICHER
MILITARY RIFLE . . . . NiB $370 Ex $287 Gd $186
Caliber: 8x52mm Hungarian. Bolt action, straight handle. Five round projecting box magazine. 24-inch bbl. Weight: 9 lbs. Adj. leaf rear sight, hooded front blade. Two-piece military-type stock. Made from 1935 to 1940.

MODEL 1943M (GERMAN GEW 98/40) MANNLICHER
MILITARY RIFLE . . . . NiB $388 Ex $322 Gd $200
Modification, during German occupation, of Model 1935M. Caliber: 7.9mm Mauser. Turned-down bolt handle and Mauser M/98-type box magazine; other differences are minor. Made from 1940 to end of war in Europe.

Husqvarna 3000
Crown Grade

Husqvarna 4100
Lightweight

Husqvarna 6000
Imperial Custom

HUSQVARNA VAPENFABRIK A.B. —
Husqvarna, Sweden

MODEL 456 LIGHTWEIGHT
FULL-STOCK SPORTER. . . . . . NiB $713 Ex $466 Gd $339
Same as Series 4000/4100 except w/sporting style full stock w/
slope-away cheekrest. Weight: 6.5 lbs. Made from 1959 to 1970.

SERIES 1000 SUPER GRADE . . NiB $572 Ex $479 Gd $339
Same as 1951 Hi-Power except w/European walnut sporter stock
w/Monte Carlo comb and cheekpiece. Made from 1952 to 1956.

SERIES 1100 DELUXE MODEL HI-POWER
BOLT-ACTION SPORTING RIFLE . . . NiB $557 Ex $468 Gd $339
Same as 1951 Hi-Power, except w/jeweled bolt, European walnut
stock. Made from 1952 to 1956.

1950 HI-POWER SPORTING RIFLE . . NiB $554 Ex $415 Gd $300
Mauser-type bolt action. Calibers: .220 Swift, .270 Win. .30-06 (see
note below), 5-round box magazine. 23.75-inch bbl. Weight: 7.75 lbs.
Sights: Open rear; hooded ramp front. Sporting stock of Arctic beech,
checkered pistol grip and forearm, swivels. Note: Husqvarna sporters
were first intro. in U.S. about 1948; earlier models were also available
in calibers 6.5x55, 8x57 and 9.3x57. Made from 1946 to 1951.

1951 HI-POWER RIFLE. . . . . . NiB $554 Ex $415 Gd $300
Same as 1950 Hi-Power except w/high-comb stock, low safety.

SERIES 3000 CROWN GRADE. NiB $643 Ex $455 Gd $300
Same as Series 3100, except w/Monte Carlo comb stock.

SERIES 3100 CROWN GRADE. NiB $643 Ex $455 Gd $300
HVA improved Mauser action. Calibers: .243, .270, 7mm, .30-06, .308
Win. Five round box magazine. 23.75-inch bbl. Weight: 7.75 lbs. Sights:
Open rear; hooded ramp front. European walnut stock, checkered, cheek-
piece, pistol-grip cap, black forend tip, swivels. Made from 1954 to 1972.
SERIES 4000 LIGHTWEIGHT RIFLE . . NiB $699 Ex $433 Gd $297

Same as Series 4100 except w/Monte Carlo comb stock and no rear sight.

SERIES 4100 LIGHTWEIGHT RIFLE . . NiB $616 Ex $423 Gd $260
HVA improved Mauser action. Calibers: .243, .270, 7mm, .30-06,
.308 Win. Five round box magazine. 20.5-inch bbl. Weight: 6.25
lbs. Sights: Open rear; hooded ramp front. Lightweight walnut stock
w/cheekpiece, pistol grip, Schnabel forend tip, checkered, swivels.
Made from 1954 to 1972.

SERIES 6000 IMPERIAL CUSTOM GRADENiB $877 Ex $633 Gd $409
Same as Series 3100 except fancy-grade stock, 3-leaf folding rear
sight, adj. trigger. Calibers: .243, .270, 7mm Rem. Mag. .308, .30-
06. Made from 1968 to 1970.

SERIES 7070 IMPERIAL
MONTE CARLO LIGHTWEIGHTNiB $920 Ex $577 Gd $400
Same as Series 4000 Lightweight except fancy-grade stock, 3-leaf
folding rear sight, adj. trigger. Calibers: .243, .270, .308, .30-06.
Made from 1968 to 1970.

MODEL 8000
IMPERIAL GRADE RIFLE . . . . . NiB $831 Ex $569 Gd $389
Same as Model 9000 except w/jeweled bolt, engraved floorplate,
deluxe French walnut checkered stock, no sights. Made 1971 to 1972.

MODEL 9000 CROWN GRADE RIFLE NiB $633 Ex $459 Gd $348
New design Husqvarna bolt action. Adj. trigger. Calibers: .270, 7mm
Rem. Mag., .30-06, .300 Win. Mag. Five round box magazine, hinged
floorplate. 23.75-inch bbl. Sights: Folding leaf rear; hooded ramp front.
Checkered walnut stock w/Monte Carlo cheekpiece, rosewood forend
tip and pistol-grip cap. Weight: 7 lbs. 3 oz. Made from 1971 to 1972.

SERIES P-3000 PRESENTATION RIFLENiB $1179 Ex $889 Gd $627
Same as Crown Grade Series 3000 except w/selected stock,
engraved action, adj. trigger. Calibers: .243, .270, 7mm Rem. Mag.,
.30-06. Made from 1968 to 1970.

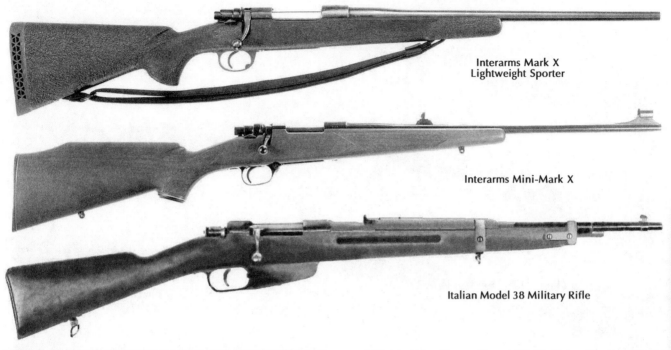

Interarms Mark X
Lightweight Sporter

Interarms Mini-Mark X

Italian Model 38 Military Rifle

INTERARMS RIFLES — Alexandria, Virginia

The following Mark X rifles are manufactured by Zavodi Crvena Zastava, Belgrade, Yugoslavia.

MARK X ALASKAN . . . . **NiB $708 Ex $447 Gd $321**
Same specs as Mark X Sporter, except chambered for .375 H&H Mag. and .458 Win. Mag. w/3-round magazine. Stock w/recoil-absorbing cross bolt and heavy duty recoil pad. Weighs 8.25 lbs. Made from 1976 to 1984.

MARK X BOLT-ACTION SPORTER SERIES
Mauser-type action. Calibers: .22-250, .243, .25-06, .270, 7x57, 7mm Rem. Mag., .308, .30-06, .300 Win. Mag. Five round magazine (3-round in magnum calibers). 24-inch bbl. Weight: 7.5 lbs. Sights: Adj. leaf rear; ramp front, w/hood. Classic-style stock of European walnut w/Monte Carlo comb and cheekpiece, checkered pistol grip and forearm, black forend tip, QD swivels. Made from 1972 to 1997.
Mark X Standard . . . . **NiB $479 Ex $355 Gd $260**
Mark X Camo (Realtree) . . . . **NiB $499 Ex $440 Gd $327**
American Field, std.
(rubber recoil pad) . . . . **NiB $570 Ex $460 Gd $368**
American Field, Magnum
(rubber recoil pad) . . . . **NiB $689 Ex $572 Gd $408**

MARK X CAVALIER . . . . **NiB $460 Ex $355 Gd $260**
Same specifications as Mark X Sporter except w/contemporary-style stock w/rollover cheekpiece, rosewood forend tip/grip cap, recoil pad. Intro. 1974; Disc.

MARK X CONTINENTAL
MANNLICHER STYLE CARBINE. . . . . **NiB $643 Ex $412 Gd $277**
Same specifications as Mark X Sporter except straight European-style comb stock w/sculptured cheekpiece. Precise double-set triggers and classic "butterknife" bolt handle. French checkering. Weight: 7.25 lbs. Disc.

MARK X LIGHTWEIGHT SPORTER . . **NiB $445 Ex $355 Gd $260**
Calibers: .22-250 Rem., .270 Win., 7mm Rem. Mag., .30-06 or 7mm Mag. Four- or 5-round magazine. 20-inch bbl. Synthenic Carbolite

stock Weight: 7 lbs. Imported from 1988-90. (Reintroduced 1994-97.)

MARK X MARQUIS
MANNLICHER-STYLE CARBINE . . . . **NiB $575 Ex $408 Gd $290**
Same specifications as Mark X Sporter except w/20-inch bbl., full-length Mannlicher-type stock w/metal forend/muzzle cap. Calibers: .270, 7x57, .308, .30-06. Imported 1976 to 1984.

MINI-MARK X BOLT-ACTION RIFLE . **NiB $448 Ex $359 Gd $260**
Miniature M98 Mauser action. Caliber: .223 Rem. Five round magazine. 20-inch bbl. 39.75 inches overall. Weight: 6.25 lbs. Adj. rear sight, hooded ramp front. Checkered hardwood stock. Imported from 1987 to 1994.

MARK X VISCOUNT . . . . **NiB $440 Ex $368 Gd $258**
Same specifications as Mark X Sporter except w/plainer field grade stock. Imported from 1974 to 1987.

AFRICAN SERIES . . . . **NiB $1035 Ex $603 Gd $422**
Mauser-type bolt-action. Calibers: .375 H&H Mag., .458 Win. Mag. Three round magazine. 24-inch bbl. Weight: 8 lbs. Sights: 3-leaf express open rear, ramp front w/hood. English-style stock of European walnut, w/cheekpiece, black forend tip, checkered pistol grip and forearm, recoil pad, QD swivels. Imported from 1974 to 1996 by Whitworth Rifle Co., England.

ITALIAN MILITARY RIFLES —
Manufactured by government plants at Brescia, Gardone, Terni, and Turin, Italy

MODEL 38 MILITARY RIFLE . . . **NiB $167 Ex $120 Gd $85**
Modification of Italian Model 1891 Mannlicher-Carcano Military Rifle w/turned-down bolt handle, detachable folding bayonet. Caliber: 7.35mm Italian Service (many arms of this model were later converted to the old 6.5mm caliber). Six round box magazine. 21.25-inch bbl. Weight: 7.5 lbs. Sights: Adj. rear-blade front. Military straight-grip stock. Adopted 1938.

Ithaca Model 49

Ithaca Model 49
Presentation

Ithaca Model 49R
Sporter

Ithaca Model 72
Saddlegun

Ithaca Model 72
Saddlegun Deluxe

ITHACA GUN COMPANY, INC. — King Ferry, New York (formerly Ithaca, NY)

**MODEL 49 SADDLEGUN LEVER ACTION
SINGLE-SHOT RIFLE. . . . . NiB $166 Ex $135 Gd $96**
Martini-type action. Hand-operated rebounding hammer. Caliber: .22 LR, Long, Short. 18-inch bbl. Open sights. Western carbine-style stock. Weight: 5.5 lbs. Made from 1961 to 1978.

MODEL 49 SADDLEGUN — DELUXE NiB $220 Ex $167 Gd $121
Same as standard Model 49 except w/gold-plated hammer and trigger, figured walnut stock, sling swivels. Made from 1962 to 1975.

MODEL 49 SADDLEGUN — MAGNUM . . .NiB $205 Ex $188 Gd $130
Same as standard Model 49 except chambered for .22 WMR cartridge. Made from 1962 to 1978.

**MODEL 49 SADDLEGUN
—PRESENTATION . . . . NiB $333 Ex $239 Gd $166**
Same as standard Model 49 Saddlegun except w/gold-plated hammer and trigger, engraved receiver, full fancy-figured walnut stock w/gold nameplate. Available in .22 LR or .22 WMR. Made from 1962 to 1974.

**MODEL 49 SADDLEGUN
— ST. LOUIS BICENTENNIAL . NiB $370 Ex $333 Gd $169**
Same as Model 49 Deluxe except w/commemorative inscription. 200 made in 1964. Top value is for rifle in new, unfired condition.

**MODEL 49R SADDLEGUN
REPEATING RIFLE . . . . NiB $298 Ex $243 Gd $154**
Similar in appearance to Model 49 Single-Shot. Caliber: .22 LR, Long, Short. Tubular magazine holds 15 LR, 17 Long, 21 Short. 20-inch bbl. Weight: 5.5 lbs. Sights: Open rear-bead front. Western-style stock, checkered grip. Made from 1968 to 1971.

Ithaca
Model LSA-65 Standard

Ithaca
Model X5-T

Ithaca
Model X-15

Ithaca
BSA CF-2

MODEL 49 YOUTH SADDLEGUN . . NiB $177 Ex $138 Gd $105
Same as standard Model 49 except shorter stock for young shooters. Made from 1961 to 1978.

REPEATING CARBINE. . . . . . NiB $379 Ex $300 Gd $208
Caliber: .22 LR, Long, Short. Tubular magazine holds 15 LR, 17 Long, 21 Short. 18.5-inch bbl. Weight: 5.5 lbs. Sights: Open rear; hooded ramp front. Receiver grooved for scope mounting. Western carbine stock and forearm of American walnut. Made 1973 to 1978.

MODEL 72 SADDLEGUN — DELUXE NiB $443 Ex $370 Gd $250
Same as standard Model 72 except w/silver-finished and engraved receiver, octagon bbl., higher grade walnut stock and forearm. Made from 1974 to 1976.

MODEL LSA-65 BOLT
ACTION STANDARD GRADE . NiB $479 Ex $443 Gd $337
Same as Model LSA-55 Standard Grade except calibers .25-06, .270, .30-06; 4-round magazine, 23-inch bbl., weight: 7 lbs. Made from 1969 to 1977.

MODEL LSA-65 DELUXE. . . . . NiB $590 Ex $531 Gd $355
Same as Model LSA-65 Standard Grade except w/special features of Model LSA-55 Deluxe. Made from 1969 to 1977.
MODEL X5-C LIGHTNING

AUTOLOADER. . . . . NiB $222 Ex $177 Gd $123
Takedown. Caliber: .22 LR. Seven round clip magazine. 22-inch bbl. Weight: 6 lbs. Sights: Open rear; Ray-bar front. Pistol-grip stock, grooved forearm. Made from 1958 to 1964.

MODEL X5-T LIGHTNING AUTOLOADER TUBULAR
REPEATING RIFLE . . . . NiB $222 Ex $177 Gd $123
Same as Model X5-C except w/16-round tubular magazine, stock w/plain forearm.

MODEL X-15 LIGHTNING
AUTOLOADER. . . . . NiB $222 Ex $177 Gd $123
Same general specifications as Model X5-C except forend is not grooved. Made from 1964 to 1967.

BSA CF-2 BOLT-ACTION
REPEATING RIFLE . . . . NiB $510 Ex $370 Gd $277
Mauser-type action. Calibers: 7mm Rem. Mag., .300 Win. Mag. Three round magazine. 23.6-inch bbl. Weight: 8 lbs. Sights: Adj. rear; hooded ramp front. Checkered walnut stock w/Monte Carlo comb, rollover cheekpiece, rosewood forend tip, recoil pad, sling swivels. Imported from 1976 to 1977. Mfd. by BSA Guns Ltd., Birmingham, England.

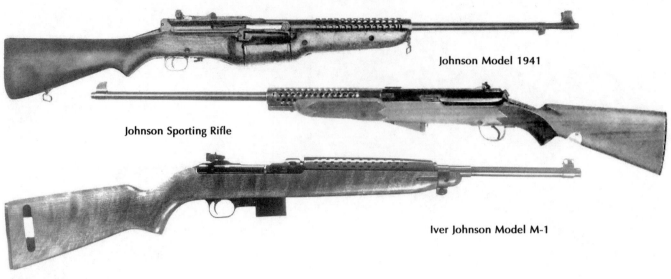

Johnson Model 1941

Johnson Sporting Rifle

Iver Johnson Model M-1

JAPANESE MILITARY RIFLES — Tokyo, Japan. Manufactured by Government Plant

MODEL 38 ARISAKA SERVICE RIFLE. NiB $656 Ex $390 Gd $220
Mauser-type bolt action. Caliber: 6.5mm Japanese. Five round box magazine. Bbl. lengths: 25.38 and 31.25 inches. Weight: 9.25 lbs. w/long bbl. Sights: fixed front, adj. rear. Military-type full stock. Adopted in 1905, the 38th year of the Meiji reign hence, the designation "Model 38."

MODEL 38 ARISAKA CARBINE NiB $656 Ex $390 Gd $220
Same general specifications as Model 38 Rifle except w/19-inch bbl., heavy folding bayonet, weight 7.25 lbs.

MODEL 44 CAVALRY CARBINE NiB $1190 Ex $690 Gd $355
Same general specifications as Model 38 Rifle except w/19-inch bbl., heavy folding bayonet, weight 8.5 lbs. Adopted in 1911, the 44th year of the Meiji reign, hence the designation, "Model 44."

MODEL 99 SERVICE RIFLE . . . NiB $577 Ex $255 Gd $200
Modified Model 38. Caliber: 7.7mm Japanese. Five round box magazine. 25.75-inch bbl. Weight: 8.75 lbs. Sights: Fixed front; adj. aperture rear; anti-aircraft sighting bars on some early models; fixed rear sight on some late WWII rifles. Military-type full stock, may have bipod. Takedown paratroop model was also made during WWII. Adopted in 1939, (Japanese year 2599) from which the designation "Model 99" is taken. Note: The last Model 99 rifles made were of poor quality; some with cast steel receivers. Value shown is for earlier type.
Sniper Rifle (with 4x scope) . . . . NiB $3900 Ex $3431 Gd $1817

JARRETT CUSTOM RIFLES — Jackson, South Carolina

**MODEL NO. 2 WALK ABOUT
BOLT-ACTION RIFLE** . . . . NiB $4788 Ex $3077 Gd $2043
Custom lightweight rifle built on Remington M707 action. Jarrett match- grade barrel cut and chambered to customer's specification in short action calibers only. McMillan fiberglass stock pillar-bedded to action. Made 1995 to 2003.

**MODEL NO. 3 CUSTOM
BOLT-ACTION RIFLE** . . . . NiB $4800 Ex $3147 Gd $2090
Custom rifle built on Remington M707 action. Jarrett match grade barrel cut and chambered to customer's specification. McMillan classic fiberglass stock pillar-bedded to action and finished to customer's preference. Made from 1989 to date.

**MODEL NO. 4 PROFESSIONAL
HUNTER BOLT-ACTION RIFLE** . . NiB $6988 Ex $5876 Gd $4490
Custom magnum rifle built on Winchester M70 "controlled feed" action. Jarrett match grade barrel cut and chambered to customer's specification in magnum calibers only. Quarter rib w/iron sights and two Leupold scopes w/Q-D rings and mounts. McMillan classic fiberglass stock fitted and finished to customer's preference.

JOHNSON AUTOMATICS, INC. — Providence, Rhode Island

**MODEL 1941 SEMIAUTO
MILITARY RIFLE** . . . . NiB $7433 Ex $5740 Gd $3328
Short-recoil operated. Removable, air-cooled, 22-inch bbl. Caliber: .30-06, 7mm Mauser. 10-round rotary magazine. Two-piece wood stock, pistol grip, perforated metal radiator sleeve over rear half of bbl. Sights: Receiver peep; protected post front. Weight: 9.5 lbs. Note: The Johnson M/1941 was adopted by the Netherlands government in 1940-41 and the major portion of the production of this rifle, 1941-43, was on Dutch orders. A quantity was also bought by the U.S. government for use by Marine Corps parachute troops (1943) and for Lend Lease. All these rifles were caliber .30-06; the 7mm Johnson rifles were made for the South American government.

SPORTING RIFLE PROTOTYPE NiB $14,000 Ex $11,500 Gd $7595
Same general specifications as military rifle except fitted w/sporting stock, checkered grip and forend. Blade front sight; receiver peep sight. Less than a dozen made prior to World War II.

IVER JOHNSON ARMS, INC. — Jacksonville, Arkansas (formerly of Fitchburg, Massachusetts, and Middlesex, New Jersey)

LI'L CHAMP BOLT-ACTION RIFLE NiB $227 Ex $146 Gd $90
Caliber: .22 Short, Long, LR. Single-shot. 16.25-inch bbl. 32.5 inches overall. Weight: 3.25 lbs. Adj. rear sight, blade front. Synthetic composition stock. Made from 1986 to 1988.

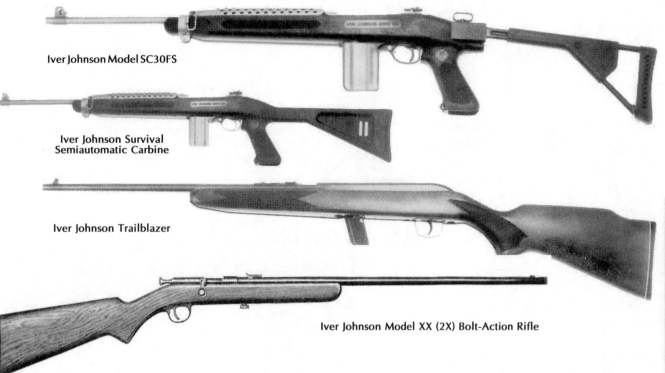

Iver Johnson Model SC30FS

Iver Johnson Survival Semiautomatic Carbine

Iver Johnson Trailblazer

Iver Johnson Model XX (2X) Bolt-Action Rifle

MODEL M-1 SEMIAUTOMATIC CARBINE

Similar to U.S. M-1 Carbine. Calibers: 9mm Parabellum 30 U.S. Carbine. 15- or 30-round magazine. 18-inch bbl. 35.5 inches overall. Weight: 6.5 lbs. Sights: blade front, w/guards; adj. peep rear. Walnut, hardwood or collapsible wire stock. Parkerized finish.

(30 cal. w/hardwood) . . . . NiB $460 Ex $340 Gd $220
(30 cal. w/walnut) . . . . NiB $506 Ex $374 Gd $242
(30 cal. w/wire) . . . . NiB $469 Ex $388 Gd $222
5.7mm or 9mm, add 30%

MODEL PM.30

SEMIAUTOMATIC CARBINE . . NiB $413 Ex $320 Gd $190
Similar to U.S. Carbine, Cal. 30 M1. 18-inch bbl. Weight: 5.5 lbs. 15- or 30-round detachable magazine. Both hardwood and walnut stock.

MODEL SC30FS

SEMIAUTOMATIC CARBINE . . NiB $466 Ex $390 Gd $233
Similar to Survival Carbine except w/folding stock. Made from 1983 to 1989.

SURVIVAL SEMIAUTOMATIC CARBINE NiB $433 Ex $399 Gd $230

Similar to Model PM.30 except in stainless steel. Made from 1983 to 1989. W/folding high-impact plastic stock add $35.

TRAILBLAZER SEMIAUTO RIFLE NiB $277 Ex $160 Gd $126

Caliber: .22 LR. 18-inch bbl. Weight: 5.5 lbs. Sights: Open rear, blade front. Hardwood stock. Made from 1983 to 1985

MODEL X BOLT-ACTION RIFLE NiB $270 Ex $189 Gd $115

Takedown, Single-shot. Caliber: .22 Short, Long and LR. 22-inch bbl. Weight: 4 lbs. Sights: Open rear; blade front. Pistol-grip stock w/knob forend tip. Made from 1928 to 1932.

MODEL XX (2X) BOLT-ACTION RIFLE NiB $323 Ex $170 Gd $100

Improved version of Model X w/heavier 24-inch bbl. larger stock (w/o knob tip), weight: 4.5 lbs. Made from 1932 to 1955.

K.B.I., INC. — Harrisburg, Pennsylvania

See listing under Armscor; Charles Daly; FEG; Liberty and I.M.I.

SUPER CLASSIC

Calibers: .22 LR, .22 Mag., RF, .22 Hornet. Five- or 10-round capacity. Bolt and semiauto action. 22.6- or 20.75-inch bbl. 41.25 or 40.5 inches overall. Weight: 6.4 to 6.7 lbs. Blue finish. Oil-finished American walnut stock w/hardwood grip cap and forend tip. Checkered Monte Carlo comb and cheekpiece. High polish blued barreled action w/damascened bolt. Dovetailed receiver and iron sights. Recoil pad. QD swivel posts.

M-1500 SC, .22 LR . . . . NiB $482 Ex $223 Gd $170
M-1500SC, .22 WMR . . . . NiB $289 Ex $233 Gd $177
M-1800-S, .22 Hornet . . . . NiB $455 Ex $380 Gd $256
M-2000 SC, semiauto, .22 LR . . . . . . NiB $290 Ex $244 Gd $179

K.D.F. INC. — Sequin, Texas

MODEL K15 BOLT-ACTION RIFLE

Calibers: (Standard) .22-250, .243 Win., 6mm Rem., .25-06, .270 Win., .280 Rem., 7mm Mag., .30-60; (Magnum) .300 Wby., .300 Win., .338 Win., .340 Wby., .375 H&H, .411 KDF, .416 Rem., .458 Win. Four round magazine (standard), 3-shot (magnum). 22-inch (standard) or 24-inch (magnum) bbl. 44.5 to 46.5 inches overall. Weight: 8 lbs. Sights optional. Kevlar composite or checkered walnut stock in Classic, European or thumbhole-style. Note: U.S. Manufacture limited to 25 prototypes and pre-production variations.

Standard model . . . . NiB $1796 Ex $1721 Gd $977
Magnum model . . . . NiB $1834 Ex $1597 Gd $1106

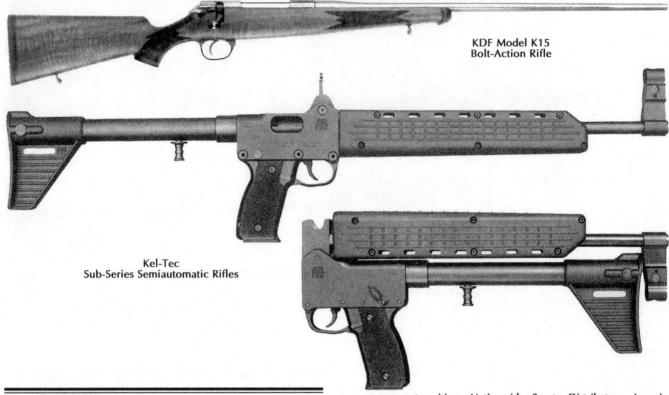

KDF Model K15
Bolt-Action Rifle

Kel-Tec
Sub-Series Semiautomatic Rifles

KEL-TEC CNC INDUSTRIES, INC. — Cocoa, FL

SUB-SERIES SEMIAUTOMATIC RIFLES

Semiautomatic blow-back action w/pivoting bbl., takedown. 9mm Parabellum or 40 S&W. Interchangeable grip assembly accepts most double column, high capacity handgun magazines. 16.1-inch bbl. 31.5 inches overall. Weight: 4.6 lbs. Hooded post front sight, flip-up rear. Matte black finish. Tubular buttstock w/grooved polymer buttplate and vented handguard. Made from 1997 to 2000.

Sub-9 model (9mm) . . . . NiB $395 Ex $333 Gd $265
Sub-40 model (.40 S&W) . . . . NiB $395 Ex $333 Gd $265

SUB-2000 . . . . NiB $380 Ex $300 Gd $200
Similar to Sub-9 and Sub-40. Accepts Glock, Beretta, S&W or SIG pistol magazines. Made 2001 to date.

SU-16A . . . . NiB $640 Ex $500 Gd $360
Semi-automatic w/pivoting bbl. Caliber: 5.56 NATO. Compatibale with AR-style magazines. 16- or 18.5-inch bbl. Weight: 4.7 lbs. Matte black, OD green or tan finish. Polymer stock. Made from 2003 to date.

KIMBER RIFLES — Manufactured by Kimber Manufacturing, Inc., Yonkers, NY(formerly Kimber of America, Inc.; Kimber of Oregon, Inc.)

Note: From 1980-91, Kimber of Oregon produced Kimber firearms. A redesigned action designated by serialization with a "B" suffix was introduced 1986. Pre-1986 production is recognized as the "A" series but is not so marked. These early models in rare configurations and limited-run calibers command premium prices from collectors. Kimber of America, in Clackamas, Oregon, acquired the Kimber trademark and resumed manufactured of Kimber rifles. During this

transition, Nationwide Sports Distributors, Inc. in Pennsylvania and Nevada became exclusive distributors of Kimber products. In 1997, Kimber Manufacturing acquired the trademark with manufacturing rights and expanded production to include a 1911-A1-style semiautomatic pistol, the Kimber Classic 45. Rifle production resumed in late 1998 with the announcement of an all-new Kimber .22 rifle and a refined Model 84 in both single-shot and repeater configurations.

MODEL 82 BOLT-ACTION RIFLE

Small action based on Kimber's "A" Model 82 rimfire receiver w/ twin rear locking lugs. Calibers: .22 LR, .22 WRF, .22 Hornet, .218 Bee, .25-20. 5- or 10-round magazine (.22 LR); 5-round magazine (22WRF); 3-round magazine (.22 Hornet). .218 Bee and .25-20 are single-shot. 18- to 25-inch bbl. 37.63 to 42.5 inches overall. Weight: 6 lbs. (Light Sporter), 6.5 lbs. (Sporter), 7.5 lbs. (Varmint); 10.75 lbs. (Target). Right- and left-hand actions are available in distinctive stock styles.

Cascade (disc. 1987) . . . . NiB $890 Ex $674 Gd $388
Classic (disc. 1988) . . . . NiB $885 Ex $674 Gd $388
Continental . . . . NiB $1482 Ex $1197 Gd $823
Custom Classic (disc. 1988) . NiB $1041 Ex $833 Gd $579
Mini Classic . . . . NiB $679 Ex $555 Gd $389
Super America . . . . NiB $1307 Ex $1165 Gd $909
Super Continental. . . . . . . NiB $2220 Ex $1390 Gd $925
All-American Match . . . . . . NiB $1978 Ex $1165 Gd $789
Deluxe Grade (disc. 1990). NiB $1388 Ex $1097 Gd $898
Hunter (w/laminated stock). . . NiB $912 Ex $833 Gd $523
Government Target. . . . . NiB $660 Ex $550 Gd $330

MODEL 82C CLASSIC BOLT-ACTION RIFLE

Caliber: .22 LR. Four- or 10-round magazine. 21-inch air-gauged bbl. 40.5 inches overall. Weight: 6.5 lbs. Receiver drilled and tapped for Warne scope mounts; no sights. Single-set trigger. Checkered Claro walnut stock w/red buttpad and polished steel grip cap. Reintroduced 1993.

Classic model. . . . . NiB $833 Ex $688 Gd $495
Left-hand model, add $100

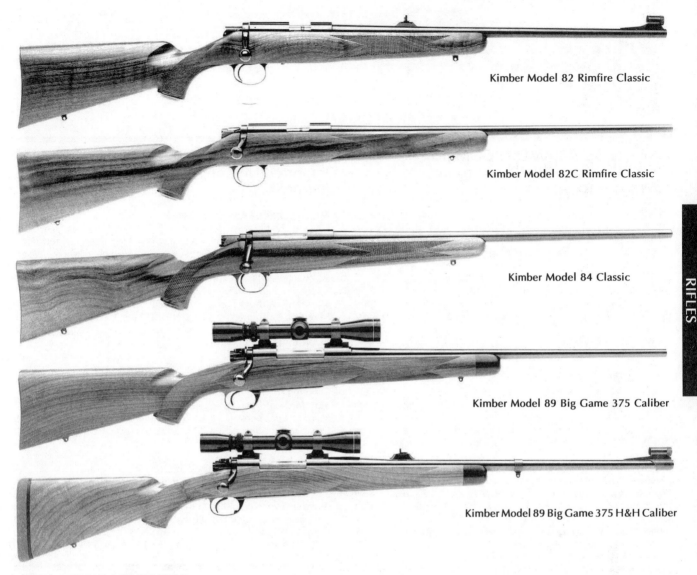

Kimber Model 82 Rimfire Classic

Kimber Model 82C Rimfire Classic

Kimber Model 84 Classic

Kimber Model 89 Big Game 375 Caliber

Kimber Model 89 Big Game 375 H&H Caliber

MODEL 84 BOLT-ACTION RIFLE

Classic (disc. 1988) Compact-medium action based on a scaled-down Mauser-type receiver, designed to accept small base centerfire cartridges. Calibers: .17 Rem., .221 Fireball, .222 Rem., .223 Rem. Five round magazine. Same general barrel and stock specifications as Model 82.

Classic (disc. 1988)	NiB $1100	Ex $821	Gd $577
Continental	NiB $1400	Ex $1098	Gd $769
Custom Classic (disc. 1988)	NiB $1410	Ex $978	Gd $713
Super America (disc. 1988)	NiB $1925	Ex $1078	Gd $757
Super Continental I(disc. 1988)	NiB $2100	Ex $1170	Gd $844
1990 Classifications			
Deluxe Grade (disc. 1990)	NiB $1310	Ex $1044	Gd $733
Hunter/Sporter (laminated stock)	NiB $1010	Ex $943	Gd $665
Super America (disc. 1991)	NiB $1988	Ex $1146	Gd $825
Super Varmint (disc. 1991)	NiB $1137	Ex $1187	Gd $825
Ultra Varmint (disc. 1991)	NiB $1189	Ex $1123	Gd $779

MODEL 89 BGR (BIG GAME RIFLE)

Large action combining the best features of the pre-64 Model 70 Winchester and the Mauser 98. Three action lengths are offered in three stock styles. Calibers: .257 Roberts, .25-06, 7x57, .270 Win., .280 Win., .30-06, 7mm Rem. Mag., .300 Win. Mag., .300 H&H, .338 Win., 35 Whelen, .375 H&H, .404 Jeffrey, .416 Rigby, .460 Wby., .505 Gibbs (.308 cartridge family to follow). Five round magazine (standard calibers); 3-round magazine (Magnum calibers). 22- to 24-inch bbl. 42 to 44 inches overall. Weight: 7.5 to 10.5 lbs. Model 89 African features express sights on contoured quarter rib, banded front sight. Barrel-mounted recoil lug w/integral receiver lug and twin recoil crosspins in stock.

BGR Long Action

Classic (disc. 1988)	NiB $944	Ex $844	Gd $588
Custom Classic (disc. 1988)	NiB $1288	Ex $1044	Gd $745
Super America	NiB $1548	Ex $1270	Gd $926
1990 Classifications			
Deluxe Grade: Featherweight	NiB $1995	Ex $1490	Gd $1044
Medium	NiB $1866	Ex $1566	Gd $1135
.375 H&H	NiB $1956	Ex $1577	Gd $1145
Hunter Grade (laminated stock)			
.270 and .30-06	NiB $1370	Ex $1105	Gd $800
.375 H&H	NiB $1676	Ex $1356	Gd $944
Super America: Featherweight	NiB $2088	Ex $1703	Gd $1213
Medium	NiB $2189	Ex $1760	Gd $1217
.375 H&H	NiB $2788	Ex $2274	Gd $1590
African — All calibers	NiB $5635	Ex $3955	Gd $2766

Krico Model 400

KNIGHT'S ARMAMENT COMPANY — Titusville, FL, formerly , Vero Beach, FL

SR-15 SEMIAUTOMATIC
MATCH RIFLE . . . . **NiB $1733 Ex $1544 Gd $1103**
AR-15 configuration. Caliber: .223 Rem. (5.56mm). Five- or 10-round magazine. 20-inch w/free-floating, match-grade bbl., 38 inches overall. Weight: 7.9 lbs. Integral Weaver-style rail. Two-stage target trigger. Matte black oxide finish. Black synthetic AR-15A2-style stock and forearm. Made from 1997 to 2008.

SR-15 M-4 SEMIAUTOMATIC CARBINE
Similar to SR-15 rifle except w/16-inch bbl. Sights and mounts optional. Fixed synthetic or collapsible buttstock. Made from 1997 to 2008.
Model SR-15 Carbine
(w/collapsible stock) . . . . . **NiB $1520 Ex $1388 Gd $1077**

SR-15 M-5
SEMIAUTOMATIC RIFLE . . **NiB $1765 Ex $1488 Gd $1165**
Caliber: .223 Rem. (5.56mm). Five- or 10-round magazine. 20-inch bbl. 38 inches overall. Weight: 7.6 lbs. Integral Weaver-style rail. Two-stage target trigger. Matte black oxide finish. Black synthetic AR-15A2-style stock and forearm. Made from 1997 to 2008.

SR-25 MATCH RIFLE
Similar to SR-25 Sporter except w/free floating 20- or 24-inch match bbl. 39.5-43.5 inches overall. Weight: 9.25 and 10.75 lbs., respectively. Integral Weaver-style rail. Sights and mounts optional. 1 MOA guaranteed. Made from 1993 to 2008.
Model SR-25 LW Match (w/20-inch bbl.)NiB $5744 Ex $3289 Gd $2665
W/RAS (Rail Adapter System), add **$350**

SR-25 SEMIAUTOMATIC CARBINE
Similar to SR-25 Sporter except w/free floating 16-inch bbl. 35.75 inches overall. Weight: 7.75 lbs. Integral Weaver-style rail. Sights and mounts optional. Made from 1995 to 2008.
Model SR-25 Carbine (w/o sights) NiB $6000 Ex $3927 Gd $1949
W/RAS (Rail Adapter System), add. **$300**

SR-25 SEMIAUTOMATIC
SPORTER RIFLE . . . . **NiB $2784 Ex $2409 Gd $1709**
AR-15 configuration. Caliber: .308 Win. (7.62 NATO). Five, 10- or 20-round magazine. 20-inch bbl. 39.5 inches overall. Weight: 8.75 lbs. Integral Weaver-style rail. Protected post front sight adjustable for elevation, detachable rear adjustable for windage. Two-stage target trigger. Matte black oxide finish. Black synthetic AR-15A2-style stock and forearm. Made from 1993 to 1997.

SR-50 SEMIAUTOMATIC LONG
RANGE PRECISION RIFLE. NiB $6833 Ex $6096 Gd $3597
Gas-operated semiautomatic action. Caliber: .50 BMG. 10-round magazine. 35.5-inch bbl. 58.5 inches overall. Weight: 31.75 lbs. Integral Weaver-style rail. Two-stage target trigger. Matte black oxide finish. Tubular-style stock. Limited production from 1996 to 2008.

KONGSBERG RIFLES — Kongsberg, Norway. Imported by Kongsberg America L.L.C., Fairfield, CT

MODEL 393 CLASSIC SPORTER
Calibers: .22-250 Rem., .243 Win., 6.5x55, .270 Win., 7mm Rem. Mag., .30-06, .308 Win. .300 Win. Mag., .338 Win. Mag. Three- or 4-round rotary magazine. 23-inch bbl. (Standard) or 26-inch bbl. (magnum). Weight: 7.5 to 8 lbs. 44 to 47 inches overall. No sights w/ dovetailed receiver or optional hooded blade front sight, adjustable rear. Blue finish. Checkered European walnut stock w/rubber buttplate. Imported from 1994 to 1998.
Standard calibers . . . . **NiB $957 Ex $779 Gd $597**
Magnum calibers . . . . **NiB $1289 Ex $1100 Gd $800**
Left-hand model, add **$150**
W/optional sights, add **$75**

MODEL 393 DELUXE SPORTER
Similar to Classic Model except w/deluxe European walnut stock. Imported from 1994 to 1998.
Standard calibers . . . . **NiB $1017 Ex $909 Gd $599**
Magnum calibers . . . . **NiB $1347 Ex $1117 Gd $809**
Left-hand model, add **$150**
W/optional sights, add **$75**

MODEL 393 THUMBHOLE SPORTER
Calibers: 22-250 Rem. or 308 Win. Four round rotary magazine. 23-inch heavy bbl. Weight: 8.5 lbs. 44 inches overall. No sights, dovetailed receiver. Blue finish. Stippled American walnut thumbhole stock w/adjustable cheekpiece. Imported from 1993 to 1998.
Right-hand model . . . . **NiB $1453 Ex $1347 Gd $650**
Left-hand model . . . . **NiB $1533 Ex $1377 Gd $800**

KRICO RIFLES — Stuttgart-Hedelfingen, Germany. Manufactured by Sportwaffenfabrik, Kriegeskorte GmbH. Imported by Northeast Arms, LLC, Ft. Fairfield, Maine (previously by Beeman Precision Arms, Inc and Mandell Shooting Supplies)

MODEL 260
SEMIAUTOMATIC RIFLE . . . . . **NiB $744 Ex $656 Gd $459**
Caliber: .22 LR. 10-round magazine. 20-inch bbl. 38.9 inches overall. Weight: 6.6 lbs. Hooded blade front sight; adj. rear. Grooved receiver. Beech stock. Blued finish. Introduced 1989. Disc.

MODEL 300 BOLT-ACTION RIFLE
Calibers: .22 LR. .22 WMR, .22 Hornet. 19.6-inch bbl. (22 LR), 23.6-inch (22 Hornet). 38.5 inches overall. Weight: 6.3 lbs. Double-set triggers. Sights: Ramped blade front, adj. open rear. Checkered walnut-finished hardwood stock. Blued finish. Introduced 1989. Disc.
Model 300 Standard . . . . **NiB $735 Ex $568 Gd $445**
Model 300 Deluxe . . . . **NiB $779 Ex $589 Gd $455**
Model 300 SA (Monte Carlo walnut stock)NiB $897 Ex $744 Gd $553
Model 300 Stutzen (full-length walnut stock)NiB $1023 Ex $864 Gd $654

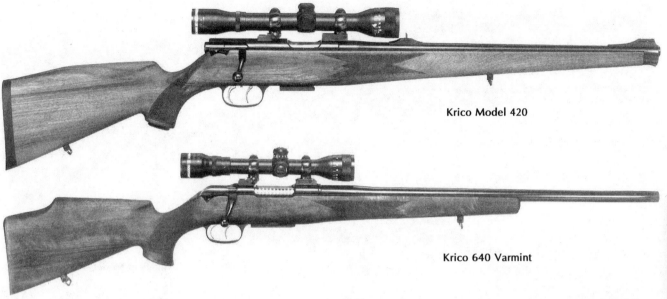

Krico Model 420

Krico 640 Varmint

MODEL 311 SMALL-BORE RIFLE
Bolt action. Caliber: .22 LR. Five or 10-round clip magazine. 22-inch bbl. Weight: 6 lbs. Single- or double-set trigger. Sights: Open rear; hooded ramp front; available w/factory-fitted Kaps 2.5x scope. Checkered stock w/cheekpiece, pistol-grip and swivels. Disc. 1962.
W/scope sight. . . . . **NiB $376 Ex $347 Gd $233**
W/iron sights only . . . . **NiB $355 Ex $333 Gd $270**

MODEL 320 BOLT-ACTION SPORTER NiB $920 Ex $622 Gd $423
Caliber: .22 LR. Five round detachable box magazine. 19.5-inch bbl. 38.5 inches overall. Weight: 6 lbs. Adj. rear sight, blade ramp front. Checkered European walnut Mannlicher-style stock w/low comb and cheekpiece. Single or double-set triggers. Imported from 1986 to 1988.

MODEL 340 METALLIC SILHOUETTE
BOLT-ACTION RIFLE . . . . **NiB $788 Ex $658 Gd $466**
Caliber: .22 LR. Five round magazine. 21-inch heavy, bull bbl. 39.5 inches overall. Weight: 7.5 lbs. No sights. Grooved receiver for scope mounts. European walnut stock in off-hand, match-style configuration. Match or double-set triggers. Imported from 1983 to 1988. Disc.

MODEL 360S BIATHLON RIFLE . . NiB $1455 Ex $1188 Gd $687
Caliber: .22 LR. Five 5-round magazines. 21.25-inch bbl. w/snow cap. 40.5 inches overall. Weight: 9.25 lbs. Straight-pull action. Match trigger w/17-oz. pull. Sights: Globe front, adj. match peep rear. Biathlon-style walnut stock w/high comb and adj. butt-plate. Imported from 1991. Disc.

MODEL 360 S2 BIATHLON RIFLE. NiB $1423 Ex $1189 Gd $655
Similar to Model 360S except w/pistol-grip activated action. Biathlon-style walnut stock w/black epoxy finish. Imported from 1991. Disc.

MODEL 400 BOLT-ACTION RIFLE . . NiB $889 Ex $766 Gd $544
Caliber: .22 Hornet. Five round detachable box magazine. 23.5-inch bbl. Weight: 6.75 lbs. Adj. open rear sight, ramp front. European walnut stock. Disc. 1990.

MODEL 420 BOLT-ACTION RIFLE . NiB $1043 Ex $833 Gd $568
Same as Model 400 except w/full-length Mannlicher-style stock and double-set triggers. Scope optional, extra. Disc. 1989.

MODEL 440 S BOLT-ACTION RIFLE . NiB $889 Ex $745 Gd $540
Caliber: .22 Hornet. Detachable box magazine. 20-inch bbl. 36.5 inches overall. Weight: 7.5 lbs. No sights. French walnut stock w/ventilated forend. Disc. 1988.

MODEL 500 MATCH RIFLE. . . . . NiB $3633 Ex $2988 Gd $1077
Caliber: .22 LR. Single-shot. 23.6-inch bbl. 42 inches overall. Weight: 9.4 lbs. Kricotronic electronic ignition system. Sights: Globe front; match micrometer aperture rear. Match-style European walnut stock w/adj. butt.

MODEL 600 BOLT-ACTION RIFLE NiB $1177 Ex $1055 Gd $733
Same general specifications as Model 707 except w/short action. Calibers: .17 Rem., .222, .223, .22-250, .243, 5.6x50 Mag. and 308. Introduced 1983. Disc.

MODEL 620 BOLT-ACTION RIFLE NiB $1206 Ex $1119 Gd $726
Same as Model 600 except w/short-action-chambered for .308 Win. only and full-length Mannlicher-style stock w/Schnabel forend tip. 20.75-inch bbl. Weight: 6.5 lbs. No longer imported.

MODEL 640 SUPER SNIPER BOLT-ACTION
REPEATING RIFLE . . . . **NiB $1863 Ex $1277 Gd $905**
Calibers: .223 Rem., .308 Win. Three round magazine. 26-inch bbl. 44.25 inches overall. Weight: 9.5 lbs. No sights drilled and tapped for scope mounts. Single or double-set triggers. Select walnut stock w/adj. cheekpiece and recoil pad. Disc. 1989.

MODEL 640 VARMINT RIFLE . . . . . . NiB $997 Ex $844 Gd $638
Caliber: .222 Rem. Four round magazine. 23.75-inch bbl. Weight: 9.5 lbs. No sights. European walnut stock. No longer imported.

MODEL 707 BOLT-ACTION RIFLE
Calibers: .17 Rem., .222, .222 Rem. Mag., .223, .22-250, 5.6x50 Mag., .243, 5.6x57 RSW, 6x62, 6.5x55, 6.5x57, 6.5x68 .270 Win., 7x64, 7.5 Swiss, 7mm Mag., .30-06, .300 Win., 8x68S, 9.3x64. 24-inch (standard) or 26-inch (magnum) bbl. 44 inches overall (standard). Weight: 7.5 lbs. Adj. rear sight; hooded ramp front. Checkered European-style walnut stock w/Bavarian cheekpiece and rosewood Schnabel forend tip. Imported from 1983 to date.
Model 707 Hunter . . . . NiB $1146 Ex $896 Gd $790
Model 707 Deluxe . . . . NiB $1244 Ex $1043 Gd $733
Model 707 Deluxe R . . . . . . NiB $1096 Ex $790 Gd $695
Model 707 Deluxe Stutzen . . NiB $1290 Ex $770 Gd $655

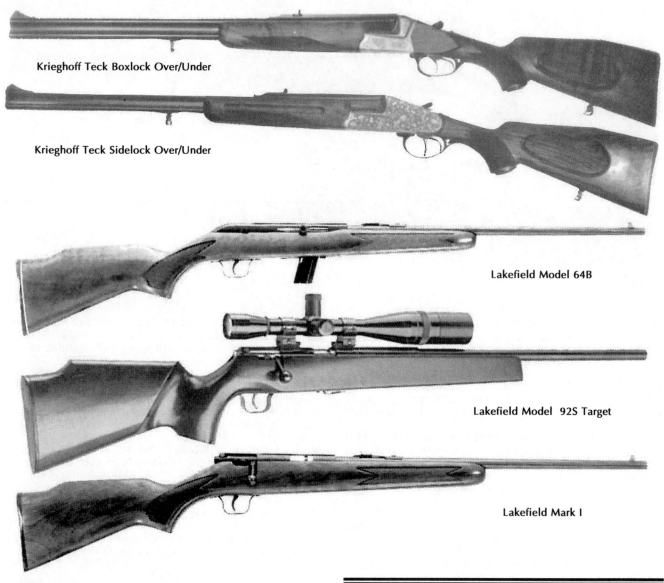

Krieghoff Teck Boxlock Over/Under

Krieghoff Teck Sidelock Over/Under

Lakefield Model 64B

Lakefield Model 92S Target

Lakefield Mark I

MODEL 720 BOLT-ACTION RIFLE
Same general specifications as Model 707 except in calibers .270 Win. and .30-06 w/full-length Mannlicher-style stock and Schnabel forend tip. 20.75-inch bbl. Weight: 6.75 lbs. Disc. importing 1990.
Sporter Model . . . . NiB $1144 Ex $1043 Gd $728
Ltd. Edition . . . . NiB $2419 Ex $2179 Gd $1188

BOLT-ACTION SPORTING RIFLE . . . NiB $733 Ex $634 Gd $438
Miniature Mauser action. Single- or double-set trigger. Calibers: .22 Hornet, .222 Rem. Four round clip magazine. 22-24- or 26-inch bbl. Weight: 6.25 lbs. Sights: Open rear; hooded ramp front. Checkered stock w/cheekpiece, pistol-grip, black forend tip, sling swivels. Imported from 1956 to 1962. Disc.

CARBINE . . . . NiB $743 Ex $637 Gd $440
Same as Krico Sporting Rifle except w/20- or 22-inch bbl., full-length Mannlicher-type stock. Disc. 1962.

SPECIAL VARMINT RIFLE . . . . NiB $743 Ex $637 Gd $440
Same as Krico Rifle except w/heavy bbl., no sights, weight: 7.25 lbs. Caliber: .222 Rem. only. Disc. 1962.

KRIEGHOFF RIFLES — Ulm (Donau), Germany. Manufactured by H. Krieghoff Jagd und Sportwaffenfabrik
See also Combination Guns under Krieghoff shotgun listings.

TECK OVER/UNDER RIFLE
Kersten action, double crossbolt, double underlugs. Boxlock. Calibers: 7x57r5, 7x64, 7x65r5, .30-30, .308 Win. .30-06, .300 Win. Mag., 9.3x74r5, .375 H&H Mag. .458 Win. Mag. 25-inch bbls. Weight: 8 to 9.5 lbs. Sights: Express rear; ramp front. Checkered walnut stock and forearm. Made from 1967. Disc.
Standard calibers . . . . NiB $8843 Ex $6953 Gd $5442
.375 H&H Mag.
(Disc. 1988)
.458 Win. Mag . . . . NiB $10650 Ex $7566 Gd $6831

ULM OVER/
UNDER RIFLE. . . . . . . NiB $14,790 Ex $11,110 Gd $6990
Same general specifications as Teck model except w/sidelocks w/ leaf Arabesque engraving. Made from 1963. Disc.

**Magnum Research Mountain Eagle
Bolt-Action Rifle**

ULM-PRIMUS OVER/UNDER RIFLE. . . . .NiB $20,244 Ex $16,277 Gd $10,550
Delux version of Ulm model, w/detachable sidelocks, higher grade engraving and stock wood. Made from 1963. Disc.

LAKEFIELD ARMS LTD. — Ontario, Canada
See also listing under Savage for production since 1994.

MODEL 64B SEMIAUTOMATIC RIFLE. NiB $150 Ex $110 Gd $85
Caliber: .22 LR. 10-round magazine. 20-inch bbl. Weight: 5.5 lbs. 40 inches overall. Bead front sight, adj. rear. Grooved receiver for scope mounts. Stamped checkering on walnut-finished hardwood stock w/Monte Carlo cheekpiece. Imported from 1990 to 1994.

**MODEL 90B
BOLT-ACTION TARGET RIFLE NiB $476 Ex $359 Gd $232**
Caliber: .22 LR. Five round magazine. 21-inch bbl. w/snow cap. 39.63 inches overall. Weight: 8.25 lbs. Adj. receiver peep sight; globe front w/colored inserts. Receiver drilled and tapped for scope mounts. Biathlon-style natural finished hardwood stock w/shooting rails, hand stop and butthook. Made from 1991 to 1994.

MODEL 91T/91TR BOLT-ACTION TARGET RIFLE
Calibers: .22 Short, Long, LR. 25-inch bbl. 43.63 inches overall. Weight: 8 lbs. Adj. rear peep sight; globe front w/inserts. Receiver drilled and tapped for scope mounts. Walnut-finished hardwood stock w/shooting rails and hand stop. Model 91TR is a 5-round clip-fed repeater. Made from 1991 to 1994.
Model 91T single-shot . . . . NiB $378 Ex $299 Gd $148
Model 91TR repeater (.22 LR only) . . NiB $416 Ex $266 Gd $171

MODEL 92S TARGET RIFLE . . NiB $300 Ex $257 Gd $184
Same general specifications as Model 90B except w/conventional target-style stock. 8 lbs. No sights, but drilled and tapped for scope mounts. Made from 1993 to 1995.

MODEL 93M BOLT ACTION. . NiB $188 Ex $157 Gd $110
Caliber: .22 WMR. Five round magazine. 20.75-inch bbl. 39.5 inches overall. Weight: 5.75 lbs. Bead front sight, adj. open rear. Receiver grooved for scope mount. Thumb-operated rotary safety. Checkered walnut-finished hardwood stock. Blued finish. Made in 1995.

MARK I BOLT-ACTION RIFLE . . . NiB $133 Ex $98 Gd $77
Calibers: .22 Short, Long, LR. Single-shot. 20.5-inch bbl. (19-inch Youth Model); available in smoothbore. Weight: 5.5 lbs. 39.5 inches overall. Bead front sight; adj. rear. Grooved receiver for scope mounts. Checkered walnut-finished hardwood stock w/Monte Carlo and pistol-grip. Blued finish. Made from 1990 to 1994.

MARK II BOLT-ACTION RIFLE
Same general specifications as Mark I except has repeating action w/10-round detachable box magazine. .22 LR. only. Made 1992 to 1994.
Mark II standard model. . . . . . NiB $137 Ex $120 Gd $80

Mark II Youth model (w/19-inch bbl.) . NiB $132 Ex $111 Gd $83
Mark II left-hand model . . . . . NiB $169 Ex $137 Gd $100

LAURONA RIFLES — Manufactured in Eibar, Spain. Imported by Galaxy Imports, Victoria, TX

MODEL 2000X O/U EXPRESS RIFLE
Calibers: .30-06, 8x57 JRS, 8x75 JR, .375 H&H, 9.3x74R Five round magazine. 24-inch separated bbls. Weight: 8.5 lbs. Quarter rib drilled and tapped for scope mount. Open sights. Matte black chrome finish. Monte Carlo-style checkered walnut buttstock; tulip forearm. Custom orders only. Imported from 1993 to date.
Standard calibers . . . . NiB $3166 Ex $2480 Gd $1723
Magnum calibers . . . . NiB $3790 Ex $3044 Gd 2133

L.A.R. MANUFACTURING, INC. — West Jordan, Utah

**BIG BOAR COMPETITOR
BOLT-ACTION RIFLE . . . . NiB $2230 Ex $1966 Gd $1429**
Single-shot, bull-pup action. Caliber: .50 BMG. 36-inch bbl. 45.5 inches overall. Weight: 28.4 lbs. Made from 1994 to date.

LUNA RIFLE — Mehlis, Germany. Manufactured by Ernst Friedr. Büchel

SINGLE-SHOT TARGET RIFLE NiB $1043 Ex $788 Gd $558
Falling block action. Calibers: .22 LR. .22 Hornet. 29-inch bbl. Weight: 8.25 lbs. Sights: Micrometer peep rear tang; open rear; ramp front. Cheekpiece stock w/full pistol-grip, semibeavertail forearm, checkered, swivels. Made before WWII.

MAGNUM RESEARCH, INC. — Minneapolis, Minnesota

MOUNTAIN EAGLE BOLT-ACTION RIFLE SERIES
Calibers: .222 Rem., .223 Rem., .270 Win., .280 Rem., 7mm Rem. Mag., 7mm STW, .30-06, .300 Win. Mag., .338 Win. Mag., .340 Wby. Mag., .375 H&H, .416 Rem. Mag. Five round (std.) or 4-round (Mag.). 24- or 26-inch bbl. 44 to 46 inches overall. Weight: 7.75 to 9.75 lbs. Receiver drilled and tapped for scope mount; no sights. Blued finish. Fiberglass composite stock. Made from 1994 to 2000.
Standard model . . . . NiB $1379 Ex $1209 Gd $744
Magnum model . . . . NiB $1997 Ex $1202 Gd $931
Varmint model (Intro. 1996) . . . . . NiB $1498 Ex $1216 Gd $938
Calibers .375 H&H, .416 Rem. Mag., add $325
Left-hand model, add $110

RIFLES

Mannlicher Model L Rifle

Mannlicher Model
M Carbine

Mannlicher Model M Professional

Mannlicher Model
M Rifle

MAGTECH — Las Vegas, Nevada. Manufactured by CBC, Brazil

MODEL MT 122.2/S BOLT-ACTION RIFLE NiB $135 Ex $121 Gd $75
Calibers: .22 Short, Long, Long Rifle. Six- or 10-round clip. Bolt action. 25-inch free-floating bbl. 43 inches overall. Weight: 6.5 lbs. Double locking bolt. Red cocking indicator. Safety lever. Brazilian hardwood finish. Double extractors. Beavertail forearm. Sling swivels. Imported from 1994. Disc.

MODEL MT 122.2/R BOLT-ACTION RIFLE NiB $140 Ex $116 Gd $88
Same as Model MT 122.2/S except adj. rear sight and post front sight. Introduced 1994. Disc.

MODEL MT 122.2T BOLT-ACTION RIFLE NiB $151 Ex $122 Gd $93
Same as Model MT 122.2/S except w/adj. micrometer-type rear sight and ramp front sight. Introduced 1994. Disc.

MANNLICHER SPORTING RIFLES — Steyr, Austria. Manufactured by Steyr-Daimler-Puch, A.-G.

NOTE: *Certain Mannlicher-Schoenauer models were produced before WWII. Manufacture of sporting rifles and carbines was resumed at the Steyr-Daimler-Puch plant in Austria in 1950 during which time the Model 1950 rifles and carbines were introduced.*

In 1967, Steyr-Daimler-Puch introduced a series of sporting rifles with a bolt action that is a departure from the Mannlicher-Schoenauer system of earlier models. In the latter, the action is locked by lugs symmetrically arranged behind the bolt head as well as by placing the bolt handle ahead of the right flank of the receiver, the rear section of which is open on top for backward movement of the bolt handle. The current action, made in four lengths to accommodate different ranges of cartridges, has a closed-top receiver; the bolt locking lugs are located toward the rear of the bolt (behind the magazine). The Mannlicher-Schoenauer rotary magazine has been redesigned as a detachable box type made of Makrolon. Imported by Gun South, Inc. Trussville, AL

MODEL L CARBINE . . . . . . NiB $1666 Ex $1189 Gd $835
Same general specifications as Model SL Carbine except w/type "L" action, weight: 6.2 lbs. Calibers same as for Model L Rifle. Imported 1968 to 1996.

**Mannlicher Model SL
Rifle w/Single-Set Trigger**

RIFLES

MODEL L RIFLE . . . . NiB $2177 Ex $1508 Gd $1009
Same general specifications as Model SL Rifle except w/type "L" action, weighs 6.3 lbs. Calibers: .22-250, 5.6x57 (disc. 1991), ..243 Win., 6mm Rem. .308 Win. Imported 1968 to 1996.

MODEL L VARMINT RIFLE . NiB $2107 Ex $1600 Gd $977
Same general specs as Model SL Varmint Rifle except w/type "L" action. Calibers: .22-250, .243 Win., .308 Win. Imported 1969 to 1996.

MODEL LUXUS BOLT-ACTION RIFLE
Same general specifications as Models L and M except w/3-round detachable box magazine and single-set trigger. Full or half-stock w/ low-luster oil or high-gloss lacquer finish. Disc. 1996.
Full stock . . . . NiB $2133 Ex $1790 Gd $1305
Half stock . . . . NiB $2733 Ex $1966 Gd $928

MODEL M CARBINE
Same general specifications as Model SL Carbine except w/type "M" action, stock w/recoil pad, weighs 6.8 lbs. Left-hand version w/additional 6.5x55 and 9.3x62 calibers intro. 1977. Imported 1969 to 1996.
Right-hand carbine . . . . . . NiB $1688 Ex $1570 Gd $909
Left-hand carbine . . . . NiB $2088 Ex $1964 Gd $1507

MODEL M PROFESSIONAL RIFLE . . NiB $1079 Ex $800 Gd $633
Same as standard Model M Rifle except w/synthetic (Cycolac) stock, weighs 7.5 lbs. Calibers: 6.5x55, 6.5x57, .270 Win., 7x57, 7x64, 7.5 Swiss, .30-06, 8x57JS, 9.3x62. Imported 1977 to 1993.

MODEL M RIFLE
Same general specifications as Model SL Rifle except w/type "M" action, stock w/forend tip and recoil pad; weighs 6.9 lbs. Calibers: 6.5x57, .270 Win., 7x57, 7x64, .30-06, 8x57JS, 9.3x62. Made 1969 to date. Left-hand version also in calibers 6.5x55 and 7.5 Swiss. Imported 1977 to 1996.
Right-hand rifle . . . . NiB $1667 Ex $1188 Gd $832
Left-hand rifle. . . . . NiB $2317 Ex $1951 Gd $1489

MODEL S RIFLE . . . . NiB $1674 Ex $1203 Gd $855
Same general specs as Model SL Rifle except w/type "S" action, 4-round magazine, 25.63-inch bbl., stock w/forend tip and recoil pad, weighs 8.4 lbs. Calibers: 6.5x68, .257 Weatherby Mag., .264 Win. Mag., 7mm Rem. Mag., .300 Win. Mag., .300 H&H Mag., .308 Norma Mag., 8x68S, .338 Win. Mag., 9.3x64, .375 H&H Mag. Imported 1970 to 1996.

MODEL SL CARBINE . . . . . NiB $1664 Ex $1176 Gd $815
Same general specifications as Model SL Rifle except w/20-inch bbl. and full-length stock, weight: 6 lbs. Imported 1968 to 1996.

MODEL SL RIFLE . . . . NiB $1744 Ex $1278 Gd $823
Steyr-Mannlicher SL bolt action. Calibers: .222 Rem., .222 Rem., .222 Rem. Mag., .223 Rem. Five round rotary magazine, detachable. 23.63-inch bbl. Weight: 6 lbs. Single- or double-set trigger (mechanisms interchangeable). Sights: Open rear; hooded ramp front. Half stock of European walnut w/Monte Carlo comb and cheekpiece, skip-checkered forearm and pistol grip, rubber buttpad, QD swivels. Imported 1967 to 1996.
MODEL SL

VARMINT RIFLE . . . . NiB $1233 Ex $1198 Gd $854
Same general specifications as Model SL Rifle except caliber .222 Rem. only, w/25.63-inch heavy bbl., no sights, weighs 7.92 lbs. Imported 1969 to 1996.

MODEL SSG MATCH TARGET RIFLE
Type "L" action. Caliber: .308 Win. (7.62x51 NATO). Five- or 10-round magazine, single-shot plug. 25.5-inch heavy bbl. Weight: 10.25 lbs. Single trigger. Sights: Micrometer peep rear; globe front. Target stock, European walnut or synthetic, w/full pistol-grip, wide forearm w/swivel rail, adj. rubber buttplate. Imported 1969 to date.
W/walnut stock . . . . NiB $2388 Ex $1956 Gd $1267
W/synthetic stock . . . . NiB $1488 Ex $1131 Gd $709

MODEL S/T RIFLE . . . . NiB $1278 Ex $1564 Gd $931
Same as Model S Rifle except w/heavy 25.63-inch bbl., weight: 9 lbs. Calibers: 9.3x64, .375 H&H Mag., .458 Win. Mag. Option of 23.63-inch bbl. in latter caliber. Imported 1975 to 1996.

MODEL 1903 BOLT-ACTION
SPORTING CARBINE . . . . NiB $2790 Ex $2133 Gd $1500
Caliber: 6.5x53mm (referred to in some European gun catalogs as 6.7x53mm, following the Austrian practice of designating calibers by bullet diameter). Five round rotary magazine. 450mm (17.7-inch) bbl. Weight: 6.5 lbs. Double-set trigger. Sights: Two-leaf rear; ramp front. Full-length sporting stock w/cheekpiece, pistol-grip, trap buttplate, swivels. Pre-WWII.

MODEL 1905 CARBINE . . . . NiB $1966 Ex $904 Gd $633
Same as Model 1903 except w/19.7-inch bbl.chambered 9x56mm and weight: 6.75 lbs. Pre-WWII.

MODEL 1908 CARBINE . . . . NiB $1910 Ex $909 Gd $640
Same as Model 1905 except calibers 7x57mm and 8x56mm Pre-WWII.

MODEL 1910 CARBINE . . . NiB $1823 Ex $1535 Gd $870
Same as Model 1905 except in 9.5x57mm. Pre-WWII.

MODEL 1924 CARBINE . . NiB $1767 Ex $1543 Gd $1067
Same as Model 1905 except caliber .30-06 (7.62x63mm). Pre-WWII.

MODEL 1950 BOLT-ACTION
SPORTING RIFLE . . . . NiB $1947 Ex $1466 Gd $590
Calibers: .257 Roberts, .270 Win., .30-06. Five round rotary magazine. 24-inch bbl. Weight: 7.25 lbs. Single trigger or double-set trigger. Redesigned low bolt handle, shotgun-type safety. Sights: Folding leaf open rear; hooded ramp front. Improved half-length stock w/cheekpiece, pistol grip, checkered, ebony forend tip, swivels. Made from 1950 to 1952.

GRADING: **NiB** = New in Box   **Ex** = Excellent or NRA 95%   **Gd** = Good or NRA 68%

271

Mannlicher-Schoenauer
Model 1950 Carbine

Mannlicher-Schoenauer
Model 1950 Carbine

Mannlicher-Schoenauer
Model 1950 Carbine

Mannlicher-Schoenauer
Model 1950 Carbine

Mannlicher-Schoenauer
Model 1950 Carbine

MODEL 1950 CARBINE . . . NiB $2065 Ex $1567 Gd $997
Same general specifications as Model 1950 Rifle except w/20-inch bbl., full-length stock, weighs 7 lbs. Made from 1950 to 1952.

MODEL 1950
6.5 CARBINE . . . . NiB $2060 Ex $1550 Gd $990
Same as other Model 1950 Carbines except caliber 6.5x53mm, w/18.25-inch bbl., weighs 6.75 lbs. Made from 1950 to 1952.

MODEL 1952
IMPROVED CARBINE . . . . NiB $1866 Ex $1444 Gd $905
Same as Model 1950 Carbine except w/swept-back bolt handle, redesigned stock. Calibers: .257, .270, 7mm, .30-06. Made 1952 to 1956.

MODEL 1952 IMPROVED
6.5 CARBINE . . . . NiB $2088 Ex $1091 Gd $623
Same as Model 1952 Carbine except caliber 6.5x53mm, w/18.25-inch bbl. Made from 1952 to 1956.

MODEL 1952 IMPROVED
SPORTING RIFLE . . . . NiB $1847 Ex $1350 Gd $896
Same as Model 1950 except w/swept-back bolt handle, redesigned stock. Calibers: .257, .270, .30-06, 9.3x62mm. Made from 1952 to 1956 and imported exclusively by Stoeger Arms Corp.
MODEL 1956 CUSTOM CARBINE . . NiB $2055 Ex $831 Gd $567

Same general specifications as Models 1950 and 1952 Carbines except w/redesigned stock w/high comb. Drilled and tapped for scope mounts. Calibers: .243, 6.5mm, .257, .270, 7mm, .30-06, .308. Made 1956 to 1960.

CARBINE, MODEL 1961-MCA . . . NiB $1867 Ex $1278 Gd $990
Same as Model 1956 Carbine except w/universal Monte Carlo design stock. Calibers: .243 Win., 6.5mm, .270, .308, .30-06. Made from 1961 to 1971.

RIFLE, MODEL 1961-MCA . NiB $2159 Ex $1389 Gd $997
Same as Model 1956 Rifle except w/universal Monte Carlo design stock. Calibers: .243, .270, .30-06. Made from 1961 to 1971.

HIGH VELOCITY BOLT-ACTION
SPORTING RIFLE . . . . NiB $2650 Ex $1630 Gd $1190
Calibers: 7x64 Brenneke, .30-06 (7.62x63), 8x60 Magnum, 9.3x62, 10.75x68mm. 23.6-inch bbl. Weight: 7.5 lbs. Sights: British-style 3-leaf open rear; ramp front. Half-length sporting stock w/cheekpiece, pistol grip, checkered, trap buttplate, swivels. Also produced in a takedown model. Pre-WWII. See illustration next page.
10.75x68mm, add 105%

M72 MODEL L/M CARBINE . NiB $1043 Ex $762 Gd $513
Same general specifications as M72 Model L/M Rifle except w/20-inch bbl. and full-length stock, weight: 7.2 lbs. Imported from 1972 to date.

**Mannlicher Schoenauer
High Velocity Bolt-Action Sporting Rifle**

Marlin Model 9 9mm Carbine

Marlin Model 9N Nickel-Teflon

M72 MODEL L/M RIFLE . . . . . NiB $906 Ex $821 Gd $600
M72 bolt-action, type L/M receiver front-locking bolt internal rotary magazine (5-round). Calibers: .22-250, 5.6x57, 6mm Rem., .243 Win., 6.5x57, .270 Win., 7x57, 7x64, .308 Win., .30-06. 23.63-inch bbl. Weight: 7.3 lbs. Single- or double-set trigger (mechanisms interchangeable). Sights: Open rear; hooded ramp front. Half stock of European walnut, checkered forearm and pistol-grip, Monte Carlo cheekpiece, rosewood forend tip, recoil pad QD swivels. Imported 1972 to 1981.

M72 MODEL S RIFLE . . . . . . NiB $876 Ex $756 Gd $544
Same general specifications as M72 Model L/M Rifle except w/ magnum action, 4-round magazine, 25.63-inch bbl., weighs 8.6 lbs. Calibers: 6.5x68, 7mm Rem. Mag., 8x68S, 9.3x64, .375 H&H Mag. Imported from 1972 to 1981.

M72 MODEL S/T RIFLE. . . . NiB $1755 Ex $1461 Gd $999
Same as M72 Model S Rifle except w/heavy 25.63-inch bbl., weighs 9.3 lbs. Calibers: .300 Win. Mag. 9.3x64, .375 H&H Mag., .458 Win. Mag. Option of 23.63-inch bbl. in latter caliber. Imported from 1975 to 1981.

MODEL SBS FORESTER RIFLE
Calibers: .243 Win., .25-06 Rem., .270 Win., .6.5x55mm, 6.5x57mm, 7x64mm, 7mm-08 Rem., .30-06, .308 Win. 9.3x64mm. Four round detachable magazine. 23.6-inch bbl. 44.5 inches overall. Weight: 7.5 lbs. No sights w/drilled and tapped for Browning A-Bolt configuration. Checkered American walnut stock w/Monte Carlo cheekpiece and Pachmayr swivels. Polished or matte blue finish. Imported from 1997 to date.

Standard calibers . . . . NiB $955 Ex $823 Gd $595
Mountain Rifle (w/20-inch bbl.) . . . . NiB $975 Ex $805 Gd $555
For magnum calibers, add. $50
For metric calibers, add $126

MODEL SBS PRO-HUNTER RIFLE
Similar to the Forester Model, except w/ASB black synthetic stock. Matte blue finish. Imported from 1997 to date.
Standard calibers . . . . NiB $1000 Ex $879 Gd $467

Mountain Rifle (w/20-inch bbl.) . . . . NiB $897 Ex $689 Gd $523
.376 Steyr . . . . NiB $887 Ex $679 Gd $513
Youth/Ladies rifle. . . . . NiB $720 Ex $689 Gd $523
For magnum calibers, add $50
For metric calibers, add $150
W/walnut stock . . . . NiB $2307 Ex $1896 Gd $1371
W/synthetic stock, add. $150

MARLIN FIREARMS CO. — formerly North Haven, Connecticut, owned by Freedom Group Inc. since 2007

MODEL 9 SEMIAUTOMATIC CARBINE
Calibers: 9mm Parabellum. 12-round magazine. 16.5-inch bbl. 35.5 inches overall. Weight: 6.75 lbs. Manual bolt hold-open. Sights: Hooded post front; adj. open rear. Walnut-finished hardwood stock w/rubber buttpad. Blued or nickel-Teflon finish. Made 1985 to 1999.
Model 9. . . . . NiB $525 Ex $387 Gd $213
Model 9N, nickel-Teflon (disc. 1994). . . NiB $475 Ex $390 Gd $146

MODEL 15Y/15YN
Bolt-action, single-shot "Little Buckaroo" rifle. Caliber: .22 Short, Long or LR. 16.25-inch bbl. Weight: 4.25 lbs. Thumb safety. Ramp front sight; adj. open rear. One-piece walnut Monte Carlo stock w/full pistol-grip. Made 1984 to 1988. Reintroduced in 1989 as Model 15YN.
Model 15Y . . . . NiB $200 Ex $130 Gd $98
Model 15YN. . . . . .NiB $215 Ex $140 Gd $110

MODEL 18 BABY SLIDE-ACTION
REPEATER . . . . NiB $1405 Ex $1105 Gd $610
Exposed hammer. Solid frame. Caliber: .22 Short, Long, LR. Tubular magazine holds 14 Short cartridges. 20-inch bbl., round or octagon. Weight: 3.75 lbs. Sights: Open rear; bead front. Plain straight-grip stock and slide handle. Made from 1906 to 1909.

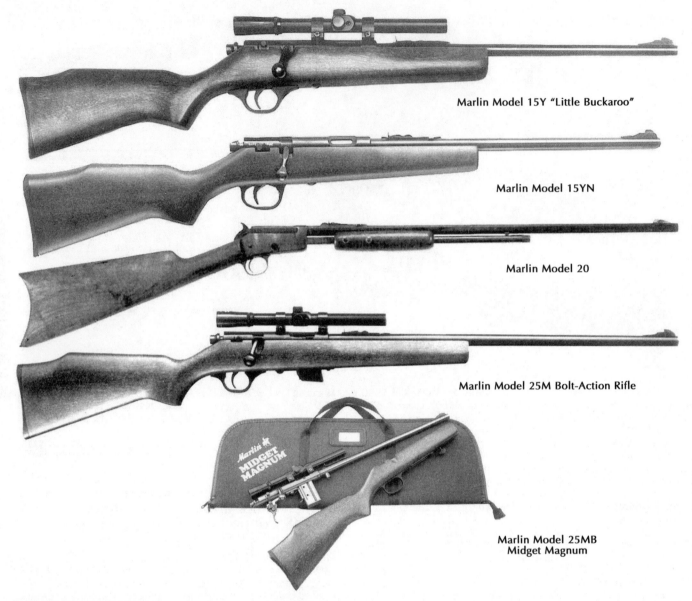

Marlin Model 15Y "Little Buckaroo"

Marlin Model 15YN

Marlin Model 20

Marlin Model 25M Bolt-Action Rifle

Marlin Model 25MB
Midget Magnum

MODEL 20 SLIDE-ACTION
REPEATING RIFLE . . . . NiB $1405 Ex $1105 Gd $605
Exposed hammer. Takedown. Caliber: .22 LR, Long, Short. Tubular magazine: Half-length holds 15 Short, 12 Long, 10 LR; full-length holds 25 Short, 20 Long, 18 LR. 24-inch octagon bbl. Weight: 5 lbs. Sights: Open rear; bead front. Plain straight-grip stock, grooved slide handle. Made from 1907 to 1922. Note: After 1920 was designated "Model 20-S."

MODEL 25MB BOLT-ACTION RIFLE . . NiB $179 Ex $110 Gd $95
Caliber: .22 Short, Long or LR; 7-round clip. 22-inch bbl. Weight: 5.5 lbs. Ramp front sight, adj. open rear. One-piece walnut Monte Carlo stock w/full pistol-grip Mar-Shield finish. Made 1984 to 1988.

MODEL 25
SLIDE-ACTION REPEATER . . . . NiB $879 Ex $540 Gd $431
Exposed hammer. Takedown. Caliber: .22 Short (also handles 22 CB caps). Tubular magazine holds 15 Short. 23-inch bbl. Weight: 4 lbs. Sights: Open rear; beaded front. Plain straight-grip stock and slide handle. Made from 1909 to 1910.
MODEL 25M BOLT ACTION W/SCOPE NiB $167 Ex $119 Gd $95

Caliber: .22 WMR. 7-round clip. 22-inch bbl. Weight: 6 lbs. Ramp front sight w/brass bead, adj. open rear. Walnut-finished stock w/Monte Carlo styling and full pistol-grip. Sling swivels. Made 1986 to 1988.

MODEL 25MB MIDGET MAGNUM . . . NiB $190 Ex $126 Gd $99
Bolt action. Caliber: .22 WMR. Seven round capacity.16.25-inch bbl. Weight: 4.75 lbs. Walnut-finished Monte Carlo-style stock w/ full pistol grip and abbreviated forend. Sights: Ramp front w/brass bead, adj. open rear. Thumb safety. Made from 1986 to 1988.

MODEL 25MG/25MN/25N/25NC BOLT-ACTION RIFLE
Caliber: .22 WMR (Model 25MN) or .22 LR. (Model 25N). Seven round clip magazine. 22-inch bbl. 41 inches overall. Weight: 5.5 to 6 lbs. Adj. open rear sight, ramp front; receiver grooved for scope mounts. One piece walnut-finished hardwood Monte Carlo stock w/pistol grip. Made from 1989 to 2003.
Model 25MG (Garden Gun) . . . . NiB $218 Ex $179 Gd $126
Model 25MN . . . . NiB $200 Ex $167 Gd $110
Model 25N. . . . . NiB $177 Ex $155 Gd $109
MODEL 25 NC (camo stock), add $50

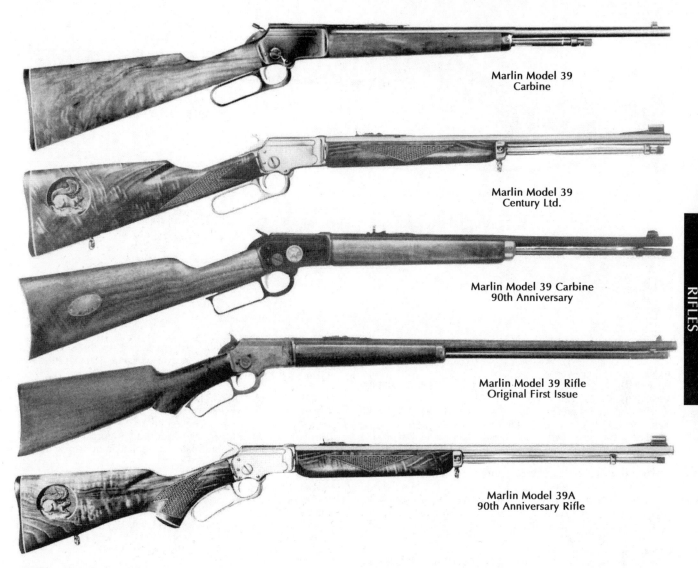

Marlin Model 39
Carbine

Marlin Model 39
Century Ltd.

Marlin Model 39 Carbine
90th Anniversary

Marlin Model 39 Rifle
Original First Issue

Marlin Model 39A
90th Anniversary Rifle

MODEL 27 SLIDE-ACTION
REPEATING RIFLE . . . . **NiB $1159 Ex $909 Gd $650**
Exposed hammer. Takedown. Calibers: .25-20, .32-20. Magazine (tubular) holds 7 rounds. 24-inch octagon bbl. Weight: 5.75 lbs. Sights: Open rear; bead front. Plain, straight-grip stock, grooved slide handle. Made from 1910 to 1916.

MODEL 27S . . . . **NiB $909 Ex $579 Gd $388**
Same as Model 27 except w/round bbl., also chambered for .25 Stevens rimfire Made from 1920 to 1932.

MODEL 29 SLIDE-ACTION REPEATER NiB $660 Ex $388 Gd $290
Similar to Model 20 w/23-inch round bbl., half magazine only, weight 5.75 lbs. Made from 1913 to 1916.

MODEL 30/30A AND 30AS LEVER-ACTION
Caliber: .30/30 Win. Six-round tubular magazine. 20-inch bbl. w/Micro-Groove rifling. 38.25 inches overall. Weight: 7 lbs. Brass bead front sight, adj. rear. Solid top receiver, offset hammer spur for scope use. Walnut-finished hardwood stock w/pistol-grip. Mar-Shield finish. Made from 1964 to 2000.
Model 30/30A . . . . **NiB $290 Ex $198 Gd $160**
Model 30AS . . . . **NiB $290 Ex $198 Gd $160**
Model 30AS w/4x scope, add **$25**
MODEL 32 SLIDE-ACTION REPEATER NiB $1154 Ex $690 Gd $533

Hammerless. Takedown. Caliber: .22 LR, Long, Short. Tubular magazine holds 15 Short, 12 Long, 10 LR; full magazine, 25 Short, 20 Long, 18 LR. 24-inch octagon bbl. Weight: 5.5 lbs. Sights: Open rear; bead front. Plain pistol-grip stock, grooved slide handle. Made from 1914 to 1915.

MODEL 36 LEVER-ACTION REPEATING CARBINE
Calibers: .30-30, .32 Special. Seven-round tubular magazine. 20-inch bbl. Weight: 6.5 lbs. Sights: Open rear; bead front. Pistol-grip stock, semibeavertail forearm w/carbine bbl. band. Early production w/ receiver, lever and hammer color casehardened and the remaining metal blued. Late production w/blued receiver. Made 1936 to 1948. Note: In 1936, this was designated "Model 1936" and was so marked on the upper tang. In 1937, the model designation was shortened to "36". An "RC" serial number suffix identifies a "Regular/Carbine".
Model 1936 CC receiver
(w/long tang, no SN prefix) . . . . **NiB $909 Ex $744 Gd $500**
Model 1936 CC receiver
(w/short tang, no SN prefix) . . . . **NiB $645 Ex $531 Gd $390**
Model 1936 CC receiver (w/SN prefix) **NiB $534 Ex $488 Gd $345**
Model 36, CC receiver (w/SN prefix). **NiB $508 Ex $433 Gd $300**
Model 36, blued receiver (w/SN prefix) **NiB $482 Ex $390 Gd $289**

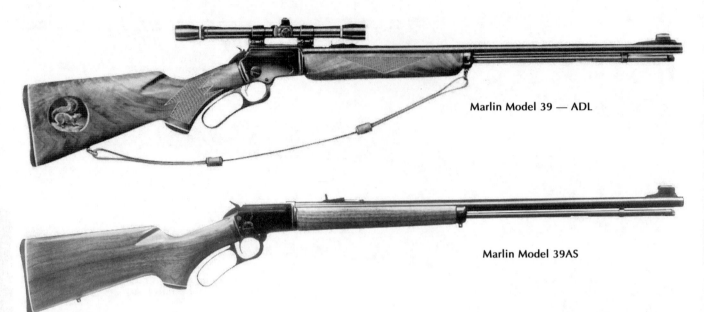

Marlin Model 39 — ADL

Marlin Model 39AS

MODEL 36 SPORTING CARBINE

Same as M36 carbine except w/6-round, (2/3 magazine) and weighs 6.25 lbs.
Model 1936, CC receiver
(w/long tang, no SN prefix) . . . . NiB $860 Ex $707 Gd $499
Model 1936, CC receiver
(w/short tang, no SN prefix) . . . . . . NiB $656 Ex $567 Gd $380
Model 1936, CC receiver (w/SN prefix)NiB $588 Ex $497 Gd $355
Model 36, CC receiver (w/SN prefix). NiB $555 Ex $457 Gd $339
Model 36, blued receiver (w/SN prefix)NiB $480 Ex $413 Gd $303

MODEL 36A/36A-DL LEVER-ACTION REPEATING RIFLE

Same as Model 36 Carbine except has 24-inch bbl. w/hooded front
sight and 2/3 magazine holding 6 cartridges. Weight: 6.75 lbs. Note:
An "A" serial number suffix identifies a Rifle while an "A-DL" suf-
fix designates a Deluxe Model w/checkered stock, semibeavertail
forearm, swivels and sling. Made from 1936 to 1948.
Model 1936, CC receiver
(w/long tang, no SN prefix) . . . . . NiB $1180 Ex $1077 Gd $790
Model 1936, CC receiver
(lw/short tang, no SN prefix) . . . . . . NiB $795 Ex $556 Gd $378
Model 1936, CC receiver (w/SN prefix)NiB $845 Ex $589 Gd $465
MODEL 36, CC receiver, (w/SN prefix)NiB $775 Ex $451 Gd $348
Model 36, blued receiver (w/SN prefix)NiB $744 Ex $440 Gd $332
ADL model, add. $25%

MODEL 37 SLIDE-ACTION

REPEATING RIFLE . . . . NiB $650 Ex $442 Gd $237
Similar to Model 29 except w/24-inch bbl. and full magazine.
Weight: 5.25 lbs. Made from 1913 to 1916.

MODEL 38 SLIDE-ACTION

REPEATING RIFLE . . . . NiB $744 Ex $418 Gd $339
Hammerless. Takedown. Caliber: .22 LR, Long, Short. 2/3 magazine (tubular) holds 15 Short, 12 Long, 10 LR. 24-inch octagon or round bbls. Weight:
5.5 lbs. Sights: Open rear; bead front. Plain shotgun-type pistol-grip buttstock w/hard rubber buttplate, grooved slide handle. Ivory bead front sight;
adj. rear. About 20,000 Model 38 rifles were made 1920 to 1930.

MODEL 39 CARBINE . . . . . . NiB $556 Ex $355 Gd $298

Same as 39M except w/lightweight bbl., 3/4 magazine (capacity: 18 Short,
14 Long, 12 LR), slimmer forearm. Weight: 5.25 lbs. Made 1963 to 1967.
MODEL 39 90TH

ANNIVERSARY CARBINE . . . NiB $1244 Ex $976 Gd $835

Carbine version of 90th Anniversary Model 39A. 500 made in 1960.
Top value is for carbine in new, unfired condition.

MODEL 39 CENTURY LTD. . . NiB $670 Ex $370 Gd $259

Commemorative version of Model 39A. Receiver inlaid w/
brass medallion, "Marlin Centennial 1870-1970." Square lever.
20-inch octagon bbl. Fancy walnut straight-grip stock and forearm; brass forend cap, buttplate, nameplate in buttstock. 35,388
made in 1970.

MODEL 39 LEVER-ACTION

REPEATER . . . . NiB $3145 Ex $1189 Gd $1018
Takedown. Casehardened receiver. Caliber: .22 LR, Long, Short.
Tubular magazine holds 25 Short, 20 Long, 18 LR. 24-inch octagon
bbl. Weight: 5.75 lbs. Sights: Open rear; bead front. Plain pistol-grip
stock and forearm. Made from 1922 to 1938.

MODEL 39A

General specifications same as Model 39 except w/blued receiver,
round bbl., heavier stock w/semibeavertail forearm, weight 6.5 lbs.
Made from 1939 to 1960.
Early model (no prefix) . . . . NiB $1500 Ex $1178 Gd $800
Late model ("B" prefix) . . . . . NiB $1166 Ex $895 Gd $650

MODEL 39A 90TH

ANNIVERSARY RIFLE . . . . . NiB $1268 Ex $1140 Gd $835
Commemorates Marlin's 90th anniversary. Same general specifications as Golden 39A except w/chrome-plated bbl. and action, stock
and forearm of select walnut-finely checkered, carved figure of a
squirrel on right side of buttstock. 500 made in 1960. Top value is
for rifle in new, unfired condition.

MODEL 39A

ARTICLE II RIFLE . . . . NiB $489 Ex $420 Gd $338
Commemorates National Rifle Association Centennial 1871-1971.
"The Right to Bear Arms" medallion inlaid in receiver. Similar to
Model 39A. Magazine capacity: 26 Short, 21 Long, 19 LR. 24-inch
octagon bbl. Fancy walnut pistol-grip stock and forearm; brass
forend cap, buttplate. 6,244 made in 1971.

Marlin Model 56

Marlin Model 57

Marlin Model 60C

Marlin Model 60SS

Marlin Model 62

GOLDEN 39A/39AS RIFLE
Same as Model 39A except w/gold-plated trigger, hooded ramp front sight, sling swivels. Made from 1960-87 (39A); Model 39AS from 1988 to date.
Golden 39A . . . . NiB $479 Ex $300 Gd $190
Golden 39AS (W/hammer block safety) NiB $479 Ex $300 Gd $190

MODEL 39A "MOUNTIE" LEVER-
ACTION REPEATING RIFLE . . . NiB $479 Ex $300 Gd $190
Same as Model 39A except w/lighter, straight-grip stock, slimmer forearm. Weight: 6.25 lbs. Made from 1953 to 1960.

MODEL 39M "MOUNTIE"
CARBINE . . . . NiB $495 Ex $300 Gd $190

MODEL 39A OCTAGON . . . . NiB $645 Ex $579 Gd $390
Same as Golden 39A except w/oct. bbl., plain bead front sight, slimmer stock and forearm, no pistol-grip cap or swivels. Made in1973. (2551 produced).

MODEL 39D . . . . NiB $440 Ex $280 Gd $200
Same as Model 39M except w/pistol-grip stock, forearm w/bbl. band. Made from 1970 to 1974.

39M ARTICLE II CARBINE. . . . NiB $488 Ex $469 Gd $300
Same as 39A Article II Rifle except w/straight-grip buttstock, square

lever, 20-inch octagon bbl., reduced magazine capacity. 3,824 units, made in 1971.

GOLDEN 39M
Calibers: .22 Short, Long and LR. Tubular magazine holds 21 Short, 16 Long or 15 LR cartridges. 20-inch bbl. 36 inches overall. Weight: 6 lbs. Gold-plated trigger. Hooded ramp front sight, adj. folding semi-buckhorn rear. Two-piece, straight-grip American black walnut stock. Sling swivels. Mar-Shield finish. Made from 1960 to 1987.
Golden 39M. . . . . NiB $445 Ex $338 Gd $266
octagonal bbl.
made 1973 only . . . . NiB $495 Ex $469 Gd $390

MODEL 39M "MOUNTIE" CARBINE
Same as Model 39A "Mountie" Rifle except w/20-inch bbl. Weight: 6 lbs. 500 made in 1960. (For values See Marlin 39 90th Anniversary Carbine)

MODEL 39TDS
CARBINE . . . . NiB $545 Ex $369 Gd $290
Same general specifications as Model 39M except takedown style w/16.5-inch bbl. and reduced magazine capacity. 32.63 inches overall. Weight: 5.25 lbs. Made from 1988 to 1995.

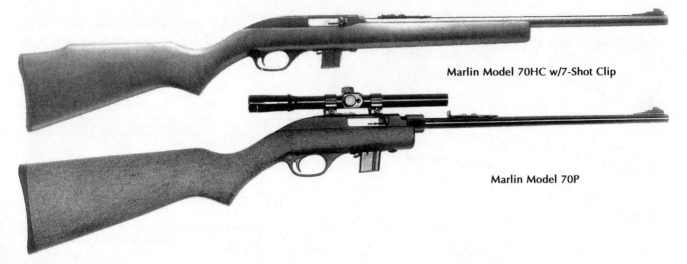

Marlin Model 70HC w/7-Shot Clip

Marlin Model 70P

MODEL 45 . . . . **NiB $390 Ex $290 Gd $198**
Semiautomatic action. Caliber: .45 Auto. Seven round clip.16.5-inch bbl. 35.5 inches overall. Weight: 6.75 lbs. Manual bolt hold-open. Sights: Ramp front sight w/brass bead, adj. folding rear. Receiver drilled and tapped for scope mount. Walnut-finished hardwood stock. Made from 1986 to 1999.

MODEL 49/49DL AUTOLOADING RIFLE
Same as Model 99C except w/two-piece stock, checkered after 1970. Made 1968-71. Model 49DL w/scrollwork on sides of receiver, checkered stock and forearm; made from 1971 to 1978.
Model 49 . . . . NiB $200 Ex $190 Gd $145
Model 49DL . . . . NiB $227 Ex $179 Gd $144

MODEL 50/50E AUTOLOADING RIFLE
Takedown. Cal.: .22 LR. Six round detachable box mag. 22 inch bbl. Wt: 6 lbs. Sights: Open rear; bead front; Mdl. 50E w/peep rear sight, hooded front. Plain pistol-grip stock, forearm w/finger grooves. Made from 1931 to 1934.
Model 50 . . . . NiB $227 Ex $190 Gd $124
Model 50E . . . . NiB $235 Ex $200 Gd $130

MODEL 56 LEVERMATIC RIFLE NiB $345 Ex $250 Gd $149
Same as Model 57 except clip-loading. Magazine holds eight rounds. Weight: 5.75 lbs. Made from 1955 to 1964.

MODEL 57 LEVERMATIC RIFLE NiB $375 Ex $227 Gd $132
Lever-action. Cal: .22 LR, 22 Long, 22 Short. Tubular mag. holds 19 LR, 21 Long, 27 Short. 22 inch bbl. Wt: 6.25 lbs. Sights: Open rear, adj. for windage and elevation; hooded ramp front. Monte Carlo-style stock w/pistol-grip. Made from 1959 to 1965.

MODEL 57M LEVERMATIC . . . NiB $415 Ex $255 Gd $148
Same as Model 57 except chambered for 22 WMR cartridge, w/24-inch bbl., 15-round magazine. Made from 1960 to 1969.

MODEL 60 SEMIAUTOMATIC RIFLE . . **NiB $227 Ex $145 Gd $90**
Caliber: .22 LR. 14-round tubular magazine. 22-inch bbl. 40.5 inches overall. Weight: 5.5 lbs. Grooved receiver. Ramp front sight w/removable hood; adj. open rear. Anodized receiver w/blued bbl. Monte Carlo-style walnut-finished hardwood stock w/Mar-Shield finish. Made 1981 to date. Note: Marketed 1960 to 1980 under Glenfield promotion logo and w/slightly different stock configuration.

MODEL 60C SELF-LOADING RIFLE . . **NiB $198 Ex $130 Gd $107**
Caliber: .22 LR. 14- round tubular mag. 22 inch Micro-Groove bbl., 40.5 inch overall. Wt: 5.5 lbs. Screw-adjustable open rear and ramp front sights. Aluminum receiver, grooved for scope mount. Hardwood Monte Carlo stock w/Mossy Oak "Break-Up" camouflage pattern. Made from 2000 to

date.

MODEL 60SS SEMIAUTOMATIC RIFLE
Same general specifications as Model 60 except w/stainless bbl. and magazine tube. Synthetic, uncheckered birch or laminated black/gray birch stock w/nickel-plated swivel studs. Made from 1993 to date.
W/uncheckered birch stock . . . . NiB $278 Ex $200 Gd $135
W/laminated birch stock . . . . NiB $270 Ex $197 Gd $126
W/fiberglass stock . . . . NiB $260 Ex $188 Gd $126

MODEL 62
LEVERMATIC RIFLE . . . . NiB $555 Ex $440 Gd $190
Lever-action. Calibers: .256 Magnum, .30 Carbine. Four round clip magazine. 23-inch bbl. Weight: 7 lbs. Sights: Open rear; hooded ramp front. Monte Carlo-style stock w/pistol-grip, swivels and sling. Made in .256 Magnum 1963 to 1966; in .30 Carbine 1963 to 1969.

MODEL 65 BOLT-ACTION
SINGLE-SHOT RIFLE . . . . NiB $139 Ex $93 Gd $70
Takedown. Caliber: .22 LR, Long, Short. 24-inch bbl. Weight: 5 lbs. Sights: Open rear; bead front. Plain pistol-grip stock w/grooved forearm. Made 1932-38. Model 65E is same as Model 65 except w/ rear peep sight and hooded front sight.

MODEL 70HC SEMIAUTOMATIC
Caliber: .22 LR. Seven and 15-round magazine. 18-inch bbl. Weight: 5.5 lbs. 36.75 inches overall. Ramp front sight; adj. open rear. Grooved receiver for scope mounts. Walnut-finished hardwood stock w/Monte Carlo and pistol-grip. Made from 1988 to 1996.
Marlin model . . . . NiB $200 Ex $155 Gd $124
Glenfield model . . . . NiB $155 Ex $126 Gd $100

MODEL 70P
SEMIAUTOMATIC . . . . NiB $290 Ex $189 Gd $100
"Papoose" takedown. Caliber: .22 LR. Seven round clip. 16.25-inch bbl. 35.25 inches overall. Weight: 3.75 lbs. Sights: Ramp front, adj. open rear. Side ejection, manual bolt hold-open. Cross-bolt safety. Walnut-finished hard-wood stock w/abbreviated forend, pistol-grip. Made 1984 to 1994.

MODEL 70PSS
SELF-LOADING CARBINE . . . NiB $338 Ex $200 Gd $175
"Papoose" takedown carbine. Caliber: .22 LR. Seven round clip. 16.25- inch bbl., 35.25 inches overall. Weight: 3.25 lbs. Ramp front and adjustable open rear sights. Automatic last-shot hold open (1996). Black fiberglass synthetic stock. Made from 1995 to date.

Marlin Model 75C

Marlin Model 80C

Marlin Model 80DL

Marlin Model 81DL

MODEL 75C
SEMIAUTOMATIC . . . . **NiB $233 Ex $158 Gd $109**
Caliber: .22 LR. 13-round tubular magazine.18-inch bbl. 36.5 inches overall. Weight: 5 lbs. Side ejection. Cross-bolt safety. Sights: Ramp-mounted blade front; adj. open rear. Monte Carlo-style walnut-finished hardwood stock w/pistol-grip. Made 1975 to 1992.

MODEL 80 BOLT-ACTION REPEATING RIFLE
Takedown. Caliber: .22 LR, Long, Short. Eight round detachable box magazine. 24-inch bbl. Weight: 6 lbs. Sights: Open rear; bead front. Plain pistol-grip stock. Made from 1934 to 1939. Model 80E, w/ peep rear sight; hooded front, made from 1934 to 1940.
Model 80 Standard . . . . **NiB $190 Ex $135 Gd $95**
Model 80E . . . . **NiB $175 Ex $110 Gd $85**

MODEL 80C/80DL
BOLT-ACTION REPEATER
Improved version of Model 80. Model 80C w/bead from sight, semibeavertail forearm; made 1940-70. Model 80DL w/peep rear sight; hooded blade front sight on ramp, swivels; made 1940 to 1965.
Model 80C . . . . **NiB $200 Ex $155 Gd $100**
Model 80DL . . . . **NiB $167 Ex $110 Gd $90**
MODEL 81/81E BOLT-ACTION REPEATER
Takedown. .22 LR, Long, Short. Tubular magazine holds 24 Short, 20 Long, 18 LR. 24-inch bbl. Weight: 6.25 lbs. Sights: Open rear, bead front. Plain pistol-grip stock. Made from 1937 to 1940. Model 81E w/peep rear sight; hooded front w/ramp.
Model 81 . . . . **NiB $220 Ex $176 Gd $110**
Model 81E . . . . **NiB $245 Ex $195 Gd $139**

MODEL 81C/81DL BOLT-ACTION REPEATER
Improved version of Model 81 w/same general specifications. Model 81C w/bead front sight, semibeavertail forearm; made 1940 to 1970. Model 81 DL w/peep rear sight, hooded front, swivels; disc. 1965.
Model 81C . . . . **NiB $239 Ex $188 Gd $100**
Model 81DL . . . . **NiB $220 Ex $199 Gd $110**

MODEL 88-C/88-DL TAKEDOWN RIFLE
Takedown. Caliber: .22 LR. Tubular magazine in buttstock holds 14 cartridges. 24-inch bbl. Weight: 6.75 lbs. Sights: Open rear; hooded front. Plain pistol-grip stock. Made from 1947-56. Model 88-DL w/received peep sight, checkered stock and sling swivels, made 1953 to 1956.
Model 88-C . . . . **NiB $200 Ex $145 Gd $100**
Model 88-DL . . . . **NiB $200 Ex $145 Gd $100**

Marlin Model 93 Musket

Marlin Model 93 Lever Action

Marlin Model 94 Sporting Carbine

MODEL 89C/89DL AUTOLOADING RIFLE
Clip magazine version of Model 88-C. Seven round clip (12-round in later models); other specifications same. Made from 1950 to 1961. Model 89-DL w/receiver peep sight, sling swivels.
Model 89-C . . . . NiB $200 Ex $145 Gd $100
Model 89-DL . . . . NiB $210 Ex $150 Gd $105

MODEL 92 LEVER-ACTION REPEATING RIFLE
Calibers: .22 Short, Long, LR. .32 Short, Long (rimfire or center-fire by changing firing pin). Tubular magazines holding 25 Short, 20 Long, 18 LR (.22); or 17 Short, 14 Long (.32); 16-inch bbl. model w/shorter magazine holding 15 Short, 12 Long, 10 LR. Bbl. lengths: 16 (.22 cal. only) 24, 26, 28 inches. Weight: 5.5 lbs. w/24-inch bbl. Sights: open rear; blade front. Plain straight-grip stock and forearm. Made 1892 to 1916. Note: Originally designated "Model 1892."
Model 92 (.22 caliber) . . . . NiB $1598 Ex $1400 Gd $883
Model 92 (.32 caliber) . . . . NiB $1554 Ex $1268 Gd $956

MODEL 93/93SC CARBINE
Same as Standard Model 93 Rifle except in calibers .30-30 and .32 Special only. Model 93 w/7-round magazine. 20-inch round bbl., carbine sights, weight: 6.75 lbs. Model 93SC magazine capacity 5 rounds, weight 6.5 lbs.
Model 93 Carbine (w/saddle ring) NiB $1689 Ex $1423 Gd $1108
Model 93 Carbine "Bull's-Eye
(w/o saddle ring) . . . . NiB $1449 Ex $1188 Gd $976
Model 93SC Sporting Carbine. . . . NiB $1377 Ex $1087 Gd $915

MODEL 93 LEVER-ACTION
REPEATING RIFLE . . . . . . NiB $2833 Ex $2022 Gd $1370
Solid frame or takedown. Calibers: .25-36 Marlin, .30-30, .32 Special, .32-40, .38-55. Tubular magazine holds 10 cartridges. 26-inch round or octagon bbl. standard; also made w/28-, 30- and 32-inch bbls. Weight: 7.25 lbs. Sights: Open rear; bead front. Plain straight-grip stock and forearm. Made from 1893 to 1936. Note: Before 1915 designated "Model 1893."

MODEL 93 MUSKET. . . . . NiB $5610 Ex $ 3766 Gd $2833
Same as Standard Model 93 except w/30-inch bbl., angular bayonet, ramrod under bbl., musket stock, full-length military-style forearm. Weight: 8 lbs. Made from 1893 to 1915.

MODEL 94 LEVER-ACTION
REPEATING RIFLE . . . . . .NiB $2655 Ex $1840 Gd $989
Solid frame or takedown. Calibers: .25-20, .32-20, .38-40, .44-40. 10-round tubular magazine. 24-inch round or octagon bbl. Weight: 7 lbs. Sights open rear; bead front. Plain straight-grip stock and forearm (also available w/pistol-grip stock). Made from 1894 to 1934. Note: Before 1906 designated "Model 1894."

MODEL 94 LEVER-ACTION COWBOY SERIES
Calibers: .357 Mag., .44-40, .44 Mag., .45 LC. 10-round magazine. 24-inch tapered octagon bbl. Weight: 7.5 lbs. 41.5 inches overall. Marble carbine front sight, adjustable semi-buckhorn rear. Blue finish. Checkered, straight-grip American black walnut stock w/hard rubber buttplate. Made from 1996 to date. Cowboy II introduced in 1997.
Cowboy model (.45 LC) . . . . NiB $833 Ex $650 Gd $466
Cowboy II model
(.357 Mag., .44-40, .44 Mag.). . . . . . NiB $854 Ex $659 Gd $572

MODEL 97 LEVER-ACTION
REPEATING RIFLE . . . . . . NiB $2590 Ex $2066 Gd $1269
Takedown. Caliber: .22 LR, Long, Short. Tubular magazine; full length holds 25 Short, 20 Long, 18 LR; half length holds 16 Short, 12 Long and 10 LR. Bbl. lengths: 16, 24, 26, 28 inches. Weight: 6 lbs. Sights: Open rear; bead front. Plain, straight-grip stock and forearm (also avail. w/pistol-grip stock). Made from 1897 to 1922. Note: Before 1905 designated "Model 1897."

MODEL 98 AUTOLOADING RIFLE . . NiB $255 Ex $138 Gd $100
Solid frame. Caliber: .22 LR. Tubular magazine holds 15 cartridges. 22-inch bbl. Weight: 6.75 lbs. Sights: Open rear; hooded ramp front. Monte Carlo stock w/cheekpiece. Made from 1950 to 1961.

MODEL 99 AUTOLOADING RIFLE . . NiB $255 Ex $138 Gd $100
Caliber: .22 LR. Tubular magazine holds 18 cartridges. 22-inch bbl. Weight: 5.5 lbs. Sights: Open rear; hooded ramp front. Plain pistol-grip stock. Made from 1959 to 1961.

MODEL 99C. . . . . NiB $209 Ex $177 Gd $119
Same as Model 99 except w/gold-plated trigger, receiver grooved for tip-off scope mounts, Monte Carlo stock (checkered in later production). Made from 1962 to 1978.

MODEL 99DL. . . . . NiB $266 Ex $255 Gd $144
Same as Model 99 except w/gold-plated trigger, jeweled breech bolt, Monte Carlo stock w/pistol-grip, swivels and sling. Made 1960 to 1965.

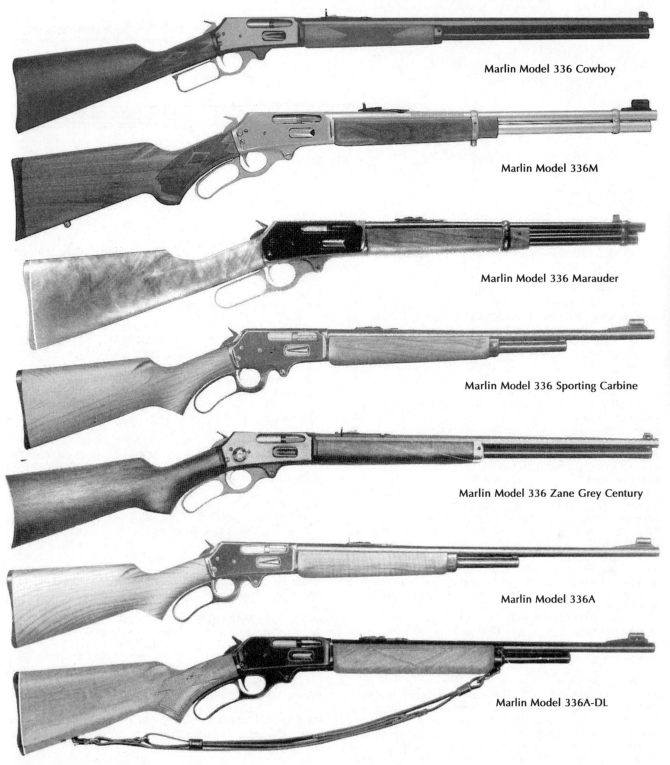

Marlin Model 336 Cowboy

Marlin Model 336M

Marlin Model 336 Marauder

Marlin Model 336 Sporting Carbine

Marlin Model 336 Zane Grey Century

Marlin Model 336A

Marlin Model 336A-DL

RIFLES

MODEL 100 BOLT-ACTION
SINGLE-SHOT RIFLE . . . . **NiB $200 Ex $123 Gd $90**
Takedown. Caliber: .22 LR, Long, Short. 24-inch bbl. Weight: 4.5 lbs. Sights: Open rear; bead front. Plain pistol-grip stock. Made 1936 to 1960.

MODEL 100SB . . . . **NiB $120 Ex $90 Gd $65**
Same as Model 100 except smoothbore for use w/22 shot cartridges, shotgun sight. Made from 1936 to 1941.

MODEL 99M1 CARBINE . . . . **NiB $200 Ex $99 Gd $80**
Same as Model 99C except styled after U.S. .30 M1 Carbine; 9-round tubular magazine, 18-inch bbl. Sights: Open rear; military-style ramp front; carbine stock w/handguard and bbl. band, sling swivels. Weight: 4.5 lbs. Made 1966 to 1979.

GRADING: **NiB** = New in Box **Ex** = Excellent or NRA 95% **Gd** = Good or NRA 68%

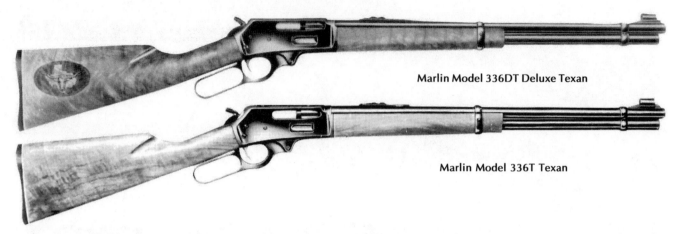

Marlin Model 336DT Deluxe Texan

Marlin Model 336T Texan

MODEL 100 TOM MIX SPECIAL . . . . NiB $315 Ex $200 Gd $146
Same as Model 100 except w/peep rear sight; hooded front; sling. Made from 1936 to 1946.

MODEL 101 . . . . NiB $100 Ex $75 Gd $55
Improved version of Model 100 w/same general specifications, except w/stock w/beavertail forearm, weighs 5 lbs. Intro. 1951. Disc.

MODEL 101 DL . . . . NiB $119 Ex $85 Gd $70
Same as Model 101 except has peep rear sight; hooded front, swivels. Disc.

MODEL 122 SINGLE-SHOT
JUNIOR TARGET RIFLE. . . . . . . NiB $135 Ex $95 Gd $75
Bolt action. Caliber: .22 LR, .22 Long, .22 Short. 22-inch bbl. Weight: 5 lbs. Sights: Open rear; hooded ramp front. Monte Carlo stock w/pistol-grip, swivels, sling. Made from 1961 to 1965.

MODEL 322 BOLT-ACTION
VARMINT RIFLE. . . . . NiB $597 Ex $390 Gd $278
Sako short Mauser action. Caliber: .222 Rem. Three round clip magazine. 24-inch medium weight bbl. Checkered stock. Sights: Two-position peep rear; hooded ramp front. Weight: 7.5 lbs. Made from 1954-57.

MODEL 336A
LEVER-ACTION RIFLE. . . . . . NiB $570 Ex $400 Gd $338
Improved version of Model 36A Rifle w/same general specifications except w/improved action w/round breech bolt. Calibers: .30-30, .32 Special (disc. 1963), .35 Rem. (intro. 1952). Made from 1948-63; reintroduced 1973, disc. 1980.

MODEL 336A-DL . . . . NiB $665 Ex $544 Gd $351
Same as Model 336A Rifle except w/deluxe checkered stock and forearm, swivels and sling. Made from 1948-63.

MODEL 336AS
LEVER-ACTION RIFLE. . . . . . NiB $475 Ex $291 Gd $139
Similar to Model 30AS. Caliber: .30-30 Win., Six round tubular magazine. 20- inch Micro-Groove bbl. 38.25 inches overall. Weight: 7 lbs. Maine birch pistol grip stock w/swivel studs and hard rubber butt plate. Tapped for scope mount and receiver sight. Screw-adjustable open rear and ramp front sight. Checkered walnut finish. Made from 1999 to date.

MODEL 336C
LEVER-ACTION CARBINE. . . . NiB $559 Ex $398 Gd $290
Improved version of Model 36 Carbine w/same general specifications except w/improved action w/round breech bolt. Original calibers: .30-30 and .32 Win. Spec. Made from 1948-83. Note: Caliber .35 Rem. intro. 1953. Caliber .32 Winchester Special disc. 1963.

MODEL 336 COWBOY
LEVER-ACTION RIFLE. . . . . . NiB $600 Ex $445 Gd $380
Calibers: .30-30 Win., or .38-55 Win., 6- round tubular magazine. 24- inch tapered octagon bbl. 42.5 inches overall. Weight: 7.5 lbs. American black walnut checkering stock. Marble carbine front sight w/solid top receiver drilled and tapped for scope mount. Mar-Shield finish. Made from 1998 to date.

MODEL 336CS
W/SCOPE. . . . . NiB $479 Ex $338 Gd $266
Lever-action w/hammer block safety. Caliber: .30/30 Win. or .35 Rem. Six round tubular magazine. 20-inch round bbl. w/Micro-Groove rifling. 38.5 inches overall. Weight: 7 lbs. Ramp front sight w/hood, adj. semi-buckhorn folding rear. Solid top receiver drilled and tapped for scope mount or receiver sight; offset hammer spur for scope use. American black walnut stock w/pistol-grip, fluted comb. Mar-Shield finish. Made from 1984 to date.

MODEL 336DT
DELUXE TEXAN . . . . NiB $500 Ex $466 Gd $359
Same as Model 336T except w/select walnut stock and forearm, hand-carved longhorn steer and map of Texas on buttstock. Made 1962 to 1964.

MODEL 336M
LEVER-ACTION RIFLE. . . . . . NiB $590 Ex $495 Gd $359
Calibers: .30-30 Win., 6- round tubular magazine. 20- inch stainless steel Micro Groove bbl., 38.5 inches overall. Weight: 7 lbs. American black walnut w/checkered pistol-grip stock. Adjustable folding semi-buckhorn rear and ramp front sight w/brass bead and removable Wide-Scan hood. Tapped for receiver sight and scope mount. Mar-Shield finish. Made from 1999 to date.

MODEL 336 MARAUDER . . . . NiB $600 Ex $485 Gd $300
Same as Model 336 Texan Carbine except w/16.25-inch bbl., weight: 6.25 lbs. Made from 1963 to 1964.

MODEL 336-MICRO GROOVE ZIPPER NiB $845 Ex $633 Gd $390
General specifications same as Model 336 Sporting Carbine except caliber .219 Zipper. Made from 1955 to 1961.

MODEL 336 OCTAGON. . . . . NiB $570 Ex $498 Gd $300
Same as Model 336T except chambered for .30-30 only w/22-inch octagon bbl. Made in 1973.

MODEL 336 SPORTING CARBINE . . NiB $845 Ex $589 Gd $445
Same as Model 336A rifle except w/20-inch bbl., weight: 6.25 lbs. Made from 1948 to 1963.

MODEL 336T TEXAN CARBINE . . . . NiB $369 Ex $277 Gd $228
Same as Model 336 Carbine except w/straight-grip stock and is not available in caliber .32 Special. Made 1953-83. Caliber .44 Magnum made 1963 to 1967.

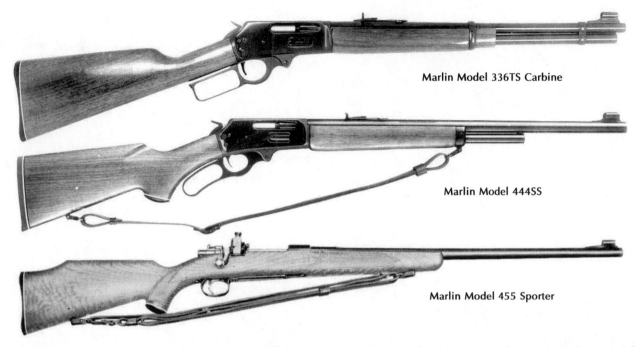

Marlin Model 336TS Carbine

Marlin Model 444SS

Marlin Model 455 Sporter

MODEL 336TS . . . . **NiB $400 Ex $333 Gd $190**
Lever-action w/hammer-block safety. Caliber: .30-30 Win. Six round tubular magazine. 18.5-inch Micro-Groove bbl. 37 inches overall. Weight: 6.5 lbs. Ramp front sight, adj. semi-buckhorn folding rear. Straight-grip American black walnut stock. Made 1983 to 1987.

MODEL 336 ZANE
GREY CENTURY . . . . **NiB $488 Ex $439 Gd $300**
Similar to Model 336A except w/22-inch octagonal bbl., caliber .30-30, Zane Grey Centennial 1872-1972 medallion inlaid in receiver; select walnut stock w/classic pistol-grip and forearm; brass buttplate, forend cap. Weight: 7 lbs. 10,000 produced (numbered ZG1 through ZG10,000). Made in 1972.

MODEL 444 LEVER-ACTION
REPEATING RIFLE . . . . **NiB $482 Ex $390 Gd $235**
Action similar to Model 336. Caliber: .444 Marlin. Four round tubular magazine. 24-inch bbl. Weigh: 7.5 lbs. Sights: Open rear; hooded ramp front. Monte Carlo stock w/straight grip, recoil pad. Carbine-style forearm w/bbl. band. Swivels, sling. Made from 1965 to 1971.

MARLIN MODEL 444 SPORTER . . . . **NiB $576 Ex $445 Gd $235**
Same as Model 444 Rifle except w/22-inch bbl., pistol-grip stock and forearm as on Model 336A, recoil pad, QD swivels and sling. Made from 1972 to 1983.

MODEL 444P (OUTFITTER)
LEVER-ACTION RIFLE . . . . . . **NiB $559 Ex $447 Gd $255**
Caliber: .444 Marlin. Five round tubular magazine. 18.5-inch ported bbl., 37 inches overall. Weight: 6.75 lbs. Ramp front and adjustable folding rear sights. Black walnut straight grip stock w/cut checkering and Mar-Shield finish. Made from 1999 to 2002.

MODEL 444SS . . . . **NiB $570 Ex $449 Gd $240**
Same general specifications as Model 444 except w/hammer safety. Made from 1984-2002. (Changed to M444 in 2001.)

MODEL 455 BOLT-ACTION SPORTER
FN Mauser action w/Sako trigger. Calibers: .30-06 or .308. Five round box magazine. 24-inch medium weight stainless-steel bbl.

Monte Carlo stock w/cheekpiece, checkered pistol grip and forearm. Lyman No. 48 receiver sight; hooded ramp front. Weight: 8.5 lbs. Made from 1957 to 1959.
.30-06 Spfd., 1079 produced . . . . . . **NiB $707 Ex $535 Gd $325**
.308 Win., 59 produced . . . . **NiB $800 Ex $610 Gd $475**

MODEL 780 BOLT-ACTION REPEATER SERIES
Caliber: .22 LR, Long, Short. Seven round clip magazine. 22-inch bbl. Weight: 5.5 to 6 lbs. Sights: Open rear; hooded ramp front. Receiver grooved for scope mounting. Monte Carlo stock w/checkered pistol-grip and forearm. Made from 1971 to 1988.
Standard model . . . . **NiB $145 Ex $100 Gd $85**
W/17-round tubular mag. . . . . **NiB $145 Ex $100 Gd $85**
.22 WMR w/swivels, sling. . . . . **NiB $145 Ex $100 Gd $85**
W/12-round tubular mag. . . . . **NiB $145 Ex $100 Gd $85**

MODEL 795 SELF-LOADING RIFLE. . **NiB $167 Ex $130 Gd $115**
Caliber: .22 LR. 10- round clip. 18- inch Micro-Groove bbl., 37 inches overall. Weight: 5 lbs. Screw-adjustable open rear and ramp front sight. Monte Carlo synthetic stock with checkering swivel studs. Made from 1999 to date.

MODEL 880/881/882/883 BOLT-ACTION REPEATER SERIES
Caliber: .22 rimfire. Seven round magazine. 22-inch bbl. 41 inches overall. Weight: 5.5 to 6 lbs. Hooded ramp front sight; adj. folding rear. Grooved receiver for scope mounts. Checkered Monte Carlo-style walnut stock w/QD studs and rubber recoil pad. Made from 1989 to 1997.
.22 LR . . . . **NiB $220 Ex $177 Gd $115**
Stainless .22 LR . . . . **NiB $269 Ex $200 Gd $150**
Squirrel .22 LR . . . . **NiB $269 Ex $223 Gd $160**
Model 881 W/7-round tubular magazine . . **NiB $244 Ex $175 Gd $110**
Model 882 (.22 WMR) . . . . **NiB $235 Ex $189 Gd $115**
W/laminated hardwood stock . . . . **NiB $277 Ex $189 Gd $120**
Stainless w/Fire sights . . . . **NiB $290 Ex $222 Gd $167**
Stainless .22 LR . . . . **NiB $195 Ex $227 Gd $170**
Model 883
(.22 WMR w/12-round tubular mag.). **NiB $235 Ex $179 Gd $120**
W/nickel-Teflon finish . . . . **NiB $279 Ex $226 Gd $180**
Stainless w/laminated stock. . . . . **NiB $297 Ex $200 Gd $177**

Marlin Model 780

Marlin Model 781

Marlin Model 783

Marlin Model 882L

Marlin Model 883N

MODEL 922 MAGNUM
SELF-LOADING RIFLE. . . . . . . NiB $390 Ex $244 Gd $160
Similar to Model 9 except chambered for .22 WMR. Seven round magazine. 20.5-inch bbl. 39.5 inches overall. Weight: 6.5 lbs. American black walnut stock w/Monte Carlo. Blued finish. Made from 1993 to 2001.

MODEL 980 .22 MAGNUM . . NiB $290 Ex $167 Gd $135
Bolt action. Caliber: .22 WMR. Eight round clip magazine. 24-inch bbl. Weight: 6 lbs. Sights: Open rear; hooded ramp front. Monte Carlo stock, swivels, sling. Made from 1962 to 1970.

MODEL 989 AUTOLOADING RIFLE . NiB $210 Ex $144 Gd $110
Caliber: .22 LR. Seven round clip magazine. 22-inch bbl. Weight: 5.5 lbs. Sights: Open rear; hooded ramp front. Monte Carlo walnut stock w/pistol grip. Made from 1962 to 1966.

MODEL 989M2
CARBINE . . . . NiB $250 Ex $145 Gd $100
Same as Model 99M1 except clip-loading, 7-round magazine. Made from 1966- to 199.

MODEL 990 SEMIAUTOMATIC
Caliber: .22 LR. 17-round tubular magazine. 22-inch bbl. 40.75 inches overall. Weight: 5.5 lbs. Side ejection. Cross-bolt safety. Ramp front sight w/brass bead; adj. semi-buckhorn folding rear. Receiver grooved for scope mount. Monte Carlo-style American black walnut stock w/checkered pistol grip and forend. Made from 1979 to 1987.
Model 990 Semiautomatic . . . . NiB $135 Ex $100 Gd $85
W/14-round mag,
laminated hardwood stock, QD swivels, black recoil pad.
Made 1992 to date) . . . . NiB $208 Ex $155 Gd $110

Marlin Model 980

Marlin Model 989

Marlin Model 989M2

Marlin Model 990

Marlin Model 990L

Marlin Model 995

RIFLES

MODEL 995 SEMIAUTOMATIC NiB $233 Ex $167 Gd $110
Caliber: .22 LR. Seven round clip magazine.18-inch bbl. 36.75 inches overall. Weight: 5 lbs. Cross-bolt safety. Sights: Ramp front w/brass bead; adj. folding semi-buckhorn rear. Monte Carlo-style American black walnut stock w/checkered pistol grip and forend. Made from 1979 to 1994.

MODEL 1870-1970 CENTENNIAL MATCHED PAIR, MODELS 336 AND 39. . . . NiB $2230 Ex $1766 Gd $1180
Presentation-grade rifles in luggage-style case. Matching serial numbers. Fancy walnut straight-grip buttstock and forearm brass buttplate and forend cap. Engraved receiver w/inlaid medallion; square lever. 20-inch octagon bbl. Model 336: .30-30, 7-round capacity; weight: 7 lbs. Model 39: .22 Short, Long, LR, tubular mag

azine holds 21 Short, 16 Long, 15 LR. 1,000 sets produced. Made in 1970. Top value is for rifles in new, unfired condition. See illustration on page 284.

MODEL 1892 LEVER-ACTION RIFLE
See Marlin Model 92 listed previously under this section.

MODEL 1893 LEVER-ACTION RIFLE
See Marlin Model 93 listed previously under this section.

MODEL 1894 LEVER-ACTION RIFLE
See Marlin Model 94 Lever-Action Rifle listed previously under this section.

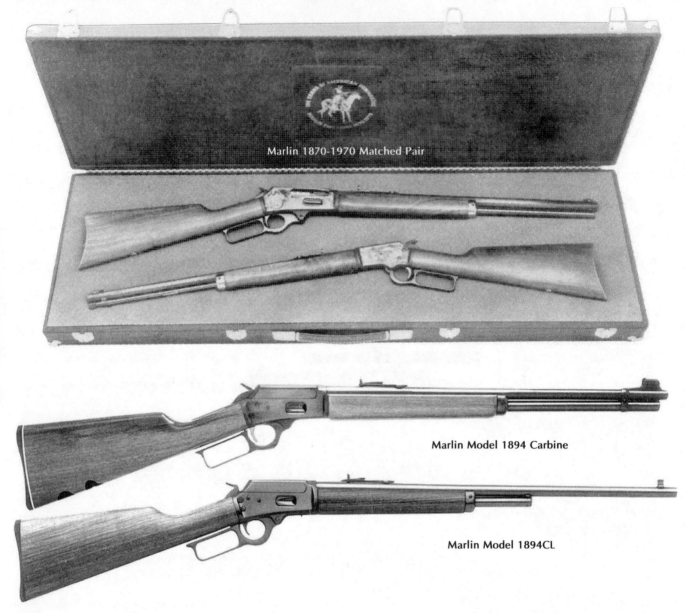

Marlin 1870-1970 Matched Pair

Marlin Model 1894 Carbine

Marlin Model 1894CL

MODEL 1894 CARBINE
Replica of original Model 94. Caliber: .44 Rem. 10-round magazine. 20-inch round bbl. Weight: 6 lbs. Sight: Open rear; ramp front. Straight-grip stock. Made from 1969 to 1984.
MODEL 1894 CARBINE . . . . **NiB $415 Ex $300 Gd $245**
Octagon bbl. (made 1973) . . . . **NiB $525 Ex $390 Gd $239**
Sporter model
(w/22-inch bbl. made 1973) . . . . . . **NiB $585 Ex $369 Gd $345**

MODEL 1894CL
CLASSIC. . . . . **NiB $743 Ex $545 Gd $355**
Calibers: .218 Bee, .25-20 Win., .32-20 Win. Six round tubular magazine. 22-inch bbl. 38.75 inches overall. Weight: 6.25 lbs. Adj. semibuckhorn folding rear sight, brass bead front. Receiver tapped for scope mounts. Straight-grip American black walnut stock w/Mar-Shield finish. Made from 1988 to 1994.
MODEL 1894CS LEVER-ACTION. . . . . **NiB $779 Ex $545 Gd $369**
Caliber: .357 Magnum, .38 Special. Nine round tubular

magazine. 18.5-inch bbl. 36 inches overall. Weight: 6 lbs. Side ejection. Hammer block safety. Square finger lever. Bead front sight, adj. semi-buckhorn folding rear. Offset hammer spur for scope use. Two-piece straight grip American black walnut stock w/white buttplate spacer. Mar-Shield finish. Made from 1984 to 2002.

MODEL 1894M LEVER-ACTION . . . . **NiB $495 Ex $443 Gd $233**
Caliber: .22 WMR.11-round tubular magazine. 20-inch bbl. Weight: 6.25 lbs. Sights: Ramp front w/brass bead and Wide-Scan hood; adj. semi-buckhorn folding rear. Offset hammer spur for scope use. Straight-grip American black walnut stock w/white buttplate spacer. Squared finger lever. Made from 1986 to 1988.

MODEL 1894S LEVER-ACTION. . . . . . **NiB $522 Ex $347 Gd $245**
Calibers: .41 Mag., .44 Rem. Mag., .44 S&W Special, .45 Colt.10-shot tubular magazine. 20-inch bbl.37.5 inches overall. Weight: 6 lbs. Sights and stock same as Model 1894M. Made 1984 to 2002.

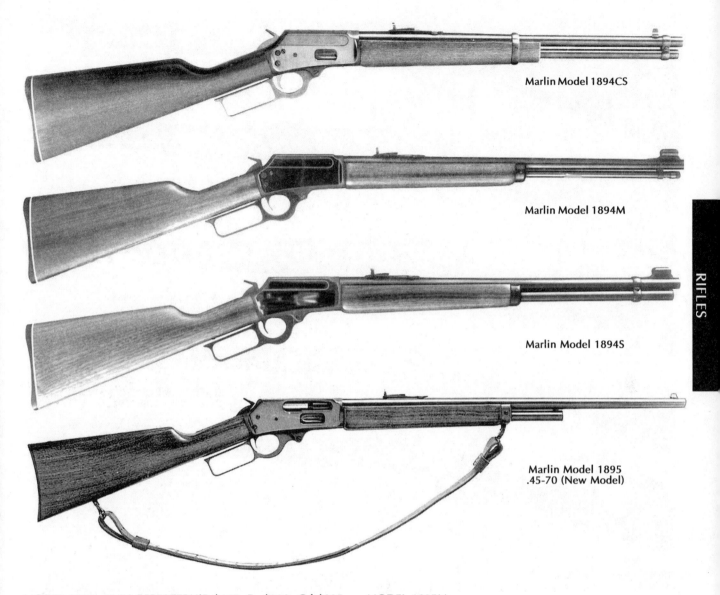

Marlin Model 1894CS

Marlin Model 1894M

Marlin Model 1894S

Marlin Model 1895
.45-70 (New Model)

RIFLES

MODEL 1895 .45-70 REPEATERNiB $445 Ex $390 Gd $235
Model 336-type action. Caliber: .45-70 Government. Four round magazine. 22-inch bbl. Weight: 7 lbs. Sights: Open rear; bead front. Straight-grip stock, forearm w/metal end cap, QD swivels, leather sling. Made 1972 to 1979.

MODEL 1895
LEVER-ACTION REPEATER . . . NiB $447 Ex $393 Gd $236
Solid frame or takedown. Calibers: .33 WCF, .38-56, .40-65, .40-70, .40-82, .45-70. Nine round tubular magazine. 24-inch round or octagongon bbl. standard (other lengths available). Weight: 8 lbs. Sights: Open rear; bead front. Plain stock and forearm (also available w/pistol-grip stock). Made 1895 to 1915.

MODEL 1895G (GUIDE GUN)
LEVER-ACTION RIFLE. . . . . . NiB $590 Ex $389 Gd $280
Caliber: .45-70 Govt., 4- round magazine. 18.5-inch ported bbl., 37 inches overall. Weight: 6.75 lbs. Ramp front and adjustable folding rear sights. Black walnut straight grip stock w/cut checkering and Mar-Shield finish. 2,500 made starting in 1998.

MODEL 1895M
LEVER-ACTION RIFLE. . . . . . NiB $448 Ex $290 Gd $144
Caliber: .450 Marlin. Four round tubular magazine., 18.5- inch ported bbl. w/Ballard-type rifling. 37 inches overall. Weight: 6.75 lbs. Genuine American black walnut straight-grip stock w/checkering. Ventilated recoil pad. Adjustable folding semi-buckhorn rear and ramp front sights. Mar-Shield finish. Made 2000 to date. Model 1895GBL (big loop). . . . . NiB $595 Ex $340 Gd $165

MODEL 1895SS
LEVER-ACTION . . . . NiB $609 Ex $448 Gd $356
Caliber: .45-70 Govt. Four round tubular magazine. 22-inch bbl. w/Micro-Groove rifling. 40.5 inches overall. Weight: 7.5 lbs. Ramp front sight w/brass bead and Wide-Scan hood; adj. semi-buckhorn folding rear. Solid top receiver tapped for scope mount or receiver sight. Off-set hammer spur for scope use. Two-piece American black walnut stock w/fluted comb, pistol-grip, sling swivels. Made 1984 to date. (Changed to M1895 in 2001.)

MODEL 1897 LEVER-ACTION RIFLE
See Marlin Model 97 listed previously under this section.

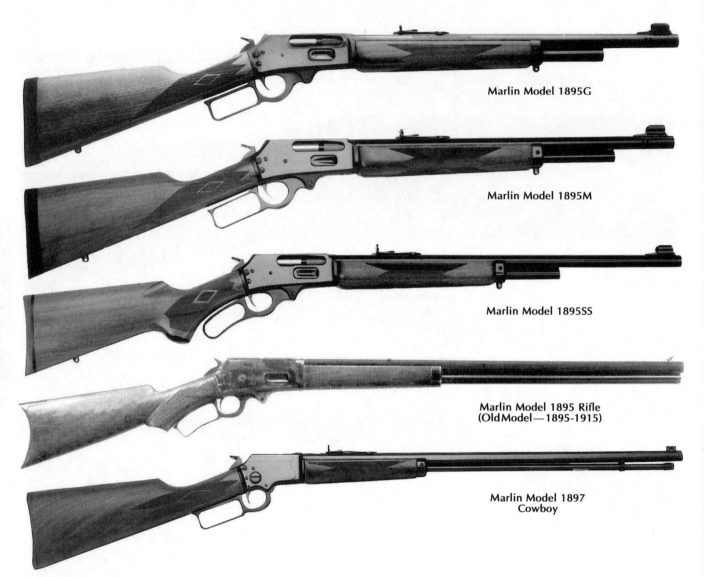

Marlin Model 1895G

Marlin Model 1895M

Marlin Model 1895SS

Marlin Model 1895 Rifle
(Old Model—1895-1915)

Marlin Model 1897
Cowboy

MODEL 1897 COWBOY
LEVER-ACTION RIFLE . . . . **NiB $643 Ex $489 Gd $369**
Caliber: .22 LR., capacity: 19 LR, 21 L, or 26 S, tubular magazine. 24-inch tapered octagon bbl., 40 inches overall. Weight: 6.5 lbs. Marble front and adjustable rear sight, tapped for scope mount. Black walnut straight grip stock w/cut checkering and Mar-Shield finish. Made from 1999 to 2001.

MODEL 1936 LEVER-ACTION CARBINE
See Marlin Model 36 listed previously under this section.

MODEL 2000 TARGET RIFLE
Bolt-action single-shot. Caliber: .22 LR. Optional 5-round adapter kit available. 22-inch bbl. 41 inches overall. Weight: 8 lbs. Globe front sight, adj. peep or aperture rear. two-stage target trigger. Textured composite Kevlar or black/gray laminated stock. Made from 1991 to 1995.
MODEL 2000 TARGET RIFLE . . . . . . **NiB $590 Ex $479 Gd $338**
W/adj. comb (made 1994 only) . . . . . **NiB $643 Ex $522 Gd $355**
W/laminated stock (intro. 1996) . . . . **NiB $654 Ex $535 Gd $429**

MODEL 7070

Caliber: .22 LR. 10-round magazine. 18-inch bbl. Weight: 5.5 lbs. Synthetic stocks. No sights; receiver grooved for scope. Semi-auto. Side ejection. Manual bolt hold-open. Cross-bolt safety. Matte finish. Made from 1997 to 2001.
Model 7070 . . . . **NiB $255 Ex $190 Gd $146**
Model 7070T . . . . **NiB $390 Ex $290 Gd $220**

MODEL A-1
AUTOLOADING RIFLE . . . . **NiB $185 Ex $110 Gd $90**
Takedown. Caliber: .22 LR. Six round detachable box magazine. 24-inch bbl. Weight: 6 lbs. Open rear sight. Plain pistol-grip stock. Made from 1935 to 1946.

MODEL A-1C
AUTOLOADING RIFLE . . . . **NiB $185 Ex $110 Gd $90**
Improved version of Model A-1 w/same general specifications, stock w/semibeavertail forend. Made from 1940 to 1946.

MODEL A-1DL . . . . **NiB $185 Ex $110 Gd $90**
Same as Model A-1C above, except w/peep rear sight; hooded front, swivels.

Marlin Model 2000

Marlin Model 2000L

Marlin Model 7000

Marlin Model 7000T

MODEL A-1E . . . . NiB $190 Ex $126 Gd $95
Same as Model A-1 except w/peep rear sight; hooded front.

MODEL MR-7 BOLT-ACTION
RIFLE . . . . NiB $555 Ex $380 Gd $277
Calibers: .25-06 Rem., .270 Win., .280 Rem., .308 Win. or .30-06.
Four round magazine. 22-inch bbl. w/ or w/o sights. 43.31 inches
overall. Weight: 7.5 lbs. Checkered American walnut or birch stock
w/recoil pad and sling-swivel studs. Jeweled bolt w/cocking indica-
tor and 3-position safety. Made from 1996 to 1999.
W/birch stock, intro. 1998 . . . . NiB $460 Ex $379 Gd $255
W/open sights, add. $50

MODEL 10. . . . . NiB $140 Ex $110 Gd $85
Same as Marlin Model 101 except w/walnut-finished hardwood
stock. Made 1966-79. Note: Later production featuring hot-
ironstamped wood pistol grip to simulate checkering/carving;
plain forend.

MODEL 20. . . . . NiB $779 Ex $439 Gd $310
Same as Marlin Model 80/780 except w/bead front sight, walnut-
finished hardwood stock. Made 1966 to 1982. Note: Recent production has stamped pistol grip; plain forend.

MODEL 30. . . . . NiB $280 Ex $133 Gd $100

Same as Marlin Model 336C except chambered for .30-30 only,
w/4-round magazine, plainer stock and forearm of walnut-finished
hardwood. Made 1966 to 1968.

MODEL 30A. . . . . NiB $279 Ex $190 Gd $139
Same as Marlin Model 336C but chambered for .30-30 only, w/
checkered walnut-finished hardwood stock. Made 1969 to 1983.

MODEL 36G . . . . NiB $879 Ex $633 Gd $260
Same as Marlin Model 336C except chambered for .30-30 only,
w/5-round magazine, plainer stock. Made 1960 to 1965.

MODEL 60. . . . . NiB $200 Ex $124 Gd $79
Same as Marlin Model 99C except w/walnut-finished hardwood
stock. Made 1960 to 1980.

MODEL 70. . . . . NiB $188 Ex $95 Gd $65
Same as Marlin Model 989M2 except w/walnut-finished hardwood
stock; no handguard. Made 1966 to 1969.

MODEL 80G . . . . NiB $100 Ex $65 Gd $45
Same as Marlin Model 80C except w/plain stock, bead front sight.
Made 1960 to 1965.

Marlin Model A-1 Autoloader

Marlin-Glenfield Model 10

Marlin-Glenfield Model 30A

Marlin-Glenfield Model 60

Marlin-Glenfield Model 70

Marlin-Glenfield Model 80G

MODEL 81G . . . . NiB $110 Ex $78 Gd $66
Same as Marlin Model 81C except w/plain stock, bead front sight.
Made from 1960 to 1965.

MODEL 99G . . . . NiB $170 Ex $75 Gd $65
Same as Marlin Model 99C except w/plain stock, bead front sight.
Made from 1960 to 1965.

MODEL 101G . . . . NiB $110 Ex $79 Gd $55
Same as Marlin Model 101 except w/plain stock. Made 1960 to 1965.

MODEL 989G
AUTOLOADING RIFLE . . . . NiB $179 Ex $110 Gd $79
Same as Marlin Model 989 except w/plain stock, bead front sight.
Made from 1962 to 1964.

MAUSER SPORTING RIFLES—Oberndorf am Neckar, Germany. Manufactured by Mauser-Werke GmbH. Imported by Brolin Arms, Pomona, CA (previously by Gun South, Inc.; Gibbs Rifle Co.; Precision Imports, Inc. and KDF, Inc.)

Before the end of WWI the name of the Mauser firm was "Waffenfabrik Mauser A.-G." Shortly after WWI it was changed to "Mauser-Werke A.-G." This information may be used to determine the age of genuine original Mauser sporting rifles made before WWII because all bear either of these firm names as well as the Mauser banner trademark.

Mauser Model ES340

Mauser Model ES350

The first four rifles listed were manufactured before WWI. Those that follow were produced between World Wars I and II. The early Mauser models can generally be identified by the pistol grip, which is rounded instead of capped, and the M/98 military-type magazine floorplate and catch. The later models have hinged magazine floorplates with lever or button release.

NOTE: *The "B" series of Mauser .22 rifles (Model ES340B, MS350B, etc.) were improved versions of their corresponding models and were introduced about 1935.*

PRE-WORLD WAR I MODELS

BOLT-ACTION SPORTING CARBINE
Calibers: 6.5x54, 6.5x58, 7x57, 8x57, 957mm. 19.75-inch bbl. Weight: 7 lbs. Full-stocked to muzzle. Other specifications same as for standard rifle.
W/20-inch bbl. (Type M). . . . . . NiB $2489 Ex $2066 Gd $1445
W/20- or 24-inch bbl. (Type S) . . NiB $2566 Ex $2155 Gd $1486

BOLT-ACTION SPORTING RIFLE
Calibers: 6.5x55, 6.5x58, 7x57, 8x57, 9x57, 9.3x62 10.75x68. Five-round box magazine, 23.5-inch bbl. Weight: 7 to 7.5 lbs. Pear-shaped bolt handle. Double-set or single trigger. Sights: Tangent curve rear; ramp front. Pistol-grip stock, forearm w/ Schnabel tip and swivels.
Type A, English export . . . . NiB $2669 Ex $2276 Gd $1559
Type B. . . . . NiB $1790 Ex $1466 Gd $1080

BOLT-ACTION SPORTING RIFLE,
MILITARY MODEL TYPE C . . . . . NiB $3854 Ex $3165 Gd $2189
So called because of stepped M/98-type bbl., military front sight and double-pull trigger. Calibers: 7x57, 8x57, 9x57mm. Other specifications same as for standard rifle.

BOLT-ACTION SPORTING RIFLE
SHORT MODEL TYPE K . . . . NiB $3856 Ex $3169 Gd $2190
Calibers: 6.5x54, 8x51mm. 19.75-inch bbl. Weight: 6.25 lbs. Other specifications same as for standard rifle.

PRE-WORLD WAR II MODELS

MODEL DSM34 BOLT-ACTION
SINGLE-SHOT SPORTING RIFLE . . . . NiB $670 Ex $445 Gd $338
Also called "Sport-model." Caliber: .22 LR. 26-inch bbl. Weight: 7.75 lbs. Sights: Tangent curve open rear; Barleycorn front. M/98 military-type stock, swivels. Intro. c. 1935.

MODEL EL320 BOLT-ACTION
SINGLE-SHOT SPORTING RIFLE . . . . NiB $556 Ex $449 Gd $339
Caliber: .22 LR. 23.5-inch bbl. Weight: 4.25 lbs. Sights: Adj. open rear; bead front. Sporting stock w/checkered pistol grip, swivels.

MODEL EN310 BOLT-ACTION
SINGLE-SHOT SPORTING RIFLE . . . . NiB $499 Ex $420 Gd $298
Caliber: .22 LR. ("22 Lang fur Buchsen.") 19.75-inch bbl. Weight: 4 lbs. Sights: Fixed open rear, blade front. Plain pistol-grip stock.

MODEL ES340 BOLT-ACTION
SINGLE-SHOT TARGET RIFLE . . . . . NiB $765 Ex $455 Gd $338
Caliber: .22 LR. 25.5-inch bbl. Weight: 6.5 lbs. Sights: Tangent curve rear; ramp front. Sporting stock w/checkered pistol-grip and grooved forearm, swivels.

MODEL ES340B BOLT-ACTION SINGLE-SHOT
TARGET RIFLE . . . . NiB $765 Ex $445 Gd $356
Caliber: .22 LR. 26.75-inch bbl. Weight: 8 lbs. Sights: Tangent curve open rear; ramp front. Plain pistol-grip stock, swivels.

MODEL ES350 BOLT-ACTION SINGLE-SHOT
TARGET RIFLE . . . . NiB $977 Ex $775 Gd $558
"Meistershaftsbuchse" (Championship Rifle). Caliber: .22 LR. 27.5-inch bbl. Weight: 7.75 lbs. Sights: Open micrometer rear; ramp front. Target stock w/checkered pistol-grip and forearm, grip cap, swivels.

MODEL ES350B BOLT-ACTION SINGLE-SHOT
TARGET RIFLE . . . . NiB $970 Ex $668 Gd $495
Same general specifications as Model MS350B except single-shot, weight: 8.25 lbs.

MODEL KKW BOLT-ACTION
SINGLE-SHOT TARGET RIFLE . . . . . . NiB $944 Ex $667 Gd $544
Caliber: .22 LR. 26-inch bbl. Weight: 8.75 lbs. Sights: Tangent curve open rear; Barleycorn front. M/98 military-type stock, swivels. Note: This rifle has an improved design Mauser 22 action w/separate nonrotating bolt head. In addition to being produced for commercial sale, this model was used as a training rifle by the German armed forces; it was also made by Walther and Gustoff. Intro. just before WWII.

MODEL MM410 BOLT-ACTION
REPEATING SPORTING RIFLE . . . . NiB $2166 Ex $1590 Gd $955
Caliber: .22 LR. Five round detachable box magazine. 23.5-inch bbl. Weight: 5 lbs. Sights: Tangent curve open rear; ramp front. Sporting stock w/checkered pistol-grip, swivels.

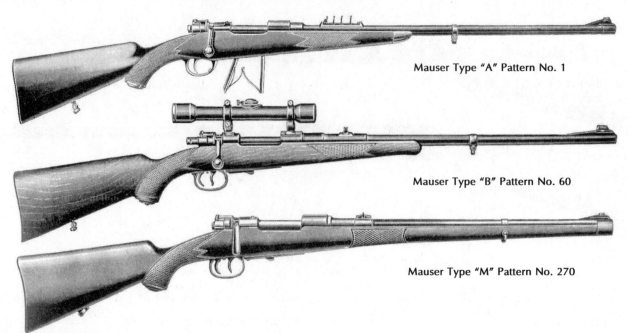

Mauser Type "A" Pattern No. 1

Mauser Type "B" Pattern No. 60

Mauser Type "M" Pattern No. 270

MODEL MM410B BOLT-ACTION
REPEATING SPORTING RIFLE.... NiB $2166 Ex $1590 Gd $955
Caliber: .22 LR. Five round detachable box magazine. 23.5-inch bbl. Weight: 6.25 lbs. Sights: Tangent curve open rear; ramp front. Lightweight sporting stock w/checkered pistol-grip, swivels.

MODEL MS350B BOLT-ACTION
REPEATING TARGET RIFLE...... NiB $1268 Ex $800 Gd $556
Caliber: .22 LR. Five round detachable box magazine. Receiver and bbl. grooved for detachable rear sight or scope. 26.75-inch bbl. Weight: 8.5 lbs. Sights: Micrometer open rear; ramp front. Target stock w/checkered pistol grip and forearm, grip cap, sling swivels.

MODEL MS420 BOLT-ACTION
REPEATING SPORTING RIFLE..... NiB $1145 Ex $879 Gd $606
Caliber: .22 LR. Five round detachable box magazine. 25.5-inch bbl. Weight: 6.5 lbs. Sights: Tangent curve open rear; ramp front. Sporting stock w/checkered pistol grip, grooved forearm swivels.

MODEL MS420B BOLT-ACTION
REPEATING TARGET RIFLE...... NiB $1156 Ex $922 Gd $633
Caliber: .22 LR. Five round detachable box magazine. 26.75-inch bbl. Weight: 8 lbs. Sights: Tangent curve open rear; ramp front. Target stock w/checkered pistol grip, grooved forearm, swivels.

STANDARD MODEL RIFLE ... NiB $339 Ex $210 Gd $159
Refined version of German Service Kar. 98k. Straight bolt handle. Calibers: 7mm Mauser (7x57mm), 7.9mm Mauser (8x57mm). Five round box magazine. 23.5-inch bbl. Weight: 8.5 lbs. Sights: Blade front; adj. rear. Walnut stock of M/98 military-type. Note: These rifles were made for commercial sale and are of the high quality found in the Oberndorf Mauser sporters. They bear the Mauser trademark on the receiver ring.

TYPE "A" BOLT-ACTION
SPORTING RIFLE .... NiB $7000 Ex $6200 Gd $3005
Special British Model. 7x57, 30-06 (7.62x63), 8x60, 9x57, 9.3x62mm. Five round box mag. 23.5-inch round bbl. Weight: 7.25 lbs. Mil.-type single trigger. Sights: Express rear; hooded ramp front. Circassian walnut sporting stock w/checkered pistol-grip and forearm, w/ or w/o cheekpiece, buffalo horn forend tip and grip cap, detachable swivels. Variations: Octagon bbl., double-set trigger, shotgun-type safety, folding peep rear sight, tangent curve rear sight, three-leaf rear sight.

TYPE "A" BOLT-ACTION SPORTING RIFLE,
MAGNUM MODEL...... NiB $5598 Ex $3473 Gd $2745
Same general specifications as standard Type "A" except w/Magnum action, weighs 7.5 to 8.5 lbs. Calibers: .280 Ross, .318 Westley Richards Express, 10.75x68mm, .404 Nitro Express.

TYPE "A" BOLT-ACTION SPORTING
RIFLE, SHORT MODEL ... NiB $6149 Ex $4144 Gd $2448
Same as standard Type "A" except w/short action, 21.5-inch round bbl., weight 6 lbs. Calibers: .250-3000, 6.5x54, 8x51mm.

TYPE "B" BOLT-ACTION SPORTING
RIFLE............... NiB $5005 Ex $4885 Gd $2544
Normal Model. Calibers: 7x57, .30-06 (7.62x63), 8x57, 8x60, 9x57, 9.3x62, 10.7568mm. Five round box magazine. 23.5-inch round bbl. Weight: 7.25 lbs. Double-set trigger. Sights: Three-leaf rear, ramp front. Fine walnut stock w/checkered pistol-grip, Schnabel forend tip, cheekpiece, grip cap, swivels. Variations: Octagon or half-octagon bbl., military-type single trigger, shotgun-type safety, folding peep rear sight, tangent curve rear sight, telescopic sight.

TYPE "K" BOLT-ACTION
SPORTING RIFLE .... NiB $8177 Ex $6805 Gd $4285
Light Short Model. Same specifications as Normal Type "B" model except w/short action, 21.5-inch round bbl., weight: 6 lbs. Calibers: .250-3000, 6.5x54, 8x51mm.

TYPE "M" BOLT-ACTION
SPORTING CARBINE .... NiB $6000 Ex $5133 Gd $3200
Calibers: 6.5x54, 7x57, .30-06 (7.62x63), 8x51, 8x60, 9x57mm. Five round box magazine. 19.75-inch round bbl. Weight: 6 to 6.75 lbs. Double-set trigger, flat bolt handle. Sights: Three-leaf rear; ramp front. Stocked to muzzle, cheekpiece, checkered pistol-grip and forearm, grip cap, steel forend cap, swivels. Variations: Military-type single trigger, shotgun-type trigger, shotgun-type safety, tangent curve rear sight, telescopic sight.

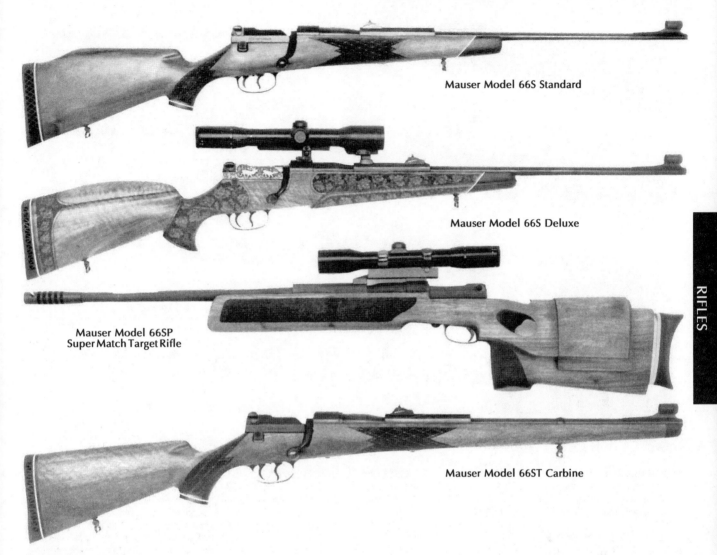

Mauser Model 66S Standard

Mauser Model 66S Deluxe

Mauser Model 66SP
Super Match Target Rifle

Mauser Model 66ST Carbine

TYPE "S" BOLT-ACTION
SPORTING CARBINE . . . . NiB $6000 Ex $5009 Gd $3005
Calibers: 6.5x54 7x57, 8x51, 8x60, 9x57mm. Five-round box magazine. 19.75-inch round bbl. Weight: 6 to 6.75 lbs. Double-set trigger. Sights: Three-leaf rear; ramp front. Stocked to muzzle, Schnabel forend tip, cheekpiece, checkered pistol-grip w/cap, swivels. Variations: Same as listed for Normal Model Type "B."

POST-WORLD WAR II MODELS

NOTE: *Production of original Mauser sporting rifles (66 series) resumed at the Oberndorf plant in 1965 by Mauser-Jagdwaffen GmbH, now Mauser-Werke Oberndorf GmbH. The Series 2000-3000-4000 rifles, however, were made for Mauser by Friedrich Wilhelm Heym Gewehrfabrik, Muennerstadt, West Germany.*

MODEL 66S BOLT-ACTION STANDARD SPORTING RIFLE
Telescopic short action. Bbls. interchangeable within cal. group. Single- or double-set trigger (interchangeable). Cal: .243 Win., 6.5x57, .270 Win., 7x64, .308 Win., .30-06. Three round mag. 23.6 inch bbl. (25.6inch in 7x64). Wt: 7.3 lbs. (7.5 lbs. in 7x64). Sights: Adj. open rear, hooded ramp front. Select Eur. walnut stock, Monte Carlo w/cheekpiece, rosewood forend tip and pistol-grip cap, skip checkering, recoil pad, sling swivels. Made from 1974 to 1995, export to U.S. disc. 1974. Note: U.S. designation, 1971 to 1973,

was "Model 660."
Model 66S . . . . NiB $4739 Ex $3054 Gd $2044
W/extra bbl. assembly, add. $600

MODEL 66S DELUXE SPORTER
Limited production special order. Model 66S rifles and carbines are available with /elaborate engraving, gold and silver inlays and carved select walnut stocks. Added value is upward of $4500.

MODEL 66S ULTRA
Same general specifications as Model 66S Standard except with 20.9-inch bbl., weight: 6.8 lbs.
Model 66S Ultra. . . . . . . NiB $1754 Ex $1644 Gd $1097
W/extra bbl. assembly, add. $600

MODEL 66SG BIG GAME
Same general specifications as Model 66S Standard except w/25.6-inch bbl., weight 9.3 lbs. Calibers: .375 H&H Mag., .458 Win. Mag. Note: U.S. designation, 1971-73, was "Model 660 Safari."
MODEL 66SG BIG GAME . NiB $3077 Ex $2100 Gd $1388
W/ extra bbl. assembly, add $600

Mauser Model 99

Mauser Model 201

Mauser Model 3000

Mauser Model 4000

MODEL 66SH HIGH PERFORMANCE . . NiB $1706 Ex $1530 Gd $1109
Same general specifications as Model 66S Standard except w/25.6-inch bbl., weighs 7.5 lbs. (9.3 lbs. in 9.3x64). Calibers: 6.5x68, 7mm Rem. Mag., 7mm S.E.v. Hoffe, .300 Win. Mag., 8x68S, 9.3x64.

MODEL 66SP SUPER MATCH
BOLT-ACTION TARGET RIFLE . . NiB $4198 Ex $3707 Gd $2033
Telescopic short action. Adj. single-stage trigger. Caliber: .308 Win. (chambering for other cartridges available on special order). Three round magazine. 27.6-inch heavy bbl. w/muzzle brake, dovetail rib for special scope mount. Weight: 12 lbs. Target stock w/wide and deep forearm, full pistol-grip, thumbhole adj. cheekpiece, adj. rubber buttplate.

MODEL 66ST CARBINE
Same general specifications as Model 66S Standard except w/20.9-inch bbl., full-length stock, weight: 7 lbs.
Model 66ST . . . . NiB $2635 Ex $1710 Gd $1277
W/extra bbl. assembly, add $600

MODEL 83 BOLT-ACTION RIFLE NiB $2215 Ex $2188 Gd $1360
Centerfire single-shot, bolt-action rifle for 300-meter competition. Caliber: .308 Win. 25.5-inch fluted bbl. Weight: 10.5 lbs. Adj. micrometer rear sight globe front. Fully adj. competition stock. Disc. 1988.

MODEL 96 . . . . NiB $677 Ex $633 Gd $455
Calibers: .25-06, .270 Win., 7x64, .308 Win., .30-06, 7mm Rem. Mag., .300 Win. Mag. 22-inch bbl.; magnums 24-inch. Weight: 6.25 lbs. No sights; drilled and tapped for scope. Walnut stock. Five-round top-loading magazine. 3-position safety.

MODEL 99 CLASSIC BOLT-ACTION RIFLE
Calibers: .243 Win., .25-06, .270 Win., .30-06, .308 Win., .257 Wby., .270 Wby., 7mm Rem. Mag., .300 Win., .300 Wby. .375 H&H. Four round magazine (standard), 3-round (Magnum). Bbl.: 24-inch (standard) or 26-inch (Magnum). 44 inches overall (standard). Weight: 8 lbs. No sights. Checkered European walnut stock w/rosewood grip cap available in Classic and Monte Carlo styles w/High-Luster or oil finish. Disc. importing 1994.
Standard Classic or
Monte Carlo (oil finish) . . . . NiB $1156 Ex $1077 Gd $710
Magnum Classic or
Monte Carlo (oil finish) . . . . NiB $1266 Ex $1109 Gd $800
Standard Classic or
Monte Carlo (H-L finish) . . . . NiB $1188 Ex $1098 Gd $775
Magnum Classic or
Monte Carlo (H-L finish) . . . . NiB $1347 Ex $1109 Gd $790

MODEL 107 BOLT-ACTION RIFLE . . NiB $369 Ex $277 Gd $210
Caliber: .22 LR. Mag. Five round magazine. 21.5-inch bbl. 40 inches overall. Weight: 5 lbs. Receiver drilled and tapped for rail scope mounts. Hooded front sight, adj. rear. Disc. importing 1994.

MODEL 201/201 LUXUS BOLT-ACTION RIFLE
Calibers: .22 LR. .22 Win. Mag. Five round magazine. 21-inch bbl. 40 inches overall. Weight: 6.5 lbs. Receiver drilled and tapped for scope mounts. Sights optional. Checkered walnut-stained beech stock w/Monte Carlo. Model 201 Luxus w/checkered European walnut stock QD swivels, rosewood forend and rubber recoil pad. Made from 1989 to 1997.
Standard model . . . . NiB $670 Ex $555 Gd $400
Magnum . . . . NiB $722 Ex $569 Gd $440
Luxus Standard model . . . . . . NiB $756 Ex $544 Gd $468
Luxus Magnum model . . . . NiB $844 Ex $633 Gd $560

Midland Model 2707 Bolt-Action Rifle

Merkel Model 220

MODEL 2000 BOLT-ACTION
SPORTING RIFLE . . . . **NiB $539 Ex $355 Gd $290**
Modified Mauser-type action. Calibers: .270 Win., .308 Win., .30-06. Five-round magazine. 24-inch bbl. Weight: 7.5 lbs. Sights: Folding leaf rear; hooded ramp front. Checkered walnut stock w/Monte Carlo comb and cheekpiece, forend tip, sling swivels. Made from 1969 to 1971. Note: Model 2000 is similar in appearance to Model 3000.

MODEL 2000 CLASSIC BOLT-ACTION SPORTING RIFLE
Calibers: .22-250 Rem., .234 Win., .270 Win., 7mm Mag., .308 Win., .30-06, .300 Win. Mag. Three or 5-round magazine. 24-inch bbl. Weight: 7.5 lbs. Sights: Folding leaf rear; hooded ramp front. Checkered walnut stock w/Monte Carlo comb and cheekpiece, forend tip, sling swivels. Imported 1998. Note: The Model 2000 Classic is designed to interchange bbl. assemblies within a given caliber group.
Classic model. . . . . .NiB $1696 Ex $1377 Gd $1044
Professional model . . . . NiB $3228 Ex $2709 Gd $1995
W/recoil compensator. . . . . NiB $3245 Ex $2730 Gd $1100
Sniper model . . . . NiB $2010 Ex $1544 Gd $1120
Varmint model . . . . .NiB $1996 Ex $1528 Gd $965
Extra bbl. assembly, add. $950

MODEL 3000 BOLT-ACTION
SPORTING RIFLE . . . . **NiB $570 Ex $440 Gd $400**
Modified Mauser-type action. Calibers: .243 Win., .270 Win., .308 Win., .30-06. Five round magazine. 22-inch bbl. Weight: 7 lbs. No sights. Select European walnut stock, Monte Carlo style w/cheek-piece, rosewood forend tip and pistol-grip cap, skip checkering, recoil pad, sling swivels. Made from 1971 to 1974.

MODEL 3000 MAGNUM . . . . **NiB $641 Ex $486 Gd $379**
Same general specifications as standard Model 3000, except w/3-round magazine, 26-inch bbl., weight: 8 lbs. Calibers: 7mm Rem. Mag., .300 Win. Mag., .375 H&H Mag.

MODEL 4000 VARMINT RIFLE NiB $466 Ex $380 Gd $269
Same general specifications as standard Model 3000, except w/ smaller action, folding leaf rear sight; hooded ramp front, rubber buttplate instead of recoil pad, weight 6.75 lbs. Calibers: .222 Rem., .223 Rem. 22-inch bbl. Select European walnut stock w/rosewood forend tip and pistol-grip cap. French checkering and sling swivels.

McMILLAN GUNWORKS—Phoenix, Arizona
See Harris Gunworks.

GEBRÜDER MERKEL — Suhl, Germany

For Merkel combination guns and drillings, see listings under Merkel shotguns.

OVER/UNDER RIFLES ("BOCK-DOPPELBÜCHSEN")
Calibers: 5.6x35 Vierling, 6.5x58r5, 7x57r5, 8x57JR, 8x60R Magnum, 9.3x53r5, 9.3x72r5, 9.3x74r5, 10.3x60R as well as most of the British calibers for African and Indian big game. Various bbl. lengths, weights. In general, specifications correspond to those of Merkel over/under shotguns. Values of these over/under rifles (in calibers for which ammunition is obtainable) are about the same as those of comparable shotgun models currently manufactured. For more specific data, see Merkel shotgun models indicated below.
Model 210 . . . . NiB $5766 Ex $4470 Gd $3210
Model 210E . . . . NiB $6630 Ex $4950 Gd $3765
Model 213 . . . . NiB $13,760 Ex $10,550 Gd $7330
Model 240E1 . . . . NiB $7113 Ex $4966 Gd $3412
Model 313E . . . . . . .NiB $19,670 Ex $16,750 Gd $10,355
Model 320E . . . . . . .NiB $15,770 Ex $12,559 Gd $9220
Model 321 . . . . .NiB $17,210 Ex $13,880 Gd $9155
Model 321E . . . . .NiB $17,998 Ex $14,760 Gd $9970
Model 322 . . . . .NiB $12,550 Ex $14,770 Gd $10,049
Model 323E . . . . . .NiB $23,760 Ex $19,210 Gd $12,960
Model 324 . . . . . . .NiB $27,650 Ex $21,880 Gd $15,330

MEXICAN MILITARY RIFLE — Manufactured by Government Arsenal, Mexico, D.F.

MODEL 1936 MAUSER MILITARY RIFLE NiB $221 Ex $169 Gd $95
Same as German Kar.98k w/minor variations and U.S. M/1903 Springfield-type knurled cocking piece.

MODEL 1936
MAUSER MILITARY RIFLE . . . . NiB $233 Ex $179 Gd $110

Mossberg Model 25

MIDLAND RIFLES — Manufactured by Gibbs Rifle Company, Inc., Martinsburg, West Virginia

MODEL 2100 BOLT-ACTION
RIFLE . . . . NiB $413 Ex $338 Gd $228
Calibers: .22-250, .243 Win., 6mm Rem., .270 Win., 6.5x55, 7x57, 7x64, .308 Win., and .30-06. Springfield 1903 action. Four-round magazine. 22-inch bbl. 43 inches overall. Weight: 7 lbs. Flip-up rear sight; hooded ramp front. Finely finished and checkered walnut stock w/pistol-grip cap and sling swivels. Steel recoil bar. Action drilled and tapped for scope mounts. Production disc.1997.

MODEL 2600 BOLT-ACTION RIFLE . NiB $445 Ex $370 Gd $220
Same general specifications as Model 2100 except no pistol-grip cap, and stock is walnut-finished hardwood. Made 1992 to 1997.

MODEL 2707 BOLT-ACTION RIFLE . NiB $443 Ex $284 Gd $220
Same general specifications as Model 2100 except the weight of this rifle as been reduced by utilizing a tapered bbl., anodized aluminum trigger housing and lightened stock. Weight: 6.5 lbs. Disc.

MODEL 2800 LIGHTWEIGHT RIFLE . NiB $466 Ex $355 Gd $269
Same general specifications as Model 2100 except w/laminated birch stock. Made from 1992 to 1994 and from 1996 to 1997.

MITCHELL ARMS. INC. — Fountain Valley, California (formerly Santa Ana, CA)

MODEL 15/22 SEMIAUTOMATIC
High Standard-style action. Caliber: .22 LR. 15-round magazine (10-round after 10/13/94). 20.5-inch bbl. 37.5 inches overall. Weight: 6.25 lbs. Ramp front sight; adj. open rear. Blued finish. Mahogany stock; Monte Carlo-style American walnut stock on Deluxe model. Made from 1994 to 1996.
NiB $300 Ex $233 Gd $179 . . . . . . NiB $300 Ex $233 Gd $179
Carbine . . . . NiB $300 Ex $233 Gd $179
Deluxe . . . . NiB $259 Ex $166 Gd $126

MODEL 9300 SERIES BOLT-ACTION RIFLE
Calibers: .22 LR. .22 Mag. Five or 10-round magazine. 22.5-inch bbl. 40.75 inches overall. Weight: 6.5 lbs. Beaded ramp front sight; adj. open rear. Blued finish. American walnut stock. Made 1994 to 1995.
Model 9302 (.22 LR
w/checkered stock, rosewood caps). . NiB $319 Ex $239 Gd $177
Model 9302 (.22 Mag.,
checkered stock, rosewood caps) . . . NiB $317 Ex $237 Gd $175
Model 9303 (.22 LR, plain stock) . . . NiB $317 Ex $237 Gd $175
Model 9304
(.22 Mag., checkered stock) . . . . NiB $266 Ex $201 Gd $177
Model 9305 (.22 LR, special stock) . . NiB $221 Ex $179 Gd $235

AK-22 SEMIAUTOMATIC RIFLE. . . . . NiB $359 Ex $248 Gd $189
Replica of AK-47 rifle. .22 LR. .22 WMR., 20-round magazine (.22 LR) 10-round (.22 WMR). 18-inch bbl. 36 inches overall. Weight: 6.5 lbs. Sights: Post front; open adj. rear. European walnut stock and forend. Matte black finish. Made from 1985 to 1994.

CAR-15 . . . . NiB $525 Ex $355 Gd $283
Replica of AR-15 CAR rifle. Caliber: .22 LR. 15-round magazine.16.25-inch bbl. 32 inches overall. Sights: Adj. post front; adj. aperture rear. Telescoping buttstock and ventilated forend. Matte black finish. Made 1990 to 1994.

GALIL 22 SEMIAUTOMATIC RIFLE . . NiB $439 Ex $289 Gd $198
Replica of Israeli Galil rifle. Calibers: .22 LR. .22 WMR., 20-round magazine (.22 LR), 10-round (.22 WMR). 18-inch bbl. 36 inches overall. Weight: 6.5 lbs. Sights: Adj. post front; rear adj. for windage. Folding metal stock w/ European walnut grip and forend. Matte black finish. Made 1987 to 1993.

M-16A 22 SEMIAUTOMATIC RIFLE. . NiB $479 Ex $266 Gd $179
Replica of AR-15 rifle. Caliber: .22 LR. 15-round magazine. 20.5-inch bbl. 38.5 inches overall. Weight: 7 lbs. Sights: Adj. post front, adj. aperture rear. Black composite stock and forend. Matte black finish. Made 1990 to 1994.

MAS 22 SEMIAUTOMATIC RIFLE . . . NiB $439 Ex $290 Gd $221
Replica of French MAS bullpup rifle. Caliber: .22 LR. 20-round magazine. 18-inch bbl. 28 inches overall. Weight: 7.5 lbs. Sights: Adj. post front, folding aperture rear. European walnut buttstock and forend. Matte black finish. Made from 1987 to 1993.

PPS SEMIAUTOMATIC RIFLE
Caliber: .22 LR. 20-round magazine, 50-round drum. 16.5-inch bbl. 33.5 inches overall. Weight: 5.5 lbs. Sights: Blade front; adj. rear. European walnut stock w/ventilated bbl. shroud. Matte black finish. Made 1989 to 1994.
Model PPS (20-round magazine)NiB $370 Ex $259 Gd $188
Model PPS/50 (50-round drum) NiB $522 Ex $402 Gd $300

O.F. MOSSBERG & SONS, INC. — North Haven, Connecticut (formerly New Haven, CT)

MODEL 10 BOLT-ACTION
SINGLE-SHOT RIFLE. . . . . . . NiB $338 Ex $190 Gd $120
Takedown. Caliber: .22 LR, Long, Short. 22-inch bbl. Weight: 4 lbs. Sights: Open rear; bead front. Plain pistol-grip stock w/swivels, sling. Made 1933 to 1935.

MODEL 14 BOLT-ACTION
SINGLE-SHOT RIFLE. . . . . . . NiB $338 Ex $190 Gd $120
Takedown. Caliber: .22 LR, Long, Short. 24-inch bbl. Weight: 5.25 lbs. Sights: Peep rear; hooded ramp front. Plain pistol-grip stock w/ semi-beavertail forearm, 1.25-inch swivels. Made 1934 to 1935.

MODEL 20 BOLT-ACTION
SINGLE-SHOT RIFLE. . . . . . . NiB $338 Ex $190 Gd $120
Takedown. Caliber: .22 LR, Long, Short. 24-inch bbl. Weight: 4.5 lbs. Sights: Open rear; bead front. Plain pistol-grip stock and forearm w/finger grooves, sling and swivels. Made from 1933 to 1935.

MODEL 25/25A BOLT-ACTION SINGLE-SHOT RIFLE
Takedown. Caliber: .22 LR, Long, Short. 24-inch bbl. Weight: 5 lbs. Sights: Peep rear; hooded ramp front. Plain pistol-grip stock w/semi-beavertail forearm. 1.25-inch swivels. Made from 1935 to 1936.
Model 25 . . . . NiB $338 Ex $190 Gd $120
Model 25A (Improved Model 25, 1936-38)NiB $325 Ex $190 Gd $120

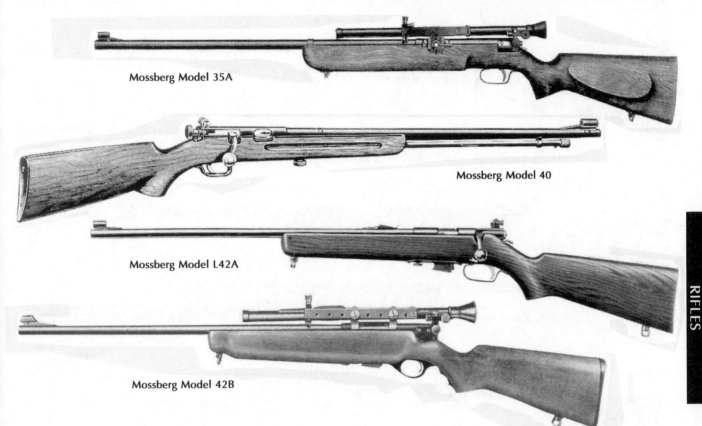

Mossberg Model 35A

Mossberg Model 40

Mossberg Model L42A

Mossberg Model 42B

MODEL 26B/26C BOLT-ACTION SINGLE-SHOT

Takedown. Caliber: .22 LR. Long, Short. 26-inch bbl. Weight: 5.5 lbs. Sights; Rear, micrometer click peep or open; hooded ramp front. Plain pistol-grip stock swivels. Made from 1938 to 1941.
Model 26B . . . . NiB $338 Ex $190 Gd $120
Model 26C
(No rear sights or sling swivels) . . . . . . NiB $250 Ex $132 Gd $91

MODEL 30 BOLT-ACTION

SINGLE-SHOT RIFLE . . . . NiB $338 Ex $190 Gd $120
Takedown. Caliber: .22 LR. Long, Short. 24-inch bbl. Weight: 4.5 lbs. Sights: Peep rear; bead front, on hooded ramp. Plain pistol-grip stock, forearm w/finger grooves. Made from 1933 to 1935.

MODEL 34 BOLT-ACTION

SINGLE-SHOT RIFLE . . . . NiB $338 Ex $190 Gd $120
Takedown. Caliber: .22 LR. Long, Short. 24-inch bbl. Weight: 5.5 lbs. Sights: Peep rear; hooded ramp front. Plain pistol-grip stock w/semibeavertail forearm, 1.25-inch swivels. Made 1934 to 1935.

MODEL 35 TARGET GRADE

BOLT-ACTION SINGLE-SHOT RIFLE . NiB $440 Ex $300 Gd $166
Caliber: .22 LR. 26-inch heavy bbl. Weight: 8.25 lbs. Sights: Micrometer click rear peep; hooded ramp front. Large target stock w/full pistol grip, cheekpiece, full beavertail forearm, 1.25-inch swivels. Made from 1935 to 1937.

MODEL 35A BOLT-ACTION

SINGLE-SHOT RIFLE . . . . NiB $440 Ex $300 Gd $166
Caliber: .22 LR. 26-inch heavy bbl. Weight: 8.25 lbs. Sights: Micrometer click peep rear; hooded front. Target stock w/cheekpiece full pistol grip and forearm, 1.25-inch sling swivels. Made from 1937 to 1938.

MODEL 35A-LS . . . . NiB $440 Ex $300 Gd $166

Caliber .22 LR. Same as Model 35A but w/Lyman No. 57 rear sight, 17A front. Target stock w/checkpiece, full pistol-grip and forearm.

MODEL 35B . . . . NiB $440 Ex $300 Gd $166

Same specifications as Model 44B except single-shot. Made from 1938 to 1940.

MODEL 40 BOLT-ACTION REPEATER NiB $222 Ex $140 Gd $100

Takedown. Caliber: .22 LR. Long, Short, 16-round tubular magazine. 24-inch bbl. Weight: 5 lbs. Sights: Peep rear; bead front, on hooded ramp. Plain pistol-grip stock, forearm w/finger grooves. Made 1933 to 1935.

MODEL 42 BOLT-ACTION REPEATER NiB $278 Ex $155 Gd $110

Takedown. Caliber: .22 LR. Long, Short. Seven-round detachable box magazine. 24-inch bbl. Weight: 5 lbs. Sights: Receiver peep, open rear; hooded ramp front. Pistol-grip stock. 1.25-inch swivels. Made 1935 to 1937.

MODEL 42A/L42A BOLT-ACTION REPEATERS

Takedown. Caliber: .22 LR. Long, Short. Seven-round detachable box magazine. 24-inch bbl. Weight: 5 lbs. Sights: Receiver peep, open rear; ramp front. Plain pistol-grip stock. Made from 1937-38. Model L42A (left-hand action) made from 1937 to 1941.
Model 42A . . . . NiB $279 Ex $169 Gd $120
Model L42A . . . . NiB $288 Ex $179 Gd $130

MODEL 42B/42C BOLT-ACTION REPEATERS

Takedown. Caliber: .22 LR. Long, Short. Five-round detachable box magazine. 24-inch bbl. Weight: 6 lbs. Sights: Micrometer click receiver peep, open rear hooded ramp front. Plain pistol-grip stock, swivels. Made from 1938 to 1941.
Model 42B . . . . NiB $289 Ex $190 Gd $100
Model 42C (No rear peep sight)NiB $235 Ex $155 Gd $110

Mossberg Model 42C

Mossberg Model L-43

Mossberg Model 43B

Mossberg Model 44US

Mossberg Model L45A
Left-Hand Model

Mossberg Model 45B

Mossberg Model L46A-LS

Mossberg Model 46B

**MODEL 42M BOLT-ACTION
REPEATER** . . . . **NiB $345 Ex $233 Gd $135**
Caliber: .22 LR, Long, Short. Seven-round detachable box magazine. 23-inch bbl. Weight: 6.75 lbs. Sights: Microclick receiver peep, open rear; hooded ramp front. Two-piece Mannlicher-type stock w/cheekpiece and pistol-grip, swivels. Made from 1940 to 1950.

**MODEL 43/L43 BOLT-ACTION
REPEATERS** . . . . **NiB $376 Ex $256 Gd $198**

Speedlock, adj. trigger pull. Caliber: .22 LR. Seven-round detachable box (magazine. 26-inch heavy bbl. Weight: 8.25 lbs. Sights: Lyman No. 57 rear; selective aperture front. Target stock w/cheekpiece, full pistol-grip, beavertail forearm, adj. front swivel. Made from 1937-38. Model L43 is same as Model 43 except w/left-hand action.

MODEL 43B . . . . **NiB $390 Ex $300 Gd $170**
Same as Model 44B except w/Lyman No. 57 receiver sight and No. 17A front sight. Made from 1938 to 1939.

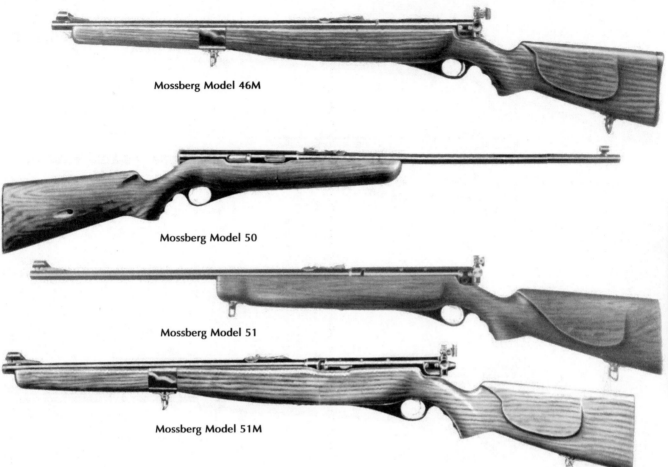

Mossberg Model 46M

Mossberg Model 50

Mossberg Model 51

Mossberg Model 51M

MODEL 44 BOLT-ACTION REPEATER NiB $397 Ex $276 Gd $160
Takedown. Caliber: .22 LR, Long, Short. Tubular magazine holds 16
LR. 24-inch bbl. Weight: 6 lbs. Sights: Peep rear; hooded ramp front.
Plain pistol-grip stock w/semi-beavertail forearm, 1.25-inch swivels.
Made from 1934 to 1935. Note: Do not confuse this rifle w/later
Models 44B and 44US, which are clip repeaters.

**MODEL 44B BOLT-ACTION
TARGET RIFLE . . . . NiB $389 Ex $266 Gd $160**
Caliber: .22 LR. Seven-round detachable box magazine. Made
from 1938 to 1941.

MODEL 44US BOLT-ACTION REPEATER
Caliber: .22 LR. Seven round detachable box magazine. 26-inch heavy
bbl. Weight: 8.5 lbs. Sights: Micrometer click receiver peep, hooded
front. Target stock, swivels. Made from 1943-48. Note: This model was
used as a training rifle by the U.S. Armed Forces during WWII.
Model 44US. . . . . NiB $395 Ex $279 Gd $145
Model 44US (marked U.S. Property) . NiB $395 Ex $279 Gd $145

MODEL 45 BOLT-ACTION REPEATER NiB $254 Ex $178 Gd $117
Takedown. Caliber: .22 LR, Long, Short. Tubular magazine holds 15 LR, 18
Long, 22 Short. 24-inch bbl. Weight: 6.75 lbs. Sights: Rear peep; hooded
ramp front. Plain pistol-grip stock, 1.25-inch swivels. Made 1935 to 1937.

MODEL 45A, L45A, 45AC BOLT-ACTION REPEATERS
Takedown. Caliber: .22 LR, Long, Short. Tubular magazine holds 15 LR,
18 Long, 22 Short. 24-inch bbl. Weight: 6.75 lbs. Sights: Receiver peep,
open rear; hooded blade front sight mounted on ramp. Plain pistol-grip
stock, 1.25-inch sling swivels. Made 1937 to 1938.

Model 45A. . . . . NiB $300 Ex $190 Gd $145
Model L45A (Left-hand action) . . . . . NiB $655 Ex $355 Gd $279
Model 45AC (No receiver peep sight) NiB $249 Ex $177 Gd $123

MODEL 45B/45C BOLT-ACTION REPEATERS
Takedown. Caliber: .22 LR, Long, Short. Tubular magazine holds
15 LR, 18 Long, 22 Short. 24-inch bbl. Weight: 6.25 lbs. Open rear
sight; hooded blade front sight mounted on ramp. Plain pistol-grip
stock w/sling swivels. Made from 1938 to 1940.
Model 45B. . . . . NiB $338 Ex $233 Gd $138
Model 45C (No sights, made 1935 to 1937)NiB $338 Ex $233 Gd $138

MODEL 46 BOLT-ACTION REPEATER NiB $338 Ex $233 Gd $138
Takedown. Caliber: .22 LR, Long, Short. Tubular magazine holds
15 LR, 18 Long, 22 Short. 26-inch bbl. Weight: 7.5 lbs. Sights:
Micrometer click rear peep; hooded ramp front. Pistol-grip stock
w/cheekpiece, full beavertail forearm, 1.25-inch swivels. Made
from 1935 to 1937.

MODEL 46A, 46A-LS, L46A-LS BOLT-ACTION REPEATERS
Takedown. Caliber: .22 LR, Long, Short. Tubular magazine holds
15 LR, 18 Long, 22 Short. 26-inch bbl. Weight: 7.25 lbs. Sights:
Micrometer click receiver peep, open rear; hooded ramp front.
Pistol-grip stock w/cheekpiece and beavertail forearm, quick-
detachable swivels. Made from 1937 to 1938.
Model 46A. . . . . NiB $338 Ex $233 Gd $138
Mdl. 46A-LS (w/Lyman No. 57 receiver sight)NiB $386 Ex $276 Gd $189
Model L46A-LS (Left-hand action). . . NiB $650 Ex $355 Gd $269

Mossberg Model 140B

Mossberg Model 140K

Mossberg Model 144LS

Mossberg Model 146B

MODEL 46B BOLT-ACTION
REPEATER . . . . **NiB $290 Ex $167 Gd $133**
Takedown. Caliber: .22 LR, Long, Short. Tubular magazine holds 15 LR, 18 Long, 22 Short. 26-inch bbl. Weight: 7 lbs. Sights: Micrometer click receiver peep, open rear, hooded front. Plain pistol-grip stock w/cheekpiece, swivels. Note: Postwar version of this model has full magazine holding 20 LR, 23 Long, 30 Short. Made 1938 to 1950.

MODEL 46BT. . . . . **NiB $347 Ex $229 Gd $176**
Same as Model 46B except w/heavier bbl. and stock. Weight: 7.75 lbs. Made from 1938 to 1939.

MODEL 46C. . . . . **NiB $347 Ex $229 Gd $176**
Same as Model 46 except w/a heavier bbl. and stock than that model. Weight: 8.5 lbs. Made from 1936 to 1937.

MODEL 46M
BOLT-ACTION REPEATER. . . . . **NiB $347 Ex $229 Gd $176**
Caliber: .22 LR, Long, Short. Tubular magazine holds 22 Short, 18 Long, 15 LR. 23-inch bbl. Weight: 7 lbs. Sights: Microclick receiver peep, open rear; hooded ramp front. Two-piece Mannlicher-type stock w/cheekpiece and pistol-grip, swivels. Made 1940 to 1952.

MODEL 50
AUTOLOADING RIFLE. . . . . **NiB $298 Ex $213 Gd $139**
Same as Model 51 except w/plain stock w/o beavertail cheekpiece, swivels or receiver peep sight. Made from 1939 to 1942.
MODEL 51 AUTOLOADING RIFLE . . **NiB $298 Ex $213 Gd $139**

Takedown. Caliber: .22 LR. Fifteen-round tubular magazine in buttstock. 24-inch bbl. Weight: 7.25 lbs. Sights: Micrometer click receiver peep, open rear; hooded ramp front. Cheekpiece stock w/ full pistol grip and beavertail forearm, swivels. Made in 1939 only.

MODEL 51M AUTOLOADING RIFLE. NiB $278 Ex $154 Gd $123
Caliber: .22 LR. Fifteen-round tubular magazine. 20-inch bbl. Weight: 7 lbs. Sights: Microclick receiver peep, open rear; hooded ramp front. Two-piece Mannlicher-type stock w/pistol-grip and cheekpiece, hard-rubber buttplate and sling swivels. Made from 1939 to 1946.

MODEL 140B SPORTER-TARGET RIFLE NiB $254 Ex $186 Gd $134
Same as Model 140K except w/peep rear sight, hooded ramp front sight. Made from 1957 to 1958.

MODEL 140K BOLT-ACTION REPEATER NiB $248 Ex $197 Gd $123
Caliber: .22 LR, .22 Long, .22 Short. Seven-round clip magazine. 24.5-inch bbl. Weight: 5.75 lbs. Sights: Open rear; bead front. Monte Carlo stock w/cheekpiece and pistol-grip, sling swivels. Made 1955 to 1958.

MODEL 142-A BOLT-ACTION
REPEATING CARBINE. . . . . . . **NiB $277 Ex $233 Gd $166**
Caliber: .22 Short Long, LR. Seven-round detachable box magazine. 18-inch bbl. Weight: 6 lbs. Sights: Peep rear, military-type front. Monte Carlo stock w/pistol-grip, hinged forearm pulls down to form hand grip; sling swivels mounted on left side of stock. Made from 1949 to 1957.

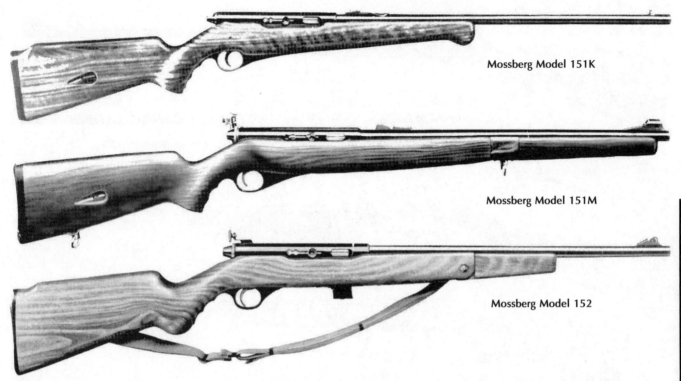

Mossberg Model 151K

Mossberg Model 151M

Mossberg Model 152

RIFLES

MODEL 142K . . . . **NiB $244 Ex $152 Gd $109**
Same as Model 142 except w/open rear sight. Made 1953 to 1957.

**MODEL 144 BOLT-ACTION
TARGET RIFLE** . . . . **NiB $390 Ex $288 Gd $215**
Caliber: .22 LR. Seven-round detachable box magazine. 26-inch heavy bbl. Weight: 8 lbs. Sights: Microclick receiver peep; hooded front. Pistol-grip target stock w/beavertail forearm, adj. hand stop, swivels. Made from 1949 to 1954. Note: This model designation was resumed c.1973 to replace Model 144LS, and then disc. again in 1985.

MODEL 144LS . . . . **NiB $385 Ex $277 Gd $205**
Same as Model 144 except w/Lyman No. 57MS or Mossberg S331 receiver sight and Lyman 17A front sight. Made from 1954 to date. Note: Since 1973, this model has been marketed as Model 144.

MODEL 146B BOLT-ACTION REPEATER NiB $347 Ex $190 Gd $139
Takedown. Caliber: .22 LR, Long, Short. Tubular magazine holds 30 Short, 23 Long, 20 LR. 26-inch bbl. Weight: 7 lbs. Sights: Micrometer click rear peep, open rear; hooded front. Plain stock w/pistol-grip, Monte Carlo comb and cheekpiece, knob forend tip, swivels. Made from 1949 to 1954.

MODEL 151K . . . . **NiB $290 Ex $193 Gd $130**
Same as Model 151M except w/24-inch bbl., weight: 6 lbs., w/o peep sight, plain stock w/Monte Carlo comb and cheekpiece, pistol-grip knob, forend tip, w/o swivels. Made from 1950 to 1951.

MODEL 151M AUTOLOADING RIFLE NiB $370 Ex $199 Gd $138
Improved version of Model 51M w/same general specifications, complete action is instantly removable w/o use of tools. Made 1946 to 1958.

MODEL 152 AUTOLOADING CARBINE NiB $276 Ex $197 Gd $135
Caliber: .22 LR. Seven-round detachable box magazine. 18-inch bbl. Weight: 5 lbs. Sights: Peep rear; military-type front. Monte Carlo stock w/pistol-grip, hinged forearm pulls down to form hand grip, sling mounted on swivels on left side of stock. Made 1948 to 1957.

MODEL 152K . . . . **NiB $233 Ex $176 Gd $121**
Same as Model 152 except w/open instead of peep rear sight. Made from 1950 to 1957.

MODEL 320B BOY SCOUT TARGET RIFLE NiB $233 Ex $176 Gd $121
Same as Model 340K except single-shot w/auto. safety. Made 1960 to 1971.

**MODEL 320K HAMMERLESS
BOLT-ACTION SINGLE-SHOT** . . **NiB $200 Ex $123 Gd $90**
Same as Model 346K except single-shot, w/drop-in loading platform, automatic safety. Weight: 5.75 lbs. Made from 1958 to 1960.

MODEL 321B . . . . **NiB $347 Ex $190 Gd $139**
Same as Model 321K except w/receiver peep sight. Made 1972 to 1975.

**MODEL 321K BOLT-ACTION
SINGLE-SHOT** . . . . **NiB $347 Ex $190 Gd $139**
Same as Model 341 except single-shot. Made from 1972 to 1980.

**MODEL 333
AUTOLOADING CARBINE** . . . . **NiB $266 Ex $180 Gd $145**
Caliber: .22 LR. 15-round tubular magazine. 20-inch bbl. Weight: 6.25 lbs. Sights: Open rear; ramp front. Monte Carlo stock w/checkered pistol grip and forearm, bbl. band, swivels. Made 1972 to 1973.

MODEL 340B TARGET SPORTER . . . **NiB $231 Ex $188 Gd $133**
Same as Model 340K except w/peep rear sight, hooded ramp front sight. Made from 1958 to 1981.

**MODEL 340K HAMMERLESS
BOLT-ACTION REPEATER** . . . . **NiB $231 Ex $188 Gd $133**
Same as Model 346K except clip type, 7-round magazine. Made from 1958 to 1971.

MODEL 340M . . . . **NiB $650 Ex $390 Gd $238**
Same as Model 340K except w/18.5-inch bbl., Mannlicher-style stock w/swivels and sling. Weight: 5.25 lbs. Made 1970 to 1971.

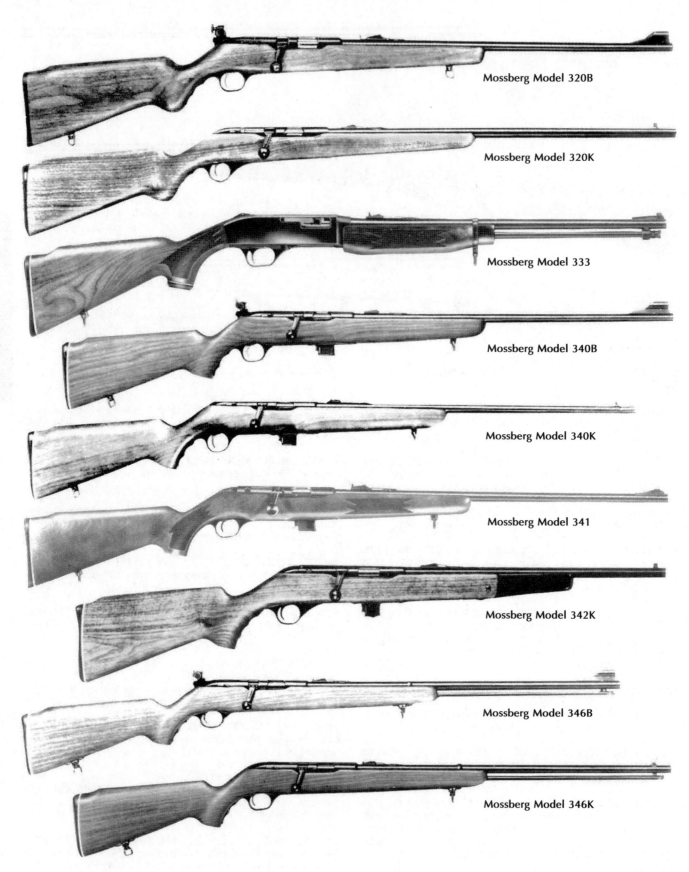

Mossberg Model 320B

Mossberg Model 320K

Mossberg Model 333

Mossberg Model 340B

Mossberg Model 340K

Mossberg Model 341

Mossberg Model 342K

Mossberg Model 346B

Mossberg Model 346K

Mossberg Model 350K
Autoloading — Clip Type

Mossberg Model 351K
Automatic Sporter

Mossberg Model 352K
Carbine

Mossberg Model 353
Carbine

Mossberg Model 377
Plinkster

MODEL 341 BOLT-ACTION REPEATERNiB $290 Ex $144 Gd $110
Caliber: .22 Short. Long, LR. Seven-round clip magazine. 24-inch bbl. Weight: 6.5 lbs. Sights: Open rear, ramp front. Monte Carlo stock w/ checkered pistol-grip and forearm, sling swivels. Made 1972 to 1985.

MODEL 342K HAMMERLESS
BOLT-ACTION CARBINE . . . . NiB $240 Ex $150 Gd $113
Same as Model 340K except w/18-inch bbl., stock w/no cheekpiece, extension forend is hinged, pulls down to form hand grip; sling swivels and web strap on left side of stock. Weight: 5 lbs. Made 1958 to 1974.

MODEL 346B . . . . NiB $240 Ex $180 Gd $113
Same as Model 346K except w/peep rear sight, hooded ramp front sight. Made from 1958 to 1967.

MODEL 346K HAMMERLESS
BOLT-ACTION REPEATER. . . . NiB $240 Ex $150 Gd $113
Caliber: .22 Short. Long, LR. Tubular magazine holds 25 Short, 20 Long, 18 LR. 24-inch bbl. Weight: 6.5 lbs. Sights: Open rear; bead front. Walnut stock w/Monte Carlo comb, cheekpiece, pistol-grip, sling swivels. Made from 1958 to 1971.

MODEL 350K AUTOLOADING
RIFLE — CLIP TYPE . . . . NiB $240 Ex $150 Gd $113
Caliber: .22 Short (High Speed), Long, LR. Seven-round clip magazine. 23.5-inch bbl. Weight: 6 lbs. Sights: Open rear; bead front. Monte

Carlo stock w/pistol-grip. Made from 1958 to 1971.

MODEL 351C
AUTOLOADING CARBINE . . . . NiB $240 Ex $150 Gd $113
Same as Model 351K except w/18.5-inch bbl., Western carbine-style stock w/barrel band and sling swivels. Weight: 5.5 lbs. Made from 1965 to 1971.

MODEL 351K AUTOLOADING
SPORTER . . . . NiB $240 Ex $150 Gd $113
Caliber: .22 LR. Fifteen-round tubular magazine in buttstock. 24-inch bbl. Weight: 6 lbs. Sights: Open rear; bead front. Monte Carlo stock w/pistol-grip. Made from 1960 to 1971.

MODEL 352K AUTOLOADING CARBINE NiB $240 Ex $150 Gd $113
Caliber: .22 Short, Long, LR. Seven-round clip magazine. 18-inch bbl. Weight: 5 lbs. Sights: Open rear; bead front. Monte Carlo stock w/pistol grip; extension forend of Tenite is hinged, pulls down to form hand grip; sling swivels, web strap. Made from 1958 to 1971.

MODEL 353 AUTOLOADING CARBINE . . . NiB $240 Ex $150 Gd $113
Caliber: .22 LR. Seven round clip magazine. 18-inch bbl. Weight: 5 lbs. Sights: Open rear; ramp front. Monte Carlo stock w/checkered pistol-grip and forearm; black Tenite extension forend pulls down to form hand grip. Made 1972 to 1985.

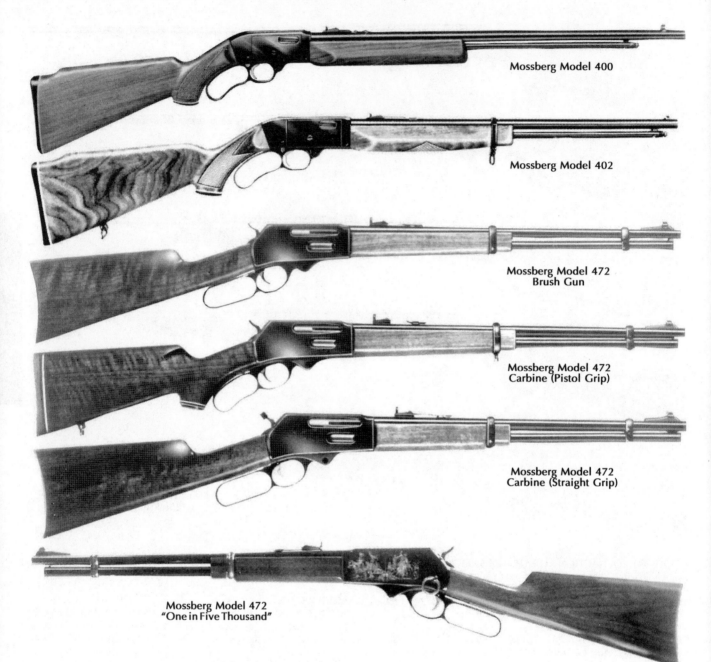

Mossberg Model 400

Mossberg Model 402

Mossberg Model 472
Brush Gun

Mossberg Model 472
Carbine (Pistol Grip)

Mossberg Model 472
Carbine (Straight Grip)

Mossberg Model 472
"One in Five Thousand"

MODEL 377 PLINKSTER AUTOLOADER NiB $278 Ex $200 Gd $155
Caliber: .22 LR. Fifteen-round tubular magazine. 20-inch bbl. Weight: 6.25 lbs. 4x scope sight. Thumbhole stock w/rollover cheekpiece, Monte Carlo comb, checkered forearm; molded of modified polystyrene foam in walnut-finish; sling swivel studs. Made 1977 to 1979.

MODEL 380 SEMIAUTOMATIC RIFLE NiB $278 Ex $200 Gd $155
Caliber: .22 LR. Fifteen-round buttstock magazine. 20-inch bbl. Weight: 5.5 lbs. Sights: Open rear; bead front. Made 1980 to 1985.

MODEL 400 PALOMINO LEVER-ACTION NiB $390 Ex $242 Gd $161
Hammerless. Caliber: .22 Short, Long, LR. Tubular magazine holds 20 Short, 17 Long, 15 LR. 24-inch bbl. Weight: 5.5 lbs. Sights: Open rear; bead front. Monte Carlo stock w/checkered pistol-grip; beavertail forearm. Made 1959 to 1964.
MODEL 402 PALOMINO CARBINE. . NiB $390 Ex $242 Gd $161

Same as Model 400 except w/18.5-inch (1961-64) or 20-inch bbl. (1964-71), forearm w/bbl. band, swivels; magazine holds two fewer rounds. Weight: 4.75 lbs. Made from 1961 to 1971.

MODEL 430 AUTOLOADING RIFLE . NiB $340 Ex $180 Gd $135
Caliber: .22 LR. Eighteen-round tubular magazine. 24-inch bbl. Weight: 6.25 lbs. Sights: Open rear; bead front. Monte Carlo stock w/checkered pistol grip; checkered forearm. Made 1970 to 1971.

MODEL 432 WESTERN-STYLE AUTO NiB $340 Ex $180 Gd $135
Same as Model 430 except w/plain straight-grip carbine-type stock and forearm, bbl. band, sling swivels. Magazine capacity: 15 cartridges. Weight: 6 lbs. Made from 1970 to 1971.

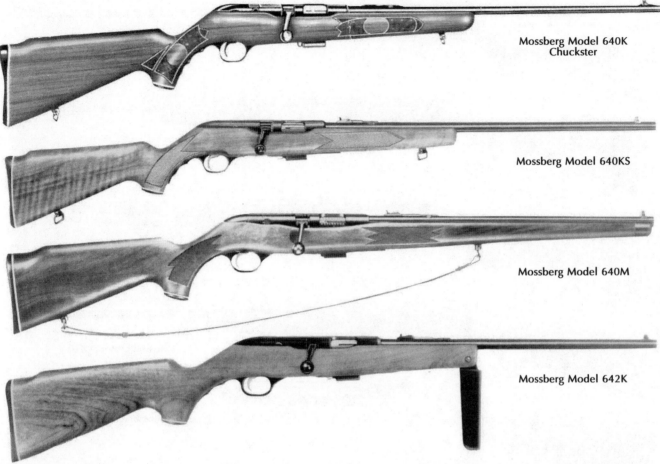

Mossberg Model 640K Chuckster

Mossberg Model 640KS

Mossberg Model 640M

Mossberg Model 642K

RIFLES

MODEL 472 BRUSH GUN . . . NiB $340 Ex $180 Gd $135
Same as Model 472 Carbine w/straight-grip stock except w/18-inch bbl., weight: 6.5 lbs. Caliber: .30-30. Magazine capacity: 5 rounds. Made from 1974 to 1976.

MODEL 472 LEVER-ACTION CARBINE NiB $340 Ex $180 Gd $135
Calibers: .30-30, .35 Rem. Six round tubular magazine. 20-inch bbl. Weight: 6.75 to 7 lbs. Sights: Open rear; ramp front. Pistol-grip or straight-grip stock, forearm w/bbl. band; sling swivels on pistol-grip model saddle ring on straight-grip model. Made from 1972 to 1979.

MODEL 472 ONE IN FIVE THOUSAND NiB $665 Ex $423 Gd $240
Same as Model 472 Brush Gun except w/Indian scenes etched on receiver; brass buttplate, saddle ring and bbl. bands, gold-plated trigger, bright blued finish, select walnut stock and forearm. Limited edition of 5,000; serial numbered 1 to 5,000. Made in 1974.

MODEL 472 RIFLE . . . . NiB $340 Ex $180 Gd $135
Same as Model 472 Carbine w/pistol-grip stock except w/24-inch bbl., 5-round magazine, weight: 7 lbs. Made from 1974 to 1976.

MODEL 479
Caliber: .30-30. Six-round tubular magazine. 20-inch bbl. Weight: 6.75 to 7 lbs. Sights: Open rear; ramp front. Made 1983 to 1985.
Model 479 Rifle . . . . NiB $340 Ex $180 Gd $135
Model 479PCA
(carbine w/20-inch bbl.) . . . . NiB $340 Ex $180 Gd $135
Model 479RR
(Roy Rogers model, 5000 Ltd. Ed.) . . NiB $665 Ex $423 Gd $240
MODEL 620K HAMMERLESS SINGLE-SHOT

BOLT-ACTION RIFLE . . . . . . NiB $290 Ex $179 Gd $133
Single shot. Caliber: .22 WMR. 24-inch bbl. Weight: 6 lbs. Sights: Open rear; bead front. Monte Carlo stock w/cheekpiece, pistol-grip, sling swivels. Made from 1959 to 1960.

MODEL 620K-A . . . . NiB $290 Ex $179 Gd $133
Same as Model 640K except w/sight modification. Made 1960 to 1968.

MODEL 640K CHUCKSTER HAMMERLESS
BOLT-ACTION RIFLE . . . . . . NiB $338 Ex $228 Gd $136
Caliber: .22 WMR. Five-round detachable clip magazine. 24-inch bbl. Weight: 6 lbs. Sights: Open rear; bead front. Monte Carlo stock w/cheekpiece, pistol grip, sling swivels. Made from 1959 to 1984.

MODEL 640KS . . . . .NiB $338 Ex $ 228 Gd $136
Deluxe version of Model 640K w/select walnut stock hand checkering; gold-plated front sight, rear sight elevator, and trigger. Made 1960 to 1964.

MODEL 640M . . . . NiB $665 Ex $423 Gd $240
Similar to Model 640K except w/heavy receiver and jeweled bolt. 20-inch bbl., full length Mannlicher-style stock w/Monte Carlo comb and cheekpiece, swivels and leather sling. 40.75 inches overall. Weight: 6 lbs. Made from 1971 to 1973.

MODEL 642K CARBINE . . . . . NiB $396 Ex $277 Gd $194
Caliber: .22 WMR. Five-round detachable clip magazine. 18-inch bbl. Weight: 5 lbs. 38.25 inches overall. Sights: Open rear; bead front. Monte Carlo walnut stock w/black Tenite forearm extension that pulls down to form hand grip. Made from 1961 to 1968.

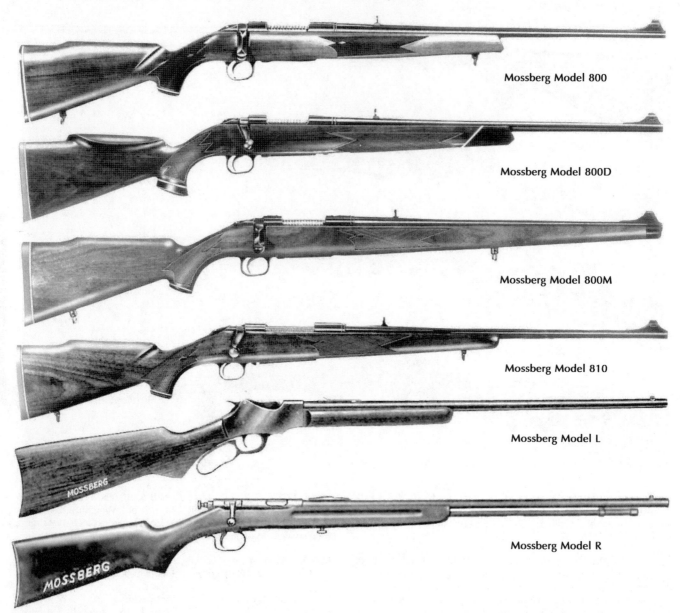

Mossberg Model 800

Mossberg Model 800D

Mossberg Model 800M

Mossberg Model 810

Mossberg Model L

Mossberg Model R

MODEL 800 BOLT-ACTION
CENTERFIRE RIFLE . . . . **NiB $455 Ex $307 Gd $200**
.222 Rem., .22-250, .243 Win., .308 Win. Four-round mag., 3-round in .222. 22-inch bbl. Weight: 7.5 lbs. Sights: Folding leaf rear; ramp front. Monte Carlo stock w/cheekpiece, checkered pistol-grip and forearm, sling swivels. Made from 1967 to 1979.

MODEL 800D SUPER GRADE. **NiB $455 Ex $307 Gd $200**
Deluxe version of Model 800 except w/stock w/rollover comb and cheekpiece, rosewood forend tip and pistol-grip cap. Weight: 6.75 lbs. Chambered for all calibers listed for the Model 800 except for .222 Rem. Sling swivels. Made from 1970 to 1973.

MODEL 800M . . . . **NiB $650 Ex $315 Gd $209**
Same as Model 800 except w/flat bolt handle, 20-inch bbl., Mannlicher-style stock. Weight: 6.5 lbs. Calibers: .22-250, .243 Win., .308 Win. Made from 1969 to 1972.

MODEL 800VT VARMINT/TARGET . . **NiB $455 Ex $307 Gd $200**
Similar to Model 800 except w/24-inch heavy bbl., no sights. Weight: 9.5 lbs. Calibers: .222 Rem., .22-250, .243 Win. Made 1968 to 1979.

MODEL 810 BOLT-ACTION CENTERFIRE RIFLE
Calibers: .270 Win., .30-06, 7mm Rem. Mag., .338 Win. Mag. Detachable box magazine (1970-75) or internal magazine w/hinged floorplate (1972 to date). Capacity: Four-round in .270 and .30-06, 3-round in Magnums. 22-inch bbl. in .270 and .30-06, 24-inch in Magnums. Weight: 7.5 to 8 lbs. Sights: Leaf rear; ramp front. Stock w/Monte Carlo comb and cheekpiece, checkered pistol-grip and forearm, grip cap, sling swivels. Made from 1970 to 1979.
Standard calibers . . . . **NiB $390 Ex $333 Gd $232**
Magnum calibers . . . . **NiB $370 Ex $316 Gd $226**

MODEL 1500 MOUNTAINEER
GRADE I CENTERFIRE RIFLE. . NiB $441 Ex $338 Gd $288
Calibers: .223, .243, .270, .30-06, 7mm Mag. 22-inch or 24-inch (7mm Mag.) bbl. Weight: 7 lbs. 10 oz. Hardwood walnut-finished checkered stock. Sights: Hooded ramp front w/gold bead; fully adj. rear. Drilled and tapped for scope mounts. Sling swivel studs. Imported from 1986 to 1987.

Musgrave Premier NR5

Musgrave RSA NR1

Musgrave Valiant NR6

Musketeer Mauser Sporter

MODEL 1500 VARMINT BOLT-ACTION RIFLE
Same as Model 1500 Grade I except w/22-inch heavy bbl. Chambered in .222, .22-250, .223 only. High-luster blued finish or Parkerized satin finished stock. Imported from Japan 1986 to 1987.
High-luster blue . . . . NiB $440 Ex $328 Gd $288
Parkerized satin finish . . . . . . NiB $455 Ex $338 Gd $298

MODEL 1707LS CLASSIC
HUNTER BOLT-ACTION RIFLE . . . . . NiB $479 Ex $369 Gd $266
Same as Model 1500 Grade I except w/checkered classic-style stock and Schnabel forend. Chambered in 243, 270, 30-06 only. Imported from Japan 1986 to 1987.

MODEL B BOLT-ACTION RIFLE**NiB $340 Ex $205 Gd $113**
Takedown. Caliber: .22 LR, Long, Short. Single-shot. 22-inch bbl. Sights: Open rear; bead front. Plain pistol-grip stock. Made from 1930 to 1932.

MODEL K SLIDE-ACTION REPEATER NiB $545 Ex $390 Gd $233
Hammerless. Takedown. Caliber: .22 LR, Long, Short. Tubular magazine holds 20 Short, 16 Long, 14 LR. 22-inch bbl. Weight: 5 lbs. Sights: Open rear; bead front. Plain, straight-grip stock. Grooved slide handle. Made from 1922 to 1931.

MODELS L42A, L43, L45A, L46A-LS
See Models 42A, 43, 45A and 46A-LS respectively; "L" refers to a left-hand version of those rifles.

MODEL L SINGLE-SHOT RIFLE . . . . . NiB $850 Ex $535 Gd $429
Martini-type falling-block lever-action. Takedown. Caliber: .22 LR, Long, Short. 24-inch bbl. Weight: 5 lbs. Sights: Open rear; bead front. Plain pistol-grip stock and forearm. Made from 1929 to 1932.

MODEL M SLIDE-ACTION REPEATER**NiB $550 Ex $ 340 Gd $227**
Specifications same as for Model K except w/24-inch octagon bbl., pistol-grip stock, weighs 5.5 lbs. Made from 1928 to 1931.

MODEL R BOLT-ACTION REPEATER. NiB $379 Ex $265 Gd $190
Takedown. Caliber: .22 LR, Long, Short. Tubular magazine. 24-inch bbl. Sights: Open rear; bead front. Plain pistol-grip stock. Made from 1930 to 1932.

MUSGRAVE RIFLES, MUSGRAVE MFRS. & DIST. (PTY) LTD. — Bloemfontein, South Africa

PREMIER NR5 BOLT-
ACTION HUNTING RIFLE . . . NiB $460 Ex $375 Gd $288
Calibers: .243 Win., .270 Win., .30-06, .308 Win., 7mm Rem. Mag. Five-round magazine. 25.5-inch bbl. Weight: 8.25 lbs. Furnished w/o sights, but drilled and tapped for scope mount. Select walnut Monte Carlo stock w/cheekpiece, checkered pistol-grip and fore-arm, contrasting pistol-grip cap and forend tip, recoil pad, swivel studs. Musgrave or Mauser action. Made from 1971 to 1976.

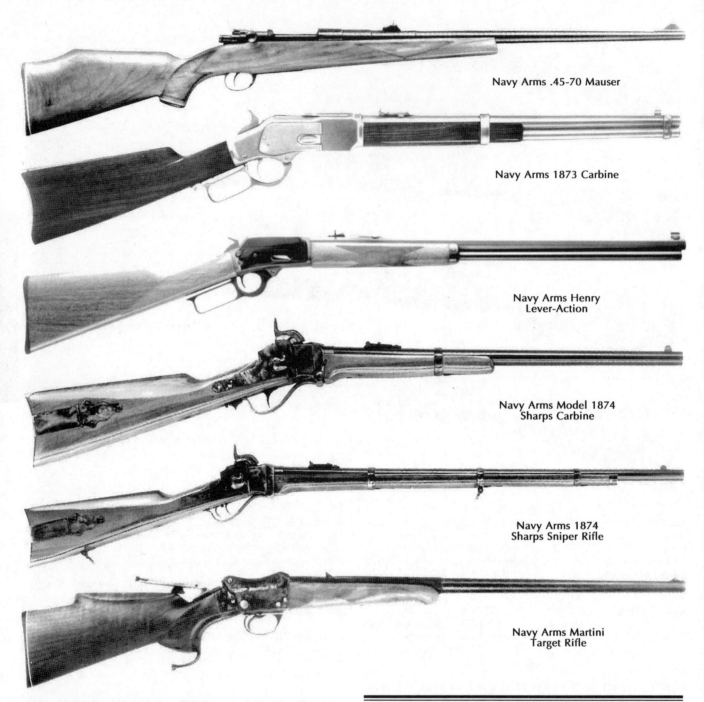

Navy Arms .45-70 Mauser

Navy Arms 1873 Carbine

Navy Arms Henry
Lever-Action

Navy Arms Model 1874
Sharps Carbine

Navy Arms 1874
Sharps Sniper Rifle

Navy Arms Martini
Target Rifle

RSA NR1 BOLT-ACTION
SINGLE-SHOT TARGET RIFLE. NiB $449 Ex $420 Gd $300
Caliber: .308 Win. (7.62mm NATO). 26.4-inch heavy bbl. Weight: 10 lbs. Sights: Aperture receiver; tunnel front. Walnut target stock w/beavertail forearm, handguard, bbl. band, rubber buttplate, sling swivels. Made from 1971 to 1976.

VALIANT NR6 HUNTING RIFLE NiB $415 Ex $369 Gd $255
Similar to Premier except w/24-inch bbl.; stock w/straight comb, skip French-style checkering, no grip cap or forend tip. Sights: Leaf rear; hooded ramp front bead sight. Weight: 7.7 lbs. Made from 1971 to 1976.

MUSKETEER RIFLES — Washington, D.C.
Manufactured by Firearms International Corp.

MAUSER SPORTER
FN Mauser bolt action. .243, .25-06, .270, .264 Mag., .308, .30-06, 7mm Mag., .300 Win. Mag. Magazine holds 5 standard, 3 Magnum cartridges. 24-inch bbl. Weight: 7.25 lbs. No sights. Monte Carlo stock w/checkered pistol-grip and forearm, swivels. Made 1963 to 1972.

	NiB	Ex	Gd
Standard Sporter	$415	$295	$255
Deluxe Sporter	$459	$380	$276
Standard Carbine	$415	$295	$255

Navy Arms
Revolving Carbine

Navy Arms
Rolling Block Baby Carbine

Navy Arms
Rolling Block Buffalo Rifle

NAVY ARMS—Importer in MArtinsburg, WV, previously Union City, NJ and Ridgefield, NJ

.45-70 MAUSER CARBINE . . . NiB $333 Ex $227 Gd $160
Same as .45-70 Mauser Rifle except w/18-inch bbl., straight-grip stock w/low comb, weight: 7.5 lbs. Disc.

.45-70 MAUSER RIFLE . . . . . . NiB $260 Ex $221 Gd $155
Siamese Mauser bolt action. Caliber: .45-70 Govt. Three-round magazine. 24- or 26-inch bbl. Weight: 8.5 lbs. w/26-inch bbl. Sights: Open rear; ramp front: Checkered stock w/Monte Carlo comb. Intoduced 1973. Disc.

**MODEL 1873 WINCHESTER
BORDER RIFLE. . . . . NiB $1077 Ex $869 Gd $378**
Replica of Winchester Model 1873 Short Rifle. Calibers: .357 Mag., .44-40, and .45 Colt. 20- inch bbl., 39.25 inches overall. Weight: 7.6 lbs. Blued full octagonal barrel, color casehardened receiver w/ walnut stocks. Made from 1999 to 2009.

MODEL 1873 CARBINE . . . . NiB $1043 Ex $756 Gd $399
Similar to Model 1873 Rifle except w/blued receiver, 10-round magazine, 19-inch round bbl. carbine-style forearm w/bbl. band, weighs 6.75 lbs. Disc. Reissued in 1991 in .44-40 or .45 Colt.

MODEL 1873 LEVER-ACTION RIFLE NiB $1043 Ex $756 Gd $399
Replica of Winchester Model 1873. Casehardened receiver. Calibers: .22 LR, .357 Magnum, .44-40. 15-round magazine. 24-inch octagon bbl. Weight: 8 lbs. Sights: Open rear; blade front. Straight-grip stock, forearm w/end cap. Disc. Reissued in 1991 in .44-40 or .45 Colt w/12-round magazine. Disc. 1994.

MODEL 1873 TRAPPER . . . . . NiB $744 Ex $560 Gd $425
Same as Model 1873 Carbine, except w/16.5-inch bbl., 8-round magazine, weighs 6.25 lbs. Disc.

MODEL 1873 SPORTING CARBINE/RIFLE
Replica of Winchester Model 1873 Sporting Rifle. Calibers: .357 Mag. (24.25-inch bbl. only), .44-40 and .45 Colt. 24.25-inch bbl. (Carbine) or 30-inch bbl. (Rifle). 48.75 to 53 inches overall. Weight: 8.14 to 9.3 lbs. Octagonal barrel, case-hardened receiver and checkered walnut pistol-grip. Made from 1999 to 2003.
Carbine model . . . . NiB $970 Ex $844 Gd $630
Rifle model . . . . NiB $1035 Ex $928 Gd $670

**MODEL 1874 SHARPS
CAVALRY CARBINE . . . . NiB $1010 Ex $733 Gd $580**

Replica of Sharps 1874 Cavalry Carbine. Similar to Sniper Model, except w/22-inch bbl. and carbine stock. Caliber: .45-70. Imported from 1997 to 2009.

MODEL 1874 SHARPS SNIPER RIFLE
Replica of Sharps 1874 Sharpshooter's Rifle. Caliber: .45-70. Falling breech, single-shot. 30-inch bbl. 46.75 inches overall. Weight: 8.5 lbs. Double-set triggers. Color casehardened receiver. Blade front sight; rear sight w/elevation leaf. Polished blued bbl. Military three-band stock w/patch box. Imported from 1994 to 2000.
Infantry model (single trigger) . . . . . . NiB $933 Ex $790 Gd $630
Sniper model (double set trigger). . NiB $2013 Ex $1118 Gd $956

ENGRAVED MODELS
Yellowboy and Model 1873 rifles are available in deluxe models w/select walnut stocks and forearms and engraving in three grades. Grade "A" has delicate scrollwork in limited areas. Grade "B" is more elaborate with 40 percent coverage. Grade "C" has highest grade engraving. Add to value:
Grade "A" . . . . NiB $1023 Ex $779 Gd $615
Grade "B" . . . . NiB $1126 Ex $986 Gd $813
Grade "C" . . . . NiB $1568 Ex $995 Gd $723

HENRY LEVER-ACTION RIFLE
Replica of the Winchester Model 1860 Henry Rifle. Caliber: .44-40. Twelve round magazine. 16.5-, 22- or 24.25-inch octagon bbl. Weight: 7.5 to 9 lbs. 35.4 to 43.25 inches overall. Sights: Blade front, adjustable ladder rear. European walnut straight grip buttstock w/bbl. and side stock swivels. Imported from 1985 to date. Brass or steel receiver. Blued or color casehardened metal.
Carbine model w/22-inch bbl. (introduced 1992)NiB$735 Ex$479 Gd $376
Military rifle model (w/brass frame). . NiB $989 Ex $688 Gd $482
Trapper model (w/brass frame) . . . . . NiB $735 Ex $479 Gd $376
Trapper model (w/iron frame) . . . . . NiB $1055 Ex $800 Gd $479
W/"A" engraving, add. $325
W/"B" engraving, add. $550
W/"C" engraving, add. $950

MARTINI TARGET RIFLE. . . . . NiB $556 Ex $379 Gd $333
Martini single-shot action. Calibers: .444 Marlin, .45-70. 26- or 30-inch half-octagon or full-octagon bbl. Weight: 9 lbs. w/26-inch bbl. Sights: Creedmoor tang peep, open middle, blade front. Stock w/cheekpiece and pistol-grip, forearm w/Schnabel tip, both checkered. Intro. 1972. Disc.

**Navy Arms
Yellowboy Carbine
.22 LR**

REVOLVING CARBINE . . . . . NiB $641 Ex $540 Gd $400
Action resembles that of Remington Model 1875 Revolver. Casehardened frame. Calibers: .357 Magnum, .44-40, .45 Colt. Six round cylinder. 20-inch bbl. Weight: 5 lbs. Sights: Open rear; blade front. Straight-grip stock brass trigger guard and buttplate. Intro. 1968. Disc.

ROLLING BLOCK BABY CARBINE. . . NiB $255 Ex $190 Gd $155
Replica of small Remington Rolling Block single-shot action. Casehardened frame, brass trigger guard. Calibers: .22 LR, .22 Hornet, .357 Magnum, .44-40. 20-inch octagon or 22-inch round bbl. Weight: 5 lbs. Sights: Open rear; blade front. Straight-grip stock, plain forearm, brass buttplate. Imported from 1968 to 1981.

ROLLING BLOCK BUFFALO CARBINE NiB $439 Ex $333 Gd $227
Same as Buffalo Rifle except w/18-inch bbl., weight: 10 lbs

ROLLING BLOCK BUFFALO RIFLE . . NiB $720 Ex $572 Gd $338
Replica Remington Rolling Block single-shot action. Casehardened frame, brass trigger guard. Calibers: .444 Marlin, .45-70, .50-70. 26- or 30-inch heavy half-octagon or full-octagon bbl. Weight: 11 to 12 lbs. Sights: Open rear; blade front. Straight-grip stock w/brass buttplate, forearm w/brass bbl. band. Made from 1971 to 2003.

ROLLING BLOCK CREEDMOOR RIFLE
Same as Buffalo Rifle except calibers .45-70 and .50-70 only, 28- or 30-inch heavy half-octagon or full-octagon bbl., Creedmoor tang peep sight.
Target model . . . . NiB $1530 Ex $1109 Gd $775
Deluxe target model (disc. 1998) . NiB $1677 Ex $1330 Gd $190

YELLOWBOY CARBINE . . . . . NiB $865 Ex $590 Gd $443
Similar to Yellowboy Rifle except w/19-inch bbl., 10-round magazine (14-round in 22 Long Rifle), carbine-style forearm. Weight: 6.75 lbs. Disc. Reissued 1991 in .44-40 only.

YELLOWBOY LEVER-ACTION REPEATER NiB $1035 Ex $567 Gd $359
Replica of Winchester Model 1866. Calibers: .38 Special, .44-40. 15-round magazine. 24-inch octagon bbl. Weight: 8 lbs. Sights: Folding leaf rear; blade front. Straight-grip stock, forearm w/end cap. Intro. 1966. Disc. Reissued 1991 in .44-40 only w/12-round magazine and adj. ladder-style rear sight.

YELLOWBOY TRAPPER'S MODEL. . . NiB $723 Ex $500 Gd $379
Same as Yellowboy Carbine except w/16.5-inch bbl., 8-round magazine, weighs 6.25 lbs. Disc.

NEW ENGLAND FIREARMS — Gardner, Massachusetts

In 1987, New England Firearms was established as an independent company producing selected H&R models under the NEF logo. In 1991, H&R 1871, Inc. was formed from the residual of the parent company and that took over the New England Firearms facility. H&R 1871 produced firearms under both its logo and the NEF brand name until 1999, when the Marlin Firearms Company acquired the assets of H&R 1871.

HANDI-RIFLE . . . . NiB $245 Ex $190 Gd $137
Single-shot, break-open action w/side-lever release. Calibers: .22 Hornet, .22-250, .223, .243, .270, .30-30, .30-06, .45-70. 22-inch bbl. Weight: 7 lbs. Sights: Ramp front; folding rear. Drilled and tapped for scope mounts. Walnut-finished hardwood or synthetic stock. Blued finish. Made from 1989 to 2008.
Synthetic . . . . NiB $290 Ex $200 Gd $128
Synthetic/Stainless . . . . NiB $325 Ex $266 Gd $159
Youth model . . . . NiB $300 Ex $233 Gd $144
10th Anniversary model . . . . . NiB $822 Ex $555 Gd $375
Trapper's Edition . . . . NiB $337 Ex $265 Gd $190

SUPER LIGHT HANDI-RIFLE . . NiB $378 Ex $229 Gd $145
Cal.: .22 Hornet, .223 Rem., .243 Win. Same as Handi Rifle but with black synthetic stock and forearm, recoil pad. Bbl.: 20-inch special contour w/rebated muzzle. .223 Rem. model includes scope base and hammer extension. Weight: 5.5 lbs. Made 1997 to 2008.

SPORTSTER . . . . NiB $218 Ex $144 Gd $90
Cal.: .17 HMR, .17 Mach 2, .22 LR, .22 Mag. Bbl.: 20 or 22 inches, Weaver-style rail, no sights. Adult or youth (.22 LR only) dimensions. Stock and forearm: Black polymer. Made 1999 to 2008.

SURVIVOR. . . . . NiB $297 Ex $195 Gd $115
Cal.: .223 Rem., .308 Win., .357 Mag., .410/.45 Long Colt. Similar to Survivor series shotgun but with removable forearm and thumbhole stock (both with ammo compartments). Bbl.: 20 or 22 inches, blue or nickel finish. Weight: 6 lbs. Made 1996 to 2008.

NEWTON SPORTING RIFLES — Buffalo, New York. Manufactured by Newton Arms Co., Charles Newton Rifles Corp. and Buffalo Newton Rifle Co.

**BUFFALO
SPORTING RIFLE** . . . . NiB $2590 Ex $1800 Gd $970
Same general specifications as Standard Model, Second Type. Made c. 1922 to 1932 by Buffalo Newton Rifle Co.

**MAUSER
SPORTING RIFLE** . . . . NiB $2125 Ex $1633 Gd $1110
Mauser (Oberndorf) action. Caliber: .256 Newton. Five round box magazine, hinged floorplate. Double-set triggers. 24-inch bbl. Open rear sight, ramp front sight. Sporting stock w/checkered pistol-grip. Weight: 7 lbs. Made c. 1914 by Newton Arms Co.

**STANDARD MODEL
SPORTING RIFLE, FIRST TYPE** . . NiB $3597 Ex $2044 Gd $1035
Newton bolt action, interrupted screw-type breech-locking mechanism, double-set triggers. Calibers: .22, .256, .280, .30, ,33, ,35 Newton; ,30-06. 24-inch bbl. Sights: Open rear or cocking-piece peep; ramp front. Checkered pistol-grip stock. Weight: 7 to 8 lbs.,depending on caliber. Made c. 1916 to 1918 by Newton Arms Co. Second type was prototype only; never manufactured.

NEWTON SPRINGFIELD . . . NiB $1568 Ex $1105 Gd $890
Kit including a Marlin-built sporting stock with .256 Newton barrel. Springfield 1903 action and sights provided by customer. Original has square-cut barrels marked "Newton Arms Co. Buffalo, NY." Mfg. 1914 to 1917.

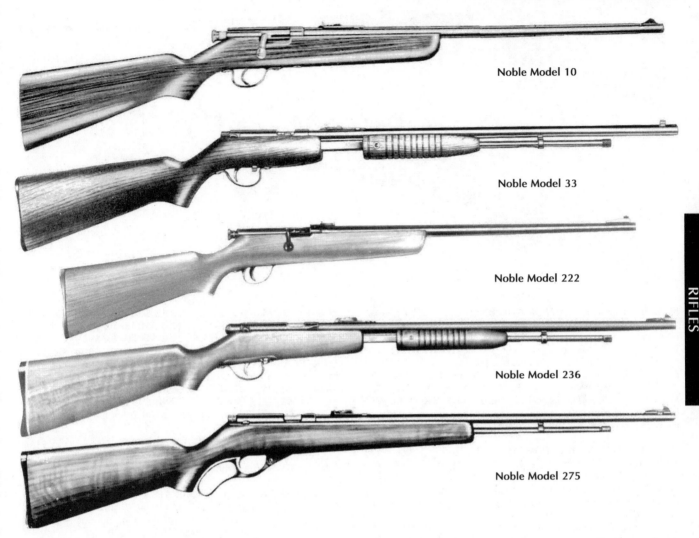

Noble Model 10

Noble Model 33

Noble Model 222

Noble Model 236

Noble Model 275

NIKKO FIREARMS, LTD. — Tochiga, Japan

See listings under Golden Eagle Rifles.

NOBLE MFG. CO. — Haydenville, Massachusetts

MODEL 10 BOLT-ACTION
SINGLE-SHOT RIFLE . . . . NiB $121 Ex $89 Gd $73
Caliber: .22 LR, Long, Short. 24-inch bbl. Plain pistol-grip stock. Sights: Open rear, bead front. Weight: 4 lbs. Made 1955 to 1958.

MODEL 20 BOLT-ACTION
SINGLE-SHOT RIFLE . . . . NiB $126 Ex $92 Gd $75
Manually cocked. Caliber: .22 LR, Long, Short. 22-inch bbl. Weight: 5 lbs. Sights: Open rear; bead front. Walnut stock w/pistol grip. Made from 1958 to 1963.

MODEL 33 SLIDE-ACTION REPEATER. NiB $230 Ex $110 Gd $80
Hammerless. Caliber: .22 LR, Long, Short. Tubular magazine holds 21 Short, 17 Long, 15 LR. 24-inch bbl. Weight: 6 lbs. Sights: Open rear; bead front. Tenite stock and slide handle. Made 1949 to 1953.

MODEL 33A . . . . NiB $115 Ex $89 Gd $69
Same general specifications as Model 33 except w/wood stock and slide handle. Made from 1953 to 1955.

MODEL 222 BOLT-ACTION
SINGLE-SHOT RIFLE . . . . NiB $240 Ex $120 Gd $80
Manually cocked. Caliber: .22 LR, Long, Short. Barrel integral w/receiver. Overall length: 38 inches. Weight: 5 lbs. Sights: Interchangeable V-notch and peep rear; ramp front. Scope mounting base. Pistol-grip stock. Made from 1958 to 1971.

MODEL 236 SLIDE-ACTION
REPEATING RIFLE . . . . NiB $159 Ex $140 Gd $97
Hammerless. Caliber: .22 Short, Long, LR. Tubular magazine holds 21 Short, 17 Long, 15 LR. 24-inch bbl. Weight: 5.5 lbs. Sights: Open rear; ramp front. Pistol-grip stock, grooved slide handle. Made from 1951 to 1971.

MODEL 278 LEVER-ACTION RIFLE . . NiB $227 Ex $139 Gd $110
Hammerless. Caliber: .22 Short, Long, LR. Tubular magazine holds 21 Short, 17 Long, 15 LR. 24-inch bbl. Weight: 5.5 lbs. Sights: Open rear; ramp front. Stock w/semipistol-grip. Made from 1958 to 1971.

NORINCO — Manufactured by Northern China Industries Corp., Beijing, China. Imported by Century International Arms; Interarms; KBI and others

Parker-Hale
Model 81 Classic

Parker-Hale
Model 87

MODEL 81S/AK SEMIAUTOMATIC RIFLE

Semiautomatic Kalashnikov style AK-47 action. Caliber: 7.62x39mm. Five, 30- or 40-round magazine. 17.5-inch bbl. 36.75 inches overall. Weight: 8.5 lbs. Hooded post front sight, 500 meters leaf rear sight. Oil-finished hardwood (military style) buttstock, pistol grip, forearm and handguard or folding metal stock. Black oxide finish. Imported 1988 to 1989.

NIdek 81S (w/wood stock) . . . . NiB $1244 Ex $965 Gd $733
Model 81S (w/folding metal stock) . . . NiB $1266 Ex $1002 Gd $753
Model 81S-5/56S-2
(w/folding metal stock) . . . . NiB $1339 Ex $1027 Gd $755

MODEL 84S/AK SEMIAUTOMATIC RIFLE

Semiautomatic Kalashnikov style AK-47 action. Caliber: .223 (5.56mm). 30-round magazine. 16.25-inch bbl. 35.5 inches overall. Weight: 8.75 lbs. Hooded post front sight, 800 meters leaf rear sight. Oil-finished hardwood (military style) buttstock, pistol grip, forearm and handguard; sporterized composite fiberglass stock or folding metal stock. Black oxide finish. Imported from 1988 to 1989.

Model 84S (w/wood stock) . . . . . . NiB $1479 Ex $1032 Gd $678
Model 84S-3 (w/folding metal stock) . . . NiB $1688 Ex $954 Gd $669
Model 84S-3 (w/composite stock) . NiB $1337 Ex $1043 Gd $645
Model 84S-5 (w/folding metal stock) . . . NiB $1613 Ex $981 Gd $687

MODEL AK-47 THUMBHOLE SPORTER

Semiautomatic AK-47 sporterized variant. Calibers: .223 (5.56mm) or 7.62x39mm. Five round magazine. 16.25-inch bbl. or 23.25-inch bbl. 35.5 or 42.5 inches overall. Weight: 8.5 to 10.3 lbs. Adj. post front sight, open adj. rear. Forged receiver w/black oxide finish. Walnut-finished thumbhole stock w/recoil pad. Imported from 1991 to 1993.

5.56mm . . . . NiB $775 Ex $466 Gd $337
7.62x39mm . . . . NiB $564 Ex $466 Gd $339

MODEL MAK 90/01 SPORT . . NiB $733 Ex $455 Gd $337

Similar to Model AK-47 Thumbhole Sporter except w/minor modifications implemented to meet importation requirements. Imported from 1994 to 1995.

OLYMPIC ARMS — Olympia, Washington

PCR SERIES

Gas-operated semi-auto action. Calibers: .17 Rem., .223, 7.62x39, 6x45, 6PPC or 9mm, .40 S&W, 4.5ACP (in carbine version only). Ten-round magazine. 16-, 20- or 24-inch bbl. Weight: 7 to 10.2 lbs. Black composite stocks. Post front, rear adj. sights; scope ready flattop. Barrel fluting. William set trigger. Made from 1994 to date.

PCR-1 Ultra Match . . . . NiB $981 Ex $760 Gd $583
PCR-2 Mult-iMatch ML-1 . . . NiB $1032 Ex $915 Gd $633
PCR-3 Multi-Match ML-2 . . . NiB $1070 Ex $959 Gd $654
PCR-4 AR-15 Match . . . . NiB $877 Ex $808 Gd $521
MCR-5 CAR-15 (.223 Rem.) . . NiB $977 Ex $803 Gd $522
PCR5 CAR-15
(9mm, 40 S&W, .45 ACP) . . . . NiB $903 Ex $794 Gd $538
PCR-5 CAR (.223 Rem.) . . . . . NiB $955 Ex $731 Gd $510
PCR-6/A-2 (7.62x39mm) . . . . NiB $895 Ex $692 Gd $486

BOLT-ACTION SAKO . . . . NiB $755 Ex $575 Gd $456
Cal.: Various from .17 Rem. to .416 Rem. Mag. Bbl.: Fluted; various stock options. Value is for base model without custom options.

ULTRA CSR TACTICAL . . . NiB $1877 Ex $1355 Gd $1043
Cal.: .308 Win. Sako action. Bbl.: Heavy, 26 inches, broach cut. Stock: Bell & Carlson black or synthetic with aluminum bedding. Harris bipod included. Made from 1996 to 2000.

COUNTER SNIPER RIFLE . NiB $1490 Ex $1266 Gd $1079
Bolt action. Cal.: .308 Win. Bbl.: Heavy, 26-inches. Stock: Camo fiberglass. Weight: 10.5 lbs. Disc. 1987.

SURVIVOR 1 . . . . NiB $455 Ex $276 Gd $264
Converts M1911 into bolt-action carbine. Cal.: .223 Rem., .45 ACP. Bbl.: 16.25 inches. Collapsible stock. Available for S&W and Browning Hi-Power. Weight: 5 lbs.

CAR 97 . . . . NiB $909 Ex $693 Gd $633
Cal.: .223 Rem., 9mm Para., 10mm, .40 S&W, .45 ACP. Similar to PCR-5 but w/ 16-inch button-rifled barrel. A2 sights, fixed CAR stock, post-ban muzzle brake. Weight: 7 lbs. Made from 1997 to 2004.
M-4 version (disc. 2004), add $75

FAR-15 . . . . NiB $1035 Ex $780 Gd $669
Featherweight model. Cal.: .223 Rem. Bbl.: 16 inches, lightweight, button-rifled, collapsible stock. Weight: 9.2 lbs. Made from 2001 to 2004.

GI-16 . . . . NiB $989 Ex $760 Gd $590
Cal.: .223 Rem. Forged aluminum receiver, matte finish. Bbl.: Match grade, 16 inches, button rifled. Collapsible stock. Weight: 7 lbs. Made 2004 and 2006.

GI-20 . . . . NiB $877 Ex $698 Gd $549
Cal. .223 Rem. Similar to GI-16 except w/20-inch heavy bbl., A-2 lower. Weight: 8.4 lbs. Made 2004.

Olympic Arms OA-93 Carbine

Olympic Arms LTF Tactical Rifle

Olympic Arms K4B

Olympic Arms K7 Eliminator

K7 ELIMINATOR. . . . . NiB $1087 Ex $800 Gd $633
Cal.: .223 Rem. Bbl.: 16 inches, stainless steel w/flash supp.; adj. A2 rear sight and front post; A2 buttstock. Weight: 7.8 lbs.

K8 TARGET MATCH. . . . . . . NiB $1087 Ex $723 Gd $572
Cal.: .223 Rem. Bbl.: 20-inch bull bbl., stainless, button rifling; Picatinny flattop upper, A2 buttstock. Weight: 8.5 lbs.

K8-MAG. . . . . NiB $1423 Ex $1150 Gd $976
Similar to Target Match model. Cal.: .223 WSSM, .243 WSSM, .25 WSSM, .300 WSM. 24-inch bbl. Weight: 9.4 lbs.

K9/K10/K40/K45 . . . . NiB $1132 Ex $955 Gd $780
Cal.: 9mm Para., 10mm Norma, .40 S&W, .45 ACP. Blow-back action. Bbl.: 16 inches w/flash suppressor and bayonet lug. Adj. A2 rear sight. Collapsible stock. Weight: 6.7 lbs.

K9GL/K40GL . . . . NiB $1188 Ex $992 Gd $694
Similar to K9 series. Cal.: 9mm Para., .40 S&W. Lower designed to accept Glock magazines. Bbl.: 16 inches; flash suppressor. Collapsible stock. No magazine furnished.
A3 upper, add $126

K16 . . . . NiB $962 Ex $710 Gd $577
Cal.: .223 Rem. Bbl.: 16 inches, free-floating, button rifled. Picatinny flattop upper; A2 buttstock. Weight: 7.5 lbs.
K30R . . . . NiB $1077 Ex $879 Gd $683
W/A3 upper, add $126

K-30 (.30 carbine) . . . . NiB $978 Ex $668 Gd $533
Cal.: 7.62x39mm. Bbl.: 16-inch stainless steel, adj. rear sight. Parkerized steel parts. Six-point collapsible stock.

K68 . . . . NiB $1198 Ex $978 Gd $645
Cal.: 6.8 Rem. SPC. Bbl.: 16-inch stainless steel, A2 upper with adj. rear sight and flash suppressor. Matte black anodized receiver, Parkerized steel parts. Six-position collapsible A2 stock w/pistol grip.
W/A3 upper, add $126

K74 . . . . NiB $1027 Ex $903 Gd $645
Cal.: 5.45x39mm. Bbl.: 16-inches, button rifling; flash suppressor and adj. front sight. Six-position collapsible stock. Weight 6.75 lbs.

OA-93 Carbine. . . . . NiB $1390 Ex $1133 Gd $976
Based on OA-93 pistol. Cal.: .223 Rem. Bbl.: 16 inches. Flattop receiver. Aluminum side folding stock, round aluminum handguard, Vortex flash supp. Weight: 7.5 lbs. Made 1998 and from 2004 to 2007.

OA-93PT . . . . NiB $1077 Ex $976 Gd $692
Similar to OA-93 carbine but with aluminum receiver, black matte anodized finish. Bbl.: 16 inches, match grade chromemoly steel with removable muzzle brake, push-button removable stock. Weight: 7 lbs. Made from 2006 to 2007.

LTF TACTICAL RIFLE . . . . . NiB $1338 Ex $1056 Gd $777
Cal. .223 Rem. Bbl.: 16 inches, fluted or non-fluted w/flash supp. Black matte anodized receiver. Firsh-type forearm, Picatinny rails, Parkerized steel parts. Tube-style stock. Weight: 6.4 lbs.
Fluted bbl., add 10%

K3B CARBINE . . . . . . NiB $1189 Ex $873 Gd $689
Cal. .223 Rem. Bbl.: 16 inches, match grade chromemoly steel w/ flash supp. A2 rear sight and buttstock; adj. front post sight.
A3 Flattop receiver, add $75
FAR carbine, add $75
M4 carbine, add. $75
A3-TC carbine, add $250

K4B/K4B68. . . . . NiB $1087 Ex $764 Gd $590
Cal.: .223 Rem., 6.8 SPC. Bbl.: 20 inches, match grade, chromemoly steel, button rifled; flash supp. Adj. A2 rear sight and front post; A2 buttstock, upper receiver and hand guard. Weight: 8.5 lbs.
Flattop receiver, add. $150

K4B-A4 . . . . NiB $1034 Ex $766 Gd $588
Cal.: .223 Rem. Bbl.: 20 inches w/A2 flash supp.; bayonet lug. Flattop receiver. Adj. post front sight. Firsh handguard, Picatinny rails. Made from 2006 to 2008.

PARKER-HALE LIMITED — Birmingham, England

MODEL 81 AFRICAN . . . . NiB $909 Ex $789 Gd $533
Same general specifications as Model 81 Classic except in caliber .375 H&H only. Sights: African Express rear; hooded blade front. Barrel-band swivel. All-steel trigger guard. Checkered European walnut stock w/pistol grip and recoil pad. Engraved receiver. Imported from 1986 to 1991.

**MODEL 81 CLASSIC
BOLT-ACTION RIFLE** . . . . NiB $745 Ex $627 Gd $439
Calibers: .22-250, .243 Win., .270 Win., 6mm Rem., 6.5x55, 7x57, 7x64, .308 Win., .30-06, .300 Win. Mag., 7mm Rem. Mag. Four round magazine. 24-inch bbl. Weight: 7.75 lbs. Sights: Adj. open rear, hooded ramp front. Checkered pistol-grip stock of European walnut. Imported from 1984 to 1991.

MODEL 85 SNIPER RIFLE . NiB $2730 Ex $2161 Gd $1578
Caliber: .308 Win. Ten or 20-round M-14-type magazine. 24.25-inch bbl. 45 inches overall. Weight: 12.5 lbs. Blade front sight, folding aperture rear. McMillan fiberglass stock w/detachable bipod. Imported from 1989 to 1991.

RIFLES

Parker-Hale Model 1100
Lightweight

Parker-Hale Model 1200
Super Clip

MODEL 87 BOLT-ACTION
REPEATING TARGET RIFLE. NiB $1425 Ex $1233 Gd $757
Calibers: .243 Win., 6.5x55, .308 Win., .30-06 Springfield, .300 Win. Mag. Five-round detachable box magazine. 26-inch bbl. 45 inches overall. Weight: 10 lbs. No sights; grooved for target-style scope mounts. Stippled walnut stock w/adj. buttplate. Sling swivel studs. Parkerized finish. Folding bipod. Imported 1988 to 1991.

MODEL 1000 STANDARD RIFLE.... NiB $460 Ex $359 Gd $248
Calibers: .22-250, .243 Win., .270 Win., 6mm Rem., .308 Win., .30-06. Four-round magazine. Bolt action. 22-inch or 24-inch (22-250) bbl. 43 inches overall. 7.25 lbs. Checkered walnut Monte Carlo-style stock w/satin finish. Imported from 1984 to 1988.

MODEL 1100 LIGHTWEIGHT
BOLT-ACTION RIFLE .... NiB $535 Ex $443 Gd $337
Same general specifications as Model 1000 Standard except w/22-inch lightweight profile bbl., hollow bolt handle, alloy trigger guard and floorplate, 6.5 lbs., Schnabel forend. Imported 1984 to 1991.

MODEL 1100M AFRICAN
MAGNUM RIFLE .... NiB $858 Ex $745 Gd $500
Same as Model 1000 Standard except w/24-inch bbl. in calibers .404 Jeffery, .458 Win. Mag. Weight: 9.5 lbs. Sights: Adj. rear; hooded post front. Imported from 1984 to 1991.

MODEL 1200 SUPER CLIP
BOLT-ACTION RIFLE .... NiB $763 Ex $555 Gd $423
Same as Model 1200 Super except w/detachable box magazine in calibers .243 Win., 6mm Rem., .270 Win. .30-06 and .308 Win., .300 Win. Mag., 7mm Rem. Mag. Imported from 1984 to 1991.

MODEL 1200 SUPER BOLT-ACTION
SPORTING RIFLE .... NiB $586 Ex $480 Gd $355
Mauser-type bolt action. Calibers: .22-250, .243 Win., 6mm Rem., .25-06, .270 Win., .30-06, .308 Win. Four round magazine. 24-inch bbl. Weight: 7.25 lbs. Sights: Folding open rear, hooded ramp front. European walnut stock w/rollover Monte Carlo cheekpiece, rosewood forend tip and pistol-grip cap, skip checkering, recoil pad, sling swivels. Imported from 1968 to 1991.

MODEL 1200 SUPER MAGNUM.... NiB $556 Ex $550 Gd $369
Same general specifications as 1200 Super except calibers 7mm Rem. Mag. and .300 Win. Mag., 3-round magazine. Imported 1988 to 1991.

MODEL 1200P PRESENTATION .... NiB $580 Ex $459 Gd $347
Same general specifications as 1200 Super except w/scroll-engraved action, trigger guard and floorplate, no sights. QD swivels. Calibers: .243 Win. and .30-06. Imported from 1969 to 1975.

MODEL 1200V VARMINT.... NiB $557 Ex $498 Gd $425
Same general specifications as 1200 Super, except w/24-inch heavy bbl., no sights, weight: 9.5 lbs. Calibers: .22-250, 6mm Rem., .25-06, .243 Win. Imported from 1969-89.

MODEL 1300C SCOUT..... NiB $733 Ex $689 Gd $550
Calibers: .243, .308 Win. 10-round magazine. 20-inch bbl. w/muzzle brake. 41 inches overall. Weight: 8.5 lbs. No sights, drilled and tapped for scope. Checkered laminated birch stock w/QD swivels. Imported in 1991.

MODEL 2100 MIDLAND
BOLT-ACTION RIFLE .... NiB $380 Ex $321 Gd $244
Calibers: .22-250, .243 Win., 6mm Rem., .270 Win., 6.5x55, 7x57, 7x64, .308 Win, .30-06. Four-round box magazine. 22-inch or 24-inch (22-250) bbl. 43-inches overall. Weight: 7 lbs. Sights: Adj. folding rear; hooded ramp front. Checkered European walnut Monte Carlo stock w/pistol-grip. Imported from 1984 to 1991.

MODEL 2707 LIGHTWEIGHT...... NiB $370 Ex $329 Gd $237
Same general specifications as Model 2100 Midland except w/ tapered lightweight bbl. and aluminum trigger guard. Weight: 6.5 lbs. Imported in 1991.

MODEL 2800 MIDLAND .... NiB $375 Ex $319 Gd $245
Same general specifications as model 2100 except w/laminated birch stock. Imported in 1991.

PEDERSEN CUSTOM GUNS — North Haven, Connecticut, Division of O.F. Mossberg & Sons, Inc.

MODEL 3000 GRADE I
BOLT-ACTION RIFLE ...... NiB $1034 Ex $809 Gd $544
Richly engraved w/silver inlays, full-fancy American black walnut stock. Mossberg Model 810 action. Calibers: .270 Win., .30-06, 7mm Rem. Mag., .338 Win. Mag. Three-round magazine, hinged floorplate. 22-inch bbl. in .270 and .30-06, 24-inch in Magnums. Weight: 7 to 8 lbs. Sights: Open rear; hooded ramp front. Monte Carlo stock w/roll-over cheekpiece, wraparound hand checkering on pistol grip and forearm, rosewood pistol-grip cap and forend tip, recoil pad or steel buttplate w/trap, detachable swivels. Imported 1973 to 1975.

MODEL 3000 GRADE II ..... NiB $733 Ex $480 Gd $380
Same as Model 3000 Grade I except less elaborate engraving, no inlays, fancy grade walnut stock w/recoil pad. Imported 1973 to 1975.

MODEL 3000 GRADE III..... NiB $579 Ex $380 Gd $299
Same as Model 3000 Grade I except no engraving or inlays, select grade walnut stock w/recoil pad. Imported from 1973 to 1974.

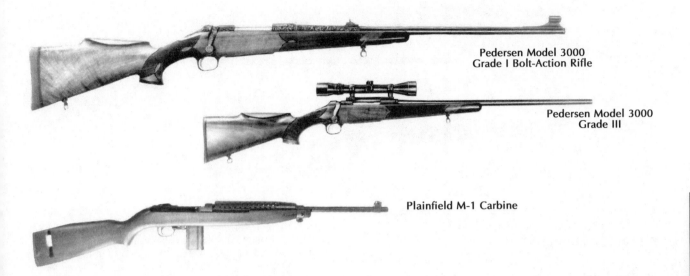

Pedersen Model 3000
Grade I Bolt-Action Rifle

Pedersen Model 3000
Grade III

Plainfield M-1 Carbine

MODEL 4707 CUSTOM

DELUXE LEVER-ACTION RIFLE . . . . . NiB $279 Ex $238 Gd $175
On Mossberg Model .472 action. Calibers: .30-30, 35 Rem. Five-round tubular magazine. 24-inch bbl. Weight: 7.5 lbs. Sights: Open rear, hooded ramp front. Hand-finished black walnut stock and beavertail forearm, barrel band swivels. Imported in 1975.

J.C. PENNEY CO., INC. — Dallas, Texas

Firearms sold under the J.C. Penney label were mfd. by Marlin, High Standard, Stevens, Savage and Springfield.

MODEL 2025 BOLT-ACTION REPEATER NiB $100 Ex $65 Gd $55
Takedown. Caliber: .22 RF. Eight round detachable box magazine. 24-inch bbl. Weight: 6 lbs. Sights: Open rear; bead front. Plain pistol-grip stock. Manufactured by Marlin.

MODEL 2035 BOLT-ACTION REPEATER NiB $100 Ex $65 Gd $55
Takedown. Caliber: .22 RF. Eight round detachable box magazine. 24-inch bbl. Weight: 6 lbs. Sights: Open rear; bead front. Plain pistol-grip stock. Manufactured by Marlin.

MODEL 2935 LEVER-ACTION RIFLE . NiB $210 Ex $170 Gd $121
Same general specifications as Marlin Model 336.

MODEL 6400 BOLT-ACTION

CENTERFIRE RIFLE . . . . NiB $210 Ex $170 Gd $110
Same general specifications as Savage Model 340.

MODEL 6660

AUTOLOADING RIFLE . . . . NiB $115 Ex $90 Gd $75
Caliber: .22 RF. Tubular magazine. 22-inch bbl. Weight: 5.5 lbs. Sights: Open rear; hooded ramp front. Plain pistol-grip stock. Manufactured by Marlin.

PLAINFIELD MACHINE COMPANY — Dunellen, New Jersey

M-1 CARBINE . . . . NiB $227 Ex $166 Gd $135
Same as U.S. Carbine, Cal. .30, M-1 except also available in caliber

5.7mm (.22 caliber w/necked-down .30 Carbine cartridge case). Current production w/ventilated metal handguard and barrel band w/o bayonet lug; earlier models have standard military-type fittings. Made from 1960 to 1977.

M-1 CARBINE,
COMMANDO MODEL . . . . NiB $232 Ex $171 Gd $145
Same as M-1 Carbine except w/paratrooper-type stock w/telescoping wire shoulderpiece. Made from 1960 to 1977.

M-1 CARBINE, MILITARY SPORTER . NiB $227 Ex $166 Gd $135
Same as M-1 Carbine except w/unslotted buttstock and wood handguard. Made from 1960 to 1977.

M-1 DELUXE SPORTER . . . . . . NiB $232 Ex $171 Gd $145
Same as M-1 Carbine except w/Monte Carlo sporting stock Made from 1960 to 1973.

POLISH MILITARY RIFLES — Manufactured by Government Arsenals at Radom and Warsaw, Poland

MODEL 1898 (KARABIN 98, K98)
MAUSER MILITARY CARBINE . . . . . . NiB $331 Ex $210 Gd $166
Same as German Kar. 98A except for minor details. First manufactured during early 1920s.

MODEL 1898 (KARABIN 98, WZ98A)
MAUSER MILITARY RIFLE . . . . NiB $289 Ex $180 Gd $145
Same as German Kar. 98 used in WWI except for minor details. Manufacture began c. 1921.

MODEL 1929 (KARABIN 29, WZ29)
MAUSER MILITARY RIFLE . . . . NiB $331 Ex $210 Gd $166
Same as Czech Model 24, mfd. 1929 thru WWII except for minor details. A similar model produced during German occupation was designated Gew. 29/40.

Polish Model 1929 Mauser

Purdey Double Rifle

Purdey Bolt-Action Rifle

WILLIAM POWELL & SON LTD. — Birmingham, England

DOUBLE-BARREL RIFLE . . . NiB $32,278 Ex $26,900 Gd $18,900
Boxlock. Made to order in any caliber during the time that rifle was manufactured. Bbls.: Made to order in any legal length, but 26 inches recommended. Highest grade French walnut buttstock and forearm w/fine checkering. Metal is elaborately engraved. Imported by Stoeger from 1938 to 1951.

BOLT-ACTION RIFLE . . . . NiB $2888 Ex $2367 Gd $1699
Mauser-type bolt action. Calibers: 6x54 through .375 H&H Magnum. Three and 4-shot magazine, depending upon chambering. 24-inch bbl. Weight: 7.5 to 8.75 lbs. Sights: Folding leaf rear; hooded ramp front. Cheekpiece stock, checkered forearm and pistol grip, swivels. Imported by Stoeger from 1938 to 1951.

PTR 91, INC. — Aynor, SC previously Bristol, CT and Farmington, CT

MODEL PTR-91F SEMI-AUTOMATIC. . . NiB $1150 Ex $900 Gd $600
Delayed roller-locked blow-back action similar to H&K G3. Caliber: .308 Win. 20-round magazine. 18-inch bbl. H&K Navy type polymer trigger group. Sights: H&K style front post and rear adj. diopter. Plastic buttstock. Matte black finish. and forearm. Made from 2005 to date.

PTR-91 AI
(match grade barrel, 2005-2008). . . NiB $1170 Ex $730 Gd $570
PTR-91 Classic
(black or wood stock, 2012) . . NiB $880 Ex $650 Gd $460
PTR-91 KC (16-in. bbl.) . . . . NiB $1160 Ex $910 Gd $600
PTR-91T (green furniture) . . . . NiB $900 Ex $850 Gd $550
PTR-MSG 91 Sniper
(18-in. fluted target bbl.). . . NiB $1980 Ex $1600 Gd $900

PUMA — Imported by Legacy Sports Int'l., Reno, NV

Model 1886 Lever Action . . . NiB $1260 Ex $880 Gd $625
Reproduction of Winchester 1886 lever action. Caliber: .45-70. 7- or 8-round tube magazine. 22- or 26-inch round or octagon bbl. Case colored receiver, Italian walnut stock. Made 2009 to date.

Model 92 Lever Action . . . . . NiB $925 Ex $710 Gd $460
Caliber: .38 Special/.357 Mag., .44 Special/.44 Mag., .45 LC, .454 Casull or .480 Ruger. Lever action, 9- or 10-round tube magazine. 20-inch round or octagon bbl. Blue, brass or case colored receiver, walnut stock. Made 2001 to date.

PPS/22 . . . . NiB $480 Ex $330 Gd $280
Caliber: .22 LR. Semi-auto action, 16-inch bbl., 10- or 50-round (drum) magazine. Made 2009 to 2010.

JAMES PURDEY & SONS LTD. — London, England

DOUBLE RIFLE
Sidelock action, hammerless, ejectors. Almost any caliber is available but the following are the most popular: .375 Flanged Magnum Nitro Express, .500/465 Nitro Express .470 Nitro Express, .577 Nitro Express. 25.5-inch bbls. (25-inch in .375). Weight: 9.5 to 12.75 lbs. Sights: Folding leaf rear; ramp front. Cheekpiece stock, checkered forearm and pistol-grip, recoil pad, swivels. Currently manufactured to individual measurements and specifications; same general specifications apply to pre-WWII model.
H&H calibers . . . . NiB $72,665 Ex $57,550 Gd $38,750
NE calibers. . . . . NiB $85,000 Ex $56,000 Gd $39,000

BOLT-ACTION RIFLE . . . . . NiB $22,800 Ex $19,970 Gd $12,770
Mauser-type bolt action. Calibers: 7x57, .300 H&H Magnum, .375 H&H Magnum, 10.75x73. Three round magazine. 24-inch bbl. Weight: 7.5 to 8.75 lbs. Sights: Folding leaf rear; hooded ramp front. Cheekpiece stock, checkered forearm and pistol-grip, swivels. Currently manufactured; same general specifications apply to pre-WWII model.

RAPTOR ARMS COMPANY, INC. — Newport, New Hampshire

BOLT-ACTION RIFLE
Calibers: .243 Win., .270 Win., .30-06 or .308 Win. Four round magazine. 22-inch sporter or heavy bbl. Weight: 7.3 to 8 lbs. 42.5 inches overall. No sights w/drilled and tapped receiver or optional blade front, adjustable rear. Blue, stainless or "Taloncote" rust-resistant finish. Checkered black synthetic stock w/Monte Carlo cheepiece and vented recoil pad. Imported from 1997 to 1999.
Raptor Sporter model . . . . NiB $255 Ex $190 Gd $155
Raptor Deluxe Peregrine model (disc. 1998)NiB $258 Ex $195 Gd $159
Raptor heavy bbl. model. . . . . NiB $277 Ex $222 Gd $195
Raptor stainless bbl. model . . . . NiB $299 Ex $257 Gd $213
W/optional sights, add $40

Remington No. 7
Target and Sporting Rifle

REMINGTON ARMS COMPANY — Ilion, New York, and Mayfield, Kentucky. Acquired by Freedom Group Inc.

To facilitate locating Remington firearms, models are grouped into four categories: Single-shot rifles, bolt-action repeating rifles, slide-action (pump) rifles, and semiautomatic rifles. For a complete listing, please refer to the index.

SINGLE-SHOT RIFLES

NO. 1 SPORTING RIFLE . . NiB $6223 Ex $3856 Gd $2210
Single-Shot, rolling-block action. Calibers: .40-50, .40-70, .44-77, .50-45, .50-70 Gov't. centerfire and .44 Long, .44 Extra Long, .45-70, .46 Long, .46 Extra Long, .50-70 rimfire. Bbl. lengths: 28- or 30-inch part octagon. Weight: 5 to 7.5 lbs. Sights: Folding leaf rear sight; sporting front, dovetail bases. Plain walnut straight stock; flanged-top, semicarbine buttplate. Plain walnut forend with thin, rounded front end. Made from 1868 to 1902.

NO. 1 1/2 SPORTING RIFLE NiB $4190 Ex $1200 Gd $1888
Single-Shot, rolling-block action. Calibers: .22 Short, Long, or Extra Long. 25 Stevens, .32, and .38 rimfire cartridges. .32-20, .38-40 and .44-40 centerfire. Bbl. lengths: 24-, 26-, 28- or 30-inch part octagon. Remaining features similar to Remington No. 1. Made from 1869 to 1902.

NO. 2 SPORTING RIFLE
Single-shot, rolling-block action. Calibers: .22, .25, .32, .38, .44 rimfire or centerfire. Bbl. lengths: 24, 26, 28 or 30 inches. Weight: 5 to 6 lbs. Sights: Open rear; bead front. Straight-grip sporting stock and knobtip forearm of walnut. Made from 1873 to 1909.
Calibers: .22, .25, .32. . . . . NiB $3575 Ex $2040 Gd $989
Calibers: .38, .44 . . . . NiB $9650 Ex $8129 Gd $5450

**NO. 3 CREEDMOOR
AND SCHUETZEN RIFLES. NiB $16,187 Ex $12,750 Gd $10,510**
Produced in a variety of styles and calibers, these are collector's items and bring far higher prices than the sporting types. The Schuetzen Special, which has an under-lever action, is especially rare — perhaps fewer than 100 have been made.

NO. 3 HIGH POWER RIFLE
Single-shot, Hepburn falling-block action w/side lever. Calibers: .30-30, .30-40, .32 Special, .32-40, .38-55, .38-72 (high-power cartridges). Bbl. lengths: 26-, 28-, 30-inch. Weight: About 8 lbs. Open sporting sights. Checkered pistol-grip stock and forearm. Made from 1893 to 1907.
Calibers: .30-30, .30-40,
.32 Special, .32-40. . . . . NiB $9775 Ex $7956 Gd $5110
Calibers: .38-55, .38-72 . . . . NiB $9688 Ex $8154 Gd $6422

NO. 3 SPORTING RIFLE . . NiB $9775 Ex $7279 Gd $6788
Single-shot, Hepburn falling-block action w/side lever. Calibers: .22 WCF, .22 Extra Long, .25-20 Stevens, .25-21 Stevens, .25-25 Stevens, .32 WCF, .32-40 Ballard & Marlin, .32-40 Rem., .38 WCF, .38-40 Rem., 38-

.38-50 Rem., .38-55 Ballard & Marlin, .40-60 Ballard & Marlin, .40-60 WCF, .40-65 Rem. Straight, .40-82 WCF, .45-70 Gov., .45-90 WCF, also was supplied on special order in bottle-necked .40-50, .40-70, .40-90, .44-77, .44-90, .44-105, .50-70 Gov., .50-90 Sharps Straight. Bbl. lengths: 26-inch (22, 25, 32 cal. only), 28-inch, 30-inch; half-octagon or full-octagon. Weight: 8 to 10 lbs. Sights: Open rear; blade front. Checkered pistol-grip stock and forearm. Made from 1880 to c. 1911.

NO. 4 SINGLE-SHOT RIFLE. . . . . NiB $1630 EX $944 Gd $755
Rolling-block action. Solid frame or takedown. Calibers: .22 Short and Long, .22 LR, .25 Stevens R.F., .32 Short and Long R.F. 22.5-inch octagon bbl., 24-inch available in .32 caliber only. Weight: About 4.5 lbs. Sights: Open rear; blade front. Plain walnut stock and forearm. Made from 1890-1933.

**NO. 4S MILITARY MODEL 22
SINGLE-SHOT RIFLE. . . . . . NiB $2650 Ex $2033 Gd $997**
Rolling-block action. Calibers: .22 Short, Long LR. 28-inch bbl. Weight: About 5 lbs. Sights: Military-type rear; blade front. Military-type stock w/handguard, stacking swivel, sling. Has a bayonet stud on the barrel; bayonet and scabbard were regularly supplied. Note: At one time the Military Model was the official rifle of the Boy Scouts of America and was called the Boy Scout Rifle. Made from 1913 to 1933.

NO. 5 SPECIAL SINGLE-SHOT RIFLE
Single-shot, rolling-block action. Calibers: 7mm Mauser, .30-30, .30-40 Krag, .303 British, .32-40, .32 Special, .38-55 (high-power cartridges). Bbl. lengths: 24, 26 and 28 inches. Weight: About 7 lbs. Open sporting sights. Plain straight-grip stock and forearm. Made 1902 to 1918. Note: Models 1897 and 1902 Military Rifles, intended for the export market, are almost identical with the No. 5, except for 30-inch bbl. full military stock and weight (about 8.5 lbs.); a carbine was also supplied. The military rifles were produced in caliber 8mm Lebel for France, 7.62mm Russian for Russia and 7mm Mauser for the Central and South American government trade. Also offered to retail buyers.
Sporting model. . . . . NiB $934 Ex $733 Gd $530
Military model . . . . NiB $731 Ex $554 Gd $400

NO. 6 TAKEDOWN RIFLE. . . . NiB $675 Ex $535 Gd $459
Single-shot, rolling-block action. Calibers: .22 Short, Long, LR; .32 Short, Long RF. 20-inch bbl. Weight: Avg. 4 lbs. Sights: Open front and rear; tang peep. Plain straight-grip stock, forearm. Made from 1901 to 1933.

NO. 7 TARGET AND SPORTING RIFLE. NiB $9707 Ex $7235 Gd $6755
Single-shot. Rolling-block Army Pistol frame. Calibers: .22 Short, .22 LR. 25-10 Stevens R.F. (other calibers available on special order). Half-octagon bbls.: 24-, 26-, 28-inch. Weight: About 6 lbs. Sights: Lyman combination rear; Beach combination front. Fancy walnut stock, Swiss buttplate available. Made from 1903 to 1911.

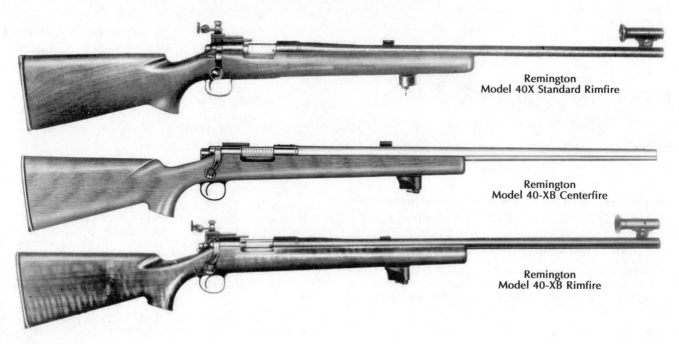

Remington
Model 40X Standard Rimfire

Remington
Model 40-XB Centerfire

Remington
Model 40-XB Rimfire

MODEL 33 BOLT-ACTION
SINGLE-SHOT RIFLE....... NiB $278 EX $190 Gd $239
Takedown. Caliber: .22 Short, Long, LR. 24-inch bbl. Weight: About 4.5 lbs. Sights: Open rear, bead front. Plain, pistol-grip stock, forearm with grasping grooves. Made from 1931 to 1936.

MODEL 33 NRA
JUNIOR TARGET RIFLE..... NiB $544 Ex $408 Gd $240
Same as Model 33 Standard except has Lyman peep rear sight, Partridge-type front sight, 0.88-inch sling and swivels, weighs about 5 lbs.

MODEL 40X
CENTERFIRE RIFLE...... NiB $2690 Ex $2044 Gd $1107
Specifications same as for Model 40X Rimfire (heavy weight). Calibers: .222 Rem., .222 Rem. Mag., 7.62mm NATO, .30-06 (others were available on special order). Made from 1961 to 1964. Value shown is for rifle w/o sights.

MODEL 40X HEAVYWEIGHT BOLT-ACTION TARGET RIFLE (RIMFIRE)
Caliber: .22 LR. Single shot. Action similar to Model 722. Click adj. trigger. 28-inch heavy bbl. Redfield Olympic sights. Scope bases. High-comb target stock bedding device, adj. swivel, rubber buttplate. Weight: 12.75 lbs. Made from 1955 to 1964.
With sights............ NiB $3370 Ex $2133 Gd $1320
Without sights .... NiB $2390 Ex $1096 Gd $675

MODEL 40-X SPORTER ....NiB $3000 Ex $1947 Gd $944
Same general specifications as Model 707 C Custom (see that listing in this section) except in caliber .22 LR. Made from 1972 to 1977.

MODEL 40X STANDARD BARREL
Same as Model 40X Heavyweight except has lighter barrel. Weight: 10.75 lbs.
With sights.............. NiB $579 Ex $416 Gd $322
Without sights .... NiB $495 Ex $338 Gd $256

MODEL 40-XB CENTERFIRE MATCH RIFLE NiB $590 Ex $466 Gd $380
Bolt-action, single-shot. Calibers: .222 Rem., .222 Rem. Mag., .223 Rem., .22-250, 6x47mm, 6mm Rem., .243 Win., .25-06, 7mm Rem. Mag., .30-06, .308 Win. (7.62mm NATO), .30-338, (7.62mm NATO), .30-338, .300 Win. Mag. 27 25-inch standard or heavy bbl. Target stock w/adj. front swivel block on guide rail, rubber buttplate. Weight w/o sights: Standard bbl., 9.25 lbs.; heavy bbl., 11.25 lbs. Value shown is for rifle without sights. Made from 1964 to date.

MODEL 40-XB RANGEMASTER CENTERFIRE RIFLE
Single-shot target rifle with same basic specifications as Model 40-XB Centerfire Match. Additional calibers in .220 Swift, 6mm BR Rem. and 7mm BR Rem., and stainless bbl. only. American walnut or Kevlar (weighs 1 lb. less) target stock with forend stop. Discontinued 1994.
right-hand model .... NiB $835 Ex $600 Gd $444
left-hand model .... NiB $835 Ex $600 Gd $444
Kevlar stock, right-hand model .. NiB $2200 Ex $2011 Gd $1077
Kevlar stock, left-hand model ... NiB $2200 Ex $2011 Gd $1077
W/2 oz. trigger, add............................... $126
Repeater model, add............................... $126

MODEL 40-XB RANGEMASTER
RIMFIRE MATCH RIFLE...... NiB $877 Ex $792 Gd $440
Bolt-action, single-shot. Caliber: .22 LR. 28-inch standard or heavy bbl. Target stock with adj. front swivel block on guide rail, rubber buttplate. Weight w/o sights: Standard bbl., 10 lbs.; heavy bbl., 11.25 lbs. Value shown is for rifle without sights. Made from 1964-74.

MODEL 40-XB
VARMINT SPECIAL RIFLE........ NiB $1367 Ex $899 Gd $466
Same general specifications as Model 40-XB Repeater except has synthetic stock (Kevlar). Made from 1987-94.

MODEL 40-XBBR BENCH REST RIFLE
Bolt action, single shot. Calibers: .222 Rem., .222 Rem. Mag., .223 Rem., 6x47mm, .308 Win. (7.62mm NATO). 20- or 26-inch unblued stainless-steel bbl. Supplied w/o sights. Weight: With 20-inch bbl., 9.25 lbs., with 26-inch bbl.,12 lbs. (Heavy Varmint class; 7.25 lbs. w/Kevlar stock (Light Varmint class). Made from 1974 to 2004; reintroduced 2007.
Model 40-XBBR (disc.) .... NiB $3550 Ex $2896 Gd $1600
Model 40-XBBR KS (Kevlar stock) NiB $3504 Ex $2973 Gd $1679

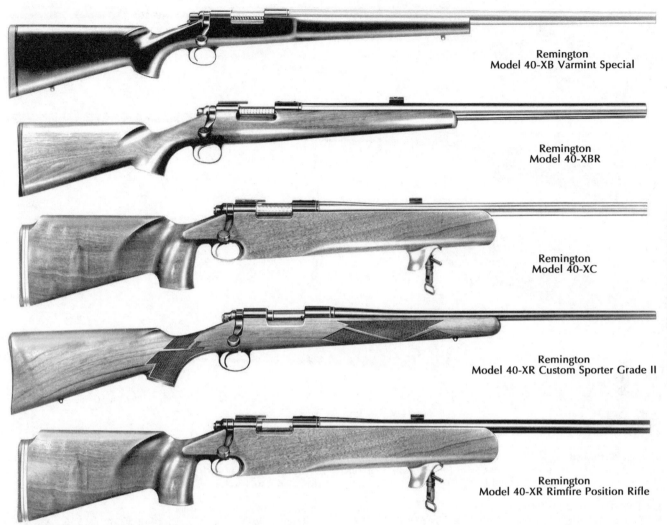

Remington
Model 40-XB Varmint Special

Remington
Model 40-XBR

Remington
Model 40-XC

Remington
Model 40-XR Custom Sporter Grade II

Remington
Model 40-XR Rimfire Position Rifle

RIFLES

MODEL 40-XC NATIONAL MATCH COURSE RIFLE
Bolt-action repeater. Caliber: .308 Win. (7.62mm NATO). Five round magazine, clip slot in receiver. 24-inch bbl. Supplied w/o sights. Weight: 11 lbs. Thumb groove stock w/adj. hand stop and sling swivel, adj. buttplate. Disc 2004, reintroduced 2006.

W/wood stock, disc.) . . . . NiB $3170 Ex $2834 Gd $1566
W/Kevlar stock, disc. 1994) . . . . NiB $3159 Ex $2833 Gd $1633

MODEL 40-XR CUSTOM SPORTER RIFLE
Caliber: .22 RF. 24-inch contoured bbl. Supplied w/o sights. Made in four grades of checkering, engraving and other custom features. Made from 1987 to date. High grade model discontinued 1991.

Grade I . . . . NiB $1233 Ex $1099 Gd $820
Grade II . . . . NiB $2270 Ex $1833 Gd $1166
Grade III . . . . NiB $3077 Ex $2100 Gd $1310
Grade IV . . . . NiB $5055 Ex $4110 Gd $2966

MODEL 40-XR RIMFIRE POSITION RIFLE
Bolt action, single shot. Caliber: .22 LR. 24-inch heavy bbl. Supplied w/o sights. Weight: 10 lbs. Position-style stock w/thumb groove, adj. hand stop and sling swivel on guide rail, adj. buttplate. Made from 1974. Discontinued 2004.

MODEL 40-XR
RIMFIRE POSITION RIFLE . . . . NiB $1266 Ex $1087 Gd $677
KS model (w/Kevlar stock) . . . . . . NiB $1387 Ex $1100 Gd $707

MODEL 41A TARGETMASTER BOLT-ACTION
SINGLE-SHOT RIFLE. . . . . NiB $296 Ex $190 Gd $137
Takedown. Caliber: .22 Short, Long, LR. 27-inch bbl. Weight: About 5.5 lbs. Sights: Open rear; bead front. Plain pistol-grip stock. Made 1936 to 1940.

MODEL 41AS. . . . . NiB $398 Ex $224 Gd $135
Same as Model 41A except chambered for .22 Remington Special (.22 W.R.F.).

MODEL 41P. . . . . NiB $323 Ex $200 Gd $135
Same as Model 41A except has peep rear sight, hooded front sight.

MODEL 41SB. . . . . NiB $439 Ex $167 Gd $154
Same as Model 41A except smoothbore for use with shot cartridges.

MODEL 510A TARGETMASTER
BOLT-ACTION SINGLE-SHOT RIFLE. NiB $255 Ex $170 Gd $130
Takedown. Caliber: 22 Short, Long, LR. 25-inch bbl. Weight: About 5.5 lbs. Sights: Open rear; bead front. Plain pistol-grip stock. Made from 1939 to 1962.

MODEL 510P. . . . . NiB $277 Ex $175 Gd $131
Same as Model 510A except has peep rear sight, Partridge front on ramp.

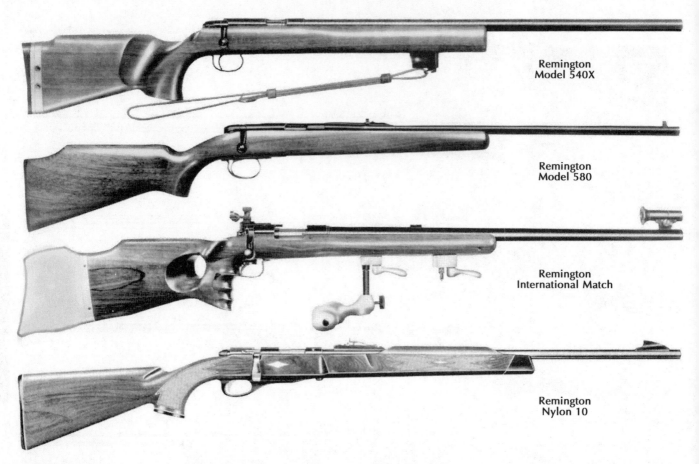

Remington
Model 540X

Remington
Model 580

Remington
International Match

Remington
Nylon 10

MODEL 510-X SB . . . . **NiB $390 Ex $248 Gd $190**
Same as Model 510A except smoothbore for use with shot cartridges, shotgun bead front sight, no rear sight.

**MODEL 510X BOLT-ACTION
SINGLE-SHOT RIFLE** . . . . **NiB $233 Ex $190 Gd $126**
Same as Model 510A except improved sights. Made from1964-66.

**MODEL 514 BOLT-ACTION
SINGLE-SHOT** . . . . **NiB $180 Ex $157 Gd $126**
Takedown. Caliber: .22 Short, Long, LR. 24-inch bbl. Weight: 4.75 lbs. Sights: Open rear; bead front. Plain pistol-grip stock. Made from1948 to 1971.

MODEL 514BC BOY'S CARBINE . . . . **NiB $227 Ex $166 Gd $129**
Same as Model 514 except has 21-inch bbl., 1-inch shorter stock. Made from1961 to 1971.

MODEL 514P . . . . **NiB $227 Ex $166 Gd $129**
Same as Model 514 except has receiver peep sight.

MODEL 540-X RIMFIRE TARGET RIFLE **NiB $455 Ex $300 Gd $141**
Bolt-action, single-shot. Caliber: .22 R. 26-inch heavy bbl. Supplied w/o sights. Weight: About 8 lbs. Target stock w/Monte Carlo cheekpiece and thumb groove, guide rail for hand stop and swivel, adj. buttplate. Made from 1969 to 1974.

MODEL 540-XR POSITION RIFLE . . . **NiB $455 Ex $300 Gd $141**
Bolt-action, single-shot. Caliber: .22 LR. 26-inch medium-weight bbl. Supplied w/o sights. Weight: 8 lbs., 13 oz. Position-style stock w/thumb groove, guide rail for hand stop and swivel, adj. buttplate. Made from 1974 to 1984.

MODEL 540-XRJR. . . . . **NiB $415 Ex $338 Gd $200**
Same as Model 540-XR except 1.75-inch shorter stock. Made from 1974 to 1984.

**MODEL 580 BOLT-ACTION
SINGLE-SHOT** . . . . **NiB $200 Ex $155 Gd $120**
Caliber: .22 Short, Long, LR. 24-inch bbl. Weight: 4.75 lbs. Sights: Bead front; U-notch rear. Monte Carlo stock. Made 1967 to 1978.

MODEL 580BR BOY'S RIFLE. . **NiB $200 EX $155 Gd $120**
Same as Model 580 except w/1-inch shorter stock. Made 1971 to 1978.

MODEL 580SB SMOOTH BORE **NiB $290 Ex $215 Gd $149**
Same as Model 580 except smooth bore for .22 Long Rifle shot cartridges. Made from 1967 to 1978.

INTERNATIONAL FREE RIFLE **NiB $1100 Ex $824 Gd $482**
Same as Model 40-XB rimfire and centerfire except has free rifle-type stock with adj. buttplate and hook, adj. palm rest, movable front sling swivel, 2-oz. trigger. Weight: About 15 lbs. Made from 1964 to 1974. Value shown is for rifle with professionally-finished stock, no sights.

**INTERNATIONAL
MATCH FREE RIFLE** . . . . **NiB $1133 Ex $1055 Gd $677**
Calibers: .22 LR, .222 Rem., .222 Rem. Mag., 7.62mm NATO, .30-06 (others were available on special order). Model 40X-type bolt-action, single-shot. 2-oz. adj. trigger. 28-inch heavy bbl. Weight: About 15.5 lbs. Free rifle-style stock with thumbhole (furnished semifinished by mfr.); interchangeable and adj. rubber buttplate and hook buttplate, adj. palm rest, sling swivel. Made 1961 to 1964. Value shown is for rifle with professionally-finished stock, no sights.

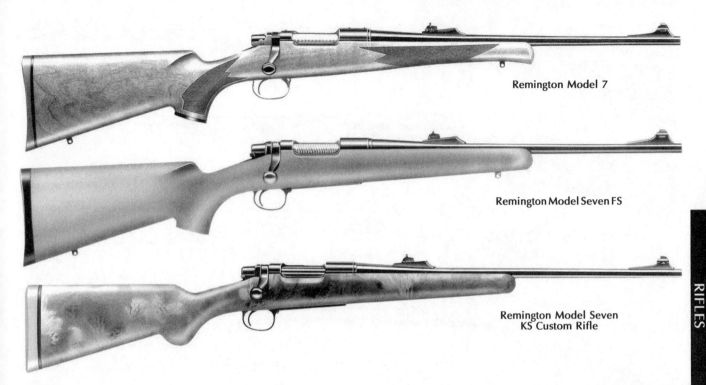

Remington Model 7

Remington Model Seven FS

Remington Model Seven
KS Custom Rifle

NYLON 10 BOLT-ACTION
SINGLE-SHOT RIFLE. . . . . . . NiB $580 Ex $475 Gd $280
Caliber: .22 Short, Long, LR. 19.13-inch bbl. Weight: 4.25 lbs. Open rear sight; ramped blade front. Receiver grooved for scope mount. Brown nylon stock. Made from 1962 to 1966.

BOLT-ACTION REPEATING RIFLES

MODEL SEVEN (7) CF BOLT-ACTION RIFLE
Calibers: .17 Rem., .222 Rem., .223 Rem., .243 Win., 6mm Rem., 7mm-08 Rem., .308 Win. Magazine capacity: 5-round in .17 Rem., .222 Rem., .223 Rem., 4-round in other calibers. 18.5-inch bbl. Weight: 6.5 lbs. Walnut stock checkering, and recoil pad. Made from 1983 to 1999. .223 Rem. added in 1984.
Standard calibers. . . . . NiB $525 Ex $459 Gd $325
.17 Rem & .222 Rem.. . . . . NiB $577 Ex $485 Gd $350

MODEL SEVEN (7)
FS RIFLE. . . . . NiB $559 Ex $495 Gd $356
Calibers: .243, 7mm-08 Rem., .308 Win. 18.5-inch bbl. 37.5 inches overall. Weight: 5.25 lbs. Hand layup fiberglass stock, reinforced with DuPont Kevlar at points of bedding and stress. Made 1987 to 1989.

MODEL SEVEN (7) KS RIFLE NiB $2269 Ex $1090 Gd $789
Calibers: .223 Rem., 7mm-08, .308, .35 Rem. and .350 Rem. Mag. 20-inch bbl. Custom-made in Remington's Custom Shop with Kevlar stock. Made from 1987 to date.

MODEL SEVEN (7) LS RIFLE . . NiB $654 Ex $495 Gd $338
Calibers: .223 Rem., .243 Win., .260 Rem., 7mm-08 and 308 Win. 20-inch matte bbl. Laminated hardwood stock w/matte brown finish. Weight: 6.5 lbs. Made from 2000 to 2005.

MODEL SEVEN (7) LSS RIFLE . NiB $645 Ex $510 Gd $355
Similar to Model 7 LS except stainless bbl. w/o sights. Calibers: .22-250 Rem., .243 Win. or 7mm-08. Made from 2000 to 2003.

MODEL SEVEN (7) MS

CUSTOM RIFLE . . . . NiB $2655 Ex $2025 Gd $1043
Similar to the standard Model 7 except fitted with a laminated full Mannlicher-style stock. Weight: 6.75 lbs. Calibers: .222 Rem., .22-250, .243, 6mm Rem.,7mm-08, .308, .350 Rem. Additional calibers available on special order. Made from 1993 to 1999.

MODEL SEVEN (7) SS RIFLE . . NiB $650 Ex $445 Gd $316
Same as Model 7 except 20-inch stainless bbl., receiver and bolt; black synthetic stock. Calibers: .243, 7mm-08 or .308. Made 1994 to 2006.

MODEL SEVEN (7) YOUTH RIFLE . . . NiB $575 Ex $370 Gd $279
Similar to the standard Model 7 except fitted with hardwood stock with a 12.19-inch pull. Calibers: .243, 6mm, 7mm-08 only. Made 1993 to 2007.

MODEL 30A BOLT-ACTION
EXPRESS RIFLE . . . . NiB $650 Ex $522 Gd $361
Standard Grade. Modified M/1917 Enfield Action. Calibers: .25, .30, .32 and .35 Rem., 7mm Mauser, .30-06. Five round box magazine. 22-inch bbl. Weight: About 7.25 lbs. Sights: Open rear; bead front. Walnut stock w/ checkered pistol grip and forearm. Made 1921 to 1940. Note: Early Model 30s had a slender forend with Schnabel tip, military-type double-pull trigger.

MODEL 30R CARBINE . . . . . . NiB $655 Ex $540 Gd $433
Same as Model 30A except has 20-inch bbl., plain stock weight about 7 lbs.

MODEL 30S SPORTING RIFLE NiB $790 Ex $650 Gd $455
Special Grade. Same action as Model 30A. Calibers: .257 Roberts, 7mm Mauser, .30-06. Five round box magazine. 24-inch bbl. Weight: About 8 lbs. Lyman No. 48 Receiver sight, bead front sight. Special high comb stock with long, full forearm, checkered. Made 1930 to 1940.

MODEL 34 BOLT-ACTION REPEATER NiB $210 Ex $166 Gd $137
Takedown. Caliber: .22 Short, Long, LR. Tubular magazine holds 22 Short, 17 Long or 15 LR. 24-inch bbl. Weight: 5.25 lbs. Sights: Open rear; bead front. Plain, pistol-grip stock, forearm w/grasping grooves. Made from 1932 to 1936.

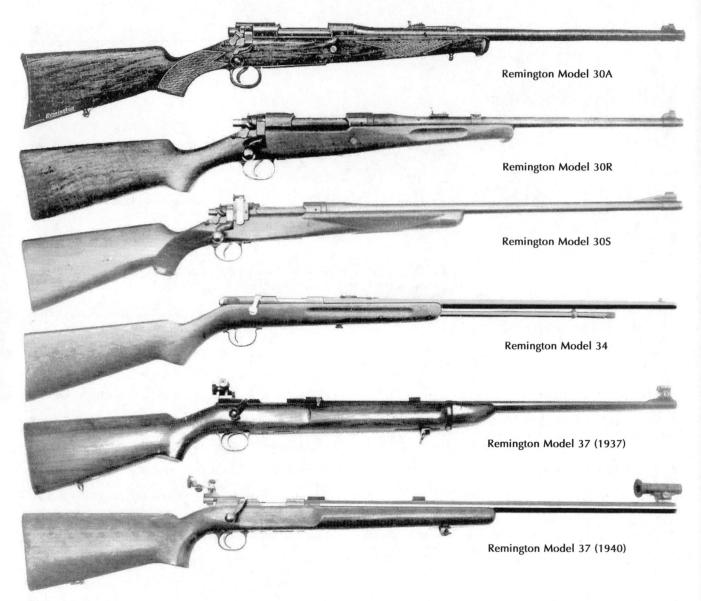

Remington Model 30A

Remington Model 30R

Remington Model 30S

Remington Model 34

Remington Model 37 (1937)

Remington Model 37 (1940)

MODEL 34 NRA TARGET RIFLE . . . . NiB $553 Ex $390 Gd $256
Same as Model 34 Standard except has Lyman peep rear sight, Partridge-type front sight, .88-inch sling and swivels, weight: About 5.75 lbs.

MODEL 37 RANGEMASTER BOLT-ACTION TARGET RIFLE (I)
Model of 1937. Caliber: .22 LR. Five round box magazine, single shot adapter also supplied as standard equipment. 28-inch heavy bbl. Weight: About 12 lbs. Remington front and rear sights, scope bases. Target stock, swivels, sling. Note: Original 1937 model had a stock with outside bbl. band similar in appearance to that of the old-style Winchester Model 52, forearm design was modified and bbl. band eliminated in 1938. Made from 1937 to 1940.
W/factory sights . . . . NiB $1190 Ex $715 Gd $380
W/out sights . . . . NiB $1010 Ex $599 Gd $338

MODEL 37 RANGEMASTER BOLT-ACTION TARGET RIFLE (II)
Model of 1940. Same as Model of 1937 except has "Miracle" trigger mechanism and Randle-design stock with high comb, full pistol-grip and wide beavertail forend. Made from 1940 to 1954.
W/factory sights . . . . NiB $1179 Ex $687 Gd $491
W/out sights . . . . NiB $977 Ex $569 Gd $338

MODEL 40-XB
CENTERFIRE REPEATER . . . . NiB $2210 Ex $1088 Gd $779
Same as Model 40-XB Centerfire except 5-round repeater. Calibers: .222 Rem., .222 Rem. Mag., .223 Rem., .22-250, 6x47mm, 6mm Rem., .243 Win., .308 Win. (7.62mm NATO). Heavy bbl. only. Discontinued.

MODEL 788 SPORTSMAN
BOLT-ACTION RIFLE . . . . NiB $496 Ex $390 Gd $322
Similar to Model 707 ADL except with straight-comb walnut-finished hardwood stock in calibers .223 Rem., .243 Win, .270 Win., .30-06 Springfield and .308 Win. 22-inch bbl. Weight: 7 lbs. Adj. sights. Made from 1967 to 1983.

MODEL 341A SPORTSMASTER
BOLT-ACTION REPEATER. . . . NiB $295 Ex $167 Gd $135
Takedown. Caliber: .22 Short, Long, LR. Tubular magazine holds 22 Short, 17 Long, 15 LR. 27-inch bbl. Weight: About 6 lbs. Sights: Open rear; bead front. Plain pistol-grip stock. Made from 1936 to 1940.

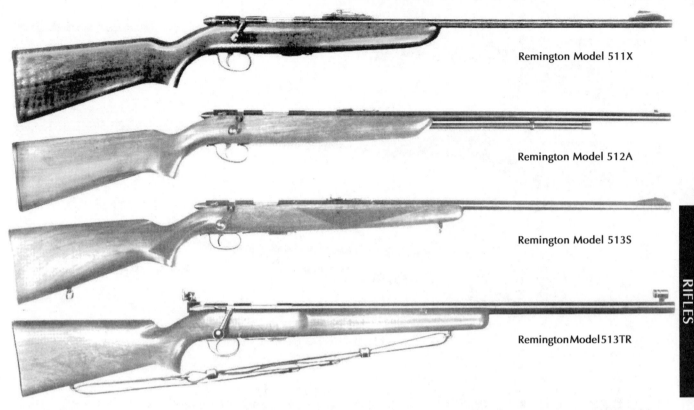

Remington Model 511X

Remington Model 512A

Remington Model 513S

RemingtonModel513TR

MODEL 341P . . . . NiB $465 Ex $220 Gd $150
Same as Model 341A except has peep rear sight, hooded front sight.

MODEL 341SB . . . . NiB $533 Ex $280 Gd $198
Same as Model 341A previously listed except smoothbore for use with shot cartridges.

MODEL 511A SCOREMASTER BOLT-ACTION
BOX MAGAZINE REPEATER . . . . NiB $266 Ex $188 Gd $145
Takedown. Caliber: 22 Short, Long, LR. Six round detachable box magazine. 25-inch bbl. Weight: About 5.5 lbs. Sights: Open rear; bead front. Plain pistol-grip stock. Made 1939 to 1962.

MODEL 511P . . . . NiB $190 Ex $201 Gd $150
Same as Model 511A except has peep rear sight, Partridge-type blade front on ramp.

MODEL 511X BOLT-ACTION REPEATERNiB $259 Ex $210 Gd $155
Clip type. Same as Model 511A except improved sights. Made from 1964 to 1966.

MODEL 512A SPORTSMASTER
BOLT-ACTION REPEATER. . . . NiB $269 EX $179 Gd $139
Takedown. Caliber: .22 Short, Long, LR. Tubular magazine holds 22 Short, 17 Long, 15 LR. 25-inch bbl. Weight: About 5.75 lbs. Sights: Open rear; bead front. Plain pistol-grip stock w/semibeavertail forend. Made from 1940 to 1962.

MODEL 512P . . . . NiB $288 Ex $227 Gd $170
Same as Model 512A except has peep rear sight, blade front, on ramp.

MODEL 512X BOLT-
ACTION REPEATER . . . . NiB $277 Ex $228 Gd $180
Tubular magazine type. Same as Model 512A except has improved sights. Made from 1964 to 1966.

MODEL 513S BOLT-ACTION RIFLE . NiB $854 Ex $492 Gd $312
Caliber: .22 LR. Six round detachable box magazine. 27-inch bbl. Weight: About 6.75 lbs. Marble open rear sight, Partridge-type front. Checkered sporter stock. Made from 1941 to 1956.

MODEL 513TR MATCHMASTER
BOLT-ACTION TARGET RIFLE NiB $450 Ex $299 Gd $211
Caliber: .22 LR. Six round detachable box magazine. 27-inch bbl. Weight: About 9 lbs. Sights: Redfield No. 75 rear; globe front. Target stock. Sling and swivels. Made from 1941 to 1969.

MODEL 521TL JUNIOR TARGET
BOLT-ACTION REPEATER. . . . NiB $398 Ex $269 Gd $191
Takedown. Caliber: .22 LR. Six round detachable box magazine. 25-inch bbl. Weight: About 7 lbs. Sights: Lyman No. 57RS rear; dovetailed blade front. Target stock. Sling and swivels. Made from 1947 to 1969.

MODEL 522 VIPER . . . . NiB $129 Ex $128 Gd $102
Calibers: .22 LR. 10-round magazine. 20-inch bbl. 40 inches overall. Weight: 4.63 lbs. Checkered black PET resin stock with beavertail forend. Dupont high-tech synthetic lightweight receiver. Matte black finish on all exposed metal. Made from 1993 to date.

MODEL 541-S CUSTOM SPORTER . . NiB $750 Ex $599 Gd $418
Bolt-action repeater. Scroll engraving on receiver and trigger guard. Caliber: .22 Short, Long, LR. Five round clip magazine. 24-inch bbl. Weight: 5.5 lbs. Supplied w/o sights. Checkered walnut stock w/rosewood-finished forend tip, pistol-grip cap and buttplate. Made from 1972 to 1984.

MODEL 541-T BOLT-ACTION RIFLE
Caliber: .22 RF. Clip-fed, Five round. 24-inch bbl. Weight: 5.88 lbs. Checkered walnut stock. Made from 1986 to date; heavy bbl. model intro. 1993.
Model 541-T Standard . . . . . . NiB $500 Ex $311 Gd $193
Model 541-T-HB heavy bbl. . . NiB $466 Ex $337 Gd $249

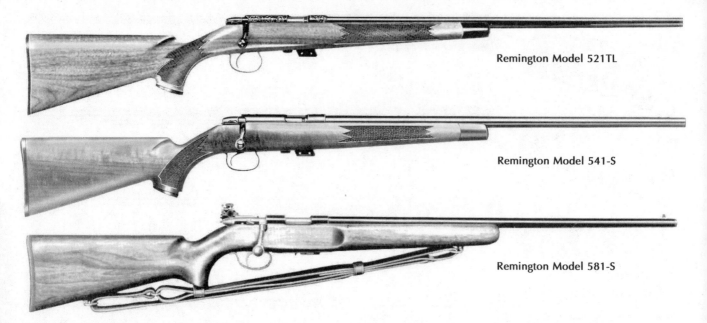

Remington Model 521TL

Remington Model 541-S

Remington Model 581-S

MODEL 581 CLIP REPEATER. . . . . . .NiB $ 259 Ex $144 Gd $120
Same general specifications as Model 580 except has 5-round clip magazine. Made from 1967 to 1984.
Model 581 (left-hand, made 1969-84) NiB $257 Ex $142 Gd $118

MODEL 581-S BOLT-ACTION RIFLE . NiB $190 Ex $157 Gd $133
Caliber: .22 RF. Clip-fed, 5-round. 24-inch bbl. Weight: 4.75 lbs. Plain walnut-colored stock. Made from 1987 to 1992.

MODEL 582 TUBULAR REPEATER . . NiB $256 Ex $179 Gd $127
Same general specifications as Model 580 except has tubular magazine holding 20 Short,15 Long,14 LR. Weight: About 5 lbs. Made from 1967 to 1984.

**MODEL 591 BOLT-ACTION
CLIP REPEATER . . . . NiB $319 Ex $210 Gd $171**
Caliber: 5mm Rimfire Magnum. Four round clip magazine. 24-inch bbl. Weight: 5 lbs. Sights: Bead front; U-notch rear. Monte Carlo stock. Made from 1970 to 1973.

MODEL 592 TUBULAR REPEATER . . NiB $278 Ex $175 Gd $128
Same as Model 591 except has tubular magazine holding 10 rounds, weight: 5.5 lbs. Made from 1970 to 1973.

MODEL 600 BOLT-ACTION CARBINE
Calibers: .222 Rem., .223 Rem., .243 Win., 6mm Rem., .308 Win., 35 Rem., 5-round magazine (6-round in .222 Rem.) 18.5-inch bbl. with ventilated rib. Weight: 6 lbs. Sights: Open rear; blade ramp front. Monte Carlo stock w/pistol-grip. Made from 1964 to 1967.
.222 Rem. . . . . NiB $550 Ex $445 Gd $333
.223 Rem . . . . NiB $1109 Ex $923 Gd $715
.35 Rem. . . . . NiB $641 Ex $540 Gd $499
Standard calibers . . . . NiB $510 Ex $390 Gd $338

MODEL 600 MAGNUM . . . . NiB $1044 Ex $800 Gd $645
Same as Model 600 except calibers 6.5mm Mag. and .350 Rem. Mag., 4-round magazine, special Magnum-type bbl. with bracket for scope back-up, laminated walnut and beech stock w/ recoil pad. QD swivels and sling; weight: About 6.5 lbs. Made 1965 to 1967.
MODEL 600 MONTANA

TERRITORIAL CENTENNIAL . . NiB $990 Ex $755 Gd $559
Same as Model 600 except has commemorative medallion embedded in buttstock. Made in 1964. Value is for rifle in new, unfired condition.

MODEL 660 STP
Calibers: .222 Rem., 6mm Rem., .243 Win., .308 Win., 5-round magazine. (6-round in .222 Rem.) 20-inch bbl. Weight: 6.5 lbs. Sights: Open rear; bead front on ramp. Monte Carlo stock, checkered, black pistol-grip cap and forend tip. Made from 1968 to 1971.
.222 Rem . . . . NiB $465 Ex $355 Gd $290
Other calibers . . . . NiB $560 Ex $443 Gd $355

MODEL 660 MAGNUM . . . . . NiB $970 Ex $766 Gd $641
Same as Model 660 except calibers 6.5mm Rem. Mag. and .350 Rem. Mag., 4-round magazine, laminated walnut-and-beech stock with recoil pad. QD swivels and sling. Made from 1968 to 1971.

MODEL 707 ADL CENTERFIRE RIFLE NiB $535 Ex $369 Gd $266
Calibers: .22-250, .222 Rem., .25-06, 6mm Rem., .243 Win., .270 Win., .30-06, .308 Win., 7mm Rem. Mag. Magazine capacity: 6-round in .222 Rem.; 4-round in 7mm Rem. Mag. Five round in other calibers. Bbl. lengths: 24-inch in .22-250, .222 Rem., .25-06, 7mm Rem. Mag.; 22-inch in other calibers. Weight: 7 lbs. standard; 7.5 lbs. in 7mm Rem. Mag. Sights: Ramp front; sliding ramp open rear. Monte Carlo stock w/cheekpiece, skip checkering, recoil pad on Magnum. Laminated stock also avail. Made from 1962 to 2005.

MODEL 707 APR BOLT-ACTION RIFL . . . NiB $2900 Ex $2290 Gd $1998
Acronym for African Plains Rifle. Calibers: 7mm Rem. Mag., 7mm STW, 300 Win. Mag., 300 Wby. Mag., 300 Rem. Ultra Mag., 338 Win. Mag., 375 H&H. Three round magazine. 26-inch bbl. on a magnum action. 46.5 inches overall. Weight: 7.75 lbs. Matte blue finish. Checkered classic-style laminated wood stock w/black magnum recoil pad. Made 1994 to 2004.

MODEL 707 AS BOLT-ACTION RIFLE
Similar to the Model 707 BDL except with non-reflective matte black metal finish, including the bolt body. Weight: 6.5 lbs. Straight comb synthetic stock made of Arylon, a fiberglass-reinforced thermoplastic resin with non-reflective matte finish. Made from 1988 to 1992.
Standard caliber . . . . NiB $555 Ex $440 Gd $339
Magnum caliber . . . . NiB $579 Ex $466 Gd $340

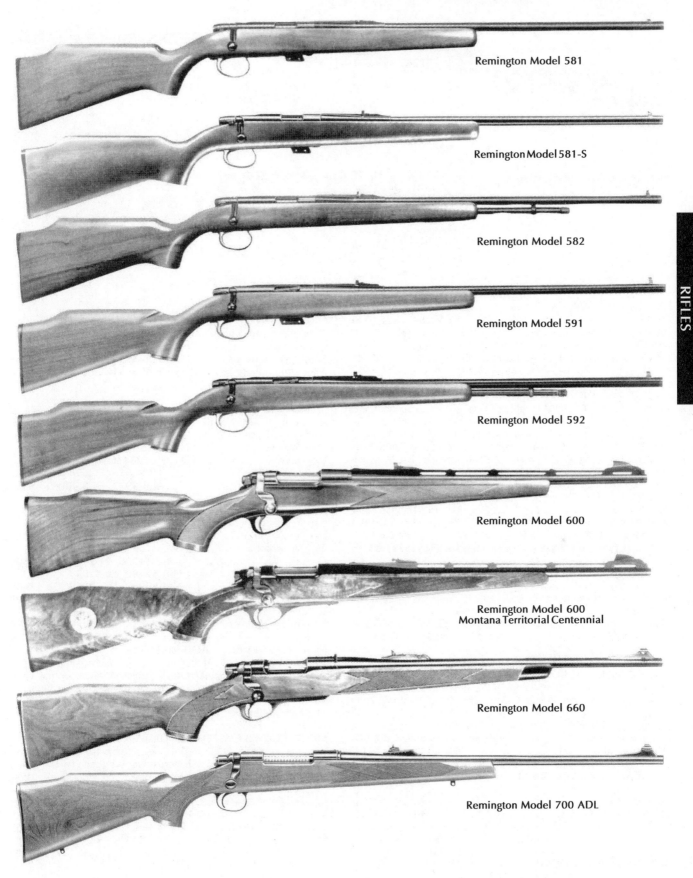

Remington Model 581

Remington Model 581-S

Remington Model 582

Remington Model 591

Remington Model 592

Remington Model 600

Remington Model 600
Montana Territorial Centennial

Remington Model 660

Remington Model 700 ADL

RIFLES

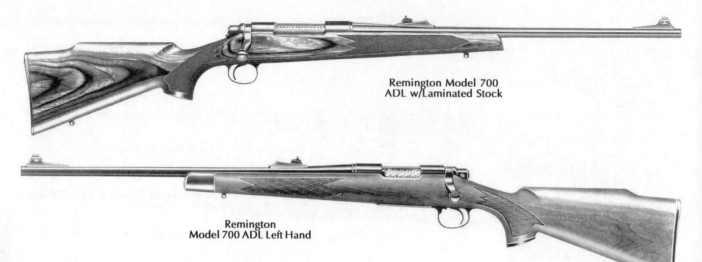

**Remington Model 700
ADL w/Laminated Stock**

**Remington
Model 700 ADL Left Hand**

MODEL 707 AWR
BOLT-ACTION RIFLE . . . . NiB $1566 Ex $1264 Gd $1090
Acronym for Alaskan Wilderness Rifle, similar to Model 707 APR except w/24-inch stainless bbl. and black chromed action. Matte gray or black Kevlar stock w/straight comb and raised cheekpiece fitted w/black magnum recoil pad. Made from 1994 to 2004.

MODEL 707 BDL CENTERFIRE RIFLE
Same as Model 707 ADL except has hinged floorplate hooded ramp front sight, stock w/black forend tip and pistol-grip cap, cut checkering, QD swivels and sling. Additional calibers: .17 Rem., .223 Rem., .264 Win. Mag., 7mm-08, .280, .300 Sav., .300 Win. Mag., 8mm Rem. Mag., .338 Win. Mag., .35 Whelen. All have 24-inch bbls. Magnums have 4-round magazine, recoil pad, weighs 7.5 lbs; .17 Rem. has 6-round magazine, weighs 7 lbs. Made 1962 to date. Made from 1973 to 2004.
Standard calibers.	NiB $810	Ex $466	Gd $333
Magnum calibers and .17 Rem.	NiB $855	Ex $555	Gd $380
Left-hand, .270 Win. And .30-06 . . .	NiB $855	Ex $469	Gd $343
Left hand, 7mm Rem. Mag. & .222 Rem.	NiB $788	Ex $559	Gd $495

MODEL 707 BDL EUROPEAN RIFLE
Same general specifications as Model 707 BDL, except has oil-finished walnut stock. Calibers: .243, .270, 7mm-08, 7mm Mag., .280 Rem., .30-06. Made from 1993 to 1995.
Standard calibers	NiB $495	Ex $422	Gd $370
Magnum calibers	NiB $579	Ex $466	Gd $357

MODEL 707 BDL SS BOLT-ACTION RIFLE
Same as Model 707 BDL except w/24-inch stainless bbl., receiver and bolt plus black synthetic stock. Calibers: .223 Rem., .243 Win., 6mm Rem., .25-06 Rem., .270 Win. .280 Rem., 7mm-08, 7mm Rem. Mag., 7mm Wby. Mag., .30-06, .300 Win., .308 Win., .338 Win. Mag. .375 H&H. Made from 1992 to 2004.
Standard calibers	NiB $625	Ex $509	Gd $347
Magnum calibers, add			$100
DM (detachable magazine), add			$50
DM-B (w/muzzle brake), add			$126

MODEL 707 BDL
VARMINT SPECIAL. . . . . NiB $695 Ex $449 Gd $315
Same as Model 707 BDL except has 24-inch heavy bbl., no sights, weighs 9 lbs. (8.75 lbs. in 308 Win.). Calibers: .22-250, .222 Rem., .223 Rem., .25-06, 6mm Rem., .243 Win., .308 Win. Made 1967 to 1994.
REMINGTON MODEL 707 CS BOLT-ACTION RIFLE

Similar to Model 707 BDL except with nonreflective matte black metal finish, including the bolt body. Straight comb synthetic stock camouflaged in Mossy Oak Bottomland pattern. Made 1992 to 1994.
Standard calibers	NiB $590	Ex $495	Gd $369
Magnum calibers	NiB $641	Ex $500	Gd $370

MODEL 707 CLASSIC
Same general specifications as Model 707 BDL except has "Classic" stock of high-quality walnut with full-pattern cut-checkering, special satin wood finish; Schnabel forend. Brown rubber buttpad. Hinged floorplate. No sights. Weight: 7 lbs. Also chambered for "Classic" cartridges such as .257 Roberts and .250-3000. Introduced in 1981.
Standard calibers	NiB $916	Ex $588	Gd $369
Magnum calibers	NiB $977	Ex $588	Gd $369

MODEL 707 CUSTOM BOLT-ACTION RIFLE
Same general specifications as Model 707 BDL except custom-built; available in choice of grades, each with higher quality wood, different checkering patterns, engraving, high-gloss blued finish. Introduced in 1965.
C Grade I	NiB $1965	Ex $1110	Gd $800
C Grade II	NiB $2490	Ex $1854	Gd $1354
C Grade III	NiB $2988	Ex $2360	Gd $1635
C Grade IV	NiB $4955	Ex $3290	Gd $2990
D Peerless Grade	NiB $2855	Ex $1590	Gd $1122
F Premier Grade	NiB $3634	Ex $2989	Gd $2190

MODEL 707 FS BOLT-ACTION RIFLE
Similar to Model 707 ADL except with straight comb fiberglass stock reinforced with DuPont Kevlar, finished in gray or gray camo with Old English-style recoil pad. Made from 1987 to 1989.
Standard calibers	NiB $600	Ex $479	Gd $259
Magnum calibers	NiB $720	Ex $590	Gd $433

MODEL 707 KS CUSTOM MOUNTAIN RIFLE
Similar to standard Model 707 MTN Rifle, except with custom Kevlar reinforced resin synthetic stock with standard or wood-grain finish. Calibers: .270 Win., .280 Rem., 7mm Rem Mag., .30-06, .300 Win. Mag., .300 Wby. Mag., 8mm Rem. Mag., .338 Win. Mag., .35 Whelen, .375 H&H. Four round magazine. 24-inch bbl. Weight: 6.75 lbs. Made from 1986 to 2008.
Standard KS stock (disc. 1993) . .	NiB $1899	Ex $1380	Gd $1079
Wood-grain KS stock	NiB $1139	Ex $899	Gd $655
Stainless synthetic (1995-97). . . .	NiB $2090	Ex $1421	Gd $1008
Left-hand model, add			$100

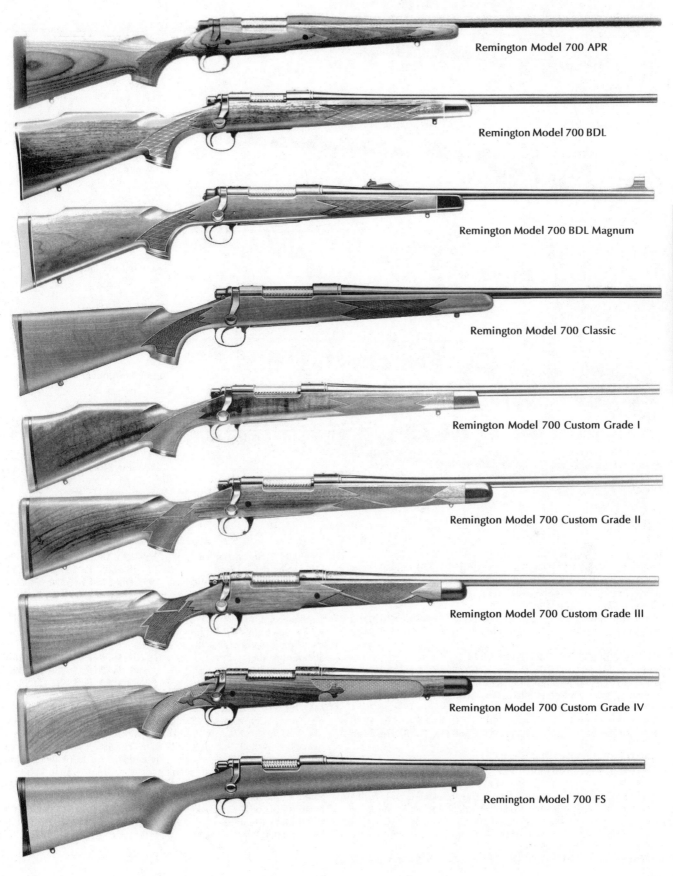

Remington Model 700 APR

Remington Model 700 BDL

Remington Model 700 BDL Magnum

Remington Model 700 Classic

Remington Model 700 Custom Grade I

Remington Model 700 Custom Grade II

Remington Model 700 Custom Grade III

Remington Model 700 Custom Grade IV

Remington Model 700 FS

RIFLES

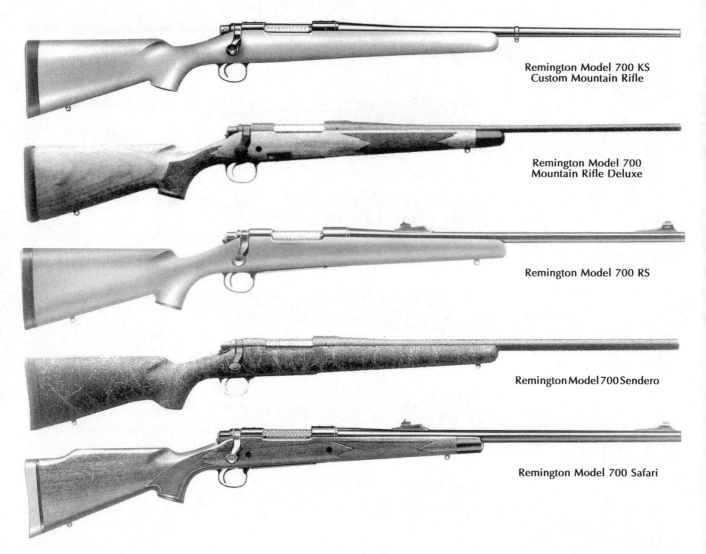

Remington Model 700 KS
Custom Mountain Rifle

Remington Model 700
Mountain Rifle Deluxe

Remington Model 700 RS

Remington Model 700 Sendero

Remington Model 700 Safari

MODEL 707 LS BOLT-ACTION RIFLE
Similar to Model 707 ADL except with checkered Monte Carlo-style laminated wood stock with alternating grain and wood color, impregnated with phenolic resin and finished with a low satin luster. Made from 1988 to 1993.
Standard calibers . . . . NiB $690 Ex $550 Gd $395
Magnum calibers . . . . NiB $779 Ex $598 Gd $443

MODEL 707 LSS BOLT-ACTION RIFLE
Similar to Model 707 BDL except with stainless steel barrel and action. Checkered Monte Carlo-style laminated wood stock with alternating grain and gray tinted color impregnated with phenolic resin and finished with a low satin luster. Made from 1996 to 2004.
Standard calibers . . . . NiB $510 Ex $440 Gd $290
Magnum calibers . . . . NiB $588 Ex $479 Gd $466

MODEL 707 MOUNTAIN RIFLE
Lightweight version of Model 707. Calibers: .243 Win., .25-06, .257 Roberts, .270 Win., 7x57, 7mm-08 Rem., .280 Rem., .30-06 and .308 Win. Four round magazine. 22-inch bbl. Weight: 6.75 lbs. Satin blue or stainless finish. Checkered walnut stock and redesigned pistol grip, straight comb, contoured cheekpiece, Old English-style recoil pad and satin oil finish or black synthetic stock with pressed checkering and blind magazine. Made from 1986 to 1994.
DM model (intro. 1995) . . . . NiB $755 Ex $488 Gd $367

SS model (stainless synthetic, disc. 1993)NiB $500 Ex $443 Gd $309
DM Model (New 1995). . . . . NiB $685 Ex $443 Gd $339
SS Model stainless synthetic (disc. 1993)NiB $450 Ex $390 Gd $287

MODEL 707 RS BOLT-ACTION RIFLE
Similar to the Model 707 BDL except with straight comb DuPont Rynite stock finished in gray or gray camo with Old English style recoil pad. Made from 1987 to 1990.
Standard calibers . . . . NiB $600 Ex $433 Gd $380
Magnum calibers . . . . NiB $677 Ex $535 Gd $390
.280 Rem. (Limited prod.) . . . . NiB $739 Ex $596 Gd $415

MODEL 707 SAFARI GRADE
Big game heavy magnum version of the Model 707 BDL. 8mm Rem. Mag., .375 H&H Mag., .416 Rem. Mag. and .458 Win. Mag. 24-inch heavy bbl. Weight: 9 lbs. Blued or stainless finish. Checkered walnut stock in synthetic/Kevlar stock with standard matte or wood-grain finish with old English style recoil pad. Made from 1962 to 2000.
Safari Classic/Monte Carlo . . . . . . NiB $1498 Ex $1044 Gd $610
Safari KS (Kevlar stock, intro. 1989)NiB $1335 Ex $1155 Gd $927
Safari KS (wood-grain stock, intro. 1992)NiB$1296 Ex$1133 Gd$909
Safari KS SS (stainless, intro. 1993)NiB $1577 Ex $1326 Gd $1055
Safari model, left-hand, add $126

Remington Model 721A Deluxe

Remington Model 722A

MODEL 707 SENDERO BOLT-ACTION RIFLE
Same as Model 707 VS except chambered in long action and magnum .25-06 Rem., .270 Win., .280 Rem., 7mm Rem. Mag., .300 Win. Made from 1994 to 2002.
Standard calibers . . . . NiB $707 Ex $589 Gd $390
Magnum calibers, add $50
SF model (stainless, fluted bbl.), add $150

MODEL 707 VLS (VARMINT LAMINATED STOCK)
BOLT-ACTION RIFLE . . . . NiB $899 Ex $555 Gd $390
Same as Model 707 BDL Varmint Special except with 26-inch polished blue barrel. Laminated wood stock with alternating grain and wood color impregnated with phenolic resin and finished with a satin luster. Calibers: .222 Rem., .223 Rem., .22-250 Rem., .243 Win., 7mm-08 Rem., .308 Win. Weight: 9.4 lbs. Made from 1995 to date.

MODEL 707 VS BOLT-ACTION RIFLE
Same as Model 707 BDL Varmint Special except w/26-inch matte blue or fluted stainless barrel. Textured black or gray synthetic stock reinforced with Kevlar, fiberglass and graphite with full length aluminum bedding block. Calibers: .22-250 Rem., .220 Swift, .223 Rem., .308 Win. Made from 1992 to date.
Model 707 VS . . . . NiB $888 Ex $559 Gd $444
Model SF (fluted bbl.) . . . . NiB $790 Ex $677 Gd $535
Model 707 VS SF/SF-P
(fluted & ported bbl.) . . . . NiB $1043 Ex $866 Gd $657

MODEL 720A BOLT-ACTION
HIGH POWER . . . . NiB $1379 Ex $1266 Gd $1108
Modified M/1917 Enfield action. .257 Roberts, .270 Win., .30-06. Five round box magazine. 22-inch bbl. Weight: About 8 lbs. Sights: Open rear; bead front, on ramp. Pistol-grip stock, checkered. Model 720R has 20-inch bbl.; Model 720S has 24-inch bbl. Made in 1941.

MODEL 721 STANDARD GRADE
BOLT-ACTION HIGH-POWER RIFLE. NiB $495 Ex $433 Gd $356
Calibers: .270 Win., .30-06. Four round box magazine. 24-inch bbl. Weight: About 7.25 lbs. Sights: Open rear; bead front, on ramp. Plain sporting stock. Made from 1948 to 1962.

MODEL 721A MAGNUM
STANDARD GRADE . . . . NiB $655 Ex $499 Gd $439
Caliber: .264 Win. Mag. or .300 H&H Mag. Same as standard model except has 26-inch bbl. Three round magazine and recoil pad. Weight: 8.25 lbs.

MODEL 721ADL/BDL DELUXE
Same as Model 721A Standard or Magnum except has deluxe checkered stock and/or select wood.
Deluxe Grade. . . . . NiB $744 Ex $548 Gd $433
.300 Win. Mag. Deluxe . . . . NiB $790 Ex $775 Gd $600
Deluxe Special Grade. . . . . NiB $844 Ex $645 Gd $500
.300 Mag. Deluxe. . . . . NiB $833 Ex $689 Gd $567

MODEL 722A STANDARD GRADE SPORTER
Same as Model 721A bolt-action except shorter action. .222 Rem. mag., .243 Win., .257 Roberts, .308 Win., .300 Savage. Four or 5-round magazine. Weight: 7-8 lbs. .222 Rem. introduced 1950; .244 Rem. introduced 1955. Made from 1948 to 1962.
.222 Rem. . . . . NiB $517 Ex $466 Gd $360
.244 Rem. . . . . NiB $500 Ex $380 Gd $278
.222 Rem. Mag. & .243 Win. . NiB $465 Ex $390 Gd $288
Other calibers . . . . NiB $466 Ex $398 Gd $270

MODEL 722ADL DELUXE GRADE
Same as Model 722A except has deluxe checkered stock.
Standard calibers . . . . NiB $590 Ex $513 Gd $398
.222 Rem. Deluxe Grade . . . . NiB $690 Ex $579 Gd $455
.244 Rem. Deluxe Grade . . . . NiB $835 Ex $733 Gd $495

MODEL 722BDL DELUXE SPECIAL GRADE
Same as Model 722ADL except select wood.
Standard calibers . . . . NiB $866 Ex $590 Gd $498
.222 Rem. Deluxe Special Grade NiB $866 Ex $590 Gd $498
.224 Rem. Deluxe Special Grade NiB $799 Ex $733 Gd $475

MODEL 725 KODIAK
MAGNUM RIFLE . . . . NiB $4200 Ex $3543 Gd $2300
Similar to Model 725ADL. Calibers: .375 H&H Mag., .458 Win. Mag. Three round magazine. 26-inch bbl. with recoil reducer built into muzzle. Weight: About 9 lbs. Deluxe, reinforced Monte Carlo stock with recoil pad, black forend tip swivels, sling. Fewer than 100 made in 1961.

MODEL 725ADL BOLT-ACTION REPEATING RIFLE
Calibers: .222, .243, .244, .270, .280, .30-06. Four round box mag. (5-round in 222). 22-inch bbl. (24-inch in .222). Weight: About 7 lbs. Sights: Open rear, hooded ramp front. Monte Carlo comb stock w/pistol-grip, checkered, swivels. Made from 1958 to 1961.
.222 Rem., .243 Win., .244 Rem NiB $855 Ex $690 Gd $505
.270 Win. . . . . NiB $767 Ex $659 Gd $467
.280 Win. . . . . NiB $977 Ex $800 Gd $509
.30-06 . . . . NiB $707 Ex $580 Gd $439

MODEL 788 CENTERFIRE BOLT-ACTION
Calibers: .222 Rem., .22-250, .223 Rem., 6mm Rem., .243 Win., 7mm-08 Rem., .308 Win., .30-30, .44 Rem. Mag. Three round clip magazine (4-round in .222 and .223 Rem.). 24-inch bbl. in .22s, 22-inch in other calibers. Weight: 7.5 lbs. with 24-inch bbl.; 7.25 lbs. with 22-inch bbl. Sights: Blade front on ramp; U-notch rear. Plain Monte Carlo stock. Made 1967 to 1984.
.22-250, .223 Rem., 6mm Rem.,
.243 Win., .308 Win. . . . . NiB $522 Ex $339 Gd $243
.30-30 Win. NiB $555 Ex $434 Gd $319
7mm-08 Rem. . . . . NiB $733 Ex $423 Gd $333
.44 Mag. . . . . NiB $650 Ex $449 Gd $339

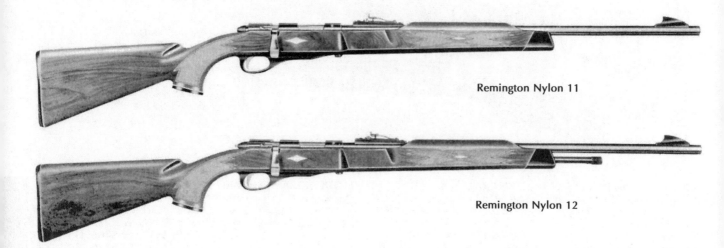

Remington Nylon 11

Remington Nylon 12

NYLON 11 BOLT-ACTION
REPEATER . . . . NiB $495 Ex $322 Gd $209
Clip type. Caliber: .22 Short, Long, LR. Six- or 10-round clip mag. 19.63-inch bbl. Weight: 4.5 lbs. Sights: Open rear; blade front. Nylon stock. Made from 1962 to 1966.

NYLON 12 BOLT-ACTION
REPEATER . . . . NiB $545 Ex $433 Gd $245
Same as Nylon 11 except has tubular magazine holding 22 Short, 17 Long, 15 LR. Made from 1962 to 1966.

SLIDE- AND LEVER-ACTION RIFLES

MODEL SIX (6) SLIDE-ACTION
REPEATER . . . . NiB $698 Ex $390 Gd $288
Hammerless. Calibers: 6mm Rem., .243 Win., .270 Win. 7mm Express Rem., .30-06, .308 Win. 22-inch bbl. Weight: 7.5 lbs. Checkered Monte Carlo stock and forearm. Made 1981 to 1988.

MODEL SIX (6) SLIDE-ACTION
REPEATER, PEERLESS GRADE . . . . NiB $1864 Ex $1607 Gd $989
Same as Model Six Standard except has engraved receiver. Three versions made from 1981 to 1988.

MODEL SIX (6) SLIDE-ACTION REPEATER, PREMIUM GRADES
Same as Model Six Standard except has engraved receiver with gold inlay. Made from 1981 to 1988.
Peerless D Grade . . . . NiB $1977 Ex $1670 Gd $1120
Premier F Grade . . . . NiB $4509 Ex $3533 Gd $2410
Premier Gold F Grade . . . . NiB $6212 Ex $4944 Gd $3490

MODEL 12A, 12B, 12C, 12CS SLIDE-ACTION REPEATERS
Standard Grade. Hammerless. Takedown. Caliber: .22 Short, Long or LR. Tubular magazine holds 15 Short, 12 Long or 10 LR cartridges. 22- or 24-inch round or octagonal bbl. Open rear sight, bead front. Plain, half-pistol-grip stock and grooved slide handle of walnut. Made from 1909 to 1936.
Model 12A . . . . NiB $600 Ex $399 Gd $278
Model 12B
(22 Short only w/octagon bbl.) . . . . . NiB $733 Ex $549 Gd $370
Model 12C
(w/24-inch octagon bbl.) . . . . NiB $623 Ex $544 Gd $355
Model 12CS
(22 WRF w/24-inch octagon bbl.) . . . NiB $570 Ex $445 Gd $315
MODEL 14A HIGH POWER

SLIDE-ACTION REPEATING RIFLE . . NiB $1077 Ex $798 Gd $643
Standard grade. Hammerless. Takedown. Calibers: .25, .30, .32 and .35 Rem. Five round tubular magazine. 22-inch bbl. Weight: About 6.75 lbs. Sights: Open rear; bead front. Plain half-pistol-grip stock and grooved slide handle of walnut. Made from 1912 to 1935.

MODEL 14R CARBINE . . . . NiB $1286 Ex $1044 Gd $590
Same as Model 14R except has 18.5-inch bbl., straight-grip stock, weight: About 6 lbs.

MODEL 14 1/2 CARBINE . . NiB $1286 Ex $1044 Gd $590
Same as Model 14A Rifle previously listed, except has 9-round magazine, 18.5-inch bbl.

MODEL 14 1/2 RIFLE . . . . . NiB $1688 Ex $1044 Gd $622
Similar to Model 14A except calibers: .38-40 and .44-40, 11-round full magazine, 22.5-inch bbl. Made from 1912 to early 1920's.

MODEL 25A SLIDE-ACTION
REPEATER . . . . NiB $1094 Ex $744 Gd $500
Standard Grade. Hammerless. Takedown. Calibers: .25-20, .32-20. 10-round tubular magazine. 24-inch bbl. Weight: About 5.5 lbs. Sights: Open rear; bead front. Plain, pistol-grip stock, grooved slide handle. Made from 1923 to 1936.

MODEL 25R CARBINE . . . . . NiB $1190 Ex $745 Gd $533
Same as Model 25A except has 18-inch bbl. Six round magazine, straight-grip stock, weight: About 4.5 lbs.

MODEL 121A FIELDMASTER
SLIDE-ACTION REPEATER . . . NiB $677 Ex $500 Gd $355
Standard Grade. Hammerless. Takedown. Caliber: .22 Short, Long, LR. Tubular magazine holds 20 Short, 15 Long or 14 LR cartridges. 24-inch round bbl. Weight: 6 lbs. Plain, pistol-grip stock and grooved semi-beavertail slide handle. Made from 1936 to 1954.

MODEL 121S . . . . NiB $599 Ex $500 Gd $443
Same as Model 121A except chambered for .22 Remington Special (.22 W.R.F.). Magazine holds 12 rounds. Disc.

MODEL 121SB . . . . NiB $707 Ex $553 Gd $439
Same as Model 121A except smoothbore. Disc.

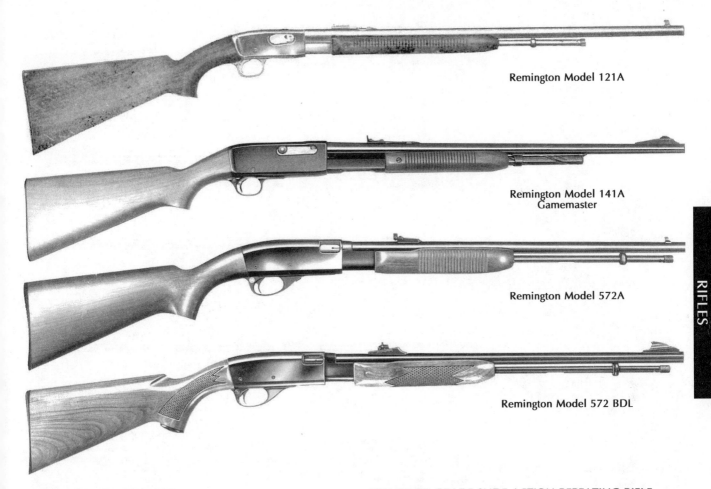

Remington Model 121A

Remington Model 141A
Gamemaster

Remington Model 572A

Remington Model 572 BDL

MODEL 141A GAMEMASTER
SLIDE-ACTION REPEATER . . . NiB $543 Ex $359 Gd $269
Standard Grade. Hammerless. Takedown. Calibers: .30, .32 and .35 Rem. Five round tubular magazine. 24-inch bbl. Weight: About 7.75 lbs. Sights: Open rear; bead front, on ramp. Plain, pistol-grip stock, semibeavertail forend (slide-handle). Made from 1936 to 1950.

MODEL 572A FIELDMASTER
SLIDE-ACTION REPEATER . . . NiB $290 Ex $179 Gd $130
Hammerless. Caliber: .22 Short, Long, LR. Tubular magazine holds 20 Short, 17 Long, 15 LR. 23-inch bbl. Weight: About 5.5 lbs. Sights: Open rear; ramp front. Pistol-grip stock, grooved forearm. Made 1955 to 1988.

MODEL 572BDL DELUXE. . . . NiB $533 Ex $444 Gd $149
Same as Model 572A except has blade ramp front sight, sliding ramp rear; checkered stock and forearm. Made from 1966 to date.

MODEL 572SB SMOOTH BORENiB $549 Ex $400 Gd $300
Same as Model 572A except smoothbore for .22 LR shot cartridges. Made from 1961 to date.

MODEL 760 BICENTENNIAL
COMMEMORATIVE . . . . NiB $556 Ex $398 Gd $265
Same as Model 760 except has commemorative inscription on receiver. Made in 1976.

MODEL 760 CARBINE . . . . . . NiB $480 Ex $390 Gd $245
Same as Model 760 Rifle except made in calibers .270 Win., .280 Rem., .30-06 and .308 Win. only, has 18.5-inch bbl., weight: 7.25 lbs. Made 1961 to 1980.
MODEL 760 GAMEMASTER

STANDARD GRADE SLIDE-ACTION REPEATING RIFLE
Hammerless. Calibers: .223 Rem., 6mm Rem., .243 Win., .257 Roberts, .270 Win. .280 Rem., .30-06, .300 Sav., .308 Win., .35 Rem. 22-inch bbl. Weight: About 7.5 lbs. Sights: Open rear; bead front, on ramp. Plain pistol-grip stock, grooved slide handle on early models; current production has checkered stock and slide handle. Made from 1952 to 1980.

	NiB	Ex	Gd
.222 Rem.	$1195	$1021	$744
.223 Rem.	$1409	$1135	$739
.257 Roberts	$933	$779	$489
Other calibers	$460	$407	$375

MODEL 760ADL
DELUXE GRADE. . . . . NiB $500 Ex $398 Gd $347
Same as Model 760 except has deluxe checkered stock, standard or high comb, grip cap, sling swivels. Made from 1953 to 1963.

MODEL 760BDL
CUSTOM DELUXE . . . . NiB $655 Ex $449 Gd $325
Same as Model 760 Rifle except made in calibers .270, .30-06 and .308 only, has Monte Carlo cheekpiece stock forearm with black tip, basket-weave checkering. Available also in left-hand model. Made from 1953 to 1980.

MODEL 760D
PEERLESS GRADE. . . . . NiB $2589 Ex $1176 Gd $925
Same as Model 760 except scroll engraved, fancy wood. Made from 1953 to 1980.

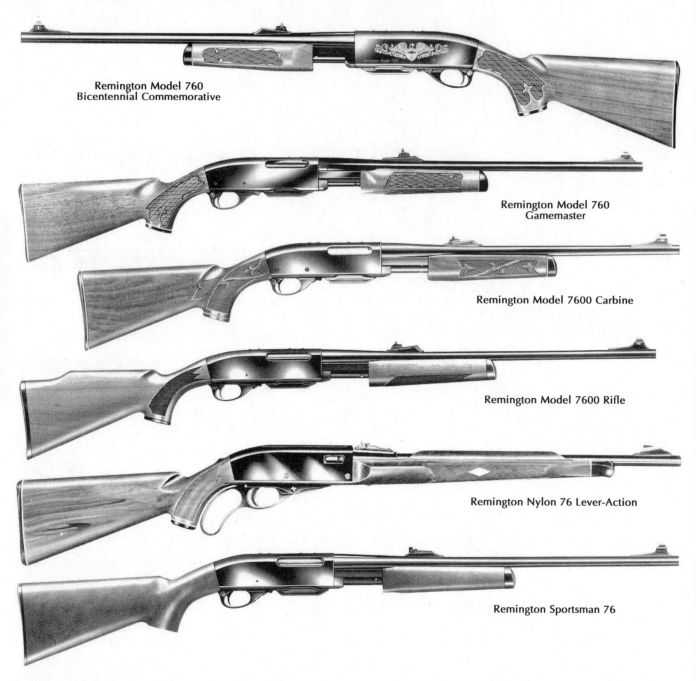

Remington Model 760
Bicentennial Commemorative

Remington Model 760
Gamemaster

Remington Model 7600 Carbine

Remington Model 7600 Rifle

Remington Nylon 76 Lever-Action

Remington Sportsman 76

MODEL 760F PREMIER GRADE
Same as Model 760 except extensively engraved with game scenes and scroll, finest grade wood. Also available with receiver inlaid with gold; adds 50 percent to value. Made from 1953 to 1980.
Premier F Grade . . . . **NiB $5200 Ex $3288 Gd $2579**
Premier Gold F Grade. . . . **NiB $7179 Ex $6088 Gd $4439**

MODEL 7600 SLIDE-ACTION
CARBINE . . . . **NiB $698 Ex $449 Gd $370**
Same general specifications as Model 7600 Rifle except has 18.5-inch bbl. and weighs 7.25 lbs. Made from 1987 to date.

MODEL 7600 SLIDE-ACTION RIFLE . **NiB $707 Ex $451 Gd $370**
Similar to Model Six except has lower grade finishes. Made from 1981 to date.
MODEL 7600 SPECIAL PURPOSE . . . **NiB $470 Ex $444 Gd $289**

Same general specification as the Model 7600, except chambered only in .270 or .30-06. Special Purpose matte black finish on all exposed metal. American walnut stock with SP non-glare finish.

NYLON 76 LEVER-ACTION REPEATER NiB $899 Ex $677 Gd $468
Short-throw lever action. Caliber: .22 LR. 14-round buttstock tubular magazine. Weight: 4 lbs. Black (add $707) or brown nylon stock and forend. Made 1962-64. Remington's only lever-action rifle.

SPORTSMAN 76 SLIDE-ACTION RIFLE NiB $375 Ex $300 Gd $200
Caliber: .30-06, 4-round magazine. 22-inch bbl. Weight: 7.5 lbs. Open rear sight; front blade mounted on ramp. Uncheckered hardwood stock and forend. Made from 1985 to 1987.

SEMIAUTOMATIC RIFLES

MODEL FOUR (4) AUTOLOADING RIFLE
Hammerless. Calibers: 6mm Rem., .243 Win., .270 Win. 7mm Express Rem., .30-06, .308 Win. 22-inch bbl. Weight: 7.5 lbs. Sights: Open rear; bead front, on ramp. Monte Carlo checkered stock and forearm. Made from 1981 to 1988.
Standard model . . . . NiB $722 Ex $465 Gd $369
Peerless Grade (engraved receiver) NiB $2219 Ex $1266 Gd $909
Premier Grade (engraved receiver) NiB $4155 Ex $3265 Gd $2200
Premier Grade,
(engraved receiver, gold inlay) . . NiB $6544 Ex $5233 Gd $3588

MODEL FOUR DIAMOND
ANNIVERSARY LTD. EDITION . . . NiB $1377 EX $1088 Gd $976
Same as Model Four Standard except has engraved receiver w/ inscription, checkered high-grade walnut stock and forend. Only 1,500 produced. Made in 1981 only. (Value for new condition.)

MODEL 8A AUTOLOADING RIFLE . . NiB $766 Ex $645 Gd $473
Standard Grade. Takedown. Calibers: .25, .30, .32 and .35 Rem. Five-round, clip-loaded magazine. 22-inch bbl. Weight: 7.75 lbs. Sights: Adj. and dovetailed open rear; dovetailed bead front. Half-moon metal buttplate on plain straight-grip walnut stock; plain walnut forearm with thin curved end. Made from 1906 to 1936.

MODEL 16 AUTOLOADING RIFLE . . NiB $755 Ex $523 Gd $390
Takedown. Closely resembles the Winchester Model 03 semiautomatic rifle. Calibers: .22 Short, .22 LR, 22 Rem. Auto. 15-round tubular magazine in buttstock. 22-inch bbl. Weight: 5.75 lbs. Sights: Open rear; dovetailed bead front. Plain straight-grip stock and forearm. Made from 1914 to 1928. Note: In 1918 this model was discontinued in all calibers except .22 Rem. Auto; specifications are for that model.

MODEL 24A AUTOLOADING RIFLE . NiB $498 Ex $343 Gd $244
Standard Grade. Takedown. Calibers: .22 Short only, .22 LR. only. Tubular magazine in buttstock, holds 15 Short or 10 LR. 21-inch bbl. Weight: About 5 lbs. Sights: Dovetailed adj. open rear; dovetailed bead front. Plain walnut straight-grip buttstock; plain walnut forearm. Made 1922 to 1935.

MODEL 81A WOODSMASTER
AUTOLOADER . . . . NiB $590 Ex $498 Gd $300
Standard Grade. Takedown. Calibers: .30, .32 and .35 Rem., .300 Sav. Five round box magazine (not detachable). 22-inch bbl. Weight: 8.25 lbs. Sights: Open rear; bead front. Plain walnut pistol-grip stock, forearm. Made from 1936 to 1950.

MODEL 141A SPEEDMASTER
AUTOLOADER . . . . NiB $500 Ex $326 Gd $249
Standard Grade. Takedown. Calibers: .22 Short only, .22 LR. only. Tubular magazine in buttstock, holds 15 Short or 10 LR. 24-inch bbl. Weight: About 6 lbs. Sights: Open rear, bead front. Plain walnut stock and forearm. Made from 1935 to 1951.

MODEL 550A AUTOLOADER . NiB $370 Ex $222 Gd $129
Has "Power Piston" or floating chamber, which permits interchangeable use of 22 Short, Long or LR cartridges. Tubular magazine holds 22 Short, 17 Long, 15 LR. 24-inch bbl. Weight: About 6.25 lbs. Sights: Open rear; bead front. Plain, one-piece pistol-grip stock. Made from 1941 to 1971.

MODEL 550P . . . . NiB $369 Ex $221 Gd $156
Same as Model 550A except has peep rear sight, blade front, on ramp.

MODEL 550-2G . . . . NiB $388 Ex $279 Gd $200
"Gallery Special." Same as Model 550A except has 22-inch bbl., screw eye for counter chain and fired shell deflector.

**Remington Sportsman 742
Canadian Centennial**

MODEL 552A SPEEDMASTER
AUTOLOADER . . . . NiB $339 Ex $229 Gd $133
Caliber: .22 Short, Long, LR. Tubular magazine holds 20 Short, 17 Long, 15 LR. 25-inch bbl. Weight: About 5.5 lbs. Sights: Open rear; bead front. Pistol-grip stock, semi-beavertail forearm. Made from 1957 to 1988.

MODEL 552BDL DELUXE . . . . NiB $533 Ex $367 Gd $290
Same as Model 552A except has checkered walnut stock and forearm. Made from 1966 to date.

MODEL 552C CARBINE . . . . . NiB $333 Ex $209 Gd $148
Same as Model 552A except has 21-inch bbl. Made 1961 to 1977.

MODEL 552GS GALLERY SPECIAL . . NiB $387 Ex $265 Gd $190
Same as Model 552A except chambered for .22 Short only. Made from 1957 to 1977.

MODEL 740A WOODSMASTER AUTOLOADER
Standard Grade. Gas-operated. Calibers: .30-06 or .308. Four round detachable box magazine. 22-inch bbl. Weight: About 7.5 lbs. Plain pistol-grip stock, semibeavertail forend with finger grooves. Sights: Open rear; ramp front. Made from 1955 to 1959.
Rifle model . . . . NiB $369 Ex $278 Gd $199
Carbine model . . . . NiB $467 Ex $443 Gd $290

MODEL 740ADL/BDL DELUXE
Same as Model 740A except has deluxe checkered stock, standard or high comb, grip cap, sling swivels. Model 740 BDL also has select wood. Made from 1955 to 1960.
Model 740 ADL Deluxe Grade . . . . . NiB $480 Ex $572 Gd $410
Model 740 BDL Deluxe Special Grade NiB $480 Ex $572 Gd $410

MODEL 742 BICENTENNIAL
COMMEMORATIVE . . . . NiB $588 Ex $380 Gd $355
Same as Model 742 Woodsmaster rifle except has commemorative inscription on receiver. Made in 1976. (Value for new condition.)

MODEL 742 CARBINE . . . . . . NiB $522 Ex $355 Gd $260
Same as Model 742 Woodsmaster Rifle except made in calibers .30-06 and .308 only, has 18.5-inch bbl., weight 6.75 lbs. Made from 1961 to 1980.

MODEL 742 WOODSMASTER
AUTOMATIC BIG GAME RIFLE . . . . . NiB $707 Ex $533 Gd $290
Gas-operated semiautomatic. Calibers: 6mm Rem., .243 Win., .280 Rem., .30-06, .308 Win. Four round clip magazine. 22-inch bbl. Weight: 7.5 lbs. Sights: Open rear; bead front, on ramp. Checkered pistol-grip stock and forearm. Made from 1960 to 1980.

RIFLES

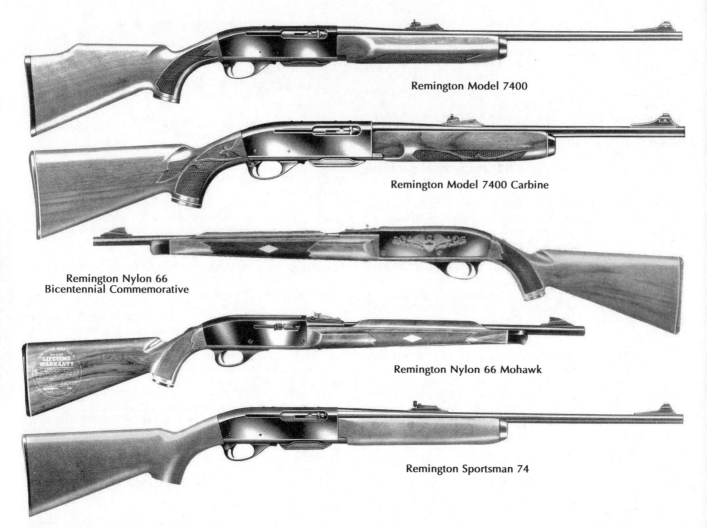

Remington Model 7400

Remington Model 7400 Carbine

Remington Nylon 66
Bicentennial Commemorative

Remington Nylon 66 Mohawk

Remington Sportsman 74

MODEL 742BDL CUSTOM DELUXE . NiB $523 Ex $433 Gd $300
Same as Model 742 Rifle except made in calibers .30-06 and
.308 only, Monte Carlo cheekpiece stock, forearm with black tip,
basket-weave checkering. Available in left-hand model. Made
from 1966 to 1980.

MODEL 742D PEERLESS GRADE... NiB $2590 Ex $2020 Gd $1100
Same as Model 742 except scroll engraved, fancy wood. Made
from 1961 to 1980.

MODEL 742F PREMIER GRADE
Same as Model 742 except extensively engraved with game scenes
and scroll, finest grade wood. Also available with receiver inlaid
with gold; adds 50 percent to value. Made from 1961 to 1980.
Premier F Grade........ NiB $5233 Ex $3288 Gd $2270
Premier Gold F Grade.... NiB $7350 Ex $5093 Gd $3466

MODEL 7400 AUTOLOADER
Similar to Model Four w/lower grade finishes. Made from 1981 to date.
Model 7400 Standard............ NiB $559 Ex $433 Gd $310
Model 7400 HG
(High gloss finish).............. NiB $559 Ex $433 Gd $310

MODEL 7400 CARBINE ..... NiB $559 Ex $433 Gd $310
Caliber: .30-06 only. Similar to the Model 7400 rifle except has
18.5-inch bbl. and weight: 7.25 lbs. Made from 1988 to date.

MODEL 7400 SPECIAL PURPOSE ... NiB $476 Ex $434 Gd $289
Same general specification as the Model 7400 except chambered
only in .270 or .30-06. Special Purpose matte black finish on metal.
American walnut stock with SP nonglare finish. Made 1993 to 1995.

NYLON 66 APACHE BLACK .. NiB $279 Ex $169 Gd $130
Same as Nylon 66 Mohawk Brown listed below except bbl. and
receiver cover chrome-plated, black stock. Made 1962 to 1984.

NYLON 66 BICENTENNIAL
COMMEMORATIVE .... NiB $597 Ex $433 Gd $259
Same as Nylon 66 Mohawk Brown listed below except has com-
memorative inscription on receiver. Made 1976 only.

NYLON 66MB AUTOLOADING RIFLE NiB $500 Ex $325 Gd $244
Similar to the early production Nylon 66 Black Apache except with
blued bbl. and receiver cover. Made from 1978 to 1987.

NYLON 66 MOHAWK
BROWN AUTOLOADER..... NiB $450 Ex $278 Gd $230
Caliber: .22 LR. Tubular magazine in buttstock holds 14 rounds.
19.5-inch bbl. Weight: About 4 lbs. Sights: Open rear; blade front.
Brown nylon stock and forearm. Made from 1959 to 1987.

NYLON 77 CLIP REPEATER .. NiB $400 Ex $295 Gd $220
Same as Nylon 66 except has 5-round clip magazine. Made 1970 to 1971.

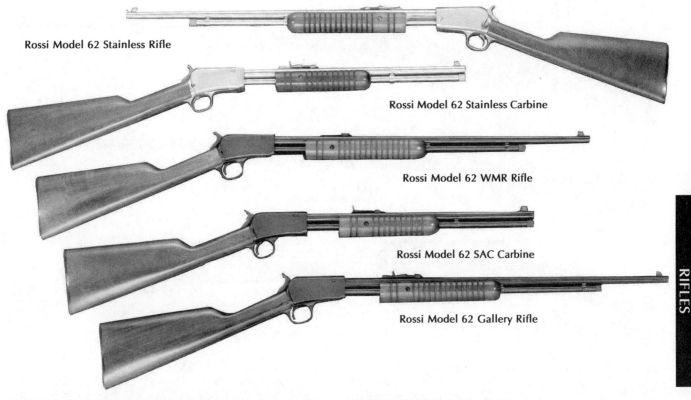

Rossi Model 62 Stainless Rifle

Rossi Model 62 Stainless Carbine

Rossi Model 62 WMR Rifle

Rossi Model 62 SAC Carbine

Rossi Model 62 Gallery Rifle

RIFLES

SPORTSMAN 74 AUTOLOADING RIFLE NiB $379 Ex $294 Gd $200
Caliber: .30-06, 4-round magazine. 22-inch bbl. Unchecked buttstock and forend. Open rear sight; ramped blade front sight. Made 1985 to 1988.

JOHN RIGBY & CO. — Paso Robles, California

MODEL 278 MAGAZINE SPORTING RIFLE NiB $6475 Ex $5144 Gd $3576
Mauser action. Caliber: .278 High Velocity or 7x57mm; 5-round box magazine. 25-inch bbl. Weight: about 7.5 lbs. Sights: Folding leaf rear; bead front. Sporting stock w/half-pistol-grip, checkered. Specifications given are those of current model; however, in general, they apply also to prewar model.

**MODEL 278 LIGHTWEIGHT
MAGAZINE RIFLE. . . . . NiB $5110 Ex $4122 Gd $2833**
Same as standard .278 rifle except has 21-inch bbl. Weight: 6.75 lbs.

**MODEL 350 MAGNUM
MAGAZINE SPORTING RIFLE. . . NiB $4332 Ex $3633 Gd $2490**
Mauser action. Caliber: .350 Magnum. Five round box magazine. 24-inch bbl. Weight: About 7.75 lbs. Sights: Folding leaf rear; bead front. Sporting stock with full pistol-grip, checkered. Currently mfd.

**MODEL 416 BIG GAME
MAGAZINE SPORTING RIFLE. . . NiB $7688 Ex $6133 Gd $4286**
Mauser action. Caliber: .416 Big Game. Four round box magazine. 24-inch bbl. Weight: 9 to 9.25 lbs. Sights: Folding leaf rear; bead front. Sporting stock with full pistol-grip, checkered. Currently mfd.

**BEST QUALITY HAMMERLESS
EJECTOR DOUBLE RIFLE . . NiB $73,675 Ex $62,000 Gd $38,550**
Sidelocks. Calibers: .278 Magnum, .350 Magnum, .470 Nitro Express. 24- to 28-inch bbls. Weight: 7.5 to 10.5 lbs. Sights: Folding leaf rear; bead front. Checkered pistol-grip stock and forearm.

**SECOND QUALITY HAMMERLESS
EJECTOR DOUBLE RIFLE . . NiB $13,600 Ex $11,290 Gd $10,375**
Same general specifications as Best Quality double rifle except boxlock.

**THIRD QUALITY HAMMERLESS
EJECTOR DOUBLE RIFLE . . . NiB $11,689 Ex $10,450 Gd $7,800**
Same as Second Quality double rifle except plainer finish and not of as high quality.

ROSS RIFLE CO. — Quebec, Canada

MODEL 1910 BOLT-ACTION SPORTING RIFLE
Straight-pull bolt-action with interrupted screw-type lugs. Calibers: .280 Ross, .303 British. Four round or 5-round magazine. Bbl. lengths: 22, 24, 26 inches. Sights: Two-leaf open rear; bead front. Checkered sporting stock. Weight: About 7 lbs. Made c. 1910 to end of World War I. Note: Most firearm authorities agree that this and other Ross models with interrupted screw-type lugs are unsafe to fire.
Military model . . . . NiB $2175 Ex $1370 Gd $989
Military Match Target model . . . . . . NiB $10,300 Ex $7227 Gd $3590

ROSSI RIFLES

MODEL 62 GALLERY SAC CARBINE
Same as standard Gallery Model except in .22 LR only with 16.25-inch bbl.; weight 5.5 lbs. Imported 1975 to 1998.
Blued finish . . . . NiB $215 Ex $159 Gd $126
Nickel finish. . . . . NiB $220 Ex $163 Gd $130
Stainless. . . . . NiB $220 Ex $163 Gd $130

MODEL 62 GALLERY MAGNUM. . . . NiB $235 Ex $200 Gd $135
Same as standard Gallery Model except chambered for .22 WMR, 10-shot magazine. Imported from 1975 to 1998.

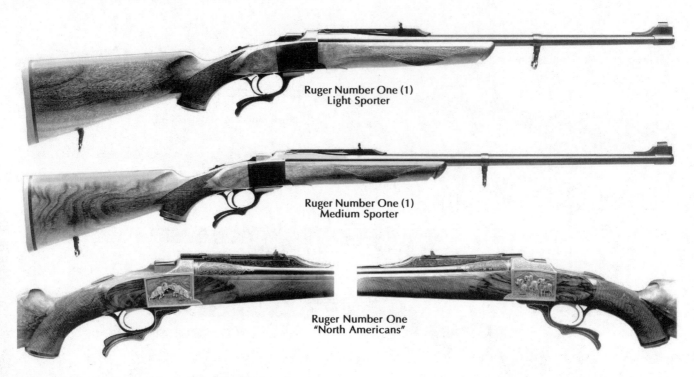

Ruger Number One (1)
Light Sporter

Ruger Number One (1)
Medium Sporter

Ruger Number One
"North Americans"

62 GALLERY MODEL SLIDE-ACTION REPEATER
Similar to Winchester Model 62. Calibers: .22 LR, Long, Short or .22 WMR. Tubular magazine holds 13 LR, 16 Long, 20 Short. 23-inch bbl. 39.25 inches overall. Weight: 5.75 lbs. Sights: Open rear; bead front. Straight-grip stock, grooved slide handle. Blued, nickel or stainless finish. Imported 1970 to 1998. Values same as SAC Model.

MODEL 65/92 LEVER-ACTION CARBINE
Similar to Winchester Model 92. Caliber: .38 Special/.357 Mag., .44 Mag., .44-40, .45 LC. 8- or 10-round magazine. 16-, 20- or 24-inch round or half-octagonal bbl. Weight: 5.5 to 6 lbs. 33.5- to 41.5-inches overall. Satin blue, chrome or stainless finish. Brazilian hardwood buttstock and forearm. Made from 1978 to 1998.

.45 LC	NiB $338	Ex $250	Gd $190
.38/.357, .44 Mag.	NiB $338	Ex $250	Gd $190
W/octagon bbl.	NiB $400	Ex $329	Gd $278
LL Lever model.	NiB $510	Ex $396	Gd $280
Engraved, add			$100
Chrome, add			$50
Stainless, add			$50

RUGER RIFLES

NUMBER ONE (1) LIGHT SPORTER NiB $1010 Ex $615 Gd $445
Same as No.1 Standard except has 22-inch bbl., folding leaf rear sight on quarter-rib and ramp front sight, Henry pattern forearm. Made from 1966 to date.

NUMBER ONE (1) MEDIUM SPORTER NiB $1010 Ex $615 Gd $445
Same as No. 1 Light Sporter except has 26-inch bbl. 22-inch in 45-70); weight: 8 lbs (7.25 lbs. in .45-70). Calibers: 7mm Rem. Mag., .300 Win. Mag., .45-70. Made from 1966 to date.

NUMBER ONE (1) "NORTH AMERICANS"
PRESENTATION RIFLE .... NiB $53,950 Ex $43,550 Gd $38,770
Same general specifications as the Ruger No. 1 Standard except highly customized with elaborate engravings, carvings, fine-line checkering and gold inlays. This was a series of 21 rifles depicting a North American big-game animal, chambered in the caliber appropriate to the game. Stock is of Northern California English walnut. Comes in trunk-style Huey case with Leupold scope and other accessories.

NUMBER ONE (1) RSI INTERNATIONAL
SINGLE-SHOT RIFLE .... NiB $1010 Ex $615 Gd $445
Similar to the No. 1 Light Sporter except with lightweight 20-inch bbl. and full Mannlicher-style forend, in calibers .243 Win., .270 Win., 7x57mm, .30-06. Weight: 7.25 lbs.

NUMBER ONE (1)
SPECIAL VARMINTER .... NiB $1010 Ex $615 Gd $445
Same as No. 1 Standard except has heavy 24-inch bbl. with target scope bases, no quarter-rib. Weight: 9 lbs. Calibers: .22-250, .25-06, 7mm Rem. Mag., .300 Win. Mag. Made from 1966 to date.

NUMBER ONE (1)
STANDARD RIFLE .... NiB $1010 Ex $615 Gd $445
Falling-block single-shot action with Farquharson-type lever. Calibers: .22-250, .243 Win., 6mm Rem., .25-06, .270 Win., .30-06, 7mm Rem. Mag., .300 Win. Mag. 26-inch bbl. Weight: 8 lbs. No sights, has quarter-rib for scope mounting. Checkered pistol-grip buttstock and semibeavertail forearm, QD swivels, rubber buttplate. Made from 1966 to date.

NUMBER ONE (1) TROPICAL RIFLE NiB $1010 Ex $615 Gd $445
Same as No. 1 Light Sporter except has heavy 24-inch bbl.; calibers are .375 H&H .404 Jeffery, .416 Rigby, and .458 Win. Mag. Weight: 8.25 to 9 lbs. Made from 1966 to date.

NUMBER THREE (3) SINGLE-SHOT
CARBINE .... NiB $800 Ex $495 Gd $355
Falling-block action with American-style lever. Calibers: .22 Hornet .223 Rem., .30-40 Krag, .357 Win., .44 Mag., .45-70. 22-inch bbl. Weight: 6 lbs. Sights: Folding leaf rear; gold bead front. Carbine-style stock w/curved buttplate, forearm with bbl. band. Made 1972 to 1987.

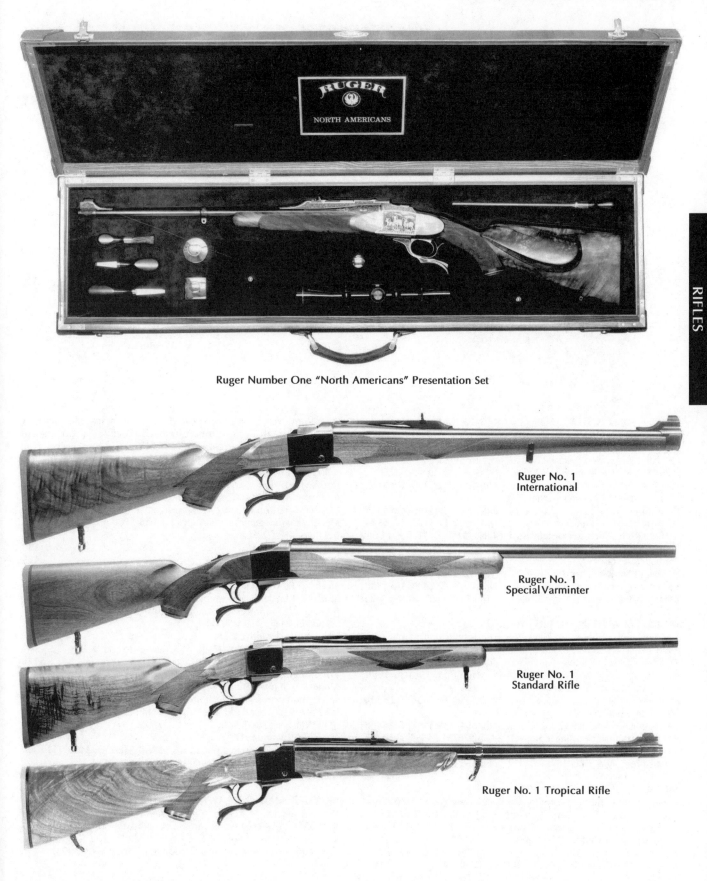

Ruger Number One "North Americans" Presentation Set

Ruger No. 1
International

Ruger No. 1
Special Varminter

Ruger No. 1
Standard Rifle

Ruger No. 1 Tropical Rifle

GRADING: **NiB** = New in Box   **Ex** = Excellent or NRA 95%   **Gd** = Good or NRA 68%   **337**

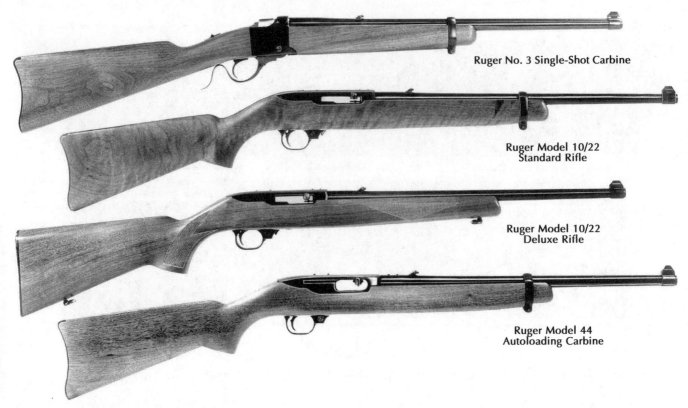

Ruger No. 3 Single-Shot Carbine

Ruger Model 10/22 Standard Rifle

Ruger Model 10/22 Deluxe Rifle

Ruger Model 44 Autoloading Carbine

MODEL 10/22 AUTOLOADING CARBINE

Caliber: .22 LR. Detachable 10-round rotary magazine. 18.5-inch bbl. Weight: 5 lbs. Sights: Folding leaf rear; bead front. Carbine-style stock with bbl. band and curved buttplate (walnut stock discontinued 1980). Made from 1964 to date. International and Sporter versions discontinued 1971.

Standard carbine w/walnut stock . . . . . . NiB $265 Ex $190 Gd $149
International, w/Mannlicher-style
stock (disc. 1971) . . . . NiB $710 Ex $497 Gd $375
RB (w/birch stock, blued finish) . . . . . . NiB $260 Ex $178 Gd $144
K-10/22 RB (w/birch stock, stainless finish)NiB $260 Ex $178 Gd $144
Sporter (w/MC stock,
flat buttplate, disc1971) . . . . NiB $260 Ex $178 Gd $144
SP Deluxe Sporter (intro. 1966) . . . . . . NiB $260 Ex $178 Gd $144
RBI International (blued, intro. 1994) . . NiB $690 Ex $488 Gd $380
RBI International (stainless, intro. 1995) . . . NiB $695 Ex $448 Gd $380

MODEL 44 AUTOLOADING CARBINE

Gas-operated. Caliber: .44 Magnum. Four round tubular magazine (with magazine release button since 1967). 18.5-inch bbl. Weight: 5.75 lbs. Sights: Folding leaf rear; gold bead front. Carbine-style stock w/bbl. band and curved buttplate. Made from 1961 to 1986. International and Sporter versions discontinued 1971.

Standard model . . . . NiB $588 Ex $434 Gd $338
Model 44 International
(w/Mannlicher-style stock) . . . . NiB $944 Ex $597 Gd $488
44 Sporter (MC stock w/finger groove) . . NiB $707 Ex $569 Gd $495
44RS Carbine
(w/peep rear sight, disc. 1978) . . . . NiB $695 Ex $487 Gd $388

MODEL 77 BOLT-ACTION RIFLE

Receiver with integral scope mount base or with round top. Short stroke or magnum length action (depending on caliber) in the former type receiver, magnum only in the latter. .22-250, .220 Swift, 6mm Rem., .243 Win., .250-3000, .25-06, .257 Roberts, 6.5 Rem. Mag., .270 Win., 7x57mm, 7mm-08 7mm Rem. Mag., .280 Rem., .284 Win., .308 Win., .30-06, .300 Win. Mag. .338 Win. Mag., .350 Rem. Mag., .458 Win. Mag. Five round magazine standard, 4-round in .220 Swift, 3-round in magnum calibers. 22 24- or 26-inch bbl. (depending on caliber). Weight: About 7 lbs.; .458 Mag. model, 8.75 lbs. Round-top model furnished w/folding leaf rear sight and ramp front; integral base model furnished w/scope rings,with or w/o open sights. Stock w/checkered pistol grip and forearm, pistol-grip cap, rubber recoil pad, QD swivel studs. Made from 1968 to 1992.

Model 77 w/integral base, no sights . . . NiB $500 Ex $408 Gd $321
6.5 Rem. Mag., add $100
.284 Win., add. $50
.338 Win. Mag., add $75
.350 Rem. Mag., add $75
Model 77RL Ultra Light, w/no sights. . . NiB $545 Ex $438 Gd $290
Model 77RL Ultra Light, w/open sights. NiB $569 Ex $454 Gd $331
MODEL 77RS w/integral base, open sights NiB $569 Ex $454 Gd $331
.338 Win. Mag., .458 Win. Mag.,
standard stock, add $100
Model 77RSC, .458 Win. Mag.,
w/walnut stock, add. $126
W/fancy grade Circassian walnut stock, add. $707
Model 77RSI International w/Mannlicher
stock, short action, 18.5-inch bbl.. . . . . NiB $675 Ex $466 Gd $339
Model 77ST w/round top, open sights . NiB $575 Ex $439 Gd $369
.338 Win. Mag., add $75
Model 77V Varmint
w/integral base, no sights. . . . . NiB $588 Ex $466 Gd $300
Model 77 NV Varmint w/integral base, no sights,
stainless steel bbl., laminated wood stockNiB $593 Ex $468 Gd $379

MODEL 77 MARK II ALL-WEATHER RIFLE NiB $535 Ex $430 Gd $315
Revised Model 77 action. Same general specifications as Model M-77 Mark II except with stainless bbl. and action. Zytel injection-molded stock. Calibers: .223, .243, .270, .308, .30-06, 7mm Mag., .300 Win. Mag., .338 Win. Mag. Made from 1999 to 2008.

Ruger Model 77 Round Top Receiver

Ruger Model 77 Ultra-Light Carbine

Ruger Model 77 International Carbine

Ruger Model 77 Varmint Rifle

Ruger Model 77 Mark II All-Weather Rifle

RIFLES

MODEL 77 MARK II BOLT-ACTION RIFLE

Revised Model 77 action. Same general specifications as Model M-77 except with new 3-position safety and fixed blade ejector system. Calibers .22 PPC, .223 Rem., 6mm PPC, 6.5x55 Swedish, .375 H&H, .404 Jeffery and .416 Rigby also available. Weight: 6 to 10.25 lbs. Made from 1989 to date.

MKIIR w/integral base, no sights . . . . NiB $545 Ex $423 Gd $314
Left-hand model, add $50
MKII RL Ultralight, no sights . . . . NiB $545 Ex $423 Gd $314
MKII RLS w/open sights . . . . NiB $545 Ex $423 Gd $314
MKII RS w/integral base, open sights. . . . . NiB $545 Ex $423 Gd $314
MKII RS Express w/fancy grade French
walnut stock, integral base,
open sights . . . . NiB $1347 Ex $1116 Gd $835
MKII RSI International Mannlicher. . . NiB $799 Ex $479 Gd $368
MKII RSM Magnum w/fancy grade Circassian
walnut stock, integral base, open sights NiB $1465 Ex $1143 Gd $870
77VT (VBZ or VTM) MKII
Varmint/Target w/stainless steel action,
laminated wood stock . . . . NiB $480 Ex $403 Gd $288

MODEL 77/.22 HORNET

BOLT-ACTION RIFLE . . . . NiB $556 EX $445 Gd $339
Mini-Sporter built on the 77/.22 action in caliber .22 Hornet. Six round rotary magazine. 20- inch bbl. 40 inches overall. Weight: 6 lbs. Receiver machined for Ruger rings (included). Beaded front sight and open adj. rear, or no sights. Blued or stainless finish. Checkered American walnut stock. Made from 1994 to date.

Model 77/.22RH (rings, no sights) . . . NiB $625 Ex $470 Gd $369
Model 77/.22RSH (rings & sights) . . . NiB $625 Ex $470 Gd $369
Model 77/.22VHZ (S/S w/
laminated wood stock) . . . . NiB $735 Ex $544 Gd $390

MODEL 77/.22 RIMFIRE BOLT-ACTION RIFLE

Calibers: .22 LR or .22 WMR. 10-shot (.22 LR) or 9-shot (.22 WMR) rotary magazine. 20-inch bbl. 39.75 inches overall. Weight: 5.75 lbs. Integral scope bases; with or w/o sights. Checkered American walnut or Zytel injection-molded stock. Stainless or blued finish. Made 1983 to date. (Blued); stainless. Introduced 1989.

77/.22R w/scope rings, no sights, walnut stock NiB $625 Ex $544 Gd $390
77/.22RS w/scope rings, sights, walnut stock. NiB $625 Ex $544 Gd $390
77/.22RP w/scope rings, no sights, synthetic stock NiB $625 Ex $544 Gd $390
77/.22RSP w/scope rings, sights, synthetic stock NiB $625 Ex $544 Gd $390
K77/.22RP w/stainless scope rings,
no sights, synthetic stock . . . . NiB $625 Ex $544 Gd $390
K77/.22RSP w/stainless scope rings,
sights, synthetic stock . . . . NiB $625 Ex $544 Gd $390
77/.22RM (.22 WMR) w/scope rings,
no sights, walnut stock . . . . NiB $625 Ex $544 Gd $390
K77/.22RSMP (.22 WMR) w/stainless
scope rings, sights, synthetic stock . . . . . NiB $735 Ex $579 Gd $437
K77/.22RMP (.22 WMR) w/stainless
scope rings, sights, synthetic stock . . . . . NiB $625 Ex $544 Gd $390
K77/.22 VBZ (.22 WMR) w/no sights,
laminated stock (intro. 1993) . . . . NiB $735 Ex $579 Gd $437

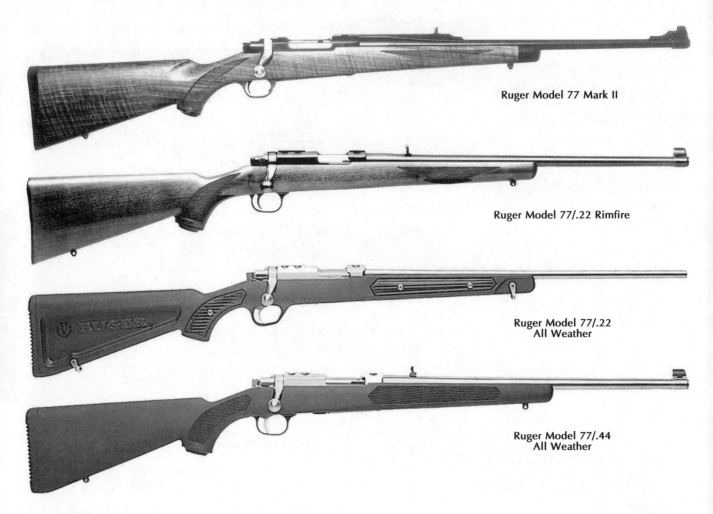

Ruger Model 77 Mark II

Ruger Model 77/.22 Rimfire

Ruger Model 77/.22 All Weather

Ruger Model 77/.44 All Weather

MODEL 77/.44 BOLT-ACTION
Short-action, carbine-style M77 similar to the 77/.22RH. Chambered .44 Rem. Mag. Four round rotary magazine. 18.5-inch bbl. 38.25 inches overall. Weight: 6 lbs. Gold bead front sight, folding adjustable rear w/integral scope base and Ruger rings. Blue or stainless finish. Synthetic or checkered American walnut stock w/rubber buttpad and swivels. Made from 1997 to 2004.

Blued finish . . . . NiB $625 Ex $544 Gd $390
Stainless finish . . . . NiB $555 Ex $350 Gd $245

MODEL 96 LEVER ACTION CARBINE
Caliber: .22 LR, .22 Mag., .44 Mag. Detachable 10-, 9- or 4-round magazine. 18.5-inch bbl. Weight: 5.25 lbs. Front gold bead sights. Drilled and tapped for scope. American hardwood stock. Made from 1996 to 2008.

.22 LR . . . . NiB $379 Ex $255 Gd $180
.22 WMR . . . . NiB $390 Ex $278 Gd $195
.44 Mag. . . . . NiB $390 Ex $278 Gd $195

MINI-14 SEMIAUTOMATIC RIFLE
Gas-operated. Caliber: .223 Rem. (5.56mm). 5-, 10- or 20-round box magazine. 18.5-inch bbl. Weight: About 6.5 lbs. Sights: Peep rear; blade front mounted on removable barrel band. Pistol-grip stock w/curved buttplate, handguard. Made from 1974 to 2004.

Blued finish . . . . NiB $725 Ex $579 Gd $375
K-Mini-14/S stainless steel. . . . . NiB $815 Ex $580 Gd $444

Mini-14/5F w/blued finish,
folding stock. . . . . NiB $1144 Ex $995 Gd $790
K-Mini-14/SF w/stainless finish,
folding stock. . . . . NiB $855 Ex $690 Gd $545
Mini-14 Ranch Rifle w/scope. . . . . . NiB $800 Ex $590 Gd $400
K-Mini-1H Ranch Rifle,
scope model, stainless . . . . NiB $1098 Ex $588 Gd $381

MINI-THIRTY (30) AUTOLOADER
Caliber: 7.62 x 39mm. 5-round detachable magazine. 18.5-inch bbl. 37.25 inches overall. Weight: 7 lbs. 3 oz. Designed for use with telescopic sights. Walnut stained stock. Sights: Peep rear; blade front mounted on bbl. band. Blued or stainless finish. Made from 1987 to 2004.

Blued. . . . . NiB $625 Ex $439 Gd $300
Stainless. . . . . NiB $815 Ex $545 Gd $360

PC SERIES SEMIAUTOMATIC CARBINES
Calibers: 9mm Parabellum or .40 S&W. 10-round magazine. 15.25-inch bbl. Weight: 6.25 lbs. Integral Ruger scope mounts with or without sights. Optional blade front sight, adjustable open rear. Matte black oxide finish. Matte black Zytel stock w/checkered pistol-grip and forearm. Made from 1997 to date.

Model PC9 (no sights). . . . . . NiB $510 Ex $440 Gd $300
Model PC4 (no sights). . . . . . NiB $545 Ex $467 Gd $333
W/adjust. sights, add. $50

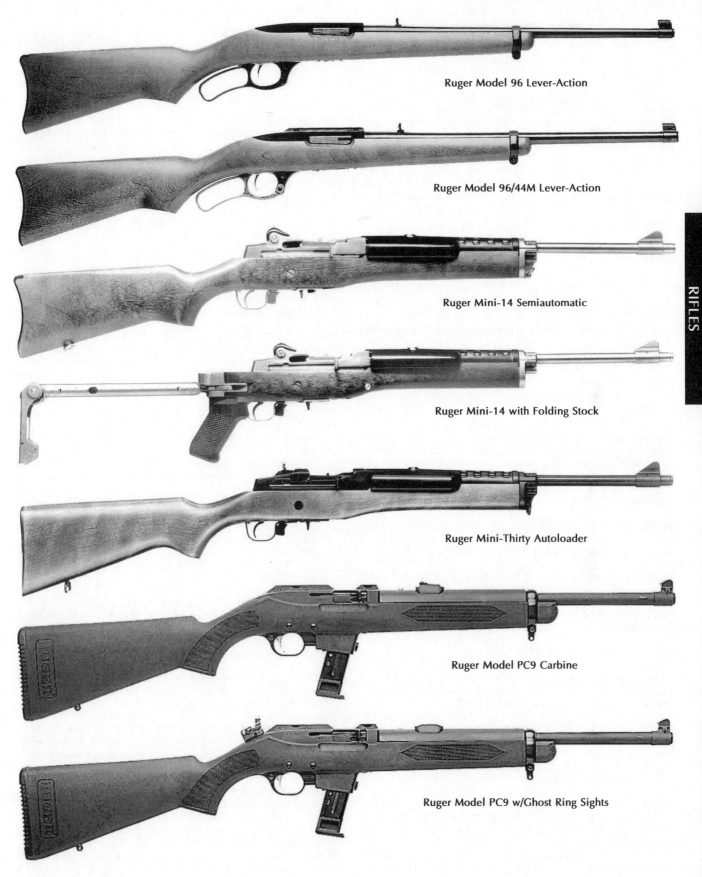

Ruger Model 96 Lever-Action

Ruger Model 96/44M Lever-Action

Ruger Mini-14 Semiautomatic

Ruger Mini-14 with Folding Stock

Ruger Mini-Thirty Autoloader

Ruger Model PC9 Carbine

Ruger Model PC9 w/Ghost Ring Sights

RIFLES

RUSSIAN MILITARY RIFLES — Principal U.S.S.R. Arms Plant, Tula

MODEL 1891
MOSIN MILITARY RIFLE . . . . **NiB $485 Ex $269 Gd $187**
Nagant system bolt action. Caliber: 7.62mm Russian. Five round box magazine. 31.5-inch bbl. Weight: About 9 lbs. Sights: Open rear; blade front. Full stock w/straight grip. Specifications given are for WWII version; earlier types differ slightly. Note: In 1916, Remington Arms Co. and New England Westinghouse Co. produced 250,000 of these rifles on a contract from the Imperial Russian Government. Few were delivered to Russia and the balance bought by the U.S. Government for training in 1918. Eventually, many of these rifles were sold to N.R.A. members for about $3 each by the Director of Civilian Marksmanship.

TOKAREV MODEL 40 SEMIAUTOMATIC
MILITARY RIFLE . . . . **NiB $844 Ex $438 Gd $270**
Gas-operated. Caliber: 7.62mm Russian. 10-round detachable box magazine. 24.5-inch bbl. Muzzle brake. Weight: About 9 lbs. Sights: Leaf rear, hooded post front. Full stock w/pistol grip. Differences among Models 1938,1940 and 1941 are minor.

SAKO RIFLES — Riihimaki, Finland. Manufactured by Sako L.T.D.

Formerly imported by Stoeger Industries, Wayne NJ (formerly by Garcia Corp.) until 2000. Imported by Beretta USA 2001 to date.

MODEL 72 . . . . **NiB $1090 Ex $865 Gd $660**
Single model designation replacing Vixen Sporter, Vixen Carbine, Vixen Heavy Barrel, Forester Sporter, Forester Carbine, Forester Heavy Barrel, Finnbear Sporter, and Finnbear Carbine, with same specifications, except all but heavy barrel models fitted with open rear sight. Values same as for corresponding earlier models. Imported from 1972 to 1974.

MODEL 73 LEVER-ACTION RIFLE . . **NiB $1670 Ex $988 Gd $690**
Same as Finnwolf except has 3-round clip magazine, flush floor-plate; stock has no cheekpiece. Imported from 1973 to 1975.

MODEL 74 CARBINE . . . . . . **NiB $1141 Ex $735 Gd $600**
Long Mauser-type bolt action. Caliber: .30-06. Five round magazine. 20-inch bbl. Weight: 7.5 lbs. No sights. Checkered Mannlicher-type full stock of European walnut, Monte Carlo cheekpiece. Imported from 1974 to 1978.

MODEL 74 HEAVY BARREL RIFLE,
LONG ACTION . . . . **NiB $1165 Ex $755 Gd $634**
Same specifications as short action except w/24-inch heavy bbl., weighs 8.75 lbs.; magnum w/4-round magazine. Calibers: .25-06, 7mm Rem. Mag. Imported from 1974 to 1978.

MODEL 74 HEAVY BARREL RIFLE,
MEDIUM ACTION . . . . **NiB $1165 Ex $755 Gd $634**
Same specifications as short action except w/23-inch heavy bbl., weighs 8.5 lbs. Calibers: .220 Swift, .22-250, .243 Win., .308 Win. Imported from 1974 to 1978.

MODEL 74 HEAVY BARREL RIFLE,
SHORT ACTION . . . . **NiB $1195 Ex $909 Gd $650**
Mauser-type bolt action. Calibers: .222 Rem., .223 Rem. Five round magazine. 23.5-inch heavy bbl. Weight: 8.25 lbs. No sights. Target-style checkered European walnut stock w/beavertail forearm. Imported from 1974 to 1978.

MODEL 74 SUPER SPORTER,
LONG ACTION . . . . **NiB $1165 Ex $755 Gd $634**
Same specifications as short action except w/24-inch bbl., weight: 8 lbs.; magnums have 4-round magazine, recoil pad. Calibers: .25-06, .270 Win. 7mm Rem. Mag., .30-06, .300 Win. Mag., .338 Win. Mag., .375 H&H Mag. Imported from 1974-78.

MODEL 74 SUPER SPORTER,
MEDIUM ACTION . . . . **NiB $1175 Ex $910 Gd $659**
Same specifications as short action except weight: 7.25 lbs. Calibers: .220 Swift, .22-250, .243 Win. Imported from 1974-78.

MODEL 74 SUPER SPORTER,
SHORT ACTION . . . . **NiB $1175 Ex $910 Gd $659**
Mauser-type bolt action. Calibers: .222 Rem., .223 Rem. Five round magazine. 23.5-inch bbl. Weight: 6.5 lbs. No sights. Checkered European walnut stock w/Monte Carlo cheekpiece, QD swivel studs. Imported 1974. Disc.

MODEL 75 DELUXE . . . . **NiB $1190 Ex $944 Gd $690**
Same specifications as Sako 75 Hunter Model except w/hinged floor plate, deluxe high gloss checkered walnut stock w/rosewood forend cap and grip cap w/silver inlay. Imported from 1998-2006. Disc.

MODEL 75 HUNTER . . . . . . **NiB $1260 Ex $833 Gd $665**
New bolt action design available in four action lengths fitted with a new bolt featuring three front locking lugs with an external extractor positioned under the bolt. Calibers: .17 Rem., .222 Rem., .223 Rem., (I); .22-250 Rem., .243 Win., 7mm-08 Rem., .308 Win., (III); .25-06 Rem., .270 Win., .280 Rem., .30-06, (IV); 7mm Rem Mag., .300 Win. Mag., .300 Wby. Mag., .338 Win. Mag. 7mm STW, .300 Wby. Mag., .340 Wby. Mag., .375 H&H Mag. and .416 Rem. Mag.,(V). 4-, 5- or 6-round magazine w/detachable magazine. 22-, 24-, and 26-inch bbls. 41.75 to 45.6 inches over all. Weight: 6.3 to 9 lbs. Sako dovetail scope base integral with receiver with no sights. Checkered high-grade walnut stock w/recoil pad and sling swivels. Made from 1997 to 2006.

MODEL 75 STAINLESS SYNTHETIC. **NiB $1279 Ex $877 Gd $685**
Similar to Model 75 Hunter except chambered for .22-250 Rem., .243 Win., .25-06 Rem., .270 Win., 7mm-08 Rem., 7mm STW, .30-06, .308 Win., 7mm Rem Mag., .300 Win. Mag., .338 Win. Mag. or .375 H&H Mag. 22-, 24-, and 26-inch bbls. Black composite stock w/soft rubber grips inserts. Matte stainless steel finish. Made from 1997 to 2006.

MODEL 75 VARMINT RIFLE . **NiB $1471 Ex $835 Gd $656**
Similar to Model 75 Hunter except chambered .17 Rem., .222 Rem., .223 Rem. and .22-250 Rem. 24-inch bbl. Matte lacquered walnut stock w/beavertail forearm. Made from 1998 to 2006.

MODEL 78 SUPER HORNET SPORTER **NiB $654 Ex $535 Gd $338**
Same specifications as Model 78 Rimfire except chambered for .22 Hornet, 4-round magazine. Imported from 1977 to 1987.

MODEL 78 SUPER RIMFIRE SPORTER **NiB $587 Ex $466 Gd $338**
Bolt action. Caliber: .22 LR. Five round magazine. 22.5-inch bbl. Weight, 6.75 lbs. No sights. Checkered European walnut stock, Monte Carlo cheekpiece. Imported from 1977 to 1986.

MODEL 85 CLASSIC BOLT-ACTION RIFLE
Calibers: .25-06 Rem., .270 Win., .30-06, .308 Win., .300 Win. Mga., .338 Win. Mag., .370 Sako Mag., .375 H&H Mag.., .270 WSM., .300 WSM., 7mm Mag. detachable mag., single stage trigger, pistol grip, checkered walnut stock. Weight: 7 lbs. New 2009,
Standard calibers . . . . . . **NiB $1937 Ex $1216 Gd $1019**
Magnum caliber, add **$126**

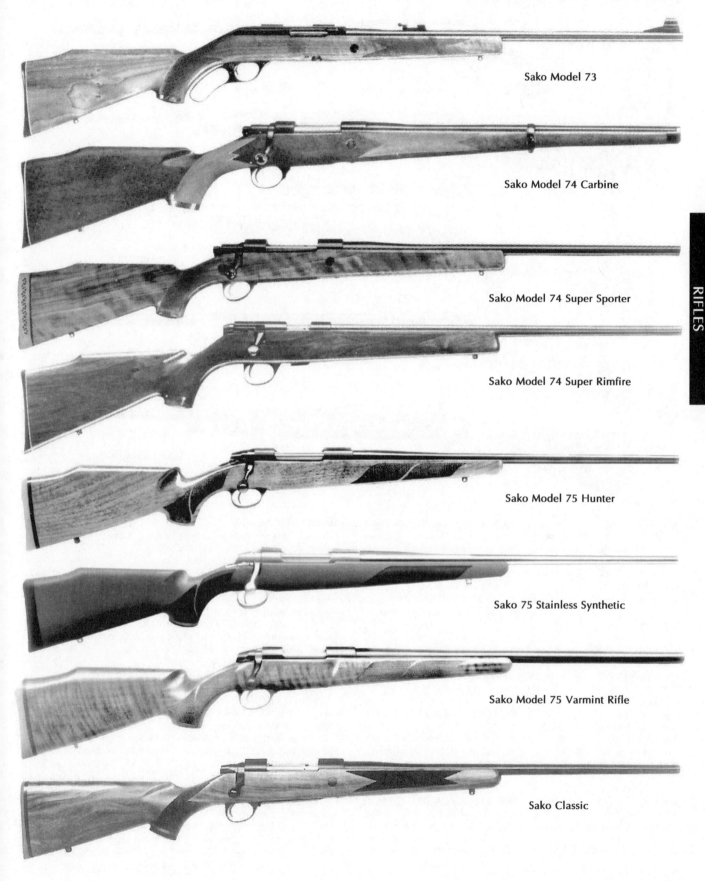

Sako Model 73

Sako Model 74 Carbine

Sako Model 74 Super Sporter

Sako Model 74 Super Rimfire

Sako Model 75 Hunter

Sako 75 Stainless Synthetic

Sako Model 75 Varmint Rifle

Sako Classic

Sako Deluxe Lightweight

Sako Fiberglass

Sako Finnfire

Sako Finnfire Heavy Barrel

Sako Finnwolf

DELUXE GRADE AI . . . . NiB $1266 Ex $870 Gd $633
Same specifications as Standard Grade except w/22 lines to the inch French checkering, rosewood grip cap and forend tip, semibeavertail forend. Disc.

DELUXE GRADE AII . . . . NiB $1145 Ex $790 Gd $556
Same specifications as Standard Grade except w/22 lines per inch French checkering, rosewood grip cap and forend tip, semi beavertail forend. Disc.

DELUXE GRADE AIII . . . . . NiB $1482 Ex $1188 Gd $766
Same specifications as w/standard except w/French checkering, rosewood grip cap and forend tip, semibeavertail forend. Disc.

**DELUXE LIGHTWEIGHT
BOLT-ACTION RIFLE** . . . . . NiB $1190 Ex $1021 Gd $699
Same general specifications as Hunter Lightweight except w/ beautifully grained French walnut stock; superb high-gloss finish, fine hand-cut checkering, rosewood forend tip and grip cap. Imported from 1985-97.

**FIBERCLASS BOLT-ACTION
RIFLE** . . . . NiB $1137 Ex $1077 Gd $650
All-weather fiberglass stock version of Sako barreled long action. Calibers: .25-06, .270, .30-06, 7mm Rem. Mag., .300 Win. Mag., .338 Win. Mag., .375 H&H Mag. Bbl. length: 22.5 inches. Overall length: 44.25 inches. Weight: 7.25 lbs. Imported 1984 to 1996.

FINNBEAR CARBINE . . . . . . NiB $1190 Ex $926 Gd $572
Same as Finnbear Sporter except w/20-inch bbl., Mannlicher-type full stock. Imported 1971. Disc.

FINNBEAR SPORTER . . . . . . NiB $1190 Ex $926 Gd $572
Long Mauser-type bolt action. Calibers: .25-06, .264 Mag. .270, .30-06, .300 Win. Mag., .338 Mag., 7mm Mag., .375 H&H Mag. Magazine holds 5 standard or 4 magnum cartridges. 24-inch bbl. Weight: 7 lbs. Hooded ramp front sight. Sporter stock w/Monte Carlo cheekpiece, checkered pistol-grip and forearm, recoil pad, swivels. Imported from 1961 to 1971.

FINNFIRE BOLT-ACTION RIFLE
Mini-Sporter built for rimfires on a scaled-down Sako design. Caliber: .22 LR. 5- or 10-round magazine. 22-inch bbl. 39.5 inches overall. Weight: 5.25 lbs. Receiver machined for 11mm dovetail scope rings. Beaded blade front sight, open adj. rear. Blued finish. Checkered European walnut stock. Imported from 1994 to 2005.
Hunter model. . . . . NiB $926 Ex $694 Gd $533
Varmint model . . . . NiB $988 Ex $696 Gd $580
Sporter model. . . . . NiB $1027 Ex $866 Gd $613

FINNWOLF LEVER-ACTION RIFLE . . . . . . .NiB $975 Ex $733 Gd $621
Hammerless. Calibers: .243 Win., .308 Win. Four round clip magazine. 23-inch bbl. Weight: 6.75 lbs. Hooded ramp front sight. Sporter stock w/Monte Carlo cheekpiece, checkered pistol-grip and forearm, swivels (available w/right- or left-hand stock). Imported 1963 to 1972.

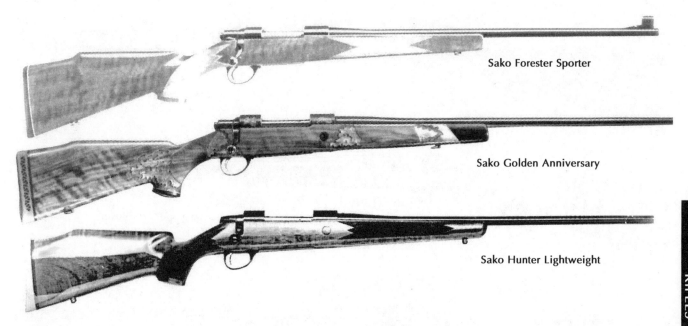

Sako Forester Sporter

Sako Golden Anniversary

Sako Hunter Lightweight

FINNSPORT 2707. . . . . **NiB $808 Ex $597 Gd $466**
Bolt-action centerfire rifle. Calibers: .270, .30-06, 7mm Rem. Mag., .300 Win. Mag. Bbl. length: 24 inches. Weight: 8 lbs. Imported 1984 to 1986.

FORESTER CARBINE. . . . . . . **NiB $1116 Ex $924 Gd $550**
Same as Forester Sporter except w/20-inch bbl., Mannlicher-type full stock. Imported from 1958 to 1971.

FORESTER HEAVY BARREL. . **NiB $1423 Ex $988 Gd $713**
Same as Forester Sporter except w/24-inch heavy bbl. Weight 7.5 lbs. Imported from 1958 to 1971.

FORESTER SPORTER. . . . . . **NiB $1141 Ex $1015 Gd $559**
Medium-length Mauser-type bolt action. Calibers: .22-250, .243 Win., .308 Win. Five round magazine. 23-inch bbl. Weight: 6.5 lbs. Hooded ramp front sight. Sporter stock w/Monte Carlo cheekpiece, checkered pistol grip and forearm, swivels. Imported 1957 to 1971.

GOLDEN ANNIVERSARY MODEL NiB $2866 Ex $2210 Gd $1570
Special presentation-grade rifle issued in 1973 to commemorate Sako's 50th anniversary. 1,000 (numbered 1 to 1,000) made. Same specifications as Deluxe Sporter: Long action, 7mm Rem. Mag. receiver, trigger guard and floorplate decorated w/gold oak leaf and acorn motif. Stock of select European walnut, checkering bordered w/hand-carved oak leaf pattern.

HIGH-POWER MAUSER SPORTING RIFLENiB $1154 Ex $1043 Gd $831
FN Mauser action. Calibers: .270, .30-06. Five round magazine. 24-inch bbl. Sights: Open rear leaf; Partridge front; hooded ramp. Checkered stock w/Monte Carlo comb and cheekpiece. Weight: 7.5 lbs. Imported from 1950 to 1957.

HUNTER LIGHTWEIGHT BOLT-ACTION RIFLE
5- or 6-round magazine. Bbl. length: 21.5 inches, AI; 22 inches, AII; 22.5 inches, AIII. Overall length: 42.25-44.5 inches. Weight: 5.75 lbs., AI; 6.75 lbs. AII; 7.25 lbs., AIII. Monte Carlo-style European walnut stock, oil finished. Hand-checkered pistol-grip and forend. Imported from 1985-97. Left-hand version intro. 1987.
AI (Short Action) .17 Rem. . . . . . **NiB $1466 Ex $1224 Gd $1018**
.222 Rem., .223 Rem.. . . . . **NiB $1088 Ex $831 Gd $589**
AII (medium action)
.22-250 Rem., .243 Win., .308 Win.. **NiB $976 Ex $798 Gd $543**
AII (Long Action) .25-06 Rem.

.270 Win., .30-06. . . . . **NiB $978 Ex $792 Gd $553**
.338 Win. Mag. . . . . **NiB $1154 Ex $976 Gd $735**
.375 H&H Mag. . . . . **NiB $1266 Ex $1044 Gd $766**
Left-hand model (standard cal.). . . **NiB $1294 Ex $1088 Gd $773**
Magnum calibers . . . . **NiB $1590 Ex $1277 Gd $945**

LAMINATED STOCK BOLT-ACTION RIFLES
Similar in style and specifications to Hunter Grade except w/stock of resin-bonded hardwood veneers. Available 18 calibers in AI (Short), AII (Medium) or AV action, left-hand version in 10 calibers, AV only. Imported from 1987 to 1995.
Short or medium action . . . . **NiB $1043 Ex $899 Gd $577**
Long action/Magnum . . . . . . **NiB $1108 Ex $902 Gd $645**

MAGNUM MAUSER . . . . . . **NiB $1588 Ex $1244 Gd $909**
Similar specifications as Standard Model except w/recoil pad and redesigned longer AIII action to handle longer magnum cartridges. Calibers: .300 H&H Magnum, .375 H&H Magnum, standard at time of introduction. Disc.

MANNLICHER-STYLE CARBINE
Similar to Hunter Model except w/full Mannlicher-style stock and 18.5-inch bbl. Weighs 7.5 lbs. Chambered in .243, .25-06, .270, .308, .30-06, 7mm Rem. Mag., .300 Win. Mag., .338 Win. Mag., .375 H&H. Intro. in 1977. Disc.
Standard calibers . . . . **NiB $1287 Ex $1021 Gd $734**
Magnum calibers (except .375). . . **NiB $1338 Ex $1055 Gd $733**
.375 H&H . . . . **NiB $1370 Ex $1094 Gd $790**

SAFARI GRADE . . . . **NiB $2576 Ex $1988 Gd $1166**
Classic bolt-action. Calibers: .300 Win. Mag., .338 Win. Mag., .375 H&H. Oil-finished European walnut stock w/hand-checkering. Barrel band swivel, express-type sight rib; satin or matte blue finish. Imported from 1980 to 1996.

SPORTER DELUXE . . . . . . **NiB $1290 Ex $1045 Gd $687**
Same as Vixen, Forester, Finnbear and Model 74 except w/fancy French walnut stock w/skip checkering, rosewood forend tip and pistol-grip cap, recoil pad, inlaid trigger guard and floorplate. Disc.

GRADING: **NiB** = New in Box   **Ex** = Excellent or NRA 95%   **Gd** = Good or NRA 68%

Sako Mannlicher-Style Carbine

Sako Sporter Deluxe

Sako TRG-21
Target Rifle

STANDARD GRADE AI. . . . . NiB $1077 Ex $823 Gd $440
Short bolt-action. Calibers: .17 Rem., .222 Rem., .223 Rem. Five round magazine. 23.5-inch bbl. Weight: 6.5 lbs. No sights. Checkered European walnut
stock w/Monte Carlo cheekpiece, QD swivel studs. Imported 1978 to 1985.

STANDARD GRADE AII . . . . NiB $1090 Ex $840 Gd $456
Medium bolt-action. Calibers: .22-250 Rem., .243 Win., .308 Win.
23.5-inch bbl. in .22-250; 23-inch bbl. in other calibers. Five round
magazine. Weight: 7.25 lbs. Checkered European walnut stock w/
Monte Carlo cheekpiece, QD swivel studs. Imported from 1978 to
1985.

STANDARD GRADE AIII. . . . NiB $1178 Ex $843 Gd $545
Long bolt action. Calibers: .25-06 Rem., .270 Win., .30-06, 7mm
Rem. Mag., .300 Win. Mag., .338 Win. Mag., .375 H&H. 24-inch
bbl. 4-round magazine. Weight: 8 lbs. Imported from 1978 to 1984.

SUPER DELUXE RIFLE. . . . NiB $2544 Ex $2210 Gd $1347
Available in AI, AII, AIII calibers. Select European walnut stock,
hand-checkered, deep oak leaf hand-engraved design. Disc.

TRG BOLT-ACTION TARGET RIFLE
Caliber: .308 Win., .330 Win. or .338 Lapua Mag. Detachable
10-round magazine. 25.75- or 27.2-inch bbl. Weight: 10.5 to 11 lbs.
Blued action w/stainless barrel. Adjustable two-stage trigger. modular
reinforced polyurethane target stock w/adj. cheekpiece and buttplate.
Options: Muzzle break; detachable bipod; QD sling swivels and scope
mounts w/1-inch or 30mm rings. Imported from 1993 to 2004.

TRG 21 .308 Win. . . . . NiB $2376 Ex $2099 Gd $1545
TRG 22 .308 Win. . . . . NiB $2459 Ex $2288 Gd $1590
TRG 41 .338 Lapua . . . . NiB $2788 Ex $2690 Gd $1877
TRG-42 (.300 Win Mag. or .338 Lapua)NiB $3154 Ex $2651 Gd $1835

TRG-S BOLT-ACTION RIFLE
Calibers: .243, 7mm-08, .270, .30-06, 7mm Rem. Mag., .300 Win.
Mag., .338 Win. Mag. Five shot magazine (standard calibers),
4-shot (magnum), 22- or 24-inch bbl. 45.5 inches overall. Weight:
7.75 lbs. No sights. Reinforced polyurethane stock w/Monte Carlo.
Introduced in 1993.
Standard calibers . . . . NiB $823 Ex $707 Gd $466
Magnum calibers . . . . NiB $880 Ex $844 Gd $545

VIXEN CARBINE. . . . . NiB $1096 Ex $954 Gd $868
Same as Vixen Sporter except w/20-inch bbl., Mannlicher-type full
stock. Imported from 1947 to 1971.

VIXEN HEAVY BARREL. . . . . NiB $1110 Ex $933 Gd $545
Same as Vixen Sporter except calibers .222 Rem., .222 Rem. Mag.,
.223 Rem., heavy bbl., target-style stock w/beavertail forearm.
Weight: 7.5 lbs. Imported from 1947-71.

VIXEN SPORTER. . . . . NiB $1100 Ex $969 Gd $546
Short Mauser-type bolt-action. Cals.: .218 Bee, .22 Hornet, .222
Rem., .222 Rem. Mag., .223 Rem. Five round magazine. 23.5-inch
bbl. Weight: 6.5 lbs. Hooded ramp front sight. Sporter stock w/
Monte Carlo cheekpiece, checkered pistol-grip and forearm, swiv-
els. Imported from 1946 to 1971.

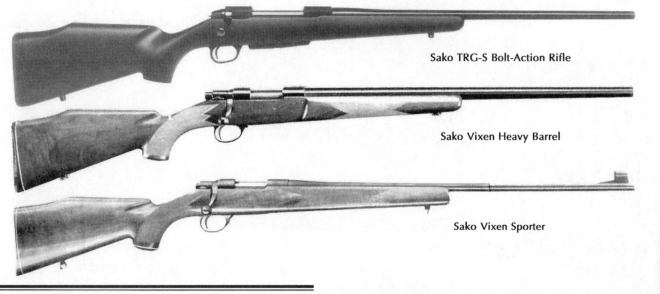

Sako TRG-S Bolt-Action Rifle

Sako Vixen Heavy Barrel

Sako Vixen Sporter

J. P. SAUER & SOHN — Eckernforde, Germany (formerly Suhl, Germany). Imported by Sigarms Exeter, NH (previously by Paul Company Inc. and G.U. Inc.)

MAUSER BOLT-ACTION
SPORTING RIFLE . . . . NiB $1457 Ex $1089 Gd $777
Calibers: 7x57 and 8x57mm most common, but these rifles were produced in a variety of calibers including most of the popular Continental calibers as well as our .30-06. Five round box magazine. 22- or 24-inch Krupp steel bbl., half-octagon w/raised matted rib. Double-set trigger. Weight: 7.5 lbs. Sights: Three-leaf open rear; ramp front. Sporting stock w/cheekpiece, checkered pistol grip, raised side-panels, Schnabel tip, swivels. Also made w/20-inch bbl. and full-length stock. Mfd. before WWII.

MODEL S-90 BOLT-ACTION RIFLES
Calibers: .243 Win., .308 Win. (Short action); .25-06, .270 Win., .30-06 (Medium action); 7mm Rem. Mag., .300 Win. Mag., .300 Wby., .338 Win., .375 H&H (Magnum action). Four round (standard) or 3-round magazine (magnum). Bbl. length: 20-inch (Stutzen), 24-inch. Weight: 7.6 to 10.75 lbs. Adjustable (Supreme) checkered Monte Carlo style stock. contrasting forend and pistol grip cap w/high-gloss finish or European (Lux) checkered Classic-style European walnut stock w/satin oil finish. Imported from 1983 to 1989.

S-90 Standard.	NiB $1154	Ex $990	Gd $587
S-90 Lux	NiB $1389	Ex $1100	Gd $654
S-90 Safari	NiB $1411	Ex $1127	Gd $665
S-90 Stutzen.	NiB $1144	Ex $994	Gd $482
S-90 Supreme.	NiB $1490	Ex $1167	Gd $800
Grade I engraving, add			$650
Grade II engraving, add			$850
Grade III engraving add			$1200
Grade IV engraving, add.			$1717

MODEL 200 BOLT-ACTION RIFLES
Calibers: .243 Win., .25-06, .270 Win., 7mm Rem Mag., .30-06, .308 Win., .300 Win. Mag., Detachable box magazine. 24-inch (American) or 26-inch (European) interchangeable bbl. Standard (steel) or lightweight (alloy) action. Weight: 6.6 to 7.75 lbs. 44 inches overall. Stock options: American Model w/checkered Monte Carlo style 2-piece stock contrasting forend and pistol grip cap w/high gloss finish and no sights. European walnut stock w/ Schnabel forend, satin oil finish and iron sights. Contemporary Model w/ synthetic carbon fiber stock. Imported from 1986 to 1993.
Standard model . . . . NiB $1266 Ex $1093 Gd $707

Lightweight model	NiB $1278	Ex $1043	Gd $580
Contemporary model	NiB $1260	Ex $1017	Gd $565
American model.	NiB $1260	Ex $1017	Gd $565
European model.	NiB $1395	Ex $1070	Gd $532
Left-hand model, add			$200
Magnum calibers, add			$130
Interchangeable barrel assembly, add			$325

MODEL 202 BOLT-ACTION RIFLES
Calibers: .243 Win., 6.5x55, 6.5x57, 6.6x68, .25-06, .270 Win., .280 7x64, .308, .30-06, Springfield, 7mm Rem. Mag., .300 Win. Mag., .300 Wby. Mag., 8x68S, .338 Win. Mag., .375 H&H Mag. Removable 3-round box magazine. 23.6- and 26-inch interchangable bbl. 44.3 and 46 inches overall. Modular receiver drilled and tapped for scope bases. Adjustable two-stage trigger w/dual release safety. Weight: 7.7 to 8.4 lbs. Stock options: Checkered Monte Carlo-style select American walnut two-piece stock; Euro-classic French walnut two-piece stock w/semi Schnabel forend and satin oil finish; Super Grade Claro walnut two-piece stock fitted w/ rosewood forend and grip cap w/high-gloss epoxy finish. Imported from 1994 to 2004.

Standard model	NiB $2660	Ex $1848	Gd $983
Euro-Classic model.	NiB $1369	Ex $897	Gd $633
Super Grade model.	NiB $1119	Ex $888	Gd $603
Left-hand model, add			$150
Magnum calibers, add			$126
Interchangeable barrel assembly, add			$295

SAVAGE INDUSTRIES — Westfield, Massachusetts (formerly Chicopee Falls, MA, and Utica, NY)

MODEL 3 BOLT-ACTION
SINGLE-SHOT RIFLE. . . . . NiB $100 Ex $61 Gd $59
Takedown. Caliber: .22 Short, Long, LR. 26-inch bbl. on prewar rifles, postwar production w/24-inch bbl. Weight: 5 lbs. Sights: Open rear; bead front. Plain pistol-grip stock. Made 1933 to 1952.

MODEL 3S. . . . . NiB $116 Ex $89 Gd $59
Same as Model 3 except w/peep rear sight, hooded front. Made 1933 to 1942.

MODEL 3ST. . . . . NiB $120 Ex $85 Gd $50
Same as Model 3S except fitted w/swivels and sling. Made from 1933 to 1942.

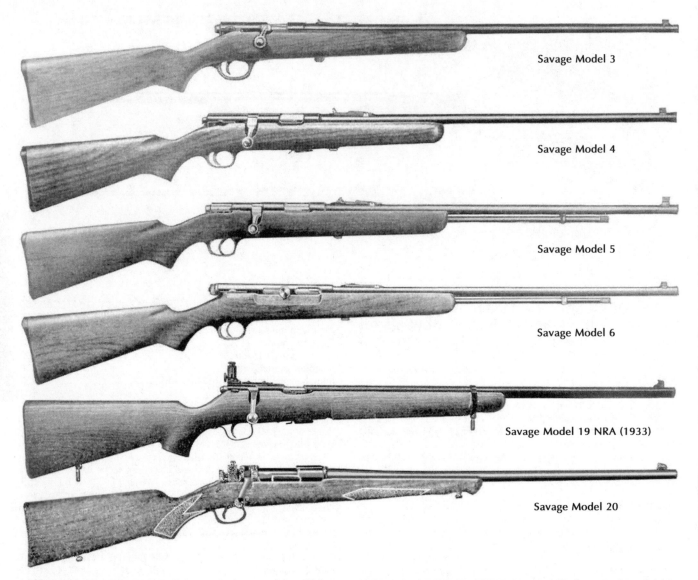

Savage Model 3

Savage Model 4

Savage Model 5

Savage Model 6

Savage Model 19 NRA (1933)

Savage Model 20

MODEL 4 BOLT-ACTION REPEATER. . . NiB $149 Ex $90 Gd $59
Takedown. Caliber: .22 Short, Long, LR. Five round detachable box magazine. 24-inch bbl. Weight: 5.5 lbs. Sights: Open rear; bead front. Checkered pistol-grip stock on prewar models, early production had grooved forearm; postwar rifles have plain stocks. Made from 193 to 1965.

MODEL 4M . . . . NiB $121 Ex $87 Gd $64
Same as Model 4 except chambered for .22 Rimfire Magnum. Made from 1961 to 1965.

MODEL 4S. . . . . NiB $130 Ex $78 Gd $47
Same as Model 4 except w/peep rear sight, hooded front. Made from 1933 to 1942.

MODEL 5 BOLT-ACTION
REPEATER . . . . NiB $126 Ex $78 Gd $57
Same as Model 4 except w/tubular magazine (holds 21 Short, 17 Long, 15 LR), weight: 6 lbs. Made from 1936 to 1961.

MODEL 5S. . . . . NiB $135 Ex $77 Gd $50
Same as Model 5 except w/peep rear sight, hooded front. Made from 1936 to 1942.

MODEL 6 AUTOLOADING RIFLE . . . . . NiB $169 Ex $94 Gd $57
Takedown. Caliber: .22 Short, Long, LR. Tubular magazine holds 21 Short, 17 Long, 15 LR. 24-inch bbl. Weight: 6 lbs. Sights: Open rear; bead front. Checkered pistol-grip stock on prewar models, postwar rifles have plain stocks. Made from 1938 to 1968.

MODEL 6S. . . . . NiB $170 Ex $95 Gd $48
Same as Model 6 except w/peep rear sight, bead front. Made from 1938 to 1942.

MODEL 7 AUTOLOADING RIFLE . . . . NiB $167 Ex $105 Gd $59
Same general specifications as Model 6 except w/5-round detachable box magazine. Made from 1939 to 1951.

MODEL 7S. . . . . NiB $167 Ex $105 Gd $62
Same as Model 7 except w/peep rear sight, hooded front. Made from 1938 to 1942.

MODEL 19 BOLT-ACTION TARGET RIFLENiB $325 Ex $270 Gd $209
Model of 1933. Speed lock. Caliber: .22 LR. Five round detachable box magazine. 25-inch bbl. Weight: 8 lbs. Adj. rear peep sight, blade front on early models, later production equipped w/extension rear sight, hooded front. Target stock w/full pistol-grip and beavertail forearm. Made from 1933 to 1946.

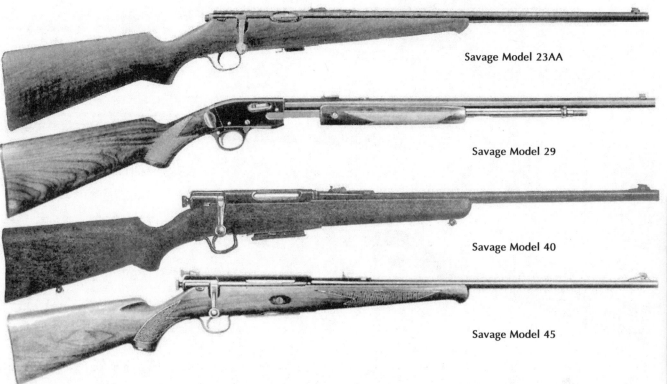

Savage Model 23AA

Savage Model 29

Savage Model 40

Savage Model 45

RIFLES

MODEL 19 NRA BOLT-ACTION
MATCH RIFLE . . . . **NiB $300 Ex $205 Gd $126**
Model of 1919. Caliber: .22 LR. Five round detachable box magazine. 25-inch bbl. Weight: 7 lbs. Sights: Adj. rear peep; blade front. Full military stock w/pistol-grip. Made from 1919 to 1933.

MODEL 19H . . . . **NiB $575 Ex $340 Gd $265**
Same as standard Model 19 (1933) except chambered for .22 Hornet, w/Model 23D-type bolt mechanism, loading port and magazine. Made from 1933 to 1942.

MODEL 19L . . . . **NiB $348 Ex $290 Gd $185**
Same as standard Model 19 (1933) except equipped w/Lyman No. 48Y receiver sight, 17A front sight. Made from 1933 to 1942.

MODEL 19M . . . . **NiB $356 Ex $465 Gd $227**
Same as standard Model 19 (1933) except w/heavy 28-inch bbl. w/ scope bases, weight: 9.25 lbs. Made from 1933 to 1942.

MODEL 20-1926
HI-POWER . . . . **NiB $944 Ex $725 Gd $420**
Same as Model 1920, listed on page 354, except w/24-inch medium weight bbl., improved stock, Lyman 54 rear peep sight, weight: 7 lbs. Made from 1926 to 1929.

MODEL 23A BOLT-ACTION
SPORTING RIFLE . . . . **NiB $270 Ex $208 Gd $177**
Caliber: 22 LR. Five round detachable box magazine. 23-inch bbl. Weight: 6 lbs. Sights: Open rear, blade or bead front. Plain pistol-grip stock w/slender forearm and Schnabel tip. Made 1923 to 1933.

MODEL 23AA . . . . **NiB $370 Ex $278 Gd $200**
Model of 1933. Improved version of Model 23A w/same general specifications except w/speed lock, improved stock, weighs 6.5 lbs. Made from 1933-42.

MODEL 23B . . . . **NiB $333 Ex $235 Gd $179**
Same as Model 23A except caliber .25-20, 25-inch bbl. Model of 1933 w/improved stock w/full forearm instead of slender forearm w/ Schnabel found on earlier production. Weight: 6.5 lbs. Made from 1923 to 1942.

MODEL 23C . . . . **NiB $389 Ex $290 Gd $175**
Same as Model 23B except caliber .32-20. Made 1923 to 1942.

MODEL 23D . . . . **NiB $415 Ex $300 Gd $220**
Same as Model 23B except caliber .22 Hornet. Made 1933 to 1947.

MODEL 25 SLIDE-ACTION REPEATER NiB $346 Ex $391 Gd $237
Takedown. Hammerless. Caliber: .22 Short, Long, LR. Tubular magazine holds 20 Short, 17 Long, 15 LR. 24-inch octagon bbl. Weight: 5.75 lbs. Sights: Open rear; blade front. Plain pistol-grip stock, grooved slide handle. Made from 1925 to 1929.

MODEL 29 SLIDE-ACTION
REPEATER . . . . **NiB $500 Ex $380 Gd $265**
Takedown. Hammerless. Caliber: .22 Short, Long, LR. Tubular magazine holds 20 Short, 17 Long, 15 LR. 24-inch bbl., octagon on prewar, round on postwar production. Weight: 5.5 lbs. Sights: Open rear; bead front. Stock w/checkered pistol grip and slide handle on prewar, plain stock and grooved forearm on postwar production. Made from 1929 to 1967.

MODEL 40 BOLT-ACTION
SPORTING RIFLE . . . . **NiB $379 Ex $280 Gd $227**
Standard Grade. Calibers: .250-3000, .300 Sav., .30-30, .30-06. Four round detachable box magazine. 22-inch bbl. in calibers .250-3000 and .30-30; 24-inch in .300 Sav. and .30-06. Weight: 7.5 lbs. Sights: Open rear; bead front, on ramp. Plain pistol-grip stock w/tapered forearm and Schnabel tip. Made 1928 to 1940.

MODEL 45 SUPER SPORTER. . **NiB $423 Ex $265 Gd $220**
Special Grade. Same as Model 40 except w/checkered pistol-grip and forearm, Lyman No. 40 receiver sight. Made 1928 to 1940.

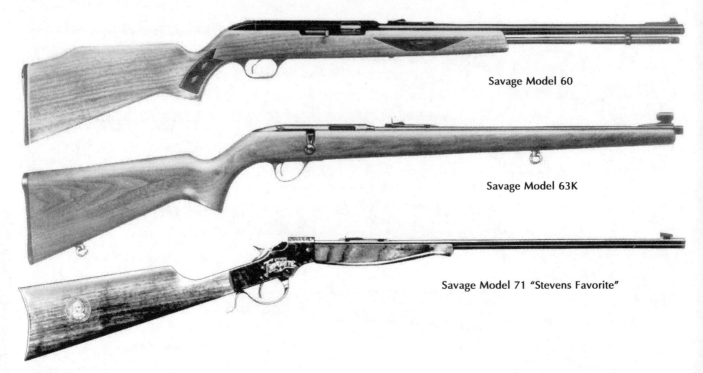

Savage Model 60

Savage Model 63K

Savage Model 71 "Stevens Favorite"

MODEL 60 AUTOLOADING RIFLE . . . . NiB $115 Ex $80 Gd $48
Caliber: .22 LR. 15-round tubular magazine. 20-inch bbl. Weight: 6 lbs. Sights: Open rear, ramp front. Monte Carlo stock of walnut w/ checkered pistol-grip and forearm. Made from 1969 to 1972.

MODEL 63K KEY LOCK BOLT-ACTION
SINGLE-SHOT RIFLE . . . . NiB $120 Ex $90 Gd $60
Trigger locked w/key. Caliber: .22 Short, Long, LR. 18-inch bbl. Weight: 4 lbs. Sights: Open rear; hooded ramp front. Full-length stock w/pistol grip, swivels. Made from 1970 to 1972.

MODEL 63KM . . . . NiB $126 Ex $98 Gd $63
Same as Model 63K except chambered for .22 WMR. Made 1970 to 1972.

MODEL 64F AUTOLOADING RIFLE . . NiB $173 Ex $128 Gd $99
Same general specifications as Model 64G except w/black graphite/ polymer stock. Weight: 5 lbs. Made from 1997 to date.

MODEL 64G AUTOLOADING RIFLE. NiB $177 Ex $126 Gd $100
Caliber: 22 LR. 10-round magazine. 20-inch bbl. Weight: 5.5 lbs. 40 inches overall. Sights: Adj. open rear; bead front. Grooved receiver for scope mounts. Stamped checkering on walnut-finished hard-wood stock w/Monte Carlo cheekpiece. Made from 1996 to date.

MODEL 71 "STEVENS FAVORITE"
SINGLE-SHOT LEVER-ACTION RIFLE . NiB $229 Ex $114 Gd $98
Replica of original Stevens Favorite issued as a tribute to Joshua Stevens, "Father of .22 Hunting." Caliber: .22 LR. 22-inch full-octagon bbl. Brass-plated hammer and lever. Sights: Open rear; brass blade front. Weight: 4.5 lbs. Plain straight-grip buttstock and Schnabel forend; brass commemorative medallion inlaid in butt-stock, brass crescent-shaped buttplate. 10,000 produced. Made in 1971 only. Top value is for new, unfired gun.

MODEL 90 AUTO-LOADING
CARBINE . . . . NiB $194 Ex $161 Gd $126
Similar to Model 60 except w/16.5-inch bbl. w/folding leaf rear sight, bead front. 10-round tubular magazine. Uncheckered, carbine-

style walnut stock w/bbl. Band and sling swivels. Weight: 5.75 lbs. Made from 1969 to 1972.

MODEL 93G BOLT-ACTION RIFLE . . NiB $227 Ex $166 Gd $126
Caliber: .22 Win Mag. 5-round magazine. 20.75-inch bbl. 39.5 inches overall. Weight: 5.75 lbs. Sights: Adj. open rear; bead front. Grooved receiver for scope mounts. Stamped checkering on walnut-finished hardwood stock w/Monte Carlo cheekpiece. Made from 1996 to date.

MODEL 93F BOLT-ACTION RIFLE . . NiB $277 Ex $124 Gd $110
Same general specifications as Model 93G except w/black graphite/ polymer stock. Weight: 5.2 lbs. Made from 1997 to date.

NOTE: MODEL 99 LEVER-ACTION REPEATER
Introduced in 1899, this model has been produced in a variety of styles and calibers. Original designation "Model 1899" was changed to "Model 99" c.1920. Earlier rifles and carbines — similar to Models 99A, 99B and 99H — were supplied in calibers .25-35, .30-30, .303 Sav., .32-40 and .38-55. Post-WWII Models 99A, 99C, 99CD, 99DE, 99DL, 99F and 99PE have top tang safety other 99s have slide safety on right side of trigger guard. Models 99C and 99CD have detachable box magazine instead of traditional Model 99 rotary magazine.

MODEL 99A (I) . . . . NiB $1015 Ex $768 Gd $545
Hammerless. Solid frame. Calibers: .30-30, .300 Sav., .303 Sav. Five-round rotary magazine. 24-inch bbl. Weight: 7.25 lbs. Sights: Open rear; bead front, on ramp. Plain straight-grip stock, tapered forearm. Made from 1920 to 1936.

MODEL 99A (II) . . . . NiB $915 Ex $668 Gd $445
Current model. Similar to original Model 99A except w/top tang safety, 22-inch bbl., folding leaf rear sight, no crescent buttplate. Calibers: .243 Win., .250 Sav., .300 Sav., .308 Win. Made from 1971 to 1982.

MODEL 99B . . . . NiB $1245 Ex $938 Gd $577
Takedown. Otherwise same as Model 99A except weight: 7.5 lbs. Made from 1920 to 1936.

Savage Model 90

Savage Model 99A 1971 Issue

Savage Model 99C

Savage Model 99CD

Savage Model 99DE

MODEL 99C . . . . **NiB $560 Ex $488 Gd $399**
Current model. Same as Model 99F except w/clip magazine instead
of rotary. Calibers: .243 Win., .284 Win., .308 Win. Four round
detachable magazine holds one round less in .284. Weight: 6.75
lbs. Made from 1965-98.

MODEL 99CD . . . . **NiB $698 Ex $599 Gd $389**
Deluxe version of Model 99C. Calibers: .243 Win., .250 Sav., .308
Win. Hooded ramp front sight. Weight: 8.25 lbs. Stock w/Monte
Carlo comb and cheekpiece, checkered pistol-grip, grooved fore-
arm, swivels and sling. Made from 1975 to 81.

MODEL 99DE CITATION GRADE . . . **NiB $955 Ex $679 Gd $495**
Same as Model 99PE except w/less elaborate engraving. Made from
1968-70.

MODEL 99DL DELUXE . . . . . . **NiB $745 Ex $576 Gd $359**
Postwar model. Calibers: .243 Win., .308 Win. Same as Model 99F,
except w/high comb Monte Carlo stock, sling swivels. Weight: 6.75
lbs. Made from 1960-73.

MODEL 99E CARBINE (I) . . . . **NiB $656 Ex $500 Gd $439**
Pre-WWII type. Solid frame. Calibers: .22 Hi-Power, .250/3000,
.30/30, .300 Sav., .303 Sav. w/22-inch bbl.; .300 Sav. 24-inch.
Weight: 7 lbs. Other specifications same as Model 99A. Made
from 1920-36.

MODEL 99E CARBINE (II) . . . . **NiB $709 Ex $505 Gd $457**
Current model. Solid frame. Calibers: .250 Sav., .243 Win., .300
Sav., .308 Win. 20- or 22-inch bbl. Checkered pistol-grip stock and
forearm. Made from 1960-89.

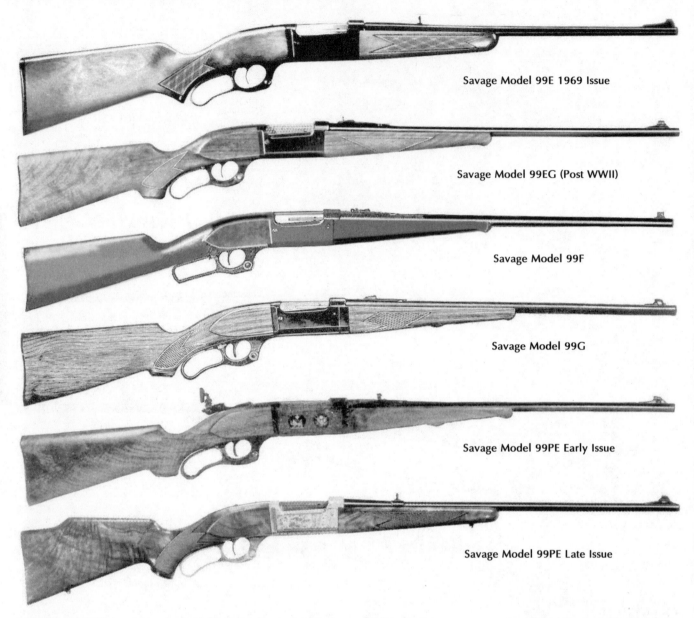

Savage Model 99E 1969 Issue

Savage Model 99EG (Post WWII)

Savage Model 99F

Savage Model 99G

Savage Model 99PE Early Issue

Savage Model 99PE Late Issue

MODEL 99EG (I) . . . . NiB $877 Ex $687 Gd $476
Pre-WWII type. Solid frame. Plain pistol-grip stock and forearm. Otherwise same as Model G. Made from 1936 to 1941.

MODEL 99EG (II) . . . . NiB $1023 Ex $799 Gd $600
Post-WWII type. Same as prewar model except w/checkered stock and forearm. Calibers: .250 Sav., .300 Sav., .308 Win. (intro. 1955), .243 Win., and .358 Win. Made from 1946 to 1960.

MODEL 99F
FEATHERWEIGHT (I) . . . . NiB $813 Ex $707 Gd $514
Pre-WWII type. Takedown. Specifications same as Model 99E, except weight: 6.5 lbs. Made 1920 to 1942. Some marked 99M.

MODEL 99F
FEATHERWEIGHT (II) . . . . NiB $945 Ex $735 Gd $567
Postwar model. Solid frame. Calibers: .243 Win., .300 Sav., .308 Win. 22-inch bbl. Checkered pistol-grip stock and forearm. Weight: 6.5 lbs. Made from 195 to 1973.

MODEL 99G . . . . NiB $1290 Ex $933 Gd $707
Takedown. Checkered pistol-grip stock and forearm. Weight: 7.25 lbs. Other specifications same as Model 99E. Made 1920 to 1942.

MODEL 99H CARBINE . . . . . NiB $926 Ex $577 Gd $4455
Solid frame. Calibers: .250/3000, .30/30, .303 Sav. 20-inch special weight bbl. Walnut carbine stock w/metal buttplate; walnut forearm w/bbl. band. Weight: 6.5 lbs. Open rear sights; ramped blade front sight. Other specifications same as Model 99A. Made 1931 to 1942.

MODEL 99K . . . . NiB $3854 Ex $2650 Gd $2128
Deluxe version of Model G w/similar specifications except w/fancy stock and engraving on receiver and bbl. Lyman peep rear sight and folding middle. Made from 1931 to 1942.

MODEL 99PE PRESENTATION GRADE . . . NiB $2055 Ex $1717 Gd $854
Same as Model 99DL except w/engraved receiver (game scenes on sides), tang and lever, fancy walnut Monte Carlo stock and forearm w/hand checkering, QD swivels. Calibers: .243, .284, .308. Made 1968 to 1970.

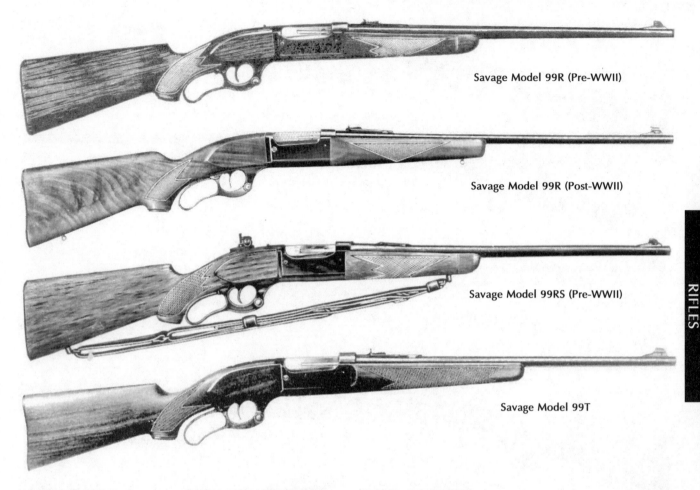

Savage Model 99R (Pre-WWII)

Savage Model 99R (Post-WWII)

Savage Model 99RS (Pre-WWII)

Savage Model 99T

MODEL 99R (I) . . . . **NiB $735 Ex $588 Gd $499**
Pre-WWII type. Solid frame. Calibers: .250-3000 (22-inch bbl.), .300 Sav. (24-inch bbl.). Weight: 7.5 lbs. Special large pistol-grip stock and forearm, checkered. General specifications same as other Model 99 rifles. Made from 1936 to 1942.

MODEL 99R (II) . . . . **NiB $689 Ex $498 Gd $356**
Post-WWII type. Same as prewar mod except w/24-inch bbl. only, w/screw eyes for sling swivels. Calibers: .250 Sav., .300 Sav., .308 Win., .243 Win. and .358 Win. Made from 1946 to 1960.

MODEL 99RS (I) . . . . **NiB $944 Ex $650 Gd $489**
Pre-WWII type. Same as prewar Model 99R except equipped w/ Lyman rear peep sight and folding middle sight, quick detachable swivels and sling. Made from 1932 to 1942.

MODEL 99RS (II) . . . . **NiB $756 Ex $600 Gd $467**
Post-WWII type. Same as postwar Model 99RS except equipped w/ Redfield 70LH receiver sight, blank in middle sight slot. Made from 1946 to 1960.

MODEL 99T . . . . **NiB $1707 Ex $1032 Gd $744**
Featherweight. Solid frame. Calibers: .22 Hi-Power, .30/30, .303 Sav. w/20-inch bbl.; .300 Sav. w/22-inch bbl. Checkered pistol-grip stock and beavertail forearm. Weight: 7 lbs. General specifications same as other Model 99 rifles. Made from 1936 to 1942.

MODEL 99-358 . . . . **NiB $1156 Ex $903 Gd $657**
Similar to current Model 99A except caliber .358 Win. has grooved forearm, recoil pad, swivel studs. Made from 1977 to 1980.

MODEL 110 SPORTER
BOLT-ACTION RIFLE . . . . . . **NiB $420 Ex $333 Gd $155**
Calibers: .243, .270, .308, .30-06. Four round box magazine. 22-inch bbl. Weight: About 6.75 lbs. Sights: Open rear; ramp front. Standard sporter stock with checkered pistol-grip. Made 1958 to 1963.

MODEL 110B BOLT-ACTION RIFLE
Same as Model 110E except with checkered select walnut Monte Carlo-style stock (early models) or brown laminated stock (late models). Calibers: .243 Win., .270 Win. .30-06, 7mm Rem. Mag., .338 Win. Mag. Made from 1976 to 1991.
Early model . . . . **NiB $423 Ex $303 Gd $227**
Laminated stock model . . . . . . **NiB $367 Ex $299 Gd $211**

MODEL 110BL . . . . **NiB $439 Ex $369 Gd $269**
Same as Model 110B except has left-hand action.

MODEL 110C
Calibers: .22-250, .243, .25-06, .270, .308, .30-06, 7mm Rem. Mag., .300 Win. Mag. Four round detachable clip magazine (3-round in Magnum calibers). 22-inch bbl. (24-inch in .22-250 Magnum calibers). Weight: 6.75 lbs., Magnum, 7.75 to 8 lbs. Sights: Open rear; ramp front. Checkered Monte Carlo-style walnut stock (Magnum has recoil pad). Made from 1966 to 1988.
Standard calibers . . . . **NiB $468 Ex $413 Gd $239**
Magnum calibers . . . . **NiB $639 Ex $455 Gd $279**

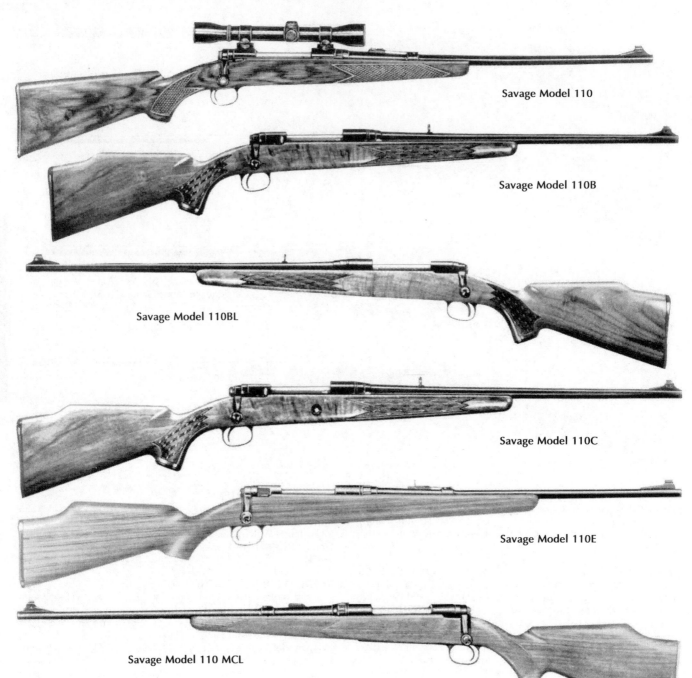

Savage Model 110

Savage Model 110B

Savage Model 110BL

Savage Model 110C

Savage Model 110E

Savage Model 110 MCL

MODEL 110CL
Same as Model 110C except has left-hand action. (Available only in
.243 Win., .30-06, .270 Win. and 7mm Mag.) Made 1963 to 1966.
Standard calibers . . . . **NiB $488 Ex $369 Gd $262**
Magnum calibers . . . . **NiB $459 Ex $350 Gd $255**

MODEL 110CY
YOUTH/LADIES RIFLE . . . . . . **NiB $466 Ex $379 Gd $228**
Same as Model 110G except with walnut-finished hardwood stock
with 12.5-inch pull. Calibers: .243 Win. and .300 Savage. Made
from 1991 to 2009.

MODEL 110D
Similar to Model 110C except has internal magazine with hinged
floorplate. Calibers: .243 Win., .270 Win., .30-06, 7mm Rem. Mag.,
.300 Win. Mag. Made from 1972 to 1988.
Standard calibers . . . . **NiB $390 Ex $310 Gd $240**
Magnum calibers . . . . **NiB $453 Ex $390 Gd $259**

MODEL 110DL
Same as Model 110D except has left-hand action. Discontinued.
Standard calibers . . . . **NiB $500 Ex $413 Gd $297**
Magnum calibers . . . . **NiB $535 Ex $430 Gd $319**

Savage Model 110P

Savage Model 110PE

MODEL 110E . . . . **NiB $379 Ex $255 Gd $198**
Calibers: .22-250, .223 Rem., .243 Win., .270 Win., .308, 7mm Rem. Mag., .30-06. Four round box magazine (3-round in Magnum). 20- or 22-inch bbl. (24-inch stainless steel in Magnum). Weight: 6.75 lbs.; Magnum, 7.75 lbs. Sights: Open rear; ramp front. Plain Monte Carlo stock on early production; current models have checkered stocks of walnut-finished hardwood (Magnum has recoil pad). Made 1963 to 1989.

MODEL 110EL . . . . **NiB $370 Ex $248 Gd $185**
Same as Model 110E except has left-hand action made in .30-06 and 7mm Rem. Mag. only. Made from 1969 to 1973.

MODEL 110F/110K BOLT-ACTION RIFLE
Same as Model 110E except Model 110F has black Rynite synthetic stock, swivel studs; made 1988 to 1993. Model 110K has laminated camouflage stock; made from 1986 to 1988.
Adj. sights . . . . NiB $770 Ex $470 Gd $359
W/out sights . . . . NiB $735 Ex $355 Gd $277
Standard calibers . . . . NiB $355 Ex $320 Gd $256
Magnum calibers . . . . NiB $520 Ex $399 Gd $287

MODEL 110FM SIERRA ULTRA LIGHT NiB $376 Ex $336 Gd $244
Calibers: .243 Win., .270 Win., .30-06, .308 Win. Five round magazine. 20-inch bbl. 41.5 inches overall. Weight: 6.25 lbs. No sights w/drilled and tapped receiver. Black graphite/fiberglass composition stock. Non-glare matte blue finish. Made 1996 to date.

MODEL 110FP POLICE RIFLE . **NiB $610 Ex $355 Gd $265**
Calibers: .223, .308 Win. Four round magazine. 24-inch bbl. 45.5 inches overall. Weight: 9 lbs. Black Rynite composite stock. Matte blue finish. Made from 1990 to date.

MODEL 110G BOLT-ACTION RIFLE
Calibers: .223, .22-250, .243 Win., .270, 7mm Rem. Mag., .308 Win., .30-06, .300 Win. Mag. Five round (standard) or 4-round magazine (magnum). 22- or 24-inch bbl. 42.38 overall (standard). Weight: 6.75 to 7.5 lbs. Ramp front sight, adj. rear. Checkered walnut-finished hardwood stock with rubber recoil pad. Made from 1989 to 1993.
Standard calibers . . . . NiB $408 Ex $309 Gd $220
Magnum calibers . . . . NiB $455 Ex $338 Gd $259
Left-hand, no sights . . . . NiB $355 Ex $369 Gd $271

MODEL 110GV VARMINT RIFLE . . . . **NiB $369 Ex $338 Gd $268**
Similar to the Model 110G except fitted with medium-weight varmint bbl. with no sights. Receiver drilled and tapped for scope mounts. Calibers .22-250 and .223 only. Made from 1989-93.

MAGNUM 110M MAGNUM . . **NiB $445 Ex $345 Gd $269**
Same as Model 110MC except calibers: 7mm Rem. Mag. .264, .300 and .338 Win. 24-inch bbl. Stock with recoil pad. Weight: 7.75 to 8 lbs. Made from 1963 to 1969.

MODEL 110MC . . . . **NiB $444 Ex $229 Gd $149**
Same as Model 110 except has Monte Carlo-style stock. Calibers: .22-250, .243 Win., .270, .308, .30-06. 24-inch bbl. in .22-250. Made from 1959 to 1969.
Model 110MCL . . . . **NiB $400 Ex $215 Gd $135**

MODEL 110P PREMIER GRADE
Calibers: .243 Win., 7mm Rem. Mag., .30-06. Four round magazine (3-round in Magnum). 22-inch bbl. (24-inch stainless steel in Magnum). Weight: 7 lbs.; Magnum, 7.75 lbs. Sights: Open rear folding leaf; ramp front. French walnut stock w/Monte Carlo comb and cheekpiece, rosewood forend tip and pistol-grip cap, skip checkering, sling swivels (Magnum has recoil pad). Made 1964 to 1970.
Calibers .243 Win. and .30-06 NiB $798 Ex $645 Gd $459
Caliber 7mm Rem. Mag . . . . . **NiB $945 Ex $765 Gd $545**

MODEL 110PE PRESENTATION GRADE
Same as Model 110P except has engraved receiver, floorplate and trigger guard, stock of choice grade French walnut. Made 1968 to 1970.
Calibers .243 Win. and .30-06 NiB $555 Ex $441 Gd $290
Caliber 7mm Rem. Mag . . . . . **NiB $600 Ex $455 Gd $347**

MODEL 110PEL PRESENTATION GRADE
Same as Model 110PE except has left-hand action.
Calibers .243 Win. and .30-06 NiB $807 Ex $654 Gd $458
Caliber 7mm Rem. Mag . . . . . **NiB $879 Ex $710 Gd $496**

MODEL 110PL PREMIER GRADE
Same as Model 110P except has left-hand action.
Calibers .243 Win. and .30-06 NiB $528 Ex $401 Gd $271
Caliber 7mm Rem. Mag . . . . . **NiB $549 Ex $401 Gd $293**

MODEL 110S/110V
Same as Model 110E except Model 110S in .308 Win. only; discontinued 1985. Model 110V in .22-250 and .223 Rem. w/heavy 2-inch barrel, 47 inches overall, weight: 9 lbs. Discontinued. 1989.
Model 110S . . . . **NiB $397 Ex $315 Gd $240**
Model 110V . . . . **NiB $416 Ex $322 Gd $248**

Savage Model 111 Chieftain

Savage Model 111F

Savage Model 112V

Savage Model 116FCSAK

MODEL 111 CHIEFTAIN BOLT-ACTION RIFLE
Calibers: .243 Win., .270 Win., 7x57mm, 7mm Rem. Mag. .30-06. 4-round clip magazine (3-round in Magnum). 22-inch bbl. (24-inch in Magnum). Weight: 7.5 lbs., 8.25 lbs. Magnum. Sights: Leaf rear; hooded ramp front. Select walnut stock w/Monte Carlo comb and cheekpiece, checkered, pistol-grip cap, QD swivels and sling. Made from 1974 to 1979.

Standard calibers . . . . NiB $444 Ex $389 Gd $259
Magnum calibers . . . . NiB $445 Ex $398 Gd $279

MODEL 111F, 11FC, 111FNS CLASSIC HUNTER RIFLE
Similar to the Model 111G except with graphite/fiberglass composite stock. Weight: 6.25 lbs. Made from 1994 to date.

Model 111F (right- or left-hand w/box mag.)NiB $498 Ex $411 Gd $238
MODEL 111FC (w/detachable mag.) . NiB $448 Ex $338 Gd $206
Model 111FNS (right- or left-hand
w/detachable mag.) . . . . NiB $469 Ex $355 Gd $228

MODEL 111G, 111GC, 111GNS CLASSIC HUNTER RIFLE
Calibers: .22-250 Rem., .223 Rem., .243 Win., .25-06 Rem. .250 Sav., .270 Win., 7mm-08 Rem., 7mm Rem. Mag., .30-06, .300 Sav., .300 Win. Mag., .308 Win., .338 Win. 22- or 24-inch bbl. Weight: 7 lbs. Ramp front sight, adj. open rear. Walnut-finished hardwood stock. Blued finish. Made from 1994 to date.

Model 111G (right- or left-hand w/box mag.)NiB $369 Ex $298 Gd $210
Model 111GC (right- or left-hand w/
detachable mag.) . . . . NiB $465 Ex $358 Gd $227
Model 111GNS (w box mag., no sights)NiB $370 Ex $300 Gd $198

MODEL 112BV,112BVSS HEAVY VARMINT RIFLES
Similar to the Model 110G except fitted with 26-inch heavy bbl. Laminated wood stock with high comb. .22-250 and .223 only.
Model 112BV (Made 1993-94) . . . . . NiB $520 Ex $378 Gd $266

Model 112BVSS (w/fluted stainless
bbl., intro. 1994) . . . . NiB $556 Ex $422 Gd $315

MODEL 112FVVS, 112FVSS VARMINT RIFLE
Similar to the Model 110G except fitted with 26-inch heavy bbl. and Dupont Rynite stock. Calibers: .22-250, .223 and .220 Swift (112FVS only). Blued or stainless finish. Made from 1991 to date.
Model 112RV (blued finish) . . . . NiB $420 Ex $355 Gd $261
Model 112FV-S (blued finish,
single-shot, disc. 1993). . . . . NiB $533 Ex $445 Gd $398
Model 112FVSS (stainless finish). . . . NiB $645 Ex $545 Gd $390
Model 112 FVSS-S (stainless finish, single-shot)NiB $645 Ex $545 Gd $390

MODEL 112V VARMINT RIFLE NiB $389 Ex $289 Gd $200
Bolt action, single shot. Caliber: .220 Swift, .222 Rem., .223 Rem., .22-250, .243 Win., .25-06. 26-inch heavy bbl. with scope bases. Supplied w/o sights. Weight: 9.25 lbs. Select walnut stock in varmint style w/checkered pistol-grip, high comb, QD sling swivels. Made from 1975 to 1979.

MODEL 114C, 114CE, 114CU RIFLES
Calibers: .270 Win., 7mm Rem. Mag., .30-06, .300 Win. Mag. 22- or 24-inch bbl. Weight: 7 lbs. Detachable 3- or 4-round magazine. Ramp front sight; adjustable, open rear; (114CU has no sights). Checkered select walnut stock w/oil finish, red butt pad. Schnabel forend and skip-line checkering (114CE). High-luster blued finish. Made from 1991 to date.
Model 114C (Classic) . . . . NiB $745 Ex $588 Gd $338
Model 114CE (Classic European). . . . NiB $533 Ex $390 Gd $300
Model 114CU (Classic Ultra) . . . . . . NiB $540 Ex $400 Gd $310

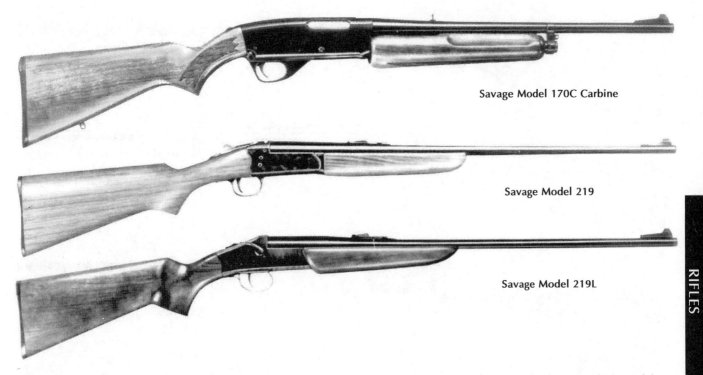

Savage Model 170C Carbine

Savage Model 219

Savage Model 219L

MODELS 116FSAK, 116FCSAK BOLT-ACTION RIFLES
Similar to the Model 116FSK except in calibers .270 Win., .30-06, 7mm Mag., .300 Win. Mag., .338 Win. Mag. Fluted 22-inch stainless bbl. w/adj. muzzle brake. Weight: 6.5 lbs. Made from 1994 to date.
Model 116FSAK . . . . NiB $590 Ex $443 Gd $338
Model 116FCSAK (detachable mag.) . NiB $645 Ex $547 Gd $379

MODELS 116FSC, 116FSS BOLT-ACTION RIFLES
Improved Model 110 with satin stainless action and bbl. Calibers: .223, .243, .270, .30-06, 7mm Rem. Mag., .300 Win. Mag., .338 Win. Mag. 22- or 24-inch bbl. Four or 5-round capacity. Weight: About 7.5 lbs. Black Rynite stock w/recoil pad and swivel studs. Receiver drilled and tapped for scope mounts, no sights. Made from 1991 to date.
Model 116FSS . . . . NiB $677 Ex $544 Gd $339
Model 116FSC, detachable magazine NiB $688 Ex $554 Gd $349

MODEL 116FSK KODIAK RIFLE . . . . NiB $535 Ex $380 Gd $278
Similar to the Model 116FSS except with 22-inch bbl. chambered for 338 Win. Mag. only. "Shock Suppressor" recoil reducer. Made from 1994 to 2000.

MODEL 116-SE, 116-US RIFLES
Calibers: .270 Win., 7mm Rem Mag., .30-06, .300 Win. Mag. (116US); .300 Win. Mag., .338 Win. mag., .425 Express, .458 Win. Mag. (116SE). 24-inch stainless barrel (with muzzle brake 116SE only). 45.5 inches overall. Weight: 7.2 to 8.5 lbs. Three round magazine. 3-leaf Express sights 116SE only. Checkered Classic style select walnut stock with ebony forend tip. Stainless finish. Made from 1994 to 2004.
Model 116SE (Safari Express) . NiB $947 Ex $788 Gd $556
Model 116US (Ultra Stainless). NiB $660 Ex $498 Gd $400

MODEL 170 PUMP-ACTION
CENTERFIRE RIFLE . . . . NiB $249 Ex $190 Gd $106
Calibers: .30-30, .35 Rem. Three round tubular magazine. 22-inch bbl. Weight: 6.75 lbs. Sights: Folding leaf rear; ramp front. Select walnut stock w/checkered pistol-grip Monte Carlo comb, grooved slide handle. Made from 1970 to 1981.

MODEL 170C CARBINE . . . . . NiB $280 Ex $322 Gd $166
Same as Model 170 Rifle except has 18.5-inch bbl., straight comb stock, weight: 6 lbs.; caliber .30-30 only. Made from 1974 to 1981.

MODEL 219 SINGLE-SHOT RIFLE NiB $227 Ex $119 Gd $67
Hammerless. Takedown. Shotgun-type action with top lever. Calibers: .22 Hornet, .25-20, .32-20, .30-30. 26-inch bbl. Weight: about 6 lbs. Sights: Open rear; bead front. Plain pistol-grip stock and forearm. Made from 1938 to 1965.
Model 219L (w/side lever, made 1965-67) NiB $155 Ex $100 Gd $70

MODEL 221-229 UTILITY GUNS
Same as Model 219 except in various calibers, supplied in combination with an interchangeable shotgun bbl. All versions discontinued.
Model 221 (.30-30,12-ga. 30-inch bbl.) NiB $155 Ex $80 Gd $55
Model 222 (.30-30,16-ga. 28-inch bbl.). NiB $155 Ex $80 Gd $55
Model 223 (.30-30, 20-ga. 28-inch bbl.) NiB $155 Ex $80 Gd $55
Model 227 (.22 Hornet, 12-ga. 30-inch bbl.) NiB $155 Ex $80 Gd $55
Model 228 (.22 Hornet, 16-ga. 28-inch bbl.) NiB $155 Ex $80 Gd $55
Model 229 (.22 Hornet, 20-ga. 28-inch bbl.) NiB $155 Ex $80 Gd $55

MODEL 340 BOLT-ACTION REPEATER
Calibers: .22 Hornet, .222 Rem., .223 Rem., .227 Win., .30-30. Clip magazine; 4-round capacity (3-round in 30-30). Bbl. lengths: Originally 20-inch in .30-30, 22-inch in .22 Hornet; later 22-inch in .30-30, 24-inch in other calibers. Weight: 6.5 to 7.5 lbs. depending on caliber and vintage. Sights: Open rear (folding leaf on recent production); ramp front. Early models had plain pistol-grip stock, checkered since 1965. Made from 1950-85. (Note: Those rifles produced between 1947-1950 were .22 Hornet Stevens Model .322 and .30-30 Model .325. The Savage model, however, was designated Model .340 for all calibers.)
Pre-1965 with plain stock. . . . NiB $266 Ex $190 Gd $105
Savage Model 340C Carbine. . NiB $278 Ex $228 Gd $140

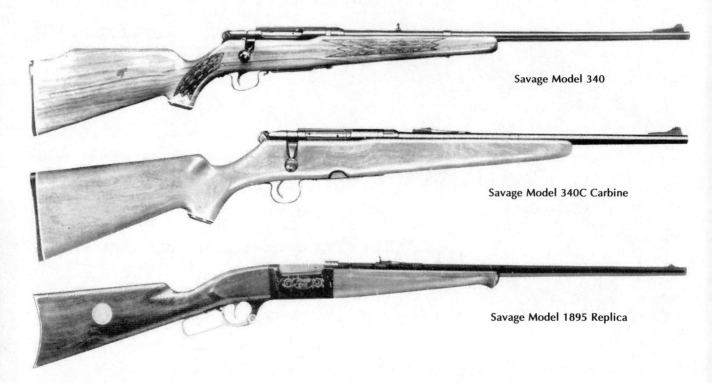

Savage Model 340

Savage Model 340C Carbine

Savage Model 1895 Replica

MODEL 340S DELUXE . . . . . . NiB $345 Ex $298 Gd $218
Same as Model 340 except has checkered stock, screw eyes for sling, peep rear sight, hooded front. Made from 1955 to 1960.

MODEL 342 . . . . NiB $345 Ex $298 Gd $218
Designation, 1950 to 1955, of Model 340 .22 Hornet.

MODEL 342S DELUXE . . . . . . NiB $355 Ex $325 Gd $227
Designation, 1950 to 1955, of Model 340S .22 Hornet.

ANNIVERSARY MODEL
1895 LEVER-ACTION . . . . NiB $6235 Ex $4589 Gd $2240
Replica of Savage Model 1895 Hammerless Lever-Action Rifle issued to commemorate the 75th anniversary (1895-1970) of Savage Arms. Caliber: .308 Win. Five round rotary magazine. 24-inch full-octagon bbl. Engraved receiver. Brass-plated lever. Sights: Open rear; brass blade front. Plain straight-grip buttstock, Schnabel-type forend; brass medallion inlaid in buttstock, brass crescent-shaped buttplate. 9,999 produced. Made in 1970 only. Top value is for new, unfired specimen.

MODEL 1903 SLIDE-ACTION
REPEATER . . . . NiB $733 Ex $549 Gd $370
Hammerless. Takedown. Caliber: .22 Short, Long, LR. Detachable box magazine. 24-inch octagon bbl. Weight: About 5 lbs. Sights: Open rear; bead front. Pistol-grip stock, grooved slide handle. Made 1903 to 1921.

MODEL 1904 BOLT-ACTION
SINGLE-SHOT RIFLE. . . . . NiB $228 Ex $140 Gd $90
Takedown. .22 Short, Long, LR. 18-inch bbl. Weight: About 3 lbs. Sights: Open rear; bead front. Plain, straight-grip, one-piece stock. Made from 1904 to 1917.

MODEL 1905 BOLT-ACTION
SINGLE-SHOT RIFLE. . . . . NiB $220 Ex $138 Gd $85
Takedown. .22 Short, Long, LR. 22-inch bbl. Weight: About 5 lbs. Sights: Open rear; bead front. Plain, straight-grip one-piece stock. Made from 1905 to 1919.

MODEL 1909 SLIDE-ACTION
REPEATER . . . . NiB $800 Ex $533 Gd $337
Hammerless. Takedown. Similar to Model 1903 except has 20-inch round bbl., plain stock and forearm, weight: Approximately 4.75 lbs. Made from 1909 to 1915.

MODEL 1912
AUTOLOADING RIFLE . . . . NiB $800 Ex $533 Gd $337
Takedown. Caliber: 22 LR. only. Seven round detachable box magazine. 20-inch bbl., plain stock and forearm. Made 1912 to 1916.

MODEL 1914 SLIDE-ACTION
REPEATER . . . . NiB $520 Ex $347 Gd $239
Hammerless. Takedown. Caliber: .22 Short, Long, LR, Tubular magazine holds 20 Short, 17 Long, 15 LR. 24-inch octagon bbl. Weight: About 5.75 lbs. Sights: Open rear; bead front. Plain pistol-grip stock, grooved slide handle. Made from 1914 to 1924.

MODEL 1920 HI-POWER BOLT-ACTION RIFLE
Short Mauser-type action. Calibers: .250/3000, .300 Sav. Five round box magazine. 22-inch bbl. in .250 cal.; 24-inch in .300 cal. Weight: About 6 lbs. Sights: Open rear; bead front. Checkered pistol-grip stock w/slender forearm and Schnabel tip. Made from 1920 to 1926.
.250-3000 Savage. . . . . NiB $1029 Ex $833 Gd $690
.300 Savage . . . . NiB $969 Ex $755 Gd $588

NOTE: *In 1965, Savage began the importation of rifles manufactured by J. G. Anschutz GmbH, Ulm, West Germany. Models designated "Savage/Anschutz" are listed in this section, those marketed in the U.S. under the "Anschutz" name are included in that firm's listings. Anschutz rifles are now distributed in the U.S. by Precision Sales Int'l., Westfield, Mass. See "Anschutz" for detailed specifications.*

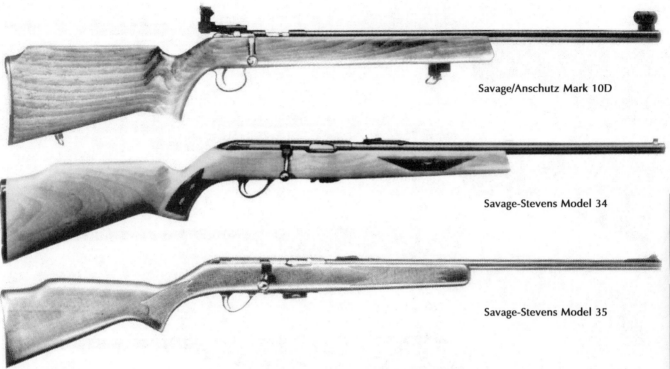

Savage/Anschutz Mark 10D

Savage-Stevens Model 34

Savage-Stevens Model 35

MARK 10 BOLT-ACTION
TARGET RIFLE . . . . **NiB $534 Ex $359 Gd $265**
Single shot. Caliber: .22 LR. 26-inch bbl. Weight: 8.5 lbs. Sights: Anschutz micrometer rear; globe front. Target stock w/full pistol-grip and cheekpiece, adj. hand stop and swivel. Made 1967 to 1972.

MARK 10D . . . . **NiB $544 Ex $369 Gd $259**
Same as Mark 10 except has redesigned stock with Monte Carlo comb, different rear sight. Weight: 7.75 lbs. Made in 1972.

MODEL 54
CUSTOM SPORTER . . . . **NiB $766 Ex $639 Gd $400**
Same as Anschutz Model 1422D.

MODEL 54M . . . . **NiB $945 Ex $670 Gd $439**
Same as Anschutz Model 1522D.

MODEL 64 BOLT-ACTION
TARGET RIFLE . . . . **NiB $655 Ex $512 Gd $338**
Same as Anschutz Model 1403.

MODEL 153 BOLT-ACTION
SPORTER . . . . **NiB $697 Ex $488 Gd $349**
Caliber: .222 Rem. Three round clip magazine. 24-inch bbl. Sights: Folding leaf open rear; hooded ramp front. Weight: 6.75 lbs. French walnut stock w/cheekpiece, skip checkering, rosewood forend tip and grip cap, swivels. Made from 1964 to 1967.

MODEL 153S . . . . **NiB $770 Ex $556 Gd $390**
Same as Model 153 except has double-set trigger. Made 1965 to 1967.

MODEL 164 CUSTOM SPORTER . . . **NiB $775 Ex $561 Gd $195**
Same as Anschutz Model 1416.

MODEL 164M . . . . **NiB $660 Ex $454 Gd $300**
Same as Anschutz Model 1516.

MODEL 184 SPORTER . . . . . . **NiB $638 Ex $484 Gd $288**
Same as Anschutz Model 1441.

NOTE: *Since J. Stevens Arms (see also separate listing) is a division of Savage Industries, certain Savage models carry the "Stevens" name.*

MODEL 34 BOLT-ACTION
REPEATER . . . . **NiB $190 Ex $126 Gd $88**
Caliber: .22 Short, Long, LR. 20-inch bbl. Weight: 4.75 lbs. Sights: Open rear; bead front. Plain pistol-grip stock. Made 1965 to 1980.

MODEL 34M . . . . **NiB $190 Ex $146 Gd $98**
Same as Model 34 except chambered for 22 WMR. Made 1969 to 1973.

MODEL 35 . . . . **NiB $190 Ex $146 Gd $98**
Bolt-action repeater. Caliber: 22 LR. Six round clip magazine. 22-inch bbl. Weight: About 5 lbs. Sights: Open rear; ramp front. Monte Carlo stock w/checkered pistol grip and forearm. Made from 1982 to 1985.

MODEL 35M . . . . **NiB $219 Ex $140 Gd $100**
Same as Model 35 except chambered for 22 WMR. Made from 1982 to 1985.

MODEL 46 BOLT-ACTION
RIFLE . . . . **NiB $190 Ex $136 Gd $100**
Caliber: .22 Short, Long, LR. Tubular magazine holds 22 Short, 17 Long, 15 LR. 20-inch bbl. Weight: 5 lbs. Plain pistol-grip stock on early production; later models have Monte Carlo stock w/checkering. Made from 1969 to 1073.

MODEL 65
BOLT-ACTION RIFLE . . . . **NiB $219 Ex $138 Gd $99**
Caliber: .22 Short, Long, LR. Five round clip magazine. 20-inch bbl. Weight: 5 lbs. Sights: Open rear; ramp front. Monte Carlo stock w/ checkered pistol grip and forearm. Made from 1969 to 1973.

Savage-Stevens Model 46

Savage-Stevens Model 65

Savage-Stevens Model 72 — Crackshot

Savage-Stevens Model 73

Savage-Stevens Model 80

MODEL 65M . . . . **NiB $200 Ex $134 Gd $90**
Same as Model 65 except chambered for .22 WMR, has 22-inch
bbl., weighs 5.25 lbs. Made from 1969 to 1981.

NOTE: *The Model 72 is a "Favorite"-type single-shot unlike the
smaller, original "Crackshot" made by Stevens from 1913 to 1939.*

**MODEL 72 CRACKSHOT SINGLE-SHOT
LEVER-ACTION RIFLE**. . . . . **NiB $190 Ex $109 Gd $79**
Falling-block action. Casehardened frame. Caliber: .22 Short, Long,
LR. 22-inch octagon bbl. Weight: 4.5lbs. Sights: Open rear; bead front.
Plain straight-grip stock and forend of walnut. Made 1972 to 1989.

MODEL 73 BOLT-ACTION SINGLE-SHOT **NiB $159 Ex $138 Gd $89**
Caliber: .22 Short, Long, LR. 20-inch bbl. Weight: 4.75 lbs. Sights:
Open rear; bead front. Plain pistol-grip stock. Made 1965 to 1980.

MODEL 73Y YOUTH MODEL. . **NiB $150 Ex $110 Gd $90**
Same as Model 73 except has 18-inch bbl., 1.5-inch shorter buttstock, weight: 4.5 lbs. Made from 1965 to 1980.

**MODEL 74
LITTLE FAVORITE**. . . . . **NiB $167 Ex $115 Gd $98**
Same as Model 72 Crackshot except has black-finished frame,
22-inch round bbl., walnut-finished hardwood stock. Weight: 4.75
lbs. Made from 1972 to 1974.

**MODEL 80
AUTOLOADING RIFLE**. . . . . **NiB $215 Ex $170 Gd $126**
Caliber: 22 LR. 15-round tubular magazine. 20-inch bbl.
Weight: 6 lbs. Sights: Open rear, bead front. Monte Carlo
stock of walnut w/checkered pistol-grip and forearm. Made
from 1976 to date. (Note: This rifle is essentially the same as
the Model 60 of 1969 to 1972 except for a different style of
checkering, side instead of top safety and plain bead instead
of ramp front sight.)

**MODEL 88
AUTOLOADING RIFLE**. . . . . **NiB $190 Ex $110 Gd $88**
Similar to Model 60 except has walnut-finished hardwood stock,
plain bead front sight. Weight: 5.75 lbs. Made from 1969 to 1972.

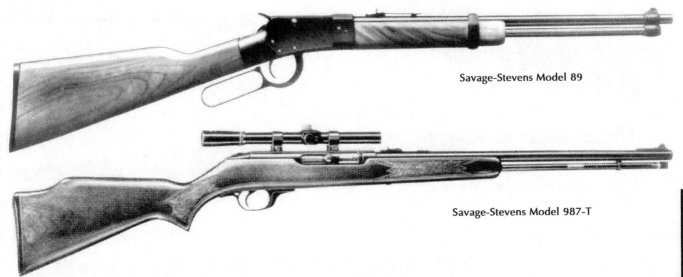

Savage-Stevens Model 89

Savage-Stevens Model 987-T

MODEL 89 SINGLE-SHOT
LEVER-ACTION CARBINE. . . . . . NiB $121 Ex $90 Gd $66
Martini-type action. Caliber: .22 Short, Long, LR. 18.5-inch bbl. Weight: 5 lbs. Sights: Open rear; bead front. Western-style carbine stock w/straight grip, forearm with bbl. band. Made 1976 to 1989.

MODEL 987-T
AUTOLOADING RIFLE. . . . . . NiB $217 Ex $166 Gd $129
Caliber: .22 LR. 15-round tubular magazine. 20-inch bbl. Weight: 6 lbs. Sights: Open rear; ramp front. Monte Carlo stock w/checkered pistol grip and forearm. Made from 1981 to 1989.

"STEVENS FAVORITE"
See Savage Model 71.

V.C. SCHILLING — Suhl, Germany

MAUSER-MANNLICHER
BOLT ACTION SPORTING RIFLENiB $938 Ex $744 Gd $539
Same general specifications as given for the Haenel Mauser-Mannlicher Sporter. See separate listing.

'88 MAUSER SPORTER. . . . . . NiB $909 Ex $722 Gd $515
Same general specifications as Haenel '88 Mauser Sporter. See separate listing.

SCHULTZ & LARSEN GEVAERFABRIK — Otterup, Denmark

MATCH RIFLE NO. 47 . . . . . . NiB $690 Ex $555 Gd $360
Caliber: .22 LR. Bolt-action, single-shot, set trigger. 28.5-inch heavy bbl. Weight: 14 lbs. Sights: Micrometer receiver, globe front. Free-rifle stock w/cheekpiece, thumbhole, adj. Schuetzen-type buttplate, swivels, palmrest.

FREE RIFLE MODEL 54 . . . . . . NiB $866 Ex $780 Gd $598
Calibers: 6.5x55mm or any standard American centerfire caliber. Schultz & Larsen M54 bolt-action, single-shot, set trigger. 27.5-inch heavy bbl. Weight: 15.5 lbs. Sights: Micrometer receiver; globe front. Free-rifle stock w/cheekpiece, thumbhole, adj. Schuetzen-type buttplate, swivels, palm rest.

MODEL 54J
SPORTING RIFLE . . . . NiB $684 Ex $528 Gd $430
Calibers: .270 Win., .30-06, 7x61 Sharpe & Hart. Schultz & Larsen bolt action. Three-round magazine. 24-inch bbl. in .270 and .30-06, 26-inch in 7x61 S&H. Checkered stock w/Monte Carlo comb and cheekpiece. Value shown is for rifle less sights.

SEARS, ROEBUCK & COMPANY — Chicago, Illinois

The most encountered brands or model designations used by Sears are J. C. Higgins and Ted Williams. Firearms sold under these designations have been mfd. by various firms including Winchester, Marlin, Savage, Mossberg, etc.

MODEL 2C
BOLT-ACTION RIFLE . . . . NiB $159 Ex $119 Gd $95
Caliber: .22RF. Seven round clip mag. 21-inch bbl. Weight: 5 lbs. Sights: Open rear; ramp front. Plain Monte Carlo stock. Mfd. by Win.

MODEL 42
BOLT-ACTION REPEATER. . . . . NiB $159 Ex $119 Gd $95
Takedown. Caliber: .22RF. Eight round detachable box magazine. 24-inch bbl. Weight: 6 lbs. Sights: Open rear; bead front. Plain pistol-grip stock. Mfd. by Marlin.

MODEL 42DL
BOLT-ACTION REPEATER. . . . . NiB $159 Ex $119 Gd $95
Same general specifications as Model 42 except fancier grade w/ peep sight, hooded front sight and swivels.

MODEL 44DL
LEVER-ACTION RIFLE. . . . . . . NiB $239 Ex $179 Gd $130
Caliber: .22RF. Tubular magazine holds 19 LR cartridges. 22-inch bbl. Weight: 6.25 lbs. Sights: Open rear; hooded ramp front. Monte Carlo-style stock w/pistol grip. Mfd. by Marlin.

MODEL 53
BOLT-ACTION RIFLE . . . . NiB $289 Ex $198 Gd $155
Calibers: .243, .270, .308, .30-06. Four-round magazine. 22-inch bbl. Weight: 6.75 lbs. Sights: Open rear; ramp front. Standard sporter stock w/pistol-grip, checkered. Mfd. by Savage.

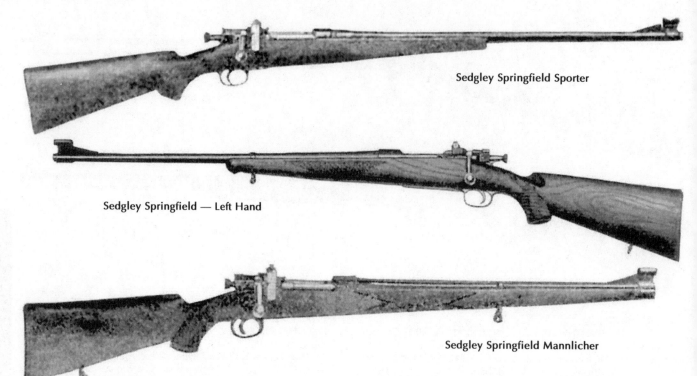

Sedgley Springfield Sporter

Sedgley Springfield — Left Hand

Sedgley Springfield Mannlicher

MODEL 54 LEVER-ACTION
RIFLE . . . . NiB $222 Ex $188 Gd $135
Similar general specifications as Winchester Model 94 carbine.
Made in .30-30 caliber only. Mfd. by Winchester.

MODEL 103 SERIES
BOLT-ACTION REPEATER. . . . . NiB $229 EX $121 Gd $98
Same general specifications as Model 103.2 w/minor changes. Mfd.
by Marlin.

MODEL 103.2 BOLT-ACTION
REPEATER . . . . NiB $145 Ex $100 Gd $90
Takedown. Caliber: .22RF. Eight-round detachable box magazine.
24-inch bbl. Weight: 6 lbs. Sights: Open rear; bead front. Plain
pistol-grip stock. Mfd. by Marlin.

R. F. SEDGLEY, INC. —
Philadelphia, Pennsylvania

SPRINGFIELD SPORTER . . . NiB $1290 Ex $1189 Gd $633
Springfield '03 bolt action. Calibers: .220 Swift, .218 Bee, .22-3000,
R, .22-4000, .22 Hornet, .25-35, .250-3000, .257 Roberts, .270
Win., 7mm, .30-06. 24-inch bbl. Weight: 7.5 lbs. Sights: Lyman No.
48 receiver; bead front on matted ramp. Checkered walnut stock,
grip cap, sling swivels. Disc. 1941.

SPRINGFIELD LEFT-HAND SPORTERNiB $1674 Ex $1412 Gd $954
Bolt-action reversed for left-handed shooter; otherwise the same as
standard Sedgley Springfield Sporter. Disc. 1941.

SEDGLEY SPRINGFIELD
MANNLICHER-TYPE SPORTER . . NiB $1515 Ex $1479 Gd $1088
Same as standard Sedgley Springfield Sporter except w/20-
inch bbl., Mannlicher-type full stock w/cheekpiece, weight:
7.75 lbs. Disc. 1941.

SHILEN RIFLES, INC. — Enis, Texas

DGA BENCHREST RIFLE. . . NiB $1529 Ex $1244 Gd $977
DGA single-shot bolt-action. Calibers as listed for Sporter. 26-inch medium-
heavy or heavy bbl. Weight: From 10.5 lbs. No sights. Fiberglass or walnut
stock, classic or thumbhole pattern. Currently manufactured.

DGA SPORTER. . . . . NiB $1567 Ex $1189 Gd $843
DGA bolt action. Calibers: .17 Rem., .222 Rem., .223 Rem. .22-250,
.220 Swift, 6mm Rem., .243 Win., .250 Sav., .257 Roberts, .284
Win., .308 Win., .358 Win. Three round blind magazine. 24-inch
bbl. Average weight: 7.5 lbs. No sights. Select Claro walnut stock w/
cheekpiece, pistol grip, sling swivel studs. Currently manufactured.

DGA VARMINTER . . . . . . NiB $1455 Ex $1209 Gd $1155
Same as Sporter except w/25-inch medium-heavy bbl. Weight: 9 lbs.

SHILOH RIFLE MFG. CO.—Big Timber, Montana

SHARPS MODEL 1874 BUSINESS RIFLENiB$1149Ex$1072Gd$698
Replica of 1874 Sharps similar to No. 3 Sporting Rifle. .32-40,
.38-55, .40-50 BN, .40-70 BN, .40-90 BN, .45-70 ST, .45-90 ST,
.50-70 ST, .50-100 ST. 28-inch round heavy bbl. Blade front sight,
buckhorn rear. Double-set triggers. Straight-grip walnut stock w/
steel crescent buttplate. Made from 1986 to date.

SHARPS MODEL 1874 LONG
RANGE EXPRESS RIFLE. . . NiB $1798 Ex $1703 Gd $1166
Replica of 1874 Sharps w/single-shot falling breech action. .32-40, .38-
55, .40-50 BN, .40-70 BN, .40-90 BN, .45-70 ST, .45-90 ST, .45-110
ST, .50-70 ST, .50-90 ST, .50-110 ST. 34-inch tapered octagon bbl. 51
inches overall. Weight: 10.75 lbs. Globe front sight, sporting tang peep
rear. Walnut buttstock w/pistol-grip and Schnabel-style forend. Color
casehardened action w/double-set triggers Made from 1986 to date.

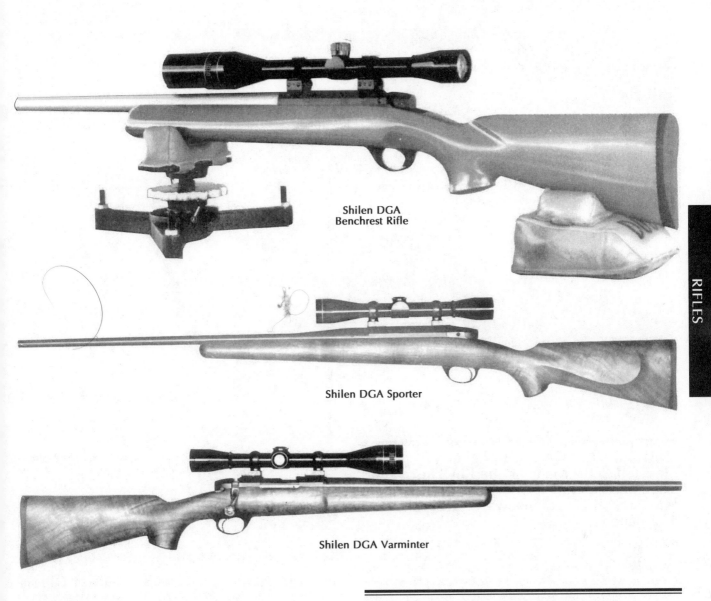

Shilen DGA
Benchrest Rifle

Shilen DGA Sporter

Shilen DGA Varminter

SHARPS MODEL 1874
SADDLE RIFLE . . . . **NiB $1267 Ex $1133 Gd $723**
Similar to 1874 Express Rifle except w/30-inch bbl., blade front sight and buckhorn rear. Made from 1986 to date.

SHARPS MODEL 1874
SPORTING RIFLE NO. 1 . . . **NiB $1355 Ex $1187 Gd $745**
Similar to 1874 Express Rifle except w/30-inch bbl., blade front sight and buckhorn rear. Made from 1986 to date.

SHARPS MODEL 1874
SPORTING RIFLE NO. 3 . . . **NiB $1150 Ex $1007 Gd $688**
Similar to 1874 Sporting Rifle No. 1 except w/straight-grip stock w/ steel crescent buttplate. Made from 1986 to date.

SHARPS MODEL 1874 MONTANA ROUGHRIDER
Similar to 1874 Sporting Rifle No. 1 except w/24- to 34-inch half-octagon or full-octagon bbl. Standard or deluxe walnut stock w/ pistol-grip or military-style buttstock. Made from 1989 to date.
Standard model . . . . **NiB $1154 Ex $715 Gd $646**
Deluxe model . . . . **NiB $1300 Ex $990 Gd $615**

SIG SWISS INDUSTRIAL COMPANY —
Neuhausen-Rhine Falls, Switzerland

AMT SEMIAUTOMATIC RIFLE . . . **NiB $4798 Ex $3270 Gd $2775**
.308 Win.(7.62 NATO). Five, 10, or 20-round magazine. 18.5-inch bbl. w/flash suppressor. Weight: 9.5 lbs. Sights: Adj. aperture rear, post front. Walnut buttstock and forend w/synthetic pistol grip. Imported 1980 to 1988.

AMT SPORTING RIFLE . . . **NiB $4876 Ex $3129 Gd $2210**
Semiautomatic version of SG510-4 automatic assault rifle based on Swiss Army SIGW57. Roller-delayed blowback action. Caliber: 7.62x51mm NATO (.308 Win.). Five, 10- and 20-round magazines. 19-inch bbl. Weight: 10 lbs. Sights, aperture rear, post front. Wood buttstock and forearm, folding bipod. Imported from 1960 to 1988.

PE-57 SEMIAUTOMATIC RIFLE . . **NiB $6596 Ex $4348 Gd $3100**
Caliber: 7.5 Swiss. 24-round magazine. 23.75-inch bbl. Weight: 12.5 lbs. Sights: Adj. aperture rear; post front. High-impact synthetic stock. Imported from Switzerland during the 1980s.

Smith & Wesson
Model 1500DL

Smith & Wesson
Model 1707 LS Classic Hunter

Springfield Armory
BM-59

SMITH & WESSON — Springfield, Massachusetts. Manufactured by Husqvarna, Vapenfabrik A.B., Huskvarna, Sweden, & Howa Machinery LTD., Shinkawa-Chonear, Nagota 452, Japan

MODEL 1500 . . . . NiB $410 Ex $339 Gd $269
Bolt-action. .243 Win., .270 Win., .30-06, 7mm Rem. Mag. 22-inch bbl. (24-inch in 7mm Rem. Mag.). Weight: 7.5 lbs. American walnut stock w/Monte Carlo comb and cheekpiece, cut checkering. Sights: Open rear, hooded ramp, gold bead-front. This model was also imported by Mossberg (see separate listings); Imported from 1979 to 1984.

MODEL 1500DL DELUXE . . . . NiB $410 Ex $339 Gd $269
Same as standard model, except w/o sights; w/engine-turned bolt, decorative scroll on floorplate, French checkering. Imported from 1983 to 1984.

MODEL 1707 LS "CLASSIC HUNTER" NiB $460 Ex $388 Gd $318
Bolt action. Calibers: .243 Win., .270 Win., .30-06, 5-round magazine. 22-inch bbl. Weight: 7.5 lbs. Solid recoil pad, no sights, Schnabel forend, checkered walnut stock. Imported 1983 to 1984.

MODEL A BOLT-ACTION RIFLE . . . . NiB $443 Ex $329 Gd $290
Similar to Husqvarna Model 9000 Crown Grade. Mauser-type bolt action. Calibers: .22-250, .243 Win., .270 Win., .308 Win., .30-06, 7mm Rem. Mag., .300 Win. Mag. Five round magazine except 3-round capacity in latter two calibers. 23.75-inch bbl. Weight: 7 lbs. Sights: Folding leaf rear; hooded ramp front. Checkered walnut stock w/Monte Carlo cheekpiece, rosewood forend tip and pistol-grip cap, swivels. Made from 1969 to 1972.
MODEL B . . . . NiB $460 Ex $367 Gd $238

Same as Model A except w/20.25-inch extra-light bbl., Monte Carlo cheekpiece w/Schnabel-style forearm, weight: 6 lbs., 10 oz. Calibers: .243 Win., .30-06.

MODEL C . . . . NiB $460 Ex $367 Gd $238
Same as Model B except w/cheekpiece stock w/straight comb.

MODEL D . . . . NiB $588 Ex $469 Gd $240
Same as Model C except w/full-length Mannlicher-style forearm.

MODEL E . . . . NiB $588 Ex $469 Gd $240
Same as Model B except w/full-length Mannlicher-style forearm.

SPRINGFIELD, INC. — Colona, Illinois (formerly Springfield Armory of Geneseo, IL)

This is a private firm not to be confused with the former U.S. Government facility in Springfield, Mass.

BM-59 SEMIAUTOMATIC RIFLE
Gas-operated. Caliber: .308 Win. (7.62mm NATO). 20-round detachable box magazine. 19.3-inch bbl. w/flash suppressor. About 43 inches overall. Weight: 9.25 lbs. Adj. military aperture rear sight, square post front; direct and indirect grenade launcher sights. European walnut stock w/handguard or folding buttstock (Alpine Paratrooper). Made from 1981 to 1990.
Standard
model . . . . NiB $1844 Ex $1329 Gd $911
Paratrooper
model . . . . NiB $2136 Ex $1779 Gd $1533

364

Springfield Armory
SAR-8 Sporter Rifle

M-1 GARAND SEMIAUTOMATIC RIFLE
Gas-operated. Calibers: .308 Win. (7.62 NATO), .30-06. Eight round stripper clip. 24-inch bbl. 43.5 inches overall. Weight: 9.5 lbs. Adj. aperture rear sight, military square blade front. Standard "Issue-grade" walnut stock or folding buttstock. Made from 1979 to 1990.
Standard model . . . . NiB $779 Ex $588 Gd $353
National Match model . . . . . . NiB $909 Ex $799 Gd $489
Ultra Match model . . . . NiB $1000 Ex $808 Gd $589
Sniper model . . . . NiB $1264 Ex $876 Gd $665
Tanker model . . . . NiB $954 Ex $677 Gd $498
Paratrooper model
(w/folding stock). . . . . . . NiB $1466 Ex $1109 Gd $1077

MATCH M1A
Same as Standard M1A except w/National Match-grade bbl. w/ modified flash suppressor, National Match sights, turned trigger pull, gas system assembly in one unit, modified mainspring guide glass-bedded walnut stock. Super Match M1A w/premium-grade heavy bbl. (weight: 10 lbs).
Match M1A . . . . NiB $1277 Ex $1879 Gd $1271
Super Match M1A. . . . . . . NiB $2695 Ex $1899 Gd $1721

STANDARD M1A SEMIAUTOMATIC
Gas-operated. Similar to U.S. M14 service rifle except w/o provision for automatic firing. Caliber: 7.65mm NATO (.308 Win.). Five, 10- or 20-round detachable box magazine. 25.13-inch bbl w/flash suppressor. Weight: 9 lbs. Sights: Adj. aperture rear; blade front. Fiberglass, birch or walnut stock, fiberglass handguard, sling swivels. Made from 1996 to 2000.
W/fiberglass or birch stock . . NiB $1198 Ex $694 Gd $645
W/walnut stock . . . . NiB $1412 Ex $1100 Gd $833

M-6 SCOUT RIFLE/SHOTGUN COMBO
Similar to (14-inch) short-barrel Survival Gun provided as backup weapon to U.S. combat pilots. Calibers: .22 LR/.410 and .22 Hornet/.410. 18.5-inch bbl. 32 inches overall. Weight: 4 lbs. Parkerized or stainless steel finish. Folding detachable stock w/storage for fifteen .22 LR cartridges and four .410 shells. Drilled and tapped for scope mounts. Intro. 1982 and imported from Czech Republic 1995 to 2004.
First Issue (no trigger guard)NiB $1709 Ex $1443 Gd $1067
Second Issue (w/trigger guard)NiB $1797 Ex $1449 Gd $1088

SAR-8 SPORTER RIFLE
Similar to H&K 911 semiautomatic rifle. Calibers: .308 Win., (7.62x51) NATO. Detachable 5- 10- or 20-round magazine. 18- or 20-inch bbl. 38.25 or 45.3 inches overall. Weight: 8.7 to 9.5 lbs. Protected front post and rotary adj. rear sight. Delayed roller-locked blow-back action w/fluted chamber. Kevlar-reinforced fiberglass thumb-hole style wood stock. Imported from 1990 to 1998.
SAR-8 w/wood stock (disc. 1994) . . NiB $1077 Ex $877 Gd $658
SAR-8 w/thumb-hole stock . . . . NiB $1127 Ex $976 Gd $679

SAR-48, SAR-4800
Similar to Browning FN FAL/LAR semiautomatic rifle. Calibers: .233 Rem. (5.56x45) and 3.08 Win. (7.62x51) NATO. Detachable 5- 10- or 20-round magazine. 18- or 21-inch chrome-lined bbl. 38.25 or 45.3 inches overall. Weight: 9.5 to 13.25 lbs. Protected post front and adj. rear sight. Forged receiver and bolt w/adj. gas system. Pistol-grip or thumb-hole style; synthetic or wood stock. Imported 1985; reintroduced 1995.
W/pistol-grip stock, disc. 1989 . . . NiB $1788 Ex $1289 Gd $990
W/wood stock, disc. 1989 . . . . . NiB $2577 Ex $2066 Gd $1500
W/folding stock, disc. 1989 . . . . NiB $2854 Ex $2310 Gd $1669
W/thumb-hole stock . . . . NiB $1329 Ex $1100 Gd $796

SQUIRES BINGHAM CO., INC. —
Makati, Rizal, Philippines

MODEL 14D DELUXE BOLT-ACTION
REPEATING RIFLE . . . . NiB $159 Ex $123 Gd $88
Caliber: .22 LR. Five round box magazine. 24-inch bbl. Sights: V-notch rear; hooded ramp front. Receiver grooved for scope mounting. Pulong Dalaga stock w/contrasting forend tip and grip cap, checkered forearm and pistol-grip. Weight: 6 lbs. Disc.

MODEL 15 . . . . NiB $189 Ex $127 Gd $115
Same as Model 14D except chambered for .22 WMR. Importation. Disc.

MODEL M16 SEMIAUTOMATIC RIFLENiB $190 Ex $166 Gd $126
Styled after U.S. M16 military rifle. Caliber: .22 LR. 15-round box magazine. 19.5-inch bbl. w/muzzle brake/flash hider. Rear sight in carrying handle, post front on high ramp. Black-painted mahogany buttstock and forearm. Weight: 6.5 lbs. Importation disc.

MODEL M20D DELUXE . . . . . NiB $277 Ex $227 Gd $131
Caliber: .22 LR. 15-round box magazine. 19.5-inch bbl. w/muzzle brake/flash hider. Sights: V-notch rear; blade front. Receiver grooved for scope mounting. Pulong Dalaga stock w/contrasting forend tip and grip cap, checkered forearm/pistol-grip. Weight: 6 lbs. Importation disc.

STANDARD ARMS COMPANY —
Wilmington, Delaware

MODEL G AUTOMATIC RIFLE NiB $815 Ex $569 Gd $355
Gas-operated. Autoloading. Hammerless. Takedown. .25-35, .30-30, .25 Rem., .30 Rem., .35 Rem. Magazine capacity: 4 rounds in .35 Rem., 5 rounds in other calibers. 22.38-inch bbl. Weight: 7.75 lbs. Sights: Open sporting rear; ivory bead front. Shotgun-type stock. Made c. 1910. Note: This was the first gas-operated rifle manufactured in the U.S. While essentially an autoloader, the gas port can be closed and the rifle may be operated as a slide-action repeater.

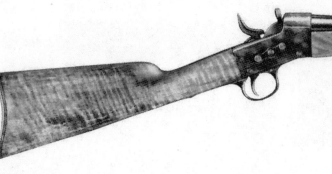

**Star
Rolling Block Carbine**

MODEL M HAND-OPERATED RIFLE . NiB $737 Ex $543 Gd $431
Slide-action repeater w/same general specifications as Model G except lacks autoloading feature. Weight: 7 lbs.

STAR — Eibar, Spain. Manufactured by Bonifacio Echeverría, S.A.

ROLLING BLOCK CARBINE . . NiB $500 Ex $337 Gd $178
Single-shot, similar to Remington Rolling Block. .30-30, .357 Mag., .44 Mag. 20-inch bbl. Weight: 6 lbs. Sights: Folding leaf rear; ramp front. Walnut straight-grip stock w/crescent buttplate, forearm w/bbl. band. Imported 1934 to 1975.

STERLING — Imported by Lanchester U.S.A., Inc., Dallas, Texas

MARK 6 SEMIAUTOMATIC CARBINENiB $1822 Ex $1177 Gd $987
Caliber: 9mm Para 34-round magazine. Bbl.: 16.1 inches. Weight: 7.5 lbs. Flip-type rear peep sight, ramp front. Folding metal skeleton stock. Made from 1983 to 1994.

J. STEVENS ARMS CO. — Chicopee Falls, Massachusetts, div. of Savage Industries, Westfield, Massachusetts

J. Stevens Arms eventually became a division of Savage Industries. Consequently, the "Stevens" brand name is used for some rifles by Savage; see separate Savage-Stevens listings under Savage.

**NO. 12 MARKSMAN
SINGLE-SHOT RIFLE . . . . .NiB $456 Ex $324 Gd $189**
Lever-action, tip-up. Takedown. Calibers: .22 LR, .25 R.F., .32 R.F. 22-inch bbl. Plain straight-grip stock, small tapered forearm.

**NO. 14 LITTLE SCOUT
SINGLE-SHOT RIFLE. . . . . NiB $455 Ex $310 Gd $180**
Caliber: .22 RF. 18-inch bbl. One-piece slab stock readily distinguishes it from the No. 14X that follows. Made from 1906 to 1910.

**NO. 14 1/2 LITTLE SCOUT
SINGLE-SHOT RIFLE. . . . . . . NiB $455 Ex $309 Gd $200**
Rolling block. Takedown. Caliber: .22 LR. 18- or 20-inch bbl. Weight: 2.75 lbs. Sights: open rear; blade front. Plain straight-grip stock, small tapered forearm.

MODEL 15 . . . . NiB $227 Ex $150 Gd $144
Same as Stevens-Springfield Model 15 except w/24-inch bbl., weight: 5 lbs., w/redesigned stock. Made from 1948 to 1965.

MODEL 15Y YOUTH'S RIFLE . NiB $221 Ex $155 Gd $127
Same as Model 15 except w/21-inch bbl., short buttstock, weight: 4.75 lbs. Made from 1958 to 1965.

**NO. 44 IDEAL
SINGLE-SHOT RIFLE. . . . . NiB $689 Ex $466 Gd $380**
Rolling block. Lever-action. Takedown. Calibers: .22 LR, .25 R.F., .32 R.F., .25-20 S.S., .32-20, .32-40, .38-40, .38-55, .44-40. Bbl. lengths: 24-inch, 26-inch (round, half-octagon, full-octagon). Weight: 7 lbs w/26-inch round bbl. Sights: Open rear; Rocky Mountain front. Plain straight-grip stock and forearm. Made from 1894 to 1932.

NO. 44 1/2 IDEAL SINGLE-SHOT RIFLENiB $990 Ex $848 Gd $578
Falling-block. Lever-action rifle. Aside from the new design action intro. 1903, specifications of this model are the same as those of Model 44. Model 44X disc. 1916.

NOS. 45-54 IDEAL SINGLE-SHOT RIFLES
These are higher-grade models, differing from the standard No. 44 and 44.5 chiefly in finish, engraving, set triggers, levers, bbls., stock, etc. The Schuetzen types (including the Stevens-Pope models) are in this series. Model Nos. 45 to 54 were intro. 1896 and originally had the No. 44-type rolling-block action, which was superseded in 1903 by the No. 44.5-type falling-block action. These models were all disc. about 1916. Generally speaking, the 45-54 series rifles, particularly the Stevens Pope and higher grade Schuetzen models are collector's items, bringing much higher prices than the ordinary No. 44 and 44.5.

**MODEL 66 BOLT-ACTION
REPEATING RIFLE . . . . NiB $255 Ex $140 Gd $121**
Takedown. Caliber: .22 Short, Long, LR. Tubular magazine holds 13 LR, 15 Long, 19 Short. 24-inch bbl. Weight: 5 lbs. Sights: Open rear, bead front. Plain pistol-grip stock w/grooved forearm. Made from 1931 to 1935.

**NO. 70 VISIBLE LOADING
SLIDE-ACTION. . . . . NiB $579 Ex $398 Gd $255**
Exposed hammer. Caliber: .22 LR, Long, Short. Tubular magazine holds 11 LR., 13 Long, 15 Short. 22-inch bbl. Weight: 4.5 lbs. Sights: Open rear; bead front. Plain straight-grip stock, grooved slide handle. Made 1907-34. Note: Nos. 702, 71, 712, 72, 722 essentially the same as No. 70, differing chiefly in bbl. length or sight tooling.

MODEL 87 AUTOLOADING RIFLE . . . NiB $167 Ex $121 Gd $90
Takedown. Caliber: .22 LR. 15-round tubular magazine. 24-inch bbl. (20-inch on current model). Weight: 6 lbs. Sights: Open rear, bead front. Pistol-grip stock. Made 1938 to date. Note: This model originally bore the "Springfield" brand name, disc. in 1948.

**MODEL 322 HI-POWER
BOLT-ACTION CARBINE . . . . NiB $487 Ex $333 Gd $202**
Caliber: .22 Hornet. 4-round detachable magazine. 21-inch bbl. Weight: 6.75 lbs. Sights: Open rear; ramp front. Pistol-grip stock. Made 1947 to 1950 (See Savage models 340, 342.)

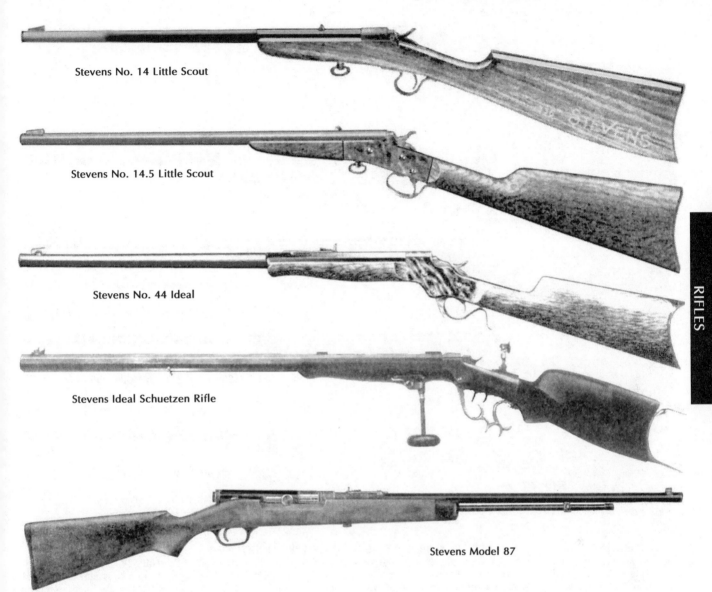

Stevens No. 14 Little Scout

Stevens No. 14.5 Little Scout

Stevens No. 44 Ideal

Stevens Ideal Schuetzen Rifle

Stevens Model 87

MODEL 322-S . . . . **NiB $479 Ex $338 Gd $200**
Same as Model 325 except w/peep rear sight. (See Savage models 340S, 342S.)

**MODEL 325 HI-POWER
BOLT-ACTION CARBINE** . . . . **NiB $479 Ex $338 Gd $200**
Caliber: .30-30. Three round detachable box magazine. 21-inch bbl. Weight: 6.75 lbs. Sights: Open rear; bead front. Plain pistol-grip stock. Made from 1947 to 1950. (See Savage Model 340.)

MODEL 325-S . . . . **NiB $479 Ex $338 Gd $200**
Same as Model 325 except w/peep rear sight. (See Savage Model 340S.)

**NO. 414 ARMORY MODEL
SINGLE-SHOT RIFLE.** . . . . **NiB $488 Ex $398 Gd $316**
No. 44-type lever-action. Calibers: .22 LR only, .22 Short only. 26-inch bbl. Weight: 8 lbs. Sights: Lyman receiver peep; blade front. Plain straight-grip stock, military-type forearm, swivels. Made from 1912 to 1932.

**MODEL 416 BOLT-ACTION
TARGET RIFLE** . . . . **NiB $159 Ex $100 Gd $77**
Caliber: .22 LR. Five round detachable box magazine. 26-inch heavy bbl. Weight: 9.5 lbs. Sights: Receiver peep; hooded front. Target stock, swivels, sling. Made from 1937 to 1949.

**NO. 419 JUNIOR TARGET MODEL
BOLT-ACTION SINGLE-SHOT RIFLE.** **NiB $433 Ex $325 Gd $255**
Takedown. Caliber: .22 LR. 26-inch bbl. Weight: 5.5 lbs. Sights: Lyman No. 55 rear peep; blade front. Plain junior target stock w/ pistol grip and grooved forearm, swivels, sling. Made 1932 to 1936.

**BUCKHORN MODEL 053 BOLT-ACTION
SINGLE-SHOT RIFLE.** . . . . **NiB $200 Ex $148 Gd $110**
Takedown. Calibers: .22 Short, Long, LR., .22 WRF. .25 Stevens R.F. 24-inch bbl. Weight: 5.5 lbs. Sights: Receiver peep; open middle; hooded front. Sporting stock w/pistol-grip and black forend tip. Made 1935 to 1948.

BUCKHORN MODEL 53 . . . . . **NiB $220 Ex $179 Gd $122**
Same as Buckhorn Model 053 except w/open rear sight and plain bead front sight.

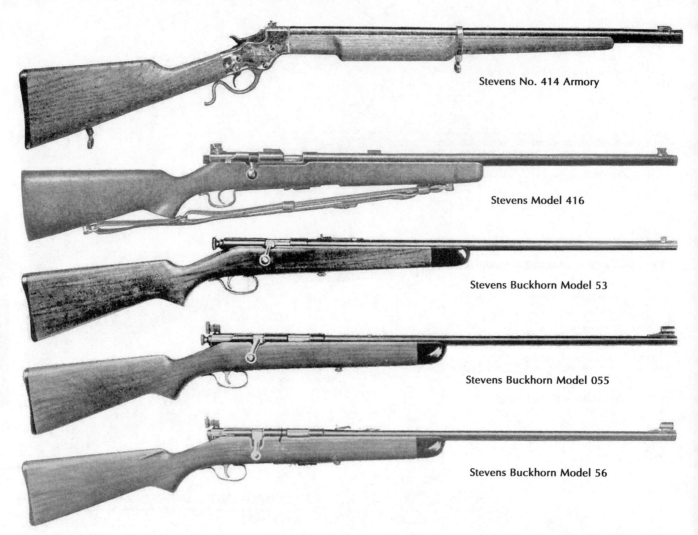

Stevens No. 414 Armory

Stevens Model 416

Stevens Buckhorn Model 53

Stevens Buckhorn Model 055

Stevens Buckhorn Model 56

BUCKHORN 055 . . . . **NiB $233 Ex $188 Gd $126**
Takedown. Same as Model 056 except in single-shot configuration. Weight: 5.5 lbs. Caliber: .22 LR, Long, Short. 24-inch bbl. Weight: 6 lbs. Sights: Receiver peep, open middle, hooded front. Made from 1935 to 1948.

BUCKHORN MODEL 056
BOLT-ACTION . . . . **NiB $230 Ex $190 Gd $131**
Takedown. Caliber: .22 LR, Long, Short. Five round detachable box magazine. 24-inch bbl. Weight: 6 lbs. Sights: Receiver peep, open middle, hooded front. Sporting stock w/pistol grip and black forend tip. Made from 1935 to 1948.

BUCKHORN
MODEL 56 . . . . **NiB $230 Ex $190 Gd $131**
Same as Buckhorn Model 056 except w/open rear sight and plain bead front sight.

BUCKHORN NO. 057 . . . . . . **NiB $233 Ex $155 Gd $120**
Same as Buckhorn Model 076 except w/5-round detachable box magazine. Made from 1939 to 1948.

BUCKHORN NO. 57 . . . . **NiB $230 Ex $155 Gd $120**
Same as Buckhorn Model 76 except w/5-round detachable box magazine. Made from 1939 to 1948.

BUCKHORN MODEL 066
BOLT-ACTION REPEATING RIFLE . . . **NiB $290 Ex $227 Gd $130**
Takedown. Caliber: .22 LR, Long, Short. Tubular magazine holds 21 Short, 17 Long, 15 LR. 24-inch bbl. Weight: 6 lbs. Sights: Receiver peep; open middle; hooded front. Sporting stock w/pistol grip and black forend tip. Made from 1935 to 1948.

BUCKHORN MODEL 66 . . . . . **NiB $219 Ex $133 Gd $210**
Same as Buckhorn Model 066 except w/open rear sight, plain bead front sight.

BUCKHORN NO. 076
AUTOLOADING RIFLE . . . . . . **NiB $227 Ex $188 Gd $135**
Takedown. Caliber: .22 LR. 15-round tubular magazine. 24-inch bbl. Weight: 6 lbs. Sights: Receiver peep; open middle; hooded front. Sporting stock w/pistol grip, black forend tip. Made 1938 to 1948.

BUCKHORN NO. 76 . . . . **NiB $227 Ex $188 Gd $135**
Same as Buckhorn No. 076 except w/open rear sight, plain bead front sight.

CRACKSHOT NO. 26
SINGLE-SHOT RIFLE . . . . **NiB $338 Ex $229 Gd $170**
Lever-action. Takedown. Calibers: .22 LR, .32 R.F. 18-inch or 22-inch bbl. Weight: 3.25 lbs. Sights: Open rear; blade front. Plain straight-grip stock, small tapered forearm. Made from 1913 to 1939.

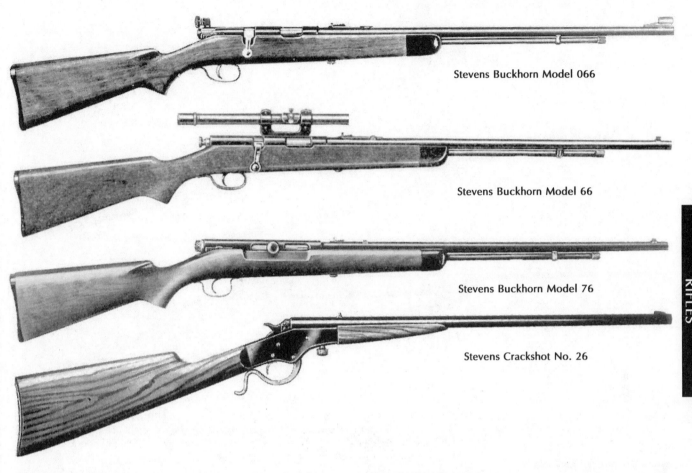

Stevens Buckhorn Model 066

Stevens Buckhorn Model 66

Stevens Buckhorn Model 76

Stevens Crackshot No. 26

CRACKSHOT NO. 26.5 . . . . . **NiB $325 Ex $220 Gd $195**
Same as Crackshot No. 26 on previous page except w/smoothbore bbl. for shot cartridges.

FAVORITE NO. 17
SINGLE-SHOT RIFLE. . . . . **NiB $333 Ex $227 Gd $200**
Lever-action. Takedown. Calibers: .22 LR, .25 R.F., .32 R.F. 24-inch round bbl; other lengths were available. Weight: 4.5 lbs. Sights: Open rear; Rocky Mountain front. Plain straight-grip stock, small tapered forearm. Made from 1894 to 1935.

FAVORITE NO. 18 . . . . **NiB $422 Ex $300 Gd $179**
Same as Favorite No. 17 except w/Vernier peep rear sight, leaf middle sight, Beach combination front sight.

FAVORITE NO. 19 . . . . **NiB $439 Ex $333 Gd $220**
Same as Favorite No. 17 except w/Lyman combination rear sight, leaf middle sight, Lyman front sight.

FAVORITE NO. 20 . . . . **NiB $420 Ex $325 Gd $215**
Same as Favorite No. 17 except w/smoothbore barrel.

FAVORITE NO. 27 . . . . **NiB $439 Ex $333 Gd $220**
Same as Favorite No. 17 except w/octagon bbl.

FAVORITE NO. 28 . . . . **NiB $439 Ex $333 Gd $220**
Same as Favorite No. 18 except w/octagon bbl.

FAVORITE NO. 29 . . . . **NiB $439 Ex $333 Gd $220**
Same as Favorite No. 19 except w/octagon bbl.

WALNUT HILL NO. 417-0
SINGLE-SHOT TARGET RIFLE . . . . . . **NiB $909 Ex $777 Gd $530**
Lever-action. Calibers: .22 LR only, .22 Short only, .22 Hornet. 28-inch heavy bbl. (extra heavy 29-inch bbl. also available). Weight: 10.5 lbs. Sights: Lyman No. 52L extension rear; 17A front, scope bases mounted on bbl. Target stock w/full pistol-grip, beavertail forearm, bbl. band, swivels, sling. Made from 1932 to 1947.

WALNUT HILL NO. 417-1 . . . **NiB $909 Ex $750 Gd $521**
Same as No. 417-0 except w/Lyman No. 48L receiver sight.

WALNUT HILL NO. 417-2 . . . **NiB $909 Ex $750 Gd $521**
Same as No. 417-0 except w/Lyman No. 144 tang sight.

WALNUT HILL NO. 417-3 . . . **NiB $909 Ex $750 Gd $521**
Same as No. 417-0 except w/o sights.

WALNUT HILL NO. 417.5
SINGLE-SHOT RIFLE. . . . . **NiB $909 Ex $750 Gd $521**
Lever-action. Calibers: .22 LR, .22 WMR, .25 R.F., .22 Hornet. 28-inch bbl. Weight: 8.5 lbs. Sights: Lyman No. 144 tang peep, folding middle; bead front. Sporting stock w/pistol-grip, semi-beavertail forearm, swivels, sling. Made from 1932 to 1940.

WALNUT HILL NO. 418
SINGLE-SHOT RIFLE. . . . . **NiB $988 Ex $768 Gd $589**
Lever-action. Takedown. Calibers: .22 LR only, .22 Short only. 26-inch bbl. Weight: 6.5 lbs. Sights: Lyman No. 144 tang peep; blade front. Pistol-grip stock, semi-beavertail forearm, swivels, sling. Made from 1932 to 1940.

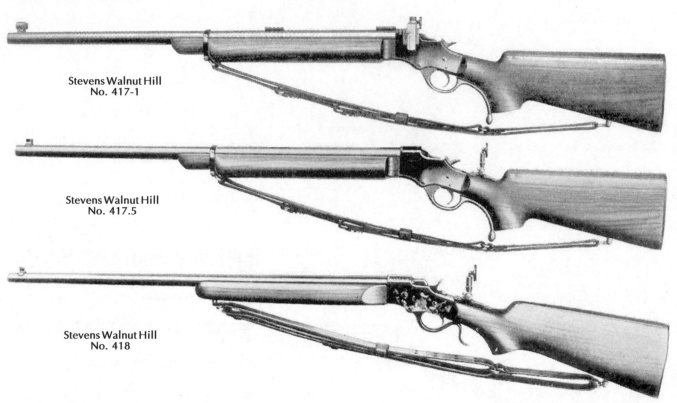

Stevens Walnut Hill
No. 417-1

Stevens Walnut Hill
No. 417.5

Stevens Walnut Hill
No. 418

WALNUT HILL NO. 418-5 . . . NiB $988 Ex $768 Gd $589
Same as No. 418 except also available in calibers .22 WRF and
.25 Stevens R.F., w/Lyman No. 2A tang peep sight, bead front sight.

**MODEL 15 SINGLE-SHOT
BOLT-ACTION RIFLE** . . . . NiB $200 Ex $155 Gd $110
Takedown. Caliber: .22 LR, Long, Short. 22-inch bbl. Weight: 4 lbs.
Sights: Open rear, bead front. Plain pistol-grip stock. Made 1937 to 1948.

**MODEL 82 BOLT-ACTION
SINGLE-SHOT RIFLE**. . . . . . . NiB $178 Ex $144 Gd $115
Takedown. Caliber: .22 LR, Long, Short. 22-inch bbl. Weight: 4 lbs.
Sights: Open rear; gold bead front. Plain pistol-grip stock w/grooved
forearm. Made from 1935 to 1939.

**MODEL 83 BOLT-ACTION
SINGLE-SHOT RIFLE**. . . . . . . NiB $200 Ex $155 Gd $110
Takedown. Calibers: .22 LR, Long, Short; .22 WRF, .25 Stevens R.F.
24-inch bbl. Weight: 4.5 lbs. Sights: Peep rear; open middle; hooded
front. Plain pistol-grip stock w/grooved forearm. Made 1935 to 1939.

MODEL 84. . . . . NiB $220 Ex $190 Gd $128
Same as Model 86 except w/5-round detachable box magazine.
Pre-1948 rifles of this model were designated Springfield Model 84,
later known as Stevens Model 84. Made from 1940 to 1965.

MODEL 84-S (084) . . . . NiB $220 Ex $190 Gd $128
Same as Model 84 except w/peep rear sight and hooded front sight.
Pre-1948 rifles of this model were designated Springfield Model
084, later known as Stevens Model 84-S. Disc.

MODEL 85. . . . . NiB $244 Ex $199 Gd $139
Same as Stevens Model 87 except w/5-round detachable box magazine. Made
1939 to date. Pre-1948 rifles of this model were designated Springfield Model
85, currently known as Stevens Model 85. Earlier models command slight
premiums.

MODEL 85-S (085) . . . . NiB $224 Ex $167 Gd $126
Same as Model 85 except w/peep rear sight and hooded front sight.
Pre-1948 models were designated Springfield Model 085; also
known as Stevens Model 85-S.

**MODEL 86
BOLT-ACTION** . . . . NiB $224 Ex $167 Gd $126
Takedown. Caliber: .22 LR, Long, Short. Tubular magazine holds
15 LR, 17 Long, 21 Short. 24-inch bbl. Weight: 6 lbs. Sights: Open
rear, gold bead front. Pistol-grip stock, black forend tip on later
production. Made 1935 to 1965. Note: The Springfield brand name
was disc. in 1948.

MODEL 86-S (086) . . . . NiB $230 Ex $172 Gd $128
Same as Model 86 except w/peep rear sight and hooded front sight.
Pre-1948 rifles of this model were designated as Springfield Model
086, later known as Stevens Model 86-S. Disc.

MODEL 87-S (087) . . . . NiB $233 Ex $215 Gd $156
Same as Stevens Model 87 except w/peep rear sight and
hooded front sight. Pre-1948 rifles of this model were designated as Springfield Model 087, later known as Stevens Model
87-S. Disc.

STEYR DAIMLER PUCH A.G. — Steyr, Austria
See also listings under Mannlicher.

**AUG-SA
SEMIAUTOMATIC RIFLE**. . . . . . NiB $4220 Ex $3370 Gd $2340
Gas-operated. Caliber: .223 Rem. (5.56mm). Thirty or 40-round
magazine. 20-inch bbl. standard; optional 16-inch or 24-inch heavy
bbl. w/folding bipod. 31 inches overall. Weight: 8.5 lbs. Sights:
Integral 1.5x scope and mount. Green high-impact synthetic stock
w/folding vertical grip.

Stevens-Springfield
Model 15

Stevens-Springfield
Model 82

Stevens-Springfield
Model 83

Stevens-Springfield
Model 84

Stevens-Springfield
Model 85

Stevens-Springfield
Model 86-S

SMALL BORE CARBINE . . . . . NiB $440 Ex $300 Gd $166
Bolt-action repeater. Caliber: .22 LR. Five round detachable box magazine. 19.5-inch bbl. Sights: Leaf rear; hooded bead front. Mannlicher-type stock, checkered, swivels. Made 1953 to 1967.

STOEGER RIFLE — Manufactured by Franz Jaeger & Co., Suhl, Germany; dist. in the U.S. by A. F. Stoeger, Inc., New York, NY

HORNET RIFLE. . . . . NiB $1388 Ex $1008 Gd $659
Same specifications as Herold Rifle, designed and built on a Miniature Mauser-type action. See listing under Herold Bolt-Action Repeating Sporting Rifle for additional specifications. Imported during the 1930s.

SURVIVAL ARMS — Orange, Connecticut

AR-7 EXPLORER. . . . . NiB $180 Ex $155 Gd $98
Caliber: .22 LR. Eight round magazine. Weight: 3 lbs. Polymer stocks. Drift adj. sights. Disassembles into five separate elements,

allowing barrel, action and magazine to fit into buttstock; assembles quickly w/o tools. Choice of camo, silvertone or black matte finishes. Made from 1992 to 1995.

THOMPSON/CENTER ARMS — (Div. of Smith & Wesson, Springfield, MA; formerly Rochester, NH)

CONTENDER CARBINE
Calibers: .22 LR, .22 Hornet, .222 Rem., .223 Rem., 7mm T.C.U., 7x30 Waters, .30-30 Win., .35 Rem., .44 Mag., .357 Rem. Max. and .410 bore. 21-inch interchangeable bbls. 35 inches overall. Adj. iron sights. Checkered American walnut or Rynite stock and forend. Made from 1986 to 2000.
Standard model (rifle calibers) NiB $466 Ex $287 Gd $198
Standard model (.410 bore). . . NiB $459 Ex $280 Gd $210
Rynite stock model
(rifle calibers). . . . . NiB $390 Ex $290 Gd $245
Rynite stock model (.410 bore) NiB $390 Ex $300 Gd $244
Youth model (all calibers). . . . NiB $495 Ex $320 Gd $235
Extra bbl. (rifle calibers), add $25
Extra bbl. (.410 bore), add $35

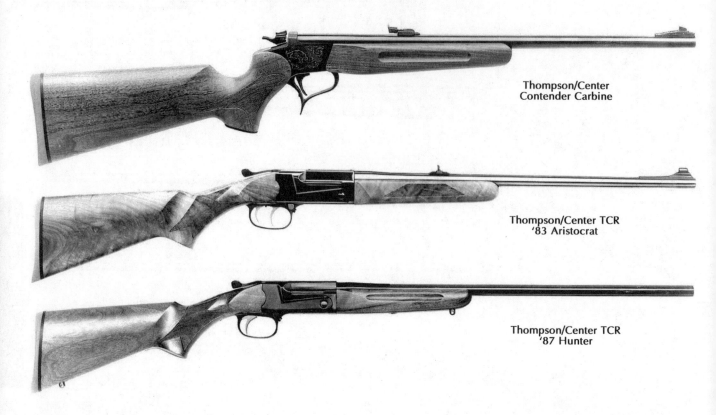

Thompson/Center
Contender Carbine

Thompson/Center TCR
'83 Aristocrat

Thompson/Center TCR
'87 Hunter

CONTENDER CARBINE
SURVIVAL SYSTEM. . . . . **NiB $655 Ex $488 Gd $370**
Similar to standard Contender Carbine w/Rynite stock and forend. Comes w/two 16.25-inch bbls. chambered in .223 and .45/.410 bore. Camo Cordura case.

STAINLESS CONTENDER CARBINE
Same as standard Contender Carbine Model, except stainless steel w/blued sights. Calibers: .22 LR, .22 Hornet, .223 Rem., 7-30 Waters, .30-30 Win., .410. Walnut or Rynite stock and forend. Made from 1993 to 2000.
Walnut stock model . . . . **NiB $445 Ex $390 Gd $325**
Rynite stock model. . . . . **NiB $495 Ex $425 Gd $300**
Youth stock model . . . . **NiB $467 Ex $388 Gd $287**
Extra bbls. (rifle calibers), add. **$25**

TCR '83/ARISTOCRAT MODEL NiB $497 Ex $445 Gd $277
Break frame, overlever action. Calibers: .223 Rem., .22/250 Rem., .243 Win., 7mm Rem. Mag., .30-06 Springfield. Interchangeable bbls.: 23 inches in length. Weight: 6 lbs., 14 oz. American walnut stock and forearm, checkered, black rubber recoil pad, cheekpiece. Made from 1983 to 1987.
Aristocrat model. . . . . **NiB $569 Ex $439 Gd $280**
Extra bbl. (rifle calibers), add **$278**

TCR '87 HUNTER RIFLE . . . . . **NiB $544 Ex $345 Gd $200**
Similar to TCR '83 except in calibers .22 Hornet, ..222 Rem., 223 Rem., .22-250 Rem., .243 Win., .270 Win., 7mm-08, .308 Win., .30-06, .32-40 Win. Also 12-ga. slug and 10- and 12-ga. field bbls. 23-inch standard or 25.88-inch heavy bbl. interchangeable. 39.5 to 43.38 inches overall. Weight: 6 lbs., 14 oz. to 7.5 lbs. Iron sights optional. Checkered American black walnut buttstock w/fluted end. Disc. 1992.

Extra bbl. (rifle calibers, 10- & 12-ga. field), add **$250**
Extra bbl. (12-ga. slug), add **$300**

ICON. . . . . **NiB $1167 Ex $855 Gd $766**
Bolt action. Cal.: .22-250 Rem., .270 Win., .30-06, .300 Win. Mag., .308 Win., .30 TC, 6.5 Creedmoor, 7mm Mag. Bbl.: 24 inches. Medium or long action, hinged floor plate (on long action). Stock: Black synthetic or RealTree camo, checkered American walnut, classic walnut or Ultra Wood; pistol grip and forearm. Adj. trigger, cocking indicator, three-shot magazine (on medium action). Jeweled bolt handle. Weaver-style bases. Weight: 7.5 pounds. Guaranteed to shoot 1-inch or less at 100 yards.
Walnut stock models, add. **$75**

ICON PRECISION HUNTER . **NiB $1355 Ex $988 Gd $778**
Bolt action. Cal.: .204 Ruger, .223 Rem., .22-250 Rem., .243 Win., 6.5 Creedmoor, .308 Win. Bbl.: 22 inches, fluted; 5R button rifling. Tactical-style bolt handle. Stock: Brown synthetic with cheekpiece and beavertail fore end. Detachable 3-round magazine with single-shot adapter. Picatinny rail, adj. trigger, sling studs.

ICON WARLORD. . . . . **NiB $1370 Ex $1127 Gd $888**
Bolt action. Cal.: .308 Win. or .338 Lapua; 5- or 10-round magazine. Bbl.: Fluted, stainless steel, hand lapped. Stock: Carbon fiber tactical style with adj. cheek piece available in OD, flat black or desert sand. Adj. trigger, Picatinny rail. Weight: 12.75 to 13.75 lbs.

VENTURE. . . . . **NiB $632 Ex $495 Gd $375**
Bolt action. Cal.: 270 Win., .30-06, 7 mm Rem. Mag., .300 Win. Mag. Bbl.: 24 inches, tapered match grade with 5R button rifling.

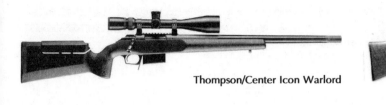

Thompson/Center Icon Warlord

Thompson/Center Model R-55 Classic

Thompson/Center Encore Katahdin

Stock: Black synthetic, sporter design, textured grip. Adj. trigger, two-position safety.

VENTURE PREDATOR . . . . . . **NiB $690 Ex $559 Gd $433**
Bolt action. Cal.: .204 Ruger, .223 Rem., .22-250 Rem. or .308 Win. Bbl.: 22 inches, fluted, 3-round magazine. Stock: Composite with 100% Realtree Max-1 camo coating; Hogue panels, Weather Shield bolt handle. Weight. 6.75 lbs.

SILVER LYNX . . . . **NiB $488 Ex $390 Gd $300**
Semi-auto. Cal.: .22 LR. Bbl.: 20 inches, match grade; 5-round magazine, stainless steel action and bbl. Stock: Black composite with Monte Carlo cheek piece. Weight: 5.5 lbs.

MODEL R-55 CLASSIC . . . . . . **NiB $629 Ex $428 Gd $326**
Semi-auto. Cal.: .17 Mach 2, .22 LR. Bbl.: 22 inches, match grade; adj. rear sight; blue finish. Blow-back action. Smooth Monte Carlo walnut stock. Weight: 5.5 lbs.
R-55 Target . . . . **NiB $677 Ex $466 Gd $389**
R-55 Sporter. . . . . **NiB $519 Ex $405 Gd $310**

ENCORE RIFLE. . . . . **NiB $788 Ex $521 Gd $379**
Single-shot, break-action. Cal.: Rimfire and centerfire from .17 Mach 2 to .45-70 Gov't. Bbl.: 24 to 16 inches, interchangeable. Hammer block safety, trigger guard opening lever. Stock: Synthetic black, Realtree camo or American walnut; smooth forearm, Monte Carlo stock w/pistol grip.; adj. rear sight.
W/extra blued bbls., add. $245
Camo models, add $150
W/thumbhole stock, add $227
.17 Mach 2, add $75
W/stainless bbl., add $400
Hunter pkg. (scope, bases, case), add $300

ENCORE KATAHDIN . . . . **NiB $633 Ex $467 Gd $379**
Same as Encore but with 18-inch blued bbl. Cal.: .444 Marlin, .450 Marlin or .45-70 Gov't. Stock: Black composite. Fiber optic sights, drilled and tapped for scope. Weight: 6.6 lbs. Made from 2002 to 2005.

PRO HUNTER RIFLE. . . . . . . **NiB $944 Ex $670 Gd $433**
Cal.: Various. Bbl.: 28 inches, stainless steel. Recoil reducing Flex-Tech stock (thumbhole option) in black or camo.

W/camo stock, add $100
W/ extra bbl., add $400

HOTSHOT (CAMO STOCK) . . **NiB $395 Ex $299 Gd $214**
W/pink camo stock, add $25
Youth model. Cal.: 22 LR. Bbl.: 19 inches. Stock: Black synthetic, Realtree AP camo or AP pink camo. Auto safety; drilled and tapped for scope. Weight: 3 lbs.

TIKKA RIFLES — Manufactured by Sako, Ltd. of Riihimaki, Finland & Armi Marocchi in Italy

Imported by Beretta USA

NOTE: *Tikka New Generation, Battue and Continental series bolt action rifles are being manufactured by Sako, Ltd., in Finland. Tikka O/U rifles (previously Valmet) are being manufactured in Italy by Armi Marocchi. For earlier importation see additional listings under Ithaca LSA and Valmet 412S models.*

T3 HUNTER . . . . **NiB $655 Ex $535 Gd $390**
Calibers:..223, .22-250, .243Win., .308 Win., .25-06, .270 Win., 6.5x55, 270 WSM, 7mm Rem. Mag., .30-06, 300 WSM, .300 Win. Mag., .338 Win. Mag., Bbl: 22 7/16 inches (24 3/8 in magnum calibers. Weight: 6 3/4 pounds. No sights. Walnut stock with rubber butt pad. Introduced 2003.

T3 LAMINATED
STAINLESS . . . . **NiB $765 Ex $689 Gd $590**
Same as T3 Hunter but with stainless barrel and action; laminated stock.

T3 LITE . . . . **NiB $555 Ex $489 Gd $410**
Similar to T3 Hunter but with synthetic stock; weight: 6 pounds, 3 ounces. Introduced 2003.

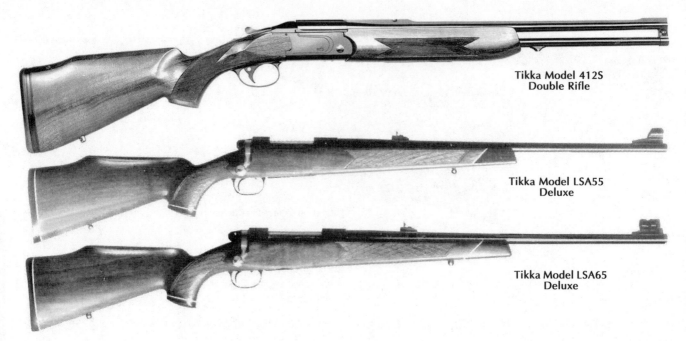

Tikka Model 412S
Double Rifle

Tikka Model LSA55
Deluxe

Tikka Model LSA65
Deluxe

T3 LITE STAINLESS . . . . NiB $589 Ex $469 Gd $370
Same as T3 Lite but with stainless barrel and action.

T3 TACTICAL . . . . NiB $1469 Ex $1210 Gd $1077
Calibers: .223, .308 Win. Similar to T3 Hunter but designed for
law enforcement. Bbl.: 20 inches. Black phosphate finish, synthetic stock with adjustable comb. Five round detachable magazine.
Picatinny rail on action, fitted for muzzle brake and bipod use.

T3 VARMINT . . . . NiB $844 Ex $707 Gd $567
Calibers: .223, .22-250, .308 Win. Similar to T3 Hunter but with
heavy bull barrel, synthetic stock, adjustable trigger. Five round
detachable magazine.

**T3 VARMINT
STAINLESS** . . . . NiB $844 Ex $707 Gd $567
Similar to T3 Varmint but with stainless barrel and action.

MODEL 412S DOUBLE RIFLE
Calibers: .308 Win., .30-06, 9.3x74R. 24-inch bbl. w/quarter rib
machined for scope mounts; automatic ejectors (9.3x74R only). 40
inches overall. Weight: 8.5 lbs. Ramp front and folding adj. rear
sight. Barrel selector on trigger. European walnut buttstock and
forearm. Model 412S was replaced by the 512S version in 1994.
Imported from 1989 to 1993.
**Model 412S
(disc. 1993)** . . . . NiB $1135 Ex $944 Gd $725
**Extra bbl. assembly
(O/U shotgun), add** $707
**Extra bbl. assembly
(O/U Combo), add** $800
**Extra bbl. assembly
(OU/rifle), add** $1050

MODEL 512S DOUBLE RIFLE
Formerly Valmet 412S. In 1994, following the joint venture of
1989, the model designation was changed to 512S. Imported from
1994 to 1997.
Model 512S . . . . .NiB $1559 Ex $1440 Gd $1100
W/extra bbl. assembly (O/U rifle), add $800

LSAFF DELUXE . . . . NiB $590 Ex $534 Gd $450
Same as LSA55 Standard except w/rollover cheekpiece, rosewood
grip cap and forend tip, skip checkering, high-luster blue. Imported
from 1965 to 1988.

LSA55 SPORTER . . . . NiB $580 Ex $482 Gd $369
Same as LSA55 except has 22.8-inch heavy bbl. w/o sights, special
stock w/beavertail forearm, not available in 6mm Rem. Weighs 9
lbs. Imported from 1965 to 1988.

**LSA55 STANDARD
BOLT-ACTION REPEATER** . . . . NiB $555 Ex $389 Gd $244
Mauser-type action. Calibers: .222 Rem., .22-250, 6mm Rem.
Mag., .243 Win., .308 Win. Three round clip magazine. 22.8-inch
bbl. Weight: 6.8 lbs. Sights: Folding leaf rear; hooded ramp front.
Checkered walnut stock w/Monte Carlo cheekpiece, swivels. Made
from 1965-88.

LSA65 DELUXE . . . . NiB $598 Ex $522 Gd $369
Same as LSA65 Standard except w/special features of LSA55
Deluxe. Imported from 1970 to 1988.

LSA65 STANDARD . . . . NiB $495 Ex $398 Gd $277
Same as LSA55 Standard except calibers: .25-06, 6.5x55 .270
Win., .30-06. Five round magazine, 22-inch bbl., weight: 7.5 lbs.
Imported 1970 to 1988.

MODEL M 55
Bolt action. Calibers: .222 Rem., .22-250 Rem., .223 Rem. .243
Win., .308 Win. (6mm Rem. and 17 Rem. available in Standard
and Deluxe models only). 23.2-inch bbl. (24.8-inch in Sporter and
Heavy Barrel models). 42.8 inches overall (44 inches in Sporter
and Heavy Barrel models). Weight: 7.25 to 9 lbs. Monte Carlo-style
stock w/pistol-grip. Sling swivels. Imported 1965 to 1988.

Continental	NiB $745	Ex $560	Gd $420
Deluxe model	NiB $808	Ex $579	Gd $443
Sporter	NiB $733	Ex $577	Gd $400
Sporter w/sights	NiB $755	Ex $572	Gd $390
Standard	NiB $669	Ex $544	Gd $367
Super Sporter	NiB $833	Ex $466	Gd $398
Super Sporter w/sights	NiB $909	Ex $478	Gd $514
Trapper	NiB $755	Ex $556	Gd $443

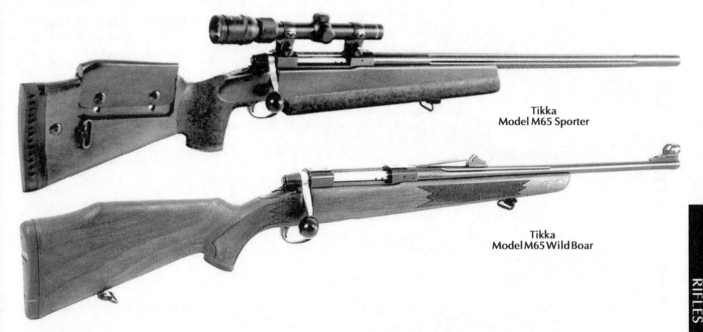

**Tikka
Model M65 Sporter**

**Tikka
Model M65 Wild Boar**

MODEL M65
Bolt action. Calibers: .25-06, .270 Win., .308 Win., .30-06, 7mm Rem. Mag., .300 Win. Mag. (Sporter and Heavy Bbl. models in .270 Win., .308 Win. and .30-06 only). 22.4-inch bbl. (24.8-inch in Sporter and Heavy Bbl. models). 43.2 inches overall (44 inches in Sporter, 44.8 inches in Heavy Bbl.). Weight: 7.5 to 9.9 lbs. Monte Carlo-style stock w/pistol-grip. Disc. 1989.

Continental	NiB $755	Ex $572	Gd $439
Deluxe Magnum	NiB $800	Ex $677	Gd $495
Deluxe model	NiB $770	Ex $587	Gd $467
Magnum	NiB $709	Ex $540	Gd $440
Sporter	NiB $579	Ex $555	Gd $398
Sporter w/sights	NiB $789	Ex $645	Gd $445
Standard	NiB $670	Ex $690	Gd $479
Super Sporter	NiB $898	Ex $690	Gd $489
Super Sporter w/sights	NiB $909	Ex $695	Gd $494
Super Sporter Master	NiB $1143	Ex $944	Gd $643

MODEL M65 WILD BOAR ... NiB $790 Ex $650 Gd $469
Same general specifications as Model M 65 except 20.8-inch bbl., overall length of 41.6 inches, weight: of 7.5 lbs. Disc. 1989.

NEW GENERATION RIFLES
Short-throw bolt available in three action lengths. Calibers: .22-250 Rem., .223 Rem., .243 Win., .308 Win., (medium action) .25-06 Rem., .270 Win., .30.06, (Long Action) 7mm Rem. Mag., .300 Win. Mag., .338 Win. Mag., (Magnum Action). 22- to 26-inch bbl. 42.25 to 46 inches overall. Weight: 7.2 to 8.5 lbs. Available w/o sights or w/hooded front and open rear sight on quarter rib. Quick-release 3- or 5-round detachable magazine w/recessed side release. Barrel selector on trigger and cocking indicators in tang. European walnut buttstock and forearm matte lacquer finish. Imported 1989 to 1994.
Standard calibers .... NiB $769 Ex $688 Gd $487
Magnum calibers, add $50

PREMIUM GRADE RIFLE
Similar to New Generation rifles except w/hand-checkered deluxe wood stock w/roll-over check-piece and rosewood grip cap and forend tip. High polished blued finish. Imported from 1989 to 1994.
Standard calibers .... NiB $923 Ex $755 Gd $488
Magnum calibers, add $50

WHITETAIL BOLT-ACTION RIFLE SERIES
New Generation design in multiple model configurations and three action lengths chambered .22-250 to .338 Win. Mag.

BATTUE MODEL
Similar to Hunter Model except designed for snapshooting w/hooded front and open rear sights on quarter rib. Blued finish. Checkered select walnut stock w/matt lacquered finish. Imported 1991 to 1997.
Battue model (standard w/sights) NiB $568 Ex $466 Gd $388
Magnum calibers, add $50

CONTINENTAL MODEL
Similar to Hunter Model except w/prone-style stock w/wider fore-arm and 26-inch heavy bbl. chambered for 17 Rem., .22-250 Rem., .223 Rem., .308 Win. (Varmint); .25-06 Rem., .270 Win., 7mm Rem. Mag., .300 Win. Mag. (Long Range). Weight: 8.6 lbs. Imported from 1991 to 2003.
Continental Long-Range model NiB $690 Ex $558 Gd $390
Continental Varmint model ... NiB $640 Ex $500 Gd $355
Magnum calibers, add 40%

SPORTER MODEL .... NiB $909 Ex $779 Gd $633
Similar to Hunter Model except 23.5-inch bbl. Five round detachable mazigine. Chambered .22-250 Rem., .223 Rem., .308 Win. Weight: 8.6 lbs. Adjustable buttplate and cheekpiece w/stippled pistol grip and forend. Imported from 1998 to 2003.

WHITETAIL HUNTER MODEL
Calibers: .22-250 Rem., .223 Rem., .243 Win., .25-06 Rem., .270 Win., 7mm Rem. Mag., .308 Win .30.06, .300 Win. Mag., .338 Win. Mag. Three or 5-round detachable box magazine. 20.5- to 24.5-inch bbl. with no sights. 42 to 44.5 inches overall. Weight: 7 to 7.5 lbs. Adj. single-stage or single-set trigger. Blued or stainless finish. All-Weather synthetic or checkered select walnut stock w/ matt lacquered finish. Imported from 1991 to 2002.
Standard model .... NiB $633 Ex $523 Gd $389
Deluxe model .... NiB $689 Ex $534 Gd $445
Synthetic model .... NiB $689 Ex $534 Gd $445
Stainless model .... NiB $689 Ex $534 Gd $445
Magnum calibers, add $50
Left-hand model, add $100

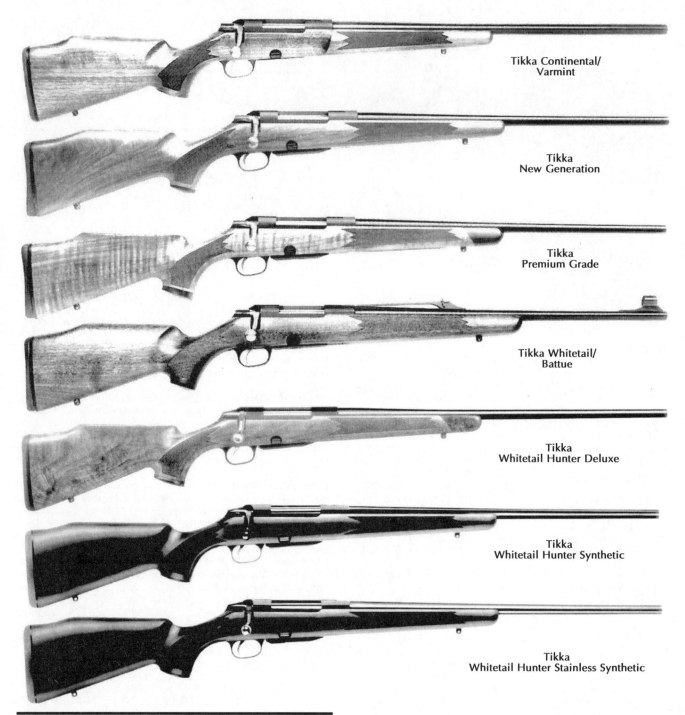

Tikka Continental/
Varmint

Tikka
New Generation

Tikka
Premium Grade

Tikka Whitetail/
Battue

Tikka
Whitetail Hunter Deluxe

Tikka
Whitetail Hunter Synthetic

Tikka
Whitetail Hunter Stainless Synthetic

UBERTI RIFLES — Lakeville, Connecticut. Manufactured By Aldo Uberti, Ponte Zanano, Italy. Imported by Stoeger Industries, Accokeek, MD

MODEL 1866 SPORTING RIFLE

Replica of Winchester Model 1866 lever-action repeater. Calibers: .22 LR, .22 WMR, .38 Spec., .44-40, .45 LC. 24.25-inch octagonal bbl. 43.25 inches overall. Weight: 8.25 lbs. Blade front sight, rear elevation leaf. Brass frame and buttplate. Bbl., magazine tube, other metal parts blued. Walnut buttstock and forearm.

Model 1866 Rifle . . . . NiB $976 Ex $667 Gd $390

Model 1866 Carbine
(19-inch round bbl.) . . . . NiB $944 Ex $600 Gd $409
Model 1866 Trapper
(16-inch bbl.)
Disc. 1989 . . . . NiB $1145 Ex $855 Gd $600
Model 1866
Rimfire
(Indian Rifle) . . . . NiB $744 Ex $523 Gd $379
Model 1866 Rimfire
(Indian Carbine) . . . . NiB $744 Ex $523 Gd $379

RIFLES

Uberti Model
1873 Carbine

MODEL 1873 SPORTING RIFLE
Replica of Winchester Model 1873 lever-action repeater. Calibers: .22 LR, .22 WMR, .38 Spec., .357 Mag., .44-40, .45 LC. 24.25- or 30-inch octagonal bbl. 43.25 inches overall. Weight: 8 lbs. Blade front sight; adj. open rear. Color case-hardened frame. Bbl., magazine tube, hammer, lever and buttplate blued. Walnut buttstock and forearm.
Model 1873 Rifle . . . . NiB $1095 Ex $809 Gd $572
Model 1873 Carbine
(19-inch round bbl.) . . . . NiB $790 Ex $666 Gd $445
Model 1873 Trapper
(16-inch bbl.,
disc. 1990) . . . . NiB $1095 Ex $809 Gd $572

HENRY RIFLE
Replica of Henry lever-action repeating rifle. Calibers: .44-40, .45 LC. 24.5-inch half-octagon bbl. 43.75 inches overall. Weight: 9.25 lbs. Blade front sight; rear sight adj. for elevation. Brass frame, buttplate and magazine follower. Bbl., magazine tube and remaining parts blued. Walnut buttstock.
Henry Rifle. . . . . NiB $1177 Ex $808 Gd $590
Henry Carbine
(22.5-inch bbl.) . . . . NiB $1177 Ex $808 Gd $590
Henry Trapper
(16- or 18-inch bbl.). . . . . . . NiB $1177 Ex $808 Gd $590
Steel frame, add $100

MODEL 1875
ARMY TARGET. . . . . NiB $455 Ex $360 Gd $300
Calibers: .357 Mag., .44-40 Colt. Six-round cylinder. Bbl.: 18 inches. Overall length: 37 inches. Weight: 4 1/2 pounds. Carbine version of Model 1875 single-action revolver. Sights: Adjustable rear, ramp front. Plain walnut stock, polished brass butt plate and trigger guard. Case-hardened frame. Blued or nickel-plated cylinder and barrel. Made in Italy. Introduced in 1987, discontinued 1989.
Nickel finish, add. $50

ROLLING BLOCK
BABY CARBINE . . . . NiB $450 Ex $380 Gd $319
Calibers: .22 LR, .22WMR, .22 Hornet, .357 Mag. Bbl.: 22 inches. Overall length: 35 1/2 inches. Weight: 4 3/4 pounds. Copy of Remington New Model No. 4 carbine featuring brass butt plate and trigger guard; blued barrel; color case-hardened frame. Introduced in 1986.

ULTRA-HI PRODUCTS COMPANY — Hawthorne, New Jersey

MODEL 2200 SINGLE-SHOT
BOLT-ACTION RIFLE . . . . NiB $235 Ex $166 Gd $120
Caliber: .22 LR, Long, Short. .23-inch bbl. Weight: 5 lbs. Sights: Open rear; blade front. Monte Carlo stock w/pistol grip. Made in Japan. Intro. 1977; Disc.

ULTRA LIGHT ARMS COMPANY—Granville, West Virginia

MODEL 20 BOLT-ACTION RIFLE
Calibers: .22-250 Rem., .243 Win., 6mm Rem., .250-3000 Savage, .257 Roberts, .257 Ack., 7mm Mauser, 7mm Ack., 7mm-08 Rem., .284 Win., .300 Savage, .308 Win., .358 Win. Box magazine. 22-inch ultra light bbl. Weight: 4.75 lbs. No sights. Synthetic stock of Kevlar or graphite finished, seven different colors. Nonglare matte or bright metal finish. Medium-length action available L.H. models. Made from 1985 to 1999.
Standard model . . . . NiB $2270 Ex $2056 Gd $1190
Left-hand model, add $150

MODEL 20S BOLT-ACTION RIFLE
Same general specifications as Model 20 except w/short action in calibers 17 Rem., .222 Rem., .223 Rem., .22 Hornet only.
Standard model . . . . NiB $2467 Ex $2144 Gd $1180
Left-hand model, add $126

MODEL 24 BOLT-ACTION RIFLE
Same general specifications as Model 20 except w/long action in calibers .25-06, .270 Win., .30-06 and 7mm Express only.
Standard model . . . . NiB $2350 Ex $2123 Gd $1179
Left-hand model, add. $126

MODEL 28 BOLT-ACTION RIFLE NiB $2709 Ex $2033 Gd $1190
Same general specifications as Model 20 except w/long magnum action in calibers .264 Win. Mag., 7mm Rem. Mag., .300 Win. Mag., .338 Win. Mag. only. Offered w/recoil arrester. Left-hand model available.

MODEL 40 BOLT-ACTION RIFLE
Similar to Model 28 except in calibers .300 Wby. and .416 Rigby. Weight: 5.5 lbs. Made from 1994 to 1999.
Standard model . . . . NiB $2770 Ex $2055 Gd $1290
Left-hand, model, add. $126

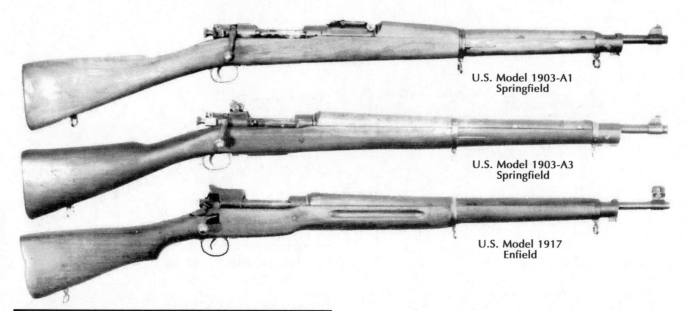

U.S. Model 1903-A1
Springfield

U.S. Model 1903-A3
Springfield

U.S. Model 1917
Enfield

UNIQUE RIFLE — Hendaye, France. Manufactured by Manufacture d'Armes des Pyrénées Francaises

T66 MATCH RIFLE . . . . NiB $469 Ex $388 Gd $289
Single-shot bolt-action rifle. Caliber: .22 LR. 25.5-inch bbl. Weight: 10.5 lbs. Sights: Micrometer aperture rear; globe front. French walnut target stock w/Monte Carlo comb, bull pistol-grip, wide and deep forearm, stippled grip surfaces, adj. swivel on accessory track, adj. rubber buttplate. Made in 1966. Disc.

U.S. MILITARY RIFLES — Manufactured by Springfield Armory, Remington Arms Co., Winchester Repeating Arms Co., Inland Mfg. Div. of G.M.C., and other contractors. See notes.

Unless otherwise indicated, the following U.S. military rifles were mfg. at Springfield Armory, Springfield, Mass.

MODEL 1898
KRAG-JORGENSEN CARBINENiB $2100 Ex $1879 Gd $1100
Same general specifications as Model 1898 Rifle except w/22-inch bbl., weight: 8 lbs., carbine-type stock. Note: The foregoing specifications apply, in general, to Carbine models 1896 and 1899, which differed from Model 1898 only in minor details.

MODEL 1898
KRAG-JORGENSEN MILITARY RIFLENiB $2100 Ex $1879 Gd $1100
Bolt action. Caliber: .30-40 Krag. Five round hinged box magazine. 30-inch bbl. Weight: 9 lbs. Sights: Adj. rear; blade front. Military-type stock, straight grip. Note: The foregoing specifications apply, in general, to Rifle models 1892 and 1896, which differed from Model 1898.

MODEL 1903 MARK I SPRINGFIELDNiB $2144 Ex $1844 Gd $945
Same as Standard Model 1903 except altered to permit use of the Pedersen Device. This device, officially designated "U.S. Automatic Pistol Model 1918," converted the M/1903 to a semiautomatic weapon firing a .30 caliber cartridge similar to .32 automatic pistol ammunition. Mark I rifles have a slot milled in the left side of the receiver to serve as an ejection port when the Pedersen Device was in

use; these rifles were also fitted w/a special sear and cut-off. Some 65,000 of these devices were manufactured and, presumably, a like number of M/1903 rifles were converted to handle them. During the early 1930s, all Pedersen Devices were ordered destroyed and the Mark I rifles were reconverted by replacement of the special sear and cut-off w/standard components. Some 20-odd specimens are known to have escaped destruction and are in government museums and private collections. Probably more are extant. Rarely is a Pedersen Device offered for sale, so a current value cannot be assigned. However, many of the altered rifles were bought by members of the National Rifle Association through the Director of Civilian Marksmanship. Value shown is for the Mark I rifle w/o the Pedersen Device.

MODEL 1903 NATIONAL
MATCH SPRINGFIELD . . . NiB $1755 Ex $1577 Gd $1109
Same general specifications as Standard Model 1903 except specially selected w/star-gauged bbl., Type C pistol-grip U.S. Model 1903 National Match Springfield (Con't) stock, polished bolt assembly; early types have headless firing pin assembly and reversed safety lock. Produced especially for target shooting.

MODEL 1903 SPRINGFIELD MILITARY RIFLE
Modified Mauser-type bolt action. Caliber: .30-06. Five round box magazine. 23.79-inch bbl. Weight: 8.75 lbs. Sights: Adj. rear; blade front. Military-type stock straight grip. Note: M/1903 rifles of Springfield manufacture w/serial numbers under 800,000 (1903 to 1918) have casehardened receivers; those between 800,000 and 1,278,767 (1918 to 1927) were double heat-treated; rifles numbered over 1,278,767 have nickle steel bolts and receivers. Rock Island production from No. 1 to 285,507 have case-hardened receivers. Improved heat treatment was adopted in May 1918 with No. 285,207; about three months later, with No. 319,921, the use of nickel steel was begun, but the production of some double-heat-treated carbon-steel receivers and bolts continued. Made 1903 to 1930 at Springfield Armory during WWI, M/1903 rifles were also made at Rock Island Arsenal, Rock Island, Ill.
W/case-hardened receiver. NiB $5566 Ex $4769 Gd $2270
W/double heat-treated receiverNiB $4410 Ex $3636 Gd $1645
W/nickel steel receiver . . . . NiB $1707 Ex $1530 Gd $977

MODEL 1903 SPRINGFIELD SPORTERNiB $1449 Ex $1978 Gd $899
Same general specifications as National Match except w/sporting design stock, Lyman No. 48 receiver sight.

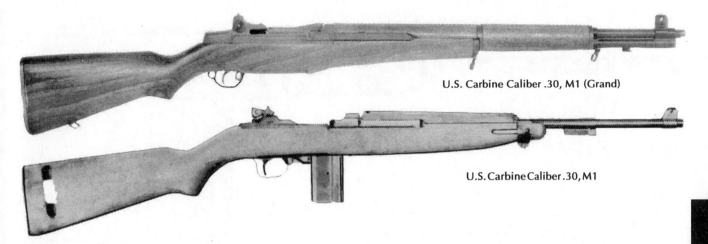

U.S. Carbine Caliber .30, M1 (Grand)

U.S. Carbine Caliber .30, M1

MODEL 1903 STYLE T
SPRINGFIELD MATCH RIFLE . . . . . NiB $1633 Ex $1290 Gd $934
Same specifications as Springfield Sporter except w/heavy bbl. (26-, 28- or 30-inch), scope bases, globe front sight, weight: 12.5 lbs. w/26-inch bbl.

MODEL 1903 TYPE A
SPRINGFIELD FREE RIFLE . NiB $1900 Ex $1544 Gd $1150
Same as Style T except made w/28-inch bbl. only, w/Swiss buttplate, weight: 13.25 lbs.

MODEL 1903 TYPE B
SPRINGFIELD FREE RIFLE . NiB $3510 Ex $2065 Gd $1400
Same as Type A, except w/cheekpiece stock, palm rest, Woodie double-set triggers, Garand fast firing pin, weight: 14.75 lbs.

MODEL 1903-A1 SPRINGFIELD
Same general specifications as Model 1903 except may have Type C pistol-grip stock adopted in 1930. The last Springfields produced at the Springfield Armory were of this type; final serial number was 1,532,878, made in 1939. Note: Late in 1941, Remington Arms Co., Ilion, N.Y., began production, under government contract, of Springfield rifles of this type w/a few minor modifications. These rifles are numbered 3,000,001-3,348,085 and were manufactured before the adoption of Model 1903-A3.
Springfield manufacture . . . NiB $1444 Ex $1266 Gd $845
Remington manufacture . . . . . NiB $955 Ex $855 Gd $577

MODEL 1903-A3 SPRINGFIELD . . NiB $1698 Ex $1492 Gd $978
Same general specifications as Model 1903-A1, except modified to permit increased production and lower cost; may have either straight-grip or pistol-grip stock, bolt is not interchangeable w/ earlier types, w/receiver peep sight, many parts are stamped sheet steel, including the trigger guard and magazine assembly. Quality of these rifles, lower than that of other 1903 Springfields, reflects the emergency conditions under which they were produced. Mfd. during WWII by Remington Arms Co. and L. C. Smith Corona Typewriters, Inc.

MODEL 1922-M1 22
SPRINGFIELD TARGET RIFLE NiB $1277 Ex $1068 Gd $788
Modified Model 1903. Caliber: .22 LR. Five round detachable box magazine. 24.5-inch bbl. Weight: 9 lbs. Sights: Lyman No. 48C receiver, blade front. Sporting-type stock similar to that of Model 1903 Springfield Sporter. Issued 1927. Note: The earlier Model 1922, which is seldom encountered, differs from the foregoing chiefly in the bolt mechanism and magazine.

M2 22 SPRINGFIELD TARGET RIFLE . . . . NiB $1370 Ex $1123 Gd $580
Same general specifications as Model 1922-M1 except w/speed-lock, improved bolt assembly adj. for headspace. Note: These improvements were later incorporated in many rifles of the preceding models (M1922, M1922MI) and arms so converted were marked "M1922M2" or "M1922MII."

NOTE: *The WWII-vintage .30-caliber U.S. Carbine was mfd. by Inland Mfg. Div. of G.M.C., Dayton, OH; Winchester Repeating Arms Co., New Haven, CT, and other contractors: International Business Machines Corp., Poughkeepsie, NY; National Postal Meter Co., Rochester, NY; Quality Hardware & Machine Co., and Rock-Ola Co., Chicago, IL; Saginaw Steering Gear Div. of G.M.C., Saginaw, MI; Standard Products Co., Port Clinton, OH; Underwood-Elliott-Fisher Co., Hartford, CT.*

CALIBER .30, M1
(GARAND) MIL. RIFLE . . . NiB $1441 Ex $1206 Gd $1166
Clip-fed, gas-operated, air-cooled semiautomatic. Uses a clip containing 8 rounds. 24-inch bbl. Weight: W/o bayonet, 9.5 lbs. Sights: Adj. peep rear; blade front w/guards. Pistol-grip stock, handguards. Made 1937-57. Note: Garand rifles have also been produced by Winchester Repeating Arms Co., Harrington & Richardson Arms Co. and International Harvester Co. Deduct 25% for arsenal-assembled mismatches.

CALIBER .30, M1,
NATIONAL MATCH . . . . . . NiB $2389 Ex $1775 Gd $730
Accurized target version of the Garand. Glass-bedded stock; match grade bbl., sights, gas cylinder. "NM" stamped on bbl. forward of handguard.

MODEL 1917 ENFIELD MILITARY RIFLE NiB $977 Ex $800 Gd $370
Modified Mauser-type bolt action. Caliber: .30-06. Five round box magazine. 26-inch bbl. Weight: 9.25 lbs. Sights: Adj. rear; blade front w/guards. Military-type stock w/semi-pistol-grip. This design originated in Great Britain as the, "Pattern 14" and was mfd. in caliber .303 for the British Government in three U.S. plants. In 1917, the U.S. Government contracted w/these firms to produce the same rifle in caliber .30-06; over two million of these Model 1917 Enfields were mfd. While no more were produced after WWI, the U.S. supplied over a million of them to Great Britain during WWII.

NOTE: *The U.S. Model 1917 Enfield was mfd. 1917 to 1918 by Remington Arms Co. of Delaware (later Midvale Steel & Ordnance Co., Eddystone, PA); Remington Arms Co., Ilion, NY; Winchester Repeating Arms Co., New Haven, CT.*

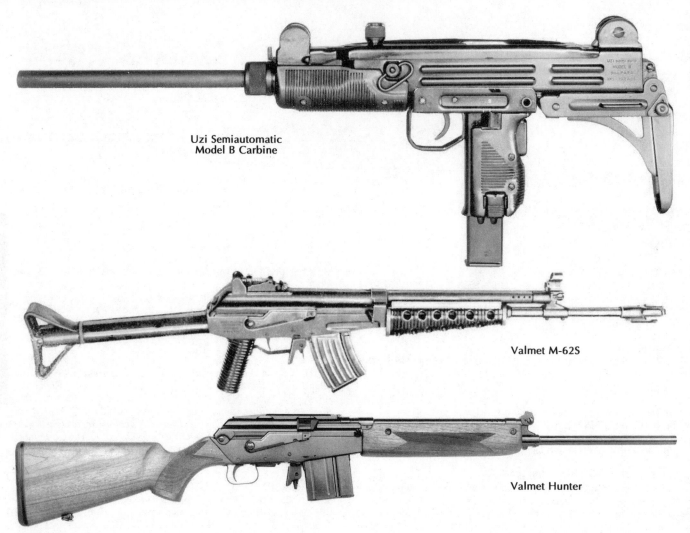

Uzi Semiautomatic
Model B Carbine

Valmet M-62S

Valmet Hunter

CARBINE,
CALIBER 30, M1 . . . . NiB $844 Ex $677 Gd $497
Gas-operated (short-stroke piston), semiautomatic. 15- or 30-round detachable box magazine. 18-inch bbl. Weight: 5.5 lbs. Sights: adj. rear; blade front sight w/guards. Pistol-grip stock w/handguard, side-mounted web sling. Made 1942 to 1945. In 1963, 150,000 surplus M1 Carbines were sold at $20 each to members of the National Rifle Assn. by the Dept. of the Army. Note: For Winchester and Rock-Ola, add 30%; for Irwin Pedersen, add 80%. Quality Hardware did not complete its production run. Guns produced by other manufacturers were marked "Unquality" & command premium prices.

U.S. REPEATING ARMS CO.

See Winchester Rifle listings.

UNIVERSAL FIREARMS, INC.—Miami, Florida

DELUXE CARBINE . . . . NiB $466 Ex $348 Gd $210
Same as standard model except also available in caliber .256, w/deluxe walnut Monte Carlo stock and handguard. Made fro 1965 to 1987.

STANDARD M-1 CARBINE . . . NiB $375 Ex $246 Gd $175
Same as U.S. Carbine, Cal. .30, M1 except may have either wood or metal handguard, bbl. band w/ or w/o bayonet lug; 5-round magazine standard. Made from 1964 to 1987.

UZI CARBINE — Manufactured by Israel Military Industries, Israel

SEMIAUTOMATIC MODEL B CARBINE
Calibers: 9mm Parabellum, .41 Action Express, .45 ACP. 20- to 50-round magazine. 16.1-inch bbl. Weight: 8.4 lbs. Metal folding stock. Front post-type sight, open rear, both adj. Imported by Action Arms 1983 to 1989. NFA (Selective Fire) models imported by UZI America, INC., 1983 to 1994.
Model B Carbine (9mm or .45 ACP)NiB $1500 Ex $1149 Gd $963
Model B Carbine (.41 AE) . . . . NiB $1500 Ex $1149 Gd $963
Centerfire conversion unit, add $215
Rimfire conversion unit, add $150

SEMIAUTOMATIC
MINI CARBINE . . . . NiB $2375 Ex $2153 Gd $1535
Similar to Uzi Model B except with 19.75-inch bbl.and chambered 9mm Parabellum only. 20-round magazine. Weight: 7.2 lbs. Imported in 1989.

**Vickers Jubilee
Single-Shot Target Rifle**

VALMET — Jyväskylä, Finland

M-62S SEMIAUTOMATIC RIFLE . NiB $2590 Ex $2088 Gd $1675
Semiautomatic version of Finnish M-62 automatic assault rifle based on Russian AK-47. Gas-operated rotating bolt action. Caliber: 7.62mmX39 Russian. 15- and 30-round magazines. 16.63-inch bbl. Weight: 8 lbs. w/metal stock. Sights: Tangent aperture rear; hooded blade front w/luminous flip-up post for low-light use. Tubular steel or wood stock. Intro. 1962. Disc.

M-71S . . . . NiB $1988 Ex $1766 Gd $1064
Same specifications as M-62S except caliber 5.56mmx45 (.223 Rem.), w/open rear sight, reinforced resin or wood stock, weight: 7.75 lbs. w/former. Made from 1971 to 1989.

M-76 SEMIAUTOMATIC RIFLE
Semiautomatic assault rifle. Gas-operated, rotating bolt action. Caliber: 223 Rem. 15- and 30-round magazines. Made 1984 to 1989.
Wood stock . . . . NiB $1788 Ex $1373 Gd $1055
Folding stock . . . . NiB $1947 Ex $1522 Gd $1140

M-78 SEMIAUTOMATIC RIFLE . . NiB $1865 Ex $1492 Gd $1170
Caliber: 7.62x51 (NATO). 24.13-inch bbl. Overall length: 43.25 inches. Weight: 10.5 lbs.

M-82 SEMIAUTOMATIC CARBINE NiB $1748 Ex $1399 Gd $1180
Caliber: .223 Rem. 15- or 30-round magazine. 17-inch bbl. 27 inches overall. Weight: 7.75 lbs.

MODEL 412 S DOUBLE RIFLE . . . NiB $1095 Ex $1077 Gd $933
Boxlock. Manual or automatic extraction. Calibers: .243, .308, .30-06, .375 Win., 9.3x74R. Bbls.: 24-inch over/under. Weight: 8.63 lbs. American walnut checkered stock and forend.

HUNTER SEMIAUTOMATIC RIFLE . . NiB $955 Ex $755 Gd $639
Similar to M-78 except in calibers .223 Rem. (5.56mm), .243 Win., .308 Win. (7.62 NATO) and .30-06. Five , 9- or 15-round magazine. 20.5-inch plain bbl. 42 inches overall. Weight: 8 lbs. Sights: Adj. combination scope mount/rear; blade front, mounted on gas tube. Checkered European walnut buttstock and extended checkered forend and handguard. Imported from 1986 to 1989.

VICKERS LTD. — Crayford, Kent, England

**JUBILEE MODEL SINGLE-SHOT-
TARGET RIFLE . . . . NiB $545 Ex $390 Gd $265**
Round-receiver Martini-type action. Caliber: .22 LR. 28-inch heavy bbl. Weight: 9.5 lbs. Sights: Parker-Hale No. 2 front; Perfection rear peep. One-piece target stock w/full forearm and pistol-grip. Made before WWII.

EMPIRE MODEL . . . . NiB $569 Ex $439 Gd $287
Similar to Jubilee Model except w/27- or 30-inch bbl., straight-grip stock, weight: 9.25 lbs. w/30-inch bbl. Made before WWII.

VOERE—Manufactured in Vohrenvach, Germany
**VEC-91 LIGHTNING
BOLT-ACTION RIFLE . . . . NiB $2765 Ex $2165 Gd $1540**
Features unique electronic ignition system to activate or fire caseless ammunition. Calibers: .5.56 UCC (.222 Cal.), 6mm UCC caseless. Five round magazine. 20-inch bbl. 39 inches overall. Weight: 6 lbs. Open adj. rear sight. Drilled and tapped for scope mounts. European walnut stock w/cheekpiece. Twin forward locking lugs. Imported from 1992 to date.

VOERE, VOELTER & COMPANY — Vaehrenbach, Germany
Mauser-Werke acquired Voere in 1987 and all models are now marketed under new designations.

MODEL 1007 BIATHLON REPEATER. NiB $466 Ex $350 Gd $254
Caliber: 22 LR. Five round magazine. 19.5-inch bbl. 39 inches overall. Weight: 5.5 lb. Sights: Adj. rear, blade front. Plain beechwood stock. Imported from 1984 to 1986.

MODEL 1013 BOLT-ACTION REPEATER NiB $766 Ex $544 Gd $389
Same as Model 1007 except w/military-style stock in 22 WMR caliber. Double-set triggers optional. Imported 1984 to 1986 by KDF, Inc.

MODEL 2107 BOLT-ACTION REPEATER
Caliber: 22 LR. Five or 8-round magazine. 19.5-inch bbl. 41 inches overall. Weight: 6 lbs. Sights: Adj. rear sight, hooded front. European hardwood Monte Carlo-style stock. Imported 1986 by KDF, Inc.
Standard model . . . . NiB $439 Ex $278 Gd $255
Deluxe model. . . . . NiB $469 Ex $347 Gd $266

WALTHER RIFLES — Mfd. by the German firms of Waffenfabrik Walther and Carl Walther Sportwaffenfabrik

The following Walther rifles were mfd. before WWII by Waffenfabrik Walther, Zella-Mehlis (Thür.), Germany.

**MODEL 1 AUTOLOADING
RIFLE (LIGHT) . . . . NiB $976 Ex $723 Gd $500**
Similar to Standard Model 2 but w/20-inch bbl., lighter stock, weight: 4.5 lbs.

MODEL 2 AUTOLOADING RIFLE . . NiB $1045 Ex $690 Gd $533
Bolt-action, may be used as autoloader, manually operated repeater or single-shot. Caliber: .22 LR. Five or 9-round detachable box magazine. 24.5-inch bbl. Weight: 7 lbs. Sights: Tangent-curve rear; ramp front. Sporting stock w/checkered pistol grip, grooved forearm, swivels. Disc.

Walther Model 1

Walther Model 2

Walther Model GX-1

Walther Model KKM-S

Walther Model U.I.T.
Super Match

OLYMPIC BOLT-ACTION
MATCH RIFLE . . . . **NiB $1354 Ex $1095 Gd $800**
Single-shot. Caliber: .22 LR. 26-inch heavy bbl. Weight: 13 lbs. Sights: Micrometer extension rear; interchangeable front. Target stock w/checkered pistol-grip, thumbhole, full beavertail forearm covered w/corrugated rubber, palm rest, adj. Swiss-type buttplate, swivels. Disc.

MODEL V BOLT-ACTION
SINGLE-SHOT RIFLE. . . . . **NiB $645 Fx $544 Gd $368**
Caliber: .22 LR. 26-inch bbl. Weight: 7 lbs. Sights: Open rear; ramp front. Plain pistol-grip stock w/grooved forearm. Disc.

MODEL V MEISTERBÜCHSE
(CHAMPION) . . . . **NiB $675 Ex $494 Gd $338**
Same as standard Model V except w/micrometer open rear sight and checkered pistol-grip. Disc.

POST WWII MODELS
The Walther rifles listed below have been manufactured since WWII by Carl Walther Sportwaffenfabrik, Ulm (Donau), Germany.

MODEL GX-1 FREE RIFLE . . **NiB $1985 Ex $1544 Gd $933**
Bolt-action, single-shot. Caliber: .22 LR. 25.5-inch heavy bbl. Weight: 15.9 lbs. Sights: Micrometer aperture rear; globe front. Thumbhole stock w/adj. cheekpiece and buttplate w/removable hook, accessory rail. Left-hand stock available. Accessories furnished include hand stop and sling swivel, palm rest, counterweight assembly.

MODEL KKJ SPORTER . . . . **NiB $1355 Ex $1108 Gd $650**
Bolt action. Caliber: .22 LR. Five round box magazine. 22.5-inch bbl. Weight: 5.5 lbs. Sights: Open rear; hooded ramp front. Stock w/cheekpiece, checkered pistol-grip and forearm, sling swivels. Disc.

MODEL KKJ-HO . . . . **NiB $1543 Ex $1337 Gd $1110**
Same as Model KKJ except chambered for .22 Hornet. Disc.

MODEL KKJ-MA . . . . **NiB $1321 Ex $1231 Gd $650**
Same as Model KKJ except chambered for .22 WMR. Disc.

MODEL KKM INTERNATIONAL
MATCH RIFLE . . . . **NiB $944 Ex $669 Gd $609**
Bolt-action, single-shot. Caliber: .22 LR. 28-inch heavy bbl. Weight: 15.5 lbs. Sights: Micrometer aperture rear; globe front. Thumbhole stock w/high comb, adj. hook buttplate, accessory rail. Left-hand stock available. Disc.

MODEL KKM-S . . . . **NiB $1000 Ex $877 Gd $641**
Same specifications as Model KKM, except w/adj. cheekpiece. Disc.

MOVING TARGET MATCH RIFLE . . **NiB $1067 Ex $833 Gd $554**
Bolt-action, single-shot. Caliber: .22 LR. 23.6-inch bbl. w/weight. Weight: 8.6 lbs. Supplied w/o sights. Thumbhole stock w/adj. cheekpiece and buttplate. Left-hand stock available.

PRONE 400 TARGET RIFLE . . . **NiB $833 Ex $715 Gd $500**
Bolt-action, single-shot. Caliber: .22 LR. 25.5-inch heavy bbl. Weight: 10.25 lbs. Supplied w/o sights. Prone stock w/adj. cheekpiece and buttplate, accessory rail. Left-hand stock available. Disc.

MODEL SSV VARMINT RIFLE . **NiB $770 Ex $697 Gd $488**
Bolt-action, single-shot. Calibers: .22 LR, .22 Hornet. 25.5-inch bbl. Weight: 6.75 lbs. Supplied w/o sights. Monte Carlo stock w/high cheekpiece, full pistol grip and forearm. Disc.

MODEL U.I.T. SPECIAL MATCH RIFLE **NiB $1187 Ex $1070 Gd $833**
Bolt-action, single-shot. Caliber: .22 LR. 25.5-inch bbl. Weight: 10.2 lbs. Sights: Micrometer aperture rear; globe front. Target stock w/high comb, adj. buttplate, accessory rail. Left-hand stock avail. Disc. 1993.

MODEL U.I.T. SUPER MATCH RIFLE **NiB $1169 Ex $1966 Gd $788**
Bolt-action, single-shot. Caliber: .22 LR. 25.5-inch heavy bbl. Weight: 10.2 lbs. Micrometer aperture rear; globe front. Target stock w/support for off-hand shooting, high comb, adj. buttplate and swivel. Left-hand stock available. Disc. 1993.

MONTGOMERY WARD — Chicago, Illinois, Western Field and Hercules Models

Firearms under the "private label" names of Western Field and Hercules are manufactured by such firms as Mossberg, Stevens, Marlin, and Savage for distribution and sale by Montgomery Ward.

MODEL 14M-497B WESTERN FIELD
BOLT-ACTION RIFLE . . . . **NiB $160 Ex $121 Gd $90**
Caliber: .22 RF. Seven round detachable box magazine. 24-inch bbl. Weight: 5 lbs. Sights: Receiver peep; open rear; hooded ramp front. Pistol-grip stock. Mfg. by Mossberg.

MODEL M771 WESTERN FIELD
LEVER-ACTION RIFLE . . . . . . **NiB $221 Ex $177 Gd $135**
Calibers: .30-30, .35 Rem. Six round tubular magazine. 20-inch bbl. Weight: 6.75 lbs. Sights: Open rear; ramp front. Pistol-grip or straight stock, forearm w/barrel band. Mfg. by Mossberg.

MODEL M772 WESTERN FIELD
LEVER-ACTION RIFLE . . . . . . **NiB $235 Ex $190 Gd $131**
Calibers: .30-30, .35 Rem. Six round tubular magazine. 20-inch bbl. Weight: 6.75 lbs. Sights: Open rear; ramp front. Pistol-grip or straight stock, forearm w/bbl. band. Mfg. by Mossberg.

MODEL M775
BOLT-ACTION RIFLE . . . . **NiB $158 Ex $139 Gd $99**
Calibers: .222 Rem., .22-250, .243 Win., .308 Win. Four round magazine. Weight: 7.5 lbs. Sights: Folding leaf rear; ramp front. Monte Carlo stock w/cheekpiece, pistol-grip. Mfg by Mossberg.

MODEL M776
BOLT-ACTION RIFLE . . . . **NiB $260 Ex $227 Gd $159**
Calibers: .222 Rem., .22-250, .243 Win., .308 Win. Four round magazine. Weight: 7.5 lbs. Sights: Folding leaf rear; ramp front. Monte Carlo stock w/cheekpiece, pistol-grip. Mfg. by Mossberg.

MODEL M778
LEVER-ACTION . . . . **NiB $255 Ex $188 Gd $138**
Calibers: .30-30, .35 Rem. Six round tubular magazine. 20-inch bbl. Weight: 6.75 lbs. Sights: Open rear; ramp front. Pistol-grip or straight stock, forearm w/bbl. band. Mfg. by Mossberg.

MODEL M780
BOLT-ACTION RIFLE . . . . **NiB $265 Ex $237 Gd $168**
Calibers: .222 Rem., .22-250, .243 Win., .308 Win. Four round magazine. Weight: 7.5 lbs. Sights: Folding leaf rear; ramp front. Monte Carlo stock w/cheekpiece, pistol grip. Mfg. by Mossberg.

MODEL M782
BOLT-ACTION RIFLE . . . . **NiB $259 Ex $233 Gd $177**
Same general specifications as Model M780.

MODEL M808 . . . . **NiB $155 Ex $133 Gd $90**
Takedown. Caliber: .22RF. Fifteen round tubular magazine. Bbls.: 20- and 24-inch. Weight: 6 lbs. Sights: Open rear; bead front. Pistol-grip stock. Mfg. by Stevens.

MODEL M832 BOLT-ACTION RIFLE . . **NiB $166 Ex $144 Gd $90**
Caliber: .22 RF. Seven round clip magazine. 24-inch bbl. Weight: 6.5 lbs. Sights: Open rear; ramp front. Mfg. by Mossberg.

MODEL M836 . . . . **NiB $169 Ex $122 Gd $95**
Takedown. Caliber: .22RF. Fifteen round tubular magazine. Bbls.: 20- and 24-inch. Weight: 6 lbs. Sights: Open rear; bead front. Pistol-grip stock. Mfg. by Stevens.

MODEL M865 LEVER-ACTION CARBINE **NiB $188 Ex $146 Gd $144**
Hammerless. Caliber: .22RF. Tubular magazine. Made w/both 18.5-inch and 20-inch bbls., forearm w/bbl. band, swivels. Weight: 5 lbs. Mfg. by Mossberg.

MODEL M894
AUTO-LOADING CARBINE . . **NiB $198 Ex $137 Gd $105**
Caliber: .22 RF. Fifteen round tubular magazine. 20-inch bbl. Weight: 6 lbs. Sights: Open rear; ramp front. Monte Carlo stock w/pistol-grip. Mfg. by Mossberg.

MODEL M-SD57 . . . . **NiB $178 Ex $133 Gd $95**
Takedown. Caliber: .22RF. 15-round tubular magazine. Bbls.: 20- and 24-inch. Weight: 6 lbs. Sights: Open rear; bead front. Pistol-grip stock. Mfg. by Stevens.

WEATHERBY, INC. — Atascadero, California (formerly South Gate, CA)

CROWN CUSTOM RIFLE . **NiB $8656 Ex $6298 Gd $4470**
Calibers: .240, .30-06, .257, .270, 7mm, .300, and .340. Bbl.: Made to order. Super fancy walnut stock. Also available w/engraved barreled action including gold animal overlay.

RIFLES

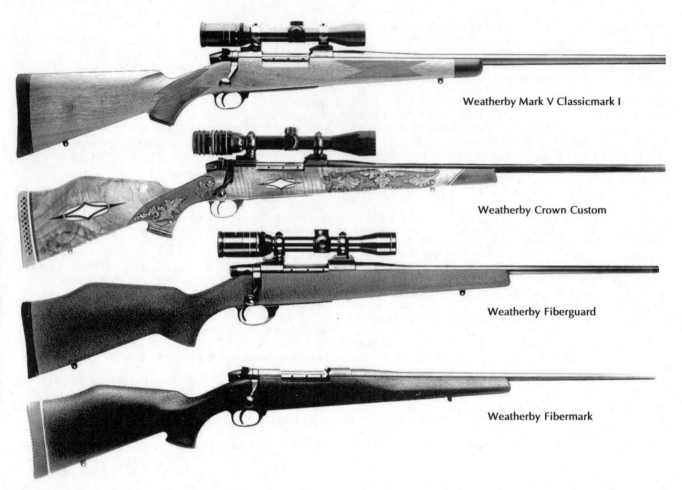

Weatherby Mark V Classicmark I

Weatherby Crown Custom

Weatherby Fiberguard

Weatherby Fibermark

DELUXE .378 MAGNUM RIFLE. . NiB $2233 Ex $2148 Gd $1490
Same general specifications as Deluxe Magnum in other calibers except caliber .378 W. M. Schultz & Larsen action; 26-inch bbl. Disc. 1958.

DELUXE MAGNUM RIFLE. NiB $1844 Ex $1623 Gd $1189
Calibers: .220 Rocket, .257 Weatherby Mag., .270 W.M. 7mm W.M., .300 W.M., .375 W.M. Specially processed FN Mauser action. 24-inch bbl. (26-inch in .375 cal.). Monte Carlo-style stock w/cheekpiece, black forend tip, grip cap, checkered pistol-grip and forearm, quick-detachable sling swivels. Value shown is for rifle w/o sights. Disc. 1958.

DELUXE RIFLE . . . . NiB $1844 Ex $1623 Gd $1189
Same general specifications as Deluxe Magnum except chambered for standard calibers such as .270, .30-06, etc. Disc. 1958.

FIBERGUARD RIFLE . . . . NiB $810 Ex $679 Gd $485
Same general specifications as Vanguard except for fiberglass stock and matte metal finish. Disc, 1988.

FIBERMARK RIFLE . . . . NiB $1377 Ex $1043 Gd $707
Same general specifications as Mark V except w/molded fiberglass stock, finished in a nonglare black wrinkle finish. The metal is finished in a non-glare matte finish. Disc. 1993.

MARK V ACCUMARK BOLT-ACTION REPEATING RIFLE
Weatherby Mark V magnum action. Calibers: .257 Wby., .270 Wby., 7mm Rem. Mag., 7mm Wby., 7mm STW, .300 Win. Mag., .300 Wby. Mag., .30-338 Wby., .30-378 Wby. and .340 Wby. 26- or 28-inch

stainless bbl. w/black oxide flutes. 46.5 or 48.5 inches overall. Weight: 8 to 8.5 lbs. No sights, drilled and tapped for scope. Stainless finish w/blued receiver. H-S Precision black synthetic stock w/aluminum bedding plate, recoil pad and sling swivels. Imported from 1996 to date.
.30-338 & .30-378 Wby. Mag. . . . NiB $1674 Ex $1198 Gd $865
All other calibers . . . . NiB $1589 Ex $1020 Gd $722
Left-hand model, add $100

MARK V ACCUMARK
LIGHT WEIGHT RIFLE . . . . NiB $1357 Ex $1154 Gd $744
Similar to the Mark V Accumark except w/LightWeight Mark V action designed for standard calibers w/sixlocking lugs rather than nine. 24-inch stainless bbl. Weight: 5.75 lbs. Gray or black Monte Carlo-style composite Kevlar/fiberglass stock w/Pachmayr "Decelerator" pad. No sights. Imported from 1997 to 2004.

MARK V CLASSICMARK I RIFLE
Same general specifications as Mark V except w/checkered select American Claro walnut stock w/oil finish and presentation recoil pad. Satin metal finish. Imported from 1992 to 1993.
Calibers .240 to .300 Wby. . . NiB $1135 Ex $884 Gd $572
Caliber .340 Wby. . . . . NiB $1135 Ex $884 Gd $572
Caliber .378 Wby. . . . . NiB $1177 Ex $944 Gd $577
Caliber .416 Wby. . . . . NiB $1150 Ex $922 Gd $535
Caliber .460 Wby. . . . . NiB $1313 Ex $1044 Gd $590

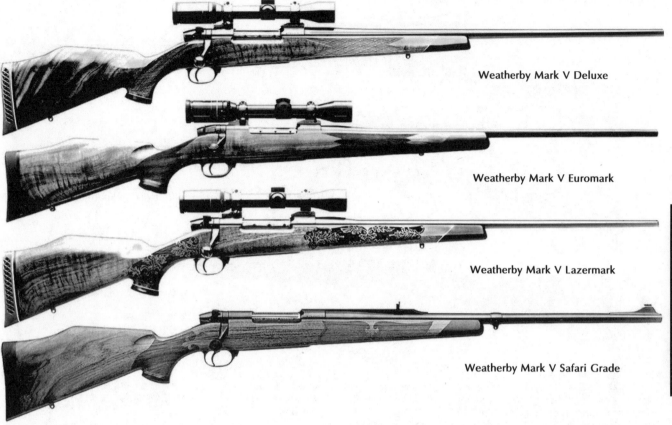

Weatherby Mark V Deluxe

Weatherby Mark V Euromark

Weatherby Mark V Lazermark

Weatherby Mark V Safari Grade

MARK V CLASSICMARK LL RIFLE

Same general specifications as Classicmark I except w/checkered select American walnut stock w/oil finish steel grip cap and Old English recoil pad. Satin metal finish. Right-hand only. Imported from 1992 to 1993.

.240 to .340 Wby. (26-inch bbl.)NiB $1589 Ex $1043 Gd $844
.378 Wby. . . . . NiB $1188 Ex $1044 Gd $909
.426 Wby. . . . . NiB $1207 Ex $1044 Gd $1032
.460 Wby. . . . . NiB $1290 Ex $1170 Gd $1056

MARK V DELUXE RIFLE . . NiB $2633 Ex $1845 Gd $1579

Similar to Mark V Sporter except w/Lightweight Mark V action designed for standard calibers w/sixlocking lugs rather than nine, 4- or 5-round magazine. 24-inch bbl. 44 inches overall. Weight: 6.75 lbs. Checkered Monte Carlo American walnut stock w/rosewood forend and pistol grip and diamond inlay. Imported from 1957 to date.

WEATHERBY MARK V DELUXE BOLT-ACTION SPORTING RIFLE

Mark V action, right or left hand. Calibers: .22-250, .30-06- .224 Weatherby Varmintmaster; .240, .257, .270, 7mm, .300, .340, .375, .378, .416, .460 Weatherby Magnums. Box magazine holds 2 to 5 cartridges depending on caliber. 24- or 26-inch bbl. Weight: 6.5 to 10.5 lbs. Monte Carlo-style stock w/cheekpiece, skip checkering, forend tip, pistol-grip cap, recoil pad, QD swivels. Values shown are for rifles w/o sights. Made in Germany 1958 to 1969; in Japan 1970 to 1994. Values shown for Japanese production.

.22-250, .224 Wby. . . . . NiB $1790 Ex $1408 Gd $956
.375 H&H Magnum . . . . NiB $1835 Ex $1079 Gd $766
.378 Wby. Mag. . . . . NiB $2239 Ex $1177 Gd $897
.416 Wby. Mag.. . . . . NiB $2210 Ex $1443 Gd $833
.460 Wby. Mag.. . . . . NiB $2633 Ex $1399 Gd $1069

MARK V EUROMARK BOLT-ACTION RIFLE

Same general specifications as other Mark V rifles except w/hand-rubbed, satin oil finish Claro walnut stock and nonglare special process blue matte barreled action. Left-hand models available. Imported from 1986 to 1993. Reintroduced in 1995.

.378 Wby. Mag. . . . . NiB $1855 Ex $1190 Gd $943
.416 Wby. Mag. . . . . NiB $1855 Ex $1190 Gd $943
.460 Wby. Mag. . . . . NiB $1896 Ex $1497 Gd $1108
Other calibers . . . . NiB $1590 Ex $800 Gd $555

MARK V LAZERMARK RIFLE

Same general specifications as Mark V except w/laser-carved stock.

.378 Wby. Mag. . . . . NiB $2022 Ex $1598 Gd $938
.416 Wby. Mag. . . . . NiB $2022 Ex $1598 Gd $938
.460 Wby. Mag. . . . . NiB $1489 Ex $1134 Gd $822
Other calibers . . . . NiB $1489 Ex $1134 Gd $822

MARK V SAFARI GRADE RIFLE . . NiB $2300 Ex $1841 Gd $1283

Same general specifications as Mark V except extra capacity magazine, bbl. sling swivel, and express rear sight typical "Safari" style.

MARK V SPORTER RIFLE

Sporter version of Mark V Magnum w/low-luster metal finish. Checkered Carlo walnut stock w/o grip cap or forend tip. No sights. Imported from 1993 to date.

Calibers .257 to .300 Wby . . NiB $1488 Ex $920 Gd $723
.340 Wby. Mag. . . . . NiB $1644 Ex $923 Gd $555
.375 H&H . . . . NiB $1588 Ex $923 Gd $555

MARK V LIGHTWEIGHT SPORTER RIFLE NiB $1041 Ex $843 Gd $498

Similar to Mark V Sporter except w/Lightweight Mark V action designed for standard calibers w/six locking lugs rather than nine. Imported from 1998 to date.

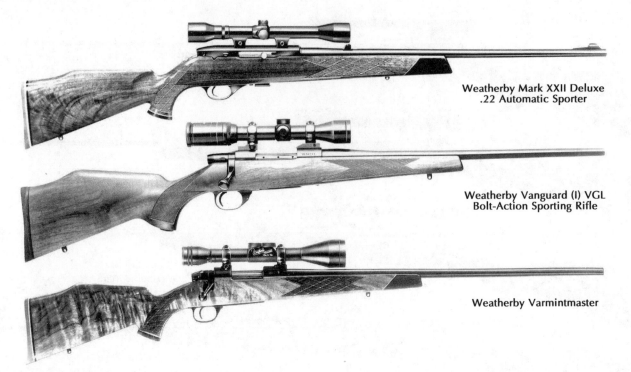

Weatherby Mark XXII Deluxe .22 Automatic Sporter

Weatherby Vanguard (I) VGL Bolt-Action Sporting Rifle

Weatherby Varmintmaster

MARK V STAINLESS RIFLE
Similar to the Mark V Magnum except in 400-series stainless steel w/bead-blasted matte finish. Weight: 8 lbs. Monte Carlo synthetic stock w/aluminum bedding block. Imported from 1997 to 2002.
.30-378 Wby Mag. . . . . NiB $1488 Ex $967 Gd $641
.375 H&H . . . . NiB $1455 Ex $975 Gd $643
All other calibers . . . . NiB $1135 Ex $800 Gd $600
W/fluted bbl., add $150

MARK V (LW) STAINLESS RIFLE . . . NiB $1146 Ex $833 Gd $500
Similar to the Mark V (standard calibers) except in 400-series stainless steel w/bead-blasted matte finish. Five round magazine. 24-inch bbl. 44 inches overall. Weight: 6.5 lbs. Monte Carlo synthetic stock w/aluminum bedding block. Imported from 1997 to 2002.

MARK V SLS RIFLE
Acronym for Stainless Laminated Sporter. Similar to the Mark V Magnum Sporter, except w/stainless 400-series action and 24- or 26-inch stainless bbl. Laminated wood stock. Weight: 8.5 lbs. Black oxide bead-blasted matte blue finish. Imported from 1997 to date.
.340 Wby. Mag. . . . . NiB $1267 Ex $1088 Gd $777
All other calibers . . . . NiB $1200 Ex $955 Gd $724

MARK V SYNTHETIC RIFLE
Similar to the Mark V Magnum except w/Monte Carlo synthetic stock w/aluminum bedding block. 24- or 26-inch standard tapper or fluted bbl. Weight: 7.75 to 8 lbs. Matte blue finish. Imported from 1995 to date.
.340 Wby. Mag. . . . . NiB $1096 Ex $790 Gd $533
.30-378 Wby. Mag. . . . . NiB $1135 Ex $823 Gd $567
All other calibers . . . . NiB $835 Ex $633 Gd $450
W/fluted bbl., add $126

MARK V ULTRA LIGHT WEIGHT RIFLE
Similar to the Mark V Magnum except w/skeletonized bolt handle. 24- or 26-inch fluted stainless bbl. chambered .257 Wby., .270 Wby., 7mm Rem. Mag., 7mm Wby., .300 Win. Mag., .300 Wby. Monte Carlo synthetic stock w/aluminum bedding block. Weight:

6.75 lbs. Imported from 1998 to date.
Standard calibers . . . . NiB $1648 Ex $1396 Gd $879
Weatherby calibers. . . . . . NiB $1866 Ex $1545 Gd $1077
Left-hand action, add $200

MARK XXII DELUXE .22 AUTOMATIC
SPORTER, CLIP-FED MODEL . . . . . . NiB $846 Ex $547 Gd $397
Semiautomatic w/single-shot selector. Caliber: .22 LR. Five and 10-round clip magazines. 24-inch bbl. Weight: 6 lbs. Sights: Folding leaf open rear; ramp front. Monte Carlo-type stock w/cheekpiece, pistol-grip, forend tip, grip cap, skip checkering, QD swivels. Intro. 1964. Made in Italy from 1964 to 1969; in Japan, from 1970 to 191981; in the U.S., from 1982 to 1990.

MARK XXII, TUBULAR
MAGAZINE MODEL . . . . NiB $844 Ex $546 Gd $397
Same as Mark XXII, clip-fed model except w/15-round tubular magazine. Made in Japan from 1973-81; in the U.S., from 1982-90.

VANGUARD (I) BOLT-ACTION SPORTING RIFLE
Mauser-type action. Calibers: .243 Win., .25-06, .270 Win., 7mm Rem. Mag., .30-06, .300 Win. Mag. Five round magazine; (3-round in Magnum calibers). 24-inch bbl. Weight: 7 lbs. 14 oz. No sights. Monte Carlo-type stock w/cheekpiece, rosewood forend tip and pistol-grip cap, checkering, rubber buttpad, QD swivels. Imported from 1970 to 1984.
Standard model . . . . NiB $495 Ex $439 Gd $298
VGL model (w/20-inch bbl.,
plain checkered stock, matte finish) . NiB $650 Ex $533 Gd $400
VGS model (w/24-inch bbl.) . . . . NiB $440 Ex $388 Gd $338
VGX model (w/higher grade finish) . . NiB $655 Ex $493 Gd $339

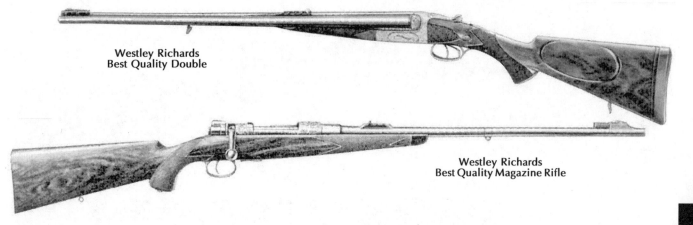

Westley Richards
Best Quality Double

Westley Richards
Best Quality Magazine Rifle

VANGUARD CLASSIC I RIFLE. NiB $555 Ex $439 Gd $321
Same general specifications as Vanguard VGX Deluxe except w/hand-checkered classic-style stock, black buttpad and satin finish. Calibers .223 Rem., .243 Win. .270 Win., 7mm-08, 7mm Rem. Mag., .30-06 and .308 Win. Imported 1989 to 1994.

VANGUARD CLASSIC II RIFLE NiB $720 Ex $587 Gd $444
Same general specifications as Vanguard VGX Deluxe except custom checkered classic-style American walnut stock w/black forend tip, grip cap and solid black recoil pad, satin finish. Imported 1989 to 1994.

VANGUARD VGX DELUXE. . . NiB $650 Ex $456 Gd $398
Calibers: .22-250 Rem., .243 Rem., .270 Wby. Mag., .270 Win., 7mm Rem. Mag., .30-06, .300 Win. Mag., .300 Wby. Mag., .338 Win. Mag. Three or 5-round capacity. 24-inch bbl. About 44 inches overall. Weight: 7 to 8.5 lbs. Custom checkered American walnut stock w/Monte Carlo and recoil pad. Rosewood forend tip and pistol-grip cap. High-luster finish. Disc. 1994.

VARMINT SPECIAL BOLT-ACTION RIFLENiB $654 Ex $447 Gd $368
Calibers: .224 Wby., .22-250, 4-round magazine. 26-inch bbl. 45 inches overall. Weight: 7.75 lbs. Checkered walnut stock. No sights. Disc.

WEATHERMARK RIFLE
Same gen. specs. as Classicmark except w/checkered blk. Weathermark composite stock. Mark V bolt act. Cal: .240, .257, .270, .300, .340, .378, .416 and .460 Weatherby Mag.; plus .270 Win., 7mm Rem. Mag., .30-06 and .375 H&H Mag. Wt: 8 to 10 lbs. Right-hand only. Imp. 1992 to 1994.
Calibers .257 to .300 Wby. Mag.NiB $798 Ex $616 Gd $452
.340 Wby. Mag. . . . . NiB $835 Ex $647 Gd $445
.375 H&H . . . . NiB $1079 Ex $835 Gd $450
Non-Wby. calibers . . . . NiB $800 Ex $577 Gd $465

WEATHERMARK ALASKAN RIFLE . . . NiB $707 Ex $544 Gd $433
Same general specifications as Weathermark except w/nonglare electroless nickel finish. Right-hand only. Imported from 1992 to 1994.

WEIHRAUCH — Melrichstadt, Germany. Imported by European American Armory, Sharpes, FL

MODEL HW 60 TARGET RIFLE NiB $677 Ex $559 Gd $445
Single-shot. Caliber: .22 LR. 26.75-inch bbl. Walnut stock. Adj. buttplate and trigger. Hooded ramp front sight. Push button safety. Imported 1995 to 1997.

MODEL HW 66 BOLT-ACTION RIFLE NiB $645 Ex $482 Gd $338
Caliber: .22 Hornet. 22.75-inch bbl. 41.75 inches overall. Weight: 6.5 lbs. Walnut stock w/cheekpiece. Hooded blade ramp front sight. Checkered pistol grip and forend. Imported from1989 to 1990.

MODEL HW 660 MATCH
BOLT-ACTION RIFLE . . . . . . NiB $942 Ex $745 Gd $500
Caliber: .22 LR. 26-inch bbl. 45.33 inches overall. Weight: 10.75 lbs. Walnut or laminated stock w/adj. cheekpiece and buttplate. Checkered pistol grip and forend. Adj. trigger. Imported 1991 to 2005.

WESTERN FIELD RIFLES

See listings under "W" for Montgomery Ward.

WESTLEY RICHARDS & CO., LTD. — London, England

BEST QUALITY
DOUBLE RIFLE. . . . . NiB $35,000 Ex $28,900 Gd $19,670
Boxlock, hammerless, ejector. Hand-detachable locks. Calibers: .30-06, .318 Accelerated Express, .375 Mag., .425 Mag. Express, .465 Nitro Express, .470 Nitro Express. 25-inch bbls. Weight: 8.5 to 11 lbs. Sights: leaf rear; hooded front. French walnut stock w/ cheekpiece, checkered pistol grip and forend.

BEST QUALITY MAGAZINE RIFLE
Mauser or Magnum Mauser action. Calibers: 7mm High Velocity, .30-06, .318 Accelerated Express, .375 Mag., .404 Nitro Express, .425 Mag. Bbl. lengths: 24-inch; 7mm, 22-inch; .425 caliber, 25-inch. Weight 7.25 to 9.25 lbs. Sights: Leaf rear; hooded front.
Standard action . . . . NiB $11,970 Ex $7295 Gd $5790
Magnum action . . . . . NiB $13,888 Ex $11,679 Gd $8957

WICHITA ARMS — Wichita, Kansas

MODEL WCR CLASSIC BOLT-ACTION RIFLE
Single-shot. Calibers: .17 Rem through .308 Win. 21-inch octagon bbl. Hand-checkered walnut stock. Drilled and tapped for scope w/no sights. Right or left-hand action w/Canjar trigger. Non-glare blued finish. Made from 1978 to date.
Right-hand model . . . . NiB $2578 Ex $2044 Gd $1760
Left-hand model . . . . NiB $3544 Ex $2967 Gd $2178

MODEL WSR SILHOUETTE BOLT-ACTION RIFLE
Single-shot, bolt action, chambered in most standard calibers. Right or left-hand action w/fluted bolt. Drilled and tapped for scope mount with no sights. 24-inch bbl. Canjar trigger. Metallic gray Fiberthane stock w/vented rubber recoil pad. Made 1983 to 1995.
Right-hand model . . . . NiB $2588 Ex $2066 Gd $1449
Left-hand model . . . . NiB $2744 Ex $2190 Gd $1633

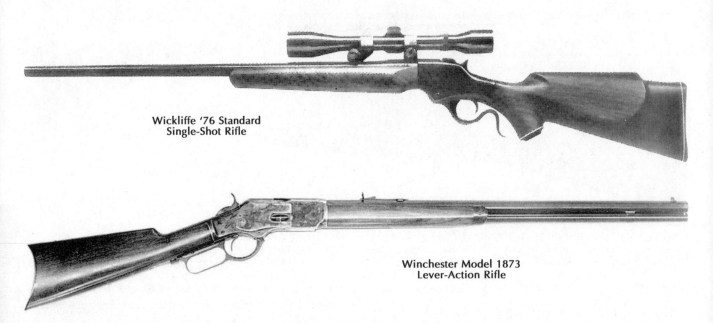

Wickliffe '76 Standard
Single-Shot Rifle

Winchester Model 1873
Lever-Action Rifle

MODEL WMR STAINLESS
MAGNUM BOLT-ACTION RIFLE. . . NiB $2275 Ex $1938 Gd $1179
Single-shot or w/blind magazine action chambered .270 Win. through .458 Win. Mag. Drilled and tapped for scope with no sights. Fully adj. trigger. 22- or 24-inch bbl. Hand-checkered select walnut stock. Made from 1980 to 1984.

MODEL WVR VARMINT RIFLE
Calibers: .17 Rem through .308 Win. Three round magazine. Right or left-hand action w/jeweled bolt. 21-inch bbl. w/o sights. Drilled and tapped for scope. Hand-checkered American walnut pistol-grip stock. Made from 1978 to 1997.
Right-hand model . . . . NiB $2577 Ex $2038 Gd $1289
Left-hand model . . . . NiB $2798 Ex $2260 Gd $1678

WICKLIFFE RIFLES — Wickliffe, Ohio. Manufactured by Triple S Development Co., Inc.

'76 COMMEMORATIVE
MODEL . . . . NiB $1169 Ex $1044 Gd $939
Limited edition of 100. Same as Deluxe Model except w/filled etching on receiver sidewalls, U.S. silver dollar inlaid in stock, 26-inch bbl. only, comes in presentation case. Made in 1976 only.

'76 DELUXE MODEL . . . . NiB $522 Ex $415 Gd $331
Same as Standard Model except w/22-inch bbl. in .30-06 only; high-luster blued finish, fancy-grade figured American walnut stock w/nickel silver grip cap.

'76 STANDARD MODEL
SINGLE-SHOT RIFLE. . . . . NiB $443 Ex $300 Gd $217
Falling-block action. Calibers: .22 Hornet, .223 Rem., .22-250, .243 Win., .25-06, .308 Win., .30-06, .45-70. 22-inch lightweight bbl. (.243 and .308 only) or 26-inch heavy sporter bbl. Weight: 6.75 or 8.5 lbs., depending on bbl. No sights. Select American walnut Monte Carlo stock w/right or left cheekpiece and pistol-grip, semi-beavertail forearm. Intro. 1976. Disc.

STINGER MODEL . . . . NiB $433 Ex $300 Gd $217
Falling block, single-shot. Calibers: .22 Hornet and .223 Rem.

.22-inch bbl. w/no sights. American walnut Monte Carlo stock w/ continental-type forend. Made from 1979-80.

TRADITIONALIST MODEL . . . NiB $441 Ex $339 Gd $200
Falling block single-shot. Calibers: .30-06, .45-70. 24-inch bbl. w/ open sights. Hand-checkered. American walnut classic-style butt-stock and forearm. Made from 1979 to 1980.

WILKINSON ARMS CO. — Covina, California

TERRY CARBINE. . . . . NiB $551 Ex $408 Gd $354
Caliber: 9mm Para. Semiautomatic. Thirty round magazine. 16-inch bbl. 30 inches overall. Weight: 6 lbs. Dovetailed receiver for scope mounting. Bolt-type safety. Ejection port w/automatic trap door. Blowback action. Fires from closed bolt. Made from 1975. Disc.

TED WILLIAMS RIFLES

See Sears, Roebuck and Company.

WINCHESTER RIFLES — Winchester Repeating Arms Company, New Haven, Connecticut

Formerly Winchester Repeating Arms Co., and then mfd. by Winchester-Western Div., Olin Corp., later by U.S. Repeating Arms Company. In 1999, production rights were acquired by Browning Arms Company.

EARLY MODELS 1873 – 1918

NOTE: *Most Winchester rifles manufactured prior to 1918 used the date of approximate manufacture as the model number. For example, the Model 1894 repeating rifle was manufactured from 1894 to 1937. When Winchester started using two-digit model numbers after 1918, the "18" was dropped and the rifle was then called the Model 94. The Model 1892 was called the Model 92, etc. In light of the recent shut-down, Winchester is no longer made at New Haven.*

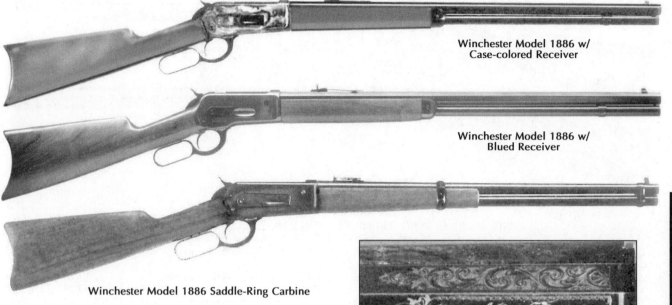

Winchester Model 1886 w/
Case-colored Receiver

Winchester Model 1886 w/
Blued Receiver

Winchester Model 1886 Saddle-Ring Carbine

At Right: Close-up barrel engraving on Winchester
Model 1873 One of One Thousand.

RIFLES

MODEL 1873 LEVER-ACTION
CARBINE . . . . NiB $4820 Ex $3933 Gd $2577
Same as Standard Model 1873 Rifle except w/20-inch bbl.,
12-round magazine, weight: 7.25 lbs.

MODEL 1873 LEVER-ACTION
RIFLE . . . . NiB $5088 Ex $3482 Gd $2100
Calibers: .32-20, .38-40, .44-40; a few were chambered for .22
rimfire. Fifteen round magazine, also made w/6-round half magazine. 24-inch bbl. (round, half-octagon, octagon). Weight: 8.5 lbs.
Sights: Open rear; bead or blade front. Plain straight-grip stock and
forearm. Made 1873 to 1924. 720,610 rifles of this model were mfd.

MODEL 1873 —
ONE OF ONE THOUSAND. NiB $196,000+ Ex $150,000 Gd $90,000
During the late 1870s, Winchester offered Model 1873 rifles
of superior accuracy and extra finish, designated "One of One
Thousand" grade, at $100. These rifles are marked "1 of 1000"
or "One of One Thousand." Only 136 of this model are known to
have been manufactured. This is one of the rarest of shoulder arms
and, because so few have been sold in recent years, it is extremely
difficult to assign a value, however, an "excellent" specimen would
probably bring a price upward of $200,000.

MODEL 1873 SPECIAL
SPORTING RIFLE . . . . NiB $11,375 Ex $10,450 Gd $7,707
Same as Standard Model 1873 Rifle except this type has receiver case-
hardened in colors, pistol-grip stock of select walnut, octagon bbl. only.

MODEL 1885 SINGLE-SHOT RIFLE
Designed by John M. Browning, this falling-block, lever-action rifle
was manufactured from 1885 to 1920 in a variety of models and
chambered for most of the popular cartridges of the period — both
rimfire and centerfire — from .22 to .50 caliber. There are two
basic styles of frames, low-wall and high-wall. The low-wall was

chambered only for the lower-powered cartridges, while the high-
wall was supplied in all calibers and made in three basic types. The
standard model for No. 3 and heavier barrels is the type commonly
encountered; the thin-walled version was supplied with No. 1 and
No. 2 light barrels and the thick-walled action in the heavier calibers. Made in both solid frame and takedown versions. Barrels were
available in five weights ranging from the lightweight No. 1 to the
extra-heavy No. 5 in round, half-octagon and full-octagon styles.
Many other variations were also offered.

MODEL 1885 HIGH-WALL
SPORTING RIFLE . . . . NiB $5335 Ex $3100 Gd $2066
Solid frame or takedown. No. 3, 30-inch bbl., standard. Weight: 9.5
lbs. Standard trigger and lever. Open rear sights; blade front sight.
Plain stock and forend.

MODEL 1885 LOW-WALL
SPORTING RIFLE . . . . NiB $1550 Ex $1466 Gd $1000
Solid frame. No. 1, 28-inch round or octagon bbl. Weight: 7 lbs.
Open rear sight; blade front sight. Plain stock and forend.

MODEL 1885
SCHUETZEN RIFLE . . . . . NiB $10,000 Ex $7860 Gd $5779
Solid frame or takedown. High-wall action. Schuetzen double-set
trigger. Spur finger lever. No. 3, 30-inch octagon bbl. Weight: 12
lbs. Vernier rear peep sight; wind-gauge front sight. Fancy walnut
Schuetzen stock with checkered pistol-grip and forend. Schuetzen
buttplate; adj. palm rest.

MODEL 1885
SPECIAL SPORTING RIFLE . . . NiB $7335 Ex $5550 Gd $5090
Same general specifications as the standard high-wall model except
with checkered fancy walnut stock and forend.

Winchester Model 1890

Winchester Model 1892

MODEL 1885 SINGLE-SHOT
MUSKET. . . . . NiB $1590 Ex $1171 Gd $878
Solid frame. Low-wall. .22 Short and Long Rifle. 28-inch round bbl. Weight: 8.6 lbs. Lyman rear peep sight; blade front sight. Military-type stock and forend. Note: The U.S. Government purchased a large quantity of these muskets during World War I for training purposes.

MODEL 1885 SINGLE-SHOT
"WINDER" MUSKET . . . . . NiB $1488 Ex $1203 Gd $1037
Solid frame or takedown. High-wall. Plain trigger. 28-inch round bbl. Weight: 8.5 lbs. Musket rear sight; blade front sight. Military-type stock and forend w/bbl. band and sling stud/rings.

MODEL 1886 LEVER-ACTION RIFLE
Solid frame or takedown. .33 Win., .38-56, .38-70, .40-65, .40-70, .40-82, .45-70, .45-90, .50-100, .50-110. The .33 Win. and .45-70 were the last calibers in which this model was supplied. Eight round tubular magaine; also 4-round half-magazine. 26-inch bbl. (round, half-octagon, octagon). Weight: 7.5 lbs. Sights: Open rear; bead or blade front. Plain straight-grip stock and forend or standard models. Made from 1886 to 1935.
Standard model . . . . NiB $7288 Ex $4399 Gd $3100
Takedown model . . . . NiB $10,270 Ex $7668 Gd $5790
Deluxe model (W/pistol grip and
high-quality walnut stock). . NiB $17,689 Ex $13,790 Gd $10,777

MODEL 1886 SADDLE-RING
CARBINE . . . . NiB $18,690 Ex $15,660 Gd $12,750
Same as standard rifle except with 22-inch bbl., carbine buttstock and forend. Carbine rear sight. Saddle ring on left side of receiver.

MODEL 1890 SLIDE-ACTION RIFLE
Visible hammer. Calibers: .22 Short, Long, LR; .22 WRF (not interchangeable). Tubular magazine holds 15 Short, 12 Long, 11 LR; 12 WRF. 24-inch octagon bbl. Weight: 5.75 lbs. Sights: Open rear; bead front. Plain straight-grip stock, grooved slide handle. Originally solid frame; after No. 15,499, all rifles of this model were takedown-type. Fancy checkered pistol-grip stock, nickel-steel bbl. supplied at extra cost, which can also increase the value by 100% or more. Made from 1890 to 1932.
WRF, blued model . . . . NiB $2079 Ex $1754 Gd $1166
.22 LR, blued model. . . . . NiB $2148 Ex $2066 Gd $1180
Color casehardened receiver. . . . NiB $6689 Ex $5349 Gd $3730

MODEL 1892 LEVER-ACTION
RIFLE . . . . NiB $3482 Ex $2210 Gd $1588
Solid frame or takedown. Calibers: .25-20, .32-20, .38-40, .44-40. Thirteen round tubular magazine; also 7-round half-magazine. 24-inch bbl. (round, octagon, half-octagon). Weight: from 6.75 lbs. up. Sights: Open rear; bead front. Plain straight-grip stock and forend. Pistol-grip fancy walnut stocks were available at extra cost and also doubles the value of the current value for standard models.

MODEL 1892 SADDLE-RING
CARBINE . . . . NiB $5321 Ex $2549 Gd $1266
Same general specifications as the Model 1892 rifle except carbine buttstock, forend and sights. 20-inch bbl. Saddle ring on left side of receiver.

MODEL 1894 LEVER-ACTION
RIFLE . . . . NiB $6530 Ex $4739 Gd $3220
Solid frame or takedown. .25-35, .30-30, .32-40, .32 Special, .38-55. Seven round tubular magazine or 4-round half-magazine. 26-inch bbl. (round, octagon, half-octagon). Weight: about 7.35 lbs. Sights: Open rear; bead front. Plain straight-grip stock and forearm on standard model; crescent-shaped or shotgun-style buttplate. Made from 1894-1937. See also Winchester Model 94 for later variations of this model.

MODEL 1894 LA DELUXE . . . NiB $12,890 Ex $10,669 Gd $8777
Same general specifications as the standard rifle except checkered pistol-grip buttstock and forend using high-grade walnut. Engraved versions are considerably higher in value.

MODEL 1894 SADDLE-RING
CARBINE . . . . NiB $2866 Ex $1806 Gd $1100
Same general specifications as the Model 1894 standard rifle except 20-inch bbl., carbine buttstock, forend, and sights. Saddle ring on left side of receiver. Weight: about 6.5 lbs.

MODEL 1894 STANDARD CARBINE NiB $6798 Ex $4890 Gd $3855
Same general specifications as Saddle-Ringle Carbine except shotgun type buttstock and plate, no saddle ring, standard open rear sight. Sometimes called "Eastern Carbine." See also Winchester Model 94 carbine.

1895 LEVER-ACTION
CARBINE . . . . NiB $4297 Ex $3037 Gd $1971
Same as Model 95 Standard Rifle except has 22-inch bbl., carbine-style buttstock and forend, weight: About 8 lbs., calibers .30-40 Krag, .30-03, .30-06 and .303, solid frame only.

MODEL 1895 LEVER-
ACTION RIFLE . . . . NiB $3364 Ex $2130 Gd $1266
Calibers: .30-40 Krag, .30-03, .30-60, .303 British, 7.62mm Russian, .35 Win., .38-72, .40-72, .405 Win. Four round box magazine except .30-40 and .303, which have 5-round magazines. Bbl. lengths: 24-, 26-, 28-inches (round, half-octagon, octagon). Weight: About 8.5 lbs. Sights: Open rear; bead or blade front. Plain straight-grip stock and forend (standard). Both solid frame and takedown models were made from1897 to 1931.

MODEL (1897) LEE BOLT-ACTION RIFLE
Straight-pull bolt-action. .236 U.S. Navy, 5-round box magazine, clip loaded. 24- and 28-inch bbl. Weight: 7.5 to 8.5 lbs. Sights: Folding leaf rear sight on musket; open sporting sight on sporting rifle.
Musket model. . . . . NiB $1939 Ex $1777 Gd $1129
Sporting rifle . . . . NiB $2000 Ex $1808 Gd $1110

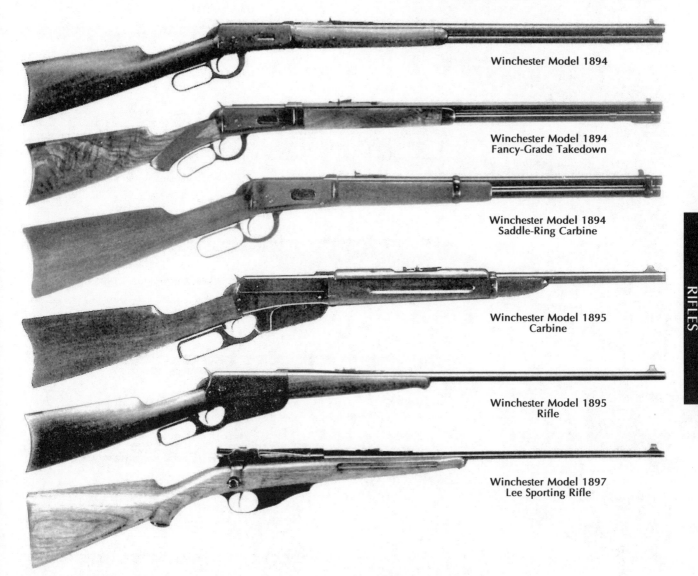

Winchester Model 1894

Winchester Model 1894
Fancy-Grade Takedown

Winchester Model 1894
Saddle-Ring Carbine

Winchester Model 1895
Carbine

Winchester Model 1895
Rifle

Winchester Model 1897
Lee Sporting Rifle

RIFLES

MODEL 1900 BOLT-ACTION
SINGLE-SHOT RIFLE.....NiB $628 Ex $499 Gd $356
Takedown. Caliber: .22 Short and Long. 18-inch bbl. Weight: 2.75 lbs. Open rear sight; blade front sight. One-piece, straight-grip stock. Made from 1899 to 1902.

MODEL 1902 BOLT-ACTION
SINGLE-SHOT RIFLE......NiB $495 Ex $369 Gd $269
Takedown. Basically the same as Model 1900 with minor improvements. Calibers: .22 Short and Long, .22 Extra Long, .22 LR. Weight: 3 lbs. Made from 1902 to 1931.

MODEL 1903
SELF-LOADING RIFLE. . . . NiB $1133 Ex $909 Gd $577
Takedown. Caliber: .22 WRA. Ten round tubular magazine in buttstock. 20-inch bbl. Weight: 5.75 lbs. Sights: Open rear; bead front. Plain straight-grip stock and forearm (fancy grade illustrated). Made from 1903 to 1936.

MODEL (1904) 99 THUMB-TRIGGER BOLT-ACTION
SINGLE-SHOT RIFLE......NiB $833 Ex $707 Gd $510
Takedown. Same as Model 1902 except fired by pressing a button behind the cocking piece. Made from 1904 to 1923.

MODEL 1904 BOLT-ACTION
SINGLE-SHOT RIFLE......NiB $469 Ex $388 Gd $269
Similar to Model 1902. Takedown. Caliber: 22 Short, Long Extra Long, LR. 21-inch bbl. Weight: 4 lbs. Made from 1904 to 1931.

MODEL 1905
SELF-LOADING RIFLE.......NiB $768 Ex $580 Gd $500
Takedown. Calibers: .32 Win. S. and L., .35 Win. S. and L. Five or 10-round detachable box magazine. 22-inch bbl. Weight: 7.5 lbs. Sights: Open rear; bead front. Plain pistol-grip stock and forearm. Made from 1905 to 1920.

MODEL 1906
SLIDE-ACTION REPEATERNiB $1590 Ex $1077 Gd $733
Takedown. Visible hammer. Caliber: .22 Short, Long, LR. Tubular magazine holds 20 Short, 16 Long or 14 LR. 20-inch bbl. Weight: 5 lbs. Sights: Open rear; bead front. Straight-grip stock and grooved forearm. Made from 1906 to 1932.

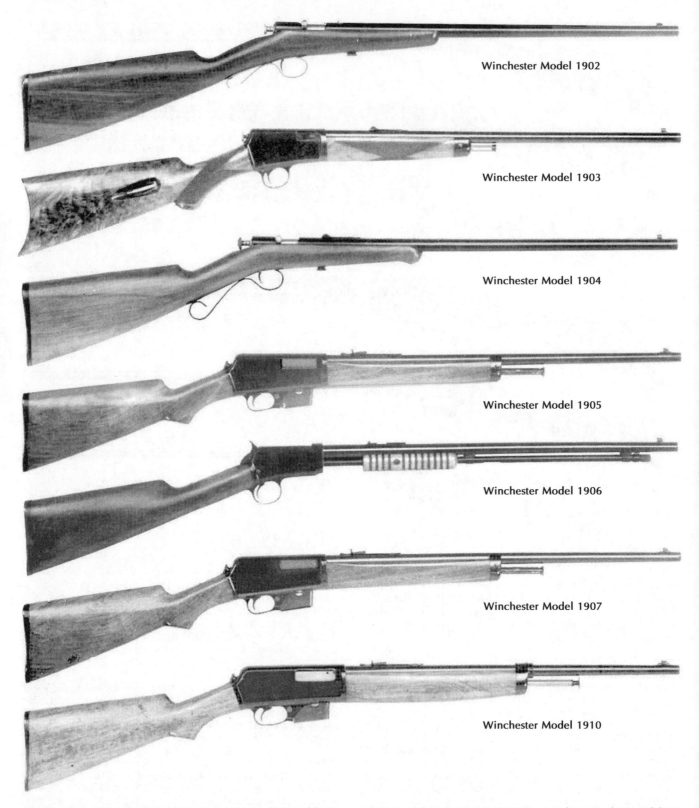

Winchester Model 1902

Winchester Model 1903

Winchester Model 1904

Winchester Model 1905

Winchester Model 1906

Winchester Model 1907

Winchester Model 1910

MODEL 1907 SELF-LOADING RIFLE. NiB $733 Ex $589 Gd $421
Takedown. Caliber: .351 Win. S. and L. Five or 10-round detachable box magazine. 20-inch bbl. Weight: 7.75 lbs. Sights: Open rear; bead front. Plain pistol-grip stock and forearm. Made 1907 to 1957.

MODEL 1910 SELF-LOADING RIFLE. NiB $910 Ex $707 Gd $533
Takedown. Caliber: .401 Win. S. and L. Four round detachable box magazine. 20-inch bbl. Weight: 8.5 lbs. Sights: Open rear; bead front. Plain pistol-grip stock and forearm. Made from 1910 to 1936.

Winchester Model 43
Special Grade

MODEL 43 BOLT-ACTION
SPORTING RIFLE . . . . **NiB $855 Ex $679 Gd $480**
Standard Grade. Calibers: .218 Bee, .22 Hornet, .25-20, .32-20 (latter two discontinued 1950). Three round detachable box magazine. 24-inch bbl. Weight: 6 lbs. Sights: Open rear, bead front on hooded ramp. Plain pistol-grip stock with swivels. Made from 1949 to 1957.

MODEL 43 SPECIAL GRADE. . **NiB $855 Ex $679 Gd $480**
Same as Standard Model 43 except has checkered pistol-grip and forearm, grip cap.

MODEL 47 BOLT-ACTION
SINGLE-SHOT RIFLE. . . . . **NiB $466 Ex $370 Gd $245**
Caliber: .22 Short, Long, LR. 25-inch bbl. Weight: 5.5 lbs. Sights: Peep or open rear; bead front. Plain pistol-grip stock. Made from 1949 to 1954.

MODEL 52 BOLT-ACTION TARGET RIFLE
Standard bbl. First type. .22 LR. Five round box magazine. 28-inch bbl. Weight: 8.75 lbs. Sights: Folding leaf peep rear; blade front sight; standard sights various other combinations available. Scope bases. Semi-military-type target stock w/pistol grip; original model has grasping grooves in forearm; higher comb and semi-beavertail forearm on later models. Numerous changes were made in this model; the most important was the adoption of the speed lock in 1929. Model 52 rifles produced before this change are generally referred to as "slow lock" models. Last arms of this type bore serial numbers followed by the letter "A." Made 1919 to 1937.
Slow Lock model . . . . **NiB $909 Ex $622 Gd $370**
Speed Lock model . . . . **NiB $733 Ex $466 Gd $379**

MODEL 52 HEAVY BARREL **NiB $1379 Ex $1008 Gd $798**
First type speed lock. Same general specifications as Standard Model 52 of this type except has heavier bbl., Lyman No. 17G front sight, weight: 10 lbs.

MODEL 52 INTERNATIONAL MATCH RIFLE
Similar to Model 52-D Heavy Barrel except has special lead-lapped bbl., laminated "free rifle"-style stock with high comb, thumbhole, hook buttplate, accessory rail, handstop/swivel assembly, palm rest. Weight: 13.5 lbs. Made from 1969 to 1978.
With standard trigger . . . . . **NiB $1577 Ex $1103 Gd $922**
With Kenyon or I.S.U. trigger, add **$350**

MODEL 52 INTERNATIONAL PRONE **NiB $1470 Ex $1133 Gd $909**
Similar to Model 52-D Heavy Barrel except has special lead-lapped bbl., prone stock with full pistol-grip, rollover cheekpiece removable for bore-cleaning. Weight 11.5 lbs. Made from 1975 to 1980.

MODEL 52 SPORTING RIFLE
First type. Same as Standard Model 52 of this type except has lightweight 24-inch bbl., Lyman No. 48 receiver sight and gold bead front sight on hooded ramp, deluxe checkered sporting stock with cheekpiece, black forend tip, etc. Weight: 7.75 lbs. Made 1934 to 1958. Reintroduced 1993.
Model 52 Sporter . . . . **NiB $4677 Ex $3200 Gd $1590**
Model 52A Sporter . . . . **NiB $3290 Ex $2733 Gd $1266**
Model 52B Sporter . . . . **NiB $4633 Ex $2479 Gd $1790**
Model 52C Sporter . . . . **NiB $5125 Ex $4120 Gd $2798**
Model 52 C Sporter
(1993 BAC re-issue) . . . . **NiB $650 Ex $500 Gd $433**

MODEL 52-B BOLT-ACTION RIFLE
Standard bbl. Extensively redesigned action. Supplied with choice of "Target" stock, an improved version of the previous Model 52 stock, or "Marksman" stock with high comb, full pistol grip and beavertail forearm. Weight: 9 lbs. Offered with a wide choice of target sight combinations (Lyman, Marble-Goss, Redfield, Vaver, Winchester), value shown is for rifle less sight equipment. Other specifications as shown for first type. Made from 1935 to 1947. Reintroduced 1997.
Target model . . . . **NiB $1270 Ex $968 Gd $755**
BAC model
(1997 BAC re-issue) . . . . **NiB $1270 Ex $968 Gd $755**
USRAC Sporting model . . . . . . **NiB $768 Ex $600 Gd $455**

MODEL 52-B BULL GUN
HEAVY BARREL . . . . **NiB $1880 Ex $1144 Gd $600**
Same specifications as Standard Model 52-B except Bull Gun has extra heavy bbl., Marksman stock only, weight: 12 lbs. Heavy Bbl. model weight: 11 lbs. Made 1940 to 1947.

MODEL 52-C BOLT-ACTION RIFLE
Improved action with "Micro-Motion" trigger mechanism and new-type "Marksman" stock. General specifications same as shown for previous models. Made from 1947 to 1961, Bull Gun from 1952. Value shown is for rifle less sights.
Bull Gun (w/extra heavy bbl.,
wt. 12 lbs.). . . . . **NiB $1877 Ex $976 Gd $694**
W/standard bbl.
(wt. 9.75 lbs.). . . . . **NiB $1466 Ex $800 Gd $659**
Target model
(w/heavy bbl.) . . . . **NiB $1455 Ex $909 Gd $689**

NOTE: *Following WWI, Winchester had financial difficulties and, like many other firearm firms of the day, failed. However, Winchester continued to operate in the hands of receivers. Then, in 1931, The Western Cartridge Co.—under the leadership of John Olin—purchased all assets of the firm. After that, Winchester leaped ahead of all other firms of the day in firearm and ammunition development. The first sporting firearm to come out of the Winchester plant after WWI was the Model 20 shotgun, but this was quickly followed by the famous Model 52 bolt-action rifle. This was also a time when Winchester dropped the four-digit model numbers and began using two-digit numbers instead. This model-numbering procedure, with one exception (Model 677), continued for the next several years.*

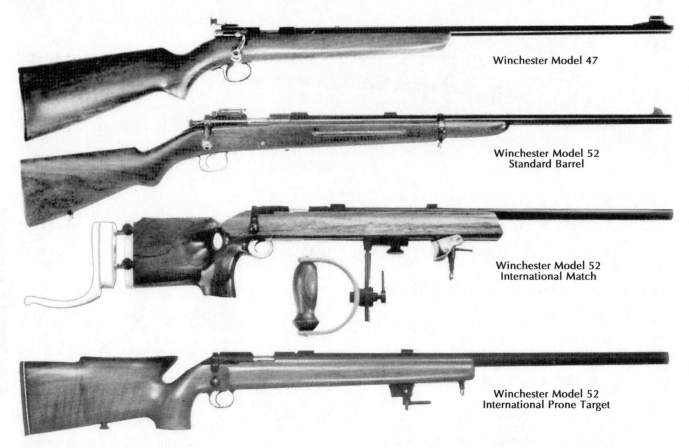

Winchester Model 47

Winchester Model 52
Standard Barrel

Winchester Model 52
International Match

Winchester Model 52
International Prone Target

MODEL 52-D BOLT-ACTION

TARGET RIFLE . . . . NiB $1377 Ex $976 Gd $488
Redesigned Model 52 action, Single-Shot. Caliber: .22 LR. 28-inch standard or heavy bbl., free-floating, with blocks for standard target scopes. Weight: With standard bbl., 9.75 lbs., with heavy barrel, 11 lbs. Restyled Marksman stock with accessory channel and forend stop, rubber buttplate. Made 1961 to 1978. Value shown is for rifle without sights.

MODEL 53 LEVER-ACTION

REPEATER . . . . NiB $2343 Ex $1869 Gd $1333
Modification of Model 92. Solid frame or takedown. Calibers: .25-20, .32-20, .44-40. Six round tubular half-magazine in solid frame model. Seven round in takedown. 22-inch nickel steel bbl. Weight: 5.5 to 6.5 lbs. Sights: Open rear; bead front. Redesigned straight-grip stock and forearm. Made from 1924 to 1932.

MODEL 54 BOLT-ACTION

HIGH POWER SPORTING RIFLE (I). NiB $1570 Ex $933 Gd $667
First type. Calibers: .270 Win., 7x57mm, .30-30, .30-06, 7.65x53mm, 9x57mm. Five round box magazine. 24-inch bbl. Weight: 7.75 lbs. Sights: Open rear; bead front. Checkered stock w/ pistol grip, tapered forearm w/Schnabel tip. This type has two-piece firing pin. Made from 1925 to 1930.

MODEL 54 BOLT-ACTION

HIGH POWER SPORTING RIFLE (II) NiB $1180 Ex $922 Gd $744
Standard Grade. Improved type with speed lock and one-piece firing pin. Calibers: .22 Hornet, .220 Swift, .250/3000, .257 Roberts, .270 Win., 7x57mm, .30-06. Five round box magazine. 24-inch bbl., 26-inch in cal. .220 Swift. Weight: About 8 lbs. Sights: Open rear, bead front on ramp. NRA-type stock w/checkered pistol-grip and forearm. Made 1930 to 1936. Add $200 for .22 Hornet caliber.

MODEL 54 CARBINE (I) . . . . NiB $1495 Ex $884 Gd $601
First type. Same as Model 54 rifle except has 20-inch bbl., plain lightweight stock with grasping grooves in forearm. Weight: 7.25 lbs.

MODEL 54 CARBINE (II). . . . NiB $1566 Ex $912 Gd $648
Improved type. Same as Model 54 Standard Grade Sporting Rifle of this type except has 20-inch bbl. Weight: About 7.5 lbs. This model may have either NRA-type stock or the lightweight stock found on the first-type Model 54 Carbine.

MODEL 54 NATIONAL

MATCH RIFLE . . . . NiB $1722 Ex $967 Gd $679
Same as Standard Model 54 except has Lyman sights, scope bases, Marksman-type target stock, weighs 9.5 lbs. Same calibers as Standard Model.

MODEL 54 SNIPER'S

MATCH RIFLE . . . . NiB $2489 Ex $1388 Gd $633
Similar to the earlier Model 54 Sniper's Rifle except has Marksman-type target stock, scope bases, weight: 12.5 lbs. Available in same calibers as Model 54 Standard Grade.

MODEL 54 SNIPER'S RIFLE NiB $2566 Ex $ 1534 Gd $770
Same as Standard Model 54 except has heavy 26-inch bbl., Lyman No. 48 rear peep sight and blade front sight semi-military stock, weight: 11.75 pounds, cal. .30-06 only.

MODEL 54 SUPER GRADE NiB $3144 Ex $2057 Gd $1166
Same as Standard Model 54 Sporter except has deluxe stock with cheekpiece, black forend tip, pistol-grip cap, quick detachable swivels, 1-inch sling strap.

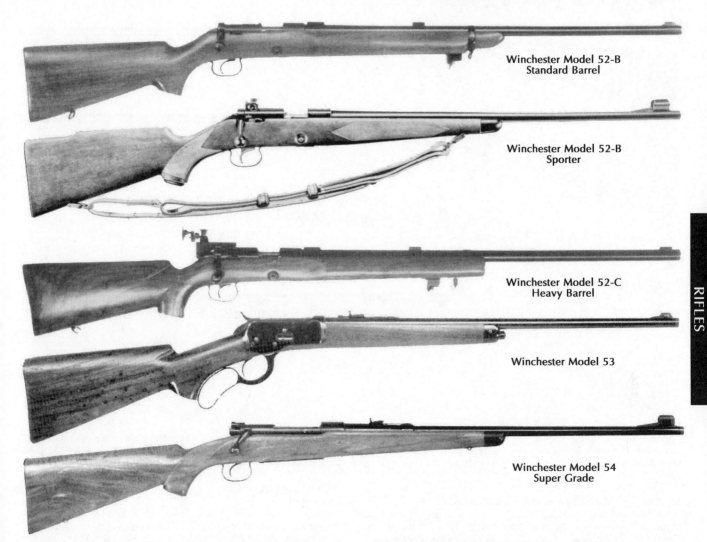

Winchester Model 52-B
Standard Barrel

Winchester Model 52-B
Sporter

Winchester Model 52-C
Heavy Barrel

Winchester Model 53

Winchester Model 54
Super Grade

RIFLES

MODEL 54 TARGET RIFLE . . . NiB $888 Ex $572 Gd $390
Same as Standard Model 54 except has 24-inch medium-weight bbl. (26-inch in cal. .220 Swift), Lyman sights, scope bases, Marksman-type target stock, weight: 10.5 lbs., same calibers as Standard Model.

MODEL 55 "AUTOMATIC"
SINGLE-SHOT . . . . NiB $379 Ex $290 Gd $210
Caliber: .22 Short, Long, LR. 22-inch bbl. Sights: Open rear, bead front. One-piece walnut stock. Weight: About 5.5 lbs. Made from 1958 to 1960.

MODEL 55 LEVER-ACTION REPEATER
Modification of Model 94. Solid frame or takedown. Calibers: .25-35, .30-30, .32 Win. Special. Three round tubular half magazine. 24-inch nickel steel bbl. Weight: About 7 lbs. Sights: Open rear; bead front. Made from 1924 to 1932.
Standard model (straight grip) . . . NiB $2133 Ex $1670 Gd $1006
Deluxe model (pistol grip) . . . . . NiB $2287 Ex $1744 Gd $1140

MODEL 56 BOLT-ACTION
SPORTING RIFLE . . . . NiB $1179 Ex $1143 Gd $707
Solid frame. Caliber: .22 LR., .22 Short. Five or 10-round detachable box magazine. 22-inch bbl. Weight: 4.75 lbs. Sights: Open rear; bead front. Plain pistol-grip with Schnabel forend. Made from 1926 to 1929.

MODEL 57 BOLT-ACTION RIFLE
Solid frame. Same as Model 56 except available (until 1929) in .22 Short as well as LR with 5- or 10-round magazine. Has semi-military style target stock, bbl. band on forend, swivels and web sling, Lyman peep rear sight, weight: 5 lbs. Made from 1926 to 1936.
Sporter model. . . . . NiB $888 Ex $654 Gd $500
Target model . . . . NiB $733 Ex $679 Gd $500

MODEL 58 BOLT-ACTION
SINGLE-SHOT . . . . NiB $1056 Ex $800 Gd $598
Similar to Model 52. Takedown. Caliber: .22 Short, Long LR. 18-inch bbl. Weight: 3 lbs. Sights, Open rear; blade front. Plain, flat, straight-grip hardwood stock. Not serial numbered. Made 1928 to 1931.

MODEL 59 BOLT-ACTION
SINGLE-SHOT . . . . NiB $1268 Ex $1009 Gd $756
Improved version of Model 58, has 23-inch bbl., redesigned stock w/pistol grip, weight: 4.5 lbs. Made in 1930.

MODEL 60, 60A BOLT-ACTION SINGLE-SHOT
Redesign of Model 59. Caliber: .22 Short, Long, LR. 23-inch bbl. (27-inch after 1933). Weight: 4.25 lbs. Sights: Open rear, blade front. Plain pistol-grip stock. Made 1930 to 1934 (60), 1932 to 1939 (60A).
Model 60 . . . . NiB $445 Ex $276 Gd $200
Model 60A. . . . . NiB $556 Ex $380 Gd $338

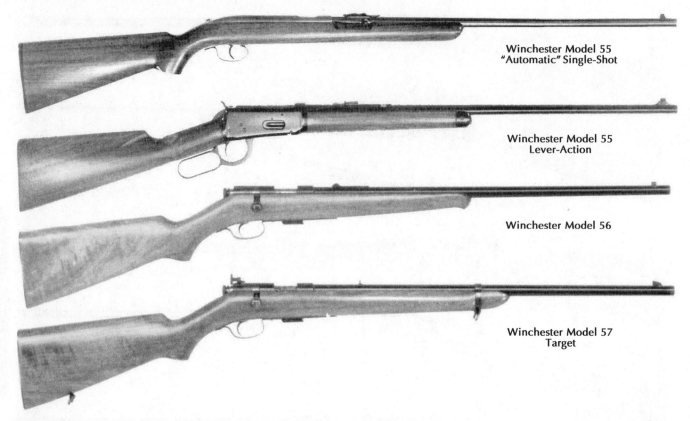

Winchester Model 55
"Automatic" Single-Shot

Winchester Model 55
Lever-Action

Winchester Model 56

Winchester Model 57
Target

MODEL 60A TARGET RIFLE . . NiB $670 Ex $448 Gd $338
Essentially the same as Model 60 except has Lyman peep rear sight and square top front sight, semi-military target stock and web sling, weight: 5.5 lbs. Made from 1932 to 1939.

MODEL 61 HAMMERLESS SLIDE-ACTION REPEATER
Takedown. Caliber: .22 Short, Long, LR. Tubular magazine holds 20 Short, 16 Long, 14 LR. 24-inch round bbl. Weight: 5.5 lbs. Sights: Open rear; bead front. Plain pistol-grip stock, grooved semi-beavertail slide handle. Also available with 24-inch full-octagon bbl. and only calibers .22 Short, .22 LR or .22 WRF. Note: Octagon barrel model discontinued 1943 to 1944; assembled 1948.
W/round bbl. . . . . NiB $1330 Ex $987 Gd $478
W/grooved receiver . . . . . . NiB $1268 Ex $1160 Gd $800
W/octagon bbl.. . . . . NiB $1766 Ex $1447 Gd $1006

MODEL 61 MAGNUM . . . NiB $2650 Ex $1854 Gd $1000
Same as Standard Model 61 except chambered for .22 WMR; magazine holds 12 rounds. Made from 1960 to 1963.

MODEL 62
VISIBLE HAMMER . . . . . . NiB $1560 Ex $1288 Gd $1043
Modernized version of Model 1890. Caliber: .22 Short, Long, LR. 23-inch bbl. Weight: 5.5 lbs. Plain straight-grip stock, grooved semi-beavertail slide handle. Also available in Gallery Model chambered for .22 Short only. Made from 1932 to 1959. Note: Pre-WWII model (small forearm) commands 25% higher price.

MODEL 63 SELF-LOADING RIFLE
Takedown. Caliber: .22 LR High Speed only. Ten round tubular magazine in buttstock. 23-inch bbl. Weight: 5.5 lbs. Sights: Open rear, bead front. Plain pistol-grip stock and forearm. Originally available with 20-inch bbl. as well as 23-inch. Made from 1933 to 1959. Reintroduced in 1997.
W/23-inch bbl. . . . . NiB $1144 Ex $996 Gd $573
W/20-inch bbl. . . . . NiB $2690 Ex $1877 Gd $1133

W/grooved receiver . . . . NiB $2711 Ex $1912 Gd $995
Grade I (1997 BAC re-issue) . . . . NiB $707 Ex $576 Gd $488
High Grade (1997 BAC re-issue) . . . . . . NiB $705 Ex $579 Gd $495

MODEL 64 DELUXE
DEER RIFLE . . . . NiB $1370 Ex $1109 Gd $777
Same as Standard Model 64 calibers .30-30 and .32 Win. Special, except has checkered pistol-grip and semi-beavertail forearm, swivels and sling, weighs 7.75 lbs. Made from 1933 to 1956.

MODEL 64 LEVER-ACTION REPEATER
Standard Grade. Improved version of Models 94 and 55. Solid frame. Calibers: .25-35, .30-30, .32 Win. Special. Five round tubular two-thirds magazine. 20- or 24-inch bbl. Weight: About 7 lbs. Sights: Open rear; bead front on ramp w/sight cover. Plain pistol-grip stock and forearm. Made from 1933 to 1956. Production resumed in 1972 (caliber .30-30, 24-inch bbl.). Discontinued in 1974.
Original model. . . . . NiB $1079 Ex $883 Gd $620
1972-74 model. . . . . NiB $495 Ex $339 Gd $216

MODEL 64 .219 ZIPPER . . NiB $4107 Ex $3054 Gd $1978
Same as Standard Grade Model 64 except has 26-inch bbl., peep rear sight. Made from 1937 to 1947.

MODEL 65 LEVER-ACTION
REPEATER . . . . NiB $5044 Ex $3200 Gd $2555
Improved version of Model 53. Solid frame. Calibers: .25-20 and .32-20. Six round tubular half-magazine. 22-inch bbl. Weight: 6.5 lbs. Sights: Open rear, bead front on ramp base. Plain pistol-grip stock and forearm. Made from 1933 to 1947.

MODEL 65 .218 BEE . . . . NiB $5051 Ex $2979 Gd $2000
Same as Standard Model 65 except has 24-inch bbl., peep rear sight. Made from 1938 ti 1947.

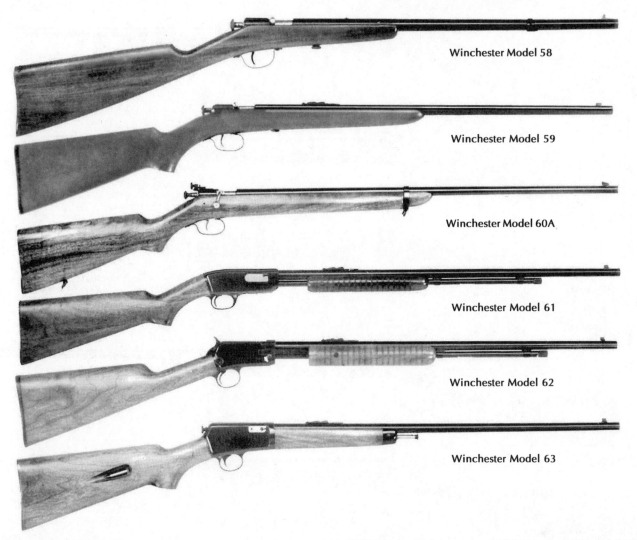

Winchester Model 58

Winchester Model 59

Winchester Model 60A

Winchester Model 61

Winchester Model 62

Winchester Model 63

MODEL 67 BOLT-ACTION
SINGLE-SHOT RIFLE. . . . . . . NiB $345 Ex $259 Gd $200
Takedown. Calibers: .22 Short, Long, LR, .22 LR round (smooth-bore), .22 WRF. 27-inch bbl. Weight: 5 lbs. Sights: Open rear, bead front. Plain pistol-grip stock (original model had grasping grooves in forearm). Made from 1934 to 1963.

MODEL 67 BOY'S RIFLE. . . . . NiB $345 Ex $259 Gd $200
Same as Standard Model 67 except has shorter stock, 20-inch bbl., weighs 4.25 lbs.

MODEL 68 BOLT-ACTION
SINGLE-SHOT . . . . NiB $345 Ex $259 Gd $200
Same as Model 67 except has rear peep sight. Made 1934 to 1946.

MODEL 69 BOLT-
ACTION RIFLE'S. . . . . NiB $450 Ex $370 Gd $200
Takedown. Caliber: .22 Short, Long, LR. Five or 10-round box magazine. 25-inch bbl. Weight: 5.5 lbs. Peep or open rear sight. Plain pistol-grip stock. Rifle cocks on closing motion of the bolt. Made from 1935 to 1937.

MODEL 69A BOLT-ACTION RIFLE
Same as the Model 69 except cocking mechanism was changed to cock the rifle by the opening motion of the bolt. Made from 1937 to 1963. Note: Models with grooved receivers command 20% higher prices.

Model 69A standard . . . . .NiB $489 Ex $397 Gd $290
Match model w/Lyman No. 57E
receiver sight . . . . .NiB $546 Ex $444 Gd $314
Target model w/Winchester
peep rear sight, swivels, sling . NiB $690 Ex $567 Gd $389

MODEL 70
Introduced in 1937, the Model 70 Bolt-Action Repeating Rifle was offered in several styles and calibers. Only minor design changes were made over a period of 27 years and more than 500,000 of these rifles were sold. The original model was dubbed "The Rifleman's Rifle." In 1964, the original Model 70 was superseded by a revised version with redesigned action, improved bolt, swaged (free-floating) barrel, restyled stock. This model again underwent major changes in 1972. Most visible: New stock with contrasting forend tip and grip cap, cut checkering (instead of impressed as in predecessor) knurled bolt handle. The action was machined from a solid block of steel with barrels made from chrome molybdenum steel. Other changes in the design and style of the Model 70 continued. The XTR models were added in 1978 along with the Model 70A, the latter omitting the white liners, forend caps and floor plates. In 1981, an XTR Featherweight Model was added to the line, beginning with serial number G1,440,000. This version featured lighter barrels, fancy-checkered stocks with Schnabel forend. After U.S. Repeating Arms took over the Winchester plant, the Model 70 went through even more changes as described under that section of Winchester rifles.

Winchester Model 64
Deer Rifle

Winchester Model 64
Standard

Winchester Model 64
1972-74 Type

Winchester Model 65

Winchester Model 67

Winchester Model 68

Winchester Model 69

Winchester Model 69 Match

Winchester Model 70
Basic Post-WWII Model

Winchester Model 70
Standard Model

Winchester Model 70
Super Grade

Winchester Model 70
African (1964)

Winchester Model 70
Deluxe (1964)

RIFLES

PRE-1964 MODEL 70

MODEL 70
AFRICAN RIFLE . . . . NiB $8000 Ex $5600 Gd $3809
Same general specifications as Super Grade Model 70 except w/25-inch bbl., 3-round magazine, Monte Carlo stock w/recoil pad. Weight: 9.5 lbs. Caliber: .458 Winchester Magnum. Made from 1956 to 1963.

MODEL 70 ALASKAN
Same as Standard Model 70 except calibers .338 Win. Mag., .375 H&H Mag.; 3-round magazine in .338, 4-round in .375 caliber; 25-inch bbl.; stock w/recoil pad. Weight: 8 lbs. in .338; 8.75 lbs. in .375 caliber. Made from 1960 to 1963.
.338 Win.
Mag. . . . . NiB $4135 Ex $2170 Gd $1166
.375 H&H Mag. . . . . NiB $4395 Ex $2100 Gd $1189

MODEL 70 BULL GUN. . . NiB $4467 Ex $3889 Gd $2356
Same as Standard Model 70 except w/heavy 28-inch bbl., scope bases, Marksman stock, weighs 13.25 lbs., caliber .300 H&H Magnum and .30-06 only. Disc. in 1963.

MODEL 70 FEATHERWEIGHT SPORTER
Same as Standard Model 70 except w/redesigned stock and 22-inch bbl., aluminum trigger guard, floorplate and buttplate. Calibers: .243 Win., .264 Win. Mag., .270 Win., .308 Win., .30-06, .358 Win. Weight: 6.5 lbs. Made from 1952 to 1963.

	NiB	Ex	Gd
.243 Win.	$1790	$1019	$707
.264 Win. Mag.	$2164	$1443	$998
.270 Win.	$1869	$1233	$854
.30-06 Springfield	$1043	$888	$596
.308 Win.	$1278	$866	$658
.358 Win.	$4566	$3000	$2043

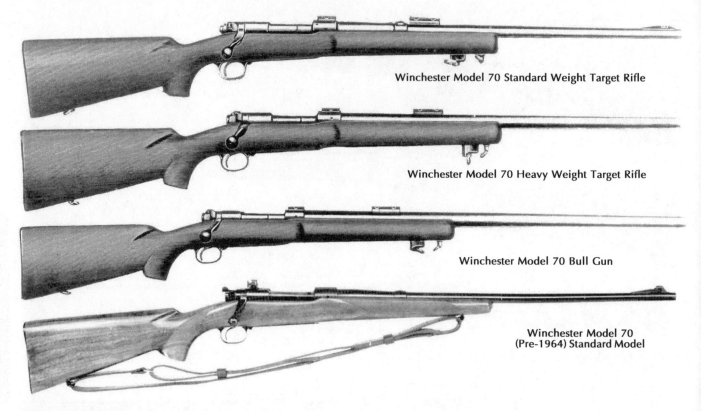

Winchester Model 70 Standard Weight Target Rifle

Winchester Model 70 Heavy Weight Target Rifle

Winchester Model 70 Bull Gun

Winchester Model 70 (Pre-1964) Standard Model

MODEL 70 NATIONAL
MATCH RIFLE . . . . NiB $3376 Ex $1943 Gd $1723
Same as Standard Model 70 except w/scope bases, Marksman-type target stock, weight: 9.5 lbs. caliber .30-06 only. Disc. 1960.

MODEL 70 STANDARD GRADE
Calibers: .22 Hornet, .220 Swift, .243 Win., .250-3000, .257 Roberts, .270 Win., 7x57mm, .30-06, .308 Win., .300 H&H Mag., .375 H&H Mag. Five round box magazine (4-round in Magnum calibers). 24-inch bbl. standard; 26-inch in .220 Swift and .300 Mag.; 25-inch in .375 Mag.; at one time a 20-inch bbl. was available. Sights: Open rear; hooded ramp front. Checkered walnut stock; Monte Carlo comb standard on later production. Weight: From 7.75 lbs. depending on caliber and bbl. length. Made from 1937 to 1963.
.22 Hornet (1937-58) . . . . NiB $3466 Ex $2033 Gd $1266
.220 Swift (1937-63). . . . . NiB $1497 Ex $1266 Gd $879
.243 Win. (1955-63). . . . . NiB $2145 Ex $1077 Gd $910
.250-3000 Sav. (1937-49) . . . . . NiB $5433 Ex $3810 Gd $2244
.257 Roberts (1937-59). . . . . . . NiB $3809 Ex $2088 Gd $1110
.264 Win. Mag. (1959-63, limited prod.) . .NiB $1988 Ex $1154 Gd $877
.270 Win. (1937-63). . . . . NiB $2588 Ex $2000 Gd $1165
7x57mm Mauser (1937-49). . . . . NiB $6970 Ex $4650 Gd $4077
7.65 Argentine (1937, limited prod.) Very Rare
.30-06 Springfield (1937-63). . . . NiB $3466 Ex $1880 Gd $1299
.308 Win. (1952-63, special order) Very Rare
.300 H&H (1937-63) . . . . NiB $3598 Ex $2079 Gd $1599
.300 Sav. (1944-50, limited prod.) Rare
.300 Win. Mag. (1962-63) . . . . . NiB $2244 Ex $1867 Gd $1265
.338 Win. Mag. (1959-63, special order only) .NiB $2144 Ex $1675 Gd $1197
.35 Rem. (1941-47, limited prod.) Very Rare
.358 Win. (1955-58) Very Rare
.375 H&H (1937-63) . . . . NiB $4676 Ex $4054 Gd $2354
.458 Win. Mag. (1956-63)
Super Grade only . . . . NiB $4000 Ex $2978 Gd $2369
9x57 Mauser (1937 only, limited prod.) Very Rare

MODEL 70 SUPER GRADE
Same as Standard Grade Model 70 except w/deluxe stock w/cheekpiece, black forend tip, pistol-grip cap, quick detachable swivels, sling. Disc. 1960. Prices for Super Grade models also reflect rarity in both production and caliber. Values are generally twice that of standard models of similar configuration.

MODEL 70 SUPER GRADE FEATHERWEIGHT
Same as Standard Grade Featherweight except w/deluxe stock w/cheekpiece, black forend tip, pistol-grip cap, quick detachable swivels, sling. Disc. 1960. Note: SG-FWs are very rare, but unless properly documented will not command premium prices. Prices for authenticated Super Grades Featherweight models are generally 4 to 5 times that of a standard production Featherweight model w/similar chambering.

MODEL 70 TARGET RIFLE
Same as Standard Model 70 except w/24-inch medium-weight bbl., scope bases, Marksman stock, weight 10.5 lbs. Originally offered in all of the Model 70 calibers, this rifle was available later in calibers .243 Win. and .30-06. Disc. 1963. Values are generally twice that of standard models of similar configuration.

MODEL 70 TARGET
HEAVY WEIGHT . . . . NiB $3160 Ex $2244 Gd $1590
Same general specifications as Standard Model 70 except w/either 24- or 26-inch heavy weight bbl. weight: 10.5 lbs. No checkering. .243 and .30-06 calibers.

MODEL 70 TARGET
BULL BARREL . . . . NiB $4466 Ex $2587 Gd $1964
Same general specifications as Standard Model 70 except 28-inch heavy weight bbl. and chambered for either .30-06 or .300 H&H Mag. Drilled and tapped for front sight base. Receiver slotted for clip loading. Weight: 13.25 lbs.

400

Winchester Model 70
International Army Match (1964)

Winchester Model 70
Mannlicher (1964)

Winchester Model 70
Standard (1964)

Winchester Model 70
Target (1964)

RIFLES

MODEL 70
VARMINT RIFLE . . . . **NiB $2388 Ex $1454 Gd $1145**
Same general specifications as Standard Model 70 except w/26-inch heavy bbl., scope bases, special varminter stock. Calibers: .220 Swift, .243 Win. Made from 1956 to 1963.

MODEL 70
WESTERNER . . . . **NiB $707 Ex $569 Gd $355**
Same as Standard Model 70 except calibers .264 Win. Mag., .300 Win. Mag.; 3-round magazine; 26-inch bbl. in former caliber, 24-inch in latter. Weight: 8.25 lbs. Made from 1960 to 1963.

1964-TYPE MODEL 70

MODEL 70 AFRICAN . . . . . . **NiB $595 Ex $397 Gd $338**
Caliber: .458 Win. Mag. Three round magazine. 22-inch bbl. Weight: 8.5 lbs. Special "African" sights. Monte Carlo stock w/ ebony forend tip, hand-checkering, twin stock-reinforcing bolts, recoil pad, QD swivels. Made from 1964 to 1971.

MODEL 70 DELUXE . . . . **NiB $790 Ex $588 Gd $445**
Calibers: .243, .270 Win., .30-06, .300 Win. Mag. Five round box magazine (3-round in Magnum). 22-inch bbl. (24-inch in Magnum). Weight: 7.5 lbs. Sights: Open rear; hooded ramp front. Monte Carlo stock w/ebony forend tip, hand-checkering, QD swivels, recoil pad on Magnum. Made from 1964 to 1971.

MODEL 70 INTERNATIONAL
ARMY MATCH RIFLE . . . . . . **NiB $1198 Ex $955 Gd $744**
Caliber: .308 Win. (7.62 NATO). Five round box magazine. 24-inch heavy barrel. Externally adj. trigger. Weight: 11 lbs. ISU stock w/ military oil finish, forearm rail for standard accessories, vertically adj. buttplate. Made in 1971. Value shown is for rifle w/o sights.

MODEL 70 MAGNUM
Calibers: 7mm Rem. Mag.; .264, .300, .338 Win. Mag.; .375 H&H Mag. Three round magazine. 24-inch bbl. Weight: 7.75 to 8.5 lbs. Sights: Open rear; hooded ramp front. Monte Carlo stock w/cheekpiece, checkering, twin stock-reinforcing bolts, recoil pad, swivels. Made from 1964 to 1971.
375 H&H Mag. . . . . **NiB $1043 Ex $787 Gd $678**
Other calibers . . . . **NiB $800 Ex $687 Gd $473**

MODEL 70 MANNLICHER . **NiB $1266 Ex $1090 Gd $789**
Calibers: .243, .270, .308 Win., .30-06. Five round box magazine. 19-inch bbl. Sights: open rear; hooded ramp front. Weight: 7.5 lbs. Mannlicher-style stock w/Monte Carlo comb and cheekpiece, checkering, steel forend cap, QD sling swivels. Made from 1969 to 1971.

MODEL 70 STANDARD . . . . . **NiB $788 Ex $577 Gd $400**
Calibers: .22-250, .222 Rem., .227, .243, .270, .308 Win., .30-06. Five round box magazine. 22-inch bbl. Weight: 7.5 lbs. Sights: Open rear; hooded ramp front. Monte Carlo stock w/cheekpiece, checkering, swivels. Made from 1964 to 1971.

Winchester Model 70
African (1972)

MODEL 70 TARGET . . . . . NiB $4200 Ex $2765 Gd $1489
Calibers: .308 Win. (7.62 NATO) and .30-06. Five round box magazine. 24-inch heavy bbl. Blocks for target scope. No factory sights installed, but drilled and tapped for front and rear sights. Weight: 10.25 lbs. High-comb Marksman-style stock, aluminum hand stop, swivels. Straight-grain, one-piece stock w/sling swivels, but no checkering. Made from 1964 to 1971.

MODEL 70 VARMINT. . . . NiB $2160 Ex $1576 Gd $1009
Same as Model 70 Standard except w/24-inch target weight bbl., blocks for target scope. No factory sights installed, but drilled and tapped for front and rear sights. Available in calibers .22-250, .222 Rem., and .243 Win. only. Weight: 9.75 lbs. Made 1964 to 1971.

1972-TYPE MODEL 70

MODEL 70 AFRICAN . . . . NiB $909 Ex $733 Gd $523
Similar to Model 70 Magnum except w/22-inch bbl. caliber .458 Win. Mag. w/special African open rear sight, reinforced stock w/ ebony forend tip, detachable swivels and sling; front sling swivel stud attached to bbl. Weight: 8.5 lbs. Made from 1972 to 1992.

MODEL 70 CLASSIC SM
Similar to Model 70 Classic Sporter except w/checkered black composite stock and matte metal finish. Made from 1994 to 1996.
MODEL 70 CLASSIC SM. . . . . NiB $765 Ex $595 Gd $355
.375 H&H . . . . NiB $944 Ex $765 Gd $535
W/BOSS, add $150
W/open sights, add. $50

MODEL 70 CLASSIC SPORTER
Similar to Model 70 Sporter except w/pre-64-style action w/con-trolled round feeding, classic-style stock. Optional open sights. Made from 1994 to 2006.
Standard model . . . . NiB $835 Ex $599 Gd $456
W/BOSS, add $150
W/open sights, add. $50

MODEL 70 CLASSIC SPORTER STAINLESS
Similar to Model 70 Classic Sporter except w/matte stainless steel finish. Weight: 7.5 lbs. No sights. Made from 1994 to 2006.
Standard model . . . . NiB $875 Ex $679 Gd $369
Magnum model . . . . NiB $845 Ex $743 Gd $498
W/BOSS, add $126

MODEL 70 CUSTOM SHARPSHOOTER
Calibers: .22-250, .223, .308 Win., .300 Win. Mag. 24- or 26-inch bbl. 44.5 inches overall (24-inch bbl.). Weight: 11 lbs. Custom-fitted, hand-honed action. McMillan A-2 target-style stock. Matte blue or stainless finish. Made from 1992 to 1996.
Blued model. . . . . NiB $2145 Ex $1598 Gd $1195
NiB $2145 Ex $1598 Gd $1195 NiB $2167 Ex $1620 Gd $2125

MODEL 70 CUSTOM SPORTING SHARPSHOOTER
Similar to Custom Sharpshooter Model except w/sporter-style gray composite stock. Stainless 24- or 26-inch bbl. w/blued receiver. Calibers: .270, 7mm STW, .300 Win. Mag. Made 1993 to 2006.
Blued model (disc. 1995) . . . . . . NiB $2155 Ex $1635 Gd $1266
Stainless model . . . . .NiB $2260 Ex $1723 Gd $1319

MODEL 70 GOLDEN 50TH ANNIVERSARY EDITION
BOLT-ACTION RIFLE . . . . NiB $1693 Ex $1279 Gd $1039
Caliber: .300 Win. Three round magazine. 24-inch bbl. 44.5 inches overall. Weight: 7.75 lbs. Checkered American walnut stock. Hand-engraved American scroll pattern on bbl., receiver, magazine cover, trigger guard and pistol-grip cap. Sights: Adj. rear; hooded front ramp. Inscription on bbl. reads "The Rifleman's Rifle 1937 to 1987." Only 500 made 1986 to 1987. (Value for guns in new condition.)

MODEL 70 FEATHERWEIGHT CLASSIC NiB $735 Ex $520 Gd $449
Similar to Model 70 XTR Featherweight except w/controlled-round feeding system. Calibers: .270, .280 and .30-06. Made 1992 to 2006.

MODEL 70 INTERNATIONAL
ARMY MATCH. . . . . NiB $1095 Ex $944 Gd $654
Caliber: .308 Win. (7.62mm NATO). Five round magazine, clip slot in receiver bridge. 24-inch heavy barrel. Weight: 11 lbs. No sights, but drilled and tapped for front and rear iron sights, and/or scope mounts. ISU target stock. Intro. 1973; disc.

MODEL 70 LIGHTWEIGHT. . . NiB $679 Ex $449 Gd $227
Calibers: .22-250 and .223 Rem.; .243, .270 and .308 Win.; .30-06 Springfield. Five round mag. capacity (6-round .223 Rem.). 22-inch barrel. 42 to 42.5 inches overall. Weight: 6 to 6.25 lbs. Checkered classic straight stock. Sling swivel studs. Made from 1986 to 1995.

MODEL 70 MAGNUM
Same as Model 70 except w/3-round magazine, 24-inch bbl., rein-forced stock w/recoil pad. Weight: 7.75 lbs. (except 8.5 lbs. in .375 H&H Mag.). Calibers: .264 Win. Mag., 7mm Rem. Mag., .300 Win. Mag., .338 Win. Mag., .375 H&H Mag. Made from 197 to 1980.
.375 H&H Magnum . . . . NiB $655 Ex $533 Gd $400
Other magnum calibers . . . . . NiB $554 Ex $495 Gd $388

MODEL 70 STANDARD . . . . . NiB $677 Ex $439 Gd $331
Same as Model 70A except w/5-round magazine, Monte Carlo stock w/cheekpiece, black forend tip and pistol-grip cap w/white spacers, checkered pistol grip and forearm, detachable sling swiv-els. Same calibers plus .227 Win. Made from 1972 to 1980.

MODEL 70 STANDARD CARBINE. . . NiB $596 Ex $437 Gd $369
Same general specifications as Standard Model 70 except 19-inch bbl. and weight: 7.25 lbs. Shallow recoil pad. Walnut stock and forend w/traditional Model 70 checkering. Swivel studs. No sights, but drilled and tapped for scope mount.

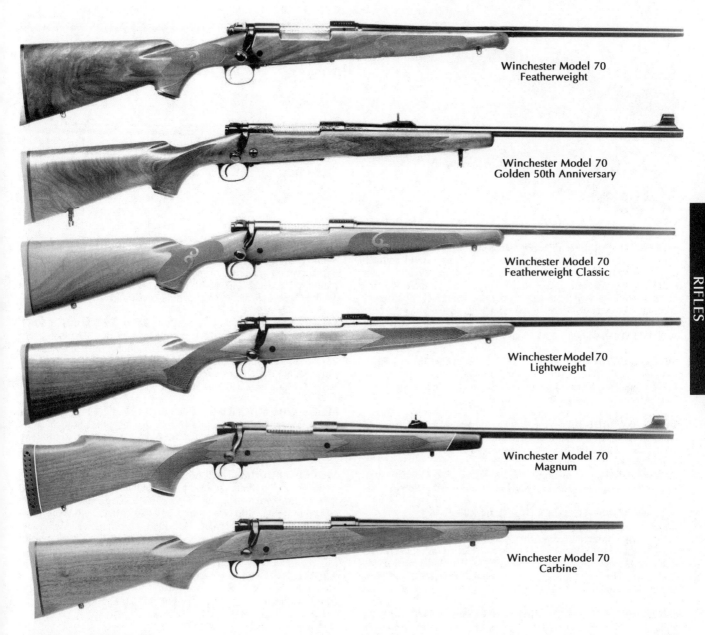

Winchester Model 70
Featherweight

Winchester Model 70
Golden 50th Anniversary

Winchester Model 70
Featherweight Classic

Winchester Model 70
Lightweight

Winchester Model 70
Magnum

Winchester Model 70
Carbine

RIFLES

MODEL 70 SPORTER DBM

Same general specifications as Model 70 Sporter SSM except w/ detachable box magazine. Calibers: .22-250 (disc. 1994), .223 (disc. 1994), .243 (disc. 1994), .270, 7mm Rem. Mag., .308 (disc. 1994), .30-06, .300 Win. Mag. Made from 1992 to 1994.
MODEL 70 SPORTER DBM . . . . NiB $755 Ex $585 Gd $359
S-model (w/iron sights) . . . . NiB $589 Ex $496 Gd $369

MODEL 70 STAINLESS

SPORTER SSM . . . . NiB $688 Ex $495 Gd $390
Same general specifications as Model 70 XTR Sporter except w/ checkered black composite stock and matte finished receiver, bbl. and other metal parts. Calibers: .270, 7mm Rem. Mag., .30-06, .300 Win. Mag., .338 Win. Mag. Weight: 7.75 lbs. Made 1992 to 1994.

MODEL 70 CLASSIC SUPER GRADE . NiB $977 Ex $857 Gd $590
Calibers: .270, 7mm Rem. Mag., .30-06, .300 Win. Mag., .338 Win.

Mag. Five round magazine (standard), 3-round (magnum). 24-inch bbl. 44.5 inches overall. Weight: 7.75 lbs. Checkered walnut stock w/sculptured cheekpiece and tapered forend. Scope bases and rings, no sights. Controlled-round feeding system. Made from 1990 to 1995. Improved in 1999. Disc. 2006.

MODEL 70 TARGET . . . . NiB $976 Ex $945 Gd $588
Calibers: .30-06 and .308 Win. (7.62mm NATO). Five round magazine. 26-inch heavy bbl. Weight: 10.5 lbs. No sights, but drilled and tapped for scope mount and open sights. High-comb Marksman-style target stock, aluminum hand stop and swivels. Intro. 1972. Disc.

MODEL 70 ULTRA MATCH . NiB $1099 Ex $976 Gd $569
Similar to Model 70 Target but custom grade w/26-inch heavy bbl. w/deep counterbore, glass bedding, externally adj. trigger. Intro. 1972. Disc.

Winchester Model 70
XTR Sporter

Winchester Model 70A

MODEL 70 VARMINT (HEAVY BARREL)
Same as Model 70 Standard except w/medium-heavy, counter-bored 26-inch bbl., no sights, stock w/less drop. Weight: 9 lbs. Calibers: .22-250 Rem., .223 Rem., .243 Win., .308 Win. Made 1972-93. Model 70 SHB, in .308 Win. only w/black synthetic stock and matte blue receiver/bbl. Made from 1992 to 1993.
Model 70 Varmint . . . . NiB $699 Ex $633 Gd $390
Model 70 SHB (synthetic stock, heavy bbl.)NiB $745 Ex $641 Gd $440

MODEL 70 WIN-CAM RIFLE. . NiB $576 Ex $488 Gd $338
Caliber: .270 Win. and .30-06 Springfield. 24-inch barrel. Camouflage one-piece laminated stock. Recoil pad. Drilled and tapped for scope. Made from 1986 to 1987.

MODEL 70 WINLITE BOLT-ACTION RIFLENiB $855 Ex $570 Gd $448
Calibers: .270 Win., .280 Rem., .30-06 Springfield, 7mm Rem., .300 Win. Mag., and .338 Win. Mag. Five round magazine; 3-round for Magnum calibers. 22-inch bbl.; 24-inch for Magnum calibers. 42.5 inches overall; 44.5, Magnum calibers. Weight: 6.25 to 7 lbs. Fiberglass stock w/rubber recoil pad, sling swivel studs. Made from 1986 to 1990.

MODEL 70 WIN-TUFF BOLT-ACTION RIFLE
Calibers: .22-250, .223, .243, .270, .308 and .30-06 Springfield. 22-inch bbl. Weight: 6.25–7 lbs. Laminated dye-shaded brown wood stock w/recoil pad. Barrel drilled and tapped for scope. Swivel studs. FWT Model made from 1986 to 1994. LW Model intro. 1992.
Featherweight model . . . . NiB $590 Ex $470 Gd $388
Lightweight model (Made 1992–93) . NiB $590 Ex $470 Gd $388

MODEL 70 XTR FEATHERWEIGHT . . NiB $590 Ex $470 Gd $388
Similar to Standard Win. Model 70 except lightweight American walnut stock w/classic Schnabel forend, checkered. 22-inch bbl., hooded blade front sight, folding leaf rear sight. Stainless-steel magazine follower. Weight: 6.75 lbs. Made from 1984 to 1994.

MODEL 70 XTR SPORTER RIFLE . . . . NiB $744 Ex $545 Gd $376
Calibers: .264 Win. Mag., 7mm Rem. Mag., .300 Win. Mag., .200 Weatherby Mag., and .338 Win. Mag. Three round magazine. 24-inch barrel. 44.5 inches overall. Weight: 7.75 lbs. Walnut Monte Carlo stock. Rubber buttpad. Receiver tapped and drilled for scope mounting. Made from 1986 to 1994.

MODEL 70 XTR SPORTER MAGNUM NiB $598 Ex $482 Gd $369
Calibers: .264 Win. Mag., 7mm Rem. Mag., .300 Win. Mag., .338 Win. Mag. Three round magazine. 24-inch bbl. 44.5 inches overall. Weight: 7.75 lbs. No sights furnished, optional adj. folding leaf rear; hooded ramp. Receiver drilled and tapped for scope. Checkered American walnut Monte Carlo-style stock w/satin finish. Made from 1986 to 1994.

MODEL 70 XTR
SPORTER VARMINT . . . . NiB $707 Ex $420 Gd $268
Same general specifications as Model 70 XTR Sporter, except in calibers .223, .22-250, .243 only. Checkered American walnut Monte Carlo-style stock w/cheekpiece. Made from 1986 to 1994.

MODEL 70A. . . . . NiB $450 Ex $316 Gd $231
Calibers: .222 Rem., .22-250, .243 Win., .25-06, .270 Win., .30-06, .308 Win. Four round magazine. 22-inch bbl. (except 24- or 26-inch in 25-06). Weight: 7.5 lbs. Sights: Open rear; hooded ramp front. Monte Carlo stock w/checkered pistol grip and forearm, sling swivels. Made from 1972 to 1978.

MODEL 70A MAGNUM . . . . . NiB $476 Ex $316 Gd $236
Same as Model 70A except w/3-round magazine, 24-inch bbl., recoil pad. Weight: 7.75 lbs. Calibers: .264 Win. Mag., 7mm Rem. Mag., .300 Win. Mag. Made from 1972 to 1978

MODEL 70 ULTIMATE CLASSIC BOLT-ACTION RIFLE
Calibers: .25-06 Rem., .264 Win., .270 Win., .270 Wby. Mag., .280 Rem., 7mm Rem. Mag., 7mm STW, .30-06, Mag., .300 Win. Mag., .300 Wby. Mag., .300 H&H Mag., .338 Win. Mag., .340 Wby. Mag., .35 Whelen, .375 H&H Mag., .416 Rem. Mag. and .458 Win. Mag. Three, 4- or 5-round magazine. 22- 24- 26-inch stainless bbl. in various configurations including: full-fluted tapered round, half round and half octagonal or tapered full octagonal. Weight: 7.75 to 9.25 lbs. Checkered fancy walnut stock. Made in 1995.
Model 70
Ultimate Classic . . . . NiB $2153 Ex $1999 Gd $1098
For Mag. calibers (.375 H&H,
.416 and .458), add $250

MODEL 70 LAMINATED STAINLESS
BOLT-ACTION RIFLE . . . . . NiB $2150 Ex $1792 Gd $952
Calibers: .270 Win., .30-06 Spfld., 7mm Rem. Mag., .300 Win. Mag., and .338 Win. Mag. Five round magazine. 24-inch bbl. 44.75 inches overall. Weight: 8 to 8.525 lbs. Gray/Black laminated stock. Made from 1998 to 1999.

MODEL 70 CHARACTERISTICS

MODEL 70 FIRST MODEL (SERIAL NUMBERS 1 – 80,000)
First manufactured in 1936; first sold in 1937. Receiver drilled for Lyman No. 57W or No. 48WJS receiver peep sights. Also drilled and tapped for Lyman or Fecker scope sight block. Weight w/24-inch bbl. in all calibers except .375 H&H Mag.: 8.25 lbs. 9 lbs. in H&H Mag. Early type safety located on bolt top. Production of this model ended in 1942 near serial number 80,000 due to World War II.

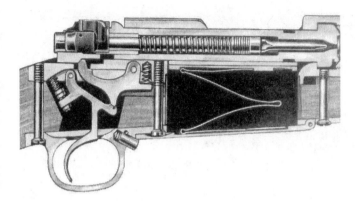

Cross-sectional view of the pre-1964 Winchester Model 70's speed lock action. This action cocks on the opening movement of the bolt with polished, smooth-functioning cams and guide lug, insuring fast and smooth operation.

MODEL 70 SECOND MODEL (SERIAL NUMBERS 80,000 – 350,000)
All civilian production of Winchester Model 70 rifles halted during World War II. Production resumed in 1947 w/improved safety and integral front-sight ramp. Serial numbers started at around 80,000. This model type was produced until 1954, ending around serial number 350,000.

MODEL 70 THIRD MODEL (SERIAL NUMBERS 350,000 – 400,000)
This variety was manufactured from 1954 to 1960 and retained many features of the Second Model except that a folding rear sight replaced the earlier type and front-sight ramps were brazed onto the bbl. rather than being an integral part of the bbl. The Model 70 Featherweight Rifle was intro. in 1954 in .308 WCF caliber. It was fitted w/light 22-inch bbl. and was also available w/either a Monte Carlo or Standard stock. The .243 Win. cartridge was added in 1955 in all grades of the Winchester Model 70 except the National Match and Bull Gun models. The .358 Win. cartridge was also intro. in 1955, along w/new Varmint Model chambered in .243 caliber only.

MODEL 70 FOURTH MODEL (SERIAL NUMBERS 400,000 – 500,000)
Different markings were inscribed on the barrels of these models and new magnum calibers were added; that is, .264 Win Mag., .338 Win. Mag, and .458 Win. Mag. All bbls. of this variation were about 0.13 inch shorter than previous ones. The .22 Hornet and .257 Roberts were disc. in 1962; the .358 Win. caliber in 1963.

MODEL 70 FIFTH MODEL (SERIAL NUMBERS 500,000 TO ABOUT 570,000)
These rifles may be recognized by slightly smaller checkering patterns and slightly smaller lightweight stocks. Featherweight bbls. were marked "Featherweight." Webbed recoil pads were furnished on magnum calibers.

POST-1964 MODEL 70 RIFLES

In 1964, the Winchester-Western Division of Olin Industries claimed that they were losing money on every Model 70 they produced. Both labor and material costs had increased to a level that could no longer be ignored. Other models followed suit. Consequently, sweeping changes were made to the entire Winchester line. Many of the older, less popular models were discontinued. Models that were to remain in production were modified for lower production costs.

**1964 WINCHESTER MODEL 70 RIFLES
SERIAL NUMBERS 570,000 TO ABOUT 707,000)**
The first version of the "New Model 70s" utilized a free-floating barrel, swaged rifle bore, new stock and sights, new type of bolt and receiver, and a different finish throughout on both the wood and metal parts. The featherweight grade was dropped, but six other grades were available in this new line:

Standard
Deluxe (Replaced Previous Super Grade)
Magnum
Varmint
Target
African

**1966 MODEL 70 RIFLES
(SERIAL NUMBERS 707,000-G TO ABOUT 1,005,000)**
In general, this group of Model 70s had fancier wood checkering, cross-bolt stock reinforcement, improved wood finish and improved action. One cross-bolt reinforcement was used on standard guns. Magnum calibers, however, used an additional forward cross-bolt and red recoil pad. The free-floating barrel clearance forward of the breech taper was reduced in thickness. Impressed checkering was used on the Deluxe models until 1968. Hand checkering was once again used on Deluxe and Carbine models in 1969; the big, red "W" was removed from all grip caps. A new, red safety-indicator and undercut cheekpiece was introduced in 1971.

**1972 MODEL 70 RIFLES
(SERIAL NUMBERS G1,005,000 TO ABOUT G1,360,000)**
Both the barrels and receivers for this variety of Model 70s were made from chrome molybdenum (C-M) steel. The barrels were tapered w/spiral rifling, ranging in length from 22 to 24 inches. Calibers .222 Rem., .227 Win. .22-250, .243 Win., .25-06, .270, .308 Win., .30-06 and .458 WM used the 22-inch length, while the following calibers used the 24-inch length: .222 Rem., .22-250, .243 Win., .264 Win. Mag., 7mm Mag., .300 and .375 H&H Mag. The .227 Win caliber was dropped in 1973; Mannlicher stocks were also disc. in 1973. The receiver for this variety of Model 70s was machined from a block of C-M steel. A new improved anti-bind bolt was introduced along with a new type of ejector. Other improvements included hand-cut checkering, pistol-grip stocks with pistol-grip and dark forend caps. An improved satin wood finish was also utilized.

**1978 MODEL 70 RIFLES
(SERIAL NUMBERS BEGAN AROUND G1,360,000)**
This variety of Model 70 was similar to the 1972 version except that a new XTR style was added which featured high-luster wood and metal finishes, fine-cut checkering, and similar embellishments. All Model 70 rifles made during this period used the XTR style; no standard models were available. In 1981, beginning with serial number G1,440,000 (approximately), a Featherweight version of the Model 70 XTR was introduced. The receiver was identical to the 1978 XTR, but lighter barrels were fitted. Stocks were changed to a lighter design with larger scroll checkering patterns and a Schnabel forend with no Monte Carlo comb. A satin sheen stock finish on the featherweight version replaced the high-luster finish used on the other XTR models. A new-style red buttplate with thick, black rubber liner was used on the Featherweight models. The grip cap was also redesigned for this model.

RIFLES

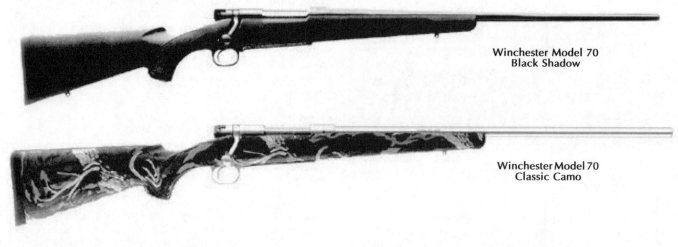

Winchester Model 70
Black Shadow

Winchester Model 70
Classic Camo

U.S. REPEATING ARMS MODEL 70 — 2006
In the early 1980s, negotiations began between Olin Industries and an employee-based corporation. The result of these negotiations ended with Olin selling all tools, machinery, supplies, etc. at the New Haven plant to the newly-formed corporation which was eventually named U.S. Repeating Arms Company. Furthermore, U.S. Repeating Arms Company purchased the right to use the Winchester name and logo. Winchester Model 70s went through very few changes the first two years after the transition. However, in 1984, the Featherweight Model 70 XTR rifles were offered in a new short action for .22-250 Rem., .223 Rem., .243 Win. and .308 Win. calibers, in addition to their standard action which was used for the longer cartridges. A new Model 70 lightweight carbine was also introduced this same year. Two additional models were introduced in 1985 — the Model 70 Lightweight Mini-Carbine Short Action and the Model 70 XTR Sporter Varmint. The Model 70 Winlite appeared in the 1986 "Winchester" catalog, along with two economy versions of the Model 70 — the Winchester Ranger and the Ranger Youth Carbine. Five or six different versions of the Winchester Model 70 had been sufficient for 28 years (1937 to 1964). Now, changes in design and the addition of new models each year seemed to be necessary to keep the rifle alive. New models were added, old models dropped, changed in design, etc., on a regular basis. Still, the Winchester Model 70 Bolt-Action Repeating Rifle — in any of its variations — is the most popular bolt-action rifle ever built.

MODEL 70 BLACK SHADOW . NiB $556 Ex $379 Gd $300
Calibers: .243 Win., .270 Win., .300 Win. Mag., .308 Win., .338 Win. Mag., .30-06 Spfld., 7mm STW., 7mm Rem. Mag. and 7mm-08 Rem. Three, 4- or 5-round magazine. 20- 24- 25- or 26-inch bbls. 39.5 to 46.75 inches overall.Weight: 6.5 to 8.25 lbs. Composite, Walnut or Gray/Black laminated stocks. Made from 1998 to 2006.

MODEL 70 CLASSIC
CAMO BOLT-ACTION RIFLE. . NiB $990 Ex $887 Gd $554
Calibers: .270 Win., 30-06 Spfld., 7mm Rem. Mag., .300 Win. Mag. Three or 5-round magazine. 24- or 26-inch bbl. 44.75 to 46.75 inches overall. Weight; 7.25 to 7.5 lbs. Mossy Oak finish and composite stock. Made from 1998 to 2006.

MODEL 70 CLASSIC COMPACT
BOLT-ACTION RIFLE . . . . NiB $3329 Ex $2221 Gd $2069
Calibers: .243 Win., .308 Win., and 7mm-08 Rem. Three round magazine. 20-inch bbl., 39.5 inches overall. Weight: 6.5 lbs. Walnut stock. Made from 1998 to 2006.

MODEL 70 CLASSIC LAREDO RANGE HUNTER
BOLT-ACTION RIFLE
Calibers: 7mm STW, 7mm Rem. mag., .300 Win. Mag. Three round magazine. 26-inch bbl. 46.75 inches overall. Weight: 9.5 lbs. Composite stock. Made from 1996 to 1999.
Classic Laredo . . . . NiB $788 Ex $675 Gd $500
W/fluted bbl. (intro. 1998) . . . . NiB $833 Ex $733 Gd $513
Bossa Classic model . . . . NiB $800 Ex $689 Gd $466

MODEL 70 COYOTE . . . . NiB $875 Ex $612 Gd $432
Calibers: .22-250 Rem., .223 Rem., and .243 Win. Five or 6-round magazine. 24- inch bbl., 44 inches overall. Weight: 9 lbs. Medium-heavy stainless steel barrel w/laminated stock. Reverse taper forend. Made from 1999. Disc.

MODEL 70 RANGER
COMPACT RIFLE . . . . NiB $555 Ex $369 Gd $257
Calibers: .22-250 Rem., .223 Rem., .243 Win., 7mm-08 Rem., Mag., and .308 Win. Five or 6-round magazine. 20- or 22-inch bbl. 41 inches overall. Weight: 6.5 lbs. Adjustable TRUGLO front and rear fiber optic sights. Push-feed action. Made from 1999 to 2000.

MODEL 70
STEALTH RIFLE . . . . NiB $920 Ex $707 Gd $449
Varminter style bolt-action rifle. Calibers: .22-250 Rem., .223 Rem., and .308 Win. Five or 6-round magazine. 26- inch bbl. 46 inches overall. Weight: 10.75 lbs. Black synthetic stock w/Pillar Plus Accu Block and full-length aluminum bedding block. Matte blue finish. Made from 1999. Disc.

MODEL 71 LEVER-ACTION REPEATER
Solid frame. Caliber: .348 Win. Four round tubular magazine. 20- or 24-inch bbl. Weight: 8 lbs. Sights: Open or peep rear; bead front on ramp w/hood. Walnut stock. Made from 1935 to 1957.
Standard Grade (no checkering, grip cap,
sling or swivels) . . . . NiB $1370 Ex $1167 Gd $789
Special Grade
(checkered pistol grip and forearm,
grip cap, QD swivels and sling) . NiB $2144 Ex $1798 Gd $1129
Special Grade carbine
(w/20-inch bbl., disc. 1940) . . . . NiB $2695 Ex $2155 Gd $1769
Standard Grade carbine
(20-inch bbl., disc. 1940) . . . . . . NiB $2266 Ex $1880 Gd $1249

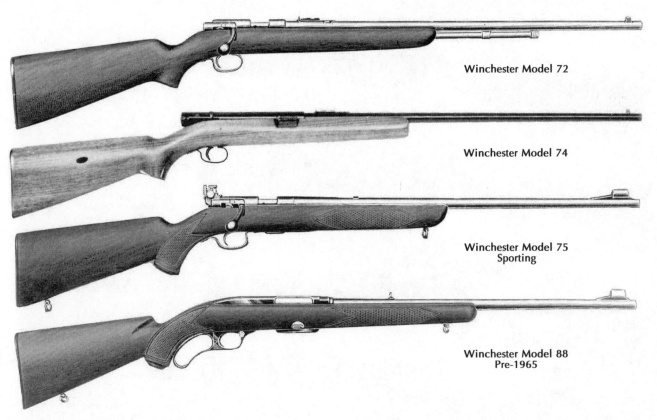

Winchester Model 72

Winchester Model 74

Winchester Model 75 Sporting

Winchester Model 88 Pre-1965

MODEL 72 BOLT-ACTION REPEATER NiB $525 Ex $266 Gd $189
Tubular magazine. Takedown. Caliber: .22 Short, Long, LR. Magazine holds 20 Short, 16 Long or 15 LR. 25-inch bbl. Weight: 5.75 lbs. Sights: Peep or open rear; bead front. Plain pistol-grip stock. Made from 1938 to 1959.

MODEL 73 LEVER-ACTION REPEATER
See Model 1873 rifles, carbines, "One of One Thousand" and other variations of this model at the beginning of Winchester Rifle Section. Note: The Winchester Model 1873 was the first lever-action repeating rifle bearing the Winchester name.

MODEL 74 SELF-LOADING RIFLE. . . NiB $389 Ex $290 Gd $198
Takedown. Calibers: .22 Short only, .22 LR only. Tubular magazine in buttstock holds 20 Short, 14 LR. 24-inch bbl. Weight: 6.25 lbs. Sights: Open rear; bead front. Plain pistol-grip stock, one-piece. Made from 1939 to 1955.

MODEL 75 SPORTING RIFLE . NiB $600 Ex $299 Gd $210
Same as Model 75 Target except has 24-inch bbl., checkered sporter stock, open rear sight; bead front on hooded ramp, weight: 5.5 lbs.

MODEL 75 TARGET RIFLE . . . NiB $600 Ex $299 Gd $210
Caliber: .22 LR. 5- or 10-round box magazine. 28-inch bbl. Weight: 8.75 lbs. Target sights (Lyman, Redfield or Winchester). Target stock w/pistol grip and semi-beavertail forearm, swivels and sling. Made from 1938 to 1959.

MODEL 77 SEMIAUTOMATIC RIFLE,
CLIP TYPE . . . . NiB $322 Ex $190 Gd $133
Solid frame. Caliber: .22 LR. Eight round clip magazine. 22-inch bbl. Weight: About 5.5 lbs. Sights: Open rear; bead front. Plain, one-piece pistol-grip stock. Made from 1955 to 1963.

MODEL 77,
TUBULAR MAGAZINE . . . . . . NiB $379 Ex $269 Gd $200
Same as Model 77. Clip type except has tubular magazine holding 15 rounds. Made from 1955 to 1963.

MODEL 86 CARBINE AND RIFLE
See Model 1886 at beginning of Winchester Rifle section.

MODEL 88 CARBINE
Same as Model 88 Rifle except has 19-inch bbl., plain carbine-style stock and forearm with bbl. band. Weight: 7 lbs. Made 1968 to 1973.
Standard calibers . . . . NiB $1335 Ex $1098 Gd $866
.284 Win. . . . . NiB $2095 Ex $1788 Gd $1077

MODEL 88 LEVER-ACTION RIFLE
Hammerless. Calibers: .243 Win., .284 Win., .308 Win., .358 Win. Four round box magazine. Three round in pre-1963 models and in .284. 22-inch bbl. Weight: About 7.25 lbs. One-piece walnut stock with pistol-grip, swivels (1965 and later models have basket-weave ornamentation instead of checkering). Made from 1955 to 1973. Note: .243 and .358 introduced 1956, later discontinued 1964; .284 introduced 1963.
Model 88 (checkered stock) . . . . . . NiB $1045 Ex $744 Gd $469
W/basketweave checkering. . . . . . . NiB $1045 Ex $744 Gd $469
.243 Win.. . . . . NiB $1269 Ex $1088 Gd $899
.284 Win.. . . . . NiB $2300 Ex $1969 Gd $1675

MODEL 1892 GRADE 1 LEVER-ACTION RIFLE
Similar to the original Model 1892. Calibers: .357 Mag., .44-40, .44 Mag., .45 LC. Ten round magazine. 24-inch round bbl. Weight: 6.25 lbs. 41.25 inches overall. Bead front sight, adjustable buckhorn rear. Etched receiver and gold trigger. Blue finish. Smooth straight-grip walnut stock and forewarn w/ metal grip cap. Made from 1997 to 1999.
Standard Rifle. . . . . NiB $677 Ex $558 Gd $425
Short Rifle (w/20-inch bbl., .44 Mag. only)NiB $669 Ex $500 Gd $488

Winchester Model 70
Coyote

Winchester Model 70
Ranger Compact

Winchester Model 70
Stealth

Winchester Model 94
Traditional

MODEL 94
ANTIQUE CARBINE . . . . NiB $588 Ex $448 Gd $290
Same as standard Post-64 Model 94 Carbine except has decorative scrollwork and casehardened receiver, brass-plated loading gate, saddle ring; caliber .30-30 only. Made from 1964 to 1984.

MODEL 94 CARBINE
Same as Model 1894 Rifle except 20-inch round bbl., 6-round full-length magazine. Weight: About 6.5 lbs. Originally made in calibers .25-35, .30-30, .32 Special and .38-55. Original version discontinued 1964.
Pre WWII (under No. 1,300,000) NiB $7250 Ex $5988 Gd $3866
Postwar, pre-1964
(under No. 2,707,000) . . . . NiB $865 Ex $707 Gd $530

MODEL 94
CLASSIC CARBINE . . . . NiB $655 Ex $443 Gd $400
Same as Canadian Centennial '67 Commemorative Carbine except without commemorative details; has scroll-engraved receiver, gold-plated loading gate. Made from 1967 to 1970.

MODEL 94
CLASSIC RIFLE . . . . NiB $6744 Ex $5467 Gd $4388
Same as Model 67 Rifle except without commemorative details; has scroll-engraved receiver, gold-plated loading gate. Made from 1968 to 1970.

MODEL 94
DELUXE CARBINE . . . . NiB $845 Ex $600 Gd $400
Caliber: .30-30 Win. Six round magazine. 20-inch bbl. 37.75 inches overall. Weight: 6.5 lbs. Semi-fancy American walnut stock with rubber buttpad, long forearm and specially cut checkering. Engraved with "Deluxe" script. Made from 1987 to 2006.

MODEL 94 LONG BARREL RIFLE . . . NiB $707 Ex $449 Gd $370
Caliber: .30-30 Win. Seven round magazine. 24-inch bbl. 41.75 inches overall. Weight: 7 lbs. American walnut stock. Blade front sight. Made from 1987 to 2006.

MODEL 94 TRAPPER . . . . NiB $779 Ex $588 Gd $430
Same as Winchester Model 94 Carbine except 16-inch bbl. and weight: 6 lbs., 2 oz. Made from 1980 to 2006.

MODEL 94 WIN-TUFF RIFLE . NiB $556 Ex $400 Gd $297
Caliber: .30-30 Win. Six round magazine. 20-inch bbl. 37.75 inches overall. Weight: 6.5 lbs. Brown laminated wood stock. Made from 198 to -2006.

MODEL 94 WRANGLER CARBINE
Same as standard Model 94 Carbine except has 16-inch bbl., engraved receiver and chambered for .32 Special & .38-55 Win.
Top-eject model (disc. 1984) . . . . . . NiB $623 Ex $414 Gd $331
Wranger II, angle-eject model
(disc. 1985) . . . . NiB $544 Ex $387 Gd $244

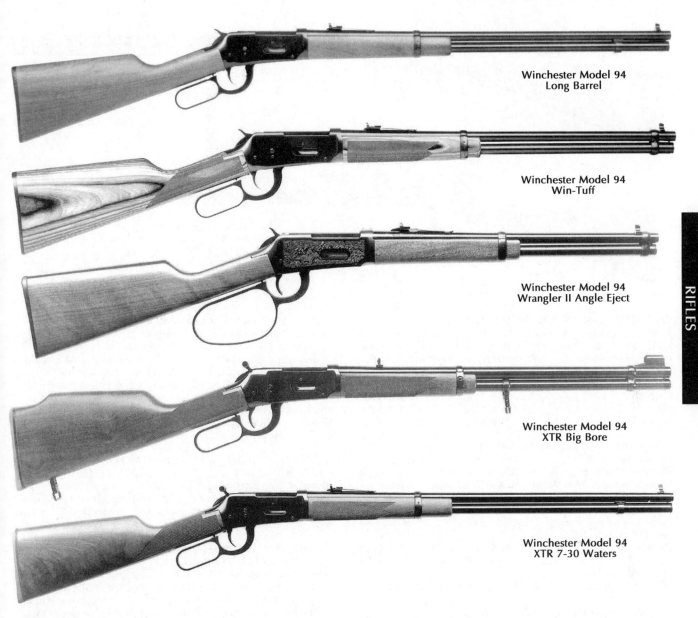

Winchester Model 94
Long Barrel

Winchester Model 94
Win-Tuff

Winchester Model 94
Wrangler II Angle Eject

Winchester Model 94
XTR Big Bore

Winchester Model 94
XTR 7-30 Waters

RIFLES

MODEL 94 XTR BIG BORE . . . NiB $745 Ex $572 Gd $445
Modified Model 94 action for added strength. Caliber: .375 Win. 20-inch bbl. Rubber buttpad. Checkered stock and forearm. Weight: 6.5 lbs. Made from 1978 to 2006.

MODEL 94 XTR
LEVER-ACTION RIFLE. . . . . . NiB $745 Ex $572 Gd $445
Same general specifications as standard Angle Eject M94 except chambered .30-30 and 7-30 Waters and has 20- or 24-inch bbl. Weight: 7 lbs. Made 1985 to 1988 by U.S. Repeating Arms.

MODEL 94 COMMEMORATIVES

MODEL 94 ANTLERED GAME. NiB $775 Ex $639 Gd $482
Standard Model 94 action. Gold-colored medallion inlaid in stock. Antique gold-plated receiver, lever tang and bbl. bands. Medallion and receiver engraved with elk, moose, deer and caribou. 20.5-inch bbl. Curved steel buttplate. In .30-30 caliber. 19,999 made in 1978.

MODEL 94 BICENTENNIAL
'76 CARBINE . . . . NiB $944 Ex $812 Gd $654
Same as Standard Model 94 Carbine except caliber .30-30 Win. only; antique silver-finished, engraved receiver; stock and forearm of fancy walnut, checkered, Bicentennial medallion embedded in buttstock, curved buttplate. 20,000 made in 1976.

MODEL 94 BUFFALO BILL COMMEMORATIVE
Same as Centennial '66 Rifle except receiver is black-chromed, scroll-engraved and bears name "Buffalo Bill"; hammer, trigger, loading gate, saddle ring, forearm cap, and buttplate are nickel-plated; Buffalo Bill Memorial Assn. commemorative medallion embedded in buttstock; "Buffalo Bill Commemorative" inscribed on bbl., facsimile signature "W.F. Cody, Chief of Scouts" on tang. Carbine has 20-inch bbl., 6-round magazine, 7-lb. weight. 112,923 made in 1968.
Carbine . . . . NiB $733 Ex $597 Gd $433
Rifle. NiB $778 Ex $650 Gd $469
Matched carbine/rifle set . NiB $1590 Ex $1370 Gd $1007

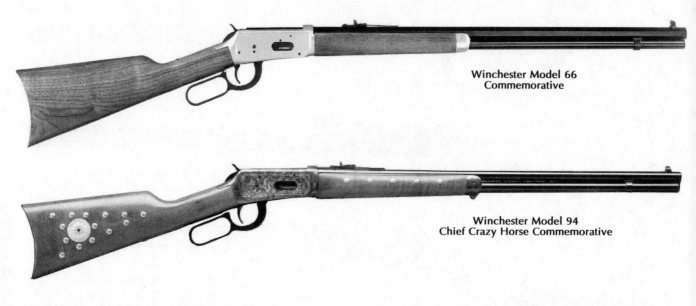

**Winchester Model 66
Commemorative**

**Winchester Model 94
Chief Crazy Horse Commemorative**

CANADIAN CENTENNIAL '67 COMMEMORATIVE
Same as Centennial '66 Rifle except receiver engraved with maple leaves and forearm cap is black-chromed, buttplate is blued, commemorative inscription in gold on barrel and top tang: "Canadian Centennial 1867–1967." Carbine has 20-inch bbl., 6-round magazine, weight: 7 lb., 90,398 made in 1967.

Carbine . . . . NiB $667 Ex $498 Gd $300
Rifle. . . . . NiB $667 Ex $498 Gd $300
Matched carbine/rifle set . . . . NiB $725 Ex $535 Gd $350

CENTENNIAL '66 COMMEMORATIVE
Commemorates Winchester's 100th anniversary. Standard Model 94 action. Caliber: .30-30. Full-length magazine holds 8 rounds. 26-inch octagon bbl. Weight: 8 lbs. Gold-plated receiver and forearm cap. Sights: Open rear; post front. Saddle ring. Walnut buttstock and forearm with high-gloss finish, solid brass buttplate. Commemorative inscription on bbl. and top tang of receiver. 100,478 made in 1966.

Carbine . . . . NiB $727 Ex $537 Gd $353
Rifle. . . . . NiB $727 Ex $537 Gd $353
Matched carbine/
rifle set . . . . NiB $1579 Ex $1355 Gd $954

MODEL 94 CHEYENNE
COMMEMORATIVE . . . . NiB $976 Ex $755 Gd $642
Available in Canada only. Same as Standard Model 94 Carbine except chambered for .44-40. 11,227 made in 1977.

MODEL 94 CHIEF CRAZY HORSE
COMMEMORATIVE . . . . NiB $888 Ex $733 Gd $521
Cailber: .38-55, 7-round tubular magazine. 24-inch bbl., 41.75 inches overall. Walnut stock with medallion of the United Sioux Tribes; buttstock and forend also decorated with brass tacks. Engraved receiver. Open rear sights; bead front sight. 19,999 made in 1983.

MODEL 94 COLT COMMEMORATIVE
CARBINE SET . . . . NiB $2689 Ex $2077 Gd $1370
Standard Model 94 action. Caliber: .44-40 Win. 20-inch bbl. Weight: 6.25 lbs. Features the horse-and-rider trademark and distinctive WC monogram in gold etching on left side of receiver. Sold in set with Colt Single Action Revolver chambered for same caliber.

MODEL 94 COWBOY COMMEMORATIVE CARBINE
Same as Standard Model 94 Carbine except caliber .30-30 only; nickel-plated receiver, tangs, lever, bbl. bands; engraved receiver, "Cowboy Commemorative" on bbl., commemorative medallion embedded in buttstock; curved buttplate. 20,915 made in 1970. Nickel-silver medallion inlaid in stock. Antique silver-plated receiver engraved with scenes of the old frontier. Checkered walnut stock and forearm. 19,999 made in 1970.

Cowboy carbine. . . . . NiB $744 Ex $588 Gd $414
1 of 300 model . . . . NiB $3278 Ex $2966 Gd $2288

MODEL 94 GOLDEN SPIKE COMMEMORATIVE
CARBINE . . . . NiB $855 Ex $670 Gd $495
Same as Standard Model 94 Carbine except caliber .30-30 only; gold-plated receiver, tangs and bbl. bands; engraved receiver, commemorative medallion embedded in stock. 64,758 made in 1969.

MODEL 94 ILLINOIS SESQUICENTENNIAL
COMMEMORATIVE CARBINE . NiB $622 Ex $398 Gd $287
Same as Standard Model 94 Carbine except caliber .30-30 only; gold-plated buttplate, trigger, loading gate, and saddle ring; receiver engraved with profile of Lincoln, commemorative inscription on receiver, bbl.; souvenir medallion embedded in stock. 31,124 made in 1968.

MODEL 94 LEGENDARY FRONTIERSMEN
COMMEMORATIVE . . . . NiB $769 Ex $655 Gd $488
Standard Model 94 action. Caliber: .39-55. 24-inch round bbl. Nickel-silver medallion inlaid in stock. Antique silver-plated receiver engraved with scenes of the old frontier. Checkered walnut stock and forearm. 19,999 made in 1979.

MODEL 94 LEGENDARY LAWMEN
COMMEMORATIVE . . . . NiB $769 Ex $655 Gd $488
Same as Standard Model 94 Carbine except .30-30 Win. only; antique silver-plated receiver engraved with action law-enforcement scenes. 16-inch Trapper bbl., antique silver-plated bbl. bands. 19,999 made in 1978.

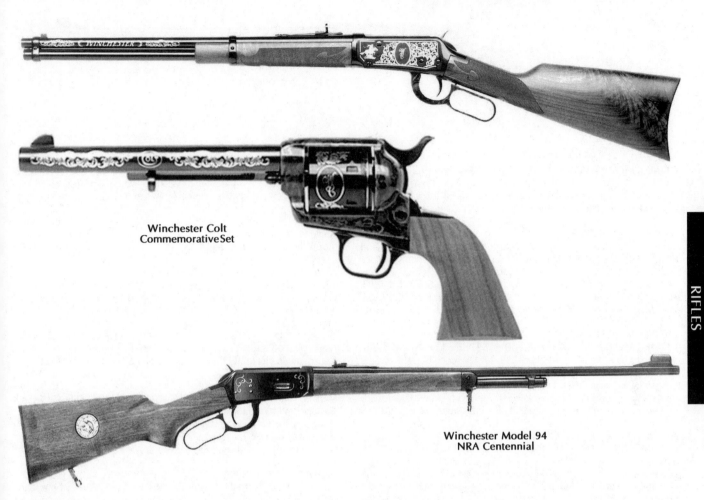

Winchester Colt
Commemorative Set

Winchester Model 94
NRA Centennial

MODEL 94 LONE STAR COMMEMORATIVE
Same as Theodore Roosevelt Rifle except yellow-gold plating; "Lone Star" engraving on receiver and bbl., commemorative medallion embedded in buttstock. 30,669 made in 1970.

Rifle or carbine . . . . NiB $754 Ex $598 Gd $449
Matched carbine/rifle set . . NiB $1499 Ex $1288 Gd $955

MODEL 94 NRA
CENTENNIAL MUSKET . . . . . . NiB $707 Ex $597 Gd $479
Commemorates 100th anniversary of National Rifle Association of America. Standard Model 94 action. Caliber: .30-30. Seven round magazine. 26-inch bbl. Sights: Military folding rear; blade front. Black chrome-finished receiver engraved "NRA 1871–1971" plus scrollwork. Barrel inscribed "NRA Centennial Musket." Musket-style buttstock and full-length forearm; commemorative medallion embedded in buttstock. Weight: 7.13 lbs. Made in 1971.

MODEL 94 NRA
CENTENNIAL RIFLE . . . . NiB $715 Ex $609 Gd $520
Same as Model 94 Rifle except has commemorative details as in NRA Centennial Musket (barrel inscribed "NRA Centennial Rifle"); caliber .30-30, 24-inch bbl., QD sling swivels. Made in 1971.

MODEL 94 NRA
CENTENNIAL MATCHED SET NiB $1400 Ex $1266 Gd $1077
Rifle and musket were offered in sets with consecutive serial numbers. Note: Production figures not available. These rifles offered in Winchester's 1972 catalog.

MODEL 94 NEBRASKA CENTENNIAL
COMMEMORATIVE CARBINE . . . . NiB $1133 Ex $933 Gd $633
Same as Standard Model 94 Carbine except caliber .30-30 only; gold-plated hammer, loading gate, bbl. band, and buttplate; souvenir medallion embedded in stock, commemorative inscription on bbl. 2,500 made in 1966.

MODEL 94 THEODORE ROOSEVELT
COMMEMORATIVE RIFLE/CARBINE
Standard Model 94 action. Caliber: .30-30. Rifle has 6-round half-magazine, 26-inch octagon bbl., weight: 7.5-lb. Carbine has 6-round full magazine, 20-inch bbl., weight: 7-lb. White gold-plated receiver, upper tang, and forend cap; receiver engraved with American Eagle, "26th President 1901–1909," and Roosevelt's signature. Commemorative medallion embedded in buttstock. Saddle ring. Half pistol-grip, contoured lever. 49,505 made in 1969.

Carbine . . . . NiB $733 Ex $560 Gd $398
Rifle. . . . . NiB $733 Ex $560 Gd $398
Matched set . . . . NiB $1415 Ex $1153 Gd $805

MODEL 94 TEXAS RANGER
ASSOCIATION CARBINE . . . . NiB $769 Ex $654 Gd $498
Same as Texas Ranger Commemorative Model 94 except special edition of 150 carbines, numbered 1 through 150, with hand-checkered full-fancy walnut stock and forearm. Sold only through Texas Ranger Association. Made in 1973.

Winchester Model 100

MODEL 94 TEXAS RANGER
COMMEMORATIVE CARBINE . . NiB $655 Ex $496 Gd $400
Same as Standard Model 94 Carbine except caliber .30-30 Win. only, stock and forearm of semi-fancy walnut, replica of Texas Ranger star embedded in buttstock, curved buttplate. 5,000 made in 1973.

MODEL 94 TRAPPER
Same as Winchester Model 94 Carbine except w/16-inch bbl. and weighs 6 lbs. 2 oz. Angle Eject introduced in 1985 also chambered for .357 Mag., .44 Mag. and .45 LC. Made from 1980 to 2006.
Top eject (disc. 1984) . . . . NiB $755 Ex $573 Gd $388
Angle eject (.30-30) . . . . NiB $445 Ex $306 Gd $200
.357 Mag., .44 mag., .45 LC, add. $50

MODEL 94 JOHN WAYNE
COMMEMORATIVE CARBINE.NiB $1597 Ex $1166 Gd $769
Standard Model 94 action. Caliber: .32-40. 18.5-inch bbl. Receiver is pewter-plated with engraving of Indian attack and cattle drive scenes. Oversized bow on lever. Nickel-silver medallion in buttstock bears a bas-relief portrait of Wayne. Selected American walnut stock with deep-cut checkering. Introduced by U.S. Repeating Arms in 1981.

MODEL 94 WELLS FARGO & CO.
COMMEMORATIVE CARBINE . . NiB $770 Ex $544 Gd $339
Same as Standard Model 94 Carbine except .30-30 Win. only; antique silver-finished, engraved receiver; stock and forearm of fancy walnut, checkered, curved buttplate. Nickel-silver stagecoach medallion (inscribed "Wells Fargo & Co. —1852–1977—125 Years") embedded in buttstock. 20,000 made in 1977.

MODEL 94 O. F. WINCHESTER
COMMEMORATIVE RIFLE. . . . . . . NiB $854 Ex $650 Gd $599
Standard Model 94 action. Caliber: .38-55. 24-inch octagonal bbl. Receiver is satin gold-plated with distinctive engravings. Stock and forearm semi-fancy American walnut with high grade checkering.

MODEL 94 WRANGLER CARBINE
Same as standard Model 94 Carbine except w/16-inch bbl., engraved receiver and chambered for .32 Special and .38-55 Win. Angle Eject introduced in 1985 as Wrangler II, also chambered for .30-30 Win., .44 Mag. and .45 LC. Made 1980 to 1986. Re-introduced in 1992.
Top eject (disc. 1984) . . . . NiB $398 Ex $290 Gd $200
Wrangler II, angle eject (.30-30). . . . . . NiB $390 Ex $285 Gd $195
.44 Mag or .45 LC, add $50

MODEL 94 WYOMING DIAMOND JUBILEE
COMMEMORATIVE CARBINE . . . . NiB $2166 Ex $1812 Gd $1347
Same as Standard Model 94 Carbine except caliber .30-30 Win. only, receiver engraved and casehardened in colors, brass saddle ring and loading gate, souvenir medallion embedded in buttstock, commemorative inscription on bbl. 1,500 made in 1964.

MODEL 94 ALASKAN PURCHASE CENTENNIAL
COMMEMORATIVE CARBINE . . . . NiB $2379 Ex $2006 Gd $1339
Same as Wyoming issue except different medallion and inscription. 1,501 made in 1967.

MODEL 94 XTR BIG BORE
Modified Model 94 action for added strength. Calibers: .307 Win., .356 Win., .375 Win. or .444 Marlin. 20-inch bbl. Six round magazine. Rubber buttpad. Checkered stock and forearm. Weight: 6.5 lbs. Made from 1978 to date.
Top eject (disc. 1984) . . . . NiB $755 Ex $577 Gd $488
Angle eject (intro. 1985) . . . . NiB $441 Ex $379 Gd $255
.356 Win. or .375 Win., add $200

MODEL 94 XTR LEVER-ACTION RIFLE
Same general specifications as standard M94 and Angle Eject M94 except chambered for .30-30 Win. and 7-30 Waters and has 20- or 24-inch bbl. Weight: 6.5 to 7 lbs. Made from 1978 to 1988 by U.S. Repeating Arms.
Top eject (disc. 1984) . . . . NiB $744 Ex $ 533 Gd $445
Angle eject (.30-30) . . . . NiB $744 Ex $533 Gd $445
Deluxe angle eject (.30-30) . . . . NiB $744 Ex $533 Gd $445
7-30 Waters, add $100

MODEL 100 AUTOLOADING RIFLE . . NiB $675 Ex $559 Gd $466
Gas-operated semiautomatic. Calibers: .243, .284, .308 Win. Four round clip magazine (3-round in .284). 22-inch bbl. Weight: 7.25 lbs. Sights: Open rear; hooded ramp front. One-piece stock w/pistol grip, basket-weave checkering, grip cap, sling swivels. Made from 1961 to 1973.

MODEL 100 CARBINE . . . . NiB $800 Ex $622 Gd $482
Same as Model 100 Rifle except has 19-inch bbl., plain carbine-style stock and forearm with bbl. band. Weight: 7 lbs. Made 1967 to 1973.

MODEL 121 DELUXE. . . . . NiB $200 Ex $126 Gd $90
Same as Model 121 Standard except has ramp front sight, stock with fluted comb and sling swivels. Made from 1967 to 1973.

MODEL 121 STANDARD
BOLT-ACTION SINGLE SHOT . . . NiB $167 Ex $100 Gd $80
Caliber: .22 Short, Long, LR. 20.75-inch bbl. Weight: 5 lbs. Sights: Open rear; bead front. Monte Carlo-style stock. Made 1967 to 1973.

MODEL 121 YOUTH . . . . NiB $200 Ex $126 Gd $90
Same as Model 121 Standard except has 1.25-inch shorter stock. Made from 1967 to 1973.

MODEL 131 BOLT-ACTION REPEATER NiB $269 Ex $227 Gd $178
Caliber: .22 Short, Long or LR. Seven round clip magazine. 20.75-inch bbl. Weight: 5 lbs. Sights: Open rear; ramp front. Plain Monte Carlo stock. Made from 1967 to 1973.

MODEL 135. . . . . NiB $244 Ex $169 Gd $155
Same as Model 131 except chambered for .22 WMR cartridge. Magazine holds 5 rounds. Made in 1967.

MODEL 141 BOLT-ACTION
TUBULAR REPEATER . . . . NiB $279 Ex $216 Gd $155
Same as Model 131 except has tubular magazine in buttstock; holds 19 Short, 15 Long, 13 LR. Made from 1967 to 1973.

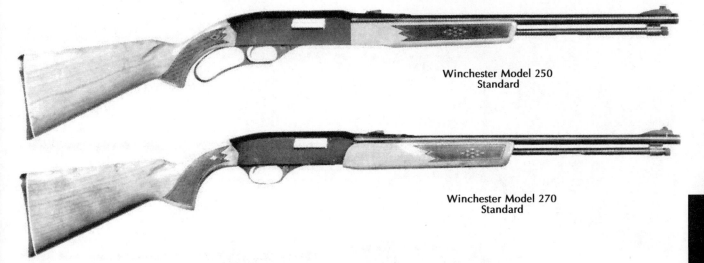

Winchester Model 250
Standard

Winchester Model 270
Standard

MODEL 145 . . . . **NiB $256 Ex $200 Gd $145**
Same as Model 141 except chambered for .22 WMR; magazine holds 9 rounds. Made in 1967.

MODEL 150 LEVER-ACTION CARBINE . **NiB $244 Ex $180 Gd $126**
Same as Model 250 except has straight loop lever, plain carbine-style straight-grip stock and forearm with bbl. band. Made from 1967 to 1973.

MODEL 190 CARBINE . . . . . . **NiB $255 Ex $195 Gd $135**
Same as Model 190 rifle except has carbine-style forearm with bbl. band. Made from 1967 to 1973.

MODEL 190 SEMIAUTOMATIC RIFLE . . **NiB $265 Ex $210 Gd $145**
Same as current Model 290 except has plain stock and forearm. Made from 1966 to 1978.

MODEL 250 DELUXE RIFLE . . **NiB $300 Ex $233 Gd $150**
Same as Model 250 Standard Rifle except has fancy walnut Monte Carlo stock and forearm, sling swivels. Made from 1965 to 1971.

**MODEL 250 STANDARD
LEVER-ACTION RIFLE**. . . . . . . **NiB $249 Ex $175 Gd $126**
Hammerless. Caliber: .22 Short, Long or LR. Tubular magazine holds 21 Short, 17 Long, 15 LR. 20.5-inch bbl. Sights: Open rear; ramp front. Weight: About 5 lbs. Plain stock and forearm on early production; later model has checkering. Made from 1963 to 1973.

MODEL 255 DELUXE RIFLE . . **NiB $338 Ex $265 Gd $175**
Same as Model 250 Deluxe Rifle except chambered for .22 WMR cartridge. Magazine holds 11 rounds. Made 1965 to 1973.

MODEL 255 STANDARD RIFLE **NiB $265 Ex $198 Gd $144**
Same as Model 250 Standard Rifle except chambered for .22 WMR cartridge. Magazine holds 11 rounds. Made from 1964 to 1970.

MODEL 270 DELUXE RIFLE . . **NiB $288 Ex $149 Gd $145**
Same as Model 270 Standard Rifle except has fancy walnut Monte Carlo stock and forearm. Made from 1965 to 1973.

**MODEL 270 STANDARD
SLIDE-ACTION RIFLE** . . . . **NiB $200 Ex $137 Gd $110**
Hammerless. Caliber: .22 Short, Long or LR. Tubular magazine holds 21 Short, 17 Long, 15 LR. 20.5-inch bbl. Sights: Open rear; ramp front. Weight: About 5 lbs. Early production had plain walnut stock and forearm (slide handle); latter also furnished in plastic (Cycolac); last model has checkering. Made from 1963 to 1973.

MODEL 278 DELUXE RIFLE . . **NiB $322 Ex $268 Gd $144**
Same as Model 270 Deluxe Rifle except chambered for .22 WMR cartridge. Tubular magazine holds 11 rounds. Made 1965–70.

**MODEL 278
STANDARD RIFLE** . . . . **NiB $266 Ex $190 Gd $133**
Same as Model 270 Standard Rifle except chambered for .22 WMR cartridge. Magazine holds 11 rounds. Made from 1964–70.

MODEL 290 DELUXE RIFLE . . **NiB $325 Ex $278 Gd $175**
Same as Model 290 Standard Rifle except has fancy walnut Monte Carlo stock and forearm. Made from 1965 to 1973.

MODEL 290 STANDARD SEMIAUTOMATIC RIFLE
Caliber: .22 Long or LR. Tubular magazine holds 17 Long, 15 LR. 20.5-inch bbl. Sights: Open rear; ramp front. Weight: About 5 lbs. Plain stock and forearm on early production; current model has checkering. Made from 1963 to 1977.
W/plain stock/forearm . . . . . . **NiB $286 Ex $227 Gd $133**
W/checkered
stock/forearm . . . . **NiB $300 Ex $255 Gd $156**

**MODEL 310 BOLT-ACTION
SINGLE SHOT** . . . . **NiB $370 Ex $300 Gd $210**
Caliber: .22 Short, Long, LR. 22-inch bbl. Weight: 5.63 lbs. Sights: Open rear; ramp front. Monte Carlo stock w/checkered pistol-grip and forearm, sling swivels. Made from 1972 to 1975.

**MODEL 320 BOLT-ACTION
REPEATER** . . . . **NiB $370 Ex $300 Gd $210**
Same as Model 310 except has 5-round clip magazine. Made from 1972 to 1974.

**MODEL 490
SEMIAUTOMATIC RIFLE**. . . . . **NiB $388 Ex $298 Gd $234**
Caliber: .22 LR. Five round clip magazine. 22-inch bbl. Weight: 6 lbs. Sights: Folding leaf rear; hooded ramp front. One-piece walnut stock w/checkered pistol grip and forearm. Made 1975 to 1977.

**MODEL 670 BOLT-ACTION
SPORTING RIFLE** . . . . **NiB $386 Ex $308 Gd $231**
Calibers: .227 Win., .243 Win., .270 Win., .30-06, .308 Win. Four round magazine. 22-inch bbl. Weight: 7 lbs. Sights: Open rear; ramp front. Monte Carlo stock w/checkered pistol-grip and forearm. Made from 1967 to 1973.

Winchester Model 310

Winchester Model 320

Winchester Model 490
Rifle

Winchester Model 670
Bolt-Action Rifle

Winchester Model 670
Magnum

Winchester Model 770

MODEL 670 CARBINE . . . . . . NiB $356 Ex $338 Gd $244
Same as Model 670 Rifle except has 19-inch bbl. Weight: 6.75
lbs. Calibers: .243 Win., .270 Win., .30-06. Made from 1967
to 1970.

MODEL 670 MAGNUM . . . . . NiB $410 Ex $356 Gd $281
Same as Model 670 Rifle except has 24-inch bbl., reinforced
stock with recoil pad with slightly different checkering pattern.
Weight: 7.25 lbs. Calibers: .264 Win. Mag., 7mm Rem. Mag.,
.300 Win. Mag. Open rear sight; ramp front sight with hood.
Made from 1967 to 1970.

MODEL 770 BOLT-ACTION
SPORTING RIFLE . . . . NiB $443 Ex $321 Gd $277
Model 70-type action. Calibers: .22-250, .222 Rem., .243, .270 Win.,
.30-06. Four round box magazine. 22-inch bbl. Sights: Open rear;
hooded ramp front. Weight: 7.13 lbs. Monte Carlo stock, checkered
pistol-grip and forend; sling swivels. Made from 1969 to 1971.

MODEL 770 MAGNUM . . . . . NiB $443 Ex $318 Gd $233
Same as Standard Model 770 except 24-inch bbl., weight: 7.25 lbs.,
recoil pad. Calibers: 7mm Rem. Mag., .264 and .300 Win. Mag.
Made from 1969 to 1971.

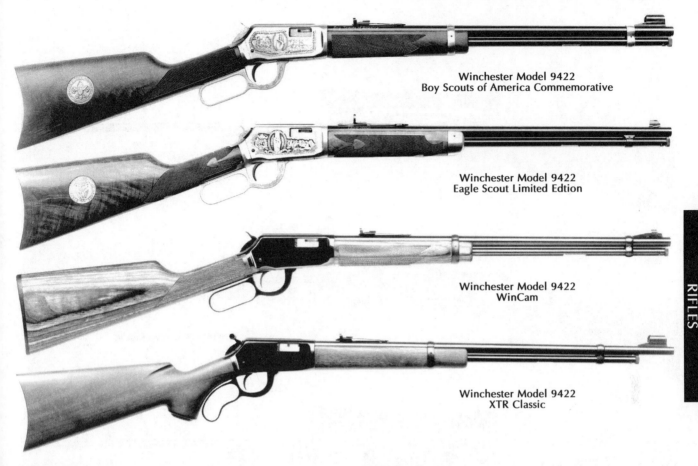

Winchester Model 9422
Boy Scouts of America Commemorative

Winchester Model 9422
Eagle Scout Limited Edtion

Winchester Model 9422
WinCam

Winchester Model 9422
XTR Classic

MODEL 9422 LEVER-ACTION RIMFIRE RIFLES

Similar to the standard Model 94 except chambered for .22 Rimfire. Calibers: .22 Short, Long, LR. (9422) or .22 WMR (9422M). Tubular magazine holds 21 or 15 Short.17 or 12 Long, 15 or 11 LR (9422 or Trapper) or 11 or 8 WRM (9422M or Trapper M). 16.5- or 20.5 inch bbl. 33.125- to 37.125 inches overall. Weight: 5.75 to 6.25 lbs. Open rear sight; hooded ramp front. Carbine-style stock and barrel-band forearm. Stock options: Walnut (Standard), laminated brown (WinTuff), laminated green (WinCam). Made from 1972. Disc.

Standard model	NiB $655	Ex $368	Gd $265
WinCam model	NiB $690	Ex $376	Gd $254
WinTuff model	NiB $533	Ex $337	Gd $233
Legacy model	NiB $844	Ex $577	Gd $300
Trapper model (16.5-inch bbl.)	NiB $765	Ex $456	Gd $268
XTR Classic model	NiB $800	Ex $587	Gd $370
High Grade Series I	NiB $1389	Ex $1085	Gd $770
High Grade Series II	NiB $1389	Ex $1985	Gd $770

25th Anniversary Edition

Grade (1 of 2,500)	NiB $860	Ex $569	Gd $447

25th Anniversary Edition

High Grade (1 of 250)	NiB $1688	Ex $1233	Gd $1044

25th Anniversary Edition

High Grade (1 of 250)	NiB $843	Ex $667	Gd $495

Eagle Scout

Commemorative (1 of 1,000)	NiB $1448	Ex $1177	Gd $988
.22 WRM, add			10%

DOUBLE XPRESS RIFLE . . NiB $3889 Ex $2866 Gd $1744

Over/under double rifle. Caliber: .30-06. 23.5-inch bbl. Weight: 8.5 lbs. Made for Olin Corp. by Olin-Kodensha in Japan. Introduced 1982.

RANGER YOUTH

BOLT-ACTION CARBINE . . . . NiB $499 Ex $338 Gd $270
Calibers: .223 (discontinued 1989), .243 Win., and .308 Win. Four and 5-round magazine. Bbl.: 20-inch. Weight: 5.75 lbs. American hardwood stock. Open rear sight. Made 1985 to 2006 by U.S. Repeating Arms.

RANGER LEVER-ACTION CARBINE. . NiB $655 Ex $398 Gd $290
Caliber: .30-30. Five round tubular magazine. Bbl.: 20-inch round. Weight: 6.5 lbs. American hardwood stock. Economy version of Model 94. Made 1985 to 2006 by U.S. Repeating Arms.

RANGER BOLT-ACTION CARBINE . . . . NiB $470 Ex $388 Gd $243
Calibers: .223 Rem., .243 Win., .270, .30-06, 7mm Rem. (discontinued 1985), Mag. Three and 4-round magazine. Bbl.: 24-inch in 7mm; 22-inch in .270 and .30-06. Open sights. American hardwood stock. Made from 1985 to 1999 by U.S. Repeating Arms.

MODEL 1892 GRADE I LEVER-ACTION RIFLE

Similar to the original Model 1892. Calibers: .357 Mag., .44-40, .44 Mag., .45 LC. 10-round magazine. 24-inch round bbl. Weight: 6.25 lbs. 41.25 inches overall. Bead front sight, adjustable buckhorn rear. Etched receiver and gold trigger. Blue finish. Smooth straight-grip walnut stock and forearm w/ metal grip cap. Made from 1997. Disc.

Standard Rifle	NiB $800	Ex $713	Gd $482

Short Rifle (w/20-inch bbl.,

.44 Mag. only)	NiB $750	Ex $495	Gd $352

MODEL 1892 GRADE

II LEVER-ACTION RIFLE . . . NiB $1388 Ex $1167 Gd $828
Similar to the Grade I Model 1892 except w/gold appointments and receiver game scene. Chambered .45 LC only. Limited production of 1,000 in 1997.

Winslow Commander Grade

Winslow Crown Grade

Winslow Regent Grade
Bushmaster Stock

WINSLOW ARMS COMPANY — Camden, South Carolina

BOLT-ACTION SPORTING RIFLE
Action: FN Supreme Mauser, Mark X Mauser, Remington 707 and 788, Sako, Winchester 70. Standard calibers: .17-222, .17-223, .222 Rem., .22-250, .243 Win., 6mm Rem., .25-06, .257 Roberts, .270 Win., 7x57, .280 Rem., .284 Win., .308 Win., .30-06, .358 Win. Magnum calibers: .17-222 Mag., .257 Wby., .264 Win., .270 Wby., 7mm Rem., 7mm Wby., .300 H&H, .300 Wby., .300 Win., .308 Norma, 8mm Rem., .338 Win., .358 Norma, .375 H&H, .375 Wby., .458 Win. Three-round magazine in standard calibers, 2-round in magnum. 24-inch barrel in standard calibers, 26-inch in magnum. Weight: With 24-inch bbl., 7 to 7.5 lbs.; with 26-inch bbl., 8 to 9 lbs. No sights. Stocks: "Bushmaster" with slender pistol-grip and beavertail forearm, "Plainsmaster" with full curl pistol-grip and flat forearm; both styles have Monte Carlo cheekpiece. Values shown are for basic rifle in each grade; extras such as special fancy wood, more elaborate carving, inlays and engraving can increase these figures considerably. Made from 1962 to 1989.

Commander Grade	NiB $1897	Ex $1565	Gd $1177
Regal Grade	NiB $2066	Ex $1590	Gd $1322
Regent Grade	NiB $2175	Ex $1698	Gd $1443
Regimental Grade	NiB $2966	Ex $2490	Gd $1788
Crown Grade	NiB $3228	Ex $2579	Gd $2188
Royal Grade	NiB $3590	Ex $2666	Gd $2077
Imperial Grade	NiB $4100	Ex $3695	Gd $3000
Emperor Grade	NiB $7070	Ex $5266	Gd $4590

ZEPHYR DOUBLE RIFLES—Manufactured by Victor Sarasqueta Company, Eibar, Spain

DOUBLE RIFLE . . . . . NiB $22,656 Ex $18,622 Gd $12,799
Boxlock. Calibers: Available in practically every caliber from .22 Hornet to .505 Gibbs. Bbls.: 22 to 28 inches standard, but any lengths were available on special order. Weight: 7 lbs. for the smaller calibers up to 12 or more lbs. for the larger calibers. Imported by Stoeger from about 1938 to 1951.

36th Edition
GUN TRADER'S GUIDE

Shotguns

American Arms
Bristol (Sterling) Over/Under

American Arms
Derby Hammerless Double

American Arms
Gentry/York Hammerless Double

American Arms
Silver Over/Under

ALDENS SHOTGUN — Chicago, Illinois

MODEL 670 CHIEFTAIN SLIDE ACTION NiB $331 Ex $239 Gd $190
Hammerless. Gauges: 12, 20 and others. Three round tubular magazine. Bbl.: 26- to 30-inch; various chokes. Weight: 6.25 to 7.5 lbs. depending on bbl. length and ga. Walnut-finished hardwood stock.

AMERICAN ARMS — N. Kansas City, Missouri

See also Franchi Shotguns.

BRISTOL (STERLING) O/U . . . . NiB $853 Ex $621 Gd $500
Boxlock w/Greener crossbolt and engraved sideplates. Single selective trigger. Selective automatic ejectors. Gauges: 12, 20; 3-inch chambers. 26-, 28-, 30-, or 32-inch vent-rib bbls. w/screw-in choke tubes (Improved Cylinder/Modified/Full). Weight: 7 lbs. Antique-silver receiver w/game scene or scroll engraving. Checkered full pistol-grip-style buttstock and forearm w/high-gloss finish. Imported 1986-88 designated Bristol; redesignated Sterling 1989 to 1990.

BRITTANY HAMMERLESS DOUBLE. . NiB $863 Ex $744 Gd $508
Boxlock w/engraved case-colored receiver. Single selective trigger. Selective automatic ejectors. Gauges: 12, 20. 3-inch chambers. Bbls.: 25- or 27-inch w/screw-in choke tubes (IC/M/F).

Weight: 6.5 lbs. (20 ga.). Checkered English-style walnut stock w/semi-beavertail forearm or pistol-grip stock w/high-gloss finish. Imported 1989 to 2000.

CAMPER SPECIAL . . . . NiB $217 Ex $166 Gd $90
Similar to the Single Barrel except takedown model w/21-inch bbl., M choke and pistol-grip stock. Made in 1989.

COMBO . . . . NiB $292 Ex $200 Gd $156
Similar to the Single-Barrel model except available w/interchangeable rifle and shotgun bbls. .22 LR/20-ga. shotgun or .22 Hornet/12-ga. shotgun. Rifle bbl. has adj. rear sights; blade-type front sight. Made in 1989.

DERBY HAMMERLESS DOUBLE

Sidelock w/engraved sideplates. Single non-selective or double triggers. Selective automatic ejectors. Gauges: 12, 20, 28 and .410. 3 inch chambers. Bbls.: 26-inch (IC/M) or 28-inch (M/F). Weight: 6 lbs. (20 ga.). Checkered English-style walnut stock and splinter forearm w/hand-rubbed oil finish. Engraved frame/sideplates w/antique silver finish. Imported 1986 to 1994.

12 or 20 ga. . . . . NiB $1254 Ex $907 Gd $677
28 ga. or .410 (disc. 1991) . . NiB $1377 Ex $979 Gd $855

American Arms
WS/SS Hammerless Double

F.S. SERIES O/U
Greener crossbolt in Trap and Skeet configuration. Single selective trigger. Selective automatic ejectors. 12 gauge only. 26-, 28-, 30-, or 32-inch separated bbls. Weight: 6.5 to 7.25 lbs. Black or chrome receiver. Checkered walnut buttstock and forearm. Imported 1986 to 1987.

Model F.S. 200 Boxlock . . . . . NiB $867 Ex $677 Gd $490
Model F.S. 300 Boxlock . . . . NiB $1099 Ex $827 Gd $568
Model F.S. 400 Sidelock . . . NiB $1386 Ex $1197 Gd $871
Model F.S. 500 Sidelock . . . NiB $1386 Ex $1197 Gd $871

GENTRY/YORK HAMMERLESS DOUBLE
Chrome, coin-silver or color casehardened boxlock receiver w/ scroll engraving. Double triggers. Extractors. Gauges: 12, 16, 20, 28, .410. 3-inch chambers (16 and 28 have 2.75-inch). Bbls.: 26-inch (IC/M) or 28-inch (M/F, 12, 16 and 20). Weight: 6.75 lbs. (12 ga.). Checkered walnut buttstock w/pistol-grip and beavertail forearm; both w/semi-gloss oil finish. Imported as York from 1986 to 1988, redesignated Gentry 1989 to 2000.

Gentry 12, or 16 or 20 ga. . . . . .NiB $733 Ex $577 Gd $428
Gentry 28 ga. or .410. . . . . .NiB $755 Ex $590 Gd $488
York 12, 16 or 20 ga. (disc. 1988) . . .NiB $690 Ex $577 Gd $433
York 20 ga. or .410 . . . . .NiB $690 Ex $577 Gd $433

GRULLA #2 HAMMERLESS DOUBLE
True sidelock w/engraved detachable sideplates. Double triggers. Extractors and cocking indicators. Gauges: 12, 20, .410 w/3-inch chambers; 28 w/2.75-inch. 26-inch bbl. Imported 1989 to 2000.

Standard model . . . . NiB $3798 Ex $2886 Gd $2166
Two-bbl. set (disc. 1995) . NiB $3876 Ex $3688 Gd $2544

SILVER I O/U
Boxlock. Single selective trigger. Extractors. Gauges: 12, 20 and .410 w/3-inch chambers; 28 w/2.75 inch. Bbls.: 26-inch (IC/M), 28-inch (M/F, 12 and 20 ga. only). Weight: 6.75 lbs. (12 ga.). Checkered walnut stock and forearm. Antique-silver receiver w/ scroll engraving. Imported 1987 to 2000.

12 or 20 ga. . . . . NiB $622 Ex $535 Gd $368
28 ga. or .410. . . . . NiB $663 Ex $590 Gd $477

SILVER II O/U
Similar to Model Silver I except w/selective automatic ejectors and 26-inch bbls. w/screw-in tubes (12 and 20 ga.). Fixed chokes (28 and .410). Made 1987 to 2000.

12 or 20 ga . . . . NiB $735 Ex $600 Gd $489
28 ga or .410 . . . . NiB $730 Ex $652 Gd $464
Upland Lite II . . . . NiB $1254 Ex $1066 Gd $855
Two-bbl. set . . . . NiB $1293 Ex $1088 Gd $867

SILVER LITE O/U
Similar to Model Silver II except w/blued, engraved alloy receiver. Available in 12 and 20 ga. only. Imported from 1990 to 1992.

Standard Model . . . . NiB $922 Ex $655 Gd $477
Two-bbl. Set . . . . NiB $1169 Ex $908 Gd $733

SILVER SKEET/TRAP . . . . NiB $855 Ex $640 Gd $569
Similar to the Silver II Model except has 28-inch (Skeet) or 30-inch (Trap) ported bbls. w/target-style rib and mid-bead sight. Imported 1992 to 1994.

SILVER SPORTING O/U . . . . NiB $966 Ex $768 Gd $633
Boxlock. Single selective trigger. Selective automatic ejectors. Gauges: 12, 2.75-inch chambers. 28-inch bbls.w/Franchoke tubes (SK, IC, M and F). Weight: 7.5 lbs. Checkered walnut stock and forearm. Special broadway rib and vented side ribs. Engraved receiver w/chrome-nickel finish. Imported from 1990 to 2000.

SINGLE-SHOT SHOTGUN
Break-open action. Gauges: 10 (3.5), 12, 20, .410, 3-inch chamber. Weight: about 6.5 lbs. Bead front sight. Walnut-finished hardwood stock w/checkered grip and forend. Made from 1988 to 1990.

10 ga. (3.5-inch). . . . . NiB $198 Ex $117 Gd $75
12 & 20 ga., .410 . . . . NiB $200 Ex $99 Gd $66
Multi-choke bbl., add $50

SLUGGER SINGLE-SHOT SHOTGUN . NiB $190 Ex $100 Gd $79
Similar to the Single-Shot model except in 12 and 20 ga. only w/24-inch slug bbl. Rifle-type sights and recoil pad. Made 1989 to 1990.

TS/OU 12 SHOTGUN . . . . NiB $744 Ex $555 Gd $490
Turkey Special. Boxlock. Single selective trigger. Selective automatic ejectors. Gauge: 12, 3.5-inch chambers. Bbls.: 24-inch O/U w/screw-in choke tubes (IC, M, F). Weight: 6 lbs. 15 oz. Checkered European walnut stock and beavertail forearm. Matte blue metal finish. Imported 1987 to 2000.

TS/SS 10 HAMMERLESS DOUBLE . . . NiB $700 Ex $533 Gd $400
Turkey Special. Same general specifications as Model WS/ SS 10, except w/26-inch side-by-side bbls., screw-in choke tubes (F/F) and chambered for 10-ga. 3.5-inch shells. Weight: 10 lbs., 13 oz. Imported 1987 to 1993.

TS/SS 12 HAMMERLESS DOUBLE . . . NiB $766 Ex $533 Gd $421
Same general specifications as Model WS/SS 10 except in 12 ga. w/26-inch side-by-side bbls. and 3 screw-in choke tubes (IC/M/F). Weight: 7 lbs., 6 oz. Imported 1987 to 2000.

WS O/U 12 SHOTGUN . . . . . NiB $644 Ex $538 Gd $377
Waterfowl Special. Boxlock. Single selective trigger. Selective automatic ejectors. Gauge: 12; 3.5-inch chambers. Bbls.: 28-inch O/U w/ screw-in tubes (IC/M/F). Weight: 7 lbs. Checkered European walnut stock and beavertail forearm. Matte blue metal finish. Imported 1987-2000.

WS/SS 10 HAMMERLESS DOUBLE . . NiB $883 Ex $671 Gd $428
Waterfowl Special. Boxlock. Double triggers. Extractors. Gauge: 10; 3.5-inch chambers. Bbls.: 32-inch side/side choked F/F. Weight: About 11 lbs. Checkered walnut stock and beavertail forearm w/ satin finish. Parkerized metal finish. Imported from 1987 to 1995.

SHOTGUNS

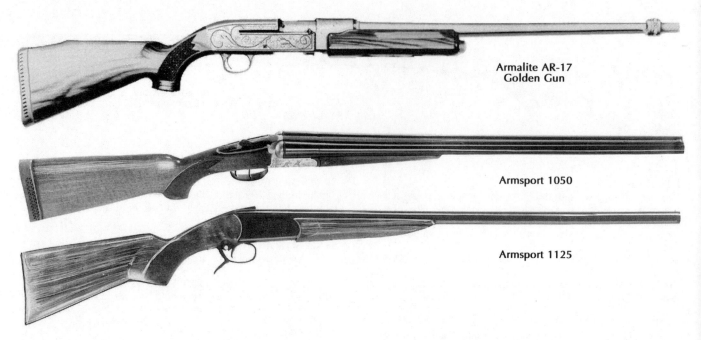

Armalite AR-17
Golden Gun

Armsport 1050

Armsport 1125

WT O/U SHOTGUN . . . . **NiB $844 Ex $657 Gd $533**
Same general specifications as Model WS/OU 12 except chambered for 10-ga. 3.5-inch shells. Extractors. Satin wood finish and matte blue metal. Imported 1987 to 2000.

ARMALITE, INC. — Costa Mesa, California

AR-17 GOLDEN GUN . . . . . . **NiB $863 Ex $643 Gd $559**
Recoil-operated semiautomatic. High-test aluminum bbl. and receiver housing. 12 ga. only. Two round capacity. 24-inch bbl. w/interchangeable choke tubes: IC/M/F. Weight: 5.6 lbs. Polycarbonate stock and forearm recoil pad. Gold-anodized finish standard, also made w/black finish. Made 1964 to 1965. Fewer than 2,000 produced.

ARMSCOR (Arms Corp.) — Manila, Philippines. Imported until 1991 by Armscor Precision, San Mateo, CA; 1991–95 by Ruko Products, Inc., Buffalo NY

MODEL M-30 FIELD PUMP SHOTGUN
Double slide-action bars w/damascened bolt. Gauge: 12 only w/3-inch chamber. Bbl.: 28-inch w/fixed chokes or choke tubes. Weight: 7.6 lbs. Walnut or walnut finished hardwood stock.
**Model M-30F (w/hard
wood stock, fixed choke)** . . . . **NiB $288 Ex $212 Gd $149**
**Model M-30F (w/hard-
wood stock and choke tubes)** . **NiB $288 Ex $212 Gd $149**
**Model M-30F/IC (w/walnut
stock and choke tubes)** . . . . . . **NiB $366 Ex $247 Gd $169**

MODEL M-30 RIOT PUMP
Double-action slide bar w/damascened bolt. Gauge: 12 only w/3-inch chamber. Bbls: 18.5 and 20-inch w/IC bore. Five- or 7-round magazine. Weight: 7 lbs, 2 ozs. Walnut finished hardwood stock.
Model M-30R6 (W/5-round magazine). NiB $190 Ex $121 Gd $90

Model M-30R8 (W/7-round magazine)NiB $219 Ex $135 Gd $100

MODEL M-30 SPECIAL COMBO
Simlar to Special Purpose Model except has detachable synthetic stock that removes to convert to pistol-grip configuration.
Model M-30C (disc. 1995) . . . **NiB $249 Ex $200 Gd $155**
Model M-30RP (disc. 1995) . . **NiB $249 Ex $200 Gd $155**

MODEL M-30 SPECIAL PURPOSE
Double-action slide bar w/damascened bolt. Seven round magazine.   Gauge: 12 only w/3-inch chamber. 20-inch bbl. w/cylinder choke. Iron sights (DG Model) or venter handguard (SAS Model). Weight: 7.5 lbs. Walnut finished hardwood stock.
Model M-30DG (Deer Gun) . . . . **NiB $266 Ex $198 Gd $137**
Model M-30SAS (Special Air Services) . . **NiB $277 Ex $218 Gd $125**

ARMSPORT, INC. — Miami, Florida

1000 SERIES HAMMERLESS DOUBLES
Side-by-side w/engraved receiver, double triggers and extractors. Gauges: 10 (3.5), 12, 20, .410- 3-inch chambers. Model 1033: 10 ga., 32-inch bbl. Model 1050/51: 12 ga., 28-inch bbl., M/F choke. Model 1052/53: 20 ga., 26-inch bbl., I/M choke. Model 1054/57: .410 ga., 26-inch bbl., I/M. Model 1055: 28 ga., Weight: 5.75 to 7.25 lbs. European walnut buttstock and forend. Made in Italy. Importation disc. 1993.
Model 1033 (10 ga., disc. 1989) . .NiB $844 Ex $690 Gd $497
Model 1050 (12 ga., disc. 1993) . .NiB $766 Ex $692 Gd $477
Model 1051 (12 ga., disc. 1985) . .NiB $503 Ex $412 Gd $326
Model 1052 (20 ga., disc. 1985) . .NiB $477 Ex $390 Gd $288
Model 1053 (20 ga., disc. 1993) . .NiB $790 Ex $666 Gd $459
Model 1054 (.410, disc. 1992) . . .NiB $888 Ex $739 Gd $522
Model 1055 (28 ga., disc. 1992) . .NiB $554 Ex $448 Gd $336
Model 1057 (.410, disc. 1985) . . .NiB $569 Ex $481 Gd $357

MODEL 1125 SINGLE-SHOT SHOTGUN NiB $196 Ex $139 Gd $98
Bottom-opening lever. Gauges: 12, 20. 3-inch chambers. Bead front sight. Plain stock and forend. Imported 1987-89.

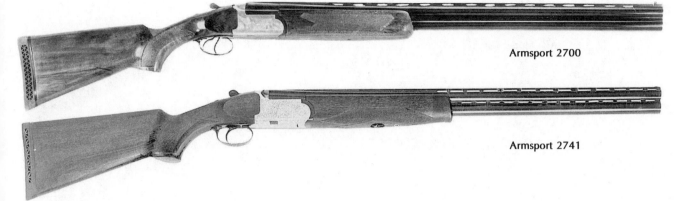

Armsport 2700

Armsport 2741

MODEL 2700 GOOSE GUN
Similar to the 2700 Standard Model except 10 ga. w/3.5-inch chambers. Double triggers w/28-inch bbl. choked IC/M or 32-inch bbl., F/F. 12mm wide vent rib. Weight: 9.5 lbs. Canada geese engraved on receiver. Antiqued silver-finished action. Checkered European walnut stock w/rubber recoil pad. Imported from Italy 1986 to 1993.

W/fixed choke . . . . NiB $1167 Ex $933 Gd $676
W/choke tubes . . . . NiB $1433 Ex $979 Gd $724

MODEL 2700 OVER/UNDER SERIES
Hammerless, takedown shotgun w/engraved receiver. Selective single or double triggers. Gauges: 10, 12, 20, 28 and .410. Bbl.: 26-or 28-inch w/fixed chokes or choke tubes. Weight: 8 lbs. Checkered European walnut buttstock and forend. Made in Italy. Importation disc. 1993.

Model 2701 12 ga. (disc. 1985) . . . . NiB $613 Ex $500 Gd $357
Model 2702 12 ga. . . . . NiB $635 Ex $525 Gd $378
Model 2703 20 ga. (disc. 1985) . . . . NiB $668 Ex $544 Gd $365
Model 2704 20 ga. . . . . NiB $655 Ex $548 Gd $400
Model 2705 (.410, DT, fixed chokes) NiB $775 Ex $638 Gd $454
Model 2730/31 (BOSS-style action,
SST Choke tubes) . . . . NiB $868 Ex $733 Gd $538
Model 2733/35 (Boss-style
action, extractors). . . . . NiB $790 Ex $644 Gd $466
Model 2741 (Boss-style
action, ejectors) . . . . NiB $678 Ex $566 Gd $412
Model 2742 Sporting Clays
(12 ga./choke tubes) . . . . NiB $835 Ex $679 Gd $555
Model 2744 Sporting Clays
(20 ga./choke tubes) . . . . NiB $855 Ex $677 Gd $499
Model 2750 Sporting Clays
(12 ga./sideplates). . . . . NiB $955 Ex $723 Gd $528
Model 2751 Sporting Clays
(20 ga./sideplates). . . . . NiB $943 Ex $759 Gd $544

MODEL 2755 SLIDE-ACTION SHOTGUN
Gauge: 12 w/3-inch chamber. Tubular magazine. Bbls.: 28- or 30-inch w/fixed choke or choke tubes. Weight: 7 lbs. European walnut stock. Made in Italy 1986 to 1987.

Standard model, fixed choke. . NiB $444 Ex $366 Gd $270
Standard model, choke tubes . NiB $579 Ex $489 Gd $355
Police model, 20-inch bbl. . . . NiB $390 Ex $333 Gd $244

MODEL 2900 TRI-BARREL (TRILLING) SHOTGUN
Boxlock. Double triggers w/top-tang bbl. selector. Extractors. Gauge: 12; 3-inch chambers. Bbls.: 28-inch (IC, M and F). Weight: 7.75 lbs. Checkered European walnut stock and forearm. Engraved silver receiver. Imported 1986 to 1987 and 1990 to 1993.

Model 2900 (W/fixed chokes)NiB $2288 Ex $1844 Gd $1307
Model 2900 (choke tubes) NiB $2945 Ex $2385 Gd $1669
Deluxe grades, add. $600

ARRIETA, S.L. — Elgoibar, Spain.
Imported by New England Arms Corp., Wingshooting Adventures Quality Arms, Griffin & Howe and Orvis

Custom double-barreled shotguns with frames scaled to individual gauges. Standard gauges are 12 and 16. Add: 5% for small gauges (20, 24, 28, 32 and .410 bore) on currently manufactured models; $900 for single trigger (most actions); 5% for matched pairs; 10% for rounded action on standard models; extra bbls., add $1375 to $2000 per set.

MODEL 557 STANDARD . . . . . . .NiB $4428 Ex $3966 Gd $2044
Gauges: 12, 16 or 20. Demi-Bloc steel barrels, detachable engraved sidelocks, double triggers, ejectors.

MODEL 570 LIEJA . . . . NiB $4949 Ex $4210 Gd $2588
Gauges: 12, 16 or 20. Non-detachable sidelocks.

MODEL 578 VICTORIA . . . . . . .NiB $6280 Ex $4366 Gd $2290
Gauges: 12, 16 or 20. Similar to Model 570 but with fine English scrollwork.

LIGERA MODEL . . . . NiB $5634 Ex $4247 Gd $3270
Available in all gauges. Lightweight 12 ga. has 2-inch chambers, lightweight or standard action. Includes unique frame engraving and Turkish wood upgrade. Wt. appox. 6 pounds.

MODEL 590 REGINA . . . . NiB $3589 Ex $3177 Gd $2229
Gauges: 12, 16 or 20. Similar to Model 570 but has more elaborate engraving.

MODEL 595 PRINCIPE . . . . . . .NiB $5579 Ex $4367 Gd $3410
Available in all gauges, sidelock, engraved hunting scenes, ejectors,double triggers.

MODEL 600 IMPERIAL . . . . .NiB $9115 Ex $5910 Gd $3588
Gauges: 12, 16 or 20. Self-opening action, very ornate engraving throughout.

MODEL 601 IMPERIAL TYRO . . .NiB $9350 Ex $6005 Gd $4337
Available in all gauges, sidelock, nickel plating, ejectors,single selective trigger, border engraving.

MODEL 801 . . . . .NiB $12,870 Ex $11,665 Gd $10,644
All gauges, detachable sidelocks, ejectors,coin-wash finish, Churchill-style engraving.

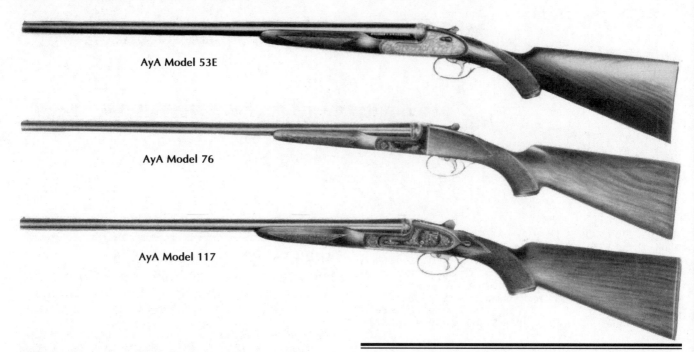

AyA Model 53E

AyA Model 76

AyA Model 117

MODEL 802 . . . . **NiB $13,669 Ex $11,544 Gd $8534**
Gauges: 12, 16 or 20. Similar to Model 801 except with non-detachable sidelocks, finest Holland-style engraving.

BOSS ROUND BODY . . . . **NiB $8799 Ex $7733 Gd $6477**
Available in all gauges, Boss pattern best quality engraving, wood upgrade.

MODEL 803 . . . . **NiB $11,333 Ex $9121 Gd $6344**
Available in all gauges. Similar to Model 801 except finest Purdey-style engraving.

MODEL 871 . . . . **NiB $7333 Ex $4144 Gd $2608**
Available in all gauges. Rounded frame sidelock action with Demi-Bloc barrels, scroll engraving, ejectors,double trigger.

MODEL 871 EXTRA FINISH. NiB $7555 Ex $4759 Gd $3977
Similar to Model 871 except with standard game scene engraving with woodcock and ruffed grouse.

MODEL 872 . . . . **NiB $16,788 Ex $13,690 Gd $11,550**
Available in all gauges, rounded frame sidelock action, Demi-Bloc barrels, elaborate scroll engraving with third lever fastener.

MODEL 873 . . . . **NiB $17,228 Ex $14,788 Gd $11,766**
Available in all gauges. Sidelock, gold line engraved action, ejectors, single selective trigger.

MODEL 874 . . . . **NiB $12,980 Ex $11,887 Gd $6,777**
Available in all gauges. Sidelock, gold line engraved action, Demi-Bloc barrels.

MODEL 875 . . . . **NiB $18,960 Ex $14,449 Gd $11,733**
Available in all gauges. Custom model built to individual specifications only, elaborate engraving, gold inlays

MODEL 931 . . . . **NiB $26,877 Ex $19,785 Gd $15,860**
Available in all gauges. Self-opening action, elaborate engraving, H&H selective ejectors.

ASTRA SHOTGUNS — Guernica, Spain. Manufactured by Unceta y Compania

MODEL 650 O/U SHOTGUN
Hammerless, takedown w/double triggers. 12 ga. w/.75-inch chambers. Bbls.: 28-inch (M/F or SK/SK); 30-inch (M/F). Weight: 6.75 lbs. Checkered European walnut buttstock and forend. Disc. 1987.
W/extractors . . . . **NiB $733 Ex $579 Gd $454**
W/ejectors . . . . **NiB $844 Ex $685 Gd $477**

MODEL 750 O/U SHOTGUN
Similar to the Model 650 except w/selective single trigger and ejectors. Made in field, skeet and trap configurations from 1980. Disc. 1987.
Field model w/extractors . . . . **NiB $779 Ex $637 Gd $500**
Field model w/ejectors . . . . . **NiB $888 Ex $755 Gd $566**
Trap or Skeet model . . . . **NiB $1099 Ex $867 Gd $559**

AYA (Aguirre Y Aranzabal) — Eibar, Spain (previously manufactured by Diarm). Imported by Armes De Chasse, Hertford, NC

MODEL 1 HAMMERLESS DOUBLE
A Holland & Holland sidelock similar to the Model 2 except in 12 and 20 ga. only, w/special engraving and exhibition-grade wood. Weight: 5-8 lbs., depending on ga. Imported by Diarm until 1987, since 1992 by Armes de Chasse.
Model 1 Standard . . . . . . **NiB $9177 Ex $5448 Gd $3229**
Model 1 Deluxe . . . . . **NiB $13,110 Ex $10,077 Gd $7470**
W/Extra set of bbls., add **$750**

AyA Matador II

AyA Model XXV Boxlock

MODEL 2 HAMMERLESS DOUBLE
Sidelock action w/selective single or double triggers automatic ejectors and safety. Gauges: 12, 20, 28, (2.75-inch chambers); .410 (3-inch chambers). Bbls.: 26- or 28-inch w/various fixed choke combinations. Weight: 7 lbs. (12 ga.). English-style straight walnut buttstock and splinter forend. Imported by Diarm until 1987, since 1992 by Armes de Chasse.

12 or 20 ga. w/double triggers NiB $4777 Ex $3178 Gd $2090
12 or 20 ga. w/single trigger NiB $4777 Ex $3178 Gd $2090
28 ga. or .410 w/double triggers NiB $4777 Ex $3178 Gd $2090
28 ga. or .410 w/single trigger NiB $3533 Ex $2970 Gd $2135
W/Extra set of bbls., add $1450

MODEL 4 HAMMERLESS DOUBLE
Lightweight Anson & Deely boxlock, scalloped frame. Gauges: 12, 16, 20, 28, and .410. Bbls.: 25- to 28-inch w/concave rib. Importation disc. 1987 and resumed in 1992 by Armes de Chasse.

12 ga. . . . . NiB $2098 Ex $1376 Gd $1099
16 ga. (early importation) . NiB $2098 Ex $1376 Gd $1099
20 ga. . . . . NiB $2098 Ex $1376 Gd $1099
28 ga. . . . . NiB $2098 Ex $1376 Gd $1099
.410 ga. . . . . NiB $2098 Ex $1376 Gd $1099
Deluxe grades, add. $700

MODEL 37 SUPER
O/U SHOTGUN . . . . NiB $3266 Ex $2279 Gd $2099
Sidelock. automatic ejectors. Selective single trigger. Made in all gauges, bbl. lengths and chokes. Vent rib bbls. Elaborately engraved. Checkered stock (w/straight or pistol grip) and forend. Disc. 1995.

MODEL 37 SUPER A
O/U SHOTGUN . . . . NiB $14,879 Ex $12,776 Gd $11,340
Similar to the Standard Model 37 Super except has nickel steel frame and is fitted w/detachable sidelocks engraved w/game scenes. Importation disc. 1987 and resumed 1992 by Armes de Chasse. Disc.

MODEL 53E . . . . NiB $6860 Ex $4950 Gd $2910
Same general specifications as Model 117 except more elaborate engraving and select figured wood. Importation disc. 1987 and resumed in 1992 by Armes de Chasse.

MODEL 56 HAMMERLESS DOUBLE
Pigeon weight Holland & Holland sidelock w/Purdey-style third lug and sideclips. Gauges: 12, 16, 20. Receiver has fine-line scroll and rosette engraving; gold-plated locks. Importation disc. 1987 and resumed 1992 by Armes de Chasse.

12 ga. . . . . NiB $10,477 Ex $7880 Gd $4610
16 ga. (early importation), add 20%
20 ga. (early importation), add 20%

MODEL 76 HAMMERLESS
DOUBLE . . . . NiB $955 Ex $838 Gd $529
Anson & Deeley boxlock. Auto ejectors. Selective single trigger. Gauges: 12, 20 (3-inch). Bbls.: 26-, 28-, 30-inch (latter in 12 ga. only), any standard choke combination. Checkered pistol-grip stock/beavertail forend. Disc.

MODEL 76 .410. . . . . NiB $1099 Ex $877 Gd $669
Same general specifications as 12 and 20 ga. Model 76 except chambered for 3-inch shells in .410, has extractors, double triggers, 26-inch bbls. only, English-style stock w/straight grip and small forend. Disc.

MODEL 117 HAMMERLESS
DOUBLE . . . . NiB $1887 Ex $1077 Gd $868
Holland & Holland-type sidelocks, hand-detachable. Engraved action. Automatic ejectors. Selective single trigger. Gauges: 12, 20 (3-inch). Bbls.: 26-, 27-, 28-, 30-inch; 27- and 30-inch in 12 ga. only; any standard choke combination. Checkered pistol-grip stock and beavertail forend of select walnut. Manufactured in 1985.

BOLERO . . . . NiB $556 Ex $479 Gd $357
Same general specifications as Matador except non-selective single trigger and extractors. Gauges: 12 16, 20, 20 Magnum (3-inch), .410 (3-inch). Note: This model, prior to 1956, was designated F. I. Model 400 by the importer. Made from 1955 to 63.

CONTENTO OVER/UNDER SHOTGUN
Boxlock w/Woodward side lugs and double internal bolts. Gauge: 12 (2.75-inch chambers). Bbls.: 26-, 28-inch field; 30-, 32-inch trap; fixed chokes as required or screw-in choke tubes. Hand-checkered European walnut stock and forend. Single selective trigger and automatic ejectors.

M.K.2. . . . . NiB $1155 Ex $897 Gd $655
M.K.3. . . . . NiB $1887 Ex $1533 Gd $1095
W/extra bbl., add $500

MATADOR HAMMERLESS
DOUBLE. . . . . NiB $619 Ex $490 Gd $339
Anson & Deeley boxlock. Selective automatic ejectors. Selective single trigger. Gauges: 12, 16, 20, 20 Magnum (3-inch). Bbls: 26-, 28-, 30-inches; any standard choke combination. Weight: 6.5 to 7.5 lbs., depending on ga. and bbl. length. Checkered pistol-grip stock and beavertail forend. Note: This model, prior to 1956, was designated F. I. Model 400E by the U. S. importer, Firearms Int'l. Corp. of Washington, D.C. Made from 1955 to 1963.

SHOTGUNS

MATADOR II . . . . **NiB $754 Ex $567 Gd $421**
Improved version of Matador w/same general specifications except has vent-rib bbls. Made 1964 to 1969.

MATADOR III. . . . . **NiB $859 Ex $744 Gd $590**
Same general specifications as AyA Matador II. Made 1970 to 1985.

MODEL XXV BOXLOCK
Anson & Deeley boxlock w/double locking lugs. Gauges: 12 and 20. 25-inch chopper lump, satin blued bbls. w/Churchill rib. Weight: 5 to 7 lbs. Double triggers. Automatic safety and ejectors. Color-casehardened receiver w/Continental-style scroll and floral engraving. European walnut stock. Imported 1979 to 1986 and 1991.
12 or 20 ga. . . . . **NiB $3190 Ex $2688 Gd $2100**
W/extra set of bbls., add **$1250**

MODEL XXV SIDELOCK
Holland & Holland-type sidelock. Gauges: 12, 20, 28 and .410; 25-, 26-, 27- 28-, 29-, and 32-inch bbls. Chopper lump, satin blued bbls. w/Churchill rib. Weight: 5 to 7 lbs. Double triggers standard or selective or non-selective single trigger optional. Automatic safety and ejectors. Cocking indicators. Color-casehardened or coin-silver-finished receiver w/Continental-style scroll and floral engraving. Select European walnut stock w/hand-cut checkering and oil finish. Imported 1979 to 1986 and 1991.
12 or 20 ga. . . . . **NiB $5975 Ex $4220 Gd $3188**
28 ga. (disc. 1997) . . . . . . **NiB $6177 Ex $5063 Gd $3580**
.410 bore (disc. 1997) . . . **NiB $6177 Ex $5063 Gd $3580**
W/single trigger, add **$100**
W/single-selective trigger, add **$200**
W/extra set of bbls., add **$2250**

BAIKAL SHOTGUNS — Izhevsk and Tula, Russia

MODEL IZH-18M SINGLE SHOT. . . **NiB $110 Ex $80 Gd $65**
Hammerless w/cocking indicator. Automatic ejector. Manual safety. Gauges: 12 , 20, 16 w/2.75-inch chamber or .410 w/3-inch chamber. Bbls.: 26-, 28-inch w/fixed chokes (IC, M, F). Weight: 5.5 to 6 lbs. Made in Russia.

MODEL IZH-27 FIELD O/U. . . **NiB $400 Ex $341 Gd $244**
Boxlock. Double triggers w/extractors. 12 ga.; 2.75-inch chambers. Bbls.: 26-inch, IC/M; 28-inch, M/F w/fixed chokes. Weight: 6.75 lbs. Made in Russia.

MODEL IZH-43 FIELD SIDE-BY-SIDE
Side-by-side; boxlock. Double triggers; extractors. 12 or 20 ga. w/2.75-inch chambers. Bbls: 20-inch cylinder bbl and 26-or 28-inch modified full bbl. Weight: 6.75 to 7 lbs. Checkered walnut stock, forend. Blued, engraved receiver. Imported 1994 to 1996.
Field model w/20-inch bbl. . . . . . **NiB $425 Ex $275 Gd $200**
Model IJ-43 Field
Field model w/26- or 28-inch bbls.. . . **NiB $425 Ex $275 Gd $200**

IZH-43 SERIES SIDE-BY-SIDE
Boxlock. Gauges: 12, 16, 20 or .410 w/2.75- or 3-inch chambers. Bbls.: 20-, 24-, 26- or 28-inch w/fixed chokes or choke tubes. Single selective or double triggers. Weight: 6.75 lbs. Checkered hardwood (standard on Hunter II Model) or walnut stock and forend (standard on Hunter Model). Blued, engraved receiver. Imported 1994 to 1996.
Model IZH-43 Hunter model
w/12 ga. w/walnut stock . . . .**NiB $544 Ex $335 Gd $260**

Model IZH-43 Hunter
Hunter model (20 & 16 ga., .410) . . .**NiB $457 Ex $366 Gd $255**
Model IZH-43 Hunter II
Hunter II model (12 ga. w/external hammers) . . **NiB $477 Ex $366 Gd $257**
Model IZH-43 Hunter II
Hunter II model (12 ga. hammerless) . . **NiB $477 Ex $366 Gd $257**
Hunter II model (12, 16 or 20 ga.) . . . .**NiB $477 Ex $366 Gd $257**
Hunter II model w/walnut stock, add. **$60**
Hunter II model w/single-selective trigger, add **$75**

MODEL IZH-27 O/U
Boxlock. Single selective trigger w/automatic ejectors or double triggers w/extractors. Gauges: 12 or 20 w/2.75-inch chambers. Bbls.: 26-inch or 28-inch w/fixed chokes. Weight: 7 lbs. Checkered European hardwood stock and forearm. Made in Russia.
Model IJ-27 (w/double
triggers and extractors.) . . . . . **NiB $400 Ex $334 Gd $171**
Model IJ-27 (single selective
trigger and ejectors) . . . . **NiB $400 Ex $334 Gd $171**

BAKER SHOTGUNS — Batavia, New York. Made 1903–1933 by Baker Gun Company

BATAVIA LEADER HAMMERLESS DOUBLE
Sidelock. Plain extractors or automatic ejectors. Double triggers. Gauges: 12, 16, 20. Bbls.: 26- to 32-inch; any standard boring. Weight: About 7.75 lbs. (12 ga. w/30-inch bbls.). Checkered pistol-grip stock and forearm.
W/extractors . . . . **NiB $1465 Ex $944 Gd $500**
W/ejectors . . . . **NiB $1600 Ex $1100 Gd $400**

BATAVIA EJECTOR . . . . **NiB $1258 Ex $1178 Gd $798**
Same general specifications as the Batavia Leader except higher quality and finer finish throughout; has Damascus or homotensile steel bbls., checkered pistol-grip stock and forearm of select walnut; automatic ejectors standard; 12 and 16 ga. only. Deduct 60% for Damascus bbls.

BATAVIA SPECIAL . . . . **NiB $2000 Ex $1230 Gd $500**
Same general specifications as the Batavia Leader except 12 and 16 ga. only; extractors, Homotensile steel bbls.

BLACK BEAUTY
Same general specifications as the Batavia Leader except higher quality and finer finish throughout; has line engraving, special steel bbls., select walnut stock w/straight, full or half-pistol-grip.
W/extractors. . . . . **NiB $2000 Ex $1200 Gd $444**
Black Beauty Special
w/extractors . . . . **NiB $2166 Ex $1790 Gd $577**
Black Beauty Special
w/ejectors . . . . **NiB $2208 Ex $1834 Gd $544**

GRADE R . . . . **NiB $4000 Ex $2833 Gd $1106**
High-grade gun w/same general specifications as the Batavia Leader except has fine Damascus or Krupp fluid steel bbls., engraving in line, scroll and game scene designs, checkered stock and forearm of fancy European walnut; 12 and 16 ga. only. Deduct 60% for Damascus bbls.

GRADE S
Same general specifications as the Batavia Leader except higher quality and finer finish throughout; has Flui-tempered steel bbls., line and scroll engraving, checkered stock w/half-pistol-grip and forearm of semi-fancy imported walnut; 10, 12 and 16 ga.
Non-ejector . . . . **NiB $3886 Ex $2013 Gd $1077**
W/ejectors . . . . **NiB $4100 Ex $2315 Gd $1366**

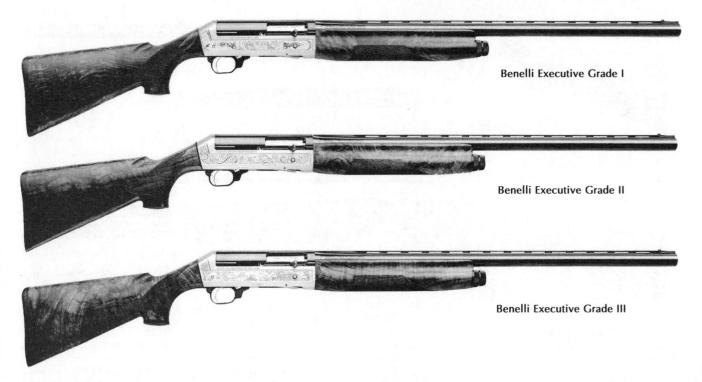

Benelli Executive Grade I

Benelli Executive Grade II

Benelli Executive Grade III

PARAGON, EXPERT AND DELUXE GRADES

Made to order only, these are the higher grades of Baker hammerless sidelock double-bbl. shotguns. After 1909, the Paragon Grade, as well as the Expert and Deluxe intro. that year, had a crossbolt in addition to the regular Baker system taper wedge fastening. There are early Paragon guns w/Damascus bbls. and some are non-ejector, but this grade was also produced w/automatic ejectors and w/the finest fluid steel bbls., in lengths to 34 inches, standard on Expert and Deluxe guns. Differences among the three models are in overall quality, finish, engraving and grade of fancy figured walnut in the stock and forearm; Expert and Deluxe wood may be carved as well as checkered. Choice of straight, full or half-pistol grip was offered. A single trigger was available in the two higher grades. The Paragon was available in 10 ga (Damascus bbls. only), and the other two models were regularly produced in 12, 16 and 20 ga.

Paragon grade, no ejector. NiB $4277 Ex $2660 Gd $2033
Paragon grade w/auto ejector NiB $4455 Ex $2978 Gd $2270
Expert grade . . . . NiB $6177 Ex $4588 Gd $2844
Deluxe grade . . . . NiB $11,477 Ex $9968 Gd $7133
W/ejectors, add $350

BELKNAP SHOTGUNS—Louisville, Kentucky

MODEL B-68 SINGLE-SHOT SHOTGUN . . . NiB $199 Ex $144 Gd $100
Takedown. Visible hammer. Automatic ejector. Gauges: 12, 16, 20 and .410. Bbls.: 26-inch to 36-inch; F choke. Weight: 6 lbs. Plain pistol-grip stock and forearm.

MODEL B-63 SINGLE-SHOT SHOTGUN . . NiB $229 Ex $135 Gd $105
Takedown. Visible hammer. Automatic ejector. Gauges: 12, 20 and .410. Bbls.: 26- to 36-inch, F choke. Weight: Average 6 lbs. Plain pistol-grip stock and forearm.

MODEL B-63E SINGLE-SHOT SHOTGUN . . . NiB $209 Ex $133 Gd $95
Same general specifications as Model B-68 except has side lever opening instead of top lever.

MODEL B-64

SLIDE-ACTION SHOTGUN . . . . NiB $339 Ex $244 Gd $225
Hammerless. Gauges: 12, 16, 20 and .410. Three round tubular magazine. Various bbl. lengths and chokes from 26-inch to 30-inch. Weight: 6.25 to 7.5 lbs. Walnut-finished hardwood stock.

MODEL B-65C

AUTOLOADING SHOTGUN. . NiB $533 Ex $400 Gd $290
Browning-type lightweight alloy receiver. 12 ga. only. Four round tubular magazine. Bbl.: plain, 28-inch. Weight: About 8.25 lbs. Disc. 1949.

BENELLI SHOTGUNS — Urbino, Italy. Imported by Benelli USA, Accokeek, MD

MODEL 121 M1 MILITARY/POLICE

AUTOLOADING SHOTGUN . . . . NiB $656 Ex $432 Gd $335
Gauge: 12. Seven round magazine. 19.75-inch bbl. 39.75 inches overall. Cylinder choke, 2.75-inch chamber. Weight: 7.4 lbs. Matte black finish and European hardwood stock. Post front sight, fixed buckhorn rear sight. Imported in 1985. Disc.

BLACK EAGLE AUTOLOADING SHOTGUN

Two-piece aluminum and steel receiver. Ga: 12; 3-inch chamber. Four round magazine. Screw-in choke tubes (SK, IC, M, IM, F). Bbls.: Ventilated rib; 21, 24, 26 or 28 inches w/bead front sight; 24-inch rifled slug. 42.5 to 49.5 inches overall. Weight: 7.25 lbs. (28-inch bbl.). Matte black lower receiver w/blued upper receiver and bbl. Checkered walnut stock w/high-gloss finish and drop adjustment. Imported from 1989 to 1990 and 1997 to 1998.
Limited edition . . . . NiB $1587 Ex $1090 Gd $965
Competition model . . . . NiB $953 Ex $755 Gd $523
Slug model (disc. 1992) . . . . NiB $815 Ex $608 Gd $466
Standard model (disc. 1990) . . . . NiB $879 Ex $770 Gd $505

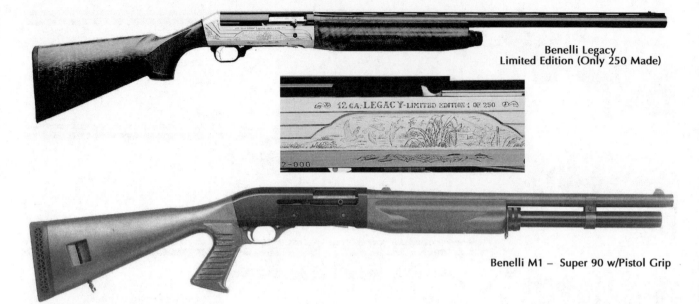

Benelli Legacy
Limited Edition (Only 250 Made)

Benelli M1 – Super 90 w/Pistol Grip

BLACK EAGLE EXECUTIVE
Custom Black Eagle Series. Montefeltro-style rotating bolt w/three locking lugs. All-steel lower receiver engraved, gold inlay by Bottega Incisione di Cesare Giovanelli. 12 ga. only. 21-, 24-, 26-, or 28-inch vent-rib bbl. w/5 screw-in choke tubes (Type I) or fixed chokes. Custom deluxe walnut stock and forend. Built to customer specifications on special order.

Grade I . . . . NiB $4190 Ex $3295 Gd $2293
Grade II . . . . NiB $4378 Ex $3566 Gd $2500
Grade III . . . . NiB $5690 Ex $4177 Gd $2960

LEGACY AUTOLOADING SHOTGUN
Gauges: 12 and 20 ga. w/3-inch chambers. 24- 26- or 28-inch bbl. 47.63 to 49.62 inches overall. Weight: 5.8 to 7.5 lbs. Four round magazine. Five screw-in choke tubes. Lower alloy receiver and upper steel reciever cover. Features Benelli's inertia recoil operating system. Imported 1998 to date.

Legacy model . . . . NiB $1292 Ex $977 Gd $877
Limited Edition . . . . NiB $1944 Ex $1620 Gd $1010

M1 FIELD AUTOLOADING SHOTGUN. . NiB $867 Ex $767 Gd $671
Gauge: 20. Chambers: 2.75 or 3 inches. Bbl. 24 or 26 inches, stepped ventilated rib and red bar sights. Stock: Synthetic, black or camo. Weight: 5.7 to 5.8 lbs. Includes set of five choke tubes. Imported from Italy.

M1 SUPER 90
AUTO-LOADING SHOTGUN . . .NiB $955 Ex $836 Gd $554
Gauge: 12. Seven round magazine. Cylinder choke. 19.75-inch bbl. 39.75 inches overall. Weight: 7 lbs., 4 oz. to 7 lbs., 10 oz. Matte black finish. Stock and forend made of fiberglass-reinforced polymer. Sights: Post front, fixed buckhorn rear, drift adj. Introduced 1985; when the model line expanded in 1989, this configuration was discontinued.

M1 SUPER 90
DEFENSE AUTOLOADER . . . NiB $1093 Ex $966 Gd $509
Same general specifications as Model Super 90 except w/pistol-grip stock. Available w/Ghost-Ring sight option. Imported 1986 to 1998.
M1 SUPER 90 FIELD
Inertia-recoil semiautomatic shotgun. Gauge: 12; 3-inch chamber. Three round magazine. Bbl.: 21, 24, 26 or 28 inches. 42.5 to 49.5 inches overall. Choke: SK, IC, M, IM, F. Matte receiver. Standard polymer stock or satin walnut (26- or 28-inch bbl. only). Bead front sight. Imported from 1990 to 2006.

W/Realtree camo stock . . . . NiB $1066 Ex $743 Gd $488
W/polymer stock . . . . NiB $766 Ex $563 Gd $447
W/walnut stock . . . . NiB $1031 Ex $660 Gd $458

M1 SUPER 90 SLUG AUTOLOADER
Same general specifications as M1 Super 90 Field except w/5-round magazine. 18.5-inch bbl. Cylinder bore. 39.75 inches overall. Weight: 6.5 lbs. Polymer standard stock. Rifle or Ghost-Ring sights. Imported 1986 to 1998.

W/rifle sights . . . . NiB $988 Ex $677 Gd $549
W/ghost-ring sights . . . . NiB $1096 Ex $786 Gd $659
W/Realtree camo finish, add $150

M1 SUPER 90 SPECIAL
SPORTING AUTOLOADER . . . NiB $877 Ex $655 Gd $589
Same general specifications as M1 Super 90 Field except w/18.5-inch bbl. 39.75 inches overall. Weight: 6.5 lbs. Ghost-ring sights. Polymer stock. Imported from 1994 to 1998.

M2 AUTOLOADER
Redesign of M1 w/ new receiver, trigger guard, safety. Imported 2004 to date.

Three Gun . . . . NiB $2350 Ex $1800 Gd $1000
Practical . . . . NiB $1196 Ex $970 Gd $480
Tacical . . . . NiB $1230 Ex $900 Gd $510

M3 SUPER 90 PUMP/AUTOLOADER
Inertia-recoil semiautomatic and/or pump action. Gauge: 12. Seven round magazine. Cylinder choke. 19.75-inch bbl. 41 inches overall (31 inches folded). Weight: 7 to 7.5 lbs. Matte black finish. Stock: standard synthetic, pistol-grip or folding tubular steel. Standard rifle or Ghost-Ring sights. Imported 1989 to date. Caution: Increasing the magazine capacity to more than 5 rounds in M3 shotguns w/pistol-grip stocks violates provisions of the 1994 Crime Bill. This model may be used legally only by the military and law-enforcement agencies.

Standard model . . . . NiB $1477 Ex $1067 Gd $799
Pistol-grip model . . . . NiB $1644 Ex $1133 Gd $990
W/folding stock . . . . NiB $1190 Ex $955 Gd $944
W/laser sight . . . . NiB $1766 Ex $1388 Gd $1100
W/ghost-ring sights, add $100

Benelli Montefeltro
Super 90 Left-Handed Model

Benelli Montefeltro Realtree Camo

M4 TACTICAL AUTOLOADER NiB $1680 Ex $1230 Gd $870
Civilian version of U.S. military M4, gas regulating system. Gauge: 12; 3-inch chamber. Four round magazine. Bbl.: 18.5 inches. 40 inches overall. Choke: M. Matte receiver. Standard and pistol grip sythetic stock. Ghost ring rear, post front sights. Imported from 2003 to date.
M1040 Limited Edition . . . . NiB $1380 Ex $960 Gd $660

MONTEFELTRO/SUPER 90 SEMIAUTOMATIC
Gauges: 12 or 20 gauge w/3-inch chamber. 21- 24- 26- or 28-inch bbl. 43.7 to 49.5 inches overall. Weight: 5.3 to 7.5 lbs. Four round magazine. Five screw-in choke tubes (C, IC, M, IM, F). High gloss or satin walnut or Realtree Camo stock. Blued metal finish. Imported 1987 to 1992.
Standard Hunter model . . . . NiB $1155 Ex $865 Gd $490
Slug model (disc. 1992) . . . . . NiB $744 Ex $639 Gd $440
Turkey model . . . . NiB $744 Ex $639 Gd $440
Uplander model . . . . NiB $744 Ex $639 Gd $440
Limited Edition (1995-96) . NiB $2077 Ex $1688 Gd $1176
20 ga. w/Realtree camo . . . . NiB $1269 Ex $988 Gd $775
20 ga. Youth Model w/short stock, add $75
Left-hand model, add $50

NOVA PUMP SHOTGUN . . . . NiB $466 Ex $368 Gd $256
Gauge: 12 or 20. Chambers: 2.75 or 3 inches; 3.5 inch chambers in 12 gauge only Four-round magazine. Bbl. 24, 26 or 28 inches; red bar sights. Stock: Synthetic,(Xtra Brown in 12 gauge or Timber HD in 20 gauge). Montefeltro rotating bolt, magazine cutoff, synthetic trigger assembly. Introduced 1999. Imported from Italy.

SL 121V SEMIAUTO
(SL-80 SERIES) . . . . Nib $466 Ex $359 Gd $270
Recoil-operated semiautomaticw/split receiver design. Gauge: 12. Five round capacity. 26-, 28- or 30-inch ventilated rib bbl. (26-inch choked M, IM, IC, 28-inch, F, M, IM; 30-inch, F choke - Mag.). Straight walnut stock w/hand-checkered pistol grip and forend. Importation disc. in 1985.

SL 121V SLUG SHOTGUN
(SL-80 SERIES) . . . . Nib $578 Ex $376 Gd $305
Same general specifications as Benelli SL 121V except designed for rifled slugs and equipped w/rifle sights. Disc. in 1985.

SL 123V SEMIAUTO
(SL-80 SERIES) . . . . NiB $500 Ex $378 Gd $297
Gauge: 12. 26- and 28-inch bbls. 26-inch choked IM, M, IC; 28-inch choked F, IM, M. Disc. in 1985.

SL 201 SEMIAUTOMATIC
(SL-80 SERIES) . . . . NiB $459 Ex $365 Gd $300
Gauge: 20. 26-inch bbl. Mod. choke. Weight: 5 lbs., 10 oz. Ventilated rib. Disc. in 1985.

SPORT AUTOLOADING. . . . NiB $1266 Ex $999 Gd $654
Similar to the Black Eagle Competition model except has one-piece matte- finished alloy receiver w/inscribed red Benelli logo. 26 or 28 inches bbl. w/2 inchangable carbon fiber vent ribs. Oil-finished checkered walnut stock w/adjustable buttpad and butt-stock. Imported 1997 to 2002.

SUPER BLACK EAGLE
AUTOLOADING SHOTGUN
Same general specifications as Black Eagle except w/3.5-inch chamber that accepts 2.75-, 3- and 3.5-inch shells. Two round magazine (3.5-inch), 3-round magazine (2.75- or 3-inch). High-gloss, satin finish or camo stock. Realtree camo, matte black or blued metal finish. Imported 1991 to 2005.
Standard model . . . . NiB $1096 Ex $933 Gd $766
Realtree camo model . . . . . NiB $1221 Ex $1099 Gd $866
Custom slug model . . . . NiB $1254 Ex $958 Gd $744
Limited edition. . . . . NiB $1979 Ex $1654 Gd $1177
W/wood stock, add. $40
Left-hand model, add $100

ULTRA LIGHT . . . . NiB $1480 Ex $1010 Gd $610
Gauges: 12, 20 or 28 gauge w/3-inch chamber. 24- or 26-inch bbl. 45.5 to 47.5 inches overall. Weight: 5.0 to 6.1 lbs. Two round magazine. Five screw-in choke tubes (C, IC, M, IM, F). High gloss WeatherCoat stock. Blued metal finish. Imported 2006 to date.

CORDOBA . . . . NiB $1800 Ex $1230 Gd $760
Gauges: 12 or 20 gauge w/3-inch chamber. 28- or 30-inch bbl. 49.7 to 51.7 inches overall. Weight: 6.3 to 7.3 lbs. Four round magazine. Five screw-in choke tubes (C, IC, M, IM, F). ComfortTech stock. Matte black finish. Imported 2005 to date.

VINCI . . . . NiB $1300 Ex $930 Gd $560
Modular construction. Gauges: 12 gauge w/3-inch chamber. 26- or 28-inch bbl. 45.7 to 49.7 inches overall. Weight: 6.7 to 6.9 lbs. Three round magazine. Five screw-in choke tubes (C, IC, M, IM, F). ComfortTech stock. Matte black finish. Imported 2009 to date.

BERETTA USA CORP.—Accokeek, Maryland. Manufactured by Fabbrica D'Armi Pietro Beretta S.P.A. in Gardone Val Trompia (Brescia), Italy. Imported by Beretta USA (previously by Garcia Corp.)

MODEL 409PB
HAMMERLESS DOUBLE . . . . . NiB $966 Ex $733 Gd $545
Boxlock. Double triggers. Plain extractors. Gauges: 12, 16, 20, 28. Bbls.: 27.5-, 28.5- and 30-inch, IC/M choke or M/F choke. Weight: from 5.5 to 7.75 lbs., depending on ga. and bbl. length. Straight or pistol-grip stock and beavertail forearm, checkered. Imported 1934 to 1964.

MODEL 410E
Same general specifications as Model 409PB except has automatic ejectors and is of higher quality throughout. Imported 1934 to 1964.
12 ga. . . . . NiB $1367 Ex $1144 Gd $922
20 ga. . . . . NiB $2882 Ex $2096 Gd $1377
28 ga. . . . . NiB $3881 Ex $3036 Gd $2456

SHOTGUNS

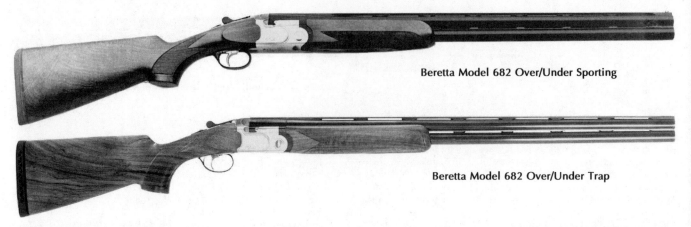

Beretta Model 682 Over/Under Sporting

Beretta Model 682 Over/Under Trap

MODEL 410 10-GA. MAGNUM...NiB $1269 Ex $945 Gd $700
Same as Model 410E except heavier construction. Plain extractors. Double triggers. 10-ga. Magnum, 3.5-inch chambers. 32-inch bbls., both F choke. Weight: about 10 lbs. Checkered pistol-grip stock and forearm, recoil pad. Imported 1934 to 1984.

MODEL 411E
Same general specifications as Model 409PB except has sideplates, automatic ejectors and is of higher quality throughout. Imported 1934 to 1964.
12 ga. . . . . NiB $2077 Ex $1700 Gd $1179
20 ga. . . . . NiB $2866 Ex $2234 Gd $1590
28 ga. . . . . NiB $4339 Ex $3977 Gd $2766

MODEL 424 HAMMERLESS
DOUBLE . . . . NiB $1288 Ex $1292 Gd $957
Boxlock. Light border engraving. Plain extractors. Gauges: 12, 20; chambers 2.75-inch in former, 3-inch in latter. Bbls.: 28-inch M/F choke, 26-inch IC/M choke. Weight: 5 lbs. 14 oz. to 6 lbs. 10 oz., depending on ga. and bbl. length. English-style straight-grip stock and forearm, checkered. Imported 1977 to 1984.

MODEL 426E . . . . NiB $1588 Ex $1233 Gd $1067
Same as Model 424 except action body is finely engraved, silver pigeon inlaid in top lever; has selective automatic ejectors and selective single trigger, stock and forearm of select European walnut. Imported 1977-84.

MODEL 450 SERIES HAMMERLESS DOUBLES
Custom English-style sidelock. Single, non-selective trigger or double triggers. Manual safety. Selective automatic ejectors. Gauge: 12; 2.75- or 3-inch chambers. Bbls.: 26, 28 or 30 inches choked to customers' specifications. Weight: 6.75 lbs. Checkered high-grade walnut stock. Receiver w/coin-silver finish. Imported 1948. Disc.
Model 450 EL (disc. 1982)...NiB $8334 Ex $6688 Gd $4731
Model 450 EELL (disc. 1982)...NiB $10,655 Ex $6798 Gd $4880
Model 451 (disc. 1987)... NiB $6443 Ex $5670 Gd $3990
Model 451 E (disc. 1989) . NiB $7125 Ex $6225 Gd $4350
Model 451 EL (disc. 1985)....NiB $17,787 Ex $14,866 Gd $11,700
Model 451 EELL (disc. 1990)..NiB $15,788 Ex $12,877 Gd $10,777
Model 452 (Intro. 1990) NiB $29,988 Ex $21,980 Gd $18,799
Model 452 EELL (intro. 1992) ..NiB $41,665 Ex $35,000 Gd $27,889
W/extra bbls, add 30%

MODEL 470 SERIES HAMMERLESS DOUBLE
Gauge: 12 and 20 ga. w/3-inch chambers. 26- or 28-inch bbl. Weight: 5.9 to 6.5 lbs. Low profile, improved box lock action w/single selective trigger. Selected walnut, checkered stock and forend. Metal front bead sight. Scroll-engraved receiver w/gold inlay and silver chrome finish. Imported 1999 to date.

Silver Hawk 12 ga. . . . . NiB $9332 Ex $6880 Gd $5440
Silver Hawk 20 ga. . . . . NiB $9566 Ex $6465 Gd $5566
EL Silver Hawk 12 ga. . . . . . . .NiB $8310 Ex $7223 Gd $5600
EL Silver Hawk 20 ga. . . . . . . .NiB $8554 Ex $6133 Gd $5477
EELL (Jubilee II) 12 ga. . . . . . .NiB $8366 Ex $6328 Gd $4790
EELL (Jubilee II) 20 ga. . . . . . .NiB $9000 Ex $7231 Gd $4889
W/extra bbls., add 30%

MODEL 625 S/S HAMMERLESS DOUBLE
Boxlock. Gauges: 12 or 20. Bbls.: 26-, 28- or 30-inch w/fixed choke combinations. Single selective or double triggers w/extractors. Checkered English-style buttstock and forend. Imported 1984 to 1987.
W/double triggers. . . . . NiB $1591 Ex $900 Gd $667
W/single selective trigger . . NiB $1880 Ex $1067 Gd $700
20 ga., add. $200

MODEL 626 S/S HAMMERLESS DOUBLE
Field Grade side-by-side. Boxlock action w/single selective trigger, extractors and automatic safety. Gauges: 12 (2.75-inch chambers); 20 (3-inch chambers). Bbls.: 26- or 28-inch w/Mobilchoke or various fixed-choke combinations. Weight: 6.75 lbs. (12 ga.). Bright chrome finish. Checkered European walnut buttstock and forend in straight English style. Imported 1985 to 1994.
Model 626 Field (disc. 1988) . . .NiB $1345 Ex $1190 Gd $700
Model 626 Onyx . . . . NiB $1779 Ex $1288 Gd $1006
Model 626 Onyx (3.5-inch
magnum, disc. 1993) . . . . NiB $1798 Ex $1388 Gd $1098
20 ga., add. 50%

MODEL 627 S/S HAMMERLESS DOUBLE
Same as Model 626 S/S except w/engraved sideplates and pistol-grip or straight English-style stock. Imported 1985 to 1994.
Model 627 EL Field . . . . . NiB $2370 Ex $2090 Gd $1550
Model 627 EL Sport . . . . . NiB $2592 Ex $2210 Gd $1776
Model 627 EELL . . . . NiB $4460 Ex $3978 Gd $2666

MODEL 682 O/U SHOTGUN
Hammerless takedown w/single selective trigger. Gauges: 12, 20, 28, .410. Bbls.: 26- to 34-inch w/fixed chokes or Mobilchoke tubes. Checkered European walnut buttstock/forend in various grades and configurations. Imported 1984 to 2000.
Comp Skeet model . . . . . NiB $1566 Ex $1160 Gd $1004
Comp Skeet Deluxe model. . . . NiB $1789 Ex $1440 Gd $1166
Comp Super Skeet . . . . NiB $2599 Ex $2055 Gd $1490
Comp Skeet model, 2-bbl.
set (disc. 1989) . . . . NiB $5100 Ex $4256 Gd $2920
Comp Skeet, 4 bbl. set (disc. 1996)NiB $5786 Ex $4670 Gd $3241
Sporting Continental. . . . . NiB $1589 Ex $1170 Gd $1097
Sporting Combo . . . . NiB $1778 Ex $1566 Gd $1180

Beretta Model 687EL

Beretta Model 687EEL

Gold Sporting . . . . NiB $1788 Ex $1266 Gd $1011
Super Sporting . . . . .NiB $1566 Ex $1365 Gd $1291
Comp Trap Gold X . . . . NiB $2269 Ex $1775 Gd $1231
Comp Trap Top Single (1986-95) . . . NiB $2177 Ex $1688 Gd $1166
Comp Trap Live Pigeon (1990-98). . . NiB $2769 Ex $2255 Gd $1568
Comp Mono/Combo Trap Gold X . . . NiB $2977 Ex $2510 Gd $1765
Comp Mono Trap (1985-88) . . . . NiB $1867 Ex $1588 Gd $1100
Super Trap Gold X (1991-95) . . . . . . NiB $2267 Ex $1880 Gd $1266
Super Trap Combo Gold X (1991-97) NiB $3166 Ex $2478 Gd $1776
Super Trap Top Single Gold X (1991-95)NiB $2265 Ex $2099 Gd $1369
Super Trap Unsingle (1992-94) . . . . . NiB $2210 Ex $2050 Gd $1319

MODEL 686 O/U SHOTGUN

Low-profile improved boxlock action. Single selective trigger. Selective automatic ejectors. Gauges: 12, 20, 28 w/3.5- 3- or 2.75-inch chambers, depending upon ga. Bbls.: 26-, 28-, 30-inch w/fixed chokes or Mobilchoke tubes. Weight: 5.75 to 7.5 lbs. Checkered American walnut stock and forearm of various qualities, depending upon model. Receiver finishes also vary, but all have blued bbls. Sideplates to simulate sidelock action on EL models. Imported 1988 to 1995.

Field Onyx. .NiB $1335 Ex $1108 Gd $733
(3.5-inch Mag., disc.
  1993 & reintro.1996) . . . . .NiB $4370 Ex $2888 Gd $2280
EL Gold Perdiz (1992-97). . . . . .NiB $2077 Ex $1576 Gd $1200
Essential (1994-96). . . . . NiB $1009 Ex $808 Gd $635
Silver Essential (1997-98) . . . . NiB $1180 Ex $966 Gd $680
Silver Pigeon Onyx (intro. 1996) . . . . . . NiB $1566 Ex $1254 Gd $870
Silver Perdiz Onyx (disc. 1996) . . . . . . .NiB $1488 Ex $1155 Gd $866
Silver Pigeon/Perdiz Onyx Combo . . . . . NiB $1133 Ex $866 Gd $633
L Silver Perdiz (disc. 1994) . . . . .NiB $1288 Ex $1007 Gd $766
Skeet Silver Pigeon (1996-98) . . . . NiB $1276 Ex $988 Gd $766
Skeet Silver Perdiz (1994-96) . . . . .NiB $1570 Ex $1288 Gd $944
Skeet Silver Pigeon/Perdiz Combo . . . .NiB $1570 Ex $1288 Gd $944
Sporting Special (1987-93) . . . . .NiB $1798 Ex $1369 Gd $1100
Sporting English (1991-92) . . . . .NiB $1820 Ex $1400 Gd $1188
Sporting Onyx
  w/fixed chokes (1991-92). . . . . .NiB $1743 Ex $1388 Gd $1014
Sporting Onyx
  w/ choke tubes (intro. 1992). . . . . . . .NiB $1344 Ex $1130 Gd $966
Sporting Onyx Gold (disc. 1993) . . . . .NiB $1879 Ex $1577 Gd $1188
Sporting Silver Pigeon (intro. 1996) . . .NiB $1598 Ex $1266 Gd $1005
Sporting Silver Perdiz (1993-96) . . . . . . NiB $1612 Ex $1288 Gd $1130
Sporting Collection Sport (1996-97) . . NiB $1188 Ex $1033 Gd $892
Sporting Combo . . . . NiB $2667 Ex $2174 Gd $1545
Trap International (1994-95) . . . . NiB $1144 Ex $967 Gd $755
Trap Silver Pigeon (intro. 1997) . . . . . NiB $1266 Ex $1057 Gd $798
Trap Top Mono (intro. 1998) . . . . NiB $1279 Ex $1088 Gd $800
Ultralight Onyx (intro. 1992) . . . . NiB $1599 Ex $1366 Gd $968
Ultralight Del. Onyx (intro. 1998) . . . . .NiB $2056 Ex $1665 Gd $1156

MODEL 687 O/U SHOTGUN

Same as Model 686 except w/decorative sideplates and varying grades of engraving and game-scene motifs.
L Onyx (disc. 1991) . . . . NiB $1460 Ex $1233 Gd $865
L Onyx Gold Field (1988-89). . . . . . NiB $1688 Ex $1344 Gd $966
L Onyx Silver Pigeon . . . . NiB $1288 Ex $1668 Gd $1208
EL Onyx (disc. 1990) . . . . NiB $2855 Ex $2344 Gd $1629
EL Gold Pigeon . . . . NiB $3266 Ex $2688 Gd $1863
EL Gold Pigeon small frame . . . . . NiB $3090 Ex $2451 Gd $1761
EL Gold Pigeon Sporting (intro 1993). . NiB $4388 Ex $3571 Gd $2510
EELL Diamond Pigeon . . . . NiB $4416 Ex $3620 Gd $2560
EELL Diamond Pigeon Skeet . . . . . . NiB $4233 Ex $3548 Gd $2480
EELL Diamond Pigeon Sporting . . . NiB $4416 Ex $3578 Gd $2560
EELL Diamond Pigeon X Trap . . . . . NiB $3966 Ex $3133 Gd $2190
EELL Diamond Pigeon Mono Trap . NiB $4088 Ex $3310 Gd $2366
EELL Diamond Pigeon Trap Combo NiB $5480 Ex $4766 Gd $3266
EELL Field Combo . . . . NiB $4570 Ex $3775 Gd $2760
EELL Skeet 4-bbl. set . . . . NiB $7588 Ex $5977 Gd $3554
EELL Gallery Special . . . . NiB $7233 Ex $5610 Gd $3798
EELL Gallery Special Combo . . . . . NiB $8235 Ex $6799 Gd $4571
EELL Gallery Special pairs . . . . NiB $17,844 Ex $14,560 Gd $10,134
Sporting English (1991-92) . . . . NiB $2247 Ex $1867 Gd $1359
Sporting Silver Pigeon (intro. 1996). . . NiB $2079 Ex $1677 Gd $1261
Sporting Silver Perdiz (1993-96) . . NiB $2255 Ex $1767 Gd $1388

MODEL 1200 SERIES SEMIAUTOLOADING SHOTGUN

Short recoil action. Gauge: 12; 2.75- or 3-inch chamber. Six round magazine. 24-, 26- or 28-inch vent-rib bbl. w/fixed chokes or Mobilchoke tubes. Weight: 7.25 lbs. Matte black finish. Adj. technopolymer stock and forend. Imported 1988 to 1990.
W/fixed choke (disc. 1989) . . . . NiB $466 Ex $359 Gd $266
Riot (disc. 1994) . . . . NiB $476 Ex $368 Gd $277
W/Mobilchoke (disc. 1994). . . . . NiB $741 Ex $577 Gd $400
Riot model . . . . NiB $805 Ex $633 Gd $451
W/Pistol-grip stock, add $65
W/Tritium sights, add $100

MODEL A-301

AUTOLOADING SHOTGUN. . NiB $644 Ex $470 Gd $356
Field Gun. Gas-operated. Scroll-decorated receiver. Gauge: 12 or 20; 2.75-inch chamber in former, 3-inch in latter. Three round magazine. Bbl.: Ventilated rib; 28-inch F or M choke, 26-inch IC. Weight: 6 lbs., 5 oz. – 6 lbs., 14 oz., depending on gauge and bbl. length. Checkered pistol-grip stock/forearm. Imported 1977 to 1982.

SHOTGUNS

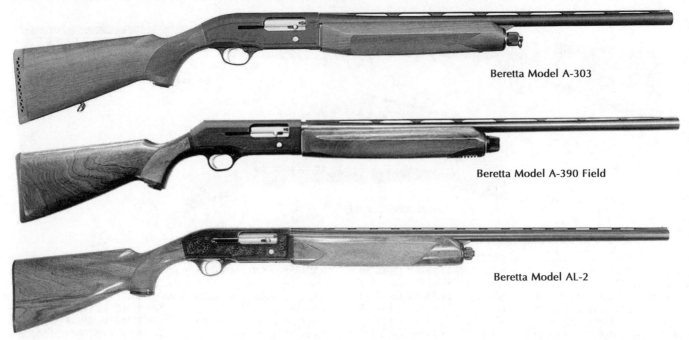

Beretta Model A-303

Beretta Model A-390 Field

Beretta Model AL-2

MODEL A-301 MAGNUM. . . . NiB $455 Ex $277 Gd $200
Same as Model A-301 Field Gun except chambered for 12 ga. Three inch Magnum shells, 30-inch F choke bbl. only, stock w/recoil pad. Weight: 7.25 lbs.

MODEL A-301 SKEET GUN . . NiB $466 Ex $300 Gd $210
Same as Model A-301 Field Gun except 26-inch bbl. SK choke only, skeet-style stock, gold-plated trigger.

MODEL A-301 SLUG GUN . . . NiB $488 Ex $287 Gd $217
Same as Model A-301 Field Gun except has plain 22-inch bbl., slug choke, w/rifle sights. Weight: 6 lbs., 14 oz.

MODEL A-301 TRAP GUN . . . NiB $466 Ex $287 Gd $233
Same as Model A-301 Field Gun except has 30-inch bbl. in F choke only, checkered Monte Carlo stock w/recoil pad, gold-plated trigger. Blued bbl. and receiver. Weight: 7 lbs., 10 oz. Imported 1978 to 1982.

MODEL A-302 SEMIAUTOLOADING SHOTGUN
Similar to gas-operated Model 301. Hammerless, takedown shotgun w/tubular magazine and Mag-Action that handles both 2.75- and 3-inch Magnum shells. Gauge: 12 or 20; 2.75- or 3-inch Mag. chambers. Bbl.: Vent or plain; 22-inch/Slug (12 ga.); 26-inch/IC (12 or 20) 28-inch/M (20 ga.), 28-inch/Multi-choke (12 or 20 ga.) 30-inch/F (12 ga.). Weight: 6.5 lbs., 20 ga.; 7.25.lbs., 12 ga. Blued/black finish. Checkered European walnut, pistol-grip stock and forend. Imported from 1983 to c. 1987.
Standard model w/fixed choke. . .NiB $466 Ex $338 Gd $254
Standard model w/multi-choke . . .NiB $490 Ex $345 Gd $258

MODEL A-302 SUPER LUSSO. . .NiB $1844 Ex $1452 Gd $1166
A custom A-302 in presentation grade w/hand-engraved receiver and custom select walnut stock.

MODEL A-303 SEMIAUTOLOADER
Similar to Model 302, except w/target specifications in Trap, Skeet and Youth configurations, and weighs 6.5 to 8 lbs. Imported from 1983 to 1996.
Field and Upland models . . . . NiB $523 Ex $400 Gd $288
Skeet and Trap (disc. 1994) . . NiB $488 Ex $366 Gd $257
Slug model (disc. 1992) . . . . . NiB $453 Ex $377 Gd $260
Sporting Clays . . . . NiB $600 Ex $453 Gd $279

Super Skeet . . . . NiB $500 Ex $433 Gd $318
Super Trap . . . . NiB $643 Ex $494 Gd $388
Waterfowl/Turkey model (disc. 1992)NiB $525 Ex $460 Gd $354
W/Mobil choke, add. $75

MODEL A-303 YOUTH GUN. . . NiB $498 Ex $376 Gd $277
Locked-breech, gas-operated action. Ga: 12 and 20; 2-round magazine. Bbls.: 24, 26, 28, 30 or 32-inches, vent rib. Weight: 7 lbs. (12 ga.), 6 lbs. (20 ga.). Crossbolt safety. Length of pull shortened to 12.5 inches. Imported 1988-96.

MODEL AL-390 SEMIAUTOMATIC SHOTGUN
Gas-operated, self-regulating action designed to handle any size load. Gauges: 12 or 20 w/ 3-inch chamber. Three round magazine. Bbl.: 24, 26, 28 or 30 inches w/vent rib and Mobilchoke tubes. Weight: 7.5 lbs. Select walnut stock w/adj. comb. Blued or matte black finish. Imported 1992-96. Superseded by AL-390 series.
Standard/Slug models . . . . . . NiB $525 Ex $377 Gd $296
Field/Silver Mallard models. . . NiB $525 Ex $377 Gd $296
Deluxe/Gold Mallard models . NiB $485 Ex $335 Gd $250
Turkey/Waterfowl model
(w/matte finish) . . . . NiB $577 Ex $366 Gd $300
20 ga., add. $75

MODEL AL-390 TARGET
Similar to the Model 390 Field except w/2.75-inch chamber. Skeet: 28-inch ported bbl. w/wide vent rib and fixed choke (SK). Trap: 30- or 32-inch w/Mobilchoke tubes. Weight: 7.5 lbs. Fully adj. buttstock. Imported from 1993 to 1996.
Sport Trap model . . . . NiB $599 Ex $367 Gd $290
Sport Skeet model . . . . NiB $479 Ex $345 Gd $266
Sporting Clays model (unported). . .NiB $700 Ex $579 Gd $421
Super Trap model (ported) . . . NiB $577 Ex $367 Gd $292
Super Skeet model (ported). . . NiB $569 Ex $355 Gd $307
W/ported bbl., add. $100
20 ga., add. $75

MODEL AL-1 FIELD GUN. . . . NiB $566 Ex $349 Gd $279
Same as Model AL-2 gas-operated Field Gun except has bbl. w/o rib, no engraving on receiver. Imported from 1971 to 1973.

Beretta Model AL-391
Urika Gold Sporting

Beretta Model AL-391
Urika Gold Trap

MODEL AL-2 AUTOLOADING SHOTGUN
Field Gun. Gas-operated. Engraved receiver (1968 version, 12 ga. only, had no engraving). Gauge: 12 or 20. 2.75-inch chamber. Three round magazine. Bbls.: Vent rib; 30-inch F choke, 28-inch F or M choke, 26-inch IC. Weight: 6.5 to 7.25 lbs, depending on ga. and bbl. length. Checkered pistol-grip stock and forearm. Imported from 1968 to 1975.

W/Plain receiver	NiB $435	Ex $315	Gd $229
W/Engraved receiver	NiB $633	Ex $500	Gd $378

MODEL AL-2 MAGNUM . . . . . NiB $515 Ex $377 Gd $255
Same as Model AL-2 Field Gun except chambered for 12 ga. 3-inch Magnum shells; 30-inch F or 28-inch M choke bbl. only. Weight: About 8 lbs. Imported from 1973 to 1975.

MODEL AL-2 SKEET GUN. . . . NiB $466 Ex $321 Gd $234
Same as Model AL-2 Field Gun except has wide rib, 26-inch bbl. in SK choke only, checkered pistol-grip stock and beavertail forearm. Imported 1973 to 1975.

MODEL AL-2 TRAP GUN . . . . NiB $445 Ex $341 Gd $246
Same as Model AL-2 Field Gun except has wide rib, 30 inch bbl. in F choke only, beavertail forearm. Monte Carlo stock w/recoil pad. Weight: About 7.75 lbs. Imported from 1973 to 1975.

MODEL AL-3
Similar to corresponding AL-2 models in design and general specifications. Imported from 1975 to 1976.

Field model	NiB $466	Ex $331	Gd $244
Magnum model	NiB $475	Ex $350	Gd $266
Skeet model	NiB $486	Ex $351	Gd $264
Trap model	NiB $453	Ex $335	Gd $266

MODEL AL-3 DELUXE TRAP GUN . . NiB $700 Ex $566 Gd $339
Same as standard Model AL-3 Trap Gun except has fully-engraved receiver, gold-plated trigger and safety, stock and forearm of premium-grade European walnut, gold monogram escutcheon inlaid in buttstock. Imported 1975 to 1976.

AL390 FIELD SHOTGUN
Lightweight version of A-390 series. Gauges: 12 or 20 ga. 22- 24-, 26-, 28-, or 30-inch bbl., 41.7 to 47.6 inches overall. Weight: 6.4 to 7.5 lbs. Imported 1992 to 1999.

Field/Silver Mallard model (12 or 20 ga.)	NiB $655	Ex $465	Gd $300
Field/Silver Mallard Youth model (20 ga.)	NiB $500	Ex $355	Gd $245
Field/Slug (12 ga. only)	NiB $525	Ex $433	Gd $266
Silver Mallard camo model	NiB $533	Ex $379	Gd $295
Silver Mallard model, synthetic stock	NiB $566	Ex $430	Gd $349
Gold Mallard (12 or 20 ga.)	NiB $800	Ex $656	Gd $445
NWTF Special model, camo	NiB $645	Ex $355	Gd $339
NTWF Special model, synthetic	NiB $600	Ex $440	Gd $322
NWTF Special Youth model	NiB $590	Ex $367	Gd $292

AL390 SPORT SPORTING SHOTGUN
Similar to Model AL-390 Sport Skeet. Gauges: 12 or 20 ga., 28- or 30-inch bbls. Weight: 6.8 to 8 lbs. Imported from 1995-1999.

Sport Sporting	NiB $566	Ex $396	Gd $300
Sport Sporting Collection	NiB $590	Ex $433	Gd $335
Sport Sporting Youth (20 ga. only)	NiB $590	Ex $454	Gd $397
Sport Gold Sporting	NiB $823	Ex $577	Gd $446
EELL Sport Diamond Sporting	NiB $2166	Ex $1488	Gd $1094
W/Ported bbl., add			$100

AL390 SPORT SKEET SHOTGUN
Gauges: 12 ga. only. 26- or 28-inch bbl. w/3-round mqagazine. Weight: 7.6 to 8 lbs. Matte finish wood and metal. Imported 1995 to 1999.

Sport Skeet	NiB $498	Ex $366	Gd $279
Sport Super Skeet	NiB $576	Ex $377	Gd $301
W/ported bbl., add			$125

AL390 SPORT TRAP SHOTGUN
Gauges: 12 ga. only. 30- or 32-inch bbl. w/3-round chamber. Weight: 7.8 to 8.25 lbs. Matte finish wood and metal. Black recoil rubber pad. Imported from 1995 to 1999.

Sport Trap	NiB $564	Ex $379	Gd $288
Sport Super Trap	NiB $688	Ex $512	Gd $360
Multi-choke bbl. (30-inch only), add			$65
W/Ported bbl., add			$125

AL391 URIKA AUTOLOADING SHOTGUN
Gauge: 12 and 20 ga. w/3-inch chambers. 28- 30- or 32-inch bbl. Weight: 6.6 to 7.7 lbs. Self-compensating gas valve. Adjustable synthetic and walnut stocks w/ five interchangeable chokes. Imported from 2001 to 2006.

Urika	NiB $923	Ex $800	Gd $655
Urika synthetic	NiB $865	Ex $758	Gd $600
Urika camo w/Realtree Hardwoods	NiB $977	Ex $844	Gd $654
Urika Gold w/black receiver	NiB $896	Ex $588	Gd $464
Urika Gold w/silver receiver	NiB $1196	Ex $974	Gd $799
Urika Youth	NiB $900	Ex $779	Gd $698
Urika Sporting	NiB $1088	Ex $965	Gd $600
Urika Gold Sporting w/black receiver	NiB $859	Ex $655	Gd $488
Urika Gold Sporting w/silver receiver	NiB $1256	Ex $1011	Gd $733
Urika Trap	NiB $1047	Ex $798	Gd $633
Urika Gold Trap	NiB $1066	Ex $881	Gd $700
Parallel Target	NiB $1066	Ex $881	Gd $700

SHOTGUNS

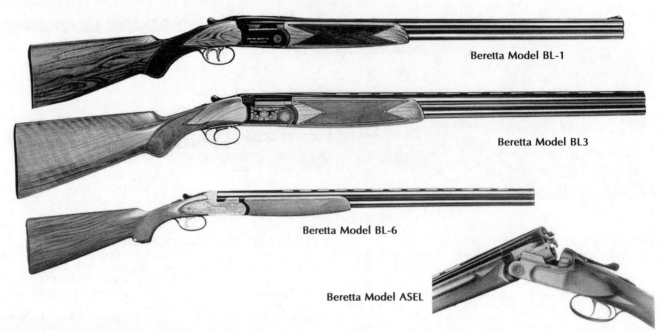

Beretta Model BL-1

Beretta Model BL3

Beretta Model BL-6

Beretta Model ASEL

MODEL ASE 90 O/U SHOTGUN
Competition-style receiver w/coin-silver finish and gold inlay featuring drop-out trigger group. Gauge: 12; 2.75-inch chamber. Bbls.: 28- or 30-inch w/fixed or Mobilchoke tubes; vent rib. Weight: 8.5 lbs. (30-inch bbl.). Checkered high-grade walnut stock. Imported 1992 to 1994.
Pigeon, Skeet, Trap models . . . NiB $3719 Ex $2466 Gd $1967
Sporting Clays model . . . . NiB $8171 Ex $6559 Gd $4577
Trap Combo model. . . NiB $13,878 Ex $10,798 Gd $8657
Deluxe model (introduced 1996)NiB $17,366 Ex $12,988 Gd $9853

MODEL ASE SERIES O/U SHOTGUN
Boxlock. Single non-selective trigger. Selective automatic ejectors. gauges: 12 and 20. Bbls. 26-, 28-, 30-inch; IC and M choke or M and F choke. Weight: about 5.75-7 lbs. Checkered pistol-grip stock and forearm. Receiver w/various grades of engraving. Imported 1947 to 1964.
Model ASE (light scroll engraving)...NiB $2366 Ex $1971 Gd $1388
Model ASEL (half coverage engraving)....NiB $3341 Ex $2679 Gd $1882
Model ASEELL (full coverage engraving)...NiB $4966 Ex $4054 Gd $2866
For 20 ga. models, add 95%

MODEL BL-1/BL-2 O/U
Boxlock. Plain extractors. Double triggers.12 gauge, 2.75-inch chambers only. Bbls.: 30-and 28-inch M/F choke, 26-inch IC/M choke. Weight: 6.75-7 lbs., depending on bbl. length. Checkered pistol-grip stock and forearm. Imported 1968 to 1973.
Model BL-1 . . . . NiB $478 Ex $339 Gd $227
Model BL-2 (single selective trigger). . . . NiB $596 Ex $487 Gd $356

MODEL BL-2/S. . . . . NiB $554 Ex $451 Gd $307
Similar to Model BL-1, except has selective "Speed-Trigger," vent-rib bbls., 2.75- or 3-inch chambers. Weight: 7-7.5 lbs. Imported 1974 to 1976.

MODEL BL-3 . . . . NiB $690 Ex $579 Gd $491
Same as Model BL-1, except has deluxe engraved receiver, selective single trigger, vent-rib bbls., 12 or 20 ga., 2.75-inch or 3-inch chambers in former, 3-inch in latter. Weight: 6-7.5 lbs. depending on ga. and bbl. length. Imported 1968 to 1976.

MODELS BL-4/BL-6
Higher grade versions of Model BL-3 w/more elaborate engraving and fancier wood; Model BL-6 has sideplates. Selective automatic ejectors standard. Imported 1968-76.
Model BL-4 . . . . NiB $966 Ex $779 Gd $633
Model BL-5 . . . . NiB $996 Ex $800 Gd $671
Model BL-6 (1973-76) . . . . NiB $1287 Ex $1108 Gd $977

SERIES BL SKEET GUNS
Models BL-3, BL-4, BL-5 and BL-6 w/standard features of their respective grades plus wider rib and skeet-style stock, 26-inch bbls. SK choked. Weight: 6-7.25 lbs. depending on ga.
Model BL-3 skeet gun . . . . . NiB $1166 Ex $877 Gd $588
Model BL-4 skeet gun . . . . . . NiB $822 Ex $658 Gd $433
Model BL-5 skeet gun . . . . . . NiB $966 Ex $700 Gd $582
Model BL-6 skeet gun . . . . NiB $1139 Ex $1076 Gd $755

SERIES BL TRAP GUNS
Models BL-3, BL-4, BL-5 and BL-6 w/standard features of their respective grades plus wider rib and Monte Carlo stock w/recoil pad; 30-inch bbls., improved M/F or both F choke. Weight: About 7.5 lbs.
Model BL-3 . . . . NiB $679 Ex $466 Gd $388
Model BL-4 . . . . NiB $733 Ex $566 Gd $452
Model BL-5 . . . . NiB $966 Ex $753 Gd $521
Model BL-6 . . . . NiB $1166 Ex $893 Gd $600

D10 TRIDENT TRAP GUNS NIB $7520 EX $5000 GD $2510
Removeable trigger group. 12 gauge, 3-inch chambers. Bbls.: 30-and 32-inch Optima choke tubes. Weight: 8.8 lbs., depending on bbl. length. Wlanut stock and forearm. Imported 2000 to 2008.
Top Single . . . . NIB $7520 EX $5000 GD $2510
Bottom Single . . . . NIB $7520 EX $5000 GD $2510
Combo . . . . NiB $9060 Ex $7200 Gd $4000
Model BL-6 . . . . NiB $1166 Ex $893 Gd $600

MODEL FS-1
FOLDING SINGLE . . . . NiB $238 Ex $167 Gd $95
Formerly "Companion." Folds to length of bbl. Hammerless. Underlever. Gauge: 12, 16, 20, 28 or .410. Bbl.: 30-inch in 12 ga., 28-inch in 16 and 20 ga.; 26-inch in 28 and .410 ga.; all F choke. Checkered semipistol-grip stock/forearm. Weight: 4.5-5.5 lbs. depending on ga. Disc. 1971.

Beretta FS-1 Folding

SHOTGUNS

MODEL GR-2 HAMMERLESS DOUBLE . . . NiB $956 Ex $788 Gd $641
Boxlock. Plain extractors. Double triggers. Gauges: 12, 20; 2.75-inch chambers in former, 3-inch in latter. Bbls.: Vent rib; 30-inch M/F choke (12 ga. only); 28-inch M/F choke, 26-inch IC/M choke. Weight: 6.5 to 7.5 lbs. depending on ga. and bbl. length. Checkered pistol-grip stock and forearm. Imported 1968 to 1976.

MODEL GR-3 . . . . NiB $1174 Ex $1021 Gd $751
Same as Model GR-2 except has selective single trigger chambered for 12-ga. Three inch or 2.75-inch shells. Magnum model has 30-inch M/F choke bbl., recoil pad. Weight: about 8 lbs. Imported 1968 to 1976.

MODEL GR-4 . . . . NiB $1359 Ex $1165 Gd $943
Same as Model GR-2 except has automatic ejectors and selective single trigger, higher grade engraving and wood. 12 ga., 2.75-inch chambers only. Imported 1968 to 1976.

GRADE 100 O/U
SHOTGUN. . . . . NiB $2134 Ex $1741 Gd $1288
Sidelock. Double triggers. Automatic ejectors. 12 ga. only. Bbls.: 26-, 28-, 30-inch, any standard boring. Weight: About 7.5 lbs. Checkered stock and forend, straight or pistol grip. Disc.

GRADE 200 . . . . NiB $2780 Ex $2284 Gd $1633
Same general specifications as Grade 00 except higher quality; bores and action parts hard chrome plated. Disc.

MARK II SINGLE-BARREL TRAP GUN . . . NiB $774 Ex $623 Gd $441
Boxlock action similar to that of Series "BL" over-and-unders. Engraved receiver. Automatic ejector. 12 ga. only. 32- or 34-inch bbl. w/wide vent rib. Weight: About 8.5 lbs. Monte Carlo stock w/ pistol grip and recoil pad, beavertail forearm. Imported 1972 to 1976.

MODEL S55B O/U
SHOTGUN. . . . . NiB $672 Ex $490 Gd $336
Boxlock. Plain extractors. Selective single trigger. Gauges: 12, 20; 2.75- or 3-inch chambers in former, 3-inch in latter. Bbls. vent rib; 30-inch M/F choke or both F choke in 12-ga. Three inch Magnum only; 28-inch M/F choke; 26 inch IC/M choke. Weight: 6.5 to 7.5 lbs. depending on ga. and bbl. length. Checkered pistol-grip stock and forearm. Introduced in 1977. Disc.

MODEL S56E . . . . NiB $853 Ex $567 Gd $356
Same as Model S55B except has scroll-engraved receiver selective automatic ejectors. Introduced in 1977. Disc.

MODEL S58 SKEET GUN . . . . NiB $855 Ex $621 Gd $443
Same as Model S56E except has 26-inch bbls. of Boehler Antinit Anticorro steel, SK choked, w/wide vent rib; skeet-style stock and forearm. Weight: 7.5 lbs. Introduced in 1977.

MODEL S58 TRAP GUN. . . . . NiB $620 Ex $494 Gd $368
Same as Model S58 Skeet Gun except has 30-inch bbls. bored IM/F Trap, Monte Carlo stock w/recoil pad. Weight: 7 lbs. 10 oz. Introduced in 1977. Disc.

SILVER HAWK FEATHERWEIGHT
HAMMERLESS DOUBLE-BARREL SHOTGUN
Boxlock. Double triggers or non-selective single trigger. Plain extractor. Gauges: 12, 16, 20, 28, 12 Mag. Bbls.: 26- to 32-inch w/ high matted rib, all standard choke combinations. Weight: 7 lbs. (12 ga. w/26-inch bbls.). Checkered walnut stock w/beavertail forearm. Disc. 1967.
W/double triggers . . . . NiB $1133 Ex $844 Gd $521
W/single trigger, add $200

Beretta S682 Gold E Trap

Beretta S682 Gold E Double Trap

SILVER SNIPE O/U SHOTGUN

Boxlock. Non-selective or selective single trigger. Plain extractor. Gauges: 12, 20, 12 Mag., 20 Mag. Bbls.: 26-, 28-, 30-inch; plain or vent rib; chokes IC/M, M/F, SK number 1 and number 2, F/F. Weight: From about 6 lbs. in 20 ga. to 8.5 lbs. in 12 ga. (Trap gun). Checkered walnut pistol-grip stock, forearm. Imported 1955 to 1967.

W/plain bbl., non-selective trigger . . NiB $779 Ex $643 Gd $448
W/vent rib bbl., non-selective
single trigger . . . . NiB $779 Ex $643 Gd $448
W/selective single trigger, add $100

GOLDEN SNIPE O/U

Same as Silver Snipe (see page 430) except has automatic ejectors, vent rib is standard feature. Imported 1959 to 1967.
W/non-selective single trigger. . . . NiB $1256 Ex $1065 Gd $645

MODEL 57E O/U

Same general specifications as Golden Snipe, but higher quality throughout. Imported 1955 to 1967.
W/non-selective single trigger NiB $977 Ex $765 Gd $545
W/selective single trigger . . . NiB $1165 Ex $996 Gd $703

MODEL SL-2 PIGEON SERIES SHOTGUN

Hammerless. Takedown.12 ga. only. Three round magazine. Bbls.: Vent rib; 30-inch F choke, 28-inch M, 26-inch IC. Weight: 7-7.25 lbs., depending on bbl. length. Receiver w/various grades of engraving. Checkered pistol-grip stock and forearm. Imported 1968 to 1971.
PUMP SHOTGUN . . . . NiB $553 Ex $442 Gd $308
Silver Pigeon . . . . NiB $466 Ex $367 Gd $377
Gold Pigeon. . . . . NiB $663 Ex $507 Gd $464
Ruby Pigeon. . . . . NiB $863 Ex $638 Gd $477

"SO" SERIES SHOTGUNS

Jubilee Series introduced in 1998. The Beretta Boxlock is made with mechanical works from a single block of hot forged, high-resistance steel. The gun is richly engraved in scroll and game scenes. All engraving is signed by master engravers. High-quality finishing on the inside with high polishing of all internal points. Sidelock. Selective automatic ejectors. Selective single trigger or double triggers. 12 ga. only, 2.75- or 3-inch chambers. Bbls.: Vent rib (wide type on skeet and trap guns); 26-, 27-, 29-, 30-inch; any combination of standard chokes. Weight: 7 to 7.75 lbs., depending on bbl. length, style of stock and density of wood. Stock and forearm of select walnut, finely checkered; straight or pistol-grip, field, skeet and trap guns have appropriate styles of stock and forearm. Models differ chiefly in quality of wood and grade of engraving. Models SO-3EL, SO-3EELL, SO4 and SO-5 have hand-detachable

locks. "SO-4" is used to designate skeet and trap models derived from Model SO-3EL, but with less elaborate engraving. Models SO3EL and SO-3EELL are similar to the earlier SO-4 and SO-5, respectively. Imported 1933 to date.
Jubilee O/U (.410, 12, 16, 20, 28 ga.). . .NiB $18,766 Ex $15,580 Gd $12,654
Jubilee II Side-by-side. . . . . NiB $20,888 Ex $16,876 Gd $13,777
Model SO-2 . . . . NiB $9121 Ex $4760 Gd $3231
Model SO-3 . . . . NiB $7786 Ex $6988 Gd $4766
Model SO-3EL . . . . .NiB $10,573 Ex $8227 Gd $5470
Model SO-3EELL . . . . NiB $12,098 Ex $10,866 Gd $8977
Model SO-4 Field, Skeet or Trap gun . . . NiB $10,677 Ex $9154 Gd $7110
Model SO-5 Sporting,
Skeet or Trap model. . . . . . NiB $12,779 Ex $10,870 Gd $8965
W/extra bbl. set, add 25%

MODELS SO-6 AND SO-9 PREMIUM GRADE SHOTGUNS

High-grade over/unders in the SO series. Gauges: 12 ga. only (SO-6); 12, 20, 28 and .410 (SO-9). Fixed or Mobilchoke (12 ga. only). Sidelock action. Silver or casehardened receiver (SO-6); English custom hand-engraved scroll or game scenes (SO-9). Supplied w/ leather case and accessories. Imported 1990 to date.
SO-6 O/U . . . . NiB $9044 Ex $6987 Gd $4733
Model SO-6 EELL O/U. . . . . NiB $8343 Ex $6865 Gd $6577
Model SO-9 O/U . . . . NiB $50,000 Ex $47,750 Gd $45,000
Model SO-9EELL
  w/custom engraving . . . NiB $110,000 Ex $95,000 Gd $80,000
W/extra bbl. set, add 25%

MODEL SO6/SO-7 S/S SHOTGUNS

Side-by-side shotgun w/same general specifications as SO Series over/unders except higher grade w/more elaborate engraving, fancier wood.
Model SO-6 (imported 1948-93) . .NiB $7254 Ex $6144 Gd $4988
Model SO-7 (imported 1948-90) . .NiB $8977 Ex $7238 Gd $6144

MODEL TR-1 SINGLE-SHOT

TRAP GUN. . . . . NiB $355 Ex $279 Gd $125
Hammerless. Underlever action. Engraved frame.12 ga. only. 32-inch bbl. w/vent rib. Weight: About 8.25 lbs. Monte Carlo stock w/pistol grip and recoil pad, beavertail forearm. Imported 1968 to 1971.

MODEL TR-2

MODEL TR-2 . . . . NiB $364 Ex $231 Gd $156
Same as Model TR-1 except has extended ventilated rib. Imported 1969-73.

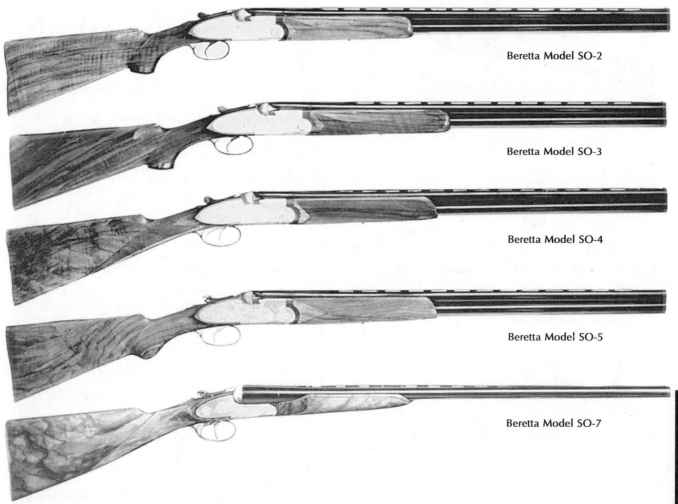

Beretta Model SO-2

Beretta Model SO-3

Beretta Model SO-4

Beretta Model SO-5

Beretta Model SO-7

VICTORIA PINTAIL (ES100) SEMIAUTOLOADER

Short Montefeltro-type recoil action. Gauge: 12 w/3-inch chamber. Bbl.: 24-inch slug, 24-, 26- or 28-inch vent rib w/Mobilchoke tubes. Weight: 7 lbs. to 7 lbs., 5 oz. Checkered synthetic or walnut buttstock and forend. Matte finish on both metal and stock. Imported 1993 and 2005.

Field model w/synthetic
stock (intro. 1998) . . . . NiB $522 Ex $320 Gd $244
Field model w/walnut stock (disc. 1998). . .NiB $733 Ex $535 Gd $431
Rifled slug model w/synthetic
stock (intro. 1998) . . . . NiB $544 Ex $378 Gd $296
Standard slug model
w/walnut stock (disc. 1998) . . . . NiB $544 Ex $378 Gd $296
Wetland Camo model (intro. 2000). . NiB $677 Ex $460 Gd $339

VINCENZO BERNARDELLI —

Gardone V.T. (Brescia), Italy. Previously imported by Armsport, Miami, FL (formerly by Magnum Research, Inc., Quality Arms, Stoeger Industries, Inc. & Action Arms, LTD).

115 SERIES O/U SHOTGUNS

Boxlock w/single trigger and ejectors. 12 ga. only. 25.5-, 26.75-, and 29.5-inch bbls. Concave top and vented middle rib. Anatomical

grip stock. Blued or coin-silver finish w/various grades of engraving. Imported 1985 to 1997.
Standard Model . . . . NiB $1844 Ex $1532 Gd $1176
Hunting Model 115E (disc. 1990) . . .NiB $2247 Ex $1993 Gd $1612
Hunting Model 115L (disc. 1990) . . NiB $2788 Ex $2391 Gd $2095
Hunting Model 115S (disc. 1990) . . .NiB $3712 Ex $3122 Gd $2210
Target Model 115 (disc. 1992). . . NiB $1977 Ex $1678 Gd $1440
Target Model 115E (disc. 1992) . . . NiB $6108 Ex $5388 Gd $3789
Target Model 115L (disc. 1992) . . . NiB $3855 Ex $3410 Gd $2377
Target Model 115S (disc. 1992) . . . NiB $6077 Ex $4129 Gd $3755
Trap/Skeet Model 115S
(imported 1996-97) . . . . NiB $3366 Ex $2581 Gd $1786
Sporting Clays Model 115S
(imported 1995-97). . . . . NiB $3944 Ex $3216 Gd $2533

BRESCIA
HAMMER DOUBLE . . . . . . NiB $1564 Ex $1096 Gd $839
Back-action sidelock. Plain extractors. Double triggers. Gauges: 12, 20. Bbls.: 27.5 or 29.5-inch M/F choke in 12 ga. 25.5-inch IC/M choke in 20 ga.. Weight: From 5.75 to 7 lbs., depending on ga. and bbl. length. English-style stock and forearm, checkered. No longer imported.

ELIO . . . . NiB $1232 Ex $1006 Gd $781
Lightweight game gun, 12 ga. only, w/same general specifications as Standard Gamecock (S. Uberto 1) except weight: About 6 to 6.25 lbs.; has automatic ejectors, fine English-pattern scroll engraving. No longer imported.

Bernardelli Gamecock

Bernardelli Standard Gamecock

Bernardelli Gardone

Bernardelli Italia

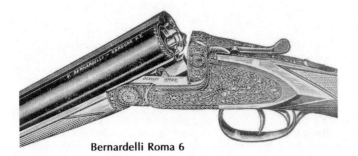

Bernardelli Roma 6

GAMECOCK, PREMIER (ROME 3)

Same general specifications as Standard Gamecock (S. Uberto 1) except has sideplates, auto ejectors, single trigger. No longer imported.

Roma 3 (disc. 1989,
Reintroduced 1993-97) . . . NiB $1790 Ex $1435 Gd $1108
Roma 3E (disc. 1950) . . . . NiB $1956 Ex $1600 Gd $1119
Roma 3M
w/single trigger (disc. 1997) . . . NiB $1956 Ex $1600 Gd $1119

GAMECOCK, STANDARD (S. UBERTO 1) HAMMERLESS
DOUBLE-BARREL SHOTGUN . . . NiB $900 Ex $766 Gd $563

Boxlock. Plain extractors. Double triggers. Gauges: 12, 16, 20; 2.75-inch chambers in 12 and 16, 3-inch in 20 ga. Bbls. 25.5-inch IC/M choke; 27.5-inch M/F choke. Weight: 5.75-6.5 lbs., depending on ga. and bbl. length. English-style straight-grip stock and forearm, checkered. No longer imported.

GARDONE HAMMER DOUBLE . . . NiB $2766 Ex $2261 Gd $1600

Same general specifications as Brescia except for higher grade engraving and wood, but not as high as the Italia. Half-cock safety. Disc. 1956.

HEMINGWAY HAMMERLESS DOUBLE

Boxlock. Single or double triggers w/hinged front. Selective automatic ejectors. Gauges: 12 and 20 w/2.75- or 3-inch chambers, 16 and 28 w/2.75-inch. Bbls.: 23.5- to 28-inch w/fixed chokes. Weight: 6.25 lbs. Checkered English-style European walnut stock. Silvered and engraved receiver.

Standard model . . . . NiB $2288 Ex $1866 Gd $1383
Deluxe model
w/sideplates (disc. 1993) . . . NiB $2698 Ex $2210 Gd $1679
W/single trigger, add $125

ITALIA . . . . NiB $1866 Ex $1044 Gd $623

Same general specifications as Brescia except higher grade engraving and wood. Disc. 1986.

ROMA 4 AND ROMA 6

Same as Premier Gamecock (Rome 3) except higher grade engraving and wood, double triggers. Disc. 1997.

Roma 4 (disc. 1989) . . . . . NiB $1847 Ex $1412 Gd $1095
Roma 4E (disc. 1997) . . . . NiB $1796 Ex $1370 Gd $1060
Roma 6 (disc. 1989) . . . . . NiB $1488 Ex $1233 Gd $1000
Roma 6E (disc. 1997) . . . NiB $2533 Ex $2000 Gd $1277

ROMA 7, 8, AND 9

Side-by-side. Anson & Deeley boxlock; hammerless. Ejectors; double triggers. 12 ga. Barrels: 27.5-or 29.5-inch. M/F chokes. Fancy hand-checkered European walnut straight or pistol-grip stock, forearm. Elaborately engraved, silver-finished sideplates. Imported 1994 to 1997.

Roma 7 . . . . NiB $3366 Ex $2160 Gd $1500
Roma 8 . . . . NiB $3866 Ex $2571 Gd $1880
Roma 9 . . . . NiB $4665 Ex $3748 Gd $2977

S. UBERTO 2 . . . . NiB $1460 Ex $1277 Gd $898

Same as Standard Gamecock (S. Uberto 1) except higher grade engraving and wood. Currently imported.

S. UBERTO F.S.

Same as Standard Gamecock except w/higher grade engraving, wood and has auto-ejectors. Disc. 1989, reintro. 1993 to 1997.

Model FS . . . . NiB $1746 Ex $1544 Gd $1100
Model V.B. Incisio . . . . . . NiB $2169 Ex $1754 Gd $1239
W/single trigger, add $100

HOLLAND V.B. SERIES SHOTGUNS
Holland & Holland-type sidelock action. Auto-ejectors. Double triggers. 12 ga. only. Bbl. length or choke to custom specification. Silver-finish receiver (Liscio) or engraved coin finish receiver (Incisio). Extra-select wood and game scene engraving (Lusso). Checkered stock (straight or pistol-grip). Imported 1992 to 1997.
Model V.B. Liscio......... NiB $11,650 Ex $10,500 Gd $8675
Model V.B. Incisio.......... NiB $12,200 Ex $9779 Gd $6755
Model V.B. Lusso............. NiB $9465 Ex $8119 Gd $5231
Model V.B. Extra......... NiB $14,766 Ex $10,877 Gd $8669
Model V.B. Gold....... NiB $49,600 Ex $44,688 Gd $37,789
W/Engraving Pattern
No. 4, add..................................... $1250
W/ ngraving Pattern
No. 12, add................................... $5000
W/Engraving Pattern No. 20, add $9500
W/Single trigger, add $700

BOSS & COMPANY — London, England

HAMMERLESS DOUBLE-BARREL
SHOTGUN....... NiB $64,887 Ex $57,955 Gd $35,898
Sidelock. Automatic ejectors. Double triggers, non-selective or selective single trigger. Made in all gauges, bbl. lengths and chokes. Checkered stock and forend, straight or pistol-grip.

HAMMERLESS O/U
SHOTGUN...... NiB $117,650 Ex $94,800 Gd $45,000
Sidelock. Automatic ejectors. Selective single trigger. Made in all gauges, bbl. lengths and chokes. Checkered stock and forend, straight or pistol-grip. Disc.

BREDA MECCANICA BRESCIANA — Brescia, Italy; formerly ERNESTO BREDA, Milan, Italy. Previously imported by Tristar (Kansas City, MO), Gryphon International (Kansas City, MO) and Diana Imports Co., (San Francisco, CA).

VEGA SPECIAL O/U SHOTGUN. . .NiB $676 Ex $543 Gd $410
12 or 20 gauge. Box lock action. Bbl. 26 or 28 inches; single trigger; ejectors. Blue only.

VEGA SPECIAL TRAP .... NiB $966 Ex $733 Gd $590
12 or 20 gauge. Box lock action. Competition triggers and lock. Bbl. 30 or 32 inches; single trigger; ejectors. Blue only.

VEGA LUSSO.......... NiB $1765 Ex $1430 Gd $1100
12 gauge only, 3-inch chambers. Scalloped box lock action, single selective trigger, ejectors. Bbl. 26 or 28 inches, ventilated rib. Coin finished receiver with light engraving. Deluxe checkered Circassian walnut stock and forearm. Imported 2001 to 2002.

SIRIO STANDARD ...... NiB $2176 Ex $1788 Gd $1354
12 or 20 gauge. Engraved box lock action. Bbl. 26 or 28 inches; single trigger; ejectors. Blue only. Also available in skeet model.

ANDROMEDA SPECIAL ..... NiB $755 Ex $665 Gd $525
Side-by-side.12 gauge, single trigger; ejectors, select checkered walnut stock; satin finish on receiver with elaborate engraving.

GOLD SERIES SEMIAUTOMATIC SHOTGUN
12 or (lightweight) 20 gauge, 2.75-inch chamber. Bbl. 25 or 27 inches; ventilated rib standard. Recoil operated

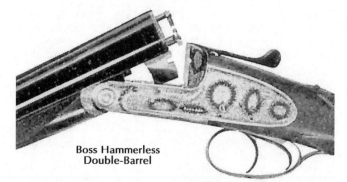
Boss Hammerless Double-Barrel

Antares Standard Model ..... NiB $543 Ex $421 Gd $336
Argus Model .... NiB $521 Ex $390 Gd $266
Aries Model .... NiB $521 Ex $390 Gd $266

STANDARD GRADE GOLD SERIES NiB $377 Ex $290 Gd $245
12 gauge, 2-3/4-inch chamber. Recoil operated. Bbl. 25 or 27 inches. Light engraving. Disc.

GRADE 1 .... NiB $644 Ex $500 Gd $336
Similar to Standard model but with fancier wood and engraving.

GRADE 2 .... NiB $756 Ex $644 Gd $500
Similar to Grade 1 but with more engraving, etc.

GRADE 3 .... NiB $966 Ex $771 Gd $654
Same as Grade 1 but with custom-quality embellishments.

MAGNUM MODEL......... NiB $546 Ex $400 Gd $297
Similar to Standard Grade but with 3-inch chambers.

ALTAIR SPECIAL.......... NiB $533 Ex $400 Gd $336
12 gauge, 2.75-inch chamber. Gas-operated. Bbl. 25 or 27 inches, ventilated rib standard. Alloy construction, blue or chrome receiver.

ASTRO.............. NiB $1126 Ex $853 Gd $700
12 gauge (disc. 2002) or 20 gauge, 3-inch chamber. Inertia action. Bbl. 22 (slug), 24, 26, 28 or 30 inches; ventilated rib. Black synthetic, Advantage camo, or Circassian walnut stock and forearm. Imported 2001.
Advantage camo model, add........................ $125

ASTROLUX .... NiB $1588 Ex $1344 Gd $1033
Similar to Astro model except has two-tone receiver with engraving and deluxe checkered Circassian walnut stock and forearm. Imported 2001 to 2002.

ERMES SERIES .... NiB $1044 Ex $788 Gd $648
12 gauge, 3-inch chamber. Semiautomatic. Inertia recoil operating system, aluminum alloy receiver, nickeel plated or blue finish on lower receiver. Bbl. 24, 26, or 28 inches. Deluxe checkered Circassian walnut stock and forearm. Imported 2001.
Ermes Silver .... NiB $1287 Ex $1095 Gd $869
Ermes Gold .... NiB $1452 Ex $1138 Gd $1009

MIRA .... NiB $880 Ex $622 Gd $500
12 gauge, 3-inch chamber. Semiautomatic, gas-operated. Aluminum alloy receiver; black or Advantage camo finish. Bbl. 22 (slug), 24, 26, 28 or 30 inches, ventilated rib. Circassian walnut or black synthetic stock and forearm. Imported 2001.
Sporting Clays model, add $50
W/black synthetic stock & forearm, deduct 10%

ARIES 2 . . . . NiB $879 Ex $793 Gd $649
12 gauge, 2-3/4-inch chamber. Semiautomatic, gas-operated. Engraved two-tone receiver. Bbl. 20 or 30 inches, ventilated rib. Deluxe checkered Circassian walnut or black synthetic stock and forearm. Imported 2001 only.

BRETTON SHOTGUNS — St. Etienne (Cedex1), France

BABY STANDARD SPRINT O/U . . . . .NiB $1088 Ex $855 Gd $687
Inline sliding breech action. 12 or 20 gauge w/2.75-inch chambers. 27.5-inch separated bbls. w/vent rib and choke tubes. Weight: 4.8 to 5 lbs. Engraved alloy receiver. Checkered walnut buttstock and forearm w/satin oil finish. Limited import.

SPRINT DELUXE O/U . . . . NiB $1077 Ex $863 Gd $700
Similar to the Standard Model except w/engraved coin-finished receiver and chambered 12, 16 and 20 ga. Limited import.

FAIR PLAY O/U . . . . NiB $1088 Ex $863 Gd $600
Lightweight action similar to the Sprint Model except w/hinged action that pivots open and is chambered 12 or 20 gauge only. Limited import.

BRNO SHOTGUNS — Brno and Uherski Brod, Czech Republic (formerly Czechoslovakia)

MODEL 500 O/U SHOTGUN . NiB $900 Ex $777 Gd $568
Hammerless boxlock w/double triggers and ejectors.12 ga. w/2.75-inch chambers. 27.5-inch bbls.. choked M/F. 44 inches overall. Weight: 7 lbs. Etched receiver. Checkered walnut stock w/classic style cheekplece. Imported from 1987 to 1991.

500 SERIES O/U COMBINATION GUNS
Similar to the 500 Series over/under shotgun above, except w/lower bbl. chambered in rifle calibers and set trigger option. Imported from 1987 to 1995.
Model 502 12 ga./.222 or .243 (disc. 1991)...NiB $2088 Ex $1256 Gd $1077
Model 502 12 ga. .308 or .30-06 (disc. 1991)... NiB $1164 Ex $1038 Gd $772
Model 571 12 ga./6x65R (disc. 1993) . . . . . NiB $853 Ex $709 Gd $587
Model 572 12 ga./7x65R (imported since 1992) . . .NiB $881 Ex $733 Gd $600
Model 584 12 ga./7x57R (imported since 1992) . . .NiB $1264 Ex $1033 Gd $800
Sport Series 4-bbl. set (disc. 1991)...NiB $3153 Ex $2571 Gd $1863

CZ 581 SOLO O/U SHOTGUN . . . . . . NiB $966 Ex $738 Gd $561
Hammerless boxlock w/double triggers, ejectors and automatic safety. 12 ga. w/2.75- or 3-inch chambers. 28-inch bbls. choked M/F. Weight: 7.5 lbs. Checkered walnut stock. Disc. 1996.

SUPER SERIES O/U SHOTGUN
Hammerless sidelock w/selective single or double triggers and ejectors. 12 ga. w/2.75- or 3-inch chambers. 27.5-inch bbls. choked M/F. 44.5 inches overall. Weight: 7.25 lbs. Etched or engraved side plates. Checkered European walnut stock w/classic-style cheekpiece. Imported from 1987 to 1991.
Super Series Shotgun (disc. 1992) . . . . . NiB $866 Ex $731 Gd $577
Super Series Combo (disc. 1992) . . . . NiB $2021 Ex $1190 Gd $977
Super Ser. 3-bbl. set (disc. 1990) . . . NiB $1993 Ex $1578 Gd $1266
Super Series engraving, add. $1350

ZH 300 SERIES O/U SHOTGUNS
Hammerless boxlock w/double triggers. Gauge: 12 or 16 w/2.75- or 3-inch chambers. Bbls.: 26, 27.5 or 30 inches; choked M/F. Weight: 7 lbs. Skip-line checkered walnut stock w/classic-style cheekpiece.

Imported from 1986-93.
Model 300 (disc. 1993) . . . . NiB $786 Ex $547 Gd $408
Model 301 Field (disc. 1991) . . . . NiB $667 Ex $582 Gd $400
Model 302 Skeet (disc. 1992) . . . . NiB $745 Ex $557 Gd $442
Model 303 Trap (disc. 1992) . . . . NiB $749 Ex $566 Gd $449

ZH 300 SERIES O/U COMBINATION GUNS
Similar to the 300 Series over/under shotgun except lower bbl. chambered in rifle calibers.
Model 300 Combo
8-bbl. Set (disc. 1991) . . . . NiB $3375 Ex $2977 Gd $2500
Model 304 12 ga./7x57R (disc. 1995) . . .NiB $846 Ex $698 Gd $535
Model 305 12 ga./5.6x52R (disc. 1993) . . . NiB $921 Ex $769 Gd $544
Model 306 12 ga./5.6x50R (disc. 1993) . . . NiB $965 Ex $798 Gd $579
Model 307 12 ga./.22 Hornet
(Imported since 1995) . . . . NiB $843 Ex $755 Gd $507
Model 324 16 ga./7x57R (disc. 1987) . . .NiB $880 Ex $742 Gd $509

ZP 149 HAMMERLESS DOUBLE
Sidelock action w/double triggers, automatic ejectors and automatic safety.12 ga. w/2.75- or 3-inch chambers. 28.5-inch bbls. choked M/F. Weight: 7.25 lbs. Checkered walnut buttstock with cheekpiece.
Standard model . . . . NiB $669 Ex $458 Gd $388
Engraved model . . . . NiB $700 Ex $477 Gd $421

BROLIN ARMS, INC. — Pomona, California

FIELD SERIES PUMP SHOTGUN
Slide-action. Gauge: 12 ga. w/3-inch chamber. 24-, 26-, 28- or 30-inch bbl. 44 and 50 inches overall. Weight: 7.3 to 7.6 lbs. Cross-bolt safety. Vent rib bbl. w/screw-in choke tube and bead sights. Non- reflective metal finish. Synthetic or oil-finished wood stock w/ swivel studs. Made from 1997 to 1998.
Synthetic stock model . . . . NiB $254 Ex $188 Gd $95
Wood stock model . . . . NiB $200 Ex $129 Gd $75

COMBO MODEL PUMP SHOTGUN
Similar to the Field Model except w/extra 18.5- or 22-inch bbl. w/ bead or rifle sight. Made from 1997 to 1998.
Synthetic stock model . . . . . . NiB $279 Ex $200 Gd $115
Wood stock model . . . . NiB $331 Ex $240 Gd $193

LAWMAN MODEL PUMP SHOTGUN
Similar to the Field Model except has 18.5-inch bbl. w/cylinder bore fixed choke. Weight: 7 lbs. Dual operating bars. Bead, rifle or ghost ring sights. Black synthetic or wood stock. Matte chrome or satin nickel finish. Made from 1997 to 1999.
Synthetic stock model . . . . NiB $217 Ex $151 Gd $90
Wood stock model . . . . NiB $217 Ex $151 Gd $90
W/rifle sights, add $35
W/ghost ring sights, add $50
W/satin nickel finish (disc. 1997), add. $50

SLUG MODEL PUMP SHOTGUN
Similar to the Field Model except has 18.5- or 22-inch bbl. w/IC fixed choke or 4-inch extended rifled choke. Rifle or ghost ring sights or optional cantilevered scope mount. Black synthetic or wood stock. Matte blued finish. Made from 1998 to 1999.
Synthetic stock model . . . . NiB $288 Ex $202 Gd $166
Wood stock model . . . . NiB $300 Ex $221 Gd $180
W/rifled bbl., add $25
W/cantilevered scope mount, add $50

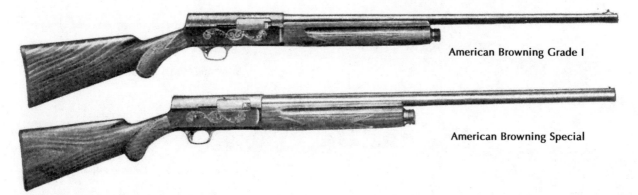

American Browning Grade I

American Browning Special

TURKEY SPECIAL PUMP SHOTGUN
Similar to the Field Model except has 22-inch vent-rib bbl. w/extended extra-full choke. Rifle or ghost ring sights or optional cantilevered scope mount. Black synthetic or wood stock. Matte blued finish. Made from 1998 to 1999.

Synthetic stock model . . . . NiB $266 Ex $190 Gd $125
Wood stock model . . . . NiB $305 Ex $237 Gd $154
W/cantilevered
scope mount, add. $50

BROWNING SHOTGUNS — Morgan (formerly Ogden), Utah

AMERICAN BROWNING SHOTGUNS

Designated "American" Browning because they were produced in Ilion, New York, the following Remington-made Brownings are almost identical to the Remington Model 11A and Sportsman and the Browning Auto-5. They are the only Browning shotguns manufactured in the U.S. during the 20th century and were made for Browning Arms when production was suspended in Belgium because of WW II.

NOTE: *Fabrique Nationale Herstal (formerly Fabrique Nationale d'Armes de Guerre) of Herstal, Belgium, is the longtime manufacturer of Browning shotguns dating back to 1900. Miroku Firearms Mfg. Co. of Tokyo, Japan, bought into the Browning company and has, since the early 1970s, undertaken some of the production. The following shotguns were manufactured for Browning by these two firms.*

GRADE I AUTOLOADER (AUTO-5)
Recoil-operated autoloader. Similar to the Remington Model 11A except w/different style engraving and identified w/the Browning logo. Gauges: 12, 16 or 20. Plain 26- to 32-inch bbl. w/any standard boring. Two or four shell tubular magazine w/magazine cut-off. Weight: About 6.88 lbs. (20 ga.) to 8 lbs. (12 ga.). Checkered pistol-grip stock and forearm. Made from 1940 to 1949.

American Browning Grade I
Auto-5, 12 or 16 ga. . . . . NiB $856 Ex $744 Gd $400
20 ga., add. 20%

SPECIAL 441
Same general specifications as Grade I except supplied w/raised matted rib or vent rib. Disc. 1949.

W/raised matted rib . . . . NiB $894 Ex $756 Gd $435
W/vent rib . . . . NiB $925 Ex $790 Gd $466
20 ga., add. 20%

SPECIAL SKEET MODEL . . . . . NiB $815 Ex $645 Gd $477
Same general specifications as Grade I except has 26-inch bbl. w/ vent rib and Cutts Compensator. Disc. 1949.

UTILITY FIELD GUN. . . . . . . NiB $608 Ex $458 Gd $339
Same general specifications as Grade I except has 28-inch plain bbl. w/Poly Choke. Disc. 1949.

MODEL 12 PUMP SHOTGUN
Special limited edition Winchester Model 12. Gauge: 20 or 28. Five-round tubular magazine. 26-inch bbl., M choke. 45 inches overall. Weight: about 7 lbs. Grade I has blued receiver, checkered walnut stock w/matte finish. Grade V has engraved receiver, checkered deluxe walnut stock w/high-gloss finish. Made from 1988 to 1992. See illustration next page.

Grade I, 20 ga. 8600 prod. . . . . NiB $866 Ex $569 Gd $449
Grade I, 28 ga. . . . . NiB $1166 Ex $912 Gd $744
Grade V, 20 ga 4000 prod.. . . NiB $1455 Ex $1187 Gd $879
Grade V, 28 ga . . . . NiB $1768 Ex $1344 Gd $961

MODEL 42 LIMITED Edition SHOTGUN
Special limited edition Winchester Model 42 pump shotgun. Same general specifications as Model 12 except w/smaller frame in .410 ga. and 3-inch chamber. Made from 1991 to 1993.
Grade I
(6000 produced) . . . . NiB $967 Ex $744 Gd $466
Grade V
(6000 produced). . . . . NiB $1590 Ex $1156 Gd $863

2000 BUCK SPECIAL . . . . NiB $588 Ex $467 Gd $355
Same as Field Model except has 24-inch plain bbl. Bored for rifled slug and buckshot, fitted w/rifle sights (open rear, ramp front). 12 ga., 2.75-inch or 3-inch chamber; 20 ga., 2.75-inch chamber. Weight: 12 ga., 7 lbs., 8 oz.; 20 ga., 6 lbs., 10 oz. Made from 1974 to 1981 by FN.

2000 GAS AUTOMATIC SHOTGUN, FIELD MODEL
Gas-operated. Gauge: 12 or 20. 2.75-inch chamber. Four-round magazine. Bbl.: 26-, 28-, 30-inch, any standard choke plain matted bbl. (12 ga. only) or vent rib. Weight: 6 lbs. 11 oz.-7 lbs. 12 oz. depending on ga. and bbl. length. Checkered pistol-grip stock/ forearm. Made from 1974 to 1981 by FN; assembled in Portugal.
W/plain matted bbl. . . . . NiB $559 Ex $468 Gd $346

2000 MAGNUM MODEL . . . . NiB $579 Ex $377 Gd $300
Same as Field Model except chambered for 3-inch shells, three-round magazine. Bbl.: 26- (20 ga. only), 28-, 30- or 32-inch (latter two 12 ga. only); any standard choke; vent rib. Weight: 6 lbs., 11 oz.-7 lbs., 13 oz. depending on ga. and bbl. Made from 1974 to 1983 by FN.

SHOTGUNS

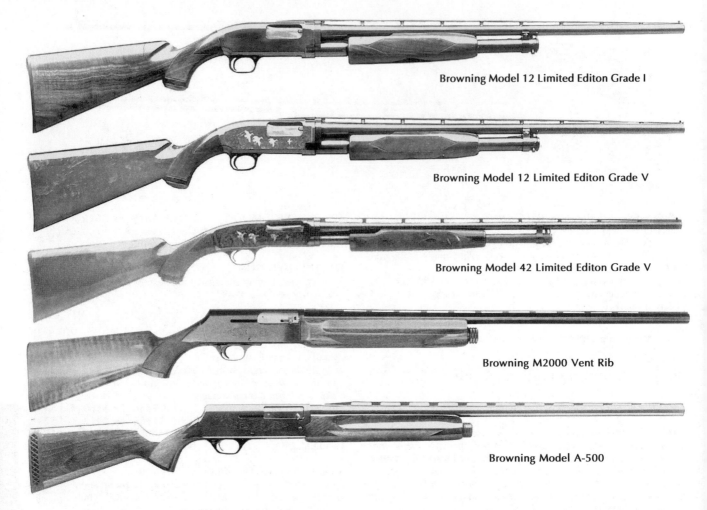

Browning Model 12 Limited Editon Grade I

Browning Model 12 Limited Editon Grade V

Browning Model 42 Limited Editon Grade V

Browning M2000 Vent Rib

Browning Model A-500

2000 SKEET MODEL . . . . **NiB $527 Ex $441 Gd $338**
Same as Field Model except has skeet-style stock w/recoil pad, 26-inch
vent-rib bbl., SK choke. 12 or 20 ga., 2.75-inch chamber. Weight: 8
lbs., 1 oz. (12 ga.); 6 lbs., 12 oz. (20 ga.) Made 1974 to 1981 by FN.

2000 TRAP MODEL . . . . **NiB $527 Ex $441 Gd $338**
Same as Field Model except has Monte Carlo stock w/recoil pad,
30- or 32-inch bbl. w/high-post vent rib and receiver extension,
M/I/F chokes. 12 ga., 2.75-inch chamber. Weight: About 8 lbs., 5
oz. Made 1974 to 1981 by FN.

A-500G GAS-OPERATED SEMIAUTOMATIC
Same general specifications as Browning Model A-500R except gas-
operated. Made 1990 to 1993.
Buck Special . . . . **NiB $590 Ex $466 Gd $339**
Hunting model . . . . **NiB $688 Ex $491 Gd $388**

A-500G SPORTING CLAYS . . . **NiB $663 Ex $490 Gd $388**
Same general specifications as Model A-500G except has matte
blued receiver w/"Sporting Clays" logo. 28- or 30-inch bbl. w/
Invector choke tubes. Made 1992 to 1993.

A-500R SEMIAUTOMATIC
Recoil-operated. Gauge: 12. 26- to 30-inch vent-rib bbls. 24-inch
Buck Special. Invector choke tube system. 2.75- or 3-inch Magnum
cartridges. Weight: 7 lbs., 3 oz.-8 lbs., 2 oz. Cross-bolt safety. Gold-
plated trigger. Scroll-engraved receiver. Gloss-finished walnut stock
and forend. Made by FN from 1987 to 1993.

Hunting model . . . . **NiB $677 Ex $476 Gd $388**
Buck Special . . . . **NiB $692 Ex $490 Gd $433**

A-BOLT SERIES SHOTGUN
Bolt-action repeating single-barrel shotgun. 12 ga. only w/3-inch
chambers, 2-round magazine. 22- or 23-inch rifled bbl., w/or w/o a
rifled invector tube. Receiver drilled and tapped for scope mounts.
Bbl. w/ or w/o open sights. Checkered walnut or graphite/fiberglass
composite stock. Matte black metal finish. Imported 1995 to 1998.
Stalker model w/
composite stock . . . . **NiB $1365 Ex $1077 Gd $867**
Hunter model w/walnut stock . . . . **NiB $1365 Ex $1077 Gd $867**
W/rifled bbl., add $200
W/open sights, add $75

AUTOLOADING SHOTGUNS, GRADES II, III & IV
These higher grade models differ from the Standard or Grade I in
general quality, grade of wood, checkering, engraving, etc., other-
wise specifications are the same. Grade IV guns, sometimes called
Midas Grade, are inlaid w/yellow and green gold. Disc. in 1940.
Grade II, plain bbl.. . . . . **NiB $1698 Ex $1390 Gd $976**
Grade III, plain bbl. . . . . **NiB $1580 Ex $1176 Gd $833**
Grade IV, plain bbl. . . . . **NiB $4469 Ex $3865 Gd $3033**
W/raised, matted rib bbl., add 15%
W/vent. rib bbl., add 30%

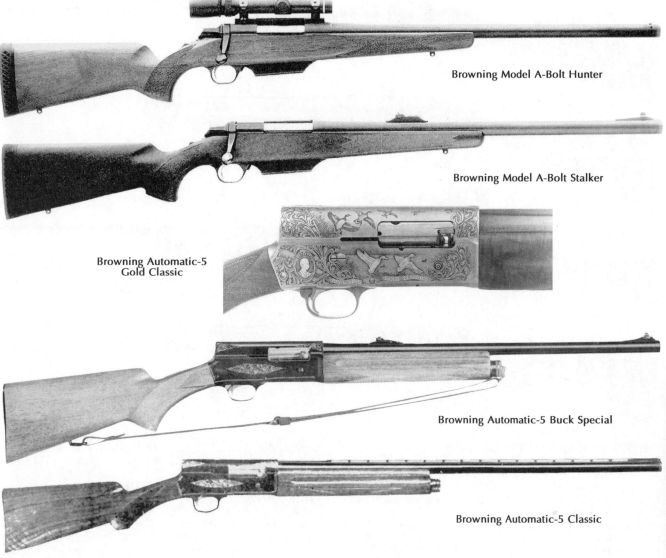

Browning Model A-Bolt Hunter

Browning Model A-Bolt Stalker

Browning Automatic-5 Gold Classic

Browning Automatic-5 Buck Special

Browning Automatic-5 Classic

AUTOMATIC-5, LIGHT 20

Same general specifications as Standard Model except lightweight and 20 ga. Bbl.: 26- or 28-inch; plain or vent rib. Weight: About 6.25-6.5 lbs. depending on bbl. Made 1958 to 1976 by FN, since then by Miroku.

FN manu., plain bbl. . . . . NiB $844 Ex $633 Gd $429
FN manu., vent. rib bbl. . . . . NiB $1267 Ex $988 Gd $687
Miroku manu., vent. rib,fixed choke NiB $965 Ex $743 Gd $846
Miroku manu., vent. rib, invectors NiB $1065 Ex $844 Gd $600

AUTOMATIC-5, BUCK SPECIAL MODELS

Same as Light 12, Magnum 12, Light 20, Magnum 20, in respective gauges, except 24-inch plain bbl. bored for rifled slug and buckshot, fitted w/rifle sights (open rear, ramp front). Weight: 6.13-8.25 lbs. depending on ga. Made 1964 to 1976 by FN, since then by Miroku.

FN manu., w/plain bbl. . . . . . NiB $1276 Ex $889 Gd $567
Miroku manu., ... NiB $966 Ex $843 Gd $544
W/3-inch mag. rec., add. $10%

AUTOMATIC-5 CLASSIC. . . . NiB $1186 Ex $983 Gd $889

Gauge: 12. 5-round capacity. 28-inch vent rib bbl./M choke. 2.75-

inch chamber. Engraved silver-gray receiver. Gold-plated trigger. Crossbolt safety. High-grade, hand-checkered select American walnut stock w/rounded pistol grip. 5,000 issued; made in Japan in 1984, engraved in Belgium.

AUTOMATIC-5 GOLD CLASSIC . NiB $9887 Ex $6690 Gd $4690

Same general specifications as Automatic-5 Classic except engraved receiver inlaid w/gold. Pearl border on stock and forend plus fine-line hand-checkering. Each gun numbered "One of Five Hundred," etc. 500 issued in 1984; made in Belgium.

AUTOMATIC-5, LIGHT 12

12 ga. only. Same general specifications as Standard Model except lightweight (about 7.25 lbs.), has gold-plated trigger. Guns w/rib have striped matting on top of bbl. Fixed chokes or Invector tubes. Made 1948 to 1976 by FN, since then by Miroku.

FN manu., plain bbl. . . . . NiB $889 Ex $655 Gd $498
FN manu., w/raised matte rib . . NiB $954 Ex $777 Gd $675
FN manu., vent. rib . . . . NiB $1098 Ex $966 Gd $676
Miroku manu., vent. rib, fixed choke . . . NiB $889 Ex $667 Gd $487
Miroku manu., vent. rib, Invectors . . . NiB $1099 Ex $776 Gd $566

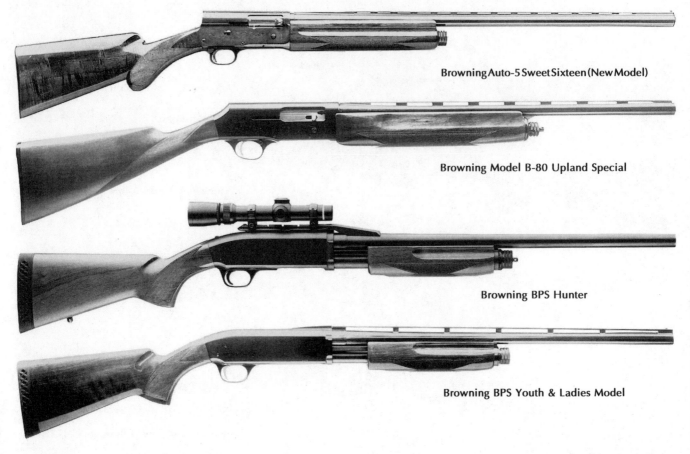

Browning Auto-5 Sweet Sixteen (New Model)

Browning Model B-80 Upland Special

Browning BPS Hunter

Browning BPS Youth & Ladies Model

AUTOMATIC-5, MAGNUM 12 GAUGE
Same general specifications as Standard Model. Chambered for 3-inch Magnum 12-ga. shells. Bbl.: 28-inch M/F, 30- or 32-inch F/F, plain or vent rib. Weight: 8.5-9 lbs. depending on bbl. Buttstock has recoil pad. Made 1958 to 1976 by FN, since then by Miroku. Fixed chokes or Invector tubes.

FN manu., plain bbl. . . . . NiB $954 Ex $779 Gd $549
FN manu., vent. rib bbl. . . . NiB $1288 Ex $977 Gd $765
Miroku manu., vent. rib, fixed chokes . . . NiB $888 Ex $645 Gd $455
Miroku manu., vent. rib, Invectors . . . . NiB $1066 Ex $707 Gd $500

AUTOMATIC-5, MAGNUM 20 GAUGE
Same general specifications as Standard Model except chambered for 3-inch Magnum 20-ga. shell. Bbl.: 26- or 28-inch, plain or vent rib. Weight: 7 lbs., 5 oz.-7 lbs., 7 oz. depending on bbl. Made 1967 to 1976 by FN, since then by Miroku.

FN manu., plain bbl. . . . . NiB $944 Ex $768 Gd $567
FN manu., vent. rib bbl. . . . NiB $1333 Ex $989 Gd $779
Miroku manu., vent. rib, Invectors NiB $989 Ex $766 Gd $590

AUTOMATIC-5, SKEET MODEL
12 ga. only. Same general specifications as Light 12. Bbl.: 26-or 28-inch, plain or vent rib, SK choke. Weight: 7 lbs., 5 oz.-7 lbs., 10 oz. depending on bbl. Made by FN prior to 1976, since then by Miroku.

FN manu., plain bbl. . . . . . . NiB $1177 Ex $956 Gd $654
FN manu., vent. rib bbl. . . NiB $1769 Ex $1166 Gd $956
Miroku manu., vent. rib bbl. . . NiB $987 Ex $766 Gd $554

AUTOMATIC-5 STALKER
Same general specifications as Automatic-5 Light and Magnum models except w/matte blue finish and black graphite fiberglass stock and forearm. Made from 1992 to 1997.

Light model . . . . NiB $966 Ex $831 Gd $664
Magnum model . . . . NiB $1031 Ex $977 Gd $689

AUTOMATIC-5, STANDARD (GRADE I)
Recoil-operated. Gauge: 12 or 16 (16-gauge guns made prior to WW II were chambered for 2-inch shells; standard 16 disc. 1964). Four shell magazine in 5-round model, prewar guns were also available in 3-round model. Bbls.: 26- to 32-inch; plain, raised matted or vent rib; choice of standard chokes. Weight: About 8 lbs., in 12 ga., 7.5 lbs., in 16 ga. Checkered pistol-grip stock and forearm. (Note: Browning Special, disc. about 1940.) Made from 1900 to 1973 by FN.

Grade I, plain bbl. . . . . NiB $844 Ex $677 Gd $544
Grade I (or Browning Special),
  w/raised matted rib. . . . . . . NiB $977 Ex $778 Gd $580
Grade I (or Browning Special), w/ vent. rib NiB $977 Ex $778 Gd $580

AUTOMATIC-5, SWEET 16
16 ga. Same general specifications as Standard Model except lightweight (about 6.75 lbs.), has gold plated trigger. Guns w/rib have striped matting on top of bbl. Made 1937 to 1976 by FN.

W/plain bbl. . . . . NiB $1189 Ex $793 Gd $555
W/raised matted or vent. rib . . . NiB $1769 Ex $1388 Gd $1012

AUTO-5, SWEET
SIXTEEN NEW MODEL . . . . NiB $1399 Ex $1156 Gd $922
Reissue of popular 16-gauge Hunting Model w/5-round capacity, 2.75-inch chamber, scroll-engraved blued receiver, high-gloss French walnut stock w/rounded pistol grip. 26- or 28-inch vent-rib bbl. F choke tube. Weight: 7 lbs., 5 oz. Reintro. 1987 to 1993.

Browning BPS
Waterfowl – Mossy Oak Shadow Grass

Browning BPS Stalker

AUTOMATIC-5, TRAP MODEL NiB $1277 Ex $965 Gd $777
12 ga. only. Same general specifications as Standard Model except has trap-style stock, 30-inch vent-rib bbl. F choke. Weight: 8.5 lbs. Disc. 1971.

MODEL B-80 GAS-OPERATED
AUTOMATIC . . . . NiB $699 Ex $577 Gd $400
Gauge: 12 or 20; 2.75-inch chamber. Four round magazine. Bbl.: 26-, 28- or 30-inch, any standard choke, vent-rib bbl. w/fixed chokes or Invector tubes. Weight: 6 lbs., 12 oz.-8 lbs., 1 oz. depending on ga. and bbl. Checkered pistol-grip stock and forearm. Made 1981 to 1988.

MODEL B-80 PLUS . . . . NiB $765 Ex $605 Gd $466
Same general specifications as Browning Model B-80 except chambered for 3-inch shotshells. Made in 1988.

MODEL B-80 SUPERLIGHT. . . NiB $689 Ex $544 Gd $432
Same as Standard Model except weighs 1 lb. less.

MODEL B-80 UPLAND SPECIAL . . NiB $698 Ex $566 Gd $433
Gauge: 12 or 20. 22-inch vent-rib bbl. Invector choke tube system. 2.75-inch chambers. 42 inches overall. Weight: 5 lbs., 7 oz. (20 ga.); 6 lbs., 10 oz. (12 ga.). German nickel silver sight bead. Crossbolt safety. Checkered walnut straight-grip stock and forend. Disc. 1988.

BPS DEER HUNTER SPECIAL . . . NiB $735 Ex $510 Gd $375
Same general specifications as Standard BPS model except has 20.5-inch bbl. w/adj. rifle-style sights. Solid scope mounting system. Checkered walnut stock w/sling swivel studs. Made from 1992 to date.

BPS GAME GUN TURKEY SPECIAL . . . NiB $498 Ex $380 Gd $295
Same general specifications as Standard BPS model except w/ matte blue metal finish and satin-finished stock. Chambered for 12 ga. 3-inch only. 20.5-inch bbl. w/extra full invector choke system. Receiver drilled and tapped for scope. Made from 1992 to 2001.

BPS PIGEON GRADE . . . . NiB $699 Ex $449 Gd $354
Same general specifications as Standard BPS model except w/select grade walnut stock and gold-trimmed receiver. Available in 12 ga. from only w/26- or 28-inch vent-rib bbl. Made 1992 to 1998.

BPS PUMP INVECTOR STALKER
Same general specifications as BPS Pump Shotgun except in 10 and 12 ga. w/Invector choke system, 22-, 26-, 28- or 30-inch bbls.; matte blue metal finish w/matte black stock. Made from 1987 to date.
12 ga. model (3-inch) . . . . NiB $577 Ex $412 Gd $290
10- & 12 ga. model (3.5-inch) . . . . . . NiB $776 Ex $600 Gd $466

BPS PUMP SHOTGUN
Takedown. Gauges: 10, 12 (3.5-inch chamber); 12, 20 and .410 (3-inch) and 28 ga. chambered 2.75-inch. Bbls.: 22-, 24-, 26-, 28-, 30-, or 32-inch; fixed choke or Invector tubes. Weight: 7.5 lbs. (w/28-inch bbl.). Checkered select walnut pistol-grip stock and semi-beavertail forearm, recoil pad. Introduced in 1977 by Miroku.

Magnum Hunter	NiB $690	Ex $589	Gd $477
Magnum Stalker.	NiB $690	Ex $589	Gd $477
Magnum Camo	NiB $779	Ex $644	Gd $546
Hunter.	NiB $690	Ex $589	Gd $477
Upland	NiB $595	Ex $490	Gd $395
Stalker (26, 28- or 30-inch bbl.).	NiB $566	Ex $477	Gd $375
Stalker 24-inch bbl	NiB $566	Ex $477	Gd $375
Game Gun - Turkey Special.	NiB $478	Ex $390	Gd $277
Game Gun - fully rifled bbl..	NiB $700	Ex $622	Gd $490
Hunter 20 ga.	NiB $600	Ex $497	Gd $400
Upland 20 ga.	NiB $600	Ex $497	Gd $400
Micro.	NiB $488	Ex $397	Gd $300
Hunter 28 ga.	NiB $590	Ex $480	Gd $400
Bore Hunter .410.	NiB $644	Ex $564	Gd $433
Buck Spec. (10 or 12 ga., 3.5-inch)	NiB $700	Ex $566	Gd $470
Buck Spec. (12 or 20 ga.).	NiB $455	Ex $330	Gd $229
Waterfowl			
(10 or 12 ga., 3.5-inch)	NiB $700	Ex $566	Gd $470
W/fixed choke, deduct.			$75

BPS YOUTH AND LADIES' MODEL
Lightweight (6 lbs., 11 oz.) version of BPS Pump Shotgun in 20 ga. w/22-inch bbl. and floating vent rib, F choke (invector) tube. Made 1986 to 2002.
Standard Invector model (disc. 1994). . . NiB $390 Ex $288 Gd $195
Invector Plus model . . . . NiB $444 Ex $300 Gd $244

BSA 10 SEMIAUTOMATIC SHOTGUN
Gas-operated short-stroke action. 10 ga.; 3.5-inch chamber. Five round magazine. Bbls.: 26-, 28-or 30-inches w/Invector tubes and vent rib. Weight: 10.5 lbs. Checkered select walnut buttstock and forend. Blued finish. Made 1993 to date. Note: Although intro. as the BSA 10, this model is now marketed as the Gold Series. See separate listing for pricing.

B-SS SIDE-BY-SIDE
Boxlock. Automatic ejectors. Non-selective single trigger (early production) or selective-single trigger (late production). Gauges: 12 or 20 w/3-inch chambers. Bbls.: 26-, 28-, or 30-inches; IC/M, M/F, or F/F chokes; matte solid rib. Weight: 7 to 7.5 lbs. Checkered straight-grip stock and beavertail forearm. Made from 1972 to 1988 by Miroku.
Standard model (early/NSST) . . . . NiB $1276 Ex $956 Gd $835
Standard model (late/SST) . . . . NiB $1276 Ex $956 Gd $835
Grade II (antique silver receiver) . . . NiB $3365 Ex $2990 Gd $2455
20 ga. models, add $650

SHOTGUNS

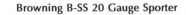

Browning B-SS 20 Gauge Sporter

Browning BT-99 Competition Trap

B-SS SIDE-BY-SIDE SIDELOCK
Same general specifications as B-SS boxlock models except sidelock version available in 26- or 28-inch bbl. lengths. 26-inch choked IC/M; 28-inch, M/F. Double triggers. Satin-grayed receiver engraved w/rosettes and scrolls. German nickel-silver sight bead. Weight: 6.25 lbs. to 6 lbs., 11 oz. 12 ga. made in 1983; 20 ga. Made in 1984. Disc. 1988.

12 ga. model . . . . NiB $3865 Ex $3077 Gd $2027
20 ga. model . . . . NiB $5277 Ex $3388 Gd $2879

B-SS S/S 20 GAUGE SPORTER . . . NiB $3241 Ex $2766 Gd $1547
Same as standard B-SS 20 ga. except has selective single trigger, straight-grip stock. Introduced 1977. Disc. 1987.

BT-99 GRADE I SINGLE BBL. TRAP . . . NiB $1087 Ex $782 Gd $554
Boxlock. Automatic ejector. 12 ga. only. 32- or 34-inch vent rib bbl., M, IM or F choke. Weight: About 8 lbs. Checkered pistol-grip stock and beavertail forearm, recoil pad. Made 1971 to 1976 by Miroku.

BT-99 MAX
Boxlock. 12 ga. only w/ejector selector and no safety. 32- or 34-inch ported bbl. w/high post vent rib. Checkered select walnut buttstock and finger-grooved forend w/high luster finish. Engraved receiver w/ blued or stainless metal finish. Made 1995 to 1996.

Blued . . . . NiB $1398 Ex $1110 Gd $790
Stainless . . . . NiB $1941 Ex $1590 Gd $1166

BT-99 PLUS
Similar to the BT-99 Competition except w/Browning Recoil Reduction System. Made 1989 to 1995.

Grade I . . . . NiB $1869 Ex $1275 Gd $1013
Pigeon grade . . . . NiB $1977 Ex $1276 Gd $912
Signature grade . . . . NiB $1877 Ex $1233 Gd $888
Stainless model . . . . NiB $2106 Ex $1433 Gd $1133
Golden Clays . . . . NiB $2926 Ex $2474 Gd $2310

BT-99 PLUS MICRO . . . . . . NiB $1277 Ex $1088 Gd $872
Same general specifications as BT-99 Plus except scaled down for smaller shooters. 30-inch bbl. w/adj. rib and Browning's recoil reducer system. Made 1991 to 1996.

BT-100 COMPETITION TRAP SPECIAL
Same as BT-99 except has super-high wide rib and standard Monte Carlo or fully adj. stock. Available w/adj. choke or Invector Plus tubes w/optional porting. Made 1976 to 2000.

Grade I w/fixed
choke (disc. 1992) . . . . NiB $1867 Ex $1233 Gd $994
Grade I w/Invectors . . . . NiB $2077 Ex $1156 Gd $1034
Grade I stainless (disc. 1994) . . . NiB $2366 Ex $1967 Gd $1256
Grade I Pigeon Grade (disc. 1994) NiB $1650 Ex $1290 Gd $1072

BT-100 SINGLE-SHOT TRAP
Similar to the BT-99 Max, except w/additional stock options and removable trigger group. Made 1995 to 2002.

Grade I blued . . . . NiB $2044 Ex $1366 Gd $1065
Stainless . . . . NiB $2366 Ex $1998 Gd $1387
Satin finish . . . . NiB $1490 Ex $1266 Gd $853
W/adj. comb, add $150
W/thumbhole stock, add $350
W/replacement trigger assembly, add $550
W/fixed choke, deduct $100

CITORI O/U HUNTING MODELS
Boxlock. Gauges: 12, 16 (disc. 1989), 20, 28 (disc. 1992) and .410 bore (disc. 1989). Bbl. lengths: 24-, 26-, 28-, or 30-inch w/vent rib. Chambered 2.75-, 3- or 3.5-inch mag. Chokes: IC/M, M/F (Fixed Chokes); Standard Invector, or Invector plus choke systems. Overall length ranges from 41-47 inches. 2.75-, 3- or 3-inch Mag. loads, depending on ga. Weight: 5.75 lbs. to 7 lbs. 13 oz. Single selective, gold-plated trigger. Medium raised German nickel-silver sight bead. Checkered, rounded pistol-grip walnut stock w/ beavertail forend. Invector Chokes and Invector Plus became standard in 1988 and 1995, respectively. Made from 1973 to date by Miroku.

Grade I (disc. 1994) . . . . NiB $1076 Ex $792 Gd $566
Grade I - 3.5-inch Mag.(1989 to date) NiB $1076 Ex $792 Gd $566
Grade II (disc. 1983) . . . . NiB $1288 Ex $1079 Gd $721
Grade III (1985-95) . . . . NiB $2077 Ex $1266 Gd $1091
Grade V (disc. 1984) . . . . NiB $2888 Ex $2069 Gd $1243
Grade VI (1985-95) . . . . NiB $2888 Ex $2069 Gd $1277
Sporting Hunter model
(12 and 20 ga., 1998 to date) . . . . NiB $1387 Ex $1176 Gd $700
Satin Hunter model
(2 ga. only, 1998 to date) . . . . . . NiB $1266 Ex $1006 Gd $744
W/o Invector choke system, deduct $150
For 3.5-inch mag., add $120
For disc. gauges (16, 28 and .410), add 15%

CITORI LIGHTNING O/U MODELS
Same general specifications as the Citori Hunting models except w/classic Browning rounded pistol-grip stock. Made from 1988 to date by Miroku.

Grade I . . . . NiB $1059 Ex $798 Gd $612
Grade III . . . . NiB $1969 Ex $1154 Gd $834
Grade VI . . . . NiB $3166 Ex $2054 Gd $1152
Gran Lightning model . . . . NiB $1998 Ex $1258 Gd $887
Feather Model (alloy receiver) . . . NiB $1577 Ex $1159 Gd $1013
Feather Combo model (2-bbl. set) . . . . NiB $3500 Ex $2745 Gd $2388
Privilege model (w/engraved sideplates) . . . NiB $4855 Ex $3966 Gd $2767
Micro model, add 10%
W/o Invector choke
system, deduct $250
28 ga. and .410, add $15%

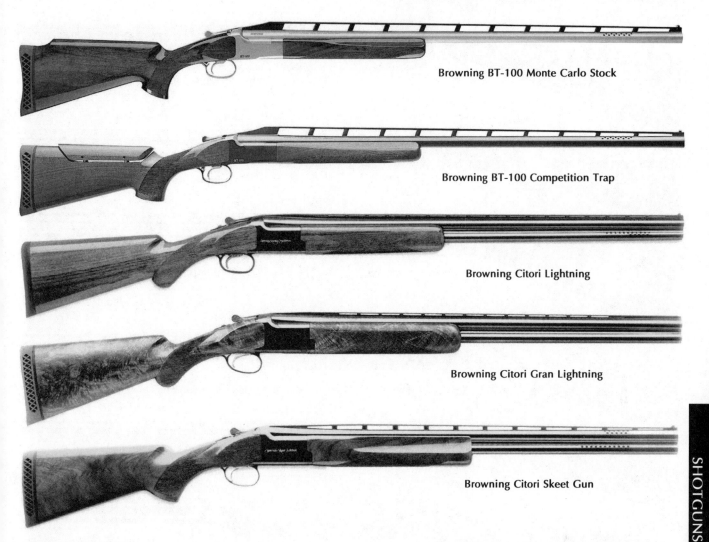

Browning BT-100 Monte Carlo Stock

Browning BT-100 Competition Trap

Browning Citori Lightning

Browning Citori Gran Lightning

Browning Citori Skeet Gun

CITORI SKEET GUN

Same as Hunting model except has skeet-style stock and forearm, 26- or 28-inch bbls., both bored SK choke. Available w/either standard vent rib or special target-type, high-post, wide vent rib. Weight (w/26-inch bbls.): 12 ga., 8 lbs., 20 ga., 7 lbs. Made 1974 to date by Miroku.

Grade I	NiB $1390	Ex $1166	Gd $990
Grade II	NiB $1690	Ex $1345	Gd $1125
Grade III	NiB $1789	Ex $1433	Gd $1093
Grade VI (disc. 1995)	NiB $2345	Ex $1765	Gd $1299
Golden Clays	NiB $2866	Ex $1889	Gd $1465
28 ga. and .410, add			15%
Grade I, 3-bbl. set (disc. 1996)	NiB $2465	Ex $2079	Gd $1500
Grade III, 3-bbl. set (disc. 1996)	NiB $3577	Ex $2260	Gd $1545
Grade VI, 3-bbl. set (disc. 1994)	NiB $3781	Ex $2477	Gd $2053
Golden Clays, 3-bbl. set (disc. 1995)	NiB $4376	Ex $3069	Gd $2210
Grade I, 4-bbl. set	NiB $3588	Ex $3066	Gd $2754
Grade III, 4-bbl. set	NiB $4361	Ex $3276	Gd $2390
Grade VI, 4-bbl. set (disc. 1994)	NiB $4733	Ex $3489	Gd $2466
Golden Clays, 4-bbl. set (disc. 1995)	NiB $5656	Ex $3892	Gd $2721

CITORI SPORTING CLAYS

Similar to the standard Citori Lightning model except Classic-style stock with rounded pistol-grip. 30-inch back-bored bbls. with Invector Plus tubes. Receiver with "Lightning Sporting Clays Edition" logo. Made from 1989 to date.

GTI model (disc. 1995)	NiB $1167	Ex $1058	Gd $821
GTI Golden Clays model (1993-94)	NiB $2455	Ex $1749	Gd $1256
Lightning model (intro. 1989)	NiB $1440	Ex $1102	Gd $866
Lightning Golden Clays (1993-98)	NiB $2736	Ex $1871	Gd $1319
Lightning Pigeon Grade (1993-94)	NiB $1622	Ex $1188	Gd $887
Micro Citori Lightning model (w/low rib)	NiB $1588	Ex $1266	Gd $1006
Special Sporting model (intro. 1989)	NiB $1590	Ex $1268	Gd $1010
Special Sporting Golden Clays (1993-98)	NiB $3231	Ex $3110	Gd $2127
Special Sporting Pigeon Grade (1993-94)	NiB $1454	Ex $1167	Gd $944
Ultra model (intro. 1995)	NiB $1661	Ex $1288	Gd $937
Ultra Golden Clays (intro. 1995)	NiB $2134	Ex $1822	Gd $1645
Model 325 (1993-94)	NiB $1292	Ex $1188	Gd $900
Model 325 Golden Clays (1993-94)	NiB $2545	Ex $1889	Gd $1438
Model 425 Grade I (intro. 1995)	NiB $1761	Ex $1216	Gd $1022
Model 425 Golden Clays (intro. 1995)	NiB $2665	Ex $2144	Gd $1977
Model 425 WSSF (intro. 1995)	NiB $1896	Ex $1459	Gd $1256
Model 802 Sporter (ES) Extended Swing (intro. 1996)	NiB $1488	Ex $1299	Gd $993
W/2 bbl. set, add			$1000
W/adj. stock, add			$250
W/high rib, add			$125
W/ported barrels, add			$100

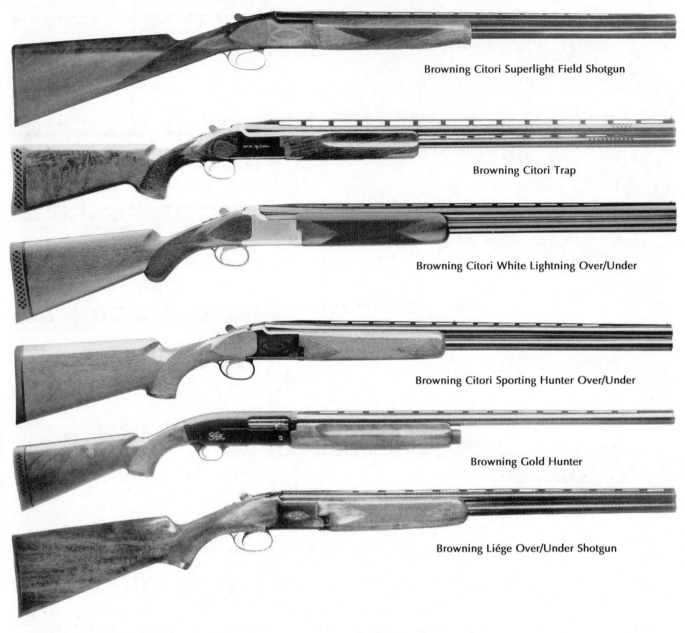

Browning Citori Superlight Field Shotgun

Browning Citori Trap

Browning Citori White Lightning Over/Under

Browning Citori Sporting Hunter Over/Under

Browning Gold Hunter

Browning Liége Over/Under Shotgun

CITORI SUPERLIGHT O/U FIELD SHOTGUNS
Similar to the Citori Hunting model except w/straight-grip stock and Schnabel forend tip. Made by Miroku 1982 to date.

Grade I . . . . NiB $1067 Ex $843 Gd $625
Grade III . . . . NiB $2066 Ex $1590 Gd $1167
Grade V (disc. 1985) . . . . NiB $3132 Ex $2398 Gd $2034
Grade VI . . . . NiB $2876 Ex $2334 Gd $1655
W/o Invectors, deduct. $300
28 ga. and .410, add 10%

CITORI TRAP GUN
Same as Hunting model except 12 ga. only, has Monte Carlo or fully adjustable stock and beavertail forend, trap-style recoil pad; 20- or 32-inch bbls.; M/F, IM/F, or F/F. Available with either standard vent rib or special target-type, high-post, wide vent rib. Weight: 8 lbs. Made from 1974 to 2001 by Miroku.

Grade I Trap . . . . NiB $1035 Ex $888 Gd $698

Grade I Trap Pigeon grade
(disc. 1994) . . . . NiB $1857 Ex $1589 Gd $1134
Grade I Trap Signature grade (disc. 1994) . . . NiB $1756 Ex $1477 Gd $1234
Grade I Plus Trap (disc. 1994) . . . . NiB $2878 Ex $2330 Gd $2099
Grade I Plus Trap
w/ported bbls. (disc. 1994) . . . NiB $1979 Ex $1488 Gd $1253
Grade I Plus Trap
Combo (disc. 1994) . . . . . NiB $2773 Ex $2078 Gd $1760
Grade I Plus Trap
Golden Clays (disc. 1994) . . . NiB $3176 Ex $2465 Gd $2200
Grade II w/HP rib (disc. 1984) . . . NiB $1989 Ex $1423 Gd $1166
Grade III Trap. . . . . NiB $1958 Ex $1688 Gd $1290
Grade V Trap (disc. 1984) . . . NiB $1890 Ex $1656 Gd $1388
Grade VI Trap (disc. 1994). . . NiB $2066 Ex $1879 Gd $1488
Grade VI Trap
Golden Clays (disc. 1994) . . . NiB $3000 Ex $2698 Gd $2365

CITORI UPLAND SPECIAL O/U SHOTGUN

A shortened version of the Hunting model fitted with 24-inch bbls. and straight-grip stock.

12, 20 ga. models. . . . . NiB $1277 Ex $1097 Gd $900
16 ga. (disc. 1989) . . . . NiB $1426 Ex $1266 Gd $954
W/o Inv. Chokes, deduct $150

CITORI WHITE LIGHTNING O/U SHOTGUN

Similar to the standard Citori Lightning model except w/silver nitride receiver w/scroll and rosette engraving. Satin wood finish w/round pistol grip. Made 1998 to 2001.

12. 20 ga. models. . . . . NiB $1769 Ex $1213 Gd $879
28 ga., .410 models (Intro. 2000). . . NiB $1887 Ex $1369 Gd $1228

CITORI WHITE UPLAND SPECIAL. . . NiB $1389 Ex $1168 Gd $879

Similar to the standard Citori Upland model except w/silver nitride receiver w/scroll and rosette engraving. Satin wood finish w/round pistol grip. Made 2000 to 2001.

CYNERY SERIES

Monolock hinge system. Gauges: 12, 20, 28 or .410 bore. Bbl. lengths: 26-, or 28-inch w/vent rib. Chambered 3-inch. Chokes: Invector Plus choke tubes. Overall length ranges from 43-45 inches. Weight: 5 to 6 lbs. Single selective, gold-plated trigger. Wood or composite stock. Silver nitride finish. Made from 2004 to date.

Field grade. . . . . NiB $2430 Ex $1810 Gd $930
Classic Field grade . . . . NiB $2360 Ex $1000 Gd $720
Euro Field grade. . . . . NiB $2300 Ex $1500 Gd $760
Feather . . . . NiB $2530 Ex $1655 Gd $960
Sporting (made 2004-2007). . . . . . NiB $1900 Ex $1410 Gd $840

DOUBLE AUTOMATIC (STEEL RECEIVER)

Short recoil system. Takedown. 12 ga. only. Two round capacity. Bbls.: 26-, 28-, 30-inches; any standard choke. Checkered pistol-grip stock and forend. Weight: About 7.75 lbs. Made 1955 to 1961.

W/plain bbl. . . . . NiB $889 Ex $679 Gd $453
W/recessed-rib bbl. . . . . . . NiB $1167 Ex $1090 Gd $756

GOLD DEER HUNTER AUTOLOADING SHOTGUN

Similar to the Standard Gold Hunter model except chambered 12 ga. only. 22-inch bbl. W/rifled bore or smooth bore w/5-inch rifled invector tube. Cantilevered scope mount. Made 1997 to 2005.

W/standard finish . . . . NiB $1000 Ex $766 Gd $591
Field model (w/Mossy Oak finish) . . . NiB $956 Ex $619 Gd $495

GOLD HUNTER SERIES

Self-cleaning, gas-operated, short-stroke action. Gauges: 10 or 12 (3.5-inch chamber); 12 or 20 (3-inch chamber). 26-, 28-, or 30-inch bbl. w/Invector or Invector Plus choke tubes. Checkered walnut stock. Polished or matte black metal finish. Made 1990 to date.

Gold Hunter (Light 10 ga. 3.5-inch
w/walnut stock) . . . . NiB $1499 Ex $1277 Gd $1108
Gold Hunter (12 ga. 3.5-inch) . . . . . NiB $977 Ex $790 Gd $559
Gold Hunter (12 or 20 ga. 3-inch) . . .NiB $1067 Ex $880 Gd $670
Gold Hunter Classic model (12 or 20 ga., 3-inch). . .NiB $921 Ex $787 Gd $600
Gold Hunter High
Grade Classic (12 or 20 ga., 3-inch). . . NiB $1690 Ex $1225 Gd $1098
Gold Deer Hunter
(12 ga. w/22-inch bbl.). . . . . NiB $1078 Ex $884 Gd $643
Gold Turkey Hunter Camo
(12 ga. /24-inch bbl.) . . . . NiB $987 Ex $699 Gd $534
Gold Waterfowl Hunter
Camo (12 ga. w/24-inch bbl.) . . . . . . NiB $987 Ex $699 Gd $534

GOLD STALKER SERIES

Self-cleaning, gas-operated, short-stroke action. Gauges: 10 or 12 (3.5-inch chamber); 12 or 20 (3-inch chamber). 26-, 28-, or 30-inch bbl. w/Invector or Invector Plus choke tubes. Graphite/fiberglass composite stock. Polished or matte black finish. Made 1998 to 2007.

Browning Over/Under Gold Classic

Gold Stalker Light (10 ga.,
3.5-inch w/composite stock) . . . . NiB $1487 Ex $1269 Gd $1109
Gold Stalker (12 ga. 3.5-inch) . . . . NiB $1048 Ex $911 Gd $500
Gold Stalker (12 or 20 ga., 3-inch) . . NiB $898 Ex $654 Gd $521
Gold Stalker Classic
Model (21 or 20 ga., 3-inch). . . . NiB $1754 Ex $1228 Gd $1067
Gold Deer Stalker
(12 ga. w/22-inch bbl.). . . . . NiB $855 Ex $529 Gd $380
Gold Turkey Stalker Camo
(12 ga. w/24-inch bbl.). . . . . NiB $799 Ex $482 Gd $355
Gold Waterfowl Stalker
Camo (12 ga. w/24-inch bbl.) . . . . . . NiB $943 Ex $667 Gd $543

GOLD SPORTING CLAYS SERIES

Similar to Gold Hunter Series except w/2.75-inch chamber and 28- or 30-inch ported bbl. w/Invector Plus chokes. Made 1996 to 2008.

Standard model . . . . NiB $1132 Ex $821 Gd $677
Sporting Clays (Youth or Ladies). . .NiB $1677 Ex $1265 Gd $1071
Sporting Clays w/engraved nickel receiver . . .NiB $1793 Ex $1277 Gd $1056

LIEGE O/U SHOTGUN (B26/27)

Boxlock. Automatic ejectors. Non-selective single trigger. 12 ga. only. Bbls.: 26.5-, 28-, or 30-inch; 2.75-inch chambers in 26.5- and 28-inch, 3-inch in 30-inch, IC/M, M/F, or F/F chokes; vent rib. Weight: 7 lbs., 4 oz.to 7 lbs., 14 oz., depending on bbls. Checkered pistol-grip stock and forearm. Made 1973 to 1975 by FN.

Liège (B-26 BAC production) . . . . NiB $1488 Ex $1161 Gd $988
Liège (B-27 FN prod., Standard Game model). . . NiB $1488 Ex $1161 Gd $988
Deluxe Game model. . . . . NiB $1522 Ex $1269 Gd $1043
Grand Delux Game model . . . . . NiB $1687 Ex $1438 Gd $1210
Deluxe Skeet model . . . . NiB $1488 Ex $1161 Gd $988
Deluxe Trap model. . . . . NiB $1488 Ex $1161 Gd $988
NRA Sporting . . . . NiB $1067 Ex $700 Gd $5254

LIGHT SPORTING 802ES . . NiB $1476 Ex $1211 Gd $989

Over/under. Invector-plus choke tubes. 12 ga. only with 28-inch bbl. Weight: 7 lbs., 5 oz.

LIGHTNING SPORTING CLAYS

Similar to the standard Citori Lightning model except Classic-style stock with rounded pistol grip. 30-inch back-bored bbls. with Invector Plus tubes. Receiver with "Lightning Sporting Clays Edition" logo. Made 1989 to 1994.

Standard model . . . . NiB $1396 Ex $1178 Gd $909
Pigeon grade . . . . NiB $1378 Ex $1161 Gd $882

O/U CLASSIC . . . . NiB $2359 Ex $2091 Gd $1389

Gauge: 20, 2.75-inch chambers. 26-inch blued bbls. choked IC/M. Gold-plated, single selective trigger. Manual, top-tang-mounted safety. Engraved receiver. High grade, select American walnut straight-grip stock with Schnabel forend. Fine-line checkering with pearl borders. High-gloss finish. 5,000 issued in 1986; made in Japan, engraved in Belgium.

O/U GOLD CLASSIC . . . . NiB $6245 Ex $4890 Gd $3179

Same general specifications as Over/Under Classic except more elaborate engravings, enhanced in gold, including profile of John M. Browning. Fine oil finish. 500 issued; made in 1986 in Belgium.

RECOILLESS TRAP SHOTGUN

The action and bbl. are driven forward when firing to achieve 72 percent less recoil. 12 ga, 2.75-inch chamber. 30-inch bbl. with Invector Plus tubes; adjustable vent rib. 51.63 inches overall. Weight: 9 lbs. Adj. checkered walnut buttstock and forend. Blued finish. Made from 1993 to 1996.

SHOTGUNS

Browning Superposed Broadway 12 Trap

Browning Superposed Grade I Lightning

Left Side

Right Side

Browning Superposed Bicentennial

Browning Superposed Grade IV Diana (Postwar)

Browning Superposed Grade V Midas (Postwar)

Standard model . . . . NiB $1088 Ex $865 Gd $644
Micro model (27-inch bbl.) . . . . . . NiB $1088 Ex $865 Gd $644
Signature model (27-inch bbl.) . . . . NiB $1088 Ex $865 Gd $644

SUPERPOSED BICENTENNIAL
COMMEMORATIVE . . . . NiB $13,650 Ex $12,790 Gd $9779
Special limited edition issued to commemorate U.S. Bicentennial.
51 guns, one for each state in the Union plus one for Washington,
D.C. Receiver with sideplates has engraved and gold-inlaid hunter
and wild turkey on right side, U.S. flag and bald eagle on left side,
together with state markings inlaid in gold, on blued background.
Checkered straight-grip stock and Schnabel-style forearm of highly-
figured American walnut. Velvet-lined wood presentation case.
Made in 1976 by FN. Value shown is for gun in new, unfired condition. See illustration next page.

SUPERPOSED
BROADWAY 12 TRAP . . . NiB $2084 Ex $1766 Gd $1460
Same as Standard Trap Gun except has 30- or 32-inch bbls. with
wider Broadway rib. Disc. 1976.

SUPERPOSED SHOTGUNS, HUNTING MODELS
Over/under boxlock. Selective automatic ejectors. Selective single
trigger; earlier models (worth 25% less) supplied w/double triggers,
twin selective triggers or non-selective single trigger. Gauges: 12, 20
(intro. 1949, 3-inch chambers in later production), 28, .410 (latter
two ga. intro. 1960). Bbls.: 26.5-, 28-, 30-, 32-inch, raised matted or
vent rib, prewar Lightning Model made w/ribbed bbl., postwar version supplied only w/vent rib; any combination of standard chokes.
Weight (w/26.5-inch vent-rib bbls.): Standard 12, 7 lbs., 11 oz.;
Lightning 12, 7 lbs., 6 oz.; Standard 20, 6 lbs., 8 oz.; Lightning 20,
6 lbs., 4 oz.; Lightning 28, 6 lbs., 7 oz.; Lightning .410, 6 lbs., 10
oz. Checkered pistol-grip stock/forearm.
Higher grades (Pigeon, Pointer, Diana, Midas, Grade VI) differ from
standard Grade I models in overall quality, engraving, wood and
checkering; otherwise, specifications are the same. Midas Grade
and Grade VI guns are richly gold inlaid. Made by FN 1928-1976.
Prewar models may be considered as disc. in 1940 when Belgium
was occupied by Germany. Grade VI offered 1955-1960. Pointer
Grade disc. in 1966, Grade I Standard in 1973, Pigeon Grade in
1974. Lightning Grade I, Diana and Midas Grades were not offered
after 1976.
Grade I standard weight . . NiB $2390 Ex $1979 Gd $1749
Grade I Lightning . . . . . . NiB $2209 Ex $1867 Gd $1428
Grade I Lightning, pre-war,
matted bbl., no rib . . . . . . NiB $2979 Ex $2255 Gd $1217
Grade II - Pigeon . . . . NiB $4400 Ex $2790 Gd $1966

Browning Superposed Ltd.
Pintail Duck Issue

Grade III - Pointer . . . . . . NiB $5000 Ex $4155 Gd $3860
Grade IV - Diana . . . . NiB $8250 Ex $6300 Gd $3760
Grade V - Midas. . . . . NiB $7300 Ex $5012 Gd $3690
Grade VI . . . . NiB $10,000 Ex $8292 Gd $6659
For 20 ga., add. 20%
For 28 ga., add. 75%
For .410, add 50%
Values shown are for models w/vent. rib.
W/raised matted rib, deduct 10%

SUPERPOSED LIGHTNING AND SUPERLIGHT MODELS (REISSUE B-25)

Reissue of popular 12-and 20-ga. Superposed shotguns. Lightning models available in 26.5- and 28-inch bbl. lengths w/2.75- or 3-inch chambering, full pistol grip. Superlight models available in 26.5-inch bbl. lengths w/2.75-inch chambering only, and straight-grip stock w/Schnabel forend. Both have hand-engraved receivers, fine-line checkering, gold-plated single selective trigger, automatic selective ejectors, manual safety. Weight: 6 to 7.5 lbs. Reintroduced 1985.
Grade I, Standard . . . . . . NiB $2377 Ex $1898 Gd $1344
Grade II, Pigeon . . . . NiB $5696 Ex $3863 Gd $3000
Grade III, Pointer . . . . NiB $8879 Ex $5770 Gd $3760
Grade IV, Diana. . . . . NiB $8009 Ex $5679 Gd $3698
Grade V, Midas . . . . NiB $13,750 Ex $11,299 Gd $10,650
W/extra bbls., add 50%

SUPERPOSED MAGNUM. . . NiB $1988 Ex $1572 Gd $1189
Same as Grade I except chambered for 12-ga. 3-inch shells, 30-inch vent-rib bbls., stock w/recoil pad. Weight: About 8.25 lbs. Disc. 1976.

SUPERPOSED BLACK
DUCK LTD. ISSUE . . . . . NiB $10,390 Ex $8977 Gd $5640
Gauge: 12. Superposed Lightning action. 28-inch vent-rib bbls. Choked M/F. 2.75-inch chambers. Weight: 7 lbs., 6 oz. Gold-inlaid receiver and trigger guard engraved w/black duck scenes. Gold-plated, single selective trigger. Top-tang mounted manual safety. Automatic, selective ejectors. Front and center ivory sights. High-grade, hand-checkered, hand-oiled select walnut stock and forend. 500 issued in 1983.

SUPERPOSED MALLARD
DUCK LTD. ISSUE . . . . . NiB $10,768 Ex $7322 Gd $5680
Same general specifications as Ltd. Black Duck issue except mallard duck scenes engraved on receiver and trigger guard, dark French walnut stock w/rounded pistol-grip. 500 issued in 1981.

SUPERPOSED PINTAIL
DUCK LTD. ISSUE . . . . . NiB $10,766 Ex $7298 Gd $5660
Same general specifications as Ltd. Black Duck issue except pintail duck scenes engraved on receiver and trigger guard. Stock is of dark French walnut w/rounded pistol-grip. 500 issued in 1982.

SUPERPOSED, PRESENTATION GRADES

Custom versions of Super-Light, Lightning Hunting, Trap and Skeet Models, w/same general specifications as those of standard guns, but of higher overall quality. The four Presentation grades differ in receiver finish (grayed or blued), engraving gold inlays, wood and checkering. Presentation 4 has sideplates. Made by FN, these models were Intro. in 1977.

Presentation 1 . . . . NiB $3475 Ex $2770 Gd $12967
Presentation 1, gold-inlaid. . .NiB $4889 Ex $3388 Gd $2491
Presentation 2 . . . . NiB $4956 Ex $3860 Gd $2709
Presentation 2, gold-inlaid. . .NiB $7900 Ex $5275 Gd $4100
Presentation 3, gold-inlaid. . .NiB $9975 Ex $7866 Gd $6077
Presentation 4 . . . . NiB $9106 Ex $7320 Gd $5863
Presentation 4, gold-inlaid . . .NiB $13,675 Ex $11,960 Gd $9989

SUPERPOSED SKEET GUNS, GRADE I

Same as standard Lightning 12, 20, 28 and .410 Hunting models, except has skeet-style stock and forearm, 26.5- or 28-inch vent-rib bbls. w/SK choke. Available also in All Gauge Skeet Set: Lightning 12 w/one removable fore-arm and three extra sets of bbls. in 20, 28 and .410 ga. in fitted luggage case. Disc. 1976. (For higher grades see listings for comparable Hunting models)
12 or 20 ga. . . . . NiB $2170 Ex $1690 Gd $1167
28 ga. or .410 . . . . NiB $2566 Ex $2278 Gd $1489
Combo skeet set (all gauges). . .NiB $6549 Ex $6000 Gd $5489

SUPERPOSED SUPER
LIGHT MODEL . . . . NiB $7101 Ex $4877 Gd $4128
Ultralight field gun version of Standard Lightning Model has classic straight-grip stock and slimmer forearm. Available only in 12 and 20 gauges (2.75-inch chambers), w/26.5-inch vent-rib bbls. Weight: 6.5 lbs., (12 ga.); 6 lbs., (20 ga.). Made 1967 to 1976.

SUPERPOSED TRAP GUN . . .NiB $5321 Ex $3867 Gd $2998
Same as Grade I except has trap-style stock, beavertail forearm, 30-inch vent-rib bbls., 12 ga. only. Disc. 1976. (For higher grades see listings for comparable hunting models)

TWELVETTE DOUBLE AUTOMATIC
Lightweight version of Double Automatic w/same general specifications except aluminum receiver. Bbl. w/plain matted top or vent rib. Weight: 6.75 to 7 lbs., depending on bbl. Receiver is finished in black w/gold engraving; 1956-1961 receivers were also anodized in gray, brown and green w/silver engraving. Made 1955 to 1971
W/plain bbl. . . . . NiB $900 Ex $600 Gd $380
W/vent. rib bbl. . . . . NiB $1000 Ex $750 Gd $476

CENTURY INTERNATIONAL ARMS, INC. — St. Albans, Vermont, and Boca Raton, Florida

ARTHEMIS . . . . NiB $522 Ex $390 Gd $259
O/U boxlock action with double triggers and extractors. 12, 20, 28 ga. or .410 bore. 3-inch chambers. 28-inch bbls. Single set trigger, extractors. Checkered wood stock and forearm. Weight: 5.3 to 7.4 lbs. Mfg. in Turkey by Khan. Disc.

ARTHEMIS O/U. . . . . NiB $475 Ex $310 Gd $245
Gauge: 12, 20, 28, .410. Bbl.: 28 inches, vent. rib, 3-inch chamber. Single selective trigger, extractors. Stock: Checkered walnut. Weight: 5.3 to 7.4 lbs. Mfg. by PAR. Imported from 2002 to 2009.

PHANTOM . . . . NiB $295 Ex $240 Gd $190
Semi-auto. Gauge: 12. 3-inch chamber. Bbl.: 24, 26 or 28 inches; vent. rib. Three choke tubes. Stock: Black synthetic. Mfg. in Turkey. Disc.

SHOTGUNS

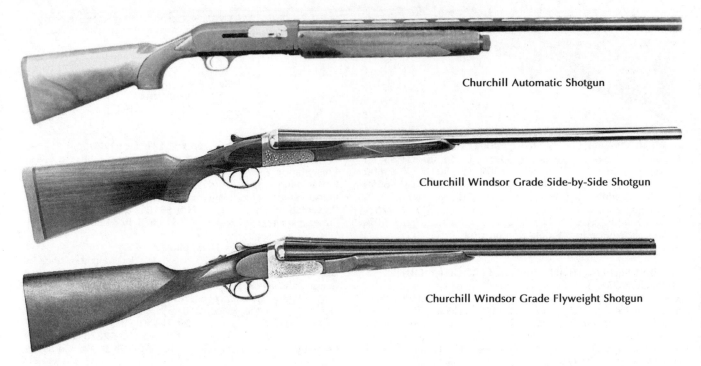

Churchill Automatic Shotgun

Churchill Windsor Grade Side-by-Side Shotgun

Churchill Windsor Grade Flyweight Shotgun

SAS-12 . . . . **NiB $250 Ex $185 Gd $100**
Semi-auto. Gauge: 12. 2.75-inch chamber. Bbl.: 22 or 23.5 inches. Detachable 3- or 5-round mag.
Ghost ring rear sight, add **$25**

COACH MODEL . . . . **NiB $325 Ex $200 Gd $140**
Side-by-side. Gauge: 12, 20, .410. Bbl.: 20 inches, exposed hammers, double trigger. Stock: Checkered walnut. Sling swivels. Mfg. in China.

MODEL IJ2 . . . . **NiB $220 Ex $155 Gd $100**
Slide-action. Gauge: 12; 2.75-inch or 3-inch chamber. Bbl.: 19 inches, fixed choke. Ghost ring rear or fiber optic sights. Weight: 7 lbs. Mfg. in China.

ULTRA 87 . . . . **NiB $255 Ex $180 Gd $110**
Slide-action. Gauge: 12. Bbl.: 19 inches. Optional heat shield and pistol grip. Side folding stock. Includes extra 28-inch bbl. Weight: 8.2 lbs.

CHURCHILL SHOTGUNS — Italy and Spain. Imported by Ellett Brothers, Inc., Chapin, SC; previously by Kassnar Imports, Inc., Harrisburg, PA

AUTOMATIC SHOTGUN
Gas-operated. Gauge: 12, 2.75- or 3-inch chambers. Five round magazine w/cutoff. Bbl.: 24-, 25-, 26-, 28-inch w/ICT choke tubes. Checkered walnut stock w/satin finish. Imported from 1990 to 1994.
Standard model . . . . **NiB $657 Ex $571 Gd $455**
Turkey model . . . . **NiB $697 Ex $586 Gd $434**

MONARCH O/U SHOTGUN
Hammerless, takedown w/engraved receiver. Selective single or double triggers. Gauges: 12, 20, 28, .410; 3-inch chambers. Bbls.: 25- or 26-inch (IC/M); 28-inch (M/F). Weight: 6.5-7.5 lbs. Checkered European walnut buttstock and forend. Made in Italy from 1986 to 1993.

W/double triggers . . . . **NiB $490 Ex $378 Gd $225**
W/single trigger . . . . **NiB $588 Ex $466 Gd $321**

REGENT O/U SHOTGUNS
Gauges: 12 or 20; 2.75-inch chambers. 27-inch bbls. w/interchangeable choke tubes and wide vent rib. Single selective trigger, selective automatic ejectors. Checkered pistol-grip stock in fancy walnut. Imported from Italy 1984 to 1988 and 1990 to 1994.
Regent V(disc. 1988) . . . . **NiB $987 Ex $680 Gd $590**
Regent VII w/sideplates (disc. 1994) . . .**NiB $873 Ex $779 Gd $544**

REGENT SKEET . . . . **NiB $873 Ex $779 Gd $544**
12 or 20 ga. w/2.75-inch chambers. Selective automatic ejectors, single-selective trigger. 26-inch over/under bbls. w/vent rib. Weight: 7 lbs. Made in Italy from 1984 to 1988.

REGENT TRAP . . . . **NiB $876 Ex $654 Gd $490**
12-ga. competition shotgun w/2.75-inch chambers. 30-inch over/under bbls. choked IM/F, vent side ribs. Weight: 8 lbs. Selective automatic ejectors, single selective trigger. Checkered Monte Carlo stock w/Supercushion recoil pad. Made in Italy 1984 to 1988.

SPORTING CLAYS O/U . . . . **NiB $945 Ex $800 Gd $575**
Same general specifications as Windsor IV except in 12 ga. only w/28-inch ported bbls. and choke tubes. Selective automatic ejectors. Weight: 7.5 lbs. Made from 1992 to 1994.

WINDSOR O/U SHOTGUNS
Hammerless, boxlock w/engraved receiver, selective single trigger. Extractors or ejectors. Gauges: 12, 20, 28 or .410; 3-inch chambers. Bbls.: 24 to 30 inches w/fixed chokes or choke tubes. Weight: 6 lbs., 3 oz. (Flyweight) to 7 lbs., 10 oz. (12 ga.). Checkered straight (Flyweight) or pistol-grip stock and forend of European walnut. Imported from Italy 1984 to 1993.
Windsor III w/fixed chokes . . . . **NiB $668 Ex $544 Gd $455**
Windsor III w/choke tubes . . . . **NiB $798 Ex $670 Gd $555**
Windsor IV w/fixed chokes (disc. 1993) . . . **NiB $768 Ex $659 Gd $455**
Windsor IV w/choke tubes . . . . **NiB $833 Ex $754 Gd $500**

WINDSOR SIDE-BY-SIDE SHOTGUNS

Boxlock action w/double triggers, ejectors or extractors and automatic safety. Gauges: 10, (3.5-inch chambers); 12, 20, 28, .410 (3-inch chambers), 16 (2.75-inch chambers). Bbls.: 23 to 32 inches w/various fixed choke or choke tube combinations. Weight: 5 lbs., 12 oz. (Flyweight) to 11.5 lbs. (10 ga.). European walnut buttstock and forend. Imported from Spain 1984 to 1990.

Windsor I 10 ga.	NiB $569	Ex $400	Gd $327
Windsor I 12 ga. thru .410. . . .	NiB $569	Ex $400	Gd $327
Windsor II 12 or 20 ga.	NiB $569	Ex $400	Gd $327
Windsor VI 12 or 20 ga.	NiB $569	Ex $400	Gd $327

E.J. CHURCHILL, LTD. —
Surrey (previously London), England

The E.J. Churchill shotguns listed below are no longer imported.

PREMIERE QUALITY HAMMERLESS DOUBLE

Sidelock. Automatic ejectors. Double triggers or selective single trigger. Gauges: 12, 16, 20, 28. Bbls.: 25-, 28- 30-, 32-inch; any degree of boring. Weight: 5-8 lbs. depending on ga. and bbl. length. Checkered stock and forend, straight or pistol-grip.

W/double triggers . . . . . . NiB $46,775 Ex $36,950 Gd $30,000
W/single selective trigger, add $10%

FIELD MODEL HAMMERLESS DOUBLE

Sidelock Hammerless ejector gun w/same general specifications as Premiere Model but of lower quality.

W/double triggers . . . NiB $10,667 Ex $9260 Gd $8110
W/single selective trigger, add .10%

PREMIERE QUALITY O/U SHOTGUN

Sidelock. Automatic ejectors. Double triggers or selective single trigger. Gauges: 12, 16, 20, 28. Bbls.: 25-, 28-, 30-, 32-inch, any degree of boring. Weight: 5-8 lbs. depending on ga. and bbl. length. Checkered stock and forend, straight or pistol-grip.

W/double triggers . . . . . . NiB $55,000 Ex $38,000 Gd $25,000
W/selective single trigger, add .10%
W/raised vent. rib, add 15%

UTILITY MODEL HAMMERLESS DOUBLE-BARREL

Anson & Deeley boxlock action. Double triggers or single trigger. Gauges: 12, 16, 20, 28, .410. Bbls.: 25-, 28-, 30-, 32-inch, any degree of boring. Weight: 4.5-8 lbs. depending on ga. and bbl. length. Checkered stock and forend, straight or pistol-grip.

W/double triggers . . . . . . NiB $7340 Ex $6077 Gd $4340
W/single selective trigger, add .10%

XXV PREMIERE

HAMMERLESS DOUBLENiB $47,000 Ex $40,000 Gd $35,000
Sidelock. Assisted opening. Automatic ejectors. Double triggers. Gauges: 12, 20. 25-inch bbls. w/narrow, quick-sighting rib; any standard choke combination. English-style straight-grip stock and forearm, checkered.

XXV IMPERIAL . . . . . NiB $14,775 Ex $12,700 Gd $9775
Similar to XXV Premiere but no assisted opening feature.

XXV HERCULES . . . . . NiB $10,750 Ex $9450 Gd $6680
Boxlock, otherwise specifications same as for XXV Premiere.

XXV REGAL . . . . NiB $6277 Ex $4988 Gd $3500
Similar to XXV Hercules but w/o assisted opening feature. Gauges: 12, 20, 28, .410.

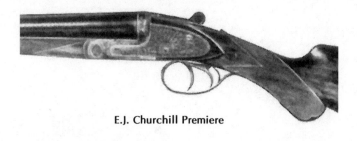

E.J. Churchill Premiere

CLASSIC DOUBLES — Tochigi, Japan
Imported by Classic Doubles International, St. Louis, MO, and previously by Olin as Winchester Models 101 and 23.

MODEL 101 O/U SHOTGUN

Boxlock. Engraved receiver w/single selective trigger, auto ejectors and combination bbl. selector and safety. Gauges: 12, 20, 28 or .410, 2.75-, 3-inch chambers, 25.5- 28- or 30-inch vent-rib bbls. Weight: 6.25 – 7.75 lbs. Checkered French walnut stock. Imported from 1987 to 1990.

Classic I Field.	NiB $1590	Ex $1488	Gd $1033
Classic II Field	NiB $1879	Ex $1540	Gd $1133
Classic Sporter	NiB $2066	Ex $1788	Gd $1233
Classic Sporter combo.	NiB $3475	Ex $2870	Gd $2035
Classic Trap	NiB $1380	Ex $1166	Gd $990
Classic Trap Single	NiB $1435	Ex $1140	Gd $1089
Classic Trap combo.	NiB $2560	Ex $2053	Gd $1498
Classic Skeet	NiB $1765	Ex $1600	Gd $1179
Classic Skeet 2-bbl. set	NiB $2867	Ex $2374	Gd $1790
Classic Skeet 4-bbl. set	NiB $4488	Ex $3972	Gd $2633
ClassicWaterfowler	NiB $1554	Ex $1266	Gd $1031
For Grade II (28 ga.), add			$900
For Grade II (.410), add.			$300

MODEL 201 SIDE-BY-SIDE SHOTGUN

Boxlock. Single selective trigger, automatic safety, selective ejectors. Gauges: 12 or 20; 3-inch chambers. 26- or 28-inch vent-rib bbl., fixed chokes or internal tubes. Weight: 6 to 7 lbs. Checkered French walnut stock and forearm. Imported 1987 to 1990.

Field model . . . . NiB $2687 Ex $1490 Gd $1264
Skeet model . . . . NiB $2687 Ex $1490 Gd $1264
With internal choke tubes, add $100

MODEL 201

SMALL BORE SET . . . . NiB $4650 Ex $3751 Gd $2975
Same general specifications as the Classic Model 201 except w/ smaller frame, in 28 ga. (IC/M) and .410 (F/M). Weight: 6-6.5 lbs. Imported from 1987 to 1990.

COGSWELL & HARRISON, LTD. —
London, England

AMBASSADOR HAMMERLESS
DOUBLE-BARREL SHOTGUN . . . NiB $6056 Ex $4533 Gd $3718
Boxlock. Sideplates w/game scene or rose scroll engraving. Automatic ejectors. Double triggers. Gauges: 12, 16, 20. Bbls.: 26-28-, 30-inch; any choke combination. Checkered straight-grip stock and forearm. Disc.

AVANT TOUT SERIES HAMMERLESS
DOUBLE-BARREL SHOTGUNS . . . NiB $2688 Ex $2133 Gd $1954
Boxlock. Sideplates (except Avant Tout III Grade). Automatic ejectors. Double triggers or single trigger (selective or non-selective). Gauges: 12, 16, 20. Bbls.: 25-, 27.5-, 30-inch, any choke combination. Checkered stock and forend, straight grip standard. Made

SHOTGUNS

Colt Auto Shotgun
Ultra Light Standard

Colt Custom
Hammerless Double

Colt Standard Pump

Cogswell & Harrison
Best Quality
HammerlessSidelock

Colt-Sauer
Drilling

in three models (Avant Tout I or Konor, Avant Tout II or Sandhurst. Avant Tout III or Rex) which differ chiefly in overall quality of engraving, grade of wood, checkering, etc. General specifications are the same. Disc.

Avant Tout I. . . . . NiB $3544 Ex $3160 Gd $2477
Avant Tout II . . . . NiB $2983 Ex $2786 Gd $1966
Avant Tout III. . . . . NiB $2254 Ex $2090 Gd $1760
W/non-selective single trigger, add $250
W/selective single trigger, add $425

BEST QUALITY HAMMERLESS
SIDELOCK DOUBLE-BARREL SHOTGUN
Hand-detachable locks. Automatic ejectors. Double triggers or single trigger (selective or non-selective). Gauges: 12, 16, 20. Bbls.: 25-, 26-, 28-, 30-inch, any choke combination. Checkered stock and forend, straight grip standard.

Victor model . . . . NiB $6570 Ex $5461 Gd $4130
Primic model (disc.). . . . . NiB $6640 Ex $5521 Gd $4200
W/non-selective single trigger, add $250
W/selective single trigger, add. $450

HUNTIC MODEL HAMMERLESS DOUBLE
Sidelock. Automatic ejectors. Double triggers or single trigger (selective or non-selective). Gauges: 12, 16, 20. Bbls.: 25-, 27.5-, 30-inch; any choke combination. Checkered stock and forend, straight grip standard. Disc.

W/double triggers . . . . NiB $4077 Ex $2986 Gd $1769
W/non-selective single trigger, add $250
W/selective single trigger, add $400

MARKOR HAMMERLESS DOUBLE
Boxlock. Non-ejector or ejector. Double triggers. Gauges: 12, 16, 20. Bbls.: 27.5 or 30-inch; any choke combination. Checkered stock and forend, straight grip standard. Disc.

Non-ejector . . . . NiB $1784 Ex $1599 Gd $1188
Ejector model, add 20%

REGENCY HAMMERLESS DOUBLE . NiB $4395 Ex $3667 Gd $2971
Anson & Deeley boxlock action. Automatic ejectors. Double triggers. Gauges: 12, 16, 20. Bbls.: 26-, 28-, 30-inch, any choke combination. Checkered straight-grip stock and forearm. Introduced in 1970 to commemorate the firm's bicentennial, this model has deep scroll engraving and the name "Regency" inlaid in gold on the rib. Disc.

COLT INDUSTRIES — Hartford, Connecticut
Auto Shotguns were made by Franchi and are similar to corresponding models of that manufacturer.

AUTO SHOTGUN — ULTRA LIGHT STANDARD
Recoil-operated. Takedown. Alloy receiver. Gauges: 12, 20. Mag. holds 4 rounds. Bbls.: plain, solid or vent rib, chrome-lined; 26-inch IC or M choke, 28-inch M or F choke, 30-inch F choke, 32-inch F choke. Weight: 12 ga., about 6.25 lbs. Checkered pistol-grip stock and forearm. Made 1964 to 1966.

W/plain bbl. . . . . NiB $400 Ex $297 Gd $200
W/solid rib bbl. . . . . NiB $450 Ex $344 Gd $250
W/vent. rib bbl. . . . . NiB $450 Ex $344 Gd $250

452

AUTO SHOTGUN — MAGNUM CUSTOM
Same as Magnum except has engraved receiver, select walnut stock and forearm. Made 1964 to 66.
W/Solid-rib bbl. . . . . NiB $544 Ex $422 Gd $300
W/vent. rib bbl. . . . . NiB $600 Ex $470 Gd $351

AUTO SHOTGUN — ULTRA LIGHT CUSTOM
Same as Standard Auto except has engraved receiver, select walnut stock and forearm. Made 1964 to 1966.
W/solid-rib bbl. . . . . NiB $544 Ex $470 Gd $366
W/vent. rib bbl. . . . . NiB $600 Ex $495 Gd $379

AUTO SHOTGUN — MAGNUM
Same as Standard Auto except steel receiver,chambered for 3-inch Magnum shells, 30- and 32-inch bbls. in 12 ga., 28-inch in 20 ga. Weight: 12 ga., about 8.25 lbs. Made 1964 to 1966.
W/plain bbl. . . . . NiB $552 Ex $447 Gd $332
W/solid-rib bbl. . . . . NiB $622 Ex $470 Gd $356
W/vent. rib bbl. . . . . NiB $644 Ex $500 Gd $371

CUSTOM HAMMERLESS DOUBLE . . NiB $766 Ex $509 Gd $446
Boxlock. Double triggers. Auto ejectors. Gauges: 12 Mag., 16. Bbls.: 26-inch IC/M; 28-inch M/F; 30-inch F/F. Weight: 12 ga., about 7.5 lbs. Checkered pistol-grip stock and beavertail forearm. Made in 1961.

COLTSMAN PUMP
SHOTGUN. . . . . NiB $489 Ex $355 Gd $269
Takedown. Gauges: 12, 16, 20. Magazine holds 4 rounds. Bbls.: 26-inch IC; 28-inch M or F choke; 30-inch F choke. Weight: About 6 lbs. Plain pistol-grip stock and forearm. Made 1961 to 1965 by Manufrance.

CUSTOM PUMP. . . . . NiB $500 Ex $377 Gd $286
Same as Standard Pump shotgun except has checkered stock, vent-rib bbl. Weight: About 6.5 lbs. Made 1961 to 1963 by Manufrance.

SAUER DRILLING. . . . . . NiB $4466 Ex $3778 Gd $2360
Three-bbl. combination gun. Boxlock. Set rifle trigger. Tang bbl. selector, automatic rear sight positioner. 12 ga. over .30-06 or .243 rifle bbl. 25-inch bbls., F and M choke. Weight: About 8 lbs. Folding leaf rear sight, blade front w/brass bead. Checkered pistol-grip stock and beavertail forearm, recoil pad. Made 1974 to 1985 by J. P. Sauer & Sohn, Eckernförde, Germany.

CONNECTICUT VALLEY CLASSICS — Westport, Connecticut

SPORTER 101 O/U
Gauge: 12; 3-inch chamber. Bbls.: 28-, 30- or 32-inch w/ screw-in tubes. Weight: 7.75 lbs. Engraved stainless or nitrided receiver; blued bbls. Checkered American black walnut buttstock and forend w/low-luster satin finish. Made from 1993 to 1998.
Classic Sporter . . . . NiB $1966 Ex $1634 Gd $1388
Stainless Classic Sporter . . NiB $2764 Ex $2259 Gd $1744

FIELD O/U
Similar to the standard Classic Sporter over/under model except w/30-inch bbls. only and non-reflective matte blued finish on both bbls. and receiver for Waterfowler; other grades w/different degrees of embellishment; Grade I the lowest and Grade III the highest. Made 1993 to 1998.
Grade I . . . . NiB $2788 Ex $2308 Gd $1683
Grade II. . . . . NiB $3166 Ex $2521 Gd $1790
Grade III . . . . NiB $3767 Ex $2866 Gd $1946
Waterfowler. . . . . NiB $2581 Ex $2264 Gd $1598

CONNENTO/VENTUR — Formerly imported by Ventura, Seal Beach, California

Model 51 . . . . NiB $456 Ex $361 Gd $295
Gauge: 12, 16, 20, 28 and .410. Double-barrel, box-lock action. Barrels: 26, 28, 30 and 32 inches; various chokes; extractors; and double triggers. Checkered walnut stock. Introduced in 1980, discontinued 1985.

Model 52 . . . . NiB $610 Ex $433 Gd $329
Same as Model 51 except in 10 gauge.

Model 53 . . . . NiB $538 Ex $449 Gd $300
Same as Model 51 except with scalloped receiver, automatic ejectors and optional single selective trigger. Discontinued in 1985.
W/single trigger, add 25%

Model 62 . . . . NiB $1132 Ex $990 Gd $760
Holland & Holland-design sidelock shotgun with various barrel lengths and chokes; automatic ejectors; cocking indicators. Floral engraved receiver, checkered walnut stock. Discontinued in 1982.

Model 64 . . . . NiB $1388 Ex $1054 Gd $877
Same as Model 62 except deluxe finish. Discontinued.

Grade I . . . . NiB $1259 Ex $988 Gd $844
Gauge: 12. Over/under shotgun. Barrels: 32 inches; screw-in choke tubes; high ventilated rib; automatic ejectors; single selective trigger standard. Checkered Monte Carlo walnut stock.
Mark II . . . . NiB $1569 Ex $1236 Gd $1006
Same as Mark I model but with an extra single barrel and fitted leather case.
Mark III . . . . NiB $1788 Ex $1469 Gd $1100
Same as Mark I model but with finely figured walnut stock and engraved metal.

Mark III Combo . . . . NiB $2877 Ex $2243 Gd $2071
Same as Mark III model above but with extra single barrel and fitted leather case.

CHARLES DALY, INC. — New York, New York

The pre-WWII Charles Daly shotguns, w/the exception of the Commander, were manufactured by various firms in Suhl, Germany. The postwar guns, except for the Novamatic series, were produced by Miroku Firearms Mfg. Co., Tokyo. Miroku ceased production in 1976 and the Daly trademark was acquired by Outdoor Sports Headquarters, in Dayton, Ohio. OSHI continued to market O/U shotguns from both Italy and Spain under the Daly logo. Automatic models were produced in Japan for distribution in the USA. In 1996, KBI, Inc. in Harrisburg, PA acquired the Daly trademark and currently imports firearms under that logo.

COMMANDER O/U SHOTGUN
Daly-pattern Anson & Deeley system boxlock action. Automatic ejectors. Double triggers or Miller selective single trigger. Gauges: 12, 16,20, 28, .410. Bbls.: 26- to 30-inch, IC/M or M/F choke. Weight: 5.25 to 7.25 lbs. depending on ga. and bbl. length. Checkered stock and forend, straight or pistol grip. The two models, 100 and 200, differ in general quality, grade of wood, checkering, engraving, etc.; otherwise specs are the same. Made in Belgium c. 1939.
Model 100 . . . . NiB $665 Ex $500 Gd $397
Model 200 . . . . NiB $866 Ex $703 Gd $511
W/Miller single trigger, add $150

Charles Daly Over/Under
Field Grade (Postwar)

HAMMERLESS DOUBLE-BARREL SHOTGUN

Daly-pattern Anson & Deeley system boxlock action. Automatic ejectors except "Superior Quality" is non-ejector. Double triggers. Gauges: 10, 12, 16, 20, 28, .410. Bbls.: 26- to 32-inch, any combination of chokes. Weight: from 4 to 8.5 lbs. depending on ga. and bbl. length. Checkered pistol-grip stock and forend. The four grades—Regent Diamond, Diamond, Empire, Superior—differ in general quality, grade of wood, checkering, engraving, etc.; otherwise specifications are the same. Disc. about 1933.

Diamond quality . . . . NiB $12,677 Ex $10,445 Gd $7869
Empire quality . . . . NiB $6133 Ex $4632 Gd $3144
Regent Diamond quality . . NiB $14,878 Ex $12,966 Gd $10,077
Superior quality . . . . NiB $1522 Ex $1292 Gd $1000

HAMMERLESS DRILLING

Daly pattern Anson & Deeley system boxlock action. Plain extractors. Double triggers, front single set for rifle bbl. Gauges: 12, 16, 20, .25-20, .25-35, .30-30 rifle bbl. Supplied in various bbl. lengths and weights. Checkered pistol-grip stock and forend. Auto rear sight operated by rifle bbl. selector. The three grades — Regent Diamond, Diamond, Superior—differ in general quality, grade of wood, checkering, engraving, etc.; otherwise, specifications are the same. Disc. 1933.

Diamond quality . . . . NiB $7235 Ex $5530 Gd $4200
Regent Diamond quality . . . NiB $14,866 Ex $11,977 Gd $9977
Superior quality . . . . NiB $3733 Ex $2988 Gd $2036

HAMMERLESS DOUBLE

EMPIRE GRADE . . . . NiB $1887 Ex $1352 Gd $1091
Boxlock. Plain extractors. Non-selective single trigger. Gauges: 12, 16, 20; 3-inch chambers in 12 and 20, 2.75-inch in 16 ga. Bbls.: vent rib; 26-, 28-, 30-inch (latter in 12 ga. only); IC/M, M/F, F/F. Weight: 6 to 7.75 lbs., depending on ga. and bbls. Checkered pistol-grip stock and beavertail forearm. Made 1968 to 1971.

1974 WILDLIFE COMMEMORATIVE NiB $2466 Ex $2167 Gd $1477
Limited issue of 500 guns. Similar to Diamond Grade over/under. 12-ga. trap and skeet models only. Duck scene engraved on right side of receiver, fine scroll on left side. Made in 1974.

NOVAMATIC LIGHTWEIGHT AUTOLOADER

Same as Breda. Recoil-operated. Takedown.12 ga., 2.75-inch chamber. Four-round tubular magazine. Bbls.: Plain vent rib; 26-inch IC or Quick-Choke w/three interchangeable tubes, 28-inch M or F choke. Weight (w/26-inch vent-rib bbl.): 7 lbs., 6 oz. Checkered pistol-grip stock and forearm. Made 1968 by Ernesto Breda, Milan, Italy.

W/plain bbl. . . . . NiB $398 Ex $277 Gd $198
W/vent rib bbl. . . . . NiB $397 Ex $260 Gd $200
W/Quick-Choke, add $50

NOVAMATIC SUPER LIGHTWEIGHT

Lighter version of Novamatic Lightweight. Gauges: 12, 20. Weight (w/26-inch vent-rib bbl.): 12 ga., 6 lbs., 10 oz., 20 ga., 6 lbs. SK choke available in 26-inch vent-rib bbl. 28-inch bbls. in 12 ga. only. Quick-Choke in 20 ga. w/plain bbl. Made 1968 by Ernesto Breda, Milan, Italy.

12 ga., plain bbl. . . . . NiB $387 Ex $288 Gd $198
12 ga., vent. rib bbl. . . . . NiB $387 Ex $288 Gd $198
20 ga., plain bbl. . . . . NiB $543 Ex $433 Gd $315
20 ga., plain bbl. w/Quick-Choke . . . . . NiB $388 Ex $335 Gd $217
20 ga., vent. rib bbl. . . . . NiB $433 Ex $290 Gd $200

NOVAMATIC SUPER LIGHTWEIGHT

20 GA. MAGNUM. . . . . NiB $377 Ex $296 Gd $200
Same as Novamatic Super Lightweight 2, except 3-inch chamber, has 3-round magazine, 28-inch vent-rib bbl., F choke.

NOVAMATIC

12 GA. MAGNUM. . . . . NiB $377 Ex $296 Gd $200
Same as Novamatic Lightweight, except chambered for 12-ga. Magnum 3-inch shell. Has 3-round magazine, 30-inch vent rib bbl., F choke, and stock w/recoil pad. Weight: 7.75 lbs.

Post-War Charles Daly shotguns were imported by Sloan's Sporting Goods trading as Charles Daly in New York. In 1976, Outdoor Sports Headquarters acquired the Daly trademark and continued to import European-made shotguns under that logo. In 1996, KBI, Inc., in Harrisburg, PA, acquired the Daly trademark and currently imports firearms under that logo.

NOVAMATIC TRAP GUN . . . . NiB $643 Ex $500 Gd $355
Same as Novamatic Lightweight except has 30-inch vent rib bbl., F choke and Monte Carlo stock w/recoil pad. Weight: 7.75 lbs.

O/U SHOTGUNS (PRE-WWII)

Daly-pattern Anson & Deeley-system boxlock action. Sideplates. Auto ejectors. Double triggers. Gauges: 12, 16, 20. Supplied in various bbl. lengths and weights. Checkered pistol-grip stock and forend. The two grades — Diamond and Empire — differ in general quality, grade of wood, checkering, engraving, etc.; otherwise specifications are the same. Disc. about 1933.

Diamond Quality . . . . NiB $6133 Ex $4965 Gd $3476
Empire Quality . . . . NiB $4771 Ex $3865 Gd $2700

O/U SHOTGUNS (POST-WWII)

Boxlock. Auto ejectors or selective auto/manual ejection. Selective single trigger. Gauges: 12, 12 Magnum (3-inch chambers), 20 (3-inch chambers), 28, .410. Bbls.: Vent rib; 26-, 28-, 30-inch; standard choke combinations. Weight: 6 to 8 lbs. depending on ga. and bbls. Select walnut stock w/pistol grip, fluted forearm checkered; Monte Carlo comb on trap guns; recoil pad on 12-ga. mag. and trap models. The various grades differ in quality of engraving and wood. Made from 1963 to 1976.

Diamond grade . . . . NiB $1588 Ex $1266 Gd $990
Field grade . . . . NiB $933 Ex $800 Gd $576
Superior grade . . . . NiB $1139 Ex $1008 Gd $853
Venture grade . . . . NiB $900 Ex $773 Gd $525

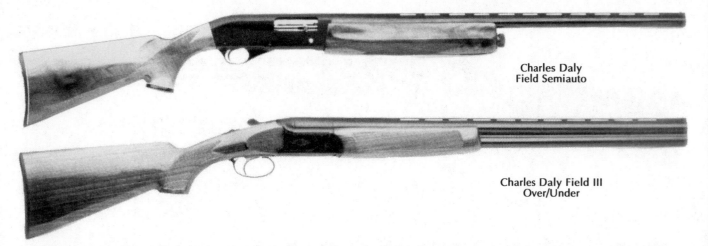

Charles Daly
Field Semiauto

Charles Daly Field III
Over/Under

SEXTUPLE MODEL SINGLE-BARREL TRAP GUN

Daly-pattern Anson & Deeley system boxlock action. Six locking bolts. Auto ejector. 12 ga. only. Bbls.: 30-, 32-, 34-inch, vent rib. Weight: 7.5 to 8.25 lbs. Checkered pistol-grip stock and forend. The two models made Empire and Regent Diamond differ in general quality, grade of wood, checkering, engraving, etc., otherwise specifications are the same. Disc. about 1933.

Regent Diamond quality (Linder) . . . NiB $2788 Ex $2188 Gd $1886
Empire quality (Linder) . . . . NiB $5300 Ex $4260 Gd $3143
Regent Diamond quality (Sauer) . NiB $3921 Ex $3288 Gd $2876
Empire quality (Sauer). . . . . NiB $2966 Ex $2377 Gd $1677

SINGLE-SHOT TRAP GUN

Daly-pattern Anson & Deeley system boxlock action. Auto ejector. 12 ga. only. Bbls.: 30-, 32-, 34-inch, vent rib. Weight: 7.5 to 8.25 lbs. Checkered pistol-grip stock and forend. This model was made in Empire Quality only. Disc. about 1933.

Empire grade (Linder) . . . . NiB $4765 Ex $3966 Gd $2960
Empire grade (Sauer). . . . . NiB $2477 Ex $2099 Gd $1776

SUPERIOR GRADE SINGLE-SHOT TRAP NiB $954 Ex $833 Gd $700

Boxlock. Automatic ejector. 12 ga. only. 32- or 34-inch vent-rib bbl., F choke. Weight: About 8 lbs. Monte Carlo stock w/pistol grip and recoil pad, beavertail forearm, checkered. Made 1968 to 1976.

DIAMOND GRADE O/U

Boxlock. Single selective trigger. Selective automatic ejectors. Gauges: 12 and 20, 3-inch chambers (2.75 target grade). Bbls.: 26, 27- or 30-inch w/fixed chokes or screw-in tubes. Weight: 7 lbs. Checkered European walnut stock and forearm w/oil finish. Engraved antique silver receiver and blued bbls. Made from 1984 to 1990.

Standard model . . . . NiB $1088 Ex $900 Gd $670
Skeet model . . . . NiB $1155 Ex $966 Gd $733
Trap model . . . . NiB $1155 Ex $966 Gd $733

DIAMOND GTX DL HUNTER O/U SERIES

Sidelock. Single selective trigger and selective auto ejectors. Gauges: 12, 20, 28 ga. or .410 bore. 26-, 28- and 30-inch bbls w/3-inch chambers (2.75-inch 28 ga.). Choke tubes (12 and 20 ga.), Fixed chokes (28 and 410). Weight: 5-8 lbs. Checkered European walnut stock w/hand-rubbed oil finish and recoil pad. Made from 1997 to 2001.

Diamond GTX DL Hunter . . . . . NiB $11,977 Ex $9478 Gd $5800
Diamond GTX EDL Hunter . . NiB $13,778 Ex $10,771 Gd $8987
Diamond GTX Sporting (12 or 20 ga.) . . . NiB $5921 Ex $4771 Gd $3380
Diamond GTX Skeet (12 or 20 ga.) . . .NiB $5540 Ex $4380 Gd $3100
Diamond GTX Trap (12 ga. only). . . .NiB $6144 Ex $4766 Gd $3200

EMPIRE DL HUNTER O/U. . NiB $1456 Ex $1277 Gd $956

Boxlock. Ejectors. Single selective trigger. Gauges:12, 20, 28 ga. and .410 bore. 26- or 28- inch bbls. w/3-inch chambers (2.75-inch 28 ga.). Choke tubes (12 and 20 ga.), Fixed chokes (28 and .410). Engraved coin-silver receiver w/game scene. Imported from 1997 to 1998.

EMPIRE EDL HUNTER SERIES

Similar to Empire DL Hunter except engraved sideplates. Made 1998 to date.

Hunter model. . . . . NiB $1477 Ex $1133 Gd $890
Sporting model. . . . . NiB $1371 Ex $1108 Gd $870
Skeet model . . . . NiB $1388 Ex $1170 Gd $880
Trap model . . . . NiB $1366 Ex $1109 Gd $853
28 ga., add. $110
.410 ga, add. $150
Multi-chokes w/Monte
Carlo stock, add $175

DSS HAMMERLESS DOUBLE . NiB $885 Ex $744 Gd $561

Boxlock. Single selective trigger. Selective automatic ejectors. Gauges: 12 and 20; 3-inch chambers. 26-inch bbls. w/screw-in choke tubes. Weight: 6.75 lbs. Checkered walnut pistol-grip stock and semi-beavertail forearm w/recoil pad. Engraved antique silver receiver and blued bbls. Made from 1990. Disc.

FIELD GRADE O/U . . . . NiB $675 Ex $570 Gd $449

Boxlock. Single selective trigger. Extractors. Gauges: 12 and 20; 3-inch chambers. Bbls.: 26-inch, IC/M; 28-inch, M/F. Weight: 6.75 lbs. (12 ga.). Checkered walnut stock and forearm w/semi-gloss finish and recoil pad. Engraved color-casehardened receiver and blued bbls. Made from 1989. Disc.

FIELD SEMIAUTO SHOTGUN . . .NiB $622 Ex $476 Gd $377

Recoil-operated. Takedown. 12-ga. and 12-ga. Magnum. Bbls.: 27- and 30-inch; vent rib. Made from 1982 to 1988.

FIELD III O/U SHOTGUN . . . . NiB $679 Ex $580 Gd $445

Boxlock. Plain extractors. Non-selective single trigger. Gauges: 12 or 20. Bbls.: vent rib; 26- and 28-inch; IC/M, M/F. Weight: 6 to 7.75 lbs. depending on ga. and bbls. Chrome-molybdenum steel bbls. Checkered pistol-grip stock and forearm. Made from 1982. Disc.

LUXIE O/U . . . . NiB $900 Ex $733 Gd $529

Similar to the Field Grade except w/selective automatic ejectors and choke tubes. Gauges: 12, 20, 28 and .410. Receiver w/antique silver finish and blued bbls. Made from 1989 to 1994.

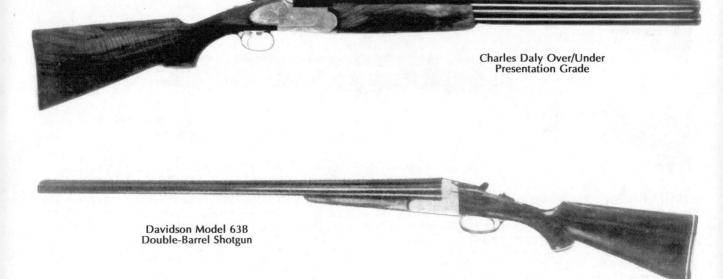

Charles Daly Over/Under
Presentation Grade

Davidson Model 63B
Double-Barrel Shotgun

MULTI-XII SELF-LOADING SHOTGUN . . . NiB $656 Ex $490 Gd $387
Similar to the gas-operated field semiauto except w/new Multi-Action gas system designed to shoot all loads w/o adjustment. 12 ga. w/3-inch chamber. 27-inch bbl. w/Invector choke tubes, vent rib. Made in Japan from 1987 to 1988.

**PRESENTATION
GRADE O/U . . . . NiB $1254 Ex $1009 Gd $770**
Purdey boxlock w/double cross-bolt. Gauges: 12 or 20. Engraved receiver w/single selective trigger and auto-ejectors. 27-inch chrome-molybdenum steel, rectified, honed and internally chromed, vent-rib bbls. Hand-checkered deluxe European walnut stock. Made from 1982 to 1986.

**SUPERIOR II
SHOTGUN O/U . . . . NiB $1064 Ex $880 Gd $602**
Boxlock. Plain extractors. Non-selective single trigger. Gauges: 12 or 20. Bbls.: chrome-molybdenum vent rib 26-, 28-, 30-inch, latter in magnum only, assorted chokes. Silver engraved receiver. Checkered pistol-grip stock and forearm. Made from 1982 to 1988

SPORTING CLAYS O/U . . . . NiB $833 Ex $644 Gd $535
Similar to the Field Grade except in 12 ga. only w/ported bbls. and internal choke tubes. Made from 1990 to 1996.

DAKOTA ARMS, INC. — Sturgis, South Dakota

**CLASSIC FIELD GRADE
S/S SHOTGUN . . . . NiB $7566 Ex $6548 Gd $4456**
Boxlock. Gauge: 20 ga. 27-inch bbl. w/fixed chokes. Double triggers. Selective ejectors. Color-casehardened receiver. Weight: 6 lbs. Checkered English walnut stock and splinter forearm w/hand-rubbed oil finish. Made from 1996 to 1998.

**PREMIER GRADE
S/S SHOTGUN . . . . . . NiB $14,765 Ex $11,466 Gd $9224**
Similar to Classic Field Grade model except w/50% engraving coverage. Exhibition grade English walnut stock. Made from 1996 to date.

**AMERICAN LEGEND
S/S SHOTGUN . . . . . NiB $16,750 Ex $15,000 Gd $11,550**
Limited edition built to customer's specifications. Gauge: 20 ga. 27-inch bbl. Double triggers. Selective ejectors. Fully engraved, coin-silver finished receiver w/gold inlays. Weight: 6 lbs. Hand checkered special-selection English walnut stock and forearm. Made from 1996 to 2005.

DARNE S.A. — Saint-Etienne, France

HAMMERLESS DOUBLE-BARREL SHOTGUNS
Sliding-breech action w/fixed bbls. Auto ejectors. Double triggers. Gauges: 12, 16, 20, 28; also 12 and 20 Magnum w/3-inch chambers. Bbls.: 27.5-inch standard, 25.5- to 31.5-inch lengths available; any standard choke combination. Weight: 5.5 to 7 lbs. depending on ga. and bbl. length. Checkered straight-grip or pistol-grip stock and forearm. The various models differ in grade of engraving and wood. Manufactured from 1881 to 1979.

Model R11
(Bird Hunter) . . . . NiB $7044 Ex $4698 Gd $2677
Model R15
(Pheasant Hunter). . . . . NiB $14,900 Ex $12,785 Gd $10,000
Model R16 (Magnum). . . . . NiB $3775 Ex $2730 Gd $2167
Model V19
(Quail Hunter) . . . . NiB $22,000 Ex $17,500 Gd $14,275
Model V22. . . . . NiB $31,000 Ex $26,800 Gd $22,975
Model V Hors Série No. 1. . NiB $77,000 Ex $58,650 Gd $46,790

DAVIDSON GUNS — Manufactured by Fabrica de Armas ILJA, Eibar, Spain; distributed by Davidson Firearms Co., Greensboro, North Carolina

MODEL 63B DOUBLE-BARREL
SHOTGUN..................NiB $433 Ex $279 Gd $200
Anson & Deeley boxlock action. Frame engraved and nickel plated. Plain extractors. Auto safety. Double triggers. Gauges: 12, 16, 20, 28, .410. Bbl. lengths: 25 (.410 only), 26, 28, 30 inches (latter 12 ga. only). Chokes: IC/ M, M/F, F/F. Weight: 5 lbs., 11 oz. (.410) to 7 lbs. (12 ga.). Checkered pistol-grip stock and forearm of European walnut. Made in 1963. Disc.

MODEL 63B MAGNUM
Similar to standard Model 63B except chambered for 10 ga. 3.5-inch, 12 and 20 ga. 3-inch Magnum shells; 10 ga. has 32-inch bbls., choked F/F. Weight: 10 lb., 10 oz. Made from 1963. Disc.
12-and 20 ga. magnum .....NiB $455 Ex $300 Gd $210
10 ga. magnum ....NiB $477 Ex $369 Gd $230

MODEL 69SL DOUBLE-BARREL
SHOTGUN...................NiB $455 Ex $400 Gd $270
Sidelock action w/detachable sideplates, engraved and nickel plated. Plain extractors. Auto safety. Double triggers. 12 and 20 ga. Bbls.: 26-inch IC/M, 28-inch M/F. Weight: 12 ga., 7 lbs., 20 ga., 6.5 lbs. Pistol-grip stock and forearm of European walnut, checkered. Made from 1963 to 1976.

MODEL 73 STAGECOACH
HAMMER DOUBLE ....NiB $331 Ex $229 Gd $130
Sidelock action w/detachable sideplates and exposed hammers. Plain extractors. Double triggers. Gauges: 12, 20, 3-inch chambers. 20-inch bbls, M/F chokes. Weight: 7 lbs., 12 ga.; 6.5 lbs., 20 ga. Checkered pistol-grip stock and forearm. Made from 1976. Disc.

DIAMOND

Currently imported by ADCO Sales, Inc, Woburn, MA. Company established circa 1981, all guns manufactured in Turkey.

GOLD SERIES (SEMIAUTOMATIC)...NiB $354 Ex $280 Gd $175
12 gauge, 3-inch chamber. Gas operated. Bbl. 24 (slug) or 28 inches. Ventilated rib with three choke tubes. Semi-humpback design, anodized alloy frame, gold etching. Rotary bolt. Black synthetic or checkered Turkish walnut forearm and stock with recoil pad. Value $50 less for slug version.

IMPERIAL SERIES ....NiB $475 Ex $345 Gd $265
Gauge: 12 (3.5-inch) or 20 (3-inch). Bbl.: 24 (12 ga. slug), 26 (20 ga.) or 28 inches; vent. rib, rotary bi-lateral bolt, deluxe checkered stock and forearm. Imported 2003.

ELITE SERIES ....NiB $445 Ex $323 Gd $200

Gauge: 12, 3-inch. Bbl.: 22 (slug), 24, 26 or 28 inches; ventilated rib, deluxe checkered walnut stock and forearm. Imported 2001. Deduct $50 for slug model.

PANTHER SERIES ....NiB $415 Ex $338 Gd $200
Gauge: 12, 3-inch. Gas-operated. Black synthetic stock and forearm. Bbl.: 20 (slug or regular) or 28 inches. Imported 2002.
Walnut stock and forearm, add $75
Slug version ....deduct $50

MARINER ....NiB $338 Ex $198 Gd $110
Gauge: 12, 3-inch. Gas operated. Bbl.: 20 (slug) or 22 inches. Vent. rib. Anodized alloy frame and receiver, satin silver finish. Checkered walnut stock and forearm. Imported 2002.
Slug model, deduct..........................$50

GOLD ELITE SERIES
(SLIDE-ACTION)............ NiB $354 Ex $260 Gd $200
12 gauge, 3-inch chamber. Bbl. 24 (slug with open sights), or 28 inches; ventilated rib. Semi-humpback design. Anodized alloy frame, synthetic black or Turkish walnut stock and forearm. Weight: 7 lbs. Imported 2001. Value $40 less for synthetic stock.

EXCEL ARMS OF AMERICA — Gardner, Massachusetts

SERIES 100 O/U SHOTGUN
Gauge: 12. Single selective trigger. Selective auto ejectors. Hand-checkered European walnut stock w/full pistol grip, tulip forend. Black metal finish. Chambered for 2.75-inch shells (Model 103 for 3-inch). Weight: 6. 88 to 7.88 lbs. Disc 1988.
Model 101 w/26-inch bbl., IC/M....NiB $465 Ex $367 Gd $266
Model 102 w/28-inch bbl., IC/M....NiB $465 Ex $367 Gd $266
Model 103 w/30-inch bbl., M/F.....NiB $465 Ex $367 Gd $266
Model 104 w/28-inch bbl., IC/M....NiB $465 Ex $367 Gd $266
Model 105, w/28-inch bbl.,
5 choke tubes.................NiB $645 Ex $480 Gd $387
Model 106, w/28-inch bbl.,
5 choke tubes...................NiB $776 Ex $689 Gd $558
Model 107 Trap, w/30-inch bbl.,
Full or 5 tubes .... NiB $776 Ex $689 Gd $558

SERIES 200 SIDE-BY-SIDE
SHOTGUN................NiB $667 Ex $496 Gd $368
Gauges: 12, 20, 28 and .410. Bbls.: 26-, 27- and 28-inch; various choke combinations. Weight: 7 lbs. average. American or European-style stock and forend. Made from 1985 to 1987.

SERIES 300 O/U
SHOTGUN............NiB $1328 Ex $1133 Gd $1033
Gauge: 12. Bbls.: 26-, 28- and 29-inch. Non-glare black-chrome matte finish. Weight: 7 lbs. average. Selective auto ejectors, engraved receiver. Hand-checkered European walnut stock and forend. Made from 1985 to 1986.

SHOTGUNS

Fox Model B

FABARM SHOTGUNS — Brescia, Italy

Currently imported by Heckler & Koch, Inc., of Sterling, VA (previously by Ithaca Acquisition Corp., St. Lawrence Sales, Inc. and Beeman Precision Arms, Inc.)

See Current listings under "Heckler & Koch."

FIAS — Fabrica Italiana Armi Sabatti Gardone Val Trompia, Italy

GRADE I O/U
Boxlock. Single selective trigger. Gauges: 12, 20, 28, .410; 3-inch chambers. Bbls.: 26-inch IC/M; 28-inch M/F; screw-in choke tubes. Weight: 6.5 to 7.5 lbs. Checkered European walnut stock and forearm. Engraved receiver and blued finish.

12 ga. model . . . . **NiB $587 Ex $480 Gd $355**
20 ga. model . . . . **NiB $633 Ex $512 Gd $367**
28 ga. and .410 . . . . **NiB $800 Ex $665 Gd $457**

FOX SHOTGUNS — Made by A. H. Fox Gun Co., Philadelphia, Pennsylvania, 1903 to 1930, and since then by Savage Arms, originally of Utica, New York, now of Westfield, Massachusetts. In 1993, Connecticut Manufacturing Co. of New Britain, Connecticut reintroduced selected models.

Values shown are for 12 and 16 ga. doubles made by A. H. Fox. Twenty gauge guns often are valued up to 75% higher. Savage-made Fox models generally bring prices 25% lower. With the exception of Model B, production of Fox shotguns was discontinued about 1942.

MODEL B HAMMERLESS DOUBLE . . **NiB $523 Ex $387 Gd $244**
Boxlock. Double triggers. Plain extractor. Gauges: 12, 16, 20, .410. 24- to 30-inch bbls., vent rib on current production; chokes: M/F, C/M, F/F (.410 only). Weight: About 7.5 lbs., 12 ga. Checkered pistol-grip stock and forend. Made about 1940 to 1985.

MODEL B-ST . . . . **NiB $644 Ex $475 Gd $350**
Same as Model B except has non-selective single trigger. Made from 1955-66.

MODEL B-DE . . . . **NiB $645 Ex $476 Gd $351**
Same as Model B-ST except frame finished in satin chrome, select walnut buttstock w/checkered pistol grip and beavertail forearm. Made from 1965 to 1966.

MODEL B-DL . . . . **NiB $678 Ex $558 Gd $421**
Same as Model B-ST except frame finished in satin chrome, select walnut buttstock w/checkered pistol grip side panels, beavertail forearm. Made from 1962 to 1966.

MODEL B-SE . . . . **NiB $922 Ex $700 Gd $531**
Same as Model B except has selective ejectors and single trigger. Made from 1966 to 1989.

HAMMERLESS DOUBLE-BARREL SHOTGUNS
The higher grades have the same general specifications as the standard Sterlingworth model, w/differences chiefly in workmanship and materials. Higher grade models are stocked in fine select walnut; quantity and quality of engraving increases w/grade and price. Except for Grade A, all other grades have auto ejectors.

Grade A . . . . **NiB $3160 Ex $1641 Gd $1895**
Grade AE . . . . **NiB $3598 Ex $2977 Gd $2110**
Grade BE . . . . **NiB $4962 Ex $3988 Gd $2860**
Grade CE . . . . **NiB $6200 Ex $5110 Gd $3628**
Grade DE . . . . **NiB $12,779 Ex $11,360 Gd $10,475**
Grade FE . . . . **NiB $22,679 Ex $18,960 Gd $13,000**
Grade XE . . . . **NiB $8634 Ex $7321 Gd $4208**
W/Kautzy selective single trigger, add **$400**
W/vent. rib, add **$500**
W/beavertail forearm, add **$300**
20 ga. model, add **60%**

SINGLE-BARREL TRAP GUNS
Boxlock. Auto ejector. 12 ga. only. 30- or 32-inch vent-rib bbl. Weight: 7.5 to 8 lbs. Trap-style stock and forearm of select walnut, checkered, recoil pad optional. The four grades differ chiefly in quality of wood and engraving; Grade M guns, built to order, have finest Circassian walnut. Stock and receiver are elaborately engraved and inlaid w/gold. Disc. 1942. Note: In 1932, the Fox Trap Gun was redesigned and those manufactured after that date have a stock w/full pistol grip and Monte Carlo comb; at the same time frame was changed to permit the rib line to extend across it to the rear.

Grade JE . . . . **NiB $3990 Ex $2367 Gd $2031**
Grade KE . . . . **NiB $5366 Ex $4979 Gd $4000**
Grade LE . . . . **NiB $6778 Ex $4789 Gd $3760**
Grade ME . . . . **NiB $15,975 Ex $12,880 Gd $9355**

"SKEETER" DOUBLE-BARREL
SHOTGUN . . . . **NiB $4990 Ex $4078 Gd $2855**
Boxlock. Gauge: 12 or 20. Bbls.: 28 inches w/full-length vent rib. Weight: Approx. 7 lbs. Buttstock and beavertail forend of select American walnut, finely checkered. Soft rubber recoil pad and ivory bead sights. Made in early 1930s.

STERLINGWORTH DELUXE
Same general specifications as Sterlingworth except 32-inch bbl. also available, recoil pad, ivory bead sights.

W/extractors . . . . **NiB $2187 Ex $1654 Gd $1100**
W/ejectors . . . . **NiB $2370 Ex $1979 Gd $1466**
20 ga., add **45%**

STERLINGWORTH HAMMERLESS DOUBLE
Boxlock. Double triggers (Fox-Kautzky selective single trigger extra). Plain extractors (auto ejectors extra). Gauges: 12,16, 20. Bbl. lengths: 26-, 28-, 30-inch; chokes F/F, M/F, C/M (any combination of C to F choke borings was available at no extra cost). Weight: 12 ga., 6.88 to 8.25 lbs.; 16 ga., 6 to 7 lbs.; 20 ga., 5.75 to 6.75 lbs. Checkered pistol-grip stock and forearm.

W/extractors . . . . **NiB $1800 Ex $1489 Gd $1000**
W/ejectors . . . . **NiB $2170 Ex $1770 Gd $1254**
W/selective single trigger, add **25%**

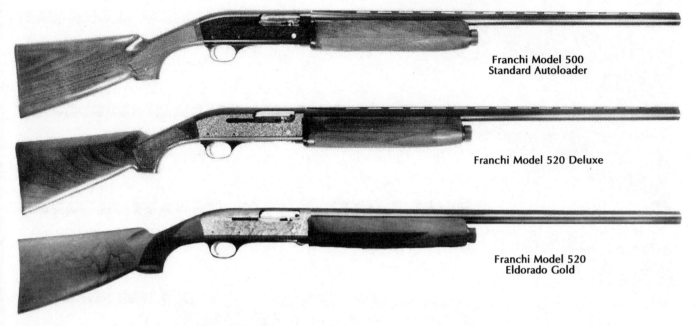

Franchi Model 500
Standard Autoloader

Franchi Model 520 Deluxe

Franchi Model 520
Eldorado Gold

STERLINGWORTH SKEET AND UPLAND GUN
Same general specifications as the standard Sterlingworth except has 26- or 28-inch bbls. w/skeet boring only, straight-grip stock. Weight: 7 lbs. (12 ga.).

W/extractors.	NiB $2588	Ex $2066	Gd $1489
W/ejectors	NiB $3000	Ex $2469	Gd $1785
20 ga., add. 45%

SUPER HE GRADE . . . . . . NiB $5863 Ex $4791 Gd $3310
Long-range gun made in 12 ga. only (chambered for 3-inch shells on order), 30- or 32-inch full choke bbls., auto ejectors standard. Weight: 8.75 to 9.75 lbs. General specifications same as standard Sterlingworth.

HAMMERLESS DOUBLE-BARREL SHOTGUNS
High-grade doubles similar to the original Fox models. 20 ga. only. 26- 28- or 30-inch bbls. Double triggers automatic safety and ejectors. Weight: 5.5 to 7 lbs. Custom Circassian walnut stock w/hand-rubbed oil finish. Custom stock configuration: straight, semi- or full pistol-grip stock w/traditional pad, hard rubber plate checkered or skeleton butt; Schnabel, splinter or beavertail forend. Made 1993 to date.

CE grade	NiB $9221	Ex $6855	Gd $4900
XE grade	NiB $9066	Ex $7221	Gd $5054
DE grade	NiB $13,788	Ex $11,650	Gd $7900
FE grade	NiB $18,977	Ex $15,220	Gd $11,760
Exhibition grade . . . NiB $27,480	Ex $22,760	Gd $14,990

LUIGI FRANCHI S.P.A. — Brescia, Italy

MODEL 48/AL ULTRA LIGHT SHOTGUN
Recoil-operated, takedown, hammerless shotgun w/tubular magazine. Gauges: 12 or 20 (2.75-inch); 12-ga. Magnum (3-inch chamber). Bbls.: 24- to 32-inch w/various choke combinations. Weight: 5 lbs., 2 oz. (20 ga.) to 6.25 lbs. (12 ga.). Checkered pistol-grip walnut stock and forend w/high-gloss finish.

Standard model	NiB $779	Ex $554	Gd $430
Hunter or magnum models . . .	NiB $977	Ex $580	Gd $476

MODEL 500 STANDARD AUTOLOADER NiB $400 Ex $288 Gd $190
Gas-operated. 12 gauge. Four round magazine. Bbls.: 26-, 28-inch; vent rib; IC, M, IM, F chokes. Weight: About 7 lbs. Checkered pistol-grip stock and forearm. Made from 1976 to 1980.

MODEL 520 DELUXE . . . . NiB $478 Ex $355 Gd $279

Same as Model 500 except higher grade w/engraved receiver. Made from 1975 to 1979.

MODEL 520 ELDORADO GOLD. . . NiB $1088 Ex $877 Gd $743
Same as Model 520 except custom grade w/engraved and gold-inlaid receiver, finer quality wood. Intro. 1977.

MODEL 610VS SEMIAUTOMATIC SHOTGUN
Gas-operated Variopress system adjustable to function w/2.75- or 3- inch shells. 12 gauge. Four round magazine. 26- or 28-inch vent rib bbls. w/Franchoke tubes. Weight: 7 lbs., 2 oz. 47.5 inches overall. Alloy receiver w/four-lug rotating bolt and loaded chamber indicator. Checkered European walnut buttstock and forearm w/ satin finish. Imported from 1997.

Standard model	NiB $766	Ex $600	Gd $445
Engraved model	NiB $800	Ex $655	Gd $500

MODEL 612 VARIOPRESS AUTOLOADING SHOTGUN
Gauge: 12 ga. Only. 24- to 28-inch bbl. 45 to 49-inches overall. Weight: 6.8 to 7 lbs. Five round magazine. Bead type sights with C, IC, M chokes. Blued, matte or Advantage camo finish. Imported from 1999 to 2004.

W/satin walnut stock, blued finish	NiB $645	Ex $559	Gd $369
W/synthetic stock, matte finish	NiB $665	Ex $590	Gd $400
W/Advantage camo finish	NiB $800	Ex $645	Gd $449
Defense model.	NiB $600	Ex $469	Gd $360
Sporting model	NiB $966	Ex $733	Gd $544

MODEL 620 VARIOPRESS AUTOLOADING SHOTGUN
Gauge: 20 ga. Only. 24- 26- or 28-inch bbl. 45 to 49-inches overall. Weight: 5.9 to 6.1 lbs. Five round magazine. Bead type sights with C, IC, M chokes. Satin walnut or Advantage camo stock. Imported from 1999 to 2004.

W/satin walnut stock, matte finish	NiB $655	Ex $498	Gd $367
W/Advantage camo finish	NiB $790	Ex $554	Gd $421
Youth model w/short stock	NiB $615	Ex $490	Gd $379

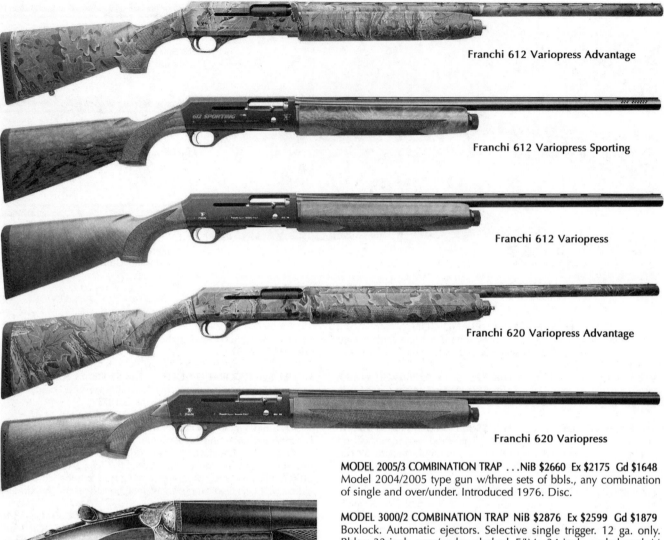

Franchi 612 Variopress Advantage

Franchi 612 Variopress Sporting

Franchi 612 Variopress

Franchi 620 Variopress Advantage

Franchi 620 Variopress

Franchi Model 2004
Trap Single Barrel

MODEL 2003 TRAP O/U . . . . . . **NiB $1355 Ex $1109 Gd $1005**
Boxlock. Auto ejectors. Selective single trigger. 12 ga. Bbls.: 30-, 32-inch
IM/F, F/F, high-vent rib. Weight (w/30-inch bbl.): 8.25 lbs. Checkered walnut
beavertail forearm and stock w/straight or Monte Carlo comb, recoil pad.
Luggage-type carrying case. Introduced 1976. Disc.

**MODEL 2004 TRAP SINGLE
BARREL TRAP** . . . . **NiB $1366 Ex $1288 Gd $915**
Same as Model 2003 except single bbl., 32- or 34-inch. Full choke.
Weight (w/32-inch bbl.): 8.25 lbs. Introduced 1976. Disc.

MODEL 2005 COMBINATION TRAP . . . **NiB $1977 Ex $1760 Gd $1233**
Model 2004/2005 type gun w/two sets of bbls., single and over/
under. Introduced 1976. Disc.

MODEL 2005/3 COMBINATION TRAP . . . **NiB $2660 Ex $2175 Gd $1648**
Model 2004/2005 type gun w/three sets of bbls., any combination
of single and over/under. Introduced 1976. Disc.

MODEL 3000/2 COMBINATION TRAP NiB $2876 Ex $2599 Gd $1879
Boxlock. Automatic ejectors. Selective single trigger. 12 ga. only.
Bbls.: 32-inch over/under choked F/IM, 34-inch underbarrel M
choke; high vent rib. Weight (w/32-inch bbls.): 8 lbs., 6 oz. Choice
of six different castoff buttstocks. Introduced 1979. Disc.

ALCIONE HAMMERLESS DOUBLE . . **NiB $763 Ex $633 Gd $544**
Boxlock. Anson & Deeley system action. Auto ejectors. Double
triggers. 12 ga. Various bbl. lengths, chokes, weights. Checkered
straight-grip stock and forearm. Made from 1940-50.

ALCIONE O/U SHOTGUN
Hammerless, takedown shotgun w/engraved receiver. Selective
single trigger and ejectors. 12 ga. w/3-inch chambers. Bbls.: 26-inch
(IC/M, 28-inch (M/F). Weight: 6.75 lbs. Checkered French walnut
buttstock and forend. Imported from Italy. 1982 to 1989.
Standard model . . . . **NiB $755 Ex $648 Gd $479**
**SL model
(disc. 1986)** . . . . **NiB $1290 Ex $1077 Gd $800**

ALCIONE FIELD (97-12 IBS) O/U
Similar to the Standard Alcione model except w/nickel-finished
receiver. 26- or 28-inch bbls. w/Franchoke tubes. Imported from
1998 to 2005.
Standard Field model . . . . **NiB $1263 Ex $1009 Gd $700**
SL Field model (w/sideplates, disc.) NiB $1296 Ex $1007 Gd $865

ALCIONE SPORT (SL IBS) O/U . . **NiB $1567 Ex $1380 Gd $1134**
Similar to the Alcione Field model except chambered for 2.75 or 3-inch shells. Ported 29-inch bbls. w/target vent rib and Franchoke tubes.

ALCIONE 2000 SX O/U SHOTGUN. . . **NiB $1790 Ex $1388 Gd $1100**
Similar to the Standard Alcione model except w/silver finished receiver and gold inlays. 28-inch bbls. w/Franchoke tubes. Weight: 7.25 lbs. Imported from 1996 to 1997.

**ARISTOCRAT FIELD
MODEL O/U** . . . . **NiB $754 Ex $600 Gd $434**
Boxlock. Selective auto ejectors. Selective single trigger. 12 ga. Bbls.: 26-inch IC/M; 28- and 30-inch M/F choke, vent rib. Weight (w/26-inch bbls.): 7 lbs. Checkered pistol-grip stock and forearm. Made from 1960 to 1969.

ARISTOCRAT DELUXE AND SUPREME GRADES
Available in Field, Skeet and Trap models w/the same general specifications as standard guns of these types. Deluxe and Supreme Grades are of higher quality, w/stock and forearm of select walnut, elaborate relief engraving on receiver, trigger guard, tang and top lever. Supreme game birds inlaid in gold. Made from 1960 to 1966.
Deluxe grade . . . . **NiB $1077 Ex $844 Gd $657**
Supreme grade . . . . **NiB $1577 Ex $1340 Gd $1098**

ARISTOCRAT IMPERIAL AND MONTE CARLO GRADES
Custom guns made in Field, Skeet and Trap models w/the same general specifications as standard for these types. Imperial and Monte Carlo grades are of highest quality w/stock and forearm of select walnut, fine engraving — elaborate on latter grade. Made 1967 to 1969.
Imperial grade . . . . **NiB $4134 Ex $2570 Gd $2160**
Monte Carlo grade . . . . . . **NiB $3677 Ex $2920 Gd $2100**

ARISTOCRAT MAGNUM MODEL . . . **NiB $765 Ex $557 Gd $469**
Same as Field Model except chambered for 3-inch shells, has 32-inch bbls. choked F/F; stock has recoil pad. Weight: About 8 lbs. Made from 1962 to 1965.

ARISTOCRAT SILVER KING . . **NiB $888 Ex $712 Gd $559**
Available in Field, Magnum, Meet and Trap models w/the same general specifications as standard guns of these types. Silver King has stock and forearm of select walnut more elaborately engraved silver-finished receiver. Made 1962 to 1969.

ARISTOCRAT SKEET MODEL . **NiB $866 Ex $754 Gd $544**
Same general specifications as Field Model except made only w/26-inch vent-rib bbls. w/SK chokes No. 1 and No. 2, skeet-style stock and forearm. Weight: About 7.5 lbs. Later production had wider (10mm) rib. Made from 1960 to 1969.

ARISTOCRAT TRAP MODEL . . **NiB $877 Ex $754 Gd $561**
Same general specifications as Field Model except made only w/30-inch vent-rib bbls., M/F choke, trap-style stock w/recoil pad, beavertail forearm. Later production had Monte Carlo comb, 10mm rib. Made from 1960 to 1969.

ASTORE HAMMERLESS DOUBLE . . **NiB $1032 Ex $866 Gd $713**
Boxlock. Anson & Deeley system action. Plain extractors. Double triggers. 12 ga. Various bbl. lengths, chokes, weights. Checkered straight-grip stock and forearm. Made 1937 to 1960.

ASTORE II . . . . **NiB $1389 Ex $1166 Gd $876**
Similar to Astore S but not as high grade. Furnished w/either plain extractors or auto ejectors, double triggers, pistol-grip stock. Bbls.: 27-inch IC/IM; 28-inch M/F chokes. Currently manufactured for Franchi in Spain.

Franchi Astore 5

ASTORE 5 . . . . **NiB $2458 Ex $1987 Gd $1466**
Same as Astore except has higher grade wood, fine engraving. automatic ejectors, single trigger, 28-inch bbl. M/F or IM/F chokes are standard on current production. Disc.

STANDARD MODEL AUTOLOADER
Recoil operated. Light alloy receiver. Gauges: 12, 20. Four round magazine. Bbls.: 26-, 28-, 30-inch; plain, solid or vent rib, IC/ M, F chokes. Weight: 12 ga., about 6.25 lbs. 20 ga., 5.13 lbs. Checkered pistol-grip stock and forearm. Made from 1950. Disc.
W/plain bbl. . . . . **NiB $490 Ex $335 Gd $260**
W/solid rib . . . . **NiB $550 Ex $512 Gd $339**
W/vent rib . . . . **NiB $560 Ex $489 Gd $368**

CROWN, DIAMOND AND IMPERIAL GRADE
Same general specifications as Standard Model except these are custom guns of the highest quality. Crown Grade has hunting scene engraving, Diamond Grade has silver-inlaid scroll engraving; Imperial Grade has elaborately engraved hunting scenes w/figures inlaid in gold. Stock and forearm of fancy walnut. Made from 1954 to 1975.
Crown grade . . . . **NiB $1670 Ex $1496 Gd $1212**
Diamond grade . . . . **NiB $2044 Ex $1760 Gd $1233**
Imperial grade . . . . **NiB $2480 Ex $2239 Gd $1799**

STANDARD MODEL MAGNUM
Same general specifications as Standard model except has 3-inch chamber, 32-inch (12 ga.) or 28-inch (20 ga.) F choke bbl., recoil pad. Weight: 12 ga., 8.25 lbs.; 20 ga., 6 lbs. Formerly designated "Superange Model." Made from 1954 to 1988.
W/plain bbl. . . . . **NiB $500 Ex $412 Gd $286**
W/vent rib . . . . **NiB $577 Ex $468 Gd $360**

DYNAMIC-12
Same general specifications and appearance as Standard Model, except 12 ga. only, has heavier steel receiver. Weight: About 7.25 lbs. Made from 1965 to 1972.
W/plain bbl. . . . . **NiB $522 Ex $430 Gd $331**
W/vent rib . . . . **NiB $550 Ex $433 Gd $330**

DYNAMIC-12 SLUG GUN . . . **NiB $578 Ex $490 Gd $354**
Same as standard gun except 12 ga. only, has heavier steel receiver. Made 1965 to 1972.

DYNAMIC-12 SKEET GUN . . . **NiB $677 Ex $549 Gd $456**
Same general specifications and appearance as Standard model except has heavier steel receiver, made only in 12 ga. w/26-inch vent-rib bbl., SK choke, stock and forearm of extra fancy walnut. Made from 1965 to 1972.

ELDORADO MODEL . . . . **NiB $588 Ex $370 Gd $355**
Same general specifications as Standard model except highest grade w/gold-filled engraving, stock and forearm of select walnut, vent-rib bbl. only. Made from 1954 to 1975.

SHOTGUNS

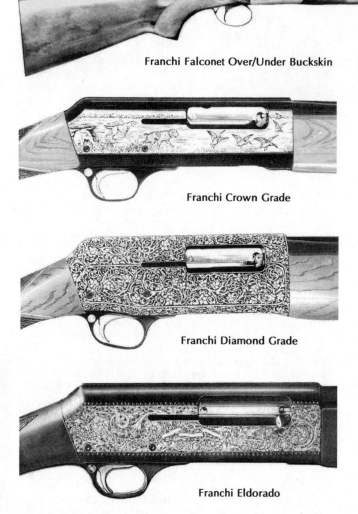

Franchi Falconet Over/Under Buckskin

Franchi Crown Grade

Franchi Diamond Grade

Franchi Eldorado

FALCONET INTERNATIONAL SKEET MODEL... NiB $1163 Ex $977 Gd $800
Similar to Standard Skeet model but higher grade. Made 1970 to 1974.

FALCONET INTERNATIONAL
TRAP MODEL. . . . . NiB $1165 Ex $980 Gd $803
Similar to Standard model but higher grade; w/straight or Monte Carlo comb stock. Made from 1970 to 1974.

FALCONET O/U FIELD MODELS
Boxlock. Auto ejectors. Selective single trigger. Gauges: 12, 16, 20, 28, .410. Bbls.: 24-, 26-, 28-, 30-inch; vent rib. Chokes: C/IC, IC/M, M/F. Weight: from about 6 lbs. Engraved lightweight alloy receiver, light-colored in Buckskin model, blued in Ebony model, pickled silver in Silver model. Checkered walnut stock and forearm. Made from 1968 to 1975.
Buckskin or Ebony model . . . NiB $655 Ex $460 Gd $449
Silver model . . . . NiB $655 Ex $460 Gd $449

FALCONET STANDARD SKEET MODEL ...NiB $1055 Ex $876 Gd $690
Same general specifications as Field models except made only w/26-inch bbls. w/SK chokes No. 1 and No. 2, wide vent rib, color-casehardened receiver skeet-style stock and forearm. Weight: 12 ga., about 7.75 lbs. Made from 1970 to 1974.

FALCONET STANDARD TRAP MODEL . . . NiB $1366 Ex $965 Gd $744
Same general specifications as Field models except made only in 12 ga. w/30-inch bbls., choked M/F, wide vent rib, color-casehardened receiver, Monte Carlo trap style stock and forearm, recoil pad. Weight: About 8 lbs. Made from 1970 to 1974.

GAS-OPERATED SEMIAUTOMATIC SHOTGUN
Gas-operated, takedown, hammerless shotgun w/tubular magazine. 12 ga. w/2.75-inch chamber. Five round magazine. Bbls.: 24 to 30 inches w/vent rib. Weight: 7.5 lbs. Gold-plated trigger. Checkered pistol-grip stock and forend of European walnut. Imported from Italy 1985 to 1990.
Prestige model . . . . NiB $677 Ex $456 Gd $449
Elite model . . . . NiB $688 Ex $571 Gd $388

HAMMERLESS SIDELOCK DOUBLES
Hand-detachable locks. Self-opening action. Auto ejectors. Double triggers or single trigger. Gauges: 12,16, 20. Bbl. lengths, chokes, weights according to customer's specifications. Checkered stock and forend, straight or pistol grip. Made in six grades — Condor, Imperiale, Imperiale S, Imperiale Montecarlo No. 5, Imperiale Montecarlo No.11, Imperiale Montecarlo Extra — which differ chiefly in overall quality, engraving, grade of wood, checkering, etc.; general specifications are the same. Only the Imperial Montecarlo Extra Grade is currently manufactured.
Condor grade . . . . NiB $7897 Ex $6200 Gd $4978
Imperial, Imperiales grades . . . . . NiB $11,776 Ex $9899 Gd $7217
Imperial Monte Carlo
grades No. 5, 11 . . . . .NiB $32,766 Ex $25,777 Gd $21,989
Imperial Monte Carlo Extra grade . Custom only. Prices start at $110,000

HUNTER MODEL
Same general specifications as Standard Model except higher grade w/ engraved receiver; w/ribbed bbl. only. Made from 1950 to 1990.
W/solid rib . . . . NiB $500 Ex $390 Gd $322
W/vent rib . . . . NiB $616 Ex $488 Gd $400

HUNTER MODEL MAGNUM . . . . . . NiB $544 Ex $454 Gd $330
Same as Standard Model Magnum except higher grade w/engraved receiver, vent rib bbl. only. Formerly designated "Wildfowler Model." Made from 1954 to 1973.

PEREGRINE MODEL 400. . . . . NiB $733 Ex $544 Gd $400
Same general specifications as Model 451 except has steel receiver. Weight (w/26.5-inch bbl.): 6 lbs., 15 oz. Made from 1975 to 1978.

PEREGRINE MODEL 451 O/U. NiB $605 Ex $451 Gd $267
Boxlock. Lightweight alloy receiver. Automatic ejectors. Selective single trigger. 12 ga. Bbls.: 26.5-, 28-inch; choked C/IC, IC/M, M/F; vent rib. Weight (w/26.5-inch bbls.): 6 lbs., 1 oz. Checkered pistol-grip stock and forend. Made from 1975 to 1978.

SKEET GUN . . . . NiB $450 Ex $320 Gd $228
Same general specifications and appearance as Standard Model except made only w/26-inch vent-rib bbl., SK choke. Stock and forearm of extra fancy walnut. Made from 1972 to 1974.

SLUG GUN . . . . NiB $435 Ex $288 Gd $190
Same as Standard Model except has 22-inch plain bbl., Cyl. bore, folding leaf open rear sight, gold bead front sight. Made 1960 to 1990. Disc.

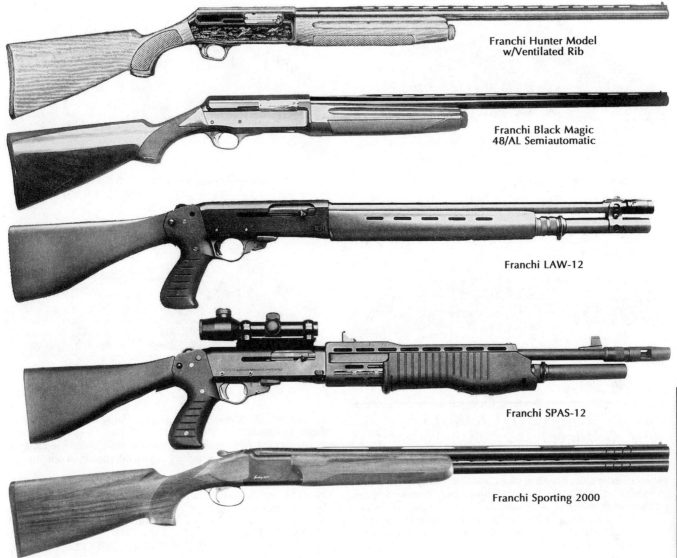

Franchi Hunter Model w/Ventilated Rib

Franchi Black Magic 48/AL Semiautomatic

Franchi LAW-12

Franchi SPAS-12

Franchi Sporting 2000

SHOTGUNS

TURKEY GUN . . . . **NiB $556 Ex $377 Gd $298**
Same as Standard Model Magnum except higher grade w/turkey scene engraved receiver, 12 ga. only, 36-inch matted-rib bbl., Extra Full choke. Made from 1963 to 1965.

BLACK MAGIC 48/AL SEMIAUTOMATIC
Similar to the Franchi Model 48/AL except w/Franchoke screw-in tubes and matte black receiver w/Black Magic logo. Gauge: 12 or 20, 2.75-inch chamber. Bbls.: 24-, 26-, 28-inch w/vent rib; 24-inch rifled slug w/sights. Weight: 5.2 lbs. (20 ga.). Checkered walnut buttstock and forend. Blued finish.
Standard model . . . . **NiB $657 Ex $543 Gd $466**
Trap model . . . . **NiB $722 Ex $596 Gd $500**

FALCONET 2000 O/U . . . . **NiB $1355 Ex $1121 Gd $967**
Boxlock. Single selective trigger. Selective automatic ejectors. Gauge: 12, 2.75-inch chambers. Bbls.: 26-inch w/Franchoke tubes; IC/M/F. Weight: 6 lbs. Checkered walnut stock and forearm. Engraved silver receiver w/gold-plated game scene. Imported from 1992 to 1993.

LAW-12 SHOTGUN . . . . **NiB $689 Ex $454 Gd $377**
Similar to the SPAS-12 Model except gas-operated semiautomatic action only, ambidextrous safety, decocking lever and adj. sights.

Made from 1983 to 1994.

SPAS-12 SHOTGUN
Selective operating system functions as a gas-operated semi-automatic or pump action. Gauge: 12, 2.75-inch chamber. Seven round magazine. Bbl.: 21.5 inches w/cylinder bore and muzzle protector or optional screw-in choke tubes, matte finish. 41 inches overall w/fixed stock. Weight: 8.75 lbs. Blade front sight, aperture rear sight. Folding or black nylon buttstock w/pistol grip and forend, non-reflective anodized finish. Made from 1983 to 1994. Limited importation.
Fixed stock model . . . . . . **NiB $5000 Ex $4500 Gd $2390**
Folding stock model . . . . . **NiB $7000 Ex $6500 Gd $3390**
W/choke tubes, add $150

SPORTING 2000 O/U . . . . . **NiB $1376 Ex $1125 Gd $966**
Similar to the Franchi Falconet 2000. Boxlock. Single selective trigger. Selective automatic ejectors. Gauge: 12; 2.75-inch chambers. Ported (1992-93) or unported 28-inch bbls., w/vent rib. Weight: 7.75 lbs. Blued receiver. Bead front sight. Checkered walnut stock and forearm; plastic composition buttplate. Imported from 1992-93 and 1997 to 1998.

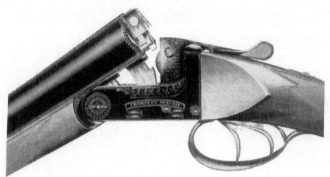

Francotte Model 8446

Francotte Model 6886

Francotte Model
10/18E628

Francotte Model 9261

AUGUSTE FRANCOTTE & CIE., S.A. — Liège, Belgium

Francotte shotguns for many years were distributed in the U.S. by Abercrombie & Fitch of New York City. This firm has used a series of model designations for Francotte guns which do not correspond to those of the manufacturer. Because so many Francotte owners refer to their guns by the A & F model names and numbers, the A & F series is included in a listing separate from that of the standard Francotte numbers.

BOXLOCK HAMMERLESS DOUBLES
Anson & Deeley system. Side clips. Greener crossbolt on models 6886, 8446, 4996 and 9261; square crossbolt on Model 6930, Greener-Scott crossbolt on Model 8537, Purdey bolt on Models 11/18E and 10/18E/628. Auto ejectors. Double triggers. Made in all standard gauges, barrel lengths, chokes, weights. Checkered stock and forend, straight or pistol-grip. The eight models listed vary chiefly in fastenings as described above, finish and engraving, etc.; custom options increase value. Disc.
Model 6886 . . . . NiB $14,688 Ex $13,879 Gd $11,776
Model 8446 (Francotte Special),
6930, 4996 . . . . NiB $15,889 Ex $14,799 Gd $14,776
Model 8537, 9261
(Francotte Original), 11/18E NiB $17,345 Ex $16,221 Gd $14,998
Model 10/18E/628 . . . . NiB $17,998 Ex $16,789 Gd $15,900

BOXLOCK HAMMERLESS DOUBLES – A & F SERIES
Boxlock, Anson & Deeley type. Crossbolt. Sideplate on all except Knockabout Model. Side clips. Auto ejectors. Double triggers. Gauges: 12, 16, 20, 28, .410. Bbls.: 26- to 32-inch in 12 ga., 26- and 28-inch in other ga.; any boring. Weight: 4.75 to 8 lbs. depending on gauge and barrel length. Checkered stock and

forend; straight, half or full pistol grip. The seven grades (No. 45 Eagle Grade, No. 30, No. 25, No. 20, No. 14, Jubilee Model, Knockabout Model) differ chiefly in overall quality, engraving, grade of wood, checkering, etc.; general specifications are the same. Disc.
Jubilee model
No. 14 . . . . NiB $4200 Ex $2633 Gd $1470
Jubilee model
No. 18 . . . . NiB $4687 Ex $3577 Gd $1890
Jubilee model
No. 20 . . . . NiB $5670 Ex $4122 Gd $2250
Jubilee model
No. 25 . . . . NiB $6245 Ex $4738 Gd $2290
Jubilee model
No. 30 . . . . NiB $7832 Ex $6110 Gd $3580
Eagle grade
No. 45 . . . . NiB $11,100 Ex $8854 Gd $5220
Knockabout
model . . . . NiB $3377 Ex $2688 Gd $1769
20 ga., add. 125%
28 ga. or .410, add. 300%

BOXLOCK HAMMERLESS DOUBLES (W/SIDEPLATES)
Anson & Deeley system. Reinforced frame w/side clips. Purdey-type bolt except on Model 8535, which has Greener crossbolt. Auto ejectors. Double triggers. Made in all standard gauges, bbl. lengths, chokes, weights. Checkered stock and forend, straight or pistol grip. Models 10594, 8535 and 6982 are of equal quality, differing chiefly in style of engraving; Model 9/40E/38321 is a higher grade gun in all details and has fine English-style engraving. Built to customer specifications.
Models 10594, 8535, 6982 . . . NiB $6044 Ex $4566 Gd $3177
Model 9/40E/3831 . . . . . . NiB $6588 Ex $5344 Gd $3889

Galef Silver Snipe Over/Under Shotgun

Galef Companion Folding Single-Barrel Shotgun

Galef Zabala Hammerless Double-Barrel Shotgun

FINE O/U SHOTGUN . . . NiB $10,566 Ex $8978 Gd $6450
Model 9/40.SE. Boxlock, Anson & Deeley system. Auto ejectors. Double triggers. Made in all standard gauges; bbl. length, boring to order. Weight: About 6.75 lbs. 12 ga. Checkered stock and forend, straight or pistol grip. Manufactured to customer specifications. Disc 1990.

FINE SIDELOCK
HAMMERLESS DOUBLE . . . . . NiB $26,350 Ex $21,789 Gd $15,680
Model 120.HE/328. Automatic ejectors. Double triggers. Made in all standard ga.; bbl. length, boring, weight to order. Checkered stock and forend, straight or pistol-grip. Manufactured to customer specifications. Disc. 1990.

HALF-FINE O/U SHOTGUN . . . . . NiB $11,656 Ex $9377 Gd $6275
Model SOB.E/11082. Boxlock, Anson & Deeley system. Auto ejectors. Double triggers. Made in all standard gauges; barrel length, boring to order. Checkered stock and forend, straight or pistol grip. Note: This model is similar to No. 9/40. SE except general quality lower. Disc. 1990.

GALEF SHOTGUNS — Manufactured for J. L. Galef & Son, Inc., New York, New York; by M. A. V. I., Gardone F. T., Italy; by Zabala Hermanos, Eiquetta, Spain; and by Antonio Zoli, Gardone V. T., Italy

SILVER SNIPE OVER/UNDER SHOTGUN . . . NiB $699 Ex $598 Gd $445
Boxlock. Plain extractors. Single trigger. Gauges: 12, 20; 3-inch chambers. Bbls: 26-, 28-, 30-inch (latter in 12 ga. only); IC/M, M/F chokes; vent rib. Weight: 12 ga. w/28-inch bbls., 6.5 lbs. Checkered walnut pistol-grip stock and forearm. Introduced by Antonio Zoli in 1968. Disc. See illustration previous page.

GOLDEN SNIPE . . . . NiB $689 Ex $570 Gd $455
Same as Silver Snipe, except has selective automatic ejectors. Made by Antonio Zoli 1968 to date.

MONTE CARLO TRAP
SINGLE-BARREL SHOTGUN . . . . NiB $356 Ex $221 Gd $177
Hammerless. Underlever. Plain extractor. 12 ga. 32-inch bbl., F choke, vent rib. Weight: About 8.25 lbs. Checkered pistol-grip stock w/Monte Carlo comb and recoil pad, beavertail forearm. Introduced by M. A. V. I. in 1968. Disc.

SILVER HAWK HAMMERLESS DOUBLE . . . NiB $565 Ex $455 Gd $300
Boxlock. Plain extractors. Double triggers. Gauges: 12, 20; 3-inch chambers. Bbls.: 26-, 28-, 30-inch (latter in 12 ga. only); IC/M, M/F chokes. Weight: 12 ga. w/26-inch bbls., 6 lbs. 6 oz. Checkered walnut pistol-grip stock and beavertail forearm. Made by Angelo Zoli 1968 to 1972.

COMPANION FOLDING SINGLE-BARREL SHOTGUN
Hammerless. Underlever. Gauges: 12 Mag., 16, 20 Mag., 28, .410. Bbls.: 26-inch (.410 only), 28-inch (12, 16, 20, 28), 30-inch (12-ga. only); F choke; plain or vent rib. Weight: 4.5 lbs. for .410 to 5 lbs., 9 oz. for 12 ga. Checkered pistol-grip stock and forearm. Made by M. A. V. I. from 1968-83.
W/plain bbl. . . . . NiB $245 Ex $179 Gd $95
W/ventilated rib . . . . NiB $270 Ex $196 Gd $110

ZABALA HAMMERLESS DOUBLE-BARREL SHOTGUN
Boxlock. Plain extractors. Double triggers. Gauges: 10 Mag., 12 Mag., 16, 20 Mag., 28, .410. Bbls.: 22-, 26-, 28-, 30-, 32-inch; IC/IC, IC/M, M/F chokes. Weight: 12 ga. w/28-inch bbls., 7.75 lbs. Checkered walnut pistol-grip stock and beavertail forearm, recoil pad. Made by Zabala from 1972-83.
10 ga. . . . . NiB $355 Ex $270 Gd $200
Other ga. . . . . NiB $244 Ex $179 Gd $115

GAMBA — Gardone V. T. (Brescia), Italy

DAYTONA COMPETITION O/U
Boxlock w/Boss-style locking system. Anatomical single trigger; optional adj., single-selective release trigger. Selective automatic ejectors. Gauge: 12 or 20; 2.75- or 3-inch chambers. Bbls.: 26.75-, 28-, 30- or 32-inch choked SK/SK, IM/F or M/F. Weight: 7.5 to 8.5 lbs. Black or chrome receiver w/blued bbls. Checkered select walnut stock and forearm w/oil finish. Imported by Heckler & Koch until 1992.
American Trap model . . . . NiB $2240 Ex $1680 Gd $1021
Pigeon, Skeet, Trap models . . . . NiB $1323 Ex $1078 Gd $877

Garbi Model 200

Sporting model. . . . . NiB $5678 Ex $4498 Gd $3123
Sideplate model . . . . NiB $11,789 Ex $9809 Gd $5977
Engraved models . . . . NiB $13,788 Ex $10,666 Gd $7477
Sidelock model . . . .NiB $28,560 Ex $23,778 Gd $19,580

GARBI SHOTGUNS — Eibar, Spain

MODEL 100
SIDELOCK SHOTGUN . . . NiB $5700 Ex $3433 Gd $2433
Gauges: 12, 16, 20 and 28. Bbls.: 25-, 28-, 30-inch. Action: Holland &
Holland pattern sidelock; automatic ejectors and double trigger. Weight:
5 lbs., 6 oz. to 7 lbs. 7 oz. English-style straight grip stock w/fine-line
hand-checkered butt; classic forend. Made from 1985 to date.

MODEL 101
SIDELOCK SHOTGUN . . . NiB $6788 Ex $4331 Gd $3000
Same general specifications as Model 100 above, except the sidelocks are handcrafted w/hand-engraved receiver; select walnut
straight-grip stock.

MODEL 102
SIDELOCK SHOTGUN . . . NiB $7175 Fx $4576 Gd $3177
Similar to the Model 101 except w/large scroll engraving. Made
from 1985 to 1993.

MODEL 103
HAMMERLESS DOUBLE
Similar to Model 100 except w/Purdey-type, higher grade engraving.
Model 103A Standard . . .NiB $14,675 Ex $11,650 Gd $9967
Model 103A Royal Deluxe. . .NiB $11,870 Ex $9443 Gd $7655
Model 103B . . . . . . .NiB $21,660 Ex $17,707 Gd $15,990
Model 103B Royal Deluxe . . .NiB $25,677 Ex $22,770 Gd $18,989

MODEL 200
HAMMERLESS DOUBLE NiB $17,766 Ex $15,221 Gd $11,488
Similar to Model 100 except w/double heavy-duty locks. Continental-
style floral and scroll engraving. Checkered deluxe walnut stock and
forearm.

GARCIA CORPORATION —
Teaneck, New Jersey

BRONCO 22/.410 O/U COMBO . . NiB $300 Ex $197 Gd $100
Swing-out action. Takedown. 18.5-inch bbls.; .22 LR over, .410 ga.
under. Weight: 4.5 lbs. One-piece stock and receiver, crackle finish.
Intro. In 1976. Disc.

BRONCO .410 SINGLE SHOT . . NiB $233 Ex $120 Gd $90
Swing-out action. Takedown. .410 ga. 18.5-inch bbl. Weight: 3.5 lbs.
One-piece stock and receiver, crackle finish. Intro. In 1967. Disc.

GOLDEN EAGLE FIREARMS INC. —
Houston, Texas. Manufactured by Nikko
Firearms Ltd., Tochigi, Japan

EAGLE MODEL 5000
GRADE I FIELD O/U . . . . NiB $989 Ex $844 Gd $659
Receiver engraved and inlaid w/gold eagle head. Boxlock. Auto
ejectors. Selective single trigger. 12, 20 ga.; 2.75- or 3-inch chambers, 12 ga., 3-inch, 20 ga. Bbls.: 26-, 28-, 30-inch (latter only in
12-ga. 3-inch Mag.); IC/M, M/F chokes; vent rib. Weight: 6.25 lbs.,
20 ga.; 7.25 lbs., 12 ga.; 8 lbs., 12-ga. Mag. Checkered pistol-grip
stock and semi-beavertail forearm. Imported 1975-82. Note: Guns
marketed 1975 to 1976 under the Nikko brand name have white
receivers; guns made since 1976 are blued.

EAGLE MODEL 5000
GRADE I SKEET . . . . NiB $954 Ex $743 Gd $522
Same as Field model except has 26- or 28-inch bbls. w/wide (11
mm) vent rib, SK choked. Imported from 1975 to 1982.

EAGLE MODEL 5000
GRADE I TRAP. . . . . NiB $954 Ex $755 Gd $569
Same as Field model except has 30-, or 32-inch bbls. w/wide (11
mm) vent rib (M/F, IM/F, F/F chokes), trap-style stock w/recoil pad.
Imported from 1975 to 1982.

EAGLE MODEL 5000
GRADE II FIELD . . . . NiB $1077 Ex $890 Gd $776
Same as Grade I Field model except higher grade w/fancier wood,
more elaborate engraving and "screaming eagle" inlaid in gold.
Imported from 1975 to 1982.

EAGLE MODEL 5000
GRADE II SKEET . . . . NiB $1100 Ex $940 Gd $800
Same as Grade I Skeet model except higher grade w/fancier wood,
more elaborate engraving and "screaming eagle" inlaid in gold;
inertia trigger, vent side ribs. Imported from 1975-82.

EAGLE MODEL 5000
GRADE II TRAP . . . . NiB $1100 Ex $940 Gd $800
Same as Grade I Trap model except higher grade w/fancier wood,
more elaborate engraving and "screaming eagle" inlaid in gold;
inertia trigger, vent side ribs. Imported from 1975 to 1982.

EAGLE MODEL 5000
GRADE III GRANDEE . . . . NiB $2760 Ex $2255 Gd $1798
Best grade, available in Field, Skeet and Trap models w/same general
specifications as lower grades. Has sideplates w/game scene engraving, scroll on frame and bbls., fancy wood (Monte Carlo comb, full
pistol-grip and recoil pad on Trap model). Made from 1976 to 1982.

Gorosabel
Model 504 Shotgun

Greener Empire Model
Hammerless

Greener
Far-Killer

GOROSABEL SHOTGUNS — Spain

MODEL 503 SHOTGUN . . . . **NiB $1088 Ex $866 Gd $735**
Gauges: 12, 16, 20 and .410. Action: Anson & Deely-style boxlock. Bbls.: 26-, 27-, and 28-inch. Select European walnut, English or pistol grip, sliver or beavertail forend, hand-checkering. Scalloped frame and scroll engraving. Intro. 1985; disc.

MODEL 504 SHOTGUN . . . . **NiB $1167 Ex $953 Gd $655**
Gauge: 12 or 20. Action: Holland & Holland-style sidelock. Bbl.: 26-, 27-, or 28-inch. Select European walnut, English or pistol grip, sliver or beavertail forend, hand-checkering. Holland-style large scroll engraving. Inro. 1985; disc.

MODEL 505 SHOTGUN . . . **NiB $1590 Ex $1266 Gd $965**
Gauge: 12 or 20. Action: Holland & Holland-style sidelock. Bbls.: 26-, 27-, or 28-inch. Select European walnut, English or pistol grip, silver or beavertail forend, hand-checkering. Purdey-style fine scroll and rose engraving. Intro. 1985; disc.

STEPHEN GRANT — Hertfordshire, England

BEST QUALITY SELF-OPENER DOUBLE-BARREL
SHOTGUN . . . . **NiB $19,870 Ex $16,920 Gd $12,612**
Sidelock, self-opener. Gauges: 12, 16 and 20. Bbls.: 25 to 30 inches standard. Highest-grade English or European walnut straight-grip butt-stock and forearm w/Greener type lever. Imported by Stoeger in the 1950s.

BEST QUALITY SIDE-LEVER DOUBLE-BARREL
SHOTGUN . . . . **NiB $13,657 Ex $11,770 Gd $9879**
Sidelock, self-lever. Gauges: 12, 16 and 20. Bbls.: 25 to 30 inches standard. Highest-grade English or European walnut straight-grip buttstock and forearm w/Greener type lever. Imported by Stoeger in the 1950s.

W. W. GREENER, LTD. — Birmingham, England

EMPIRE MODEL HAMMERLESS DOUBLES
Boxlock. Non-ejector or w/automatic ejectors. Double triggers. 12 ga. only (2.75-inch or 3-inch chamber). Bbls.: 28- to 32-inch; any choke combination. Weight: from 7.25 to 7.75 lbs. depending on bbl. length. Checkered stock and forend, straight- or half-pistol grip. Also furnished in "Empire Deluxe Grade," this model has same general specs, but deluxe finish.
Empire model, non-ejector. . .NiB $1887 Ex $1671 Gd $1388
Empire model, ejector. . . . NiB $1955 Ex $1771 Gd $1480
Empire Deluxe model, non-ejector . .NiB $2088 Ex $1933 Gd $1387
Empire Deluxe model, ejector . . .NiB $2677 Ex $2200 Gd $1588

FARKILLER MODEL GRADE F35
HAMMERLESS DOUBLE-BARREL SHOTGUN
Boxlock. Non-ejector or w/automatic ejectors. Double triggers. Gauges: 12 (2.75-inch or 3-inch), 10, 8. Bbls.: 28-, 30- or 32-inch. Weight: 7.5 to 9 lbs. in 12 ga. Checkered stock, forend; straight or half-pistol grip.
Non-ejector, 12 ga. . . . . . . NiB $1577 Ex $1122 Gd $909
Ejector, 12 ga. . . . . NiB $3897 Ex $3138 Gd $2217
Non-ejector, 10 or 8 ga. . . NiB $2886 Ex $2231 Gd $1977
Ejector, 10 or 8 ga.. . . . . . NiB $5500 Ex $4230 Gd $3110

G. P. (GENERAL PURPOSE)
SINGLE BARREL . . . . NiB $444 Ex $358 Gd $229
Greener Improved Martini Lever Action. Takedown. Ejector. 12 ga. only. Bbl. lengths: 26-, 30-, 32-inch. M or F choke. Weight: 6.25 to 6.75 lbs. depending on bbl. length. Checkered straight-grip stock and forearm.

HAMMERLESS EJECTOR DOUBLE-BARREL SHOTGUNS
Boxlock. Auto ejectors. Double triggers, non-selective or selective single trigger. Gauges: 12, 16, 20, 28, .410 (two latter gauges not supplied in Grades DH40 and DH35). Bbls.: 26-, 28-, 30-inch; any choke combination. Weight: From 4.75 to 8 lbs. Depending on ga. and bbl. length. Checkered stock and forend, straight- or half-pistol grip. The Royal, Crown, Sovereign and Jubilee models differ in quality, engraving, grade of wood, checkering, etc. General specifications are the same.
Royal Model Grade DH75 . . .NiB $4170 Ex $3008 Gd $2166
Crown Model Grade DH55 NiB $5166 Ex $3188 Gd $2270
Sovereign Model Grade DH40. . NiB $5277 Ex $4866 Gd $3900
Jubilee Model Grade DH35 . .NiB $4197 Ex $3145 Gd $2176
W/selective single trigger, add $400
W/non-selective single trigger, add $300
W/vent. rib, add $425
W/single trigger, add $455

SHOTGUNS

GRADING: **NiB** = New in Box   **Ex** = Excellent or NRA 95%   **Gd** = Good or NRA 68%

Greifelt Grade No. 1
Over-and-Under Shotgun

W/solid matted-rib bbl.,
.410 & 28 ga . . . . NiB $3844 Ex $3208 Gd $2300
W/ventilated rib, add $125
W/single trigger, add $550

GRADE NO. 3 O/U SHOTGUN
Same general specifications as Grade No. 1 except less fancy
engraving. Manufactured prior to World War II.
W/solid matted-rib bbl.,
except .410 & 28 ga. . . . . NiB $2987 Ex $2379 Gd $1979
W/solid matted-rib bbl.,
.410 & 28 ga. . . . . NiB $5187 Ex $4156 Gd $3110
W/ventilated rib, add $125
W/single trigger, add $450

MODEL 22
HAMMERLESS DOUBLE . . . . NiB $2288 Ex $1843 Gd $1244
Anson & Deeley boxlock. Plain extractors. Double triggers. Gauges:
12 and 16. Bbls.: 28- or 30-inch, M/F choke. Checkered stock and
forend, pistol grip and cheekpiece standard, English-style stock also
supplied. Manufactured since World War II.

MODEL 22E
HAMMERLESS DOUBLE . . . NiB $2866 Ex $2430 Gd $1832
Same as Model 22 except has automatic ejectors.

MODEL 103
HAMMLERLESS DOUBLE . . . NiB $2100 Ex $1821 Gd $1292
Anson & Deeley boxlock. Plain extractors. Double triggers. Gauges:
12 and 16. Bbls.: 28- or 30-inch, M and F choke. Checkered stock
and forend, pistol grip and cheekpiece standard, English-style stock
also supplied. Manufactured since World War II.

MODEL 103E
HAMMERLESS DOUBLE . . . NiB $2200 Ex $1727 Gd $1224
Same as Model 103 except has automatic ejectors.

MODEL 143E O/U SHOTGUN
General specifications same as pre-war Grade No. 1 Over-and-Under, except
this model is not supplied in 28 and .410 ga. or w/32-inch bbls. Model 143E
is not as high quality as the Grade No. 1 gun. Mfd. Since World War II.
W/raised matted rib,
double triggers . . . . NiB $2571 Ex $2068 Gd $1563
W/vent. rib, single
selective trigger . . . . NiB $2860 Ex $2276 Gd $1865

HAMMERLESS DRILLING (THREE-BARREL
COMBINATION GUN) . . . NiB $3677 Ex $3220 Gd $2179
Boxlock. Plain extractors. Double triggers, front single set for rifle
bbl. Gauges: 12, 16, 20; rifle bbl. in any caliber adapted to this type
of gun. 26-inch bbls. Weight: About 7.5 lbs. Auto rear sight operated
by rifle bbl. selector. Checkered stock and forearm, pistol-grip and
cheekpiece standard. Manufactured prior to WW II. Note: Value
shown is for guns chambered for cartridges readily obtainable. If
rifle bbl. is an odd foreign caliber, value will be considerably less.

O/U COMBINATION GUN
Similar in design to this maker's over-and-under shotguns. Gauges:
12, 16, 20, 28, .410; rifle bbl. in any caliber adapted to this type
of gun. Bbls.: 24- or 26-inch, solid matted rib. Weight: From 4.75
to 7.25 lbs. Folding rear sight. Manufactured prior to WWII. Note:
Values shown are for gauges other than .410 w/rifle bbl. Chambered
for a cartridge readily obtainable; if in an odd foreign caliber, value
will be considerably less. .410 ga. increases in value by about 50%.
W/non-automatic ejector . . . NiB $5477 Ex $4651 Gd $3822
W/automatic ejector . . . . . NiB $6055 Ex $5310 Gd $4430

GREIFELT & COMPANY — Suhl, Germany

GRADE NO. 1 O/U SHOTGUN
Anson & Deeley boxlock, Kersten fastening. Auto ejectors. Double
triggers or single trigger. Elaborately engraved. Gauges: 12, 16, 20,
28, .410. Bbls.: 26- to 32-inch, any combination of chokes, vent or
solid matted rib. Weight: 4.25 to 8.25 lbs. depending on ga. and
bbl. length. Straight- or pistol-grip stock, Purdey-type forend, both
checkered. Manufactured prior to World War II.
W/solid matted-rib bbl.,
except .410 & 28 ga. . . . . NiB $3797 Ex $3166 Gd $2280

HARRINGTON & RICHARDSON ARMS COMPANY — Gardner, Massachusetts; now H&R 1871, Inc.

Formerly Harrington & Richardson Arms Co. of Worcester, Mass. One of the oldest and most distinguished manufacturers of handguns, rifles and shotguns, H&R suspended operations on January 24, 1986. In 1987, New England Firearms was established as an independent company producing selected H&R models under the NEF logo. In 1991, H&R 1871, Inc. was formed from the residual of the parent company and then took over the New England Firearms facility. H&R 1871 produced firearms under both their logo and the NEF brand name until 1999, when the Marlin Firearms Company acquired the assets of H&R 1871.

NO. 3 HAMMERLESS
SINGLE-SHOT SHOTGUN. . . . NiB $230 Ex $115 Gd $85
Takedown. Automatic ejector. Gauges: 12, 16, 20, .410. Bbls.: plain, 26- to 32-inch, F choke. Weight: 6.5 to 7.25 lbs. depending on ga. and bbl. length. Plain pistol-grip stock and forend. Discontinued 1942.

NO. 5 STANDARD LIGHTWEIGHT
HAMMER SINGLE. . . . . NiB $227 Ex $120 Gd $90
Takedown. Auto ejector. Gauges: 24, 28, .410. Bbls.: 26- or 28-inch, F choke. Weight: About 4 to 4.75 lbs. Plain pistol-grip stock/forend. Discontinued 1942.

NO. 6 HEAVY BREECH SINGLE-SHOT
HAMMER SHOTGUN . . . . NiB $244 Ex $135 Gd $90
Takedown. Automatic ejector. Gauges: 10, 12, 16, 20. Bbls.: Plain, 28- to 36-inch, F choke. Weight: About 7 to 7.25 lbs. Plain stock and forend. Discontinued 1942.

NO. 7 & 9 BAY STATE SINGLE-SHOT
HAMMER SHOTGUN . . . . NiB $235 Ex $140 Gd $95
Takedown. Automatic ejector. Gauges: 12, 16, 20, .410. Bbls.: Plain 26- to 32-inch, F choke. Weight: 5.5 to 6.5 lbs. depending on ga. and bbl. length. Plain pistol-grip stock and forend. Discontinued 1942.

NO. 8 STANDARD SINGLE-SHOT
HAMMER SHOTGUN . . . . NiB $255 Ex $145 Gd $98
Takedown. Automatic ejector. Gauges: 12, 16, 20, 24, 28, .410. Bbl.: plain, 26- to 32-inch, F choke. Weight: 5.5 to 6.5 lbs. depending on ga. and bbl. length. Plain pistol-grip stock and forend. Made from 1908 to 1942.

MODEL 348 GAMESTER
BOLT-ACTION SHOTGUN . . . NiB $217 Ex $117 Gd $88
Takedown. 12 and 16 ga. Two round tubular magazine, 28-inch bbl, F choke. Plain pistol-grip stock. Weight: About 7.5 lbs. Made from 1949 to 1954.

MODEL 349 GAMESTER DELUXE . . NiB $220 Ex $115 Gd $85
Same as Model 348 except has 26-inch bbl. W/adj. choke device, recoil pad. Made from 1953 to 1955.

MODEL 351 HUNTSMAN
BOLT-ACTION SHOTGUN . . . NiB $239 Ex $200 Gd $125
Takedown. 12 and 16 ga. Two round tubular magazine. Pushbutton safety. 26-inch bbl. w/H&R variable choke. Weight: About 6.75 lbs. Monte Carlo stock w/recoil pad. Made from 1956 to 1958.

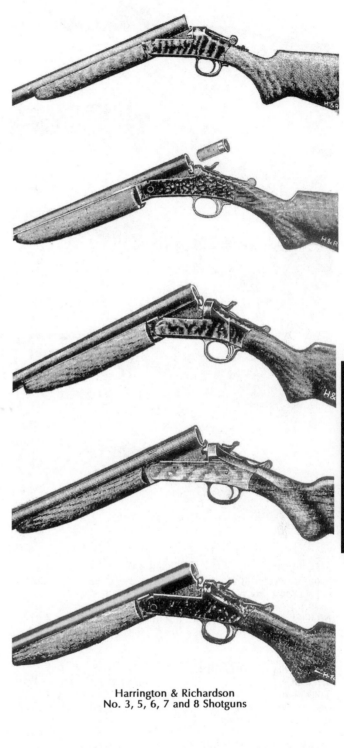

Harrington & Richardson
No. 3, 5, 6, 7 and 8 Shotguns

MODEL 400 PUMP . . . . NiB $335 Ex $254 Gd $180
Hammerless. Gauges: 12, 16, 20. Tubular magazine holds 4 shells. 28-inch bbl., F choke. Weight: About 7.25 lbs. Plain pistol-grip stock (recoil pad in 12 and 16 ga.), grooved slide handle. Made from 1955 to 1967.

SHOTGUNS

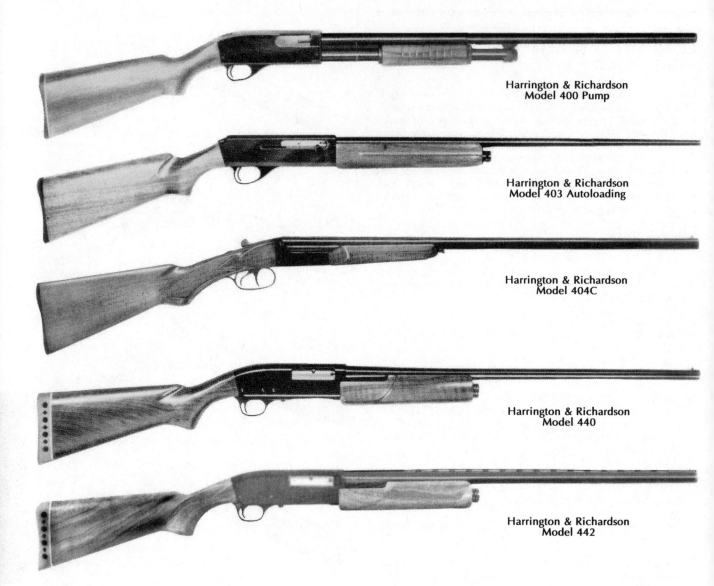

Harrington & Richardson
Model 400 Pump

Harrington & Richardson
Model 403 Autoloading

Harrington & Richardson
Model 404C

Harrington & Richardson
Model 440

Harrington & Richardson
Model 442

MODEL 401 . . . . **NiB $335 Ex $240 Gd $190**
Same as Model 400 on previous page, except has H&R variable choke. Made from 1956-63.

MODEL 402 . . . . **NiB $315 Ex $220 Gd $170**
Similar to Model 400 except .410 ga., weight: About 5.5 lbs. Made from 1959-67.

**MODEL 403 AUTOLOADING
SHOTGUN** . . . . **NiB $338 Ex $300 Gd $210**
Takedown. .410 ga. Tubular magazine holds four shells. 26-inch bbl., F choke. Weight: About 5.75 lbs. Plain pistol-grip stock and forearm. Made in 1964.

**MODEL 404/404C PUMP
SHOTGUN** . . . . **NiB $366 Ex $275 Gd $209**
Boxlock. Plain extractors. Double triggers. Gauges: 12, 20, .410. Bbls.: 28-inch in 12 ga. (M/F choke), 26-inch in 20 ga. (IC/M and .410 (F/F). Weight: 5.5 to 7.25 lbs. Plain walnut-finished hardwood stock and forend on Model 404; 404C checkered. Made in Brazil by Amadeo Rossi from 1969-1972.

MODEL 440 PUMP SHOTGUN . . . **NiB $255 Ex $194 Gd $145**
Hammerless. Gauges: 12, 16, 20. 2.75-inch chamber in 16 ga., 3-inch in 12 and 20 ga. Three round magazine. Bbls.: 26-, 28-, 30-inch; IC, M, F choke. Weight: 6.25 lbs. Plain pistol-grip stock and slide handle, recoil pad. Made from 1968-73.

MODEL 442 PUMP SHOTGUN . . . **NiB $320 Ex $254 Gd $188**
Same as Model 440 except has vent rib bbl., checkered stock and forearm, weight: 6.75 lbs. Made from 1969-73.

ULTRA SLUG SERIES . . . . **NiB $287 Ex $220 Gd $175**
Singel shot 12 or 20 ga w/3-inch chamber w/heavy-wall 24-inch fully rifled bbl. w/scope . Weight: 9 lbs. Walnut-stained Monte Carlo stock, sling swivels, black nylon sling. Made from 1995 to date.

MODEL 1212 FIELD . . . . **NiB $435 Ex $321 Gd $250**
Boxlock. Plain extractors. Selective single trigger. 12 ga., 2.75-inch chambers. 28-inch bbls., IC/IM, vent rib. Weight: 7 lbs. Checkered walnut pistol-gip stock and fluted forearm. Made 1976-80 by Lanber Arms S. A., Zaldibar (Vizcaya), Spain.

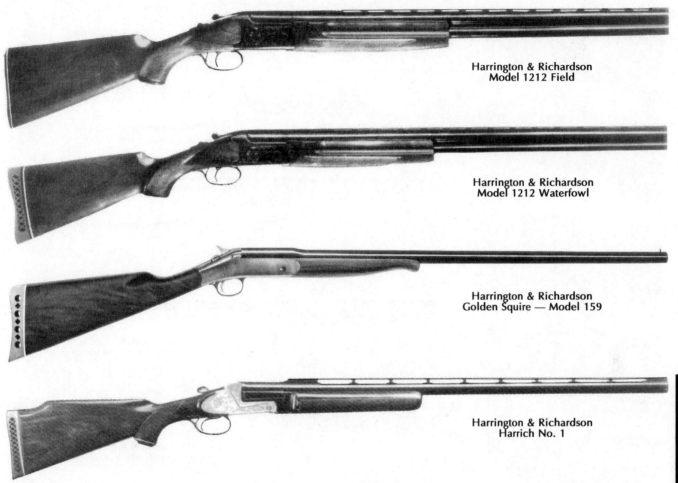

Harrington & Richardson
Model 1212 Field

Harrington & Richardson
Model 1212 Waterfowl

Harrington & Richardson
Golden Squire — Model 159

Harrington & Richardson
Harrich No. 1

SHOTGUNS

MODEL 1212
WATERFOWL GUN . . . . **NiB $544 Ex $368 Gd $277**
Same as Field Gun except chambered for 12-ga, 3-inch mag. shells, has 30-inch bbls., M/F chokes, stock and recoil pad, weight: 7.5 lbs. Made from 1976 to 1980.

MODEL 1908
SINGLE-SHOT SHOTGUN . . . **NiB $244 Ex $177 Gd $100**
Takedown. Automatic ejector. Gauges: 12, 16, 24 and 28. Bbls.: 26- to 32-inch, F choke. Weight: 5.25 to 6.5 lbs. depending on ga. and bbl. length. Casehardened receiver. Plain pistol-grip stock. Bead front sight. Made from 1908 to 1934.

MODEL 1908 .410 (12MM)
SINGLE-SHOT SHOTGUN . . . **NiB $233 Ex $177 Gd $120**
Same general specifications as standard Model 1908 except chambered for .410 or 12mm shot cartridge w/bbl. milled down at receiver to give a more pleasing contour.

MODEL 1915 SINGLE-SHOT SHOTGUN
Takedown. Both non-auto and auto-ejectors available. Gauges: 24, 28, .410, 14mm and 12mm. Bbls.: 26- or 28-inch, F choke. Weight: 4 to 4.75 lbs. depending on ga. and bbl. length. Plain black walnut stock w/semi pistol-grip.
24 ga. . . . . **NiB $390 Ex $275 Gd $190**
28, .410 ga. . . . . **NiB $390 Ex $275 Gd $190**

FOLDING GUN . . . . **NiB $320 Ex $210 Gd $165**
Single bbl. hammer shotgun hinged at the front of the frame, the bbl. folds down against the stock. Light Frame model: gauges — 28, 14mm, .410; 22-inch bbl.; weighs about 4.5 lbs. Heavy Frame model: gauges — 12, 16, 20, 28, .410; 26-inch bbl.; weighs from 5.75 to 6.5 lbs. Plain pistol-grip stock and forend. Disc. 1942.

GOLDEN SQUIRE MODEL 159 SINGLE-BARREL
HAMMER SHOTGUN . . . . . . **NiB $265 Ex $170 Gd $121**
Hammerless. Side lever. Automatic ejection. Gauges: 12, 20. Bbls: 30-inch in 12 ga., 28-inch in 20 ga., both F choke. Weight: About 6.5 lbs. Straight-grip stock w/recoil pad, forearm w/Schnabel. Made from 1964 to 1966.

GOLDEN SQUIRE JR.
MODEL 459 . . . . **NiB $255 Ex $170 Gd $125**
Same as Model 159 except gauges 20 and .410, 26-inch bbl., youth stock. Made in 1964.

HARRICH NO. 1 SINGLE-BARREL
TRAP GUN. . . . . **NiB $1733 Ex $1456 Gd $974**
Anson & Deeley-type locking system w/Kersten top locks and double underlocking lugs. Sideplates engraved w/hunting scenes. 12 ga. Bbls.: 32-, 34-inch; F choke; high vent rib. Weight: 8.5 lbs. Checkered Monte Carlo stock w/pistol-grip and recoil pad, beavertail forearm, of select walnut. Made in Austria 1971 to 1975.

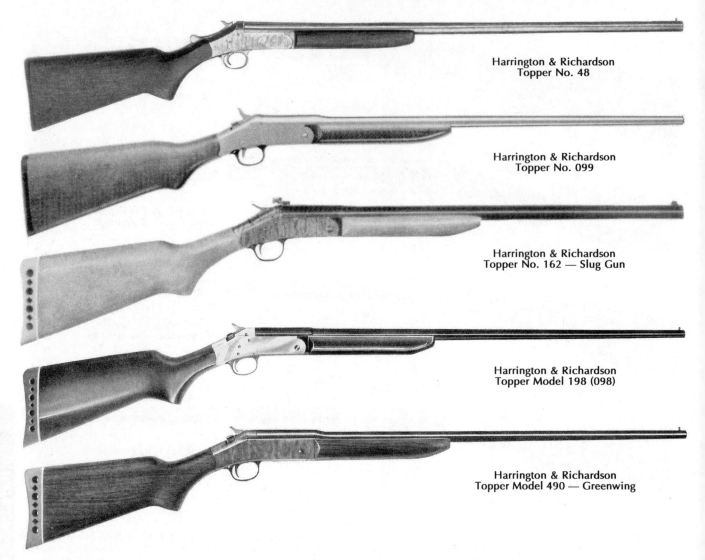

Harrington & Richardson
Topper No. 48

Harrington & Richardson
Topper No. 099

Harrington & Richardson
Topper No. 162 — Slug Gun

Harrington & Richardson
Topper Model 198 (098)

Harrington & Richardson
Topper Model 490 — Greenwing

"TOP RIB"
SINGLE-BARREL SHOTGUN . . . . NiB $335 Ex $265 Gd $190
Takedown. Auto ejector. Gauges: 12, 16 and 20. Bbls.: 28- to 30-inch, F choke w/full-length matted top rib. Weight: 6.5 to 7 lbs. depending on ga. and bbl. length. Black walnut pistol-grip stock (capped) and forend; both checkered. Flexible rubber buttplate. Made during 1930s.

TOPPER NO. 48 SINGLE-BARREL
HAMMER SHOTGUN . . . . . . NiB $280 Ex $195 Gd $145
Similar to old Model 8 Standard. Takedown. Top lever. Auto ejector. Gauges: 12, 16, 20, .410. Bbls.: plain; 26- to 30-inch; M or F choke. Weight: 5.5 to 6.5 lbs. depending on ga. and bbl. length. Plain pistol-grip stock and forend. Made from 1946 to 1957.

TOPPER MODEL 099 DELUXE. . .NiB $244 Ex $155 Gd $110
Same as Model 158 except has matte nickel finish, semipistol grip walnut-finished American hardwood stock; semibeavertail forearm; 12, 16, 20, and .410 ga. Made from 1982 to 1986.

TOPPER MODEL 148 SINGLE-SHOT
HAMMER SHOTGUN . . . . . . NiB $200 Ex $177 Gd $120
Takedown. Side lever. Auto-ejection. Gauges: 12, 16, 20, .410. Bbls.: 12 ga.,30-, 32- and 36-inch; 16 ga., 28- and 30-inch; 20 and .410 ga., 28-inch; F choke. Weight: 5 to 6.5 lbs. Plain pistol-grip stock and forend, recoil pad. Made from 1958 to 1961.

TOPPER MODEL 158 (058) SINGLE-SHOT
HAMMER SHOTGUN . . . . . . NiB $245 Ex $165 Gd $120
Takedown. Side lever. Automatic ejection. Gauges: 12, 20, .410 (2.75-inch and 3-inch shells); 16 (2.75-inch). bbl. length and choke combinations: 12 ga., 36-inch/F, 32-inch/F, 30-inch/F, 28-inch/F or M; .410, 28-inch/F. Weight: about 5.5 lbs. Plain pistol-grip stock and forend, recoil pad. Made from 1962 to 1981. Note: Designation changed to 058 in 1974.

TOPPER MODEL 162
SLUG GUN . . . . NiB $300 Ex $221 Gd $165
Same as Topper Model 158 except has 24-inch bbl., Cyl. bore, w/ rifle sights. Made from 1968 to 1986.

TOPPER MODEL 176 10 GA.
MAGNUM . . . . NiB $280 Ex $185 Gd $145
Similar to Model 158, but has 36-inch heavy bbl. chambered for 3.5-inch 10- ga. Mag. shells, weight: 10 lbs.; stock w/Monte Carlo comb and recoil pad, longer and fuller forearm. Made from 1977 to 1986.

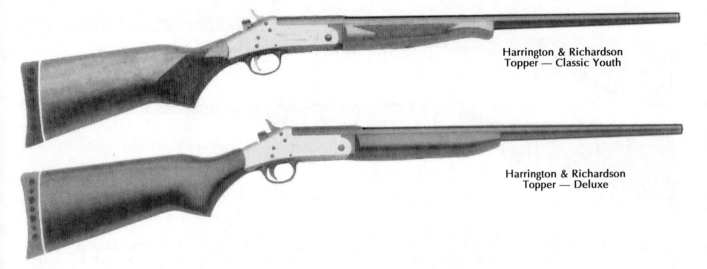

Harrington & Richardson
Topper — Classic Youth

Harrington & Richardson
Topper — Deluxe

TOPPER MODEL 188 DELUXE. . .NiB $265 Ex $200 Gd $145
Same as standard Topper Model 148 except has chromed frame, stock and forend in black, red, yellow, blue, green, pink, or purple colored finish. .410 ga. only. Made from 1958 to 1961.

TOPPER MODEL 198 (098) DELUXE. . .NiB $244 Ex $180 Gd $130
Same as Model 158 except has chrome-plated frame, black finished stock and forend; 12, 20 and .410 ga. Made 1962 to 1981. Note: Designation changed to 098 in 1974.

TOPPER JR. MODEL 480 . . . . NiB $236 Ex $165 Gd $100
Similar to No. 48 Topper except has youth-size stock, 26-inch bbl, .410 ga. only. Made from 1958-61.

TOPPER NO. 488 DELUXE . . . NiB $254 Ex $179 Gd $115
Same as standard No. 48 Topper except chrome-plated frame, black lacquered stock and forend, recoil pad. Disc. 1957.

TOPPER MODEL 490 . . . . NiB $245 Ex $185 Gd $135
Same as Model 158 except has youth-size stock (3 inches shorter), 26-inch bbl.; 20 and 28 ga. (M choke), .410 (F). Made 1962 to 1986.

TOPPER MODEL 490 GREENWING . . .NiB $266 Ex $190 Gd $140
Same as the Model 490 except has a special high-polished finish. Made from 1981 to 1986.

TOPPER JR. MODEL 580 . . . . NiB $210 Ex $166 Gd $100
Same as Model 480 except has colored stocks as on Model 188. Made from 1958 to 1961.

TOPPER MODEL 590 . . . . NiB $210 Ex $166 Gd $100
Same as Model 490 except has chrome-plated frame, black finished stock and forend. Made from 1962 to 1963.

The following models are manufactured and distributed by the reorganized company of H&R 1871, Inc.

MODEL 098 TOPPER CLASSIC YOUTH . . . NiB $200 Ex $155 Gd $100
Same as Topper Junior except also available in 28 ga. and has checkered American black walnut stock/forend w/satin finish and recoil pad. Made from 1991 to date.

MODEL 098 TOPPER DELUXE. . .NiB $200 Ex $155 Gd $100
Same as Model 098 Single Shot Hammer except in 12 ga., 3-inch chamber only. 28-inch bbl.; Mod. choke tube. Made from 1992 to date.

MODEL 098 TOPPER
DELUXE RIFLED SLUG GUN . . .NiB $217 Ex $125 Gd $95
Same as Topper Deluxe Shotgun except has compensated 24-inch rifled slug bbl. Nickel plated receiver and blued bbl. Black finished hardwood stock. Made from 1996 to date.

MODEL 098 TOPPER HAMMER
SINGLE-SHOT SHOTGUN . . . . NiB $165 Ex $115 Gd $88
Side lever. Automatic ejector. Gauges: 12, 20 and .410; 3-inch chamber. Bbls.: 28-inch, (12 ga./M); 26-inch, (20 ga./M); 26-inch (.410/F). Weight: 5 to 6 lbs. Satin nickel receiver, blued bbl. Plain pistol-grip stock and semibeavertail forend w/black finish. Re-Intro. 1992.

MODEL 098 TOPPER JUNIOR . . . NiB $200 Ex $129 Gd $90
Same as Model 098 except has youth-size stock and 22-inch bbl. 20 or .410 ga. only. Made 1991 to date.

MODEL .410 TAMER SHOTGUNNiB $200 Ex $145 Gd $100
Takedown. Topper-style single-shot, side lever action w/auto ejector. Gauge: .410; 3-inch chamber. 19.5-inch bbl. 33 inches overall. Weight: 5.75 lbs. Black polymer thumbhole stock designed to hold 4 extra shotshells. Matte nickel finish. Made from 1994 to date.

MODEL N.W.T.F. TURKEY MAG
Same as Model 098 Single-Shot Hammer except has 24-inch bbl. chambered 10 or 12 ga. w/3.5-inch chamber w/screw-in choke tube. Weight: 6 lbs. American hardwood stock, Mossy Oak camo finish. Made from 1991 to 1996.
NWTF 10 ga. Turkey Mag (Made 1996) . . . NiB $200 Ex $125 Gd $90
NWTF 12 ga. Turkey Mag (Made 1991-95). . .NiB $200 Ex $125 Gd $90

MODEL N. W. T. F.
YOUTH TURKEY GUN. . . . . . NiB $195 Ex $115 Gd $88
Same as Model N.W.T.F. Turkey Mag except has 22-inch bbl. chambered in 20 ga. w/3-inch chamber and fixed full choke. Realtree camo finish. Made from 1994 to 1995.

MODEL SB1-920
ULTRA SLUG HUNTER. . . . . . NiB $275 Ex $198 Gd $155
Special 12 ga. action w/12 ga. bbl. blank underbored to 20 ga. to form a fully rifled slug bbl. Gauge: 20 w/3 inch chamber. 24-inch bbl. Weight: 8.5 lbs. Satin nickel receiver, blued bbl. Walnut finished hardwood Monte Carlo stock. Made from 1996 to 1998.

SHOTGUNS

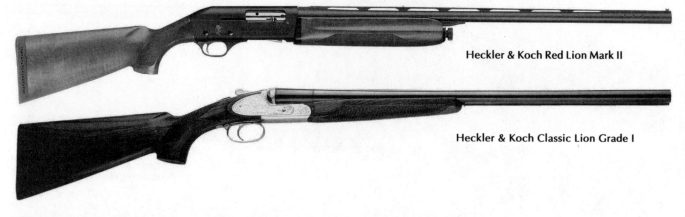

Heckler & Koch Red Lion Mark II

Heckler & Koch Classic Lion Grade I

MODEL ULTRA SLUG HUNTER. . .NiB $275 Ex $219 Gd $175
12 or 20 ga. w/3-inch chamber. 22- or 24-inch rifled bbl. Weight: 9 lbs. Matte black receiver and bbl. Walnut finished hardwood Monte Carlo stock. Made from 1997 to date.

MODEL ULTRA SLUG HUNTER DELUXE . . .NiB $335 Ex $210 Gd $155
Similar to Ultra Slug Hunter model except with compensated bbl. Made from 1997 to date.

HECKLER & KOCH FABARM SHOTGUNS — Oberndorf am Neckar, Germany, and Sterling, Virginia

CLASSIC LION SIDE-BY-SIDE SHOTGUN
12 ga. only. 28- or 30-inch non-ported Tribor bbl. w/3-inch chamber. 46.5 to 48.5-inches overall. Weight: 7 to 7.2 lbs. Five choke tubes; C, IC, M, IM, F. Traditional boxlock design. Oil-finished walnut forearms and stocks w/diamond-cut checkering. Imported from 1999 to date.
Classic Lion Grade I . . . . . . NiB $1456 Ex $1288 Gd $890
Classic Lion Grade II . . .   NiB $2177 Ex $1766 Gd $1292

CAMO LION SEMI-AUTO SHOTGUN. . .NiB $988 Ex $853 Gd $679
12 ga. Only. 24 to 28-inches Tribor bbl. 44.25-48.25-inches overall. Weight: 7-7.2 lbs. 3 inch chamber w/5 choke tubes - C, IC, M, IM, F. Two round mag. Camo covered walnut stock w/rear front bar sights. Imp. 1999 to date.

MAX LION O/U SHOTGUN. . .NiB $1977 Ex $1660 Gd $1000
12 or 20 ga. 26- 28- or 30-inch TriBore system bbls. 42.5-47.25-inches overall. Weight: 6.8-7.8 lbs. 3-inch chamber w/5 choke tubes - C, IC, M, IM, F. Single selective adj. trigger and auto ejectors. Side plates w/high-grade stock and rubber recoil pad. Made from 1999 to date.

RED LION MARK II SEMI-AUTO
SHOTGUN. NiB $954 Ex $700 Gd $544
12 ga. Only. 24- 26- or 28-inch TriBore system bbls. 44.25 to 48.25-inches overall. Weight: 7 to 7.2 lbs. 3-inch chamber w/five choke tubes- C, IC, M, IM, F. Two round magazine. Matte finish w/walnut wood stock. Rubber vented recoil pad w/leather cover. Made from 1999 to date.

SILVER LION O/U SHOTGUN. . . . NiB $1388 Ex $1097 Gd $766
12 or 20 ga. 26- 28- or 30-inch TriBore system bbls. 43.25-47.25 inches overall. 3-inch chamber w/5 choke tubes - C, IC, M, IM, F. Single selective trig. and auto ejectors. Wal. stock w/rubber recoil pad. Made from 1999 to date.

SPORTING CLAY LION
SEMI-AUTO SHOTGUN . . . . NiB $1087 Ex $944 Gd $644
12 ga. only. 28- or 30-inch bbl. w/3-inch chamber and ported Tribore system barrel. Matte finish w/gold plated trigger and carrier release button. Made from 1999 to date.

HERCULES SHOTGUNS

See Listings under "W" for Montgomery Ward.

HEYM SHOTGUNS — Münnerstadt, Germany

MODEL 22S "SAFETY" SHOTGUN/
RIFLE COMBINATION . . . . NiB $3798 Ex $2889 Gd $2250
16 and 20 ga. Cal: .22 Mag., .22 Hornet, .222 Rem., .222 Rem. Mag., 5.6x50R Mag., 6.5x57R, 7x57R, .243 Win. 24-inch bbls. 40 inches overall. Weight: About 5.5 lbs. Single-set trigger. Left-side bbl. selector. Integral dovetail base for scope mounting. Arabesque engraving. Walnut stock. Disc. 1993.

MODEL 55 BF SHOTGUN/
RIFLE COMBO . . . . NiB $7045 Ex $5370 Gd $4398
12, 16 and 20 ga. Calibers: 5.6x50R Mag., 6.5x57R, 7x57R, 7x65R, .243 Win., .308 Win., .30-06. 25-inch bbls., 42 inches overall. Weight: About 6.75 lbs. Black satin-finished, corrosion-resistant bbls. of Krupp special steel. Hand-checkered walnut stock w/long pistol-grip. Hand-engraved leaf scroll. German cheekpiece. Disc. 1988.

J. C. HIGGINS

See Sears, Roebuck & Company.

HUGLU HUNTING FIREARMS — Huglu, Turkey. Imported by Turkish Firearms Corp.

MODEL 101 B 12 AT-DT
COMBO O/U TRAP . . . . NiB $2387 Ex $1885 Gd $1444
Over/Under boxlock. 12 ga. w/3-inch chambers. Combination 30- or 32-inch top single & O/U bbls. w/fixed chokes or choke tubes. Weight: 8 lbs. Automatic ejectors or extractors. Single selective trigger. Manual safety. Circassian walnut Monte Carlo trap stock w/palm-swell grip and recoil pad. Silvered frame w/engraving. Imported from 1993 to 1997.

Heym Model 22S
"Safety" Shotgun/Rifle Combination Gun

Heym Model 55
BF Shotgun/Rifle

MODEL 101 B 12 ST O/U TRAP...NiB $1577 Ex $1377 Gd $937
Same as Model 101 AT-DT except in 32-inch O/U configuration only. Imported from 1994 to 1996.

MODEL 103 B 12 ST O/U
Boxlock. Gauges: 12, 16, 20, 28 or .410. 28-inch bbls. w/fixed chokes. Engraved action w/inlaid game scene and dummy sideplates. Double triggers, extractors and manual safety. Weight: 7.5 lbs. Circassian walnut stock. Imported 1995 to 1996.
Model 103B w/extractors .... NiB $954 Ex $733 Gd $496
28 ga. and .410, add $125

MODEL 103 C 12 ST O/U
Same general specs as Model 103 B 12 S except w/extractors or ejectors. 12 or 20 ga. w/3-inch chambers. Black receiver w/50% engraving coverage. Imported from 1995 to 1097.
Model 103C w/extractors .... NiB $920 Ex $733 Gd $578
Model 103C w/ejectors...... NiB $979 Ex $766 Gd $634

MODEL 103 D 12 ST O/U
Same gen. specs as Mdl. 103 B 12 ST except stand. boxlock. Ext. or eject. 12 or 20 ga. w/3-inch chambers. 80% engraving coverage. Imp. from 1995 to 1997.
Model 103D w/extractors ... NiB $920 Ex $733 Gd $578
Model 103D w/ejectors ..... NiB $979 Ex $766 Gd $634

MODEL 103 F 12 ST O/U
Same as Model 103 B except extractors or ejectors. 12 or 20 ga. only. 100% engraving coverage. Imported from 1996 to 1997.
Model 103F w/extractors ... NiB $1000 Ex $835 Gd $657
Model 103F w/ejectors .... NiB $1154 Ex $1010 Gd $745

MODEL 104 A 12 ST O/U
Boxlock. Gauges: 12, 20, 28 or .410. 28-inch bbls. w/fixed chokes or choke tubes. Silvered, engraved receiver w/15% engraving coverage. Double triggers, manual safety and extractors or ejectors. Weight: 7.5 lbs. Circassian walnut stock w/field dimensions. Imported 1995 to 1997.
Model 104A w/extractors ....NiB $777 Ex $688 Gd $545

Model 104A w/ejectors...... NiB $790 Ex $700 Gd $600
28 ga. and .410, add $150
W/Choke Tubes, add $75

MODEL 200 SERIES DOUBLE
Boxlock. Gauges: 12, 20, 28, or .410 w/3-inch chambers. 28-inch bbls. w/fixed chokes. Silvered, engraved receiver. Extractors, manual safety, single selective trigger or double triggers. Weight: 7.5 lbs. Circassion walnut stock. Imported from 1995 to 1997.
Model 200 (w/15%
engraving coverage, SST) ... NiB $1033 Ex $878 Gd $633
Model 201 (w/30%
engraving coverage, SST) .. NiB $1277 Ex $1100 Gd $955
Model 202 (w/Greener
cross bolt, DT) .... NiB $888 Ex $645 Gd $469
28 ga. and .410, add $125

HIGH STANDARD SPORTING ARMS — East Hartford, Connecticut; formerly High Standard Mfg. Corp. of Hamden, CT

In 1966, High Standard introduced new series of Flite-King Pumps and Supermatic autoloaders, both readily identifiable by the damascened bolt and restyled checkering. To avoid confusion, these models are designated "Series II" in this text. This is not an official factory designation. Operation of this firm was discontinued in 1984.

FLITE-KING FIELD
PUMP—12 GA. .... NiB $256 Ex $180 Gd $110
Hammerless. Magazine holds five rounds. Bbls.: 26-inch IC, 28-inch M or F, 30-inch F choke. Weight: 7.25 lbs. Plain pistol-grip stock and slide handle. Made from 1960 to 1966.

FLITE-KING BRUSH—12 GA... NiB $285 Ex $245 Gd $170
Same as Flite-King Field 2 except has 18- or 20-inch bbl. (cylinder bore) w/rifle sights. Made from 1962 to 1964.

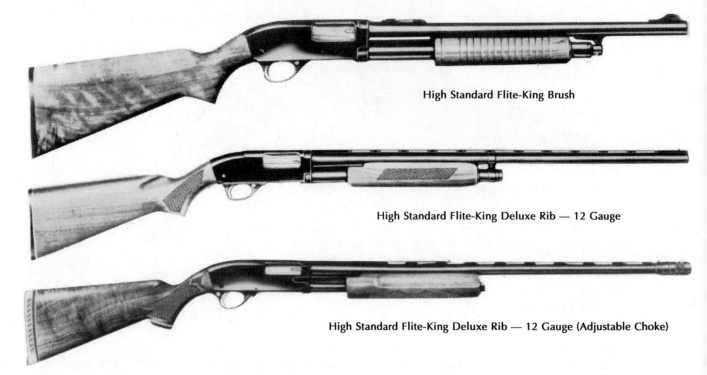

High Standard Flite-King Brush

High Standard Flite-King Deluxe Rib — 12 Gauge

High Standard Flite-King Deluxe Rib — 12 Gauge (Adjustable Choke)

FLITE-KING BRUSH DELUXE . . . NiB $275 Ex $190 Gd $120
Same as Flite-King Brush except has adj. peep rear sight, checkered pistol grip, recoil pad, fluted slide handle, swivels and sling. Not available w/18-inch bbl. Made from 1964 to 1966.

FLITE-KING BRUSH (SERIES II). . .NiB $275 Ex $190 Gd $120
Same as Flite-King Deluxe 12 (II) except has 20-inch bbl., cylinder bore, w/rifle sights. Weight: 7 lbs. Made from 1966 to 1975.

FLITE-KING BRUSH DELUXE (II). . .NiB $290 Ex $200 Gd $135
Same as Flite-King Brush (II) except has adj. peep rear sight, swivels and sling. Made from 1966-75.

FLITE-KING DELUXE 12 GA. (SERIES II)
Hammerless. Five round magazine. 27-inch plain bbls.w/adj. choke. 26-inch IC, 28-inch M or F. 30-inch F choke. Weight: About 7.25 lbs. Checkered pistol-grip stock and forearm, recoil pad. Made from 1966 to 1975.
W/adj. choke . . . . **NiB $245 Ex $170 Gd $110**
W/fixed choke . . . . **NiB $245 Ex $170 Gd $110**

FLITE-KING DELUXE
20, 28, .410 GA. (SERIES II) . . .NiB $255 Ex $178 Gd $120
Same as Flite-King Deluxe 12 (II) except chambered for 20 and .410 ga. 3-inch shell, 28 ga. 2.75-inch shell w/20- or 28-inch plain bbl. Weight: About 6 lbs. Made from 1966 to 1975.

FLITE-KING DELUXE RIB 12 GA. . .NiB $280 Ex $200 Gd $155
Same as Flite-King Field 12 except vent rib bbl. (28-inch M or F. 30-inch F). Checkered stock and forearm. Made from 1961-66.

FLITE-KING DELUXE RIB 12 GA. (II)
Same as Flite-King Deluxe 12 (II) except has vent rib bbl., available in 27-inch w/adj. choke, 28-inch M or F, 30-inch F choke. Made from 1966 to 1975.
W/adj. choke . . . . **NiB $292 Ex $217 Gd $175**
W/fixed choke . . . . **NiB $292 Ex $217 Gd $175**

FLITE-KING DELUXE RIB 20 GA. NiB $265 Ex $198 Gd $125
Same as Flite-King Field 20 except vent-rib bbl. (28 inch M or F), checkered stock and slide handle. Made from 1962 to 1966.

FLITE-KING DELUXE RIB 20, 28, .410 GA. (SERIES II)
Same as Flite-King Deluxe 20, 28, .410 (II) except 20 ga. available w/27-inch adj. choke, 28-inch M or F choke. Weight: about 6.25 lbs. Made from 1966 to 1975.
W/adj. choke . . . . **NiB $265 Ex $198 Gd $125**
W/O adj. choke . . . . **NiB $265 Ex $198 Gd $125**

FLITE-KING DELUXE SKEET GUN
12 GA. (SERIES II). . . . . NiB $544 Ex $423 Gd $318
Same as Flite-King Deluxe Rib 12 (II) except available only w/26-inch vent rib bbl., SK choke, recoil pad optional. Made from 1966 to 1975.

FLITE-KING DELUXE SKEET GUN
20, 28, .410 GA. (SERIES II) . . . NiB $454 Ex $39 Gd $243
Same as Flite-King Deluxe Rib 20, 28, .410 (II) except available only w/26-inch vent-rib bbl., SK choke. Made 1966 to 1975.

FLITE-KING DELUXE TRAP
GUN (SERIES II)). . . . . NiB $338 Ex $265 Gd $129
Same as Flite-King Deluxe Rib 12 (II) except available only w/30-inch vent-rib bbl., F choke; trap-style stock. Made 1966 to 1975.

FLITE-KING FIELD PUMP 20 GA. . .NiB $250 Ex $175 Gd $135
Hammerless. Chambered for 3-inch Magnum shells, also handles 2.75-inch. Magazine holds four rounds. Bbls.: 26-inch IC, 28-inch M or F choke. Weight: About 6 lbs. Plain pistol-grip stock and slide handle. Made from 1961 to 1966.

FLITE-KING PUMP
SHOTGUN 16 GA . . . . **NiB $250 Ex $175 Gd $135**
Same general specifications as Flite-King 12 except not available in Brush, Skeet and Trap Models or 30-inch bbl. Values same as for 12-ga. guns. Made from 1961 to 1965.

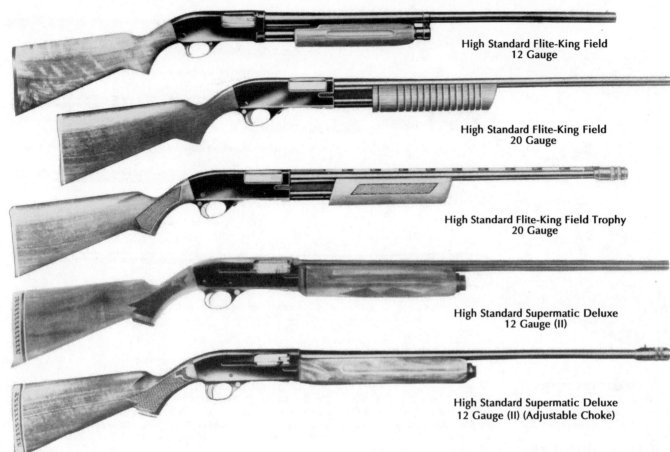

High Standard Flite-King Field
12 Gauge

High Standard Flite-King Field
20 Gauge

High Standard Flite-King Field Trophy
20 Gauge

High Standard Supermatic Deluxe
12 Gauge (II)

High Standard Supermatic Deluxe
12 Gauge (II) (Adjustable Choke)

FLITE-KING PUMP
SHOTGUN (.410) . . . . **NiB $350 Ex $275 Gd $235**
Same general specifications as Flite-King 20 except not available in Special and Trophy Models, or w/other than 26-inch choke bbl. Add $100 to 20 gauge price. Made from 1962 to 1966.

FLITE-KING SKEET
12 GA. . . . . **NiB $330 Ex $225 Gd $170**
Same as Flite-King Deluxe Rib except 26-inch vent rib bbl., w/SK choke. Made from 1962 to 1966.

FLITE-KING SPECIAL 12 GA. . . **NiB $250 Ex $175 Gd $135**
Same as Flite-King Field 12 except has 27-inch bbl. w/adj. choke. Made from 1960 to 1966.

FLITE-KING SPECIAL 20 GA. . . **NiB $250 Ex $175 Gd $135**
Same as Flite-King Field 20 except has 27-inch bbl. w/adj. choke. Made from 1961 to 1966.

FLITE-KING TRAP 12 GA. . . . . . **NiB $330 Ex $225 Gd $140**
Same as Flite-King Deluxe Rib 12 except 30-inch vent rib bbl., F choke, special trap stock w/recoil pad. Made from 1962 to 1966.

FLITE-KING TROPHY 12 GA. . . **NiB $290 Ex $200 Gd $105**
Same as Flite-King Deluxe Rib 12 except has 27-inch vent rib bbl. w/adj. choke. Made from 1960 to 1966.

FLITE-KING TROPHY 20 GA. . . **NiB $290 Ex $200 Gd $105**
Same as Flite-King Deluxe Rib 20 except has 27-inch vent rib bbl. w/adj. choke. Made from 1962 to 1966.

SUPERMATIC DEER GUN . . . . **NiB $345 Ex $165 Gd $100**
Same as Supermatic Field 12 except has 22-inch bbl. (cylinder bore) w/rifle sights, checkered stock and forearm, recoil pad. Weight: 7.75 lbs. Made in 1965.

SUPERMATIC DELUXE 12 GA. (SERIES II)
Gas-operated autoloader. Four round magazine. Bbls.: Plain; 27-inch w/adj. choke (disc. about 1970); 26-inch IC, 28-inch M or F. 30-inch F choke. Weight: About 7.5 lbs. Checkered pistol-grip stock and forearm, recoil pad. Made from 1966 to 1975.
W/adj. choke . . . . **NiB $375 Ex $195 Gd $120**
W/vent. rib, add **$40**

SUPERMATIC DELUXE 20 GA. (SERIES II)
Same as Supermatic Deluxe 12 (II) except chambered for 20 ga. Three inch shell; bbls. available in 27-inch w/adj. choke (disc. about 1970), 26-inch IC, 28-inch M or F choke. Weight: About 7 lbs. Made from 1966 to 1975.
W/adj. choke . . . . **NiB $315 Ex $199 Gd $99**
Vent Rib, add **$20**

SUPERMATIC DELUXE DEER GUN
(SERIES II) . . . . **NiB $345 Ex $165 Gd $100**
Same as Supermatic Deluxe 12 (II) except has 22-inch bbl., cylinder bore, w/rifle sights. Weight: 7.75 lbs. Made from 1966 to 1974.

SUPERMATIC DELUXE DUCK
12 GA. MAGNUM (SERIES II). . . **NiB $335 Ex $227 Gd $140**
Same as Supermatic Deluxe 12 (II) except chambered for 3-inch magnum shells, 3-round magazine, 30-inch plain bbl., F choke. Weight: 8 lbs. Made from 1966 to 1974.

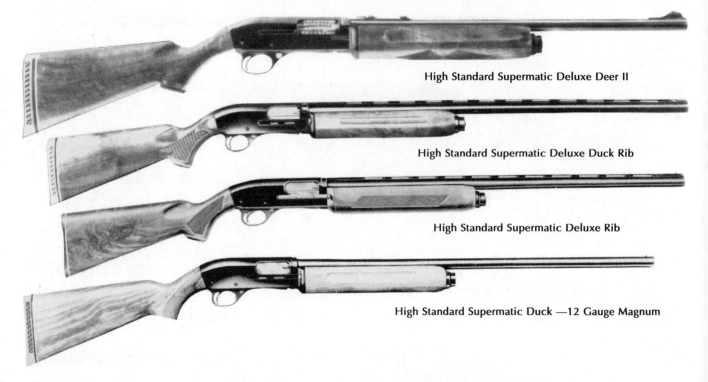

High Standard Supermatic Deluxe Deer II

High Standard Supermatic Deluxe Duck Rib

High Standard Supermatic Deluxe Rib

High Standard Supermatic Duck —12 Gauge Magnum

SUPERMATIC DELUXE RIB
12 GA.. . . . . NiB $335 Ex $227 Gd $140
Same as Supermatic Field 12 except vent rib bbl. (28-inch M or F, 30-inch F), checkered stock and forearm. Made from 1961 to 1966.

SUPERMATIC DELUXE RIB 12 GA. (II)
Same as Supermatic Deluxe 12 (II) except has vent rib bbl.; available in 27-inch w/adj. choke, 28-inch M or F, 30-inch F choke. Made from 1966 to 1975.
W/adj. choke . . . . NiB $335 Ex $227 Gd $140
W/vent. rib, add. $50

SUPERMATIC DELUXE RIB
20 GA.. . . . . NiB $377 Ex $265 Gd $180
Same as Supermatic Field 20 except vent rib bbl. (28-inch M or F), checkered stock and forearm. Made from 1963 to 1966.

SUPERMATIC DELUXE RIB 20 GA. (II)
Same as Supermatic Deluxe 20 (II) except has vent rib bbl. Made from 1966 to 1975.
W/adj. choke . . . . NiB $377 Ex $265 Gd $180
W/ vent. rib, add $50

SUPERMATIC DELUXE SKEET GUN
12 GA. (SERIES II). . . . . NiB $380 Ex $275 Gd $190
Same as Supermatic Deluxe Rib 12 (II) except available only w/26-inch vent rib bbl., SK choke. Made from 1966 to 1975.

SUPERMATIC DELUXE SKEET GUN
20 GA. (SERIES II) . . . . NiB $370 Ex $285 Gd $200
Same as Supermatic Deluxe Rib 20 (II) except available only w/26-inch vent rib bbl., SK choke. Made from 1966 to 1975.

SUPERMATIC DELUXE
TRAP GUN (SERIES II) . . . . . . NiB $315 Ex $239 Gd $177
Same as Supermatic Deluxe Rib 12 (II) except available only w/30-inch vent rib bbl., full choke; trap-style stock. Made 1966 to 1975.

SUPERMATIC DELUXE DUCK RIB
12 GA. MAG. (SERIES II) . . . . NiB $375 Ex $265 Gd $180
Same as Supermatic Deluxe Rib 12 (II) except chambered for 3-inch magnum shells, 3-round magazine; 30-inch vent rib bbl., F choke. Weight: 8 lbs. Made from 1966 to 1975.

SUPERMATIC DUCK 12 GA. MAG. . . NiB $355 Ex $241 Gd $188
Same as Supermatic Field 12 except chambered for 3-inch Magnum shell, 30-inch F choke bbl., recoil pad. Made from 1961 to 1966.

SUPERMATIC TROPHY 12 GA. . . NiB $300 Ex $198 Gd $140
Same as Supermatic Deluxe Rib 12 except has 27-inch vent-rib bbl. w/adj. choke. Made from 1961 to 1966.

SUPERMATIC DUCK RIB 12 GA. MAG. . . NiB $355 Ex $241 Gd $188
Same as Supermatic Duck 12 Magnum except has vent rib bbl., checkered stock and forearm. Made from 1961 to 1966.

SUPERMATIC FIELD AUTOLOADING
SHOTGUN 12 GA. . . . . NiB $270 Ex $197 Gd $110
Gas-operated. Magazine holds four rounds. Bbls.: 26-inch IC, 28-inch M or F choke, 30-inch F choke. Weight: About 7.5 lbs. Plain pistol-grip stock and forearm. Made from 1960 to 1966.

SUPERMATIC FIELD AUTOLOADING
SHOTGUN 20 GA.. . . . . NiB $290 Ex $217 Gd $156
Gas-operated. Chambered for 3-inch mag. shells, also handles 2.75-inch. Magazine holds three rounds. Bbls.: 26-inch IC, 28-inch M or F choke. Weight: About 7 lbs. Plain pistol-grip stock and forearm. Made from 1963 to 1966.

SUPERMATIC SHADOW AUTOMATIC. . . NiB $455 Ex $265 Gd $200
Gas-operated. Ga.: 12, 20, 2.75- or 3-inch chamber in 12 ga., 3-inch in 20 ga. Mag. holds four 2.75-inch shells, three 3-inch. Bbls.: Full-size airflow rib; 26-inch (IC or SK choke), 28-inch (M, IM or F), 30-inch (trap or F choke), 12-ga. 3-inch Mag. available only in 30-inch F choke; 20 ga. not available in 30-inch. Weight: 12 ga., 7 lbs. Checkered walnut stock and forearm. Made 1974 to 1975 by Caspoll Int'l., Inc., Tokyo.

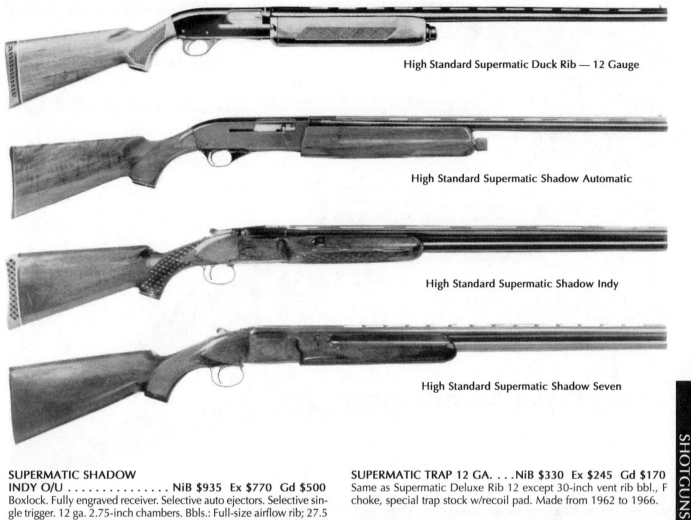

High Standard Supermatic Duck Rib — 12 Gauge

High Standard Supermatic Shadow Automatic

High Standard Supermatic Shadow Indy

High Standard Supermatic Shadow Seven

SUPERMATIC SHADOW

INDY O/U . . . . NiB $935 Ex $770 Gd $500
Boxlock. Fully engraved receiver. Selective auto ejectors. Selective single trigger. 12 ga. 2.75-inch chambers. Bbls.: Full-size airflow rib; 27.5 inch both SK choke, 29.75-inch IM/F or F/F. Weight: W/29.75-inch bbls., 8 lbs. 2 oz. Pistol-grip stock w/recoil pad, ventilated forearm, skip checkering. Made 1974 to 1975 by Caspoll Int'l., Inc., Tokyo.

SUPERMATIC SHADOW SEVEN. . .NiB $755 Ex $533 Gd $400
Same general specifications as Shadow Indy except has conventional vent rib, less elaborate engraving, standard checkering forearm is not vented, no recoil pad. 27.5-inch bbls.; also available in IC/M, M/F choke. Made from 1974 to 1975.

SUPERMATIC SKEET 12 GA. . . NiB $344 Ex $245 Gd $177
Same as Supermatic Deluxe Rib 12 except 26-inch vent-rib bbl. w/ SK choke. Made from 1962 to 1966.

SUPERMATIC SKEET 20 GA. . . NiB $390 Ex $277 Gd $217
Same as Supermatic Deluxe Rib 20 except 26-inch vent-rib bbl. w/ SK choke. Made from 1964 to 1966.

SUPERMATIC SPECIAL 12 GA. . . NiB $290 Ex $190 Gd $145
Same as Supermatic Field 12 except has 27-inch bbl. w/adj. choke. Made from 1960 to 1966.

SUPERMATIC SPECIAL 20 GA. . .NiB $315 Ex $220 Gd $145
Same as Supermatic Field 20 except has 27-inch bbl. w/adj. choke. Made from 1963 to 1966.

SUPERMATIC TRAP 12 GA. . . .NiB $330 Ex $245 Gd $170
Same as Supermatic Deluxe Rib 12 except 30-inch vent rib bbl., F choke, special trap stock w/recoil pad. Made from 1962 to 1966.

SUPERMATIC TROPHY 20 GA. . .NiB $360 Ex $275 Gd $190
Same as Supermatic Deluxe Rib 20 except has 27-inch vent rib bbl. w/adj. choke. Made from 1963 to 1966.

HOLLAND & HOLLAND, LTD. —
London, England

BADMINTON HAMMERLESS DOUBLE-BARREL SHOTGUN, ORIGINAL NO. 2 GRADE
General specifications same as Royal Model except without self-opening action. Made as a game gun or pigeon and wildfowl gun. Introduced in 1902. Disc.
W/double triggers. . . NiB $27,875 Ex $22,500 Gd $18,975
W/single trigger . . . . NiB $28,875 Ex $24,000 Gd $19,600
20 ga., add. 25%
28 ga., add. 40%
.410, add 65%

CENTENARY MODEL HAMMERLESS DOUBLE-BARREL SHOTGUN
Lightweight (5.5 lbs.). 12 ga. game gun designed for 2-inch shell. Made in four grades — Model Deluxe, Royal, Badminton, Dominion. Values: Add 35% to prices shown for standard guns in those grades. Disc. 1962.

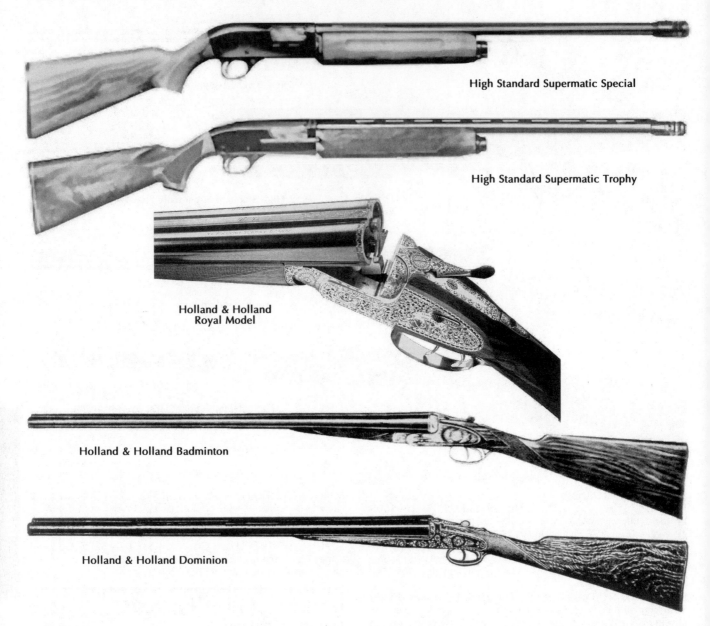

High Standard Supermatic Special

High Standard Supermatic Trophy

Holland & Holland
Royal Model

Holland & Holland Badminton

Holland & Holland Dominion

DOMINION MODEL HAMMERLESS
DOUBLE-BBL. SHOTGUN . . . NiB $7355 Ex $6121 Gd $3896
Game Gun. Sidelock. Auto ejectors. Double triggers. Gauges: 12, 16, 20. bbls. 25- to 30-inch, any standard boring. Checkered stock and forend, straight grip standard. Disc. 1967.

DELUXE HAMMERLESS DOUBLE
Same as Royal Model except has special engraving and exhibition grade stock and forearm. Currently manufactured.
W/double triggers . . . NiB $44,579 Ex $41,960 Gd $34,590
W/single trigger . . . NiB $66,800 Ex $53,980 Gd $40,676

NORTHWOOD MODEL HAMMERLESS
DOUBLE-BARREL SHOTGUN. . . NiB $6154 Ex $4944 Gd $4000
Anson & Deeley system boxlock. Auto ejectors. Double triggers. Gauges: 12, 16, 20, 28 in Game Model; 28 ga. not offered in Pigeon Model; Wildfowl Model in 12 ga. only (3-inch chambers available). Bbls.: 28-inch standard in Game and Pigeon Models, 30-inch in

Wildfowl Model; other lengths, any standard choke combination available. Weight: From 5 to 7.75 lbs. depending on ga. and bbls. Checkered straight-grip or pistol-grip stock and forearm. Disc. 1990.

RIVIERA MODEL
PIGEON GUN . . . . . NiB $32,877 Ex $25,788 Gd $19,900
Same as Badminton Model but supplied w/two sets of bbls., double triggers. Disc. 1967.

ROYAL MODEL HAMMERLESS DOUBLE
Self-opening. Sidelocks hand-detachable. Auto ejectors. Double triggers or single trigger. Gauges: 12, 16, 20, 28 .410. Built to customer's specifications as to bbl. length, chokes, etc. Made as a Game Gun or Pigeon and Wildfowl Gun, the latter having treble-grip action and side clips. Checkered stock and forend, straight grip standard. Made from 1885, disc. 1951.
W/double triggers . . . NiB $39,900 Ex $31,676 Gd $28,800
W/single trigger . . . . NiB $44,980 Ex $42,600 Gd $36,700

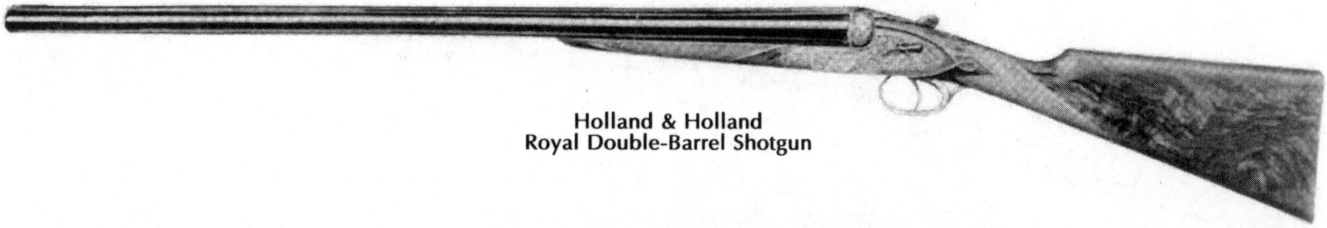

Holland & Holland
Royal Double-Barrel Shotgun

IGA Coach Gun

ROYAL MODEL O/U
Sidelocks, hand-detachable. Auto-ejectors. Double triggers or single trigger. 12 ga. Built to customer's specifications as to bbl. length, chokes, etc. Made as a Game Gun or Pigeon and Wildfowl Gun. Checkered stock and forend, straight grip standard. Note: In 1951 Holland & Holland introduced its New Model Under/Over w/an improved, narrower action body. Disc. 1960.
New model
(double triggers) ...NiB $40,770 Ex $32,550 Gd $21,900
New model
(single trigger) .....NiB $41,800 Ex $33,750 Gd $22,500
Old model
(double triggers) ...NiB $33,970 Ex $27,600 Gd $20,550
Old model
(single trigger) .....NiB $36,975 Ex $29,500 Gd $21,880

SINGLE-SHOT SUPER TRAP GUN
Anson & Deeley system boxlock. Auto-ejector. No safety. 12 ga. Bbls.: Wide vent rib, 30- or 32-inch, w/Extra Full choke. Weight: About 8.75 lbs. Monte Carlo stock w/pistol grip and recoil pad, full beavertail forearm. Models differ in grade of engraving and wood used. Disc.
Standard
grade...............NiB $4890 Ex $2988 Gd $1598
Deluxe
grade...............NiB $7355 Ex $6355 Gd $3559
Exhibition
grade...............NiB $9677 Ex $7355 Gd $4977

SPORTING O/U .... NiB $31,750 Ex $24,776 Gd $17,870
Blitz action. Auto ejectors; single selective trigger. Gauges: 12 or 20 w/2.75-inch chambers. Barrels: 28- to 32-inch w/screw-in choke tubes. Hand-checkered European walnut straight-grip or pistol grip stock, forearm. Made from 1993 to 2003   .

SPORTING O/U
DELUXE.........NiB $38,875 Ex $32,669 Gd $23,670
Same general specs as Sporting O/U except better engraving and select wood. Made from 1993 to date.

HUNTER ARMS COMPANY —
Fulton, New York

FULTON HAMMERLESS DOUBLE-BARREL SHOTGUN
Boxlock. Plain extractors. Double triggers or non-selective single trigger. Gauges: 12 16, 20. Bbls.: 26- to 32-inch various choke combinations. Weight: about 7 lbs. Checkered pistol-grip stock and forearm. Disc. 1948.
W/double triggers .... NiB $775 Ex $450 Gd $375
W/single trigger .... NiB $990 Ex $700 Gd $555

SPECIAL HAMMERLESS DOUBLE-BARREL SHOTGUN
Boxlock. Plain extractors. Double triggers or non-selective single trigger. Gauges: 12,16, 20. Bbls.: 26- to 30-inch various choke combinations. Weight: 6.5 to 7.25 lbs. depending on bbl. length and ga. Checkered full pistol-grip stock and forearm. Disc. 1948.
W/double triggers .... NiB $933 Ex $655 Gd $500
W/single trigger .... NiB $1155 Ex $820 Gd $600

IGA SHOTGUNS — Veranopolis, Brazil.
Imported by Stoeger Industries, Inc. Accokeek, Maryland

COACH GUN
Side-by-side double. Gauges: 12, 20 and .410. 20-inch bbls. w/3-inch chambers. Fixed chokes (standard model) or screw-in tubes (deluxe model). Weight: 6.5 lbs. Double triggers. Ejector and automatic safety. Blued or nickel finish. Hand-rubbed oil-finished pistol grip stock and forend w/hand checkering (hardwood on standard model or Brazilian walnut (deluxe). Imported from 1983 to 2000.
Standard Coach Gun (blued finish)NiB $400 Ex $295 Gd $200
Standard Coach Gun (nickel finish)NiB $465 Ex $377 Gd $259
Standard Coach Gun
(engraved stock)...........NiB $445 Ex $335 Gd $225
Deluxe Coach Gun (intro. 1997)...NiB $400 Ex $290 Gd $195
W/choke tubes................................$75

SHOTGUNS

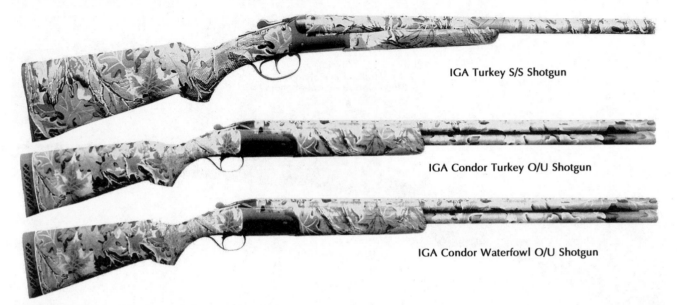

IGA Turkey S/S Shotgun

IGA Condor Turkey O/U Shotgun

IGA Condor Waterfowl O/U Shotgun

CONDOR I O/U SINGLE-TRIGGER SHOTGUN

Gauges: 12 or 20. 26- or 28-inch bbls. of chrome-molybdenum steel. Chokes: Fixed — M/F or IC/M; screw-in choke tubes (12 and 20 ga.). Three inch chambers. Weight: 6.75 to 7 lbs. Sighting rib w/ anti-glare surface. Hand-checkered hardwood pistol-grip stock and forend. Imported from 1983 to 1985.

W/fixed choke . . . . NiB $420 Ex $377 Gd $210
W/screw-in tubes . . . . NiB $510 Ex $441 Gd $350

CONDOR II O/U DOUBLE-TRIGGER

SHOTGUN. . . . . NiB $477 Ex $365 Gd $290
Same general specifications as the Condor I O/U except w/double triggers and fixed chokes only; 26-inch bbls., IC/M; 28-inch bbls., M/F.

CONDOR SUPREME. . . . . . . NiB $655 Ex $545 Gd $477

Same general specifications as Condor I except upgraded w/fine-checkered Brazilian walnut buttstock and forend, a matte-laquered finish, and a massive monoblock that joins the bbls. in a solid one-piece assembly at the breech end. Bbls. w/recessed interchangeable choke tubes formulated for use w/steel shot. Automatic ejectors. Imported from 1995 to 2000.

CONDOR TURKEY MODEL

O/U SHOTGUN . . . . NiB $755 Ex $600 Gd $445
12 gauge only. 26-inch vent-rib bbls. w/3-inch chambers fitted w/ recessed interchangeable choke tubes. Weight: 8 lbs. Mechanical single trigger. Ejectors and automatic safety. Advantage camouflage on stock and bbls. Made from 1997 to 2000.

CONDOR WATERFOWL MODEL . . . NiB $770 Ex $605 Gd $475

Similar to Condor Turkey-Advantage camo model except w/30-inch bbls. Made from 1998 to 2000.

DELUXE HUNTER CLAYS

SHOTGUN. . . . . .NiB $700 Ex $552 Gd $435
Same general specifications and values as IGA Condor Supreme. Imported from 1997 to 1999.

MODEL 2000 SHOTGUN . . . . NiB $500 Ex $379 Gd $290

Gauge: 12 w/3-inch chambers. 26- or 28-inch bbls. of chrome-molybdenum steel w/screw-in choke tubes. Extractors. Manual safety. (Mechanical triggers.) Weight: 7 lbs. Checkered Brazilian hardwood stock w/oil finish. Imported from 1992 to 1995.

REUNA SINGLE-SHOT SHOTGUN

Visible hammer. Under-lever release. Gauges: 12, 20 and .410; 3-inch chambers. 26- or 28-inch bbls. w/fixed chokes or screw-in choke tubes (12 ga. only). Extractors. Weight: 5.25 to 6.5 lbs. Plain Brazilian hardwood stock and semi-beavertail forend. Imported from 1992 to1998.

W/fixed choke . . . . NiB $210 Ex $155 Gd $90
W/choke tubes . . . . NiB $275 Ex $190 Gd $145

UPLANDER SIDE-BY-SIDE SHOTGUN

Gauges: 12, 20, 28 and .410. 26- or 28-inch bbls. of chrome-molybdenum steel. Various fixed-choke combinations; screw-in choke tubes (12 and 20 ga.). Three inch chambers (2.75-inch in 28 ga.). Weight: 6.25 to 7 lbs. Double triggers. Automatic safety. Matte-finished solid sighting rib. Hand checkered pistol-grip or straight stock and forend w/hand-rubbed, oil-finish. Imported from 1997 to 2000.

Upland w/fixed chokes. . . . . NiB $390 Ex $275 Gd $225
Upland w/screw-in tubes . . . . NiB $420 Ex $345 Gd $290
English model (straight grip) . . NiB $500 Ex $395 Gd $290
Ladies model . . . . NiB $477 Ex $365 Gd $300
Supreme model . . . . NiB $610 Ex $477 Gd $325
Youth model . . . . NiB $477 Ex $345 Gd $270

UPLANDER TURKEY MODEL

DOUBLE-BARREL SHOTGUN . . . NiB $588 Ex $440 Gd $379
12 gauge only. 24-inch solid rib bbls. w/3-inch chambers choked F&F. Weight: 6.75 lbs. Double triggers. Automatic safety. Advantage camouflage on stock and bbls. Made from 1997 to 2000.

ITHACA GUN COMPANY — King Ferry (formerly Ithaca), New York; Ithaca Acquisition Corp./Ithaca Gun Co.

MODEL 37 BICENTENNIAL

COMMEMORATIVE . . . . NiB $645 Ex $553 Gd $445
Limited to issue of 1976. Similar to Model 37 Supreme except has special Bicentennial design etched on receiver, fancy walnut stock and slide handle. Serial numbers U.S.A. 0001 to U.S.A. 1976. Originally issued w/presentation case w/cast-pewter belt buckle. Made in 1976. Best value is for gun in new, unfired condition.

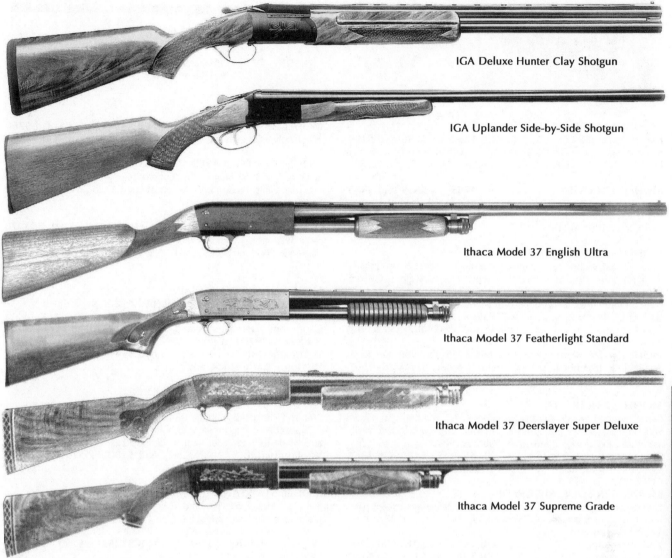

IGA Deluxe Hunter Clay Shotgun

IGA Uplander Side-by-Side Shotgun

Ithaca Model 37 English Ultra

Ithaca Model 37 Featherlight Standard

Ithaca Model 37 Deerslayer Super Deluxe

Ithaca Model 37 Supreme Grade

SHOTGUNS

MODEL 37 DEERSLAYER DELUXE

Formerly "Model 87 Deerslayer Deluxe" reintroduced under the original Model 37 designation w/the same specifications. Available w/smooth bore or rifled bbl. Reintroduced 1996. Disc.

Deluxe model (smoothbore) . . NiB $575 Ex $490 Gd $335
Deluxe model (rifled bbl.). . . . NiB $608 Ex $522 Gd $370

MODEL 37 DEERSLAYER II. . . NiB $608 Ex $522 Gd $370

Gauges: 12 or 20 ga. Five round capacity. 20- or 25-inch rifled bbl. Weight: 7 lbs. Monte Carlo checkered walnut stock and forearm. Receiver drilled and tapped for scope mount. Made 1996 to 2000.

MODEL 37 DEERSLAYER STANDARD. . . NiB $355 Ex $280 Gd $225

Same as Model 37 Standard except has 20- or 26-inch bbl. bored for rifled slugs, rifle-type open rear sight and ramp front sight. Weight: 5.75 to 6.5 lbs. depending on ga. and bbl. length. Made from 1959-86.

MODEL 37 DEERSLAYER

SUPER DELUXE . . . . NiB $465 Ex $344 Gd $220
Formerly "Deluxe Deerslayer." Same as Model 37 Standard Deerslayer except has stock and slide handle of fancy walnut. Made 1962 to 1986.

MODEL 37 ENGLISH ULTRALIGHT. . . NiB $635 Ex $500 Gd $400

Same general specifications as Model 37 Ultralite except straight buttstock, 25-inch Hot Forged vent-rib bbl. Made 1984 to 1987.

MODEL 37 FEATHERLIGHT STANDARD GRADE
SLIDE-ACTION REPEATING SHOTGUN

Adaptation of the earlier Remington Model 17, a Browning design patented in 1915. Hammerless. Takedown. Gauges: 12, 16 (disc. 1973), 20. Four round magazine. Bbl. lengths: 26-, 28-, 30-inch (the latter in 12 ga. only); standard chokes. Weight: From 5.75 to 7.5 lbs. depending on ga. and bbl. length. Checkered pistol-grip stock and slide handle. Some guns made in the 1950s and 1960s have grooved slide handle; plain or checkered pistol-grip. Made 1937 to 1984.

Standard model w/checkered
pistol grip. . . . . NiB $675 Ex $390 Gd $300
W/plain stock. . . . . NiB $325 Ex $229 Gd $190
Mdl 37D Deluxe (1954-77). . . NiB $675 Ex $390 Gd $300
Mdl 37DV Deluxe vent rib (1962-84) . . . NiB $675 Ex $390 Gd $300
Mdl 37R Deluxe
solid rib (1955-61) . . . . NiB $675 Ex $390 Gd $300
Mdl 37V Standard
vent rib (1962-84) . . . . NiB $315 Ex $244 Gd $148

**Ithaca Model 51
Deluxe Trap**

MODEL 37 FIELD GRADE
MAG. W/TUBES . . . . NiB $355 Ex $298 Gd $199
Same general specifications as Model 37 Featherlight except 32-inch bbl. and detachable choke tubes. Vent rib bbl. Made 1984 to 1987.

MODEL 37 CLASSIC . . . . NiB $755 Ex $555 Gd $465
Ggs: 12 or 20 ga. 20- or 28-inch vent rib bbl. w/choke tubes. Knuckle-cut receiver and orig. style "ring-tail" forend. Lim. prod. Made from 1998 to 2005.

MODEL 37 $1000 GRADE
Custom built, elaborately engraved and inlaid w/gold, hand-finished working parts, stock and forend of select figured walnut. General specifications same as standard Model 37. Note: Designated The $1000 Grade prior to World War II. Made 1937 to 1967.
$1000 grade . . . . NiB $5988 Ex $4776 Gd $3987
$5000 grade . . . . NiB $5588 Ex $4487 Gd $3960

MODEL 37 SUPREME GRADE . . . NiB $955 Ex $588 Gd $535
Available in Skeet or Trap Gun, similar to Model 37T. Made 1967-86 and 1997. Subtract $225 for newer models.

MODEL 37 ULTRALITE
Same general specifications as Model 37 Featherlight except streamlined forend, gold trigger, Sid Bell grip cap and vent rib. Weight: 5 to 5.75 lbs. Made from 1984 to 1987.
Standard . . . . NiB $559 Ex $400 Gd $363
W/choke tubes, add $150

MODEL 37R SOLID RIB GRADE
Same general specifications as the Model 37 Featherlight except has a raised solid rib, adding about .25 pounds of weight. Made 1937 to 1967.
W/checkered grip
and slide handle . . . . NiB $400 Ex $310 Gd $200
W/plain stock . . . . NiB $292 Ex $195 Gd $145

MODEL 37S SKEET GRADE . . . NiB $565 Ex $455 Gd $335
Same general specifications as the Model 37 Featherlight except has vent rib and large extension-type forend; weight: About .5 lb. more. Made from 1937 to 1955.

MODEL 37T TARGET GRADE . . NiB $545 Ex $376 Gd $255
Same general specifications as Model 37 Featherlight except has vent-rib bbl., checkered stock and slide handle of fancy walnut (choice of skeet- or trap-style stock). Note: This model replaced Model 37S Skeet and Model 37T Trap. Made from 1955- to 191.

MODEL 37T TRAP GRADE . . . NiB $545 Ex $376 Gd $255
Same gen. specs. as Mdl. 37S except has straighter trap-style stock of select walnut, recoil pad; weight: About .5 lb. more. Made 1937-55.

MODEL 37 TURKEYSLAYER
Gauges: 12 ga. (Standard) or 20 ga. (youth). Slide action. 22-inch bbl. Extended choke tube. Weight: 7 lbs. Advantage camouflage or Realtree pattern. Made from 1996 to 2005.
Standard model . . . . NiB $425 Ex $260 Gd $190
Youth model(intro. 1998) . . . . NiB $555 Ex $456 Gd $345

MODEL 37 WATERFOWLER . . . NiB $490 Ex $375 Gd $260
12 ga. only w/28-inch bbl. Wetlands camouflage. Made 1998 to 2005.

MODEL 51 DEERSLAYER . . . . NiB $400 Ex $279 Gd $200
Same as Model 51 Standard except has 24-inch plain bbl. w/slug boring, rifle sights, recoil pad. Weight: About 7.25 lbs. Made from 1972 to 1984.

MODEL 51 SUPREME SKEET GRADE . . NiB $525 Ex $390 Gd $270
Same as Model 51 Standard except 26-inch vent-rib bbl. only, SK choke, skeet-style stock, semi-fancy wood. Weight: About 8 lbs. Made from 1970 to 1987.

MODEL 51 SUPREME TRAP
Same as Model 51 Standard except 12 ga. only, 30-inch bbl. w/ broad floating rib, F choke, trap-style stock w/straight or Monte Carlo comb, semifancy wood, recoil pad. Weight: About 8 lbs. Made from 1970 to 1987.
W/straight stock . . . . NiB $544 Ex $390 Gd $295
W/Monte Carlo stock, add $75

MODEL 51 FEATHERLITE STANDARD
Gas-operated. Gauges: 12, 20. Three round. Bbls.: Plain or vent rib, 30-inch F choke (12 ga. only), 28-inch F or M, 26-inch IC. Weight: 7.25-7.75 lbs. depending on ga. and bbl. Checkered pistol-grip stock, forearm. Made 1970 to 1980. Avail. in 12 and 20 ga., 28-inch M choke only.
W/plain barrel . . . . NiB $300 Ex $197 Gd $121
W/vent rib, add $65

MODEL 51A STANDARD MAGNUM
Same as Model 51 Standard except has 3-inch chamber, handles Magnum shells only; 30-inch bbl. in 12 ga., 28-inch in 20 ga., F or M choke, stock w/recoil pad. Weight: 7.75-8 lbs. Made 1972 to 1982.
W/plain bbl. (disc. 1976) . . . . NiB $375 Ex $290 Gd $200
W/camo finish, add $65

MODEL 51A TURKEY GUN . . . NiB $455 Ex $300 Gd $217
Same general specifications as standard Model 51 Magnum except 26-inch bbl. and matte finish. Disc. 1986.

MODEL 66 LONG TOM . . . . . NiB $210 Ex $155 Gd $100
Same as Model 66 Standard except has 36-inch F choke bbl., 12 ga. only, checkered stock and recoil pad standard. Made 1969 to 1974.

MODEL 66 STANDARD SUPER SINGLE LEVER
Single shot. Hand-cocked hammer. Gauges: 12 (disc. 1974), 20, .410, 3-inch chambers. Bbls.: 12 ga., 30-inch F choke, 28-inch F or M; 20 ga., 28-inch F or M; .410, 26-inch F. Weight: About 7 lbs. Plain or checkered straight-grip stock, plain forend. Made from 1963 to 1978.
Standard model . . . . NiB $220 Ex $115 Gd $90
Vent. rib model (20 ga., 1969-74) . . . NiB $225 Ex $159 Gd $135
Youth model (1965-78) . . . . NiB $250 Ex $179 Gd $130

MODEL 66RS BUCKBUSTER . . . NiB $279 Ex $200 Gd $155
Same as Model 66 Standard except has 22-inch bbl. cylinder bore w/rifle sights, later version has recoil pad. Originally offered in 12 and 20 ga.; the former was disc. in 1970. Made from 1967 to 1978.

Ithaca Model
66RS Buckbuster

Previously issued as the Ithaca Model 37, the Model 87 guns listed below were made available through the Ithaca Acquisition Corp. From 1986-95. Production of the Model 37 resumed under the original logo in 1996.

MODEL 87 DEERLSLAYER SHOTGUN
Gauges: 12 or 20, 3-inch chamber. Bbls.: 18.5-, 20- or 25-inch (w/special or rifled bore). Weight: 6 to 6.75 lbs. Ramp blade front sight, adj. rear. Receiver grooved for scope. Checkered American walnut pistol-grip stock and forearm. Made from 1988 to 1996.

Basic model	NiB $445	Ex $355	Gd $225
Basic Field Combo (w/extra 28-inch bbl.)	NiB $475	Ex $390	Gd $280
Deluxe model	NiB $480	Ex $395	Gd $290
Deluxe Combo (w/extra 28-inch bbl.)	NiB $635	Ex $460	Gd $339
DSPS (8-round model)	NiB $554	Ex $400	Gd $290
Field model	NiB $433	Ex $330	Gd $287
Monte Carlo model	NiB $448	Ex $356	Gd $255
Ultra model (disc. 1991) . .	NiB $500	Ex $398	Gd $325

MODEL 87 DEERSLAYER II
RIFLED SHOTGUN . . . . NiB $600 Ex $433 Gd $310
Similar to Standard Deerslayer except w/solid frame construction and 25-inch rifled bbl. Monte Carlo stock. Made 1988 to 1996.

MODEL 87 ULTRALITE
FIELD PUMP SHOTGUN . . . NiB $490 Ex $387 Gd $260
Gauges: 12 and 20; 2.75-inch chambers. 25-inch bbl. w/choke tube. Weight: 5 to 6 lbs. Made from 1988 to 1990.

MODEL 87 FIELD GRADE
Gauge: 12 or 20.; 3-inch chamber. Five round magazine. Fixed chokes or screw-in choke tubes (IC, M, F). Bbls.: 18.5-inch (M&P); 20- and 25-inch (Combo); 26-, 28-, 30-inch vent rib. Weight: 5 to 7 lbs. Made from 1988 to 1996.

Basic field model (disc. 1993)	NiB $446	Ex $270	Gd $210
Camo model.	NiB $490	Ex $339	Gd $260
Deluxe model.	NiB $505	Ex $340	Gd $280
Deluxe Combo model	NiB $590	Ex $493	Gd $377
English model.	NiB $490	Ex $339	Gd $260
Hand grip model (w/polymer pistol-grip)	NiB $533	Ex $425	Gd $315
M&P model (disc. 1995) . . .	NiB $466	Ex $380	Gd $279
Supreme model.	NiB $720	Ex $589	Gd $400
Turkey model	NiB $445	Ex $365	Gd $256
Ultra Deluxe model (disc. 1992). . .	NiB $400	Ex $356	Gd $260

HAMMERLESS DOUBLE-BARREL SHOTGUNS
Boxlock. Plain extractors, auto ejectors standard on the "E" grades. Double triggers, non-selective or selective single trigger extra. Gauges: Magnum 10, 12; 12, 16, 20, 28, .410. Bbls.: 26- to 32-inch, any standard boring. Weight: 5.75 (.410) to 10.5 lbs. (Magnum 10). Checkered pistol-grip stock and forearm standard. Higher grades differ from Field Grade in quality of workmanship, grade of wood, checkering, engraving, etc.; general specifications are the same. Ithaca doubles made before 1925 (serial number 425,000) the rotary bolt and a stronger frame were adopted. Values shown are for this latter type; earlier models valued about 50% lower. Smaller gauge guns may command up to 75% higher. Disc. 1948.

Field grade.	NiB $1088	Ex $900	Gd $677
No. 1 grade	NiB $1377	Ex $1099	Gd $890
No. 2 grade	NiB $2480	Ex $2077	Gd $1100
No. 3 grade	NiB $2456	Ex $1866	Gd $1376
No. 4E grade (ejector). . .	NiB $6225	Ex $3688	Gd $2977
No. 5E grade (ejector). . .	NiB $5235	Ex $3767	Gd $4400

Extras:

Magnum 10 or 12 ga. (in other than the four highest grades), add	20%
Automatic ejectors (grades No. 1, 2, 3, w/ejectors designated No. 1E, 2E, 3E), add	35%
Selective single trigger, add.	$250
Non-selective single trigger, add	$200
Beavertail forend (Field No. 1 or 2), add	$200
Beavertail forend (No. 3 or 4), add	$200
Beavertail forend (No. 5, 7 or $2000 grade), add . . .	$200
Ventilated rib (No. 4, 5, 7 or $2000 grade), add. . . .	$400
Ventilated rib (lower grades), add	$250

LSA-55 TURKEY GUN . . . . . NiB $935 Ex $700 Gd $590
Over/under shotgun/rifle combination. Boxlock. Exposed hammer. Plain extractor. Single trigger. 12 ga./222 Rem. 24.5-inch ribbed bbls. (rifle bbl. has muzzle brake). Weight: About 7 lbs. Folding leaf rear sight, bead front sight. Checkered Monte Carlo stock and forearm. Made 1970 to 1977 by Oy Tikkakoski AB, Finland.

MAG-10 AUTOMATIC SHOTGUN
Gas-operated. 10 ga. 3.5-inch Magnum. Three round capacity. 32-inch plain (Standard Grade only) or vent-rib bbl. F choke. Weight: 11 lbs., plain bbl.; 11.5 lbs., vent rib. Standard grade has plain stock and forearm. Deluxe and Supreme Grades have checkering, semi-fancy and fancy wood respectively, and stud swivel. All have recoil pad. Deluxe and Supreme grades made 1974 to 191982. Standard Grade intro. in 1977. All grades disc. 1986.

Camo model.	NiB $735	Ex $555	Gd $379
Deluxe grade	NiB $890	Ex $774	Gd $522
Roadblocker.	NiB $855	Ex $740	Gd $533
Standard grade, plain bbl.. .	NiB $744	Ex $610	Gd $477
Standard grade w/vent. rib	NiB $844	Ex $633	Gd $530
Standard grade, w/choke tubes . .	NiB $988	Ex $755	Gd $544
Supreme grade	NiB $1044	Ex $856	Gd $600

SHOTGUNS

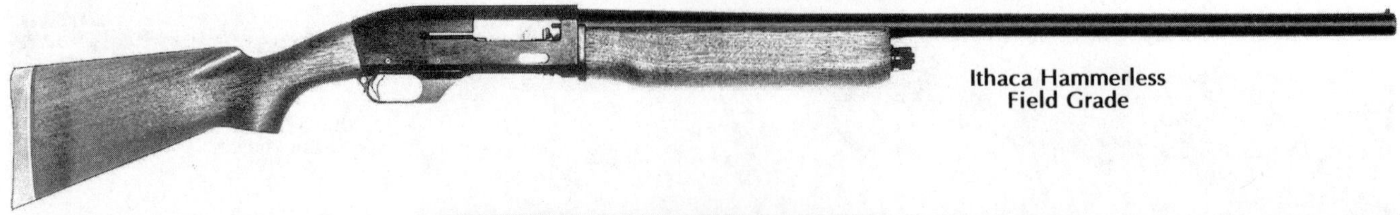

Ithaca Hammerless
Field Grade

Ithaca Hammerless
No. 2

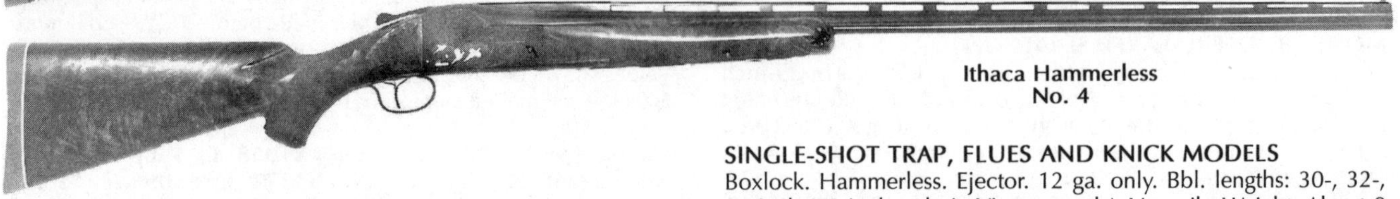

Ithaca Hammerless
No. 4

Ithaca Hammerless
Field Grade

Ithaca Model 5-E

Ithaca Single-Shot Trap
"Dollar Grade"

SINGLE-SHOT TRAP, FLUES AND KNICK MODELS

Boxlock. Hammerless. Ejector. 12 ga. only. Bbl. lengths: 30-, 32-, 34-inch (32-inch only in Victory grade). Vent rib. Weight: About 8 lbs. Checkered pistol-grip stock and forend. Grades differ only in quality of workmanship, engraving, checkering, wood, etc. Flues Model, serial numbers under 400,000, made 1908 to 1921. Triple-bolted Knick Model, serial numbers above 400,000, made since 1921. Victory Model disc. in 1938, No. 7-E in 1964, No. 4-E in 1976, No. 5-E in 1986, Dollar Grade in 1991. Values shown are for Knick Model; Flues models about 50% lower.

Victory grade . . . . NiB $1379 Ex $1100 Gd $925
No. 4-E . . . . NiB $3766 Ex $3470 Gd $1790
No. 5-E . . . . NiB $5000 Ex $4766 Gd $2128
No. 6-E (rare) . . . . .NiB $16,980 Ex $14,700 Gd $10,000
No. 7-E (rare) . . . . NiB $7445 Ex $6000 Gd $4655
$2,000 grade . . . . .NiB $9,500 Ex $8500 Gd $6650
Pre-war $1000 grade . . . . .NiB $10,000 Ex $9577 Gd $6650
Sousa grade (rare) . . . . NiB $14,500+ Ex $12,700+ Gd $9000+

NOTE: *The following Ithaca-Perazzi shotguns were manufactured by Manifattura Armi Perazzi, Brescia, Italy. See also separate Perazzi listings.*

PERAZZI COMPETITION I SKEET . . . . . .NiB $14,877 Ex $13,900 Gd $11,270
Boxlock. Auto ejectors. Single trigger. 12 ga. 26.75-inch vent-rib bbls. SK choke w/integral muzzle brake. Weight: About 7.75 lbs. Checkered skeet-style pistol-grip buttstock and forearm; recoil pad. Made from 1969 to 1974.

PERAZZI COMPETITION
TRAP I O/U . . . . .NiB $14,889 Ex $13,679 Gd $11,650
Boxlock. Auto ejectors. Single trigger. 12 ga. 30- or 32-inch vent-rib bbls. IM/F choke. Weight: About 8.5 lbs. Checkered pistol-grip stock, forearm; recoil pad. Made from 1969 to 1974.

PERAZZI COMPETITION I
TRAP SINGLE BARREL . . . . .NiB $11,770 Ex $9455 Gd $7655
Boxlock. Auto ejection. 12 ga. 32- or 34-inch bbl., vent rib, F choke. Weight: 8.5 lbs. Checkered Monte Carlo stock and beavertail forearm, recoil pad. Made from 1973 to 1978.

PERAZZI COMPETITION IV
TRAP GUN . . . . .NiB $13,890 Ex $11,870 Gd $10,000
Boxlock. Auto ejection. 12 ga. 32- or 34-inch bbl. With high, wide vent rib, four interchangeable choke tubes (Extra Full, F, IM, M). Weight: About 8.75 lbs. Checkered Monte Carlo stock and beavertail forearm, recoil pad. Fitted case. Made from 1977 to 1978.

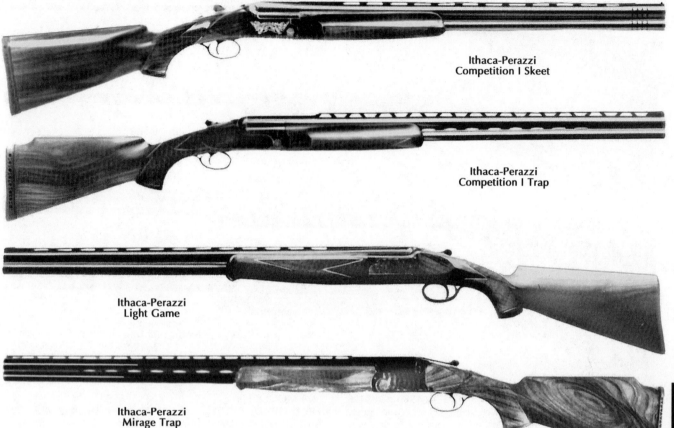

Ithaca-Perazzi
Competition I Skeet

Ithaca-Perazzi
Competition I Trap

Ithaca-Perazzi
Light Game

Ithaca-Perazzi
Mirage Trap

PERAZZI LIGHT GAME
O/U FIELD . . . . NiB $15,800 Ex $14,790 Gd $13,955
Boxlock. Auto ejectors. Single trigger. 12 ga. 27.5-inch vent rib bbls., M/F or IC/M choke. Weight: 6.75 lbs. Checkered field-style stock and forearm. Made from 1972 to 74.

PERAZZI MIRAGE
. . . . NiB $6987 Ex $4677 Gd $2700
Same as Mirage Trap except has 28-inch bbls., M and Extra Full choke, special stock and forearm for live bird shooting. Weight: About 8 lbs. Made from 1973 to 1978.

PERAZZI MIRAGE SKEET
. . . NiB $4350 Ex $3866 Gd $2789
Same as Mirage Trap except has 28-inch bbls. w/integral muzzle brakes, SK choke, skeet-stype stock and forearm. Weight: About 8 lbs. Made from 1973 to 1978.

PERAZZI MIRAGE TRAP
. . . NiB $4365 Ex $3900 Gd $2820
Same general specifications as MX-8 Trap except has tapered rib. Made from 1973 to 1978.

PERAZZI MT-6 SKEET
. . . . NiB $4233 Ex $3380 Gd $2770
Same as MT-6 Trap except has 28-inch bbls. w/two skeet choke tubes instead of Extra Full and F, skeet-style stock and forearm. Weight: About 8 lbs. Made from 1976 to 1978.

PERAZZI MT-6 TRAP COMBO
. . . NiB $5377 Ex $4260 Gd $3100
MT-6 w/extra single under bbl. w/high-rise aluminum vent rib, 32- or 34-inch; seven interchanageable choke tubes (IC through Extra Full). Fitted case. Made from 1977 to 1978.

PERAZZI MT-6
TRAP O/U . . . . NiB $3700 Ex $2566 Gd $2044
Boxlock. Auto selective ejectors. Non-selective single trigger. 12 ga. Barrels separated, wide vent rib, 30-or 32-inch, five interchange-able choke tubes (Extra full, F, IM, M, IC). Weight: About 8.5 lbs. Checkered pistol-grip stock/forearm, recoil pad. Fitted case. Made from 1976 to 1978.

PERAZZI MX
8 TRAP COMBO. . . . . . . NiB $5688 Ex $4355 Gd $2460
MX-8 w/extra single bbl., vent rib, 32- or 34-inch, F choke, forearm; two trigger groups included. Made from 1973 to 1978.

PERAZZI MX-8 TRAP
O/U . . . . NiB $4356 Ex $3879 Gd $2889
Boxlock. Auto selective ejectors. Non-selective single trigger. 12 ga. Bbls.: High vent rib; 30- or 32-inch, IM/F choke. Weight: 8.25 to 8.5 lbs. Checkered Monte Carlo stock and forearm, recoil pad. Made from 1969 to 1978.

PERAZZI SINGLE-BARREL
TRAP GUN. . . . . NiB $3350 Ex $2459 Gd $2000
Boxlock. Auto ejection. 12 ga. 34-inch vent rib bbl., F choke. Weight: Abaout 8.5 lbs. Checkered pistol-grip stock, forearm; recoil pad. Made from 1971 to 1972.

The following Ithaca-SKB shotguns, manufactured by SKB Arms Company, Tokyo, Japan, were distributed in the U.S. by Ithaca Gun Company from 1966-1976. See also listings under SKB.

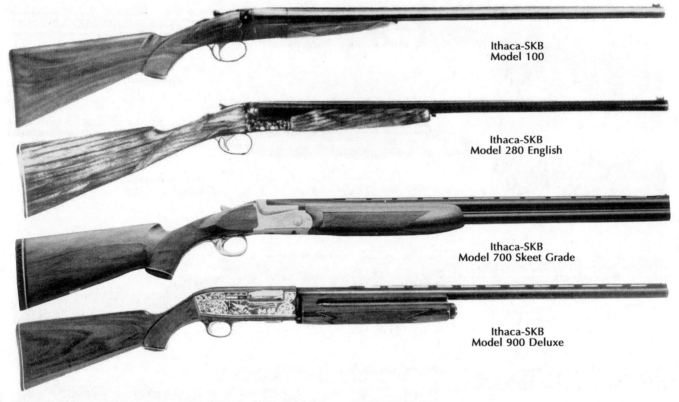

Ithaca-SKB
Model 100

Ithaca-SKB
Model 280 English

Ithaca-SKB
Model 700 Skeet Grade

Ithaca-SKB
Model 900 Deluxe

SKB MODEL 100 SIDE-BY-SIDE . . . NiB $779 Ex $580 Gd $490
Boxlock. Plain extractors. Selective single trigger. Auto safety. Gauges: 12 and 20; 2.75-inch and 3-inch chambers respectively. Bbls.: 30-inch, F/F (12 ga. only); 28-inch, F/M; 26-inch, IC/M (12 ga. only); 25-inch, IC/M (20 ga. only). Weight: 12 ga., about 7 lbs.; 20 ga., about 6 lbs. Checkered stock and forend. Made 1966 to 1976.

SKB MODEL 150 FIELD GRADE . . . NiB $770 Ex $600 Gd $488
Same as Model 100 except has fancier scroll engraving, beavertail forearm. Made from 1972 to 1974.

SKB 200E FIELD GRADE S/S . . . NiB $1077 Ex $767 Gd $580
Same as Model 100 except auto selective ejectors, engraved and silver-plated frame, gold-plated nameplate and trigger, beavertail forearm. Made from 1966 to 1976.

SKB MODEL 200E SKEET GUN . . . NiB $995 Ex $687 Gd $485
Same as Model 200E Field Grade except 26-inch (12 ga.) and 25-inch (20 ga./2.75-inch chambers) bbls., SK choke; nonautomatic safety and recoil pad. Made from 1966 to 1976.

SKB MODEL 200 ENGLISH . . . NiB $1154 Ex $990 Gd $759
Same as Model 200E except has scrolled game scene engraving on frame, English-style straight-grip stock; 30-inch bbls. not available; special quail gun in 20 ga. has 25-inch bbls., both bored IC. Made from 1971 to 1976.

SKB MODEL 300 STANDARD AUTOMATIC SHOTGUN
Recoil-operated. Gauges: 12, 20 (3-inch). Five round capacity. Bbls.: plain or vent rib; 30-inch F choke (12 ga. only), 28-inch F or M, 26-inch IC. Weight: about 7 lbs. Checkered pistol-grip stock and forearm. Made from 1968 to 1972.
W/plain barrel . . . . NiB $1088 Ex $765 Gd $490
20 ga, add 30%

**SKB MODEL 500
FIELD GRADE O/U . . . . NiB $665 Ex $455 Gd $323**
Boxlock. Auto selective ejectors. Selective single trigger. Non-automatic safety. Gauges: 12 and 20; 2.75-inch and 3-inch chambers respectively. Vent-rib bbls.: 30-inch M/F (12 ga. only); 28-inch M/F; 26-inch IC/M. Weight: 12 ga., about 7.5 lbs; 20 ga., about 6.5 lbs. Checkered stock and forearm. Made from 1966 to 1976.

SKB MODEL 500 MAGNUM . . . NiB $639 Ex $455 Gd $344
Same as Model 500 Field Grade except chambered for 3-inch 12 ga. shells, has 30-inch bbls., IM/F choke. Weight: About 8 lbs. Made 1973 to 1976.

SKB MODEL 600 DOUBLES GUN . . NiB $1096 Ex $766 Gd $500
Same as Model 600 Trap Grade except specially choked for 21-yard first target, 30-yard second. Made from 1973 to 1975.

SKB MODEL 600 FIELD GRADE . . NiB $1100 Ex $775 Gd $525
Same as Model 500 except has silver-plated frame, higher grade wood. Made from 1969 to 1976.

SKB MODEL 600 MAGNUM . . . NiB $1125 Ex $800 Gd $550
Same as Model 600 Field Grade except chambered for 3-inch 12 ga. shells; has 30-inch bbls., IM/F choke. Weight: 8.5 lbs. Made from 1969 to 1972.

SKB MODEL 600 SKEET GRADE
Same as Model 500 except also available in 28 and .410 ga., has silver-plated frame, higher grade wood, recoil pad, 26- or 28-inch bbls. (28-inch only in 28 and .410), SK choke. Weight: 7 to 7.75 lbs. depending on ga. and bbl. length. Made from 1966 to 1976.
12 or 20 ga. . . . . NiB $1155 Ex $830 Gd $575
28 ga. or .410 . . . . NiB $1500 Ex $1266 Gd $1077

SKB MODEL 600 SKEET SET . . . NiB $2866 Ex $2249 Gd $1545
Model 600 Skeet Grade w/matched set of 20, 28 and .410 ga. bbls., 28-inch, fitted case. Made from 1970-76.

Ithaca-SKB Century Trap

Ithaca-SKB Century II Trap

Ithaca-SKB Model XL300

SKB MODEL 600
TRAP GRADE O/U . . . . NiB $1055 Ex $700 Gd $533
Same as Model 500 except 12 ga. only, has silver-plated frame, 30- or 32-inch bbls. choked F/F or F/IM, choice of Monte Carlo or straight stock of higher grade wood, recoil pad. Weight: About 8 lbs. Made from 1966 to 1976.

SKB MODEL 680 ENGLISH. NiB $1388 Ex $1055 Gd $775
Same as Model 600 Field Grade except has intricate scroll engraving, English-style straight-grip stock and forearm of extra-fine walnut; 30-inch bbls. not available. Made from 1973 to 1976.

SKB MODEL 700
SKEET COMBO SET . . . . . NiB $3988 Ex $2970 Gd $2175
Model 700 Skeet Grade w/matched set of 20, 28 and .410 ga. bbls., 28-inch fitted case. Made from 1970 to 1971.

SKB MODEL 700 SKEET GRADE. . .NiB $955 Ex $779 Gd $575
Same as Model 600 Skeet Grade except not available in 28 and .410 ga., has more elaborate scroll engraving, extra-wide rib, higher grade wood. Made from 1969 to 1975.

SKB MODEL 700 TRAP GRADE . . .NiB $945 Ex $665 Gd $544
Same as Model 600 Trap Grade except has more elaborate scroll engraving, extra-wide rib, higher grade wood. Made 1969 to 1975.

SKB MODEL 700
DOUBLES GUN . . . . NiB $866 Ex $744 Gd $559
Same as Model 700 Trap Grade except choked for 21-yard first target, 30-yard second target. Made from 1973 to 1975.

SKB MODEL 900
DELUXE AUTOMATIC . . . . . . NiB $475 Ex $359 Gd $255
Same as Model 30 except has game scene etched and gold-filled on receiver, vent rib standard. Made 1968 to 1972.

SKB MODEL 900 SLUG GUN . . .NiB $350 Ex $264 Gd $190
Same as Model 900 Deluxe except has 24-inch plain bbl. w/slug boring, rifle sights. Weight: About 6.5 lbs. Made 1970 to 1972.

SKB CENTURY SINGLE-SHOT
TRAP GUN. . . . . NiB $689 Ex $500 Gd $356
Boxlock. Auto ejector. 12 ga. Bbls.: 32- or 34-inch, vent rib, F choke.

Weight: About 8 lbs. Checkered walnut stock w/pistol grip, straight or Monte Carlo comb, recoil pad, beavertail forearm. Made 1973 to 1974.

SKB CENTURY II TRAP . . . . . . NiB $700 Ex $495 Gd $400
Boxlock. Auto ejector. 12 ga. Bbls: 32- or 34-inch, vent rib, F choke. Weight: 8.25 lbs. Improved version of Century. Same general specifications except has higher comb on checkered stock stock, reverse-taper beavertail forearm w/redesigned locking iron. Made from 1975 to 1976.

SKB MODEL XL300 STANDARD AUTOMATIC
Gas-operated. Gauges: 12, 20 (3-inch). Five round capacity. Bbls.: Plain or vent rib; 30-inch F choke (12 ga. only), 28-inch F or M, 26-inch IC. Weight: 6 to 7.5 lbs. depending on ga. and bbl. Checkered pistol-grip stock, forearm. Made from 1972 to 1976.
W/plain barrel . . . . NiB $389 Ex $296 Gd $210
W/ventilated rib . . . . NiB $365 Ex $283 Gd $205

SKB MODEL XL900
DELUXE AUTOMATIC . . . . . . NiB $379 Ex $335 Gd $260
Same as Model XL300 except has game scene finished in silver on receiver, vent rib standard. Made from 1972 to 1976.

SKB MODEL XL
900 SKEET GRADE . . . . NiB $490 Ex $377 Gd $315
Gas-operated. Gauges: 12, 20 (3-inch). Five round tubular magazine. Same as Model XL900 Deluxe except has scrolled receiver finished in black chrome, 26-inch bbl. only, SK choke, skeet-style stock. Weight: 7 or 7.5 lbs. depending on ga. Made from 1972 to 1976.

SKB MODEL XL
900 SLUG GUN . . . . NiB $445 Ex $377 Gd $290
Same as Model XL900 Deluxe except has 24-inch plain bbl. w/slug boring, rifle sights. Weight: 6.5 or 7 lbs. depending on ga. Made from 1972 to 1976.

SKB MODEL
XL900 TRAP GRADE. . . . . NiB $488 Ex $358 Gd $290
Same as Model XL900 Deluxe except 12 ga. only, has scrolled receiver finished in black chrome, 30-inch bbl. only, IM or F choke, trap style w/straight or Monte Carlo comb, recoil pad. Weight: About 7.75 lbs. Made from 1972 to 1976.

SHOTGUNS

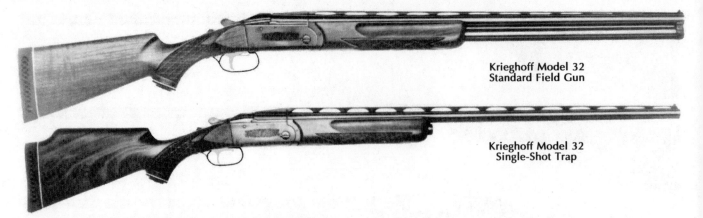

Krieghoff Model 32
Standard Field Gun

Krieghoff Model 32
Single-Shot Trap

IVER JOHNSON ARMS & CYCLE WORKS — Fitchburg, Massachusetts; currently a division of the American Military Arms Corp., Jacksonville, Arkansas

CHAMPION GRADE TOP SNAP

Auto ejector. Gauges: 12,16, 20, 28 and .410. Bbls.: 26- to 36-inch, F choke. Weight: 5.75 to 7.5 lbs. depending on ga. and bbl.length. Plain pistol-grip stock and forend. Extras include checkered stock and forend, pistol-grip cap and knob forend. Known as Model 36. Also made in a Semi-Octagon Breech, Top Matted and Jacketed Breech (extra heavy) models. Made in Champion Lightweight as Model 39 in gauges 24, 28, 32 and .410, .44 and .45 caliber, 12 and 14mm w/same extras. $200; add $100 in the smaller and obsolete gauges. Made from 1909 to 1973.

Standard model . . . . NiB $377 Ex $290 Gd $100
Semi-octagon breech . . . . . . NiB $466 Ex $351 Gd $229
Top matted rib (disc. 1948). . . NiB $398 Ex $297 Gd $195

HERCULES GRADE HAMMERLESS DOUBLE

Boxlock. (Some made w/false sideplates.) Plain extractors and auto ejectors. Double or Miller single triggers (both selective or non-selective). Gauges: 12, 16, 20 and .410. Bbl. lengths: 26- to 32-inch, all chokes. Weight: 5.75 to 7.75 lbs. depending on ga. and bbl. length. Checkered stock and forend. Straight grip in .410 ga. w/ both 2.5- and 3-inch chambers. Extras include Miller single trigger, Jostam Anti-Flinch recoil pad and Lyman ivory sights at extra cost. Disc. 1946.

W/double triggers, extractors . . NiB $1166 Ex $955 Gd $760
W/double triggers, ejectors, add 30%
W/non-selective single trigger, add $50
W/selective single trigger, add $50
.410 ga., add 100%

MATTED RIB SINGLE-SHOT HAMMER SHOTGUN
IN SMALLER GAUGES. . . . . . . NiB $400 Ex $355 Gd $210
Same general specifications as Champion Grade except has solid matted top rib, checkered stock and forend. Weight: 6 to 6.75 lbs. Disc. 1948.

MODEL 412/422 SILVER SHADOW O/U SHOTGUN

Boxlock. Plain extractors. Double triggers or non-selective single trigger. 12 ga., 3-inch chambers. Bbls.: 26-inch IC/M; 28-inch IC/M, 28-inch M/F; 30-inch both F choke; vent rib. Weight: w/28-inch bbls., 7.5 lbs. Checkered pistol-grip stock/forearm. Made by F. Marocchi, Brescia, Italy from 1973 to 1977.

Model 412 w/double triggers . . NiB $590 Ex $455 Gd $387
Model 422 w/single trigger . . . NiB $754 Ex $600 Gd $445

SKEETER MODEL HAMMERLESS DOUBLE

Boxlock. Plain extractors or selective auto ejectors. Double triggers or Miller single trigger (selective or non-selective). Gauges: 12, 16, 20, 28 and .410. 26- or 28-inch bbls., skeet boring standard. Weight: About 7.5 lbs.; less in smaller gauges. Pistol- or straight-grip stock and beavertail forend, both checkered, of select fancy-figured black walnut. Extras include Miller single trigger, selective or non-selective, Jostam Anti-Flinch recoil pad and Lyman ivory rear sight at additional cost. Disc. 1942.

W/double triggers,
plain extractors . . . . NiB $2298 Ex $1987 Gd $1133
W/double triggers,
automatic ejectors, add. 20%
W/non-selective
single trigger, add. 20%
W/selective single
trigger, add 50%
20 ga,add. 30%
28 ga., add 90%
.410 ga., add 100%

SPECIAL TRAP SINGLE-SHOT
HAMMER SHOTGUN . . . . . . NiB $500 Ex $365 Gd $298
Auto ejector. 12 ga. only. 32-inch bbl. w/vent rib, F choke. Checkered pistol-grip stock and forend. Weight: about 7.5 lbs. Disc. 1942.

SUPER TRAP HAMMERLESS DOUBLE

Boxlock. Plain extractors. Double trigger or Miller single trigger (selective or non-selective), 12 ga. only, F choke 32-inch bbl., vent rib. Weight: 8.5 lbs. Checkered pistol-grip stock and beavertail forend, recoil pad, Disc. 1942.

W/double triggers. . . . . NiB $1756 Ex $1170 Gd $990
W/non-selective
single trigger, add. $150
W/selective single trigger, add $150

KBI INC. SHOTGUNS

See listings under Armscor, Baikal, Charles Daly, Fias, & Omega

KESSLER ARMS CORP. — Deggendorf, Germany

LEVER-MATIC REPEATING
SHOTGUN . . . . NiB $335 Ex $227 Gd $179
Lever action. Takedown. Gauges: 12, 16, 20; three-round magazine. Bbls.: 26-, 28-, 30-inch; F choke. Plain pistol-grip stock, recoil pad. Weight: 7 to 7.75 lbs. Disc. 1953.

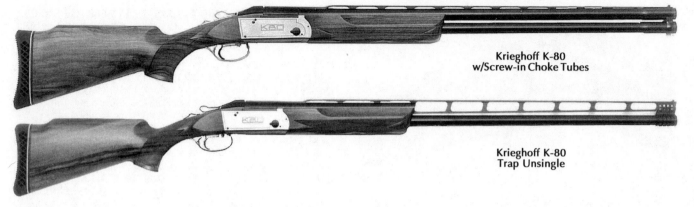

Krieghoff K-80
w/Screw-in Choke Tubes

Krieghoff K-80
Trap Unsingle

Three Shot Bolt-Action Repeater . . NiB $200 Ex $138 Gd $90
Takedown. Gauges: 12, 16, 20. Two-round detachable box magazine. Bbls.: 28-inch in 12 and 16 ga.; 26-inch in 20 ga.; F choke.
Weight: 6.25 to 7.25 lbs. depending on ga. and bbl. length. Plain
one-piece pistol-grip stock recoil pad. Made from 1951 to 1953.

H. KRIEGHOFF JAGD UND SPORTWAFFENFABRIK — Ulm (Donau), Germany

MODEL 32 FOUR-BARREL SKEET SET
Over/under w/four sets of matched bbls.: 12, 20, 28 and .410 ga., in
fitted case. Available in six grades that differ in quality of engraving
and wood. Disc. 1979.

Standard grade	NiB $9344	Ex $7120	Gd $4688
München grade	NiB $10,077	Ex $8767	Gd $6233
San Remo grade	NiB $13,876	Ex $11,990	Gd $10,550
Monte Carlo grade . .	NiB $20,000	Ex $17,890	Gd $14,650
Crown grade	NiB $27,700	Ex $22,800	Gd $15,660
Super Crown grade . .	NiB $29,000	Ex $24,770	Gd $17,600
Exhibition grade	NiB $32,000	Ex $28,900	Gd $23,750

MODEL 32 STANDARD GRADE O/U
Similar to prewar Remington Model 23. Boxlock. Auto ejector. Single
trigger. Gauges: 12, 20, 28, .410. Bbls.: Vent rib, 26.5- to 32-inch,
any chokes. Weight: 12 ga. Field gun w/28-inch bbls., about 7.5 lbs.
Checkered pistol-grip stock and forearm of select walnut; available
in field, skeet and trap styles. Made from 1958 to 1981.

W/one set of bbls.	NiB $3125	Ex $2460	Gd $2099
Low-rib two-bbl. trap combo . . .	NiB $4166	Ex $3550	Gd $2779
Vandalia (high-rib) two- bbl. trap combo . . .	NiB $5355	Ex $4288	Gd $3150

MODEL 32 STANDARD GRADE
SINGLE-SHOT TRAP GUN . . . NiB $4160 Ex $3277 Gd $3080
Same action as over/under. 28 ga.or .410 bore w/low vent rib on
bbl.; M, IM, or F choke. Checkered Monte Carlo buttstock w/thick
cushioned recoil pad, beavertail forearm. Disc. 1979.

MODEL K-80
Refined and enhanced version of the Mdl. 32. Single selective
mech. trig., adj. for position; release trigger optional. Fixed chokes
or screw-in choke tubes. Interchangeable front bbl. Hangers to
adjust point of impact. Quick-removable stock. Color casehardened
or satin grey fin. rec.; alum. alloy rec. on lightweight models. Avail.
in stand. plus 5 engraved grades. Made from 1980 to date. Standard
grade shown except where noted.

SKEET MODELS
Skeet International . . . . . . NiB $9160 Ex $5375 Gd $3853

Skeet Special	NiB $9277	Ex $6659	Gd $4390
Skeet standard model	NiB $9000	Ex $4788	Gd $3360
Skeet w/choke tubes . . .	NiB $12,776	Ex $9879	Gd $5780

SKEET SETS - Disc. 1999.

Standard grade 2-bbl. set . . .	NiB $12,769	Ex $10,000	Gd $6690
Standard grade 4-bbl. set . . .	NiB $14,879	Ex $11,890	Gd $9877
Bavaria grade 4-bbl. set . . .	NiB $11,900	Ex $9388	Gd $7710
Danube grade 4-bbl. set . . .	NiB $23,998	Ex $20,600	Gd $17,000
Gold Target grade 4-bbl. set. . .	NiB $31,800	Ex $24,800	Gd $17,955

SPORTING MODELS

Pigeon	NiB $9980	Ex $6654	Gd $4135
Sporting Clays	NiB $9566	Ex $5760	Gd $4400

TRAP MODELS

Trap Combo, add			. . . . .30%
Trap Single, add			. . . . $600
Trap Standard.	NiB $10,550	Ex $7677	Gd $4612
Trap Unsingle.	NiB $11,880	Ex $9678	Gd $6389
RT models (removable trigger), add			. $1500

KRIEGHOFF MODEL KS-5 SINGLE-BARREL TRAP
Boxlock w/no sliding top-latch. Adjustable or optional release
trigger. Gauge: 12; 2.75-inch chamber. Bbl.: 32-, 34-inch w/fixed
choke or screw-in tubes. Weight: 8.5 lbs. Adjustable or Monte Carlo
European walnut stock. Blued or nickel receiver. Made from 1985 to
1999. Redesigned and streamlined in 1993.

Standard model w/fixed chokes. . .	NiB $2650	Ex $1887	Gd $1109
Standard model w/tubes, add			. $250
Special model w/adj. rib & stock, add			. $250
Special model w/adj. rib & stock, choke tubes, add.			. $500

TRUMPF DRILLING . . . NiB $14,987 Ex $13,677 Gd $10,880
Boxlock. Steel or Dural receiver. Split extractor or ejector for
shotgun bbls. Double triggers. Gauges: 12, 16, 20; latter w/either
2.75- or 3-inch chambers. Calibers: .243, 6.5x57r5, 7x57r5,
7x65r5, .30-06; other calibers available. 25-inch bbls. w/solid rib,
folding leaf rear sight, post or bead front sight; rifle bbl. soldered or
free floating. Weight: 6.6 to 7.5 lbs. depending on type of receiver,
ga. and caliber. Checkered pistol-grip stock w/cheekpiece and
forearm of figured walnut, sling swivels. Made from 1953 to 2003.

NEPTUN DRILLING . . NiB $14,988 Ex $11,987 Gd $9000
Same general specifications as Trumpf model except has sidelocks
w/hunting scene engraving. Disc. 2003.

NEPTUN-PRIMUS
DRILLING . . . . NiB $19,800 Ex $16,779 Gd $13,980
Deluxe version of Neptun model; has detachable sidelocks, higher
grade engraving and fancier wood. Disc. 2003.

SHOTGUNS

Krieghoff
Neptun Drilling

Krieghoff ULM
Over/Under

TECK O/U

RIFLE-SHOTGUN . . . . **NiB $9788 Ex $5780 Gd $4466**
Boxlock. Kersten dble. crossbolt system. Steel or Dural receiver. Split extractor or eject. for shotgun bbl. Single or double triggers. Gauges: 12, 16, 20; latter w/either 2.75- or 3-inch chamber. Cal.: .22 Hornet, .222 Rem., .222 Rem. Mag., 7x57r5, 7x64, 7x65r5, .30-30, .300 Win. Mag., .30-06, .308, 9.3x74R. 25-inch bbls. With solid rib, folding leaf rear sight, post or bead front sight; over bbl. is shotgun, under bbl. rifle (later fixed or interchangeable; ext. rifle bbl., $175). Wt: 7.9-9.5 lbs. depending on type of rec. and caliber. Checkered pistol-grip stock w/cheekpiece and semi-beavertail forearm of fig. walnut, sling swivels. Made from 1967 to 2004. Note: This comb. gun is similar in appearance to the same model shotgun.

TECK O/U SHOTGUN . . . NiB $7354 Ex $5678 Gd $4000
Boxlock. Kersten double crossbolt system. Auto ejector. Single or double triggers. Gauges: 12, 16, 20; latter w/either 2.75- or 3-inch chambers. 28-inch vent-rib bbl., M/F choke. Weight: About 7 lbs. Checkered walnut pistol-grip stock and forearm. Made 1967 to 1989.

ULM O/U

RIFLE-SHOTGUN . . . NiB $16,228 Ex $12,876 Gd $10,336
Same general specifications as Teck model except has sidelocks w/leaf Arabesque engraving. Made from 1963-2004. Note: This combination gun is similar in appearance to the same model shotgun.

ULM O/U SHOTGUN . . . NiB $13,899 Ex $11,679 Gd $8445
Same general specifications as Teck model except has sidelocks w/ leaf Arabesque engraving. Made from 1958 to 2004.

ULM-P LIVE PIGEON GUN
Sidelock. Gauge: 12. 28- and 30-inch bbls. Chokes: F/IM. Weight: 8 lbs. Oil-finished, fancy English walnut stock w/semi-beavertail forearm. Light scrollwork engraving. Tapered, vent rib. Made from 1983 to 2004.
Standard . . . . **NiB $19,577 Ex $15,890 Gd $11,088**
Dural . . . . **NiB $13,776 Ex $11,087 Gd $9459**

ULM-PRIMUS O/U . . **NiB $19,779 Ex $17,888 Gd $13,090**
Deluxe version of Ulm model; detachable sidelocks, higher grade engraving and fancier wood. Made from 1958 to 2004.

ULM-PRIMUS O/U
RIFLE-SHOTGUN . . . NiB $21,870 Ex $18,744 Gd $15,877
Deluxe version of Ulm model; has detachable sidelocks, higher grade engraving and fancier wood. Made 1963 to 2004. Note: This combination gun is similar in appearance to the same model shotgun.

ULM-S SKEET GUN
Sidelock. Gauge: 12. Bbl.: 28-inch. Chokes: Skeet/skeet. Other specifications similar to the Model ULM-P. Made from 1983-86.
Bavaria . . . . **NiB $13,789 Ex $11,132 Gd $9000**
Standard . . . . **NiB $1188 Ex $9131 Gd $7330**

ULM-P O/U LIVE TRAP GUN
Over/under sidelock. Gauge: 12. 30-inch bbl. Tapered vent rib. Chokes: IM/F; optional screw-in choke. Custom grade versions command a higher price. Disc. 1986.
Bavaria . . . . **NiB $18,966 Ex $15,980 Gd $12,776**
Standard . . . . **NiB $15,660 Ex $13,000 Gd $10,100**

ULTRA TS RIFLE-SHOTGUN
Deluxe Over/Under combination w/25-inch vent-rib bbls. Chambered 12 ga. only and various rifle calibers for lower bbl. Kickspanner design permits cocking w/thumb safety. Satin receiver. Weight: 6 lbs. Made from 1985 to 1995 Disc.
Ultra O/U combination . . . **NiB $4220 Ex $3670 Gd $2800**
Ultra B w/selective front trigger . . . **NiB $5589 Ex $4498 Gd $4000**

LANBER SHOTGUNS — Zaldibar, Spain

MODEL 82 O/U SHOTGUN . . . NiB $577 Ex $459 Gd $390
Boxlock. Gauge: 12 or 20; 3-inch chambers. 26- or 28-inch vent-rib bbls. w/ejectors and fixed chokes. Weight: 7 lbs., 2 oz. Double or single-selective trigger. Engraved silvered receiver. Checkered European walnut stock and forearm. Imported 1994.

MODEL 87 DELUXE . . . . NiB $875 Ex $760 Gd $555
Over/Under; boxlock. Single selective trigger. 12 or 20 gauge w/3-inch chambers. Barrels: 26- or 28-inch w/choke tubes. Silvered engraved receiver. Imported 1994 only.

MODEL 97 SPORTING CLAYS. . . NiB $998 Ex $790 Gd $566
Over/Under; boxlock. Single selective trigger. 12 ga. w/2.75-inch chambers. Bbls: 28-inch w/choke tubes. European walnut stock, forend. Engraved receiver. Imported 1994 only.

MODEL 844 MST MAGNUM O/U. . . NiB $533 Ex $448 Gd $360
Field grade. Gauge: 12. 3-inch Mag. chambers. 30-inch flat vent-rib bbls. Chokes: M/F. Weight: 7 lbs., 7 oz. Single selective trigger. Blued bbls. and engraved receiver. European walnut stock w/hand-checkered pistol grip and forend. Imported from 1984 to 1986.

MODEL 2004 LCH O/U . . . . . NiB $669 Ex $490 Gd $370
Field grade. Gauge: 12. 2.75-inch chambers. 28-inch flat vent-rib bbls. 5 interchangeable choke tubes: Cyl, IC, M, IM, F. Weight: About 7 lbs. Single selective trigger. Engraved silver receiver w/fine-line scroll. Walnut stock w/checkered pistol-grip and forend. Rubber recoil pad. Imported from 1984 to 1986.

MODEL 2004 LCH O/U SKEET . . . NiB $855 Ex $659 Gd $544
Same as Model 2004 LCH except 28-inch bbls. w/5 interchangeable choke tubes. Imported from 1984 to 1986.

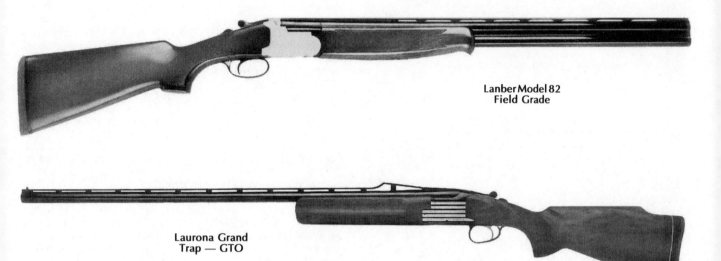

Lanber Model 82
Field Grade

Laurona Grand
Trap — GTO

MODEL 2004
LCH O/U TRAP . . . . **NiB $764 Ex $520 Gd $413**
Gauge: 12. 30-inch vent-rib bbls. Three interchangeable choke tubes: M, IM, F. Manual safety. Other specifications same as Model 2004 LCH O/U. Imported from 1984 to 1986.

CHARLES LANCASTER — London, England

"TWELVE-TWENTY" DOUBLE-BARREL
SHOTGUN. . . . . . . **NiB $16,788 Ex $14,990 Gd $10,880**
Sidelock, self-opener. Gauge: 12. Bbls.: 24 to 30 inches standard. Weight: About 5.75 lbs. Elaborate metal engraving. Highest quality English or French walnut buttstock and forearm. Imported by Stoeger in the 1950s.

JOSEPH LANG & SONS — London, England

HIGHEST QUALITY
O/U SHOTGUN . . . . **NiB $31,900 Ex $27,678 Gd $20,980**
Sidelock. Gauges: 12, 16, 20, 28 and .410. Bbls.: 25 to 30 inches standard. Highest grade English or French walnut buttstock and forearm. Selective single trigger. Imported by Stoeger in 1950s.

LAURONA SHOTGUNS — Eibar, Spain

MODEL 300 SERIES
Same general specifications as Model 300 Super Series except supplied w/29-inch over/under bbls. and beavertail forearms. Disc. 1992.
Trap model . . . . **NiB $1377 Ex $1190 Gd $921**
Sporting Clays model . . . . **NiB $1389 Ex $1440 Gd $1000**

SILHOUETTE 300 O/U
Boxlock. Single selective trigger. Selective automatic ejectors. Gauge: 12; 2.75-, 3- or 3.5-inch chambers. 28- or 29-inch vent-rib bbls. w/ flush or knurled choke tubes. Weight: 7.75 to 8 lbs. Checkered pistol-grip European walnut stock and beavertail forend. Engraved receiver w/silvered finish and black chrome bbls. Made from 1988 to 1992.
Model 300 Sporting Clays. . **NiB $1498 Ex $1277 Gd $900**
Model 300 Trap, single. . . . **NiB $1577 Ex $1264 Gd $900**
Model 300 Ultra-Magnum. **NiB $1599 Ex $1300 Gd $1055**

SUPER MODEL O/U SHOTGUNS
Boxlock. Single selective or twin single triggers. Selective automatic ejectors. Gauges: 12 or 20; 2.75- or 3-inch chambers. 26-, 28- or 29-inch vent-rib bbls. w/fixed chokes or screw-in choke tubes. Weight: 7 to 7.25 lbs. Checkered pistol-grip European walnut stock. Engraved receiver w/silvered finish and black chrome bbls. Made from 1985 to 1989.
Model 82 Super Game (disc.) . **NiB $688 Ex $500 Gd $395**
Model 83 MG Super Game . . **NiB $1090 Ex $800 Gd $707**
Model 84 S Super Trap . . . . **NiB $1366 Ex $1150 Gd $986**
Model 85 MS Super Game . . **NiB $1098 Ex $833 Gd $727**
Model 85 MS 2-bbl. set . . **NiB $2200 Ex $1789 Gd $1340**
Model 85 MS Special Sporting (disc.) **NiB $1390 Ex $1173 Gd $999**
Model 85 MS Super Trap . . **NiB $1386 Ex $1160 Gd $974**
Model 85 MS Pigeon . . . . **NiB $1409 Ex $1190 Gd $1034**
Model 85 MS Super Skeet. **NiB $1409 Ex $1190 Gd $1034**

LEBEAU-COURALLY SHOTGUNS—Belgium

BOXLOCK SIDE
BY-SIDE SHOTGUNS NiB $19,000 Ex $15,870 Gd $10,477
Gauges: 12, 16, 20 and 28. 26- to 30-inch bbls. Weight: 6.5 lbs. average. Checkered, hand-rubbed, oil-finished, straight-grip stock of French walnut. Classic forend. Made from 1986 to 1988 and 1993.

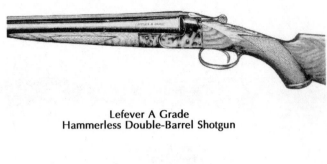

Lefever A Grade
Hammerless Double-Barrel Shotgun

LEFEVER ARMS COMPANY —
Syracuse and Ithaca, New York

Lefever sidelock hammerless double-barrel shotguns were made by Lefever Arms Company of Syracuse, New York from about 1885-1915 (serial numbers 1 to 70,000) when the firm was sold to Ithaca Gun Company of Ithaca, New York. Production of these models was continued at the Ithaca plant until 1919 (serial numbers 70,001 to 72,000). Grades listed are those that appear in the last catalog of the Lefever Gun Company, Syracuse. In 1921, Ithaca introduced the boxlock Lefever Nitro Special double, followed in 1934 by the Lefever Grade A; there also were two single-barrel Lefevers made from 1927-42. Manufacture of Lefever brand shotguns was disc. in 1948. Note: "New Lefever" boxlock shotguns made circa 1904 to 1906 by D. M. Lefever Company, Bowling Green, Ohio, are included in a separate listing.

GRADE A HAMMERLESS DOUBLE-BARREL SHOTGUN
Boxlock. Plain extractors or auto ejector. Single or double triggers. Gauges: 12, 16, 20, .410. Bbls.: 26-32 inches, standard chokes. Weight: About 7 lbs. in 12 ga. Checkered pistol-grip stock and forearm. Made from 1934 to 1942.
W/plain extractors,
double triggers . . . . NiB $1198 Ex $955 Gd $773
W/automatic ejector, add 33%
W/single trigger, add 10%
W/Beavertail Forearm, add $100
16 ga., add 25%
20 ga., add 80%
.410 ga., add 200%

GRADE A SKEET MODEL
Same as A Grade except standard features include auto ejector, single trigger, beavertail forearm; 26-inch bbls., skeet boring. Disc. 1942.
A Grade Skeet model, 12 ga. . . . . NiB $1699 Ex $1188 Gd $880
16 ga., add 40%
20 ga., add 80%
.410 ga., add 200%

HAMMERLESS SINGLE-SHOT
TRAP GUN . . . . NiB $766 Ex $600 Gd $477
Boxlock. Ejector. 12 ga. only. 26- or 32-inch bbl.; Full choke. Weight: About 8 lbs. Checkered pistol-grip stock. Auto ejector; boxlock. Made from 1904 to 1906. Rare.

LONG RANGE HAMMERLESS
SINGLE-BARREL FIELD GUN . NiB $500 Ex $394 Gd $277
Boxlock. Plain extractor. Gauges: 12, 16, 20, .410. Bbl. lengths: 26-32 inches. Weight: 5.5 to 7 lbs. depending on ga. and bbl. length. Checkered pistol-grip stock and forend. Made from 1927 to 1942.

NITRO SPECIAL HAMMERLESS DOUBLE
Boxlock. Plain extractors. Single or double triggers. Gauges: 12, 16, 20, .410. Bbls.: 26- to 32-inch, standard chokes. Weight: about 7 lbs. in 12 ga. Checkered pistol-grip stock and forend. Made 1921 to 1948.
Nitro Special W/
double triggers . . . . NiB $855 Ex $522 Gd $377
Nitro Special W/
single trigger . . . . NiB $933 Ex $654 Gd $433
16 ga., add 25%
20 ga., add 50%
.410 ga., add 200%

SIDELOCK HAMMERLESS DOUBLES
Plain extractors or auto ejectors. Boxlock. Double triggers or selective single trigger. Gauges: 10, 12, 16, 20. Bbls.: 26-32 inches; standard choke combinations. Weight: 5.75 to 10.5 lbs. depending on ga. and bbl. length. Checkered walnut straight-grip or pistol-grip stock and forearm. Grades differ chiefly in quality of workmanship, engraving, wood, checkering, etc.; general specifications are the same. DS and DSE Grade guns lack the cocking indicators found on all other models. Suffix "E" means model has auto ejector; also standard on A, AA, Optimus, and Thousand Dollar Grade guns.

Grade	NiB	Ex	Gd
H grade	NiB $2266	Ex $1770	Gd $1480
HE grade	NiB $3270	Ex $2266	Gd $1780
G grade	NiB $2288	Ex $1998	Gd $1440
GE grade	NiB $3388	Ex $2771	Gd $1880
F grade	NiB $2566	Ex $1966	Gd $1276
FE grade	NiB $3360	Ex $2770	Gd $1866
E grade	NiB $3790	Ex $2690	Gd $2210
EE grade	NiB $5750	Ex $3880	Gd $2547
D grade	NiB $4980	Ex $3777	Gd $2869
DE grade	NiB $7132	Ex $4971	Gd $4111
DS grade	NiB $1754	Ex $1530	Gd $1129
DSE grade	NiB $2184	Ex $1788	Gd $1290
C grade	NiB $7443	Ex $4270	Gd $2988
CE grade	NiB $9112	Ex $8445	Gd $6110
B grade	NiB $10,500	Ex $8667	Gd $6330
BE grade	NiB $10,580	Ex $8777	Gd $6580
A grade	NiB $19,880	Ex $17,900	Gd $16,888
AA grade	NiB $28,566	Ex $23,667	Gd $21,876
Optimus grade	NiB $47,900	Ex $42,870	Gd $37,980
Thousand Dollar grade	NiB $78,980	Ex $46,888	Gd $36,890

W/single trigger, add 10%
10 ga., add 15%
16 ga., add 45%
20 ga., add 90%

D. M. LEFEVER COMPANY —
Bowling Green, Ohio

In 1901, D. M. "Uncle Dan" Lefever, founder of the Lefever Arms Company, withdrew from that firm to organize D. M. Lefever, Sons & Company (later D. M. Lefever Company) to manufacture the "New Lefever" boxlock double- and single-barrel shotguns. These were produced at Bowling Green, Ohio, from about 1904-1906, when Dan Lefever died and the factory closed permanently. Grades listed are those that appear in the last catalog of D. M. Lefever Co.

HAMMERLESS DOUBLE-BARREL SHOTGUNS

"New Lefever." Boxlock. Auto ejector standard on all grades except O Excelsior, which was regularly supplied w/plain extractors (auto ejector offered as an extra). Double triggers or selective single trigger (latter standard on Uncle Dan Grade, extra on all others). Gauges: 12, 16, 20. Bbls.: Any length and choke combination. Weight: 5.5 to 8 lbs. depending on ga. and bbl. length. Checkered walnut straight-grip or pistol-grip stock and forearm. Grades differ chiefly in quality of workmanship, engraving, wood, checkering, etc. General specifications are the same.

O Excelsior grade w/plain extractors	NiB $2889	Ex $2255	Gd $1989
O Excelsior grade w/automatic ejectors	NiB $3244	Ex $2990	Gd $2469
No. 9, F grade	NiB $3277	Ex $2929	Gd $2240
No. 8, E grade	NiB $4240	Ex $3888	Gd $2377
No. 7, D grade	NiB $5277	Ex $4766	Gd $3698
No. 6, C grade	NiB $7000	Ex $4590	Gd $3667
No. 5, B grade	NiB $6722	Ex $4588	Gd $3292
No. 4, AA grade	NiB $10,770	Ex $8857	Gd $5497
Uncle Dan grade	Very rare: $165,000+		
W/single trigger, add	10%		
16 ga., add	45%		
20 ga., add	15%		

D. M. LEFEVER SINGLE-BARREL TRAP GUN

Boxlock. Auto ejector. 12 ga. only. Bbls.: 26- to 32 inches, F choke. Weight: 6.5 to 8 lbs. depending on bbl. length. Checkered walnut pistol-grip stock and forearm. Made 1904 to 1906. Extremely rare.

MAGTECH SHOTGUNS—San Antonio, Texas.
Manufactured by CBC in Brazil

MODEL 586-2 SLIDE-ACTION SHOTGUN

Gauge: 12; 3-inch chamber. 19-, 26- or 28-inch bbl.; fixed chokes or integral tubes. 46.5 inches overall. Weight: 8.5 lbs. Double-action slide bars. Brazilian hardwood stock. Polished blued finish. Imported 1992 to 1995.

Model 586.2F (28-inch bbl., fixed choke)	NiB $288	Ex $147	Gd $100
Model 586.2P (19-inch plain bbl., cyl. bore)	NiB $244	Ex $165	Gd $99
Model 586.2 S (24-inch bbl., rifle sights, cyl. bore)	NiB $290	Ex $155	Gd $125
Model 586.2 VR (vent rib w/tubes)	NiB $275	Ex $198	Gd $135

MARLIN FIREARMS CO. — North Haven (formerly New Haven), Connecticut

MODEL 16 VISIBLE HAMMER SLIDE-ACTION REPEATER

Takedown. 16 ga. Five round tubular magazine. Bbls.: 26- or 28-inch, standard chokes. Weight: About 6.25 lbs. Pistol-grip stock, grooved slide handle; checkering on higher grades. Difference among grades is in quality of wood, engraving on Grades C and D. Made from 1904 to 1910.

Grade A	NiB $400	Ex $322	Gd $297
Grade B	NiB $590	Ex $477	Gd $388
Grade C	NiB $722	Ex $466	Gd $388
Grade D	NiB $1496	Ex $1377	Gd $947

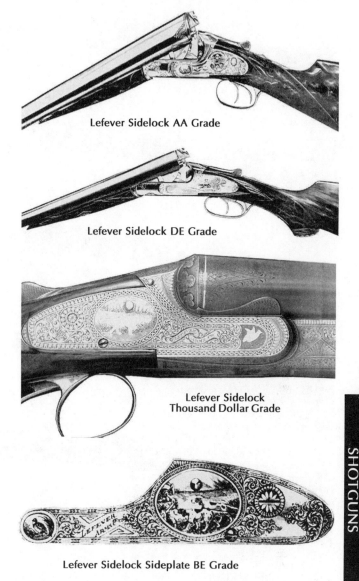

Lefever Sidelock AA Grade

Lefever Sidelock DE Grade

Lefever Sidelock
Thousand Dollar Grade

Lefever Sidelock Sideplate BE Grade

Lefever Sidelock Sideplate CE Grade

Lefever Sidelock Optimus Grade

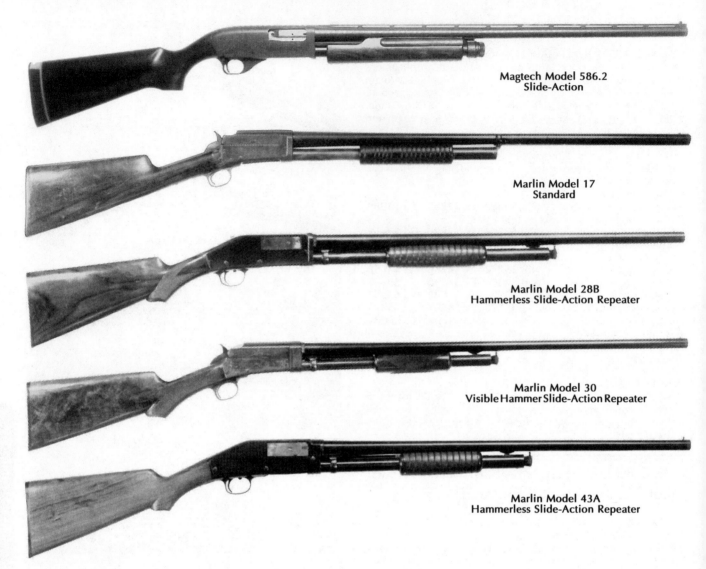

Magtech Model 586.2
Slide-Action

Marlin Model 17
Standard

Marlin Model 28B
Hammerless Slide-Action Repeater

Marlin Model 30
Visible Hammer Slide-Action Repeater

Marlin Model 43A
Hammerless Slide-Action Repeater

MODEL 17 BRUSH GUN . . . . NiB $389 Ex $297 Gd $190
Same as Model 17 Standard except has 26-inch bbl., cylinder bore.
Weight: About 7 lbs. Made from 1906 to 1908.

MODEL 17 RIOT GUN . . . . . . NiB $480 Ex $308 Gd $200
Same as Model 17 Standard except has 20-inch bbl., cylinder bore.
Weight: About 6.88 lbs. Made from 1906 to 1908.

MODEL 17 STANDARD VISIBLE HAMMER
SLIDE-ACTION REPEATER . . . . NiB $422 Ex $290 Gd $188
Solid frame.12 ga. Five round tubular magazine. Bbls.: 30- or
32-inch, F choke. Weight: About 7.5 lbs. Straight-grip stock,
grooved slide handle. Made from 1906 to 1908.

MODEL 19 VISIBLE HAMMER SLIDE-ACTION REPEATER
Similar to Model 1898 but improved, lighter weight, w/two extrac-
tors, matted sighting groove on receiver top. Weight: About 7 lbs.
Made from 1906-07.

Grade A	NiB $466	Ex $390	Gd $277
Grade B	NiB $566	Ex $448	Gd $339
Grade C	NiB $744	Ex $390	Gd $244
Grade D	NiB $1396	Ex $1087	Gd $944

MODEL 21 TRAP VISIBLE HAMMER
SLIDE-ACTION REPEATER
Similar to Model 19 w/same general specifications except has
straight-grip stock. Made from 1907 to 1909.

Grade A	NiB $433	Ex $290	Gd $197
Grade B	NiB $580	Ex $450	Gd $344
Grade C	NiB $788	Ex $590	Gd $445
Grade D	NiB $1488	Ex $1116	Gd $977

MODEL 24 VISIBLE HAMMER SLIDE-ACTION REPEATER
Similar to Model 19 but has improved takedown system and auto
recoil safety lock, solid matted rib on frame. Weight: About 7.5 lbs.
Made from 1908 to 1915.

Grade A	NiB $376	Ex $190	Gd $112
Grade B	NiB $448	Ex $277	Gd $156
Grade C	NiB $766	Ex $500	Gd $410
Grade D.	NiB $1500	Ex $1399	Gd $1177

MODEL 26
BRUSH GUN . . . . NiB $388 Ex $270 Gd $135
Same as Model 26 Standard except has 26-inch bbl., cylinder bore.
Weight: About 7 lbs. Made from 1909 to 1915.

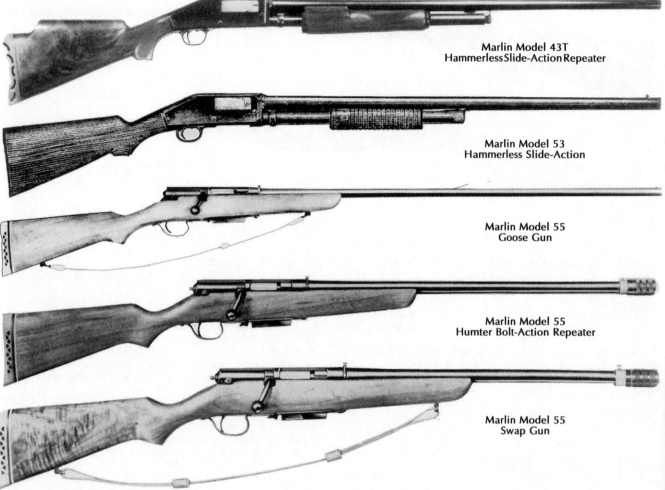

Marlin Model 43T
Hammerless Slide-Action Repeater

Marlin Model 53
Hammerless Slide-Action

Marlin Model 55
Goose Gun

Marlin Model 55
Humter Bolt-Action Repeater

Marlin Model 55
Swap Gun

MODEL 26 RIOT GUN . . . . . . NiB $360 Ex $266 Gd $131
Same as Model 26 Standard except has 20-inch bbl., cylinder bore.
Weight: About 6.88 lbs. Made from 1909 to 1915.

MODEL 26 STANDARD VISIBLE HAMMER
SLIDE-ACTION REPEATER . . . NiB $366 Ex $298 Gd $199
Similar to Model 24 Grade A except solid frame and straight-grip stock. 30-
or 32-inch full choke bbl. Weight: About 7.13 lbs. Made from 1909-15.

MODEL 28 HAMMERLESS SLIDE-ACTION REPEATER
Takedown. 12 ga. Five round tubular magazine. Bbls.: 26-, 28-,
30-, 32-inch, standard chokes; matted-top bbl. except on Model
28D, which has solid matted rib. Weight: About 8 lbs. Pistol-grip
stock, grooved slide handle; checkering on higher grades. Grades
differ in quality of wood, engraving on Models 28C and 28D.
Made 1913 to 1922; all but Model 28A disc. in 1915.
Model 28A . . . . NiB $433 Ex $288 Gd $165
Model 28B . . . . NiB $577 Ex $458 Gd $313
Model 28C . . . . NiB $755 Ex $544 Gd $340
Model 28D . . . . NiB $1480 Ex $1198 Gd $955

MODEL 28T TRAP GUN . . . . . NiB $789 Ex $566 Gd $449
Same as Model 28 except has 30-inch matted-rib bbl., Full choke,
straight-grip stock w/high-fluted comb of fancy walnut, checkered. Made
in 1915.

MODEL 28TS
TRAP GUN . . . . NiB $588 Ex $400 Gd $378
Same as Model 28T except has matted-top bbl., plainer stock. Made
in 1915.

MODEL 30 FIELD GUN . . . . . NiB $466 Ex $355 Gd $245
Same as Model 30 Grade B except has 25-inch bbl., Mod. choke,
straight-grip stock. Made from 1913 to 1914.

MODEL 30 VISIBLE HAMMER SLIDE-ACTION REPEATER
Similar to Model 16 but w/Model 24 improvements. Made from
1910-14. See illustration previous page.
Grade A . . . . NiB $460 Ex $388 Gd $210
Grade B . . . . NiB $660 Ex $433 Gd $309
Grade C . . . . NiB $777 Ex $566 Gd $363
Grade D . . . . NiB $1488 Ex $1177 Gd $1065

MODELS 30A, 30B, 30C, 30D
Same as Model 30; designations were changed in 1915. Also available
in 20 ga. w/25- or 28-inch bbl., matted-top bbl. on all grades. Suffixes
"A," "B," "C" and "D" correspond to former grades. Made in 1915.
Model 30A . . . . NiB $412 Ex $290 Gd $188
Model 30B . . . . NiB $576 Ex $445 Gd $310
Model 30C . . . . NiB $756 Ex $554 Gd $39
Model 30D . . . . NiB $1421 Ex $1131 Gd $1070

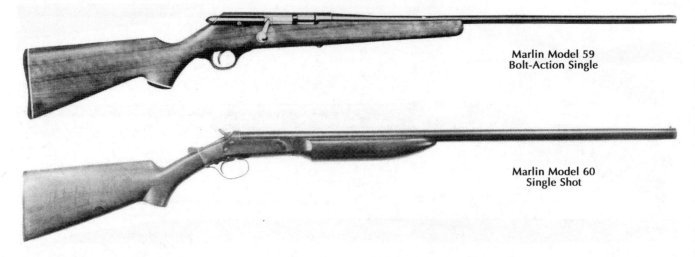

Marlin Model 59
Bolt-Action Single

Marlin Model 60
Single Shot

MODEL 31 HAMMERLESS SLIDE-ACTION REPEATER
Similar to Model 28 except scaled down for 16 and 20 ga. Bbls.: 25-inch (20 ga. only), 26-inch (16 ga. only), 28-inch, all w/matted top, standard chokes. Weight: 16 ga., about 6.75 lbs.; 20 ga., about 6 lbs. Pistol-grip stock, grooved slide handle; checkering on higher grades; straight-grip stock optional on Model 31D. Made from 1915 to 1917; Model 31A until 1922.
Model 31A . . . . NiB $476 Ex $355 Gd $254
Model 31B . . . . NiB $598 Ex $455 Gd $389
Model 31C . . . . NiB $766 Ex $644 Gd $490
Model 31D . . . . NiB $1498 Ex $1154 Gd $990

MODEL 31F FIELD GUN . . . . NiB $488 Ex $366 Gd $271
Same as Model 31B except has 25-inch bbl., M choke, straight- or pistol-grip stock. Made from 1915 to 1917.

MODEL 42A VISIBLE HAMMER
SLIDE-ACTION REPEATER . . . NiB $498 Ex $366 Gd $288
Similar to pre-World War I Model 24 Grade A w/same general specifications but not as high quality. Made from 1922-34.

MODEL 43 HAMMERLESS SLIDE-ACTION REPEATER
Similar to pre-World War I Models 28A, 28T and 28TS, w/same general specifications but not as high quality. Made from 1923 to 1930.
Model 43A . . . . NiB $355 Ex $200 Gd $144
Model 43TS . . . . NiB $665 Ex $400 Gd $228

MODEL 44 HAMMERLESS SLIDE-ACTION REPEATER
Similar to pre-World War I Model 31A w/same general specifications but not as high quality. 20 ga. only. Model 44A is a standard-grade field gun. Model 44S Special Grade has checkered stock and slide handle of fancy walnut. Made from 1923 to 1935.
Model 44A . . . . NiB $466 Ex $381 Gd $222
Model 44S . . . . NiB $622 Ex $476 Gd $338

MODEL 49 VISIBLE HAMMER SLIDE-
ACTION REPEATING SHOTGUN NiB $566 Ex $449 Gd $367
Economy version of Model 42A, offered as a bonus on the purchase of four shares of Marlin stock. About 3000 made 1925 to 1928.

MODEL 50DL BOLT
ACTION SHOTGUN . . . . NiB $388 Ex $229 Gd $131
Gauge: 12 w/3-inch chamber. Two round magazine. 28-inch bbl. w/ modified choke. 48.75 inches overall. Weight: 7.5 lbs. Checkered black synthetic stocks w/ventilated rubber recoil pad. Made 1997 to 1999.

MODEL 53 HAMMERLESS
SLIDE-ACTION REPEATER . . . NiB $480 Ex $200 Gd $144
Similar to Model 43A w/same general specifications. Made 1929 to 1930.

MODEL 55 GOOSE GUN
Same as Model 55 Hunter except chambered for 12-ga. 3-inch Magnum shell, has 36-inch bbl., F choke, swivels and sling. Weight: About 8 lbs. Walnut stock (standard model) or checkered black synthetic stock w/ ventilated rubber recoil pad (GDL model). Made from 1962 to 1996.
Model 55 Goose Gun . . . . . . NiB $335 Ex $266 Gd $195
Model 55GDL Goose Gun
(intro. 1997) . . . . NiB $398 Ex $297 Gd $239

MODEL 55 HUNTER BOLT-ACTION REPEATER
Takedown. Gauges: 12, 16, 20. Two round clip magazine. 28-inch bbl. (26-inch in 20 ga.), F or adj. choke. Plain pistol-grip stock; 12 ga. has recoil pad. Weight: About 7.25 lbs.; 20 ga., 6.5 lbs. Made 1954 to 1965.
W/plain bbl. . . . . NiB $120 Ex $70 Gd $50
W/adj. choke . . . . NiB $155 Ex $99 Gd $75

MODEL 55 SWAMP GUN . . . . . NiB $225 Ex $179 Gd $90
Same as Model 55 Hunter except chambered for 12-ga. 3-inch Magnum shell, has shorter 20.5-inch bbl. w/adj. choke, sling swivels and slightly better-quality stock. Weight: About 6.5 lbs. Made from 1963 to 1965.

MODEL 55S SLUG GUN . . . . . . NiB $200 Ex $99 Gd $75
Same as Model 55 Goose Gun except has 24-inch bbl., cylinder bore, rifle sights. Weight: About 7.5 lbs. Made from 1974 to 1979.

MODEL 59 AUTO-SAFE
BOLT-ACTION SINGLE . . . . . . NiB $244 Ex $176 Gd $95
Takedown. Auto thumb safety, .410 ga. 24-inch bbl., F choke. Weight: About 5 lbs. Plain pistol-grip stock. Made 1959 to 1961.

MODEL 60 SINGLE-SHOT
SHOTGUN . . . . NiB $210 Ex $145 Gd $95
Visible hammer. Takedown. Boxlock. Automatic ejector. 12 ga. 30- or 32-inch bbl., F choke. Weight: About 6.5 lbs. Pistol-grip stock, beavertail forearm. Note: Only about 600 were produced in 1923.

MODEL 63 HAMMERLESS SLIDE-ACTION REPEATER
Similar to Models 43A and 43T w/same general specifications. Model 63TS Trap Special is same as Model 63T Trap Gun except stock style and dimensions to order. Made from 1931-35.
Model 63A . . . . NiB $466 Ex $355 Gd $200
Model 63T or 63TS . . . . NiB $484 Ex $355 Gd $241

Marlin Model 90
Standard Over-and-Under

Marlin Model 120
Magnum Slide-Action Repeater

Marlin Model 410
Lever-Action Repeater

Marlin Model 512
Slugmaster

Marlin Model 55-10
Super Goose 10

Marlin Premier Mark I
Slide-Action Repeater

Marlin Premier Mark IV

Marlin-Glenfield
Model 50 Bolt-Action Repeater

SHOTGUNS

Marocchi Conquista
Sporting Clays

MODEL 90 STANDARD O/U SHOTGUN
Hammerless. Boxlock. Double triggers; non-selective single trigger was available as an extra on pre-war guns except .410. Gauges: 12, 16, 20, .410. Bbls.: Plain; 26-, 28- or 30-inch; chokes IC/M or M/F; bbl. design changed in 1949, eliminating full-length rib between bbls. Weight: 12 ga., about 7.5 lbs.; 16 and 20 ga., about 6.25 lbs. Checkered pistol-grip stock and forearm, recoil pad standard on prewar guns. Postwar production: Model 90-DT (double trigger), Model 90-ST (single trigger). Made from 1937 to 1958.

W/double triggers	NiB $566	Ex $400	Gd $245
W/single trigger	NiB $670	Ex $555	Gd $435
Combination model	NiB $2879	Ex $1976	Gd $1777
16 ga., deduct			10%
20 ga., add			15%
.410, add			30%

MODEL 120 MAGNUM
SLIDE-ACTION REPEATER ... NiB $354 Ex $230 Gd $155
Hammerless. Takedown. 12 ga. (3-inch). Four round tubular magazine. Bbls.: 26-inch vent rib, IC; 28-inch vent rib M choke; 30-inch vent rib, F choke; 38-inch plain, F choke; 40-inch plain, F choke; 26-inch slug bbl. w/rifle sights, IC. Weight: About 7.75 lbs. Checkered pistol-grip stock and forearm, recoil pad. Made from 1971 to 1985.

MODEL 120 SLUG GUN .... NiB $344 Ex $265 Gd $175
Same general specifications as Model 120 Magnum except w/20-inch bbl. and about .5 lb. lighter in weight. No vent rib. Adj. rear rifle sights; hooded front sight. Disc. 1990.

MODEL 410 LEVER-ACTION REPEATER
Action similar to that of Marlin Model 93 rifle. Visible hammer. Solid frame. .410 ga. (2.5-inch shell). Five round tubular magazine. 22- or 26-inch bbl., F choke. Weight: About 6 lbs. Plain pistol-grip stock and grooved beavertail forearm. Made from 1929-32.

Model 410 w/22-inch bbl.	NiB $1546	Ex $1463	Gd $1320
Model 410 w/26-inch bbl.	NiB $1470	Ex $1355	Gd $1110
Deluxe model, add			30%

MODEL 512 SLUGMASTER SHOTGUN
Bolt-action repeater. Gauge: 12; 3-inch chamber, 2-round magazine. 21-inch rifled bbl. w/adj. open sight. Weight: 8 lbs. Walnut-finished birch stock (standard model) or checkered black synthetic stock w/ ventilated rubber recoil pad (GDL model). Made from 1994 to 1999.

Model 512 Slugmaster	NiB $466	Ex $338	Gd $243
Model 512DL Slugmaster (intro. 1998)	NiB $390	Ex $278	Gd $176
Model 512P Slugmaster w/ported bbl. (intro. 1999)	NiB $447	Ex $366	Gd $260

MODEL 1898 VISIBLE HAMMER SLIDE-ACTION REPEATER
Takedown. 12 ga. Five shell tubular magazine. Bbls.: 26-, 28-, 30-, 32-inch; standard chokes. Weight: About 7.25 lbs. Pistol-grip stock, grooved slide handle; checkering on higher grades. Difference among grades is in quality of wood, engraving on Grades C and D. Made 1898 to 1905. Note: This was the first Marlin shotgun.

Grade A (Field)	NiB $387	Ex $270	Gd $190
Grade B	NiB $558	Ex $400	Gd $294
Grade C	NiB $700	Ex $554	Gd $449
Grade D	NiB $2170	Ex $1799	Gd $954

MODEL 5510 SUPER GOOSE ..... NiB $292 Ex $225 Gd $179
Similar to Model 55 Goose Gun except chambered for 10 ga. 3.5-inch Magnum shell, has 34-inch heavy bbl., F choke. Weight: About 10.5 lbs. Made from 1976 to 1985.

PREMIER MARK I
SLIDE-ACTION REPEATER ... NiB $255 Ex $198 Gd $110
Hammerless. Takedown. 12 ga. Magazine holds 3 shells. Bbls.: 30-inch F choke, 28-inch M, 26-inch IC or SK choke. Weight: About 6 lbs. Plain pistol-grip stock and forearm. Made in France from 1960-63.

PREMIER MARK II & IV
Same action and mechanism as Premier Mark except engraved receiver (Mark IV is more elaborate), checkered stock and forearm, fancier wood, vent rib and similar refinements. Made 1960 to 1963.

Premier Mark II	NiB $356	Ex $265	Gd $200
Premier Mark IV (plain barrel)	NiB $389	Ex $339	Gd $233
Premier Mark IV (vent rib barrel)	NiB $400	Ex $370	Gd $280

GLENFIELD MODEL 50
BOLT-ACTION REPEATER.... NiB $320 Ex $255 Gd $175
Similar to Model 55 Hunter except chambered for 12-or 20-ga., 3-inch Magnum shell; has 28-inch bbl. in 12 ga., 26-inch in 20 ga., F choke. Made from 1966 to 1974.

GLENFIELD 778 SLIDE-ACTION
REPEATER .... NiB $325 Ex $255 Gd $180
Hammerless. 12 ga. 2.75-inch or 3-inch. Four round tubular magazine. Bbls.: 26-inch IC, 28-inch M, 30-inch F, 38-inch MXR, 20-inch slug bbl. Weight: 7.75 lbs. Checkered pistol-grip. Made from 1979 to 1984.

MAROCCHI SHOTGUNS — Brescia, Italy. Imported by Precision Sales International of Westfield, MA

CONQUISTA MODEL O/U SHOTGUN
Boxlock. Gauge: 12; 2.75-inch chambers. 28-, 30- or 32-inch vent rib bbl. Fixed choke or internal tubes. 44.38 to 48 inches overall. Weight: 7.5 to 8.25 lbs. Adj. single-selective trigger. Checkered American walnut stock w/recoil pad. Imported 1994 to 2003.

Lady Sport Grade I	NiB $1978	Ex $1754	Gd $1288
Lady Sport Grade II	NiB $2144	Ex $1788	Gd $1488
Lady Sport Grade III	NiB $3577	Ex $2875	Gd $2290
Skeet Model Grade I	NiB $1895	Ex $1544	Gd $1154
Skeet Model Grade II	NiB $2250	Ex $1863	Gd $1455
Skeet Model Grade III	NiB $3598	Ex $3210	Gd $2240
Sporting Clays Grade I	NiB $1890	Ex $1669	Gd $1275
Sporting Clays Grade II	NiB $2200	Ex $1790	Gd $1376
Sporting Clays Grade III	NiB $3550	Ex $2977	Gd $2169
Trap Model Grade I	NiB $1890	Ex $1588	Gd $1300
Trap Model Grade II	NiB $2170	Ex $1877	Gd $1470
Trap Model Grade III	NiB $3588	Ex $3120	Gd $2260
Left-handed model, add			10%

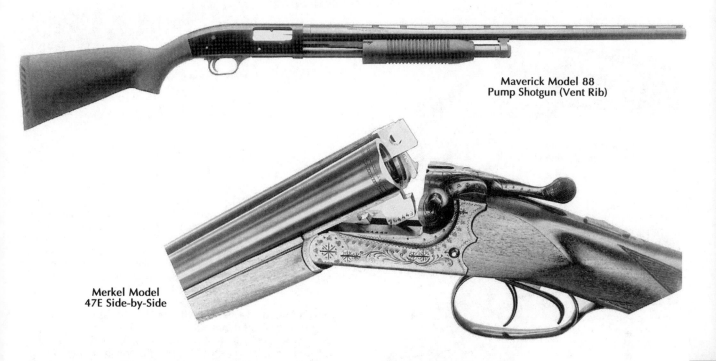

Maverick Model 88
Pump Shotgun (Vent Rib)

Merkel Model
47E Side-by-Side

MAVERICK ARMS, INC. — Eagle Pass, Texas

MODEL 88 BULLPUP . . . . . . **NiB $265 Ex $190 Gd $110**
Gauge: 12; 3-inch chamber. Bbl.: 18.5-inch w/fixed choke, blued. Weight: 9.5 lbs. Dual safeties: Grip style and crossbolt. Fixed sights in carrying handle. High-impact black synthetic stock; trigger-forward bullpup configuration w/twin pistol-grip design. Made 1990 to 1995.

MODEL 88 DEER GUN. . . . . . **NiB $377 Ex $241 Gd $176**
Crossbolt safety and dual slide bars. Cylinder bore choke. Gauge: 12 only w/3-inch chamber. Bbl.: 24-inch. Weight: 7 lbs. Synthetic stock and forearm. Disc. 1995.

MODEL 88 PUMP SHOTGUN
Gauge: 12; 2.75- or 3-inch chamber. Bbl.: 28 inches/M or 30 inches/F w/fixed choke or screw-in integral tubes; plain or vent rib, blued. Weight: 7.25 lbs. Bead front sight. Black synthetic or wood buttstock and forend; forend grooved. Made from 1989 to date.
**Synthetic stock
w/plain bbl.** . . . . **NiB $287 Ex $228 Gd $175**
**Synthetic stock
w/vent-rib bbl.** . . . . **NiB $300 Ex $238 Gd $195**
**Synthetic Combo
w/18.5 inch bbl.** . . . . **NiB $321 Ex $220 Gd $184**
**Wood stock
w/vent-rib bbl./tubes.** . . . . **NiB $300 Ex $225 Gd $179**
Wood Combo w/vent-rib bbl./tubes NiB $255 Ex $200 Gd $162

MODEL 88 SECURITY . . . . . . **NiB $275 Ex $190 Gd $145**
Crossbolt safety and dual slide bars. Optional heat shield. Cylinder bore choke. Gauge: 12 only w/3-inch chamber. Bbl.: 18.5-inches. Weight: 6 lbs., 8 ozs. Synthetic stock and forearm. Made 1993 to date.

MODEL 91 PUMP SHOTGUN
Same as Model 88, except w/2.75-, 3- or 3.5-inch chamber, 28-inch bbl. W/ACCU-F choke, crossbolt safety and synthetic stock only. Made from 1991 to 1995.
Synthetic stock w/plain bbl. . . **NiB $330 Ex $256 Gd $180**
Synthetic stock w/vent-rib bbl. **NiB $335 Ex $270 Gd $195**

MODEL 95 BOLT-ACTION . . . **NiB $255 Ex $190 Gd $140**
Modified, fixed choke. Built-in two round magazine. Gauge: 12 only. Bbl.: 25-inch. Weight: 6.75 lbs. Bead sight. Synthetic stock and rubber recoil pad. Made from 1995 to 1997.

GEBRÜDER MERKEL — Suhl, Germany. Manufactured by Suhler Jagd-und Sportwaffen GmbH. Imported by GSI, Inc., Trussville, AL (previously by Armes de Chasse)

**MODEL 8 HAMMERLESS
DOUBLE.** . . . . **NiB $1522 Ex $1190 Gd $955**
Anson & Deeley boxlock action w/Greener double-bbl. hook lock. Double triggers. Extractors. Automatic safety. Gauges: 12, 16, 20; 2.75- or 3-inch chambers. 26-or 28-inch bbls. w/fixed standard chokes. Checkered European walnut stock, pistol-grip or English-style w/or w/o cheekpiece. Scroll-engraved receiver w/tinted marble finish.

SIDE-BY-SIDE MODEL 47E NiB $4000 Ex $3200 Gd $1890
Hammerless boxlock similar to Model 8 except w/automatic ejectors and cocking indicators. Double hook bolting. Single selective or double triggers. 12, 16 or 20 ga. w/2.75-inch chambers. Standard bbl lengths, choke combos. Hand-checkered European walnut stock, forearm; pistol-grip and cheekpiece or straight English style; sling swivels.

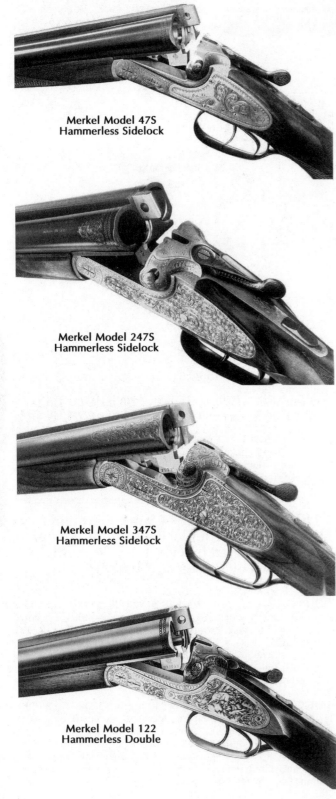

Merkel Model 47LSC
Sporting Clay

Merkel Model 47S
Hammerless Sidelock

Merkel Model 247S
Hammerless Sidelock

Merkel Model 347S
Hammerless Sidelock

Merkel Model 122
Hammerless Double

MODEL 47LSC
SPORTING CLAYS S/S . . NiB $3100 Ex $2500 Gd $1789
Anson & Deeley boxlock action w/single-selective adj. trigger, cocking indicators and manual safety. Gauge: 12; 3-inch chambers. 28-inch bbls. w/Briley choke tubes and H&H-style ejectors. Weight: 7.25 lbs. Color case-hardened receiver w/Arabesque engraving. Checkered select-grade walnut stock, beavertail forearm. Imported from 1993 to 1994.

MODELS 47SL, 147SL, 247SL, 347SL, 447SL
HAMMERLESS SIDELOCKS
Same general specifications as Model 147E except has sidelocks engraved w/Arabesques, borders, scrolls or game scenes in varying degrees of elaborateness.

Model 47SL	. . . . NiB $8350	Ex $5780	Gd $4200
Model 147SL	. . . . NiB $10,099	Ex $7988	Gd $6754
Model 147SSL	. . . . NiB $9655	Ex $6130	Gd $4200
Model 247SL	. . . . NiB $8360	Ex $5110	Gd $3966
Model 347SL	. . . . NiB $7229	Ex $5263	Gd $3800
Model 447SL	. . . . NiB $10,450	Ex $8550	Gd $5110
28 ga. .410, add 20%			

NOTE: Merkel over/under guns were often supplied with accessory barrels, interchangeable to convert the gun into an arm of another type; for example, a set might consist of one pair each of shotgun, rifle and combination gun barrels. Each pair of interchangeable barrels has a value of approximately one-third that of the gun with which they are supplied.

MODEL 100 O/U SHOTGUN
Hammerless. Boxlock. Greener crossbolt. Plain extractor. Double triggers. Gauges: 12, 16, 20. Made w/plain or ribbed bbls. in various lengths and chokes. Plain finish, no engraving. Checkered forend and stock w/pistol grip and cheekpiece or English-style. Made prior to WWII.
W/plain bbl. . . . . . NiB $1964 Ex $1771 Gd $1333
W/ribbed bbl. . . . . NiB $2175 Ex $1890 Gd $1377

MODELS 101 AND 101E O/U
Same as Model 100 except ribbed bbl. standard, has separate extractors (ejectors on Model 101E), English engraving. Made prior to World War II.
Model 101 . . . . NiB $2210 Ex $1879 Gd $1360
Model 101E . . . . NiB $2330 Ex $1968 Gd $1466

MODEL 122
HAMMERLESS DOUBLE. NiB $3965 Ex $3177 Gd $2300
Similar to the Model 147S except w/nonremovable sidelocks in gauges 12, 16 or 20. Imported since 1993.

MODEL 122E
HAMMERLESS SIDELOCK . . . . **NiB $4865 Ex $3850 Gd $2700**
Similar to the Model 122 except w/removable sidelocks and cocking indicators. Importation disc. 1992.

MODEL 126E
HAMMERLESS SIDELOCK . . . .**NiB $25,788 Ex $22,650 Gd $18,700**
Holland & Holland system, hand-detachable locks. Auto ejectors. Double triggers. 12, 16 or 20 gauge w/standard bbl. lengths and chokes. Checkered forend and pistol-grip stock; available w/cheekpiece or English-style buttstock. Elaborate game scenes and engraving. Made prior to WW II.

MODEL 127E
HAMMERLESS SIDELOCK . . . .**NiB $24,849 Ex $21,939 Gd $16,374**
Similar to the Model 126E except w/elaborate scroll engraving on removable sidelocks w/cocking indicators. Made prior to WW II.

MODEL 128E HAMMERLESS
BOXLOCK DOUBLE . . . .**NiB $28,679 Ex $22,167 Gd $16,954**
Scalloped Anson & Deeley action w/hinged floorplate and removable sideplates. Auto-ejectors. Double triggers. Elaborate hunting scene or Arabesque engraving. 12, 16 or 20 gauge w/various bbl. lengths and chokes. Checkered forend and stock w/pistol grip and cheekpiece or English-style. Made prior to WW II.

MODEL 130 HAMMERLESS
BOXLOCK DOUBLE . . . .**NiB $21,400 Ex $18,560 Gd $16,450**
Similar to Model 128E except w/fixed sideplates. Auto ejectors. Double triggers. Elaborate hunting scene or Arabesque engraving. Made prior to WW II.

MODESL 147 & 147E HAMMERLESS
BOXLOCK DOUBLE-BARREL SHOTGUN
Anson & Deeley system w/extractors or auto ejectors. Single selective or double triggers. Gauges: 12, 16, 20 or 28 ga. (Three-inch chambers available in 12 and 20 ga.). Bbls.: 26-inch standard, other lengths available w/any standard choke combination. Weight: 6.5 lbs. Checkered straight-grip stock and forearm. Disc. 1998.
Model 147 w/extractors . . **NiB $2588 Ex $2254 Gd $1899**
Model 147E w/ejectors . . . **NiB $5540 Ex $3770 Gd $2840**

Merkel Model 147E
Hammerless Boxlock Double-Barrel Shotgun

MODELS 200, 200E, 201, 201E,
202, 202E & 202EL O/U SHOTGUNS
Hammerless. Boxlock. Kersten double crossbolt. Scalloped frame. Sideplates on Models 202 and 202E. Arabesque or hunting engraving supplied on all except Models 200 and 200E. "E" models have ejectors, others have separate extractors, signal pins, double triggers. Gauges: 12, 16, 20, 24, 28, 32 (last three not available in postwar guns). Ribbed bbls. in various lengths and chokes. Weight: 5.75 to 7.5 lbs. depending on bbl. length and gauge. Checkered forend and stock w/pistol grip and cheekpiece or English-style. The 200, 201, and 202 differ in overall quality, engraving, wood, checkering, etc.; aside from the faux sideplates on Models 202 and 202E, general specifications are the same. Models 200, 201, 202, and 202E, all made before WW II, are disc. Models 201E &202E in production w/revised 2000 series nomenclature.
Model 200 . . . . **NiB $2920 Ex $2255 Gd $1730**
Model 200E . . . . **NiB $3688 Ex $2987 Gd $2116**
Model 200 ES Skeet . . . . **NiB $4760 Ex $4200 Gd $2977**
Model 200ET Trap . . . . **NiB $4660 Ex $4189 Gd $3255**
Model 200 SC Sporting Clays . . . . . . **NiB $6930 Ex $4599 Gd $3238**
Model 201 (disc.) . . . . **NiB $3400 Ex $2566 Gd $1888**
Model 201E (Pre-WW II) . . . . **NiB $7335 Ex $4990 Gd $3288**
Model 201E (Post-WW II) . . . . **NiB $5100 Ex $3991 Gd $2977**
Model 201 ES Skeet . . . . **NiB $8100 Ex $6655 Gd $5133**
Model 201 ET Trap . . . . **NiB $7661 Ex $6255 Gd $4409**
Model 202 (disc.) . . . . **NiB $8255 Ex $5588 Gd $3577**
Model 202E (Pre-WW II) . . . . **NiB $8255 Ex $4967 Gd $3886**
Model 202E (Post-WWII & 202EL) . . **NiB $7091 Ex $5897 Gd $3994**

Merkel Model 200E
O/U Shotgun

Merkel Model 203E
Sidelock O/U Shotgun

SHOTGUNS

Merkel Model 303E
O/U Shotgun

MODEL 203E SIDELOCK O/U SHOTGUNS
Hammerless action w/hand-detachable sidelocks. Kersten double cross bolt, auto ejectors and double triggers. Gauges: 12 or 20 (16, 24, 28 and 32 disc.). 26.75- or 28-inch vent rib bbls. Arabesque engraving standard or hunting engraving optional on coin-finished receiver. Checkered English or pistol-grip stock and forend.
Model 203E sidelock (disc. 1998)NiB $10,335 Ex $8556 Gd $5830
Model 203ES skeet
(imported 1993-97). . NiB $12,450 Ex $12,330 Gd $10,245
Model 203ET trap (disc. 1997)NiB $13,770 Ex $12,560 Gd $10,665

MODEL 204E
O/U SHOTGUN . . . . NiB $8843 Ex $6751 Gd $4766
Similar to Model 203E; has Merkel sidelocks, fine English engraving. Made prior to World War II.

MODEL 210E
SIDE-LOCK O/U SHOTGUN NiB $7239 Ex $5340 Gd $3882
Kersten double cross-bolt, scroll-engraved, casehardened receiver. 12, 16 or 20 ga. Double-triggers; pistol-grip stock w/cheekpiece.

MODEL 211E
SIDE-LOCK O/U SHOTGUN NiB $6865 Ex $5388 Gd $4488
Same specifications as Model 210E except w/engraved hunting scenes on silver-gray receiver.

MODELS 300, 300E, 301, 301E AND 302 O/U
Merkel-Anson system boxlock. Kersten double crossbolt, two underlugs, scalloped frame, sideplates on Model 302. Arabesque or hunting engraving. "E" models and Model 302 have auto ejectors, others have separate extractors. Signal pins. Double triggers. Gauges: 12, 16, 20, 24, 28, 32. Ribbed bbls. in various lengths and chokes. Checkered forend and stock w/pistol grip and cheekpiece or English-style. Grades 300, 301 and 302 differ in overall quality, engraving, wood, checkering, etc.; aside from the dummy sideplates on Model 302, general specifications are the same. Manufactured prior to World War II.
Model 300 . . . . NiB $5865 Ex $3579 Gd $2988
Model 300E . . . . NiB $8155 Ex $6888 Gd $5224
Model 301 . . . . NiB $6960 Ex $4977 Gd $3200
Model 301E . . . . NiB $8235 Ex $6276 Gd $5004
Model 302 . . . . NiB $14,998 Ex $12,688 Gd $10,097

MODEL 303EL O/USHOTGUN NiB $29,880 Ex $25,609 Gd $21,223
Similar to Model 203E. Has Kersten crossbolt, double underlugs, Holland & Holland-type hand-detachable sidelocks, auto-ejectors. This is a finer gun than Model 203E. Currently manufactured. Special order items.

MODEL 304E O/U
SHOTGUN. . . . . NiB $24,770 Ex $19,760 Gd $13,010
Special version of the Model 303E-type, but higher quality throughout. This is the top grade Merkel over/under. Currently manufactured. Special order items.

MODELS 400, 400E, 401, 401E O/U
Similar to Model 101 except have Kersten double crossbolt, Arabesque engraving on Models 400 and 400E, hunting engraving on Models 401 and 401E, finer general quality. "E" models have Merkel ejectors, others have separate extractors. Made prior to World War II.
Model 400 . . . . NiB $2190 Ex $1993 Gd $1465
Model 400E . . . . NiB $2433 Ex $2254 Gd $1934
Model 401 . . . . NiB $2798 Ex $2170 Gd $1588
Model 401E . . . . NiB $4366 Ex $3757 Gd $2486

O/U COMBINATION GUNS ("BOCKBÜCHSFLINTEN")
Shotgun bbl. over, rifle bbl. under. Gauges: 12, 16, 20; calibers: 5.6x35 Vierling, 7x57r5, 8x57JR, 8x60R Mag., 9.3x53r5, 9.3x72r5, 9.3x74R and others including domestic calibers from .22 Hornet to .375 H&H. Various bbl. lengths, chokes and weights. Other specifications and values correspond to those of Merkel over/under shotguns listed below. Currently manufactured. Model 210 & 211 series disc. 1992.
Models 410, 410E, 411E (see shotgun models 400, 400E, 401, 401E)
Models 210, 210E, 211, 211E, 212, 212E
(see shotgun models 200, 200E, 201, 201E, 202, 202E)

MODEL 2000EL O/U SHOTGUNS
Kersten double cross-bolt. Gauges: 12 and 20. 26.75- or 28-inch bbls. Weight: 6.4 to 7.28 lbs. Scroll engraved silver-gray receiver. Automatic ejectors and single selective or double triggers. Checkered forend and stock w/pistol grip and cheekpiece or English-style stock w/luxury grade wood. Imported from 1998 to 2005.
Model 2000EL Standard . NiB $5733 Ex $4560 Gd $3288
Model 2000EL Sporter . . . NiB $5980 Ex $4677 Gd $3455

MODEL 2001EL O/U SHOTGUNS
Gauges: 12, 16, 20 and 28; Kersten double cross-bolt lock receiver. 26.75- or 28-inch IC/mod, mod/full bbls. Weight: 6.4 to 7.28 lbs. Three-piece forearm, automatic ejectors and single selective or double triggers. Imported from 1993 to 2005.
Model 2001EL 12 ga. . . . NiB $6566 Ex $5270 Gd $3880
Model 2001EL 16 ga.
(disc. 1997) . . . . NiB $6400 Ex $5277 Gd $3760
Model 2001EL 20 ga. . . . NiB $6400 Ex $5277 Gd $3760
Model 2001EL 28 ga.
(made 1995) . . . . NiB $7200 Ex $5933 Gd $4200

MODEL 2002EL . . . . NiB $11,990 Ex $8530 Gd $6177
Same specifications as Model 2000EL except hunting scenes w/ Arabesque engraving.

ANSON DRILLINGS
Three-bbl. combination guns; usually made w/double shotgun bbls., over rifle bbl., although "Doppelbüchsdrillingen" were made w/two rifle bbls. over and shotgun bbl. under. Hammerless.

Miida Model 612
Field Grade O/U

Boxlock. Anson & Deeley system. Side clips. Plain extractors. Double triggers. Gauges: 12, 16, 20; rifle calibers: 7x57r5, 8x57JR and 9.3x74R are most common, but other calibers from 5.6mm to 10.75mm available. Bbls.: standard drilling 25.6 inches; short drilling, 21.6 inches. Checkered pistol-grip stock and forend. The three models listed differ chiefly in overall quality, grade of wood, etc.; general specifications are the same. Made prior to WW II.

Model 142 Engraved . . . . . NiB $5698 Ex $4887 Gd $3366
Model 142 Standard . . . . NiB $4880 Ex $3688 Gd $2588
Model 145 Field . . . . NiB $3865 Ex $3200 Gd $2365

MIIDA SHOTGUNS — Manufactured for Marubeni America Corp., New York, by Olin-Kodensha Co., Tochigi, Japan

MODEL 612 FIELD GRADE O/U NiB $863 Ex $665 Gd $400
Boxlock. Auto ejectors. Selective single trigger. 12 ga. Bbls.: Vent rib; 26-inch, IC/M; 28-inch, M/F choke. Weight: W/26-inch bbl., 6 lbs., 11 oz. Checkered pistol-grip stock and forearm. Made 1972 to 1974.

MODEL 2100 SKEET GUN . . . NiB $954 Ex $749 Gd $488
Similar to Model 612 except has more elaborate engraving on frame (50 percent coverage), skeet-style stock and forearm of select grade wood; 27-inch vent-rib bbls., SK choke. Weight: 7 lbs., 11 oz. Made from 1972 to 1974.

**MODEL 2200T TRAP GUN,
MODEL 2200S SKEET GUN** . . NiB $925 Ex $691 Gd $541
Similar to Model 612 except more elaborate engraving on frame (60 percent coverage), trap- or skeet-style stock and semi-beavertail forearm of fancy walnut, recoil pad on trap stock. Bbls.: Wide vent rib; 29.75-inch, IM/F choke on Trap Gun; 27-inch, SK choke on Skeet Gun. Weight: Trap, 7 lbs., 14 oz.; Skeet, 7 lbs., 11 oz. Made 1972 to 1974.

**MODEL 2200 TRAP
& SKEET MODELS** . . . . NiB $1088 Ex $766 Gd $594
Same as models 2200T and 2200S except more elaborate engraving on frame (70% coverage). Made from 1972 to 1974.

**GRANDEE MODEL GRT/IRS
TRAP/SKEET GUN** . . . . . . NiB $2655 Ex $2390 Gd $1866
Boxlock w/sideplates. Frame, breech ends of bbls., trigger guard and locking lever fully engraved and gold inlaid. Auto ejectors. Selective single trigger. 12 ga. Bbls.: Wide vent rib; 29-inch, F choke on Trap Gun; 27-inch, SK choke on Skeet Gun. Weight: Trap, 7 lbs., 14 oz.; Skeet, 7 lbs., 11 oz. Trap- or skeet-style stock and semi-beavertail forearm of extra fancy wood, recoil pad on trap stock. Made 1972 to 1974.

MITCHELL ARMS — Santa Ana, California

MODEL 9104/9105 PUMP SHOTGUNS
Slide action in Field/Riot configuration. Gauge: 12; 5-round tubular magazine. 20-inch bbl.; fixed choke or screw-in tubes. Weight: 6.5 lbs. Plain walnut stock. Made from 1994 to 1996.

Model 9104 (w/plain bbl.) . . . NiB $299 Ex $288 Gd $188
Model 9105 (w/rifle sight) . . . . NiB $299 Ex $288 Gd $188
W/choke tubes, add $40

MODEL 9108/9109 PUMP SHOTGUN
Slide action in Military/Police/Riot configuration. Gauge: 12, 7-round tubular magazine. 20-inch bbl.; fixed choke or screw-in tubes. Weight: 6.5 lbs. Plain walnut stock and grooved slide handle w/brown, green or black finish. Blued metal. Made from 1994 to 1996.

Model 9108 (w/plain bbl.) . . . NiB $292 Ex $225 Gd $196
Model 9109 (w/rifle sights) . . . NiB $292 Ex $225 Gd $196
W/choke tubes, add $40

MODEL 9111/9113 PUMP SHOTGUN
Slide action in Military/Police/Riot configuration. Gauge: 12; 6-round tubular magazine. 18.5-inch bbl.; fixed choke or screw-in tubes. Weight: 6.5 lbs. Synthetic or plain walnut stock and grooved slide handle w/brown, green or black finish. Blued metal. Made from 1994 to 1996.

Model 9111 (w/plain bbl.) . . . NiB $292 Ex $225 Gd $196
Model 9113 (w/rifle sights) . . . NiB $292 Ex $225 Gd $196
W/choke tubes, add $40

MODEL 9114/9114FS
Slide action in Military/Police/Riot configuration. Gauge: 12; 7-round tubular magazine. 20-inch bbl.; fixed choke or screw-in tubes. Weight: 6.5-7 lbs. Synthetic pistol-grip or folding stock. Blued metal. Made from 1994 to 1996.

Model 9114 . . . . NiB $345 Ex $245 Gd $169
Model 9114FS . . . . NiB $345 Ex $245 Gd $169

**MODEL 9115/9115FS
PUMP SHOTGUN** . . . . NiB $366 Ex $240 Gd $159
Slide action in Military/Police/Riot configuration. Gauge: 12; 6-round tubular magazine. 18.5-inch bbl. w/heat-shield handguard. Weight: 7 lbs. Gray synthetic stock and slide handle. Parkerized metal. Made from 1994 to 1996.

MONTGOMERY WARD

See shotgun listings under "W"

MORRONE SHOTGUN — Manufactured by Rhode Island Arms Company, Hope Valley, Rhode Island

STANDARD MODEL 46 O/U NiB $1366 Ex $890 Gd $677
Boxlock. Plain extractors. Non-selective single trigger. Gauges: 12, 20. Bbls.: Plain, vent rib; 26-inch IC/M; 28-inch M/F choke. Weight: About 7 lbs., 12 ga.; 6 lbs., 20 ga. Checkered straight- or pistol-grip stock and forearm. Made 1949-53. Note: Fewer than 500 of these guns were produced, about 50 in 20 ga.. A few had vent-rib bbls. Value shown is for 12 ga. w/plain bbls.. The rare 20 ga. and vent-rib types should bring considerably more.

SHOTGUNS

Mossberg Model 83D

Mossberg Model 85D
Bolt-Action Repeating Shotgun

Mossberg Model 183K

Mossberg Model 185K

Mossberg Model 200K
Slide-Action Repeater

Mossberg Model 395K
Bolt-Action Repeater

O.F. MOSSBERG & SONS, INC. —
North Haven, Connecticut;
formerly New Haven, Connecticut

MODEL 83D & 183D . . . . NiB $217 Ex $121 Gd $95
3-round. Takedown. .410 ga. only. Two shell fixed top-loading magazine. 23-inch bbl. w/two interchangeable choke tubes (M/F). Later production had 24-inch bbl. Plain one-piece pistol-grip stock. Weight: about 5.5 lbs. Originally designated Model 83D, changed in 1947 to Model 183D. Made from 1940 to 1971.

**MODEL 85D & 185D BOLT-ACTION
REPEATING SHOTGUN . . . . . . NiB $217 Ex $121 Gd $95**
Takedown. Three-round. 20 ga. only. Two-shell detachable box magazine. 25-inch bbl., three interchangeable choke tubes (F, M,

IC). Later production had 26-inch bbl. w/F/IC choke tubes. Weight: About 6.25 lbs. Plain one-piece, pistol-grip stock. Originally designated Model 85D, changed in 1947 to Model 185D. Made from 1940 to 1971.

MODEL 183K . . . . NiB $240 Ex $131 Gd $100
Same as Model 183D except has 25-inch bbl. w/variable C-Lect-Choke instead of interchangeable choke tubes. Made 1953 to 1986.

MODEL 185K . . . . NiB $240 Ex $131 Gd $100
Same as Model 185D except has variable C-Lect-Choke instead of interchangeable choke tubes. Made from 1950 to 1963.

MODEL 190D . . . . NiB $240 Ex $131 Gd $100
Same as Model 185D except in 16 ga. Weight: About 6 lbs. Made from 1955 to 1971.

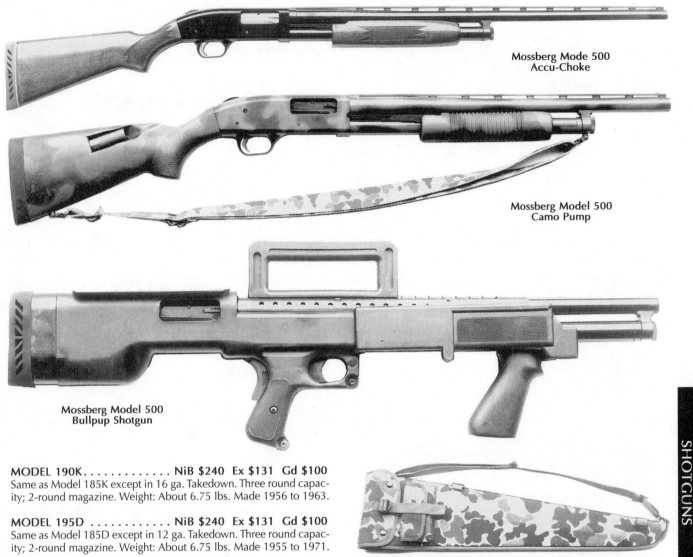

Mossberg Mode 500
Accu-Choke

Mossberg Model 500
Camo Pump

Mossberg Model 500
Bullpup Shotgun

MODEL 190K . . . . NiB $240 Ex $131 Gd $100
Same as Model 185K except in 16 ga. Takedown. Three round capacity; 2-round magazine. Weight: About 6.75 lbs. Made 1956 to 1963.

MODEL 195D . . . . NiB $240 Ex $131 Gd $100
Same as Model 185D except in 12 ga. Takedown. Three round capacity; 2-round magazine. Weight: About 6.75 lbs. Made 1955 to 1971.

MODEL 195K . . . . NiB $240 Ex $131 Gd $100
Same as Model 185K except in 12 ga. Takedown. Three round capacity; 2-round magazine. Weight: About 7.5 lbs. Made 1956 to 1963.

MODEL 200D . . . . NiB $355 Ex $240 Gd $125
Same as Model 200K except w/two interchangeable choke tubes instead of C-Lect choke. Made from 1955 to 1959.

MODEL 200K
SLIDE-ACTION REPEATER . . . . NiB $355 Ex $190 Gd $120
12 ga. 3-round detachable box magazine. 28-inch bbl. C-Lect choke. Plain pistol-grip stock. Black nylon slide handle. Weight: About 7.5 lbs. Made from 1955 to 1959.

MODEL 395K BOLT-ACTION REPEATER NiB $255 Ex $155 Gd $120
Takedown. Three round (detachable-clip magazine holds two rounds).12 ga. (3-inch chamber). 28-inch bbl. w/C-Lect-Choke. Weight: About 7.5 lbs. Monte Carlo stock w/recoil pad. Made 1963 to 1983.

MODEL 385K . . . . NiB $240 Ex $131 Gd $100
Same as Model 395K except 20 ga. (3-inch), 26-inch bbl. w/C-Lect-Choke. Weight: About 6.25 lbs.

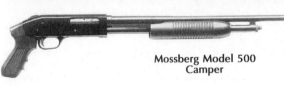

Mossberg Model 500
Camper

MODEL 390K . . . . NiB $240 Ex $131 Gd $100
Same as Model 395K except 16 ga. (2.75-inch). Made 1963 to 1974.

MODEL 395S SLUGSTER . . . . NiB $240 Ex $131 Gd $100
Same as Model 395K except has 24-inch bbl., cylinder bore, rifle sights, swivels and web sling. Weight: About 7 lbs. Made from 1968 to 1981.

MODEL 500 ACCU-CHOKE SHOTGUN NiB $290 Ex $231 Gd $125
Pump-action. Gauge: 12. 24- or 28-inch bbl. Weight: 7.25 lbs. Checkered walnut-finished wood stock w/ventilated recoil pad. Available w/synthetic field or Speed-Feed stocks. Drilled and tapped receivers, swivels and camo sling on camo models. Made from 1987 to date.

Mossberg Model 500
Persuader Law Enforcement

Mossberg Model 500
Mariner

MODEL 500 BANTAM SHOTGUN
Same as Model 500 Sporting Pump except 20 or .410 ga. only. 22-inch w/ACCU-Choke tubes or 24-inch w/F choke; vent rib. Scaled-down checkered hardwood or synthetic stock w/standard or Realtree camo finish. Made from 1990 to 1996 and 1998 to 1999.
Bantam Model (hardwood stock).... NiB $255 Ex $198 Gd $130
Bantam Model (synthetic stock) .... NiB $330 Ex $229 Gd $165
Bantam Model (Realtree camo), add $75

MODEL 500 BULLPUP SHOTGUN . . NiB $722 Ex $486 Gd $344
Pump. Gauge: 12. Six or 8-round capacity. Bbl.: 18.5 to 20 inches. 26.5 and 28.5 inches overall. Weight: About 9.5 lbs. Multiple independent safety systems. Dual pistol grips, rubber recoil pad. Fully enclosed rifle-type sights. Synthetic stock. Ventilated bbl. heat shield. Made from 1987 to 1990.

MODEL 500 CAMO PUMP
Same as Model 500 Sporting Pump except 12 ga. only. Receiver drilled and tapped. QD swivels and camo sling. Special camouflage finish.
Standard model .... NiB $390 Ex $255 Gd $200
Combo model (w/ext. Slugster bbl.) NiB $409 Ex $270 Gd $220

MODEL 500 CAMPER...... NiB $290 Ex $210 Gd $175
Same general specifications as Model 500 Field Grade except .410 bore, 6-round magazine, 18.5-inch plain cylinder bore bbl. Synthetic pistol grip and camo carrying case. Made 1986 to 1990.

MODEL 500 FIELD GRADE HAMMERLESS SLIDE-ACTION REPEATER
Pre-1977 type. Takedown. Gauges: 12, 16, 20, .410. Three inch chamber (2.75-inch in 16 ga.). Tubular magazine holds five 2.75-inch rounds or four three-inch. Bbls.: Plain- 30-inch regular or heavy Magnum, F choke (12 ga. only); 28-inch, M or F; 26-inch, IC or adj. C-Lect-Choke; 24-inch Slugster, cylinder bore, w/rifle sights. Weight: 5.75 to lbs. Plain pistol-grip stock w/ recoil pad, grooved slide handle. After 1973, these guns have checkered stock and slide handles; Models 500AM and 500AS have receivers etched w/game scenes. The latter has swivels and sling. Made from 1962 to 1976.
Model 500A, 12 ga., ... NiB $310 Ex $225 Gd $170
Model 500AM, 12 ga., hvy. Mag. bbl. NiB $310 Ex $225 Gd $170
Model 500AK, 12 ga., C-Lect-Choke NiB $335 Ex $250 Gd $190
Model 500AS, 12 ga., Slugster .... NiB $359 Ex $250 Gd $195
Model 500B 16 ga., ... NiB $369 Ex $275 Gd $205
Model 500BK, 16 ga., C-Lect-Choke NiB $300 Ex $220 Gd $145
Model 500BS, 16 ga., Slugster ..... NiB $359 Ex $250 Gd $195
Model 500C 20 ga., ... NiB $360 Ex $275 Gd $160
Model 500CK, 20 ga., C-Lect-Choke NiB $335 Ex $250 Gd $190
Model 500CS, 20 ga., Slugster ..... NiB $330 Ex $239 Gd $180
Model 500E, .410 ga., ... NiB $300 Ex $220 Gd $140
Model 500EK, .410 ga., C-Lect-Choke NiB $350 Ex $275 Gd $165

MODEL 500 "L" SERIES
"L" in model designation. Same as pre-1977 Model 500 Field Grade except not available in 16 ga., has receiver etched w/different game scenes; Accu-

Choke w/three interchangeable tubes (IC, M, F) standard, restyled stock and slide handle. Bbls.: plain or vent rib; 30- or 32-inch, heavy, F choke (12 ga. Magnum and vent rib only); 28-inch, Accu-Choke (12 and 20 ga.); 26-inch F choke (.410 bore only); 18.5-inch (12 ga. only), 24-inch (12 and 20 ga.) Slugster w/rifle sights, cylinder bore. Weight: 6 to 8.5 lbs. Intro. 1977.
Model 500ALD, 12 ga.,
plain bbl. (disc. 1980) .... NiB $275 Ex $195 Gd $110
Model 500ALDR, 12 ga., vent rib ... NiB $300 Ex $220 Gd $131
Model 500ALMR, 12 ga.,
Heavy Duck Gun (disc. 1980) ..... NiB $325 Ex $240 Gd $165
Model 500CLD, 20 ga.,
plain bbl. (disc. 1980) .... NiB $355 Ex $265 Gd $185
Model 500CLDR, 20 ga., vent rib ... NiB $310 Ex $235 Gd $135
Model 500CLS, 20 ga.,
Slugster (disc. 1980) .... NiB $355 Ex $265 Gd $185
Model 500EL, .410 ga.,
plain bbl. (disc. 1980) .... NiB $295 Ex $200 Gd $125
Model 500ELR, .410 ga., vent rib ... NiB $325 Ex $240 Gd $135

MODEL 500 MARINER SHOTGUN . . NiB $500 Ex $390 Gd $277
Slide action. Gauge: 12. 18.5 or 20-inch bbl. Six round and 8-round respectively. Weight: 7.25 lbs. High-strength synthetic buttstock and forend. Available in extra round-carrying Speed Feed synthetic buttstock. All metal treated for protection against saltwater corrosion. Intro. 1987.

MODEL 500 MUZZLELOADER COMBO. . NiB $390 Ex $275 Gd $190
Same as Model 500 Sporting Pump except w/extra 24-inch rifled .50-caliber muzzleloading bbl. w/ramrod. Made 1991 to 1996.

MODEL 500 PERSUADER LAW ENFORCEMENT
Similar to pre-1977 Model 500 Field Grade except 12 ga. only, 6- or 8-round capacity, has 18.5- or 20-inch plain bbl., cylinder bore, either shotgun or rifle sights, plain pistol-grip stock and grooved slide handle, sling swivels. Special Model 500ATP8-SP has bayonet lug, Parkerized finish. Intro. 1995.
Model 500ATP6, 6-round, 18.5-inch
bbl., shotgun sights............. NiB $410 Ex $275 Gd $190
Model 500ATP6CN, 6-round,
nickle finish "Cruiser" pistol-grip. . . NiB $440 Ex $300 Gd $225
Model 500ATP6N, 6-round, nickel
finish, 2.75- or 3-inch Mag. shells . . NiB $410 Ex $275 Gd $190
Model 500ATP6S, 6-round,
18.5-inch bbl., rifle sights .... NiB $410 Ex $275 Gd $190
Model 500ATP8, 8-round,
20-inch bbl., shotgun sights .... NiB $440 Ex $300 Gd $225
Model 500ATP8S, 8-round,
20-inch bbl., rifle sights .... NiB $450 Ex $315 Gd $240
Model 500ATP8-SP Spec. Enforcement NiB $391 Ex $313 Gd $226
Model 500 Bullpup .... NiB $690 Ex $500 Gd $345
Model 500 Intimidator w/laser sight, blued NiB $644 Ex $470 Gd $329
Model 500 Intimidator w/laser sight,
parkerized .... NiB $425 Ex $320 Gd $190
Model 500 Security combo pack ... NiB $345 Ex $270 Gd $185
Model 500 Cruiser w/pistol grip .... NiB $440 Ex $325 Gd $220

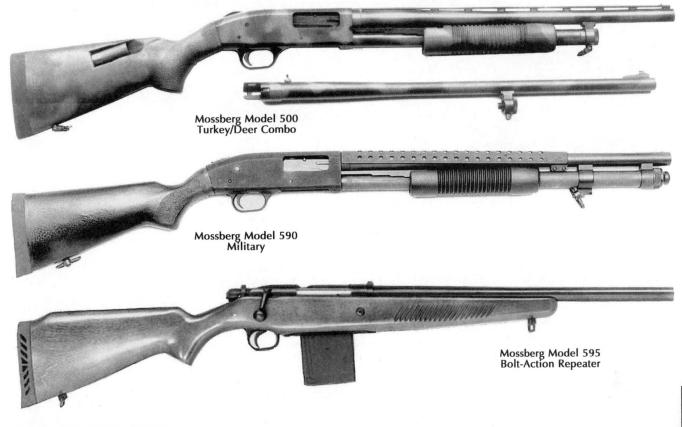

Mossberg Model 500
Turkey/Deer Combo

Mossberg Model 590
Military

Mossberg Model 595
Bolt-Action Repeater

MODEL 500 PIGEON GRADE

Same as Model 500 Super Grade except higher quality w/fancy wood, floating vent rib; field gun hunting dog etching, trap and skeet guns have scroll etching. Bbls.: 30-inch, F choke (12 ga. only); 28-inch, M choke; 26-inch, SK choke or C-Lect-Choke. Made from 1971 to 1975.
Model 500APR, 12 ga., field, trap or skeet NiB $510 Ex $409 Gd $320
Model 500APKR, 12 ga.
field gun, C-Lect-Choke.............NiB $455 Ex $279 Gd $144
Model 500 APTR, 12 ga.,
Trap gun, Monte Carlo stock.........NiB $475 Ex $300 Gd $165
Model 500CPR, 20 ga., field or skeet gun NiB $365 Ex $279 Gd $180
Model 500EPR, .410 ga.
field or skeet gun..................NiB $345 Ex $292 Gd $190

MODEL 500 CAMO COMBO SHOTGUN NiB $440 Ex $335 Gd $255
Gauges: 12 and 20. 24- and 28-inch bbl. w/adj. rifle sights. Weight: 7 to 7.25 lbs. Available w/blued or camo finish. Drilled and tapped receiver w/sling swivels and camo web sling. Made from 1987 to 1998.

MODEL 500 PUMP SLUGSTER SHOTGUN

Gauges: 12 or 20 w/3-inch chamber. 24-inch smoothbore or rifled bbl. w/adj. rifle sights or intregral scope mount and optional muzzle break (1997 porting became standard). Weight: 7 to 7.25 lbs. Wood or synthetic stock w/standard or Woodland Camo finish. Blued, matte black or Marinecote metal finish. Drilled and tapped receiver w/camo sling and swivels. Made 1987 to date.
Slugster (w/cyl. bore, rifle sights)......NiB $335 Ex $245 Gd $190
Slugster (w/rifled bore, ported).......NiB $415 Ex $335 Gd $240
Slugster (w/rifled bore, unported)......NiB $320 Ex $219 Gd $190
Slugster (w/rifled bore, ported,
integral scope mount)..............NiB $320 Ex $219 Gd $190
Slugster (w/Marinecote and
synthetic stock), add..................................$100
Slugster (w/Truglo fiber optics), add........................$50

MODEL 500 REGAL SLIDE-ACTION REPEATER

Similar to regular Model 500 except higher quality workmanship throughout. Gauges: 12 and 20. Bbls.: 26- and 28-inch w/various chokes, or Accu-Choke. Weight: 6.75 to 7.5 lbs. Checkered walnut stock and forearm. Made from 1985 to 1987.
Model 500 w/Accu-Choke ... NiB $320 Ex $219 Gd $190
Model 500 w/fixed choke ... NiB $300 Ex $200 Gd $165

MODEL 500 SPORTING PUMP

Gauges: 12, 20 or .410, 2.75- or 3-inch chamber. Bbls.: 22 to 28 inches w/fixed choke or screw-in tubes; plain or vent rib. Weight: 6.25 to 7.25 lbs. White bead front sight, brass mid-bead. Checkered hardwood buttstock and forend w/walnut finish.
Standard model ....NiB $345 Ex $275 Gd $190
Field combo (w/extra Slugster bbl.) ....NiB $440 Ex $325 Gd $240

MODEL 500 SUPER GRADE

Same as pre-1977 Model 500 Field Grade except not made in 16 ga., has vent rib bbl., checkered pistol grip and slide handle. Made from 1965- to 1976.
Model 500AR, 12 ga. ....NiB $400 Ex $299 Gd $221
Model 500AMR, 12 ga.,
heavy magnum bbl. ....NiB $400 Ex $299 Gd $221
Model 500AKR, 12 ga., C-Lect-Choke .. NiB $425 Ex $315 Gd $235
Model 500CR 20 ga. ....NiB $400 Ex $299 Gd $221
Model 500CKk, 20 ga., C-Lect-Choke .. NiB $425 Ex $315 Gd $235
Model 500ER, .410 ga. ....NiB $400 Ex $299 Gd $221
Model 500EKR, .410 ga., C-Lect-Choke NiB $425 Ex $315 Gd $235

MODEL 500 TURKEY/DEER COMBO... NiB $425 Ex $315 Gd $235
Pump (slide action). Gauge: 12. 20- and 24-inch bbls. Weight: 7.25 lbs. Drilled and tapped receiver, camo sling and swivels. Adj. rifle sights and camo finish. Vent rib. Made from 1987 to 1997.

Mossberg Model 1000
Junior Autoloading

Mossberg Model 5500
Guardian

MODEL 500 TURKEY GUN. . . NiB $465 Ex $325 Gd $254
Same as Model 500 Camo Pump except w/24-inch ACCU-Choke bbl. w/extra full choke tube and ghost ring sights. Made 1992 to 1997.

MODEL 500 VIKING PUMP SHOTGUN
Gauges: 12 or 20 w/3-inch chamber. 24-, 26- or 28-inch bbls. available in smoothbore w/Accu-Choke and vent rib or rifled bore w/iron sights and optional muzzle brake (1997 porting became standard). Optional optics: Slug Shooting System (SSS). Weight: 6.9 to 7.2 lbs. Moss-green synthetic stock. Matte black metal finish. Made from 1996 to 1998.
Mdl. 500 Viking
(w/VR & choke tubes, unported) . . . . NiB $300 Ex $225 Gd $144
Mdl. 500 Viking (w/rifled bore, ported)NiB $390 Ex $295 Gd $240
Mdl. 500 Viking
(w/rifled bore, SSS & ported). . . . . NiB $390 Ex $295 Gd $240
Mdl. 500 Viking
(w/rifled bore, unported). . . . . NiB $300 Ex $225 Gd $144
Mdl. 500 Viking Turkey
(w/VR, tubes, ported) . . . . NiB $300 Ex $225 Gd $144

MODEL 500
WATERFOWL/DEER COMBO . . . . . . NiB $455 Ex $350 Gd $285
Same general specifications as the Turkey/Deer combo except w/either 28- or 30-inch bbl. along w/the 24-inch bbl. Made from 1987 to date.

MODEL 500 ATR SUPER
GRADE TRAP . . . . NiB $400 Ex $310 Gd $225
Same as pre-1977 Model 500 Field Grade except 12 ga. only w/ vent-rib bbl.; 30-inch F choke, checkered Monte Carlo stock w/ recoil pad, beavertail slide handle. Made from 1968 to 1971.

MODEL 500DSPR DUCK STAMP
COMMEMORATIVE . . . . NiB $600 Ex $465 Gd $300
Limited edition of 1000 to commemorate the Migratory Bird Hunting Stamp program. Same as Model 500DSPR Pigeon Grade 12-Gauge Magnum Heavy Duck Gun w/heavy 30-inch vent-rib bbl., F choke; receiver has special wood duck etching. Gun accompanied by a special wall plaque. Made in 1975.

MODEL 590 BULLPUP . . . . . . NiB $745 Ex $449 Gd $335
Same general specifications as the Model 500 Bullpup except 20-inch bbl. and 9-round magazine. Made from 1989 to 1990.

MODEL 590 MARINER PUMP
Same general specifications as the Model 590 Military Security except has Marinecote metal finish and field configuration synthetic stock w/pistiol-grip conversion included. Made 1989 to 1999.
Model 590 Mariner (w/18.5-inch bbl.)NiB $645 Ex $554 Gd $470
Model 590 Mariner (w/20-inch bbl.) . NiB $645 Ex $554 Gd $470
Model 590 Mariner (w/grip conversion), add. $40
Model 590 Mariner (w/ghost ring sight), add $75

MODEL 590 MILITARY SECURITY. . . NiB $544 Ex $389 Gd $290
Same general specifications as the Model 590 Military except there

is no heat shield and gun has short pistol-grip style instead of butt-stock. Weight: About 6.75 lbs. Made from 1987 to 1993.

MODEL 590 MILITARY SHOTGUN
Slide-action. Gauge: 12. 9-round capacity. 20-inch bbl. Weight: About 7 lbs. Synthetic or hardwood buttstock and forend. Ventilated bbl. heat shields. Equipped w/bayonet lug. Blued or Parkerized finish. Made from 1987 to date.
Synthetic model, blued . . . . . NiB $465 Ex $377 Gd $260
Synthetic model Parkerized . NiB $490 Ex $400 Gd $280
Speedfeed model, blued . . . . NiB $475 Ex $380 Gd $285
Speedfeed model, Parkerized NiB $475 Ex $ 380 Gd $285
Intimidator model
w/laser sight, blued . . . . NiB $640 Ex $500 Gd $365
Intimidator model
w/laser sight, Parkerized . . . . NiB $665 Ex $515 Gd $380
For ghost ring sight, add $100

MODEL 595/595K
BOLT-ACTION REPEATER. . . . NiB $425 Ex $260 Gd $159
12 ga. only. Four round detachable magazine. 18.5-inch bbl. Weight: About 7 lbs. Walnut finished stock w/recoil pad and sling swivels. Made 1985 to 1986.

MODEL 695 BOLT-ACTION SLUGSTER
Gauge: 12 w/3-inch chamber. Two round detachable magazine. 22-inch fully rifled and ported bbl. w/blade front and folding leaf rear sights. Receiver drilled and tapped for Weaver style scope bases. Available w/1.5x-4.5x scope or fiber optics installed. Weight: 7.5 lbs. Black synthetic stock w/swivel studs and recoil pad. Made 1996 to 2002.
Model 695 (w/ACCU-choke bbl.)NiB $300 Ex $220 Gd $175
Model 695
(w/open sights). . . . . NiB $380 Ex $296 Gd $207
Model 695
(w/1.5x-4.5x Bushnell scope) . NiB $390 Ex $310 Gd $219
Model 695 (w/Truglo fiber optics) NiB $385 Ex $305 Gd $210
Model 695 OFM Camo. . . . . . . NiB $355 Ex $280 Gd $196

MODEL 695 BOLT-ACTION TURKEY GUN NiB $375 Ex $265 Gd $195
Similar to 695 Slugster Model except has smoothbore 22-inch bbl. w/extra-full turkey Accu-choke tube. Bead front and U-notch rear sights. Full OFM camo finish. Made from 1996 to 2002.

MODEL 712 AUTOLOADING SHOTGUN
Gas-operated, takedown, hammerless shotgun w/5-round (4-round w/3-inch chamber) tubular magazine. 12 ga. Bbls.: 28-inch vent rib or 24-inch plain bbl. Slugster w/rifle sights. Fixed choke or ACCU-choke tube system. Weight: 7.5 lbs. Plain alloy receiver w/top-mounted ambidextrous safety. Checkered. stained hardwood stock w/recoil pad. Imported from Japan 1986 to 1990.
Mdl. 712 w/fixed chokes . . . . NiB $369 Ex $237 Gd $185
Mdl. 712 w/ACCU-Choke tube system   NiB $390 Ex $275 Gd $219
Mdl. 712 Regal w/ACCU-Choke tube systemNiB $390 Ex $275 Gd $219
Mdl. 712 Regal w/ACCU-Choke II tube sys.NiB $390 Ex $275 Gd $219

MODEL 835 FIELD PUMP SHOTGUN

Similar to the Model 9600 Regal except has walnut-stained hardwood stock and one ACCU-Choke tube only.

Standard model	NiB $365	Ex $220	Gd $154
Turkey model	NiB $365	Ex $220	Gd $154
Combo model (24- & 28-inch bbls.)	NiB $390	Ex $250	Gd $180

MODEL 835 "NWTF" ULTI-MA SHOTGUN

National Wild Turkey Federation pump-action. Gauge: 12, 3.5-inch chamber. 24-inch vent-rib bbl. w/four ACCU-MAG chokes. Realtree camo finish. QD swivel and post. Made from 1989 to 1993.

Limited Edition model	NiB $470	Ex $366	Gd $239
Special Edition model	NiB $400	Ex $325	Gd $225

MODEL 835 REGAL ULTI-MAG PUMP

Gauge: 12, 3.5-inch chamber. Bbls.: 24- or 28-inch vent-rib w/ACCU-Choke screw-in tubes. Weight: 7.75 lbs. White bead front, brass mid-bead. Checkered hardwood or synthetic stock w/camo finish. Made 1991 to 1996.

Special model	NiB $400	Ex $350	Gd $235
Standard model	NiB $509	Ex $377	Gd $295
Camo Synthetic model	NiB $490	Ex $375	Gd $299
Combo model	NiB $528	Ex $420	Gd $310

MODEL 835 VIKING PUMP SHOTGUN

Gauge: 12 w/3-inch chamber. 28-inch smoothbore bbl. w/Accu-Choke, vent rib and optional muzzle brake (in 1997 porting became standard). Weight: 7.7 lbs. Green synthetic stock. Matte black metal finish. Made from 1996 to 1998.

Model 835 Viking (w/VR and choke tubes, ported)	NiB $300	Ex $217	Gd $175
Model 835 Viking (w/VR and choke tubes, unported)	NiB $445	Ex $270	Gd $210

MODEL 1000 AUTOLOADING SHOTGUN

Gas-operated, takedown, hammerless shotgun w/tubular magazine. Gauges: 12, 20; 2.75- or 3-inch chamber. Bbls.: 22- to 30-inch vent rib w/fixed choke or ACCU-Choke tubes; or 22-inch plain bbl, Slugster w/rifle sights. Weight: 6.5 to 7.5 lbs. Scroll-engraved alloy receiver, crossbolt-type safety. Checkered walnut buttstock and forend. Imported from Japan 1986 to 1987.

Junior model, 20 ga., 22-inch bbl.	NiB $555	Ex $435	Gd $320
Standard model w/fixed choke	NiB $555	Ex $435	Gd $320
Standard model w/choke tubes	NiB $555	Ex $435	Gd $320

MODEL 1000 SUPER AUTOLOADING SHOTGUN

Similar to Model 1000, but in 12 ga. only w/3-inch chamber and new gas metering system. Bbls.: 26-, 28- or 30-inch vent rib w/ACCU-Choke tubes.

Standard model w/choke tubes	NiB $555	Ex $435	Gd $320
Waterfowler model (Parkerized)	NiB $590	Ex $466	Gd $380

MODEL 1000S SUPER SKEET . NiB $655 Ex $500 Gd $422

Similar to Model 1000 in 12 or 20 ga., except w/all-steel receiver and vented jug-type choke for reduced muzzle jump. Bright-point front sight and brass mid-bead. 1 and 2 oz. forend cap weights.

MODEL 5500 AUTOLOADING SHOTGUN

Gas-operated. Takedown. 12 ga. only. Four round magazine (3-round w/3-inch shells). Bbls.: 18.5- to 30-inch; various chokes. Checkered walnut finished hardwood. Made from 1985 to 1986.

Model 5500 w/ACCU-Choke	NiB $300	Ex $210	Gd $148
Model 5500 modified junior	NiB $300	Ex $210	Gd $148
Model 5500 Slugster	NiB $355	Ex $209	Gd $155
Model 5500 12 ga. Mag	NiB $335	Ex $254	Gd $190
Model 5500 Guardian	NiB $330	Ex $250	Gd $180

MODEL 5500 MKII AUTOLOADING SHOTGUN

Same as Model 5500 except equipped w/two Accu-Choke bbls.: 26-inch ported for non-Magnum 2.75-inch shells; 28-inch for magnum loads. Made from 1988 to 1993.

Standard model	NiB $330	Ex $209	Gd $135
Camo model	NiB $366	Ex $270	Gd $198
NWTF Mossy Oak model	NiB $415	Ex $330	Gd $225
USST model (1991-92)	NiB $370	Ex $292	Gd $217

MODEL 6000 AUTO SHOTGUN NiB $320 Ex $231 Gd $198

Similar to the Model 9200 Regal except has 28-inch vent-rib bbl. w/mod. ACCU-Choke tube only. Made 1993 only.

MODEL 9200 CAMO SHOTGUN

Similar to the Model 9200 Regal except has synthetic stock and forend and is completely finished in camouflage pattern (incl. bbl.). Made from 1993 to date.

Standard model (OFM camo)	NiB $500	Ex $415	Gd $306
Turkey model (Mossy Oak camo)	NiB $475	Ex $429	Gd $360
Turkey model (Shadow Branch camo)	NiB $615	Ex $490	Gd $376
Comb. model (24 & 28-inch bbls. w/OFM camo)	NiB $635	Ex $515	Gd $390

MODEL 9200 CROWN (REGAL) AUTOLOADER

Gauge: 12; 3-inch chamber. Bbls.: 18.5- to 28-inch w/ACCU-Choke tubes; plain or vent rib. Weight: 7.25 to 7.5 lbs. Checkered hardwood buttstock and forend w/walnut finish. Made from 1992 to 2001.

Model 9200 Bantam (w/1-inch shorter stock)	NiB $500	Ex $433	Gd $329
Model 9200 w/ACCU-Choke	NiB $500	Ex $433	Gd $329
Model 9200 w/rifled bbl.	NiB $500	Ex $433	Gd $329
Model 9200 Combo (w/extra Slugster bbl.)	NiB $550	Ex $493	Gd $379
Model 9200 SP (w/matte blue finish, 18.5-inch bbl.)	NiB $500	Ex $433	Gd $329

MODEL 9200 PERSUADER . . . NiB $500 Ex $443 Gd $329

Similar to the Model 9200 Regal except has 18.5-inch plain bbl. w/fixed mod. choke. Parkerized finish. Black synthetic stock w/sling swivels. Made from 1996 to 2001.

MODEL 9200 A1 JUNGLE GUN NiB $665 Ex $533 Gd $347

Similar to the Model 9200 Persuader except has mil-spec heavy wall 18.5-inch plain bbl. w/cyl. bore designed for 00 Buck shot. 12 ga. w/2.75-inch chamber. Five round magazine. 38.5 inches overall. Weight: 7 lbs. Black synthetic stock. Parkerized finish. Made from 1998 to 2001.

MODEL 9200 SPECIAL HUNTER NiB $555 Ex $435 Gd $365

Similar to the Model 9200 Regal except has 28-inch vent-rib bbl. w/ACCU-Choke tubes. Parkerized finish. Black synthetic stock. Made from 1998 to 2001.

MODEL 9200 TROPHY

Similar to the Model 9200 Regal except w/24-inch rifled bbl. or 24- or 28-inch vent-rib bbl. w/ACCU-Choke tubes. Checkered walnut stock w/sling swivels. Made from 1992 to 1998.

Trophy (w/vent rib bbl.)	NiB $650	Ex $583	Gd $479
Trophy (w/rifled bbl. & cantilever scope mount)	NiB $675	Ex $609	Gd $495
Trophy (w/rifled bbl. & rifle sights)	NiB $635	Ex $570	Gd $460

MODEL 9200 USST AUTOLOADER . . NiB $525 Ex $390 Gd $295

Similar to the Model 9200 Regal except has 26-inch vent-rib bbl. w/ACCU-Choke tubes. "United States Shooting Team" engraved on receiver. Made from 1993 to date.

SHOTGUNS

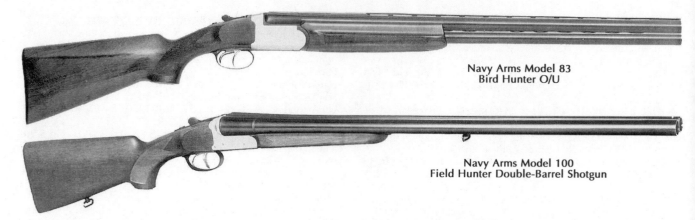

Navy Arms Model 83
Bird Hunter O/U

Navy Arms Model 100
Field Hunter Double-Barrel Shotgun

MODEL 9200
VIKING AUTOLOADER . . . . . NiB $425 Ex $330 Gd $290
Gauge: 12 w/3-inch chamber. 28-inch smoothbore bbl. W/Accu-Choke and vent rib. Weight: 7.7 lbs. Green synthetic stock. Matte black metal finish. Made from 1996 to 1998.

MODEL HS410
HOME SECURITY PUMP SHOTGUN
Gauge: .410; 3-inch chamber. Bbl.: 18.5-inch w/muzzle brake; blued. Weight: 6.25 lbs. Synthetic stock and pistol-grip slide. Optional laser sight. Made from 1990 to date. A similar version of this gun is marketed by Maverick Arms under the same model designation.
Standard model . . . . NiB $345 Ex $270 Gd $195
Laser model . . . . NiB $544 Ex $396 Gd $277

LINE LAUNCHER . . . . NiB $1066 Ex $833 Gd $545
Gauge: 12 w/blank cartridge. Projectile travels from 250 to 275 feet.

"NEW HAVEN BRAND" SHOTGUNS
Promotional models, similar to their standard guns but plainer in finish, are marketed by Mossberg under the "New Haven" brand name. Values generally are about 20 percent lower than for corresponding standard models.

NAVY ARMS SHOTGUNS —
Ridgefield, New Jersey

MODEL 83/93 BIRD HUNTER O/U
Hammerless. Boxlock, engraved receiver. Gauges: 12 and 20; 3-inch chambers. Bbls.: 28-inch chrome lined w/double vent-rib construction. Checkered European walnut stock and forearm. Gold plated triggers. Imported 1984 to 1990.
Model 83 w/extractors . . . . . . NiB $355 Ex $285 Gd $200
Model 93 w/ejectors . . . . NiB $379 Ex $339 Gd $255

MODEL 95/96 O/U SHOTGUN
Same as the Model 83/93 except w/five interchangeable choke tubes. Imported 1984 to 1990.
Model 95 w/extractors . . . . . . NiB $448 Ex $355 Gd $210
Model 96 w/ejectors . . . . NiB $555 Ex $376 Gd $280

MODEL 100/150 FIELD HUNTER DOUBLE-BARREL SHOTGUN
Boxlock. Gauges: 12 and 20. Bbls.: 28-inch chrome lined. Checkered European walnut stock and forearm. Imported 1984 to 1990.
Model 100 . . . . NiB $460 Ex $390 Gd $288
Model 150 (auto ejectors) . . . NiB $510 Ex $355 Gd $290

MODEL 100 O/U SHOTGUN . NiB $277 Ex $169 Gd $109
Hammerless, takedown shotgun w/engraved chrome receiver. Single trigger. 12, 20, 28, or .410 ga. w/3-inch chambers. Bbls.: 26-inch (F/F or SK/SK); vent rib. Weight: 6.25 lbs. Checkered European walnut buttstock and forend. Imported 1986 to 1990.

NEW ENGLAND FIREARMS —
Gardner, Massachusetts

In 1987, New England Firearms was established as an independent company producing selected H&R models under the NEF logo after Harrington & Richardson suspended operations on January 24, 1986. In 1991, H&R 1871, Inc. was formed from the residual of the parent H&R company and then took over the New England Firearms facility. H&R 1871 produced firearms under both their logo and the NEF brand name until 1999, when the Marlin Firearms Company acquired the assets of H&R 1871.

NEW ENGLAND FIREARMS NWTF TURKEY SPECIAL
Similar to Turkey and Goose models except 10 or 20 gauge w/22- or 24-inch plain bbl. w/screw-in full-choke tube. Mossy Oak camo finish on entire gun. Made from 1992 to 1996.
Turkey Special 10 ga. . . . . NiB $265 Ex $177 Gd $98
Turkey Special 20 ga. . . . . . . NiB $335 Ex $219 Gd $189

NRA FOUNDATION YOUTH . NiB $190 Ex $155 Gd $100
Smaller scale version of Pardner Model chambered for 20, 28 or .410 w/22- inch plain bbl. High luster blue finish. NRA Foundation logo laser etched on stock. Made from 1999 to 2002.

PARDNER SHOTGUN
Takedown. Side lever. Single bbl. Gauges: 12, 20 and .410 w/3-inch chamber; 16 and 28 w/2.75-inch chamber. 26-, 28- or 32-inch, plain bbl. w/fixed choke. Weight: 5-6 lbs. Bead front sight. Pistol grip-style hardwood stock w/walnut finish. Made from 1988 to date.
Standard model . . . . NiB $255 Ex $185 Gd $99
Youth model . . . . NiB $255 Ex $185 Gd $99
Turkey model . . . . NiB $323 Ex $217 Gd $110
W/32-inch bbl., add $40

PARDNER SPECIAL PURPOSE 10-GA SHOTGUN
Similar to the standard Pardner model except chambered 10 ga. only w/3.5-inch chamber. 24- or 28-inch, plain bbl. w/full choke tube or fixed choke. Weight: 9.5 lbs. Bead front sight. Pistol-grip-style hardwood stock w/camo or matte black finish. Made from 1989 to date.
Special Purpose model w/fixed choke NiB $315 Ex $220 Gd $125
W/camo finish, add $40
W/choke tube, add $25
W/24-inch bbl. turkey option, add $50

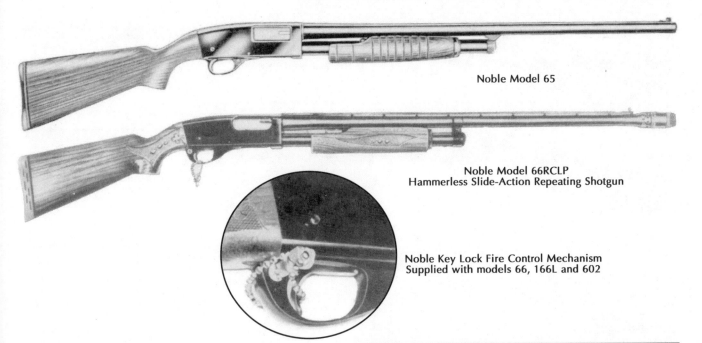

Noble Model 65

Noble Model 66RCLP
Hammerless Slide-Action Repeating Shotgun

Noble Key Lock Fire Control Mechanism
Supplied with models 66, 166L and 602

PARDNER SPECIAL PURPOSE
WATERFOWL SINGLE-SHOT . NiB $255 Ex $190 Gd $129
Similar to Special Purpose 10 Ga. model except w/32-inch bbl. Mossy Oak camo stock w/swivel and sling. Made from 1988 to date.

PARDNER TURKEY GUN
Similar to Pardner model except chambered in 12 ga. w/3.0- or 3.5-inch chamber. 24-inch plain bbl. W/turkey full-choke tube or fixed choke. Weight: 9.5 lbs. American hardwood stock w/camo or matte black finish. Made from 1999 to date.
Standard Turkey model . . . . . . NiB $200 Ex $110 Gd $85
Camo Turkey model . . . . NiB $200 Ex $110 Gd $85

SURVIVOR SERIES
Takedown single bbl. shotgun w/side lever release, Automatic ejector and patented transfer-bar safety. Gauges: 12, 20, and .410/.45 ACP w/3-inch chamber. 22-inch bbl. w/modified choke and bead sight. Weight: 6 lbs. Polymer stock and forend w/hollow cavity for storage. Made 1992 to 1993 and 1995 to date.
12 or 20 ga.
w/blued finish . . . . NiB $220 Ex $144 Gd $98
12 or 20 ga.
w/nickel finish . . . . NiB $260 Ex $177 Gd $120
.410/.45 LC add $75

TRACKER SLUG GUN
Similar to Pardner model except in 10, 12 or 20 ga. w/24-inch w/cylinder choke or rifled slug bbl. (Tracker II). Weight: 6 lbs. American hardwood stock w/walnut or camo finish, Schnabel forend, sling swivel studs. Made from 1992 to 2001.
Tracker Slug
(10 ga.) . . . . NiB $180 Ex $110 Gd $79
Tracker Slug
(12 or 20 ga.) . . . . NiB $219 Ex $120 Gd $85
Tracker II (rifled bore) . . . . NiB $219 Ex $120 Gd $85

NIKKO FIREARMS LTD. — Tochigi, Japan

See listings under Golden Eagle Firearms, Inc.

NOBLE MANUFACTURING COMPANY — Haydenville, Massachusetts

Series 602 and 70 are similar in appearance to the corresponding Model 66 guns.

MODEL 40 HAMMERLESS SLIDE-ACTION
REPEATING SHOTGUN . . . . . NiB $255 Ex $190 Gd $130
Solid frame. 12 ga. only. Five round tubular magazine. 28-inch bbl. w/ventilated Multi-Choke. Weight: About 7.5 lbs. Plain pistol-grip stock, grooved slide handle. Made from 1950 to 1955.

MODEL 50
SLIDE-ACTION . . . . NiB $266 Ex $190 Gd $125
Same as Model 40 except w/o Multi-Choke. M or F choke bbl. Made from 1953 to 1955.

MODEL 60 HAMMERLESS SLIDE-ACTION
REPEATING SHOTGUN . . . . . NiB $325 Ex $255 Gd $159
Solid frame. 12 and 16 ga. Five round tubular magazine. 28-inch bbl. w/adj. choke. Plain pistol-grip stock w/recoil pad, grooved slide handle. Weight: About 7.5 lbs. Made from 1955 to 1966.

MODEL 65 . . . . NiB $300 Ex $225 Gd $165
Same as Model 60 except without adj. choke and recoil pad. M or F choke bbl. Made from 1955 to 1966.

MODEL 66CLP . . . . NiB $235 Ex $185 Gd $135
Same as Model 66RCLP except has plain bbl. Introduced in 1967. Disc.

MODEL 66RCLP HAMMERLESS SLIDE-ACTION
REPEATING SHOTGUN . . . . . NiB $339 Ex $235 Gd $176
Solid frame. Key lock fire control mechanism. Gauges: 12, 16. 3-inch chamber in 12 ga. Five round tubular magazine. 28-inch bbl., vent rib, adj. choke. Weight: About 7.5 lbs. Checkered pistol-grip stock and slide handle, recoil pad. Made from 1967 to 1970.

MODEL 66RLP . . . . NiB $329 Ex $225 Gd $165
Same as Model 66RCLP except w/F or M choke. Made 1967 to 1970.

SHOTGUNS

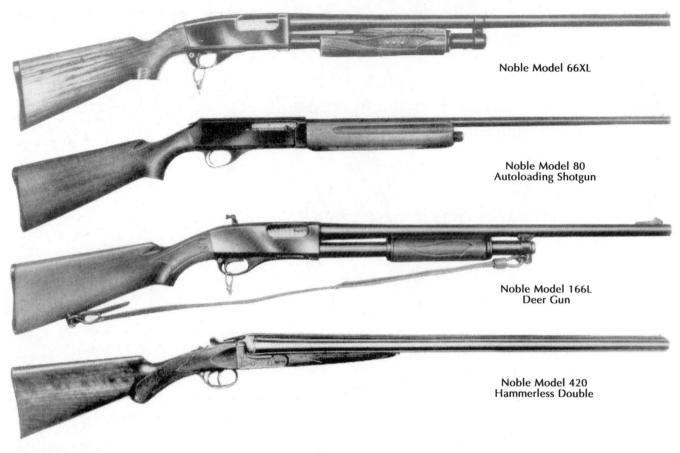

Noble Model 66XL

Noble Model 80
Autoloading Shotgun

Noble Model 166L
Deer Gun

Noble Model 420
Hammerless Double

MODEL 66XL . . . . **NiB $245 Ex $185 Gd $129**
Same as Model 66RCL except has plain bbl., F or M choke, slide
handle only checkered, no recoil pad. Made from 1967 to 1970.

**MODEL 70CLP HAMMERLESS SLIDE-ACTION
REPEATING SHOTGUN** . . . . . **NiB $277 Ex $198 Gd $145**
Solid frame. .410 gauge. Magazine holds 5 rounds. 26-inch bbl. w/
adj. choke. Weight: About 6 lbs. Checkered buttstock and forearm,
recoil pad. Made from 1958 to 1970.

MODEL 70RCLP . . . . **NiB $280 Ex $199 Gd $149**
Same as Model 70CLP except has vent rib. Made 1967 to 1970.

MODEL 70RLP . . . . **NiB $278 Ex $199 Gd $145**
Same as Model 70CLP except has vent rib and no adj. choke. Made
from 1967 to 1970.

MODEL 70XL . . . . **NiB $255 Ex $160 Gd $110**
Same as Model 70CLP except without adj. choke and checkering on
buttstock. Made from 1958 to 1970.

**MODEL 80
AUTOLOADING SHOTGUN. . NiB $344 Ex $265 Gd $196**
Recoil-operated. .410 ga. Magazine holds three 3-inch shells, four
2.5-inch shells. 26-inch bbl., full choke. Weight: About 6 lbs. Plain
pistol-grip stock and fluted forearm. Made from 1964 to 1966.

MODEL 166L DEER GUN . . . . **NiB $355 Ex $270 Gd $199**
Solid frame. Key lock fire control mechanism. 12 ga. 2.75-inch
chamber. Five round tubular magazine. 24-inch plain bbl., specially
bored for rifled slug. Lyman peep rear sight, post ramp front sight.
Receiver dovetailed for scope mounting. Weight: About 7.25 lbs.

Checkered pistol-grip stock and slide handle, swivels and carrying
strap. Made from 1967 to 1970.

**MODEL 420
HAMMERLESS DOUBLE** . . . . **NiB $466 Ex $361 Gd $255**
Boxlock. Plain extractors. Double triggers. Gauges: 12 ga.
3-inch mag.; 16 ga.; 20 ga. 3-inch mag.; .410 ga. Bbls.: 28-inch,
except .410 in 26-inch, M/F choke. Weight: About 6.75 lbs.
Engraved frame. Checkered walnut stock and forearm. Made
from 1958 to 1970.

**MODEL 450E
HAMMERLESS DOUBLE** . . . . **NiB $490 Ex $376 Gd $290**
Boxlock. Engraved frame. Selective auto ejectors. Double trig-
gers. Gauges: 12, 16, 20. 3-inch chambers in 12 and 20 ga.
28-inch bbls., M/F choke. Weight: About 6 lbs., 14 oz., 12 ga.
Checkered pistol-grip stock and beavertail forearm, recoil pad.
Made from 1967 to 1970.

MODEL 602CLP . . . . **NiB $366 Ex $255 Gd $235**
Same as Model 602RCLP except has plain barrel. Made from
1958 to 1970.

**MODEL 602RCLP HAMMERLESS SLIDE-ACTION
REPEATING SHOTGUN** . . . . . **NiB $355 Ex $255 Gd $190**
Solid frame. Key lock fire control mechanism. 20 ga. 3-inch
chamber. Five round tubular magazine. 28-inch bbl., vent rib, adj.
choke. Weight: About 6.5 lbs. Checkered pistol-grip stock/slide
handle, recoil pad. Made from 1967 to 1970.

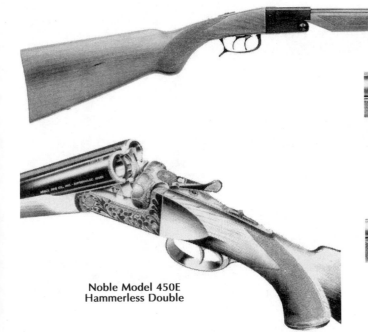

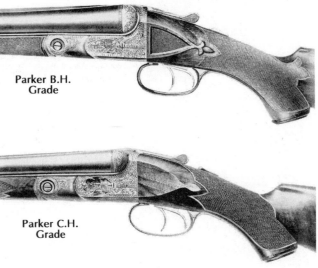

Omega Deluxe Side-by-Side Shotgun

Parker B.H.
Grade

Parker C.H.
Grade

Noble Model 450E
Hammerless Double

MODEL 602RLP . . . . NiB $315 Ex $233 Gd $157
Same as Model 602RCLP except without adj. choke, bored F or M choke. Made from 1967 to 1970.

MODEL 602XL . . . . NiB $285 Ex $177 Gd $145
Same as Model 602RCL except has plain bbl., F or M choke, slide handle only checkered, no recoil pad. Made from 1958 to 1970.

MODEL 662 . . . . NiB $308 Ex $244 Gd $165
Same as Model 602CLP except has aluminum receiver and bbl. Weight: About 4.5 lbs. Made from 1966 to 1970.

OMEGASHOTGUNS—Brescia, Italy, and Korea

FOLDING OVER/UNDER STANDARD SHOTGUN
Hammerless Boxlock. Gauges: 12, 20, 28 w/2.75-inch chambers or .410 w/3-inch chambers. Bbls.: 26- or 28-inch vent-rib w/fixed chokes (IC/M, M/F or F/F (.410). Automatic safety. Single trigger. 40.5 inches overall (42.5 inches, 20 ga., 28-inch bbl.). Weight: 6 to 7.5 lbs. Checkered European walnut stock and forearm. Imported from 1984 to 1994.
Standard model (12 ga.) . . . . NiB $475 Ex $355 Gd $298
Standard model (20 ga.) . . . . NiB $475 Ex $355 Gd $298
Standard model (28 ga. & .410) . . . . NiB $475 Ex $355 Gd $298

O/U DELUXE SHOTGUN . . . . NiB $390 Ex $287 Gd $200
Gauges: 20, 28 and .410. 26- or 28-inch vent-rib bbls. 40.5 inches overall (42.5 inches, 20 ga., 28-inch bbl.). Chokes: IC/M, M/F or F/F (.410). Weight: About 5.5-6 lbs. Single trigger. Automatic safety. European walnut stock w/checkered pistol grip and tulip forend. Imported from Italy 1984 to 1990.

OMEGA DELUXE
SIDE-BY-SIDE SHOTGUN . . . . NiB $290 Ex $225 Gd $165
Same general specifications as the Standard Side-by-Side except has checkered European walnut stock and low bbl. rib. Made in Italy from 1984 to 1989.

STANDARD SIDE-BY-SIDE SHOTGUN, NiB $245 Ex $135 Gd $90
Gauge: .410. 26-inch bbl. 40.5 inches overall. Choked F/F. Weight: 5.5 lbs. Double trigger. Manual safety. Checkered beechwood stock and semi-pistol grip. Imported from Italy 1984 to 1989.

STANDARD SINGLE-SHOT SHOTGUN
Gauges: 12, 16, 20, 28 and .410. Bbl. lengths: 26-, 28- or 30-inches. Weight: 5 lbs., 4 oz. to 5 lbs., 11 oz. Indonesian walnut stock. Matte-chromed receiver and top lever break. Imported from 1984 to 1987.
Standard fixed . . . . NiB $155 Ex $90 Gd $65
Standard folding . . . . NiB $175 Ex $110 Gd $75
Deluxe folding . . . . NiB $255 Ex $185 Gd $95

DELUXE SINGLE-SHOT SHOTGUN . . NiB $229 Ex $145 Gd $99
Same general specifications as the Standard single bbl. except has checkered walnut stock, top lever break, fully-blued receiver, vent rib. Imported from Korea 1984 to 1987.

PARKER BROTHERS—Meriden, Connecticut

This firm was taken over by Remington Arms Company in 1934 and its production facilities moved to Remington's Ilion, New York, plant. In 1984, Winchester took over production until 1999.

HAMMERLESS DOUBLE-BARREL SHOTGUNS
Grades V.H. through A-1 Special. Boxlock. Auto ejectors. Double triggers or selective single trigger. Gauges: 10, 12, 16, 20, 28, .410. Bbls.: 26- to 32-inch, any standard boring. Weight: 6.88-8.5 lbs., 12 ga. Stock and forearm of select walnut, checkered; straight, half-or full-pistol grip. Grades differ only in quality of workmanship, grade of wood, engraving, checkering, etc. General specifications are the same for all. Disc. about 1940.
V.H. grade, 12 or 16 ga. . . . . NiB $5733 Ex $4187 Gd $2266
V.H. grade, 20 ga. . . . . NiB $9455 Ex $6077 Gd $3145
V.H. grade, 28 ga. . . . . NiB $28,998 Ex $27,966 Gd $26,778
V.H. grade, .410. . . . . NiB $34,669 Ex $25,766 Gd $21,560
G.H. grade, 12 ga. . . . . NiB $7566 Ex $3998 Gd $2779
G.H. grade, 16 ga. . . . . NiB $8120 Ex $4233 Gd $2988

SHOTGUNS

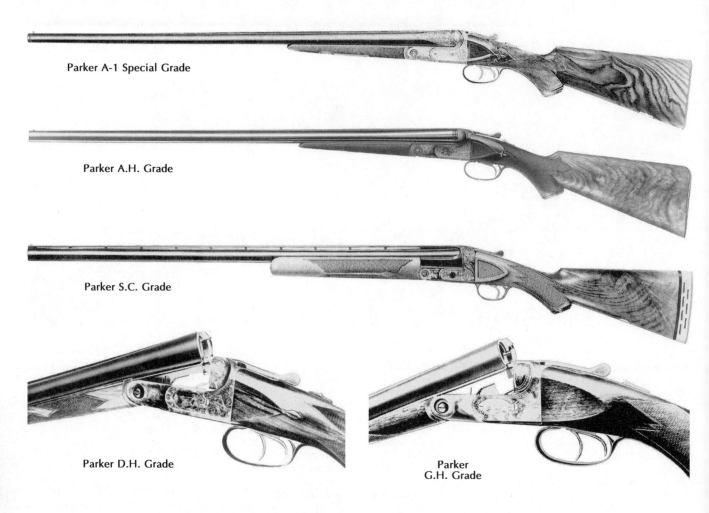

Parker A-1 Special Grade

Parker A.H. Grade

Parker S.C. Grade

Parker D.H. Grade

Parker
G.H. Grade

G.H. grade, 20 ga.. . . . . NiB $12,960 Ex $10,679 Gd $7789
G.H. grade, 28 ga.. . . . . .NiB $33,790 Ex $29,645 Gd $27,889
G.H. grade, .410. . . . . .NiB $45,890 Ex $39,955 Gd $27,987
D.H. grade, 12 or 16 ga. . . . . . . .NiB $10,440 Ex $7866 Gd $4350
D.H. grade, 20 ga.. . . . . .NiB $16,777 Ex $13,790 Gd $11,556
D.H. grade, 28 ga.. . . . . .NiB $43,088 Ex $39,655 Gd $32,200
D.H. grade, .410. . . . . .NiB $72,799 Ex $48,950 Gd $37,788
C.H. grade, 12 or 16 ga. . . . . .NiB $17,300 Ex $13,988 Gd $10,996
C.H. grade, 20 ga. . . . . .NiB $25,779 Ex $20,099 Gd $17,376
C.H. grade, 28 ga. . . . . .NiB $73,588 Ex $60,977 Gd $52,411
B.H. grade, 12 or 16 ga. . . . . .NiB $21,689 Ex $18,933 Gd $16,900
B.H. grade, 20 ga.. . . . . .NiB $31,889 Ex $22,765 Gd $17,766
B.H. grade, 28 ga.. . . . . .NiB $40,550 Ex $33,980 Gd $24,665
A.H. grade, 12 or 16 ga. . . . . .NiB $92,778 Ex $80,000 Gd $66,789
A.H. grade, 20 ga. . . . . .NiB $57,778 Ex $40,099 Gd $30,277
A.H. grade, 28 ga.. . . . . . . .NiB $104,000 Ex $88,987 Gd $67,033
A.A.H. grade, 12 or 16 ga. . . .NiB $57,980 Ex $52,077 Gd $37,773
A.A.H. grade, 20 ga. . . . . . . .NiB $83,672 Ex $62,955 Gd $43,900
A.A.H. grade, 28 ga. . . . . .NiB $200,000 Ex $175,000 Gd $155,000
A-1 Special grade,
12 or 16 ga.. . . . . .NiB $100,000 Ex $80,000 Gd $60,000
A-1 Special grade, 20 ga. . . . .NiB $82,000 Ex $65,000 Gd $45,000
A-1 Special grade, 28 ga. .NiB $200,000 Ex $165,000 Gd $110,000
W/selective-single trigger, add 20%
W/vent. rib, add. 35%
Non-ejector models, deduct .30%

SINGLE-SHOT TRAP GUNS
Hammerless. Boxlock. Ejector. 12 ga. only. Bbl. lengths: 30-, 32-, 34-inch, any boring, vent rib. Weight: 7.5-8.5 lbs. Stock and forearm of select walnut, checkered; straight, half-or full-pistol grip. The five grades differ only in quality of workmanship, grade of wood, checkering, engraving, etc. General specifications same for all. Disc. about 1940.
S.C. grade . . . . NiB $9355 Ex $7088 Gd $5167
S.B. grade . . . . .NiB $11,870 Ex $7279 Gd $6344
S.A. grade . . . . NiB $17,500 Ex $14,223 Gd $11,989
S.A.1 Special (rare). . NiB $42,000 Ex $31,000 Gd $27,000

SKEET GUN
Same as other Parker doubles from Grade V.H.E. up except selective single trigger and beavertail forearm are standard on this model, as are 26-inch bbls., SK choke. Discontinued about 1940. Values are 35 percent higher.

TROJAN HAMMERLESS DOUBLE-BARREL SHOTGUN
Boxlock. Plain extractors. Double trigger or single trigger. Gauges: 12, 16, 20. Bbls.: 30-inch both F choke (12 ga. only), 26- or 28-inch M and F choke. Weight: 6.25-7.75 lbs. Checkered pistol-grip stock and forearm. Disc. 1939.
12 ga. . . . . NiB $5444 Ex $4249 Gd $2677
16 ga. . . . . NiB $6077 Ex $4488 Gd $3210
20 ga. . . . . NiB $6898 Ex $4539 Gd $3556

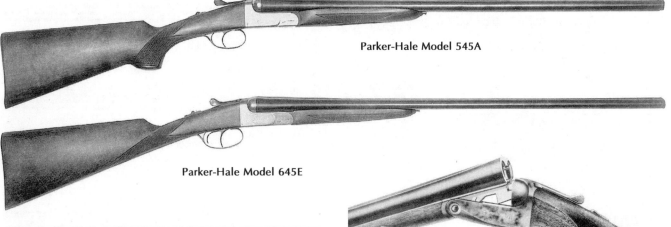

Parker-Hale Model 545A

Parker-Hale Model 645E

Parker Trojan Hammerless
Double-Barrel Shotgun

PARKER REPRODUCTIONS — Middlesex, New Jersey

HAMMERLESS DOUBLE-BARREL SHOTGUNS

Reproduction of the original Parker boxlock. Single selective trigger or double triggers. Selective automatic ejectors. Automatic safety. Gauges: 12, 16, 20, 28 or .410 w/2.75- or 3-inch chambers. Bbls.: 26- or 28-inch w/fixed or internal screw choke tubes SK/SK, IC/M, M/F. Weight: 5.5-7 lbs. Checkered English-style or pistol-grip American walnut stock w/beavertail or splinter forend and checkered skeleton buttplate. Color casehardened receiver with game scenes and scroll engraving. Produced in Japan by Olin Kodensha from 1984-88.

DHE grade, 12 ga.	NiB $4250	Ex $3288	Gd $1366
DHE grade, 12 ga Sporting Clays	NiB $4466	Ex $3890	Gd $2877
DHE grade, 20 ga.	NiB $4866	Ex $3989	Gd $2977
DHE grade, 28 ga.	NiB $5433	Ex $3200	Gd $2366
DHE grade 2-barrel set (16 & 20 ga.)	NiB $6590	Ex $4880	Gd $3588
DHE grade 2-barrel set (28 & .410)	NiB $7377	Ex $5433	Gd $3980
DHE grade 3-barrel set	NiB $10,000	Ex $6566	Gd $5080
B grade Bank Note Lim. Ed., 12 ga.	NiB $5799	Ex $4765	Gd $3499
B grade Bank Note Lim. Ed., 20 ga.	NiB $7352	Ex $6088	Gd $4139
B grade Bank Note Lim. Ed., 28 ga.	NiB $12,000	Ex $9898	Gd $7455
B grade Bank Note Lim. Ed., .410 ga.	NiB $13,900	Ex $10,000	Gd $8894
A-1 Special grade, 12 ga.	NiB $10,877	Ex $8871	Gd $6000
A-1 Special grade, 16 ga.	NiB $12,433	Ex $10,770	Gd $7379
A-1 Special grade, 20 ga.	NiB $10,665	Ex $8932	Gd $6281
A-1 Special grade, 28 ga.	NiB $14,933	Ex $12,966	Gd $9855
A-1 Special gr. 2-barrel set	NiB $13,770	Ex $10,433	Gd $7791
A-1 Special gr. 3-barrel set	NiB $29,650	Ex $23,991	Gd $17,498
A-1 Special gr. custom engraved	NiB $17,888	Ex $14,699	Gd $10,000
A-1 Special gr. custom 2-barrel set	NiB $14,600	Ex $10,553	Gd $7699
W/extra bbl. set, add			$500

PARKER-HALE SHOTGUNS — Manufactured by Ignacio Ugartechea, Spain

MODEL 645A (AMERICAN)

SIDE-BY-SIDE SHOTGUN . . . . NiB $1344 Ex $1116 Gd $844
Gauges: 12, 16 and 20. Boxlock action. 26- and 28-inch bbls. Chokes: IC/M, M/F. Weight: 6 lbs. average. Single non-selective trigger. Automatic safety. Hand-checkered pistol grip walnut stock w/beavertail forend. Raised matted rib. English scroll-design engraved receiver. Discontinued 1990.

MODEL 645E (ENGLISH) SIDE-BY-SIDE SHOTGUN

Same general specifications as the Model 645A except double trig-

gers, straight grip, splinter forend, checkered butt and concave rib. Disc. 1990.

12, 16, 20 ga. with 26- or 28-inch bbl. NiB $1388 Ex $1166 Gd $898
28, .410 ga. with 27-inch bbl. . . . . . NiB $1800 Ex $1490 Gd $1128

MODEL 645E-XXV

12, 16, 20 ga. with 25-inch bbl. . . . . NiB $1288 Ex $1189 Gd $900
28, .410 ga. with 25-inch bbl. . . . . NiB $1698 Ex $1377 Gd $1110

PEDERSEN CUSTOM GUNS — North Haven, Connecticut; div. of O.F. Mossberg & Sons, Inc.

MODEL 1000 O/U HUNTING SHOTGUN

Boxlock. Auto ejectors. Selective single trigger. Gauges: 12, 20. 2.75-inch chambers in 12 ga., 3-inch in 20 ga. Bbls.: Vent rib; 30-inch M/F (12 ga. only); 28-inch IC/M (12 ga. only), M/F; 26-inch IC/M. Checkered pistol-grip stock and forearm. Grade I is the higher quality gun with custom stock dimensions, fancier wood, more elaborate engraving, silver inlays. Made from 1973 to 1975.

Grade I . . . . NiB $2366 Ex $1969 Gd $1449
Grade II . . . . NiB $2210 Ex $1781 Gd $1290

MODEL 1000 MAGNUM

Same as Model 1000 Hunting Gun except chambered for 12-ga. Magnum 3-inch shells, 30-inch bbls., IM/F choke. Made 1973 to 1975.

Grade I . . . . NiB $2809 Ex $2277 Gd $1677
Grade II . . . . NiB $2400 Ex $1900 Gd $1378

MODEL 1000 SKEET GUN

Same as Model 1000 Hunting Gun except has skeet-style stock; 26- and 28-inch bbls. (12 ga. only), SK choke. Made from 1973 to 1975.

Grade I . . . . NiB $2433 Ex $1977 Gd $1698
Grade II . . . . NiB $1998 Ex $1569 Gd $1062

MODEL 1000 TRAP GUN

Same as Model 1000 Hunting Gun except 12 ga. only, has Monte Carlo trap-style stock, 30- or 32-inch bbls., M/F or IM/F choke. Made from 1973 to 1975.

Grade I . . . . NiB $2287 Ex $1862 Gd $1300
Grade II . . . . NiB $1844 Ex $1477 Gd $1106

SHOTGUNS

Pedersen Model 1000 Grade I

Pedersen Model 1000 Grade II

MODEL 1500 O/U
HUNTING SHOTGUN . . . . . . NiB $790 Ex $676 Gd $478
Boxlock. Auto ejectors. Selective single trigger. 12 ga. 2.75- or 3-inch chambers. Bbls.: vent rib; 26-inch IC/M; 28- and 30-inch M/F; Magnum has 30-inch, IM/F choke. Weight: 7-7.5 lbs., depending on bbl. length. Checkered pistol-grip stock and forearm. Made from 1973 to 1975.

MODEL 1500 SKEET GUN . . . NiB $833 Ex $690 Gd $569
Same as Model 1500 Hunting Gun except has skeet-style stock, 27-inch bbls., SK choke. Made from 1973 to 1975.

MODEL 1500 TRAP GUN. . . . NiB $788 Ex $648 Gd $520
Same as Model 1500 Hunting Gun except has Monte Carlo trap-style stock, 30- or 32-inch bbls., M/F or IM/F chokes. Made 1973 to 1975.

MODEL 2000 HAMMERLESS DOUBLE
Boxlock. Auto ejectors. Selective single trigger. Gauges: 12, 20. 2.75-inch chambers in 12 ga., 3-inch in 20 ga. Bbls.: Vent rib; 30-inch M/F (12 ga. only); 28-inch M/F, 26-inch IC/M choke. Checkered pistol-grip stock and forearm. Grade I is the higher quality gun w/custom dimensions, fancier wood, more elaborate engraving, silver inlays. Made from 1973 to 1974.
Grade I . . . . NiB $2887 Ex $2260 Gd $1740
Grade II . . . . NiB $2389 Ex $2276 Gd $1578

MODEL 2500
HAMMERLESS DOUBLE . . . . . NiB $780 Ex $655 Gd $356
Boxlock. Auto ejectors. Selective single trigger. Gauges: 12, 20. 2.75-inch chambers in 12 ga., 3-inch in 20 ga. Bbls.: Vent rib; 28-inch M/F; 26-inch IC/M choke. Checkered pistol-grip stock and forearm. Made 1973 to 1974.

MODEL 4000 HAMMERLESS SLIDE-ACTION
REPEATING SHOTGUN . . . . . NiB $597 Ex $440 Gd $375
Custom version of Mossberg Model 500. Full-coverage floral engraving on receiver. Gauges: 12, 20, .410. Three-inch chamber. Bbls.: Vent rib; 26-inch IC or SK choke; 28-inch F or M; 30-inch F. Weight: 6-8 lbs. depending on ga. and bbl. Checkered stock and slide handle of select wood. Made in 1975.

MODEL 4000 TRAP GUN. . . . NiB $590 Ex $466 Gd $265
Same as standard Model 4000 except 12 ga. only, has 30-inch F choke bbl., Monte Carlo trap-style stock w/recoil pad. Made in 1975.

MODEL 4500. . . . . NiB $500 Ex $390 Gd $335
Same as Model 4000 except has simpler scroll engraving. Made in 1975.

MODEL 4500 TRAP GUN. . . . NiB $525 Ex $420 Gd $366
Same as Model 4000 Trap Gun except has simpler scroll engraving. Made in 1975.

J. C. PENNEY CO., INC. — Dallas, Texas

MODEL 4011
AUTOLOADING SHOTGUN. . NiB $377 Ex $290 Gd $197
Hammerless. Five round magazine. Bbls.: 26-inch IC; 28-inch M or F; 30-inch F choke. Weight: 7.25 lbs. Plain pistol-grip stock and slide handle.

MODEL 6610
SINGLE-SHOT SHOTGUN . . . . NiB $205 Ex $100 Gd $75
Hammerless. Takedown. Auto ejector. Gauges: 12, 16, 20 and .410. Bbl. length: 28-36 inches. Weight: About 6 lbs. Plain pistol-grip stock and forearm.

MODEL 6630
BOLT-ACTION SHOTGUN . . . NiB $254 Ex $179 Gd $115
Takedown. Gauges: 12, 16, 20. Two round clip magazine. 26- and 28-inch bbl. lengths; with or without adj. choke. Plain pistol-grip stock. Weight: About 7.25 lbs.

MODEL 6670
SLIDE-ACTION SHOTGUN . . . NiB $260 Ex $188 Gd $140
Hammerless. Gauges: 12, 16, 20, and .410. Three round tubular magazine. Bbls.: 26- to 30-inch; various chokes. Weight: 6.25-7.25 lbs. Walnut finished hardwood stock.

MODEL 6870 SLIDE-ACTION
SHOTGUN. . . . . NiB $315 Ex $225 Gd $178
Hammerless. Gauges: 12, 16, 20, .410. Four round magazine. Bbls.: Vent rib; 26- to 30-inch, various chokes. Weight: Average 6.5 lbs. Plain pistol-grip stock.

PERAZZI SHOTGUNS — Manufactured by Manifattura Armi Perazzi, Brescia, Italy

See also listings under Ithaca-Perazzi.

DB81 O/U TRAP . . . . NiB $5266 Ex $4300 Gd $3450
Gauge: 12; 2.75-inch chambers. 29.5- or 31.5-inch bbls. w/ wide vent rib; M/F chokes. Weight: 8 lbs., 6 oz. Detachable and interchangeable trigger with flat V-springs. Bead front sight. Interchangeable and custom-made checkered stock; beavertail forend. Imported 1988 to 1994.

DB81 SINGLE-SHOT TRAP NiB $5300 Ex $4277 Gd $3389
Same general specifications as the DB81 over/under except in single bbl. version w/32- or 34-inch wide vent-rib bbl., F choke. Imported 1988 to 1994.

Perazzi — DB81 Over/Under Trap

Perazzi — Mirage Over/Under Shotgun

Perazzi — MX3 Over/Under Shotgun

Perazzi — MX8 Over/Under Shotgun

GRAND AMERICAN 88 SPECIAL SINGLE TRAP
Same general specifications as MX8 Special Single Trap except w/ high ramped rib. Fixed choke or screw-in choke tubes.
Model 88 standard . . . . . NiB $4988 Ex $3988 Gd $2777
Model 88 w/interchangeable
choke tubes . . . . NiB $4990 Ex $4100 Gd $3099

MIRAGE O/U SHOTGUN
Gauge: 12; 2.75-inch chambers. Bbls.: 27.63-, 29.5- or 31.5-inch vent-rib w/fixed chokes or screw-in choke tubes. Single selective trigger. Weight: 7 to 7.75 lbs. Interchangeable and custom-made checkered buttstock and forend.
Competition Trap,
Skeet, Pigeon, Sporting . . NiB $6400 Ex $5440 Gd $3200
Skeet 4-barrel sets . . NiB $14,680 Ex $12,890 Gd $9800
Competition Special (w/adj. 4-position trigger) add . . . $500

MX-1 O/U SHOTGUN
Similar to Model MX8 except w/ramp-style, tapered rib and modified stock configuration.
Competition Trap, Skeet,
Pigeon & Sporting . . . . . . NiB $6799 Ex $5240 Gd $3390
MXlC (w/choke tubes) . . . NiB $3698 Ex $3288 Gd $2298
MXlB (w/flat low rib) . . . . NiB $3467 Ex $2980 Gd $2098

MX-2 O/U SHOTGUN
Similar to Model MX8 except w/broad high-ramped competition rib.
Competition-Trap, Skeet,
Pigeon & Sporting . . . . . . NiB $6780 Ex $3544 Gd $3589
MX2C (w/choke tubes) . . . NiB $4988 Ex $3998 Gd $2766

MX-3 O/U SHOTGUN
Similar to Model MX8 except w/ramp-style, tapered rib and modified stock configuration.

Competition Trap, Skeet,
Pigeon & Sporting . . . . NiB $48,988 Ex $42,998 Gd $35,999
Competition Special (w/adj. 4-position trigger) add . . $400
Game models . . . . NiB $4478 Ex $3659 Gd $2699
Combo O/U plus SB . . . . NiB $5563 Ex $4478 Gd $3380
SB Trap 32- or 34-inch . . NiB $3987 Ex $3166 Gd $2267
Skeet 4-bbl. sets . . . . NiB $12,888 Ex $10,099 Gd $7789
Skeet Special 4-bbl. sets NiB $13,066 Ex $11,288 Gd $8,996

MX-3 SPECIAL PIGEON SHOTGUN NiB $5344 Ex $4276 Gd $3110
Gauge: 12; 2.75-inch chambers. 29.5- or 31.5-inch vent rib bbl.; IC/M and extra full chokes. Weight: 8 lbs., 6 oz. Detachable and interchangeable trigger group w/flat V-springs. Bead front sight. Interchangeable and custom-made checkered stock for live pigeon shoots; splinter forend. Imported 1991 to 1992.

MX-4 O/U SHOTGUN
Similar to Model MX3 in appearance and shares the MX8 locking system. Detachable, adj. 4-position trigger standard. Interchangeable choke tubes optional.
Competition Trap,
Skeet, Pigeon & Sporting . . . . . NiB $4487 Ex $4089 Gd $3124
MX4C (w/choke tubes) . . . NiB $5388 Ex $4500 Gd $3787

MX-5 O/U GAME GUN
Similar to Model MX8 except in hunting configuration, chambered in 12 or 20 ga. Non-detachable single selective trigger.
MX5 Standard . . . . NiB $3977 Ex $2886 Gd $2066
MX5C (w/choke tubes) . . . NiB $4264 Ex $3188 Gd $2200

MX-6 AMER.
TRAP SINGLE-BARREL . . . . NiB $4302 Ex $2677 Gd $1988
Single shot. Removable trigger group. 12 ga. Barrels: 32- or 34-inch with fixed or choke tubes. Raised vent rib. Checkered European walnut Monte Carlo stock, beavertail forend. Imported 1995 to 1998.

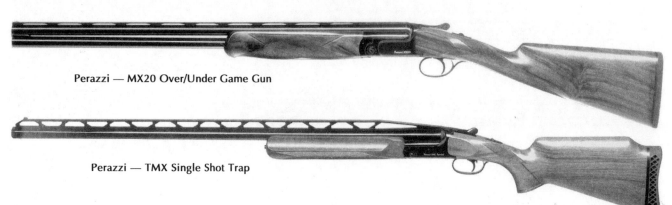

Perazzi — MX20 Over/Under Game Gun

Perazzi — TMX Single Shot Trap

MX-6 SKEET O/U . . . . . . NiB $4277 Ex $3100 Gd $2250
Same general specs as MX6 American Trap single barrel except over/under; boxlock. Barrels: 26.75- or 27.50-inch. Imported 1995 to 1998.

MX-6 SPORTING O/U . . . NiB $4277 Ex $3100 Gd $2250
Same specs as MX6 American Trap single barrel except over/under; boxlock. Single selective trigger; external selector. Barrels: 28.38-, 29.50-, or 31.50-inch. Imported 1995 to 1998.

MX-6 TRAP O/U . . . . NiB $4350 Ex $2929 Gd $1877
Same general specs as MX6 American Trap single barrel except over/under; boxlock. Barrels: 29.50-, 30.75-, or 31.50-inch. Imported 1995 to 1998.

MX-7 O/U SHOTGUN . . . NiB $4188 Ex $3755 Gd $2690
Similar to Model MX12 except w/MX3-style receiver and top-mounted trigger selector. Bbls.: 28.73-, 2.5-, 31.5-inch w/vent rib; screw-in choke tubes. Imported 1992 to 1998.

MX-8 O/U SHOTGUN
Gauge: 12, 2.75-inch chambers. Bbls.: 27.63-, 29.5- or 31.5-inch vent-rib w/fixed chokes or screw-in choke tubes. Weight: 7 to 8.5 lbs. Interchangeable and custom-made checkered stock; beavertail forend. Special models have detachable and interchangeable 4-position trigger group w/flat V-springs. Imported 1968 to date.
MX-8 Standard . . . . NiB $8099 Ex $4133 Gd $2377
MX-8 Special (adj. 4-pos. trigger) NiB $4229 Ex $3378 Gd $2490
MX-8 Special single
(32-or 34-inch bbl.) . . . . . NiB $8380 Ex $7121 Gd $4365
MX-8 Special combo . . . . NiB $8009 Ex $6355 Gd $4682

MX-8/20 O/U SHOTGUN   NiB $4155 Ex $3370 Gd $2499
Similar to the Model MX8 except w/smaller frame and custom stock. Available in sporting or game configurations with fixed chokes or screw-in tubes. Imported 1993 to date.

MX-9 O/U SHOTGUN . . . NiB $6880 Ex $5672 Gd $4200
Gauge: 12; 2.75-inch chambers. Bbls.: 29.5- or 30.5-inch w/choke tubes and vent side rib. Selective trigger. Checkered walnut stock w/adj. cheekpiece. Available in single bbl., combo, O/U trap, skeet, pigeon and sporting models. Imported 1993 to 1994.

MX-10 O/U SHOTGUN . NiB $8293 Ex $5760 Gd $34,105
Similar to the Model MX9 except w/fixed chokes and different rib configuration. Imported 1993.

MX-10 PIGEON-ELECTROCIBLES O/UNiB $8996 Ex $6133 Gd $4400
Over/Under; boxlock. Removable trigger group; external selector. 12 gauge. Barrels: 27.50- or 29.50-inch. Checkered European walnut adjustable stock, beavertail forend. Imported 1995 to date.

MX–11 AMERICAN TRAP COMBO . . . .NiB $5440 Ex $4688 Gd $3277
Over/Under; boxlock. External selector. Removable trigger group; single selective trigger. 12 ga. Bbls: 29-1/2- to 34-inch with fixed or choke tubes; vent rib. European walnut Monte Carlo adjustable stock, beavertail forend. Imported 1995 to date.

**MX-11 AMERICAN TRAP
SINGLE BARREL** . . . . NiB $5155 Ex $4309 Gd $2879
Same general specs as MX11 American Trap combo except 32- or 34-inch single bbl. Imported 1995 to 1996.

MX-11 PIGEON-ELECTROCIBLES O/UNiB $5331 Ex $4277 Gd $3100
Same specs as MX11 American Trap combo except 27.50 O/U bbls. Checkered European walnut pistol grip adjustable stock, beavertail forend. Imported 1995 to 1996.

MX-11 SKEET O/U . . . . . . NiB $5390 Ex $4369 Gd $3122
Same general specs as MX11 American Trap combo except 26.75 or 27.50-inch O/U bbls. Checkered European walnut pistol-grip adjustable stock, beavertail forend. Imported 1995 to 1996.

MX-11 SPORTING O/U . . NiB $5344 Ex $4766 Gd $3409
Same general specs as MX11 American Trap combo except 28.38, 29.50-, or 31.50-inch O/U bbls. Checkered European walnut pistol-grip adjustable stock, beavertail forend. Imported 1995 to 1996.

MX-11 TRAP O/U . . . . NiB $5293 Ex $4266 Gd $3109
Same general specs as MX11 American Trap combo except 29.50,-30.75, or 31.50-inch O/U bbls. Checkered European walnut pistol-grip adjustable stock, beavertail forend. Imported 1995 to 1996.

MX-12 O/U GAME GUN
Gauge: 12, 2.75-inch chambers. Bbls.: 26-, 27.63-, 28.38- or 29.5-inch, vent rib, fixed chokes or screw-in choke tubes. Non-detachable single selective trigger group w/coil springs. Weight: 7.25 lbs. Interchangeable and custom-made checkered stock; Schnabel forend.
MX12 Standard . . . . NiB $7966 Ex $4312 Gd $3100
MX12C (w/choke tubes) . . NiB $7994 Ex $4366 Gd $3180

**MX-14 AMERICAN TRAP
SINGLE-BARREL** . . . . NiB $6892 Ex $3677 Gd $2573
Single shot. Removable trigger group; unsingle configuration. 12 ga. Bbl: 34-inch with fixed or choke tubes; vent rib. Checkered European walnut Monte Carlo adjustable stock, beavertail forend. Imported 1995 to 1996.

**MX-15 AMERICAN TRAP
SINGLE-BARREL** . . . . NiB $6654 Ex $4138 Gd $2998
Full choke. Detachable trigger group. Gauge: 12 only with 2.75-inch chamber. Bbls: 32 and 34-inch. Weight: 8 lbs., 6 oz.

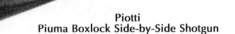

**Piotti
Piuma Boxlock Side-by-Side Shotgun**

**Powell No. 7
Aristocrat Grade Double**

MX-20 O/U GAME GUN
Gauges: 20, 28 and .410; 2.75- or 3-inch chambers. 26-inch vent-rib bbls., M/F chokes or screw-in chokes. Auto selective ejectors. Selective single trigger. Weight: 6 lbs., 6 oz. Non-detachable coil-spring trigger. Bead front sight. Interchangeable and custom-made checkered stock w/Schnabel forend. Imported from 1988 to date.
Standard grade . . . . NiB $5311 Ex $4255 Gd $2987
Standard grade
w/gold outline . . . . NiB $8991 Ex $7200 Gd $5102
MX20C w/choke tubes . . . NiB $5886 Ex $4480 Gd $3171
SC3 grade . . . . NiB $9766 Ex $7764 Gd $5433
SCO grade . . . . NiB $13,978 Ex $11,888 Gd $9166

MX-28 O/U GAME GUN
NiB $15,660 Ex $12,987 Gd $9821
Similar to the Model MX12 except chambered in 28 ga. w/26-inch bbls. fitted to smaller frame. Imported from 1993 to date.

MX-410 O/U GAME GUN
NiB $15,890 Ex $13,298 Gd $10,350
Similar to the Model MX12 except in .410 bore w/3-inch chambers, 26-inch bbls. fitted to smaller frame. Imported from 1993 to date.

TM1 SPECIAL
SINGLE-SHOT TRAP. . . . . NiB $3150 Ex $2770 Gd $2000
Gauge: 12- 2.75-inch chambers. 32- or 34-inch bbl. w/wide vent rib; full choke. Weight: 8 lbs., 6 oz. Detachable and interchangeable trigger group with coil springs. Bead front sight. Interchangeable and custom-made stock w/checkered pistol grip and beavertail forend. Imported from 1988 to 1995.

TMX SPECIAL
SINGLE-SHOT TRAP. . . . . NiB $3890 Ex $2553 Gd $1966
Same general specifications as Model TM1 Special except w/ultra-high rib. Interchangeable choke tubes optional.

PIOTTI SHOTGUNS — Italy

BOSS O/U . . . . NiB $58,998 Ex $50,000 Gd $35,965
Over/Under; sidelock. Gauges: 12 or 20. Barrels: 26- to 32-inch. Standard chokes. Best quality walnut. Custom-made to customer's specifications. Imported from 1993 to date.

KING NO. 1 SIDELOCK
NiB $35,866 Ex $29,821 Gd $19,670
Gauges: 10, 12, 16, 20, 28 and .410. 25- to 30-inch bbls. (12 ga.), 25- to 28-inch (other ga.). Weight: About 5 lbs. (.410) to 8 lbs. (12 ga.) Holland & Holland pattern sidelock. Double triggers standard. Coin finish or color casehardened. Level file-cut rib. Full-coverage scroll engraving, gold inlays. Hand-rubbed, oil-finished, straight-grip stock with checkered butt, splinter forend.

KING EXTRA SIDE-BY-SIDE
SHOTGUN. . . . . . . NiB $77,850 Ex $52,290 Gd $42,777
Same general specifications as the Piotti King No. 1 except has choice of engraving, gold inlays, plus stock is of exhibition-grade wood.

LUNIK SIDE-LOCK
SHOTGUN. . . . . . . NiB $35,660 Ex $31,299 Gd $26,000
Same general specifications as the Monte Carlo model except has level, file-cut rib. Renaissance-style, large scroll engraving in relief, gold crown in top lever, gold name, and gold crest in forearm, finely figured wood.

MONTE CARLO
SIDE-LOCK SHOTGUN. . NiB $11,488 Ex $9889 Gd $7577
Gauges: 10, 12, 16, 20, 28 or .410. Bbls.: 25- to 30-inch. Holland & Holland pattern sidelock. Weight: 5-8 lbs. Automatic ejectors. Double triggers. Hand-rubbed oil-finished straight-grip stock with checkered butt. Choice of Purdey-style scroll and rosette or Holland & Holland-style large scroll engraving.

PIUMA BOXLOCK
SIDE-BY-SIDE SHOTGUN
NiB $18,667 Ex $12,933 Gd $10,011
Same general specifications as the Monte Carlo model except has Anson & Deeley boxlock action w/demi-bloc bbls., scalloped frame. Standard scroll and rosette engraving. Hand-rubbed, oil-finished straight-grip stock.

WILLIAM POWELL & SON, LTD. —
Birmingham, England

NO. 1 BEST GRADE DOUBLE-BARREL
SHOTGUN. . . . . . . NiB $42,777 Ex $38,698 Gd $31,033
Sidelock. Gauges: Made to order with 12, 16 and 20 the most common. Bbls.: Made to order in any length but 28 inches was recommended. Highest grade French walnut buttstock and forearm with fine checkering. Metal elaborately engraved. Imported by Stoeger from about 1938 to 1951.

NO. 2 BEST GRADE
DOUBLE-BARREL . . NiB $29,766 Ex $24,761 Gd $16,888
Same general specifications as the Powell No. 1 except plain finish without engraving. Imported by Stoeger from about 1938 to 1951.

NO. 6 CROWN GRADE
DOUBLE-BARREL . . NiB $15,999 Ex $12,733 Gd $10,111
Boxlock. Gauges: Made to order with 12, 16 and 20 the most common. Bbls.: Made to order, but 28 inches was recommended. Highest grade French walnut buttstock and forearm with fine checkering. Metal elaborately engraved. Uses Anson & Deeley locks. Imported by Stoeger from about 1938 to 1951.

NO. 7 ARISTOCRAT GRADE DOUBLE-BARREL
SHOTGUN. . . . . NiB $9022 Ex $6988 Gd $4766
Same general specifications as the Powell No. 6 Crown Grade Double-Barrel above, except with lower quality wood and metal engraving.

SHOTGUNS

Premier Ambassador
Field Grade

Premier Continental
Field Grade

PRECISION SPORTS SHOTGUNS —
Cortland, New York; manufactured by
Ignacio Ugartechea, Spain

600 SERIES AMERICAN HAMMERLESS DOUBLES

Boxlock. Single selective trigger. Selective automatic ejectors. Automatic safety. Gauges: 12, 16, 20, 28, .410; 2.75- or 3-inch chambers. Bbls.: 26-,27- or 28-inch w/raised matte rib; choked IC/M or M/F. Weight: 5.75-7 lbs. Checkered pistol-grip walnut buttstock with beavertail forend. Engraved silvered receiver with blued bbls. Imported from 1986 to 1994.
640A (12, 16, 20 ga. w/extractors) . NiB $1177 Ex $909 Gd $677
640A (28 ga., .410 w/extractors) . NiB $1288 Ex $1067 Gd $779
640 Slug Gun (12 ga. w/extractors) NiB $1277 Ex $1059 Gd $723
645A (12, 16, 20 ga. w/ejectors) . . NiB $1177 Ex $909 Gd $677
645A (28 ga., .410, two-bbl. set) . NiB $1488 Ex $1176 Gd $877
645A (20/28 ga. two-bbl. set) . . . . NiB $1563 Ex $1253 Gd $919
650A (12 ga. w/extractors, choke tubes) NiB $1165 Ex $977 Gd $710
655A (12 ga. w/ejectors, choke tubes) NiB $1288 Ex $1022 Gd $766

600 SERIES ENGLISH HAMMERLESS DOUBLES

Boxlock. Same general specifications as American 600 series except w/double triggers and concave rib. Checkered English-style walnut stock w/splinter forend, straight grip and oil finish.
640E (12, 16, 20 ga. w/extractors) . . NiB $956 Ex $790 Gd $622
640E (28 ga., .410 w/extractors) . . . NiB $1088 Ex $900 Gd $644
640 Slug Gun (12 ga. w/extractors) NiB $1297 Ex $1044 Gd $780
645E (12, 16, 20 ga. w/ejectors) . . NiB $1300 Ex $1066 Gd $800
645E (28 ga., .410 w/ejectors) . . . NiB $1266 Ex $1022 Gd $776
645E (20/28 ga. two-bbl. set) . . . NiB $1545 Ex $1296 Gd $1000
650E (12 ga. w/extractors, choke tubes) NiB $1178 Ex $938 Gd $715
655E (12 ga. w/ejectors, choke tubes) NiB $1190 Ex $980 Gd $750

MODEL 640M MAGNUM 10 HAMMERLESS DOUBLE

Similar to Model 640E except in 10 ga. w/3.5-inch Mag. chambers. Bbls.: 26-, 30-, 32-inch choked F/F.
Model 640M Big Ten, Turkey NiB $1106 Ex $933 Gd $700
Model 640M Goose Gun . . . NiB $1133 Ex $955 Gd $735

MODEL 645E-XXV HAMMERLESS DOUBLE

Similar to Model 645E except w/25-inch bbl. and Churchill-style rib.
645E-XXV (12, 16, 20 ga. w/ejectors) NiB $1160 Ex $982 Gd $755
645E-XXV (28, .410 ga. w/ejectors) NiB $1366 Ex $1093 Gd $835

PREMIER SHOTGUNS

Premier shotguns have been produced by various gunmakers in Europe.

AMBASSADOR MODEL FIELD GRADE HAMMERLESS
DOUBLE-BARREL SHOTGUN . NiB $544 Ex $466 Gd $377

Sidelock. Plain extractors. Double triggers. Gauges: 12, 16, 20, .410. 3-inch chambers in 20 and .410 ga., 2.75- inch in 12 and 16 ga. Bbls.: 26-inch in .410 ga., 28 inch in other ga.; choked M/F. Weight: 6 lbs., 3 oz.-7 lbs., 3 oz. depending on gauge. Checkered pistol-grip stock and beavertail forearm. Intro. in 1957; disc.

BRUSH KING . . . . NiB $440 Ex $330 Gd $255

Same as standard Regent model except chambered for 12 (2.75-inch) and 20 ga. (3-inch) only; has 22-inch bbls., IC/M choke, straight-grip stock. Weight: 6 lbs., 3 oz. in 12 ga.; 5 lbs., 12 oz. in 20 ga. Introduced in 1959; disc.

CONTINENTAL MODEL FIELD GRADE HAMMER
DOUBLE-BARREL SHOTGUN . NiB $577 Ex $426 Gd $300

Sidelock. Exposed hammers. Plain extractors. Double triggers. Gauges: 12, 16, 20, .410. Three inch chambers in 20 and .410 ga., 2.75-inch in 12 and 16 ga. Bbls.: 26-inch in .410 ga.; 28-inch in other ga.; choked M/F. Weight: 6 lbs., 3 oz.-7 lbs., 3 oz. depending on gauge. Checkered pistol-grip stock and English-style forearm. Introduced in 1957; disc.

MONARCH SUPREME GRADE HAMMERLESS
DOUBLE-BARREL SHOTGUN . NiB $667 Ex $487 Gd $367

Boxlock. Auto ejectors. Double triggers. Gauges: 12, 20. 2.75-inch chambers in 12 ga., 3-inch in 20 ga. Bbls.: 26-inch IC/M choke. Weight: 6 lbs., 6 oz., 7 lbs., 2 oz. depending on gauge and bbl. Checkered pistol-grip stock and beavertail forearm of fancy walnut. Introduced in 1959; disc.

PRESENTATION
CUSTOM GRADE . . . . NiB $1488 Ex $1109 Gd $856

Similar to Monarch model but made to order of higher quality with hunting scene engraving, gold and silver inlay, fancier wood. Introduced in 1959; disc.

REGENT 10 GA.
MAGNUM EXPRESS . . . . NiB $665 Ex $431 Gd $345

Same as standard Regent model except chambered for 10-ga. Magnum 3.5-inch shells, has heavier construction, 32-inch bbls. choked F/F, stock with recoil pad. Weight: 11.25 lbs. Introduced in 1957; disc.

REGENT 12 GA.
MAGNUM EXPRESS . . . . NiB $465 Ex $388 Gd $290

Same as standard Regent model except chambered for 12-ga. Magnum 3-inch shells, has 30-inch bbls. choked F and F, stock with recoil pad. Weight: 7.25 lbs. Introduced in 1957; disc.

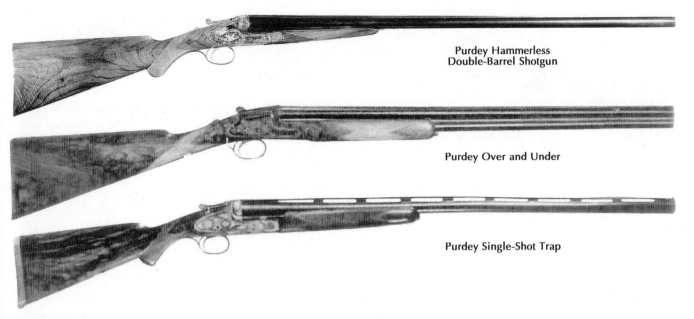

Purdey Hammerless
Double-Barrel Shotgun

Purdey Over and Under

Purdey Single-Shot Trap

REGENT FIELD GRADE
HAMMERLESS
DOUBLE-BARREL SHOTGUN. NiB $477 Ex $355 Gd $271
Boxlock. Plain extractors. Double triggers. Gauges: 12,16, 20, 28, .410. Three inch chambers in 20 and .410 ga., 2.75-inch in other gauges. Bbls.: 26-inch IC/M, M/F (28 and .410 ga. only); 28-inch M/F; 30-inch M/F (12 ga. only). Weight: 6 lbs., 2 oz.-7 lbs., 4 oz. depending on gauge and bbl. Checkered pistol-grip stock and beavertail forearm. Introduced in 1955; disc.

JAMES PURDEY & SONS, LTD. — London, England

HAMMERLESS DOUBLE-BARREL SHOTGUN
Sidelock. Auto ejectors. Single or double triggers. Gauges: 12, 16, 20. Bbls.: 26-, 27-, 28-, 30-inch (latter in 12 ga. only);any boring, any shape or style of rib. Weight: 5.25-5.5 lbs. depending on model, gauge and bbl length. Checkered stock and forearm, straight grip standard, pistol-grip also available. Purdey guns of this type have been made from about 1880 to date. Models include: Game Gun, Featherweight Game Gun, Two-Inch Gun (chambered for 12 ga. 2-inch shells), Pigeon Gun (w/3rd fastening and side clips), values of all models are the same.
With double triggers NiB $62,700 Ex $54,890 Gd $44,782
With single trigger, add $1000

OVER/UNDER SHOTGUN
Sidelock. Auto ejectors. Single or double triggers. Gauges: 12 16, 20. Bbls.: 26-, 27-, 28-, 30-inch (latter in 12 ga. only); any boring, any style rib. Weight: 6-7.5 pounds depending on gauge and bbl. length. Checkered stock and forend, straight or pistol grip. Prior to WW II, the Purdey Over/Under Gun was made with a Purdey action; since the war James Purdey & Sons have acquired the business of James Woodward & Sons and all Purdey over/under guns are now built on the Woodward principle. General specifications of both types are the same.
With Purdey action,
double triggers . . . . .NiB $78,880 Ex $52,609 Gd $24,655
With Woodward action,
double triggers, add $3000
W/single trigger, add 10%

SINGLE-BARREL
TRAP GUN. . . . . .NiB $12,775 Ex $10,560 Gd $8,300
Sidelock. Mechanical features similar to those of the over/under model with Purdey action. 12 ga. only. Built to customer's specifications. Made prior to World War II.

REMINGTON ARMS CO. — Ilion, New York

Eliphalet Remington Jr. began making long arms with his father in 1816. In 1828 they moved their facility to Ilion, N.Y., where it remained a family-run business for decades. As the family began to diminish, other people bought controlling interests and today, still a successful gunmaking company, it is a subsidiary of the DuPont Corporation.

MODEL 10A STANDARD GRADE
SLIDE-ACTION REPEATING SHOTGUN . . . .NiB $420 Ex $335 Gd $255
Hammerless. Takedown. Six-round capacity. 12 ga. only. Five shell tubular magazine. Bbls.: Plain; 26- to 32-inch; choked F, M or Cyl. Weight: About 7.5 lbs. Plain pistol-grip stock, grooved slide handle. Made from 1907 to 1929.

MODEL 11 SPECIAL, TOURNAMENT, EXPERT AND PREMIER GRADE GUNS
These higher grade models differ from the Model 11A in general quality, grade of wood, checkering, engraving, etc. General specifications are the same.
Model 11B Special grade . . . . .NiB $788 Ex $609 Gd $466
Model 11D Tournament grade . . .NiB $1388 Ex $1122 Gd $866
Model 11E Expert grade . . . . . . .NiB $1880 Ex $1455 Gd $1090
Model 11F Premier grade . . . . .NiB $2998 Ex $2356 Gd $1800

MODEL 11A STANDARD GRADE AUTOLOADER
Hammerless Browning type. Five round capacity. Takedown. Gauges: 12, 16, 20. Tubular magazine holds four rounds. Bbls.: Plain, solid or vent rib, lengths from 26-32 inches, F, M, IC, Cyl., SK chokes. Weight: About 8 lbs., 12 ga.; 7.5 lbs., 16 ga.; 7.25 lbs., 20 ga. Checkered pistol grip and forend. Made from 1905 to 1949.
With plain barrel . . . . .NiB $355 Ex $260 Gd $229
With solid-rib barrel . . . . .NiB $477 Ex $339 Gd $366
With ventilated-rib barrel . . . . . . .NiB $544 Ex $420 Gd $367

SHOTGUNS

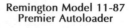

**Remington Model 11-87
Premier Autoloader**

MODEL 11R RIOT GUN. . . . . NiB $445 Ex $300 Gd $195
Same as Model 11A Standard grade except has 20-inch plain barrel, 12 ga. only. Remington Model 11-48. (See Remington Sportsman-48 Series.)

MODEL 11-87 PREMIER AUTOLOADER
Gas-operated. Hammerless. Gauge: 12; 3-inch chamber. Bbl.: 26-, 28- or 30-inch with REMChoke. Weight: 8.13- 8.38 lbs., depending on bbl. length. Checkered walnut stock and forend in satin finish. Made from 1987 to date.

Premier Deer Gun . . . . NiB $755 Ex $566 Gd $440
Premier Deer Gun w/cant-
ilever scope mount . . . . NiB $855 Ex $654 Gd $477
Premier Skeet . . . . NiB $740 Ex $535 Gd $420
Premier Sporting Clays . . . . NiB $866 Ex $700 Gd $509
Premier Sporting Clays SCNP (nickel plated)NiB $890 Ex $735 Gd $533
Premier Standard Autoloader . . . . . . NiB $766 Ex $598 Gd $455
Premier Trap . . . . NiB $844 Ex $707 Gd $510
Left-hand models, add $125

MODEL 11-87 SPECIAL PURPOSE MAGNUM
Same general specifications as Model 11-87 Premier except with non-reflective wood finish and Parkerized metal. 21-, 26- or 28-inch vent-rib bbl. with REMChoke tubes. Made from 1987 to 1993.
Model 11-87 SP Field Magnum . . .NiB $855 Ex $745 Gd $533
Model 11-87 SP Deer Gun (w/21-inch bbl.)NiB $755 Ex $607 Gd $498
Model 11-87 SP Deer Gun
w/cantilever scope mount . . . . . . .NiB $866 Ex $677 Gd $580

MODEL 11-87 SPS MAGNUM
Same general specifications as Model 11-87 Special Purpose Magnum except with synthetic buttstock and forend. 21-, 26- or 28-inch vent-rib bbl. with REMChoke tubes. Matte black or Mossy Oak camo finish (except NWTF turkey gun). Made from 1990 to date.
Model 11-87 SPS Magnum (matte black) NiB $733 Ex $643 Gd $471
Model 11-87 SPS Camo (Mossy Oak camo) NiB $760 Ex $622 Gd $479
Model 11-87 SPS Deer Gun (w/21 inch bbl.)NiB $696 Ex $494 Gd $358
Model 11-87 SPS Deer Gun w/cant. scope mt. NiB $859 Ex $633 Gd $490
Model 11-87 NWTF Turkey Gun
(Brown Trebark) disc. 1993 . . . . NiB $775 Ex $690 Gd $510
Model 11-87 NWTF Turkey Gun
(Greenleaf) disc. 1996 . . . . NiB $725 Ex $650 Gd $479
Model 11-87 NWTF Turkey
Gun (Mossy Oak) disc. 1996. . . . . . . NiB $730 Ex $655 Gd $485
Model 11-87 NWTF Turkey Gun
(Mossy Oak Breakup) introduced 1999NiB $730 Ex $655 Gd $485
Model 11-87 NWTF 20 ga. Turkey Gun
(Mossy Oak Breakup)1998 only . . . . NiB $730 Ex $655 Gd $485
Model 11-87 SPST Turkey Gun (matte bl.) NiB $730 Ex $655 Gd $485

MODEL 11-96 EURO LIGHTWEIGHT
AUTOLOADING SHOTGUN. . . . . . NiB $800 Ex $644 Gd $500
Lightweight version of Model 11-87 w/reprofiled receiver. 12 ga.

only w/3-inch chamber. 26- or 28-inch bbl. w/6mm vent rib and REM Choke tubes. Semi-fancy Monte Carlo walnut buttstock and forearm. Weight: 6.8 lbs. w/26-inch bbl. Made in 1996 only.

MODEL 17A STANDARD GRADE SLIDE-ACTION REPEATING SHOTGUN
Hammerless. Takedown. Five round capacity. 20 ga. only. Four round tubular magazine. Bbls.: plain; 26- to 32-inch; choked F, M or Cyl. Weight: About 5.75 lbs. Plain pistol-grip stock, grooved slide handle. Made 1921-33. Note: The present Ithaca Model 37 is an adaptation of this Browning design.
Plain barrel . . . . NiB $422 Ex $292 Gd $190
Solid rib. . . . . NiB $490 Ex $400 Gd $290

MODEL 29A STANDARD GRADE
SLIDE-ACTION REPEATING SHOTGUNNiB $390 Ex $300 Gd $287
Hammerless. Takedown. Six round capacity. 12 ga. only. Five round tubular magazine. Bbls.: plain- 26- to 32-inch, choked F, M or Cyl. Weight: About 7.5 lbs. Checkered pistol-grip stock and slide handle. Made from 1929 to 1933.

MODEL 29T TARGET GRADE . NiB $600 Ex $490 Gd $377
Same general specifications as Model 29A except has trap-style stock with straight grip, extension slide handle, vent rib bbl. Disc. 1933.

MODEL 31/31L SKEET GRADE
Same general specifications as Model 31A except has 26-inch bbl. with raised solid or vent rib, SK choke, checkered pistol-grip stock and beavertail forend. Weight: About 8 lbs., 12 ga. Made from 1932 to 1939.
Model 31 Standard w/raised solid rib NiB $477 Ex $290 Gd $200
Model 31 Standard w/ventilated rib NiB $566 Ex $408 Gd $335
Model 31L Lightweight w/raised solid rib NiB $455 Ex $330 Gd $245
Model 31L Lightweight w/ventilated rib NiB $555 Ex $350 Gd $287

MODEL 31D SPECIAL, TOURNAMENT,
EXPERT AND PREMIER GRADE GUNS
These higher grade models differ from the Model 31A in general quality, grade of wood, checkering, engraving, etc. General specifications are the same.
Model 31B Special grade . . . . NiB $745 Ex $600 Gd $477
Model 31D Tournament grade NiB $1688 Ex $1099 Gd $722
Model 31E Expert grade . . . NiB $1890 Ex $1266 Gd $977
Model 31F Premier grade   NiB $3100 Ex $2013 Gd $1544

MODEL 31S TRAP SPECIAL/31TC TRAP GRADE
Same general specifications as Model 31A except 12 ga. only, has 30- or 32-inch vent-rib bbl., F choke, checkered trap stock with full pistol grip and recoil pad, checkered extension beavertail forend. Weight: About 8 lbs. (Trap Special has solid-rib bbl., half pistol-grip stock with standard walnut forend).
Model 31S Trap Special . . . . . NiB $655 Ex $490 Gd $423
Model 31TC Trap grade   . . . . NiB $955 Ex $677 Gd $590

Remington Model 11-87 SPS

Remington Model 11-87 SPS Camo

Remington Model 11-87 SP Walnut Stock

Remington Model SP-10 Magnum Camo

MODEL 31A SLIDE-ACTION REPEATER
Hammerless. Takedown. 3- or 5-round capacity. Gauges: 12, 16, 20. Tubular magazine. Bbls.: Plain, solid or vent rib; lengths from 26 -32 inches; F, M, IC, C or SK choke. Weight: About 7.5 lbs., 12 ga.; 6.75 lbs., 16 ga.; 6.5 lbs., 20 ga. Earlier models have checkered pistol-grip stock and slide handle; later models have plain stock and grooved slide handle. Made from 1931 to 1949.

Model 31A with plain barrel . NiB $479 Ex $366 Gd $244
Model 31A with solid rib barrel NiB $565 Ex $443 Gd $300
Model 31A with vent rib barrel NiB $580 Ex $465 Gd $335
Model 31H Hunter
w/sporting-style stock . . . . . . NiB $440 Ex $292 Gd $222
Model 31R Riot Gun w/20-
inch plain bbl., 12 ga. . . . . . . NiB $509 Ex $388 Gd $287

MODEL 32A STANDARD GRADE O/U
Hammerless. Takedown. Auto ejectors. Early model had double triggers, later built with selective single trigger only. 12 ga. only. Bbls.: Plain, raised matted solid or vent rib; 26-, 28-, 30-, 32-inch; F/M choke standard, option of any combination of F, M, IC, C, SK choke. Weight: About 7.75 lbs. Checkered pistol-grip stock and forend. Made from 1932 to 1942.
With double triggers. . . . . NiB $2165 Ex $1800 Gd $1287
With selective single triggerNiB $2466 Ex $2100 Gd $1533
With raised solid rib, add 10%
With ventilated rib, add 20%

MODEL 32 TOURNAMENT, EXPERT AND PREMIER GRADE GUNS
These higher-grade models differ from the Model 32A in general quality, grade of wood, checkering, engraving, etc. General specifications are the same. Made from 1932 to 1942.
Model 32D Tournament grade . . NiB $4377 Ex $3310 Gd $2560
Model 32E Expert grade . . NiB $4598 Ex $4166 Gd $3000
Model 32F Premier grade   NiB $6986 Ex $5809 Gd $3976

MODEL 32 SKEET GRADE . . . . . NiB $2200 Ex $1798 Gd $1433
Same general specifications as Model 32A except 26- or 28-inch bbl., SK choke, beavertail forend, selective single trigger only. Weight: About 7.5 lbs. Made from 1932 to 1942.

MODEL 32TC
TARGET (TRAP) GRADE . . NiB $3233 Ex $2866 Gd $1974
Same general specifications as Model 32A except 30- or 32-inch vent-rib bbl., F choke, trap-style stock with checkered pistol-grip and beavertail forend. Weight: About 8 lbs. Made from 1932 to 1942.

MODEL 89 (1889) . . . . . . NiB $2133 Ex $1788 Gd $1141
Hammers. Circular action. Gauges: 10, 12, 16, 28- to 32-inch bls.; steel or Damascus twist. Weight 7-10 lbs. Made from 1889 to 1908.

MODEL 90-T SINGLE-SHOT TRAP NiB $1988 Ex $1790 Gd $1377
Gauge: 12; 2.75-inch chambers. 30-, 32- or 34-inch vent-rib bbl. with fixed chokes or screw-in REMChokes; ported or non-ported. Weight: 8.25 lbs. Checkered American walnut standard or Monte Carlo stock with low-luster finish. Engraved sideplates and drop-out trigger group optional. Made from 1990 to 1997.

MODEL 105 CTI AUTOLOADERun NiB $1230 Ex $880 Gd $600
Gas-operated. Titanium and carbon fiber receiver. Gauge: 12; 3-inch chamber. Bbl.: 26- or 28-inch with REMChoke. Weight: 7 lbs., depending on bbl. length. Checkered walnut stock and forend in satin finish. Made from 2006 to 2008.
105 CTi-II . . . . NiB $1230 Ex $880 Gd $600

MODEL 396 O/U
Boxlock. 12 ga. only w/2.75-inch chamber. 28- and 30-inch blued bbls. w/Rem chokes. Weight: 7.50 lbs. Nitride-grayed, engraved receiver, trigger guard, tang, hinge pins and forend metal. Engraved sideplates. Checkered satin-finished American walnut stock w/target style forend. Made from 1996 to 1998.
Sporting Clays . . . . NiB $1933 Ex $1658 Gd $1277
396 Skeet. . . . . NiB $1855 Ex $1544 Gd $1153

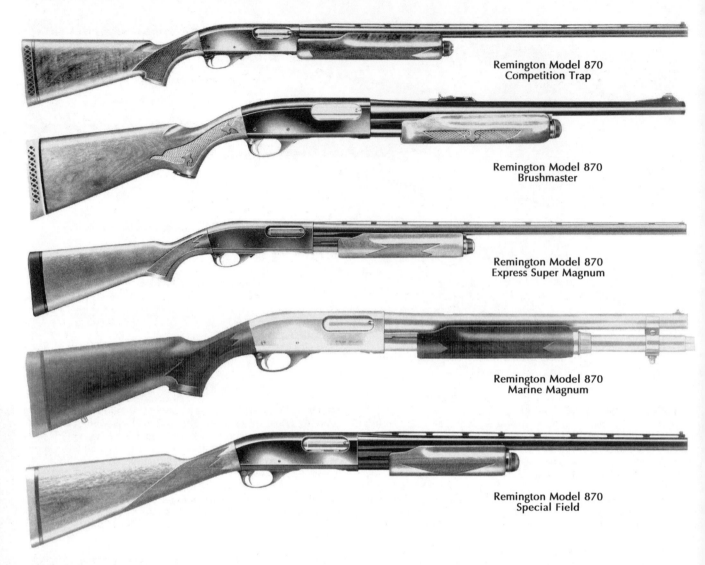

Remington Model 870
Competition Trap

Remington Model 870
Brushmaster

Remington Model 870
Express Super Magnum

Remington Model 870
Marine Magnum

Remington Model 870
Special Field

MODEL 870

"ALL AMERICAN" TRAP GUN NiB $1277 Ex $1073 Gd $777
Same as Model 870TB except custom grade with engraved receiver, trigger guard and bbl.; Monte Carlo or straight-comb stock and forend of fancy walnut; available only with 30-inch F choke bbl. Made from 1972 to 1977.

MODEL 870 COMPETITION TRAP NiB $766 Ex $555 Gd $439
Based on standard Model 870 receiver except is single-shot with gas-assisted recoil-reducing system, new choke design, a high step-up vent rib and redesigned stock, forend with cut checkering and satin finish. Weight: 8.5 lbs. Made from 1981 to 1987.

MODEL 870 STANDARD . . . . NiB $566 Ex $444 Gd $339
Same as Model 870 Wingmaster Riot Gun, on page 524, except has rifle-type sights.

MODEL 870 BRUSHMASTER DELUXE
Same as Model 870 Standard except available in 20 ga. as well as 12, has cut-checkered, satin-finished American walnut stock and forend, recoil pad.
Right-hand model . . . . NiB $559 Ex $477 Gd $366
Left-hand model . . . . NiB $659 Ex $490 Gd $380

MODEL 870 EXPRESS
Same general specifications Model 870 Wingmaster except has low-luster walnut-finished hardwood stock with pressed checkering and black recoil pad. Gauges: 12, 20 or .410, 3-inch chambers. Bbls.: 26- or 28-inch vent-rib with REMChoke; 25-inch vent-rib with fixed choke (.410 only). Black oxide metal finish. Made from 1987 to date.
Model 870 Express
(12 or20 ga., REMChoke) . . . . NiB $355 Ex $290 Gd $200
Model 870 Express
(.410 w/fixed choke). . . . . NiB $455 Ex $300 Gd $225
Express Combo (w/extra
20-inch deer bbl.) . . . . NiB $465 Ex $387 Gd $290

MODEL 870 EXPRESS DEER GUN
Same general specifications as Model 870 Express except in 12 ga. only, 20-inch bbl. with fixed IC choke, adj. rifle sights and Monte Carlo stock. Made from 1991 to date.
Express Deer Gun
w/standard barrel . . . . .NiB $433 Ex $297 Gd $200
Express Deer Gun
w/rifled barrel . . . . NiB $450 Ex $310 Gd $220

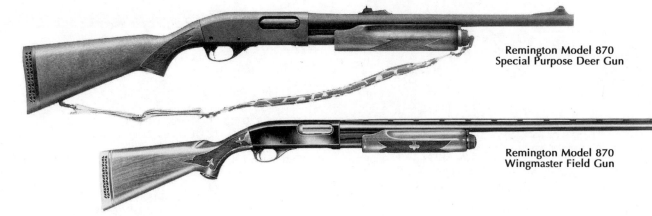

Remington Model 870
Special Purpose Deer Gun

Remington Model 870
Wingmaster Field Gun

MODEL 870 ESM (EXPRESS MAGNUM)
Similar to Model 870 Express except chambered for 12 ga. mag. w/3.5-inch chamber. Bbls.: 23-, 26- or 28-inch vent rib w/REM Choke. Checkered low-luster walnut-finished hardwood, black synthetic or camo buttstock and forearm. Matte black oxide metal finish or full camo finish. Made from 1998 to date.

Model 870 ESM
(w/hardwood stock) . . . . NiB $455 Ex $310 Gd $225
Model 870 ESM
(w/black synthetic stock) . . . . NiB $455 Ex $310 Gd $225
Model 870 ESM
(w/camo synthetic stock) . . . . NiB $488 Ex $395 Gd $259
Model 870 ESM Synthetic
Turkey (w/synthetic stock) . . . NiB $488 Ex $395 Gd $259
Model 870 ESM camo
Turkey (w/full camo) . . . . NiB $488 Ex $395 Gd $259
Model 870 ESM combo
(w/full camo, extra bbl.) . . . . NiB $509 Ex $400 Gd $323

MODEL 870 EXPRESS
SYNTHETIC HOME DEFENSE . NiB $422 Ex $300 Gd $200
Slide action, hammerless, takedown. 12 ga. only. 18-inch bbl. w/ cylinder choke and bead front sight. Positive checkered synthetic stock and forend with non-reflective black finish. Made from 1995 to date.

MODEL 870 EXPRESS TURKEY GUN NiB $448 Ex $290 Gd $210
Same general specifications as Model 870 Express except has 21-inch vent-rib bbl. and Turkey Extra-Full REMChoke. Made from 1991 to date.

MODEL 870 EXPRESS YOUTH GUN NiB $391 Ex $248 Gd $181
Same general specifications as Model 870 Express except has scaled-down stock with 12.5-inch pull and 21-inch vent rib bbl. with REMChoke. Made from 1991 to date.

MODEL 870 LIGHTWEIGHT
Same as standard Model 870 but with scaled-down receiver and lightweight mahogany stock; 20 ga. only. 2.75-inch chamber. Bbls.: plain or vent rib; 26-inch, IC; 28-inch, M or F choke. REMChoke available from 1987. Weight 5.75 lbs. w/26-inch plain bbl. American walnut stock and forend with satin or Hi-gloss finish. Made from 1972 to 1994.
With plain barrel . . . . NiB $477 Ex $366 Gd $290
With ventilated rib barrel . . . . NiB $490 Ex $380 Gd $315
With REMChoke barrel . . . . . NiB $566 Ex $435 Gd $335

MODEL 870 LIGHTWEIGHT MAGNUM
Same as Model 870 Lightweight but chambered for 20 ga. Magnum 3-inch shell; 28-inch bbl., plain or vent rib, F choke. Weight: 6 lbs. with plain bbl. Made from 1972 to 1994.

With plain barrel . . . . NiB $477 Ex $377 Gd $292
With ventilated rib barrel . . . . NiB $580 Ex $455 Gd $422

MODEL 870 MAGNUM DUCK GUN
Same as Model 870 Field Gun except has 3-inch chamber 12 and 20 gauge Magnum only. 28- or 30-inch bbl., plain or vent rib, M or F choke, recoil pad. Weight: About 7 or 6.75 lbs. Made from 1964 to date.
With plain barrel . . . . NiB $310 Ex $225 Gd $179
With ventilated rib barrel . . . . NiB $655 Ex $430 Gd $335

MODEL 870
MARINE MAGNUM . . . . NiB $735 Ex $496 Gd $359
Same general specifications as Model 870 Wingmaster except with 7-round magazine, 18-inch plain bbl. with fixed IC choke, bead front sight and nickel finish. Made from 1992 to date.

MODEL 870
SA SKEET GUN, SMALL GAUGE . . . NiB $875 Ex $677 Gd $529
Similar to Wingmaster Model 870SA except chambered for 28 and .410 ga. (2.5-inch chamber for latter); 25-inch vent rib bbl., SK choke. Weight: 6 lbs., 28 ga.; 6.5 lbs., .410. Made from 1969 to 1982.

MODEL 870 MISSISSIPPI
MAGNUM DUCK GUN . . . . . NiB $865 Ex $667 Gd $520
Same as Remington Model 870 Magnum duck gun except has 32-inch bbl. "Ducks Unlimited" engraved receiver, Made in 1983.

MODEL 870
SPECIAL FIELD SHOTGUN . . . . NiB $466 Ex $322 Gd $245
Pump action. Hammerless. Gauge: 12 or 20. 21-inch vent-rib bbl. with REMChoke. 41.5 inches overall. Weight: 6-7 lbs. Straight-grip checkered walnut stock and forend. Made from 1987 to 1995.

MODEL 870 SPECIAL PURPOSE DEER GUN
Similar to Special Purpose Magnum except with 20-inch IC choke, rifle sights. Matte black oxide and Parkerized finish. Oil-finished, checkered buttstock and forend with recoil pad. Made from 1986 to date.
Model 870 SP Deer Gun . . . . NiB $744 Ex $488 Gd $333
Model 870 SP Deer Gun,
cant. scope mt.. . . . . NiB $800 Ex $523 Gd $366

MODEL 870 SPECIAL
PURPOSE MAGNUM . . . . NiB $735 Ex $555 Gd $467
Similar to the 870 Magnum duck gun except with 26-, 28- or 30-inch vent rib REMChoke bbl.12 ga. only; 3-inch chamber. Oil-finished field-grade stock with recoil pad, QD swivels and Cordura sling. Made from 1985 to date.

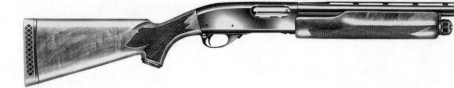

Remington Model 870TC
Wingmaster Trap

MODEL 870SPS MAGNUM
Same general specifications Model 870 Special Purpose Magnum except with synthetic stock and forend. 26- or 28-inch vent-rib bbl. with REMChoke tubes. Matte black or Mossy Oak camo finish. Made from 1991 to date.
70 SPS Mag. (black syn. stock) NiB $688 Ex $455 Gd $325
870 SPS-T Camo (Mossy Oak camo) . NiB $866 Ex $533 Gd $400

MODEL 870 WINGMASTER FIELD GUN
Same general specifications as Model 870AP except checkered stock and forend. Later models have REMChoke systems in 12 ga. Made from 1964 to date.
With plain barrel . . . . NiB $366 Ex $264 Gd $155
With ventilated rib barrel . . . . NiB $665 Ex $439 Gd $266

MODEL 870 WINGMASTER FIELD GUN, SMALL GAUGE
Same as standard Model 870 except w/scaled-down lightweight receivers. Gauges: 28 and .410. Plain or vent rib 25-inch bbl. choked IC, M or F. Weight: 5.5-6.25 lbs. depending on gauge and bbl. Made 1969 to 1994.
With plain barrel . . . . NiB $775 Ex $600 Gd $445
With ventilated-rib barrel . . . . NiB $808 Ex $625 Gd $465

MODEL 870 WINGMASTER
MAGNUM DELUXE GRADE . . NiB $667 Ex $559 Gd $400
Same as Model 870 Magnum standard grade except has checkered stock and extension beavertail forearm, bbl. with matted top surface. Disc. in 1963.

MODEL 870 WINGMASTER
MAGNUM STANDARD GRADE NiB $633 Ex $479 Gd $365
Same as Model 870AP except chambered for 12 ga. 3-inch Magnum, 30-inch F choke bbl., recoil pad. Weight: About 8.25 lbs. Made 1955 to 1963.

MODEL 870 WINGMASTER REMCHOKE SERIES
Slide action, hammerless, takedown with blued all-steel receiver. Gauges: 12, 20; 3-inch chamber. Tubular magazine. Bbls.: 21-, 26-, 28-inch vent-rib with REM Choke. Weight: 7.5 lbs. (12 ga.). Satin-finished, checkered walnut buttstock and forend with recoil pad. Right- or left-hand models. Made from 1986 to date.
Standard model, 12 ga. . . . . . NiB $500 Ex $377 Gd $266
Standard model, 20 ga. . . . . . NiB $535 Ex $400 Gd $288
Youth model, 21-inch barrel . . NiB $500 Ex $377 Gd $321

MODEL 870ADL WINGMASTER DELUXE GRADE
Same general specifications as Wingmaster Model 870AP except has pistol-grip stock and extension beavertail forend, both finely checkered; matted top surface or vent-rib bbl. Made 1950 to 1963.
With matted top-surface barrel NiB $488 Ex $365 Gd $288
With ventilated-rib barrel . . . . NiB $509 Ex $412 Gd $300

MODEL 870AP WINGMASTER STANDARD GRADE
Hammerless. Takedown. Gauges: 12, 16, 20. Tubular magazine holds four rounds. Bbls.: Plain, matted top surface or vent rib; 26-inch IC, 28-inch M or F choke, 30-inch F choke (12 ga. only). Weight: About 7 lbs., 12 ga.; 6.75 lbs., 16 ga.; 6.5 lbs., 20 ga. Plain pistol-grip stock, grooved forend. Made 1950 to 1963.
With plain barrel . . . . NiB $359 Ex $300 Gd $209
With matted surface barrel . . . NiB $435 Ex $335 Gd $225
With ventilated rib barrel . . . . NiB $466 Ex $372 Gd $260
Left-hand model . . . . NiB $489 Ex $400 Gd $265

MODEL 870DL WINGMASTER DELUXE SPECIAL
Same as Model 870ADL except select American walnut stock and forend. Made from 1950 to 1963.
With matted surface barrel . . . NiB $665 Ex $445 Gd $310
With ventilated-rib barrel . . . . NiB $715 Ex $477 Gd $349

MODEL 870D, 870F WINGMASTER
TOURNAMENT AND PREMIER GRADE GUNS
These higher-grade models differ from the Model 870AP in general quality, grade of wood, checkering, engraving, etc. General operating specifications are essentially the same. Made from 1950 to date.
Model 870D Tournament grade . NiB $3139 Ex $2288 Gd $1660
Model 870F Premier grade NiB $6445 Ex $4753 Gd $3465
Model 870F Premier gr. w/gold inlay NiB $10,098 Ex $7517 Gd $5237

MODEL 870R
WINGMASTER RIOT GUN . . . NiB $375 Ex $280 Gd $210
Same as Model 870AP except 20-inch bbl., IC choke, 12 ga. only.

MODEL 870 SA WINGMASTER SKEET GUN
Same general specifications as Model 870AP except has 26-inch vent-rib bbl., SK choke, ivory bead front sight, metal bead rear sight, pistol-grip stock and extension beavertail forend. Weight: 6.75 to 7.5 lbs. depending on gauge. Made 1950 to 1982.
Model 870SA Skeet grade (disc. 1982) NiB $677 Ex $395 Gd $288
Model 870SC Skeet Target
grade (disc. 1980) . . . . NiB $795 Ex $549 Gd $400

MODEL 870TB WINGMASTER
TRAP SPECIAL . . . . NiB $633 Ex $500 Gd $388
Same general specifications as Model 870AP Wingmaster except has 28- or 30-inch vent rib bbl., F choke, metal bead front sight, no rear sight. "Special" grade trap-style stock and forend, both checkered, recoil pad. Weight: About 8 lbs. Made from 1950 to 1981.

REMINGTON MODEL
870TC TRAP GRADE . . . . NiB $795 Ex $554 Gd $400
Same as Model 870 Wingmaster TC except has tournament-grade walnut in stock and forend w/satin finish. Over-bored 30-inch vent rib bbl. w/ 2.75-inch chamber and RemChoke tubes. Reissued in 1996. See separate listing for earlier model.

MODEL 870TC WINGMASTER TRAP GRADE
Same as Model 870TB except higher-grade walnut in stock and forend, has both front and rear sights. Made 1950-79. Model 870 TC reissued in 1996. See separate listing for later model.
Model 870 TC Trap (Standard) NiB $515 Ex $466 Gd $325
Model 870 TC Trap (Monte Carlo) NiB $545 Ex $480 Gd $366

MODEL 878A AUTOMASTER . NiB $376 Ex $266 Gd $195
Gas-operated Autoloader. 12 ga., 3-round magazine. Bbls.: 26-inch IC, 28-inch M choke, 30-inch F choke. Weight: About 7 lbs. Plain pistol-grip stock and forearm. Made from 1959-62.

NOTE: *New stock checkering patterns and receiver scroll markings were incorporated on all standard Model 1100 field, magnum, skeet and trap models in 1979.*

Remington Model 1100
Field w/Ventilated Rib

Remington Model 1100
Deer Gun

Remington Model 1100
SA Skeet Gun

MODEL 1100 AUTO FIELD GUN
Gas-operated. Hammerless. Takedown. Gauges: 12, 16, 20. Bbls.: plain or vent. rib; 30-inch F, 28-inch M or F, 26-inch IC; or REMChoke tubes. Weight: Average 7.25-7.5 lbs. depending on ga. and bbl. length. Checkered walnut pistol-grip stock and forearm in high-gloss finish. Made 1963 to 1988. 16 ga. discontinued 1980.

With plain barrel . . . . NiB $380 Ex $291 Gd $200
With ventilated-rib barrel   . . . NiB $422 Ex $356 Gd $239
REMChoke model . . . . NiB $466 Ex $390 Gd $292
REMChoke, Left-hand action . NiB $744 Ex $544 Gd $356

MODEL 1100 DEER GUN. . . . NiB $515 Ex $386 Gd $265
Same as Model 1100 Field Gun except has 22-inch barrel, IC, with rifle-type sights; 12 and 20 ga. only; recoil pad. Weight: About 7.25 lbs. Made from 1963 to 1998.

MODEL 1100 DUCKS UNLIMITED
ATLANTIC COMMEMORATIVENiB $1188 Ex $987 Gd $766
Limited production for one year. Similar specifications to Model 1100 Field except with 32-inch F choke, vent rib bbl. 12-ga. Magnum only. Made in 1982.

MODEL 1100 DUCKS UNLIMITED "THE CHESAPEAKE"
COMMEMORATIVE . . . . NiB $878 Ex $753 Gd $555
Limited edition 1 to 2400. Same general specifications as Model 1100 Field except sequentially numbered with markings "The Chesapeake." 12 ga. Magnum with 30-inch F choke, vent rib bbl. Made in 1981.

MODEL 1100 FIELD GRADE, SMALL BORE
Same as standard Model 1100 but scaled down. Gauges: 28, .410. 25-inch bbl., plain or vent rib; IC, M or F choke. Weight: 6.25-7 lbs. depending on gauge and bbl. Made from 1969 to 1994.

With plain barrel . . . . NiB $669 Ex $533 Gd $435
With ventilated rib . . . . NiB $866 Ex $677 Gd $480

MODEL 1100 LIGHTWEIGHT
Same as standard Model 1100 but scaled-down receiver and lightweight mahogany stock; 20 ga. only, 2.75-inch chamber. Bbls.: Plain or vent rib; 26-inch IC; 28-inch M and F choke. Weight: 6.25 lbs. Made from 1970 to 1976.

With plain barrel . . . . NiB $654 Ex $500 Gd $390
With ventilated rib . . . . NiB $735 Ex $566 Gd $408

MODEL 1100 LIGHTWEIGHT MAGNUM
Same as Model 1100 Lightweight but chambered for 20 gauge Magnum 3-inch shell; 28-inch bbl., plain or vent rib, F choke. Weight: 6.5 lbs. Made from 1977 to 1998.

With plain barrel . . . . NiB $688 Ex $544 Gd $422
With ventilated rib   . . . . NiB $788 Ex $590 Gd $466
With choke tubes . . . . NiB $855 Ex $598 Gd $466

MODEL 1100 LT-20 DUCKS UNLIMITED
SPECIAL COMMEMORATIVENiB $1486 Ex $1156 Gd $844
Limited edition 1 to 2400. Same general specifications as Model 1100 Field except sequentially numbered with markings, "The Chesapeake." 20 ga. only. 26-inch IC, vent-rib bbl. Made in 1981.

MODEL 1100 LT-20 SERIES
Same as Model 1100 Field Gun except in 20 ga. with shorter 23-inch vent rib bbl., straight-grip stock. REMChoke series has 21-inch vent rib bbl., choke tubes. Weight: 6.25 lbs. Checkered grip and forearm. Made from 1977 to 1995.

Model 1100
LT-20 Special . . . . NiB $588 Ex $498 Gd $377
Model 1100
LT-20 Deer Gun . . . . NiB $490 Ex $399 Gd $295
Model 1100
LT-20 Youth . . . . NiB $585 Ex $444 Gd $300

MODEL 1100 MAGNUM . . . . NiB $598 Ex $499 Gd $378
Limited production. Similar to the Model 1100 Field except with 26-inch F choke, vent rib bbl. and 3-inch chamber. Made in 1981.

MODEL 1100 MAGNUM DUCK GUN
Same as Model 1100 Field Gun except has 3-inch chamber,12 and 20 ga. Mag. only. 30-inch plain or vent rib bbl. in 12 ga., 28-inch in 20 ga.; M or F choke. Recoil pad. Weight: About 7.75 lbs. Made from 1963 to 1988.

With plain barrel . . . . NiB $555 Ex $399 Gd $324
With ventilated
rib barrel . . . . NiB $575 Ex $435 Gd $355

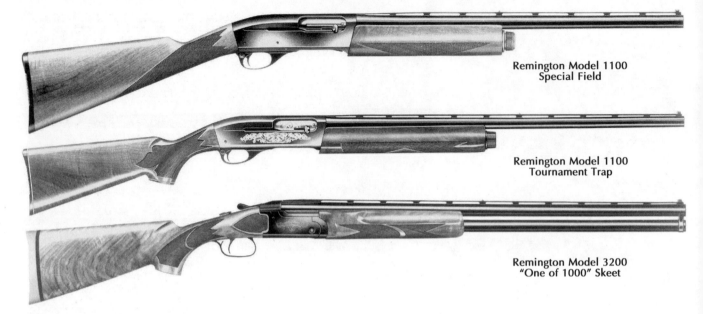

Remington Model 1100
Special Field

Remington Model 1100
Tournament Trap

Remington Model 3200
"One of 1000" Skeet

MODEL 1100
ONE OF 3000 FIELD . . . . . . **NiB $1210 Ex $966 Gd $790**
Limited edition, numbered 1 to 3000. Similar to Model 1100 Field except with fancy wood and gold-trimmed etched hunting scenes on receiver. 12 gauge with 28-inch Mod., vent rib bbl. Made in 1980.

MODEL 1100 SA SKEET GUN
Same as Model 1100 Field Gun, 12 and 20 ga. except has 26-inch vent-rib bbl., SK choke or with Cutts Compensator. Weight: 7.25-7.5 lbs. Made from 1963 to 1994.
**With skeet-
choked barrel** . . . . **NiB $977 Ex $644 Gd $388**
With Cutts Comp, add **$200**
Left-hand action, add **$75**

MODEL 1100 SA
LIGHTWEIGHT SKEET . . . . . . **NiB $655 Ex $497 Gd $366**
Same as Model 1100 Lightweight except has skeet-style stock and forearm, 26-inch vent-rib bbl., SK choke. Made from 1971 to 1997.

MODEL 1100 SA
SKEET SMALL BORE . . . . **NiB $625 Ex $443 Gd $311**
Similar to standard Model 1100SA except chambered for 28 and .410 ga. (2.5-inch chamber for latter); 25-inch vent-rib bbl., SK choke. Weight: 6.75 lbs., 28 ga.; 7.25 lbs., .410. Made from 1969 to 1994.

MODEL 1100 SB
LIGHTWEIGHT SKEET . . . . . . **NiB $644 Ex $433 Gd $310**
Same as Model 1100SA Lightweight except has select wood. Introduced in 1977.

MODEL 1100
SB SKEET GUN . . . . **NiB $654 Ex $443 Gd $319**
Same specifications as Model 1100SA except has select wood. Made from 1963 to 1997.

MODEL 1100
SPECIAL FIELD SHOTGUN . . . **NiB $600 Ex $492 Gd $388**
Gas-operated. Five round capacity. Hammerless. Gauges: 12 and 20. 21-inch vent-rib bbl. with REMChoke. Weight: 6.5-7.25 lbs. Straight-grip checkered walnut stock and forend. Made from 1983 to 1999.

MODEL 1100 SP MAGNUM
Same as Model 1100 Field except 12 ga. only with 3-inch chambers. Bbls.: 26- or 30-inch F choke; or 26-inch with REM Choke tubes; vent rib. Non-reflective matte black, Parkerized bbl. and receiver. Satin-finished stock and forend. Made 1986.
With fixed choke . . . . **NiB $475 Ex $397 Gd $321**
With REMChoke . . . . **NiB $490 Ex $417 Gd $344**

MODEL 1100 TOURNAMENT/PREMIER
These higher grade guns differ from standard models in overall quality, grade of wood, checkering, engraving, gold inlays, etc. General specs are the same. Made 1963 to 1994; 1997 to 1999; 2003.
**Model 1100D
Tournament** . . . . **NiB $966 Ex $633 Gd $577**
**Model 1100F
Premier** . . . . **NiB $1266 Ex $1059 Gd $833**
**Model 1100F Premier
with gold inlay** . . . . **NiB $10,332 Ex $7833 Gd $4460**

MODEL 1100
TOURNAMENT SKEET . . . . . . **NiB $977 Ex $738 Gd $490**
Similar to Model 1100 Field except with 26-inch bbl. SK choke. Gauges: 12, LT-20, 28, and .410. Features select walnut stocks and new cut-checkering patterns. Made from 1979- to 1999.

MODEL 1100TA TRAP GUN . . **NiB $529 Ex $417 Gd $330**
Similar to Model 1100TB Trap Gun except with regular-grade stocks. Available in both left- and right-hand versions. Made 1979 to 1986.

MODEL 1100TB TRAP GUN
Same as Model 1100 Field Gun except has special trap stock, straight or Monte Carlo comb, recoil pad; 30-inch vent-rib bbl., F or M trap choke; 12 ga. only. Weight: 8.25 lbs. Made 1963 to 1979.
With straight stock . . . . **NiB $588 Ex $460 Gd $339**
With Monte Carlo stock . . . . **NiB $599 Ex $443 Gd $360**

MODEL 1900
HAMMERLESS DOUBLE . . **NiB $1889 Ex $1366 Gd $1177**
Improved version of Model 1894. Boxlock. Auto ejector. Double triggers. Gauges: 10, 12, 16. Bbls.: 28 to 32 inches. Value shown is for standard grade with ordnance steel bbls. Made 1900 to 1910.

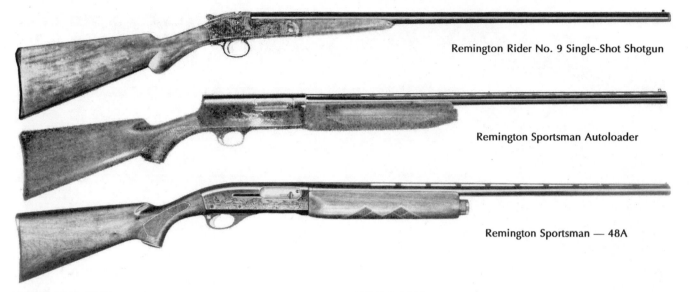

Remington Rider No. 9 Single-Shot Shotgun

Remington Sportsman Autoloader

Remington Sportsman — 48A

MODEL 3200 FIELD
GRADE O/U . . . . .NiB $1388 Ex $1178 Gd $900
Boxlock. Auto ejectors. Selective single trigger. 12 ga. 2.75-inch chambers. Bbls.: Vent rib, 26- and 28-inch M/F; 30-inch IC/M. Weight: About 7.75 lbs. with 26-inch bbls. Checkered pistol-grip stock/forearm. Made from 1973 to 1978.

MODEL 3200
COMPETITION SKEET GUN NiB $1799 Ex $1588 Gd $1165
Same as Model 3200 Skeet Gun except has gilded scrollwork on frame, engraved forend, latch plate and trigger guard, select fancy wood. Made from 1973 to 1984.

MODEL 3200
COMPETITION SKEET SET NiB $5733 Ex $4790 Gd $3300
Similar specifications to Model 3200 Field. 12-ga. O/U with additional, interchangeable bbls. in 20, 28, and .410 ga. Cased. Made from 1980 to 1984.

MODEL 3200
COMPETITION TRAP GUN NiB $1598 Ex $1266 Gd $1177
Same as Model 3200 Trap Gun except has gilded scrollwork on frame, engraved forend, latch plate and trigger guard, select fancy wood. Made from 1973 to 1984.

MODEL 3200
FIELD GRADE MAGNUM . NiB $1766 Ex $1588 Gd $1177
Same as Model 3200 Field except chambered for 12 ga. mag. 3-inch shells 30-inch bbls., M and F or both F choke. Made from 1975 to 1984.

MODEL 3200
"ONE OF 1000" SKEET . . . NiB $2088 Ex $1577 Gd $1288
Same as Model 3200 "One of 1000" Trap except has 26- or 28-inch bbls., SK choke, skeet-style stock and forearm. Made in 1974.

MODEL 3200
"ONE OF 1000" TRAP . . . NiB $2170 Ex $1660 Gd $1375
Limited edition numbered 1 to 1000. Same general specifications as Model 3200 Trap Gun but has frame, trigger guard and forend latch elaborately engraved (designation "One of 1,000" on frame side), stock and forearm of high grade walnut. Supplied in carrying case. Made in 1973.

MODEL 3200 SKEET GUN NiB $1779 Ex $1398 Gd $1055
Same as Model 3200 Field Grade except skeet-style stock and full beavertail forearm, 26- or 28-inch bbls., SK choke. Made from 1973-80.

MODEL 3200
SPECIAL TRAP GUN . . . . . . NiB $1598 Ex $1366 Gd $988
Same as Model 3200 Trap Gun except has select fancy-grade wood and other minor refinements. Made from 1973 to 1984.

MODEL 3200 TRAP GUN . NiB $1499 Ex $1262 Gd $1077
Same as Model 3200 Field Grade except trap-style stock w/Monte Carlo or straight comb, select wood, beavertail forearm, 30- or 32-inch bbls. w/ventilated rib, IM/F or F/F chokes. Made 1973 to 1977.

RIDER NO. 9
SINGLE-SHOT SHOTGUN . . . NiB $555 Ex $433 Gd $335
Improved version of No. 3 Single Barrel Shotgun made in the late 1800s. Semi-hammerless. Gauges 10, 12, 16, 20, 24, 28. 30- to 32-inch plain bbl. Weight: About 6 lbs. Plain pistol-grip stock and forearm. Auto ejector. Made from 1902 to 1910.

SP-10
MAGNUM AUTOLOADER . . NiB $1133 Ex $888 Gd $677
Takedown. Gas-operated with stainless steel piston. 10 ga., 3.5-inch chamber. Bbls.: 26- or 30-inch vent-rib with REMChoke screw-in tubes. Weight: 11 to 11.25 lbs. Metal bead front. Checkered walnut stock with satin finish. Made from 1989 to date.

SP-10
MAGNUM TURKEY COMBO NiB $1397 Ex $1121 Gd $989
Same general specifications as Model SP-10 Magnum except has extra 22-inch REMChoke bbl. with M, F and Turkey extra-full tubes. Rifle sights. QD swivels and camo sling. Made from 1991 to 1994.

PEERLESS O/U . . . . NiB $1165 Ex $966 Gd $788
Boxlock action and removable, engraved sideplates. Gauge: 12 only with 3-inch chambers. Barrels: 26-, 28-, or 30-inch with vent rib and REMChoke system. Automatic safety and single selective trigger. Weight: 7.25 lbs. to 7.5 lbs. Blued receiver and bbls. Checkered American walnut stock. Made from 1993 to 1998.

SPORTSMAN A STANDARD GRADE AUTOLOADER
Same general specifications as Model 11A except magazine holds two shells. Also available in "B" Special Grade, "D" Tournament Grade, "E" Expert Grade, "F" Premier Grade. Made from 1931 to 1948. Same values as for Model 11A.
48D . . . . NiB $445 Ex $321 Gd $226

SHOTGUNS

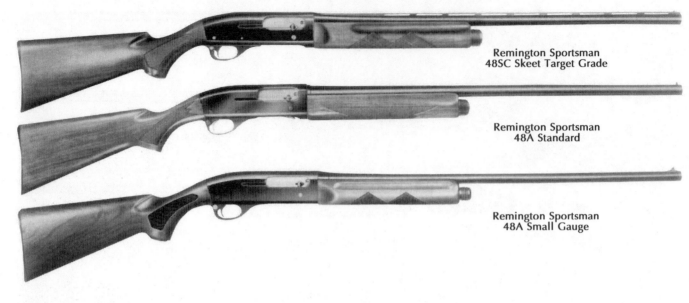

Remington Sportsman
48SC Skeet Target Grade

Remington Sportsman
48A Standard

Remington Sportsman
48A Small Gauge

SPORTSMAN SKEET GUN
Same general specifications as the Sportsman A except has 26-inch bbl. (plain, solid or vent rib), SK choke, beavertail forend. Disc. in 1949.
With plain barrel . . . . NiB $408 Ex $320 Gd $255
With solid-rib barrel . . . . NiB $408 Ex $320 Gd $255
With ventilated rib barrel . . . NiB $475 Ex $355 Gd $290

MODEL 48 MOHAWK SPORTSMAN AUTO
Streamlined receiver. Hammerless. Takedown. Gauges: 12, 16, 20. Tubular magazine holds two rounds. Bbls.: Plain, matted top surface or vent rib; 26-inch IC, 28-inch M or F choke, 30-inch F choke (12 ga. only). Weight: About 7.5 lbs., 12 ga.; 6.25 lbs., 16 ga.; 6.5 lbs., 20 ga. Pistol-grip stock, grooved forend, both checkered. Made from 1949 to 1959.
With plain bbl. . . . . NiB $376 Ex $270 Gd $198
With matted top-surface bbl. . . NiB $466 Ex $355 Gd $290
With ventilated rib bbl. . . . . . NiB $566 Ex $477 Gd $379

SPORTSMAN MODEL 48 B, D, F,
SELECT, TOURNAMENT & PREMIER GRADE GUNS
These higher grade models differ from the Sportsman-48A in general quality, grade of wood, checkering, engraving, etc. General specifications are the same. Made from 1949 to 1959.
Sportsman-48B Select grade . . NiB $490 Ex $330 Gd $225
Sportsman-48D Tournament grade NiB $1688 Ex $1178 Gd $988
Sportsman-48F Premier grade NiB $6355 Ex $3988 Gd $2500

MODEL 48SA SPORTSMAN SKEET GUN
Same general specifications as Sportsman-48A except has 26-inch bbl. with matted top surface or vent rib, SK choke, ivory bead front sight, metal bead rear sight. Made from 1949 to 1960.
With plainbarrel . . . . NiB $377 Ex $279 Gd $200
With ventilated rib barrel . . . . NiB $466 Ex $344 Gd $229
Sportsman-48SC Skeet . . . . . . NiB $577 Ex $466 Gd $355
Tournament grade . . . . . . NiB $1688 Ex $1299 Gd $1100
Sportsman-48SF Skeet
Premier grade. . . . . NiB $6220 Ex $4014 Gd $2444

MODEL 11-48A RIOT GUN . . NiB $420 Ex $322 Gd $276
Same as Model 11-48A except 20-inch plain barrel and 12 ga. only. Disc. in 1969.

MODEL 11-48A STANDARD
GRADE 4-ROUND AUTOLOADER .410 & 28 GAUGE
Same general specifications as Sportsman-48A except gauge, 3-round magazine, 25-inch bbl. Weight: About 6.25 lbs. 28 ga. introduced 1952, .410 in 1954. Disc. in 1969. Values same as shown for Sportsman-48A.

MODEL 11-48A STANDARD GRADE AUTOLOADER
Same general specifications as Sportsman-48A except magazine holds four rounds, forend not grooved. Also available in Special Grade (11-48B), Tournament Grade (11-48D) and Premier Grade (11-48F). Made 1949 to 1969. Values same as for Sportsman-48A.

MODEL 11-48SA SKEET
28 GA. AND .410 . . . . NiB $398 Ex $300 Gd $233
Same general specifications as Model 11-48A 28 gauge except has 25-inch vent rib bbl., SK choke. 28 ga. introduced 1952, .410 in 1954.

MODEL 58 SKEET, TARGET, TOURNAMENT
AND PREMIER GRADES
These higher grade models differ from the Sportsman-58SA in general quality, grade of wood, checkering, engraving, and other refinements. General operating and physical specifications are the same.
Sportsman-58C Skeet Gun . . . NiB $544 Ex $397 Gd $322
Sportsman-58D Tournament . . NiB $1656 Ex $1267 Gd $1100
Sportsman-58SF Premier . . NiB $6222 Ex $3566 Gd $2924

SPORTSMAN-58 TOURNAMENT AND PREMIER
These higher grade models differ from the Sportsman-58ADL with vent-rib bbl. in general quality, grade of wood, checkering, engraving, etc. General specifications are the same.
Sportsman-58D Tournament . NiB $1099 Ex $824 Gd $590
Sportsman-58F Premier. . . NiB $1889 Ex $1488 Gd $1051

MODEL 58ADL AUTOLOADER
Deluxe grade. Gas-operated. 12 ga. Three round magazine. Bbls.: plain or vent rib, 26-, 28- or 30-inch; IC, M or F choke, or Remington Special Skeet choke. Weight: About 7 lbs. Checkered pistol-grip stock and forearm. Made from 1956 to 1964.
With plain barrel . . . . NiB $366 Ex $267 Gd $188
With ventilated rib barrel . . . NiB $433 Ex $320 Gd $221

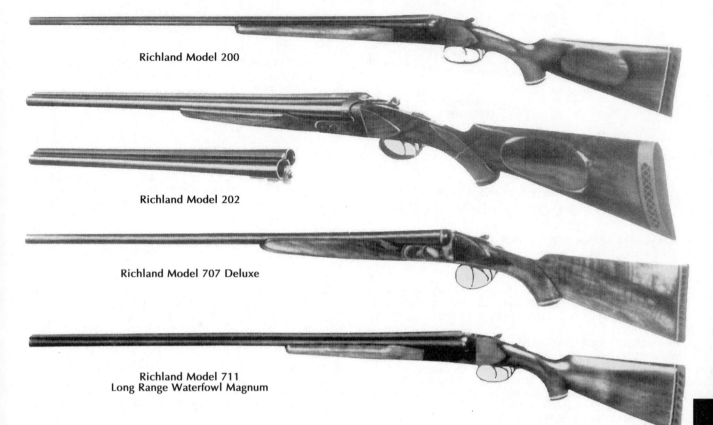

Richland Model 200

Richland Model 202

Richland Model 707 Deluxe

Richland Model 711
Long Range Waterfowl Magnum

MODEL 58BDL DELUXE SPECIAL GRADE
Same as Model 58ADL except select grade wood.
With plain barrel . . . . **NiB $544 Ex $422 Gd $338**
With ventilated rib barrel . . **NiB $577 Ex $476 Gd $390**

MODEL 58SADL
SKEET GRADE . . . . **NiB $588 Ex $432 Gd $338**
Same general specifications as Model 58ADL with vent-rib bbl.
except special skeet stock and forearm.

REVELATION SHOTGUNS

See Western Auto listings.

RICHLAND ARMS COMPANY — Blissfield, Michigan; manufactured in Italy and Spain

MODEL 200
FIELD GRADE DOUBLE . . . . . **NiB $400 Ex $294 Gd $179**
Hammerless, boxlock, Anson & Deeley-type. Plain extractors. Double
triggers. Gauges: 12, 16, 20, 28, .410 (3-inch chambers in 20 and .410;
others have 2.75-inch). Bbls.: 28-inch M/F choke, 26-inch IC/M; .410
with 26-inch M/F only; 22-inch IC/M in 20 ga. only. Weight: 6 lbs.,
2 oz. to 7 lbs., 4 oz. Checkered walnut stock with cheekpiece, pistol
grip, recoil pad; beavertail forend. Made in Spain from 1963 to 1985.

MODEL 202
ALL PURPOSE FIELD GUN . . . **NiB $554 Ex $348 Gd $245**
Hammerless, boxlock, Anson & Deeley-type. Same as Model 200

except has two sets of barrels same gauge. 12 ga.: 30-inch bbls.
F/F, 3-inch chambers; 26-inch bbls. IC/M, 2.75-inch chambers. 20
gauge: 28-inch bbls. M/F; 22-inch bbls. IC/M, 3-inch chambers.
Made from 1963. Disc.

MODEL 707
DELUXE FIELD GUN . . . . . . **NiB $433 Ex $266 Gd $180**
Hammerless, boxlock, triple bolting system. Plain extractors.
Double triggers. Gauges: 12, 2.75-inch chambers; 20, 3-inch
chambers. Bbls.: 12 ga., 28-inch M/F, 26-inch IC/M; 20 ga.,
30-inch F/F, 28-inch M/F, 26-inch IC/M. Weight: 6 lbs., 4 oz. to 6
lbs., 15 oz. Checkered walnut stock and forend, recoil pad. Made
from 1963 to 1972.

MODEL 711 LONG-RANGE WATERFOWL MAGNUM DOUBLE-BARREL SHOTGUN
Hammerless, boxlock, Anson & Deeley-type, Purdey triple lock.
Plain extractors. Double triggers. Auto safety. Gauges: 10, 3.5-
inch chambers; 12, 3-inch chambers. Bbls.: 10 ga., 32-inch; 12
ga., 30-inch; F/F. Weight: 10 ga., 11 pounds; 12 ga., 7.75 lbs.
Checkered walnut stock and beavertail forend; recoil pad. Made
in Spain from 1963 to 1985.
10 ga. magnum . . . . **NiB $545 Ex $356 Gd $280**
12 ga. magnum . . . . **NiB $566 Ex $377 Gd $300**

MODEL 808
O/U SHOTGUN . . . . **NiB $559 Ex $394 Gd $290**
Boxlock. Plain extractors. Non-selective single trigger. 12 ga. only.
Bbls. (Vickers steel): 30-inch F/F; 28-inch M/F; 26-inch IC/M. Weight:
6 lbs., 12 oz. to 7 lbs., 3 oz. Checkered walnut stock/forend. Made in
Italy from 1963 to 1968.

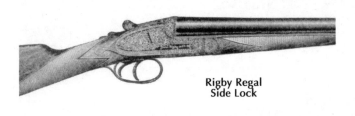

Rigby Regal
Side Lock

JOHN RIGBY & CO. — London, England

HAMMERLESS BOXLOCK DOUBLE-BARREL SHOTGUN
Auto ejectors. Double triggers. Made in all gauges, barrel lengths
and chokes. Checkered stock and forend, straight grip standard.
Made in two grades: Sackville and Chatsworth. These guns differ
in general quality, engraving, etc.; specifications are the same.
Sackville grade . . . . . . .NiB $6450 Ex $4255 Gd $3790
Chatsworth grade . . . . .NiB $4779 Ex $4109 Gd $3200

HAMMERLESS SIDELOCK DOUBLE-BARREL SHOTGUN
Auto ejectors. Double triggers. Made in all gauges, barrel
lengths and chokes. Checkered stock and forend, straight
grip standard. Made in two grades: Regal (best quality) and
Sandringham; these guns differ in general quality, engraving,
etc., specifications are the same.
Regal grade . . . . NiB $13,677 Ex $11,773 Gd $9892
Sandringham grade . . . NiB $11,088 Ex $9000 Gd $5698

RIZZINI, BATTISTA — Marcheno, Italy

*Rizzini was purchased by San Swiss AG IN 2002. Imported in the
U.S. by SIB Arms, Exeter, New Hampshire; William Larkin Moore &
Co., Scottsdale, Arizona; and New England Arms Co., Kittery, Maine*

AURUM O/U . . . . .NiB $2770 Ex $2243 Gd $2016
Gauge: 12, 16 and 20. Boxlock action, light engraving. Case
included. Introduced 1996.

AURUM LIGHT . . . . .NiB $4088 Ex $2867 Gd $2390
Similaar to Aurum but 16 gauge only. Imported beginning in
2000.

ARTEMIS . . . . .NiB $2733 Ex $2270 Gd $1966
Similarf to Aurum but with improved engraving and gold inlays.

ARTEMIS DELUXE . . . . .NiB $6777 Ex $3861 Gd $3223
Similar to Artemis but with detailed game scene engraving.
Available in all gauges

ARTEMIS EL . . . . NiB $17,776 Ex $14,600 Gd $12,980
Same as Artemis Deluxe. Custom gun with superior quality wood
and detailed hand engraving. Disc. 2000.

MODEL 780 FIELD . . . . NiB $2140 Ex $1088 Gd $977
Gauge: 10, 12 or 16. Boxlock action, double triggers, extractors,
walnut stock and forearm. Disc. 2000.
10 gauge, add. $625
Ejector model (S780EL), add $200
Single selective trigger with ejectors, add. $250
SST, ejectors and upgraded stock, add $425

MODEL S780 EMEL . . . . .NiB $14,900 Ex $13,655 Gd $11,330
Same as Model 780 Field but with special engraving and hand finished.

MODEL 780 COMPETITION . . . . . . NiB $1488 Ex $1276 Gd $1099
Same as Model 780 Field but with skeet, trap or sporting clays
features. Disc.1998.

MODEL 780
SMALL GAUGE SERIES . . . . NiB $1388 Ex $1164 Gd $889
Same as Model 780 Field but in 20, 28, or 36 gauge. Double trig-
gers, ejectors. Disc. 1998.

MODEL 782 EM FIELD . . . . NiB $1566 Ex $1275 Gd $1074
Gauge: 12 or 16. Boxlock action with sideplates, single selective trig-
ger, ejectors and extractors, walnut stock and forearm. Disc. 1998.
Model 782 EM Slug, add $550
Model 782 EML, add $450

MODEL S7820 EMEL . . . . . . .NiB $14,990 Ex $11,860 Gd $10,066
Same as Model 782 EM Field but specially engraved and hand finished.

MODEL S782 EMEL DELUXE .NiB $13,899 Ex $11,776 Gd $10,066
Gauge: 10, 12, 16, 20, 28, 36 and .410. Barrel:28-inch ventilated rib
with choke tubes (except .410); coin-finish engraving; gold inlaids;
fine scroll borders; Deluxe English walnut stock. Imported 1994.

MODEL 790 COMPETITION . . . . . . NiB $1877 Ex $1687 Gd $1261
Gauge: 12 or 20. Available in trap, skeet or sporting clays models.
Black frame outlined with gold line engraving. Disc. 1999.
20 ga. Sporting (sideplates and QD stock), add $1200
Trap model, 20 gauge, subtract $200

MODEL 790 SMALL GAUGE . . . . . NiB $1499 Ex $1179 Gd $1088
Similar to Model 790 Competition but in 20, 29, or 36 guages.
Single selective trigger, ejectors. Disc. 2000.

MODEL 790 EL . . . . NiB $7088 Ex $4977 Gd $3766
Same as Model 790 but hand finished with 18k gold inlays, hand
engraving.

MODEL 790 EL . . . . NiB $7132 Ex $4460 Gd $3477
Same as Model 790 but with multiple chokes, fitted case. Disc. 2000.

MODEL S790 EMEL DELUXE . . NiB $12,970 Ex $10,088 Gd $8990
Guages: All. Custom gun with 27.5-inch ventilated-rib bbls. choke
tubes (except .410); color case-hardened or coin-finished receiver;
ornate engraving with Rizzini crest. Stock is deluxe English walnut;
leather case included.

MODEL 792 SMALL GAUGE MAGNUM NiB $1791 Ex $1476 Gd $1199
Gauge: 20, 28, or 36. Magnum chambers. Single selective trigger;
ejectors; engraved sideplates. Disc. 1998.

MODEL 792 EMEL DELUXE . . . . . . NiB $9133 Ex $8093 Gd $6166
Same as Model 793 but hand finished with 18k gold inlays and
hand engraving.

MODEL S792 EMEL . . . . .NiB $14,000 Ex $11,980 Gd $10,760
Guages: All. Custom gun with 27.5-inch ventilated-rib bbls. choke
tubes (except .410); coin-finished receiver; sideplates with fine
game scene engraving and scroll borders; deluxe English walnut
stock; leather case included. Imported 1994.

MODEL 2000 TRAP . . . . NiB $1798 Ex $1448 Gd $1190
Guage: 12 only. Nickel-finished receiver; sideplates; gold trigger; ventilated-
rib bbls.. Disc 1998.

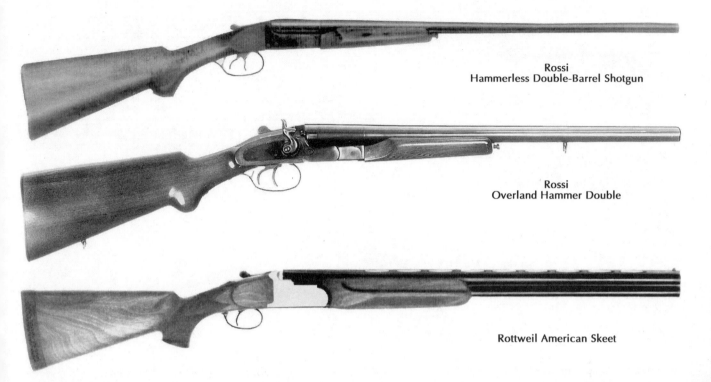

Rossi
Hammerless Double-Barrel Shotgun

Rossi
Overland Hammer Double

Rottweil American Skeet

MODEL 2000

TRAP EL . . . . NiB $5477 Ex $4100 Gd $3110
Same as Model 2000 Trap but hand finished with 18k gold inlays and ornate hand engraving.

MODEL 2000-SP . . . . NiB $3210 Ex $2976 Gd $2241
Guage: 12 only. Bbls.: 26, 29.5, or 32 inches. Over-bored barrels with choke tubes. Engraved sideplates, semi-fancy select QD stock. Case included. Imported 1994 to 1998.

PREMIER SPORTING . . . . NiB $2669 Ex $2280 Gd $1881
Guages: 12 or 20. Bbls.: 28, 29.5 or 32 inches five chokes per bbl.. Custom built on request. Imported 1994

SPORTING EL . . . . NiB $3126 Ex $2390 Gd $2177
Same as Premier model but includes multiple chokes and fitted case. Disc. 2000.

UPLAND EL . . . . NiB $2793 Ex $2277 Gd $1965
Guages: All. Custom gun with 27.5-inch ventilated-rib bbls. choke tubes (except .410); case-hardened receiver; deluxe walnut stock. Hard case included. Imported 1994.

AMADEO ROSSI, S.A. — Sao Leopoldo, Brazil

SQUIRE HAMMERLESS DOUBLE-

BARREL SHOTGUN . . . . NiB $435 Ex $333 Gd $245
Boxlock. Plain extractors. Double triggers. 12 and 20 ga., .410. Three-inch chambers. Bbls.: 20-, 26-inch IC/M; 28-inch M/F choke. Weight: 7 to 7.5 lbs. Pistol-grip hardwood stock and beavertail forearm, uncheckered. Made 1985 to 1990.

OVERLUND

HAMMER DOUBLE . . . . NiB $380 Ex $244 Gd $179
Sidelock. Plain extractors. Double triggers. Gauges: 12, .410;

3-inch chambers. Bbls.: 20-inch, IC/M in 12 g.; 26-inch, F/F choke in .410. Weight: 7 lbs. (12 ga.); 6 lbs. (.410). Pistol-grip stock and beavertail forearm, uncheckered. Note: Because of its resemblance to the short-barreled doubles carried by guards riding shotgun on 19th-century stagecoaches, the 12 ga. version originally was called the "Coach Gun." Made 1968 to 1989.

ROTTWEIL SHOTGUNS — Germany

MODEL 72 O/U

SHOTGUN . . . . NiB $1988 Ex $1687 Gd $1277
Hammerless, takedown with engraved receiver. 12 ga.; 2.75-inch chambers. 26.75-inch bbls. with SK/SK chokes. Weight: 7.5 lbs. Interchangeable trigger groups and butt-stocks. Checkered French walnut buttstock and forend. Imported from Germany.

MODEL 650 FIELD

O/U SHOTGUN . . . . NiB $888 Ex $675 Gd $544
Breech action. Gauge: 12. 28-inch bbls. Six screw-in choke tubes. Automatic ejectors. Engraved receiver. Checkered pistol grip stock. Made from 1984 to 1986.

AMERICAN SKEET . . . . . NiB $2010 Ex $1798 Gd $1288
Boxlock action. Gauge: 12. 27-inch vent-rib bbls. 44.5 inches overall. SK chokes. Weight: 7.5 lbs. Designed for tube sets. Hand-checkered European walnut stock with modified forend. Made from 1984 to 1987.

INTERNATIONAL

TRAP SHOTGUN . . . . . NiB $2066 Ex $1799 Gd $1263
Box lock action. Gauge: 12. 30-inch bbls. 48.5 inches overall. Weight: 8 lbs. Choked IM/F. Selective single trigger. Metal bead front sight. Checkered European walnut stock w/pistol grip. Engraved action. Made from 1984 to 1987.

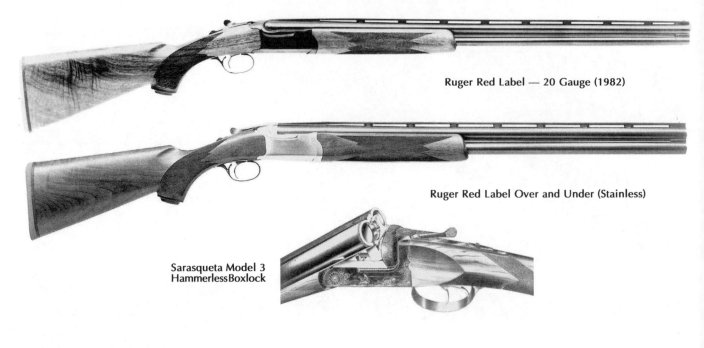

Ruger Red Label — 20 Gauge (1982)

Ruger Red Label Over and Under (Stainless)

Sarasqueta Model 3
Hammerless Boxlock

STURM, RUGER & COMPANY, INC. — Southport, Connecticut

RED LABEL O/U STANDARD GRADE
Boxlock. Auto ejectors. Selective single trigger. 12, 20 or 28 ga. w/2.75- or 3-inch chambers. 26-inch vent-rib bbl., IC/M or SK choke. Single selective trigger. Selective automatic ejectors. Automatic top safety. Standard gold bead front sight. Pistol-grip or English-style American walnut stock and forearm w/hand-cut checkering. The 20 ga. Model was introduced in 1977; 12 ga. version in 1982 and the stainless receiver became standard in 1985. Choke tubes were optional in 1988 and standard in 1990. Weight: 7.0 to 7.5 lbs.
Red Label w/fixed chokes NiB $1733 Ex $1388 Gd $1077
Red Label w/screw-in tubes NiB $1760 Ex $1410 Gd $1100
Red Label w/grade 1 engravingNiB $1893 Ex $1421 Gd $1107
Red Label w/grade 2 engraving NiB $2298 Ex $2100 Gd $1733
Red Label w/grade 3 engraving NiB $2798 Ex $2255 Gd $2100

RED LABEL O/U ALL-WEATHER STAINLESS
Gauges: 12 ga. Only. Bbls.: 26- 28- or 30-inch w/various chokes, fixed or screw-in tubes. Stainless receiver and barrel. Checkered black synthetic stock and forearm. Weight: 7.5 lbs. Made 1999 to 2006.
All-weather stainless model NiB $1387 Ex $1189 Gd $900
W/30-inch bbl., add $200

RED LABEL WOODSIDE O/U
Similar to the Red Label O/U Stainless except in 12 ga. only with wood sideplate extensions. Made from 1995 to 2002. Disc.
Standard Woodside . . . . . NiB $1687 Ex $1445 Gd $1110
Engraved Woodside . . . . . NiB $2389 Ex $1955 Gd $1533

RED LABEL SPORTING CLAYS O/U
Similar to the standard Red Label model except chambered 12 or 20 ga. only w/30-inch vent-rib bbls., no side ribs; back-bored w/screw-in choke tubes (not interchangeable w/other Red Label O/U models). Brass front and mid-rib beads. Made from 1992 to date.
Standard Sporting Clays . . . NiB $1766 Ex $1288 Gd $998
Engraved Sporting Clays . . NiB $2680 Ex $2110 Gd $1590

RED LABEL "WILDLIFE FOREVER" SPECIAL Edition
Limited edition commemorating the 50th Wildlife Forever anniversary. Similar to the standard Red Label model except chambered 12 ga. only w/engraved receiver enhanced w/gold mallard and pheasant inlays. 300 produced in 1993.
Special edition . . . . NiB $1690 Ex $1655 Gd $1299
Special edition w/hard case, add. $200

GOLD LABEL SIDE-BY-SIDE . . . . . NiB $3650 EX $2288 GD $1060
Boxlock. Auto ejectors. Selective single trigger. 12 ga. w/ 3-inch chambers. 28-inch solid-rib bbl., choke tubes. Top safety. Pistol-grip or English-style American walnut stock and forearm w/hand-cut checkering. Stainless receiver. Made from 2002 to 2008.

VICTOR SARASQUETA, S. A. — Eibar, Spain

MODEL 3 HAMMERLESS
BOXLOCK DOUBLE-BARREL SHOTGUN
Plain extractors or auto ejectors. Double triggers. Gauges: 12, 16, 20. Made in various bbl. lengths, chokes and weights. Checkered stock and forend, straight grip standard. Imported from 1985-87.
Model 3, plain extractors . . . . NiB $599 Ex $445 Gd $329
Model 3E, automatic ejectors . NiB $655 Ex $500 Gd $435

HAMMERLESS SIDELOCK DOUBLES
Automatic ejectors (except on Models 4 and 203 which have plain extractors). Double triggers. Gauges: 12, 16, 20. Barrel lengths, chokes and weights made to order. Checkered stock and forend, straight grip standard. Models differ chiefly in overall quality, engraving, grade of wood, checkering, etc.; general specifications are the same. Imported from 1985 to 1987.

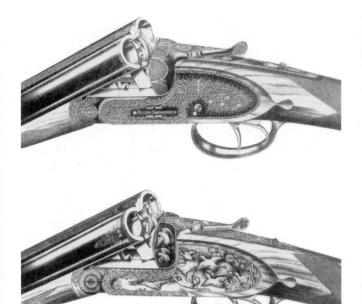

Sarasqueta Models 6E, 11E and 12E

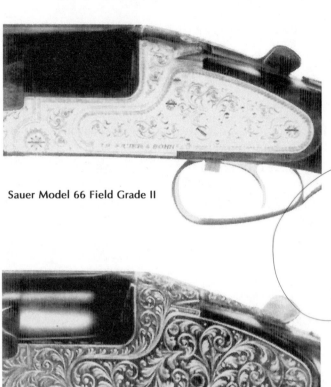

Sauer Model 66 Field Grade II

Sauer Model 66 Field Grade III

Model 4	NiB $779	Ex $643	Gd $441
Model 4E	NiB $879	Ex $754	Gd $570
Model 203	NiB $744	Ex $600	Gd $435
Model 203E	NiB $800	Ex $632	Gd $544
Model 6E	NiB $1388	Ex $1108	Gd $700
Model 7E	NiB $1443	Ex $1156	Gd $965
Model 10E	NiB $2588	Ex $2188	Gd $1966
Model 11E	NiB $2800	Ex $2577	Gd $2234
Model 12E	NiB $3110	Ex $2770	Gd $2369

J. P. SAUER & SOHN — Eckernförde, Germany; formerly Suhl, Germany

MODEL 66 O/U FIELD GUN

Purdey-system action with Holland & Holland-type sidelocks. Selective single trigger. Selective auto ejectors. Automatic safety. Available in three grades of engraving. 12 ga. only. Krupp special steel bbls. w/vent rib 28-inch, M/F choke. Weight: About 7.25 lbs. Checkered walnut stock and forend; recoil pad. Made from 1966 to 1975.

Grade I	NiB $2377	Ex $2120	Gd $1798
Grade II	NiB $3256	Ex $2460	Gd $2190
Grade III	NiB $4100	Ex $3712	Gd $2644

MODEL 66 O/U SKEET GUN

Same as Model 66 Field Gun except 26-inch bbls. with wide vent rib, SK choked- skeet-style stock and ventilated beavertail forearm; non-automatic safety. Made from 1966 to 1975.

Grade I	NiB $2312	Ex $2198	Gd $1655
Grade II	NiB $3270	Ex $2980	Gd $2110
Grade III	NiB $3988	Ex $3655	Gd $2980

MODEL 66 O/U TRAP GUN

Same as Model 66 Skeet Gun except has 30-inch bbls. choked F/F or M/F; trap-style stock. Values same as for Skeet model. Made from1966 to 1975.

MODEL 3000E DRILLING

Combination rifle and double barrel shotgun. Blitz action with Greener crossbolt, double underlugs, separate rifle cartridge extractor, front set trigger, firing pin indicators, Greener side safety, sear slide selector locks right shotgun bbl. for firing rifle bbl. Gauge/calibers12 ga. (2.75-inch chambers); .222, .243, .30-06, 7x65R. 25-inch Krupp-Special steel bbls.; M/F choke automatic folding leaf rear rifle sight. Weight: 6.5 to 7.25 lbs. depending on rifle caliber. Checkered walnut stock and forend; pistol grip, Monte Carlo comb and cheekpiece, sling swivels. Standard model with Arabesque engraving; Deluxe model with hunting scenes engraved on action. Currently manufactured. Note: Also see listing under Colt.

Standard model	NiB $4490	Ex $3891	Gd $2776
Deluxe model	NiB $5782	Ex $4669	Gd $3533

ARTEMIS DOUBLE-BARREL SHOTGUN
Holland & Holland-type sidelock with Greener crossbolt double underlugs, double sear safeties, selective single trigger, selective auto ejectors. Grade I with fine-line engraving, Grade II with full English Arabesque engraving. 12 ga. (2.75-inch chambers). Krupp special steel bbls., 28-inch, M/F choke. Weight: About 6.5 lbs. Checkered walnut pistol-grip stock and beavertail forend; recoil pad. Made from1966 to 1977.

Grade I . . . . NiB $5698 Ex $4766 Gd $4133
Grade II . . . . NiB $6880 Ex $5744 Gd $4500

BBF 54 O/U COMBINATION RIFLE/SHOTGUN
Blitz action with Kersten lock, front set trigger fires rifle bbl., slide-operated sear safety. Gauge/calibers: 16 ga.; .30-30, .30-06, 7x65R, 25-inch Krupp special steel bbls.; shotgun bbl. F choke, folding-leaf rear sight. Weight: About 6 lbs. Checkered walnut stock and forend; pistol grip, mod. Monte Carlo comb and cheekpiece, sling swivels. Standard model with Arabesque engraving; Deluxe model with hunting scenes engraved on action. Currently manufactured.

Standard model . . . . NiB $2977 Ex $2455 Gd $1766
Deluxe model . . . . NiB $3566 Ex $3088 Gd $2655

ROYAL DOUBLE-BARREL SHOTGUNS
Anson & Deeley action (boxlock) with Greener crossbolt, double underlugs, signal pins, selective single trigger, selective auto ejectors, auto safety. Scalloped frame with Arabesque engraving. Krupp special steel bbls. Gauges: 12, 2.75-inch chambers, 20, 3-inch chambers. Bbls.: 30-inch (12 ga. only) and 28-inch, M/F- 26-inch (20 ga. only), IC/M. Weight: 12 ga., about 6.5 lbs.; 20 ga., 6 lbs. Checkered walnut pistol-grip stock and beavertail forend; recoil pad. Made from 1955 to 1977.

Standard model . . . . NiB $1790 Ex $1533 Gd $1206
20 ga. add 20%

SAVAGE ARMS — Westfield, Massachusetts. Formerly located in Utica, New York

MODEL 24C .22/.410 O/U
COMBINATION . . . . NiB $570 Ex $388 Gd $245
Same as Stevens No. 22-.410 with walnut stock and forearm. Made from 1950 to 1965.

MODEL 24C
CAMPER'S COMPANION . . . . NiB $675 Ex $466 Gd $290
Same as Model 24FG except made in .22 Magnum/20 ga. only; has 20-inch bbls., shotgun tube Cyl. bore. Weight: 5.75 lbs. Trap in butt provides ammunition storage; comes with carrying case. Made 1972 to 1989.

MODEL 24 FIELD . . . . NiB $498 Ex $277 Gd $190
Same as Models 24DL and 24MDL except frame has black or casehardened finish. Game scene decoration of frame eliminated in 1974; forearm uncheckered after 1976. Made from 1970 to 1989.

MODEL 24DL . . . . NiB $400 Ex $366 Gd $243
Same general specifications as Model 24S except top-lever opening; satin-chrome-finished frame decorated with game scenes, checkered Monte Carlo stock and forearm. Made from 1962 to 1965.

MODEL 24F-12T TURKEY GUN NiB $700 Ex $488 Gd $337
12- or 20-ga. shotgun bbl./.22 Hornet, .223 or .30-30 caliber rifle. 24-inch blued bbls., 3-inch chambers, extra removable F choke tube. Hammer block safety. Color casehardened frame. DuPont Rynite camo stock. Swivel studs. Made from 1989 to 2007.

Sauer Model 3000E
Drilling

Sauer BBF 54 Combination Rifle/
Shotgun

Sauer Royal
Double-Barrel Shotgun

MODEL 24FG FIELD GRADE . NiB $525 Ex $433 Gd $276
Same general specifications as Model 24S except top lever opening. Made 1972. Disc.

MODEL 24MDL . . . . NiB $577 Ex $400 Gd $229
Same as Model 24DL except rifle bbl. chambered for 22 WMR. Made 1962 to 1969.

MODEL 24MS . . . . NiB $690 Ex $535 Gd $389
Same as Model 24S except rifle bbl. chambered for 22 WMR. Made from 1964 to 1971.

Savage Model 24
.22-/.410 O/U Combination

Savage Model 24-VS
Camper/Survival/Centerfire Rifle/Shotgun

MODEL 24S O/U
COMBINATION . . . . NiB $477 Ex $339 Gd $225
Boxlock. Visible hammer. Side lever opening. Plain extractors. Single trigger. 20 ga. or .410 bore shotgun bbl. under 22 LR bbl., 24-inch. Open rear sight, ramp front, dovetail for scope mounting. Weight: About 6.75 lbs. Plain pistol-grip stock and forearm. Made from 1964 to 1971.

MODEL 24V. . . . . NiB $588 Ex $379 Gd $298
Similar to Model 24D except 20 ga. under .222 Rem., .22 Rem., .357 Mag., .22 Hornet or .30-30 rifle bbl. Made 1967 to 1989.

MODEL 24-CS CAMPER'S COMPANION
CENTERFIRE RIFLE/SHOTGUN NiB $680 Ex $389 Gd $319
Caliber: .22 LR over 20 ga. Nickel finish full-length stock and accessory pistol-grip stock. Overall length: 36 inches with full stock; 26 inches w/pistol grip. Weight: About 5.75 lbs. Made 1972 to 1988.
.357 Mag./20 ga., add $50

MODEL 28A STANDARD GRADE
SLIDE-ACTION REPEATING SHOTGUN NiB $445 Ex $398 Gd $300
Hammerless. Takedown. 12 ga. Five round tubular magazine. Plain bbl., lengths: 26-,28-, 30-, 32-inches, choked C/M/F. Weight: About 7.5 lbs. with 30-inch bbl. Plain pistol-grip stock, grooved slide handle. Made from 1928 to 1931.

MODEL 28B. . . . . NiB $366 Ex $287 Gd $245
Raised matted rib; otherwise the same as Model 28A.

MODEL 28D TRAP GRADE. . . NiB $366 Ex $287 Gd $245
Same general specifications as Model 28A except has 30-inch F choke bbl. w/matted rib, trap-style stock w/checkered pistol grip, checkered slide handle of select walnut.

MODEL 30 SOLID FRAME HAMMERLESS
SLIDE-ACTION SHOTGUN. . . NiB $290 Ex $221 Gd $175
Gauges: 12, 16, 20, .410. 2.75-inch chamber in 16 ga., 3- inch in other ga. Magazine holds four 2.75-inch shells or three 3-inch shells. Bbls.: Vent rib; 26-, 28-, 30-inch; IC, M, F choke. Weight: Average 6.25 to 6.75 lbs. depending on ga. Plain pistol-grip stock (checkered on later production), grooved slide handle. Made from 1958 to 1970.

MODEL 30 TAKEDOWN SLUG GUN NiB $255 Ex $175 Gd $125
Same as Model 30FG except 21-inch cyl. bore bbl. with rifle sights. Made from 1971 to 1979.

MODEL 30AC SOLID FRAME . NiB $379 Ex $288 Gd $179
Same as Model 30 Solid Frame except has 26-inch bbl. with adj. choke; 12 ga. only. Made from 1959 to 1970.

MODEL 30AC TAKEDOWN . . NiB $366 Ex $265 Gd $160
Same as Model 30FG except has 26-inch bbl. with adj. choke; 12 and 20 ga. only. Made from 1971 to 1972.

MODEL 30D TAKEDOWN . . . NiB $277 Ex $200 Gd $167
Deluxe Grade. Same as Model 30FG except has receiver engraved with game scene, vent rib bbl., recoil pad. Made from 1971. Disc.

MODEL 30FG TAKEDOWN HAMMERLESS
SLIDE-ACTION SHOTGUN. . . . NiB $265 Ex $180 Gd $95
Field Grade. Gauges: 12, 20, .410. Three-inch chamber. Magazine holds four 2.75-inch shells or three 3-inch shells. Bbls.: plain; 26-inch F choke (.410 ga. only); 28-inch M/F choke; 30-inch F choke (12 ga. only). Weight: Average 7 to 7.75 lbs. depending on gauge. Checkered pistol-grip stock, fluted slide handle. Made 1970 to 1979.

MODEL 30L SOLID FRAME . . NiB $300 Ex $241 Gd $176
Same as Model 30 Solid Frame except left-handed model with ejection port and safety on left side; 12 ga. only. Made 1959 to 1970.

MODEL 30T SOLID FRAME
TRAP AND DUCK . . . . NiB $377 Ex $288 Gd $190
Same as Model 30 Solid Frame except only in 12 ga. w/30-inch F choke bbl.; has Monte Carlo stock with recoil pad, weight: About 8 lbs. Made from 1963 to 1970.

MODEL 30T TAKE DOWN
TRAP GUN. . . . . NiB $335 Ex $292 Gd $197
Same as Model 30D except only in 12 ga. w/30-inch F choke bbl. Monte Carlo stock with recoil pad. Made from 1970 to 1973.

MODEL 69-RXL SLIDE-ACTION
SHOTGUN. . . . . NiB $366 Ex $256 Gd $190
Similar to Model 67 (law enforcement configuration). Hammerless, side ejection top tang safe for left- or right-hand use. 12 ga. chambered for 2.75- and 3-inch magnum shells. 18.25-inch bbl. Tubular magazine holds 6 rounds (one less for 3-inch mag). Walnut finish hardwood stock with recoil pad and grooved operating handle. Weight: About 6.5 lbs. Made from 1982 to 1989.

MODEL 210F BOLT-ACTION
SLUG GUN . . . . NiB $490 Ex $377 Gd $290
Built on Savage 110 action. Gauge: 12 w/3-inch chamber. Two round detachable magazine. 24-inch fully rifled bbl. Receiver drilled and tapped for scope mounts w/no sights. Weight: 7.5 lbs. Checkered black synthetic stock w/swivel studs and recoil pad. Made from 1997 to 2000.

MODEL 210FT BOLT-ACTION SHOTGUN NiB $599 Ex $459 Gd $335
Similar to Model 210F except has smoothbore 24-inch bbl. w/choke tubes. Bead front and U-notch rear sights. Advantage Camo finish. Made from 1997 to 2000.

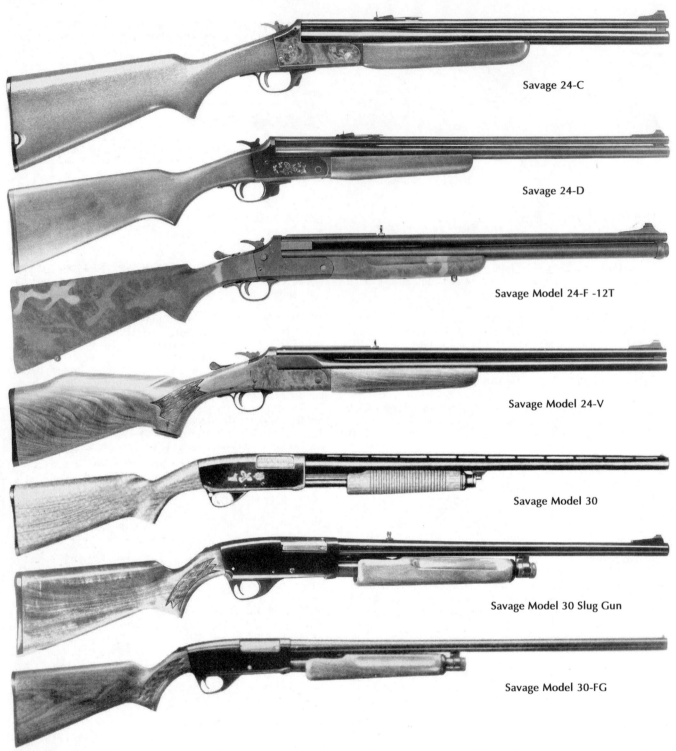

Savage 24-C

Savage 24-D

Savage Model 24-F -12T

Savage Model 24-V

Savage Model 30

Savage Model 30 Slug Gun

Savage Model 30-FG

**MODEL 220 SINGLE-BARREL
SHOTGUN** . . . . **NiB $590 Ex $386 Gd $265**
Hammerless. Takedown. Auto ejector. Gauges: 12,16, 20 .410. Single
shot. Bbl. lengths: 12 ga., 28- to 36-inch, 16 ga., 28- to 32-inch; 20 ga.,
26- to 32-inch; .410 bore, 26- and 28-inch. F choke. Weight: about 6
lbs. Plain pistol-grip stock and wide forearm. Made 1938 to 1965.

MODEL 220AC. . . . . **NiB $490 Ex $255 Gd $190**
Same as Model 220 except has Savage adj. choke.

MODEL 220L . . . . **NiB $490 Ex $388 Gd $229**
Same general specifications as Model 220 except has side lever
opening instead of top lever. Made from 1965 to 1972.

MODEL 220P . . . . **NiB $490 Ex $388 Gd $229**
Same as Model 220 except has PolyChoke bbl., made in 12 ga.
with 30-inch bbl., 16 and 20 ga. with 28-inch bbl., no .410 bore;
recoil pad.

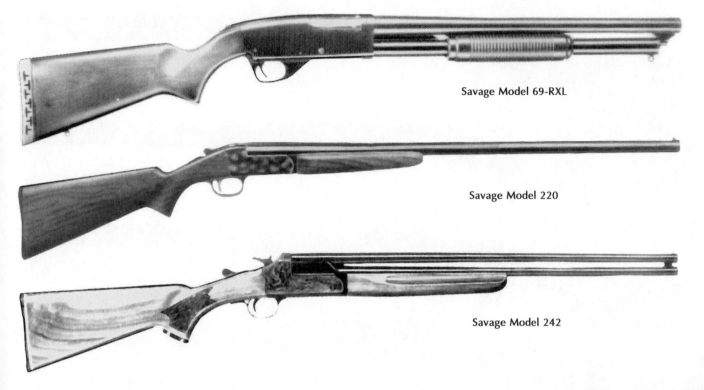

Savage Model 69-RXL

Savage Model 220

Savage Model 242

MODEL 242 O/U SHOTGUN . NiB $498 Ex $376 Gd $292
Similar to Model 24D except both bbls. .410 bore, F choke. Weight: About 7 lbs. Made from 1977 to 1980.

MODEL 312 FIELD GRADE O/UNiB $688 Ex $554 Gd $400
Gauge: 12; 2.75- or 3-inch chambers. 26- or 28-inch bbls. w/vent rib; F/M/IC chokes. 43 or 45 inches overall. Weight: 7 lbs. Internal hammers. Top tang safety. American walnut stock with checkered pistol grip and recoil pad. Made from 1990 to 1993.

MODEL 312 SPORTING CLAYS O/U. NiB $688 Ex $578 Gd $445
Same as Model 312 Field Grade except furnished with number 1 and number 2 Skeet tubes and 28-inch bbls. only. Made 1990 to 1993.

MODEL 312 TRAP O/U . . . . . NiB $756 Ex $600 Gd $477
Same as Model 312 Field Grade except with 30-inch bbls. only, Monte Carlo buttstock, weight: 7.5 lbs. Made from 1990 to 1993.

MODEL 330 O/U SHOTGUN . NiB $589 Ex $477 Gd $398
Boxlock. Plain extractors. Selective single trigger. Gauges: 12, 20. 2.75-inch chambers in 12 ga., 3-inch in 20 gauge. Bbls.: 26-inch IC/M; 28-inch M/F; 30-inch M/F choke (12 ga. only). Weight: 6.25 to 7.25 lbs., depending on gauge. Checkered pistol-grip stock and forearm. Made from 1969 to 1978.

MODEL 333 O/U SHOTGUN
Boxlock. Auto ejectors. Selective single trigger. Gauges: 12, 20. 2.75-inch chambers in 12 ga., 3-inch in 20 ga. Bbls.: vent rib; 26-inch SK choke, IC/M; 28-inch M/F; 30-inch M/F choke (12 ga. only). Weight: Average 6.25 to 7.25 lbs. Checkered pistol-grip stock and forearm. Made from 1973 to 1979.
Model 333 12 ga. . . . . NiB $598 Ex $467 Gd $366
Model 333 20 ga., add 30%

MODEL 333T TRAP GUN . . . . NiB $654 Ex $498 Gd $396
Similar to Model 330 except only in 12 ga. with 30-inch vent-rib bbls., IM/F choke; Monte Carlo stock w/recoil pad. Weight: 7.75 lbs. Made from 1972 to 1979.

MODEL 420 O/U SHOTGUN
Boxlock. Hammerless. Takedown. Automatic safety. Double triggers or non-selective single trigger. Gauges: 12, 16, 20. Bbls.: Plain, 26- to 30-inch (the latter in 12 ga. only); choked M/F, C/IC. Weight with 28-inch bbls.: 12 ga., 7.75 lbs.; 16 ga., 7.5 lbs.; 20 ga., 6.75 lbs. Plain pistol-grip stock and forearm. Made from 1938 to 1942.
With double triggers . . . . NiB $589 Ex $477 Gd $300
With single trigger . . . . NiB $633 Ex $498 Gd $376

MODEL 430
Same as Model 420 except has matted top bbl., checkered stock of select walnut with recoil pad, checkered forearm. Made from 1938 to 1942.
With double triggers . . . . NiB $677 Ex $544 Gd $390
With single trigger . . . . NiB $677 Ex $559 Gd $443

MODEL 440 O/U SHOTGUN . NiB $635 Ex $490 Gd $387
Boxlock. Plain extractors. Selective single trigger. Gauges: 12, 20. 2.75-inch chambers in 12 ga., 3-inch in 20 ga. Bbls.: Vent rib; 26-inch SK choke, IC/M; 28-inch M/F; 30-inch M/F choke (12 ga. only). Weight: Average 6 to 6.5 lbs. depending on ga. Made from 1968 to 1972.

MODEL 440T TRAP GUN . . . . NiB $598 Ex $488 Gd $392
Similar to Model 440 except only in 12 ga. with 30-inch bbls., extra-wide vent rib, IM/F choke. Trap-style Monte Carlo stock and semibeavertail forearm of select walnut, recoil pad. Weight: 7.5 lbs. Made from 1969 to 1972.

MODEL 444 DELUXE
O/U SHOTGUN . . . . NiB $687 Ex $500 Gd $369
Similar to Model 440 except has auto ejectors, select walnut stock and semi-beavertail forearm. Made from 1969 to 1972.

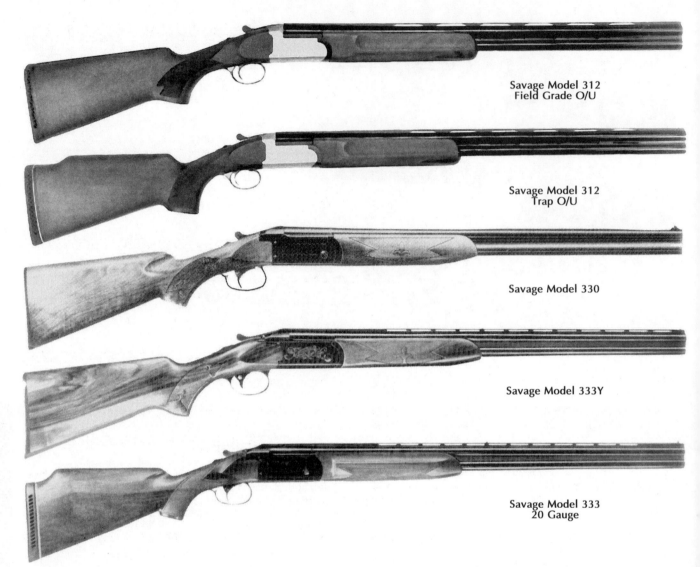

Savage Model 312
Field Grade O/U

Savage Model 312
Trap O/U

Savage Model 330

Savage Model 333Y

Savage Model 333
20 Gauge

MODEL 550
HAMMERLESS DOUBLE .... **NiB $355 Ex $290 Gd $200**
Boxlock. Auto ejectors. Non-selective single trigger. Gauges: 12, 20. 2.75-inch chamber in 12 ga., 3-inch in 20 ga. Bbls.: Vent rib; 26-inch IC/M; 28-inch M/F; 30-inch M/F choke (12 ga. only). Weight: 7 to 8 lbs. Checkered pistol-grip stock and semi-beavertail forearm. Made 1971 to 1973.

MODEL 720 STANDARD GRADE 5 SHOT AUTOLOADING
SHOTGUN. .... **NiB $335 Ex $269 Gd $200**
Browning type. Takedown. 12 and 16 ga. Four round tubular magazine. Bbl.: plain; 26- to 32-inch (the latter in 12 ga. only); choked IC, M, F. Weight: About 8.25 lbs., 12 ga. with 30-inch bbl.; 16 ga., about .5 lb. lighter. Checkered pistol-grip stock and forearm. Made from 1930 to 1949.

MODEL 726 UPLAND SPORTER AUTO
SHOTGUN. .... **NiB $377 Ex $292 Gd $233**
Same as Model 720 except has 2-round magazine capacity. Made from 1931 to 1949.

MODEL 740C
SKEET GUN .... **NiB $410 Ex $300 Gd $237**
Same as Model 726 except has special skeet stock and full beavertail forearm, equipped with Cutts Compensator. Bbl. length overall with spreader tube is about 24.5 inches. Made from 1936 to 1949.

MODEL 745 LIGHT-WEIGHT
AUTOLOADER. .... **NiB $377 Ex $266 Gd $198**
Three- or five-round models. Same general specifications as Model 720 except has lightweight alloy receiver, 12 ga.only, 28-inch plain bbl. Weight: About 6.75 lbs. Made from 1940 to 1949.

MODEL 750
AUTO SHOTGUN .... **NiB $355 Ex $287 Gd $239**
Browning-type autoloader. Takedown. 12 ga. Four round tubular magazine. Bbls.: 28-inch F or M choke; 26-inch IC. Weight: About 7.25 lbs. Checkered walnut pistol-grip stock and grooved forearm. Made from 1960 to 1967.

MODEL 750-AC
.... **NiB $377 Ex $280 Gd $210**
Same as Model 750 except has 26-inch bbl. with adj. choke. Made from 1964 to 1967.

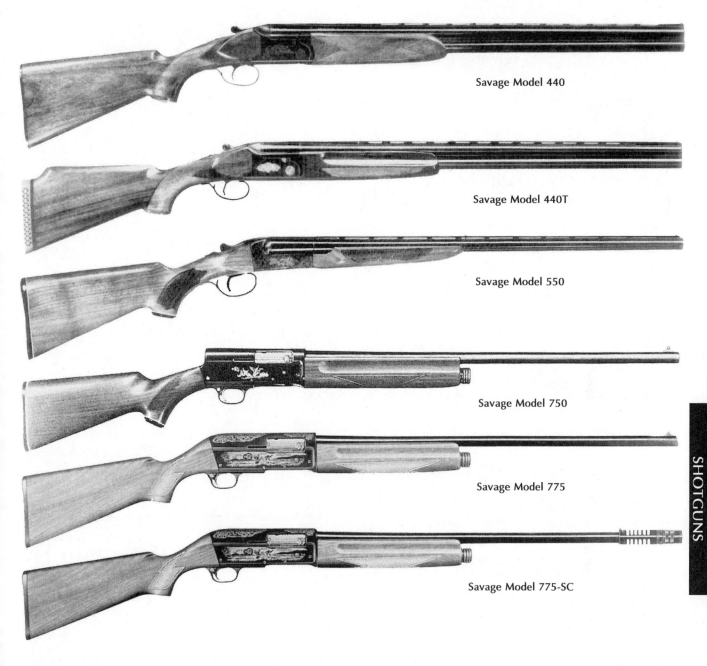

Savage Model 440

Savage Model 440T

Savage Model 550

Savage Model 750

Savage Model 775

Savage Model 775-SC

SHOTGUNS

MODEL 750-SC . . . . NiB $368 Ex $267 Gd $198
Same as Model 750 except has 26-inch bbl. with Savage Super Choke. Made from 1962 to 1963.

**MODEL 755 STANDARD
GRADE AUTOLOADER.** . . . . . NiB $389 Ex $297 Gd $245
Streamlined receiver. Takedown.12 and 16 ga. Four round tubular magazine (a three-round model with magazine capacity of two rounds was also produced until 1951). Bbl.: Plain, 30-inch F choke (12 ga. only), 28-inch F or M, 26-inch IC. Weight: About 8.25 lbs., 12 ga. Checkered pistol-grip stock and forearm. Made from 1949 to 1958.

MODEL 755-SC . . . . NiB $389 Ex $297 Gd $245
Same as Model 755 except has 26-inch bbl. w/recoil-reducing, adj. Savage Super Choke.

MODEL 775 LIGHTWEIGHT . . NiB $389 Ex $297 Gd $245
Same general specifications as Model 755 except has lightweight alloy receiver, weight: About 6.73 lbs. Made from 1950 to 1965.

MODEL 775-SC . . . . NiB $410 Ex $300 Gd $255
Same as Model 775 except has 26-inch bbl. with Savage Super Choke.

**MODEL 2400 O/U
COMBINATION** . . . . NiB $775 Ex $577 Gd $450
Boxlock action similar to that of Model 330. Plain extractors. Selective single trigger. 12-ga. (2.75-inch chamber) shotgun bbl., F choke over .308 Win. or .222 Rem. rifle bbl.; 23.5-inch; solid matted rib with blade front sight and folding leaf rear, dovetail for scope mounting. Weight: About 7.5 lbs. Monte Carlo stock w/pistol grip and recoil pad, semibeavertail forearm, checkered. Made 1975 to 1979 by Valmet.

Savage Model 2400
O/U Combination Gun

SEARS, ROEBUCK & COMPANY — Chicago, Illinois. (J. C. Higgins and Ted Williams Models)

Although they do not correspond to specific models below, the names Ted Williams and J. C. Higgins have been used to designate various Sears shotguns at various times.

MODEL 18
BOLT-ACTION REPEATER. . . . . NiB $200 Ex $125 Gd $90
Takedown. Three round top-loading magazine. Gauge: .410 only. Bbl.: 25-inch w/variable choke. Weight: About 5.75 lbs.

MODEL 20 SLIDE-ACTION REPEATER NiB $300 Ex $210 Gd $155
Hammerless. Five round magazine. Bbls.: 26- to 30-inch w/various chokes. Weight: 7.25 lbs. Plain pistol-grip stock and slide handle.

MODEL 21 SLIDE-ACTION REPEATER NiB $320 Ex $235 Gd $190
Same general specifications as the Model 20 except vent rib and adustable choke.

MODEL 30 SLIDE-ACTION REPEATER NiB $305 Ex $220 Gd $175
Hammerless. Gauges: 12, 16, 20 and .410. Four round magazine. Bbls.: 26- to 30-inch, various chokes. Weight: 6.5 lbs. Plain pistol-grip stock, grooved slide handle.

MODEL 97 SINGLE-SHOT SHOTGUN NiB $165 Ex $100 Gd $79
Takedown. Visible hammer. Automatic ejector. Gauges: 12, 16, 20 and .410. Bbls.: 26- to 36-inch, F choke. Weight: Average 6 lbs. Plain pistol-grip stock and forearm.

MODEL 97-AC SINGLE-SHOT SHOTGUN NiB $190 Ex $121 Gd $89
Same general specifications as Model 97 except fancier stock and forearm.

MODEL 101.7 DOUBLE-BARREL
SHOTGUN. . . . . NiB $335 Ex $229 Gd $175
Boxlock. Double triggers. Gauges: 12, 16, 20, .410. Bbls.: 26- to 32-inch, choked M and F. Weight: From 6 to 7.5 lbs. Plain stock and forend.

MODEL 101.7C DOUBLE-BARREL
SHOTGUN. . . . . NiB $345 Ex $239 Gd $185
Same general specifications as Model 101.7 except checkered stock and forearm.

MODEL 101.25 BOLT-ACTION SHOTGUN NiB $220 Ex $125 Gd $90
Takedown. .410 gauge. Five round tubular magazine. 24-inch bbl., F choke. Weight: About 6 lbs. Plain, one-piece pistol-grip stock.

MODEL 101.40 SINGLE-SHOT SHOTGUN NiB $175 Ex $105 Gd $80
Takedown. Visible hammer. Automatic ejector. Gauges: 12, 16, 20 and .410. Bbls.: 26- to 36-inch, F choke. Weight: Average 6 lbs. Plain pistol-grip stock and forearm.

MODEL 101.1120 BOLT-ACTION REPEATER NiB $170 Ex $119 Gd $88
Takedown. .410 ga. 24-inch bbl., F choke. Weight: About 5 lbs. Plain one-piece pistol-grip stock.

MODEL 101.1380
BOLT-ACTION REPEATER . . . . NiB $195 Ex $130 Gd $95
Takedown. Gauges: 12, 16, 20. Two round detachable box magazine. 26-inch bbl., F choke. Weight: About 7 lbs. Plain one-piece pistol-grip stock.

MODEL 101.1610 DOUBLE-BARREL
SHOTGUN. . . . . NiB $495 Ex $322 Gd $275
Boxlock. Double triggers. Plain extractors. Gauges: 12, 16, 20 and .410. Bbls.: 24- to 30-inch. Various chokes, but mostly M and F. Weight: About 7.5 lbs, 12 ga. Checkered pistol-grip stock and forearm.

MODEL 101.1701 DOUBLE-BARREL
SHOTGUN. . . . . NiB $420 Ex $335 Gd $240
Same general specifications as Model 101.1610 except satin chrome frame and select walnut stock and forearm.

MODEL 101.5350-D
BOLT-ACTION REPEATER. . . . . NiB $229 Ex $120 Gd $89
Takedown. Gauges: 12, 16, 20. Two round detachable box magazine. 26-inch bbl., F choke. Weight: About 7.25 lbs. Plain one piece pistol-grip stock.

MODEL 101.5410
BOLT-ACTION REPEATER. . . . . NiB $200 Ex $115 Gd $90
Same general specifications as Model 101.5350-D.

SKB ARMS COMPANY — Tokyo, Japan. Imported by G.U. Inc., Omaha, Nebraska

MODEL 385
SIDE-BY-SIDE . . . . NiB $2200 Ex $1790 Gd $1176
Boxlock action w/double locking lugs. Gauges: 12, 20 and 28 w/2.75- and 3-inch chambers. 26- or 28-inch bbls. w/Inter-Choke tube system. Single selective trigger. Selective automatic ejectors and automatic safety. Weight: 6 lbs., 10 oz. Silver nitride receiver w/engraved scroll and game scene. Solid rib w/flat matte finish and metal front bead sight. Checkered American walnut English or pistol-grip stock. Imported from 1992.

MODELS 300 AND 400 SIDE-BY-SIDE SHOTGUNS
Similar to Model 200E except higher grade. Models 300 and 400 differ in that the latter has more elaborate engraving and fancier wood.
Model 300 . . . . NiB $1077 Ex $900 Gd $635
Model 400 . . . . NiB $1566 Ex $1309 Gd $1187

MODEL 400 SKEET. . . . . . NiB $1566 Ex $1309 Gd $1187
Similar to Model 200E Skeet except higher grade with more elaborate engraving and full fancy wood.

MODEL 480 ENGLISH . . . NiB $1766 Ex $1510 Gd $1377
Similar to Model 280 English except higher grade with more elaborate engraving and full fancy wood.

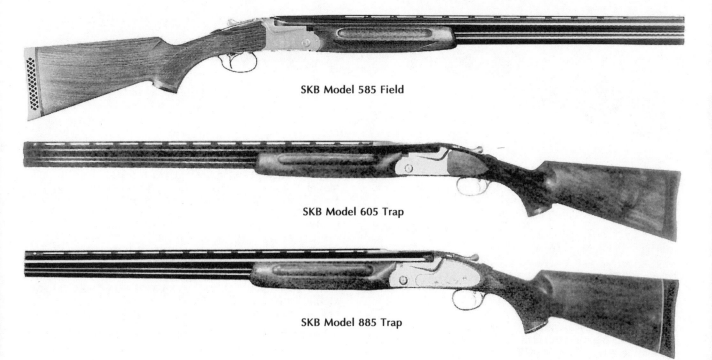

SKB Model 585 Field

SKB Model 605 Trap

SKB Model 885 Trap

MODEL 500 SERIES O/U SHOTGUN

Boxlock. Gauges: 12 and 20 w/2.75-or 3-inch chambers. Bbls.: 26-, 28- or 30-inch with vent rib; fixed chokes. Weight: 7.5 to 8.5 lbs. Single selective trigger. Selective automatic ejectors. Manual safety. Checkered walnut stock. Blue finish with scroll engraving. Imported 1967 to 1980.

500 Field, 12 ga. . . . . NiB $1000 Ex $750 Gd $415
500 Field, 20 ga, add. 20%
500 Magnum, 12 ga, add. 25%

MODEL 500 SMALL

GAUGE O/U SHOTGUN . . . . NiB $884 Ex $652 Gd $466
Similar to Model 500 except gauges 28 and .410; has 28-inch vent-rib bbls., M/F chokes. Weight: About 6.5 lbs.

MODEL 505 O/U SHOTGUN

Blued boxlock action. Gauge: 12, 20, 28 and .410. Bbls.: 26-, 28, 30-inch; IC/M, M/F or inner choke tubes. 45.19 inches overall. Weight: 6.6 to 7.4 lbs. Hand checkered walnut stock. Metal bead front sight, ejectors, single selective trigger and ejectors. Introduced 1988.

Standard Field, Skeet or Trap grade NiB $1365 Ex $1188 Gd $765
Standard Two-bbl. Field set NiB $1590 Ex $1277 Gd $1006
Skeet grade, three-bbl. set NiB $1904 Ex $1888 Gd $1301
Sporting Clays . . . . NiB $1189 Ex $977 Gd $668
Trap grade two-bbl. set . . . . . NiB $965 Ex $800 Gd $652

MODEL 585 O/U SHOTGUN

Boxlock. Gauges: 12, 20, 28 and .410; 2.75-or 3-inch chambers. Bbls.: 26-, 28-, 30-, 32- or 34-inch with vent rib; fixed chokes or Inter-choke tubes. Weight: 6.5 to 8.5 lbs. Single selective trigger. Selective automatic ejectors. Manual safety. Checkered walnut stock in standard or Monte Carlo style. Silver nitride finish with engraved game scenes. Made from 1992 to 2008.

Field, Skeet, Trap grades . . NiB $1477 Ex $1211 Gd $933
Field grade, two-bbl. set . NiB $2376 Ex $1969 Gd $1387
Skeet set (20, 28, .410 ga.) NiB $2933 Ex $2460 Gd $1977
Sporting Clays . . . . NiB $1700 Ex $1390 Gd $1054
Trap Combo (two-bbl. set) NiB $2433 Ex $1976 Gd $1366

MODEL 600 SERIES O/U SHOTGUN

Similar to 500 Series except w/silver nitride receiver. Checkered deluxe walnut stock in both Field and Target Grade configurations . Imported from 1969 to 1980.

600 Field, 12 ga. . . . . NiB $1093 Ex $773 Gd $540
600 Field, 20 ga. . . . . NiB $1100 Ex $977 Gd $650
600 Magnum, 12 ga.
3-inch chambers. . . . . NiB $1100 Ex $977 Gd $650
600 Skeet or Trap grade . . NiB $1154 Ex $1008 Gd $690
600 Trap Doubles model . . NiB $1154 Ex $1008 Gd $690

MODEL 600 SMALL GAUGE. NiB $1210 Ex $945 Gd $650

Same as Model 500 Small Gauge except higher grade with more elaborate engraving and fancier wood.

MODEL 605 SERIES O/U SHOTGUN

Similar to the Model 505 except w/engraved silver nitride receiver and deluxe wood. Introduced 1988.

Field, Skeet, Trap grade . . . NiB $1233 Ex $1026 Gd $779
Skeet three-bbl. set . . . . . NiB $2290 Ex $2003 Gd $1544
Sporting Clays . . . . NiB $1266 Ex $1033 Gd $780

MODEL 680 ENGLISH O/U SHOTGUN

Similar to 600 Series except w/English style select walnut stock and fine scroll engraving. Imported from 1973 to 1977.

680 English, 12 ga.. . . . . NiB $1477 Ex $1179 Gd $993
680 English, 20 ga. . . . . NiB $1788 Ex $1165 Gd $1055

MODEL 685 DELUXE O/U

Similar to the 585 Deluxe except with semi-fancy American walnut stock. Gold trigger and jeweled barrel block. Silvered receiver with fine engraving.

Field, Skeet, Trap grade . . NiB $1477 Ex $1319 Gd $1066
Field grade, two-bbl. set . NiB $1977 Ex $1819 Gd $1566
Skeet set . . . . NiB $1977 Ex $1819 Gd $1566
Sporting Clays . . . . NiB $1477 Ex $1319 Gd $1066
Trap Combo, two-bbl. set. NiB $2189 Ex $1844 Gd $1360

Sile Field Master II

MODEL 800 SKEET/TRAP O/U
Similar to Model 700 Skeet and Trap except higher grade with more elaborate engraving and fancier wood.
Skeet model . . . . NiB $1329 Ex $1166 Gd $973
Trap model . . . . NiB $1266 Ex $1090 Gd $945

MODEL 880 SKEET/TRAP
Similar to Model 800 Skeet except has sideplates.
Skeet model . . . . NiB $1688 Ex $1470 Gd $1137
Trap model . . . . NiB $1859 Ex $1466 Gd $1123

MODEL 885 DELUXE O/U
Similar to the 685 Deluxe except with engraved sideplates.
Field, Skeet, Trap grade . . NiB $1779 Ex $1456 Gd $1160
Field grade, two-bbl. set . NiB $2665 Ex $2167 Gd $1800
Skeet Set . . . . NiB $1782 Ex $1693 Gd $1366
Sporting Clays . . . . NiB $1834 Ex $1500 Gd $1220
Trap Combo. . . . . NiB $2591 Ex $2277 Gd $1989

The following SKB shotguns were distributed by Ithaca Gun Co. from 1966-76. For specific data, see corresponding listings under Ithaca.

CENTURY SINGLE-BARREL TRAP GUN
The SKB catalog does not differentiate between Century and Century II; however, specifications of current Century are those of Ithaca-SKB Century II.
Century (505). . . . . NiB $966 Ex $831 Gd $634
Century II (605) . . . . NiB $1190 Ex $1006 Gd $798

GAS-OPERATED AUTOMATIC SHOTGUNS
Model XL300 with plain barrel NiB $365 Ex $247 Gd $180
Model XL300 with vent rib . . . NiB $400 Ex $365 Gd $217
Model XL900 . . . . NiB $449 Ex $300 Gd $198
Model XL900 Trap . . . . NiB $487 Ex $376 Gd $221
Model XL900 Skeet. . . . . NiB $510 Ex $375 Gd $266
Model XL900 Slug . . . . NiB $488 Ex $370 Gd $259
Model 1300 Upland, Slug. . . . NiB $598 Ex $455 Gd $290
Model 1900 Field, Trap, Slug . NiB $588 Ex $443 Gd $376

SKB OVER/UNDER SHOTGUNS
Model 500 Field . . . . NiB $677 Ex $489 Gd $389
Model 500 Magnum . . . . NiB $690 Ex $500 Gd $421
Model 600 Field . . . . NiB $1070 Ex $883 Gd $600
Model 600 Magnum . . . . NiB $1165 Ex $955 Gd $690
Model 600 Trap . . . . NiB $1190 Ex $975 Gd $710
Model 600 Doubles . . . . NiB $1190 Ex $975 Gd $710
Model 600 Skeet—12 or 20 ga.. . . . NiB $1190 Ex $975 Gd $710
Model 600 Skeet—28 or .410. . . NiB $1595 Ex $1266 Gd $1065
Model 600 Skeet Combo. . . . . . . NiB $2651 Ex $2210 Gd $2085
Model 600 English . . . . NiB $1190 Ex $975 Gd $710
Model 700 Trap . . . . NiB $950 Ex $844 Gd $630
Model 700 Doubles . . . . NiB $877 Ex $600 Gd $490
Model 700 Skeet . . . . NiB $988 Ex $765 Gd $633
Model 700 Skeet Combo. . . . . . . NiB $2690 Ex $2166 Gd $1650

SKB RECOIL-OPERATED AUTOMATIC SHOTGUNS
Model 300—with plain barrel NiB $477 Ex $370 Gd $269
Model 300—with vent rib . . . NiB $554 Ex $425 Gd $335
Model 900 . . . . NiB $559 Ex $400 Gd $298
Model 900 Slug . . . . NiB $573 Ex $455 Gd $360

SKB SIDE-BY-SIDE DOUBLE-BARREL SHOTGUNS
Model 100 . . . . NiB $795 Ex $650 Gd $425
Model 150 . . . . NiB $795 Ex $650 Gd $425
Model 200E . . . . NiB $1179 Ex $900 Gd $808
Model 200E Skeet . . . . NiB $1179 Ex $900 Gd $808
Model 280 English . . . . NiB $1280 Ex $1006 Gd $922

SIG SAUER — (SIG) Schweizerische Industrie-Gesellschaft, Neuhausen, Switzerland

MODEL SA3 O/U SHOTGUN
Monobloc boxlock action. Single selective trigger. Automatic ejectors. Gauges: 12 or 20 w/3- inch chambers. 26-, 28- or 30-inch vent rib bbls. w/choke tubes. Weight: 6.8 to 7.1 lbs. Checkered select walnut stock and forearm. Satin nickel-finished receiver w/game scene and blued bbls. Imported from 1997-98.
Field model . . . . NiB $1294 Ex $1126 Gd $966
Sporting Clays model . . . . NiB $1500 Ex $1398 Gd $1225

MODEL SA5 O/U SHOTGUN
Similar to SA3 Model except w/detachable sideplates. Gauges: 12 or 20 w/3- inch chambers. 26.5-, 28- or 30-inch vent rib bbls. w/choke tubes. Imported from 1997 to 1999.
Field model . . . . NiB $2288 Ex $2055 Gd $1530
Sporting Clays model . . . . NiB $2455 Ex $2160 Gd $1880

SILE SHOTGUNS — Sile Distributors, New York, New York

FIELD MASTER II O/U SHOTGUN. . . . . NiB $735 Ex $615 Gd $479
Gauge: 12, 3-inch chambers. 28-inch bbl., IC, M, IM, F choke tubes. 45.25 inches overall. Weight: 7.25 lbs. Satin-finished walnut, checkered stock and forend. Introduced 1989.

L. C. SMITH SHOTGUNS—Made 1890–1945 by Hunter Arms Company, Fulton, New York 1946–51 and 1968–73 and 2004 by Marlin Firearms Company, New Haven, Connecticut

L. C. SMITH DOUBLE-BARREL SHOTGUNS
Values shown are for L. C. Smith doubles made by Hunter. Those of 1946-51 Marlin manufacture generally bring prices about 1/3 lower. Smaller gauge models, especially in the higher grades, command premium prices: Up to 50 percent more for 20 gauge, up to 400 percent for .410.

L.C. Smith Crown

L.C. Smith Field

Crown grade, double triggers,
automatic ejectors . . . . . NiB $11,650 Ex $9000 Gd $7750
Crown grade, selective single trigger,
automatic ejectors . . . NiB $12,275 Ex $10,200 Gd $9976
Deluxe grade, selective single trigger,
automatic ejectors . . NiB $80,000 Ex $65,000 Gd $44,000
Eagle grade, double triggers,
automatic ejectors . . . . . . NiB $7450 Ex $6600 Gd $3540
Eagle grade, selective
single trigger . . . . NiB $8433 Ex $7210 Gd $4450
Field grade, double trigger
plain extractors . . . . NiB $1877 Ex $1659 Gd $1200
Field grade, double triggers
auto. ej. . . . . NiB $2400 Ex $2175 Gd $1765
Field grade, non-selective single trigger,
plain extractors . . . . NiB $1788 Ex $1489 Gd $1016
Field grade, selective single trigger,
automatic ejectors . . . . . . NiB $2276 Ex $1998 Gd $1688
Ideal grade, double triggers,
plain extractors . . . . NiB $2698 Ex $2100 Gd $1933
Ideal grade, double triggers,
auto. ej. . . . . NiB $3355 Ex $2288 Gd $1987
Ideal grade, selective single trigger,
automatic ejectors . . . . . NiB $2979 Ex $2466 Gd $2132
Monogram grade, selective single trigger,
automatic ejectors . NiB $17,800 Ex $15,888 Gd $11,880
Olympic grade, selective single trigger,
automatic ejectors . . . . . NiB $7225 Ex $5179 Gd $3889
Premier grade, selective single trigger
automatic ejectors . NiB $42,975 Ex $33,670 Gd $25,000
Skeet Special, non-selective single trigger,
automatic ejectors . . . . . NiB $4055 Ex $3329 Gd $2165
Skeet Special, selective single trigger,
auto ejectors . . . . NiB $4070 Ex $3360 Gd $2185
.410 ga. . . . . NiB $14,887 Ex $11,965 Gd $9865
Specialty grade, double triggers,
auto ejectors . . . . NiB $4177 Ex $3688 Gd $3245
Specialty grade, selective single trigger,
automatic ejectors . . . . . . NiB $3866 Ex $3390 Gd $2788
Trap grade, sel. single trigger,
auto ej. . . . . NiB $3687 Ex $3255 Gd $2877

L. C. SMITH HAMMERLESS DOUBLE-BARREL SHOTGUNS

Sidelock. Auto ejectors standard on higher grades, extra on Field and Ideal Grades. Double triggers or Hunter single trigger (non-selective or selective). Gauges: 12, 16, 20, .410. Bbls.: 26- to 32-inch, any standard boring. Weight: 6.5 to 8.25 lbs., 12 ga. Checkered stock and forend; choice of straight, half or full pistol grip, beavertail or standard-type forend. Grades differ only in quality of workmanship, wood, checkering, engraving, etc. Same general specifications apply to all. Manufacture of these L. C. Smith guns

was discontinued in 1951. Production of Field Grade 12 ga. was resumed 1968-73. Note: L. C. Smith Shotguns manufactured by the Hunter Arms Co. 1890-13 were designated by numerals to indicate grade with the exception of Pigeon and Monogram.

00 grade	NiB $1577	Ex $1369	Gd $1100
0 grade	NiB $1735	Ex $1575	Gd $1244
1 grade	NiB $2170	Ex $1876	Gd $1390
2 grade	NiB $3533	Ex $2177	Gd $1566
3 grade	NiB $4480	Ex $3066	Gd $2200
Pigeon	NiB $5250	Ex $3688	Gd $2531
4 grade	NiB $6244	Ex $5187	Gd $4966
5 grade	NiB $10,300	Ex $8879	Gd $6610
Monogram	NiB $13,975	Ex $11,755	Gd $10,000
A1	NiB $7225	Ex $4488	Gd $3240
A2.	NiB $14,779	Ex $11,960	Gd $10,066
A3	NiB $42,600	Ex $37,988	Gd $32,776

HAMMERLESS DOUBLE
MODEL 1968 FIELD GRADE. NiB $1165 Ex $980 Gd $644
Re-creation of the original L. C. Smith double. Sidelock. Plain extractors. Double triggers. 12 ga. 28-inch vent-rib bbls., M/F choke. Weight: About 6.75 lbs. Checkered pistol-grip stock and forearm. Made from 1968 to 1973.

HAMMERLESS DOUBLE
MODEL 1968 DELUXE . . . . NiB $1688 Ex $1076 Gd $884
Same as 1968 Field Grade except has Simmons floating vent rib, beavertail forearm. Made from 1971 to 1973.

SINGLE-SHOT TRAP GUNS
Boxlock. Hammerless. Auto ejector.12 gauge only. Bbl. lengths: 32- or 34-inch. Vent rib. Weight: 8 to 8.25 lbs. Checkered pistol-grip stock and forend, recoil pad. Grades vary in quality of workmanship, wood, engraving, etc.; general specifications are the same. Disc. 1951. Note: Values shown are for L. C. Smith single-barrel trap guns made by Hunter. Those of Marlin manufacture generally bring prices about one-third lower.

Olympic grade	NiB $3188	Ex $2677	Gd $2190
Specialty grade	NiB $3598	Ex $3200	Gd $2560
Crown grade	NiB $4488	Ex $3900	Gd $2677
Monogram grade	NiB $8865	Ex $6231	Gd $4997
Premier grade. . . . . Very rare (Three or fewer manufactured)			
Deluxe grade . . . . . . Very rare (Four or fewer manufactured)			

SMITH & WESSON SHOTGUNS —
Springfield, Massachusetts

Sold several times, currently Saf-T-Hammer.

SHOTGUNS

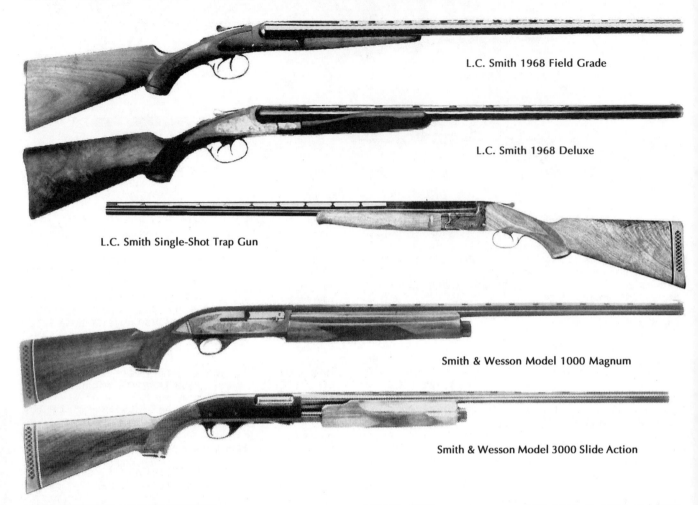

L.C. Smith 1968 Field Grade

L.C. Smith 1968 Deluxe

L.C. Smith Single-Shot Trap Gun

Smith & Wesson Model 1000 Magnum

Smith & Wesson Model 3000 Slide Action

MDEL 916 SLIDE-ACTION REPEATER
Hammerless. Solid frame. Gauges: 12, 16, 20. Three inch chamber in 12 and 20 ga. Five round tubular magazine. Bbls.: plain or vent rib; 20-inch C (12 ga., plain only); 26-inch IC- 28-inch M or F; 30-inch F choke (12 ga. only). Weight: With 28-inch plain bbl., 7.25 lbs. Plain pistol-grip stock, fluted slide handle. Made 1972 to 1981.
With plain bbl. . . . . **NiB $225 Ex $170 Gd $110**
With ventilated rib bbl. . . . . . **NiB $255 Ex $185 Gd $120**

MODEL 916T
Same as Model 916 except takedown, 12 ga. only. Not available with 20-inch bbl. Made from 1976 to 1981.
With plain bbl. . . . . **NiB $250 Ex $180 Gd $115**
With ventilated rib bbl. . . . . . **NiB $275 Ex $200 Gd $140**

MODEL 1000 AUTOLOADER . **NiB $433 Ex $355 Gd $240**
Gas-operated. Takedown. Gauges: 12, 20. 2.75-inch chamber in 12 ga., 3-inch in 20 ga. Four round magazine. Bbls.: Vent rib, 26-inch SK choke, IC; 28-inch M or F; 30-inch F choke (12 ga. only). Weight: With 28-inch bbl., 6.5 lbs. in 20 ga.,7.5 lbs. in 12 ga. Checkered pistol-grip stock and forearm. Made from 1972. Disc.

MODEL 3000
SLIDE ACTION . . . . **NiB $425 Ex $295 Gd $190**
Hammerless. 20-ga. Bbls.: 26-inch IC; 28-inch M or F. Chambered for 3-inch magnum and 2.75-inch loads. American walnut stock and forearm. Checkered pistol grip and forearm. Introduced 1982.

MODEL 1000 . . . . **NiB $425 Ex $295 Gd $190**
Same as Model 3000 but an earlier version.

MODEL 1000 MAGNUM . . . . **NiB $595 Ex $445 Gd $398**
Same as standard Model 1000 except chambered for 12 ga. magnum, 3-inch shells; 30-inch bbl. only, M or F choke; stock with recoil pad. Weight: About 8 lbs. Introduced in 1977.

SPRINGFIELD ARMS — Built by Savage Arms Company, Utica, New York

SPRINGFIELD DOUBLE-BARREL
HAMMER SHOTGUN . . . . **NiB $588 Ex $439 Gd $366**
Gauges: 12 and 16. Bbls.: 28 to 32 inches. In 12 ga., 32-inch model, both bbls. have F choke. All other gauges and barrel lengths are left barrel, Full; right barrel, Mod. Weight: 7.25 to 8.25 lbs., depending on gauge and barrel length. Black walnut checkered buttstock and forend. Disc. 1934.

SQUIRES BINGHAM CO., INC. — Makati, Rizal, Philippines

MODEL 30
PUMP SHOTGUN . . . . **NiB $366 Ex $255 Gd $175**
Hammerless. 12 ga. Five round magazine. Bbl.: 20-inch Cyl.; 28-inch M; 30-inch F choke. Weight: About 7 lbs. Pulong Dalaga stock and slide handle. Currently manufactured.

Squires Bingham Model 30 Pump Shotgun

J. STEVENS ARMS COMPANY — Chicopee Falls, Massachusetts; division of Savage Arms Corporation

NO. 20 "FAVORITE" SHOTGUN NiB $325 Ex $217 Gd $140
Calibers: .22 and .32 shot. Smoothbore bbl. Blade front sight; no rear. Made from 1893 to 1939.

**NO. 39 NEW MODEL
POCKET SHOTGUN** . . . . NiB $800 Ex $605 Gd $490
Gauge: .410. Calibers: .38-40 shot, .44-40 shot. Bbls.: 10, 12, 15 or 18 inches, half-octagonal smoothbore. Shotgun sights. Made 1895 to 1906.

NO. 22-.410 O/U COMBINATION GUN
.22 caliber rifle barrel over .410 ga. shotgun barrel. Visible hammer. Takedown. Single trigger. 24-inch bbls., shotgun bbl. F choke. Weight: About 6 lbs. Open rear sight and ramp front sight of sporting rifle type. Plain pistol-grip stock and forearm; originally supplied with walnut stock and forearm. "Tenite" (plastic) was used in later production. Made 1939 to 1950. Note: This gun is now manufactured as the Savage Model 24.
**With wood stock and forearm NiB $545 Ex $435 Gd $300
With Tenite stock and forearm NiB $525 Ex $460 Gd $345**

**MODEL 51 BOLT-ACTION
SHOTGUN** . . . . NiB $235 Ex $154 Gd $95
Single shot. Takedown. .410 ga. 24-inch bbl., F choke. Weight: About 4.75 lbs. Plain one-piece pistol-grip stock. checkered on later models. Made from 1962 to 1971.

**MODEL 58 BOLT-ACTION
REPEATER** . . . . NiB $254 Ex $165 Gd $120
Takedown. Gauges: 12, 16, 20. Two round detachable box magazine. 26-inch bbl., F choke. Weight: About 7.25 lbs. Plain one piece pistol-grip stock on early models w/takedown screw on bottom of forend. Made 1933-81. Note: Later production models have 3-inch chamber in 20 ga., checkered stock with recoil pad.

**MODEL 58-.410 BOLT-ACTION
REPEATER** . . . . NiB $225 Ex $130 Gd $95
Takedown. .410 ga. Three round detachable box magazine. 24-inch bbl., F choke. Weight: About 5.5 lbs. Plain one piece pistol-grip stock, checkered on later production. Made from 1937 to 1981.

**MODEL 59 BOLT-ACTION
REPEATER** . . . . NiB $255 Ex $190 Gd $135
Takedown. .410 ga. Five round tubular magazine. 24-inch bbl., F choke. Weight: About 6 lbs. Plain, one piece pistol-grip stock, checkered on later production. Made from 1934 to 1973.

MODEL 67 PUMP SHOTGUN
Hammerless, side-ejection solid-steel receiver. Gauges: 12, 20 and .410, 2.75- or 3-inch shells. Bbls.: 21-, 26-, 28- 30-inch with fixed chokes or interchangeable choke tubes, plain or vent rib. Weight: 6.25 to 7.5 lbs. Optional rifle sights. Walnut-finished hardwood stock with corncob-style forend.

Standard model, plain bbl. . . . NiB $245 Ex $195 Gd $120
Standard model, vent rib   . . . NiB $255 Ex $205 Gd $125
Standard model, w/choke tubes NiB $275 Ex $220 Gd $155
Slug model w/rifle sights . . . . NiB $255 Ex $205 Gd $125
Lobo model, matte finish   . . . NiB $255 Ex $205 Gd $125
Youth model, 20 ga. . . . . NiB $260 Ex $210 Gd $130
Camo model. w/choke tubes . NiB $275 Ex $220 Gd $155

MODEL 67 WATERFOWL SHOTGUN NiB $335 Ex $200 Gd $135
Hammerless. Gauge: 12. Three round tubular magazine. Walnut finished hardwood stock. Weight: About 7.5 lbs. Made 1972 to 1989.

MODEL 77 SLIDE-ACTION REPEATER. NiB $225 Ex $130 Gd $95
Solid frame. Gauges: 12, 16, 20. Five round tubular magazine. Bbls.: 26-inch IC, 28-inch M or F choke. Weight: About 7.5 lbs. Plain pistol-grip stock with recoil pad, grooved slide handle. Made from 1954 to 1971.

MODEL 77-AC . . . . NiB $217 Ex $125 Gd $95
Same as Model 77 except has Savage Super Choke.

MODEL 79-VR SUPER VALUE. NiB $355 Ex $265 Gd $190
Hammerless, side ejection. Bbl.: Chambered for 2.75-inch and 3-inch mag. shells. 12, 20, and .410 ga. vent rib. Walnut finished hardwood stock with checkering on grip. Weight: 6.75-7 lbs. Made 1979 to 1990.

MODEL 94 SINGLE-SHOT SHOTGUN NiB $165 Ex $95 Gd $70
Takedown. Visible hammer. Auto ejector. Gauges: 12, 16, 20, 28, .410. Bbls.: 26-, 28-, 30-, 32-, 36-inch, F choke. Weight: About 6 lbs. depending on gauge and barrel. Plain pistol-grip stock and forearm. Made from 1939 to 1961.

MODEL 94C. . . . . NiB $165 Ex $95 Gd $70
Same as Model 94 except has checkered stock, fluted forearm on late production. Made from 1965 to 1990.

MODEL 94Y YOUTH GUN. . . . . NiB $165 Ex $95 Gd $70
Same as Model 94 except made in 20 and .410 ga. only; has 26-inch F choke bbl., 12.5-inch buttstock with recoil pad; checkered pistol grip and fluted forend on late production. Made from 1959 to 1990.

MODEL 95 SINGLE-SHOT SHOTGUN NiB $200 Ex $140 Gd $95
Solid frame. Visible hammer. Plain extractor. 12 ga. Three-inch chamber. Bbls.: 28-inch M- 30-inch F choke. Weight: About 7.25 lbs. Plain pistol-grip stock, grooved forearm. Made 1965 to 1969.

**MODEL 107 SINGLE-SHOT
HAMMER SHOTGUN** . . . . NiB $217 Ex $129 Gd $95
Takedown. Auto ejector. Gauges: 12, 16, 20, .410. Bbl. lengths: 28- and 30-inch (12 and 16 ga.), 28-inch (20 ga.), 26-inch (.410); F choke only. Weight: About 6 lbs., 12 bore ga. Plain pistol-grip stock and forearm. Made from about 1937 to 1953.

**MODEL 124
BOLT-ACTION REPEATER.** . . . . . .NiB $265 Ex $198 Gd $155
Hammerless. Solid frame. 12 ga. only. Two round tubular magazine. 28-inch bbl.; IC, M or F choke. Weight: About 7 lbs. Tenite stock and forearm. Made from 1947 to 1952.

SHOTGUNS

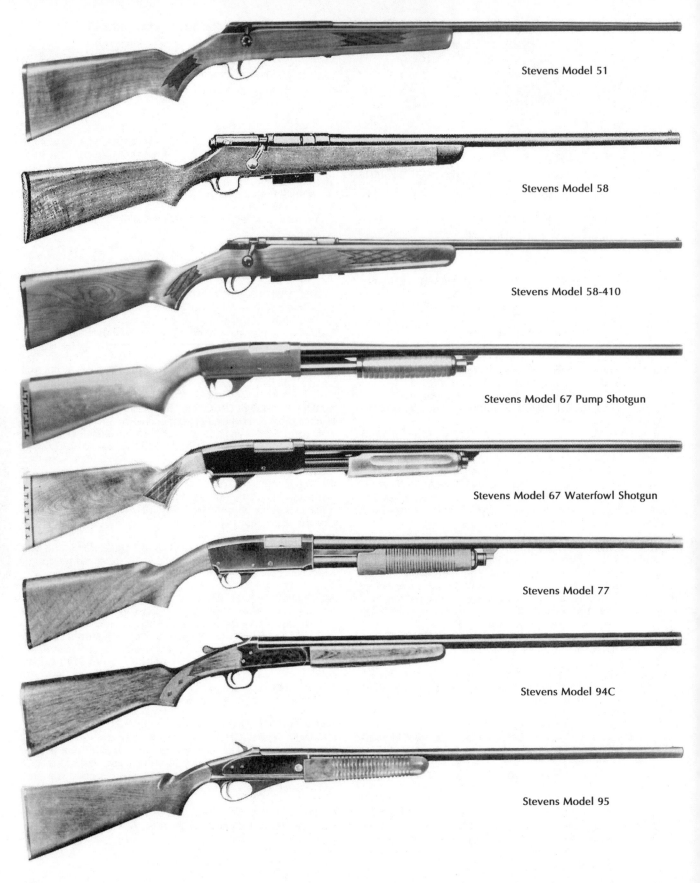

Stevens Model 51

Stevens Model 58

Stevens Model 58-410

Stevens Model 67 Pump Shotgun

Stevens Model 67 Waterfowl Shotgun

Stevens Model 77

Stevens Model 94C

Stevens Model 95

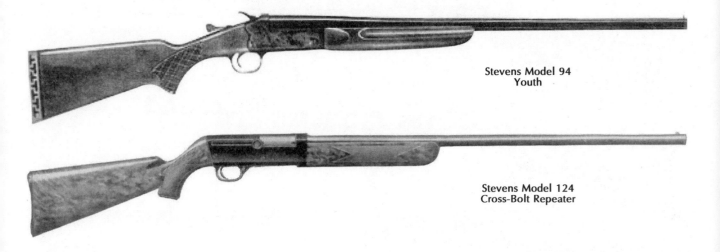

Stevens Model 94
Youth

Stevens Model 124
Cross-Bolt Repeater

MODEL 240 O/U SHOTGUN . NiB $448 Ex $375 Gd $270
Visible hammer. Takedown. Double triggers. .410 ga. 26-inch bbls., F choke. Weight: 6 lbs. Tenite (plastic) pistol-grip stock and forearm. Made from 1940 to 1949.

MODEL 258 BOLT-ACTION
REPEATER . . . . NiB $290 Ex $174 Gd $100
Takedown. 20-gauge. Two round detachable box magazine. 26-inch barrel, Full choke. Weight: About 6.25 lbs. Plain, one piece pistol-grip stock. Made from 1937 to 1965.

MODEL 311 SPRINGFIELD HAMMERLESS DOUBLE
Same general specifications as Stevens Model 530 except earlier production has plain stock and forearm; checkered on current guns. Originally produced as a "Springfield" gun, this model became a part of the Stevens line in 1948 when the Springfield brand name was discontinued. Made from 1931 to 1989.
Pre-WWII . . . . NiB $675 Ex $450 Gd $325
Post-WWII . . . . NiB $335 Ex $200 Gd $125

MODEL 311-R
HAMMERLESS DOUBLE . . . . . NiB $300 Ex $225 Gd $145
Same general specifications as Stevens Model 311 except compact design for law enforcement use. Bbls.: 18.25-inch 12 gauge with solid rib, chambered for 2.75 and 3-inch Mag. shells. Double triggers and auto top tang safety. Walnut finished hardwood stock with recoil pad and semi-beavertail forend. Weight: About 6.75 lbs. Made from 1982 to 1989.

MODEL 530
HAMMERLESS DOUBLE . . . . NiB $335 Ex $245 Gd $200
Boxlock. Double triggers. Gauges: 12, 16, 20, .410. Bbl. lengths: 26- to 32-inch; choked M/F, C/M, F/F. Weight: 6 to 7.5 pounds depending on gauge and barrel length. Checkered pistol-grip stock and forearm; some early models with recoil pad. Made from 1936 to 1954.

MODEL 530M . . . . NiB $339 Ex $255 Gd $210
Same as Model 530 except has Tenite (plastic) stock and forearm. Disc. about 1947.

MODEL 530ST DOUBLE GUN NiB $339 Ex $255 Gd $210
Same as Model 530 except has non-selective single trigger. Disc.

MODEL 620 HAMMERLESS SLIDE-ACTION
REPEATING SHOTGUN . . . . . NiB $400 Ex $255 Gd $180
Takedown. Gauges: 12, 16, 20. Five round tubular magazine. Bbl. lengths: 26-, 28-, 30-, 32-inch; choked F, M IC, C. Weight: About 7.75 lbs., 12 ga.; 7.25 lbs., 16 ga.- 6 lbs., 20 ga. Checkered pistol-grip stock and slide handle. Made from 1927 to 1953.

MODEL 620-C . . . . NiB $365 Ex $255 Gd $160
Same specifications as Model 620 except equipped with Cutts Compensator and two choke tubes.

MODEL 620-P . . . . NiB $288 Ex $200 Gd $155
Same specifications as Model 620 equipped with Aero-Dyne PolyChoke and 27-inch bbl.

MODEL 620-PV . . . . NiB $280 Ex $190 Gd $155
Same specifications as Model 620 except equipped with ventilated PolyChoke and 27-inch bbl.

MODEL 621 . . . . NiB $359 Ex $210 Gd $155
Same as Model 620 except has raised solid matted-rib barrel. Disc.

MODEL 820 HAMMERLESS
REPEATING SHOTGUN . . . . . NiB $388 Ex $266 Gd $190
Solid frame. 12 gauge only. Five round tubular magazine. 28-inch barrel; IC, M or F choke. Weight: About 7.5 lbs. Plain pistol-grip stock, grooved slide handle. Early models furnished w/Tenite butt-stock and forend. Made from 1949 to 1954.

MODEL 820-SC . . . . NiB $400 Ex $330 Gd $217
Same as Model 820 except has Savage Super Choke.

MODEL 940 SINGLE-
SHOT SHOTGUN. . . . . NiB $256 Ex $138 Gd $110
Same general specifications as Model 94 except has side lever opening instead of top lever. Made from 1961 to 1970.

MODEL 940Y
YOUTH GUN. . . . . NiB $265 Ex $155 Gd $115
Same general specifications as Model 94Y except has side lever opening instead of top lever. Made from 1961 to 1970.

SHOTGUNS

Stevens Model 258

Stevens Model 311

Stevens Model 530

Stevens Model 620

Stevens Model 620-P

Stevens Model 820

MODEL 9478 . . . . **NiB $145 Ex $90 Gd $65**
Takedown. Visible hammer. Automatic ejector. Gauges: 12, 20, .410. Bbls.: 26-, 28-, 30-, 36-inch; Full choke. Weight: Average 6 pounds depending on gauge and barrel. Plain pistol-grip stock and forearm. Made from 1978 to 1985.

MODEL 5151 SPRINGFIELD . . **NiB $556 Ex $435 Gd $300**
Same specifications as the Stevens Model 311 except with checkered grip and forend; equipped with recoil pad and two ivory sights.

STOEGER SHOTGUNS

See IGA and Tikka Shotguns

TAR-HUNT CUSTOM RIFLES, INC. — Bloomsburg, Pennsylvania

MODEL RSG-12 MATCHLESS
BOLT-ACTION SLUG GUN NiB $2366 Ex $2165 Gd $1590
Similar to Professional model except has McMillan Fibergrain stock and deluxe blue finish. Made from 1995 to 2004.

MODEL RSG-12 PEERLESS
BOLT-ACTION SLUG GUN NiB $2944 Ex $2577 Gd $2320
Similar to Professional model except has McMillan Fibergrain stock and deluxe NP-3 (Nickel/Teflon) metal finish. Made from 1995 to 2004.

MODEL RSG-12 PROFESSIONAL
BOLT-ACTION SLUG GUN
Bolt action 12 ga. w/2.75-inch chamber, 2-round detachable magazine, 21.5-inch fully rifled bbl. w/ or w/o muzzle brake. Receiver drilled and tapped for scope mounts w/no sights. Weight: 7.75 lbs. 41.5 inches overall. Checkered black McMillan fiberglass stock w/swivel studs and Pachmayr Deacelerator pad. Made from 1991 to 2004.

RSG-12 model
W/O muzzle brake (disc. 1993)NiB $2688 Ex $2320 Gd $1997
RSG-12 model
W/muzzle brake .... NiB $2700 Ex $2375 Gd $2044

MODEL RSG-20 MOUNTAINEER
BOLT ACTION SLUG GUN NiB $2276 Ex $1966 Gd $1433
Similar to Professional model except 20 ga. w/2.75 inch chamber. Black McMillan synthetic stock w/blind magazine. Weight: 6.5 lbs. Made from 1997 to 2004.

TECNI-MEC SHOTGUNS—Italy. Imported by RAHN Gun Work, Inc., Hastings, MI

MODEL SPL 640 FOLDING SHOTGUN
Gauges: 12, 16, 20, 24, 28, 32 and .410 bore. 26-inch bbl. Chokes: IC/IM. Weight: 6.5 lbs. Checkered walnut pistol-grip stock and forend. Engraved receiver. Available with single or double triggers. Imported from 1988 to 1994.
640 w/single trigger .... NiB $596 Ex $477 Gd $369
640 w/double trigger .... NiB $655 Ex $498 Gd $388

THOMPSON/CENTER ARMS—Rochester, New Hampshire, and Springfield, Massachusetts

Purchased by Smith & Wesson in 2006.

CONTENDER
.410 CARBINE .... NiB $500 Ex $387 Gd $279
Gauge: .410 smoothbore. 21-inch vent rib bbl. 34.75 inches overall. Weight: About 5.25 lbs. Bead front sight. Rynite stock and forend. Made 1991 to date.

ENCORE 20 GA. SHOTGUN
Gauge: 20 smoothbore w/rifled slug bbl. or 26-inch vent-rib bbl. w/ three internal screw choke tubes, 38 to 40.5 inches overall. Weight: About 5.25 to 6 lbs. Bead or fiber optic sights. Walnut stock and forend. Made from 1998 to date.
Encore 20 ga.
W/vent rib .... NiB $485 Ex $390 Gd $275
Encore 20 ga.
w/rifled slug bbl. .... NiB $522 Ex $421 Gd $300
W/extra
bbl., add $325

HUNTER SHOTGUN MODEL . NiB $580 Ex $466 Gd $355
Single shot. Gauge: 10 or 12, 3.5-inch chamber, 25-inch field bbl. with F choke. Weight: 8 lbs. Bead front sight. American black walnut stock with recoil pad. Made from 1987 to 1992.

HUNTER SLUG MODEL ..... NiB $580 Ex $466 Gd $355
Gauge: 10 (3.5-inch chamber) or 12 (3-inch chamber). Same general specifications as Model '87 Hunter Shotgun except with 22-inch slug (rifled) bbl. and rifle sights. Made from 1987 to 1992.

TIKKA SHOTGUNS—Manufactured by Sako, Ltd. in Armi Marocchi, Italy

M 07 SHOTGUN/
RIFLE COMBINATION .... NiB $1287 Ex $1009 Gd $766
Gauge/caliber: 12/.222 Rem. Shotgun bbl.: About 25 inches; rifled bbl.: About 22.75 inches. 40.66 inches overall. Weight: About 7 lbs. Dovetailed for telescopic sight mounts Single trigger with selector between the bbls. Vent rib. Monte Carlo-style walnut stock with checkered pistol grip and forend. Made from 1965 to 1987.

M 77 O/U SHOTGUN .... NiB $1345 Ex $1265 Gd $950
Gauge: 12. 27-inch vent-rib bbls., approx. 44 inches overall, weight: About 7.25 lbs. Bbl. selector. Ejectors. Monte Carlo-style walnut stock with checkered pistol grip and forend; rollover cheekpiece. Made from 1977 to 1987.

M 77K SHOTGUN/ RIFLE
COMBINATION. .... NiB $1733 Ex $1388 Gd $1009
Gauge: 12/70. Calibers: .222 Rem., 5.6x52r5, 6.5x55, 7x57r5, 7x65r5, .308 Win. Vent-rib bbls.: About 25 inches (shotgun); 23 inches (rifle), 42.3 inches overall. Weight: About 7.5 lbs. Double triggers. Monte Carlo-style walnut stock with checkered pistol grip and forend; rollover cheekpiece. Made from 1977 to 1986.

412S/512S SHOOTING SYSTEM
Boxlock action with both under lug and sliding top latch locking mechanism designed to accept interchangeable monobloc barrels, including O/U shotgun, combination and double rifle configurations. Blued or satin nickel receiver w/cocking indicators. Selective single trigger design w/barrel selector incorporated into the trigger (double triggers available). Blued barrels assemblies w/extractors or auto ejectors as required. Select American walnut stock with checkered pistol grip and forend. Previously produced in Finland (same as the former Valmet Model 412) but currently manufactured in Italy by joint venture arrangement with Armi Marocchi. From 1990-93, Stoeger Industries imported this model as the 412/S. In 1993 the nomenclature of this shooting system was changed to 512/S. Disc. 1997. Note: For double rifle values, see Tikka Rifles.

MODEL 412S/512S O/U SHOTGUN
Gauge: 12 w/3-inch chambers. 24-, 26-, 28- or 30-inch chrome-lined bbls. w/blued finish and integral stainless steel choke tubes. Weight: 7.25 to 7.5 lbs. Blue or matte nickel receiver. Select American walnut from stock with checkered pistol grip and forend. Imported 1990 to 1997.
Standard Field model .... NiB $1145 Ex $989 Gd $766
Standard Trap model .... NiB $1277 Ex $1050 Gd $766
Premium Field model .... NiB $1688 Ex $1279 Gd $1100
Premium Trap model .... NiB $1688 Ex $1279 Gd $1100
Sporting Clays model .... NiB $1233 Ex $1054 Gd $866
W/extra O/U shotgun bbl., add $700
W/extra O/U combo bbl., add $800
W/extra O/U rifle bbl., add $1025

MODEL 412S/512S OVER/UNDER COMBINATION
Gauge: 12 w/3-inch chamber. Calibers: .222 Rem., .30-06 or .308 Win. Blue or matte nickel receiver, 24-inch chrome-lined bbls. w/ extractors and blued finish. Weight: 7.25 to 7.5 lbs. Select American walnut stock with checkered pistol grip and forend. Imported from 1990 to 1997.
Standard Combination model ... NiB $1598 Ex $1335 Gd $1109
Premium Combination model ... NiB $1622 Ex $1365 Gd $1135
Extra barrel options, add......................... $800

TRADITIONS PERFORMANCE FIREARMS — Importers of shotguns produced by Fausti Stefano of Brescia, Italy, and ATA Firearms, Turkey

FIELD HUNTER MODEL . . . . . . .NiB $825 Ex $630 Gd $535
Same as Field I except 12 and 20 gauge, 3-inch chambers, screw-in chokes and extractors.

CLASSIC SERIES, FIELD I O/U . . .NiB $853 Ex $677 Gd $545
Available in 12, 20, 28 (2 3/4-inch chamber) and .410 gauge, 26- or 28-inch vent rib bbls. W/fixed chokes and extractors. Weight: 6 3/4 to 7 1/4 lbs. Blued finish, silver receiver engraved with game birds. Single, selective trigger. Brass bead front sight. European walnut stock. Overall length 43 to 45 inches. Intro. 2000.

FIELD II MODEL . . . . .NiB $945 Ex $679 Gd $555
Same as Field I except with screw-in chokes and automatic ejectors.

FIELD III GOLD MODEL . . . . .NiB $1217 Ex $1109 Gd $998
Same as Field I model except 12 gauge only, high-grade, oil-finish walnut, coin-finish receiver with engraved pheasants and woodcock, deep blue finish on barrels, automatic ejectors and non-slip recoil pad.

SPORTING CLAY II MODEL . . .NiB $1165 Ex $977 Gd $620
Same as Sporting Clay III model but with European walnut stocks, cut checkering and extended choke tubes. Overall length: 47 inches. Weight: 7 3/4 lbs.

CLASSIC SERIES O/U
SPORTING CLAY III . . . . . . .NiB $1200 Ex $1095 Gd $985
Available in 12 and 20 gauge, 3-inch chambers, high grade walnut stock, oil-satin finish, palm swell Schnabel forend. 28- and 30-inch bbls. with 3/8-inch top and middle vent rib, red target front bead sight. Automatic ejectors, extended choke tubes. Weight: 8 1/4 lbs. Intro. 2000.

UPLAND II MODEL . . . . .NiB $1065 Ex $775 Gd $546
Same as Upland III model except with English walnut straight-grip stock and Schnabel forend, 24- and 26-inch vent rib bbls., floral engraving on blued receiver, automatic ejectors.

UPLAND III MODEL . . . . .NiB $1187 Ex $977 Gd $755
Same as Sporting Clay III model but round pistol grip and Schnabel forend, blued receiver with engraved upland scene, weight: 7 1/2 lbs.

MAG 350 SERIES TURKEY II O/U . . .NiB $1144 Ex $942 Gd $700
Magnum 3 1/2-inch chambers in 12 gauge only, 24- and 26-inch bbls., screw-in flush fitting chokes: F and XF. Matte finish, engraved receiver, Mossy Oak or Realtree camo. Intro. 2000.

WATERFOWL II MODEL . . . . .NiB $1159 Ex $910 Gd $715
Same as Turkey II model except with Advantage Wetlands camo stock and barrels, weight: 8 lbs., overall length 45 inches. Waterfowl model has 28-inch bbls.

MAG HUNTER II . . . . .NiB $1159 Ex $910 Gd $715
Same as Turkey II model except blued engraved receiver and matte finish walnut stocks, 3 1/2-inch chambers, 28-inch bbls. with screw-in chokes.

ELITE HUNTER . . . . .NiB $1256 Ex $1044 Gd $770
Same as Elite Field model except 12 and 20 gauge, European walnut stock, beavertail forend, screw-in choke tubes, extractors, three-inch chambers. Blued finish. Vent-rib, tang safety. Weight: 6 1/2 pounds.

ELITE FIELD I DT. . . . . .NiB $1006 Ex $853 Gd $600
Same as Elite Field I except with double triggers, fixed chokes, extractors. Available in 12, 20, 28 (2 3/4-inch chambers) and .410. Bbls: 26 inches, fixed IC/M chokes. Weight: 5 1/2 to 6 1/4 lbs

ELITE FIELD I ST . . . . .NiB $1118 Ex $1065 Gd $790
Same as Elite Field III except single trigger, fixed chokes, extractors; European walnut stock. Available in 12, 20, 28 (2 3/4-inch chambers) and .410 gauge; fixed IC/M chokes. Weight: 5 3/4 to 6 1/2 lbs.

ELITE FIELD III ST . . . . .NiB $1967 Ex $1689 Gd $1333
Checkered English walnut straight stock, splinter forend, fixed chokes. Available in 28 and .410 gauge, 26-inch chrome-lined bbls., Cylinder and Modified chokes. Silver trigger guard and receiver with hand-finished engraving of upland game scenes with gold inlays. Automatic ejectors. Brass front sight bead. Weight: About 6 1/2 lbs. Intro. 2000.

AL 2100 SEMI-AUTO SHOTGUNS
FIELD SERIES, WALNUT MODEL . . .NiB $366 Ex $245 Gd $190
Gas-operated, 12 and 20 gauge, 3-inch chambers, cut-checkered Turkish walnut stock and forend, blued 26- and 28-inch vent rib bbls., multi-choke system, chrome bore lining. Weight: About 6 lbs. Rifled barrel with cantilever mount available Intro. 2001.

SYNTHETIC STOCK MODEL . . . .NiB $350 Ex $290 Gd $225
Same as the ALS 2100 Walnut model except with synthetic stock, matted finish on receiver and bbl., weight: About 6 lbs.

YOUTH MODEL . . . . .NiB $344 Ex $229 Gd $175
Same as ALS 2100 Walnut model except with a shorter walnut stock (length of pull: 13 1/2 inches). Available in 12 or 20 gauge with 24-inch vent rib barrel, weight: 5 1/2 to 6 lbs.

HUNTER COMBO MODEL
Same as ALS 2100 Walnut model except comes with two bbls. (28-inch vent rib and 24-inch slug), TruGlo adjustable sights and cantilever mount. Available with Turkish walnut or synthetic stock with matte barrel finish. Weight: 6 1/2 lbs.
W/walnut stock. . . . . .NiB $500 Ex $377 Gd $210
W/synthetic stock .NiB $475 Ex $339 Gd $220

SLUG HUNTER MODEL . . . . . . .NiB $355 Ex $245 Gd $190
Same as ALS 2100 Walnut except with fully-rifled barrel, choice of walnut or synthetic stocks, matte or blue finish; rifle or TruGlo adjustable sights. Weight: About 6 1/4 lbs.

TURKEY HUNTER/
WATERFOWL MODEL . . . . .NiB $375 Ex $265 Gd $220
Same as ALS 2100 Walnut except with synthetic stock, 3-inch chambers, 26-inch vent rib bbl., screw-in chokes, Mossy Oak or Realtree camo stocks.

HOME SECURITY MODEL . . . . .NiB $335 Ex $260 Gd $190
Same as ALS 2100 Walnut but with 20-inch cylinder-bore bbl., synthetic stock, 3-inch chambers, six-round capacity with 2 3/4-inch shells. Weight: About 6 lbs.

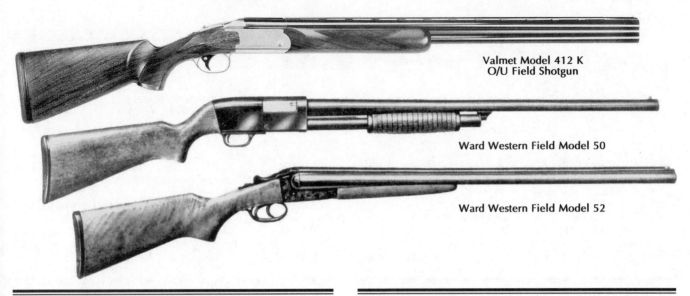

Valmet Model 412 K
O/U Field Shotgun

Ward Western Field Model 50

Ward Western Field Model 52

TRISTAR SPORTING ARMS — North Kansas City, Missouri

MODEL 1887 LEVER-ACTION REPEATER. . . NiB $765 Ex $580 Gd $445
Copy of John Browning's Winchester Model 1887 lever-action shotgun. 12 ga. only. 30-inch bbl. which may be cut down to any desired length of 18 inches or more. Version shown has 20-inch bbl. Imported from 1997 to 1999.

MODEL 300 O/U SHOTGUN . NiB $465 Ex $335 Gd $199
Similar to the Model 333 except 12 ga. only w/3-inch chambers, 26- or 28-inch vent rib bbls. w/extractors and fixed chokes. Etched receiver w/double triggers and standard walnut stock. Imported 1994 to 1998.

MODEL 311 SIDE-BY-SIDE SHOTGUN
Boxlock action w/underlug and Greener cross bolt. 12 or 20 ga. w/3-inch chambers, 20, 28- or 30-inch bbls. w/choke tubes or fixed chokes (311R). Double triggers. Extractors. Black chrome finish. Checkered Turkish walnut buttstock and forend. Weight: 6.9 to 7.2 lbs. Imported from 1994 to 1997.
311 Model (w/extractors and choke tubes)NiB $575 Ex $476 Gd $390
311R Model
(w/20-inch bbls. and fixed chokes). . . . . NiB $445 Ex $355 Gd $235

MODEL 330 O/U SHOTGUN
Similar to the Model 333 except 12 ga. only w/3-inch chambers. 26-, 28- or 30-inch vent rib bbls w/extractors or ejectors and fixed chokes or choke tubes. Etched receiver and standard walnut stock. Imported from 1994 to 1999.
330 model (w/ extractor and fixed chokes)NiB $545 Ex $420 Gd $300
330 D model (w/ejectors and choke tubes)NiB $733 Ex $567 Gd $488

MODEL 333 O/U SHOTGUN
Boxlock action. 12 or 20 ga. w/3-inch chambers. 26-, 28- or 30-inch vent rib bbls. w/choke tubes. Single selective trigger. Selective automatic ejectors. Engraved receiver w/satin nickel finish. Checkered Turkish fancy walnut buttstock and forend. Weight: 7.5 to 7.75 lbs. Imported from 1994 to 1998.
Field model . . . . .NiB $844 Ex $700 Gd $545
Sporting Clays model (1994-97). . . . NiB $900 Ex $755 Gd $580
TRL Ladies Field model. . . . . .NiB $800 Ex $675 Gd $550
SCL Ladies Sporting Clays model
(1994-97). . . . . .NiB $900 Ex $755 Gd $580

SHOTGUNS OF ULM — Ulm, Germany

See listings under Krieghoff.

U.S. REPEATING ARMS CO. — New Haven, Connecticut

See also Winchester Shotgun listings.

VALMET — Jyväskylä, Finland

NOTE: In 1987, Valmet and Sako merged and the Valmet production facilities were moved to Riihimaki, Finland. In 1989 a joint venture agreement was made with Armi Marocchi, and when production began in Italy, the Valmet name was changed to Tikka (Oy Tikkakoski Ab).

See also Savage Models 330, 333T, 333 and 2400, which were produced by Valmet.

VALMET LION O/U SHOTGUN . . . NiB $475 Ex $388 Gd $293
Boxlock. Selective single trigger. Plain extractors. 12 ga. only. Bbls.: 26-inch IC/M; 28-inch M/F, 30-inch M/F, F/F. Weight: About 7 lbs. Checkered pistol-grip stock and forearm. Imported 1947 to 1968.

MODEL 412 S O/U FIELD SHOTGUN NiB $955 Ex $744 Gd $535
Hammerless. 12-ga., 3-inch chamber, 36-inch bbl., F/F chokes. American walnut Monte Carlo stock. Disc 1989.

MODEL 412 S SHOTGUN RIFLE
COMBINATION . . . . NiB $1135 Ex $956 Gd $745
Similar to model 412 K except bottom bbl. chambered for .222 Rem., .223 Rem., .243 Win., .308 Win. or .30-06. 12-ga. shotgun bbl. with IM choke. Monte Carlo American walnut stock, recoil pad.

MODEL 412 O/U
FIELD SHOTGUN. . . . . NiB $866 Ex $723 Gd $587
12-ga. chambered for 2.75-inch shells. 26-inch bbl., IC/M chokes; 28-inch bbl., M/F chokes; 12-ga. chambered for 3-inch shells, 30-inch bbl., M/F chokes. 20-ga. (3-inch shells); 26-inch bbl., IC/M chokes; 28-inch bbl., M/ F chokes. American walnut Monte Carlo stock.

SHOTGUNS

Weatherby Model 82
Autoloading Shotgun

MODEL 412 ST SKEET . . . . . NiB $1176 Ex $922 Gd $766
Similar to Model 412 K except skeet stock and chokes. 12 and 20 ga. Disc. 1989.

MODEL 412 SE TRAP . . . . . NiB $1176 Ex $922 Gd $766
Similar to Model 412 K Field except trap stock, recoil pad. 30-inch bbls., IM/F chokes. Disc.1989.
W/EXTRA BBL., add $500

MONTGOMERY WARD — Chicago, Illinois; Western Field and Hercules Models

Although they do not correspond to specific models below, the names Western Field and Hercules have been used to designate various Montgomery Ward shotguns at various times.

MODEL 25 SLIDE-ACTION REPEATER . NiB $337 Ex $228 Gd $178
Solid frame. 12 ga. only. Two- or 5-round tubular magazine. 28-inch bbl., various chokes. Weight: About 7.5 lbs. Plain pistol-grip stock, grooved slide handle.

MODEL 40 O/U SHOTGUN . . NiB $866 Ex $700 Gd $522
Hammerless. Boxlock. Double triggers. Gauges: 12, l6, 20, .410. Bbls.: Plain; 26- to 30-inch, various chokes. Checkered pistol-grip stock and forearm.

**MODEL 40N
SLIDE-ACTION REPEATER** . . . NiB $329 Ex $233 Gd $179
Same general specifications as Model 25.

(WESTERN FIELD) MODEL 50 PUMPGUN . . . NiB $300 Ex $244 Gd $178
Solid frame. Gauges: 12 and 16. Two- and 5-round magazine. 26-, 28- or 30-inch bbl., 48 inches overall w/28-inch bbl. Weight: 7.25 - 7.75 lbs. Metal bead front sight. Walnut stock and grooved forend.

**(WESTERN FIELD) MODEL 52
DOUBLE-BARREL SHOTGUN** . NiB $388 Ex $277 Gd $191
Hammerless coil-spring action. Gauges: 12, 16, 20 and .410. 26-, 28-, or 30-inch bbls., 42 to 46 inches overall, depending upon bbl. length. Weight: 6 (.410 ga. w/26-inch bbl.) to 7.25 lbs. (12 ga. w/30-inch bbls.), depending upon gauge and bbl. length. Casehardened receiver; blued bbls. Plain buttstock and forend. Made circa 1954.

MODEL 172 BOLT-ACTION SHOTGUN . NiB $217 Ex $139 Gd $95
Takedown. Two-round detachable clip magazine.12 ga. 28-inch bbl. with variable choke. Weight: About 7.5 lbs. Monte Carlo stock with recoil pad.

MODEL 550A SLIDE-ACTION REPEATER . . . NiB $367 Ex $265 Gd $190
Takedown. Gauges: 12, 16, 20, .410. Five-round tubular magazine. Bbls.: Plain, 26- to 30-inch, various chokes. Weight: 6 (.410 ga. w/26-inch bbl.) to 8 lbs. (12 ga. w/30-inch bbls.). Plain pistol-grip stock and grooved slide handle.
MODEL SB300 DOUBLE-BARREL

SHOTGUN . . . . NiB $376 Ex $298 Gd $220
Same general specifications as Model SD52A.

MODEL SB312 DOUBLE-BARREL SHOTGUN . . . NiB $421 Ex $337 Gd $244
Boxlock. Double triggers. Plain extractors. Gauges: 12, 16, 20, .410. Bbls.: 24- to 30-inch. Various chokes. Weight: About 7.5 lbs. in 12 ga.; 6.5 lbs in .410 ga. Checkered pistol-grip stock and forearm.

MODEL SD52A DOUBLE-BARREL SHOTGUN . . . .NiB $344 Ex $255 Gd $200
Boxlock. Double triggers. Plain extractors. Gauges: 12, 16, 20, .410. Bbls.: 26- to 32-inch, various chokes. Plain forend and pistol-grip buttstock. Weight: 6 (.410 ga., 26-inch bbls.) to 7.5 lbs. (12 ga., 32-inch bbls.).

WEATHERBY, INC. — Pasa Robles, California

MODEL 82 AUTOLOADING SHOTGUN . . . NiB $556 Ex $435 Gd $332
Hammerless, gas-operated. 12 ga. only. Bbls.: 22- to 30-inch, various integral or fixed chokes. Weight: 7.5 lbs. Checkered walnut stock and forearm. Imported from 1982 to 1989.
**BuckMaster Auto Slug
w/rifle sights (1986-90)** . . . . NiB $570 Ex $455 Gd $355
W/fixed choke, deduct. $50

**MODEL 92 SLIDE-ACTION
SHOTGUN** . . . . NiB $390 Ex $288 Gd $217
Hammerless, short-stroke action. 12 ga.; 3-inch chamber. Tubular magazine. Bbls.: 22-, 26-, 28-, 30-inch with fixed choke or IMC choke tubes; plain or vent rib with rifle sights. Weight: 7.5 lbs. Engraved, matte black receiver and blued barrel. Checkered high-gloss buttstock and forend. Imported from Japan since 1982.
Standard Model 92 . . . . NiB $330 Ex $261 Gd $195
**BuckMaster Pump Slug
w/rifle sights, (intro. 1986)** . . . NiB $420 Ex $315 Gd $235

ATHENA O/U SHOTGUN
Engraved boxlock action with Greener crossbolt and sideplates. Gauges: 12, 20, 28 and .410; 2.75- or 3.5-inch chambers. Bbls.: 26-, 28-, 30- or 32-inch with fixed or IMC Multi-choke tubes. Weight: 6.75 to 7.38 lbs. Single selective trigger. Selective auto ejectors. Top tang safety. Checkered Claro walnut stock and forearm with high-luster finish. Imported from 1982 to 2002.
**Field Model w/IMC multi-chokes,
12 or 20 ga.** . . . . NiB $2177 Ex $1898 Gd $1635
Field Model W/fixed chokes, 28 ga. or .410NiB $1976 Ex $1645 Gd $1389
Skeet Model w/fixed chokes, 12 or 20 ga.NiB $1766 Ex $1432 Gd $1255
Skeet Model w/fixed chokes, 28 ga. or .410NiB $3320 Ex $2888 Gd $2366
Master Skeet tube set . . . . NiB $3155 Ex $2776 Gd $2388
Trap Model w/IC tubes. . . . . NiB $2388 Ex $1977 Gd $1677
Grade V (1993 to date) . . . . NiB $3566 Ex $3100 Gd $2665

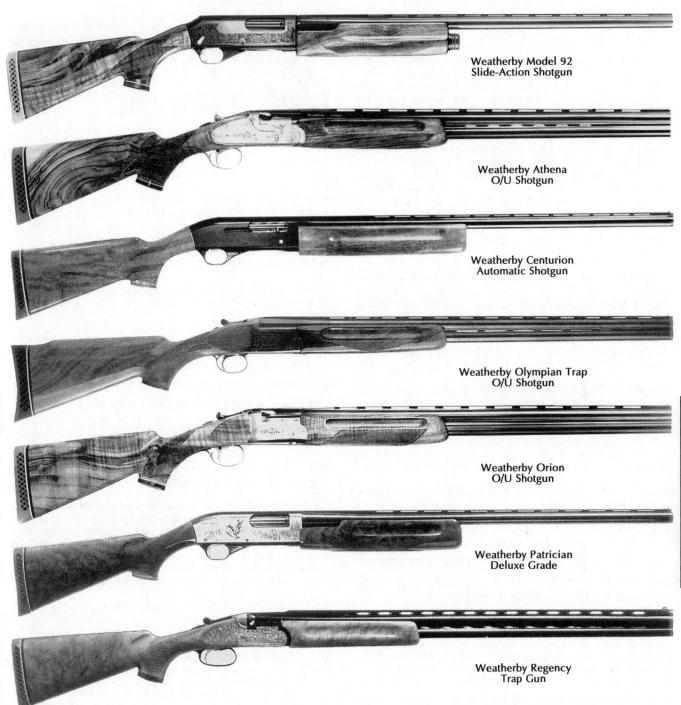

Weatherby Model 92
Slide-Action Shotgun

Weatherby Athena
O/U Shotgun

Weatherby Centurion
Automatic Shotgun

Weatherby Olympian Trap
O/U Shotgun

Weatherby Orion
O/U Shotgun

Weatherby Patrician
Deluxe Grade

Weatherby Regency
Trap Gun

CENTURION AUTOMATIC SHOTGUN

Gas-operated. Takedown. 12 ga. 2.75-inch chamber. Three round magazine. Bbls.: Vent ribs; 26-inch SK, IC or M 28-inch M or F; 30-inch Full choke. Weight: With 28-inch bbl., 7 lbs. 10.5 oz. Checkered pistol-grip stock and forearm, recoil pad. Made in Japan from 1972 to 1981.

Field Grade . . . . NiB $398 Ex $288 Gd $219
Trap Gun (30-inch full-choke bbl.)NiB $435 Ex $377 Gd $235
Deluxe model (etched receiver,
fancy wood stock) . . . . NiB $525 Ex $425 Gd $265

OLYMPIAN O/U SHOTGUN

Gauges: 12 and 20. 2.75- (12 ga.) and 3-inch (20 ga.) chambers. Bbls.: 26-, 28-, 30, and 32-inch. Weight: 6.75 - 8.75 lbs. American walnut stock and forend.

Field
Model . . . . NiB $988 Ex $700 Gd $577
Skeet
Model . . . . NiB $1033 Ex $800 Gd $690
Trap
Model . . . . NiB $995 Ex $745 Gd $650

ORION O/U SHOTGUN

Boxlock with Greener crossbolt. Gauges: 12, 20, 28 and .410; 2.75- or 3-inch chambers. Bbls.: 26-, 28, 30-, 32- or 34-inch with fixed or IMC Multi-Choke tubes. Weight: 6.5 to 9 lbs. Single selective trigger. Selective auto ejectors. Top tang safety. Checkered, high-gloss pistol-grip Claro walnut stock and forearm. Finish: Grade I, plain blued receive; Grade II, engraved blued receiver; Grade III, silver gray receiver. Imported from 1982 and 2002.

Orion I Field w/IC (12 or 20 ga.) . . . . NiB $1456 Ex $1188 Gd $975
Orion II Field w/IC (12 or 20 ga.) . . . . NiB $1155 Ex $965 Gd $743
Orion II Classic w/IC (12, 20 or 28 ga.)NiB $1644 Ex $1388 Gd $1166
Orion II Sporting Clays w/IC (12 ga.) NiB $1997 Ex $1688 Gd $1388
Orion III Field w/IC (12 or 20 ga.) . . NiB $1688 Ex $1397 Gd $1188
Orion III Classic w/IC (12 or 20 ga.) NiB $1988 Ex $1669 Gd $1367
Orion III English Field w/IC (12 or 20 ga.)NiB $1733 Ex $1448 Gd $1244
Orion Upland w/IC (12 or 20 ga.) . . . NiB $1376 Ex $1133 Gd $976
Skeet II w/fixed chokes . . . . NiB $1355 Ex $1125 Gd $950
Super Sporting Clays . . . . NiB $1988 Ex $1743 Gd $1129

PATRICIAN SLIDE-ACTION SHOTGUN

Hammerless. Takedown. 12 ga. 2.75-inch chamber. Four round tubular magazine. Bbls.: Vent rib; 26-inch, SK, IC M; 28-inch, M F; 30-inch, F choke. Weight: With 28-inch bbl., 7 lbs., 7 oz. Checkered pistol-grip stock and slide handle, recoil pad. Made in Japan from 1972 to 1982.

Field Grade . . . . NiB $369 Ex $248 Gd $125
Deluxe model (etched receiver,
fancy grade stock) . . . . NiB $455 Ex $329 Gd $260
Trap Gun (w/30-inch full-choke bbl.). . . NiB $399 Ex $255 Gd $190

REGENCY FIELD GRADE O/U SHOTGUN NiB $1387 Ex $1266 Gd $885

Boxlock with sideplates, elaborately engraved. Auto ejectors. Selective single trigger. Gauges: 12, 20. 2.75-inch chamber in 12 ga., 3-inch in 20 ga. Bbls.: Vent rib; 26-inch SK, IC/M, M/F (20 ga. only); 28-inch SK, IC/M, M/F; 30-inch M/F (12 ga only). Weight with 28-inch bbls.: 7 lbs., 6 oz., 12 ga.; 6 lbs., 14 oz., 20 ga. Checkered pistol-grip stock and forearm of fancy walnut. Made in Italy from 1965 to 1982.

REGENCY TRAP GUN . . . . . . NiB $990 Ex $823 Gd $688

Similar to Regency Field Grade except has trap-style stock with straight or Monte Carlo comb. Bbls. have vent side ribs and high, wide vent top rib; 30- or 32-inch, M/F, IM/F or F/F chokes. Weight: With 32-inch bbls., 8 lbs. Made in Italy from 1965 to 1982.

WESTERN ARMS CORP. — Ithaca, New York; division of Ithaca Gun Company

LONG RANGE HAMMERLESS DOUBLE

Boxlock. Plain extractors. Single or double triggers. Gauges: 12, 16, 20, .410. Bbls.: 26- to 32-inch, M/F choke standard. Weight: 7.5 lbs., 12 ga. Plain pistol-grip stock and forend. Made 1929 to 1946.

With double triggers . . . . . . NiB $398 Ex $244 Gd $165
With single trigger . . . . NiB $400 Ex $295 Gd $188

WESTERN AUTO SHOTGUNS — Kansas City, Missouri

MODEL 300H SLIDE-ACTION REPEATER NiB $435 Ex $300 Gd $255

Gauges: 12,16, 20, .410. Four round tubular magazine. Bbls.: 26- to 30-inch, various chokes. Weight: About 7 lbs. Plain pistol-grip stock, grooved slide handle.

MODEL 310A SLIDE-ACTION REPEATER NiB $366 Ex $270 Gd $200

Takedown. 12 ga. Five round tubular magazine. Bbls.: 28- and 30-inch. Weight: About 7.5 lbs. Plain pistol-grip stock.

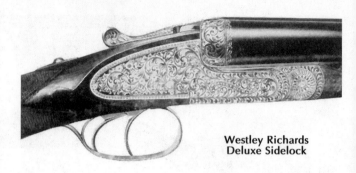

**Westley Richards
Deluxe Sidelock**

MODEL 310B SLIDE-ACTION REPEATER NiB $377 Ex $245 Gd $190

Same general specifications as Model 310A except chambered for 16 ga.

MODEL 310C SLIDE-ACTION REPEATER NiB $365 Ex $269 Gd $180

Same general specifications as Model 310A except chambered for 20 ga.

MODEL 310E SLIDE-ACTION REPEATER NiB $425 Ex $366 Gd $229

Same general specifications as Model 310A except chambered for .410 bore.

MODEL 325BK BOLT-ACTION REPEATER NiB $276 Ex $190 Gd $125

Takedown. Two round detachable clip magazine. 20 ga. 26-inch bbl. with variable choke. Weight: 6.25 lbs.

WESTERN FIELD SHOTGUNS

See "W" for listings under Montgomery Ward.

WESTLEY RICHARDS & CO., LTD. — Birmingham, England

The Pigeon and Wildfowl gun, available in all of the Westley Richards models except the Ovundo, has the same general specifications as the corresponding standard field gun except has magnum action of extra strength and treble bolting, chambered for 12 gauge only (2.75- or 3-inch); 30-inch full choke barrels standard. Weight: About 8 lbs. The manufacturer warns that 12-gauge magnum shells should not be used in their standard weight double-barrel shotguns.

BEST QUALITY BOXLOCK HAMMERLESS DOUBLE-BARREL SHOTGUN

Boxlock. Hand-detachable locks and hinged cover plate. Selective ejectors. Double triggers or selective single trigger. Gauges: 12, 16, 20. Barrel lengths and boring to order. Weight: 5.5 to 6.25 lbs. depending on ga. and bbl. length. Checkered stock and forend, straight or half-pistol grip. Also supplied in Pigeon and Wildfowl models with same values. Made from 1899 to date.

W/double triggers . . . . NiB $22,975 Ex $18,990 Gd $14,270
W/selective single trigger . . . . . NiB $26,790 Ex $21,998 Gd $14,880

BEST QUALITY SIDELOCK HAMMERLESS DOUBLE-BARREL SHOTGUN

Hand-detachable sidelocks. Selective ejectors. Double triggers or selective single trigger. Gauges: 12, 16, 20, 28, .410. Bbl. lengths and boring to order. Weight: 4.75 to 6.75 lbs., depending on ga. and bbl. length. Checkered stock and forend, straight or half-pistol grip. Also supplied in Pigeon and Wildfowl models with same values. Currently manufactured.

W/double triggers . . . . NiB $29,669 Ex $26,766 Gd $22,880
W/selective single trigger . . . . . NiB $30,000 Ex $27,898 Gd $24,550

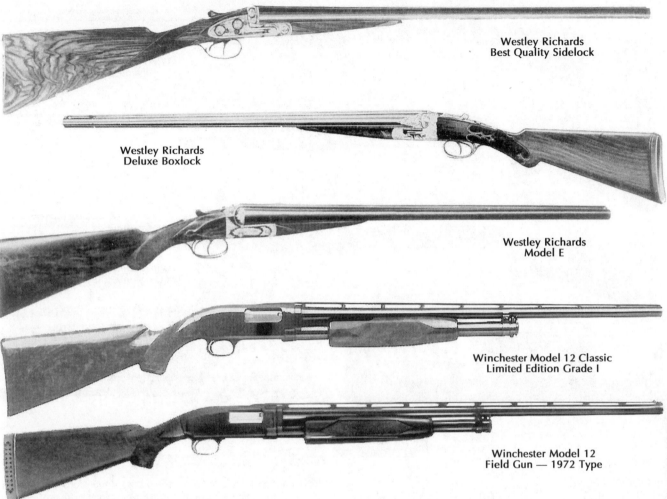

Westley Richards
Best Quality Sidelock

Westley Richards
Deluxe Boxlock

Westley Richards
Model E

Winchester Model 12 Classic
Limited Edition Grade I

Winchester Model 12
Field Gun — 1972 Type

DELUXE MODEL BOXLOCK
HAMMERLESS DOUBLE-BARREL SHOTGUN
Same general specifications as standard Best Quality gun except higher quality throughout. Has Westley Richards top-projection and treble-bite lever-work, hand-detachable locks. Also supplied in Pigeon and Wildfowl models with same values. Currently manufactured.
W/double trigger . . . . NiB $12,767 Ex $10,433 Gd $8998
W/selective
single trigger . . . . .NiB $32,880 Ex $30,880 Gd $13,990

DELUXE MODEL SIDELOCK
Same as Best Quality Sidelock except higher grade engraving and wood. Currently manufactured.
W/double triggers. . . NiB $27,889 Ex $22,999 Gd $14,887
W/single trigger . . . . NiB $31,998 Ex $26,999 Gd $18,998

MODEL E HAMMERLESS DOUBLE
Anson & Deeley-type boxlock action. Selective ejector or non-ejector. Double triggers. Gauges: 12, 16, 20. Barrel lengths and boring to order. Weight: 5.5 to 7.25 lbs. depending on type, ga. and bbl. length. Checkered stock and forend, straight or half-pistol grip. Also supplied in Pigeon and Wildfowl models with same values. Currently manufactured.
Ejector model . . . . NiB $5388 Ex $4378 Gd $2990
Non-ejector model . . . . . NiB $4998 Ex $3788 Gd $3277
OVUNDO (O/U) . . . . .NiB $19,677 Ex $16,999 Gd $12,998
Hammerless. Boxlock. Hand-detachable locks. Dummy sideplates.

Selective ejectors. Selective single trigger. 12 ga. Barrel lengths and boring to order. Checkered stock/forend, straight or half-pistol grip. Mfd. before WW II.

TED WILLIAMS SHOTGUNS

See Sears shotguns.

WINCHESTER SHOTGUNS —
New Haven, Connecticut

Formerly Winchester Repeating Arms Co., and then mfd. by Winchester-Western Div., Olin Corp., later by U.S. Repeating Arms Company. In 1999, production rights were acquired by Browning Arms Company.

MODEL 12 CLASSIC LIMITED Edition
Gauge: 20; 2.75-inch chamber. Bbl.: 26-inch vent rib; IC. Weight: 7 lbs. Checkered walnut buttstock and forend. Polished blue finish (Grade I) or engraved with gold inlays (Grade IV). Made from 1993 to 1995.
Grade I (4000) . . . . NiB $1100 Ex $889 Gd $656
Grade IV (1000) . . . . NiB $1700 Ex $1308 Gd $998

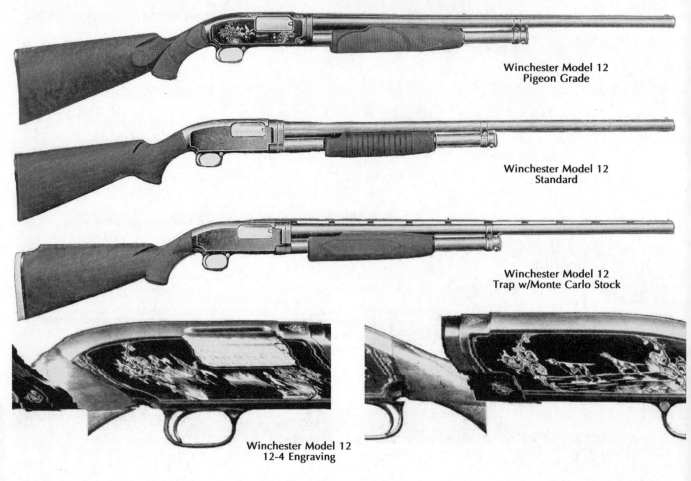

Winchester Model 12
Pigeon Grade

Winchester Model 12
Standard

Winchester Model 12
Trap w/Monte Carlo Stock

Winchester Model 12
12-4 Engraving

MODEL 12
FEATHERWEIGHT . . . . **NiB $688 Ex $577 Gd $555**
Same as Model 12 Standard w/plain barrel except has alloy trigger guard. Modified takedown w/redesigned magazine tube, cap and slide handle. 12 ga. only. Bbls.: 26-inch IC; 28-inch M or F; 30-inch F choke. Serial numbers with "F" prefix. Weight: About 6.75 lbs. Made from 1959 to 1962.

MODEL 12 FIELD GUN, 1972 TYPE . NiB $800 Ex $685 Gd $522
Same general specifications as Standard Model 12 but 12 ga. only, 26- 28- or 30-inch vent rib bbl., standard chokes. Engine-turned bolt and carrier. Hand-checkered stock/slide handle of semifancy walnut. Made from 1972 to 1975.

MODEL 12 HEAVY DUCK GUN
Same general specifications as Standard Grade except 12 ga. only chambered for 3-inch shells. 30- or 32-inch plain, solid or vent rib bbl. w/full choke only. Three round magazine. Checkered slide handle and pistol-grip walnut buttstock w/recoil pad. Weight: 8.5 to 8.75 lbs. Made from 1935 to 1963.
W/plain bbl. ` . . . . NiB $1366 Ex $890 Gd $644
W/solid rib (disc. 1959) . . . . NiB $1977 Ex $1288 Gd $876
W/vent. rib . . . . NiB $3288 Ex $2810 Gd $2466

MODEL 12 PIGEON GRADE
Deluxe versions of the regular Model 12 Standard or Field Gun, Duck Gun, Skeet Gun and Trap Gun made on special order. This grade has finer finish throughout, hand-smoothed action, engine-turned breech bolt and carrier, stock and extension slide handle of

high grade walnut, fancy checkering, stock dimensions to individual specifications. Engraving and carving available at extra cost ranging from about $135 to over $1000. Disc. 1965.

Field Gun, plain bbl.	NiB $4233	Ex $3698	Gd $3166
Field Gun, vent rib	NiB $2255	Ex $1987	Gd $1459
Skeet Gun, matted rib	NiB $2255	Ex $1987	Gd $1459
Skeet Gun, vent rib	NiB $3889	Ex $3350	Gd $3180
Skeet Gun, Cutts Compensator. . . .	NiB $1755	Ex $1398	Gd $1100
Trap Gun, matted rib	NiB $2233	Ex $1966	Gd $1399
Trap Gun, vent rib	NiB $2288	Ex $2190	Gd $2008
16 ga. (Field), add			100%
16 ga. (Skeet), add			100%
20 ga. (Field), add			175%
20 ga. (Skeet), add			175%
28 ga. (Skeet), add			550%

MODEL 12 RIOT GUN . . . . . . NiB $977 Ex $844 Gd $600
Same general specifications as plain barrel Model 12 Standard except has 20-inch cylinder bore bbl.,12 gauge only. Made from 1918 to 1963.

MODEL 12 SKEET GUN . . NiB $2200 Ex $1977 Gd $1488
Gauges: 12, 16, 20, 28. Five round tubular magazine. 26-inch matted rib bbl., SK choke. Weight: About 7.75 lbs., 12 ga.; 6.75 lbs., other gauges. Bradley red or ivory bead front sight. Winchester 94B middle sight. Checkered pistol-grip stock and extension slide handle. Disc. after WWII.

Winchester Model 21
Custom Grade

Winchester Model 21
Pigeon Grade

**MODEL 12 SKEET GUN,
CUTTS COMPENSATOR** . . . . NiB $1233 Ex $1000 Gd $766
Same general specifications as standard Model 12 Skeet Gun except has
plain bbl. fitted with Cutts Compensator, 26 inches overall. Disc. 1954.

MODEL 12 SKEET GUN, PLAIN-BARREL NiB $2099 Ex $1887 Gd $1650
Same general specifications as standard Model 12 Skeet except w/no rib.

MODEL 12 SKEET GUN, VENT RIB . NiB $4288 Ex $3760 Gd $3290
Same general specifications as standard Model 12 Skeet Gun except
has 26-inch bbl. with vent rib, 12 and 20 ga. Disc. in 1965.

MODEL 12 SKEET GUN, 1972 TYPE . . NiB $1288 Ex $909 Gd $663
Same gen. specifications as Standard Model 12 but 12 ga. only. 26-inch vent
rib bbl., SK choke. Engine-turned bolt and carrier. Hand-checkered skeet-
style stock and slide handle of choice walnut, recoil pad. Made from 1972
to 1975.

MODEL 12 STANDARD GR., MATTED RIB . NiB $835 Ex $579 Gd $443
Same general specifications as plain bbl. Model 12 Standard except
has solid raised matted rib. Disc. after World War II.

MODEL 12 STANDARD GR., VENT RIB NiB $866 Ex $571 Gd $400
Same general specifications as plain barrel Model 12 Standard except
has vent rib. 26.75- or 30-inch bbl.,12 ga. only. Disc. after World War II.

MODEL 12 STANDARD SLIDE-ACTION REPEATER
Hammerless. Takedown. Gauges: 12, 16, 20, 28. Six round tubular
magazine. Plain bbl. Lengths: 26- to 32-inches; choked F to Cyl. Weight:
About 7.5 lbs., 12 ga. 30-inch, 6.5 lbs. in other ga. with 28-inch bbl.
Plain pistol-grip stock, grooved slide handle. Made from 1912 to 1964.
12 ga., 28-inch bbl., Full choke . . . . NiB $870 Ex $733 Gd $534
16 ga. . . . . NiB $966 Ex $881 Gd $533
20 ga. . . . . NiB $1277 Ex $855 Gd $633
28 ga. . . . . NiB $5767 Ex $3488 Gd $2499

MODEL 12 SUPER PIGEON GRADE NiB $4329 Ex $3887 Gd $3176
Custom version of Model 12 with same general specifications as
standard models. 12 ga. only. 26-, 28- or 30-inch vent-rib bbl.,
any standard choke. Engraved receiver. Hand-smoothed and fitted
action. Full fancy walnut stock and forearm made to individual
order. Made from 1965 to 1972.

MODEL 12 TRAP GUN
Same general specifications as Standard Model 12 except has
straighter stock, checkered pistol grip and extension slide handle,
recoil pad, 30-inch matted-rib bbl., F choke, 12 ga. only. Disc. after
World War II; vent rib model disc. 1965.
Matted rib bbl. . . . . NiB $2210 Ex $1966 Gd $1544
With straight stock, vent rib NiB $2299 Ex $2178 Gd $1933
With Monte Carlo stock, vent rib NiB $2175 Ex $2000 Gd $1865

MODEL 12 TRAP GUN, 1972 TYPE. . NiB $1299 Ex $1077 Gd $669
Same general specifications as Standard Model 12 but 12 gauge only.
30-inch vent-rib bbl., F choke. Engine-turned bolt and carrier. Hand-
checkered trap-style stock (straight or Monte Carlo comb) and slide
handle of select walnut, recoil pad. Intro. in 1972. Disc.

MODEL 20 SINGLE-SHOT HAMMER GUN NiB $1577 Ex $1266 Gd $1008
Takedown. .410 bore. 2.5-inch chamber. 26-inch bbl., F choke.
Checkered pistol-grip stock and forearm. Weight: About 6 lbs. Made
from 1919 to 1924.

**ORIGINAL MODEL 21 DOUBLE-BARREL SHOTGUNS
(ORIGINAL PRODUCTION SERIES - 1930 to 1959)**
Hammerless. Boxlock. Automatic safety. Double triggers or selective
single trigger, selective or non-selective ejection (all postwar Model
21 shotguns have selective single trigger and selective ejection).
Gauges: 12, 16, 20, 28 and .410 bore. Bbls.: Raised matted rib or
vent rib; 26-, 28-, 30-, 32-inch, the latter in 12 ga. only; F, IM, M,
IC, SK chokes. Weight: 7.5 lbs., 12 ga. w/30-inch bbl.; about 6.5 lbs.
16 or 20 ga. w/28-inch bbl. Checkered pistol- or straight-grip stock,
regular or beavertail forend. Made from 1930 to 1959.
Standard Grade, 12 ga. . . . NiB $7344 Ex $6100 Gd $4350
Standard Grade, 16. Ga. . . . NiB $9000 Ex $5466 Gd $4000
Standard Grade, 20 ga. . NiB $10,008 Ex $6355 Gd $3988
**Tournament Grade, 12 ga.
(1933-34)**. . . . . .NiB $5733 Ex $5000 Gd $3889
**Tournament Grade, 16 ga.
(1933-34)**. . . . . .NiB $6893 Ex $6324 Gd $4388
**Tournament Grade, 20 ga.
(1933-34)**. . . . . .NiB $8244 Ex $6887 Gd $4632
Trap Grade, 12 ga. (1940-59) .NiB $5689 Ex $5000 Gd $4277
Trap Grade, 16 ga. (1940-59) .NiB $6044 Ex $4988 Gd $3776
Trap Grade, 20 ga. (1940-59) .NiB $7768 Ex $6322 Gd $3200
Skeet Grade, 12 ga. (1936-59) NiB $5463 Ex $4465 Gd $3100
Skeet Grade, 16 ga. (1936-59) NiB $6200 Ex $4988 Gd $3677
Skeet Grade, 20 ga. (1936-59) NiB $7100 Ex $5998 Gd $4325
Duck Gun, 12 ga., 3-inch (1940-52) NiB $5980 Ex $4966 Gd $3544
Magnum, 12 ga., 3-inch) (1953-59) NiB $5688 Ex $4765 Gd $3300
Magnum, 20 ga., 3-inch (1953-59) NiB $6900 Ex $5779 Gd $4200
**Cust. Deluxe grade,
12 ga. (1993-59)**. . . . . NiB $8634 Ex $6892 Gd $4855
**Cust. Deluxe grade,
16 ga., (1933-59)**. . . . . . NiB $10,339 Ex $8833 Gd $6450
**Cust. Deluxe grade,
20 ga. (1933-59)**. . . . . . . NiB $11,880 Ex $9893 Gd $6588
Cust. Deluxe grade, 28 ga. (1933-59) Very Rare NiB $30,000+
Cust. Deluxe grade, .410 (1933-59) Very Rare NiB $35,000+
*Fewer than 100 sm. bore models (28 ga. and .410) were built, which pre-
cludes accurate pricing, but projected values could exceed $30,000. Such
rare specimens should be authenticated by factory letter and/or independent
appraisals.

SHOTGUNS

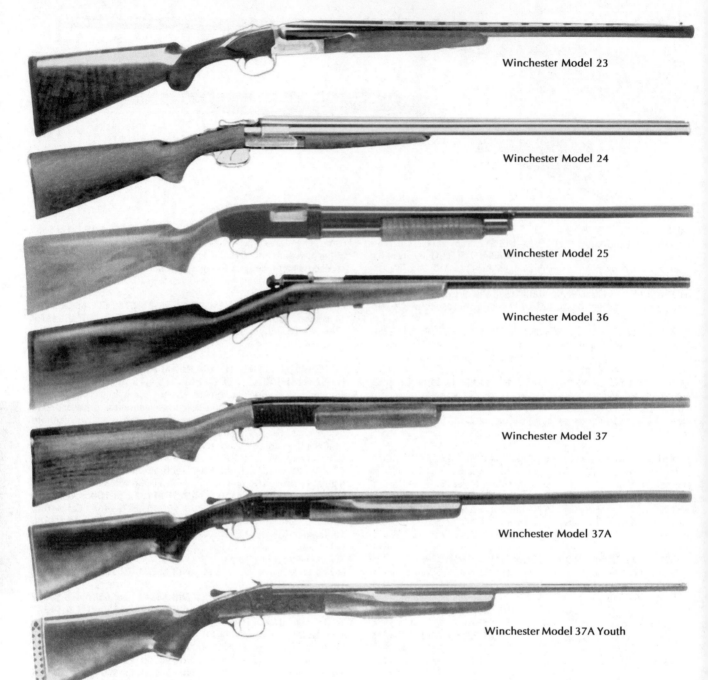

Winchester Model 23

Winchester Model 24

Winchester Model 25

Winchester Model 36

Winchester Model 37

Winchester Model 37A

Winchester Model 37A Youth

W/vent. rib,12 ga. models, add $900
W/vent. rib, 16 ga. models, add. $1825
W/vent. rib, 20 ga. models, add $1375
W/double triggers & extractors, deduct 30%
W/double triggers, selective ejection, deduct. 20%
W/Custom engraving:
No.1 pattern, add 25%
No. 2 pattern, add 35%
No. 3 pattern, add 50%
No. 4 pattern, add 35%
No. 5 pattern, add 65%
No. 6 pattern, add 75%

MODEL 21 CUSTOM, PIGEON, GRAND AMERICAN (CUSTOM SHOP SERIES - PRODUCTION 1959 TO 1981)

Since 1959 the Model 21 has been offered through the Custom Shop in deluxe models. (Custom, Pigeon, Grand American) on special order. General specifications same as for Model 21 standard models except these custom guns have full fancy American walnut stock and forearm with fancy checkering, finely polished and hand-smoothed working parts, etc.; engraving inlays, carved stocks and other extras are available at additional cost. Made 1959 to 1981.
Custom grade, 12 ga.. . . . . .NiB $11,980 Ex $9876 Gd $6759
Custom grade, 16 ga.. . . . . . . .NiB $17,544 Ex $13,977 Gd $10,655
Custom grade, 20 ga.. . . . . NiB $14,677 Ex $11,877 Gd $8321

Winchester Model 40 Skeet

Winchester Model 41 Deluxe

Pigeon grade, 12 ga.	NiB $17,889	Ex $14,670	Gd $10,300
Pigeon grade, 16 ga.	NiB $22,889	Ex $18,987	Gd $13,770
Pigeon grade, 20 ga.	NiB $21,800	Ex $19,880	Gd $14,800
Grand American, 12 ga.	NiB $25,700	Ex $19,900	Gd $14,600
Grand American, 16 ga.	NiB $39,600	Ex $31,877	Gd $22,955
Grand American, 20 ga.	NiB $30,888	Ex $27,888	Gd $20,556
Grand American 3-barrel Set	NiB $42,750	Ex $35,799	Gd $25,799

Small Bore Models

28 ga. and .410 (fewer than 20 made), ... $35,000+

*Fewer than 20 Small Bore models (28 ga. and .410) were built during this period, which precludes accurate pricing, but projected values could exceed $35,000. Such rare specimens should be authenticated by factory letter and/or independent appraisals. For Custom Shop Engraving from this period:

#1 Pattern, add	10%
#2 Pattern, add	15%
#3 Pattern, add	25%
#4 Pattern, add	35%
#5 Pattern, add	45%
#6 Pattern, add	50%

MODEL 21 U.S.R.A. CUSTOM SERIES (CUSTOM SHOP PRODUCTION 1982 TO DATE)

Individual model designations for the Model 21 (made from 1931 to 1982) were changed when U. S. Repeating Arms Company assumed production. The new model nomenclature for the Custom/Built catagory, includes: Standard Custom, Special Custom and Grand American — all of which are available on special order through the Custom Shop. General specifications remained the same on these consolidated model variations and included the addition of a Small Bore 2-Barrel Set (28/.410) and a 3-Barrel Set (20/28/.410). Made 1982 to date.

Standard custom model	NiB $6988	Ex $5570	Gd $4000
Special Custom model	NiB $8000	Ex $6500	Gd $4666
Grand American model	NiB $14,880	Ex $12,980	Gd $9660
Grand American model, 2-bb. set	NiB $48,900	Ex $38,790	Gd $26,998
Grand American, 3-bbl. set	NiB $72,877	Ex $59,988	Gd $26,800

The values shown above represent the basic model in each catagory. Since many customers took advantage of the custom built options, individual gun appointments vary and values will need to be adjusted accordingly. For this reason, individual appraisals should be obtained on all subject firearms.

MODEL 23 SIDE-BY-SIDE SHOTGUN

Boxlock. Single trigger. Automatic safety. Gauges: 12, 20, 28, .410. Bbls.: 25.5-, 26-, 28-inch with fixed chokes or Winchoke tubes.

Weight: 5.88 to 7 lbs. Checkered American walnut buttstock and forend. Made in 1979 for Olin at its Olin-Kodensha facility, Japan.

Classic 23 (gold inlay, engraved)	NiB $2779	Ex $2466	Gd $2365
Custom 23 (plain receiver, Winchoke)	NiB $1477	Ex $1155	Gd $966
Heavy Duck 23, Standard	NiB $2768	Ex $2398	Gd $2077
Lightweight 23, Classic	NiB $2188	Ex $1808	Gd $1266
Light Duck 23, Standard	NiB $2987	Ex $2665	Gd $2240
Light Duck 23, 12 ga. Golden Quail	NiB $2877	Ex $2549	Gd $2266
Light Duck 23, .410 Golden Quail	NiB $4577	Ex $4328	Gd $3972
Custom Set 23, 20 & 28 ga.	NiB $6988	Ex $5100	Gd $3766

MODEL 24 HAMMERLESS DOUBLE

Boxlock. Double triggers. Plain extractors. Auto safety. Gauges: 12, 16, 20. Bbls.: 26-inch IC/M; 28-inch M/F (also IC/M in 12 ga. only); 30-inch M and F in 12 ga. only. Weight: About 7.5 lbs., 12 ga. Metal bead front sight. Plain pistol-grip stock, semi-beavertail forearm. Made from 1939 to 1957.

12 ga. model	NiB $966	Ex $733	Gd $544
16 ga. model	NiB $1088	Ex $800	Gd $623
20 ga. model	NiB $1221	Ex $945	Gd $711

MODEL 25 RIOT GUN

MODEL 25 RIOT GUN . . . . . . NiB $677 Ex $455 Gd $390

Same as Model 25 Standard except has 20-inch cylinder bore bbl., 12 ga. only. Made from 1949 to 1955.

MODEL 25 7550

MODEL 25 7550 . . . . Ex $404 Gd $358

Hammerless. Solid frame. 12 ga. only. Four round tubular magazine. 28-in. Plain bbl.; IC, M or F choke. Weight: About 7.5 lbs. Metal bead front sight. Plain pistol-grip stock, grooved slide handle. Made from 1949 to 1955.

MODEL 36 SINGLE-SHOT

BOLT ACTION . . . . NiB $1893 Ex $1688 Gd $1477

Takedown. Uses 9mm Short or Long shot or ball cartridges interchangeably. 18-inch bbl. Plain stock. Weight: About 3 lbs. Made from 1920 to 1927.

MODEL 37 SINGLE-SHOT SHOTGUN

Semi-hammerless. Auto ejection. Takedown. Gauges: 12, 16, 20, 28, .410. Bbl. lengths: 28-, 30-, 32-inch in all gauges except .410; 26- or 28-inch in .410; all barrels plain with F choke. Weight: About 6.5 pounds, 12 ga. Made from 1937 to 1963.

12, 16, 20 ga. models	NiB $559	Ex $438	Gd $315
Youth model (20 ga. w/red dot indicator)	NiB $559	Ex $438	Gd $315
.410 model	NiB $769	Ex $588	Gd $437
28 ga. model ("Red Letter" version)	NiB $2687	Ex $2531	Gd $2033
Other "Red Letter" models, add			20%
W/32-inch bbl., add			15%

SHOTGUNS

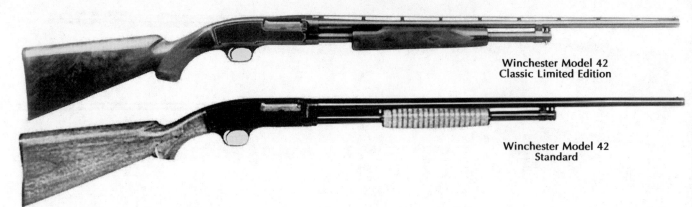

**Winchester Model 42
Classic Limited Edition**

**Winchester Model 42
Standard**

MODEL 37A SINGLE-SHOT SHOTGUN
Similar to Model 370 except has engraved receiver and gold trigger, checkered pistol-grip stock, fluted forearm; 16 ga. available with 30-inch bbl. only. Made from 1973 to 1980.

12, 16 or 20 ga. models	NiB $579	Ex $300	Gd $219
28 ga. model	NiB $2590	Ex $2331	Gd $2268
.410 model	NiB $754	Ex $559	Gd $366
W/32-inch bbl., add			$50

MODEL 37A YOUTH . . . . NiB $566 Ex $397 Gd $244
Similar to Model 370 Youth except has engraved receiver and gold trigger, checkered pistol-grip stock, fluted forearm. Made 1973 to 1980.

MODEL 40 STANDARD AUTOLOADER NiB $977 Ex $721 Gd $533
Streamlined receiver. Hammerless. Takedown. 12 ga. only. Four round tubular magazine. 28- or 30-inch bbl.; M or F choke. Weight: About 8 lbs. Bead sight on ramp. Plain pistol-grip stock, semi-beavertail forearm. Made from 1940 to 1941.

MODEL 40 SKEET GUN . . . . NiB $1188 Ex $966 Gd $700
Same general specifications as Model 40 Standard except has 24-inch plain bbl. w/Cutts Compensator and screw-in choke tube, checkered forearm and pistol grip, grip cap. Made 1940 to 1941.

MODEL 41 SINGLE-SHOT BOLT ACTION
Takedown. .410 bore. 2.5-inch chamber (chambered for 3-inch shells after 1932). 24-inch bbl., F choke. Plain straight stock standard. Also made in deluxe version. Made from 1920 to 1934.

Standard model	NiB $800	Ex $618	Gd $509
Deluxe model	NiB $954	Ex $732	Gd $600

MODEL 42 STANDARD GRADE
Hammerless. Takedown. .410 bore (3- or 2.5-inch shell). Tubular magazine holds five 3-inch or six 2.5-inch shells. 26- or 28-inch plain or solid-rib bbl.; cylinder bore, M or F choke. Weight: 5.8 to 6.5 lbs. Plain pistol-grip stock; grooved slide handle. Made from 1933 to 1963.

W/plain bbl.	NiB $2675	Ex $2143	Gd $1609
Model 42 Standard w/solid rib	NiB $3750	Ex $3396	Gd $3184

MODEL 42 CLASSIC LTD. Edition NiB $1886 Ex $1599 Gd $1179
Gauge: .410 with 2.75-inch chamber. Bbl.: 26-inch vent rib; F choke. Weight: 7 lbs. Checkered walnut buttstock and forend. Engraved blue with gold inlays. Limited production of 850. Made from 1993.

MODEL 42 DELUXE NiB $22,700 Ex $19,745 Gd $17,998
Same general specifications as the Model 42 Trap Grade except available w/vent rib after 1955. Finer finish throughout w/hand-smoothed action, engine-turned breech bolt and carrier, stock and extension slide handle of high grade walnut, fancy checkering, stock dimensions to individual specifications. Engraving and carving were offered at extra cost. Made 1940-63. Note: Exercise caution on VR models not marked "DELUXE" on the bottom of the receiver. A factory letter will insure that the rib was installed during the initial manufacturing process. Unfortunately, factory authentication is not always possible due to missing or destroyed records. To further complicate this matter, not all VR ribs were installed by Winchester. From 1955-63, both Deluxe and Skeet Grade models were available with Simmons style ribs. After-market rib installations are common.

MODEL 42 PIGEON GRADE
This higher-grade designation is similar to the Deluxe grade and is available in all configurations. May be identified by engraved Pigeon located at the base of the magazine tube. Most production occurred in the late 1940's. *NOTE: To determine the value of any Model 42 Pigeon Grade, add 50 % to value listed under the specified Model 42 configuration.*

MODEL 42 SKEET GUN
Same general specifications as Model 42 Standard except has checkered straight or pistol-grip stock and extension slide handle, 26- or 28-inch plain, solid-rib or vent-rib bbl. May be choked F., Mod., Imp. Cyl. or Skeet. Note: Some Model 42 Skeet Guns are chambered for 2.5-inch shells only. Made from 1933 to 1963.

W/plain bbl.	NiB $6277	Ex $4500	Gd $3769
W/solid rib	NiB $6277	Ex $4500	Gd $3769
W/vent. rib	NiB $6833	Ex $5971	Gd $4948
W/ 2.5-inch chamber, add			35%

MODEL 42 TRAP GRADE
This higher grade designation was available in both field and skeet configurations and is fitted w/deluxe wood w/trap grade checkering pattern and marked "TRAP" on bottom of receiver. Made 1934 to 1939. Superseded by the Deluxe model in 1940.

W/plain bbl.	NiB $27,977	Ex $24,770	Gd $22,665
W/solid rib	NiB $27,977	Ex $24,770	Gd $22,665
W/vent. rib	NiB $27,855	Ex $25,693	Gd $23,449

MODEL 50 FIELD GUN, VENT RIB NiB $766 Ex $541 Gd $396
Same as Model 50 Standard except has vent rib.

MODEL 50 SKEET GUN . . NiB $1422 Ex $1269 Gd $1031
Same as Model 50 Standard except has 26-inch vent-rib bbl. with SK choke, skeet-style stock of select walnut.

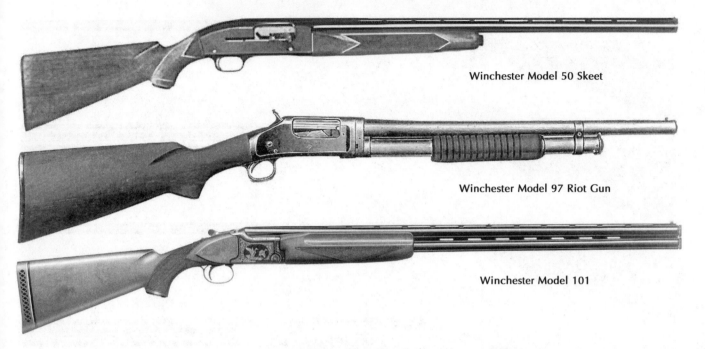

Winchester Model 50 Skeet

Winchester Model 97 Riot Gun

Winchester Model 101

MODEL 50 STANDARD GRADE NiB $779 Ex $500 Gd $388
Non-recoiling bbl. and independent chamber. Gauges: 12 and 20. Two round tubular magazine. Bbl.: 12 ga. — 26-, 28-, 30-inch; 20 ga. — 26-, 28-inch; IC, SK, M, F choke. Checkered pistol-grip stock and forearm. Weight: About 7.75 lbs. Made from 1954 to 1961.

MODEL 50 TRAP GUN. . . NiB $1466 Ex $1284 Gd $1066
Same as Model 50 Standard except 12 ga. only, has 30-inch vent-rib bbl. with F choke, Monte Carlo stock of select walnut.

MODEL 59 AUTO-LOADING SHOTGUN NiB $878 Ex $655 Gd $555
Gauge: 12. Magazine holds two rounds. Alloy receiver. Win-Lite steel and fiberglass bbl.: 26-inch IC, 28-inch M or F choke, 30-inch F choke; also furnished with 26-inch bbl. with Versalite choke (interchangeable F, M, IC tubes; one supplied with gun). Weight: About 6.5 lbs. Checkered pistol-grip stock and forearm. Made 1959 to 1965.

MODEL 1897 BUSH GUN
Takedown or solid frame. Same general specifications as standard Model 97 except w/26-inch cylinder bore bbl. Made 1897 to 1931.
W/solid frame. . . . . NiB $995 Ex $700 Gd $554
Takedown model . . . . NiB $1299 Ex $1056 Gd $800

MODEL 1897 RIOT GUN
Takedown or solid frame. Same general specifications as standard Model 97 except 12 ga. only, 20-inch cylinder bore bbl. Made from 1898 to 1935.
W/solid frame. . . . . NiB $1544 Ex $1187 Gd $900
Takedown model . . . . NiB $1390 Ex $1055 Gd $773

MODEL 1897 TRAP, TOURNAMENT & PIGEON GRADES
These higher grade models offer higher overall quality than the standard grade. Made from 1897 to 1939.
Standard Trap grade . . . . . NiB $2600 Ex $2208 Gd $1188
Special Trap grade . . . . . . NiB $1794 Ex $1566 Gd $1180
Tournament grade
(Black Diamond) . . . . NiB $2971 Ex $2387 Gd $1698
Pigeon grade . . . . NiB $11,000 Ex $9533 Gd $3000

MODEL 1897 TRENCH GUN NiB $4800 Ex $3693 Gd $2138
Solid frame. Same as Model 1897 Riot Gun except has handguard and
is equipped with a bayonet. World War I government issue, from 1917 to 1918.
w/military markings, add 20%

MODEL 1897 SLIDE-ACTION REPEATER
Standard Grade. Takedown or solid frame. Gauges: 12 and 16. Five-round tubular magazine. Bbl.: Plain; 26 to 32 inches, the latter in 12 ga. only; choked F to Cyl. Weight: About 7.75 lbs. (12 ga. w/28-inch barrel). Plain pistol-grip stock, grooved slide handle. Made from 1897 to 1957.
12 ga. w/solid frame. . . . . . . NiB $1110 Ex $855 Gd $675
16 ga. w/solid frame. . . . . . . NiB $1110 Ex $855 Gd $675
12 ga., takedown model . . . NiB $1356 Ex $1108 Gd $888
16 ga., takedown model . . . NiB $1356 Ex $1108 Gd $888

NOTE: All Winchester Model 101s are mfd. for Olin Corp. at its Olin-Kodensha facility in Tochigi, Japan. Production for Olin Corp. stopped in Nov. 1987. Importation of Model 101s was continued by Classic Doubles under that logo until 1990. See separate heading for additional data.

MODEL 101 DIAMOND
GRADE TARGET. . . . . . . NiB $1978 Ex $1596 Gd $1180
Similar to Model 101 Standard except silvered frame and Winchoke interchangeable choke tubes. Made from 1981 to 1990.

MODEL 101 O/U FIELD GUN
Boxlock. Engraved receiver. Auto ejectors. Single selective trigger. Combination bbl. selector and safety. Gauges: 12 and 28, 2.75-inch chambers; 20 and .410, 3-inch chambers. Vent rib bbls.: 30- (12 ga. only) and 26.5-inch, IC/M. Weight: 6.25 to 7.75 lbs. depending on gauge and bbl. length. Hand-checkered French walnut and forearm. Made from 1963 to 1981. Gauges other than 12 introduced 1966.
12 and 20 ga.. . . . . NiB $1099 Ex $882 Gd $723
28 and .410 ga. . . . . NiB $1622 Ex $1244 Gd $977
12 and 20 ga. mag. . . . . . . NiB $1288 Ex $1077 Gd $766

SHOTGUNS

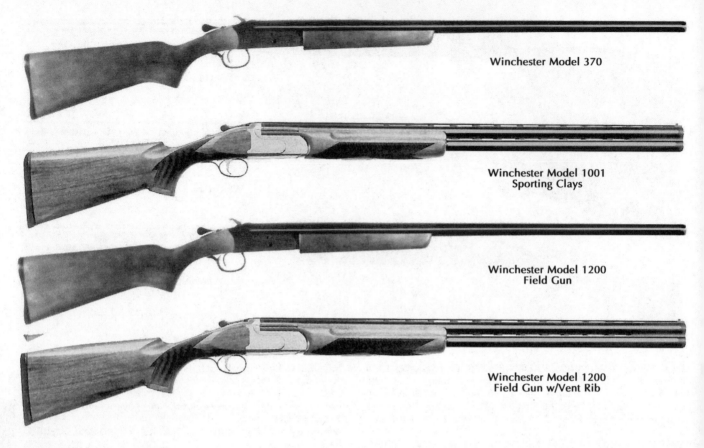

Winchester Model 370

Winchester Model 1001
Sporting Clays

Winchester Model 1200
Field Gun

Winchester Model 1200
Field Gun w/Vent Rib

MODEL 101 QUAIL SPECIAL
Same specifications as small-frame Model 101 except in 28 and .410 ga. with 3-inch chambers. 25.5-inch bbls. with choke tubes (28 ga.) or M/F chokes (.410). Imported from Japan in 1984 to 1987.

12 ga. model	NiB $3155	Ex $2926	Gd $2554
20 ga.	NiB $3599	Ex $3466	Gd $3200
28 ga. model	NiB $5799	Ex $4933	Gd $4200
.410 model	NiB $4733	Ex $4122	Gd $3888

MODEL 101 SHOTGUN/RIFLE
COMBINATION GUN. . . . NiB $2983 Ex $2777 Gd $2369
12-ga. Winchoke bbl. on top and rifle bbl. chambered for .30-06 on bottom (over/under). 25-inch bbls. Engraved receiver. Hand checkered walnut stock and forend. Weight: 8.5 lbs. Mfd. for Olin Corp. in Japan.

MODEL 370
SINGLE-SHOT SHOTGUN . . . . NiB $245 Ex $200 Gd $99
Visible hammer. Auto ejector. Takedown. Gauges: 12, 16, 20, 28, .410. 2.75-inch chambers in 16 and 28 ga., 3-inch in other ga. Bbls.: 12 ga., 30-, 32- or 36-inch,16 ga; 30- or 32-inch; 20 and 28 ga., 28-inch; .410 bore, 26-inch, all F choke. Weight: 5.5-6.25 lbs. Plain pistol-grip stock and forearm. Made from 1968 to 1973.

MODEL 370 YOUTH MODEL
Same as standard Model 370 except has 26-inch bbl. and 12.5-inch stock with recoil pad; 20 gauge with IM choke, .410 bore with F choke. Made from 1968 to 1973.

12, 16 or 20 ga. models	NiB $244	Ex $190	Gd $121
20 ga. model	NiB $300	Ex $221	Gd $165
.410 model	NiB $355	Ex $220	Gd $175

MODEL 1001 O/U SHOTGUN

Boxlock. 12 ga., 2.75- or 3-inch chambers. Bbls.: 28- or 30-inch vent rib; WinPlus choke tubes. Weight: 7-7.75 lbs. Checkered walnut buttstock and forend. Blued finish with scroll engraved receiver. Made from 1993 to 1998.
Field model

(28-inch bbl., 3-inch)	NiB $1133	Ex $978	Gd $726
Sporting Clays model	NiB $1166	Ex $1044	Gd $863
Sporting Clays Lite model . . .	NiB $1187	Ex $990	Gd $734

MODEL 1200
DEER GUN. . . . . NiB $398 Ex $221 Gd $155
Same as standard Model 1200, except has special 22-inch bbl. with rifle-type sights, for rifled slug or buckshot; 12 ga. only. Weight: 6.5 lbs. Made from 1965 to 1974.

MODEL 1200 DEFENDER SERIES
SLIDE-ACTION SECURITY SHOTGUNS
Hammerless. 12 ga. w/3-inch chamber. 18-inch bbl. w/cylinder bore and metal front bead or rifle sights. Four- or 7-round magazine. Weight: 5.5 to 6.75 lbs. 25.6 inches (PG Model) or 38.6 inches overall. Matte blue finish. Synthetic pistol grip or walnut finished hardwood buttstock w/grooved synthetic or hardwood slide handle. NOTE: Even though the 1200 series was introduced in 1964 and was supplanted by the Model 1300 in 1978, the Security series (including the Defender model) was marketed under 1200 series alpha-numeric product codes (G1200DM2R) until 1989. In 1990, the same Defender model was marketed under a 4-digit code (7715) and was then advertised in the 1300 series.

Winchester Model 1300
Deer Series — Black Shadow
Synthetic Stock

Winchester Model 1300
Deer Series — Advantage
Full Camo Pattern

Winchester Model 1300
Defender Series — Stainless
Marine Synthetic Stock

Defender
w/hardwood stock,bead sight . NiB $325 Ex $233 Gd $188
Defender
W/hardwood stock, rifle sights NiB $325 Ex $233 Gd $188
Defender model w/pistol-grip stockNiB $325 Ex $233 Gd $188
Defender Combo model
W/extra 28-inch plain bbl. . . . NiB $345 Ex $290 Gd $239
Defender Combo model
W/extra 28-inch vent rib bbl. . NiB $425 Ex $344 Gd $239

MODEL 1200 MAGNUM FIELD GUN
Same as standard Model 1200 except chambered for 3-inch 12 and 20 ga. magnum shells; plain or vent-rib bbl., 28- or 30-inch, F choke. Weight: 7.38 to 7.88 lbs. Made from 1964 to 1983.
W/plain bbl. . . . . NiB $325 Ex $240 Gd $179
W/vent. rib bbl. . . . . NiB $350 Ex $265 Gd $190
W/recoil reduction system, add. $100

MODEL 1200 RANGER
SLIDE-ACTION SHOTGUN. . . NiB $400 Ex $285 Gd $195
Hammerless. 12 and 20 ga.; 3-inch chambers. Walnut finished hardwood stock, ribbed forearm. 28-inch vent-rib bbl.; Winchoke system. Weight: 7.25 lbs. Made from 1982 to 1990 by U. S. Repeating Arms.

MODEL 1200 RANGER YOUTH
SLIDE-ACTION SHOTGUN. . . NiB $400 Ex $285 Gd $195
Same general specifications as standard Ranger Slide-Action except chambered for 20 ga. only, has Four round magazine, recoil pad on buttstock, weight: 6.5 lbs. Mfd. by U. S. Repeating Arms.

MODEL 1200 RANGER SLIDE-ACTION FIELD GUN
Front-locking rotary bolt. Takedown. Four round magazine. Gauges: 12, 16, 20 (2.75-inch chamber). Bbl.: Plain or vent rib; 26-, 28-, 30-inch; IC, M, F choke or with Winchoke (interchangeable tubes IC-M-F). Weight: 6.5 to 7.25 lbs. Checkered pistol-grip stock and fore arm (slide handle), recoil pad; also avail. 1966 to 1970 w/

Winchester recoil reduction system (Cycolac stock). Made from 1964 to 1983.
W/plain bbl. . . . . NiB $400 Ex $285 Gd $195
W/vent. rib bbl. . . . . NiB $420 Ex $305 Gd $217
W/recoil reduction system, add $100
W/Winchoke, add $50

MODEL 1200 STAINLESS MARINE SERIES SLIDE-ACTION SECURITY SHOTGUN
Similar to Model 1200 Defender except w/6-round magazine. 18-inch bbl. of ordnance stainless steel w/cylinder bore and rifle sights. Weight: 7 lbs. Bright chrome finish. Synthetic pistol grip or walnut finished hardwood buttstock w/grooved synthetic or hardwood slide handle.Made from 1984 to 1990.
W/hardwood stock . . . . NiB $325 Ex $235 Gd $175
W/pistol-grip stock . . . . NiB $325 Ex $235 Gd $175

MODEL 1200 STAINLESS POLICE SERIES SLIDE-ACTION SECURITY SHOTGUN
Similar to Model 1200 Defender except w/6-round magazine. 18-inch bbl. of ordnance stainless steel w/cylinder bore and rifle sights. Weight: 7 lbs. Matte chrome finish. Synthetic pistol grip or walnut- finished hardwood buttstock w/grooved synthetic or hardwood slide handle.Made from 1984-90.
Police model w/hardwood stockNiB $255 Ex $202 Gd $125
Police model w/pistol grip stockNiB $255 Ex $202 Gd $125

MODEL 1200 TRAP GUN
Same as standard Model 1200 except 12 gauge only. Has 2-round magazine, 30-inch vent-rib bbl., Full choke or 28-inch with Winchoke. Semi-fancy walnut stock, straight Made from 1965-73. Also available 1966 to 1970 w/Winchester recoil reduction system.
W/straight trap stock. . . . . . . NiB $425 Ex $260 Gd $180
W/Monte Carlo stock . . . . NiB $425 Ex $260 Gd $180
W/Recoil reduction system, add $100
W/Winchoke, add $50

Winchester Model 1300
Lady Defender — Synthetic Full Stock

Winchester Model 1300
Lady Defender — Synthetic Pistol Grip Stock

Winchester Model 1300
Defender 5-Shot Combo

Winchester Model 1300
Turkey Gun

Winchester Model 1300
XTR w/Winchoke

Winchester Model 1300
Magnum Waterfowl

MODEL 1200 RANGER
COMBINATION SHOTGUN . . NiB $440 Ex $300 Gd $217
Same as Ranger Deer combination except has one 28-inch vent-rib bbl. with M choke and one 18-inch Police Cyl. bore bbl. Made 1987 to 1990.

MODEL 1200 SKEET GUN . . . NiB $450 Ex $310 Gd $225
Same as standard Model 1200 except 12 and 20 ga. only; has 2-round magazine, specially tuned trigger, 26-inch vent-rib bbl. SK choke, semi-fancy walnut stock and forearm. Weight: 7.25 to 7.5 lbs. Made 1965 to 1973. Also avail. 1966 to 1970 with Winchester recoil reduction system (add $50 to value).

MODEL 1300 CAMOPACK . . . NiB $465 Ex $390 Gd $279
Gauge: 12.3-inch Magnum. Four round magazine. Bbls.: 30-and 22-inch with Winchoke system. Weight: 7 lbs. Laminated stock with Win-Cam camouflage green, cut checkering, recoil pad, swivels and sling. Made from 1987-88.

MODEL 1300 DEER SERIES
Similar to standard Model 1300 except 12 or 20 ga. only w/special 22-inch cyl. bore or rifled bbl. and rifle-type sights. Weight: 6.5 lbs. Checkered walnut or synthetic stock w/satin walnut, black or Advantage Full Camo Pattern finish. Matte blue or full-camo metal finish. Made from 1994 to 2006.
W/walnut stock (intro. 1994). . NiB $425 Ex $360 Gd $265
Black Shadow Deer model
w/synthetic stock (intro. 1994) NiB $400 Ex $298 Gd $220
Advantage Camo model (1995-98)NiB $445 Ex $377 Gd $280
Deer Combo
Deer Combo w/22- and
28-inch bbls. (1994-98) . . . . . . .NiB $515 Ex $455 Gd $390
W/rifled bbl. (intro. 1996), add $75

MODEL 1300 DEFENDER SERIES
Gauges: 12 or 20 ga. 18- 24- 28-inch vent rib bbl. w/3-inch chamber. Four-, 7- or 8- round magazine. Weight: 5.6 to 7.4 lbs. Blued, chrome or matte stainless finish. Wood or synthetic stock. Made from 1985 to 2006.
Combo model . . . . NiB $490 Ex $375 Gd $277
Hardwood stock model. . . . . . NiB $365 Ex $299 Gd $200
Synthetic pistol-grip model . . . NiB $270 Ex $283 Gd $203
Synthetic stock model. . . . . . . NiB $335 Ex $279 Gd $225
Lady Defender synthetic
stock (made 1996) . . . . NiB $320 Ex $255 Gd $210
Lady Defender synthetic
Pistol-grip (made 1996). . . . . . NiB $320 Ex $255 Gd $210
Stainless marine
model w/synthetic stock . . . . . NiB $555 Ex $435 Gd $290

MODEL 1300 DELUXE SLIDE-ACTION
Gauges: 12 and 20 w/3-inch chamber. Four round magazine. Bbl.:22, 26 or 28 inch vent rib bbl. w/Winchoke tubes. Weight: 6.5 lbs. Checkered walnut buttstock and forend w/high luster finish. Polished blue metal finish with roll-engraved receiver. Made from 1984 to 2006.
Model 1300 Deluxe
w/high gloss finish . . . . NiB $500 Ex $390 Gd $292
Model 1300 Ladies/Youth model
w/22-inch bbl., (disc. 1992) . . NiB $455 Ex $360 Gd $258

MODEL 1300 FEATHERWEIGHT SLIDE-ACTION SHOTGUN
Hammerless. Takedown. Four round magazine. Gauges: 12 and 20 (3-inch chambers). Bbls: 22, 26 or 28 inches w/plain or vent rib w/ Winchoke tubes. Weight: 6.38 to 7 lbs. Checkered walnut buttstock, grooved slide handle. Made from 1978 to 1994.
W/plain bbl. . . . . NiB $400 Ex $365 Gd $290
W/vent. rib . . . . NiB $400 Ex $365 Gd $290
XTR model . . . . NiB $400 Ex $365 Gd $290

MODEL 1300 RANGER SERIES
Gauges: 12 or 20 ga. w/3-inch chamber. Five round magazine. 22-(Rifled), 26- or 28-inch vent-rib bbl. w/Winchoke tubes. Weight: 7.25 lbs. Blued finish. Walnut-finished hardwood buttstock and forend. Made from 1984 to 2006.
Standard model . . . . NiB $377 Ex $366 Gd $270
Combo model . . . . NiB $465 Ex $399 Gd $280
Ranger Deer combo
(D&T w/rings & bases) . . . . . . NiB $455 Ex $380 Gd $265
Ranger Ladies/Youth. . . . . NiB $366 Ex $255 Gd $190

MODEL 1300 SLIDE-ACTION FIELD GUN
Takedown w/front-locking rotary bolt. Gauges: 12, 20 w/3-inch chamber. Four round magazine. Bbl.: Vent rib; 26-, 28-, 30-inch w/ Win-choke tubes IC-M-F). Weight: 7.25 lbs. Checkered walnut or synthetic stock w/standard, black or Advantage Full Camo Pattern finish. Matte blue or full-camo metal finish. Made from 1994 to 2006.
Standard Field w/walnut stock NiB $445 Ex $320 Gd $266
Black Shadow w/black
synthetic stock . . . . NiB $365 Ex $275 Gd $200
Advantage Camo model . . . . . NiB $455 Ex $375 Gd $290

MODEL 1300 SLUG HUNTER SERIES
Similar to standard Model 1300 except chambered 12 ga. only w/ special 22-inch smoothbore w/sabot-rifled choke tube or fully rifled bbl. w/rifle-type sights. Weight: 6.5 lbs. Checkered walnut, hardwood or laminated stock w/satin walnut or WinTuff finish. Matte blue metal finish. Made from 1988 to 1994.
W/hardwood stock . . . . NiB $465 Ex $365 Gd $250
W/laminated stock . . . . NiB $515 Ex $400 Gd $290
W/walnut stock . . . . NiB $500 Ex $380 Gd $265
Whitetails Unlimited model
w/beavertail forend . . . . NiB $475 Ex $396 Gd $300
W/sabot-rifled choke tubes, add $50

MODEL 1300 TURKEY SERIES
Gauges: 12 or 20 ga. 22-inch bbl. w/3-inch chamber. Four round magazine. 43 inches overall. Weight: 6.4 to 6.75 lbs. Buttstock and magazine cap, sling studs w/Cordura sling. Drilled and tapped to accept scope base. Checkered walnut, synthetic or laminated wood stock w/low luster finish. Matte blue or full camo finish. Made from 1985 to 2006.
W/Advantage camo . . . . .NiB $390 Ex $285 Gd $216
W/Realtree All-Purpose camo . . . . . . NiB $488 Ex $369 Gd $275
W/Realtre Gray All-Purpose camo NiB $500 Ex $405 Gd $325
W/Realtree All-Purpose
camo (matte finish). . . . . .NiB $525 Ex $420 Gd $355
W/Black Shadow synthetic stock. .NiB $355 Ex $285 Gd $190
W/Win-Cam green laminate stock . . . .NiB $445 Ex $365 Gd $225
Win-Cam combo
(22- or 30-inch bbl.). . . . . .NiB $465 Ex $420 Gd $350
Win-Cam NWTF model
(22- or 30-inch bbl.). . . . . .NiB $525 Ex $375 Gd $285
Win-Cam Youth/Ladies
model (20 ga.). . . . . .NiB $565 Ex $435 Gd $310
Win-Tuf model w/brown
laminated wood stock. . . . . .NiB $490 Ex $388 Gd $265

MODEL 1300 WATERFOWL SLIDE-ACTION SHOTGUN
Similar to 1300 Standard model except has 28- or 30-inch vent rib bbl. w/Winchoke tubes. Weight: 7 lbs. Matte blue metal finish. Checkered walnut finished hardwood or brown laminated Win-Tuffwood stock w/camo sling, swivels and recoil pad. Made from 1984 to 1992.
W/hardwood stock. . . . . NiB $435 Ex $300 Gd $220
W/laminated stock. . . . . NiB $435 Ex $300 Gd $220

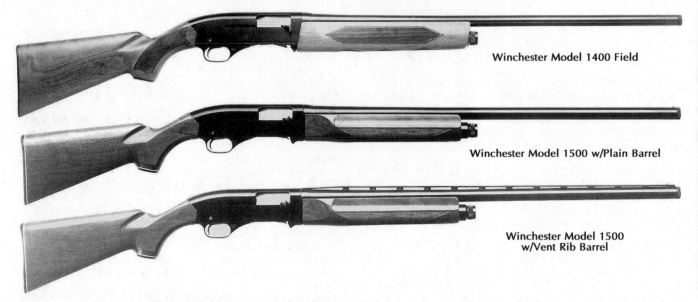

Winchester Model 1400 Field

Winchester Model 1500 w/Plain Barrel

Winchester Model 1500
w/Vent Rib Barrel

MODEL 1300 XTR SLIDE-ACTION NiB $550 Ex $455 Gd $3209
Hammerless. Takedown. Four shot magazine. Gauges: 12 and 20 (3-inch chambers). Bbl.: Plain or vent rib; 28-inch bbls.; Winchoke (interchangeable tubes IC-M-F). Weight: About 7 lbs. Disc. 2006.

MODEL 1400 AUTOMATIC FIELD GUN
Gas-operated. Front-locking rotary bolt. Takedown. Two round magazine. Gauges: 12, 16, 20 (2.75-inch chamber). Bbl.: Plain or vent rib; 26-, 28-, 30-inch; IC, M, F choke, or with Winchoke (interchangeable tubes IC-M-F). Weight: 6.5 to 7.25 lbs. Checkered pistol-grip stock and forearm, recoil pad, also available with Winchester recoil reduction system (Cycolac stock). Made from 1964 to 1968.

W/plain bbl. . . . . NiB $355 Ex $244 Gd $190
W/vent. rib bbl. . . . . NiB $390 Ex $244 Gd $196
W/recoil reduction system, add. $125
W/Winchoke, add $50

MODEL 1400 DEER GUN . . . . NiB $369 Ex $255 Gd $190
Same as standard Model 1400 except has special 22-inch bbl. with rifle-type sights, for rifle slug or buckshot; 12 ga. only. Weight: 6.25 lbs. Made from 1965 to 1968.

MODEL 1400
MARK II DEER GUN . . . . NiB $460 Ex $345 Gd $290
Same general specifications as Model 1400 Deer Gun. Made from 1968-73.

MODEL 1400 MARK II FIELD GUN
Same general specifications as Model 1400 Field Gun, except not chambered for 16 gauge; Winchester Recoil Reduction System not available after 1970. Only 28-inch barrels w/Winchoke offered after 1973. Made from 1968 to 1978.

W/plain bbl. . . . . NiB $450 Ex $365 Gd $287
W/plain bbl. and Winchoke . . NiB $475 Ex $388 Gd $315
W/ vent. rib bbl. . . . . NiB $544 Ex $390 Gd $290
W/vent. rib bbl. and Winchoke NiB $566 Ex $445 Gd $390
Add for Winchester recoil reduction system $150

MODEL 1400 MARK II
SKEET GUN . . . . NiB $535 Ex $423 Gd $356
Same general specifications as Model 1400 Skeet Gun. Made from 1968 to 1973.
MODEL 1400 MARK II TRAP GUN

Same general specifications as Model 1400 Trap Gun except also furnished with 28-inch bbl. and Winchoke. Winchester recoil reduction system not available after 1970. Made from 1968 to 1973.
W/straight stock . . . . NiB $655 Ex $475 Gd $353
W/Monte Carlo stock . . . . NiB $657 Ex $525 Gd $400
W/recoil reduction system, add $150
W/Winchoke, add $50

MODEL 1400 MARK II UTILITY SKEET NiB $590 Ex $445 Gd $355
Same general specifications as Model 1400 Mark II Skeet Gun except has stock and forearm of field grade walnut. Made 1970 to 1973.

MODEL 1400 MARK II UTILITY TRAP NiB $590 Ex $445 Gd $355
Same as Model 1400 Mark II Trap Gun except has Monte Carlo stock/forearm of field grade walnut. Made from 1970 to 1973.

MODEL 1400 RANGER
SEMIAUTOMATIC SHOTGUN NiB $566 Ex $365 Gd $255
Gauges: 12, 20. Two round magazine. 28-inch vent rib bbl. with F choke. Overall length: 48.63 inches. Weight: 7 to 7.25 lbs. Walnut finish, hardwood stock and forearm with cut checkering. Made from 1984 to 1990 by U. S. Repeating Arms.

MODEL 1400 RANGER SEMIAUTOMATIC
DEER SHOTGUN . . . . NiB $500 Ex $369 Gd $255
Same general specifications as Ranger Semiautomatic except 24.13-inch plain bbl. with rifle sights. Mfd. by U.S. Repeating Arms.

MODEL 1400 SKEET GUN . . . NiB $525 Ex $420 Gd $375
Same as standard Model 1400 except 12 and 20 ga. only, 26-inch vent-rib bbl., SK choke, semi-fancy walnut stock and forearm. Weight: 7.25 to 7.5 lbs. Made from 1965 to 1968. Also available with Winchester recoil reduction system (add $50 to value).

MODEL 1400 TRAP GUN
Same as standard Model 1400 except 12 ga. only with 30-inch vent-rib bbl., F choke. Semi-fancy walnut stock, straight or Monte Carlo trap style. Also available with Winchester recoil reduction system. Weight: About 8.25 lbs. Made from 1965 to 1968.
W/straight stock . . . . NiB $435 Ex $320 Gd $220
W/Monte Carlo stock . . . . NiB $455 Ex $340 Gd $245
W/recoil reduction system, add. $150

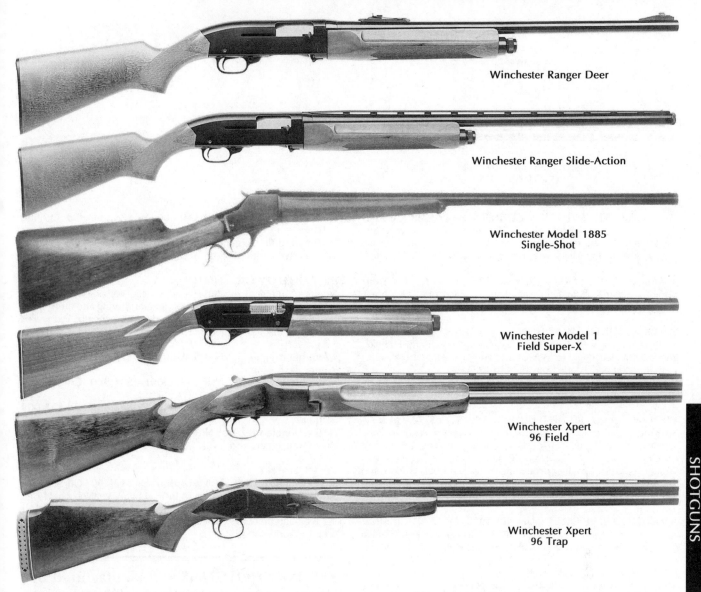

Winchester Ranger Deer

Winchester Ranger Slide-Action

Winchester Model 1885
Single-Shot

Winchester Model 1
Field Super-X

Winchester Xpert
96 Field

Winchester Xpert
96 Trap

MODEL 1500 XTR SEMIAUTOMATIC NiB $465 Ex $300 Gd $290
Gas-operated. Gauges: 12 and 20 (2.75-inch chambers). Bbl.: Plain or vent rib; 28-inch; WinChoke (interchangeable tubes IC-M-F). American walnut stock and forend; checkered grip and forend. Weight: 7.25 lbs. Made from 1978 to 1982.

MODEL 1885
SINGLE-SHOT SHOTGUN NiB $4377 Ex $3554 Gd $2566
Falling-block action, same as Model 1885 Rifle. Highwall receiver. Solid frame or takedown. 20 ga. 3-inch chamber. 26-inch bbl.; plain, matted or matted rib; Cyl. bore, M or F choke. Weight: About 5.5 lbs. Straight-grip stock and forearm. Made from 1914 to 1916.

MODEL 1887 LEVER-ACTION SHOTGUN
First of John Browning's patent shotgun designs produced by Winchester. 10 or 12 ga. on caseharded frame fitted w/20-inch blued, cylinder bore or full choke 30- or 32-inch bbl. Plain or checkered walnut stock and forend. Made from 1887 to 1901.
10 or 12 ga. Standard model.... NiB $4188 Ex $3765 Gd $3287
10 or 12 ga. Deluxe model...NiB $9233 Ex $8977 Gd $6450
10 or 12 ga. Riot Gun .... NiB $2770 Ex $2256 Gd $1656
W/.70-150 Ratchet rifled bbl.

.70 cal. rifle/87 produced) NiB $4350 Ex $3000 Gd $2275
W/3 or 4 blade Del. Damascus bbl., add. 20%

MODEL 1901 LEVER-ACTION SHOTGUN
Same general specifications as Model 1887, of which this is a redesigned version. 10 ga. only. Made from 1901 to 1920.
Standard model . . . . NiB $4379 Ex $3988 Gd $3500
Deluxe model . . . . NiB $6100 Ex $4988 Gd $3360

MODEL 1911 AUTO-
LOADING SHOTGUN . . . . . . NiB $755 Ex $655 Gd $500
Hammerless. Takedown. 12 gauge only. Four round tubular magazine. Bbl.: plain, 26- to 32-inch, standard borings. Weight: About 8.5 lbs. Plain or checkered pistol-grip stock and forearm. Made from 1911 to 1925.

RANGER DEER COMBINATION NiB $455 Ex $365 Gd $245
Gauge: 12, 3-inch Magnum. Three round magazine. Bbl.: 24-inch Cyl. bore deer bbl. and 28-inch vent rib bbl. with WinChoke system. Weight: 7.25 lbs. Made from 1987 to 1990.

Woodward
Single-Shot Trap

Woodward O/U
Special Trap Grade

SUPER-X MODEL I AUTO FIELD GUN NiB $390 Ex $280 Gd $245
Gas-operated. Takedown.12 ga. 2.75-inch chamber Four round magazine. Bbl.: Vent rib 26-inch IC; 28-inch M or F; 30-inch F choke. Weight: About 7 lbs. Checkered pistol-grip stock. Made 1974 to 1984.

SUPER-X MODEL I SKEET GUN NiB $977 Ex $755 Gd $590
Same as Super-X Field Gun except has 26-inch bbl., SK choke, skeet-style stock and forearm of select walnut. Made 1974 to 1984.

SUPER-X MODEL I TRAP GUN
Same as Super-X Field Gun except has 30-inch bbl., IM or F choke, trap-style stock (straight or Monte Carlo comb) and forearm of select walnut, recoil pad. Made from 1974 to 1984.
W/straight stock . . . . NiB $790 Ex $588 Gd $425
W/Monte Carlo stock . . . . . . NiB $875 Ex $655 Gd $470

XPERT MODEL 96 O/U FIELD GUN . NiB $975 Ex $770 Gd $677
Boxlock action similar to Model 101. Plain receiver. Auto ejectors. Selective single trigger. Gauges: 12, 20. 3-inch chambers. Bbl.: Vent rib; 26-inch IC/M; 28-inch M/F, 30-inch F/F choke (12 ga. only). Weight: 6.25 to 8.25 lbs. depending on ga. and bbls. Checkered pistol-grip stock and forearm. Made from 1976-81 for Olin Corp. at its Olin-Kodensha facility in Japan.

XPERT MODEL 96 SKEET GUN NiB $975 Ex $770 Gd $677
Same as Xpert Field Gun except has 2.75-inch chambers, 27-inch bbls., SK choke, skeet-style stock and forearm. Made 1976 to 1981.

XPERT MODEL 96 TRAP GUN
Same as Xpert Field Gun except 12 ga. only, 2.75-inch chambers, has 30-inch bbls., IM/F or F/F choke, trap-style stock (straight or Monte Carlo comb) with recoil pad. Made from 1976 to 1981.
W/straight stock . . . . NiB $975 Ex $770 Gd $677
W/Monte Carlo stock . . . . . NiB $1133 Ex $990 Gd $697

JAMES WOODWARD & SONS — London, England

James Woodward & Sons was acquired by James Purdey & Sons after World War II.

BEST QUALITY HAMMERLESS DOUBLE
Sidelock. Automatic ejectors. Double triggers or single trigger. Built to order in all standard gauges, bbl. lengths, boring and other specifications. Made as a field gun, pigeon and wildfowl gun, skeet gun or trap gun. Manufactured prior to World War II.
12 ga.
w/double triggers . . . NiB $30,000 Ex $22,700 Gd $18,900
20 ga.
w/double triggers . . . NiB $33,000 Ex $26,890 Gd $18,700
28 ga.

w/double triggers . . . NiB $40,600 Ex $33,560 Gd $25,000
.410 ga.
.410 w/double triggers NiB $45,000 Ex $36,900 Gd $25,000
W/selective single trigger, add 10%

BEST QUALITY O/U SHOTGUN
Sidelock. Automatic ejectors. Double triggers or single trigger. Built to order in all standard gauges, bbl. lengths, boring and other specifications, including Special Trap Grade with vent rib. Woodward introduced this type of gun in 1908. Made until World War II.
12 ga.
w/double triggers . . . NiB $31,660 Ex $25,850 Gd $20,000
20 ga.
w/double triggers . . . NiB $42,500 Ex $35,980 Gd $25,500
28 ga.
w/double triggers . . . NiB $55,000 Ex $44,900 Gd $32,000
.410 ga.
.410 w/double triggers NiB $63,000 Ex $49,800 Gd $35,000
W/single trigger, add 10%

BEST QUALITY
SINGLE-SHOT TRAP NiB $14,860 Ex $12,790 Gd $10,000
Sidelock. Mechanical features of the O/U gun. Vent rib bbl. 12 ga. only. Built to customer's specifications and measurements, including type and amount of checkering, carving and engraving. Made prior to World War II.

ZEPHYR SHOTGUNS — Manufactured by Victor Sarasqueta Company, Eibar, Spain

MODEL 1
O/U SHOTGUN . . . . NiB $1341 Ex $1083 Gd $778
Same general specifications as Field Model O/U except with more elaborate engraving, finer wood and checkering. Imported by Stoeger 1930s- to 1951.

MODEL 2
O/U SHOTGUN . . . . NiB $1746 Ex $1393 Gd $994
Sidelock. Auto ejectors. Gauges: 12, 16, 20, 28 and .410. Bbls.: 25 to 30 inches most common. Modest scroll engraving on receiver and sideplates. Checkered, straight-grain select walnut buttstock and forend. Imported by Stoeger 1930s to 1951.

MODEL 3
O/U SHOTGUN . . . . NiB $2369 Ex $1888 Gd $1337
Same general specifications as Zephyr Model 2 O/U except with more elaborate engraving, finer wood and checkering. Imported by Stoeger 1930s to 1951.

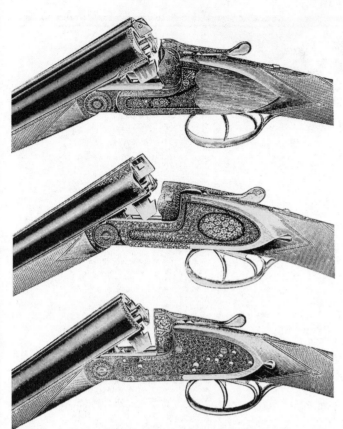

Zephyr Crown, Premier and Royal Grades

MODEL 400E FIELD GRADE DOUBLE-BARREL SHOTGUN
Anson & Deeley boxlock system. Gauges: 12 16, 20, 28 and .410. Bbls.: 25 to 30 inches. Weight: 4.5 lbs. (.410) to 6.25 lbs. (12 ga.). Checkered French walnut buttstock and forearm. Modest scroll engraving on bbls., receiver and trigger guard. Imported by Stoeger 1930s to 1950s.

12, 16 or 20 ga.	NiB $2166	Ex $1388	Gd $1000
28 g. or .410	NiB $1877	Ex $1497	Gd $1000
W/selective single trigger, add			$250

MODEL 401 E SKEET GRADE DOUBLE-BARREL SHOTGUN
Same general specifications as Field Grade except with beavertail forearm. Bbls.: 25 to 28 inches. Imported by Stoeger 1930s to 1950s.

12, 16 or 20 ga.	NiB $1954	Ex $1600	Gd $1216
28 ga., or .410	NiB $2144	Ex $1698	Gd $1277
W/selective single trigger, add			$450
W/non-selective single trigger, add			$300

MODEL 402E DELUXE
DOUBLE-BARREL SHOTGUN NiB $2455 Ex $2089 Gd $1466
Same general specifications as Model 400E Field Grade except for custom refinements. The action was carefully hand-honed for smoother operation; finer, elaborate engraving throughout, plus higher quality wood in stock and forearm. Imported by Stoeger 1930s to 1950s.

CROWN GRADE .... NiB $1800 Ex $1498 Gd $1056
Boxlock. Gauges: 12, 16, 20, 28 and .410. Bbls.: 25 to 30 inches standard but any lengths could be ordered. Weight: 6 lbs., 4 oz. (.410) to 7 lbs., 4 oz. (12 ga.). Checkered Spanish walnut stock and beavertail forearm. Receiver engraved with scroll patterns. Imported by Stoeger 1938 to 1951.

FIELD MODEL
O/U SHOTGUN .... NiB $988 Ex $745 Gd $566
Anson & Deeley boxlock. Auto ejectors. Gauges: 12, 16 and 20. Bbls.: 25 to 30 inches standard- full-length matt rib. Double triggers. Checkered buttstock and forend. Light scroll engraving on receiver. Imported by Stoeger 1930s to 1951.

HONKER SINGLE-SHOT SHOTGUN . NiB $676 Ex $580 Gd $390
Sidelock. Gauge: 10; 3.5-inch magnum. 36-inch vent rib barrel w/F choke. Weight: 10.5 lbs. Checkered select Spanish walnut buttstock and beavertail forend; recoil pad. Imported by Stoeger 1950s to 1972.

PINEHURST
DOUBLE-BARREL SHOTGUN NiB $1388 Ex $1190 Gd $800
Boxlock. Gauges: 12, 16, 20, 28 and .410. Bbls.: 25 to 28 inches most common. Checkered, select walnut buttstock and forend. Selective single trigger and auto ejectors. Imported by Stoeger 1950s to 1972.

PREMIER GRADE
DOUBLE-BARREL SHOTGUN NiB $2870 Ex $2300 Gd $1560
Sidelock. Gauges: 12, 16, 20, 28 and .410. Bbls.: Any length, but 25 to 30 inches most popular. Weight: 4.5 lbs. (.410) to 7 lbs. (12 ga.). Checkered high-grade French walnut buttstock and forend. Imported by Stoeger 1930s to 1951.

ROYAL GRADE
DOUBLE-BARREL SHOTGUN NiB $4388 Ex $2287 Gd $2077
Same general specifications as the Premier Grade except with more elaborate engraving, finer checkering and wood. Imported by Stoeger 1930s to 1951.

STERLINGWORTH II
DOUBLE-BARREL SHOTGUN NiB $1000 Ex $790 Gd $678
Genuine sidelocks with color-casehardened sideplates. Gauges: 12, 16, 20 and .410. Bbls.: 25 to 30 inches. Weight: 6 lbs., 4 oz. (.410) to 7 lbs., 4 oz. (12 ga.). Select Spanish walnut buttstock and beavertail forearm. Light scroll engraving on receiver and sideplates. Automatic, sliding-tang safety. Imported by Stoeger 1950s to 1972.

THUNDERBIRD
DOUBLE-BARREL SHOTGUN NiB $1221 Ex $900 Gd $755
Sidelock. Gauges: 12 and 10 Magnum. Bbls.: 32-inch, both F choke. Weight: 8 lbs., 8 oz. (12 ga.), 12 lbs. (10 ga.). Receiver elaborately engraved with waterfowl scenes. Checkered select Spanish walnut buttstock and beavertail forend. Plain extractors, double triggers. Imported by Stoeger 1950 to 1972.

UPLAND KING
DOUBLE-BARREL SHOTGUN NiB $1290 Ex $1066 Gd $886
Sidelock. Gauges: 12, 16, 20, 28 and .410. Bbls.: 25 to 28 inches most popular. Checkered buttstock and forend of select walnut. Selective single trigger and auto ejectors. Imported by Stoeger 1950 to 1972.

UPLANDER 4E
DOUBLE-BARREL SHOTGUN NiB $900 Ex $688 Gd $525
Same general specifications as the Zephyr Sterlingworth II except with selective auto ejectors and highly polished sideplates. Imported by Stoeger 1951 to 1972.

WOODLANDER II
DOUBLE-BARREL SHOTGUN NiB $645 Ex $465 Gd $377
Boxlock. Gauges: 12, 20 and .410. Bbls.: 25 to 30 inches. Weight: 6 lbs., 4 oz. (.410) to 7 lbs., 4 oz. (12 ga.). Checkered Spanish walnut stock and beavertail forearm. Engraved receiver. Imported by Stoeger 1950 to 1972.

SHOTGUNS

Index

INDEX

INDEX

INDEX

INDEX

INDEX

INDEX

GRADING: NiB = New in Box   Ex = Excellent or NRA 95%   Gd = Good or NRA 68%

GRADING: **NiB** = New in Box   **Ex** = Excellent or NRA 95%   **Gd** = Good or NRA 68%

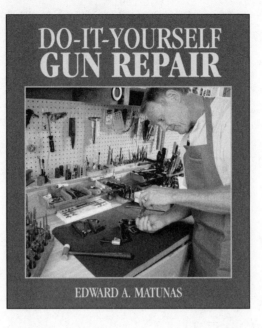

Do-It-Yourself Gun Repair
Gunsmithing at Home
By Edward A. Matunas

Diagnose and repair a broad selection of popular hunting firearms in the convenience of your home workshop and save money, too. *Do-It-Yourself Gun Repair* is an authoritative guide to maintaining, repairing, and improving rifles, shotguns, and handguns. Many of the repairs professional gunsmiths make involve replacing broken or worn parts, and you'll learn to identify and correct these common problems quickly, safely, and easily by following the detailed instructions and illustrations of gunsmithing expert Edward A. Matunas.

A unique feature of this book is a section covering disassembly, repair, and reassembly of seven of the most popular firearms: Remington 700, Remington 1100, Remington 870, Winchester 94, Savage 110, Marlin 336, and Marlin 70. The instructions are fully illustrated with photos and drawings as well as exploded views and parts lists, and much of this information can be applied to other guns with similar actions.

$19.95 Paperback • ISBN 978-1-62087-696-1